PEARSON
Chemistry

Antony C. Wilbraham • Dennis D. Staley • Michael S. Matta • Edward L. Waterman

Boston, Massachusetts • Chandler, Arizona • Glenview, Illinois • Upper Saddle River, New Jersey

Print Components

Student Edition

Teacher's Edition

Reading and Study Workbook

Reading and Study Workbook, Teacher's Edition

Technology Components

Online Student Edition

Online Teacher's Edition

Math Support:
- Math Diagnostic and Remediation
- Online Problem Sets

Tutorials:
- ChemTutor
- MathTutor

Animations:
- Concepts in Action Animations
- Kinetic Art Animations
- Directed Virtual ChemLabs

Videos:
- Untamed Science® Videos

Editable Resources:
- Lab Manual
- Small-Scale Lab Manual
- Probeware Lab Manual
- Lab Practicals
- Reading and Study Workbook
- Assessment Workbook
- PowerPoint® Presentations

CD-ROM and DVD-ROM

ExamView® CD-ROM

Classroom Resource DVD-ROM

Virtual ChemLab CD-ROM

Credits appear on pages R156–R157, which constitute an extension of this copyright page.

Copyright © 2012 Pearson Education, Inc., or its affiliates. All Rights Reserved. Printed in the United States of America. This publication is protected by copyright, and permission should be obtained from the publisher prior to any prohibited reproduction, storage in a retrieval system, or transmission in any form or by any means, electronic, mechanical, photocopying, recording, or likewise. For information regarding permissions, write to Rights Management & Contracts, Pearson Education, Inc., One Lake Street, Upper Saddle River, New Jersey 07458.

Pearson, Prentice Hall, and Pearson Prentice Hall are trademarks, in the U.S. and/or other countries, of Pearson Education, Inc., or its affiliates.

ExamView® is a registered trademark of eInstruction Corporation. Molecular Workbench® is a registered trademark of the Concord Consortium. Untamed Science® is a registered trademark of EcoMedia LLC. ACT® is a registered trademark of ACT, Inc. PowerPoint® is a registered trademark of Microsoft Corporation in the U.S. and/or other countries. SAT® is a registered trademark of the College Entrance Examination Board. Use of the trademarks implies no relationship, sponsorship, endorsement, sale, or promotion on the part of Pearson Education, Inc., or its affiliates.

Certain materials herein are adapted from *Understanding by Design, 2nd Edition,* by Grant Wiggins & Jay McTighe © 2005 ASCD. Used with permission.

UNDERSTANDING BY DESIGN® and UbD™ are trademarks of ASCD, and are used under license.

ISBN-13: 978-0-13-252576-3
ISBN-10:　　 0-13-252576-3

8 9 10 V011 17 16 15 14

Dennis Staley

earned a Master of Science in chemistry at Southern Illinois University Edwardsville. As an Instructor in the Department of Chemistry and the Office of Science and Math Education at Southern Illinois University Edwardsville, he taught high school and college-level chemistry and also led teacher workshops. Mr. Staley has been writing high school and college-level chemistry textbooks for over 30 years. He currently enjoys gardening, bicycling, sharing hands-on science with kids, and traveling to visit his grandchildren.

Antony Wilbraham

spent the majority of his career at Southern Illinois University Edwardsville, where he currently holds the position of Emeritus Professor of Chemistry. He is a member of several professional societies. For more than 30 years, he has been writing high school and college-level chemistry textbooks and has published extensively in scientific journals. Professor Wilbraham enjoys traveling, woodworking, gardening, and making toys for his granddaughters.

Michael Matta

earned a Bachelor of Science in chemistry at the University of Dayton and a Doctor of Philosophy in chemistry at Indiana University. He spent most of his career at Southern Illinois University Edwardsville, where he was most recently an Emeritus Professor. Dr. Matta developed and wrote high school and college-level chemistry textbooks and related ancillaries for over 30 years and published extensively in scientific journals. He was a member of several professional societies. In his spare time, he enjoyed woodworking, watercolor painting, and playing with his six grandchildren.

Michael Matta died shortly after the onset of this program. While he is greatly missed by his many friends throughout the chemistry community, his coauthors remain inspired by his visionary dedication to education, and they are committed to searching for even better ways to engage students in the wonders of chemistry.

Edward Waterman

taught chemistry and advanced placement chemistry from 1976 to 2007 at Rocky Mountain High School in Fort Collins, Colorado. He now conducts workshops for teachers on inquiry, differentiation, small-scale chemistry, AP chemistry and virtual chemistry laboratory. He also presents photo-essay lectures about the natural history of molecules, engaging the general public in the appreciation for and understanding of chemistry. Mr. Waterman holds a Bachelor of Science degree in chemistry from Montana State University and a Master of Science degree in chemistry from Colorado State University. In his free time, he enjoys exploring wild places in the Rocky Mountains and on the Colorado Plateau by hiking, kayaking, and cross-country skiing.

Consultants/Reviewers

Grant Wiggins, Ed.D., is a co-author with Jay McTighe of *Under-standing by Design, 2nd Edition* (ASCD 2005). His approach to instructional design provides teachers with a disciplined way of thinking about curriculum design, assessment, and instruction that moves teaching from covering content to ensuring understanding.

BIGIDEA Big Ideas are one of the core components of the Understanding by Design® methodology in **Pearson Chemistry**. These Big Ideas, such as The Mole and Quantifying Matter, establish a conceptual framework for the program.

Each chapter in the Student Edition provides opportunities to link back to the Big Ideas. Since the Understanding by Design® methodology is by nature a teaching tool, additional applications of this philosophy can be found in the Teacher's Edition.

UNDERSTANDING BY DESIGN® and UbD™ are trademarks of ASCD, and are used under license.

Teacher Advisory Board

Linda Dearth-Monroe
Warren Central High School
Indianapolis, Indiana

Jason Gilley
Cypress Creek High School
Orlando, Florida

Kenneth A. Greathouse
Parkway Central High School
Chesterfield, Missouri

Paul Holloman
Rocky Mount High School
Rocky Mount, North Carolina

George "Rod" Larsen
West Orange High School
Winter Garden, Florida

Stephanie C. LeGrone
Mary G. Montgomery High School
Semmes, Alabama

Christopher Schrempp
Los Osos High School
Rancho Cucamonga, California

Content Reviewers

Matthew Asplund, Ph.D.
Department of Chemistry
    and Biochemistry
Brigham Young University
Provo, Utah

Regina M. Barrier
Western Outreach Coordinator
The Science House
North Carolina State University
Lenoir, North Carolina

J. Phillip Bowen, Ph.D.
Department of Chemistry
    and Biochemistry
University of North Carolina
Greensboro, North Carolina

Alison J. Frontier, Ph.D.
Department of Chemistry
University of Rochester
Rochester, New York

David J. Merkler, Ph.D.
Department of Chemistry
University of South Florida
Tampa, Florida

Gregory S. Owens, Ph.D.
Department of Chemistry
University of Utah
Salt Lake City, Utah

Eric T. Sevy, Ph.D.
Department of Chemistry
    and Biochemistry
Brigham Young University
Provo, Utah

William H. Steinecker, Ph.D.
Miami University
Oxford, Ohio

Harry A. Stern, Ph.D.
Department of Chemistry
University of Rochester
Rochester, New York

Mark E. Welker, Ph.D.
Department of Chemistry
Wake Forest University
Winston-Salem, North Carolina

Teacher Reviewers

Jeff Bilyeu
West Linn High School
West Linn, Oregon

Mary Chuboff
Athens Academy
Athens, Georgia

Linda Dearth-Monroe
Warren Central High School
Indianapolis, Indiana

Jason Gilley
Cypress Creek High School
Orlando, Florida

Stella Glogover
Head-Royce School
Oakland, California

Paul Holloman
Rocky Mount High School
Rocky Mount, North Carolina

Laura McGregor
Marist School
Atlanta, Georgia

Nancy Monson
West Linn High School
West Linn, Oregon

Daniel R. Mullaney
Walpole High School
Walpole, Massachusetts

Michael Roadruck, Ph.D.
Department of Chemistry
University of Toledo
Toledo, Ohio

Michelle Tindall
Birmingham Groves High School
Beverly Hills, Michigan

Safety Consultant

Kenneth R. Roy, Ph.D.
Director of Science and Safety
Glastonbury Public Schools
Glastonbury, Connecticut

All the Elements for Success

The new **Pearson Chemistry** program combines proven content with cutting-edge digital support and a variety of lab investigations to help ensure your success in chemistry.

In your new program, you'll find:

- **Personalized learning** opportunities to support your unique learning style.

- **Connections to the real world** relate abstract concepts and processes to your every day life.

- **Cutting-edge technology** that is integrated throughout the program providing options for you to interact with the content in multiple ways.

- **Rich lab explorations** and **study support** provide numerous opportunities to practice and reinforce essential chemistry skills.

In the following pages, you'll see just a few of the elements contained in your **Pearson Chemistry** program that will lead to your success!

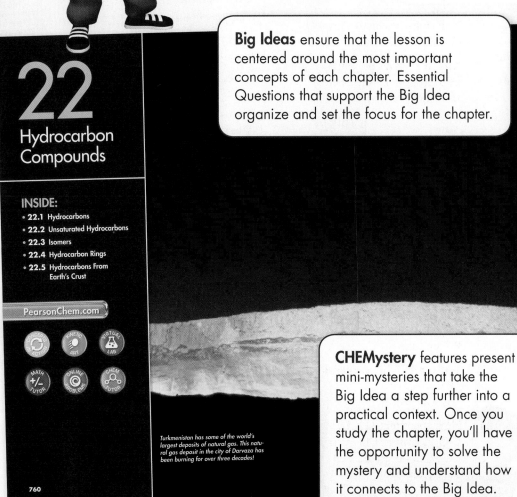

22
Hydrocarbon Compounds

INSIDE:
- 22.1 Hydrocarbons
- 22.2 Unsaturated Hydrocarbons
- 22.3 Isomers
- 22.4 Hydrocarbon Rings
- 22.5 Hydrocarbons From Earth's Crust

PearsonChem.com

Turkmenistan has some of the world's largest deposits of natural gas. This natural gas deposit in the city of Darvaza has been burning for over three decades!

Big Ideas ensure that the lesson is centered around the most important concepts of each chapter. Essential Questions that support the Big Idea organize and set the focus for the chapter.

BIG IDEA

CARBON CHEMISTRY

Essential Questions:
1. How are hydrocarbons named?
2. What are the general properties of hydrocarbons?

CHEMYSTERY

Nose for Hire

Walking home from school one day, Anthony spotted a poster soliciting participants for a smell test. The poster offered participants "$50 for less than an hour of your time." So he decided to go for it.

When Anthony reported for the study, after filling out some paperwork, a researcher asked him to smell two chemical samples. The first one smelled like a freshly cut orange. The second had an odor that reminded him of pine trees.

Anthony was curious. "What am I smelling?" he asked. "Limonene," the researcher answered. "What about the second one?" Anthony asked. The researcher gave the same reply: "Limonene." Anthony was perplexed. How could two substances, both with the name limonene, smell so different?

▶ Connect to the **BIG IDEA** As you read about hydrocarbons, think about what could make this phenomenon possible.

NATIONAL SCIENCE EDUCATION STANDARDS
A-1, A-2, B-2, D-3, E-1, E-2, F-3, F-4, F-5, F-6, G-1, G-3

CHEMystery features present mini-mysteries that take the Big Idea a step further into a practical context. Once you study the chapter, you'll have the opportunity to solve the mystery and understand how it connects to the Big Idea.

Personalized Learning

Each student approaches learning in a variety of ways. **Pearson Chemistry** provides all the tools to support your unique style to help you build the skills you need to succeed. Sample chemistry problems and math support are just a few examples.

Math Tune-Up pages at the end of selected chapters help you quickly reference how to solve a problem—and are also a great way to review before a test!

Sample Problems guide you step-by-step through complicated chemistry problems. Look for the orange button for an online animated tutorial and more practice problems.

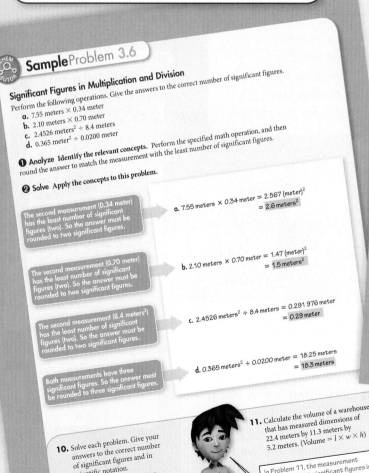

Sample Problem 3.6

Significant Figures in Multiplication and Division

Perform the following operations. Give the answers to the correct number of significant figures.
a. 7.55 meters × 0.34 meter
b. 2.10 meters × 0.70 meter
c. 2.4526 meters² ÷ 8.4 meters
d. 0.365 meter² ÷ 0.0200 meter

❶ **Analyze Identify the relevant concepts.** Perform the specified math operation, and then round the answer to match the measurement with the least number of significant figures.

❷ **Solve Apply the concepts to this problem.**

The second measurement (0.34 meter) has the least number of significant figures (two). So the answer must be rounded to two significant figures.

a. 7.55 meters × 0.34 meter = 2.567 (meter)²
= 2.6 meters²

The second measurement (0.70 meter) has the least number of significant figures (two). So the answer must be rounded to two significant figures.

b. 2.10 meters × 0.70 meter = 1.47 (meter)²
= 1.5 meters²

The second measurement (8.4 meters²) has the least number of significant figures (two). So the answer must be rounded to two significant figures.

c. 2.4526 meters² ÷ 8.4 meters = 0.291 976 meter
= 0.29 meter

Both measurements have three significant figures. So the answer must be rounded to three significant figures.

d. 0.365 meters² ÷ 0.0200 meter = 18.25 meters
= 18.3 meters

10. Solve each problem. Give your answers to the correct number of significant figures and in scientific notation.
a. 8.3 meters × 2.22 meters
b. 8432 meters² ÷ 12.5 meters
c. 35.2 seconds × $\frac{1 \text{ minute}}{60 \text{ seconds}}$

11. Calculate the volume of a warehouse that has measured dimensions of 22.4 meters by 11.3 meters by 5.2 meters. (Volume = $l \times w \times h$)

In Problem 11, the measurement with the fewest significant figures is 5.2 meters. What does this tell you?

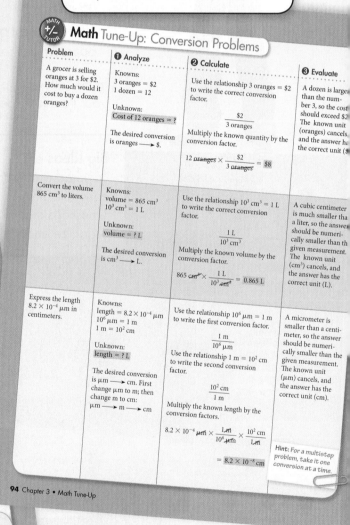

Math Tune-Up: Conversion Problems

Problem	❶ Analyze	❷ Calculate	❸ Evaluate
A grocer is selling oranges at 3 for $2. How much would it cost to buy a dozen oranges?	Knowns: 3 oranges = $2, 1 dozen = 12. Unknown: Cost of 12 oranges = ?. The desired conversion is oranges ⟶ $.	Use the relationship 3 oranges = $2 to write the correct conversion factor. $\frac{\$2}{3 \text{ oranges}}$ Multiply the known quantity by the conversion factor. 12 oranges × $\frac{\$2}{3 \text{ oranges}}$ = $8	A dozen is larger than the number 3, so the cost should exceed $2. The known unit (oranges) cancels, and the answer has the correct unit ($).
Convert the volume 865 cm³ to liters.	Knowns: volume = 865 cm³, 10³ cm³ = 1 L. Unknown: volume = ? L. The desired conversion is cm³ ⟶ L.	Use the relationship 10³ cm³ = 1 L to write the correct conversion factor. $\frac{1 \text{ L}}{10^3 \text{ cm}^3}$ Multiply the known volume by the conversion factor. 865 cm³ × $\frac{1 \text{ L}}{10^3 \text{ cm}^3}$ = 0.865 L	A cubic centimeter is much smaller than a liter, so the answer should be numerically smaller than the given measurement. The known unit (cm³) cancels, and the answer has the correct unit (L).
Express the length 8.2×10^{-4} μm in centimeters.	Knowns: length = 8.2×10^{-4} μm, 10^6 μm = 1 m, 1 m = 10^2 cm. Unknown: length = ? L. The desired conversion is μm ⟶ cm. First change μm to m; then change m to cm: μm ⟶ m ⟶ cm	Use the relationship 10^6 μm = 1 m to write the first conversion factor. $\frac{1 \text{ m}}{10^6 \text{ μm}}$ Use the relationship 1 m = 10^2 cm to write the second conversion factor. $\frac{10^2 \text{ cm}}{1 \text{ m}}$ Multiply the known length by the conversion factors. 8.2×10^{-4} μm × $\frac{1 \text{ m}}{10^6 \text{ μm}}$ × $\frac{10^2 \text{ cm}}{1 \text{ m}}$ = 8.2×10^{-8} cm	A micrometer is smaller than a centimeter, so the answer should be numerically smaller than the given measurement. The known unit (μm) cancels, and the answer has the correct unit (cm).

Hint: For a multistep problem, take it one conversion at a time.

Connecting Chemistry to your World

Chemistry connections are all around you. **Pearson Chemistry** provides examples of chemistry in daily life, connecting content to familiar examples and experiences in your world.

22.1 Hydrocarbo...

Chemistry & You intros begin each lesson with an engaging question to help spark your curiosity and guide your learning.

Chemistry & You features throughout your book showcase exciting real world applications of chemistry in technology, the environment, and in numerous careers.

CHEMISTRY & YOU

Q: *Why are some fossil fuels gases, some liquids, and some solids?* The gasoline used to fuel this motorcycle is a liquid at STP. So are the diesel fuel used in trucks and buses, and the kerosene used in lanterns. Other fuels are gases or solids. For example, the fuel used in a furnace might be natural gas or a solid such as coal. All these fuels contain mixtures of compounds called hydrocarbons. In this lesson, you will learn about the structure and properties of hydrocarbons.

Key Questions

Why does a carbon atom form four covalent bonds?

What are two possible arrangements of carbon atoms in an alkane?

Vocabulary

- hydrocarbon
- alkane
- straight-chain alkane
- homologous series
- condensed structural formula
- substituent
- alkyl group
- branched-chain alkane

Organi...
and Hy...

Why d...

Fewer than 2...
could synthe...
compounds ...
these compo...
thought tha...
bon compo...
refuted this...
to synthesi...
organic ch...
pounds, r...

Introduc...
erties of ...
longer th...
compou...
pounds ...
at least t...
contains...
are met...

Me...
times ...
on dec...
and te...
of dige...

CHEMISTRY & YOU: TECHNOLOGY

Bioremediation

Oil and water don't mix. You may have witnessed this fact watching footage of an oil spill in the news. Oil spills can lead to the deaths of seabirds and marine mammals and can contaminate soil and drinking water.

One tool being used to clean up spilled oil is a relatively new technology called bioremediation. The technology uses "oil-eating" microbes—particularly bacteria—to remedy the spill. For these microbes, the hydrocarbons in crude oil are not a contaminant but a food source. During the digestion process, harmful hydrocarbons are converted to less harmful products—mainly carbon dioxide and water. Bioremediation is a safe, simple, and relatively inexpensive method of dealing with spilled oil. However, the process takes time to work. In addition, it is usually only effective on residual oil on shorelines, after part of the spill has been removed by other means.

Take It Further

1. Describe Two hydrocarbons found in crude oil spills are methylbenzene and methylcyclopentane. Draw structural formulas for these two compounds.

2. Research a Problem Another technology called a dispersion agent is often used to remedy oil spills. Research this technology and compare it to bioremediation.

HIGH-TECH . . . AND ALIVE The degradation of petroleum in the marine environment is carried out by diverse microorganisms, including the *Pseudomonas* species shown here.

Integrating Chemistry and Technology

Pearson Chemistry comes alive online with numerous ways to practice, tutors to step through chemistry and math problems, online labs, interactive art, animations and much more to expand your learning beyond the classroom. The buttons throughout the text direct you to exciting and helpful online activities on PearsonChem.com.

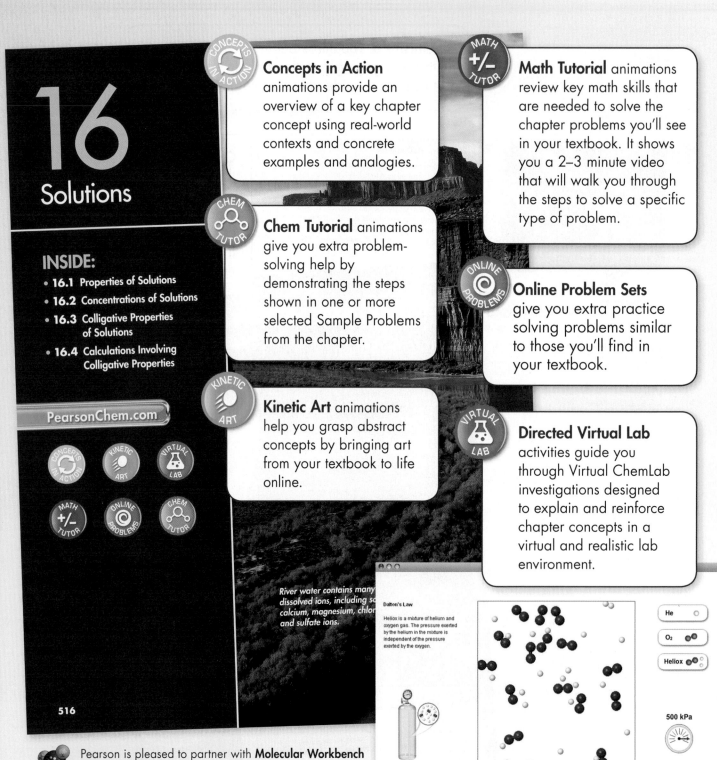

16
Solutions

INSIDE:
- **16.1** Properties of Solutions
- **16.2** Concentrations of Solutions
- **16.3** Colligative Properties of Solutions
- **16.4** Calculations Involving Colligative Properties

PearsonChem.com

Concepts in Action animations provide an overview of a key chapter concept using real-world contexts and concrete examples and analogies.

Chem Tutorial animations give you extra problem-solving help by demonstrating the steps shown in one or more selected Sample Problems from the chapter.

Kinetic Art animations help you grasp abstract concepts by bringing art from your textbook to life online.

Math Tutorial animations review key math skills that are needed to solve the chapter problems you'll see in your textbook. It shows you a 2–3 minute video that will walk you through the steps to solve a specific type of problem.

Online Problem Sets give you extra practice solving problems similar to those you'll find in your textbook.

Directed Virtual Lab activities guide you through Virtual ChemLab investigations designed to explain and reinforce chapter concepts in a virtual and realistic lab environment.

River water contains many dissolved ions, including so... calcium, magnesium, chlor... and sulfate ions.

Dalton's Law

Heliox is a mixture of helium and oxygen gas. The pressure exerted by the helium in the mixture is independent of the pressure exerted by the oxygen.

He
O₂
Heliox

500 kPa

516

Pearson is pleased to partner with **Molecular Workbench** for all Kinetic Art animations.

Lab Investigations and Study Tools

Laboratory Investigations and Study Tools extend your understanding of chemistry concepts by providing you with hands-on practice and extra study support in the areas you need most.

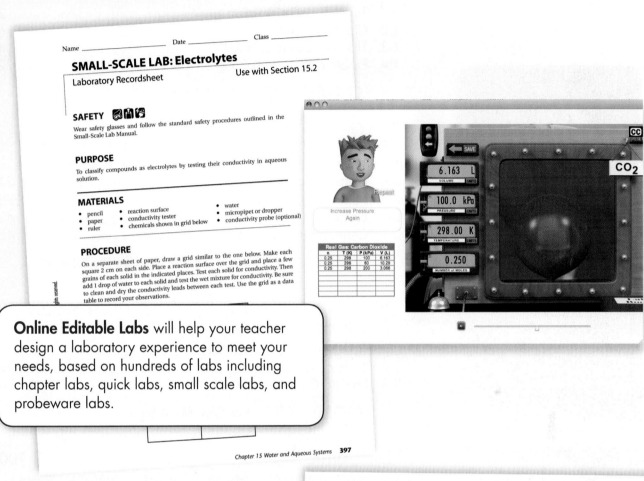

Name _____ Date _____ Class _____

SMALL-SCALE LAB: Electrolytes
Laboratory Recordsheet   Use with Section 15.2

SAFETY
Wear safety glasses and follow the standard safety procedures outlined in the Small-Scale Lab Manual.

PURPOSE
To classify compounds as electrolytes by testing their conductivity in aqueous solution.

MATERIALS
- pencil
- paper
- ruler
- reaction surface
- conductivity tester
- chemicals shown in grid below
- water
- micropipet or dropper
- conductivity probe (optional)

PROCEDURE
On a separate sheet of paper, draw a grid similar to the one below. Make each square 2 cm on each side. Place a reaction surface over the grid and place a few grains of each solid in the indicated places. Test each solid for conductivity. Then add 1 drop of water to each solid and test the wet mixture for conductivity. Be sure to clean and dry the conductivity leads between each test. Use the grid as a data table to record your observations.

Real Gas: Carbon Dioxide

n	T (K)	P (kPa)	V (L)
0.25	298	100	6.163
0.25	298	60	10.29
0.25	298	200	3.066

6.163 L — VOLUME / UNITS
100.0 kPa — PRESSURE / UNITS
298.00 K — TEMPERATURE / UNITS
0.250 — NUMBER of MOLES

Increase Pressure Again

CO₂

Online Editable Labs will help your teacher design a laboratory experience to meet your needs, based on hundreds of labs including chapter labs, quick labs, small scale labs, and probeware labs.

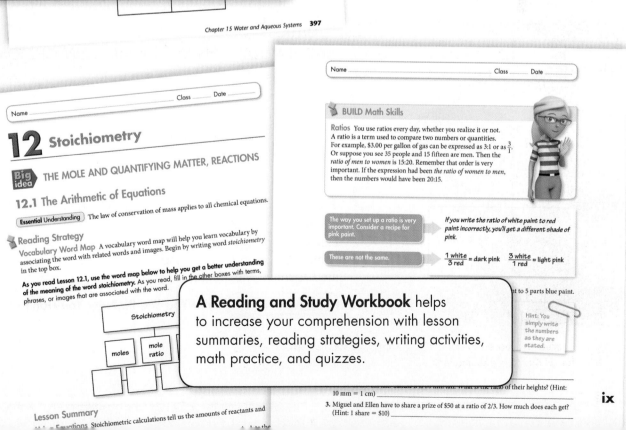

Name _____ Class _____ Date _____

12 Stoichiometry

Big idea THE MOLE AND QUANTIFYING MATTER, REACTIONS

12.1 The Arithmetic of Equations

Essential Understanding The law of conservation of mass applies to all chemical equations.

Reading Strategy
Vocabulary Word Map A vocabulary word map will help you learn vocabulary by associating the word with related words and images. Begin by writing word *stoichiometry* in the top box.

As you read Lesson 12.1, use the word map below to help you get a better understanding of the meaning of the word *stoichiometry*. As you read, fill in the other boxes with terms, phrases, or images that are associated with the word.

Stoichiometry

moles | mole ratio

Name _____ Class _____ Date _____

BUILD Math Skills

Ratios You use ratios every day, whether you realize it or not. A ratio is a term used to compare two numbers or quantities. For example, $3.00 per gallon of gas can be expressed as 3:1 or as $\frac{3}{1}$. Or suppose you see 35 people and 15 fifteen are men. Then the *ratio of men to women* is 15:20. Remember that order is very important. If the expression had been *the ratio of women to men*, then the numbers would have been 20:15.

The way you set up a ratio is very important. Consider a recipe for pink paint.

These are not the same.

If you write the ratio of white paint to red paint incorrectly, you'll get a different shade of pink.

$\frac{1\ white}{3\ red}$ = dark pink $\frac{3\ white}{1\ red}$ = light pink

... to 5 parts blue paint.

Hint: You simply write the numbers as they are stated.

A Reading and Study Workbook helps to increase your comprehension with lesson summaries, reading strategies, writing activities, math practice, and quizzes.

10 mm = 1 cm)

3. Miguel and Ellen have to share a prize of $50 at a ratio of 2/3. How much does each get? (Hint: 1 share = $10)

Lesson Summary
Stoichiometric calculations tell us the amounts of reactants and

Contents

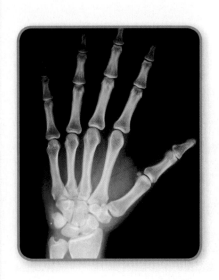

CHEMYSTERY

Enhance your understanding by exploring a chemical mystery that connects to each chapter's Big Idea. For example, you'll learn how less expensive jewelry can appear to be made of pure gold.

PearsonChem.com

What's Online

Your chemistry book comes alive online at **PearsonChem.com.**
Anytime you spot one of these icons on a page, you can visit
PearsonChem.com for an online activity, tutorial, or practice
problem that helps reinforce the concepts introduced in the book.

Small-Scale Lab

Use readily available materials and easy procedures to produce reliable lab results.

Quick Lab

Apply chemistry concepts and skills with these quick, effective hands-on opportunities.

Probe or sensor versions available in the Probeware Lab Manual.

Interpret Graphs

Visualize chemical data in graphical form and improve your critical-thinking skills.

Real Gases Deviate From the Ideal

Interpret Data

Organize and interpret data while building critical-thinking skills.

Feature Pages

Learn more about how chemistry applies to real-world situations. You'll read about the societal and environmental impact of chemical technologies, and survey some interesting careers that apply chemistry. Some features include fun experiments that you can do on your own or with classmates.

Sample Problem

Take advantage of these stepped-out problems to guide your solving process.

1

Introduction to Chemistry

INSIDE:

PearsonChem.com

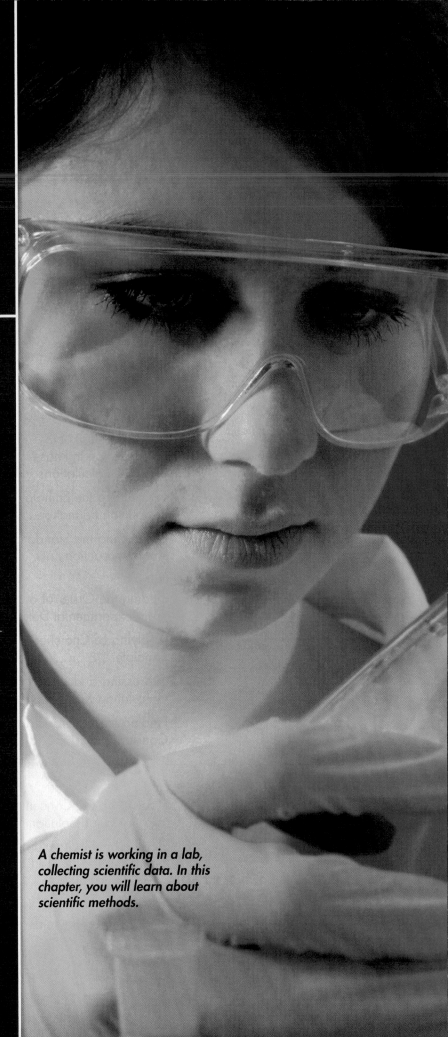

A chemist is working in a lab, collecting scientific data. In this chapter, you will learn about scientific methods.

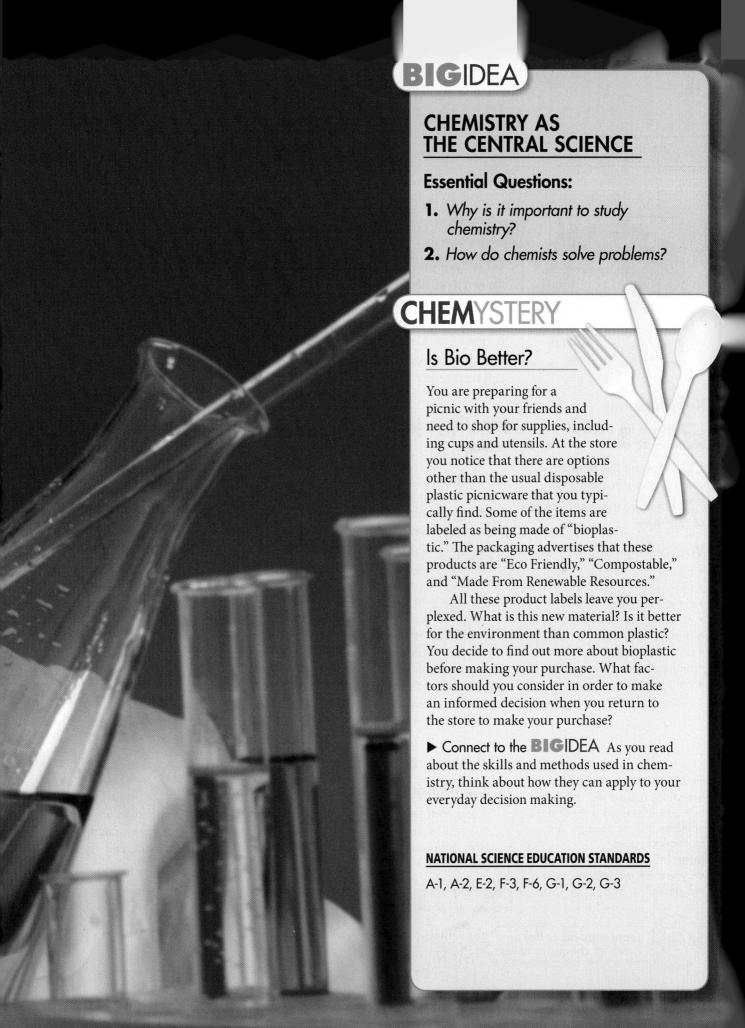

CHEMISTRY AS THE CENTRAL SCIENCE

Essential Questions:

1. *Why is it important to study chemistry?*
2. *How do chemists solve problems?*

CHEMYSTERY

Is Bio Better?

You are preparing for a picnic with your friends and need to shop for supplies, including cups and utensils. At the store you notice that there are options other than the usual disposable plastic picnicware that you typically find. Some of the items are labeled as being made of "bioplastic." The packaging advertises that these products are "Eco Friendly," "Compostable," and "Made From Renewable Resources."

All these product labels leave you perplexed. What is this new material? Is it better for the environment than common plastic? You decide to find out more about bioplastic before making your purchase. What factors should you consider in order to make an informed decision when you return to the store to make your purchase?

▶ Connect to the **BIG**IDEA As you read about the skills and methods used in chemistry, think about how they can apply to your everyday decision making.

NATIONAL SCIENCE EDUCATION STANDARDS

A-1, A-2, E-2, F-3, F-6, G-1, G-2, G-3

1.1 The Scope of Chemistry

Q: *Why might this creature interest you if you were a chemist?* Fugu, also known as puffer fish, is a sushi delicacy that can also be lethal. Puffer fish contain a powerful toxin that can kill an adult a few hours after ingestion. Sushi chefs who prepare fugu must be specially trained because any contamination of the toxin-free areas of the fish can be deadly. Recently this toxin has been put to good use, as scientists have discovered that a purified form of it can treat severe pain in cancer patients.

Key Questions

⚷ Why is the scope of chemistry so vast?

⚷ What are five traditional areas of study in chemistry?

⚷ What are the central themes of chemistry?

Vocabulary

• matter
• chemistry
• organic chemistry
• inorganic chemistry
• biochemistry
• analytical chemistry
• physical chemistry
• pure chemistry
• applied chemistry

What Is Chemistry?

⚷ Why is the scope of chemistry so vast?

Look around you. This book you are reading, the chair you sit in, and the computer you use are all made of matter. Matter is the general term for all the things that can be described as materials, or "stuff." **Matter** is anything that has mass and occupies space. The trees, the water, and the buildings you see in Figure 1.1 are all examples of matter. However, you don't have to be able to see something for it to qualify as matter. The air you breathe is an example of matter that you cannot see with the naked eye.

Have you ever wondered how some creatures can survive deep in the ocean where there is no light? Why some foods taste sweet and some taste bitter? Chemistry answers these questions and the many other questions you may have about the world you live in. **Chemistry** is the study of the composition of matter and the changes that matter undergoes. ⚷ **Chemistry affects all aspects of life and most natural events because all living and nonliving things are made of matter.** Chemistry is also known as the central science, because it is fundamental to the understanding of the other sciences.

Areas of Study

⚷ What are five traditional areas of study in chemistry?

The scope of chemistry is vast, so individual chemists tend to focus on one area of study. ⚷ **Five traditional areas of study are organic chemistry, inorganic chemistry, biochemistry, analytical chemistry, and physical chemistry.**

Figure 1.1 Matter Around You
Everything around you is made of matter. Chemistry is the study of matter and the changes that matter undergoes.
Infer *What changes in matter do you think are happening in this photo?*

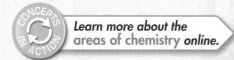
Learn more about the areas of chemistry **online**.

Most chemicals found in organisms contain carbon. Therefore, organic chemistry was originally defined as the study of the carbon-based chemicals found in organisms. Today, with few exceptions, **organic chemistry** is defined as the study of all chemicals containing carbon. The study of chemicals that, in general, do not contain carbon is called **inorganic chemistry.** Many inorganic chemicals are found in non-living things, such as rocks. The study of processes that take place in living organisms is **biochemistry.** These processes include muscle contraction and digestion. The area of study that focuses on the composition of matter is **analytical chemistry.** A task that would fall into this area of chemistry is measuring the level of carbon dioxide in the atmosphere. **Physical chemistry** is the area that deals with the mechanism, rate, and energy transfer that occurs when matter undergoes a change.

The boundaries between the five areas are not firm. A chemist is likely to be working in more than one area of chemistry at any given time. For example, an organic chemist uses analytical chemistry to determine the composition of an organic chemical. Figure 1.1 shows examples of the types of research different chemists do.

Some chemists do research on fundamental aspects of chemistry. This type of research is sometimes called pure chemistry. **Pure chemistry** is the pursuit of chemical knowledge for its own sake. The chemist doesn't expect that there will be any immediate practical use for the knowledge. However, most chemists do research that is designed to answer a specific question. **Applied chemistry** is research that is directed toward a practical goal or application. In practice, pure chemistry and applied chemistry are often linked. Pure research can lead directly to an application, but an application can exist before research is done to explain how it works.

CHEMISTRY & YOU

Q: *Why would you study a puffer fish if you were a biochemist? If you were an organic chemist?*

Analytical Chemistry
An analytical chemist might test the air for the presence of pollutants.

Physical Chemistry
A physical chemist might study factors that affect the rate of photosynthesis in trees.

Inorganic Chemistry
An inorganic chemist might develop metal materials that provide strong structural parts for buildings.

Biochemistry
A biochemist might study how the energy used for the contraction of muscles is produced and stored.

Organic Chemistry
An organic chemist might develop new lightweight plastics for flying disks.

Big Ideas in Chemistry

 **What are the central themes of chemistry?**

This book contains many ideas in the science of chemistry. One of the goals of your course in chemistry is to help you understand these ideas so you can use them to explain real situations that you may encounter in your life, such as the one shown in Figure 1.2. Fortunately, most of the topics of interest in chemistry are connected by a relatively few organizing principles, or "big ideas." **Some of chemistry's big ideas are as follows: chemistry as the central science, electrons and the structure of atoms, bonding and interactions, reactions, kinetic theory, the mole and quantifying matter, matter and energy, and carbon chemistry.**

BIGIDEA **Chemistry As the Central Science** Chemistry overlaps with all of the other sciences. Many physicists, biologists, astronomers, geologists, environmental scientists, and others use chemistry in their work.

BIGIDEA **Electrons and the Structure of Atoms** Carbon, oxygen, and copper are all examples of elements. Elements are composed of particles called atoms, and every atom contains a nucleus and one or more electrons. The type of products obtained in a chemical reaction is largely determined by the electrons in the reacting chemicals.

BIGIDEA **Bonding and Interactions** Most elements exist in chemical compounds, which are collections of two or more elements held together by relatively strong attractive forces. These forces, called chemical bonds, greatly influence the properties of compounds. Weak bonds between the particles of an element or compound can also contribute to the properties of the material.

Figure 1.2 Big Ideas
The big ideas in chemistry can help you understand the world around you. For example, all matter is made up of atoms, which are held together in compounds by chemical bonds. The fire is a result of a chemical reaction between the carbon-containing compounds in the wood and the oxygen in the air. The fire gives off energy in the form of heat and light. The gas particles in the air around the fire begin to move faster as the air heats up.
Predict *Marshmallows are made up of mostly sugar, a carbon-containing compound. What do you think happens when the sugar is heated by the fire?*

BIGIDEA **Reactions** Chemical reactions involve processes in which reactants produce products. When you strike a match, the compounds in the head of the match combine with oxygen in the air to produce a flame. New compounds, along with light and heat, are formed. The compounds in the match head and oxygen are the reactants, and the new compounds are the products. Chemical reactions are important to the chemistry of living and nonliving things.

BIGIDEA **Kinetic Theory** The particles in matter are in constant motion. The ways in which these motions vary with changes in temperature and pressure determine whether a substance will be a solid, liquid, or gas.

BIGIDEA **The Mole and Quantifying Matter** In many aspects of chemistry, it is vital to know the amount of material with which you are dealing. In conducting a chemical reaction, you would want to use just the right amount of the reacting material so none is wasted. This measurement is possible using the mole, the chemist's invaluable unit for specifying the amount of material. Other concepts in chemistry also rely on the mole unit.

BIGIDEA **Matter and Energy** Every chemical process uses or produces energy, often in the form of heat. The heat changes that occur in chemical reactions are easy to measure. Changes in a quantity called free energy allow you to predict whether a reaction will actually occur under the given conditions.

BIGIDEA **Carbon Chemistry** There are about 10 million carbon-containing compounds, with new ones being prepared each day. Many of these compounds, including plastics and synthetic fibers, are produced from petroleum. Carbon compounds are the basis of life in all living organisms.

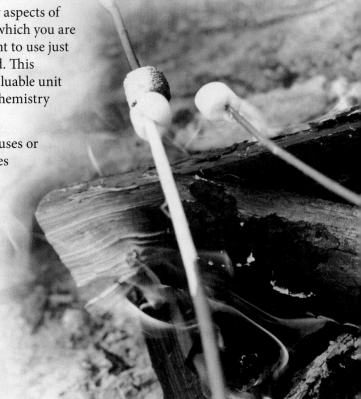

1.1 LessonCheck

1. 🔑 **Explain** Why does chemistry affect all aspects of life and most natural events?

2. 🔑 **List** Name the five traditional areas into which chemistry can be divided.

3. 🔑 **Review** What are the "big ideas" of chemistry?

4. **Describe** What is the relationship between pure and applied chemistry?

5. **Infer** Why might a geologist ask an analytical chemist to help identify the minerals in a rock?

6. **Apply Concepts** Workers digging a tunnel through a city find some ancient pots decorated with geometric designs. Which of the following tasks might they ask a chemist to do? Explain.
   a. Determine the materials used to make the pots.
   b. Explain what the designs on the pots represent.
   c. Recommend how to store the pots to prevent further damage.

BIGIDEA CHEMISTRY AS THE CENTRAL SCIENCE

7. Why would a student who wants to be a doctor need to study chemistry?

1.2 Chemistry and You

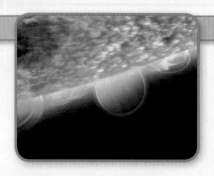

Q: *How is chemistry used to study worlds other than your own?* The Hubble Space Telescope has provided detailed views of celestial objects. Scientists who know chemistry have also used the telescope to discover water and compounds containing carbon on a planet located 63 light years from Earth. Such compounds are necessary for life on Earth. However, the planet, designated HD189733b, is much too hot to support life. Perhaps the Hubble Space Telescope or its successors will someday be used to find evidence of life on planets with atmospheres more like that of Earth.

Key Questions

⬡ What are three general reasons to study chemistry?

⬡ What are some outcomes of modern research in chemistry?

Vocabulary

- technology

Why Study Chemistry?

⬡ **What are three general reasons to study chemistry?**

You may not realize it, but chemistry can answer many questions you have about the world around you. Should you use hot water or cold water to remove a grass stain from a shirt? How could you prepare for a career in nursing, firefighting, or journalism? If your local government wanted to build a solid waste incinerator in your town, what questions would you ask about the project? ⬡ **Chemistry can be useful in explaining the natural world, preparing people for career opportunities, and producing informed citizens.**

Explaining the Natural World You were born with a curiosity about your world. Chemistry can help you satisfy your natural desire to understand how things work. For example, chemistry can be seen in all aspects of food preparation. Chemistry can explain why cut apples, such as the one shown in Figure 1.3, turn brown upon exposure to air. It can explain why the texture of eggs changes from runny to firm as eggs are boiled. Chemistry can explain why water expands as it freezes, why sugar dissolves faster in hot water than in cold water, and why yeast makes bread dough rise. After you study this textbook, you will know the answers to these questions and many more.

Preparing for a Career Being a chemist can be rewarding. Chemists contribute to society in many ways. In this book, you will find features on careers that require knowledge of chemistry. Some of the choices may surprise you. You do not need to have the word *chemist* in your job title to benefit from understanding chemistry. For example, a reporter may be asked to interview a chemist to gather background for a story. Turf managers have the important task of keeping the grass on golf courses, lawns, and soccer fields, such as the one shown in Figure 1.4a, healthy. This job requires an understanding of soil chemistry. Figure 1.4b shows a firefighter, who must know which chemicals to use to fight different types of fires.

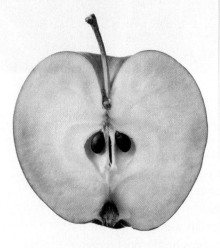

Figure 1.3 Chemistry and Food
When cut apples are exposed to air, a chemical reaction takes place, which causes the color to change to brown.

Figure 1.4 Careers
Many careers require a knowledge of chemistry. **a.** Turf managers must know how the soil and other conditions affect grass. **b.** Firefighters must choose the correct chemicals to extinguish different types of fires.
Infer *What are some factors that may affect the health and appearance of the grass on a soccer field?*

Being an Informed Citizen Industry, private foundations, and the federal and state governments all provide funds for scientific research. The availability of funding can influence the direction of research. Those who distribute funds have to balance the importance of a goal against the cost. Areas of research often compete for funds because there is limited money available.

For example, space exploration research could not take place without federal funding. Critics argue that the money spent on space exploration would be better spent on programs such as cancer research. Those who support space exploration point out that NASA research has led to the development of many items used on Earth. These include smoke detectors, scratch-resistant plastic lenses, heart monitors, and flat-screen televisions. What if all the money spent on space exploration was used to find a cure for cancer? Are there enough valid avenues of research to take advantage of the extra funding? Would there be qualified scientists to do the research?

Like the citizen shown in Figure 1.5, you will need to make choices that will influence the direction of scientific research. You may vote directly on some issues through ballot initiatives or indirectly through the officials you elect. You may speak at a public hearing, write a letter to the editor, or sign a petition. When it comes to scientific research, there is no one correct answer. However, knowledge of chemistry and other sciences can help you evaluate the data presented, arrive at an informed opinion, and take appropriate action.

Figure 1.5 Voting
Through voting, citizens have a say in the decisions their government makes. Those decisions include how much money to provide for scientific research.

Figure 1.6 Plastics packaging includes soft-drink and water bottles, milk and water jugs, and other plastic containers.

a. Read Graphs How much plastics packaging was in U.S. waste in 2007?

b. Calculate How much more plastics packaging was in U.S. waste in 2000 than in 1990?

c. Predict Do you think that the amount of plastics packaging in U.S. waste will increase or decrease in the next 10 years? Explain.

Plastics Packaging in U.S. Waste

Note: The amount of plastics packaging in U.S. waste includes plastics packaging that is to be recycled.

Chemistry, Technology, and Society

What are some outcomes of modern research in chemistry?

You have probably heard the term *high tech* used when describing the latest gadgets and inventions, such as computers that are the size of your watch, or cars that can drive themselves. However, you may not realize that many of the basic items you use every day, such as the sneakers you wear or the cereal you eat, are products of technology. **Technology** is the means by which a society provides its members with those things needed and desired. Technology allows humans to do some things more quickly or with less effort. It also allows people to do things that would be otherwise impossible, such as traveling to the moon. **Modern research in chemistry can lead to technologies that aim to benefit the environment, conserve and produce energy, improve human life, and expand our knowledge of the universe.**

Materials and the Environment Chemists don't just study matter—they also use what they know about the structure and properties of matter to make new materials with different or improved properties. Take plastics, for example. If you have ever consumed bottled water, eaten a salad with a disposable fork, or put on your helmet before riding your bike, you have used plastics. Chemistry has played a large role in developing plastics for different uses.

Most plastics are made using petrochemicals, which are chemical products derived from petroleum. Although plastics are a part of most of our daily lives, there is concern that their use is taking a toll on the environment and on natural resources. The supply of petrochemicals is limited, and the manufacture of plastics uses large amounts of energy. Unrecycled plastics end up in landfills, where they remain for hundreds of years. Figure 1.6 shows the amount of plastics packaging in U.S. waste. Understandably, there has been a demand for plastics that are better for the environment. Figure 1.7 describes a new technology that offers an alternative to petroleum-based plastics.

Figure 1.7 Bioplastic
Polylactic acid (PLA) is known as a bioplastic. Made from corn, PLA can be used to manufacture many items that are typically made out of petroleum-based plastics, including cups, utensils, containers and packaging for food, and bags.

Corn is grown, harvested, and ground. A sugar called glucose is extracted.

Bacteria are added to convert glucose into **lactic acid.**

Lactic acid is also found in your muscle tissue when you exercise.

Lactic acid molecules are linked into long chains called **polymers.**

Plastics are made out of **polymers.** Polymers are long chains of molecules that are chemically bonded to one another.

The polylactic acid (PLA) polymer is formed into small pellets. The pellets can be spun into fibers or melted to take almost any form.

Pros & Cons

Advantages of PLA

✔ **Made from renewable resources** PLA can be made from corn and other crops, which can be grown year after year.

✔ **Less energy** The production of PLA uses less energy than the production of conventional plastics.

✔ **Better for the environment** Fewer greenhouse gases, such as carbon dioxide, are produced in the production of PLA than in the production of other plastics. Also, PLA can be broken down into compounds found in nature.

Disadvantages of PLA

✘ **Melts at low temperatures** Since PLA melts at temperatures lower than other common plastics, it doesn't have as many applications.

✘ **Made from corn** The fields used to grow corn for PLA could be used to grow food for Earth's growing population. There is also concern that the corn used to produce PLA is genetically modified.

✘ **Difficult to dispose of** PLA must be taken to special compost facilities in order to ensure that the material breaks down. Products made from PLA cannot be recycled with other plastics.

Energy The needs of any modern society require energy to power homes, factories, and transportation. With population growth and more industrialization around the globe, the demand for energy is on the rise. There are only two ways to meet the demand for energy—conserve it or produce more of it. Chemistry plays an essential role in both of these options.

Gasoline-electric hybrid cars play a substantial role in the conservation of energy. They have greater fuel efficiencies than gasoline-powered vehicles. Hybrids use both a gasoline engine and a set of batteries to run the car. A knowledge of chemistry was necessary to develop these batteries. In an effort to produce more energy, sustainable energy sources are important to consider. Unlike fossil fuels, the sun is a renewable energy source. Chemists help design materials that collect energy from the sun that is then converted to electricity.

Medicine and Biotechnology Chemistry supplies the medicines, materials, and technology that doctors use to treat their patients. Biochemists work with biologists and doctors to understand the structure of matter found in the human body and the chemical changes that occur in cells.

There are more than 10,000 prescription drugs, which have been designed to treat various conditions including infections, high blood pressure, and depression. Other drugs, such as aspirin and antacids, can be sold without a prescription. Many drugs are effective because they interact in a specific way with chemicals in cells. Chemists who develop these drugs must have knowledge of the structure and function of these target chemicals in order to design safe and effective drugs. Chemistry can also develop materials to repair or replace body parts. Diseased arteries can be replaced with plastic tubes. Artificial hips and knees made from metals and plastics can replace worn-out joints and allow people to walk again without pain.

Figure 1.8a shows a model of a small piece of DNA. Segments of DNA, called genes, store the information that controls changes that take place in cells. Biotechnology applies science to the production of biological products or processes. It uses techniques that can alter the DNA in living organisms. It may depend on the transfer of genes from one organism to another. When genes from humans are inserted into bacteria, the bacteria act as factories that produce chemicals of importance to humans, such as insulin. Production takes place in large versions of the bioreactors shown in Figure 1.8b.

Figure 1.8 Biotechnology
The discovery of the structure of DNA led to the development of biotechnology. **a.** This computer graphics model shows a small segment of DNA. **b.** The conditions in a bioreactor are controlled so that the bacteria produce as much of the product as possible.

The Universe Scientists assume that the methods used to study Earth can be applied to other objects in the universe. To study the universe, chemists gather data from afar and analyze matter that is brought back to Earth.

In the early 1800s, scientists began to study the composition of stars by analyzing the light they transmitted to Earth. In 1868, Pierre Janssen discovered a gas on the sun's surface that was not known on Earth. Joseph Norman Lockyer named the gas helium from the Greek word *helios,* meaning "sun." In 1895, William Ramsay discovered helium on Earth.

The moon and the planets do not emit light, so scientists must use other methods to gather data about these objects. The methods used depend on matter brought back to Earth by astronauts or on probes that can analyze matter in space. Chemists have analyzed more than 850 pounds of moon rocks that were brought back to Earth. The rocks were similar to rocks formed by volcanoes on Earth, suggesting that vast oceans of molten lava once covered the moon's surface. Figure 1.9 is a drawing of the robotic vehicle *Opportunity*. The vehicle was designed to determine the chemical composition of rocks and soil on Mars. Data collected at the vehicle's landing site indicated that the site was once drenched with water.

Figure 1.9 Space Exploration
With help from NASA, chemists study matter from other bodies in the solar system. This drawing shows the robotic vehicle *Opportunity* on the surface of Mars.

Q: *How can chemistry be used to find evidence of life on other planets?*

1.2 LessonCheck

8. 🔑 **List** What are three reasons for studying chemistry?

9. 🔑 **Review** How has modern research in chemistry impacted society?

10. Describe How do chemists study the universe?

11. Form an Opinion Do the advantages of substituting the bioplastic PLA for conventional plastics outweigh the disadvantages? Would you use products made out of PLA? Why or why not?

12. Explain How can a knowledge of chemistry help you be a more informed citizen?

BIGIDEA
CHEMISTRY AS THE CENTRAL SCIENCE

13. A friend tells you that she doesn't think it is important to learn chemistry. What would be your response?

Accidental Chemistry

Typically, chemists direct their research toward a practical goal or application. However, sometimes scientists accidentally stumble upon a discovery that they didn't intend to find.

Polytetrafluoroethylene In 1938, Roy J. Plunkett was researching new refrigerants, which are compounds used in refrigerators and air conditioners. In preparation for an experiment, Plunkett stored a compound called tetrafluoroethylene gas (TFE) in cylinders at a low temperature overnight.

When Plunkett was ready to use the TFE the next day, he found that none of the gas came out. He opened a cylinder to find a white, waxy solid that was very slippery and did not react with any other chemicals.

The substance that Plunkett accidentally made, called polytetrafluoroethylene (PTFE) has many uses that you may be familiar with, such as insulation for electrical cables, soil and stain repellents for fabrics, and coatings for nonstick cookware.

Saccharin In 1879, Constantine Fahlberg was looking for new uses for coal tar and forgot to wash his hands after working one day in the lab. When he went home to eat dinner that night he noticed that his bread tasted sweet. He realized that the sweet taste was coming from his unwashed hands.

The substance on his hands was saccharin, which is the oldest artificial sweetener. Saccharin was initially sold in tablet form from the late 1890s to the 1940s. In 1957, it was introduced in granulated form.

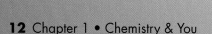

Sticky Notes In 1968, a chemist named Spencer Silver developed an adhesive that was only slightly sticky. However, Silver didn't have an application for his discovery. Several years later, in 1974, Silver's co-worker, Art Fry, was singing in his church choir. He thought that Silver's adhesive would be useful for sticking bookmarks in his hymnal. In 1980, sticky notes were introduced around the world.

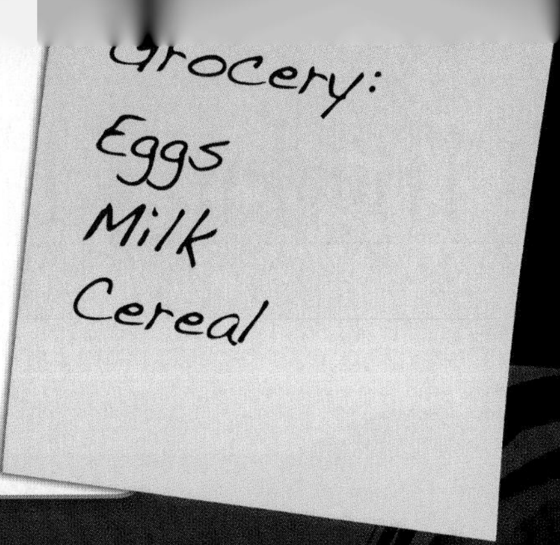

Grocery:
Eggs
Milk
Cereal

Vulcanized Rubber When rubber was introduced in the early 1830s, it was not very useful. It froze in the winter and melted into a glue-like substance in the summer. Charles Goodyear, a hardware merchant from Philadelphia was on a quest to improve the properties of the substance. After countless failed experiments, Goodyear began using sulfur in his rubber formulations. In the winter of 1839, a chunk of his rubber-sulfur formulation landed on top of a hot stove. Instead of melting, the rubber charred. The mixture had hardened but it was still elastic.

Thomas Hancock, an Englishman, saw a sample of Goodyear's rubber and re-invented it in 1843. He named the processes "vulcanization," after Vulcan, the Roman god of fire.

Take It Further

1. Identify Coal tar contains carbon. What type of chemistry was the focus of Fahlberg's research?

2. Classify Were the inventors in these examples performing pure or applied research when they made their discoveries? Explain.

3. Infer When Plunkett couldn't get the TFE gas out of the cylinders, he weighed them and found that they weighed the same as they did the night before. What was the significance of this finding?

4. Form an Opinion Are the inventions described examples of technology? Why or why not?

1.3 Thinking Like a Scientist

Q: *How do you think Alexander Fleming tested his hypothesis?* In 1928, Alexander Fleming, a Scottish scientist, noticed that a bacteria he was studying did not grow in the presence of a yellow-green mold. Other scientists had made the same observation, but Fleming was the first to recognize its importance. He assumed that the mold had released a chemical that prevented the growth of the bacteria. That chemical was penicillin, which can kill a wide range of harmful bacteria.

Key Questions

📧 How did Lavoisier help to transform chemistry?

📧 What procedures are at the core of scientific methodology?

📧 What role do collaboration and communication play in science?

Vocabulary

- observation
- hypothesis
- experiment
- independent variable
- dependent variable
- model
- theory
- scientific law

An Experimental Approach to Science

📧 How did Lavoisier help to transform chemistry?

The word *chemistry* comes from the word *alchemy*. Long before there were chemists, alchemists were studying matter. Alchemy arose independently in many regions of the world. It was practiced in China and India as early as 400 B.C. In the eighth century, Arabs brought alchemy to Spain, and from there it spread quickly to other parts of Europe.

You may have heard that alchemists were concerned with searching for a way to change other metals, such as lead, into gold. Although alchemists did not succeed with this quest, the work they did spurred the development of chemistry. Alchemists developed the tools and techniques for working with chemicals. For example, alchemists developed processes for separating mixtures and purifying chemicals. They designed equipment that is still used today, including beakers, flasks, tongs, funnels, and the mortar and pestle, which is shown in Figure 1.10. What they did not do was provide a logical set of explanations for the changes in matter that they observed. Chemists would accomplish that task many years later.

Figure 1.10 Mortar and Pestle
Pharmacists still use a bowl-shaped mortar and club-shaped pestle to mix drugs for patients. The mortar and pestle in this photograph are made of porcelain, which is a hard material.
Infer *What may be some other uses of a mortar and pestle?*

By the 1500s in Europe, there was a shift from alchemy to science. Science flourished in Britain in the 1600s, partly because King Charles II was a supporter of the sciences. With his permission, some scientists formed the Royal Society of London for the Promotion of Natural Knowledge. The scientists met to discuss scientific topics and conduct experiments. The society's aim was to encourage scientists to base their conclusions about the natural world on experimental evidence, not on philosophical debates.

In France, Antoine-Laurent Lavoisier did work in the late 1700s that would revolutionize the science of chemistry. **Lavoisier helped to transform chemistry from a science of observation to the science of measurement that it is today.** To make careful measurements, Lavoisier designed a balance that could measure mass to the nearest 0.0005 gram.

One of the many things Lavoisier accomplished was to settle a long-standing debate about how materials burn. The accepted explanation was that materials burn because they contain phlogiston, which is released into the air as a material burns. To support this explanation, scientists had to ignore the evidence that metals can gain mass as they burn. By the time Lavoisier did his experiments, he knew that there were two main gases in air—oxygen and nitrogen. Lavoisier was able to show that oxygen is required for a material to burn. Lavoisier's wife Marie Anne, shown in Figure 1.11, helped with his scientific work. She made drawings of his experiments and translated scientific papers from English.

Figure 1.11 Antoine Lavoisier
This portrait of Antoine Lavoisier and his wife Marie Anne was painted by Jacques Louis David in 1788.

Scientific Methodology

What procedures are at the core of scientific methodology?

Scientists have a powerful tool that they use to produce valuable results. Like all scientists, the biochemist shown in Figure 1.12 is using scientific methodology. Scientific methodology is a general style of investigation with a logical, systematic approach to the solution of a scientific problem. **Scientific methodology involves making observations, proposing and testing hypotheses, and developing theories.**

Making Observations Scientific methodology is useful for solving many kinds of problems. Suppose you try to turn on a flashlight and you notice that it does not light. When you use your senses to obtain information, you make an **observation.** An observation can lead to a question: What is wrong with the flashlight?

Figure 1.12 Observing With a Microscope
Observation is an essential step in scientific methodology.

Figure 1.13 Computer Models
This scientist is using a computer to model complex molecules, which are difficult to study with experiments alone.

KINETIC ART
See scientific models online.

Testing Hypotheses If you guess that the batteries in the flashlight are dead, you are making a hypothesis. A **hypothesis** is a proposed explanation for an observation. You can test your hypothesis by putting new batteries in the flashlight. Replacing the batteries is an **experiment,** a procedure that is used to test a hypothesis. If the flashlight lights, you can be fairly certain that your hypothesis was true. What if the flashlight does not work after you replace the batteries? A hypothesis is useful only if it accounts for what is actually observed. When experimental data does not fit a hypothesis, the hypothesis must be changed. A new hypothesis might be that the light bulb is burnt out. An experiment to test this new hypothesis is to replace the bulb.

When you design experiments, you deal with variables, or factors that can change. The variable that you change during an experiment is the **independent variable,** also called the manipulated variable. The variable that is observed during the experiment is the **dependent variable,** also called the responding variable. If you keep other factors that can affect the experiment from changing during the experiment, you can relate any change in the dependent variable to changes in the independent variable. For the results of an experiment to be accepted, the experiment must produce the same result no matter how many times it is repeated, or by whom. This is why scientists are expected to publish a description of their procedures along with their results.

Sometimes the experiment a scientist must perform to test a hypothesis is difficult or impossible. For example, atoms and molecules, which are some of the smallest units of matter, cannot be easily seen. In these situations, scientists often turn to models to gain more understanding of a problem. A **model** is a representation of an object or event. Figure 1.13 shows a scientist working with computer models of complex biological molecules. Chemists may also use models to study chemical reactions and processes.

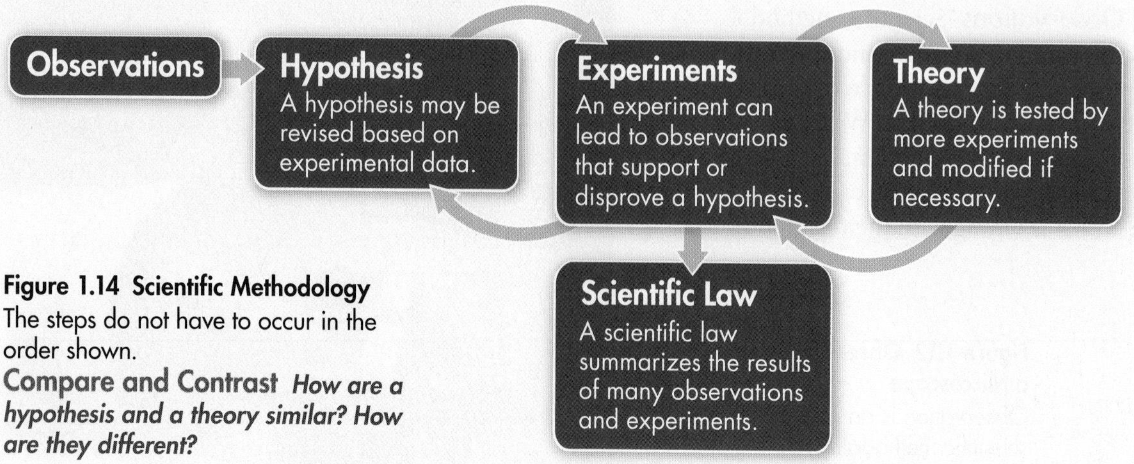

Observations → **Hypothesis**
A hypothesis may be revised based on experimental data.

Experiments
An experiment can lead to observations that support or disprove a hypothesis.

Theory
A theory is tested by more experiments and modified if necessary.

Scientific Law
A scientific law summarizes the results of many observations and experiments.

Figure 1.14 Scientific Methodology
The steps do not have to occur in the order shown.
Compare and Contrast *How are a hypothesis and a theory similar? How are they different?*

Developing Theories Figure 1.14 shows one way the procedures in scientific methodology can fit together. Once a hypothesis meets the test of repeated experimentation, it may be raised to a higher level of ideas. It may become a theory. A **theory** is a well-tested explanation for a broad set of observations. Some of the theories in chemistry are very useful because they help you form mental pictures of objects or processes that cannot be seen. Other theories allow you to predict the behavior of matter.

When scientists say that a theory can never be proved, they are not saying that a theory is unreliable. They are simply leaving open the possibility that a theory may need to be changed at some point in the future to explain new observations or experimental results.

Scientific Laws Figure 1.14 shows how scientific experiments can lead to laws as well as theories. A **scientific law** is a concise statement that summarizes the results of many observations and experiments. In Chapter 14, you will study laws that describe how gases behave. One law describes the relationship between the volume of a gas in a container and its temperature. If all other variables are kept constant, the volume of the gas increases as the temperature increases. The law doesn't try to explain the relationship it describes. That explanation requires a theory.

CHEMISTRY & YOU

Q: *What was Alexander Fleming's hypothesis? How could he test his hypothesis?*

Quick Lab

Purpose To test the hypothesis that bubble making can be affected by adding sugar or salt to a bubble-blowing mixture

Materials
- 3 plastic drinking cups
- measuring cup and spoons
- liquid dish detergent
- water
- table sugar
- table salt
- drinking straw

Bubbles!

Procedure

1. Label three drinking cups 1, 2, and 3. Measure and add one teaspoon of liquid dish detergent to each cup.

2. Use the measuring cup to add two-thirds cup of water to each drinking cup. Then swirl the cups to form a clear mixture. **CAUTION** *Wipe up any spills immediately so that no one will slip and fall.*

3. Add a half teaspoon of table sugar to cup 2 and a half teaspoon of table salt to cup 3. Swirl each cup for one minute.

4. Dip the drinking straw into cup 1, remove it, and blow gently into the straw to make the largest bubble you can. Practice making bubbles until you feel you have reasonable control over your bubble production.

5. Repeat Step 4 with the mixtures in cups 2 and 3.

Analyze and Conclude

1. Observe Did you observe any differences in your ability to produce bubbles using the mixtures in cup 1 and cup 2?

2. Observe Did you observe any differences in your ability to produce bubbles using the mixtures in cup 1 and cup 3?

3. Draw Conclusions What can you conclude about the effects of table sugar and table salt on your ability to produce bubbles?

4. Design an Experiment Propose another hypothesis related to bubble making. Design an experiment to test your hypothesis.

Figure 1.15 Teamwork
For a volleyball team to win, the players must work together.

Collaboration and Communication

What role do collaboration and communication play in science?

No matter how talented the players on a team may be, one player cannot ensure victory for the team. Individuals must collaborate, or work together, for the good of the team. Think about the volleyball players in Figure 1.15. In volleyball, the person who spikes the ball depends on the person who sets the ball. Unless the ball is set properly, the spiker will have limited success. Many sports recognize the importance of collaboration by keeping track of assists. During a volleyball game, the players also communicate with one another so it is clear who is going to do which task. Strategies that are successful in sports can work in other fields, such as science. **When scientists collaborate and communicate with one another, they increase the likelihood of a successful outcome.**

Collaboration Scientists choose to collaborate for different reasons. For example, some research problems are so complex that no one person could have all the knowledge, skills, and resources to solve the problem. It is often necessary to bring together individuals from different disciplines. Each scientist will typically bring different knowledge and, perhaps, a different approach to a problem. Just talking with a scientist from another discipline may provide insights that are helpful.

There may be a practical reason for collaboration. For example, an industry may give a university funding for pure research in an area of interest to the industry. Scientists at the university get the equipment and financing required to do the research. In exchange, the scientists provide ideas and expertise. The industry may profit from its investment by marketing applications based on the research.

Collaboration isn't always a smooth process. Conflicts can arise about use of resources, amount of work, who is to receive credit, and when and what to publish. Like the students in Figure 1.16, you will likely work in pairs or on a team in the laboratory. If so, you may face some challenges. However, you can also experience the benefits of a successful collaboration.

Figure 1.16 Lab Partners
Working in pairs or in a group can be challenging, but it can also be rewarding.
Apply Concepts *What procedure of scientific methodology are these students using?*

Communication The way scientists communicate with each other and with the public has changed over the centuries. In earlier centuries, scientists exchanged ideas through letters. They also formed societies to discuss the latest work of their members. When societies began to publish journals, scientists could use the journals to keep up with new discoveries.

Today, many scientists, like those in Figure 1.17, work as a team. They can communicate face to face. They also can exchange ideas with other scientists by e-mail, by phone, and at local and international conferences. Scientists still publish their results in scientific journals, which are the most reliable source of information about new discoveries. Most journals are now published online and are readily accessible. Articles are published only after being reviewed by experts in the author's field. Reviewers may find errors in experimental design or challenge the author's conclusions. This review process is good for science because work that is not well founded is usually not published.

The Internet is a major source of information. One advantage of the Internet is that anyone can get access to information. One disadvantage is that anyone can post information on the Internet without first having that information reviewed. To judge the reliability of information you find on the Internet, you have to consider the source. This same advice applies to articles in newspapers and magazines or the news you receive from television. If a media outlet has a reporter who specializes in science, chances are better that a report will be accurate.

Figure 1.17 Communication
Scientists often get together at professional meetings and workshops to discuss their findings and share ideas.

1.3 LessonCheck

14. 🔑 **Review** How did Lavoisier revolutionize the science of chemistry?

15. 🔑 **List** What does scientific methodology involve?

16. 🔑 **Explain** Why are collaboration and communication important in science?

17. Describe What did alchemists contribute to the development of chemistry?

18. Explain How did Lavoisier's wife help him to communicate the results of his experiments?

19. Describe What process takes place before an article is published in a scientific journal?

20. Explain Why is it important for scientists to publish a description of their procedures along with the results of their experiments?

21. Infer Why should a hypothesis be developed before experiments take place?

22. Compare What is the difference between a theory and a hypothesis?

23. Classify In Chapter 2, you will learn that matter is neither created nor destroyed in any chemical change. Is this statement a theory or a law? Explain your answer.

BIGIDEA
CHEMISTRY AS THE CENTRAL SCIENCE

24. Do the steps in scientific methodology always need to be followed in the same order? Explain.

Laboratory Safety

Purpose
To demonstrate your knowledge of safe laboratory practices

Procedure

While doing the chemistry experiments in this textbook, you will work
with equipment similar to the equipment shown in the photograph.
Your success, and your safety, will depend on following instructions and
using safe laboratory practices. To test your knowledge of these practices, answer the question after each safety symbol. Refer to the safety
rules in Appendix C and any instructions provided by your teacher.

If you accidentally spill water near electrical equipment, what should you do?

After you clean up your work area, what should you do before leaving the laboratory?

Q: *How does having a plan make solving problems easier?* Have you ever tried to solve a crossword puzzle? If so, you may have found it helpful to develop a strategy before you begin. For example, you may try to fill in all the "down" clues before attempting the "across" clues. Or, you may first try to complete the fill-in-the-blank clues before moving on to the more difficult clues. In chemistry, it is helpful to develop a strategy to solve both numeric and non-numeric problems.

Key Questions

🔑 **What is a general approach to solving a problem?**

🔑 **What are the steps for solving numeric problems?**

🔑 **What are the steps for solving nonnumeric problems?**

Skills Used in Solving Problems

🔑 **What is a general approach to solving a problem?**

Problem solving is a skill you use all the time. You are in a supermarket. Do you buy a name brand or the store brand of peanut butter? Do you buy the 1-liter bottle or the 2-liter bottle of a carbonated beverage? Do you choose the express line if there are five customers ahead of you or the non-express line with a single shopper who has a lot of items?

When you solve a problem, you may have a data table, a graph, or another type of visual to refer to. The shopper in Figure 1.18 is reading the label on a container while trying to decide whether to buy the item. She may need to avoid certain ingredients because of a food allergy. She may also want to know the number of Calories per serving.

The skills you use to solve a word problem in chemistry are not that different from those you use while shopping, cooking, or planning a party. 🔑 **Effective problem solving always involves developing a plan and then implementing that plan.**

Figure 1.18 Problem Solving
A shopper must make many decisions. Some of those decisions are based on data, such as the information on a food label.

Solving Numeric Problems

🔑 What are the steps for solving numeric problems?

Most word problems in chemistry require math because measurement is such an important part of chemistry. The techniques used in this book to solve numeric problems are conveniently organized into a three-step, problem-solving approach. This approach has been shown to be very helpful and effective. We recommend that you follow this approach when working on numeric problems in this textbook. 🔑 **The steps for solving a numeric word problem are analyze, calculate, and evaluate.** Figure 1.19 summarizes the three-step process, and Sample Problem 1.1 on the next page shows how the steps work in solving a numeric problem.

❶ Analyze To solve a word problem, you must first determine where you are starting from (identify what is known) and where you are going (identify what is unknown). What is known may be a measurement or an equation that shows a relationship between measurements. If you expect the answer (the unknown) to be a number, you need to determine what unit(s) the answer should have before you do any calculations.

After you identify the known and the unknown, you need to make a plan for using what is known to arrive at the unknown. Planning is at the heart of successful problem solving. As part of planning, you might draw a diagram that helps you visualize a relationship between the known and the unknown. You might need to use a table or graph to identify data or to identify a relationship between a known quantity and the unknown. You may need to select an equation that you can use to calculate the unknown.

❷ Calculate If you make an effective plan, doing the calculations is usually the easiest part of the process. For some problems, you will have to convert a measurement from one unit to another. For other problems, you may need to rearrange an equation before you can solve for an unknown. You will be taught these math skills as needed.

❸ Evaluate After you calculate an answer, you should evaluate it. Is the answer reasonable? Does it make sense? If not, reread the word problem. Did you copy the data correctly? Did you choose the right equations?

Check that your answer has the correct unit(s) and the correct number of significant figures. You may need to use scientific notation in your answer. You will study significant figures and scientific notation in Chapter 3.

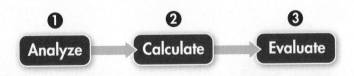

Figure 1.19 Solving Numeric Problems
This flowchart summarizes the steps for solving a numeric problem.
Identify *In which step do you make a plan for getting from what is known to what is unknown?*

READING SUPPORT

Build Reading Skills:
Main Ideas Under the heading Solving Numeric Problems, there are three main ideas presented as subheads. *What are two details that support each main idea?*

SampleProblem 1.1

Estimating Walking Time

You are visiting Indianapolis for the first time. It is a nice day, so you decide to walk from the Indiana State Capital to the Murat Centre for an afternoon performance. According to the map in Figure 1.20 on the next page, the shortest route from the capital to the theater is eight blocks. How many minutes will the trip take if you can walk one mile in 20 minutes? Assume that ten blocks equals one mile.

❶ Analyze List the knowns and the unknown.

This problem is an example of what is typically called a conversion problem. In a conversion problem, one unit of measure (in this case, blocks) must be expressed in a different unit (in this case, minutes).

Divide the distance to be traveled (in blocks) by the number of blocks in one mile to get the distance of the trip in miles. Then multiply the number of miles by the time it takes to walk one mile.

> KNOWNS
> distance to be traveled = 8 blocks
> walking speed = 1 mile/20 minutes
> 1 mile = 10 blocks
>
> UNKNOWN
> time of trip = ? minutes

❷ Calculate Solve for the unknown.

> The relationship 1 mile = 10 blocks can be interpreted as "1 mile per 10 blocks."

Divide the number of blocks to be traveled by the number of blocks in one mile.

$$8\ \text{blocks} \times \frac{1\ \text{mile}}{10\ \text{blocks}} = 0.8\ \text{mile}$$

Multiply the number of miles by the time it takes to walk one mile.

$$0.8\ \text{mile} \times \frac{20\ \text{minutes}}{1\ \text{mile}} = 16\ \text{minutes}$$

> Notice how the units cancel.

❸ Evaluate Does the result make sense?

The answer seems reasonable, 16 minutes to walk eight blocks. The answer has the correct unit. The relationships used are correct.

25. There is an ice cream shop six blocks north of your hotel. How many minutes will it take to walk there and back? Use the information in the sample problem.

> In Problem 25, you must account for both the distance to and from the ice cream shop.

26. Using the information in the sample problem, how many blocks can be walked in 48 minutes?

> In Problem 26, first determine how many miles can be walked in 48 minutes. Then, convert miles to blocks.

Figure 1.20 Reading a Map
Refer to this map of Indianapolis, Indiana, while you do Sample Problem 1.1.

Solving Nonnumeric Problems

🔑 *What are the steps for solving nonnumeric problems?*

Not every word problem in chemistry requires calculations. Some problems ask you to apply the concepts you are studying to a new situation. To solve a nonnumeric problem, you still need to identify what is known and what is unknown. Most importantly, you still need to make a plan for getting from the known to the unknown. If your answer is not a number, you do not need to check the units, make an estimate, or check your calculations.

The three-step problem-solving approach is modified for nonnumeric problems. 🔑 **The steps for solving a nonnumeric problem are analyze and solve.** Problem-solving methods, such as drawing a diagram, creating a flowchart, or building a model, may be useful. Figure 1.21 summarizes the process, and Sample Problem 1.2 on the next page shows how the steps work in an actual problem.

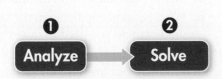

CHEMISTRY & YOU

Q: *Pick a game you like to play or a type of puzzle you enjoy solving. How does having a plan make playing the game or solving the puzzle easier?*

Figure 1.21 Solving Nonnumeric Problems
This flowchart summarizes the steps for solving a nonnumeric problem.
Compare *With a nonnumeric problem, why is the second step called* solve, *rather than* calculate?

SampleProblem 1.2

Scheduling Classes

Manny needs to schedule his classes for next year. The school day is divided into seven periods, and he must take Algebra II, Art, Chemistry, English, History, and Physical Education. Using the information from the course catalog, find a way for Manny to schedule all his classes.

✔ Algebra II is offered during either 1st or 2nd period.
✔ Art is offered during 2nd period only.
✔ Chemistry is offered during either 3rd or 6th period.
✔ English is offered during either 6th or 7th period.
✔ History is offered during either 4th or 7th period.
✔ Physical Education is offered during 4th period only.
✔ Lunch is scheduled for 5th period.

❶ Analyze Identify the relevant concepts.
Manny must take lunch during 5th period. Art is only available during 2nd period. Physical Education is only available during 4th period.

❷ Solve Apply the concepts to this problem.

> Since Art is only available during 2nd period, Manny must take Algebra II during 1st period. Since P.E. is only available during 4th period, he must take History during 7th period.

Place lunch, Art, and Physical Education into Manny's schedule.

Manny's Schedule	
1st period	
2nd period	Art
3rd period	
4th period	P.E.
5th period	Lunch
6th period	
7th period	

Fit the remainder of the classes into Manny's schedule.

Manny's Schedule	
1st period	Algebra II
2nd period	Art
3rd period	Chemistry
4th period	P.E.
5th period	Lunch
6th period	English
7th period	History

27. How would Manny's schedule change if Art was available during 1st period, instead of 2nd period?

28. Would Manny's schedule change if Algebra II was available during 1st, 2nd, and 3rd periods? Explain.

1.4 LessonCheck

29. 🔑 **Review** What are the two general steps in successful problem solving?

30. 🔑 **List** What are the three steps for solving numeric problems?

31. 🔑 **List** What are the two steps for solving nonnumeric problems?

32. Compare and Contrast How are the processes for solving numeric and nonnumeric problems similar? In what way are they different?

33. Calculate Read the following conversion problem, and then answer the questions. "There are 3600 seconds in an hour. How many seconds are there in one day?"

a. Identify the known and the unknown.

b. What relationship between the known and unknown do you need to solve the problem?

c. Calculate the answer to the problem.

d. Evaluate your answer and explain why your answer makes sense.

1 Study Guide

BIG IDEA
CHEMISTRY AS THE CENTRAL SCIENCE

It is important to study chemistry because chemistry is fundamental to the understanding of the other sciences. Chemistry is relevant to many professions. A knowledge of chemistry can help you become an informed citizen. Chemists use scientific methodology to solve problems and develop theories about the natural world.

1.1 The Scope of Chemistry

Chemistry affects all aspects of life and most natural events because all living and nonliving things are made of matter.

Five traditional areas of study are organic chemistry, inorganic chemistry, biochemistry, analytical chemistry, and physical chemistry.

Some of chemistry's big ideas are as follows: chemistry as the central science, electrons and the structure of atoms, bonding and interactions, reactions, kinetic theory, the mole and quantifying matter, matter and energy, and carbon chemistry.

- matter (2)
- chemistry (2)
- organic chemistry (3)
- inorganic chemistry (3)
- biochemistry (3)
- analytical chemistry (3)
- physical chemistry (3)
- pure chemistry (3)
- applied chemistry (3)

1.2 Chemistry and You

Chemistry can be useful in explaining the natural world, preparing people for career opportunities, and producing informed citizens.

Modern research in chemistry can lead to technologies that aim to benefit the environment, conserve and produce energy, improve human life, and expand our knowledge of the universe.

- technology (8)

1.3 Thinking Like a Scientist

Lavoisier helped to transform chemistry from a science of observation to the science of measurement that it is today.

Scientific methodology involves making observations, proposing and testing hypotheses, and developing theories.

When scientists collaborate and communicate with one another, they increase the likelihood of a successful outcome.

- observation (15)
- hypothesis (16)
- experiment (16)
- independent variable (16)
- dependent variable (16)
- model (16)
- theory (17)
- scientific law (17)

1.4 Problem Solving in Chemistry

Effective problem solving always involves developing a plan and then implementing that plan.

The steps for solving a numeric word problem are analyze, calculate, and evaluate.

The steps for solving a nonnumeric problem are analyze and solve.

Lesson by Lesson

1.1 The Scope of Chemistry

34. Explain why air is classified as matter.

⋆**35.** The Chinese characters for chemistry literally mean "change study." Why are these appropriate characters to represent chemistry?

36. Describe the main difference between inorganic chemistry and organic chemistry.

⋆**37.** Is a scientist who is studying cancer with the goal of finding an effective treatment doing pure research or applied research?

1.2 Chemistry and You

⋆**38.** Why would a firefighter or a reporter need to understand chemistry?

39. What are some products that could be made from the bioplastic polylactic acid (PLA)?

40. How do chemists help doctors treat patients?

41. What is the overall goal of biochemists who work in the field of medicine?

⋆**42.** How can scientists study the composition of distant stars?

1.3 Thinking Like a Scientist

43. What did the scientists who founded the Royal Society of London have in common with Lavoisier?

⋆**44.** What is the most powerful tool that any scientist can have?

45. What is the purpose of an experiment?

⋆**46.** Which of the following is not involved in scientific methodology?
  a. hypothesis　　**c.** guess
  b. experiment　　**d.** theory

47. How do an independent variable and a dependent variable differ?

⋆**48.** You perform an experiment and get unexpected results. According to scientific methodology, what should you do next?

⋆**49.** Explain how the results of many experiments can lead to both a theory and a scientific law.

50. List two general reasons why scientists are likely to collaborate.

1.4 Problem Solving in Chemistry

⋆**51.** Identify the statements that correctly describe good problem solvers.
  a. read a problem only once
  b. check their work
  c. look up missing facts
  d. look for relationships among the data

52. What do effective problem-solving strategies have in common?

53. In which step of the three-step problem-solving approach for numeric problems is a problem-solving strategy developed?

⋆**54.** On average, a baseball team wins two out of every three games it plays. How many games will this team lose in a 162-game season?

55. If your heart beats at an average rate of 72 times per minute, how many times will your heart beat in an hour? In a day?

⋆**56.** How many days would it take you to count a million pennies if you could count one penny each second?

Understand Concepts

⋆**57.** Match each area of chemistry with a numbered statement.
  a. physical chemistry　　**d.** inorganic chemistry
  b. organic chemistry　　　**e.** biochemistry
  c. analytical chemistry

  (1) measure the level of lead in blood
  (2) study non-carbon-based chemicals in rocks
  (3) investigate changes that occur as food is digested in the stomach
  (4) study carbon-based chemicals in coal
  (5) explain the energy transfer that occurs when ice melts

Use this photograph of the runner to answer Questions 58 and 59.

*58. Explain how chemistry has affected the ability of this athlete to compete.

59. What type of chemist might study how an athlete uses energy during a competition? Give a reason for your answer.

60. Explain why chemistry might be useful in a career you are thinking of pursuing.

*61. A doctor examines a patient's sore throat and suggests that the patient has strep throat. She takes a sample to test for the bacteria that cause strep throat. What procedures of scientific methodology is the doctor applying?

*62. You perform an experiment and find that the results do not agree with an accepted theory. Should you conclude that you made an error in your procedure? Explain.

63. A student is planning a science fair project called "Does Temperature Affect How High a Basketball Can Bounce?"
   a. Based on the project title, identify the independent variable and the dependent variable.
   b. Name at least two factors that would need to be kept constant during the experiment.

64. Describe a situation in which you used at least two procedures of scientific methodology to solve a problem.

*65. Pure water freezes at 0°C. A student wanted to test the effect of adding table salt to the water. The table shows the data that was collected.

Effect of Salt on Freezing Point of Water	
Salt Added	**Freezing Point**
5 g	−4.8°C
10 g	−9.7°C
15 g	−15.1°C
20 g	−15.0°C

   a. What was the independent variable?
   b. What was the dependent variable?
   c. Why must the volume of water be the same for each test?
   d. Based on the data, the student hypothesized, "As more salt is added to water, the temperature at which water freezes decreases." Is this hypothesis supported by the data? Explain.

*66. In the time a person on a bicycle travels 4 miles, a person in a car travels 30 miles. Assuming a constant speed, how far will the car travel while the bicycle travels 40 miles?

Think Critically

67. **Compare and Contrast** How is the study of chemistry similar to the study of a language? How is it different?

68. **Infer** Comment on the idea that science accepts what works and rejects what does not work.

69. **Apply Concepts** You are asked to design an experiment to answer the question: "Which paper towel is the best?"
   a. What is the independent variable in your experiment?
   b. List three possible dependent variables that could be used to define "best."
   c. Pick one of the dependent variables and rewrite the question as a hypothesis.
   d. List at least five factors that must be kept constant when you test the hypothesis.

*70. **Compare** Important discoveries in science are sometimes the result of an accident. Louis Pasteur said, "Chance favors the prepared mind." Explain how both of these statements can be true.

*71. **Calculate** Four beakers have a total weight of 2.0 lb. Each beaker weighs 0.5 lb. Describe two different methods you could use to calculate the weight of two beakers. Then try both methods and compare the answers.

*72. **Apply Concepts** Explain what is wrong with the statement, "Theories are proven by experiments."

*73. **Interpret Diagrams** The air you breathe is composed of about 20% oxygen and 80% nitrogen. Use your problem-solving skills to decide which drawing best represents a sample of air. Explain your choice.

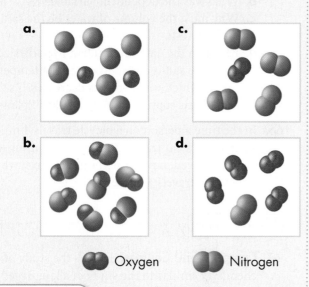

Oxygen   Nitrogen

Enrichment

74. **Calculate** A certain ball, when dropped from any height, bounces one-half the original height. If the ball was dropped from a height of 60 inches and allowed to bounce freely, what is the total distance the ball has traveled when it hits the ground for the third time? Assume the ball bounces straight up and down.

*75. **Calculate** Eggs are shipped from a farm to a market by truck. They are packed 12 eggs to a carton and 20 cartons to a box. Four boxes are placed in each crate. Crates are stacked on a truck 5 crates wide, 6 crates deep, and 5 crates high. How many eggs are on the truck?

76. **Analyze Data** An oil tanker containing 4,000,000 barrels of oil is emptied at the rate of 5000 gallons per minute. What information do you need to figure out how long it would take to empty the tanker?

*77. **Calculate** A crate of envelopes sells for $576.00. A package of envelopes contains 250 envelopes. Six packages are packed inside a carton. Twelve cartons are packed in a box. Eight boxes are packed in a crate.
   a. What does a package of envelopes cost?
   b. What fact given in the problem was not needed to calculate the answer?

Write About Science

78. **Explain** Pick one activity that you can do faster or with less effort because of technology. Write a paragraph in which you describe the activity, identify the technology, and explain how the technology affects the activity.

79. **Relate Cause and Effect** Write a paragraph explaining how you can learn about the research that is done by scientists. Then explain how this information could help you be an informed citizen.

CHEMYSTERY

Is Bio Better?

When you return home from the store, you go online and search for "bioplastics." You learn that the products you found at the store were most likely made from polylactic acid (PLA). You like that the PLA products come from natural resources, such as corn, and that less energy is used in making PLA than other plastics. However, you are concerned that it would be difficult to find a facility that would be able to compost the cups and utensils when you and your friends are finished with them.

*80. **Relate Cause and Effect** What factors will affect your decision as to whether to purchase the picnic products made from PLA? Explain.

81. **Connect to the BIGIDEA** How would a knowledge of chemistry help you make an informed decision?

Standardized Test Prep

Select the choice that best answers each question or completes each statement.

1. The branch of chemistry that studies chemicals containing carbon is _____ chemistry.
   (A) physical
   (B) inorganic
   (C) analytical
   (D) organic

2. An analytical chemist is most likely to
   (A) explain why paint is stirred before it is used.
   (B) explain what keeps paint attached to the steel frame of an automobile.
   (C) identify the type of paint chips found at the scene of a hit-and-run accident.
   (D) investigate the effect of leaded paint on the development of a young child.

3. Chemists who work in the biotechnology field are most likely to work with
   (A) X-ray technicians.
   (B) geologists.
   (C) physicians.
   (D) physicists.

Respond to each statement in Questions 4–6.

4. Someone who wears contact lenses does not have to wear safety goggles in the lab.

5. Eating food that is left over from an experiment is an alternative to discarding the food.

6. For a student who has read the procedure, the teacher's pre-lab instructions are unnecessary.

Use the flowchart to answer Question 7.

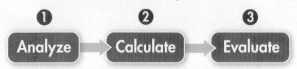

7. What should you do before you calculate an answer to a numeric problem, and what should you do after you calculate the answer?

Use this paragraph to answer Questions 8–10.

(A) One day, your car doesn't start. (B) You say, "The battery is dead!" (C) Your friend uses a battery tester and finds that the battery has a full charge. (D) Your friend sees rust on the battery terminals. (E) Your friend says, "Maybe rust is causing a bad connection in the electrical circuit, preventing the car from starting." (F) Your friend cleans the terminals, and the car starts.

8. Which statements are observations?

9. Which statements are hypotheses?

10. Which statements describe experiments?

Tips for Success

True-False Questions When the word *because* is placed between two statements, you must first decide if the statements are both true, both false, or if one statement is true and the other false. If both are true, you must decide if the second statement is a correct explanation for the first.

For each question, there are two statements. Decide whether each statement is true or false. Then decide whether Statement II is a correct explanation for Statement I.

Statement I		Statement II
11. A hypothesis may be rejected after an experiment.	BECAUSE	Experiments are used to test hypotheses.
12. Theories help you make mental models of objects that cannot be seen.	BECAUSE	Theories summarize the results of many observations and experiments.
13. All Internet sites that provide scientific information are equally reliable.	BECAUSE	All information on these sites is reviewed by qualified scientists.

If You Have Trouble With . . .

Question	1	2	3	4	5	6	7	8	9	10	11	12	13
See Lesson	1.1	1.1	1.2	1.3	1.3	1.3	1.4	1.3	1.3	1.3	1.3	1.3	1.3

2

Matter and Change

INSIDE:

- **2.1** Properties of Matter
- **2.2** Mixtures
- **2.3** Elements and Compounds
- **2.4** Chemical Reactions

PearsonChem.com

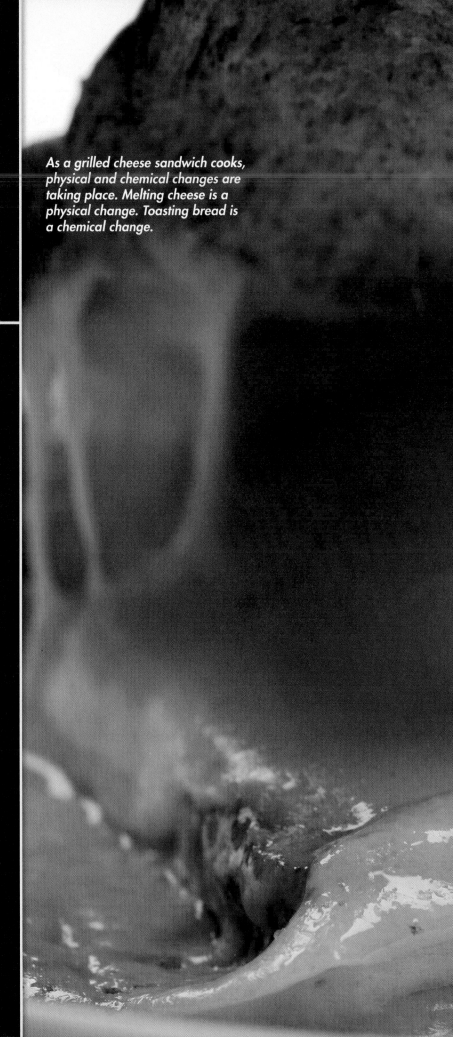

As a grilled cheese sandwich cooks, physical and chemical changes are taking place. Melting cheese is a physical change. Toasting bread is a chemical change.

CHEMYSTERY

Which One Is Not Like the Others?

In Yellowstone National Park, there are more than 300 geysers. If you are able to witness a geyser erupting, you will see water and steam shooting out of the ground.

In Glacier National Park, the bottoms of glaciers go through melting and freezing cycles. These cycles produce valleys that are scoured into a U-shape and are flanked by steep sides of earth.

In Acadia National Park, the leaves on the deciduous trees change color each fall. The leaves go from green to red, orange, or yellow.

All three of these sights are amazing to see. They all result from changes. Are they physical or chemical changes? One of them is not like the others. But which one is different, and why?

▶ **Connect to the BIGIDEA** As you read about matter, think about how matter is altered by physical and chemical changes.

NATIONAL SCIENCE EDUCATION STANDARDS

A-1, B-2, B-3, E-2, G-3

2.1 Properties of Matter

Q: *Why are windows made of glass?* When you think of a window, you probably think of something that you can look through. Most windows are made of glass and are transparent, meaning you can see through them. If you found a piece of broken glass on the ground, you would probably recognize it as glass. It is hard, yet easy to shatter, and it is heat resistant. In this lesson, you will learn how properties can be used to classify and identify matter.

Key Questions

🔑 Why do all samples of a substance have the same intensive properties?

🔑 What are three states of matter?

🔑 How can physical changes be classified?

Vocabulary

- mass
- volume
- extensive property
- intensive property
- substance
- physical property
- solid
- liquid
- gas
- vapor
- physical change

Describing Matter

🔑 **Why do all samples of a substance have the same intensive properties?**

Understanding matter begins with observation, and what you observe when you look at a particular sample of matter is its properties. Is a solid shiny or dull? Does a liquid flow quickly or slowly? Is a gas odorless, or does it have a smell? Properties used to describe matter can be classified as extensive or intensive properties.

Extensive Properties Recall that matter is anything that has mass and takes up space. The **mass** of an object is a measure of the amount of matter the object contains. The mass of the basketball in Figure 2.1 is greater than the mass of the golf ball. There is also a difference in the volume of the balls. The **volume** of an object is a measure of the space occupied by the object. The volume of the basketball is greater than the volume of the golf ball. Mass and volume are both examples of extensive properties. An **extensive property** is a property that depends on the amount of matter in a sample.

Intensive Properties Basketballs may appear to be all the same. But, there are properties to consider when selecting a basketball besides mass and volume. The outer covering may be made of leather, rubber, or a synthetic composite. Each of these materials has different properties which make the basketballs suitable for different playing situations. For example, leather balls are suitable for indoor play but not outdoor play. Leather balls absorb water and dirt more than rubber balls. Absorbancy is an example of an intensive property. An **intensive property** is a property that depends on the type of matter in a sample, not the amount of matter.

Figure 2.1 Extensive Properties
Golf balls and basketballs have different masses and different volumes.

Identifying a Substance Each object in Figure 2.2 has a different chemical makeup, or composition. The soda can is mainly aluminum. The watering can is mainly copper. Matter that has a uniform and definite composition is called a **substance.** Aluminum and copper are examples of substances, which are also referred to as *pure substances.* 🔑 **Every sample of a given substance has identical intensive properties because every sample has the same composition.**

Aluminum and copper have some properties in common, but there are differences besides their distinctive colors. Aluminum is highly reflective and is often used in silver paints. Pure copper can scratch the surface of pure aluminum because copper is harder than aluminum. Copper is better than aluminum as a conductor of heat or electric current. Copper and aluminum are both malleable, which means they can be hammered into sheets without breaking. Hardness, color, conductivity, and malleability are examples of physical properties. A **physical property** is a quality or condition of a substance that can be observed or measured without changing the substance's composition.

Table 2.1 lists physical properties for some substances. The states of the substances are given at room temperature. (Although scientists use room temperature to refer to a range of temperatures, in this book it will be used to refer to a specific temperature, 20°C.) Physical properties can help chemists identify substances. For example, a colorless substance that was found to boil at 100°C and melt at 0°C would likely be water. A colorless substance that boiled at 78°C and melted at −117°C would definitely not be water. Based on Table 2.1, it would likely be ethanol.

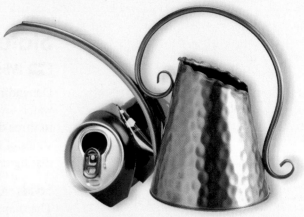

Figure 2.2 Aluminum and Copper
This soda can is made almost entirely of a thin sheet of aluminum. The watering can is made of copper, which has been hammered to give its textured appearance.
Analyze Data *Which of the properties listed in Table 2.1 could not be used to distinguish copper from aluminum?*

Q: *Glass is often used to make windows, while copper is often used in electrical wires. What properties of glass make it a desirable material to use for windows?*

Interpret Data

Physical Properties of Some Substances				
Substance	**State**	**Color**	**Melting point (°C)**	**Boiling point (°C)**
Neon	Gas	Colorless	−249	−246
Oxygen	Gas	Colorless	−218	−183
Chlorine	Gas	Greenish-yellow	−101	−34
Ethanol	Liquid	Colorless	−117	78
Mercury	Liquid	Silvery-white	−39	357
Bromine	Liquid	Reddish-brown	−7	59
Water	Liquid	Colorless	0	100
Sulfur	Solid	Yellow	115	445
Aluminum	Solid	Silver	660	2519
Sodium chloride	Solid	White	801	1413
Gold	Solid	Yellow	1064	2856
Copper	Solid	Reddish-yellow	1084	2562

Table 2.1 A substance can be described and identified by its physical properties.
a. Identify Which property can most easily distinguish chlorine from the other gases?
b. Identify A colorless liquid boils at 40°C. Is the substance water? Why or why not?
c. Calculate Which of the liquid substances has the highest melting point? The lowest boiling point?
d. Draw Conclusions Which of the properties would be the most helpful in identifying an unknown substance?

States of Matter

What are three states of matter?

Depending on the circumstances, you use three different words to refer to water—water, ice, and steam. Water, which is a common substance, exists in three different physical states. So can most other substances. **Three states of matter are solid, liquid, and gas.** Certain characteristics that can distinguish these three states of matter are summarized in Figure 2.3.

Solids A **solid** is a form of matter that has a definite shape and volume. The shape of a solid doesn't depend on the shape of its container. The particles in a solid are packed tightly together, often in an orderly arrangement, as shown in Figure 2.3a. As a result, solids are almost incompressible; that is, it is difficult to squeeze a solid into a smaller volume. In addition, solids expand only slightly when heated.

Liquids Look at Figure 2.3b. The particles in a liquid are in close contact with one another, but the arrangement of particles in a liquid is not rigid or orderly. Because the particles in a liquid are free to flow from one location to another, a liquid takes the shape of the container in which it is placed. However, the volume of the liquid doesn't change as its shape changes. The volume of a liquid is fixed or constant. Thus, a **liquid** is a form of matter that has an indefinite shape, flows, yet has a fixed volume. Liquids are almost incompressible, but they tend to expand slightly when heated.

Figure 2.3
The arrangement of particles is different in solids, liquids, and gases.
Relate Cause and Effect *Use the arrangements of their particles to explain the general shape and volume of solids and gases.*

See states of matter animated online.

KINETIC ART

Solid In a solid, the particles are packed closely together in a rigid arrangement.

Liquid In a liquid, the particles are close together, but they are free to flow past one another.

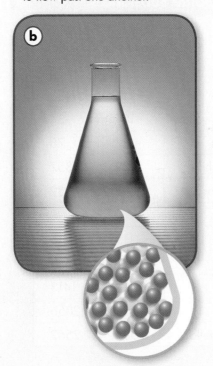

Gas In a gas, the particles are relatively far apart and can move freely.

Gases Like a liquid, a gas takes the shape of its container. But unlike a liquid, a gas can expand to fill any volume. A **gas** is a form of matter that takes both the shape and volume of its container. Look back at Figure 2.3c. As shown in the model, the particles in a gas are usually much farther apart than the particles in a liquid. Because of the space between particles, gases are easily compressed into a smaller volume.

The words *vapor* and *gas* are sometimes used interchangeably. But there is a difference. The term *gas* is used for substances, like oxygen, that exist in the gaseous state at room temperature. (*Gaseous* is the adjective form of *gas.*) **Vapor** describes the gaseous state of a substance that is generally a liquid or solid at room temperature, as in *water vapor.*

Physical Changes

🗝 *How can physical changes be classified?*

The melting point of gallium metal is 30°C. Figure 2.4 shows how heat from a person's hand can melt a sample of gallium. The shape of the sample changes during melting as the liquid begins to flow, but the composition of the sample does not change. Melting is a physical change. During a **physical change,** some properties of a material change, but the composition of the material does not change.

Words such as *boil, freeze, melt,* and *condense* are used to describe physical changes. So are words such as *break, split, grind, cut,* and *crush.* However, there is a difference between these two sets of words. Each set describes a different type of physical change. 🗝 **Physical changes can be classified as reversible or irreversible.** Melting is an example of a reversible physical change. If a sample of liquid gallium is cooled below its melting point, the liquid will become a solid. All physical changes that involve a change from one state to another are reversible. Cutting hair, filing nails, and cracking an egg are examples of irreversible physical changes.

Figure 2.4 Physical Change
The silvery substance in the photograph is gallium, which has a melting point of 30°C.
Infer *What can you infer about the temperature of the hand holding the gallium?*

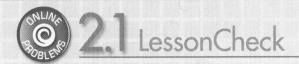

2.1 LessonCheck

1. 🗝 **Explain** Explain why all samples of a given substance have the same intensive properties.

2. 🗝 **Identify** Name three states of matter.

3. 🗝 **Describe** Describe the two categories used to classify physical changes.

4. **Identify** Name two categories used to classify properties of matter.

5. **Interpret Tables** Which property in Table 2.1 can most easily distinguish sodium chloride from the other solids?

6. **Compare and Contrast** In what way are liquids and gases alike? In what way are liquids and solids different?

7. **Explain** Is the freezing of mercury a reversible or irreversible physical change? Explain your answer.

8. **Explain** Explain why samples of platinum and copper can have the same extensive properties but not the same intensive properties.

BIGIDEA
CHEMISTRY AS THE CENTRAL SCIENCE

9. How would understanding the properties of matter be helpful in other fields of study besides chemistry?

2.2 Mixtures

Q: *Why aren't there coffee grounds in a cup of coffee?* Coffee is often brewed by mixing hot water with ground coffee beans. But when people drink coffee, the grounds are usually not in their mug. In this lesson, you will learn how to classify and separate mixtures.

Key Questions

🔑 How can mixtures be classified?

🔑 How can mixtures be separated?

Vocabulary

• mixture
• heterogeneous mixture
• homogeneous mixture
• solution
• phase
• filtration
• distillation

Classifying Mixtures

🔑 *How can mixtures be classified?*

A salad bar, like the one in Figure 2.5, provides a range of items, such as lettuce, tomatoes, cheese, and green peppers. Customers choose which items to use in their salads and how much of each item to use. So each salad mixture has different types and amounts of components. A **mixture** is a physical blend of two or more components.

Most samples of matter are mixtures. Some mixtures are easier to recognize than others. You can easily recognize chicken noodle soup as a mixture of chicken, noodles, and broth. Recognizing air as a mixture of gases is more difficult. But the fact that air can be drier or more humid shows that the amount of one component of air—water vapor—can vary. Chicken noodle soup and air represent two different types of mixtures. 🔑 **Based on the distribution of their components, mixtures can be classified as heterogeneous mixtures or as homogeneous mixtures.**

**Figure 2.5
Salads Are Mixtures**
You can choose the amount of each item you select from a salad bar. So your salad is unlikely to have the same composition as other salads containing the same items.

Quick Lab

Purpose To separate a mixture using paper chromatography

Materials

- green marking pen
- filter paper strip
- metric ruler
- clear plastic tape
- pencil
- rubbing alcohol
- clear plastic drinking cup
- clear plastic wrap

Separating Mixtures

Procedure

1. Use the marking pen to draw a line across a strip of filter paper, as shown in the drawing. The line should be 2 cm from one end of the strip.

2. Tape the unmarked end of the filter paper to the center of a pencil so that the strip hangs down when the pencil is held horizontally, as shown in the diagram below.

3. Working in a well-ventilated room, pour rubbing alcohol into a plastic cup to a depth of 1 cm.

4. Rest the pencil on the rim of the cup so that the ink end of the strip touches the rubbing alcohol but does not extend below its surface. Use plastic wrap to cover the top of the cup.

5. Observe the setup for 15 minutes.

Analyze and Conclude

1. Identify How did the appearance of the filter paper change during the procedure?

2. Analyze Data What evidence is there that green ink is a mixture?

3. Apply Concepts How could you use this procedure to identify an unknown type of green ink?

Heterogeneous Mixtures In chicken noodle soup, the ingredients in the soup are not evenly distributed throughout the mixture. There is likely to be different amounts of chicken and noodles in each spoonful. A mixture in which the composition is not uniform throughout is a **heterogeneous mixture.**

Homogeneous Mixtures The substances in the olive oil in Figure 2.6 are evenly distributed throughout the mixture. So, olive oil doesn't look like a mixture. The same is true for vinegar. Vinegar is a mixture of water and acetic acid, which dissolves in the water. Olive oil and vinegar are homogeneous mixtures. A **homogeneous mixture** is a mixture in which the composition is uniform throughout. Another name for a homogeneous mixture is a **solution.** Many solutions are liquids. But some are gases, like air, and some are solids, like stainless steel, which is a mixture of iron, chromium, and nickel.

The term **phase** is used to describe any part of a sample with uniform composition and properties. By definition, a homogeneous mixture consists of a single phase. A heterogeneous mixture consists of two or more phases. When oil and vinegar are mixed, they form a heterogeneous mixture with two layers, or phases. As shown in Figure 2.6, the oil phase floats on the water, or vinegar, phase.

Figure 2.6 Homogeneous Mixtures
Olive oil and vinegar are homogeneous mixtures. The substances in these mixtures are evenly distributed. When olive oil and vinegar are mixed, they form a heterogeneous mixture with two distinct phases.

Separating Mixtures

How can mixtures be separated?

If you have a salad containing an ingredient you don't like, you can use a fork to remove the pieces of the unwanted ingredient. Many mixtures are not as easy to separate. To separate a mixture of olive oil and vinegar, for example, you could decant, or pour off, the oil layer. Or you might cool the mixture until the oil turned solid. The first method takes advantage of the fact that oil floats on water. The second method takes advantage of a difference in the temperatures at which the olive oil and vinegar freeze. **Differences in physical properties can be used to separate mixtures.**

Filtration The coffee filter in Figure 2.7 can separate ground coffee beans from brewed coffee. The liquid brewed coffee passes through the paper filter, but the solid coffee grounds cannot pass through the filter. Filter paper used in a laboratory is similar to coffee filters. Filter paper is often placed in a funnel. Then the mixture is poured into the funnel. Solid particles that cannot pass through the filter remain in the funnel. The rest of the particles in solution pass through the filter paper. The process that separates a solid from the liquid in a heterogeneous mixture is called **filtration.**

Distillation Tap water is a homogeneous mixture of water and substances that are dissolved in the water. One way to separate water from the other components in tap water is through a process called distillation. During a **distillation,** a liquid is boiled to produce a vapor that is then condensed into a liquid. Figure 2.8 shows an apparatus that can be used to perform a small-scale distillation.

As water in the distillation flask is heated, water vapor forms, rises in the flask, and passes into a glass tube in the condenser. The tube is surrounded by cold water, which cools the vapor to a temperature at which it turns back into a liquid. The liquid water is collected in a second flask. The solid substances that were dissolved in the water remain in the distillation flask because their boiling points are much higher than the boiling point of water.

Figure 2.7 Filtration
A filter is used to separate ground coffee beans from brewed coffee. This process is a type of filtration.

Q: *Brewing coffee is a mixture of ground coffee beans and water. What process is used to separate ground coffee beans from brewed coffee?*

Figure 2.8 Distillation
A distillation can be used to remove impurities from water. As liquid water changes into water vapor, substances dissolved in the water are left behind in the distillation flask.

See distillation *animated online.*

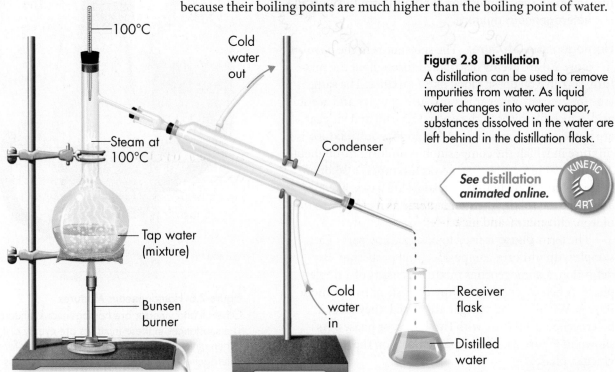

Sample Problem 2.1

Separating a Heterogeneous Mixture

How could a mixture of aluminum nails and iron nails be separated?

❶ Analyze **Identify the relevant concepts.** In order to identify how to separate aluminum and iron nails, the properties of both aluminum and iron must be known.

❷ Solve **Apply concepts to this situation.**

List the properties of each substance in the mixture.

Aluminum
- metal
- gray color
- doesn't dissolve in water
- not attracted to magnet

Iron
- metal
- gray color
- doesn't dissolve in water
- attracted to magnet

Identify a property that can be used to separate different substances from each other.

The ability to be attracted by a magnet is a property that iron and aluminum do not share. You could use a magnet to remove the iron nails from a mixture of iron and aluminum.

10. What physical properties could be used to separate iron filings from table salt?

11. Air is mainly a mixture of nitrogen and oxygen, with small amounts of other gases such as argon and carbon dioxide. What property could you use to separate the gases in air?

2.2 LessonCheck

12. 🔑 **Identify** How are mixtures classified?

13. 🔑 **List** What type of properties can be used to separate mixtures?

14. **Explain** Explain the term *phase* as it relates to homogeneous and heterogeneous mixtures.

15. **Classify** Classify each of the following as a homogeneous or heterogeneous mixture.
   a. food coloring
   b. ice cubes in liquid water
   c. mouthwash
   d. mashed, unpeeled potatoes

16. **Compare and Contrast** How are a substance and a solution similar? How are they different?

17. **Apply Concepts** In general, when would you use filtration to separate a mixture? When would you use distillation to separate a mixture?

18. **Explain** Describe a procedure that could be used to separate a mixture of sand and table salt.

BIGIDEA

CHEMISTRY AS THE CENTRAL SCIENCE

19. Give three examples of when you have separated mixtures at home.

2.3 Elements and Compounds

Q: *Why does burned toast taste so bad?* Bread that is toasted to a nice golden brown makes for a tasty addition to breakfast. But most people would agree that bread that is cooked so long that it is burned and black is not tasty.

Distinguishing Elements and Compounds

🔑 *How are elements and compounds different?*

Substances can be classified as elements or compounds. An **element** is the simplest form of matter that has a unique set of properties. Oxygen and hydrogen are two of the more than 100 known elements. A **compound** is a substance that contains two or more elements chemically combined in a fixed proportion. For example, carbon, oxygen, and hydrogen are chemically combined in the compound sucrose. Sometimes sucrose is called table sugar to distinguish it from other sugar compounds. In every sample of sucrose, there are twice as many hydrogen particles as oxygen particles. The proportion of hydrogen particles to oxygen particles in sucrose is fixed. There is a key difference between elements and compounds. 🔑 **Compounds can be broken down into simpler substances by chemical means, but elements cannot.**

Breaking Down Compounds Physical methods that are used to separate mixtures cannot be used to break a compound into simpler substances. Boil liquid water and you get water vapor, not the oxygen and hydrogen that water contains. Dissolve a sugar cube in water and you still have sucrose, not oxygen, carbon, and hydrogen. This result does not mean that sucrose or water cannot be broken down into simpler substances. But the methods must involve a chemical change.

Key Questions

🔑 How are elements and compounds different?

🔑 How can substances and mixtures be distinguished?

🔑 What do chemists use to represent elements and compounds?

🔑 Why is a periodic table useful?

Vocabulary

- element
- compound
- chemical change
- chemical symbol
- periodic table
- period
- group

**Figure 2.9
Chemical Changes**
When table sugar is heated, it goes through a series of chemical changes. The final products of these changes are solid carbon and water vapor.

A **chemical change** is a change that produces matter with a different composition than the original matter. Heating is one of the processes used to break down compounds into simpler substances. The layer of sugar in Figure 2.9 is heated in a skillet until it breaks down into solid carbon and water vapor. Can the substances that are produced also be broken down?

There is no chemical process that will break down carbon into simpler substances because carbon is an element. Heat will not cause water to break down, but electricity will. When an electric current passes through water, oxygen gas and hydrogen gas are produced. The following diagram summarizes the overall process.

CHEMISTRY & YOU

Q: *What happens to the compounds in bread when it is overcooked that causes the changes to the taste of the bread?*

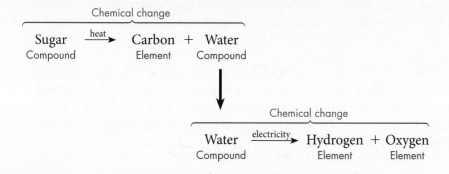

Chemical change

Sugar $\xrightarrow{\text{heat}}$ Carbon + Water
Compound   Element   Compound

Chemical change

Water $\xrightarrow{\text{electricity}}$ Hydrogen + Oxygen
Compound   Element   Element

Properties of Compounds In general, the properties of compounds are quite different from those of their component elements. Sugar is a sweet-tasting, white solid, but carbon is a black, tasteless solid. Hydrogen is a gas that burns in the presence of oxygen—a colorless gas that supports burning. The product of this chemical change is water, a liquid that can stop materials from burning. Figure 2.10 shows samples of table salt (sodium chloride), sodium, and chlorine. When the elements sodium and chlorine combine chemically to form sodium chloride, there is a change in composition and a change in properties. Sodium is a soft, gray metal. Chlorine is a pale yellow-green poisonous gas. Sodium chloride is a white solid.

Figure 2.10 Properties of Compounds and Their Elements Compounds and the elements from which they form have different properties. The elements sodium and chlorine have different properties from each other and from the compound sodium chloride.
Observe *Based on the photographs, describe two physical properties of sodium and two of chlorine.*

Sodium is stored under oil to keep it from reacting with oxygen or water vapor in air. Sodium vapor produces the light in some street lamps.

Chlorine is used to make compounds that kill harmful organisms in swimming pools.

Sodium chloride (commonly known as table salt) is a compound used to season or preserve food.

Distinguishing Substances and Mixtures

🔑 How can substances and mixtures be distinguished?

Deciding whether a sample of matter is a substance or a mixture based solely on appearance can be difficult. After all, homogeneous mixtures and substances will both appear to contain only one kind of matter. Sometimes you can decide by considering whether there is more than one version of the material in question. For example, you can buy whole milk, low-fat milk, no-fat milk, light cream, or heavy cream. From this information, you can conclude that milk and cream are mixtures. You might infer that these mixtures differ in the amount of fat they contain. Most gas stations offer at least two blends of gasoline. The blends have different octane ratings and different costs per gallon, with premium blends costing more than regular blends. So gasoline must be a mixture.

You can use their general characteristics to distinguish substances from mixtures. 🔑 **If the composition of a material is fixed, the material is a substance. If the composition of a material may vary, the material is a mixture.** Figure 2.11 summarizes the general characteristics of elements, compounds, and mixtures.

Figure 2.11 Element, Compound, or Mixture?
The flowchart summarizes the process for classifying matter. Any sample of matter is either an element, a compound, or a mixture.
Interpret Diagrams
What is the key difference between a substance and a solution?

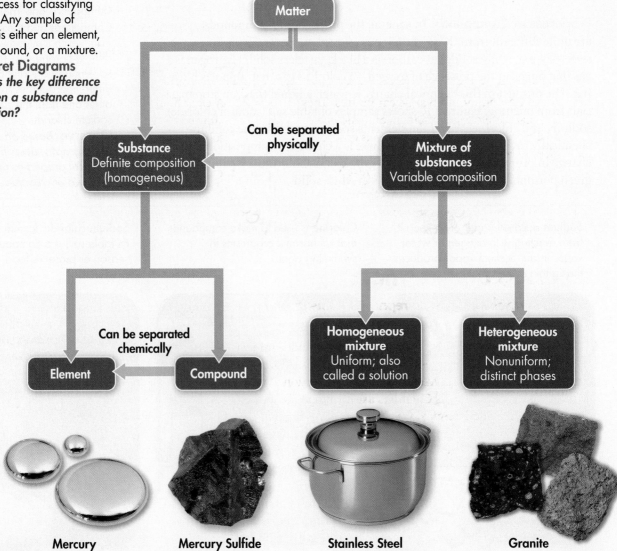

Matter

Can be separated physically

Substance
Definite composition (homogeneous)

Mixture of substances
Variable composition

Can be separated chemically

Element

Compound

Homogeneous mixture
Uniform; also called a solution

Heterogeneous mixture
Nonuniform; distinct phases

Mercury

Mercury Sulfide

Stainless Steel

Granite

Sample Problem 2.2

Classifying Materials

When a certain blue-green solid is heated, a colorless gas and a black solid form. All three materials are substances. Is it possible to classify these substances as elements or compounds?

1 Analyze **Identify the relevant concepts.** A compound can be broken down into simpler substances by a chemical change, but an element cannot. Heating can cause a chemical change.

A compound is made of two or more elements that are chemically combined.

2 Solve **Apply concepts to this situation.**

| List the known facts and relevant concepts. | → | • A blue-green solid is heated. |

| Determine if the substances are elements or compounds. | → | • A colorless gas and a black solid appear. Before heating, there was one substance. After heating, there were two substances. The blue-green solid must be a compound. Based on the information given, it isn't possible to know if the colorless gas and the black solid are elements or compounds. |

20. Liquid A and Liquid B are clear liquids. They are placed in open containers and allowed to evaporate. When evaporation is complete, there is a white solid in container B but no solid in container A. From these results, what can you infer about the two liquids?

21. A clear liquid in an open container is allowed to evaporate. After three days, a solid is left in the container. Was the clear liquid an element, a compound, or a mixture? How do you know?

Symbols and Formulas

🔑 What do chemists use to represent elements and compounds?

The common names *water* and *table salt* do not provide information about the chemical composition of these substances. Also, words are not ideal for showing what happens to the composition of matter during a chemical change. 🔑 **Chemists use chemical symbols to represent elements, and chemical formulas to represent compounds.**

Using symbols to represent different kinds of matter is not a new idea. For thousands of years, alchemists used symbols, such as the ones in Figure 2.12, to represent elements. The symbols used today for elements are based on a system developed by a Swedish chemist, Jöns Jacob Berzelius (1779–1848). He based his symbols on the Latin names of elements. Each element is represented by a one- or two-letter **chemical symbol.** The first letter of a chemical symbol is always capitalized. When a second letter is used, it is lowercase.

Figure 2.12 Element Symbols The symbols used to represent elements have changed over time. Alchemists and the English chemist John Dalton (1766–1844) both used drawings to represent chemical elements. Today, elements are represented by one- or two-letter symbols.

Table 2.2

Symbols and Latin Names for Some Elements

Name	Symbol	Latin name
Sodium	Na	*natrium*
Potassium	K	*kalium*
Antimony	Sb	*stibium*
Copper	Cu	*cuprum*
Gold	Au	*aurum*
Silver	Ag	*argentum*
Iron	Fe	*ferrum*
Lead	Pb	*plumbum*
Tin	Sn	*stannum*

If the English name and the Latin name of an element are similar, the symbol will appear to have been derived from the English name. Examples include Ca for calcium, N for nitrogen, and S for sulfur. Table 2.2 shows examples of elements for which the symbols do not match the English names. Chemical symbols provide a shorthand way to write the chemical formulas of compounds. The symbols for hydrogen, oxygen, and carbon are H, O, and C. The formula for water is H_2O. The formula for sucrose, or table sugar, is $C_{12}H_{22}O_{11}$. Subscripts in chemical formulas tell you how many of each type of element are in the compound. For example, the subscript 2 in H_2O indicates that there are always two parts of hydrogen for each part of oxygen in water. Because a compound has a fixed composition, the formula for a compound is always the same.

The Periodic Table—A Preview

🔑 *Why is a periodic table useful?*

All the known elements are organized in a special table called the periodic table. A **periodic table** is an arrangement of elements in which the elements are separated into groups based on a set of repeating properties. 🔑 **The periodic table allows you to easily compare the properties of one element (or a group of elements) to another element (or group of elements).**

Figure 2.13 shows the most commonly used form of the modern periodic table, sometimes called the long form. Each element is identified by its symbol placed in a square. The elements are listed in order from left to right and top to bottom by atomic number, a number that is unique to each element. The atomic number of the element is shown centered above the symbol. You will learn more about atomic numbers in Chapter 4. Hydrogen (H), the lightest element, is in the top left corner. Helium (He), atomic number 2, is at the top right. Lithium (Li), atomic number 3, is at the left end of the second row.

Each horizontal row of the periodic table is called a **period.** There are seven periods in the periodic table. The number of elements per period ranges from 2 (hydrogen and helium) in Period 1 to 32 in Period 6. Within a period, the properties of the elements vary as you move across the period. This pattern of properties then repeats as you move to the next period.

Each vertical column of the periodic table is called a **group,** or family. Elements within a group have similar chemical and physical properties. Note that each group is identified by a number and the letter A or B. For example, Group 2A contains the elements beryllium (Be), magnesium (Mg), calcium (Ca), strontium (Sr), barium (Ba), and radium (Ra). You will learn more about specific trends in the periodic table in Chapter 6.

Figure 2.13 The Periodic Table
Elements are arranged in the modern periodic table in order of atomic number.
Interpret Diagrams *How many elements are in Period 2? In Group 2A?*

	1A																	8A
1	1 H	2A											3A	4A	5A	6A	7A	2 He
2	3 Li	4 Be											5 B	6 C	7 N	8 O	9 F	10 Ne
3	11 Na	12 Mg	3B	4B	5B	6B	7B	8B	8B	8B	1B	2B	13 Al	14 Si	15 P	16 S	17 Cl	18 Ar
4	19 K	20 Ca	21 Sc	22 Ti	23 V	24 Cr	25 Mn	26 Fe	27 Co	28 Ni	29 Cu	30 Zn	31 Ga	32 Ge	33 As	34 Se	35 Br	36 Kr
5	37 Rb	38 Sr	39 Y	40 Zr	41 Nb	42 Mo	43 Tc	44 Ru	45 Rh	46 Pd	47 Ag	48 Cd	49 In	50 Sn	51 Sb	52 Te	53 I	54 Xe
6	55 Cs	56 Ba	71 Lu	72 Hf	73 Ta	74 W	75 Re	76 Os	77 Ir	78 Pt	79 Au	80 Hg	81 Tl	82 Pb	83 Bi	84 Po	85 At	86 Rn
7	87 Fr	88 Ra	103 Lr	104 Rf	105 Db	106 Sg	107 Bh	108 Hs	109 Mt	110 Ds	111 Rg	112 Cn	113 Uut	114 Fl	115 Uup	116 Lv	117 Uus	118 Uuo

57 La	58 Ce	59 Pr	60 Nd	61 Pm	62 Sm	63 Eu	64 Gd	65 Tb	66 Dy	67 Ho	68 Er	69 Tm	70 Yb
89 Ac	90 Th	91 Pa	92 U	93 Np	94 Pu	95 Am	96 Cm	97 Bk	98 Cf	99 Es	100 Fm	101 Md	102 No

2.3 LessonCheck

ONLINE PROBLEMS

22. 🔗 **Compare** How is a compound different from an element?

23. 🔗 **Compare** How can you distinguish a substance from a mixture?

24. 🔗 **Identify** What are chemical symbols and chemical formulas used for?

25. 🔗 **Explain** What makes the periodic table such a useful tool?

26. Identify Name two methods that can be used to break down compounds into simpler substances.

27. Classify Classify each of these samples of matter as an element, a compound, or a mixture.
   a. table sugar   **c.** cough syrup
   b. tap water   **d.** nitrogen

28. Identify Write the chemical symbol for each of the following elements:
   a. lead   **c.** silver   **e.** hydrogen
   b. oxygen   **d.** sodium   **f.** aluminum

29. Identify Name the chemical elements represented by the following symbols:
   a. C   **c.** K   **e.** Fe
   b. Ca   **d.** Au   **f.** Cu

30. Identify What elements make up the pain reliever acetaminophen, chemical formula $C_8H_9O_2N$? Which element is present in the greatest proportion by number of particles?

31. Identify Name two elements that have properties similar to those of the element calcium (Ca).

2.4 Chemical Reactions

CHEMISTRY & YOU

Q: *What happened to the match?* Matches are often used to light candles on a cake. A match is usually lit at the tip and then burns down the match. So you better be quick, or your fingers will be burned by the lit match. A lit match is different than an unlit match. In this lesson, you will learn to recognize whether the burning match is a chemical change or physical change.

Key Questions

🔑 **What always happens during a chemical change?**

🔑 **What are four possible clues that a chemical change has taken place?**

🔑 **How are the mass of the reactants and the mass of the products of a chemical reaction related?**

Vocabulary

- chemical property
- chemical reaction
- reactant
- product
- precipitate
- law of conservation of mass

READING SUPPORT

Build Study Skills: *Preview Visuals* Before you start reading the lesson, preview the visuals in Figure 2.16. Then write two questions you have about the visuals. After you finish reading, answer your questions.

Chemical Changes

🔑 **What always happens during a chemical change?**

The compound formed when iron rusts is iron oxide (Fe_2O_3). Words such as *burn, rot, rust, decompose, ferment, explode,* and *corrode* usually signify a chemical change. The ability of a substance to undergo a specific chemical change is called a **chemical property.** Iron is able to combine with oxygen to form rust. So the ability to rust is a chemical property of iron. Chemical properties can be used to identify a substance. But chemical properties can be observed only when a substance undergoes a chemical change.

Figure 2.14 compares a physical change and a chemical change that can occur in a sample of charcoal. When charcoal is broken into smaller pieces, the change is a physical change. The substances present before the change are the same substances present after the change, although the charcoal pieces are not as large. Recall that during a physical change, the composition of matter never changes. 🔑 **During a chemical change, the composition of matter always changes.** When the charcoal is heated and burned, a chemical change occurs. The substances in charcoal react with oxygen in the air to form other substances.

A chemical change is also called a chemical reaction. One or more substances change into one or more new substances during a **chemical reaction.** A substance present at the start of the reaction is a **reactant.** A substance produced in the reaction is a **product.** In the burning of charcoal, carbon and oxygen are the main reactants, and carbon dioxide is the main product.

Figure 2.14
Physical and Chemical Changes
Charcoal is used as a fuel in charcoal grills. **a.** Breaking the charcoal into smaller pieces is a physical change. **b.** Burning the charcoal is a chemical change.

Figure 2.15 Chemical Change
Clues to chemical change often have practical applications.

Learn more about physical and chemical changes *online.*

Production of a Gas
Bubbles of carbon dioxide gas form when an antacid tablet is dropped into a glass of water.

Color Change
When a test strip is dipped in a solution, the color change is used to determine the pH of the solution.

Formation of a Precipitate
One step in the production of cheese is a reaction that causes milk to separate into solid curds and liquid whey.

Recognizing Chemical Changes

🔑 **What are four possible clues that a chemical change has taken place?**

How can you tell whether a chemical change has taken place? There are four clues that can serve as a guide. 🔑 **Possible clues to chemical change include a transfer of energy, a change in color, the production of a gas, or the formation of a precipitate.**

Every chemical change involves a transfer of energy. For example, energy stored in natural gas is used to cook food. When the methane in natural gas chemically combines with oxygen in the air, energy is given off in the form of heat and light. Some of this energy is transferred to and absorbed by food that is cooking over a lit gas burner. The energy causes chemical changes to take place in the food. The food may change color and brown as it cooks, which is another clue that chemical changes are occurring.

You can observe two other clues to chemical change while cleaning a bathtub. The ring of soap scum that can form in a bathtub is an example of a precipitate. A **precipitate** is a solid that forms and settles out of a liquid mixture. Some bathroom cleaners that you can use to remove soap scum start to bubble when you spray them on the scum. The bubbles are produced because a gas is released during the chemical change that is taking place in the cleaner.

If you observe a clue to chemical change, you cannot be certain that a chemical change has taken place. The clue may be the result of a physical change. For example, energy is always transferred when matter changes from one state to another. Bubbles form when you boil water or open a carbonated drink. The only way to be sure that a chemical change has occurred is to test the composition of a sample before and after the change. Figure 2.15 shows examples of practical situations in which different clues to chemical change are visible.

CHEMISTRY & YOU

Q: *Are the changes that happen to a burning match chemical changes or physical changes? How do you know?*

Conservation of Mass

🔑 *How are the mass of the reactants and the mass of the products of a chemical reaction related?*

When wood burns, substances in the wood combine with oxygen from the air. As the wood burns, a sizable amount of matter is reduced to a small pile of ashes. The reaction seems to involve a reduction in the amount of matter. But appearances can be deceiving. 🔑 **During any chemical reaction, the mass of the products is always equal to the mass of the reactants.** Two of the products of burning wood—carbon dioxide gas and water vapor—are released into the air. When the mass of these gases is considered, the amount of matter is unchanged. Careful measurements show that the total mass of the reactants (wood and the oxygen consumed) equals the total mass of the products (carbon dioxide, water vapor, and ash).

Mass also holds constant during physical changes. For example, when 10 grams of ice melt, 10 grams of liquid water are produced. Similar observations have been recorded for all chemical and physical changes studied. The scientific law that reflects these observations is the law of conservation of mass. The **law of conservation of mass** states that in any physical change or chemical reaction, mass is conserved. Mass is neither created nor destroyed. The conservation of mass is more easily observed when a change occurs in a closed container, as in Figure 2.16.

Figure 2.16
Conservation of Mass
When the liquids in **a.** are mixed, they react. The products are shown in **b.** None of the products are gases.
Analyze Data *How do you know that a reaction took place and that mass was conserved during the reaction?*

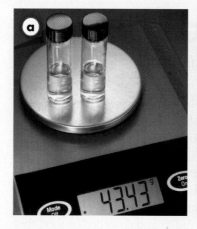

 ## 2.4 LessonCheck

32. 🔑 **Explain** How does a chemical change affect the composition of matter?

33. 🔑 **List** Name four possible clues that a chemical change has taken place.

34. 🔑 **Compare** In a chemical reaction, how does the mass of the reactants compare with the mass of the products?

35. Compare What is the main difference between physical changes and chemical changes?

36. Classify Classify the following changes as physical or chemical changes.
  a. Water boils. **c.** Milk turns sour.
  b. Salt dissolves in water. **d.** A metal rusts.

37. Explain According to the law of conservation of mass, when is mass conserved?

38. Calculate Hydrogen and oxygen react chemically to form water. How much water would form if 4.8 grams of hydrogen reacted with 38.4 grams of oxygen?

Small-Scale Lab

1 + 2 + 3 = Black!

Purpose
To make macroscopic observations of chemical reactions and use them to solve problems

Materials
- paper
- metric ruler
- reaction surface
- materials shown in grid
- pipette, medicine droppers, and spatulas

Procedure
1. Draw two copies of the grid on separate sheets of paper. Make each square in the grid 2 cm on each side.
2. Place a reaction surface over one of the grids. Use the second grid as a data table to record your observations.
3. Use the column and row labels to determine which materials belong in each square. Depending on the material, add one drop, one piece, or a few grains.
4. Stir each mixture by forcing air from an empty pipette as directed by your teacher.

	NaClO	H₂O₂	CuSO₄
KI			
KI + Starch			
KI + Paper			
KI + Cereal			

Analyze
Using your experimental data, record the answers to the following questions below your data table.
1. Describe What color is a mixture of sodium hypochlorite (NaClO) and potassium iodide (KI)?
2. Describe What happens when you mix NaClO, KI, and starch?
3. Compare What do NaClO, H₂O₂, and CuSO₄ have in common?
4. Compare What substance is found in both paper and cereal? How do you know?
5. Predict If you used NaClO instead of CuSO₄ in reactions other than the reaction with KI and starch, would you expect the results to always be identical? Explain your answer.

You're the Chemist
The following small-scale activities allow you to develop your own procedures and analyze the results.
1. Analyze Data NaClO is a bleaching agent. Such agents are used to whiten clothes and remove stains. Use different color marker pens to draw several lines on a piece of white paper. Add one drop of NaClO to each line. What happens? Try inventing a technique that you can use to make "bleach art."
2. Design an Experiment Design and carry out an experiment to see which foods contain starch.
3. Design an Experiment Read the label on a package of iodized salt. How much KI does iodized salt contain? Design an experiment to demonstrate the presence of KI in iodized salt and its absence in salt that is not iodized.
4. Design an Experiment Antacid tablets often contain starch as a binder to hold the ingredients in the tablet together. Design and carry out an experiment to explore various antacid tablets to see if they contain starch.

Recycled Mixtures

You may be used to sorting recyclables into separate bins. But now, a new process known as single-stream recycling allows you to put all recyclables into a single container. The separation is then done at a plant known as a Material Recovery Facility (MRF), which uses machines to separate paper, glass, metal, and plastics based on their properties.

1. FEEDER Unsorted paper, glass, plastic, and metal are loaded onto a conveyer belt. In some locations, workers pull any mixed-in trash off the belt and discard it.

2. SCREENING MACHINES A series of fast, rotating rubber blades, called star screens, separate out cardboard, newspaper, and other paper from the rest of the material. The plastic, glass, and metals fall through the screens onto another conveyer belt.

3. ELECTROMAGNET Heavy-duty electro-magnets grab items made of ferrous metals, such as iron and steel, off the conveyer belt.

4. EDDY CURRENT A rotating magnetic field creates an eddy current that repels nonmagnetic metals, such as aluminum, and ejects them from the rest of the materials.

5. GLASS CRUSHER The remaining materials move through another series of screens designed to break glass and remove it from the stream.

6. OPTICAL SCANNER Optical scanners use infrared technology to recognize different types or colors of plastics and can trigger blasts of air to separate the plastics into bins.

Take It Further

1. Identify What are three properties of matter that are used to help sort materials during the single-stream recycling process?

2. Describe What are some possible benefits of single-stream recycling vs. regular recycling?

CARDBOARD, PAPER AND NEWSPAPER BALER

FERROUS METALS BALER

ALUMINUM BALER

GLASS BALER

PLASTICS BALER

7. BALERS After the products are separated, they're stored and fed into balers, which bundle the materials together. The materials are then shipped out to recycling plants, where they will be made into new products.

2 Study Guide

BIGIDEA
CHEMISTRY AS THE CENTRAL SCIENCE

Physical properties, such as melting point and boiling point, and chemical properties, such as whether a substance will corrode or burn, are used to describe matter. Matter may be made of elements or compounds. Elements and compounds are pure substances but can be physically combined to make heterogenous or homogeneous mixtures. These different forms of matter may undergo physical or chemical changes.

2.1 Properties of Matter

🔑 Every sample of a given substance has identical intensive properties because every sample has the same composition.

🔑 Three states of matter are solid, liquid, and gas.

🔑 Physical changes can be classified as reversible or irreversible.

- mass (34)
- volume (34)
- extensive property (34)
- intensive property (34)
- substance (35)
- physical property (35)
- solid (36)
- liquid (36)
- gas (37)
- vapor (37)
- physical change (37)

2.2 Mixtures

🔑 Mixtures can be classified as heterogeneous mixtures or as homogeneous mixtures, based on the distribution of their components.

🔑 Differences in physical properties can be used to separate mixtures.

- mixture (38)
- heterogeneous mixture (39)
- homogeneous mixture (39)
- solution (39)
- phase (39)
- filtration (40)
- distillation (40)

2.3 Elements and Compounds

🔑 Compounds can be broken down into simpler substances by chemical means, but elements cannot.

🔑 If the composition of a material is fixed, the material is a substance. If the composition may vary, the material is a mixture.

🔑 Chemists use chemical symbols to represent elements, and chemical formulas to represent compounds.

🔑 The periodic table allows you to easily compare the properties of one element (or a group of elements) to another element (or group of elements).

- element (42)
- compound (42)
- chemical change (43)
- chemical symbol (45)
- periodic table (46)
- period (46)
- group (47)

2.4 Chemical Reactions

🔑 During a chemical change, the composition of matter always changes.

🔑 Four possible clues to chemical change include a transfer of energy, a change in color, the production of a gas, or the formation of a precipitate.

🔑 During any chemical reaction, the mass of the products is always equal to the mass of the reactants.

- chemical property (48)
- chemical reaction (48)
- reactant (48)
- product (48)
- precipitate (49)
- law of conservation of mass (50)

2 Assessment

Lesson by Lesson

2.1 Properties of Matter

39. Describe the difference between an extensive property and an intensive property and give an example of each.

40. List three physical properties of copper.

41. Name two physical properties that could be used to distinguish between water and ethanol.

★42. Name one physical property that could not be used to distinguish chlorine from oxygen.

43. What is the physical state of each of these materials at room temperature?

   a. gold
   b. gasoline
   c. oxygen
   d. neon
   e. olive oil
   f. sulfur
   g. mercury

★44. Fingernail-polish remover (mostly acetone) is a liquid at room temperature. Would you describe acetone in the gaseous state as a vapor or a gas? Explain your answer.

45. Compare the arrangements of individual particles in solids, liquids, and gases.

46. Use Table 2.1 to identify four substances that undergo a physical change if the temperature is reduced from 50°C to −50°C. What is the physical change that takes place in each case?

★ 47. Explain why sharpening a pencil is a different type of physical change than freezing water to make ice cubes.

2.2 Mixtures

48. What is the difference between homogeneous mixtures and heterogeneous mixtures?

49. How many phases does a solution have? Explain your answer.

★50. Classify each of the following as a homogeneous or heterogeneous mixture.

   a. chocolate-chip ice cream
   b. green ink
   c. cake batter
   d. cooking oil
   e. granite rock
   f. salt water
   g. paint
   h. a silver ring

51. What is the goal of a distillation? Describe briefly how this goal is accomplished.

2.3 Elements and Compounds

52. How could you distinguish an element from a compound?

★53. Classify the following materials as an element, compound, or mixture. Give reasons for your answers.

   a. table salt (NaCl)
   b. salt water
   c. sodium (Na)

54. Describe the relationship between the three items in each of the following groups. Identify each item as an element, compound, or mixture.

   a. hydrogen, oxygen, and water
   b. nitrogen, oxygen, and air
   c. sodium, chlorine, and table salt
   d. carbon, water, and table sugar

55. Name the elements found in each of the following compounds.

   a. ammonia (NH_3)
   b. potassium oxide (K_2O)
   c. sucrose ($C_{12}H_{22}O_{11}$)
   d. calcium sulfide (CaS)

56. Not all element names come from English or Latin words. The symbol for tungsten is W from the German word *wolfram*. The symbol for mercury is Hg from the Greek word *hydragyrum*. Use the symbols W and Hg to explain the system of symbols for elements.

★ 57. What does the formula H_2O tell you about the composition of water?

58. Look up the word *periodic* in the dictionary. Propose a reason for the naming of the periodic table.

2.4 Chemical Reactions

59. Use the word equation below to explain how a chemical change differs from a physical change.

$$\text{iron} + \text{sulfur} \xrightarrow{\text{heat}} \text{iron sulfide}$$

*60. Classify each of the following as a physical or chemical change. For any chemical change, list at least one clue to support your answer.

a. A copper wire is bent.
b. Charcoal burns in a grill.
c. Bread dough rises when yeast is added.
d. Sugar dissolves in water.

61. Which type of property cannot be observed without changing the composition of a substance?

*62. When ammonium nitrate (NH_4NO_3) explodes, the products are nitrogen, oxygen, and water. When 40 grams of ammonium nitrate explode, 14 grams of nitrogen and 8 grams of oxygen form. How many grams of water form?

Understand Concepts

Use the data table to answer Questions 63–66.

Substance	Color	Melting point (°C)	Boiling point (°C)
Bromine	Red-brown	−7	59
Chlorine	Green-yellow	−101	−34
Ethanol	Colorless	−117	78
Mercury	Silvery-white	−39	357
Neon	Colorless	−249	−246
Sulfur	Yellow	115	445
Water	Colorless	0	100

63. Which colorless substance is a liquid at −30°C?

64. Which colorless substance is a gas at 60°C?

65. Which substance is a solid at 7°C?

*66. As the temperature rises, which solid will melt before mercury boils?

*67. Explain why mass cannot be used as a property to identify a sample of matter.

68. Is malleability an extensive property or an intensive property? Explain.

69. The state of a substance can change when the substance is heated or cooled. So what does it mean to say that a certain substance is a solid, liquid, or gas?

*70. Use the arrangement of particles in solids and gases to explain why solids are not as easy to compress as gases.

71. You are standing in a kitchen and then in the middle of a park. When you view your surroundings in each location, do you see mostly elements, compounds, or mixtures?

72. Identify each of the following items as a mixture or compound. Classify the mixtures as homogeneous or heterogeneous.

a. raw egg
b. ice
c. gasoline
d. blood

73. Classify the following properties of the element silicon as chemical or physical properties:

a. blue-gray color
b. brittle
c. doesn't dissolve in water
d. melts at 1410°C
e. reacts vigorously with fluorine

74. How are the items in each of the following pairs similar? How are they different?

a. copper and silver
b. distilled water and salt water
c. table sugar and table salt

75. Identify each of the following as an element, compound or mixture.

a. iron
b. distilled water
c. laundry detergent
d. sulfur
e. chicken broth
f. sodium fluoride

76. Describe clues you might observe during the following events that could support the conclusion that a chemical change is occurring.

   a. An antacid tablet is dropped into water.
   b. A ring of scum forms around a bathtub.
   c. Iron rusts.
   d. A firecracker explodes.
   e. Bubbles form when hydrogen peroxide is poured onto an open wound.
   f. A hamburger cooks.

77. In photograph A, a coil of zinc metal is in a solution of sulfuric acid. In photograph B, a yellow solution of sodium chromate is being added to a colorless solution of silver nitrate. What clues in the photographs indicate that a chemical change is probably occurring?

A.    **B.**

78. Classify each of the following as a chemical change or a physical change.

   a. Plastic drink bottles are burned in an incinerator to generate electricity.
   b. Digesting a cereal bar.
   c. Water in a rain puddle evaporates.
   d. Slicing a tomato for a sandwich.
   e. Plastic drink bottles are recycled to make fiberfill for ski jackets.

79. Explain why the production of a gas does not always mean that a chemical reaction has occurred.

★80. The wax seems to disappear as a candle burns. How can the law of conservation of mass apply to this reaction?

(**Think Critically**)

★81. Apply Concepts Devise a way to separate sand from a mixture of charcoal, sand, sugar, and water.

82. Sequence Assume that water, mercury, and gallium are all at 40°C. As the temperature drops, which substance will freeze first? Which will be the last to freeze?

83. Apply Concepts A change in odor can also be a clue that a chemical change has occurred. Describe at least one situation in which you might be likely to detect such a change in odor in a kitchen.

84. Explain Explain why this statement is false. "Because there is no change in composition during a physical change, the appearance of the substance will not change."

★85. Interpret Graphs The mass of the elements iron and oxygen in four samples of a rust-colored substance was measured in grams (g). The amount of iron and oxygen in each sample is shown on the graph.

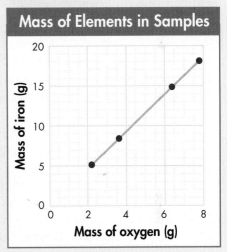

Mass of Elements in Samples

   a. Do you think all four samples are the same compound? Explain.
   b. Another sample of similar material was found to contain 9.9 grams of iron and 3.4 grams of oxygen. Is this sample the same substance as the other four samples? Explain.

86. Explain When powdered iron is left exposed to the air, it rusts. Explain why the mass of the rust is greater than the mass of the powdered iron.

87. Explain Discuss the statement "A gas requires a container, but a solid is its own container."

*88. **Interpret Graphs** Five elements make up 98% of the mass of the human body. These elements are oxygen (61%), carbon (23%), hydrogen (10.0%), nitrogen (2.6%), and calcium (1.4%). Compare these data with those in the pie graph below, which shows the five most abundant elements by mass in Earth's crust, oceans, and atmosphere.

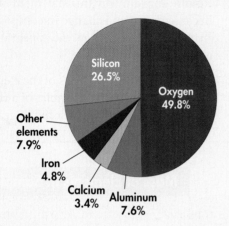

Silicon 26.5%

Oxygen 49.8%

Other elements 7.9%

Iron 4.8%

Calcium 3.4%

Aluminum 7.6%

a. Which elements are abundant both in the human body and Earth's crust, oceans, and atmosphere?

b. Which elements are abundant in Earth's crust, oceans, and atmosphere, but not in the human body?

c. Would you expect the compounds found in the human body to be the same as or different from those found in rocks, seawater, and air? Use the data to explain your answer.

89. **Evaluate** Each day you encounter some chemical changes that are helpful and some that are harmful to humans or the environment. Cite three examples of each type. For each example, list the clues that identified the change as a chemical change.

90. **Interpret Tables** Use Table 2.1 on page 35 to answer this question.

a. Which substances in the table are in the liquid state at 125°C?

b. Use the physical properties of one of these substances to explain how you figured out the answer to Question 90a.

c. The substances in the table are listed in order of increasing melting point. Propose another way that these data could be arranged.

91. **Explain** Write a paragraph in support of this statement: "Dry tea is a mixture, not a substance." Include at least two pieces of evidence to support your argument.

92. **Explain** Lavoisier proposed the law of conservation of mass in 1789. Write a paragraph describing, in general, what Lavoisier must have done before he proposed this law. Use what you have learned about the scientific method.

93. **Connect to the BIGIDEA** Compare elements and compounds by saying how they are alike. Contrast elements and compounds by describing how they are different.

CHEMYSTERY

Which One Is Not Like the Others?

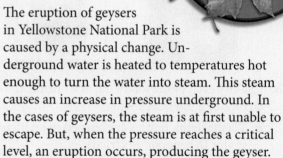

The eruption of geysers in Yellowstone National Park is caused by a physical change. Underground water is heated to temperatures hot enough to turn the water into steam. This steam causes an increase in pressure underground. In the cases of geysers, the steam is at first unable to escape. But, when the pressure reaches a critical level, an eruption occurs, producing the geyser.

The shaping of valleys by melt-refreeze cycles is also a physical change. The melting and refreezing of water is a physical change, and as the earth underneath the glacier is broken apart and moved, this is also a physical change.

The changing of the color of leaves is a chemical change. As the temperature and hours of sunlight change in the fall, chemical changes occur. Therefore, leaves changing color, a chemical change, is not like the physical changes of geysers erupting or glaciers moving.

94. **Identify** Are the physical changes in the mystery reversible or irreversible physical changes? Explain your answer.

95. **Connect to the BIGIDEA** Why would it be important for rangers at national parks to have knowledge of physical and chemical changes?

Standardized Test Prep

Select the choice that best answers each question or completes each statement.

1. Which of the following is not a chemical change?
   (A) paper being shredded
   (B) steel rusting
   (C) charcoal burning
   (D) a newspaper yellowing in the sun

2. Which phrase best describes an apple?
   (A) heterogeneous mixture
   (B) homogeneous compound
   (C) heterogeneous substance
   (D) homogeneous mixture

3. Which element is paired with the wrong symbol?
   (A) sulfur, S
   (B) potassium, P
   (C) nitrogen, N
   (D) calcium, Ca

4. Which of these properties could not be used to distinguish between table salt and table sugar?
   (A) boiling point
   (B) melting point
   (C) density
   (D) color

5. The state of matter characterized by a definite volume and an indefinite shape is a
   (A) solid.   (C) mixture.
   (B) liquid.   (D) gas.

The lettered choices below refer to Questions 6–9. A lettered choice may be used once, more than once, or not at all.
   (A) compound
   (B) heterogeneous mixture
   (C) element
   (D) homogeneous mixture

Which description correctly identifies each of the following materials?

6. air

7. carbon monoxide

8. zinc

9. mushroom pizza

Tips for Success

Using Models To answer some test questions, you will be asked to use visual models. At first the models may look very similar. Decide which information will help you answer the question. The number of particles, their colors, or their shapes may or may not be important.

Use the atomic windows to answer Question 10.

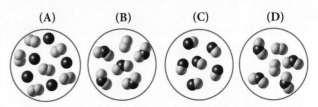

(A)   (B)   (C)   (D)

10. The species in window A react. Use the law of conservation of mass to determine which window best represents the reaction products.

Use the data table to answer Questions 11–14.

Mass of magnesium (g)	Mass of oxygen (g)	Mass of magnesium oxide (g)
5.0	3.3	8.3
6.5	(a)	10.8
13.6	9.0	(b)
(c)	12.5	31.5

11. Magnesium metal burns vigorously in oxygen to produce the compound magnesium oxide. Use the law of conservation of mass to identify the masses labeled (a), (b), and (c) in the table.

12. Use the data in the completed table to construct a graph with mass of magnesium on the *x*-axis and mass of magnesium oxide on the *y*-axis.

13. How many grams of magnesium oxide form when 8.0 g of magnesium are burned?

14. How many grams of magnesium and oxygen react to form 20.0 g of magnesium oxide?

If You Have Trouble With . . .

Question	1	2	3	4	5	6	7	8	9	10	11	12	13	14
See Lesson	2.4	2.2	2.3	2.1	2.1	2.3	2.3	2.3	2.3	2.4	2.4	2.4	2.4	2.4

3

Scientific Measurement

INSIDE:

- **3.1** Using and Expressing Measurements
- **3.2** Units of Measurement
- **3.3** Solving Conversion Problems

PearsonChem.com

A surveyor in Antarctica uses a device called a theodolite to measure the landscape for a future airstrip.

QUANTIFYING MATTER

Essential Questions:

1. *How do scientists express the degree of uncertainty in their measurements?*

2. *How is dimensional analysis used to solve problems?*

CHEMYSTERY

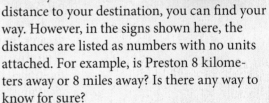

Just Give Me a Sign

While traveling in a foreign country, you happen to get lost, as many tourists do. But then you spot these signs along the road. If you know the distance to your destination, you can find your way. However, in the signs shown here, the distances are listed as numbers with no units attached. For example, is Preston 8 kilometers away or 8 miles away? Is there any way to know for sure?

▶ **Connect to the BIGIDEA** As you read the chapter, try to familiarize yourself with common metric units used in science.

NATIONAL SCIENCE EDUCATION STANDARDS

A-1, E-2

3.1 Using and Expressing Measurements

Q: *How do you measure a photo finish?* You probably know that a 100-meter dash is timed in seconds. But if it's a close finish, measuring each runner's time to the nearest second will not tell you who won. That's why sprint times are often measured to the nearest hundredth of a second (0.01 s). Chemistry also requires making accurate and often very small measurements.

Key Questions

🔑 How do you write numbers in scientific notation?

🔑 How do you evaluate accuracy and precision?

🔑 Why must measurements be reported to the correct number of significant figures?

Vocabulary

- measurement
- scientific notation
- accuracy • precision
- accepted value
- experimental value
- error • percent error
- significant figures

Scientific Notation

🔑 **How do you write numbers in scientific notation?**

Everyone makes and uses measurements. A **measurement** is a quantity that has both a number and a unit. Your height (66 inches), your age (15 years), and your body temperature (37°C) are examples of measurements.

Measurements are fundamental to the experimental sciences. For that reason, it is important to be able to make measurements and to decide whether a measurement is correct. In chemistry, you will often encounter very large or very small numbers. A single gram of hydrogen, for example, contains approximately 602,000,000,000,000,000,000,000 hydrogen atoms. The mass of an atom of gold is 0.000 000 000 000 000 000 000 327 gram. Writing and using such large and small numbers is cumbersome. You can work more easily with these numbers by writing them in scientific notation.

In **scientific notation,** a given number is written as the product of two numbers: a coefficient and 10 raised to a power. For example, the number 602,000,000,000,000,000,000,000 can be written in scientific notation as 6.02×10^{23}. The coefficient in this number is 6.02. The power of 10, or exponent, is 23. 🔑 **In scientific notation, the coefficient is always a number greater than or equal to one and less than ten. The exponent is an integer.** A positive exponent indicates how many times the coefficient must be multiplied by 10. A negative exponent indicates how many times the coefficient must be divided by 10. Figure 3.1 shows a magnified view of a human hair, which has a diameter of about 0.00007 m, or 7×10^{-5} m.

When writing numbers greater than ten in scientific notation, the exponent is positive and equals the number of places that the original decimal point has been moved to the left.

$$6{,}300{,}000. = 6.3 \times 10^6 \qquad 94{,}700. = 9.47 \times 10^4$$

Numbers less than one have a negative exponent when written in scientific notation. The value of the exponent equals the number of places the decimal has been moved to the right.

$$0.000\ 008 = 8 \times 10^{-6} \qquad 0.00736 = 7.36 \times 10^{-3}$$

Figure 3.1 Just a Hair
A hair's width expressed in meters is a very small measurement.

$$0.00007 \text{ m} = 7 \times 10^{-5} \text{ m}$$

Decimal point moves 5 places to the right.   Exponent is −5

Multiplication and Division To multiply numbers written in scientific notation, multiply the coefficients and add the exponents.

$$(3 \times 10^4) \times (2 \times 10^2) = (3 \times 2) \times 10^{4+2} = 6 \times 10^6$$

$$(2.1 \times 10^3) \times (4.0 \times 10^{-7}) = (2.1 \times 4.0) \times 10^{3+(-7)} = 8.4 \times 10^{-4}$$

To divide numbers written in scientific notation, divide the coefficients and subtract the exponent in the denominator from the exponent in the numerator.

$$\frac{3.0 \times 10^5}{6.0 \times 10^2} = \left(\frac{3.0}{6.0}\right) \times 10^{5-2} = 0.5 \times 10^3 = 5.0 \times 10^2$$

Addition and Subtraction If you want to add or subtract numbers expressed in scientific notation and you are not using a calculator, then the exponents must be the same. In other words, the decimal points must be aligned before you add or subtract the numbers. For example, when adding 5.4×10^3 and 8.0×10^2, first rewrite the second number so that the exponent is a 3. Then add the numbers.

$$(5.4 \times 10^3) + (8.0 \times 10^2) = (5.4 \times 10^3) + (0.80 \times 10^3)$$
$$= (5.4 + 0.80) \times 10^3$$
$$= 6.2 \times 10^3$$

Sample Problem 3.1

Using Scientific Notation

Solve each problem and express the answer in scientific notation.
a. $(8.0 \times 10^{-2}) \times (7.0 \times 10^{-5})$ **b.** $(7.1 \times 10^{-2}) + (5 \times 10^{-3})$

❶ Analyze Identify the relevant concepts. To multiply numbers in scientific notation, multiply the coefficients and add the exponents. To add numbers in scientific notation, the exponents must match. If they do not, then adjust the notation of one of the numbers.

❷ Solve Apply the concepts to this problem.

Multiply the coefficients and add the exponents.	**a.** $(8.0 \times 10^{-2}) \times (7.0 \times 10^{-5}) = (8.0 \times 7.0) \times 10^{-2 + (-5)}$
	$= 56 \times 10^{-7}$
	$= 5.6 \times 10^{-6}$

Rewrite one of the numbers so that the exponents match. Then add the coefficients.	**b.** $(7.1 \times 10^{-2}) + (5 \times 10^{-3}) = (7.1 \times 10^{-2}) + (0.5 \times 10^{-2})$
	$= (7.1 + 0.5) \times 10^{-2}$
	$= 7.6 \times 10^{-2}$

1. Solve each problem and express the answer in scientific notation.
  a. $(6.6 \times 10^{-8}) + (5.0 \times 10^{-9})$
  b. $(9.4 \times 10^{-2}) - (2.1 \times 10^{-2})$

2. Calculate the following and write your answer in scientific notation:
$$\frac{6.6 \times 10^6}{(8.8 \times 10^{-2}) \times (2.5 \times 10^3)}$$

Accuracy, Precision, and Error

How do you evaluate accuracy and precision?

Your success in the chemistry lab and in many of your daily activities depends on your ability to make reliable measurements. Ideally, measurements should be both correct and reproducible.

Accuracy and Precision Correctness and reproducibility relate to the concepts of accuracy and precision, two words that mean the same thing to many people. In chemistry, however, their meanings are quite different. **Accuracy** is a measure of how close a measurement comes to the actual or true value of whatever is measured. **Precision** is a measure of how close a series of measurements are to one another, irrespective of the actual value. **To evaluate the accuracy of a measurement, the measured value must be compared to the correct value. To evaluate the precision of a measurement, you must compare the values of two or more repeated measurements.**

Darts on a dartboard illustrate accuracy and precision in measurement. Let the bull's-eye of the dartboard in Figure 3.2 represent the true, or correct, value of what you are measuring. The closeness of a dart to the bull's-eye corresponds to the degree of accuracy. The closer it comes to the bull's-eye, the more accurately the dart was thrown. The closeness of several darts to one another corresponds to the degree of precision. The closer together the darts are, the greater the precision and the reproducibility.

Figure 3.2 Accuracy vs. Precision
The distribution of darts illustrates the difference between accuracy and precision.
Use Analogies *Which outcome describes a scenario in which you properly measure an object's mass three times using a balance that has not been zeroed?*

Good Accuracy, Good Precision
Closeness to the bull's-eye indicates a high degree of accuracy. The closeness of the darts to one another indicates high precision.

Poor Accuracy, Good Precision
Precision is high because of the closeness of grouping—thus, the high level of reproducibility. But the results are inaccurate.

Poor Accuracy, Poor Precision
The darts land far from one another and from the bull's-eye. The results are both inaccurate and imprecise.

Determining Error Suppose you use a thermometer to measure the boiling point of pure water at standard pressure. The thermometer reads 99.1°C. You probably know that the true or accepted value of the boiling point of pure water at these conditions is actually 100.0°C.

There is a difference between the **accepted value,** which is the correct value for the measurement based on reliable references, and the **experimental value,** the value measured in the lab. The difference between the experimental value and the accepted value is called the **error.**

$$\text{Error} = \text{experimental value} - \text{accepted value}$$

Error can be positive or negative, depending on whether the experimental value is greater than or less than the accepted value. For the boiling-point measurement, the error is 99.1°C − 100.0°C, or −0.9°C.

The magnitude of the error shows the amount by which the experimental value differs from the accepted value. Often, it is useful to calculate the relative error, or percent error. The **percent error** of a measurement is the absolute value of the error divided by the accepted value, multiplied by 100%.

$$\text{Percent error} = \frac{|\text{error}|}{\text{accepted value}} \times 100\%$$

READING SUPPORT

Build Reading Skills: *Inference*
As you read, try to identify some of the factors that cause experimental error. *What factors might result in inaccurate measurements? What factors might result in imprecise measurements?*

Sample Problem 3.2

Calculating Percent Error
The boiling point of pure water is measured to be 99.1°C. Calculate the percent error.

❶ Analyze List the knowns and unknown.
The accepted value for the boiling point of pure water is 100°C. Use the equations for error and percent error to solve the problem.

KNOWNS

Experimental value = 99.1°C
Accepted value = 100.0°C

UNKNOWN

Percent error = ?

❷ Calculate Solve for the unknown.

Start with the equation for percent error.

$$\text{Percent error} = \frac{|\text{error}|}{\text{accepted value}} \times 100\%$$

Substitute the equation for error, and then plug in the known values.

$$\text{Percent error} = \frac{|\text{experimental value} - \text{accepted value}|}{\text{accepted value}} \times 100\%$$

$$= \frac{|99.1°C - 100.0°C|}{100.0°C} \times 100\%$$

$$= \frac{0.9°C}{100.0°C} \times 100\% = 0.9\%$$

❸ Evaluate Does the result make sense? The experimental value was off by about 1°C, or $\frac{1}{100}$ of the accepted value (100°C). The answer makes sense.

3. A student measures the depth of a swimming pool to be 2.04 meters at its deepest end. The accepted value is 2.00 m. What is the student's percent error?

Think about it: Using the absolute value of the error means that percent error will always be a positive value.

Figure 3.3 Degrees Celsius
The temperature shown on this Celsius thermometer can be reported to three significant figures.

Significant Figures

🔑 *Why must measurements be reported to the correct number of significant figures?*

Look at the reading of the thermometer shown in Figure 3.3. If you use a liquid-filled thermometer that is calibrated in 1°C intervals, you can easily read the temperature to the nearest degree. With the same thermometer, however, you can also estimate the temperature to about the nearest tenth of a degree by noting the closeness of the liquid inside to the calibrations. Looking at Figure 3.3, suppose you estimate that the temperature lies between 22°C and 23°C, at 22.9°C. This estimated number has three digits. The first two digits (2 and 2) are known with certainty. But the rightmost digit (9) has been estimated and involves some uncertainty. These reported digits all convey useful information, however, and are called significant figures. The **significant figures** in a measurement include all of the digits that are known, plus a last digit that is estimated. 🔑 **Measurements must always be reported to the correct number of significant figures because calculated answers often depend on the number of significant figures in the values used in the calculation.**

Instruments differ in the number of significant figures that can be obtained from their use and thus in the precision of measurements. The three meter sticks in Figure 3.4 can be used to make successively more precise measurements.

0.8 m

1m

0.77 m

10   20   30   40   50   60   70   80   90   1m

0.772 m

10   20   30   40   50   60   70   80   90   1m

> *More on* precision in measurements *online.*

KINETIC ART

Figure 3.4 Increasing Precision
Three differently calibrated meter sticks are used to measure a door's width. A meter stick calibrated in 0.1-m (1 dm) intervals is more precise than one calibrated in a 1-m interval but less precise than one calibrated in 0.01-m (1 cm) intervals. **Measure** *How many significant figures are reported in each measurement?*

Determining Significant Figures in Measurements To determine whether a digit in a measured value is significant, you need to apply the following rules.

1. Every nonzero digit in a reported measurement is assumed to be significant.

24.7 meters
0.743 meter
714 meters

Each of these measurements has three significant figures.

---

2. Zeros appearing between nonzero digits are significant.

7003 meters
40.79 meters
1.503 meters

Each of these measurements has four significant figures.

---

3. Leftmost zeros appearing in front of nonzero digits are not significant. They act as placeholders. By writing the measurements in scientific notation, you can eliminate such placeholding zeros.

$$0.0071 \text{ meter} = 7.1 \times 10^{-3} \text{ meter}$$
$$0.42 \text{ meter} = 4.2 \times 10^{-1} \text{ meter}$$
$$0.000099 \text{ meter} = 9.9 \times 10^{-5} \text{ meter}$$

Each of these measurements has only two significant figures.

---

4. Zeros at the end of a number and to the right of a decimal point are always significant.

43.00 meters
1.010 meters
9.000 meters

Each of these measurements has four significant figures.

---

5. Zeros at the rightmost end of a measurement that lie to the left of an understood decimal point are not significant if they serve as placeholders to show the magnitude of the number.

300 meters (one significant figure)
7000 meters (one significant figure)
27,210 meters (four significant figures)

The zeros in these measurements are not significant.

If such zeros were known measured values, however, then they would be significant. Writing the value in scientific notation makes it clear that these zeros are significant.

$$300 \text{ meters} = 3.00 \times 10^2 \text{ meters}$$
(three significant figures)

The zeros in this measurement are significant.

---

6. There are two situations in which numbers have an unlimited number of significant figures. The first involves counting. A number that is counted is exact.

23 people in your classroom

This measurement is a counted value, so it has an unlimited number of significant figures.

The second situation involves exactly defined quantities such as those found within a system of measurement.

60 min = 1 hr
100 cm = 1 m

Each of these numbers has an unlimited number of significant figures.

Counting Significant Figures in Measurements

How many significant figures are in each measurement?

a. 123 m

b. 40,506 mm

c. 9.8000×10^4 m

d. 22 meter sticks

e. 0.070 80 m

f. 98,000 m

> Make sure you understand the rules for counting significant figures (on the previous page) before you begin, okay?

❶ Analyze **Identify the relevant concepts.** The location of each zero in the measurement and the location of the decimal point determine which of the rules apply for determining significant figures. These locations are known by inspecting each measurement value.

❷ Solve **Apply the concepts to this problem.**

Apply the rules for determining significant figures. All nonzero digits are significant (rule 1). Use rules 2 through 6 to determine if the zeros are significant.

a. three (rule 1)

b. five (rule 2)

c. five (rule 4)

d. unlimited (rule 6)

e. four (rules 2, 3, 4)

f. two (rule 5)

---

4. Count the significant figures in each measured length.

a. 0.057 30 meter

b. 8765 meters

c. 0.000 73 meter

d. 40.007 meters

5. How many significant figures are in each measurement?

a. 143 grams

b. 0.074 meter

c. 8.750×10^{-2} gram

d. 1.072 meters

CHEMISTRY & YOU

Q: *Suppose that the winner of a 100-meter dash finishes the race in 9.98 seconds. The runner in second place has a time of 10.05 seconds. How many significant figures are in each measurement? Is one measurement more accurate than the other? Explain your answer.*

Significant Figures in Calculations Suppose you use a calculator to find the area of a floor that measures 7.7 meters by 5.4 meters. The calculator would give an answer of 41.58 square meters. However, each of the measurements used in the calculation is expressed to only two significant figures. As a result, the answer must also be reported to two significant figures (42 m²). In general, a calculated answer cannot be more precise than the least precise measurement from which it was calculated. The calculated value must be rounded to make it consistent with the measurements from which it was calculated.

Rounding To round a number, you must first decide how many significant figures the answer should have. This decision depends on the given measurements and on the mathematical process used to arrive at the answer. Once you know the number of significant figures your answer should have, round to that many digits, counting from the left. If the digit immediately to the right of the last significant digit is less than 5, it is simply dropped and the value of the last significant digit stays the same. If the digit in question is 5 or greater, the value of the digit in the last significant place is increased by 1.

Rounding Measurements

Round off each measurement to the number of significant figures shown in parentheses. Write the answers in scientific notation.

- **a.** 314.721 meters (four)
- **b.** 0.001 775 meter (two)
- **c.** 8792 meters (two)

❶ Analyze **Identify the relevant concepts.** Using the rules for determining significant figures, round the number in each measurement. Then apply the rules for expressing numbers in scientific notation.

❷ Solve **Apply the concepts to this problem.**

> Starting from the left, count the first four digits that are significant. The arrow points to the digit immediately following the last significant digit.

a. 314.721 meters

2 is less than 5, so you do not round up.

314.7 meters = 3.147×10^2 meters

> Starting from the left, count the first two digits that are significant. The arrow points to the digit immediately following the second significant digit.

b. 0.001 775 meters

7 is greater than 5, so round up.

0.0018 meter = 1.8×10^{-3} meter

> Starting from the left, count the first two digits that are significant. The arrow points to the digit immediately following the second significant digit.

c. 8792 meters

9 is greater than 5, so round up.

8800 meters = 8.8×10^3 meters

---

6. Round each measurement to three significant figures. Write your answers in scientific notation.
- **a.** 87.073 meters
- **b.** 4.3621×10^8 meters
- **c.** 0.01552 meter
- **d.** 9009 meters
- **e.** 1.7777×10^{-3} meter
- **f.** 629.55 meters

7. Round each measurement in Problem 6 to one significant figure. Write each of your answers in scientific notation.

> If you're already familiar with rounding numbers, you can skip to Sample Problems 3.5 and 3.6.

Addition and Subtraction The answer to an addition or subtraction calculation should be rounded to the same number of decimal places (not digits) as the measurement with the least number of decimal places. Sample Problem 3.5 gives examples of rounding in addition and subtraction.

Multiplication and Division In calculations involving multiplication and division (such as those in Sample Problem 3.6), you need to round the answer to the same number of significant figures as the measurement with the least number of significant figures. The position of the decimal point has nothing to do with the rounding process when multiplying and dividing measurements. The position of the decimal point is important only in rounding the answers of addition or subtraction problems.

Sample Problem 3.5

Significant Figures in Addition and Subtraction

Perform the following addition and subtraction operations. Give each answer to the correct number of significant figures.

- **a.** 12.52 meters + 349.0 meters + 8.24 meters
- **b.** 74.626 meters − 28.34 meters

❶ Analyze Identify the relevant concepts. Perform the specified math operation, and then round the answer to match the measurement with the least number of decimal places.

❷ Solve Apply the concepts to this problem.

Align the decimal points and add the numbers.

a.
$$\begin{array}{r} 12.52 \text{ meters} \\ 349.0 \text{ meters} \\ + \quad 8.24 \text{ meters} \\ \hline 369.76 \text{ meters} \end{array}$$

The second measurement (349.0 meters) has the least number of digits (one) to the right of the decimal point. So the answer must be rounded to one digit after the decimal point.

$369.8 \text{ meters} = 3.698 \times 10^2 \text{ meters}$

Align the decimal points and subtract the numbers.

b.
$$\begin{array}{r} 74.626 \text{ meters} \\ - \quad 28.34 \text{ meters} \\ \hline 46.286 \text{ meters} \end{array}$$

The second measurement (28.34 meters) has the least number of digits (two) to the right of the decimal point. So the answer must be rounded to two digits after the decimal point.

$46.29 \text{ meters} = 4.629 \times 10^1 \text{ meters}$

---

8. Perform each operation. Express your answers to the correct number of significant figures.
- **a.** 61.2 meters + 9.35 meters + 8.6 meters
- **b.** 9.44 meters − 2.11 meters
- **c.** 1.36 meters + 10.17 meters
- **d.** 34.61 meters − 17.3 meters

9. Find the total mass of three diamonds that have masses of 14.2 grams, 8.73 grams, and 0.912 gram.

SampleProblem 3.6

Significant Figures in Multiplication and Division

Perform the following operations. Give the answers to the correct number of significant figures.

- **a.** 7.55 meters $\times$ 0.34 meter
- **b.** 2.10 meters $\times$ 0.70 meter
- **c.** 2.4526 meters^2 $\div$ 8.4 meters
- **d.** 0.365 meter^2 $\div$ 0.0200 meter

❶ Analyze **Identify the relevant concepts.** Perform the specified math operation, and then round the answer to match the measurement with the least number of significant figures.

❷ Solve **Apply the concepts to this problem.**

> The second measurement (0.34 meter) has the least number of significant figures (two). So the answer must be rounded to two significant figures.

a. 7.55 meters $\times$ 0.34 meter = 2.567 (meter)^2
= **2.6 meters^2**

> The second measurement (0.70 meter) has the least number of significant figures (two). So the answer must be rounded to two significant figures.

b. 2.10 meters $\times$ 0.70 meter = 1.47 (meter)^2
= **1.5 meters^2**

> The second measurement (8.4 meters) has the least number of significant figures (two). So the answer must be rounded to two significant figures.

c. 2.4526 meters^2 $\div$ 8.4 meters = 0.291 976 meter
= **0.29 meter**

> Both measurements have three significant figures. So the answer must be rounded to three significant figures.

d. 0.365 meters^2 $\div$ 0.0200 meter = 18.25 meters
= **18.3 meters**

10. Solve each problem. Give your answers to the correct number of significant figures and in scientific notation.

- **a.** 8.3 meters $\times$ 2.22 meters
- **b.** 8432 meters^2 $\div$ 12.5 meters
- **c.** 35.2 seconds $\times \dfrac{1\ \text{minute}}{60\ \text{seconds}}$

11. Calculate the volume of a warehouse that has measured dimensions of 22.4 meters by 11.3 meters by 5.2 meters. (Volume $= l \times w \times h$)

> In Problem 11, the measurement with the fewest significant figures is 5.2 meters. What does this tell you?

Purpose To measure the dimensions of an object as accurately and precisely as possible and to apply rules for rounding answers calculated from the measurements

Materials
• 3-inch × 5-inch index card
• metric ruler

Accuracy and Precision

Procedure

1. Use a metric ruler to measure in centimeters the length and width of an index card as accurately as you can. The hundredths place in your measurement should be estimated.

2. Calculate the area ($A = l \times w$) and the perimeter [$P = 2 \times (l + w)$] of the index card. Write both your unrounded answers and your correctly rounded answers on the chalkboard.

Analyze and Conclude

1. Identify How many significant figures are in your measurements of length and of width?

2. Compare How do your measurements compare with those of your classmates?

3. Explain How many significant figures are in your calculated value for the area? In your calculated value for the perimeter? Do your rounded answers have as many significant figures as your classmates' measurements?

4. Evaluate Assume that the correct (accurate) length and width of the card are 12.70 cm and 7.62 cm, respectively. Calculate the percent error for each of your two measurements.

3.1 LessonCheck

12. 🔑 **Review** How can you express a number in scientific notation?

13. 🔑 **Review** How are accuracy and precision evaluated?

14. 🔑 **Explain** Why must a given measurement always be reported to the correct number of significant figures?

15. Calculate A technician experimentally determined the boiling point of octane to be 124.1°C. The actual boiling point of octane is 125.7°C. Calculate the error and the percent error.

16. Evaluate Determine the number of significant figures in each of the following measurements:

    a. 11 soccer players
    b. 0.070 020 meter
    c. 10,800 meters
    d. 0.010 square meter
    e. 5.00 cubic meters
    f. 507 thumbtacks

17. Calculate Solve the following and express each answer in scientific notation and to the correct number of significant figures.

    a. $(5.3 \times 10^4) + (1.3 \times 10^4)$
    b. $(7.2 \times 10^{-4}) \div (1.8 \times 10^3)$
    c. $10^4 \times 10^{-3} \times 10^6$
    d. $(9.12 \times 10^{-1}) - (4.7 \times 10^{-2})$
    e. $(5.4 \times 10^4) \times (3.5 \times 10^9)$

BIGIDEA QUANTIFYING MATTER

18. Write a brief paragraph explaining the differences between the accuracy, precision, and error of a measurement.

Watch What You Measure

Just because you live in a digital age doesn't mean that you no longer have to do things by hand. In fact, manually measuring quantities remains an important everyday skill in a number of professions and activities. For example, chefs measure volumes of ingredients in cups (C) or liters (L). Tailors use a tape measure calibrated in inches (in. or ″) to measure length, while biologists use metric rulers or calipers calibrated in centimeters (cm). A ship's navigator uses a sextant to measure the angle between the sun and the horizon. The angle is expressed in degrees (°) and minutes (′).

The next time you make a measurement in lab, keep in mind that lots of other measurers are rounding and noting significant figures, just like you are.

$7\frac{3}{4}$″

7.92 cm

42° 31.4′

Take It Further

1. Measure What is the measured height of the tomato shown above? How many significant figures does your answer have?

2. Identify What are some other activities that involve measurements done by hand? What units and measuring tools are used?

3.2 Units of Measurement

Q: *What's the forecast for tomorrow—hot or cold?* In the weather forecast shown here, the temperatures are in degrees, but without a temperature scale. Will the high temperature tomorrow be 28°C, which is very warm? Or 28°F, which is very cold? Without the correct units, you can't be sure. When you make a measurement, you must assign the correct units to the number. Without the units, it's impossible to communicate the measurement clearly to others.

Key Questions

🔑 **What makes metric units easy to use?**

🔑 **What temperature units do scientists commonly use?**

🔑 **What determines the density of a substance?**

Vocabulary

- International System of Units (SI)
- meter (m) • liter (L)
- kilogram (kg) • gram (g)
- weight • energy
- joule (J) • calorie (cal)
- temperature • Celsius scale
- Kelvin scale • absolute zero
- density

Learn more about SI units online.

Using SI Units

🔑 **What makes metric units easy to use?**

All measurements depend on units that serve as reference standards. The standards of measurement used in science are those of the metric system. The metric system is important because of its simplicity and ease of use.

🔑 **All metric units are based on multiples of 10. As a result, you can convert between units easily.** The metric system was originally established in France in 1795. The **International System of Units** (abbreviated **SI**, after the French name, *Le Système International d'Unités*) is a revised version of the metric system. The SI was adopted by international agreement in 1960. There are seven SI base units, which are listed in Table 3.1. From these base units, all other SI units of measurement can be derived. Derived units are used for measurements such as volume, density, and pressure.

All measured quantities can be reported in SI units. Sometimes, however, non-SI units are preferred for convenience or for practical reasons. In this textbook you will learn about both SI and non-SI units.

Table 3.1

SI Base Units		
Quantity	SI base unit	Symbol
Length	meter	m
Mass	kilogram	kg
Temperature	kelvin	K
Time	second	s
Amount of substance	mole	mol
Luminous intensity	candela	cd
Electric current	ampere	A

Table 3.2

		Commonly Used Metric Prefixes	
Prefix	Symbol	Meaning	Factor
mega	M	1 million times larger than the unit it precedes	10^6
kilo	k	1000 times larger than the unit it precedes	10^3
deci	d	10 times smaller than the unit it precedes	10^{-1}
centi	c	100 times smaller than the unit it precedes	10^{-2}
milli	m	1000 times smaller than the unit it precedes	10^{-3}
micro	μ	1 million times smaller than the unit it precedes	10^{-6}
nano	n	1 billion times smaller than the unit it precedes	10^{-9}
pico	p	1 trillion times smaller than the unit it precedes	10^{-12}

Units of Length Size is an important property of matter. In SI, the basic unit of length, or linear measure, is the **meter (m).** All measurements of length can be expressed in meters. (The length of a page in this book is about one fourth of a meter.) For very large and very small lengths, however, it may be more convenient to use a unit of length that has a prefix. Table 3.2 lists the prefixes in common use. For example, the prefix *milli-* means 1/1000 (one-thousandth), so a millimeter (mm) is 1/1000 of a meter, or 0.001 m. A hyphen (-) measures about 1 mm.

For large distances, it is usually most appropriate to express measurements in kilometers (km). The prefix *kilo-* means 1000, so 1 km equals 1000 m. A standard marathon distance race of about 42,000 m is more conveniently expressed as 42 km (42 × 1000 m). Table 3.3 summarizes the relationships among metric units of length.

button diameter = 1 cm

dime thickness = 1 mm

Table 3.3

		Metric Units of Length	
Unit	Symbol	Relationship	Example
Kilometer	km	1 km = 10^3 m	length of about five city blocks ≈ 1 km
Meter	m	base unit	height of doorknob from the floor ≈ 1 m
Decimeter	dm	10^1 dm = 1 m	diameter of large orange ≈ 1 dm
Centimeter	cm	10^2 cm = 1 m	diameter of shirt button ≈ 1 cm
Millimeter	mm	10^3 mm = 1 m	thickness of dime ≈ 1 mm
Micrometer	μm	10^6 μm = 1 m	diameter of bacterial cell ≈ 1 μm
Nanometer	nm	10^9 nm = 1 m	thickness of RNA molecule ≈ 1 nm

Figure 3.5 Volumetric Units
The volume of 20 drops of liquid from a medicine dropper is about 1 mL. This is the same volume as that of a sugar cube, which is 1 cm on each edge; $1 \text{ cm}^3 = 1 \text{ mL}$. A liter bottle has a volume of 1 L, or 1000 mL.
Describe *What is the volume of a 2-L bottle in cubic centimeters?*

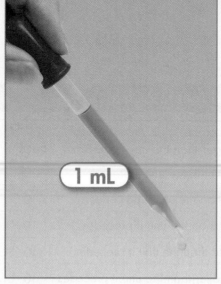
1 mL

1 cm^3

1 L

Units of Volume The space occupied by any sample of matter is called its volume. You calculate the volume of any cubic or rectangular solid by multiplying its length by its width by its height. The unit for volume is thus derived from units of length. The SI unit of volume is the amount of space occupied by a cube that is 1 m along each edge. This volume is a cubic meter (m^3). An automatic dishwasher has a volume of about 1 m^3.

A more convenient unit of volume for everyday use is the liter, a non-SI unit. A **liter (L)** is the volume of a cube that is 10 centimeters (10 cm) along each edge (10 cm $\times$ 10 cm $\times$ 10 cm = 1000 cm^3 = 1 L). A decimeter (dm) is equal to 10 cm, so 1 L is also equal to 1 cubic decimeter (dm^3). A smaller non-SI unit of volume is the milliliter (mL); 1 mL is 1/1000 of a liter. Thus, there are 1000 mL in 1 L. Because 1 L is defined as 1000 cm^3, 1 mL and 1 cm^3 are the same volume. The units milliliter and cubic centimeter are thus used interchangeably. Figure 3.5 gives you some idea of the relative sizes of a liter and a milliliter. Table 3.4 summarizes the relationships among common metric units of volume.

There are many devices for measuring liquid volumes, including graduated cylinders, pipets, burets, volumetric flasks, and syringes. Note that the volume of any solid, liquid, or gas will change with temperature (although the change is much more dramatic for gases). Consequently, accurate volume-measuring devices are calibrated at a given temperature—usually 20 degrees Celsius (20°C), which is about normal room temperature.

Table 3.4

Metric Units of Volume			
Unit	**Symbol**	**Relationship**	**Example**
Liter	L	base unit	quart of milk ≈ 1 L
Milliliter	mL	$10^3 \text{ mL} = 1 \text{ L}$	20 drops of water ≈ 1 mL
Cubic centimeter	cm^3	$1 \text{ cm}^3 = 1 \text{ mL}$	cube of sugar ≈ 1 cm^3
Microliter	μL	$10^6 \text{ μL} = 1 \text{ L}$	crystal of table salt ≈ 1 μL

Table 3.5

Metric Units of Mass

Unit	Symbol	Relationship	Example
Kilogram (base unit)	kg	$1 \text{ kg} = 10^3 \text{ g}$	small textbook ≈ 1 kg
Gram	g	$1 \text{ g} = 10^{-3} \text{ kg}$	dollar bill ≈ 1 g
Milligram	mg	$10^3 \text{ mg} = 1 \text{ g}$	ten grains of salt ≈ 1 mg
Microgram	μg	$10^6 \text{ μg} = 1 \text{ g}$	particle of baking powder ≈ 1 μg

Units of Mass The mass of an object is measured in comparison to a standard mass of 1 **kilogram (kg),** which is the basic SI unit of mass. A kilogram was originally defined as the mass of 1 L of liquid water at 4°C. A cube of water at 4°C measuring 10 cm on each edge would have a volume of 1 L and a mass of 1000 grams (g), or 1 kg. A **gram (g)** is 1/1000 of a kilogram; the mass of 1 cm^3 of water at 4°C is 1 g. The relationships among units of mass are shown in Table 3.5.

You can use a platform balance to measure the mass of an object. The object is placed on one side of the balance, and standard masses are added to the other side until the balance beam is level. The unknown mass is equal to the sum of the standard masses. Laboratory balances range from very sensitive instruments with a maximum capacity of only a few milligrams to devices for measuring quantities in kilograms. An analytical balance is used to measure objects of less than 100 g and can determine mass to the nearest 0.0001 g (0.1 mg).

Weight is a force that measures the pull on a given mass by gravity. Weight, a measure of force, is different from mass, which is a measure of the quantity of matter. The weight of an object can change with its location. For example, an astronaut on the surface of the moon weighs one sixth of what he weighs on Earth. The reason for this difference is that the force of Earth's gravity is about six times greater than that of the moon. The astronaut in Figure 3.6 is in free fall as he orbits Earth and is therefore weightless. Although it's possible for an object to become weightless, it can never become massless.

Figure 3.6 Weightlessness
An astronaut in orbit is weightless, but not massless. The astronaut's mass remains constant regardless of location or motion.

Units of Energy The capacity to do work or to produce heat is called **energy.** Like any other quantity, energy can be measured. The SI unit of energy is the **joule (J),** named after the English physicist James Prescott Joule (1818–1889). A common non-SI unit of energy is the calorie. One **calorie (cal)** is the quantity of heat that raises the temperature of 1 g of pure water by 1°C. Conversions between joules and calories can be carried out using the following relationships:

$$1 \text{ J} = 0.2390 \text{ cal} \qquad 1 \text{ cal} = 4.184 \text{ J}$$

In this book, you will see energy values expressed in both joules and calories, as well as kilojoules (kJ) and kilocalories (kcal). A kilojoule is 1000 joules; a kilocalorie is 1000 calories.

Temperature Scales

🔑 What temperature units do scientists commonly use?

When you hold a glass of hot water, the glass feels hot because heat transfers from the glass to your hand. When you hold an ice cube, it feels cold because heat transfers from your hand to the ice cube. **Temperature** is a measure of how hot or cold an object is. An object's temperature determines the direction of heat transfer. When two objects at different temperatures are in contact, heat moves from the object at the higher temperature to the object at the lower temperature. In Chapter 13, you will learn how the temperature of an object is related to the energy and motion of particles.

Almost all substances expand with an increase in temperature and contract as the temperature decreases. (A very important exception is water.) These properties are the basis for the common bulb thermometer. The liquid in the thermometer expands and contracts more than the volume of the glass, producing changes in the column height of liquid. Figure 3.7 shows two different types of thermometers.

Several temperature scales with different units have been devised. 🔑 **Scientists commonly use two equivalent units of temperature, the degree Celsius and the kelvin.** The Celsius scale of the metric system is named after the Swedish astronomer Anders Celsius (1701–1744). It uses two readily determined temperatures as reference temperature values: the freezing point and the boiling point of water. The **Celsius scale** sets the freezing point of water at 0°C and the boiling point of water at 100°C. The distance between these two fixed points is divided into 100 equal intervals, or degrees Celsius (°C).

Another temperature scale used in the physical sciences is the Kelvin, or absolute, scale. This scale is named for Lord Kelvin (1824–1907), a Scottish physicist and mathematician. On the **Kelvin scale,** the freezing point of water is 273.15 kelvins (K), and the boiling point is 373.15 K. Notice that with the Kelvin scale, the degree sign is not used.

Figure 3.7 Thermometers
A bulb thermometer contains a liquid such as alcohol or mineral spirits. A dial thermometer, often used to measure the cooking temperature of meats, contains a coiled bimetallic strip.

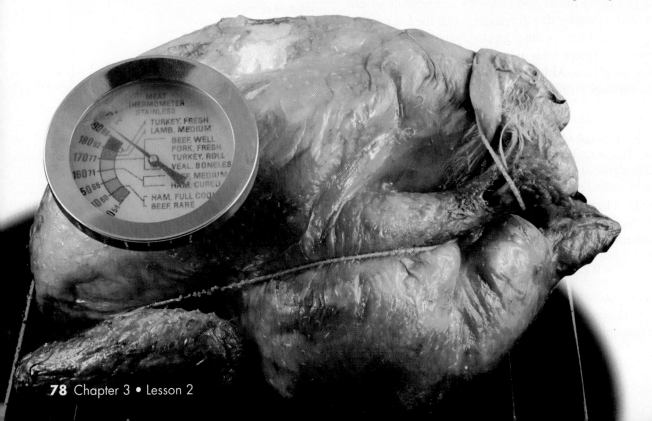

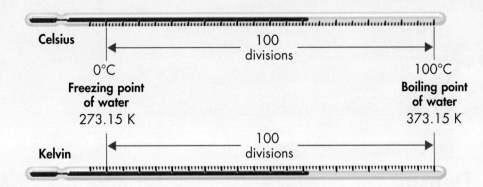

Celsius

0°C
Freezing point
of water
273.15 K

100 divisions

100°C
Boiling point
of water
373.15 K

100 divisions

Kelvin

Figure 3.8 Temperature Scales
A 1°C change on the Celsius scale is equal to a 1 K change on the Kelvin scale.
Interpret Diagrams *What is a change of 10°C equivalent to on the Kelvin scale?*

Figure 3.8 compares the Celsius and Kelvin scales. A change of one degree on the Celsius scale is equivalent to one kelvin on the Kelvin scale. The zero point on the Kelvin scale, 0 K, or **absolute zero,** is equal to −273.15°C. For problems in this text, you can round −273.15°C to −273°C. Because one degree on the Celsius scale is equivalent to one kelvin on the Kelvin scale, converting from one temperature to another is easy. You simply add or subtract 273, as shown in the following equations:

$$K = °C + 273$$
$$°C = K - 273$$

CHEMISTRY & YOU

Q: *In a few countries, such as the United States, metric units are not commonly used in everyday measurements. What temperature units are used for a typical weather forecast in the United States? What about for a country that uses the metric system, such as Australia or Japan?*

SampleProblem 3.7

Converting Between Temperature Scales

Normal human body temperature is 37°C. What is this temperature in kelvins?

❶ Analyze **List the known and the unknown.**
Use the known value and the equation K = °C + 273 to calculate the temperature in kelvins.

KNOWN
Temperature in °C = 37°C

UNKNOWN
Temperature in K = ? K

❷ Calculate **Solve for the unknown.**

Substitute the known value for the Celsius temperature into the equation and solve.

$$K = °C + 273 = 37 + 273 = 310 \text{ K}$$

❸ Evaluate **Does the result make sense?** You should expect a temperature in this range, since the freezing point of water is 273 K and the boiling point of water is 373 K; normal body temperature is between these two values.

19. The element silver melts at 960.8°C and boils at 2212°C. Express these temperatures in kelvins.

20. Liquid nitrogen boils at 77.2 K. What is this temperature in degrees Celsius?

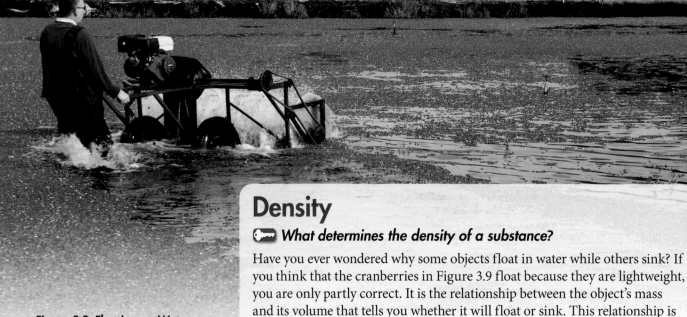

Density

What determines the density of a substance?

Have you ever wondered why some objects float in water while others sink? If you think that the cranberries in Figure 3.9 float because they are lightweight, you are only partly correct. It is the relationship between the object's mass and its volume that tells you whether it will float or sink. This relationship is called density. **Density** is the ratio of the mass of an object to its volume.

Figure 3.9 Floating on Water
Cranberries are less dense than water, so they float. Farmers make use of this property when it's time to harvest the crop.

$$\text{Density} = \frac{\text{mass}}{\text{volume}}$$

A 10.0-cm^3 piece of lead, for example, has a mass of 114 g. You can calculate the density of lead by substituting into the equation above.

$$\frac{114 \text{ g}}{10.0 \text{ cm}^3} = 11.4 \text{ g/cm}^3$$

Note that when mass is measured in grams, and volume in cubic centimeters, density has units of grams per cubic centimeter (g/cm^3). The SI unit of density is kilograms per cubic meter (kg/m^3).

Figure 3.10 compares the density of four substances: lithium, water, aluminum, and lead. Why does each 10-g sample have a different volume? The volumes vary because the substances have different densities. **Density is an intensive property that depends only on the composition of a substance, not on the size of the sample.** With a mixture, density can vary because the composition of a mixture can vary.

Figure 3.10 Comparing Densities
A 10-g sample of pure water has less volume than 10 g of lithium, but more volume than 10 g of lead or 10 g of aluminum. The faces of the cubes are shown actual size.
Predict *Which of the solids shown will sink in water?*

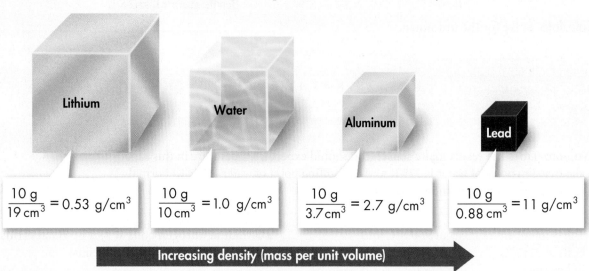

Lithium

Water

Aluminum

Lead

$$\frac{10 \text{ g}}{19 \text{ cm}^3} = 0.53 \text{ g/cm}^3$$

$$\frac{10 \text{ g}}{10 \text{ cm}^3} = 1.0 \text{ g/cm}^3$$

$$\frac{10 \text{ g}}{3.7 \text{ cm}^3} = 2.7 \text{ g/cm}^3$$

$$\frac{10 \text{ g}}{0.88 \text{ cm}^3} = 11 \text{ g/cm}^3$$

Increasing density (mass per unit volume)

| Densities of Some Common Materials | | | |
| Solids and Liquids | | Gases | |
Material	Density at 20°C (g/cm³)	Material	Density at 20°C (g/L)
Gold	19.3	Chlorine	2.95
Mercury	13.6	Carbon dioxide	1.83
Lead	11.3	Argon	1.66
Aluminum	2.70	Oxygen	1.33
Table sugar	1.59	Air	1.20
Corn syrup	1.35–1.38	Nitrogen	1.17
Water (4°C)	1.000	Neon	0.84
Corn oil	0.922	Ammonia	0.718
Ice (0°C)	0.917	Methane	0.665
Ethanol	0.789	Helium	0.166
Gasoline	0.66–0.69	Hydrogen	0.084

Table 3.6 Density is the mass per unit volume of a material.

a. Compare Why do you think the densities of the gases are reported in units that are different from those used for the densities of the solids and liquids?

b. Predict Would a balloon filled with carbon dioxide sink or rise in air? Explain.

c. Infer Why are the densities of corn syrup and gasoline expressed as a range of values?

Note the units here: Densities of the solids and liquids are expressed in g/cm³. Densities of the gases are expressed in g/L.

What do you think will happen if corn oil is poured into a container of water? Using Table 3.6, you can see that the density of corn oil is less than the density of water. For that reason, the oil floats on top of the water. Figure 3.11 shows different liquids forming distinct layers in a container due to differences in density. For example, the corn syrup (colored red), sinks below the water (colored green) because the density of corn syrup is greater than the density of water.

You have probably seen a helium-filled balloon rapidly rise to the ceiling when it is released. Whether a gas-filled balloon will sink or rise when released depends on how the density of the gas compares with the density of air. Helium is less dense than air, so a helium-filled balloon rises. The densities of various gases are listed in Table 3.6.

What happens to the density of a substance as its temperature increases? Experiments show that the volume of most substances increases as the temperature increases. Meanwhile, the mass remains the same despite the temperature and volume changes. Remember that density is the ratio of an object's mass to its volume. So if the volume changes with temperature (while the mass remains constant), then the density must also change with temperature. The density of a substance generally decreases as its temperature increases. As you will learn in Chapter 15, water is an important exception. Over a certain range of temperatures, the volume of water increases as its temperature decreases. Ice, or solid water, floats because it is less dense (0.917 g/cm³) than liquid water (1.000 g/cm³).

Figure 3.11 Liquid Layers
Because of differences in density, the liquids separate into layers.
Compare *Is the blue-colored liquid more or less dense than water?*

Sample Problem 3.8

Calculating Density

A copper penny has a mass of 3.1 g and a volume of 0.35 cm³. What is the density of copper?

❶ Analyze List the knowns and the unknown.
Use the known values and the equation for density to solve the problem.

KNOWNS	UNKNOWN
mass = 3.1 g	density = ? g/cm³
volume = 0.35 cm³	

❷ Calculate Solve for the unknown.

Start with the equation for density.

$$\text{Density} = \frac{\text{mass}}{\text{volume}}$$

The calculated answer must be rounded to two significant figures.

Substitute the known values for mass and volume and then calculate.

$$\text{Density} = \frac{3.1 \text{ g}}{0.35 \text{ cm}^3} = 8.8571 \text{ g/cm}^3 = \boxed{8.9 \text{ g/cm}^3}$$

❸ Evaluate Does the result make sense? A piece of copper with a volume of about 0.3 cm³ has a mass of about 3 grams. About three times that volume of copper, 1 cm³, should have a mass three times larger, about 9 grams. This estimate is close to the calculated result.

---

21. A student finds a shiny piece of metal that she thinks is aluminum. In the lab, she determines that the metal has a volume of 245 cm³ and a mass of 612 g. Calculate the density. Is the metal aluminum?

22. A bar of silver has a mass of 68.0 g and a volume of 6.48 cm³. What is the density of silver?

3.2 LessonCheck

23. 🔑 **Review** Why are metric units easy to use?

24. 🔑 **Identify** What temperature units do scientists commonly use?

25. 🔑 **Review** What determines density?

26. **Identify** Write the name and symbol of the SI units for mass, length, volume, and temperature.

27. **Define** Write the symbol and meaning of each prefix below.
   a. *milli-*   **b.** *nano-*   **c.** *deci-*   **d.** *centi-*

28. **List** Arrange the following units in order from largest to smallest: m³, mL, cL, µL, L, dL.

29. **Calculate** What is the volume of a paperback book 21 cm tall, 12 cm wide, and 3.5 cm thick?

30. **Compare** State the difference between mass and weight.

31. **Calculate** Surgical instruments may be sterilized by heating at 170°C for 1.5 hr. Convert 170°C to kelvins.

32. **Calculate** A weather balloon is inflated to a volume of 2.2 × 10³ L with 374 g of helium. What is the density of helium in grams per liter?

33. **Apply Concepts** A 68-g bar of gold is cut into three equal pieces. How does the density of each piece compare to the density of the original gold bar?

34. **Interpret Data** Look up the densities of the elements in Group 1A on page R2. Which Group 1A elements are less dense than pure water at 4°C?

35. **Explain** How does density vary with temperature?

Carbon Footprints

To measure a footprint, you might use units such as centimeters or inches. But what about a carbon footprint? A carbon footprint is a measure of how much greenhouse gas is released into the atmosphere by a person, country, or industry. Greenhouse gases, such as carbon dioxide (CO_2) and methane (CH_4), are gases that contribute to global warming.

Any activity that involves the burning of fossil fuels results in carbon dioxide emissions. Car travel, air travel, home heating and cooling, and electricity usage all add to an individual's carbon footprint. Your own carbon footprint is the total mass of CO_2 that you put into the atmosphere over the course of a year. This quantity can be expressed in metric tons (t) of CO_2 per year. A metric ton equals 1000 kg. So, the units of your carbon footprint can be abbreviated as: t CO_2/yr or 10^3 kg CO_2/yr.

CARBON COSTS Your choices affect the size of your carbon footprint. For example, using a clothes dryer consumes electricity, but hanging wet laundry on a clothesline does not. The things you buy also contribute to your carbon footprint. Not only is energy required to make these goods, but the goods themselves (such as TVs) may consume energy.

FOOTPRINT UNITS The carbon footprint of fresh produce can be expressed in g CO_2 per serving. Cars require different units: kg CO_2 per gallon of gasoline. For planes, the units are kg CO_2 per passenger mile.

Take It Further

1. Calculate A car emits 8.6 kg of CO_2 per gallon of unleaded gas. How much CO_2 is produced if the car burns 2.5 gal of fuel?

2. Infer What factors do you think determine the carbon footprint of an apple? Why might the carbon footprints of two apples in the same store differ substantially?

3.3 Solving Conversion Problems

CHEMISTRY & YOU

Q: *How can you convert U.S. dollars to euros?* Perhaps you have traveled to another country or are planning to do so. If so, you know (or will soon discover) that different countries have different currencies. As a tourist, exchanging money is an important part of having a good trip. After all, you often must use cash to pay for meals, transportation, and souvenirs. Because each country's currency compares differently with the U.S. dollar, knowing how to convert currency units correctly is essential. Conversion problems are readily solved by a problem-solving approach called dimensional analysis.

Key Questions

🔑 What happens when a measurement is multiplied by a conversion factor?

🔑 What kinds of problems can you solve using dimensional analysis?

Vocabulary

- conversion factor
- dimensional analysis

Conversion Factors

🔑 **What happens when a measurement is multiplied by a conversion factor?**

If you think about any number of everyday situations, you will realize that a quantity can usually be expressed in several different ways. For example, consider the monetary amount $1.

$$1 \text{ dollar} = 4 \text{ quarters} = 10 \text{ dimes} = 20 \text{ nickels} = 100 \text{ pennies}$$

These are all expressions, or measurements, of the same amount of money. The same thing is true of scientific quantities. For example, consider a distance that measures exactly 1 meter.

$$1 \text{ meter} = 10 \text{ decimeters} = 100 \text{ centimeters} = 1000 \text{ millimeters}$$

These are different ways to express the same length.

Whenever two measurements are equivalent, a ratio of the two meaurements will equal 1, or unity. For example, you can divide both sides of the equation 1 m = 100 cm by 1 m or by 100 cm.

$$\frac{1\text{m}}{1\text{m}} = \frac{100 \text{ cm}}{1 \text{ m}} = 1 \qquad \text{or} \qquad \frac{1 \text{ m}}{100 \text{ cm}} = \frac{100 \text{ cm}}{100 \text{ cm}} = 1$$

conversion factors

The ratios 100 cm/1 m and 1 m/100 cm are examples of conversion factors. A **conversion factor** is a ratio of equivalent measurements. The measurement in the numerator (on the top) is equivalent to the measurement in the denominator (on the bottom). The conversion factors shown above are read "one hundred centimeters per meter" and "one meter per hundred centimeters."

1 meter

100 centimeters

$$1 \text{ m} = \begin{array}{|c|c|c|c|c|c|c|c|c|} 10 & 20 & 30 & 40 & 50 & 60 & 70 & 80 & 90 \end{array}$$

Smaller number ➡ $\dfrac{1 \quad \text{m}}{100 \quad \text{cm}}$ ⬅ Larger unit

Larger number ➡ ⬅ Smaller unit

Figure 3.12 Conversion Factor
The two parts of a conversion factor, the numerator and the denominator, are equal.

See conversion factors *animated online.*

KINETIC ART

Figure 3.12 illustrates another way to look at the relationships in a conversion factor. Notice that the smaller number is part of the measurement with the larger unit. That is, a meter is physically larger than a centimeter. The larger number is part of the measurement with the smaller unit.

Conversion factors are useful in solving problems in which a given measurement must be expressed in some other unit of measure. ⚷ **When a measurement is multiplied by a conversion factor, the numerical value is generally changed, but the actual size of the quantity measured remains the same.** For example, even though the numbers in the measurements 1 g and 10 dg (decigrams) differ, both measurements represent the same mass. In addition, conversion factors within a system of measurement are defined quantities or exact quantities. Therefore, they have an unlimited number of significant figures and do not affect the rounding of a calculated answer.

Here are some additional examples of pairs of conversion factors written from equivalent measurements. The relationship between grams and kilograms is 1000 g = 1 kg. The conversion factors are

$$\frac{1000 \text{ g}}{1 \text{ kg}} \quad \text{and} \quad \frac{1 \text{ kg}}{1000 \text{ g}}$$

Figure 3.13 shows a scale that can be used to measure mass in grams or kilograms. If you read the scale in terms of grams, you can convert the mass to kilograms by multiplying by the conversion factor 1 kg/1000 g.

The relationship between nanometers and meters is given by the equation $10^9 \text{ nm} = 1 \text{ m}$. The possible conversion factors are

$$\frac{10^9 \text{ nm}}{1 \text{ m}} \quad \text{and} \quad \frac{1 \text{ m}}{10^9 \text{ nm}}$$

Common volumetric units used in chemistry include the liter and the microliter. The relationship $1 \text{ L} = 10^6 \text{ }\mu\text{L}$ yields the following conversion factors:

$$\frac{1 \text{ L}}{10^6 \text{ }\mu\text{L}} \quad \text{and} \quad \frac{10^6 \text{ }\mu\text{L}}{1 \text{ L}}$$

Based on what you have learned about metric prefixes, you should easily be able to write conversion factors that relate equivalent metric quantities.

Figure 3.13 Measuring Mass
This scale is calibrated to measure mass to the nearest 20 g.
Interpret Photos *What is the scale showing in grams? In kilograms?*

Dimensional Analysis

🔑 **What kinds of problems can you solve using dimensional analysis?**

Some problems are best solved using algebra. For example, converting a kelvin temperature to Celsius can be done by using the equation $°C = K - 273$. Many problems in chemistry are conveniently solved using dimensional analysis. **Dimensional analysis** is a way to analyze and solve problems using the units, or dimensions, of the measurements. The best way to explain this technique is to use it to solve an everyday situation, as in Sample Problem 3.9.

As you read Sample Problem 3.10, you might see how the same problem could be solved algebraically but is more easily solved using dimensional analysis. In either case, you should choose the problem-solving method that works best for you. Try to be flexible in your approach to problem solving, as no single method is best for solving every type of problem.

SampleProblem 3.9

Using Dimensional Analysis

How many seconds are in a workday that lasts exactly eight hours?

❶ **Analyze List the knowns and the unknown.**
To convert time in hours to time in seconds, you'll need two conversion factors. First you must convert hours to minutes: h ⟶ min. Then you must convert minutes to seconds: min ⟶ s. Identify the proper conversion factors based on the relationships 1 h = 60 min and 1 min = 60 s.

KNOWNS	UNKNOWN
time worked = 8 h	seconds worked = ? s
1 hour = 60 min	
1 minute = 60 s	

❷ **Calculate Solve for the unknown.**

The first conversion factor is based on 1 h = 60 min. The unit hours must be in the denominator so that the known unit will cancel.

$$\frac{60 \text{ min}}{1 \text{ h}}$$

The second conversion factor is based on 1 min = 60 s. The unit minutes must be in the denominator so that the desired units (seconds) will be in your answer.

$$\frac{60 \text{ s}}{1 \text{ min}}$$

Before you do the actual arithmetic, it's a good idea to make sure that the units cancel and that the numerator and denominator of each conversion factor are equal to each other.

Multiply the time worked by the conversion factors.

$$8 \text{ h} \times \frac{60 \text{ min}}{1 \text{ h}} \times \frac{60 \text{ s}}{1 \text{ min}} = 28,800 \text{ s} = 2.8800 \times 10^4 \text{ s}$$

❸ **Evaluate Does the result make sense?** The answer has the desired unit (s). Since the second is a small unit of time, you should expect a large number of seconds in 8 hours. The answer is exact since the given measurement and each of the conversion factors is exact.

36. How many minutes are there in exactly one week?

37. How many seconds are in an exactly 40-hour work week?

Sample Problem 3.10

Using Dimensional Analysis

The directions for an experiment ask each student to measure 1.84 g of copper (Cu) wire. The only copper wire available is a spool with a mass of 50.0 g. How many students can do the experiment before the copper runs out?

❶ Analyze List the knowns and the unknown.

From the known mass of copper, use the appropriate conversion factor to calculate the number of students who can do the experiment. The desired conversion is mass of copper ⟶ number of students.

KNOWNS

mass of copper available = 50.0 g Cu
Each student needs 1.84 grams of copper.

UNKNOWN

number of students = ?

❷ Calculate Solve for the unknown.

The experiment calls for 1.84 grams of copper per student. Based on this relationship, you can write two conversion factors.

$$\frac{1.84 \text{ g Cu}}{1 \text{ student}} \quad \text{and} \quad \frac{1 \text{ student}}{1.84 \text{ g Cu}}$$

Note that because students cannot be fractional, the answer is rounded down to a whole number.

Because the desired unit for the answer is students, use the second conversion factor. Multiply the mass of copper by the conversion factor.

$$50.0 \text{ g Cu} \times \frac{1 \text{ student}}{1.84 \text{ g Cu}} = 27.174 \text{ students} = \boxed{27 \text{ students}}$$

❸ Evaluate Does the result make sense? The unit of the answer (students) is the one desired. You can make an approximate calculation using the following conversion factor.

$$\frac{1 \text{ student}}{2 \text{ g Cu}}$$

Multiplying the above conversion factor by 50 g Cu gives the approximate answer of 25 students, which is close to the calculated answer.

38. An experiment requires that each student use an 8.5-cm length of magnesium ribbon. How many students can do the experiment if there is a 570-cm length of magnesium ribbon available?

Here's a tip: The equalities needed to write a particular conversion factor may be given in the problem. In other cases, you'll need to know or look up the necessary equalities.

39. A 1.00-degree increase on the Celsius scale is equivalent to a 1.80-degree increase on the Fahrenheit scale. If a temperature increases by 48.0°C, what is the corresponding temperature increase in °F?

40. An atom of gold has a mass of 3.271×10^{-22} g. How many atoms of gold are in 5.00 g of gold?

Q: *Look up the exchange rate between U.S. dollars and euros on the Internet. Write a conversion factor that allows you to convert from U.S. dollars to euros. How many euros could you buy with $50?*

Simple Unit Conversions In chemistry, as in everyday life, you often need to express a measurement in a unit different from the one given or measured initially. 🔑 **Dimensional analysis is a powerful tool for solving conversion problems in which a measurement with one unit is changed to an equivalent measurement with another unit.** Sample Problems 3.11 and 3.12 walk you through how to solve simple conversion problems using dimensional analysis.

Sample Problem 3.11

Converting Between Metric Units

Express 750 dg in grams. (Refer to Table 3.2 if you need to refresh your memory of metric prefixes.)

❶ Analyze List the knowns and the unknown.
The desired conversion is decigrams ⟶ grams. Multiply the given mass by the proper conversion factor.

KNOWNS	UNKNOWN
mass = 750 dg	mass = ? g
1 g = 10 dg	

❷ Calculate Solve for the unknown.

Use the relationship 1 g = 10 dg to write the correct conversion factor.

$$\frac{1\,g}{10\,dg}$$

Multiply the known mass by the conversion factor.

$$750\,dg \times \frac{1\,g}{10\,dg} = 75\,g$$

> Note that the known unit (dg) is in the denominator and the unknown unit (g) is in the numerator.

❸ Evaluate Does the result make sense? Because the unit gram represents a larger mass than the unit decigram, it makes sense that the number of grams is less than the given number of decigrams. The answer has the correct unit (g) and the correct number of significant figures.

41. Using tables from this chapter, convert the following:
   a. 0.044 km to meters
   b. 4.6 mg to grams
   c. 0.107 g to centigrams

42. Convert the following:
   a. 15 cm^3 to liters
   b. 7.38 g to kilograms
   c. 6.7 s to milliseconds
   d. 94.5 g to micrograms

Sample Problem 3.12

Using Density as a Conversion Factor

What is the volume of a pure silver coin that has a mass of 14 g? The density of silver (Ag) is 10.5 g/cm³.

❶ Analyze List the knowns and the unknown.
You need to convert the mass of the coin into a corresponding volume. The density gives you the following relationship between volume and mass: 1 cm³ Ag = 10.5 g Ag. Multiply the given mass by the proper conversion factor to yield an answer in cm³.

KNOWNS	UNKNOWN
mass = 14 g	volume of coin = ? cm³
density of silver = 10.5 g/cm³	

❷ Calculate Solve for the unknown.

Use the relationship 1 cm³ Ag = 10.5 g Ag to write the correct conversion factor.

$$\frac{1\ cm^3\ Ag}{10.5\ g\ Ag}$$

Notice that the known unit (g) is in the denominator and the unknown unit (cm³) is in the numerator.

Multiply the mass of the coin by the conversion factor.

$$14\ g\ Ag \times \frac{1\ cm^3\ Ag}{10.5\ g\ Ag} = 1.3\ cm^3\ Ag$$

❸ Evaluate Does the result make sense? Because a mass of 10.5 g of silver has a volume of 1 cm³, it makes sense that 14.0 g of silver should have a volume slightly larger than 1 cm³. The answer has two significant figures because the given mass has two significant figures.

---

43. Use dimensional analysis and the given densities to make the following conversions:
  a. 14.8 g of boron to cm³ of boron. The density of boron is 2.34 g/cm³.
  b. 4.62 g of mercury to cm³ of mercury. The density of mercury is 13.5 g/cm³.

44. Rework the preceding problems by applying the following equation:
$$\text{Density} = \frac{\text{mass}}{\text{volume}}$$

45. What is the mass, in grams, of a sample of cough syrup that has a volume of 50.0 cm³? The density of cough syrup is 0.950 g/cm³.

Density can be used to write two conversion factors. To figure out which one you need, consider the units of your given quantity and the units needed in your answer.

Multistep Problems Many complex tasks in your life are best handled by breaking them down into smaller, manageable parts. For example, if you were cleaning a car, you might first vacuum the inside, then wash the exterior, then dry the exterior, and finally put on a fresh coat of wax. Similarly, many complex word problems are more easily solved by breaking the solution down into steps.

When converting between units, it is often necessary to use more than one conversion factor. Sample Problems 3.13 and 3.14 illustrate the use of multiple conversion factors.

SampleProblem 3.13

Converting Between Metric Units

The diameter of a sewing needle is 0.073 cm. What is the diameter in micrometers?

1 Analyze List the knowns and the unknown.
The desired conversion is centimeters $\longrightarrow$ micrometers. The problem can be solved in a two-step conversion. First change centimeters to meters; then change meters to micrometers: centimeters $\longrightarrow$ meters $\longrightarrow$ micrometers.

KNOWNS	UNKNOWN
diameter = 0.073 cm = 7.3×10^{-2} cm	diameter = ? μm
10^2 cm = 1 m	
1 m = 10^6 μm	

2 Calculate Solve for the unknown.

Use the relationship 10^2 cm = 1 m to write the first conversion factor.

$$\frac{1 \text{ m}}{10^2 \text{ cm}}$$

Each conversion factor is written so that the unit in the denominator cancels the unit in the numerator of the previous factor.

Use the relationship 1 m = 10^6 μm to write the second conversion factor.

$$\frac{10^6 \text{ } \mu\text{m}}{1 \text{ m}}$$

Multiply the known length by the conversion factors.

$$7.3 \times 10^{-2} \text{ cm} \times \frac{1 \text{ m}}{10^2 \text{ cm}} \times \frac{10^6 \text{ } \mu\text{m}}{1 \text{ m}} = 7.3 \times 10^2 \text{ } \mu\text{m}$$

3 Evaluate Does the result make sense? Because a micrometer is a much smaller unit than a centimeter, the answer should be numerically larger than the given measurement. The units have canceled correctly, and the answer has the correct number of significant figures.

46. The radius of a potassium atom is 0.227 nm. Express this radius in the unit centimeters.

47. The diameter of Earth is 1.3×10^4 km. What is the diameter expressed in decimeters?

SampleProblem 3.14

Converting Ratios of Units

The density of manganese, a metal, is 7.21 g/cm³. What is the density of manganese expressed in units of kg/m³?

❶ Analyze List the knowns and the unknown.

The desired conversion is g/cm³ ⟶ kg/m³. The mass unit in the numerator must be changed from grams to kilograms: g ⟶ kg. In the denominator, the volume unit must be changed from cubic centimeters to cubic meters: cm³ ⟶ m³. Note that the relationship 10^6 cm³ = 1 m³ was derived by cubing the relationship 10^2 cm = 1 m. That is, $(10^2$ cm$)^3 = (1$ m$)^3$, or 10^6 cm³ = 1 m³.

> **KNOWNS**
>
> density of manganese = 7.21 g/cm³
> 10^3 g = 1 kg
> 10^6 cm³ = 1 m³
>
> **UNKNOWN**
>
> density of manganese = ? kg/m³

❷ Calculate Solve for the unknown.

> Multiply the known density by the correct conversion factors.

$$\frac{7.21 \text{ g}}{1 \text{ cm}^3} \times \frac{1 \text{ kg}}{10^3 \text{ g}} \times \frac{10^6 \text{ cm}^3}{1 \text{ m}^3} = 7.21 \times 10^3 \text{ kg/m}^3$$

❸ Evaluate Does the result make sense?

Because the physical size of the volume unit m³ is so much larger than cm³ (10^6 times), the calculated value of the density should be larger than the given value even though the mass unit is also larger (10^3 times). The units cancel, the conversion factors are correct, and the answer has the correct ratio of units.

48. Gold has a density of 19.3 g/cm³. What is the density in kilograms per cubic meter?

49. There are 7.0×10^6 red blood cells (RBCs) in 1.0 mm³ of blood. How many red blood cells are in 1.0 L of blood?

3.3 LessonCheck

50. 🔑 **Review** What happens to the numerical value of a measurement that is multiplied by a conversion factor? What happens to the actual size of the quantity?

51. 🔑 **Review** What types of problems can be solved using dimensional analysis?

52. Identify What conversion factor would you use to convert between these pairs of units?

  a. minutes to hours

  b. grams to milligrams

  c. cubic decimeters to milliliters

53. Calculate Make the following conversions. Express your answers in scientific notation.

  a. 14.8 g = ? μg   **d.** 7.5×10^4 J = ? kJ

  b. 3.72 g = ? kg   **e.** 3.9×10^5 mg = ? dg

  c. 66.3 L = ? cm³   **f.** 2.1×10^{-4} dL = ? μL

54. Calculate What is the mass, in kilograms, of 14.0 L of gasoline? (Assume that the density of gasoline is 0.680 g/cm³.)

55. Apply Concepts Light travels at a speed of 3.00×10^{10} cm/s. What is the speed of light in kilometers/hour?

Small-Scale Lab

Now What Do I Do?

Purpose

To solve problems by making accurate measurements and applying mathematics

Materials

- pencil
- paper
- meter stick
- balance
- pair of dice
- aluminum can
- calculator
- small-scale pipet
- water
- a pre-1982 penny
- a post-1982 penny
- 8-well strip
- plastic cup

Procedure

1. Determine the mass, in grams, of one drop of water. To do this, measure the mass of an empty cup. Add 50 drops of water from a small-scale pipet to the cup and measure its mass again. Subtract the mass of the empty cup from the mass of the cup with water in it. To determine the average mass in grams of a single drop, divide the mass of the water by the number of drops (50). Repeat this experiment until your results are consistent.

2. Determine the mass of a pre-1982 penny and a post-1982 penny.

Analyze

Using your experimental data, record the answers to the following questions.

1. Calculate What is the average mass of a single drop of water in milligrams? (1 g = 1000 mg)

2. Calculate The density of water is 1.00 g/cm³. Calculate the volume of a single drop in cm^3 and mL. (1 mL = 1 cm^3) What is the volume of a drop in microliters (μL)? (1000 μL = 1 mL)

3. Calculate What is the density of water in units of mg/cm^3 and mg/mL? (1 g = 1000 mg)

4. Calculate Pennies made before 1982 consist of 95.0% copper and 5.0% zinc. Calculate the mass of copper and the mass of zinc in the pre-1982 penny.

5. Calculate Pennies made after 1982 are made of zinc with a thin copper coating. They are 97.6% zinc and 2.4% copper. Calculate the mass of copper and the mass of zinc in the newer penny.

6. Explain Why does one penny have less mass than the other?

You're the Chemist

The following small-scale activities allow you to develop your own procedures and analyze the results.

1. Design an Experiment Design an experiment to determine if the size of drops varies with the angle at which they are delivered from the pipet. Try vertical (90°), horizontal (0°), and halfway between (45°). Repeat until your results are consistent.

2. Analyze Data What is the best angle to hold a pipet for ease of use and consistency of measurement? Explain. Why is it important to expel the air bubbles before you begin the experiment?

3. Design an Experiment Make the necessary measurements to determine the volume of aluminum used to make an aluminum soda can. *Hint:* Look up the density of aluminum in your textbook.

4. Design an Experiment Design and carry out some experiments to determine the volume of liquid that an aluminum soda can will hold.

5. Design an Experiment Measure a room and calculate the volume of air it contains. Estimate the percent error associated with not taking into account the furniture in the room.

6. Design an Experiment Make the necessary measurements and do the necessary calculations to determine the volume of a pair of dice. First, ignore the volume of the dots on each face, and then account for the volume of the dots. What is your error and percent error when you ignore the holes?

3 Study Guide

BIGIDEA QUANTIFYING MATTER

Scientists express the degree of uncertainty in their measurements and calculations by using significant figures. In general, a calculated answer cannot be more precise than the least precise measurement from which it was calculated. Dimensional analysis is a problem-solving method that involves analyzing the units of the given measurement and the unknown to plan a solution.

3.1 Using and Expressing Measurements

🔑 In scientific notation, the coefficient is always a number greater than or equal to one and less than ten. The exponent is an integer.

🔑 To evaluate accuracy, the measured value must be compared to the correct value. To evaluate the precision of a measurement, you must compare the values of two or more repeated measurements.

🔑 Measurements must always be reported to the correct number of significant figures because calculated answers often depend on the number of significant figures in the values used in the calculation.

- measurement (62)
- scientific notation (62)
- accuracy (64)
- precision (64)
- accepted value (65)
- experimental value (65)
- error (65)
- percent error (65)
- significant figures (66)

Key Equations

$$\text{Error} = \text{experimental value} - \text{accepted value}$$

$$\text{Percent error} = \frac{|\text{error}|}{\text{accepted value}} \times 100\%$$

3.2 Units of Measurement

🔑 All metric units are based on multiples of 10. As a result, you can convert between units easily.

🔑 Scientists commonly use two equivalent units of temperature, the degree Celsius and the kelvin.

🔑 Density is an intensive property that depends only on the composition of a substance, not on the size of the sample.

- International System of Units (SI) (74)
- meter (m) (75)
- liter (L) (76)
- kilogram (kg) (77)
- gram (g) (77)
- weight (77)
- energy (77)
- joule (J) (77)
- calorie (cal) (77)
- temperature (78)
- Celsius scale (78)
- Kelvin scale (78)
- absolute zero (79)
- density (80)

Key Equations

$$K = °C + 273$$
$$°C = K - 273$$

$$\text{Density} = \frac{\text{mass}}{\text{volume}}$$

3.3 Solving Conversion Problems

🔑 When a measurement is multiplied by a conversion factor, the numerical value is generally changed, but the actual size of the quantity measured remains the same.

🔑 Dimensional analysis is a powerful tool for solving conversion problems in which a measurement with one unit is changed to an equivalent measurement with another unit.

- conversion factor (84)
- dimensional analysis (86)

Math Tune-Up: Conversion Problems

Problem	❶ Analyze	❷ Calculate	❸ Evaluate
A grocer is selling oranges at 3 for $2. How much would it cost to buy a dozen oranges?	**Knowns:** 3 oranges = $2 1 dozen = 12 **Unknown:** Cost of 12 oranges = ? The desired conversion is oranges ⟶ $.	Use the relationship 3 oranges = $2 to write the correct conversion factor. $$\frac{\$2}{3 \text{ oranges}}$$ Multiply the known quantity by the conversion factor. $$12 \text{ oranges} \times \frac{\$2}{3 \text{ oranges}} = \$8$$	A dozen is larger than the number 3, so the cost should exceed $2. The known unit (oranges) cancels, and the answer has the correct unit ($).
Convert the volume 865 cm³ to liters.	**Knowns:** volume = 865 cm^3 10^3 cm^3 = 1 L **Unknown:** volume = ? L The desired conversion is cm^3 ⟶ L.	Use the relationship 10^3 cm^3 = 1 L to write the correct conversion factor. $$\frac{1 \text{ L}}{10^3 \text{ cm}^3}$$ Multiply the known volume by the conversion factor. $$865 \text{ cm}^3 \times \frac{1 \text{ L}}{10^3 \text{ cm}^3} = 0.865 \text{ L}$$	A cubic centimeter is much smaller than a liter, so the answer should be numerically smaller than the given measurement. The known unit (cm^3) cancels, and the answer has the correct unit (L).
Express the length 8.2×10^{-4} μm in centimeters.	**Knowns:** length = 8.2×10^{-4} μm 10^6 μm = 1 m 1 m = 10^2 cm **Unknown:** length = ? L The desired conversion is μm ⟶ cm. First change μm to m; then change m to cm: μm ⟶ m ⟶ cm	Use the relationship 10^6 μm = 1 m to write the first conversion factor. $$\frac{1 \text{ m}}{10^6 \text{ μm}}$$ Use the relationship 1 m = 10^2 cm to write the second conversion factor. $$\frac{10^2 \text{ cm}}{1 \text{ m}}$$ Multiply the known length by the conversion factors. $$8.2 \times 10^{-4} \text{ μm} \times \frac{1 \text{ m}}{10^6 \text{ μm}} \times \frac{10^2 \text{ cm}}{1 \text{ m}}$$ $$= 8.2 \times 10^{-8} \text{ cm}$$	A micrometer is smaller than a centimeter, so the answer should be numerically smaller than the given measurement. The known unit (μm) cancels, and the answer has the correct unit (cm). Hint: For a multistep problem, take it one conversion at a time.

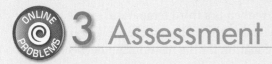
Lesson by Lesson

3.1 Using and Expressing Measurements

56. Three students made multiple weighings of a copper cylinder, each using a different balance. Describe the accuracy and precision of each student's measurements if the correct mass of the cylinder is 47.32 g.

Mass of Cylinder (g)			
	Colin	Lamont	Kivrin
Weighing 1	47.13	47.45	47.95
Weighing 2	47.94	47.39	47.91
Weighing 3	46.83	47.42	47.89
Weighing 4	47.47	47.41	47.93

57. How many significant figures are in each underlined measurement?

a. <u>60 s</u> = 1 min
b. <u>47.70 g</u> of copper
c. 1 km = <u>1000 m</u>
d. <u>25 computers</u>
e. <u>9 innings</u> in a baseball game
f. <u>0.0950 m</u> of gold chain

58. Round off each of these measurements to three significant figures.

a. 98.473 L
b. 0.000 763 21 cg
c. 57.048 m
d. 12.17°C
e. 0.007 498 3 × 10⁴ mm
f. 1764.9 mL

⋆**59.** Round off each of the answers correctly.

a. 8.7 g + 15.43 g + 19 g = 43.13 g
b. 4.32 cm × 1.7 cm = 7.344 cm²
c. 853.2 L − 627.443 L = 225.757 L
d. 38.742 m² ÷ 0.421 m = 92.023 75 m
e. 5.40 m × 3.21 m × 1.871 m = 32.431 914 m³
f. 5.47 m³ + 11 m³ + 87.300 m³ = 103.770 m³

⋆**60.** Express each of the rounded-off answers in Problems 58 and 59 in scientific notation.

61. How are the *error* and the *percent* error of a measurement calculated?

3.2 Units of Measurement

62. Write the SI base unit of measurement for each of these quantities.

a. time
b. length
c. temperature
d. mass
e. energy
f. amount of substance

⋆**63.** Order these units from smallest to largest: cm, μm, km, mm, m, nm, dm, pm. Then give each measurement in terms of meters.

64. Measure each of the following dimensions using a unit with the appropriate prefix.

a. the height of this letter I
b. the width of Table 3.3
c. the height of this page

65. State the relationship between degrees Celsius and kelvins.

⋆**66.** The melting point of silver is 962°C. Express this temperature in kelvins.

67. What equation is used to determine the density of an object?

68. Would the density of a person be the same on the surface of Earth and on the surface of the moon? Explain.

⋆**69.** A shiny, gold-colored bar of metal weighing 57.3 g has a volume of 4.7 cm³. Is the bar of metal pure gold?

70. Three balloons filled with neon, carbon dioxide, and hydrogen are released into the atmosphere. Using the data in Table 3.6 on page 81, describe the movement of each balloon.

3.3 Solving Conversion Problems

71. What is the name given to a ratio of two equivalent measurements?

72. What must be true for a ratio of two measurements to be a conversion factor?

73. How do you know which unit of a conversion factor must be in the denominator?

*74. Make the following conversions:
   a. 157 cs to seconds
   b. 42.7 L to milliliters
   c. 261 nm to millimeters
   d. 0.065 km to decimeters
   e. 642 cg to kilograms
   f. 8.25×10^2 cg to nanograms

*75. Make the following conversions:
   a. 0.44 mL/min to microliters per second
   b. 7.86 g/cm^2 to milligrams per square millimeter
   c. 1.54 kg/L to grams per cubic centimeter

76. How many milliliters are contained in 1 m^3?

*77. Complete this table so that all the measurements in each row have the same value.

mg	g	cg	kg
a. _____	b. _____	28.3	c. _____
6.6×10^3	d. _____	e. _____	f. _____
g. _____	2.8×10^{-4}	h. _____	i. _____

Understand Concepts

78. List two possible reasons for reporting precise, but inaccurate, measurements.

79. Rank these numbers from smallest to largest.
   a. 5.3×10^4 d. 0.0057
   b. 57×10^3 e. 5.1×10^{-3}
   c. 4.9×10^{-2} f. 0.0072×10^2

80. Comment on the accuracy and precision of these basketball free-throw shooters.
   a. 99 of 100 shots are made.
   b. 99 of 100 shots hit the front of the rim and bounce off.
   c. 33 of 100 shots are made; the rest miss.

81. Fahrenheit is a third temperature scale. Plot the data in the table and use the graph to derive an equation for the relationship between the Fahrenheit and Celsius temperature scales.

Example	°C	°F
Melting point of selenium	221	430
Boiling point of water	100	212
Normal body temperature	37	98.6
Freezing point of water	0	32
Boiling point of chlorine	−34.6	−30.2

82. Which would melt first, germanium with a melting point of 1210 K or gold with a melting point of 1064°C?

83. A piece of wood floats in ethanol but sinks in gasoline. Give a range of possible densities for the wood.

84. A plastic ball with a volume of 19.7 cm^3 has a mass of 15.8 g. Would this ball sink or float in a container of gasoline?

85. Write six conversion factors involving these units of measure: 1 g = 10^2 cg = 10^3 mg.

*86. A 2.00-kg sample of bituminous coal is composed of 1.30 kg of carbon, 0.20 kg of ash, 0.15 kg of water, and 0.35 kg of volatile (gas-forming) material. Using this information, determine how many kilograms of carbon are in 125 kg of this coal.

*87. The density of dry air measured at 25°C is 1.19×10^{-3} g/cm^3. What is the volume of 50.0 g of air?

88. What is the mass of a cube of aluminum that is 3.0 cm on each edge? The density of aluminum is 2.7 g/cm^3.

*89. A flask that can hold 158 g of water at 4°C can hold only 127 g of ethanol at the same temperature. What is the density of ethanol?

*90. A watch loses 0.15 s every minute. How many minutes will the watch lose in 1 day?

*91. A tank measuring 28.6 cm by 73.0 mm by 0.72 m is filled with olive oil. The oil in the tank has a mass of 1.38×10^4 g. What is the density of olive oil in kilograms per liter?

92. Alkanes are a class of molecules that have the general formula C_nH_{2n+2}, where n is an integer (whole number). The table below gives the boiling points for the first five alkanes with an odd number of carbon atoms. Using the table, construct a graph with the number of carbon atoms on the x-axis.

Boiling point (°C)	Number of carbon atoms
−162.0	1
−42.0	3
36.0	5
98.0	7
151.0	9

a. What are the approximate boiling points for the C_2, C_4, C_6, and C_8 alkanes?
b. Which of these nine alkanes are gases at room temperature (20°C)?
c. How many of these nine alkanes are liquids at 350 K?
d. What is the approximate increase in boiling point per additional carbon atom in these alkanes?

✶93. Earth is approximately 1.5×10^8 km from the sun. How many minutes does it take light to travel from the sun to Earth? The speed of light is 3.0×10^8 m/s.

✶94. The average density of Earth is 5.52 g/cm³. Express this density in units of kg/dm³.

95. How many kilograms of water (at 4°C) are needed to fill an aquarium that measures 40.0 cm by 20.0 cm by 30.0 cm?

Think Critically

96. Explain Is it possible for an object to lose weight but at the same time not lose mass? Explain your answer.

✶97. Calculate One of the first mixtures of metals, called amalgams, used by dentists for tooth fillings, consisted of 26.0 g of silver, 10.8 g of tin, 2.4 g of copper, and 0.8 g of zinc. How much silver is in a 25.0 g sample of this amalgam?

✶98. Calculate A cheetah can run 112 km/h over a 100-m distance. What is this speed in meters per second?

99. Evaluate You are hired to count the number of ducks on three northern lakes during the summer. In the first lake, you estimate 500,000 ducks, in the second 250,000 ducks, and in the third 100,000 ducks. You write down that you have counted 850,000 ducks. As you drive away, you see 15 ducks fly in from the south and land on the third lake. Do you change the number of ducks that you report? Justify your answer.

100. Describe What if ice were more dense than water? It would certainly be easier to pour water from a pitcher of ice cubes and water. Can you think of situations of more consequence?

101. Graph Plot these data that show how the mass of sulfur increases with an increase in volume. Determine the density of sulfur from the slope of the line.

Volume of sulfur (cm³)	Mass of sulfur (g)
11.4	23.5
29.2	60.8
55.5	115
81.1	168

102. Analyze Data At 20°C, the density of air is 1.20 g/L. Nitrogen's density is 1.17 g/L. Oxygen's density is 1.33 g/L.

a. Will balloons filled with oxygen and balloons filled with nitrogen rise or sink in air?
b. Air is mainly a mixture of nitrogen and oxygen. Which gas is the main component? Explain.

*103. **Calculate** The mass of a cube of iron is 355 g. Iron has a density of 7.87 g/cm³. What is the mass of a cube of lead that has the same dimensions?

*104. **Calculate** Sea water contains 8.0×10^{-1} cg of the element strontium per kilogram of sea water. Assuming that all the strontium could be recovered, how many grams of strontium could be obtained from one cubic meter of sea water? Assume the density of sea water is 1.0 g/mL.

105. **Calculate** The density of dry air at 20°C is 1.20 g/L. What is the mass of air, in kilograms, of a room that measures 25.0 m by 15.0 m by 4.0 m?

106. **Graph** Different volumes of the same liquid were added to a flask on a balance. After each addition of liquid, the mass of the flask with the liquid was measured. Graph the data using mass as the dependent variable. Use the graph to answer these questions.

Volume (mL)	Mass (g)
14	103.0
27	120.4
41	139.1
55	157.9
82	194.1

  a. What is the mass of the flask?
  b. What is the density of the liquid?

*107. **Predict** A 34.5-g gold nugget is dropped into a graduated cylinder containing water. By how many milliliters does the measured volume increase if the nugget is completely covered by water? The density of water is 1.0 g/mL. The density of gold is 19.3 g/cm³.

108. **Predict** Equal amounts of mercury, water, and corn oil are added to a beaker. Use Table 3.6 to help you anwer the following questions.

  a. Describe the arrangement of the layers of liquids in the beaker.
  b. A small sugar cube is added to the beaker. Describe its location.
  c. What change will occur to the sugar cube over time?

Write About Science

109. **Describe** For one of the topics below, write a short paragraph that identifies both metric and nonmetric units that are commonly used to communicate information.

  a. measurements used in cooking
  b. measurements used in sports
  c. measurements used in transportation

110. **Connect to the BIGIDEA** Explain how the three-step problem-solving approach defined in Chapter 1 (*Analyze, Calculate, Evaluate*) applies to problems that involve dimensional analysis.

CHEMYSTERY

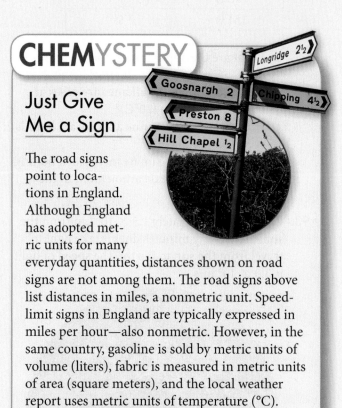

Just Give Me a Sign

The road signs point to locations in England. Although England has adopted metric units for many everyday quantities, distances shown on road signs are not among them. The road signs above list distances in miles, a nonmetric unit. Speed-limit signs in England are typically expressed in miles per hour—also nonmetric. However, in the same country, gasoline is sold by metric units of volume (liters), fabric is measured in metric units of area (square meters), and the local weather report uses metric units of temperature (°C).

111. **Calculate** The relationship between kilometers and miles (mi) is 1 km = 0.621 mi. How far is it to Chipping in kilometers?

112. **Calculate** Suppose you encounter the road signs above while cycling. If your average speed is 18 km/h, how many minutes will it take you to reach Preston?

113. **Connect to the BIGIDEA** Describe two ways in which the road signs above might be considered examples of "uncertainty in measurement."

Standardized Test Prep

Select the choice that best answers each question or completes each statement.

1. Which of these series of units is ordered from smallest to largest?
   (A) μg, cg, mg, kg
   (B) mm, dm, m, km
   (C) μs, ns, cs, s
   (D) nL, mL, dL, cL

2. Which answer represents the measurement 0.00428 g rounded to two significant figures?
   (A) 4.28×10^3 g
   (B) 4.3×10^3 g
   (C) 4.3×10^{-3} g
   (D) 4.0×10^{-3} g

3. An over-the-counter medicine has 325 mg of its active ingredient per tablet. How many grams does this mass represent?
   (A) 325,000 g
   (B) 32.5 g
   (C) 3.25 g
   (D) 0.325 g

4. If 10^4 μm = 1 cm, how many μm^3 = 1 cm^3?
   (A) 10^4
   (B) 10^6
   (C) 10^8
   (D) 10^{12}

5. If a substance contracts when it freezes, its
   (A) density will remain the same.
   (B) density will increase.
   (C) density will decrease.
   (D) change in density cannot be predicted.

For Questions 6–7, identify the known and the unknown. Include units in your answers.

6. The density of water is 1.0 g/mL. How many deciliters of water will fill a 0.5-L bottle?

7. A graduated cylinder contains 44.2 mL of water. A 48.6-g piece of metal is carefully dropped into the cylinder. When the metal is completely covered with water, the water rises to the 51.3-mL mark. What is the density of the metal?

Tips for Success

Interpret Diagrams Before you answer questions about a diagram, study the diagram carefully. Ask: What is the diagram showing? What does it tell me?

Use the diagrams below to answer Questions 8 and 9.

The atomic windows represent particles of the same gas occupying the same volume at the same temperature. The systems differ only in the number of gas particles per unit volume.

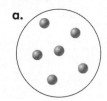 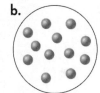 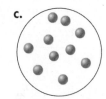

8. List the windows in order of decreasing density.

9. Compare the density of the gas in window (a) to the density of the gas in window (b).

For each question, there are two statements. Decide whether each statement is true or false. Then decide whether Statement II is a correct explanation for Statement I.

	Statement I		Statement II
10.	There are five significant figures in the measurement 0.00450 m.	BECAUSE	All zeros to the right of a decimal point in a measurement are significant.
11.	Precise measurements will always be accurate measurements.	BECAUSE	A value that is measured 10 times in a row must be accurate.
12.	A temperature in kelvins is always numerically larger than the same temperature in degrees Celsius.	BECAUSE	A temperature in kelvins equals a temperature in degrees Celsius plus 273.

If You Have Trouble With . . .

Question	1	2	3	4	5	6	7	8	9	10	11	12
See Lesson	3.2	3.1	3.3	3.3	3.2	3.3	3.2	3.2	3.2	3.1	3.1	3.2

4

Atomic Structure

INSIDE:

- **4.1** Defining the Atom
- **4.2** Structure of the Nuclear Atom
- **4.3** Distinguishing Among Atoms

PearsonChem.com

A scanning electron microscope was used to produce this color-enhanced image of nickel atoms.

ELECTRONS AND THE STRUCTURE OF ATOMS

Essential Questions:

1. *What components make up an atom?*

2. *How are atoms of one element different from atoms of another element?*

CHEMYSTERY

Artifact or Artifake?

Crystal skulls are shaped like a human skull and carved from quartz crystal. Crystal skulls are thought to have originated from pre-Columbian Central American cultures. If so, then crystal skulls would have been carved several hundred or even thousands of years ago. They would probably have been carved using primitive stone, wooden, and bone tools.

Although crystal skulls are displayed in museums throughout the world, none of them were found in an actual archaeological dig. This unusual circumstance has led to some debate about the history of the skulls. People have questioned whether crystal skulls were ever carved by people from ancient civilizations. Are these sculptures true artifacts that were carved in the pre-Columbian era, or are they just fakes?

▶ Connect to the **BIG**IDEA As you read about the structure of atoms, think about how scientists could identify whether a crystal skull is from an ancient civilization or is just a fake.

NATIONAL SCIENCE EDUCATION STANDARDS

B-1, E-1, G-1

4.1 Defining the Atom

Q: *How do you study something that you cannot see?* It is sometimes fun to try to figure out what is inside a present before opening it. You could look at the shape or weight of the box. Or maybe you would shake the box a little to find out if anything moved around or made noise inside the box. Similar to how you might study a giftwrapped present, scientists often study things that cannot be seen with the naked eye. In this lesson, you will learn how scientists obtained information about the atoms that they couldn't see.

Key Questions

🔑 How did the concept of the atom change from the time of Democritus to the time of John Dalton?

🔑 What instruments are used to observe individual atoms?

Vocabulary

• atom
• Dalton's atomic theory

READING SUPPORT

Build Vocabulary: *Word Origins* *Atom* comes from the Greek word *atomos,* meaning "indivisible." *How does the word origin of* atom *relate to Dalton's atomic theory?*

Early Models of the Atom

🔑 *How did the concept of the atom change from the time of Democritus to the time of John Dalton?*

Using your unaided eyes, you cannot see the tiny fundamental particles that make up matter. Yet, all matter is composed of such particles, which are called atoms. An **atom** is the smallest particle of an element that retains its identity in a chemical reaction.

The concept of the atom intrigued a number of early scholars. Although these philosophers and scientists could not observe individual atoms, they still were able to propose ideas about the structure of atoms.

Democritus's Atomic Philosophy The Greek philosopher Democritus (460 B.C.–370 B.C.) was among the first to suggest the existence of atoms. 🔑 **Democritus reasoned that atoms were indivisible and indestructible.** Although Democritus's ideas agreed with later scientific theory, they did not explain chemical behavior. They also lacked experimental support because Democritus's approach was not based on the scientific method.

Dalton's Atomic Theory The real nature of atoms and the connection between observable changes and events at the atomic level were not established for more than 2000 years after Democritus's death. The modern process of discovery regarding atoms began with John Dalton (1766–1844), an English chemist and schoolteacher. 🔑 **By using experimental methods, Dalton transformed Democritus's ideas on atoms into a scientific theory.** Dalton studied the ratios in which elements combine in chemical reactions.

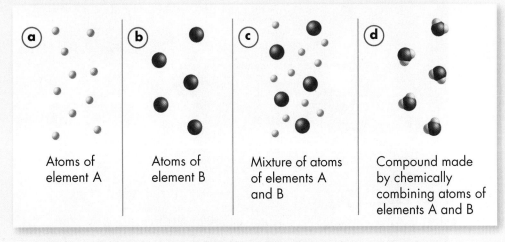

(a) Atoms of element A

(b) Atoms of element B

(c) Mixture of atoms of elements A and B

(d) Compound made by chemically combining atoms of elements A and B

Figure 4.1
Dalton's Atomic Theory
According to Dalton's atomic theory, an element is composed of only one kind of atom, and a compound is composed of particles that are chemical combinations of different kinds of atoms. **Interpret Diagrams** *How does a mixture of atoms of different elements differ from a compound?*

Based on the results of his experiments, Dalton formulated hypotheses and theories to explain his observations. The result of his work is known as **Dalton's atomic theory,** which includes the ideas illustrated in Figure 4.1 and listed below.

1. All elements are composed of tiny indivisible particles called atoms.

2. Atoms of the same element are identical. The atoms of any one element are different from those of any other element.

3. Atoms of different elements can physically mix together or can chemically combine in simple whole-number ratios to form compounds.

4. Chemical reactions occur when atoms are separated from each other, joined, or rearranged in a different combination. Atoms of one element, however, are never changed into atoms of another element as a result of a chemical reaction.

Sizing up the Atom

What instruments are used to observe individual atoms?

The liquid mercury in Figure 4.2 illustrates Dalton's concept of the atom. Whether the size of the drop of mercury is large or small, all drops have the same properties because they are all made of the same kind of atoms.

A coin the size of a penny and composed of pure copper (Cu) is another example. If you were to grind the copper coin into a fine dust, each speck in the small pile of shiny red dust would still have the properties of copper. If by some means you could continue to make the copper dust particles smaller, you would eventually come upon a particle of copper that could no longer be divided and still have the chemical properties of copper. This final particle is an atom.

Atoms are very small. A pure copper coin the size of a penny contains about 2×10^{22} atoms. By comparison, Earth's population is only about 7×10^9 people. There are about 3×10^{12} times as many atoms in the coin as there are people on Earth. If you could line up 100,000,000 copper atoms side by side, they would produce a line only 1 cm long!

Q: *How was John Dalton able to study atoms even though he couldn't observe them directly? What evidence did he use to formulate his atomic theory?*

Figure 4.2 Drops of Mercury
This petri dish contains drops of liquid mercury. Every drop, no matter its size, has the same properties. Even if you could make a drop the size of one atom, it would still have the chemical properties of mercury.

Figure 4.3 Model of a Nanocar
These nanocars are each made of a single molecule. Each nanocar is only about 2 nanometers across. A light-activated paddle wheel on the car propels the car so it can move. The arrow represesents the direction the nanocar moves.

Learn more about the size of the atom *online*.

The radii of most atoms fall within the range of 5×10^{-11} m to 2×10^{-10} m. Does seeing individual atoms seem impossible? **Despite their small size, individual atoms are observable with instruments such as scanning electron microscopes.** In scanning electron microscopes, a beam of electrons is focused on the sample. Electron microscopes are capable of much higher magnifications than light microscopes.

With the help of electron microscopes, individual atoms can even be moved around and arranged in patterns. The ability to move individual atoms holds future promise for the creation of atomic-sized electronic devices, such as circuits and computer chips. An example of a device made from individual atoms is the nanocar shown in Figure 4.3. This atomic-scale, or "nanoscale," technology could become essential to future applications in medicine, communications, solar energy, and space exploration.

4.1 LessonCheck

1. **Review** How did Democritus characterize atoms?

2. **Explain** How did Dalton advance the atomic philosophy proposed by Democritus?

3. **Identify** What instrument can be used to observe individual atoms?

4. Explain In your own words, explain the main ideas of Dalton's atomic theory.

5. Evaluate Explain why the ideas on atoms proposed by Dalton constitute a theory, while the ideas proposed by Democritus do not.

6. Identify What is the range of the radii of most atoms in nanometers (nm)?

7. Calculate A sample of copper with a mass of 63.5 g contains 6.02×10^{23} atoms. Calculate the mass of a single copper atom.

BIGIDEA
ELECTRONS AND THE STRUCTURE OF ATOMS

8. According to Dalton's theory, is it possible to convert atoms of one element into atoms of another? Explain.

4.2 Structure of the Nuclear Atom

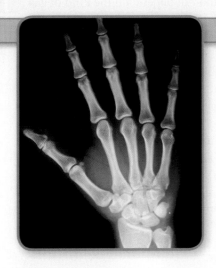

Key Questions

🔑 What are three kinds of subatomic particles?

🔑 How can you describe the structure of the nuclear atom?

Vocabulary

- electron
- cathode ray
- proton
- neutron
- nucleus

Figure 4.4
Cathode-Ray Tube
In a cathode-ray tube, electrons travel as a ray from the cathode (−) to the anode (+). Televisions used to be made with a specialized type of cathode-ray tube.

CHEMISTRY & YOU

Q: *You can X-ray a person's hand to see inside it—but how can you see inside an atom?* You may have seen X-rays like the one of the hand shown here. Doctors often use X-rays to see bones and other structures that cannot be seen through the skin. Scientists tried to figure out what was inside an atom without being able to see inside the atom. In this lesson, you will learn the methods scientists used to "see" inside an atom.

Subatomic Particles

🔑 **What are three kinds of subatomic particles?**

Much of Dalton's atomic theory is accepted today. One important change, however, is that atoms are now known to be divisible. They can be broken down into even smaller, more fundamental particles, called subatomic particles. 🔑 **Three kinds of subatomic particles are electrons, protons, and neutrons.**

Electrons In 1897, the English physicist J. J. Thomson (1856–1940) discovered the electron. **Electrons** are negatively charged subatomic particles. Thomson performed experiments that involved passing electric current through gases at low pressure. He sealed the gases in glass tubes fitted at both ends with metal disks called electrodes. The electrodes were connected to a source of electricity, as shown in Figure 4.4. One electrode, the anode, became positively charged. The other electrode, the cathode, became negatively charged. The result was a glowing beam, or **cathode ray,** that traveled from the cathode to the anode.

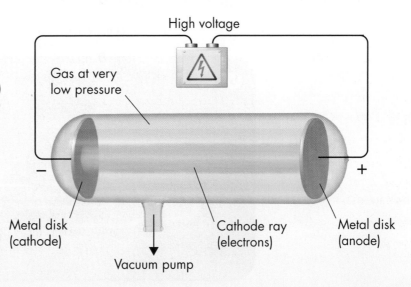

High voltage

Gas at very low pressure

Metal disk (cathode)

Vacuum pump

Cathode ray (electrons)

Metal disk (anode)

Thomson found that a cathode ray is deflected by electrically charged metal plates, as in Figure 4.5a. A positively charged plate attracts the cathode ray, while a negatively charged plate repels it. Thomson knew that opposite charges attract and like charges repel, so he hypothesized that a cathode ray is a stream of tiny negatively charged particles moving at high speed. Thomson called these particles corpuscles; later they were named electrons.

To test his hypothesis, Thomson set up an experiment to measure the ratio of an electron's charge to its mass. He found this ratio to be constant. Also, the charge-to-mass ratio of electrons did not depend on the kind of gas in the cathode-ray tube or the type of metal used for the electrodes. Thomson concluded that electrons are a component of the atoms of all elements.

The U.S. physicist Robert A. Millikan (1868–1953) carried out experiments to find the quantity of an electron's charge. In his oil-drop experiment, Millikan suspended negatively charged oil droplets between two charged plates. He then changed the voltage on the plates to see how this affected the droplets' rate of fall. From his data, he found that the charge on each oil droplet was a multiple of 1.60×10^{-19} coulomb, meaning this must be the charge of an electron. Using this charge value and Thomson's charge-to-mass ratio of an electron, Millikan calculated an electron's mass. Millikan's values for electron charge and mass are similar to those accepted today. An electron has one unit of negative charge, and its mass is 1/1840 the mass of a hydrogen atom.

Figure 4.5
Thomson's Experiment
a. Thomson found that cathode rays are attracted to metal plates that have a positive electrical charge. **b.** A cathode ray can also be deflected by a magnet.
Infer *If a cathode ray is attracted to a positively charged plate, what can you infer about the charge of the particles that make up the cathode ray?*

See cathode-ray tubes animated online.

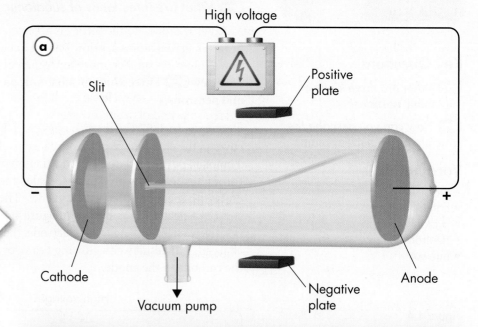

High voltage

Slit

Positive plate

Cathode

Vacuum pump

Negative plate

Anode

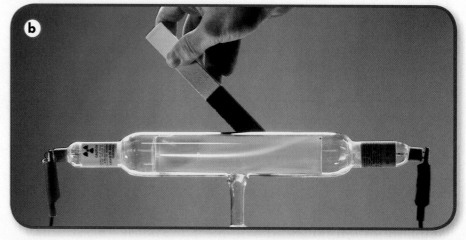

Table 4.1

Properties of Subatomic Particles				
Particle	Symbol	Relative charge	Relative mass (mass of proton = 1)	Actual mass (g)
Electron	e^-	1−	1/1840	9.11×10^{-28}
Proton	p^+	1+	1	1.67×10^{-24}
Neutron	n^0	0	1	1.67×10^{-24}

Protons and Neutrons If cathode rays are electrons given off by atoms, what remains of the atoms that have lost the electrons? For example, after a hydrogen atom (the lightest kind of atom) loses an electron, what is left? You can think through this problem using four simple ideas about matter and electric charges. First, atoms have no net electric charge; they are electrically neutral. (One important piece of evidence for electrical neutrality is that you do not receive an electric shock every time you touch something!) Second, electric charges are carried by particles of matter. Third, electric charges always exist in whole-number multiples of a single basic unit; that is, there are no fractions of charges. Fourth, when a given number of negatively charged particles combines with an equal number of positively charged particles, an electrically neutral particle is formed.

Considering all of this information, it follows that a particle with one unit of positive charge should remain when a typical hydrogen atom loses an electron. Evidence for such a positively charged particle was found in 1886, when Eugen Goldstein (1850–1930) observed a cathode-ray tube and found rays traveling in the direction opposite to that of the cathode rays. He called these rays canal rays and concluded that they were composed of positive particles. Such positively charged subatomic particles are called **protons.** Each proton has a mass about 1840 times that of an electron.

In 1932, the English physicist James Chadwick (1891–1974) confirmed the existence of yet another subatomic particle: the neutron. **Neutrons** are subatomic particles with no charge but with a mass nearly equal to that of a proton. Table 4.1 summarizes the properties of these subatomic particles. Although protons and neutrons are exceedingly small, theoretical physicists believe that they are composed of yet smaller subnuclear particles called *quarks*.

The Atomic Nucleus

🔑 *How can you describe the structure of the nuclear atom?*

When subatomic particles were discovered, scientists wondered how the particles were put together in an atom. This question was difficult to answer, given how tiny atoms are. Most scientists—including J. J. Thomson, discoverer of the electron—thought it likely that electrons were evenly distributed throughout an atom filled uniformly with positively charged material. In Thomson's atomic model, known as the "plum-pudding model," electrons were stuck into a lump of positive charge, similar to raisins stuck in dough. This model of the atom turned out to be short-lived, however, due to the work of a former student of Thomson, Ernest Rutherford (1871–1937), shown in Figure 4.6.

Figure 4.6 Ernest Rutherford
Born in New Zealand, Rutherford was awarded the Nobel Prize in Chemistry in 1908. His portrait appears on the New Zealand $100 bill.

Rutherford's Gold-Foil Experiment In 1911, Rutherford and his co-workers at the University of Manchester, England, wanted to test the existing plum-pudding model of atomic structure. So, they devised the gold-foil experiment. Their test used alpha particles, which are helium atoms that have lost their two electrons and have a double positive charge because of the two remaining protons. In the experiment, illustrated in Figure 4.7, a narrow beam of alpha particles was directed at a very thin sheet of gold foil. According to the prevailing theory, the alpha particles should have passed easily through the gold, with only a slight deflection due to the positive charge thought to be spread out in the gold atoms.

Rutherford's results were that most alpha particles went straight through the gold foil, or were slightly deflected. However, what was surprising is that a small fraction of the alpha particles bounced off the gold foil at very large angles. Some even bounced straight back toward the source. Rutherford later recollected, "This is almost as incredible as if you fired a 15-inch shell at a piece of tissue paper and it came back and hit you."

The Rutherford Atomic Model Based on his experimental results, Rutherford suggested a new theory of the atom. He proposed that the atom is mostly empty space, thus explaining the lack of deflection of most of the alpha particles. He concluded that all the positive charge and almost all the mass are concentrated in a small region that has enough positive charge to account for the great deflection of some of the alpha particles. He called this region the nucleus. The **nucleus** is the tiny central core of an atom and is composed of protons and neutrons.

Figure 4.7 Rutherford's Experiment
Rutherford's gold-foil experiment yielded evidence of the atomic nucleus.

a. Rutherford and his co-workers aimed a beam of alpha particles at a sheet of gold foil surrounded by a fluorescent screen. Most of the particles passed through the foil with no deflection at all. A few particles were greatly deflected.

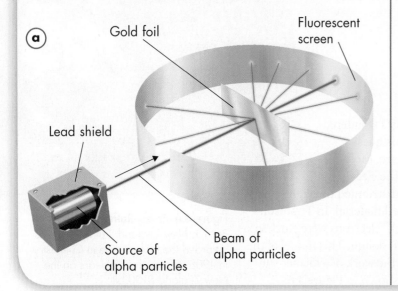

b. Rutherford concluded that most of the alpha particles pass through the gold foil because the atom is mostly empty space. The mass and positive charge are concentrated in a small region of the atom. Rutherford called this region the nucleus. Particles that approach the nucleus closely are greatly deflected.

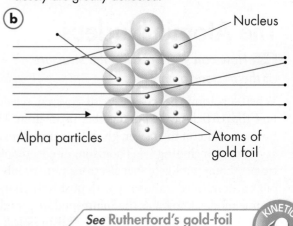

See Rutherford's gold-foil experiment *animated online.*

The Rutherford atomic model is known as the nuclear atom. In the nuclear atom, the protons and neutrons are located in the positively charged nucleus. The electrons are distributed around the nucleus and occupy almost all the volume of the atom. According to this model, the nucleus is tiny and densely packed compared with the atom as a whole. If an atom were the size of a football stadium, the nucleus would be about the size of a marble.

Although it was an improvement over Thomson's model of the atom, Rutherford's model turned out to be incomplete. In Chapter 5, you will learn how the Rutherford atomic model had to be revised in order to explain the chemical properties of elements.

Quick Lab

Purpose To determine the shape of a fixed object inside a sealed box without opening the box

Materials
• box containing a regularly shaped object fixed in place and a loose marble

Using Inference: The Black Box

Procedure
1. Do not open the box.
2. Manipulate the box so that the marble moves around the fixed object.
3. Gather data (clues) that describe the movement of the marble.
4. Sketch a picture of the object in the box, showing its shape, size, and location within the box.
5. Repeat this activity with a different box containing a different object.

Analyze and Conclude
1. Compare Find a classmate who had a box with the same letter as yours, and compare your findings.
2. Apply Concepts Think about the experiments that have contributed to a better understanding of the atom. Which experiment does this activity remind you of?

4.2 LessonCheck

9. Review What are three types of subatomic particles?

10. Explain How does the Rutherford model describe the structure of atoms?

11. Review What are the charges and relative masses of the three main subatomic particles?

12. Explain Describe Thomson's and Millikan's contributions to atomic theory.

13. Compare and Contrast Compare Rutherford's expected outcome of the gold-foil experiment with the actual outcome.

14. Analyze Data What experimental evidence led Rutherford to conclude that an atom is mostly empty space?

15. Compare and Contrast How did Rutherford's model of the atom differ from Thomson's?

Electron Microscopy

Within 30 years of J. J. Thomson's discovery of the electron, scientists were studying how to produce images of objects by using an electron beam. In 1931, German scientists Ernst Ruska and Max Knoll built the first electron microscope. There are two types of electron microscopes, scanning electron microscopes (SEM) and transmission electron microscopes (TEM). The images shown here are from SEMs. In an SEM, a beam of electrons is focused down to a very small diameter and scanned across the sample. Most materials eject electrons when the electron beam hits them. The location of the ejected electrons is detected and used to produce an image.

A typical light microscope is capable of magnifying an object 1000 times. An electron microscope can magnify an object over 100,000 times. Another advantage of electron microscopes is their higher resolution. Resolution is the ability to differentiate two objects that are very close to each other. So, an electron microscope has the ability to produce a clearer image than a light microscope at the same magnification. Electron microscopes do not produce color images. The color images shown here have false color that has been added to the images. Electron microscopes are useful in chemistry, but also in other fields, such as archeolology, pharmacology and quality assurance testing.

SEM This microscope is a scanning electron microscope. The image from the microscope is seen by using a computer screen.

BIOLOGY This diatom is a single-celled organism that lives in the water. The image shown above is a dust mite on a piece of fabric.

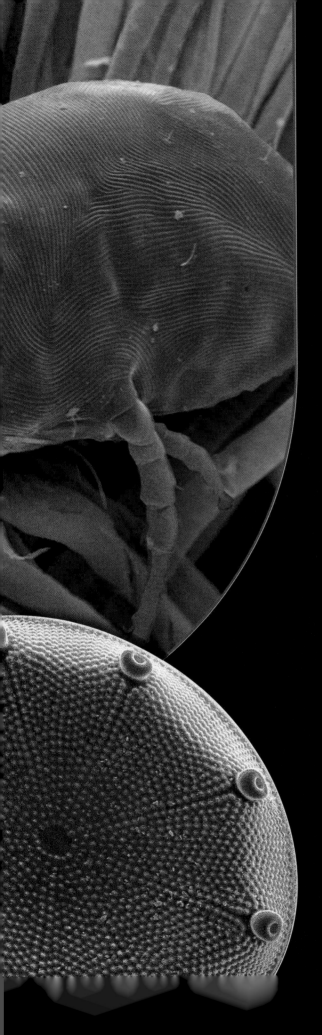

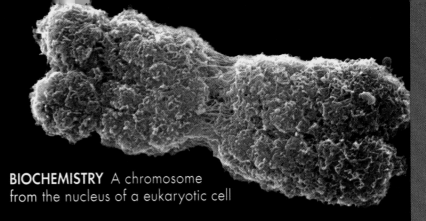

BIOCHEMISTRY A chromosome from the nucleus of a eukaryotic cell

FORENSICS The image on the left is from a light microscope, the image on the right from an SEM. The SEM image shows a clearer image of the fingerprint left on the page because oil from our fingers produces a different intensity of ejected electrons than paper or the ink.

MATERIALS SCIENCE A tip of a pencil is pointing to a tiny pressure sensor (mauve square) used in a car's air bag. When the sensors detect rapid deceleration, they trigger the inflation of the air bag.

Take It Further

1. Infer Why would a forensic investigator want to analyze gunshot residue using an electron microscope?

2. Compare Research the differences between an SEM and a TEM.

4.3 Distinguishing Among Atoms

Q: *How can there be different varieties of atoms?* Some things exist in many different varieties. For example, dogs can differ in many ways, such as color, size, ear shape, and length of hair. Just as there are many types of dogs, atoms come in different varieties, too.

Key Questions

⬤ What makes one element different from another?

⬤ How do isotopes of an element differ?

⬤ How do you calculate the atomic mass of an element?

Vocabulary

• atomic number • mass number
• isotope • atomic mass unit (amu)
• atomic mass

Atomic Number and Mass Number

⬤ **What makes one element different from another?**

Atoms are composed of protons, neutrons, and electrons. Protons and neutrons make up the nucleus. Electrons surround the nucleus. How, then, are atoms of hydrogen, for example, different from atoms of oxygen?

Atomic Number Look at Table 4.2. Notice that a hydrogen atom has one proton, but an oxygen atom has eight protons. ⬤ **Elements are different because they contain different numbers of protons.** An element's **atomic number** is the number of protons in the nucleus of an atom of that element. Since all hydrogen atoms have one proton, the atomic number of hydrogen is 1. All oxygen atoms have eight protons, so the atomic number of oxygen is 8. The atomic number identifies an element. For each element listed in Table 4.2, the number of protons equals the number of electrons. Remember that atoms are electrically neutral. Thus, the number of electrons (negatively charged particles) must equal the number of protons (positively charged particles).

Table 4.2

Atoms of the First Ten Elements						
Name	Symbol	Atomic number	Protons	Neutrons*	Mass number	Electrons
Hydrogen	H	1	1	0	1	1
Helium	He	2	2	2	4	2
Lithium	Li	3	3	4	7	3
Beryllium	Be	4	4	5	9	4
Boron	B	5	5	6	11	5
Carbon	C	6	6	6	12	6
Nitrogen	N	7	7	7	14	7
Oxygen	O	8	8	8	16	8
Fluorine	F	9	9	10	19	9
Neon	Ne	10	10	10	20	10

* Number of neutrons in the most abundant isotope. Isotopes are introduced later in Lesson 4.3.

Sample Problem 4.1

Understanding Atomic Number

The element nitrogen (N) has an atomic number of 7. How many protons and electrons are in a neutral nitrogen atom?

❶ **Analyze Identify the relevant concepts.** The atomic number gives the number of protons, which in a neutral atom equals the number of electrons.

❷ **Solve Apply the concepts to this problem.**

| Identify the atomic number. Then use the atomic number to find the number of protons and electrons. | ➜ | The atomic number of nitrogen is 7. So, a neutral nitrogen atom has 7 protons and 7 electrons. |

16. How many protons and electrons are in each atom?
   a. fluorine (atomic number = 9)
   b. calcium (atomic number = 20)
   c. aluminum (atomic number = 13)
   d. potassium (atomic number = 19)

17. Complete the table.

Element	Atomic number	Protons	Electrons
S	16	a. ___	b. ___
V	c. ___	23	d. ___
e. ___	f. ___	g. ___	5

Mass Number Most of the mass of an atom is concentrated in its nucleus and depends on the number of protons and neutrons. The total number of protons and neutrons in an atom is called the **mass number.** For example, a helium atom has two protons and two neutrons, so its mass number is 4. A carbon atom has six protons and six neutrons, so its mass number is 12.

If you know the atomic number and mass number of an atom of any element, you can determine the atom's composition. The number of neutrons in an atom is the difference between the mass number and atomic number.

> **Number of neutrons = mass number − atomic number**

Table 4.2 shows that a fluorine atom has an atomic number of 9 and a mass number of 19. Since the atomic number equals the number of protons, which equals the number of electrons, a fluorine atom has nine protons and nine electrons. The mass number of fluorine is equal to the number of protons plus the number of neutrons. So the fluorine atom has ten neutrons, which is the difference between the mass number and the atomic number ($19 - 9 = 10$).

The composition of any atom can be represented in shorthand notation using the atomic number and mass number, as in Figure 4.8. The chemical symbol for gold, Au, appears with two numbers written to its left. The atomic number is the subscript. The mass number is the superscript. You can also refer to atoms by using the mass number and the name of the element. For example, $^{197}_{79}\text{Au}$ may be written as gold-197.

Figure 4.8 Chemical Symbol
Au is the chemical symbol for gold.
Apply Concepts *How many electrons does a gold atom have?*

SampleProblem 4.2

Determining the Composition of an Atom

How many protons, electrons, and neutrons are in each atom?
a. $^{9}_{4}Be$ **b.** $^{20}_{10}Ne$ **c.** $^{23}_{11}Na$

KNOWNS	UNKNOWNS
• Beryllium (Be)	number of:
atomic number = 4	protons = ?
mass number = 9	
• Neon (Ne)	electrons = ?
atomic number = 10	
mass number = 20	neutrons = ?
• Sodium (Na)	
atomic number = 11	
mass number = 23	

❶ **Analyze** **List the knowns and the unknowns.** Use the definitions of atomic number and mass number to calculate the numbers of protons, electrons, and neutrons.

❷ **Calculate** **Solve for the unknowns.**

Use the atomic number to find the number of protons.	atomic number = number of protons **a.** 4 **b.** 10 **c.** 11
Use the atomic number to find the number of electrons.	atomic number = number of electrons **a.** 4 **b.** 10 **c.** 11
Use the mass number and atomic number to find the number of neutrons.	number of neutrons = mass number − atomic number **a.** number of neutrons = 9 − 4 = 5 **b.** number of neutrons = 20 − 10 = 10 **c.** number of neutrons = 23 − 11 = 12

❸ **Evaluate** **Do the results make sense?** For each atom, the mass number equals the number of protons plus the number of neutrons. The results make sense.

18. How many neutrons are in each atom?

    a. $^{80}_{35}Br$ **b.** $^{32}_{16}S$ **c.** $^{108}_{47}Ag$ **d.** $^{207}_{82}Pb$

19. Use Table 4.2 to express the composition of each atom below in shorthand form.

    a. carbon-12   **c.** beryllium-9
    b. boron-11   **d.** oxygen-16

Q: *How are atoms of one element different from the atoms of another element? How are isotopes of the same element different?*

Isotopes

🔑 How do isotopes of an element differ?

Figure 4.9 shows that there are three different kinds of neon atoms. How do these atoms differ? All have the same number of protons (10) and electrons (10), but they each have different numbers of neutrons. **Isotopes** are atoms that have the same number of protons but different numbers of neutrons. 🔑 **Because isotopes of an element have different numbers of neutrons, they also have different mass numbers.** Despite these differences, isotopes are chemically alike because they have identical numbers of protons and electrons, which are the subatomic particles responsible for chemical behavior. Remember the dogs at the beginning of the lesson. Their color or size doesn't change the fact that they are all dogs. Similarly, the number of neutrons in isotopes of an element doesn't change which element it is because the atomic number doesn't change.

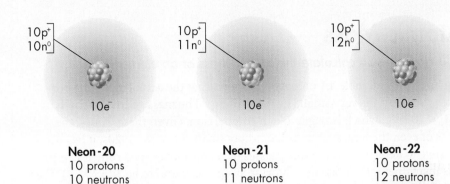

Figure 4.9 Isotopes
Neon-20, neon-21, and neon-22 are three isotopes of neon.
Compare and Contrast
How are these isotopes different? How are they similar?

Neon-20
10 protons
10 neutrons
10 electrons

Neon-21
10 protons
11 neutrons
10 electrons

Neon-22
10 protons
12 neutrons
10 electrons

There are three known isotopes of hydrogen. Each isotope of hydrogen has one proton in its nucleus. The most common hydrogen isotope has no neutrons. It has a mass number of 1 and is called hydrogen-1 ($_1^1H$) or hydrogen. The second isotope has one neutron and a mass number of 2. It is called either hydrogen-2 ($_1^2H$) or deuterium. The third isotope has two neutrons and a mass number of 3. This isotope is called hydrogen-3 ($_1^3H$) or tritium.

SampleProblem 4.3

Writing Chemical Symbols for Isotopes

Diamonds are a naturally occurring form of elemental carbon. Two stable isotopes of carbon are carbon-12 and carbon-13. Write the symbol for each isotope using superscripts and subscripts to represent the mass number and the atomic number.

❶ Analyze Identify the relevant concepts. Isotopes are atoms that have the same number of protons but different numbers of neutrons. The composition of an atom can be expressed by writing the chemical symbol, with the atomic number as a subscript and the mass number as a superscript.

❷ Solve Apply the concepts to this problem.

Use Table 4.2 to identify the symbol and the atomic number for carbon.	→	The symbol for carbon is C. The atomic number of carbon is 6.
Look at the name of the isotope to find the mass number.	→	For carbon-12, the mass number is 12. For carbon-13, the mass number is 13.
Use the symbol, atomic number, and mass number to write the symbol of the isotope.	→	For carbon-12, the symbol is $_6^{12}C$. For carbon-13, the symbol is $_6^{13}C$.

20. Three isotopes of oxygen are oxygen-16, oxygen-17, and oxygen-18. Write the symbol for each, including the atomic number and mass number.

21. Three chromium isotopes are chromium-50, chromium-52, and chromium-53. How many neutrons are in each isotope, given that chromium has an atomic number of 24?

Atomic Mass

🔑 *How do you calculate the atomic mass of an element?*

A glance back at Table 4.1 on page 107 shows that the actual mass of a proton or a neutron is very small (1.67×10^{-24} g). The mass of an electron is 9.11×10^{-28} g, which is negligible in comparison. Given these values, the mass of even the largest atom is incredibly small. Since the 1920s, it has been possible to determine these tiny masses by using a mass spectrometer. With this instrument, the mass of a fluorine atom was found to be 3.155×10^{-23} g, and the mass of an arsenic atom was found to be 1.244×10^{-22} g. Such data about the actual masses of individual atoms can provide useful information, but in general, these values are inconveniently small and impractical to work with. Instead, it is more useful to compare the relative masses of atoms using a reference isotope as a standard. The reference isotope chosen is carbon-12. This isotope of carbon has been assigned a mass of exactly 12 atomic mass units. An **atomic mass unit (amu)** is defined as one twelfth of the mass of a carbon-12 atom. Using these units, a helium-4 atom has one third the mass of a carbon-12 atom. On the other hand, a nickel-60 atom has five times the mass of a carbon-12 atom.

Interpret Data

Natural Percent Abundance of Stable Isotopes of Some Elements				
Name	Symbol	Natural percent abundance	Mass (amu)	Atomic mass
Hydrogen	$_{1}^{1}$H $_{1}^{2}$H $_{1}^{3}$H	99.985 0.015 negligible	1.0078 2.0141 3.0160	1.0079
Helium	$_{2}^{3}$He $_{2}^{4}$He	0.0001 99.9999	3.0160 4.0026	4.0026
Carbon	$_{6}^{12}$C $_{6}^{13}$C	98.89 1.11	12.000 13.003	12.011
Nitrogen	$_{7}^{14}$N $_{7}^{15}$N	99.63 0.37	14.003 15.000	14.007
Oxygen	$_{8}^{16}$O $_{8}^{17}$O $_{8}^{18}$O	99.759 0.037 0.204	15.995 16.995 17.999	15.999
Sulfur	$_{16}^{32}$S $_{16}^{33}$S $_{16}^{34}$S $_{16}^{36}$S	95.002 0.76 4.22 0.014	31.972 32.971 33.967 35.967	32.06
Chlorine	$_{17}^{35}$Cl $_{17}^{37}$Cl	75.77 24.23	34.969 36.966	35.453

Table 4.3 The atomic mass of an element is calculated using the percent abundance and mass of its isotopes.

a. Identify Which isotope of oxygen is the most abundant?

b. Describe How could you use the atomic mass of helium to determine which isotope of helium is most abundant?

Hint: The natural percent abundance of hydrogen-3 is "negligible" because the amount of naturally occurring hydrogen-3 is so small that it doesn't affect the atomic mass of hydrogen.

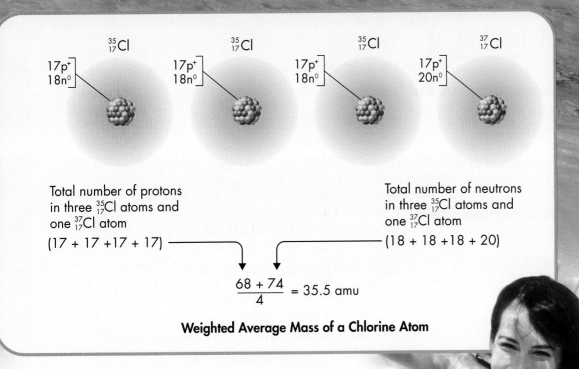

$^{35}_{17}$Cl $\qquad$ $^{35}_{17}$Cl $\qquad$ $^{35}_{17}$Cl $\qquad$ $^{37}_{17}$Cl

17p$^+$
18n^0 $\qquad$ 17p$^+$
18n^0 $\qquad$ 17p$^+$
18n^0 $\qquad$ 17p$^+$
20n^0

Total number of protons in three $^{35}_{17}$Cl atoms and one $^{37}_{17}$Cl atom

$(17 + 17 + 17 + 17)$

Total number of neutrons in three $^{35}_{17}$Cl atoms and one $^{37}_{17}$Cl atom

$(18 + 18 + 18 + 20)$

$$\frac{68 + 74}{4} = 35.5 \text{ amu}$$

Weighted Average Mass of a Chlorine Atom

A carbon-12 atom has six protons and six neutrons in its nucleus, and its mass is set as 12 amu. The six protons and six neutrons account for nearly all of this mass. Therefore, the mass of a single proton or a single neutron is about one twelfth of 12 amu, or about 1 amu. Because the mass of any single atom depends mainly on the number of protons and neutrons in the nucleus of the atom, you might predict that the atomic mass of an element should be a whole number. However, that is not usually the case.

In nature, most elements occur as a mixture of two or more isotopes. Each isotope of an element has a fixed mass and a natural percent abundance. Consider the three isotopes of hydrogen discussed earlier in this section. According to Table 4.3, almost all naturally occurring hydrogen (99.985 percent) is hydrogen-1. The other two isotopes are present in trace amounts. Notice that the atomic mass of hydrogen listed in Table 4.3 (1.0079 amu) is very close to the mass of hydrogen-1 (1.0078 amu). The slight difference takes into account the larger masses, but much smaller amounts, of the other two isotopes of hydrogen.

Now consider the two stable isotopes of chlorine listed in Table 4.3: chlorine-35 and chlorine-37. If you calculate the arithmetic mean of these two masses ((34.969 amu + 36.966 amu)/2), you get an average atomic mass of 35.968 amu. However, this value is higher than the actual value of 35.453. To explain this difference, you need to know the natural percent abundance of the isotopes of chlorine. Chlorine-35 accounts for 75 percent of the naturally occurring chlorine atoms; chlorine-37 accounts for only 25 percent. See Figure 4.10. The **atomic mass** of an element is a weighted average mass of the atoms in a naturally occurring sample of the element. A weighted average mass reflects both the mass and the relative abundance of the isotopes as they occur in nature.

Figure 4.10 Isotopes of Chlorine
Chlorine is a reactive element used to disinfect swimming pools. Chlorine occurs as two isotopes: chlorine-35 and chlorine-37. Because there is more chlorine-35 than chlorine-37 in nature, the atomic mass of chlorine, 35.453 amu, is closer to 35 than to 37.
Evaluate *How does a weighted average differ from an arithmetic mean?*

SampleProblem 4.4

Understanding Relative Abundance of Isotopes

The atomic mass of copper is 63.546 amu. Which of copper's two isotopes is more abundant: copper-63 or copper-65?

1 Analyze **Identify the relevant concepts.** The atomic mass of an element is the weighted average mass of the atoms in a naturally occurring sample of the element.

2 Solve **Apply the concepts to this problem.**

Compare the atomic mass to the mass of each isotope.	The atomic mass of 63.546 amu is closer to 63 than it is to 65.
Determine the most abundant isotope based on which isotope's mass is closest to the atomic mass.	Because the atomic mass is a weighted average of the isotopes, copper-63 must be more abundant than copper-65.

22. Boron has two isotopes: boron-10 and boron-11. Which is more abundant, given that the atomic mass of boron is 10.81 amu?

23. There are three isotopes of silicon; they have mass numbers of 28, 29, and 30. The atomic mass of silicon is 28.086 amu. Comment on the relative abundance of these three isotopes.

Now that you know that the atomic mass of an element is a weighted average of the masses of its isotopes, you can determine atomic mass based on relative abundance. To do this, you must know three things: the number of stable isotopes of the element, the mass of each isotope, and the natural percent abundance of each isotope. **To calculate the atomic mass of an element, multiply the mass of each isotope by its natural abundance, expressed as a decimal, and then add the products.** The resulting sum is the weighted average mass of the atoms of the element as they occur in nature. You can calculate the atomic masses listed in Table 4.3 based on the given masses and natural abundances of the isotopes for each element.

For example, carbon has two stable isotopes: carbon-12, which has a natural abundance of 98.89 percent, and carbon-13, which has a natural abundance of 1.11 percent. The mass of carbon-12 is 12.000 amu; the mass of carbon-13 is 13.003 amu. The atomic mass of carbon is calculated as follows:

$$\text{Atomic mass of carbon} = (12.000 \text{ amu} \times 0.9889) + (13.003 \text{ amu} \times 0.0111)$$

$$= (11.867 \text{ amu}) + (0.144 \text{ amu})$$

$$= 12.011 \text{ amu}$$

SampleProblem 4.5

Calculating Atomic Mass

Element X has two naturally occurring isotopes. The isotope with a mass of 10.012 amu (^{10}X) has a relative abundance of 19.91 percent. The isotope with a mass of 11.009 amu (^{11}X) has a relative abundance of 80.09 percent. Calculate the atomic mass of element X.

❶ **Analyze** **List the knowns and the unknown.** The mass each isotope contributes to the element's atomic mass can be calculated by multiplying the isotope's mass by its relative abundance. The atomic mass of the element is the sum of these products.

> To find all the knowns, change the percent abundance to decimals. A percent is a shorthand way of expressing a fraction whose denominator is 100. 19.91% is equivalent to 19.91/100 or 0.1991.

KNOWNS
- isotope ^{10}X:
  mass = 10.012 amu
  relative abundance = 19.91% = 0.1991
- isotope ^{11}X:
  mass = 11.009 amu
  relative abundance = 80.09% = 0.8009

UNKNOWN
atomic mass of X = ?

❷ **Calculate** **Solve for the unknown.**

Use the atomic mass and the decimal form of the percent abundance to the find the mass contributed by each isotope.

for ^{10}X: 10.012 amu × 0.1991 = 1.993 amu
for ^{11}X: 11.009 amu × 0.8009 = 8.817 amu

Add the atomic mass contributions for all the isotopes.

For element X, atomic mass = 1.993 amu + 8.817 amu
= 10.810 amu

❸ **Evaluate** **Does the result make sense?** The calculated value is closer to the mass of the more abundant isotope, as would be expected.

---

24. The element copper has naturally occurring isotopes with mass numbers of 63 and 65. The relative abundance and atomic masses are 69.2% for mass = 62.93 amu, and 30.8% for mass = 64.93 amu. Calculate the atomic mass of copper.

25. Calculate the atomic mass of bromine. The two isotopes of bromine have atomic masses and relative abundance of 78.92 amu (50.69%) and 80.92 amu (49.31%).

4.3 LessonCheck

26. 🔒 **Explain** What distinguishes the atoms of one element from the atoms of another?

27. 🔒 **Compare and Contrast** How do the isotopes of a given element differ from one another?

28. 🔒 **Explain** How is atomic mass calculated?

29. **Identify** What equation tells you how to calculate the number of neutrons in an atom?

30. **Compare** How is atomic number different from mass number?

31. **Use Models** What does the number represent in the isotope platinum-194?

32. **Explain** The atomic masses of elements are generally not whole numbers. Explain why.

33. **Identify** Which of argon's three isotopes is most abundant: argon-36, argon-38, or argon-40? (*Hint:* the atomic mass of argon is 39.948 amu.)

34. **Calculate** List the number of protons, neutrons, and electrons in each pair of isotopes.
  a. $^{6}_{3}$Li, $^{7}_{3}$Li   **b.** $^{42}_{20}$Ca, $^{44}_{10}$Ca   **c.** $^{78}_{34}$Se, $^{80}_{34}$Se

Small-Scale Lab

The Atomic Mass of "Candium"

Purpose

To analyze the isotopes of "candium" and to calculate its atomic mass

Materials

- sample of candium
- balance

Procedure

Obtain a sample of "candium" that contains three different brands of round, coated candy. Treat each brand of candy as an isotope of candium. Separate the three isotopes into groups labeled A, B, and C, and measure the mass of each isotope. Count the number of atoms in each sample. Make a table similar to the one below to record your measured and calculated data.

	A	B	C	Totals
Total mass (grams)				
Number				
Average mass (grams)				
Relative abundance				
Percent abundance				
Relative mass				

Analyze

Using the experimental data, record the answers to the following questions below your data table.

1. Calculate Calculate the average mass of each isotope by dividing its total mass by the number of particles of that isotope.

2. Calculate Calculate the relative abundance of each isotope by dividing its number of particles by the total number of particles.

3. Calculate Calculate the percent abundance of each isotope by multiplying the relative abundance from Step 2 by 100.

4. Calculate Calculate the relative mass of each isotope by multiplying its relative abundance from Step 2 by its average mass.

5. Calculate Calculate the weighted average mass of all candium particles by adding the relative masses. This weighted average mass is the atomic mass of candium.

6. Explain What is the difference between percent abundance and relative abundance? What is the result when you total the individual relative abundances? The individual percent abundances?

7. Identify The percent abundance of each kind of candy tells you how many of each kind of candy there are in every 100 particles. What does relative abundance tell you?

8. Analyze Data Compare the total values for rows 3 and 6 in the table. Explain why the totals differ and why the value in row 6 best represents atomic mass.

9. Analyze Data Explain any differences between the atomic mass of your candium sample and that of your neighbor. Explain why the difference would be smaller if larger samples were used.

You're the Chemist

The following small-scale activity allows you to develop your own procedures and analyze the results.

1. Analyze Data Determine the atomic mass of a second sample of candium. How does it compare with the first? Suggest reasons for any differences between the samples.

4 Study Guide

BIGIDEA ELECTRONS AND THE STRUCTURE OF ATOMS

Atoms are the smallest particles of an element that still have the chemical properties of that element. Atoms have positively charged protons and neutral neutrons inside a nucleus, and negatively charged electrons outside the nucleus. Atoms of the same element have the same number of protons, which is equal to an atom's atomic number. But atoms of the same element can have different numbers of neutrons. Atoms of the same element with different numbers of neutrons are isotopes.

4.1 Defining the Atom

🔑 Democritus reasoned that atoms were indivisible and indestructible. By using experimental methods, Dalton transformed Democritus's ideas on atoms into a scientific theory.

🔑 Scientists can observe individual atoms by using instruments such as scanning electron microscopes.

- atom (102)
- Dalton's atomic theory (103)

4.2 Structure of the Nuclear Atom

🔑 Three kinds of subatomic particles are electrons, protons, and neutrons.

🔑 In the nuclear atom, the protons and neutrons are located in the nucleus. The electrons are distributed around the nucleus and occupy almost all the volume of the atom.

- electron (105)
- cathode ray (105)
- proton (107)
- neutron (107)
- nucleus (108)

4.3 Distinguishing Among Atoms

🔑 Elements are different because they contain different numbers of protons.

🔑 Because isotopes of an element have different numbers of neutrons, they also have different mass numbers.

🔑 To calculate the atomic mass of an element, multiply the mass of each isotope by its natural abundance, expressed as a decimal, and then add the products.

- atomic number (112)
- mass number (113)
- isotope (114)
- atomic mass unit (amu) (116)
- atomic mass (117)

Key Equation

$$\text{number of neutrons} = \text{mass number} - \text{atomic number}$$

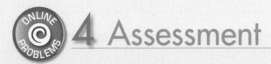 4 **Assessment**

✳ Solutions appear in Appendix E

Lesson by Lesson

4.1 Defining the Atom

35. What is an atom?

36. What were the limitations of Democritus's ideas about atoms?

37. With which of these statements would John Dalton have agreed in the early 1800s? For each, explain why or why not.

   a. Atoms are the smallest particles of matter.
   b. The mass of an iron atom is different from the mass of a copper atom.
   c. Every atom of silver is identical to every other atom of silver.
   d. A compound is composed of atoms of two or more different elements.

38. Use Dalton's atomic theory to describe how atoms interact during a chemical reaction.

4.2 Structure of the Nuclear Atom

39. What experimental evidence did Thomson have for each statement?

   a. Electrons have a negative charge.
   b. Atoms of all elements contain electrons.

✳**40.** Would you expect two electrons to attract or repel each other?

41. How do the charge and mass of a neutron compare to the charge and mass of a proton?

42. Why does it make sense that if an atom loses electrons, it is left with a positive charge?

43. Describe the location of the electrons in Thomson's "plum-pudding" model of the atom.

✳**44.** How did the results of Rutherford's gold-foil experiment differ from his expectations?

45. What is the charge, positive or negative, of the nucleus of every atom?

46. In the Rutherford atomic model, which subatomic particles are located in the nucleus?

4.3 Distinguishing Among Atoms

47. Why is an atom electrically neutral?

48. What does the atomic number of each atom represent?

49. How many protons are in the nuclei of the following atoms?

   a. phosphorus (P)   **d.** cadmium (Cd)
   b. molybdenum (Mo)   **e.** chromium (Cr)
   c. aluminum (Al)   **f.** lead (Pb)

50. What is the difference between the mass number and the atomic number of an atom?

✳**51.** Complete the following table.

Atomic number	Mass number	Number of protons	Number of neutrons
9	a. _____	b. _____	10
c. _____	d. _____	14	15
e. _____	47	f. _____	25
g. _____	55	25	h. _____

52. Name two ways that isotopes of an element differ.

✳**53.** Lithium has two isotopes, lithium-6 (atomic mass = 6.015, relative abundance = 7.5%) and lithium-7 (atomic mass = 7.016, relative abundance = 92.5%). Calculate the atomic mass of lithium.

Understand Concepts

✳**54.** How can there be more than 1000 different atoms when there are only about 100 different elements?

55. What data must you know about the isotopes of an element to calculate the atomic mass of the element?

56. How is an average mass different from a weighted average mass?

57. What is the atomic mass of an element?

58. Characterize the size of an atom.

59. Compare the size and density of an atom with its nucleus.

✳**60.** You are standing on the top of a boron-11 nucleus. Describe the numbers and kinds of subatomic particles you see looking down into the nucleus, and those you see looking out from the nucleus.

61. What parts of Dalton's atomic theory no longer agree with the current picture of the atom?

62. Millikan measured the quantity of charge carried by an electron. How did he then calculate the mass of an electron?

63. How is the atomic mass of an element calculated from isotope data?

✱64. The four isotopes of lead are shown below, each with its percent by mass abundance and the composition of its nucleus. Using these data, calculate the approximate atomic mass of lead.

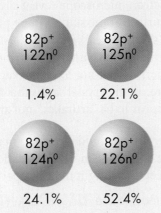

82p⁺ 122n⁰	82p⁺ 125n⁰
1.4%	22.1%
82p⁺ 124n⁰	82p⁺ 126n⁰
24.1%	52.4%

65. Dalton's atomic theory was not correct in every detail. Should this be taken as a criticism of Dalton as a scientist? Explain.

✱66. The following table shows some of the data collected by Rutherford and his colleagues during their gold-foil experiment.

Angle of deflection (degrees)	Number of deflections
5	8,289,000
10	502,570
15	120,570
30	7800
45	1435
60	477
75	211
>105	198

a. What percentage of the alpha particle deflections were 5° or less?

b. What percentage of the deflections were 15° or less?

c. What percentage of the deflections were 60° or greater?

✱67. Using the data for nitrogen listed in Table 4.3, calculate the weighted average atomic mass of nitrogen. Show your work.

68. What characteristics of cathode rays led Thomson to conclude that the rays consisted of negatively charged particles?

69. If you know the atomic number and mass number of an atom of an element, how can you determine the number of protons, neutrons, and electrons in that atom?

70. What makes isotopes of the same element chemically alike?

71. If isotopes are chemically alike, but physically different, propose which subatomic particles are responsible for determining an element's chemical reactivity.

Think Critically

72. Interpret Diagrams The diagram below shows gold atoms being bombarded with fast-moving alpha particles.

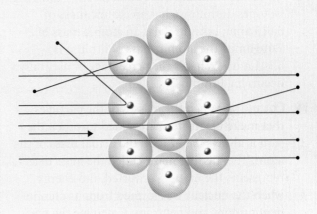

a. The large yellow spheres represent gold atoms. What do the small gray spheres represent?

b. List at least two characteristics of the small gray spheres.

c. Which subatomic particle cannot be found in the area represented by the gray spheres?

73. Evaluate and Revise How could you modify Rutherford's experimental procedure to determine the relative sizes of different nuclei?

74. Explain Rutherford's atomic theory proposed a dense nucleus surrounded by very small electrons. This structure implies that atoms are composed mainly of empty space. If all matter is mainly empty space, why is it impossible to walk through walls or pass your hand through your desk?

75. Explain This chapter illustrates the scientific method in action. What happens when new experimental results cannot be explained by the existing theory?

76. Apply Concepts The law of conservation of mass was introduced in Chapter 2. Use Dalton's atomic theory to explain this law.

77. Infer Diamond and graphite are both composed of carbon atoms. The density of diamond is 3.52 g/cm^3. The density of graphite is 2.25 g/cm^3. In 1955, scientists successfully made diamond from graphite. Using the relative densities, consider what happens at the atomic level when this change occurs. Then suggest how this synthesis may have been accomplished.

★78. Calculate Lithium has two naturally occurring isotopes. Lithium-6 has an atomic mass of 6.015 amu; lithium-7 has an atomic mass of 7.016 amu. The atomic mass of lithium is 6.941 amu. What is the percentage of naturally occurring lithium-7?

★79. Calculate When the masses of the particles that make up an atom are added together, the sum is always larger than the actual mass of the atom. The missing mass, called the mass defect, represents the matter converted into energy when the nucleus was formed from its component protons and neutrons. Calculate the mass defect of a chlorine-35 atom by using the data in Table 4.1. The actual mass of a chlorine-35 atom is 5.81×10^{-23} g.

Write About Science

80. Communicate Explain how Rutherford's gold-foil experiment yielded new evidence about atomic structure. *Hint:* First, describe the setup of the experiment. Then, explain how Rutherford interpreted his experimental data.

81. Connect to the BIGIDEA Choose two atoms from Table 4.2. Compare and contrast the structure of the two atoms.

CHEMYSTERY

Artifacts or Artifakes?

There are currently no crystal skulls that have been proven to be from ancient civilizations. The Linnean Society of London is a research institute specializing in taxonomy and natural history. They have used electron microscopy to view the surface of crystal skulls, including a crystal skull that is part of the Smithsonian collection. Images from the scanning electron microscope reveal circular patterns on the surface of the skulls. These patterns indicate the skulls were likely carved using a modern carving device with a rotary wheel. Ancient civilizations would not have had such devices. Therefore, all the crystal skulls that are known today appear to be "artifakes," not artifacts.

82. Infer Why would electron microscopes be able to provide more information about an object than a light microscope?

83. Connect to the BIGIDEA How has knowledge of atomic structure aided in the development of the electron microscope?

Cumulative Review

84. How does a scientific law differ from a scientific theory?

85. Classify each as an element, a compound, or a mixture.
   a. sulfur   **c.** newspaper
   b. salad oil   **d.** orange

★86. Oxygen and hydrogen react explosively to form water. In one reaction, 6 g of hydrogen combines with oxygen to form 54 g of water. How much oxygen was used?

87. An aquarium measures 54.0 cm × 31.10 m × 80.0 cm. How many cubic centimeters of water will this aquarium hold?

★88. What is the mass of 4.42 cm^3 of platinum? The density of platinum is 22.5 g/cm^3.

If You Have Trouble With . . .				
Question	84	85	86	87	88
See Chapter	1	2	2	3	3

Standardized Test Prep

Select the choice that best answers each question or completes each statement.

1. The smallest particle of an element that retains its identity in a chemical reaction is a
   (A) proton.
   (B) neutron.
   (C) atom.
   (D) compound.

2. Which of these descriptions is *incorrect*?
   (A) proton: positive charge, in nucleus, mass of ≈1 amu
   (B) electron: negative charge, mass of ≈0 amu, in nucleus
   (C) neutron: mass of ≈1 amu, no charge

3. Thallium has two isotopes, thallium-203 and thallium-205. Thallium's atomic number is 81, and its atomic mass is 204.38 amu. Which statement about the thallium isotopes is true?
   (A) There is more thallium-203 in nature.
   (B) Atoms of both isotopes have 81 protons.
   (C) Thallium-205 atoms have fewer neutrons.
   (D) The most common atom of thallium has a mass of 204.38 amu.

4. Which atom is composed of 16 protons, 16 electrons, and 16 neutrons?
   (A) $^{48}_{16}S$ (C) $^{32}_{16}S$
   (B) $^{16}_{32}Ge$ (D) $^{16}_{32}S$

Use the art to answer Question 5.

5. How many nitrogen-14 atoms (^{14}N) would you need to place on the right pan to balance the three calcium-42 atoms (^{42}Ca) on the left pan of the "atomic balance" below? Describe the method you used to determine your answer, including any calculations.

Tips for Success

Connectors Sometimes two phrases in a true/false question are connected by a word such as *because* or *therefore*. These words imply a relationship between one part of the sentence and another. Statements that include such words can be false even if both parts of the statement are true by themselves.

For each question below, there are two statements. Decide whether each statement is true or false. Then decide whether Statement II is a correct explanation for Statement I.

Statement I		Statement II
6. Every aluminum-27 atom has 27 protons and 27 electrons.	BECAUSE	The mass number of aluminum-27 is 27.
7. Isotopes of an element have different atomic masses.	BECAUSE	The nuclei of an element's isotopes contain different numbers of protons.
8. An electron is repelled by a negatively charged particle.	BECAUSE	An electron has a negative charge.
9. In an atom, the number of neutrons is generally equal to or greater than the number of protons.	BECAUSE	The mass number is generally equal to or greater than the atomic number.

If You Have Trouble With . . .

Question	1	2	3	4	5	6	7	8	9
See Lesson	4.1	4.2	4.3	4.3	4.3	4.3	4.3	4.2	4.2

5

Electrons
in Atoms

INSIDE:

- **5.1** Revising the Atomic Model
- **5.2** Electron Arrangement in Atoms
- **5.3** Atomic Emission Spectra and the Quantum Mechanical Model

PearsonChem.com

The brilliant colors of fireworks are produced by using compounds containing different elements. In this chapter, you will learn how elements can emit light of different colors.

ELECTRONS AND THE STRUCTURE OF ATOMS

Essential Questions:

1. *How does the quantum mechanical model describe the arrangement of electrons in atoms?*

2. *What happens when electrons in atoms absorb or release energy?*

CHEMYSTERY

Now You See It... Now You Don't

Young Liam loves to go outside at night and gaze at the stars. For his birthday, his parents gave him glow-in-the-dark star stickers so that he could look at the stars from the comfort of his bed.

That night, Liam looked at the constellations he had created on his ceiling while he drifted off to sleep. A few hours later, Liam woke up very disturbed. The stars were no longer glowing even though it was still dark in his room. He turned on his bedroom light and ran down the hall to wake his parents. However, when Liam brought his parents back to his room and turned off the light, the stars were glowing again. Why did the stars cease to glow and then light up again later?

▶ Connect to the **BIG**IDEA As you read about electrons in atoms, think about how glow-in-the-dark stickers might work.

NATIONAL SCIENCE EDUCATION STANDARDS

A-1, A-2, B-1, B-6, E-2, G-1, G-2, G-3

5.1 Revising the Atomic Model

Q: *Why do scientists use mathematical models to describe the position of electrons in atoms?* Wind tunnels and models are often used to simulate the forces from the moving air on a design. Shown here is a life-sized model of a speed skier. It is a physical model. However, not all models are physical. In fact, the current model of the atom is a mathematical model.

Key Questions

🗝 What did Bohr propose in his model of the atom?

🗝 What does the quantum mechanical model determine about the electrons in an atom?

🗝 How do sublevels of principal energy levels differ?

Vocabulary

• energy level
• quantum
• quantum mechanical model
• atomic orbital

Energy Levels in Atoms

🗝 **What did Bohr propose in his model of the atom?**

Thus far, the atomic model presented in this textbook has considered atoms as consisting of protons and neutrons making up a nucleus surrounded by electrons. After discovering the atomic nucleus, Rutherford used existing ideas about the atom and proposed an atomic model in which the electrons move around the nucleus like the planets move around the sun.

Limitations of Rutherford's Atomic Model Rutherford's atomic model explained only a few simple properties of atoms. It could not explain the chemical properties of elements. For example, Rutherford's model could not explain why metals or compounds of metals give off characteristic colors when heated in a flame. It also could not explain why an object such as the iron scroll shown in Figure 5.1 first glows dull red, then yellow, and then white when heated to higher and higher temperatures. Explaining what leads to the chemical properties of elements required a model that better described the behavior of electrons in atoms.

Figure 5.1 Glowing Metal
Rutherford's model failed to explain why objects change color when heated. As the temperature of this iron scroll is increased, it first appears black, then red, then yellow, and then white. The observed behavior could be explained only if the atoms in the iron gave off light in specific amounts of energy. A better atomic model was needed to explain this observation.

The Bohr Model In 1913, Niels Bohr (1885–1962), a young Danish physicist and a student of Rutherford, developed a new atomic model. He changed Rutherford's model to incorporate newer discoveries about how the energy of an atom changes when the atom absorbs or emits light. He considered the simplest atom, hydrogen, which has one electron. **Bohr proposed that an electron is found only in specific circular paths, or orbits, around the nucleus.**

Each possible electron orbit in Bohr's model has a fixed energy. The fixed energies an electron can have are called **energy levels.** The fixed energy levels of electrons are somewhat like the rungs of the ladder in Figure 5.2a. The lowest rung of the ladder corresponds to the lowest energy level. A person can climb up or down the ladder by stepping from rung to rung. Similarly, an electron can move from one energy level to another. A person on the ladder cannot stand between the rungs. Similarly, the electrons in an atom cannot exist between energy levels. To move from one rung to another, a person climbing the ladder must move just the right distance. To move from one energy level to another, an electron must gain or lose just the right amount of energy. A **quantum** of energy is the amount of energy required to move an electron from one energy level to another energy level. The energy of an electron is therefore said to be quantized.

READING SUPPORT

Build Vocabulary: *Latin Word Origins Quantum* comes from the Latin word *quantus,* meaning "how much." *What other commonly used English word comes from this root?*

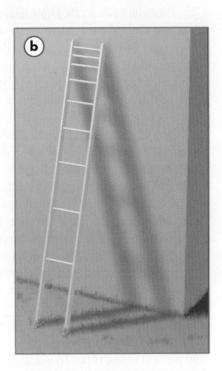

Figure 5.2 Energy Levels
The rungs of a ladder are somewhat like the energy levels in Bohr's model of the atom. **a.** In an ordinary ladder, the rungs are equally spaced. **b.** The energy levels in atoms are unequally spaced, like the rungs in this unusual ladder. The higher energy levels are closer together.
Compare *For the ladder in* **b,** *compare the amount of energy it would take to move from the first rung to the second rung with the amount of energy it would take to move from the second rung to the third rung.*

The amount of energy an electron gains or loses in an atom is not always the same. Like the rungs of the strange ladder in Figure 5.2b, the energy levels in an atom are not equally spaced. The higher energy levels are closer together. It takes less energy to climb from one rung to another near the top of the ladder in Figure 5.2b, where the rungs are closer. Similarly, the higher the energy level occupied by an electron, the less energy it takes the electron to move from that energy level to the next higher energy level.

The Bohr model provided results in agreement with experiments using the hydrogen atom. However, the Bohr model failed to explain the energies absorbed and emitted by atoms with more than one electron.

The Quantum Mechanical Model

What does the quantum mechanical model determine about the electrons in an atom?

The Rutherford model and the Bohr model of the atom described the path of a moving electron as you would describe the path of a large moving object. Later theoretical calculations and experimental results were inconsistent with describing electron motion this way. In 1926, the Austrian physicist Erwin Schrödinger (1887–1961) used these calculations and results to devise and solve a mathematical equation describing the behavior of the electron in a hydrogen atom. The modern description of the electrons in atoms, the **quantum mechanical model,** came from the mathematical solutions to the Schrödinger equation.

Like the Bohr model, the quantum mechanical model of the atom restricts the energy of electrons to certain values. Unlike the Bohr model, however, the quantum mechanical model does not specify an exact path the electron takes around the nucleus. **The quantum mechanical model determines the allowed energies an electron can have and how likely it is to find the electron in various locations around the nucleus of an atom.**

Probability describes how likely it is to find an electron in a particular location around the nucleus of an atom. If you placed three red marbles and one green marble into a box and then picked a marble without looking, the probability of picking the green marble would be one in four, or 25 percent. This percentage means that if you put the four marbles in a box and picked one, and repeated this many times, you would pick a green marble in 25 percent of your tries.

The quantum mechanical model description of how electrons move around the nucleus is similar to a description of how the blades of a windmill rotate. The windmill blades in Figure 5.3a have some probability of being anywhere in the blurry region they produce in the picture, but you cannot predict their exact locations at any instant. In the quantum mechanical model of the atom, the probability of finding an electron within a certain volume of space surrounding the nucleus can be represented as a fuzzy cloudlike region, as shown in Figure 5.3b. The cloud is more dense where the probability of finding the electron is high and is less dense where the probability of finding the electron is low. There is no boundary to the cloud because there is a slight chance of finding the electron at a considerable distance from the nucleus. Therefore, attempts to show probabilities as a fuzzy cloud are usually limited to the volume in which the electron is found 90 percent of the time. To visualize an electron probability cloud, imagine that you could mold a sack around the cloud so that the electron was inside the sack 90 percent of the time. The shape of the sack would then give you a picture of the shape of the cloud.

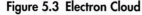

Electron cloud

Figure 5.3 Electron Cloud
The electron cloud of an atom can be compared to a photograph of spinning windmill blades. **a.** The windmill blades are somewhere in the blurry region they produce in this picture, but the picture does not tell you their exact positions at any instant. **b.** Similarly, the electron cloud of an atom represents the locations where an electron is likely to be found, but it is not possible to know where an electron is in the cloud at any instant.

Atomic Orbitals

How do sublevels of principal energy levels differ?

Solutions to the Schrödinger equation give the energies, or energy levels, an electron can have. For each energy level, the Schrödinger equation also leads to a mathematical expression, called an **atomic orbital,** describing the probability of finding an electron at various locations around the nucleus. An atomic orbital is represented pictorially as a region of space in which there is a high probability of finding an electron.

The energy levels of electrons in the quantum mechanical model are labeled by principal quantum numbers (n). These numbers are assigned the values $n = 1, 2, 3, 4$, and so forth. For each principal energy level greater than 1, there are several orbitals with different shapes and at different energy levels. These energy levels within a principal energy level constitute energy sublevels. **Each energy sublevel corresponds to one or more orbitals of different shapes. The orbitals describe where an electron is likely to be found.**

Different atomic orbitals are denoted by letters. As shown in Figure 5.4a, s orbitals are spherical, and p orbitals are dumbbell-shaped. The probability of finding an electron at a given distance from the nucleus in an s orbital does not depend on direction because of its spherical shape. The three kinds of p orbitals have different orientations in space. Figure 5.4b shows the shapes of d orbitals. Four of the five kinds of d orbitals have cloverleaf shapes. The shapes of f orbitals are more complicated than the shapes of d orbitals.

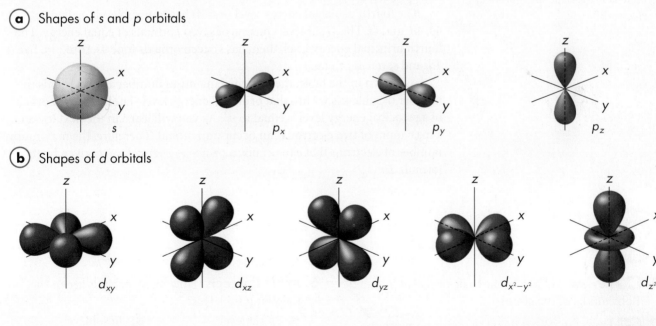

(a) Shapes of s and p orbitals

s p_x p_y p_z

(b) Shapes of d orbitals

d_{xy} d_{xz} d_{yz} $d_{x^2-y^2}$ d_{z^2}

Figure 5.4 Atomic Orbitals
Solutions to the Schrödinger equation give rise to atomic orbitals. **a.** For a given principal energy level greater than 1, there is one s orbital and three p orbitals. **b.** Four of the five d orbitals have the same shape but different spatial orientations.
Interpret Diagrams *How are the orientations of the d_{xy} and $d_{x^2-y^2}$ orbitals similar? How are they different?*

See atomic orbitals animated online.

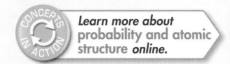

Learn more about probability and atomic structure *online*.

Table 5.1

Summary of Principal Energy Levels and Sublevels

Principal energy level	Number of sublevels	Type of sublevel	Maximum number of electrons
$n = 1$	1	1s (1 orbital)	2
$n = 2$	2	2s (1 orbital), 2p (3 orbitals)	8
$n = 3$	3	3s (1 orbital), 3p (3 orbitals), 3d (5 orbitals)	18
$n = 4$	4	4s (1 orbital), 4p (3 orbitals), 4d (5 orbitals), 4f (7 orbitals)	32

As shown in Table 5.1, the numbers and types of atomic orbitals depend on the principal energy level. The lowest principal energy level ($n = 1$) has only one sublevel, called 1s. The second principal energy level ($n = 2$) has two sublevels, 2s and 2p. The 2p sublevel is of higher energy than the 2s sublevel and consists of three p orbitals of equal energy. Thus the second principal energy level has four orbitals (one 2s and three 2p orbitals).

The third principal energy level ($n = 3$) has three sublevels. These are called 3s, 3p, and 3d. The 3d sublevel consists of five d orbitals of equal energy. Thus the third principal energy level has nine orbitals (one 3s, three 3p, and five 3d orbitals).

The fourth principal energy level ($n = 4$) has four sublevels, called 4s, 4p, 4d, and 4f. The 4f sublevel consists of seven f orbitals of equal energy. The fourth principal energy level, then, has sixteen orbitals (one 4s, three 4p, five 4d, and seven 4f orbitals).

As shown in the table, the principal quantum number always equals the number of sublevels within that principal energy level. The number of orbitals in a principal energy level is equal to n^2. As you will learn in the next lesson, a maximum of two electrons can occupy an orbital. Therefore, the maximum number of electrons that can occupy a principal energy level is given by the formula $2n^2$.

CHEMISTRY & YOU

Q: *Previous models of the atom were physical models based on the motion of large objects. Why do scientists no longer use physical models to describe the motion of electrons?*

5.1 LessonCheck

1. Review What was the basic proposal in the Bohr model of the atom?

2. Describe What does the quantum mechanical model determine about electrons in atoms?

3. Review How do two sublevels of the same principal energy level differ from each other?

4. Describe How can electrons in an atom move from one energy level to another?

5. Explain The energies of electrons are said to be quantized. Explain what this means.

6. Apply Concepts How many orbitals are in the following sublevels?
   a. 3p sublevel
   b. 2s sublevel
   c. 4p sublevel
   d. 3d sublevel
   e. 4f sublevel

BIG IDEA

ELECTRONS AND THE STRUCTURE OF ATOMS

7. How do the Bohr model and the quantum mechanical model differ in the way they describe the arrangement of electrons in atoms?

Development of Atomic Models

The atomic model has changed as scientists learned more about the atom's structure through experiments and calculations.

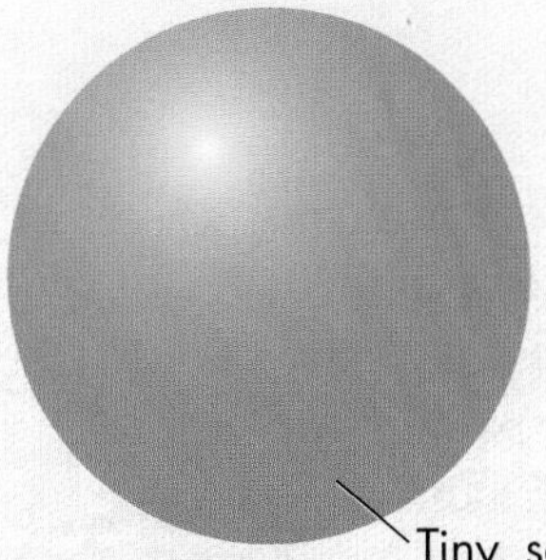

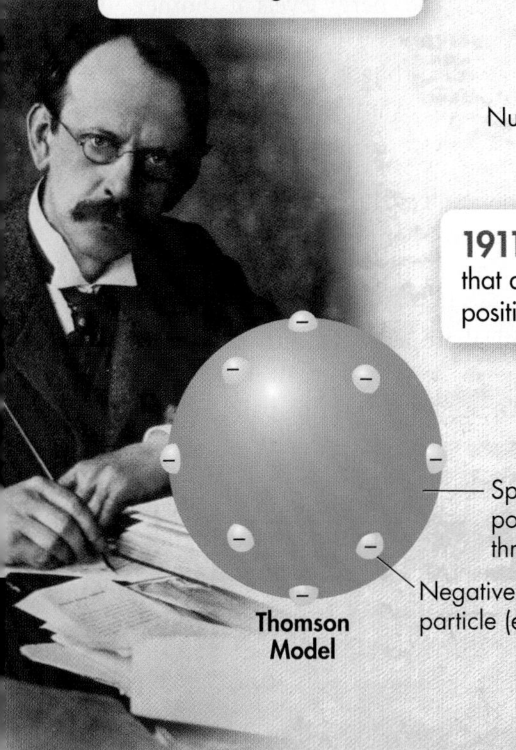

1904 Hantaro Nagaoka suggests that an atom has a central nucleus. Electrons move in orbits like the rings around Saturn.

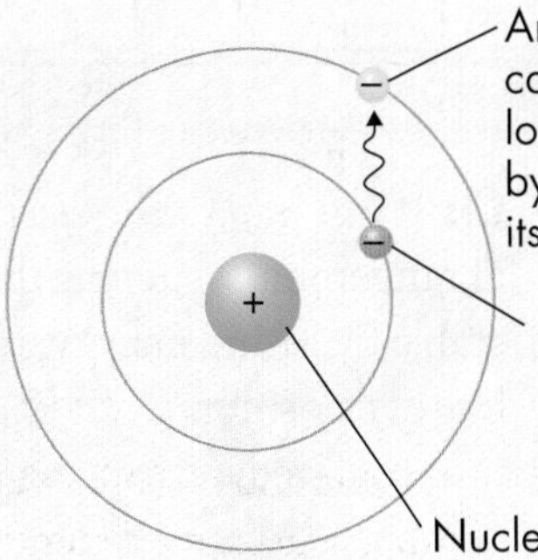

1923 Louis de Broglie proposes that moving particles like electrons have some properties of waves.

Tiny, solid sphere

Dalton Model

An electron can gain or lose energy by changing its orbit.

Electron

Nucleus

Bohr Model

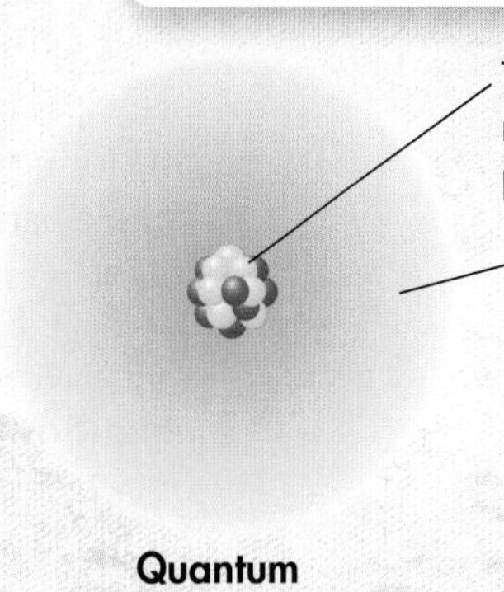

1932 James Chadwick confirms the existence of neutrons, which have no charge. Atomic nuclei contain neutrons and positively charged protons.

1803 John Dalton pictures atoms as tiny, indestructible particles.

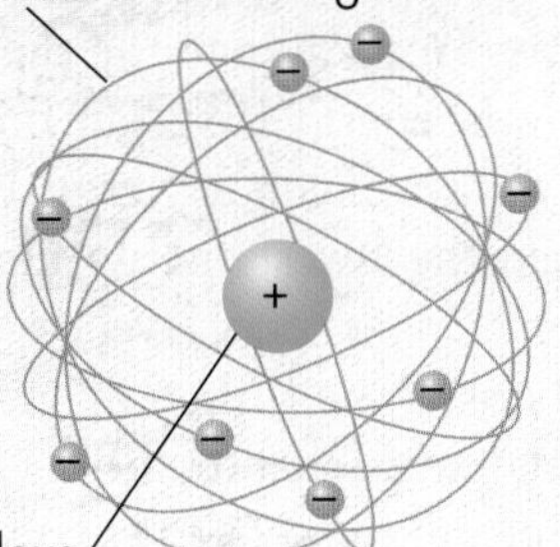

1913 In Niels Bohr's model, the electron moves in a circular orbit at fixed distances from the nucleus.

| 1800 | 1805 | 1895 | 1900 | 1905 | 1910 | 1915 | 1920 | 1925 | 1930 | 1935 |

1897 J.J. Thomson discovers the electron. He pictures electrons embedded in a sphere of positive electrical charge.

Path of a moving electron

Nucleus

Rutherford Model

1911 Ernest Rutherford finds that an atom has a small, dense, positively charged nucleus.

1926 Erwin Schrödinger develops mathematical equations to describe the motion of electrons in atoms, which leads to the quantum mechanical model.

The positively charged nucleus contains protons and neutrons.

The electron cloud is a visual model of the probable locations of electrons in an atom. The probability of finding an electron is higher in the denser regions of the cloud.

Quantum Mechanical Model

Sphere with positive charge throughout

Negatively charged particle (electron)

Thomson Model

Take It Further

1. Summarize List a major contribution of each of these scientists to the understanding of the atom: Dalton, Thomson, Rutherford, Bohr, and Schrödinger.

2. Describe Have you ever needed to identify something you could not see? Explain.

5.2 Electron Arrangement in Atoms

Q: *What makes the electron configuration of an atom stable?* Unstable arrangements, such as the yoga position shown here, tend to become more stable by losing energy. If the yogi were to fall, she would have less energy, but her position would be more stable. Energy and stability play an important role in determining how electrons are configured in an atom.

Key Question

🔑 What are the three rules for writing the electron configurations of elements?

Vocabulary

- electron configuration
- aufbau principle
- Pauli exclusion principle
- spin
- Hund's rule

Electron Configurations

🔑 **What are the three rules for writing the electron configurations of elements?**

In an atom, electrons and the nucleus interact to make the most stable arrangement possible. The ways in which electrons are arranged in various orbitals around the nuclei of atoms are called **electron configurations.** 🔑 **Three rules—the aufbau principle, the Pauli exclusion principle, and Hund's rule—tell you how to find the electron configurations of atoms.** The three rules are as follows.

Aufbau Principle According to the **aufbau principle,** electrons occupy the orbitals of lowest energy first. The orbitals for any sublevel of a principal energy level are always of equal energy. Within a principal energy level, the *s* sublevel is always the lowest-energy sublevel. However, the range of energy levels within a principal energy level can overlap the energy levels of another principal level. Look at the aufbau diagram in Figure 5.5. Each box represents an atomic orbital. Notice that the filling of atomic orbitals does not follow a simple pattern beyond the second energy level. For example, the 4*s* orbital is lower in energy than a 3*d* orbital.

Pauli Exclusion Principle According to the **Pauli exclusion principle,** an atomic orbital may describe at most two electrons. For example, either one or two electrons can occupy an *s* orbital or a *p* orbital. To occupy the same orbital, two electrons must have opposite spins; that is, the electron spins must be paired. **Spin** is a quantum mechanical property of electrons and may be thought of as clockwise or counterclockwise. A vertical arrow indicates an electron and its direction of spin (↑ or ↓). An orbital containing paired electrons is written as ↑↓.

Hund's Rule According to **Hund's rule,** electrons occupy orbitals of the same energy in a way that makes the number of electrons with the same spin direction as large as possible. For example, three electrons would occupy three orbitals of equal energy as follows: ↑ ↑ ↑ . Electrons then occupy each orbital so that their spins are paired with the first electron in the orbital.

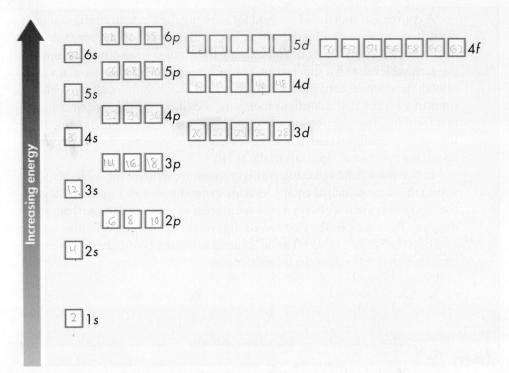

Figure 5.5 Aufbau Diagram
This aufbau diagram shows the relative energy levels of the various atomic orbitals. Orbitals of greater energy are higher on the diagram.
Interpret Tables *Which is of higher energy, a 4d orbital or a 5s orbital?*

Look at the orbital filling diagrams of the atoms listed in Table 5.2. An oxygen atom contains eight electrons. The orbital of lowest energy, 1s, has one electron, then a second electron of opposite spin. The next orbital to fill is 2s. It also has one electron, then a second electron of opposite spin. One electron then occupies each of the three 2p orbitals of equal energy. The remaining electron now pairs with an electron occupying one of the 2p orbitals. The other two 2p orbitals remain only half filled, with one electron each.

Table 5.2

Electron Configurations of Selected Elements

Element	1s	2s	$2p_x$	$2p_y$	$2p_z$	3s	Electron configuration
H	↑						$1s^1$
He	↑↓						$1s^2$
Li	↑↓	↑					$1s^2 2s^1$
C	↑↓	↑↓	↑	↑			$1s^2 2s^2 2p^2$
N	↑↓	↑↓	↑	↑	↑		$1s^2 2s^2 2p^3$
O	↑↓	↑↓	↑↓	↑	↑		$1s^2 2s^2 2p^4$
F	↑↓	↑↓	↑↓	↑↓	↑		$1s^2 2s^2 2p^5$
Ne	↑↓	↑↓	↑↓	↑↓	↑↓		$1s^2 2s^2 2p^6$
Na	↑↓	↑↓	↑↓	↑↓	↑↓	↑	$1s^2 2s^2 2p^6 3s^1$

Q: *Explain why the correct electron configuration of oxygen is $1s^2\,2s^2\,2p^4$ and not $1s^2\,2s^2\,2p^3\,3s^1$.*

A convenient shorthand method for showing the electron configuration of an atom involves writing the energy level and the symbol for every sublevel occupied by an electron. You indicate the number of electrons occupying each sublevel with a superscript. For hydrogen, with one electron in a $1s$ orbital, the electron configuration is written $1s^1$. For helium, with two electrons in a $1s$ orbital, the configuration is $1s^2$. For oxygen, with two electrons in a $1s$ orbital, two electrons in a $2s$ orbital, and four electrons in $2p$ orbitals, the electron configuration is $1s^2\,2s^2\,2p^4$. Note that the sum of the superscripts equals the number of electrons in the atom.

In this book, when electron configurations are written, the sublevels within the same principal energy level are generally written together. These configurations are not always in the same order as shown on the aufbau diagram. For example, the electron configuration of bromine is written as $1s^2\,2s^2\,2p^6\,3s^2\,3p^6\,3d^{10}\,4s^2\,4p^5$. The $3d$ sublevel is written before the $4s$ sublevel, even though the $4s$ sublevel has lower energy.

Sample Problem 5.1

Writing Electron Configurations

The atomic number of phosphorus is 15. Write the electron configuration of a phosphorus atom.

❶ **Analyze   Identify the relevant concepts.** Phosphorus has 15 electrons. There is a maximum of two electrons per orbital. Electrons do not pair up within an energy sublevel (orbitals of equal energy) until each orbital already has one electron.

> When writing electron configurations, the sublevels within the same principal energy level are written together.

❷ **Solve   Apply the concepts to this problem.**

| Use the aufbau diagram in Figure 5.5 to place electrons in the orbital with the lowest energy ($1s$) first. Continue placing electrons in each orbital with the next higher energy level. |

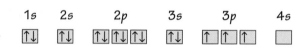

| Write the electron configuration. |

The electron configuration of phosphorus is $1s^2\,2s^2\,2p^6\,3s^2\,3p^3$. The superscripts add up to the number of electrons.

---

8. Write the electron configuration for each atom.
   a. carbon
   b. argon
   c. nickel

9. Write the electron configuration for each atom. How many unpaired electrons does each atom have?
   a. boron
   b. silicon
   c. sulfur

Exceptional Electron Configurations Copper, which is shown in Figure 5.6, has an electron configuration that is an exception to the aufbau principle. You can obtain correct electron configurations for the elements up to vanadium (atomic number 23) by following the aufbau diagram for orbital filling. If you were to continue in that fashion, however, you would assign chromium and copper the following incorrect configurations.

$$Cr\ 1s^2\,2s^2\,2p^6\,3s^2\,3p^6\,3d^4\,4s^2$$
$$Cu\ 1s^2\,2s^2\,2p^6\,3s^2\,3p^6\,3d^9\,4s^2$$

The correct electron configurations are as follows:

$$Cr\ 1s^2\,2s^2\,2p^6\,3s^2\,3p^6\,3d^5\,4s^1$$
$$Cu\ 1s^2\,2s^2\,2p^6\,3s^2\,3p^6\,3d^{10}\,4s^1$$

These arrangements give chromium a half-filled d sublevel and copper a filled d sublevel. Filled energy sublevels are more stable than partially filled sublevels. Some actual electron configurations differ from those assigned using the aufbau principle because although half-filled sublevels are not as stable as filled sublevels, they are more stable than other configurations. This tendency overcomes the small difference between the energies of the $3d$ and $4s$ sublevels in copper and chromium.

At higher principal quantum numbers, energy differences between some sublevels (such as $5f$ and $6d$, for example) are even smaller than in the chromium and copper examples. As a result, there are other exceptions to the aufbau principle. Although it is worth knowing that exceptions to the aufbau principle occur, it is more important to understand the general rules for determining electron configurations in the many cases in which the aufbau principle applies.

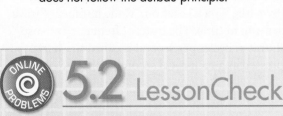

Figure 5.6 Copper
Copper is a shiny metal that can be molded into different shapes. The electron configuration of copper does not follow the aufbau principle.

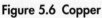 **5.2** LessonCheck

10. List What are the three rules for writing the electron configurations of elements?

11. **Sequence** Use Figure 5.5 to arrange the following sublevels in order of decreasing energy: $2p$, $4s$, $3s$, $3d$, and $3p$.

12. **Explain** Why do the actual electron configurations for some elements differ from those assigned using the aufbau principle?

13. Infer Why does one electron in a potassium atom go into the fourth energy level instead of squeezing into the third energy level along with the eight already there?

14. **Apply Concepts** The atomic number of arsenic is 33. What is the electron configuration of an arsenic atom?

5.3 Atomic Emission Spectra and the Quantum Mechanical Model

Q: *What gives gas-filled lights their colors?* If you walk in the evening along a busy street lined with shops and theaters, you are likely to see lighted advertising signs. The signs are formed from glass tubes bent in various shapes. An electric current passing through the gas in each glass tube makes the gas glow with its own characteristic color.

Key Questions

▸ What causes atomic emission spectra?

▸ How did Einstein explain the photoelectric effect?

▸ How are the frequencies of light emitted by an atom related to changes of electron energies?

▸ How does quantum mechanics differ from classical mechanics?

Vocabulary

- amplitude • wavelength
- frequency • hertz
- electromagnetic radiation
- spectrum
- atomic emission spectrum
- Planck's constant
- photoelectric effect • photon
- ground state
- Heisenberg uncertainty principle

Light and Atomic Emission Spectra

▸ What causes atomic emission spectra?

The previous sections in this chapter introduced you to some ideas about how electrons in atoms are arranged in orbitals, each with a particular energy level. You also learned how to write electron configurations for atoms. You will now get a closer look into what led to the development of Schrödinger's equation and the quantum mechanical model of the atom.

The Nature of Light Rather curiously, the quantum mechanical model grew out of the study of light. Isaac Newton (1642–1727) tried to explain what was known about the behavior of light by assuming that light consists of particles. By the year 1900, however, there was enough experimental evidence to convince scientists that light consists of waves. Figure 5.7 illustrates some of the properties of waves. As shown, each complete wave cycle starts at zero on the y-axis, increases to its highest value, passes through zero to reach its lowest value, and returns to zero again. The **amplitude** of a wave is the wave's height from zero to the crest, as shown in Figure 5.7. The **wavelength**, represented by λ (the Greek letter lambda), is the distance between the crests. The **frequency**, represented by ν (the Greek letter nu), is the number of wave cycles to pass a given point per unit of time. The units of frequency are usually cycles per second. The SI unit of cycles per second is called the **hertz** (Hz). A hertz can also be expressed as a reciprocal second (s^{-1}).

Figure 5.7 Light Waves
The frequency (ν) and wavelength (λ) of light waves are inversely related. As the wavelength decreases, the frequency increases.

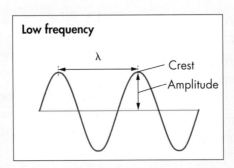

Low frequency

λ
Crest
Amplitude

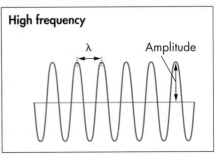

High frequency

λ
Amplitude

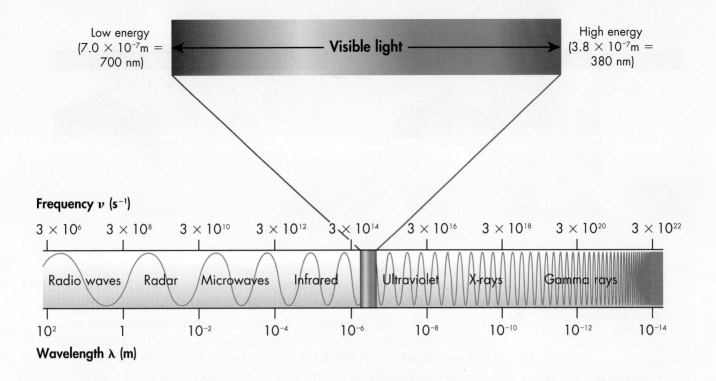

Low energy
(7.0 × 10⁻⁷m = 700 nm)

Visible light

High energy
(3.8 × 10⁻⁷m = 380 nm)

Frequency ν (s⁻¹)

3×10^6 3×10^8 3×10^{10} 3×10^{12} 3×10^{14} 3×10^{16} 3×10^{18} 3×10^{20} 3×10^{22}

Radio waves Radar Microwaves Infrared Ultraviolet X-rays Gamma rays

10^2 1 10^{-2} 10^{-4} 10^{-6} 10^{-8} 10^{-10} 10^{-12} 10^{-14}

Wavelength λ (m)

Figure 5.8 Electromagnetic Spectrum
The electromagnetic spectrum consists of radiation over a broad range of wavelengths. The visible light portion is very small. It is in the 10^{-7} m wavelength range and 10^{15} Hz (s⁻¹) frequency range.
Interpret Diagrams *What types of nonvisible radiation have wavelengths close to those of red light? To those of blue light?*

The product of frequency and wavelength equals a constant (*c*), the speed of light.

$$c = \lambda \nu$$

The wavelength and frequency of light are inversely proportional to each other. As the wavelength of light increases, the frequency decreases.

According to the wave model, light consists of electromagnetic waves. **Electromagnetic radiation** includes radio waves, microwaves, infrared waves, visible light, ultraviolet waves, X-rays, and gamma rays. All electromagnetic waves travel in a vacuum at a speed of 2.998×10^8 m/s.

The sun and incandescent light bulbs emit white light, which consists of light with a continuous range of wavelengths and frequencies. As you can see from Figure 5.8, the wavelength and frequency of each color of light are characteristic of that color. When sunlight passes through a prism, the different wavelengths separate into a **spectrum** of colors. A rainbow is an example of this phenomenon. Each tiny droplet of water acts as a prism to produce a spectrum. Each color blends into the next in the order red, orange, yellow, green, blue, and violet. As can be seen in Figure 5.8, red light has the longest wavelength and the lowest frequency in the visible spectrum.

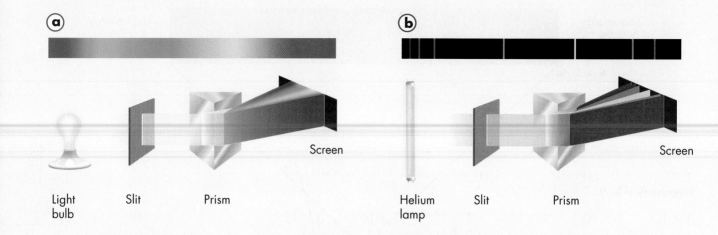

Screen

Light bulb   Slit   Prism

Screen

Helium lamp   Slit   Prism

Figure 5.9 Comparing Spectra
A prism separates light into the colors it contains. **a.** White light produces a rainbow of colors. **b.** Light from a helium lamp produces discrete lines.
Identify *Which color of the rainbow has the highest frequency?*

Atomic Emission Spectra When an electric current is passed through a gaseous element, or through the vapor of a liquid or solid element, the electrons of the atoms of the gas or vapor are energized. This energy causes them to emit light. **When atoms absorb energy, their electrons move to higher energy levels. These electrons lose energy by emitting light when they return to lower energy levels.** The energy absorbed by an electron for it to move from its current energy level to a higher energy level is identical to the energy of the light emitted by the electron as it drops back to its original energy level. Figure 5.9a shows the visible spectrum of white light. Notice that all the wavelengths of visible light are blurred together as in a rainbow. However, when the light emitted by the energized electrons of a gaseous element is passed through a prism, as shown in Figure 5.9b, the spectrum consists of a limited number of narrow lines of light. The wavelengths of these spectral lines are characteristic of the element, and they make up the **atomic emission spectrum** of the element.

Each spectral line in an atomic emission spectrum of an element corresponds to exactly one wavelength of light emitted by the electrons of that element. Figure 5.9b shows the visible portion of the atomic emission spectrum of helium.

The atomic emission spectrum of each element is like a person's fingerprint. Just as no two people have the same fingerprints, no two elements have the same atomic emission spectrum. In the same way that fingerprints identify people, atomic emission spectra are useful for identifying elements. Figure 5.10 shows the characteristic colors emitted by sodium and by mercury. Much of the knowledge about the composition of the universe comes from studying the atomic emission spectra of the stars, which are hot glowing bodies of gases.

**Figure 5.10
Atomic Emission Spectra**
No two elements have the same atomic emission spectrum.
a. Sodium vapor lamps produce a yellow glow. **b.** Mercury vapor lamps produce a blue glow.

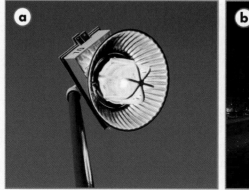

SampleProblem 5.2

Calculating the Wavelength of Light

Calculate the wavelength of the yellow light emitted by a sodium lamp if the frequency of the radiation is 5.09×10^{14} Hz ($5.09 \times 10^{14}/s$).

❶ Analyze **List the knowns and the unknown.** Use the equation $c = \lambda v$ to solve for the unknown wavelength.

> KNOWNS
>
> frequency (v) = $5.09 \times 10^{14}/s$
> $c = 2.998 \times 10^8$ m/s
>
> UNKNOWN
>
> wavelength (λ) = ? m

❷ Calculate **Solve for the unknown.**

Write the expression that relates the frequency and wavelength of light.	$c = \lambda v$
Rearrange the equation to solve for λ.	$\lambda = \dfrac{c}{v}$
Substitute the known values for v and c into the equation and solve.	$\lambda = \dfrac{2.998 \times 10^8 \text{ m/s}}{5.09 \times 10^{14}/s} = 5.89 \times 10^{-7}$ m

> Solve for λ by dividing both sides by v:
>
> $\dfrac{c}{v} = \dfrac{\lambda v}{v}$

❸ Evaluate **Does the result make sense?** The magnitude of the frequency is much larger than the numerical value of the speed of light, so the answer should be much less than 1. The answer should have three significant figures.

15. What is the wavelength of radiation with a frequency of 1.50×10^{13} Hz? Does this radiation have a longer or shorter wavelength than red light?

> In Problem 15, solve for wavelength.

16. What is the frequency of radiation with a wavelength of 5.00×10^{-8} m? In what region of the electromagnetic spectrum is this radiation?

> In Problem 16, solve for frequency.

Quick Lab

Purpose To determine the identity of the metal in an unknown solution based on its characteristic color in a flame

Materials

- 6 small test tubes
- sodium chloride (NaCl) solution
- calcium chloride (CaCl₂) solution
- lithium chloride (LiCl) solution
- copper(II) chloride (CuCl₂) solution
- potassium chloride (KCl) solution
- unknown solution
- 6 cotton swabs
- gas burner

Flame Tests

Procedure

1. Make a two-column data table. Label the columns Metal and Flame Color. Enter the metal's name for each solution in the first column.

2. Label each of five test tubes with the name of a solution; label the sixth tube Unknown. Add 1 mL of each solution to the appropriately labeled test tube.

3. Dip one of the cotton ends of a cotton swab into the sodium chloride solution and then hold it briefly in the burner flame.

Record the color of the flame. Do not leave the swab in the flame too long or the plastic will melt.

4. Repeat Step 3 for each of the remaining solutions using a new cotton swab each time.

5. Perform a flame test with the unknown solution. Note the color of the flame.

Analyze and Conclude

1. Identify What is the metal in the unknown?

2. Draw Conclusions Each solution produces a unique color. Would you expect this result based on the modern view of the atom? Explain.

3. Analyze Data Some commercially available fireplace logs burn with a red and/or green flame. What elements could be responsible for these colored flames?

4. Predict Aerial fireworks contain gunpowder and chemicals that produce colors. What element would you include to produce crimson red? Yellow?

The Quantum Concept and Photons

⚡ How did Einstein explain the photoelectric effect?

According to the laws of classical physics, the atomic emission spectrum of an element should be continuous. Thus, classical physics does not explain the emission spectra of atoms, which consist of lines.

The Quantization of Energy Recall the iron scroll in Figure 5.1 that changed color when heated. In 1900, the German physicist Max Planck (1858–1947) was trying to describe why such a body first appears black, then red, then yellow, and then white as its temperature increases. Planck found that he could explain the color changes if he assumed that the energy of a body changes only in small discrete units, or quanta. Planck showed mathematically that the amount of radiant energy (E) of a single quantum absorbed or emitted by a body is proportional to the frequency of radiation (ν).

$$E \propto \nu \text{ or } E = h\nu$$

The constant (h), which has a value of 6.626×10^{-34} J·s, (J is the joule, the SI unit of energy) is called **Planck's constant.** The energy of a quantum equals $h\nu$. A small energy change involves the emission or absorption of low-frequency radiation. A large energy change involves the emission or absorption of high-frequency radiation.

The Photoelectric Effect A few years after Planck presented his theory on the quantization of energy, scientists began to use it to explain many experimental observations that could not be explained by classical physics. In 1905, Albert Einstein (1879–1955), then a patent examiner in Bern, Switzerland, used Planck's quantum theory to explain the photoelectric effect, which is illustrated in Figure 5.11. In the **photoelectric effect,** electrons are ejected when light shines on a metal. Not just any frequency of light will cause the photoelectric effect. For example, red light will not cause potassium to eject electrons, no matter how intense the light. Yet a very weak yellow light shining on potassium begins the effect.

The photoelectric effect could not be explained by classical physics. Although classical physics correctly described light as a form of energy, it assumed that under weak light of any wavelength, an electron in a metal should eventually collect enough energy to be ejected. The photoelectric effect presented a serious problem for the classical wave theory of light.

🔑 **To explain the photoelectric effect, Einstein proposed that light could be described as quanta of energy that behave as if they were particles.** These light quanta are called **photons.** The energy of photons is quantized according to the equation $E = h\nu$. Einstein recognized that there is a threshold value of energy below which the photoelectric effect does not occur. According to $E = h\nu$, all the photons in a beam of monochromatic light (light of only one frequency) have the same energy. If the frequency, and therefore the energy, of the photons is too low, then no electrons will be ejected. It does not matter whether a single photon or a steady stream of low-energy photons strikes an electron in the metal. Only if the frequency of light is above the threshold frequency will the photoelectric effect occur.

Einstein's theory that light behaves as a stream of particles explains the photoelectric effect and many other observations. However, light also behaves as waves in other situations. Therefore, we must consider that light possesses both wavelike and particle-like properties.

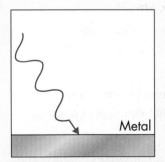

No electrons are ejected because the frequency of the light is below the threshold frequency.

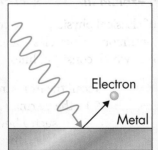

If the light is at or above the threshold frequency, electrons are ejected.

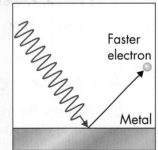

If the frequency is increased, the ejected electrons will travel faster.

Figure 5.11
Photoelectric Effect
Einstein explained the photoelectric effect by proposing that light behaves as particles.
Predict *What will happen if ultraviolet light shines on the metal?*

Calculating the Energy of a Photon

What is the energy of a photon of microwave radiation with a frequency of 3.20×10^{11}/s?

KNOWNS

frequency $(\nu) = 3.20 \times 10^{11}$/s

$h = 6.626 \times 10^{-34}$ J·s

UNKNOWN

energy $(E) = ?$ J

❶ Analyze **List the knowns and the unknown.** Use the equation $E = h\nu$ to calculate the energy of the photon.

❷ Calculate **Solve for the unknown.**

Write the expression that relates the energy of a photon of radiation and the frequency of the radiation.

$E = h\nu$

Substitute the known values for ν and h into the equation and solve.

$E = (6.626 \times 10^{-34} \text{ J·s}) \times (3.20 \times 10^{11}/\text{s})$

$\quad = 2.12 \times 10^{-22}$ J

❸ Evaluate **Does the result make sense?** Individual photons have very small energies, so the answer seems reasonable.

In Problem 18, use the equation $c = \lambda\nu$ to calculate the frequency of light from the wavelength. Then, calculate the energy.

17. Calculate the energy of a quantum of radiant energy with a frequency of 5.00×10^{11}/s.

18. The threshold photoelectric effect in tungsten is produced by light of a wavelength 260 nm. Give the energy of a photon of this light in joules.

An Explanation of Atomic Spectra

🔑 *How are the frequencies of light emitted by an atom related to changes of electron energies?*

Atomic emission spectra were known before Bohr proposed his model of the hydrogen atom. Bohr applied quantum theory to electron energy levels in atoms to explain the atomic emission spectrum of hydrogen. Bohr's model not only explained why the atomic emission spectrum of hydrogen consists of specific frequencies of light, but it also predicted specific values of these frequencies that agreed with the experimental results.

In the Bohr model, the lone electron in the hydrogen atom can have only certain specific energies. When the electron has its lowest possible energy, the atom is in its **ground state.** In the ground state, the principal quantum number (n) is 1. Excitation of the electron by absorbing energy raises the atom to an excited state with $n = 2, 3, 4, 5,$ or 6, and so forth. A quantum of energy in the form of light is emitted when the electron drops back to a lower energy level. The emission occurs in a single step, called an electronic transition. Bohr already knew that this quantum of energy E is related to the frequency v of the emitted light by the equation $E = hv$. **The light emitted by an electron moving from a higher to a lower energy level has a frequency directly proportional to the energy change of the electron.** Therefore, each transition produces a line of a specific frequency in the spectrum.

Figure 5.12 shows the three groups of lines in the emission spectrum of hydrogen atoms. The lines at the ultraviolet end of the hydrogen spectrum are the Lyman series. These lines are due to the transitions of electrons from higher energy levels to the lowest energy level, $n = 1$. The lines in the visible spectrum are the Balmer series. These lines result from transitions from higher energy levels to $n = 2$. These transitions generally involve a smaller change in electron energy than transitions to $n = 1$. Transitions to $n = 3$ from higher energy levels produce the Paschen series. The energy changes of the electron are generally smaller still. The lines are in the infrared range. Spectral lines for the transitions from higher energy levels to $n = 4$ and $n = 5$ also exist. Note that the spectral lines in each group become more closely spaced at increased values of n because the energy levels become closer together. There is an upper limit to the frequency of emitted light for each set of lines because an electron with enough energy completely escapes the atom.

Bohr's model explained the atomic emission spectrum of hydrogen but not the emission spectra of atoms with more than one electron. Also, it did not help in understanding how atoms bond to form molecules. Eventually the quantum mechanical model displaced the Bohr model of the atom.

CHEMISTRY & YOU

Q: *The glass tubes in lighted signs contain helium, neon, argon, krypton, or xenon gas, or a mixture of these gases. Why do the colors of the light depend on the gases that are used?*

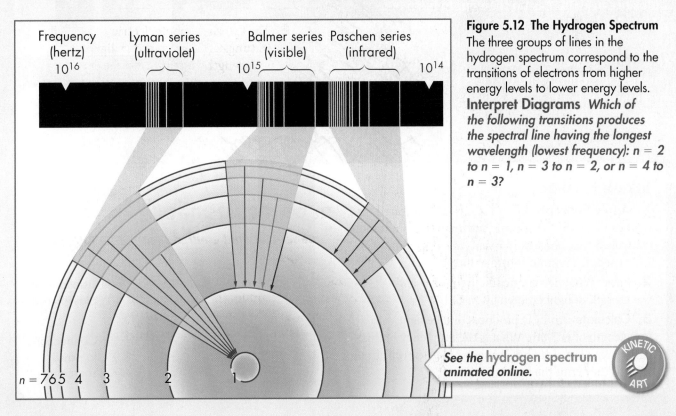

Figure 5.12 The Hydrogen Spectrum
The three groups of lines in the hydrogen spectrum correspond to the transitions of electrons from higher energy levels to lower energy levels.
Interpret Diagrams *Which of the following transitions produces the spectral line having the longest wavelength (lowest frequency): n = 2 to n = 1, n = 3 to n = 2, or n = 4 to n = 3?*

See the hydrogen spectrum animated online.

KINETIC ART

Light Emitting Diodes

Although they are small, you may have seen light emitting diodes, or LEDs, several times today. These tiny light bulbs may form the numbers on your digital clock, light up your watch, or illuminate the traffic light you stopped at on your way to school. You may have even watched television on a giant screen made out of LEDs.

Light from a typical incandescent bulb is generated when the filament inside the bulb is heated. Light from an LED is generated in a different way. A diode is made out of two materials with different properties. The electrons in one of the materials are at a higher energy level than the electrons in the other material. When a voltage, supplied by a battery or other power supply, is applied to the diode, electrons flow across the boundary between the two materials. The electrons at the higher energy level flow into the other material, fall to a lower energy level, and emit light.

LEDs last much longer than incandescent light bulbs because there is no filament to burn out. Also, a large amount of the energy that is used to produce light in an incandescent bulb is wasted as heat. However, LEDs produce very little heat, so they use less energy and cost less to operate than incandescent lights.

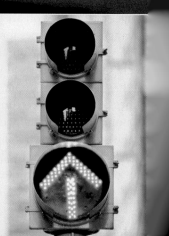

Take It Further

1. Apply Concepts LEDs that produce infrared light can be used to transmit information from remote controls. What range of frequencies of light would an LED used in a remote control emit?

2. Infer What determines the frequency and wavelength of light emitted by an LED?

3. Calculate An LED produces orange light with a wavelength of 605 nm. What is the frequency of this light? What is the energy change of the electrons in the LED as they emit the light?

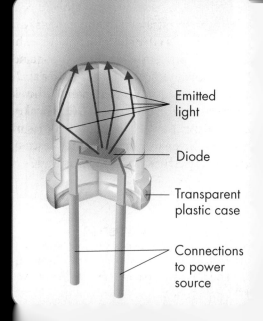

Emitted light

Diode

Transparent plastic case

Connections to power source

Quantum Mechanics

🔑 How does quantum mechanics differ from classical mechanics?

In 1924, Louis de Broglie (1892–1987), a French graduate student, asked an important question: Given that light behaves as waves and particles, can particles of matter behave as waves? De Broglie referred to the wavelike behavior of particles as matter waves. His reasoning led him to a mathematical expression for the wavelength of a moving particle.

The Wavelike Nature of Matter The proposal that matter moves in a wavelike way would not have been accepted unless experiments confirmed its validity. Only three years later, experiments by Clinton Davisson and Lester Germer at Bell Labs in New Jersey did just that. The two scientists had been studying the bombardment of metals with beams of electrons. They noticed that the electrons reflected from the metal surface produced curious patterns. The patterns were like those obtained when X-rays (which are electromagnetic waves) reflect from metal surfaces. The electrons, which were believed to be particles, were reflected as if they were waves! De Broglie was awarded the Nobel prize for his work on the wave nature of matter. Davisson also received the Nobel prize for his experiments demonstrating the wave nature of electrons.

Today, the wavelike properties of beams of electrons are useful in viewing objects that cannot be viewed with an optical microscope. The electrons in an electron microscope have much smaller wavelengths than visible light. These smaller wavelengths allow a much clearer enlarged image of a very small object, such as the pollen grain in Figure 5.13, than is possible with an ordinary microscope.

De Broglie's equation predicts that all moving objects have wavelike behavior. Why are you unable to observe the effects of this wavelike motion for ordinary objects like baseballs and trains? The answer is that the mass of the object must be very small in order for its wavelength to be large enough to observe. For example, a 50-gram golf ball traveling at 40 m/s (about 90 mi/h) has a wavelength of only 3×10^{-34} m, which is much too small to detect experimentally. On the other hand, an electron has a mass of only 9.11×10^{-28} g. If it were moving at a velocity of 40 m/s, it would have a wavelength of 2×10^{-5} m, which is comparable to infrared radiation and is readily measured.

De Broglie's prediction that matter exhibits both wave and particle properties set the stage for a new way of describing the motions of subatomic particles and atoms. The newer theory is called quantum mechanics; the older theory is called classical mechanics. **🔑 Classical mechanics adequately describes the motions of bodies much larger than atoms, while quantum mechanics describes the motions of subatomic particles and atoms as waves.**

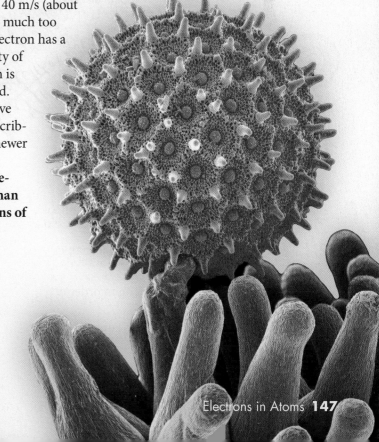

Figure 5.13 Electron Micrograph
An electron microscope can produce sharp images of a very small object, such as this pollen grain, because of the small wavelength of a moving electron compared with that of light.

The Heisenberg Uncertainty Principle German physicist Werner Heisenberg examined another feature of quantum mechanics. The **Heisenberg uncertainty principle** states that it is impossible to know both the velocity and the position of a particle at the same time. This limitation is critical when dealing with small particles such as electrons, but it does not matter for ordinary-sized objects such as cars or airplanes.

Consider how you determine the location of an object. To locate a set of keys in a dark room you can use a flashlight. You see the keys when the light bounces off them and strikes your eyes. To locate an electron, you might strike it with a photon of light, as shown in Figure 5.14. However, the electron has such a small mass that striking it with a photon affects its motion in a way that cannot be predicted accurately. The very act of measuring the position of the electron changes its velocity, making its velocity uncertain.

The discovery of matter waves led the way for Schrödinger's quantum mechanical description of electrons in atoms. Schrödinger's theory leads to the concept of electron orbitals and includes the uncertainty principle.

Figure 5.14 Heisenberg Uncertainty Principle
According to the Heisenberg uncertainty principle, it is impossible to know exactly both the velocity and the position of a particle at the same time.

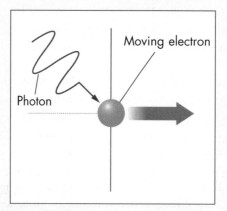

Before collision A photon strikes an electron during an attempt to observe the electron's position.

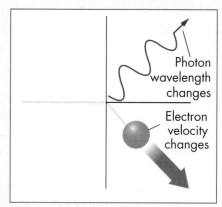

After collision The impact changes the electron's velocity, making it uncertain.

5.3 LessonCheck

19. **Describe** What is the origin of the atomic emission spectrum of an element?

20. **Review** What was Einstein's explanation for the photoelectric effect?

21. **Explain** How is the change in electron energy related to the frequency of light emitted in electronic transitions?

22. **Explain** How does quantum mechanics differ from classical mechanics?

23. **Sequence** Arrange the following in order of decreasing wavelength.
  a. infrared radiation from a heat lamp
  b. dental X-rays
  c. signal from a shortwave radio station

24. **Calculate** A hydrogen lamp emits several lines in the visible region of the spectrum. One of these lines has a wavelength of 6.56×10^{-5} cm. What is the frequency of this radiation?

25. **Calculate** What is the energy of a photon of blue light with a wavelength of 460 nm?

BIGIDEA
ELECTRONS AND THE STRUCTURE OF ATOMS

26. When a strontium compound is heated in a flame, red light is produced. When a barium compound is heated in a flame, yellow-green light is produced. Explain why these colors are emitted.

Small-Scale Lab

Atomic Emission Spectra

Purpose
To build a spectroscope and use it to measure the wavelengths, frequencies, and energies of atomic emission lines

Materials
- black construction paper
- tape
- cereal box
- scissors
- white notebook paper
- diffraction grating
- ruler

Procedure

Tape together two 2.0 cm × 10 cm strips of black construction paper so that they are parallel and form a narrow slit about 2 mm wide. Remove the top of a cereal box and tape the construction paper slit as shown. Cover the rest of the opening with white notebook paper. Cut a square hole (approximately 2 cm per side) and tape a diffraction grating over the hole as shown. Point the spectroscope toward a fluorescent light. Tape up any light leaks. Your lab partner should mark the exact positions of all the colored emission lines you see on the notebook paper. Measure the distances between the violet line and the other lines you have marked.

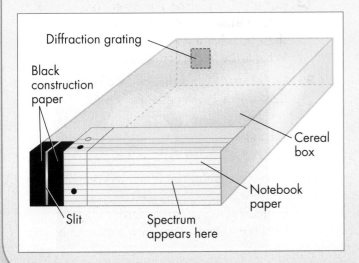

Diffraction grating

Black construction paper

Slit

Spectrum appears here

Cereal box

Notebook paper

Analyze and Conclude

1. Observe List the number of distinct lines that you see as well as their colors.

2. Measure Each line you see has a wavelength. The prominent violet line has a wavelength of 436 nm and the prominent green line has a wavelength of 546 nm. How many mm apart are these lines on the paper? By how many nm do their wavelengths differ? How many nanometers of wavelength are represented by each millimeter you measured?

3. Calculate Using the nm/mm value you calculated and the mm distance you measured for each line from the violet reference line, calculate the wavelengths of all the other lines you see.

4. Calculate Use the wavelength value of each line to calculate its frequency given that $\nu = c/\lambda$ where $c = 2.998 \times 10^{17}$ nm/s (2.998×10^{8} m/s).

5. Calculate The energy E of a quantum of light an atom emits is related to its frequency ν by $E = h\nu$. Use the frequency value for each line and $h = 6.626 \times 10^{-34}$ J·s to calculate its corresponding energy.

You're the Chemist

1. Design an Experiment Design and carry out an experiment to measure the longest and shortest wavelengths you can see in daylight. Use your spectroscope to observe light from daylight reflected off a white piece of paper. **CAUTION** *Do not look directly at the sun!* Describe the differences in daylight and fluorescent light.

2. Design an Experiment Design and carry out an experiment to determine the effect of colored filters on the spectrum of fluorescent light or daylight. For each filter, tell which colors are transmitted and which are absorbed.

3. Analyze Data Use your spectroscope to observe various atomic emission discharge tubes provided by your teacher. Note and record the lines you see and measure their wavelengths.

5 Study Guide

BIGIDEA ELECTRONS AND THE STRUCTURE OF ATOMS

The quantum mechanical model of the atom comes from the solutions to the Schrödinger equation. Solutions to the Schrödinger equation give the energies an electron can have and the atomic orbitals, which describe the regions of space where an electron may be found. Electrons can absorb energy to move from one energy level to a higher energy level. When an electron moves from a higher energy level back down to a lower energy level, light is emitted.

5.1 Revising the Atomic Model

🔑 Bohr proposed that an electron is found only in specific circular paths, or orbits, around the nucleus.

🔑 The quantum mechanical model determines the allowed energies an electron can have and how likely it is to find the electron in various locations around the nucleus of an atom.

🔑 Each energy sublevel corresponds to one or more orbitals of different shapes. The orbitals describe where an electron is likely to be found.

- energy level (129)
- quantum (129)
- quantum mechanical model (130)
- atomic orbital (131)

5.2 Electron Arrangement in Atoms

🔑 Three rules—the aufbau principle, the Pauli exclusion principle, and Hund's rule—tell you how to find the electron configurations of atoms.

- electron configuration (134)
- aufbau principle (134)
- Pauli exclusion principle (134)
- spin (134)
- Hund's rule (134)

5.3 Atomic Emission Spectra and the Quantum Mechanical Model

🔑 When atoms absorb energy, their electrons move to higher energy levels. These electrons lose energy by emitting light when they return to lower energy levels.

🔑 To explain the photoelectric effect, Einstein proposed that light could be described as quanta of energy that behave as if they were particles.

🔑 The light emitted by an electron moving from a higher to a lower energy level has a frequency directly proportional to the energy change of the electron.

🔑 Classical mechanics adequately describes the motions of bodies much larger than atoms, while quantum mechanics describes the motions of subatomic particles and atoms as waves.

- amplitude (138)
- wavelength (138)
- frequency (138)
- hertz (138)
- electromagnetic radiation (139)
- spectrum (139)
- atomic emission spectrum (140)
- Planck's constant (143)
- photoelectric effect (143)
- photon (143)
- ground state (145)
- Heisenberg uncertainty principle (148)

Key Equations

$$c = \lambda \nu$$

$$E = h\nu$$

Math Tune-Up: Atomic Emission Spectra and Photons

Problem

Calculate the wavelength of radiation with a frequency of 8.43×10^9 Hz (8.43×10^9/s). In what region of the electromagnetic spectrum is this radiation?

What is the energy of a photon of X-ray radiation with a frequency of 7.49×10^{18}/s?

① Analyze

Knowns:
$v = 8.43 \times 10^9$/s
$c = 2.998 \times 10^8$ m/s

Unknown:
$\lambda = ?$ m

Use the equation that relates the frequency and wavelength of light:
$c = \lambda v$

Knowns:
$v = 7.49 \times 10^{18}$/s
$h = 6.626 \times 10^{-34}$ J·s

Unknown:
$E = ?$ J

Use the equation that relates the energy of a photon of radiation and the frequency of the radiation:
$E = hv$

② Calculate

Solve for λ and calculate.

$$\lambda = \frac{c}{v}$$

$$\lambda = \frac{2.998 \times 10^8 \text{ m/\cancel{s}}}{8.43 \times 10^9 \text{/\cancel{s}}}$$

$$\lambda = 3.56 \times 10^{-2} \text{ m}$$

The radiation is in the radar region of the electromagnetic spectrum.

Substitute the known values for v and h into the equation and calculate.

$$E = (6.626 \times 10^{-34} \text{ J·\cancel{s}}) \times (7.49 \times 10^{18} \text{/\cancel{s}})$$

$$E = 4.96 \times 10^{-15} \text{ J}$$

If you are given the wavelength of the radiation, first calculate frequency using $c = \lambda v$, and then use $E = hv$ to calculate energy.

③ Evaluate

The magnitude of the frequency of the radiation is larger than the value for the speed of light, so the answer should be less than 1.

Individual photons have very small energies, so the answer is reasonable.

Hint: Review Sample Problem 5.2 if you have trouble with converting between wavelength and frequency.

 **5** Assessment

Lesson by Lesson

5.1 Revising the Atomic Model

27. Why was Rutherford's model of the atom known as the planetary model?

★**28.** What did Bohr assume about the motion of electrons?

29. Describe Rutherford's model of the atom and compare it with the model proposed by his student Niels Bohr.

★**30.** What is the significance of the boundary of an electron cloud?

31. What is an atomic orbital?

32. Sketch 1s, 2s, and 2p orbitals using the same scale for each.

★**33.** How many orbitals are in the 2p sublevel?

★**34.** How many sublevels are contained in each of these principal energy levels?

   a. $n = 1$ **c.** $n = 3$
   b. $n = 2$ **d.** $n = 4$

5.2 Electron Arrangement in Atoms

★**35.** What are the three rules that govern the filling of atomic orbitals by electrons?

★**36.** Arrange the following sublevels in order of increasing energy:
3d, 2s, 4s, 3p.

★**37.** Which of these orbital designations are invalid?

   a. 4s   **c.** 3f
   b. 2d   **d.** 3p

38. What is the maximum number of electrons that can go into each of the following sublevels?

   a. 2s   **e.** 3p
   b. 4s   **f.** 3d
   c. 4p   **g.** 5s
   d. 4f   **h.** 5p

★**39.** What is meant by $3p^3$?

40. Write electron configurations for the elements that are identified by these atomic numbers:

   a. 7   **c.** 12
   b. 9   **d.** 36

41. Give electron configurations for atoms of these elements:

   a. Na   **c.** I
   b. K   **d.** Ne

★**42.** How many electrons are in the highest occupied energy level of these atoms?

   a. barium   **c.** sodium
   b. aluminum   **d.** oxygen

43. How many electrons are in the second energy level of an atom of each element?

   a. chlorine
   b. phosphorus
   c. potassium

★**44.** Write electron configurations for atoms of these elements:

   a. selenium   **c.** vanadium
   b. titanium   **d.** calcium

5.3 Atomic Emission Spectra and the Quantum Mechanical Model

45. Use a diagram to illustrate each term for a wave.

   a. wavelength
   b. amplitude
   c. cycle

46. What is meant by the frequency of a wave? What are the units of frequency? Describe the relationship between frequency and wavelength.

★**47.** Consider the following regions of the electromagnetic spectrum: (i) ultraviolet, (ii) X-ray, (iii) visible, (iv) infrared, (v) radio wave, (vi) microwave.

   a. Use Figure 5.8 to arrange them in order of decreasing wavelength.
   b. How does this order differ from that of decreasing frequency?

48. List the colors of the visible spectrum in order of increasing wavelength.

49. How did Planck influence the development of modern atomic theory?

★**50.** Explain the difference between a photon and a quantum.

★**51.** What has more energy, a photon of infrared light or a photon of ultraviolet light?

52. What is the energy of a photon of green light with a frequency of 5.80×10^{14}/s?

53. Explain the difference between the energy lost or gained by an atom according to the laws of classical physics and according to the quantum model of the atom.

54. What happens when a hydrogen atom absorbs a quantum of energy?

55. The transition of electrons from higher energy levels to the $n = 2$ energy level results in the emission of light from hydrogen atoms. In what part of the spectrum is the emitted light, and what is the name given to this transition series?

Understand Concepts

56. Give the symbol for the atom that corresponds to each electron configuration.
  a. $1s^2 2s^2 2p^6 3s^2 3p^6$
  b. $1s^2 2s^2 2p^6 3s^2 3p^6 3d^{10} 4s^2 4p^6 4d^7 5s^1$
  c. $1s^2 2s^2 2p^6 3s^2 3p^6 3d^{10} 4s^2 4p^6 4d^{10} 4f^7 5s^2 5p^6 5d^1 6s^2$

57. Write the electron configuration for an arsenic atom. Calculate the total number of electrons in each energy level and state which energy levels are not full.

58. How many paired electrons are there in an atom of each element?
  a. helium   **c.** boron
  b. sodium   **d.** oxygen

59. An atom of an element has two electrons in the first energy level and five electrons in the second energy level. Write the electron configuration for this atom and name the element. How many unpaired electrons does an atom of this element have?

60. Give the symbols and names of the elements that correspond to these configurations of an atom.
  a. $1s^2 2s^2 2p^6 3s^1$
  b. $1s^2 2s^2 2p^3$
  c. $1s^2 2s^2 2p^6 3s^2 3p^2$
  d. $1s^2 2s^2 2p^4$
  e. $1s^2 2s^2 2p^6 3s^2 3p^6 4s^1$
  f. $1s^2 2s^2 2p^6 3s^2 3p^6 3d^2 4s^2$

61. What is the maximum number of electrons that can be found in any orbital of an atom?

62. Suppose your favorite AM radio station broadcasts at a frequency of 1150 kHz. What is the wavelength, in centimeters, of the radiation from the station?

63. A mercury lamp, such as the one below, emits radiation with a wavelength of 4.36×10^{-7} m.

  a. What is the wavelength of this radiation in centimeters?
  b. In what region of the electromagnetic spectrum is this radiation?
  c. Calculate the frequency of this radiation.

64. Sodium vapor lamps are used to illuminate streets and highways. The very bright light emitted by these lamps is actually due to two closely spaced emission lines in the visible region of the electromagnetic spectrum. One of these lines has a wavelength of 5.890×10^{-7} m, and the other line has a wavelength of 5.896×10^{-7} m.
  a. What are the wavelengths of these radiations in centimeters?
  b. Calculate the frequencies of these radiations.
  c. In what region of the visible spectrum do these lines appear?

65. What will happen if the following occur?
  a. Monochromatic light shining on cesium metal is just above the threshold frequency.
  b. The intensity of the light increases, but the frequency remains the same.
  c. Monochromatic light of a shorter wavelength is used.

66. Calculate the energy of a photon of red light with a wavelength of 6.45×10^{-5} cm. Compare your answer with the answer to Question 52. Is red light of higher or lower energy than green light?

67. State the Heisenberg uncertainty principle.

68. Describe how the wavelength of a wave changes if the frequency of the wave is multiplied by 1.5.

∗69. Indicate whether each of the following electron transitions emits energy or requires the absorption of energy.

  a. $3p$ to $3s$ **c.** $2s$ to $2p$
  b. $3p$ to $4p$ **d.** $1s$ to $2s$

∗70. White light is viewed in a spectroscope after passing through sodium vapor too cool to emit light. The spectrum is continuous except for a dark line at 589 nm. How can you explain this observation? (*Hint:* Recall from Sample Problem 5.2 that the atomic emission spectrum of sodium exhibits a strong yellow line at 589 nm.)

71. You use a microwave oven to heat your dinner. The frequency of the radiation is $2.37 \times 10^9\,s^{-1}$. What is the energy of one photon of this radiation?

∗72. Calculate the following energies:

  a. One photon of infrared radiation, if $\lambda = 1.2 \times 10^{-4}$ m.
  b. One photon of visible radiation, if $\lambda = 5.1 \times 10^{-7}$ m.
  c. One photon of ultraviolet radiation, if $\lambda = 1.4 \times 10^{-8}$ m.

  What do the answers indicate about the relationship between the energy of light and its wavelength?

Think Critically

∗73. **Compare** Explain the difference between an orbit in the Bohr model and an orbital in the quantum mechanical model of the atom.

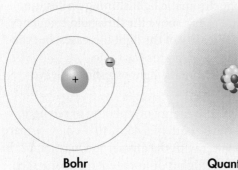

Bohr model   Quantum mechanical model

74. **Apply Concepts** Identify the elements whose electrically neutral atoms have the following electron configurations.

  a. $1s^2 2s^2 2p^5$
  b. $1s^2 2s^2 2p^6 3s^2 3p^6 3d^{10} 4s^2 4p^2$
  c. $1s^2 2s^2 2p^6 3s^2 3p^6 3d^3 4s^2$

∗75. **Predict** Traditional cooking methods make use of infrared radiation (heat). Microwave radiation cooks food faster. Could radio waves be used for cooking? Explain.

76. **Draw Conclusions** Think about the currently accepted models of the atom and of light. In what ways do these models seem strange to you? Why are these models not exact or definite?

77. **Evaluate and Revise** Orbital diagrams for the ground states of two elements are shown below. Each diagram shows something that is incorrect. Identify the error in each diagram and then draw the correct diagram.

  a. Nitrogen

  $1s$ $2s$ $2p$
  ⟨↑↓⟩ ⟨↑↓⟩ ⟨↑↓⟩⟨↑⟩⟨ ⟩

  b. Magnesium

  $1s$ $2s$ $2p$ $3s$
  ⟨↑↓⟩ ⟨↑↓⟩ ⟨↑↓⟩⟨↑↓⟩⟨↑↓⟩ ⟨ ⟩

∗78. **Infer** Picture two hydrogen atoms. The electron in the first hydrogen atom is in the $n = 1$ level. The electron in the second atom is in the $n = 4$ level.

  a. Which atom has the ground state electron configuration?
  b. Which atom can emit electromagnetic radiation?
  c. In which atom is the electron in a larger orbital?
  d. Which atom has the lower energy?

∗79. **Infer** Which of the following is the ground state of an atom? Which is its excited state? Which is an impossible electron configuration? Identify the element and briefly explain your choices.

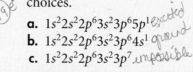

  a. $1s^2 2s^2 2p^6 3s^2 3p^6 5p^1$ excited
  b. $1s^2 2s^2 2p^6 3s^2 3p^6 4s^1$ ground
  c. $1s^2 2s^2 2p^6 3s^2 3p^7$ impossible

80. **Relate Cause and Effect** Why do electrons occupy equal energy orbitals singly before beginning to pair up?

★**81. Graph** The energy of a photon is related to its frequency and its wavelength.

Energy of photon (J)	Frequency (s^{-1})	Wavelength (cm)
3.45×10^{-21}	v_1_____	5.77×10^{-3}
2.92×10^{-20}	v_2_____	6.82×10^{-4}
6.29×10^{-20}	v_3_____	3.16×10^{-4}
1.13×10^{-19}	v_4_____	1.76×10^{-4}
1.46×10^{-19}	v_5_____	1.36×10^{-4}
3.11×10^{-19}	v_6_____	6.38×10^{-5}

  a. Complete the table above.
  b. Plot the energy of the photon (*y*-axis) versus the frequency (*x*-axis).
  c. Determine the slope of the line.
  d. What is the significance of this slope?

82. Calculate The average distance between Earth and Mars is about 2.08×10^8 km. How long would it take to transmit television pictures from Mars to Earth?

★**83. Calculate** Bohr's atomic theory can be used to calculate the energy required to remove an electron from an orbit of a hydrogen atom or an ion (an atom that has lost or gained electrons) containing only one electron. This number is the ionization energy for that atom or ion. The formula for determining the ionization energy (*E*) is

$$E = Z^2 \times \frac{k}{n^2}$$

where Z is the atomic number, k is 2.18×10^{-18} J, and n is the energy level. What is the energy required to eject an electron from a hydrogen atom when the electron is in the ground state ($n = 1$)? In the second energy level? How much energy is required to eject a ground state electron from the species Li^{2+} (a lithium atom that has lost two electrons)?

84. Draw Conclusions In a photoelectric experiment, a student shines light on the surface of a metal. The frequency of the light is greater than the threshold frequency of the metal. The student observes that after a long time, the maximum energy of the ejected electrons begins to decrease. Explain this observation.

★**85. Explain** Write a brief description of how trying to place two bar magnets pointing in the same direction alongside each other is like trying to place two electrons into the same orbital.

86. Connect to the BIGIDEA The late 1800s and early 1900s were significant times for the rapid development of chemistry. Bohr improved on Rutherford's model of the atom, then Schrödinger developed the quantum mechanical model of the atom. Explain why a model of the atom is crucial to understanding chemistry and in explaining the behavior of matter.

CHEMYSTERY

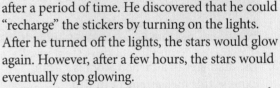

Now You See It... Now You Don't

Liam eventually realized that his star stickers would always stop glowing after a period of time. He discovered that he could "recharge" the stickers by turning on the lights. After he turned off the lights, the stars would glow again. However, after a few hours, the stars would eventually stop glowing.

Glow-in-the-dark objects contain compounds that react with light. When these objects are exposed to light, the electrons in the compounds absorb energy and become excited. As the electrons drop back down to a lower energy level, they emit light. This process, called phosphorescence, occurs more slowly in the compounds contained in glow-in-the-dark objects than in other compounds.

87. Infer Do Liam's glow-in-the-dark stars glow when the lights are on? Explain.

★**88. Connect to the BIGIDEA** Light emitted from an incandescent light bulb is in the visible region of the electromagnetic spectrum (300 nm to 700 nm). What does this information tell you about the energy of the photons absorbed by the electrons in glow-in-the dark objects?

89. Classify each of the following as homogeneous or heterogeneous:
 a. a page of this textbook
 b. a banana split
 c. the water in bottled water

90. Hamburger undergoes a chemical change when cooked on a grill. All chemical changes are subject to the law of conservation of mass. Yet, a cooked hamburger will weigh less than the uncooked meat patty. Explain.

91. Homogeneous mixtures and compounds are both composed of two or more elements. How do you distinguish between a homogeneous mixture and a compound?

92. The photo shows a magnified view of a piece of granite. Is granite a substance or a mixture?

93. The diameter of a carbon atom is 77 pm. Express this measurement in μm.

94. A silver bar has a mass of 368 g. What is the volume, in cm^3, of the bar? The density of silver is 19.5 g/cm^3.

95. Which has more mass, a 28.0-cm^3 piece of lead or a 16.0-cm^3 piece of gold? The density of lead is 11.3 g/cm^3; the density of gold is 19.3 g/cm^3.

96. Express the following measurements in scientific notation.
 a. 0.000039 kg
 b. 784 L
 c. 0.0830 g
 d. 9,700,000 ng

97. Which of these quantities or relationships are exact?
 a. 10 cm = 1 dm
 b. There are 9 baseball players on the field.
 c. A diamond has a mass of 12.4 g.
 d. The temperature is 21°C.

98. A one-kilogram steel bar is brought to the moon. How are its mass and its weight each affected by this change in location? Explain.

99. When a piece of copper with a mass of 36.4 g is placed into a graduated cylinder containing 20.00 mL of water, the water level rises to 24.08 mL, completely covering the copper. What is the density of copper?

100. The density of gold is 19.3 g/cm^3. What is the mass, in grams, of a cube of gold that is 2.00 cm on each edge? In kilograms?

101. A balloon filled with helium will rise upward when released. What does this result show about the relative densities of helium and air?

102. Explain the difference between the accuracy of a measurement and the precision of a measurement.

103. Give the number of protons and electrons in each of the following:
 a. Cs
 b. Ag
 c. Cd
 d. Se

104. Which of these was an essential part of Dalton's atomic model?
 a. indivisible atoms
 b. electrons
 c. atomic nuclei
 d. neutrons

105. How do neon-20 and neon-21 differ from each other?

106. The mass of an atom should be very nearly the sum of the masses of its protons and neutrons. The mass of a proton and the mass of a neutron are each very close to 1 amu. Why is the atomic mass of chlorine, 35.453 amu, so far from a whole number?

If You Have Trouble With . . .

Question	89	90	91	92	93	94	95	96	97	98	99	100	101	102	103	104	105	106
See Chapter	2	2	2	2	3	3	3	3	3	3	3	3	3	3	4	4	4	4

Standardized Test Prep

Select the choice that best answers each question or completes each statement.

Tips for Success

Eliminate Wrong Answers If you don't know which response is correct, start by eliminating those you know are wrong. If you can rule out some choices, you'll have fewer left to consider and you'll increase your chances of choosing the correct answer.

1. Select the correct electron configuration for silicon, atomic number 14.
   (A) $1s^2 2s^2 2p^2 3s^2 3p^2 3d^2 4s^2$
   (B) $1s^2 2s^2 2p^4 3s^2 3p^4$
   (C) $1s^2 2s^6 2p^6$
   (D) $1s^2 2s^2 2p^6 3s^2 3p^2$

2. Which two orbitals have the same shape?
   (A) $2s$ and $2p$
   (B) $2s$ and $3s$
   (C) $3p$ and $3d$
   (D) More than one is correct.

3. Which of these statements characterize the nucleus of every atom?
   I. It has a positive charge.
   II. It is very dense.
   III. It is composed of protons, electrons, and neutrons.
   (A) I and II only
   (B) II and III only
   (C) I and III only
   (D) I, II, and III

4. As the wavelength of light increases,
   (A) the frequency increases.
   (B) the speed of light increases.
   (C) the energy decreases.
   (D) the intensity increases.

5. In the third energy level of an atom,
   (A) there are two energy sublevels.
   (B) the f sublevel has 7 orbitals.
   (C) there are three s orbitals.
   (D) a maximum of 18 electrons are allowed.

The lettered choices below refer to Questions 6–10. A lettered choice may be used once, more than once, or not at all.

   (A) $s^2 p^6$ (b) $s^2 p^2$ (C) s^2 (D) $s^4 p^1$ (E) $s^2 p^4$

Which configuration is the configuration of the highest occupied energy level for each of these elements?

6. sulfur

7. germanium

8. beryllium

9. krypton

10. strontium

Use the drawings to answer Questions 11–14. Each drawing represents an electromagnetic wave.

Waves

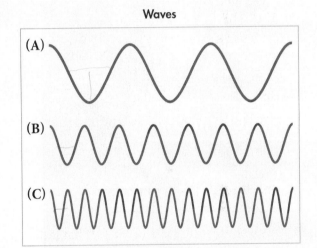

11. Which wave has the longest wavelength?

12. Which wave has the highest energy?

13. Which wave has the lowest frequency?

14. Which wave has the highest amplitude?

Write a short essay to answer Question 15.

15. Explain the rules that determine how electrons are arranged around the nuclei of atoms.

If You Have Trouble With . . .

Question	1	2	3	4	5	6	7	8	9	10	11	12	13	14	15
See Lesson	5.2	5.1	5.1	5.3	5.1	5.2	5.2	5.2	5.2	5.2	5.3	5.3	5.3	5.3	5.2

6

The Periodic Table

INSIDE:

- **6.1** Organizing the Elements
- **6.2** Classifying the Elements
- **6.3** Periodic Trends

PearsonChem.com

These beads are organized by color and shape. In the periodic table, elements are organized into groups with similar properties.

ELECTRONS AND THE STRUCTURE OF ATOMS

Essential Questions:

1. *What information does the periodic table provide?*
2. *How can periodic trends be explained?*

CHEMYSTERY

Made in the USA

Only 90 elements in the periodic table are known to occur naturally. You might ask then, "Why are there more than a hundred elements listed in the periodic table?"

Between the years of 1940 and 1958, nine of these "unnatural" elements were discovered by the American scientist Glenn Seaborg and his colleagues at the University of California at Berkeley. Later in 1974, Seaborg and his team discovered yet another element. Several other "unnatural" elements were discovered by Russian and German scientists.

How do these elements compare to other elements in the periodic table?

▶ **Connect to the BIGIDEA** As you read about the periodic table, keep an eye out for elements that do not occur naturally.

NATIONAL SCIENCE EDUCATION STANDARDS

A-1, A-2, B-1, B-2, E-2, G-1, G-2, G-3

6.1 Organizing the Elements

Key Questions

🔑 How did chemists begin to organize the known elements?

🔑 How did Mendeleev organize his periodic table?

🔑 How is the modern periodic table organized?

🔑 What are three broad classes of elements?

Vocabulary

• periodic law • metal
• nonmetal • metalloid

Figure 6.1 Triad in Dobereiner's System
Chlorine, bromine, and iodine formed one triad. These elements have similar chemical properties.

Q: *How can you organize and classify elements?* If you have ever played a card game, then you have probably organized your cards. Maybe you classified them by color or number. Elements can also be classified. In this lesson, you will learn how elements are arranged in the periodic table and what that arrangement reveals about the elements.

Searching for an Organizing Principle

🔑 **How did chemists begin to organize the known elements?**

A few elements, including copper, silver, and gold, have been known for thousands of years. Yet, there were only 13 elements identified by the year 1700. Chemists suspected that other elements existed. They had even assigned names to some of these elements, but they were unable to isolate the elements from their compounds. As chemists began to use scientific methods to search for elements, the rate of discovery increased. In one decade (1765–1775), chemists identified five new elements, including three colorless gases, hydrogen, nitrogen, and oxygen. Was there a limit to the number of elements? How would chemists know when they had discovered all the elements? To begin to answer these questions, chemists needed to find a logical way to organize the elements.

🔑 **Early chemists used the properties of elements to sort them into groups.** In 1829, a German chemist, J. W. Dobereiner (1780–1849), published a classification system. In his system, the known elements were grouped into triads. A triad is a set of three elements with similar properties. The elements in Figure 6.1 formed one triad. Chlorine, bromine, and iodine may look different, but they have very similar chemical properties. For example, they react easily with metals. Unfortunately, all the known elements could not be grouped into triads.

Dobereiner noted a pattern in his triads. One element in each triad tended to have properties with values that fell midway between those of the other two elements. For example, the average of the atomic masses of chlorine and iodine is [(35.453 1 + 126.90)/2] or 81.18 amu. This value is close to the atomic mass of bromine, which is 79.904 amu.

но въ ней, мнѣ кажется, уже ясно выражается примѣнимость вы ставллемаго мною начала ко всей совокупности элементовъ, пай которыхъ извѣстенъ съ достовѣрностію. На этотъ разъ я и желалъ преимущественно найдти общую систему элементовъ. Вотъ этотъ опытъ:

			Ti=50	Zr=90	?=180.
			V=51	Nb=94	Ta=182.
			Cr=52	Mo=96	W=186.
			Mn=55	Rh=104,4	Pt=197,4
			Fe=56	Ru=104,4	Ir=198.
		Ni=Co=59		Pl=106,6	Os=199.
H=1			Cu=63,4	Ag=108	Hg=200.
	Be=9,4	Mg=24	Zn=65,2	Cd=112	
	B=11	Al=27,4	?=68	Ur=116	Au=197?
	C=12	Si=28	?=70	Sn=118	
	N=14	P=31	As=75	Sb=122	Bi=210
	O=16	S=32	Se=79,4	Te=128?	
	F=19	Cl=35,5	Br=80	I=127	
Li=7	Na=23	K=39	Rb=85,4	Cs=133	Tl=204
		Ca=40	Sr=87,6	Ba=137	Pb=207.
		?=45	Ce=92		
		?Er=56	La=94		
		?Yt=60	Di=95		
		?In=75,6	Th=118?		

Figure 6.2
Mendeleev's Periodic Table
In this early version of the periodic table, Mendeleev (shown on the stamp below) arranged elements with similar properties in the same row.
Identify *Which element is grouped with chlorine (Cl), bromine (Br), and (I) iodine?*

Mendeleev's Periodic Table

🔑 How did Mendeleev organize his periodic table?

From 1829 to 1869, different systems for organizing the elements were proposed, but none of them gained wide acceptance. In 1869, a Russian chemist and teacher, Dmitri Mendeleev, published a table of the elements. Later that year, a German chemist, Lothar Meyer, published a nearly identical table. Mendeleev was given more credit than Meyer because he published his table first and because he was better able to explain its usefulness.

Mendeleev developed his table while working on a textbook for his students. He needed a way to show the relationships among more than 60 elements. He wrote the properties of each element on a separate note card. This approach allowed him to move the cards around until he found an organization that worked. The organization he chose was a periodic table. Elements in a periodic table are arranged into groups based on a set of repeating properties. 🔑 **Mendeleev arranged the elements in his periodic table in order of increasing atomic mass.**

Figure 6.2 is an early version of Mendeleev's periodic table. Look at the column that starts with Ti = 50. Notice the two question marks between the entries for zinc (Zn) and arsenic (As). Mendeleev left these spaces in his table because he knew that bromine belonged with chlorine and iodine. He predicted that elements would be discovered to fill those spaces, and he predicted what their properties would be based on their locations in the table. The elements between zinc and arsenic were gallium and germanium, which were discovered in 1875 and 1886, respectively. There was a close match between the predicted properties and the actual properties of these elements. This match helped convince scientists that Mendeleev's periodic table was a powerful tool.

See more about organizing information.

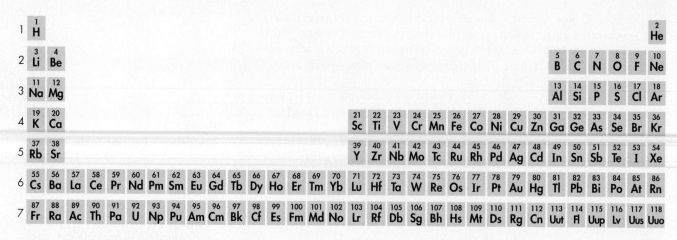

Figure 6.3 Modern Periodic Table
In the modern periodic table, the elements are arranged in order of increasing atomic number.
Interpret Diagrams *How many elements are in the second period?*

READING SUPPORT

Build Vocabulary: *Word Origins*
Periodic comes from the Greek roots *peri*, meaning "around" and *hodos*, meaning "path." In a periodic table, properties repeat from left to right across each period. *If the Greek word* metron *means "measure," what does* perimeter *mean?*

Today's Periodic Table

How is the modern periodic table organized?

The atomic mass of iodine (I) is 126.90. The atomic mass of tellurium (Te) is 127.60. In a periodic table based on atomic mass, iodine should come before tellurium since iodine has a smaller atomic mass than tellurium does. However, based on its chemical properties, iodine belongs in a group with bromine and chlorine. Mendeleev broke his rule about placing elements in strict order of atomic mass and placed tellurium before iodine in his periodic table. He assumed that the atomic masses for iodine and tellurium were incorrect, but they were not. A similar problem occurred with other pairs of elements. The problem wasn't with the atomic masses but with using atomic mass to organize the periodic table.

Mendeleev developed his table before scientists knew about the structure of atoms. He didn't know that the atoms of each element contain a unique number of protons. Recall that the number of protons is the atomic number. In 1913, a British physicist, Henry Moseley, determined an atomic number for each known element. Tellurium's atomic number is 52 and iodine's is 53, so it makes sense for iodine to come after tellurium in the periodic table. **In the modern periodic table, elements are arranged in order of increasing atomic number.**

The elements in Figure 6.3 are arranged in order of atomic number, starting with hydrogen, which has atomic number 1. There are seven rows, or periods, in the table. Period 1 has 2 elements, Period 2 has 8 elements, Period 4 has 18 elements, and Period 6 has 32 elements. Each period corresponds to a principal energy level. There are more elements in higher numbered periods because there are more orbitals in higher energy levels. (Recall the rules you studied in Chapter 5 for how electrons fill orbitals.)

The properties of the elements within a period change as you move across a period from left to right. However, the pattern of properties within a period repeats as you move from one period to the next. This pattern gives rise to the **periodic law:** When elements are arranged in order of increasing atomic number, there is a periodic repetition of their physical and chemical properties. The arrangement of the elements into periods has an important consequence. Elements that have similar chemical and physical properties end up in the same column in the periodic table.

"Elemental" Trivia

Did you know that the stench of a skunk's spray is largely due to compounds that contain the element sulfur, or that rubies are red because of small amounts of chromium? Discover more fun facts about other elements as you read this page.

ANTIMONY The element antimony is often used to increase the hardness and strength of pewter figurines.

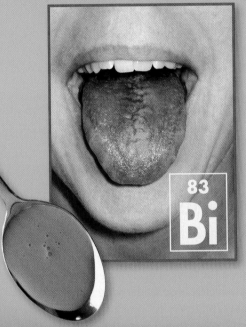

BISMUTH A compound containing bismuth is commonly used to treat indigestion. The bismuth can combine with sulfur in saliva and temporarily turn a person's tongue black!

83
Bi

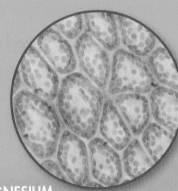

12
Mg

MAGNESIUM Magnesium is a component of chlorophyll, the green pigment in plants that allows photosynthesis to occur.

106
Sg

SEABORGIUM In 1974, this element was created by a team of scientists that included Glenn T. Seaborg. It was the first element to be named after a living person.

1
H

HYDROGEN Hydrogen is the most abundant element in the universe and, among other places, is found in stars and auroras.

Take It Further

1. Explain In elemental form, antimony (Sb) and bismuth (Bi) are both brittle, crystalline solids at room temperature. They are also poor conductors of heat and electricity. How does the periodic law support this observation? Use Figure 6.3 to explain your answer.

2. Classify Look ahead to Figure 6.4. Use the figure to classify the five elements above as metals, nonmetals, or metalloids.

Periodic Table (Figure 6.4)

Legend: Metals | Metalloids | Nonmetals

Group labels (black / red / blue):
- 1 / IA / 1A
- 2 / IIA / 2A
- 3 / IIIA / 3B, 4 / IVA / 4B, 5 / VA / 5B, 6 / VIA / 6B, 7 / VIIA / 7B, 8–10 / VIIIA / 8B, 11 / IB / 1B, 12 / IIB / 2B
- 13 / IIIB / 3A, 14 / IVB / 4A, 15 / VB / 5A, 16 / VIB / 6A, 17 / VIIB / 7A
- 18 / VIIIB / 8A

Period																		
1	1 H																	2 He
2	3 Li	4 Be											5 B	6 C	7 N	8 O	9 F	10 Ne
3	11 Na	12 Mg											13 Al	14 Si	15 P	16 S	17 Cl	18 Ar
4	19 K	20 Ca	21 Sc	22 Ti	23 V	24 Cr	25 Mn	26 Fe	27 Co	28 Ni	29 Cu	30 Zn	31 Ga	32 Ge	33 As	34 Se	35 Br	36 Kr
5	37 Rb	38 Sr	39 Y	40 Zr	41 Nb	42 Mo	43 Tc	44 Ru	45 Rh	46 Pd	47 Ag	48 Cd	49 In	50 Sn	51 Sb	52 Te	53 I	54 Xe
6	55 Cs	56 Ba	71 Lu	72 Hf	73 Ta	74 W	75 Re	76 Os	77 Ir	78 Pt	79 Au	80 Hg	81 Tl	82 Pb	83 Bi	84 Po	85 At	86 Rn
7	87 Fr	88 Ra	103 Lr	104 Rf	105 Db	106 Sg	107 Bh	108 Hs	109 Mt	110 Ds	111 Rg	112 Cn	113 Uut	114 Fl	115 Uup	116 Lv	117 Uus	118 Uuo

Lanthanides: 57 La, 58 Ce, 59 Pr, 60 Nd, 61 Pm, 62 Sm, 63 Eu, 64 Gd, 65 Tb, 66 Dy, 67 Ho, 68 Er, 69 Tm, 70 Yb

Actinides: 89 Ac, 90 Th, 91 Pa, 92 U, 93 Np, 94 Pu, 95 Am, 96 Cm, 97 Bk, 98 Cf, 99 Es, 100 Fm, 101 Md, 102 No

Figure 6.4 Classifying Elements
Periodic tables are sometimes color-coded to classify certain types of elements. This periodic table classifies elements as metals (yellow), nonmetals (blue), and metalloids (green).

Figure 6.5 Metals
The metals aluminum, copper, and iron have many important uses. The properties of the metal determine how it is used.

Metals, Nonmetals, and Metalloids

🔑 *What are three broad classes of elements?*

Most periodic tables are laid out like the one in Figure 6.4. Notice some elements from Periods 6 and 7 are placed beneath the table. This arrangement makes the periodic table more compact. It also reflects an underlying structure of the periodic table, which you will study in Lesson 6.2. Each column, or group, in this table has three labels. Scientists in the United States primarily use the labels shown in red. Scientists in Europe use the labels shown in blue.

For scientists to communicate clearly, they need to agree on the standards they will use. The International Union of Pure and Applied Chemistry (IUPAC) is an organization that sets standards for chemistry. In 1985, IUPAC proposed a new system for labeling groups in the periodic table. They numbered the groups from left to right 1 through 18 (the black labels in Figure 6.4). The large periodic table in Figure 6.9 includes the IUPAC system and the system used in the United States.

Dividing the elements into groups is not the only way to classify them based on their properties. The elements can be grouped into three broad classes based on their general properties. 🔑 **Three classes of elements are metals, nonmetals, and metalloids.** Across a period, the properties of elements become less metallic and more nonmetallic.

Copper (Cu)
Copper is ductile and second only to silver as a conductor of electric current. The copper used in electrical cables must be 99.99 percent pure.

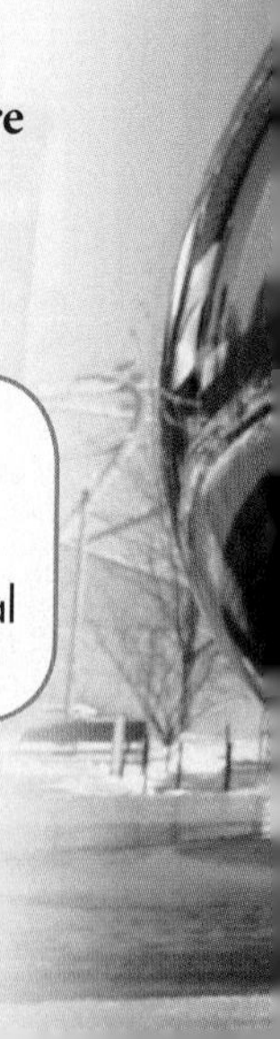

Aluminum (Al)
Aluminum is one of the metals that can be shaped into a thin sheet, or foil.

Metals The number of yellow squares in Figure 6.4 shows that most elements are metals—about 80 percent. **Metals** are generally good conductors of heat and electric current. A freshly cleaned or cut surface of a metal will have a high luster, or sheen. The sheen is caused by the metal's ability to reflect light. All metals are solids at room temperature, except for mercury (Hg). Many metals are ductile, meaning that they can be drawn into wires. Most metals are malleable, meaning that they can be hammered into thin sheets without breaking. Figure 6.5 shows how the properties of metals can determine how metals are used.

Nonmetals In Figure 6.4, blue is used to identify the nonmetals. With the exception of hydrogen, these elements are in the upper-right corner of the periodic table. There is a greater variation in physical properties among nonmetals than among metals. Most nonmetals are gases at room temperature, including the main components of air—nitrogen and oxygen. A few are solids, such as sulfur and phosphorus. One nonmetal, bromine, is a dark-red liquid. Some examples of nonmetals are shown in Figure 6.6.

The variation among nonmetals makes it difficult to describe one set of general properties that will apply to all nonmetals. However, nonmetals tend to have properties that are opposite to those of metals. In general, **nonmetals** are poor conductors of heat and electric current. Carbon, in the form of graphite, is an exception to this rule. Solid nonmetals tend to be brittle, meaning that they will shatter if hit with a hammer.

Figure 6.6 Nonmetals
The properties of nonmetals vary.

Carbon (C) and Phosphorus (P)
A diamond, which is composed of carbon, is very hard. Some match heads are coated with phosphorus, a brittle solid.

Iron (Fe)
Cloud Gate in Chicago, Illinois, is covered in stainless steel, which contains iron and chromium (Cr). The steel is shiny, malleable, and strong. It also resists rusting.

Test properties of metals *online.*

VIRTUAL LAB

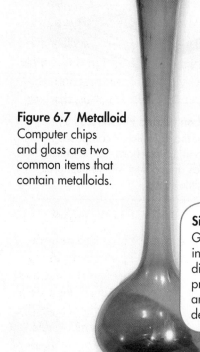

6.2 Classifying the Elements

CHEMISTRY & YOU

Q: *What can you learn about each element from the periodic table?*
Many people carry a form of identification, such as a driver's license. An ID contains information specific to a particular person, such as the person's name, address, height, eye color, and weight. The periodic table contains a square for each element that supplies information about that element. In this lesson, you will learn the types of information that are usually listed in a periodic table.

Key Questions

 What information can be displayed in a periodic table?

 How can elements be classified based on electron configurations?

Vocabulary

- alkali metal
- alkaline earth metal
- halogen
- noble gas
- representative element
- transition metal
- inner transition metal

Atomic number — **13**

Electrons in each energy level — 2 8 3

Element symbol — **Al**

Element name — **Aluminum**

Atomic mass — 26.982

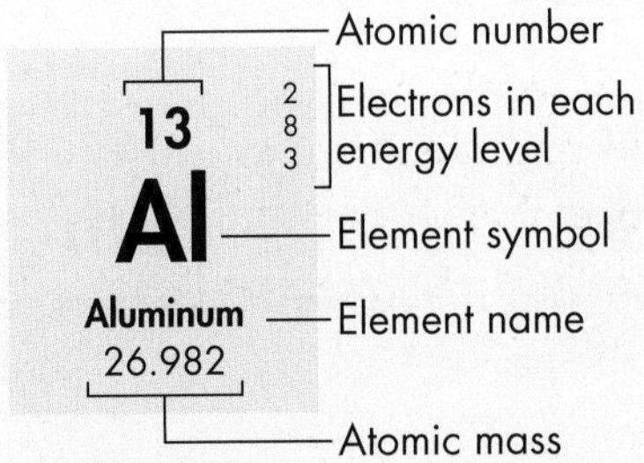

Figure 6.8 Periodic Table Square
This is the element square for aluminum from the periodic table in Figure 6.9.
Interpret Diagrams *What does the data in the square tell you about the structure of an aluminum atom?*

Reading the Periodic Table

 What information can be displayed in a periodic table?

The periodic table is a very useful tool in chemistry. **The periodic table usually displays the symbols and names of the elements, along with information about the structure of their atoms.** Figure 6.8 shows one square from the detailed periodic table of the elements in Figure 6.9 on page 168. In the center of the square is the symbol for aluminum (Al). The atomic number for aluminum (13) is above the symbol. The element name and atomic mass are below the symbol. There is also a vertical column with the numbers 2, 8, and 3, which indicate the number of electrons in each occupied energy level of an aluminum atom.

The symbol for aluminum is printed in black because aluminum is a solid at room temperature. In Figure 6.9, the symbols for gases are in red. The symbols for the two elements that are liquids at room temperature, mercury and bromine, are in blue. The symbols for some elements in Figure 6.9 are printed in grey. These elements are not found in nature. In Chapter 25, you will learn how scientists produce these elements.

The background colors in the squares are used to distinguish groups of elements in the periodic table. For example, two shades of orange are used for the metals in Groups 1A and 2A. The elements in Group 1A are called **alkali metals.** The elements in Group 2A are called **alkaline earth metals.** The name alkali comes from the Arabic *al aqali,* meaning "the ashes." Wood ashes are rich in compounds of the alkali metals sodium and potassium. Some groups of nonmetals also have special names. The nonmetals of Group 7A are called **halogens.** The name *halogen* comes from the combination of the Greek word *hals,* meaning "salt," and the Latin word *genesis,* meaning "to be born." There is a general class of compounds called salts, which include the compound called table salt. Chlorine, bromine, and iodine, the most common halogens, can be prepared from their salts.

Periodic Table of the Elements

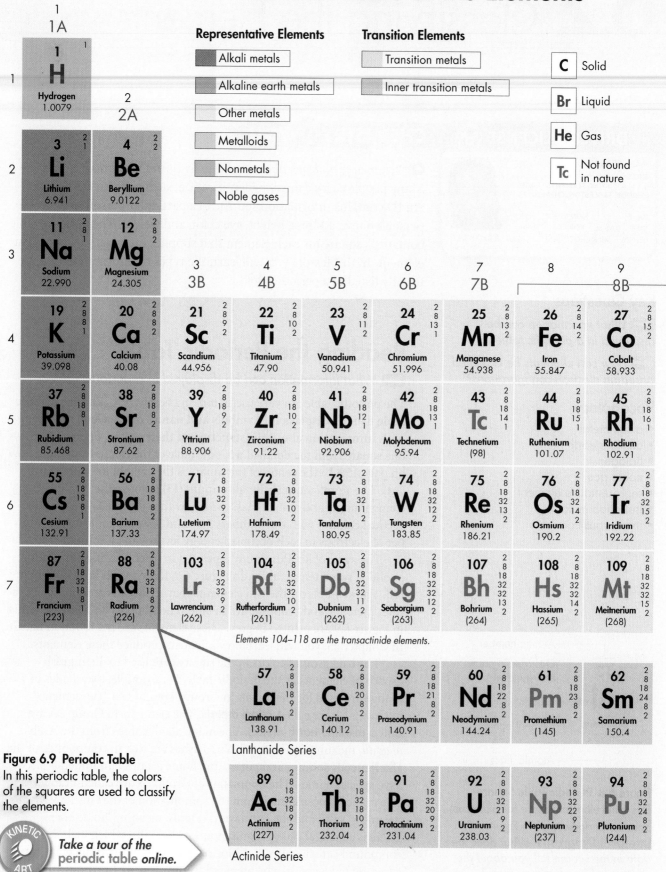

Figure 6.9 Periodic Table
In this periodic table, the colors of the squares are used to classify the elements.

Take a tour of the periodic table online.

Legend (example element):

Atomic number	13
Electrons in each energy level	2 8 3
Element symbol	Al
Element name	Aluminum
Atomic mass†	26.982

†The atomic masses in parentheses are the mass numbers of the longest-lived isotope of elements for which a standard atomic mass cannot be defined.

Group headers:

13 3A | 14 4A | 15 5A | 16 6A | 17 7A | 18 8A

10 | 11 1B | 12 2B

| 2 / He / Helium / 4.0026 (2) |

| 5 B Boron 10.81 (2,3) | 6 C Carbon 12.011 (2,4) | 7 N Nitrogen 14.007 (2,5) | 8 O Oxygen 15.999 (2,6) | 9 F Fluorine 18.998 (2,7) | 10 Ne Neon 20.179 (2,8) |

| 13 Al Aluminum 26.982 (2,8,3) | 14 Si Silicon 28.086 (2,8,4) | 15 P Phosphorus 30.974 (2,8,5) | 16 S Sulfur 32.06 (2,8,6) | 17 Cl Chlorine 35.453 (2,8,7) | 18 Ar Argon 39.948 (2,8,8) |

| 28 Ni Nickel 58.71 (2,8,16,2) | 29 Cu Copper 63.546 (2,8,18,1) | 30 Zn Zinc 65.38 (2,8,18,2) | 31 Ga Gallium 69.72 (2,8,18,3) | 32 Ge Germanium 72.59 (2,8,18,4) | 33 As Arsenic 74.922 (2,8,18,5) | 34 Se Selenium 78.96 (2,8,18,6) | 35 Br Bromine 79.904 (2,8,18,7) | 36 Kr Krypton 83.80 (2,8,18,8) |

| 46 Pd Palladium 106.4 (2,8,18,18) | 47 Ag Silver 107.87 (2,8,18,18,1) | 48 Cd Cadmium 112.41 (2,8,18,18,2) | 49 In Indium 114.82 (2,8,18,18,3) | 50 Sn Tin 118.69 (2,8,18,18,4) | 51 Sb Antimony 121.75 (2,8,18,18,5) | 52 Te Tellurium 127.60 (2,8,18,18,6) | 53 I Iodine 126.90 (2,8,18,18,7) | 54 Xe Xenon 131.30 (2,8,18,18,8) |

| 78 Pt Platinum 195.09 (2,8,18,32,17,1) | 79 Au Gold 196.97 (2,8,18,32,18,1) | 80 Hg Mercury 200.59 (2,8,18,32,18,2) | 81 Tl Thallium 204.37 (2,8,18,32,18,3) | 82 Pb Lead 207.2 (2,8,18,32,18,4) | 83 Bi Bismuth 208.98 (2,8,18,32,18,5) | 84 Po Polonium (209) (2,8,18,32,18,6) | 85 At Astatine (210) (2,8,18,32,18,7) | 86 Rn Radon (222) (2,8,18,32,18,8) |

| 110 Ds Darmstadtium (269) (2,8,18,32,32,17,1) | 111 Rg Roentgenium (272) (2,8,18,32,32,18,1) | 112 Cn Copernicium (277) (2,8,18,32,32,18,2) | *113 Uut Ununtrium (284) (2,8,18,32,32,18,3) | 114 Fl Flerovium (289) (2,8,18,32,32,18,4) | *115 Uup Ununpentium (288) (2,8,18,32,32,18,5) | 116 Lv Livermorium (293) (2,8,18,32,32,18,6) | *117 Uus Ununseptium (294) (2,8,18,32,32,18,7) | *118 Uuo Ununoctium (299) (2,8,18,32,32,18,8) |

*Discovery reported but not verified

Lanthanide/Actinide rows:

| 63 Eu Europium 151.96 (2,8,18,25,8,2) | 64 Gd Gadolinium 157.25 (2,8,18,25,9,2) | 65 Tb Terbium 158.93 (2,8,18,27,8,2) | 66 Dy Dysprosium 162.50 (2,8,18,28,8,2) | 67 Ho Holmium 164.93 (2,8,18,29,8,2) | 68 Er Erbium 167.26 (2,8,18,30,8,2) | 69 Tm Thulium 168.93 (2,8,18,31,8,2) | 70 Yb Ytterbium 173.04 (2,8,18,32,8,2) |

| 95 Am Americium (243) (2,8,18,25,8,2) | 96 Cm Curium (247) (2,8,18,32,25,9,2) | 97 Bk Berkelium (247) (2,8,18,32,27,8,2) | 98 Cf Californium (251) (2,8,18,32,28,8,2) | 99 Es Einsteinium (252) (2,8,18,32,29,8,2) | 100 Fm Fermium (257) (2,8,18,32,30,8,2) | 101 Md Mendelevium (258) (2,8,18,32,31,8,2) | 102 No Nobelium (259) (2,8,18,32,32,8,2) |

Electron Configurations in Groups

 *How can elements be classified based on electron configurations?*

Electrons play a key role in determining the properties of elements, so there should be a connection between an element's electron configuration and its location in the periodic table. **Elements can be sorted into noble gases, representative elements, transition metals, or inner transition metals based on their electron configurations.** You may want to refer to the periodic table as you read about these classes of elements.

The Noble Gases The photos in Figure 6.10 show uses of helium, neon, and argon. Helium, neon, and argon are examples of **noble gases,** the elements in Group 8A of the periodic table. These nonmetals are sometimes called the inert gases because they rarely take part in a reaction. The electron configurations for the first four noble gases in Group 8A are listed below.

Helium (He)	$1s^2$
Neon (Ne)	$1s^2 2s^2 2p^6$
Argon (Ar)	$1s^2 2s^2 2p^6 3s^2 3p^6$
Krypton (Kr)	$1s^2 2s^2 2p^6 3s^2 3p^6 3d^{10} 4s^2 4p^6$

Look at the description of the highest occupied energy level for each element, which is highlighted in yellow. The s and p sublevels are completely filled with electrons—two electrons in the s sublevel and six electrons in the p sublevel. Chapter 7 will explain how this arrangement of electrons is related to the relative inactivity of the noble gases.

Figure 6.10 Noble Gases
The noble gases are unique because their highest occupied energy levels are completely filled.
Infer *Helium-filled balloons rise in air. What does this tell you about the density of helium?*

Helium (He), Neon (Ne), and Argon (Ar)
Balloons are often filled with helium to give them "lift." The noble gases neon and argon produce the colors in this neon sign.

The Representative Elements Figure 6.11 shows the portion of the periodic table containing Groups 1A through 7A. Elements in Groups 1A through 7A are often referred to as **representative elements** because they display a wide range of physical and chemical properties. Some elements in these groups are metals, some are nonmetals, and some are metalloids. Most of them are solids, but a few are gases at room temperature, and one, bromine, is a liquid.

In atoms of representative elements, the *s* and *p* sublevels of the highest occupied energy level are not filled. Look at the electron configurations for lithium, sodium, and potassium below. In atoms of these Group 1A elements, there is only one electron in the highest occupied energy level. The electron is in an *s* sublevel.

Lithium (Li)	$1s^2 2s^1$
Sodium (Na)	$1s^2 2s^2 2p^6 3s^1$
Potassium (K)	$1s^2 2s^2 2p^6 3s^2 3p^6 4s^1$

In atoms of the Group 4A elements carbon, silicon, and germanium, there are four electrons in the highest occupied energy level.

Carbon (C)	$1s^2 2s^2 2p^2$
Silicon (Si)	$1s^2 2s^2 2p^6 3s^2 3p^2$
Germanium (Ge)	$1s^2 2s^2 2p^6 3s^2 3p^6 3d^{10} 4s^2 4p^2$

For any representative element, its group number equals the number of electrons in the highest occupied energy level.

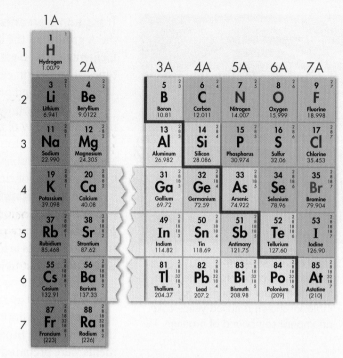

Figure 6.11 Representative Elements Some of the representative elements exist in nature as elements. Others are found only in compounds.

Tin (Sn)
Artisans often coat objects made of other metals with tin because tin resists corrosion.

Lithium (Li)
Batteries in many electronic devices, including this personal vehicle, use lithium to generate electrical energy.

Sulfur (S)
Some volcanos release high amounts of sulfur vapors. The sulfur cools and is deposited as a solid yellow powder.

Figure 6.12 Uranium
Nuclear power plants use the inner transition metal uranium as fuel. The material shown is called yellowcake, an impure compound of uranium.

Transition Elements In the periodic table, the B group elements separate the A groups on the left side of the table from the A groups on the right side. Elements in the B groups are referred to as transition elements. There are two types of transition elements—transition metals and inner transition metals. They are classified based on their electron configurations.

The **transition metals** are the Group B elements that are usually displayed in the main body of a periodic table. Copper, silver, gold, and iron are transition metals. In atoms of a transition metal, the highest occupied *s* sublevel and a nearby *d* sublevel contain electrons. These elements are characterized by the presence of electrons in *d* orbitals.

The **inner transition metals** are the elements that appear below the main body of the periodic table. In atoms of these elements, the highest occupied *s* sublevel and a nearby *f* sublevel generally contain electrons. The inner transition metals are characterized by the presence of electrons in *f* orbitals. Uranium, an example of an inner transition metal, is shown in Figure 6.12.

Before scientists knew much about inner transition metals, people referred to them as rare-earth elements. This name is misleading because some inner transition metals are more abundant than other elements. Notice that some of the inner transition metals are not found in nature. These elements were prepared in laboratories using methods presented in Chapter 25.

Blocks of Elements If you consider both the electron configurations and the positions of the elements in the periodic table, another pattern emerges. In Figure 6.13, the periodic table is divided into sections, or blocks, that correspond to the highest occupied sublevels. The *s* block contains the elements in Groups 1A and 2A and the noble gas helium. The *p* block contains the elements in Groups 3A, 4A, 5A, 6A, 7A, and 8A, with the exception of helium. The transition metals belong to the *d* block, and the inner transition metals belong to the *f* block.

You can use Figure 6.13 to help determine electron configurations of elements. Each period on the periodic table corresponds to a principal energy level. Suppose an element is located in Period 3. You know that the *s* and *p* sublevels in energy levels 1 and 2 are filled with electrons. You then read across Period 3 from left to right to complete the configuration. For transition elements, electrons are added to a *d* sublevel with a principal energy level that is one less than the period number. For the inner transition metals, the principal energy level of the *f* sublevel is two less than the period number. This procedure gives the correct electron configurations for most atoms.

Figure 6.13 Electron Configurations
This diagram classifies elements into blocks according to sublevels that are filled or are filling with electrons.
Interpret Diagrams *In the highest occupied energy level of a halogen atom, how many electrons are in the p sublevel?*

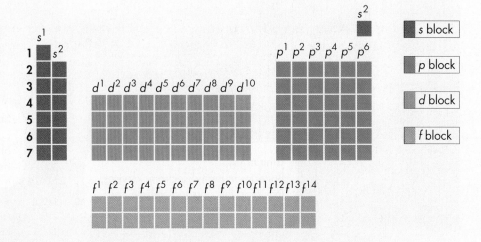

SampleProblem 6.1

Using Energy Sublevels to Write Electron Configurations

Use Figure 6.9 and Figure 6.13 to write the electron configuration for nickel (Ni).

❶ Analyze **Identify the relevant concepts.** For all elements, the atomic number is equal to the total number of electrons. For a representative element, the highest occupied energy level is the same as the number of the period in which the element is located. You can tell how many electrons are in this energy level from the group in which the element is located.

❷ Solve **Apply the concepts to this problem.**

Use Figure 6.9 to identify where the atom is in the periodic table and the number of electrons in the atom.	Nickel is located in the fourth period and has 28 electrons.
Use Figure 6.13 to determine the electron configuration.	In nickel, the s and p sublevels in the first three energy levels are full, so the configuration begins with $1s^2 2s^2 2p^6 3s^2 3p^6$. Next is $4s^2$ and $3d^8$. Put it all together: $1s^2 2s^2 2p^6 3s^2 3p^6 3d^8 4s^2$

9. Use Figure 6.9 and Figure 6.13 to write the electron configurations of the following elements:
  a. carbon
  b. strontium
  c. vanadium

Remember that the principal energy level number for elements in the *d* block is always one less than the period number.

10. List the symbols for all the elements whose electron configurations end as follows. *Note:* Each *n* represents an energy level.
  a. $ns^2 np^1$
  b. $ns^2 np^5$
  c. $ns^2 np^6 nd^2 (n+1)s^2$

6.2 LessonCheck

11. 🔑 **Identify** What types of information can be included in a periodic table?

12. 🔑 **List** Into what four classes can elements be sorted based on their electron configurations?

13. **Explain** Why do the elements potassium and sodium have similar chemical properties?

14. **Classify** Identify each element as an alkali metal, an alkaline earth metal, or a halogen:
  a. barium   **c.** lithium
  b. chlorine   **d.** beryllium

15. **Classify** Based on the following electron configurations, identify each element as a representative element, transition metal, or noble gas.
  a. $1s^2 2s^2 2p^6 3s^2 3p^6 3d^{10} 4s^2 4p^6$
  b. $1s^2 2s^2 2p^6 3s^2 3p^6 3d^6 4s^2$
  c. $1s^2 2s^2 2p^6 3s^2 3p^2$

16. **Describe** How many electrons are in the highest occupied energy level of an element in Group 5A?

17. **Identify** Which of these elements are transition metals: Cu, Sr, Cd, Au, Al, Ge, Co?

6.3 Periodic Trends

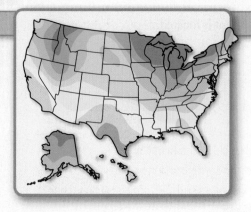

Q: *How are trends in the weather similar to trends in the properties of elements?* Although the weather changes from day to day. The weather you experience is related to your location on the globe. For example, Florida has an average temperature that is higher than Minnesota's. Similarly, a rain forest receives more rain than a desert. These differences are attributable to trends in the weather. In this lesson, you will learn how a property such as atomic size is related to the location of an element in the periodic table.

Key Questions

What are the trends among the elements for atomic size?

How do ions form?

What are the trends among the elements for first ionization energy, ionic size, and electronegativity?

Vocabulary

• atomic radius
• ion
• cation
• anion
• ionization energy
• electronegativity

Trends in Atomic Size

What are the trends among the elements for atomic size?

One way to think about atomic size is to look at the units that form when atoms of the same element are joined to one another. These units are called molecules. Figure 6.14 shows models of molecules (molecular models) for seven nonmetals. Because the atoms in each molecule are identical, the distance between the nuclei of these atoms can be used to estimate the size of the atoms. This size is expressed as an atomic radius. The **atomic radius** is one half of the distance between the nuclei of two atoms of the same element when the atoms are joined.

The distances between atoms in a molecule are extremely small. So the atomic radius is often measured in picometers (pm). Recall that there are one trillion, or 10^{12}, picometers in a meter. The molecular model of iodine in Figure 6.14 is the largest. The distance between the nuclei in an iodine molecule is 280 pm. Because the atomic radius is one half the distance between the nuclei, a value of 140 pm (280/2) is assigned as the radius of the iodine atom. **In general, atomic size increases from top to bottom within a group and decreases from left to right across a period.**

Figure 6.14 Atomic Radii
This diagram compares the atomic radii of seven nonmetals.

Distance between nuclei

Nucleus

Atomic radius

Hydrogen (H₂)
30 pm

Oxygen (O₂)
66 pm

Nitrogen (N₂)
70 pm

Fluorine (F₂)
62 pm

Chlorine (Cl₂)
102 pm

Bromine (Br₂)
120 pm

Iodine (I₂)
140 pm

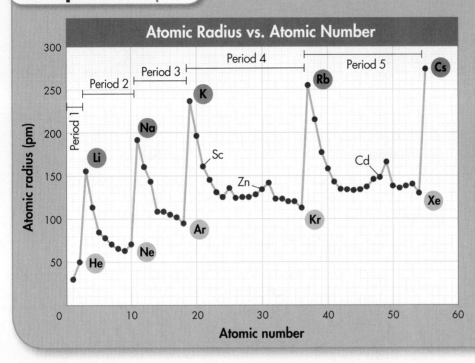

Atomic Radius vs. Atomic Number

Atomic radius (pm) vs *Atomic number*

Period 1, Period 2, Period 3, Period 4, Period 5

He, Li, Na, Ne, Ar, K, Sc, Zn, Kr, Rb, Cd, Xe, Cs

Figure 6.15 This graph plots atomic radius versus atomic number for elements with atomic numbers from 1 to 55.
a. Read Graphs Which alkali metal has an atomic radius of 238 pm?
b. Draw Conclusions Based on the data for alkali metals and noble gases, how does atomic size change within a group?
c. Predict Is an atom of barium, atomic number 56, smaller or larger than an atom of cesium (Cs)?

Group Trends in Atomic Size Look at the data for the alkali metals and noble gases in Figure 6.15. The atomic radius within these groups increases as the atomic number increases. This increase is an example of a trend.

As the atomic number increases within a group, the charge on the nucleus increases and the number of occupied energy levels increases. These variables affect atomic size in opposite ways. The increase in positive charge draws electrons closer to the nucleus. The increase in the number of occupied orbitals shields electrons in the highest occupied energy level from the attraction of protons in the nucleus. The shielding effect is greater than the effect of the increase in nuclear charge, so the atomic size increases.

Period Trends in Atomic Size Look again at Figure 6.15. With increasing atomic number, each element has one more proton and one more electron than the preceding element. Across a period, the electrons are added to the same principal energy level. The shielding effect is constant for all the elements in a period. The increasing nuclear charge pulls the electrons in the highest occupied energy level closer to the nucleus, and the atomic size decreases. Figure 6.16 summarizes the group and period trends in atomic size.

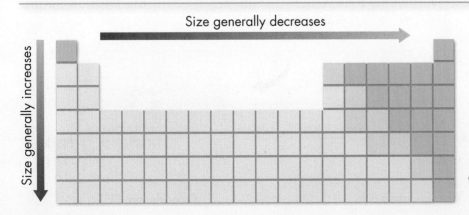

Size generally decreases

Size generally increases

Figure 6.16 Trends in Atomic Size The size of atoms tends to decrease from left to right across a period and increase from top to bottom within a group.
Predict *If a halogen and an alkali metal are in the same period, which one will have the larger radius?*

See periodic trends *animated online.*

KINETIC ART

Figure 6.17 Cation Formation
When a sodium atom loses an electron, it becomes a positively charged ion.

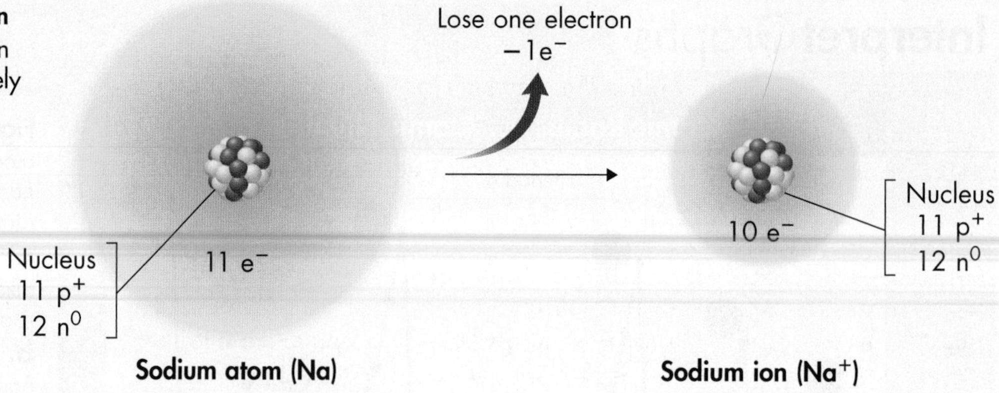

Lose one electron
$-1e^-$

Nucleus
11 p^+
12 n^0

11 e^-

10 e^-

Nucleus
11 p^+
12 n^0

Sodium atom (Na)

Sodium ion (Na⁺)

Ions

How do ions form?

Some compounds are composed of particles called ions. An **ion** is an atom or group of atoms that has a positive or negative charge. An atom is electrically neutral because it has equal numbers of protons and electrons. For example, an atom of sodium (Na) has 11 positively charged protons and 11 negatively charged electrons. The net charge on a sodium atom is zero $[(+11) + (-11) = 0]$.

Positive and negative ions form when electrons are transferred between atoms. Atoms of metals, such as sodium, tend to form ions by losing one or more electrons from their highest occupied energy levels. Figure 6.17 compares the atomic structure of a sodium atom and a sodium ion. In the sodium ion, the number of electrons (10) is not equal to the number of protons (11). Because there are more positively charged protons than negatively charged electrons, the sodium ion has a net positive charge. An ion with a positive charge is called a **cation.** The charge for a cation is written as a number followed by a plus sign. If the charge is 1, the number in 1+ is usually omitted from the symbol for the ion. For example, Na^{1+} is written as Na^+. Atoms of nonmetals, such as chlorine, tend to form ions by gaining one or more electrons. Figure 6.18 compares the atomic structure of a chlorine atom and a chloride ion. In a chloride ion, the number of electrons (18) is not equal to the number of protons (17). Because there are more negatively charged electrons than positively charged protons, the chloride ion has a net negative charge. An ion with a negative charge is called an **anion.** The charge for an anion is written as a number followed by a minus sign.

Figure 6.18 Anion Formation
When a chlorine atom gains an electron, it becomes a negatively charged ion.
Interpret Diagrams *What happens to the protons and neutrons during this change?*

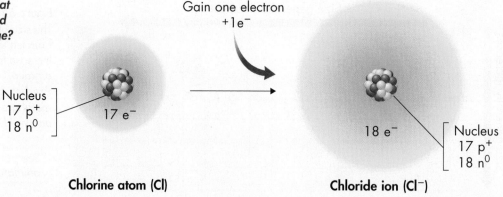

Gain one electron
$+1e^-$

Nucleus
17 p^+
18 n^0

17 e^-

18 e^-

Nucleus
17 p^+
18 n^0

Chlorine atom (Cl)

Chloride ion (Cl⁻)

Trends in Ionization Energy

What are the trends among the elements for first ionization energy?

Recall that electrons can move to higher energy levels when atoms absorb energy. Sometimes the electron has enough energy to overcome the attraction of the protons in the nucleus. The energy required to remove an electron from an atom is called **ionization energy.** This energy is measured when an element is in its gaseous state. The energy required to remove the first electron from an atom is called the first ionization energy. The cation produced has a 1+ charge. **First ionization energy tends to decrease from top to bottom within a group and increase from left to right across a period.**

Ionization energies can help you predict what ions an element will form. Look at the data in Table 6.1 for lithium (Li), sodium (Na), and potassium (K). The increase in energy between the first and second ionization energies is large. It is relatively easy to remove one electron from a Group 1A metal atom, but it is difficult to remove a second electron. This difference indicates that Group 1A metals tend to form ions with a 1+ charge.

Interpret Data

Ionization Energies of First 20 Elements (kJ/mol*)

Symbol	First	Second	Third
H	1312		
He (noble gas)	2372	5247	
Li	520	7297	11,810
Be	899	1757	14,840
B	801	2430	3659
C	1086	2352	4619
N	1402	2857	4577
O	1314	3391	5301
F	1681	3375	6045
Ne (noble gas)	2080	3963	6276
Na	496	4565	6912
Mg	738	1450	7732
Al	578	1816	2744
Si	786	1577	3229
P	1012	1896	2910
S	999	2260	3380
Cl	1256	2297	3850
Ar (noble gas)	1520	2665	3947
K	419	3069	4600
Ca	590	1146	4941

*An amount of matter equal to the atomic mass in grams

Table 6.1 The table compares ionization energies for elements with atomic numbers 1 through 20.

a. Read Tables What are the values for the first, second, and third ionization energies for sodium and aluminum?

b. Compare Is it easier to remove an electron from a sodium (Na) or aluminum (Al) atom? From Na^+ or Al^+? From Na^{2+} or Al^{2+}?

c. Draw Conclusions Which ion is more common— Na^{3+} or Al^{3+}?

Note: The second ionization energy is the energy needed to remove an electron from an ion with a 1+ charge. This produces an ion with a 2+ charge. The third ionization energy is the energy needed to remove an electron from an ion with a 2+ charge. This produces an ion with a 3+ charge.

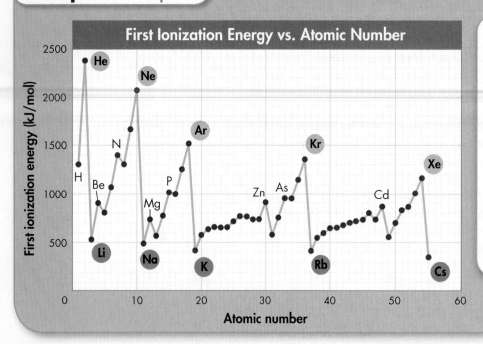

First Ionization Energy vs. Atomic Number

Figure 6.19 This graph reveals group and period trends for ionization energy.

a. Read Graphs Which element in Period 2 has the lowest first ionization energy? In Period 3?

b. Describe What are the group trends for first ionization energy for noble gases and alkali metals?

c. Predict If you drew a graph for second ionization energy, which element would you have to omit? Explain.

Group Trends in Ionization Energy Figure 6.19 is a graph of first ionization energy versus atomic number. Look at the data for the noble gases and the alkali metals. In general, first ionization energy decreases from top to bottom within a group. Recall that the atomic size increases as the atomic number increases within a group. As the size of the atom increases, nuclear charge has a smaller effect on the electrons in the highest occupied energy level. Less energy is required to remove an electron from this energy level, and the first ionization energy is lower.

Period Trends in Ionization Energy In general, the first ionization energy of representative elements tends to increase from left to right across a period. This trend can be explained by the nuclear charge and the shielding effect. The nuclear charge increases across the period, but the shielding effect remains constant. As a result, there is an increase in the attraction of the nucleus for an electron. Thus, it takes more energy to remove an electron from an atom. Figure 6.20 summarizes the group and period trends for first ionization energy.

Figure 6.20
Trends in First Ionization Energy
First ionization energy tends to increase from left to right across a period and decrease from top to bottom within a group.
Predict *Which element would have the larger first ionization energy— an alkali metal in Period 2 or an alkali metal in Period 4?*

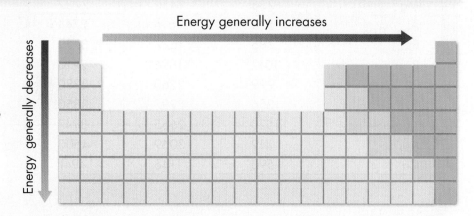

Energy generally increases

Energy generally decreases

Trends in Ionic Size

🔑 *What are the trends among the elements for ionic size?*

During reactions between metals and nonmetals, metal atoms tend to lose electrons and nonmetal atoms tend to gain electrons. This transfer of electron has a predictable effect on the size of the ions that form. Cations are always smaller than the atoms from which they form. Anions are always larger than the atoms from which they form. 🔑 **Ionic size tends to increase from top to bottom within a group. Generally, the size of cations and anions decrease from left to right across a period.**

Group Trends in Ionic Size Figure 6.21 compares the relative sizes of the atoms and ions for three metals in Group 1A—lithium (Li), sodium (Na), and potassium (K). For each of these elements, the ion is much smaller than the atom. For example, the radius of a sodium ion (95 pm) is about half the radius of a sodium atom (191 pm). When a sodium atom loses an electron, the attraction between the remaining electrons and the nucleus is increased. As a result, the electrons are drawn closer to the nucleus. Metals that are representative elements tend to lose all their outermost electrons during ionization. Therefore, the ion has one fewer occupied energy level.

The trend is the opposite for nonmetals, like the halogens in Group 7A. Look at Figure 6.21, and compare the relative sizes of the atoms and ions for fluorine (F), chlorine (Cl), and bromine (Br). For each of these elements, the ion is much larger than the atom. For example, the radius of a fluoride ion (133 pm) is more than twice the radius of a fluorine atom (62 pm). As the number of electrons increases, the attraction of the nucleus for any one electron decreases.

Period Trends in Ionic Size Look ahead at Figure 6.23. From left to right across a period, two trends are visible—a gradual decrease in the size of the positive ions (cations), followed by a gradual decrease in the size of the negative ions (anions). Figure 6.22 summarizes the group and period trends in ionic size.

Figure 6.21
Comparing Atomic and Ionic Sizes
This diagram compares the relative sizes of atoms and ions for selected alkali metals (Group 1A) and halogens (Group 7A). The numbers are measurements of the radii given in picometers (pm).

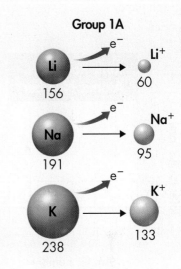

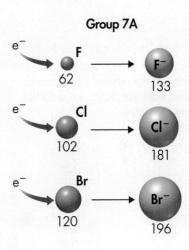

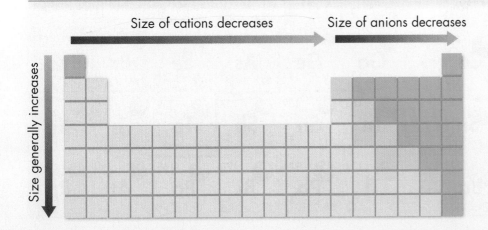

Size of cations decreases   Size of anions decreases

Size generally increases

Figure 6.22 Trends in Ionic Size
The ionic radii for cations and anions decrease from left to right across periods and increase from top to bottom within groups.

Quick Lab

Purpose To use a graph to identify period and group trends

Materials
- graph paper
- pencil

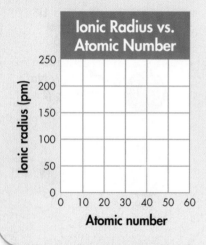

Ionic Radius vs. Atomic Number

Ionic radius (pm): 0, 50, 100, 150, 200, 250

Atomic number: 0, 10, 20, 30, 40, 50, 60

Periodic Trends in Ionic Radii

Procedure
Use the data presented in Figure 6.23 to plot ionic radius versus atomic number.

Analyze and Conclude
1. Compare How does the size change when an atom forms a cation and when an atom forms an anion?

2. Describe How do the ionic radii vary within a group of metals? How do they vary within a group of nonmetals?

3. Describe What is the shape of a portion of the graph that corresponds to one period?

4. Compare and Contrast Is the trend across a period similar or different for Periods 2, 3, 4, and 5?

5. Explain Propose explanations for the trends you have described for ionic radii within groups and across periods.

Figure 6.23 Atomic and Ionic Radii
Atomic and ionic radii are an indication of the relative size of atoms and ions. The data listed are reported in picometers (pm).

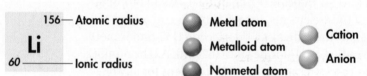

156 — Atomic radius
Li
60 — Ionic radius

● Metal atom
● Metalloid atom
● Nonmetal atom
○ Cation
○ Anion

Trends in Electronegativity

In Chapters 7 and 8, you will study two types of bonds that can exist in compounds. Electrons are involved in both types of bonds. There is a property that can be used to predict the type of bond that will form during a reaction. This property is called electronegativity. **Electronegativity** is the ability of an atom of an element to attract electrons when the atom is in a compound. Scientists use factors such as ionization energy to calculate values for electronegativity.

Table 6.2 lists electronegativity values for representative elements in Groups 1A through 7A. The elements are arranged in the same order as in the periodic table. The noble gases are omitted because they do not form many compounds. The data in Table 6.2 is expressed in Pauling units. Linus Pauling won a Nobel Prize in Chemistry for his work on chemical bonds. He was the first to define electronegativity.

In general, electronegativity values decrease from top to bottom within a group. For representative elements, the values tend to increase from left to right across a period. Metals at the far left of the periodic table have low values. By contrast, nonmetals at the far right (excluding noble gases) have high values. The electronegativity values among the transition metals are not as regular.

The least electronegative element in the table is cesium, with an electronegativity value of 0.7. It has the least tendency to attract electrons. When it reacts, it tends to lose electrons and form cations. The most electronegative element is fluorine, with a value of 4.0. Because fluorine has such a strong tendency to attract electrons, when it is bonded to any other element it either attracts the shared electrons or forms an anion.

Figure 6.24, on the next page, summarizes several trends that exist among the elements. Refer to this figure as you study the periodic trends presented in this chapter.

Table 6.2

Electronegativity Values for Selected Elements

H 2.1						
Li 1.0	Be 1.5	B 2.0	C 2.5	N 3.0	O 3.5	F 4.0
Na 0.9	Mg 1.2	Al 1.5	Si 1.8	P 2.1	S 2.5	Cl 3.0
K 0.8	Ca 1.0	Ga 1.6	Ge 1.8	As 2.0	Se 2.4	Br 2.8
Rb 0.8	Sr 1.0	In 1.7	Sn 1.8	Sb 1.9	Te 2.1	I 2.5
Cs 0.7	Ba 0.9	Tl 1.8	Pb 1.9	Bi 1.9		

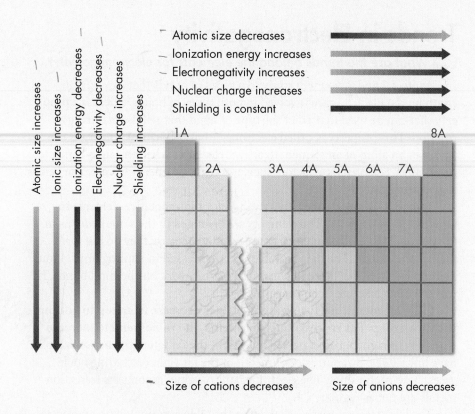

Atomic size increases
Ionic size increases
Ionization energy decreases
Electronegativity decreases
Nuclear charge increases
Shielding increases

Atomic size decreases
Ionization energy increases
Electronegativity increases
Nuclear charge increases
Shielding is constant

1A 2A 3A 4A 5A 6A 7A 8A

Size of cations decreases   Size of anions decreases

Q: *You are familiar with using a weather map to identify trends in the weather. For example, certain areas are typically warmer than other areas. What trends in the properties of elements can you identify with the help of the periodic table?*

Figure 6.24 Summary of Periodic Trends
Trends for atomic size, ionization energy, ionic size, and electronegativity vary within groups and across periods. The trends that exist among these properties can be explained by variations in atomic structure. The increase in nuclear charge within groups and across periods explains many trends. Within groups, an increase in the number of occupied energy levels and an increase in shielding both have a significant effect on each trend.

Interpret Diagrams *Which properties tend to decrease across a period? Which properties tend to decrease down a group?*

6.3 LessonCheck

ONLINE PROBLEMS

18. 🗝 **Review** How does atomic size change within groups and across periods?

19. 🗝 **Explain** When do ions form?

20. 🗝 **Summarize** How do first ionization energies vary within groups and across periods?

21. 🗝 **Describe** Compare the size of ions to the size of the atoms from which they form.

22. 🗝 **Review** How do electronegativity values vary within groups and across periods?

23. Explain In general, how can the periodic trends displayed by elements be explained?

24. Sequence Arrange these elements in order of decreasing atomic size: sulfur, chlorine, aluminum, and sodium. Does your arrangement demonstrate a periodic trend or a group trend?

25. Identify Which element in each pair has the larger first ionization energy?
  a. sodium, potassium
  b. magnesium, phosphorus

Elements of Life

Like everything else in the universe, your body is made up of elements. Your body uses these elements for different functions. Roughly 97 percent of the human body consists of just four elements: oxygen, carbon, hydrogen, and nitrogen. The remaining 3 percent contains about 20 other elements that are essential to life.

CIRCULATORY SYSTEM Iron and oxygen are critical to the circulatory system—the system that carries blood throughout the body. Iron, which is contained in red blood cells, helps transport oxygen from the lungs to other cells in your body. Two other elements—copper and cobalt—are necessary for the formation of red blood cells.

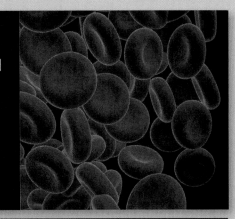

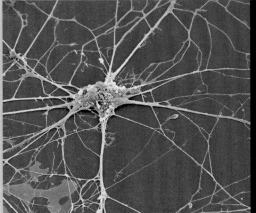

NERVOUS SYSTEM Sodium and potassium are essential to the nervous system, in particular the nerve cells. These elements allow your brain to communicate with other tissues in your body. Other elements that are important for proper nervous system function include calcium, chlorine, zinc, and magnesium.

SKELETAL SYSTEM Your bones and teeth—two components of the skeletal system—are largely comprised of calcium and phosphorus, which give bones and teeth their strength. Fluorine, boron, magnesium, and silicon are also important for bone growth and for maintaining bone strength.

Take It Further

1. Describe Use the information provided on page R1 to estimate the composition of the human body in terms of metals, nonmetals, and metalloids.

2. Predict The elements sodium, magnesium, potassium, and calcium are the most abundant metals in the human body and are present as ions. What is the charge of each of these ions?

3. Sequence Use Figure 6.23 to list the ions in Question 2 from smallest to largest.

Small-Scale Lab

Periodicity in Three Dimensions

Purpose
To build three-dimensional models for periodic trends

Materials
- 96-well spot plate
- straws
- scissors
- metric ruler
- permanent fine-line marker

Procedure

1. Measure the depth of a well in the spot plate by inserting a straw into a well and holding the straw upright as shown in the photograph. Make a mark on the straw at the point where the straw meets the surface of the plate. Measure the distance from the end of the straw to the mark in centimeters (cm). Record this distance as well depth.

2. Cut the straw to a length that is 4.0 cm plus well depth. The straw will extend exactly 4.0 cm above the surface of the plate.

3. Fluorine has an electronegativity value of 4.0. On a scale of 1.0 cm equals 1.0 unit of electronegativity, the portion of the straw that extends above the surface of the plate represents the electronegativity value for fluorine. Using the same scale, cut straws to represent the electronegativity values for all the elements listed in Table 6.2. Remember to add the well depth to the electronegativity value before cutting a straw. As you cut the straws, mark each straw with the chemical symbol of the element that the straw represents.

4. Arrange the straws in the spot plate in rows and columns to match the locations of the elements in the periodic table.

Analyze and Conclude

1. Use Models Which element represented in your model is the most electronegative?

2. Use Models Based on your model, what is the general trend in electronegativity from left to right across a period?

3. Interpret Diagrams Relate the trend in electronegativity across a period to the location of metals and nonmetals in the periodic table.

4. Use Models Based on your model, what is the general trend in electronegativity within a group? Are there any notable exceptions?

5. Explain Why do you think that the electronegativity value for hydrogen is so high given its location in the periodic table?

You're the Chemist

1. Design an Experiment Construct a similar three-dimensional model for first ionization energies. Use the data in Table 6.1 to construct the model. Use a scale of 1.0 cm equals 300 kJ/mol.

2. Design an Experiment Design and construct a three-dimensional model that shows trends in atomic and ionic radii for the elements in Groups 1A and 7A. Devise a way to display both ionic and atomic radii in the same model.

3. Analyze Data Xenon has an electronegativity value of 2.6. Cut and place a straw in your first model to represent xenon. Does xenon support the trend for electronegativity across a period? Is xenon likely to form compounds? Explain your answers.

6 Study Guide

BIGIDEA ELECTRONS AND THE STRUCTURE OF ATOMS

Periodic tables may contain each element's name, symbol, atomic number, atomic mass, and number of electrons in each energy level. The electron configuration of an element can be determined based on the location of an element in the periodic table. Atomic size, ionization energy, ionic size, and electronegativity are trends that vary across periods and groups of the periodic table. These trends can be explained by variations in atomic structure. The increase in nuclear charge within groups and across periods explains many trends. Within groups, an increase in electron shielding has a significant effect on these trends.

6.1 Organizing the Elements

🔑 Early chemists used the properties of elements to sort them into groups.

🔑 Mendeleev arranged the elements in his periodic table in order of increasing atomic mass.

🔑 In the modern periodic table, elements are arranged in order of increasing atomic number.

🔑 Three classes of elements are metals, nonmetals, and metalloids.

• periodic law (162)
• metal (165)
• nonmetal (165)
• metalloid (166)

6.2 Classifying the Elements

🔑 The periodic table usually displays the symbols and names of elements, along with information about the structure of their atoms.

🔑 Elements can be sorted into noble gases, representative elements, transition metals, or inner transition metals based on their electron configurations.

• alkali metal (167)
• alkaline earth metal (167)
• halogen (167)
• noble gas (170)
• representative element (171)
• transition metal (172)
• inner transition metal (172)

6.3 Periodic Trends

🔑 In general, atomic size increases from top to bottom within a group and decreases from left to right across a period.

🔑 Positive and negative ions form when electrons are transferred between atoms.

🔑 First ionization energy tends to decrease from top to bottom within a group and increase from left to right across a period.

🔑 Ionic size tends to increase from top to bottom within a group. Generally, the size of cations and anions decrease from left to right across a period.

🔑 In general, electronegativity values decrease from top to bottom within a group. For representative elements, the values tend to increase from left to right across a period.

• atomic radius (174)
• ion (176)
• cation (176)
• anion (176)
• ionization energy (177)
• electronegativity (181)

 **6 Assessment**

Lesson by Lesson

6.1 Organizing the Elements

26. Why did Mendeleev leave spaces in his periodic table?

★ **27.** What effect did the discovery of gallium have on the acceptance of Mendeleev's table?

28. What pattern is revealed when the elements are arranged in a periodic table in order of increasing atomic number?

29. Based on their locations in the periodic table, would you expect carbon and silicon to have similar properties? Explain your answer.

30. Identify each property below as more characteristic of a metal or a nonmetal.

   a. a gas at room temperature
   b. brittle
   c. malleable
   d. poor conductor of electric current
   e. shiny

31. In general, how are metalloids different from metals and nonmetals?

6.2 Classifying the Elements

32. Where are the alkali metals, the alkaline earth metals, the halogens, and the noble gases located in the periodic table?

33. Which of the following are symbols for representative elements: Na, Mg, Fe, Ni, Cl?

★ **34.** Which noble gas does not have eight electrons in its highest occupied energy level?

35. Which of these metals isn't a transition metal?

   a. aluminum   **c.** iron
   b. silver   **d.** zirconium

36. Use Figure 6.13 to write the electron configurations of these elements.

   a. boron   **c.** fluorine   **e.** aluminum
   b. arsenic   **d.** zinc

37. Write the electron configurations of these elements.

   a. the noble gas in Period 3
   b. the metalloid in Period 3
   c. the alkali earth metal in Period 3

6.3 Periodic Trends

★ **38.** Which element in each pair has atoms with a larger atomic radius?

   a. sodium, lithium
   b. strontium, magnesium
   c. carbon, germanium
   d. selenium, oxygen

39. Explain the difference between the first and second ionization energy of an element.

40. Which element in each pair has a greater first ionization energy?

   a. lithium, boron
   b. magnesium, strontium
   c. cesium, aluminum

41. Arrange the following groups of elements in order of increasing ionization energy:

   a. Be, Mg, Sr   **b.** Bi, Cs, Ba   **c.** Na, Al, S

42. Why is there a large increase between the first and second ionization energies of the alkali metals?

★ **43.** How does the ionic radius of a typical metal compare with its atomic radius?

44. Which particle has the larger radius in each atom/ion pair?

   a. Na, Na^+ **c.** I, I^-
   b. S, S^{2-} **d.** Al, Al^{3+}

45. Which element in each pair has a higher electronegativity value?

   a. Cl, F   **c.** Mg, Ne
   b. C, N   **d.** As, Ca

46. Why are noble gases not included in Table 6.2?

★ **47.** When the elements in each pair are chemically combined, which element in each pair has a greater attraction for electrons?

   a. Ca or O   **c.** H or O
   b. O or F   **d.** K or S

48. For which of these properties does lithium have a larger value than potassium?

   a. first ionization energy
   b. atomic radius
   c. electronegativity
   d. ionic radius

49. The bar graph shows how many elements were discovered before 1750 and in each 50-year period between 1750 and 2000.

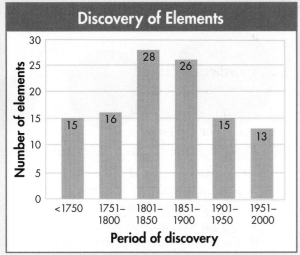

Discovery of Elements

Number of elements vs *Period of discovery*

- <1750: 15
- 1751–1800: 16
- 1801–1850: 28
- 1851–1900: 26
- 1901–1950: 15
- 1951–2000: 13

a. In which 50-year period were the most elements discovered?

b. How did Mendeleev's work contribute to the discovery of elements?

c. What percent of these elements were discovered by 1900?

50. Write the symbol of the element or elements that fit each description.

a. a nonmetal in Group 4A

b. the inner transition metal with the lowest atomic number

c. all of the nonmetals for which the atomic number is a multiple of five

d. a metal in Group 5A

✶**51.** In which pair of elements are the chemical properties of the elements most similar? Explain your reasoning.

a. sodium and chlorine

b. nitrogen and phosphorus

c. boron and oxygen

52. Explain why fluorine has a smaller atomic radius than both oxygen and chlorine.

53. Would you expect metals or nonmetals in the same period to have higher ionization energies? Give a reason for your answer.

54. In each pair, which ion is larger?
a. Ca^{2+}, Mg^{2+} **b.** Cl^-, P^{3-} **c.** Cu^+, Cu^{2+}

55. Use the graph in Figure 6.15 to estimate the atomic radius of the indium atom.

✶**56.** List the symbols for all the elements with electron configurations that end as follows. *Note:* Each n represents an energy level.

a. ns^1 **b.** ns^2np^4 **c.** ns^2nd^{10}

57. Explain why there should be a connection between an element's electron configuration and its location on the periodic table.

58. Which equation represents the first ionization of an alkali metal atom?

a. $Cl \longrightarrow Cl^+ + e^-$

b. $Ca \longrightarrow Ca^+ + e^-$

c. $K \longrightarrow K^+ + e^-$

d. $H \longrightarrow H^+ + e^-$

59. What trend is demonstrated by the following series of equations?

$$Li + 520 \text{ kJ/mol} \longrightarrow Li^+ + e^-$$
$$O + 1314 \text{ kJ/mol} \longrightarrow O^+ + e^-$$
$$F + 1681 \text{ kJ/mol} \longrightarrow F^+ + e^-$$
$$Ne + 2080 \text{ kJ/mol} \longrightarrow Ne^+ + e^-$$

✶**60.** There is a large jump between the second and third ionization energies of magnesium. There is a large jump between the third and fourth ionization energies of aluminum. Explain these observations.

61. The bar graph shows the relationship between atomic and ionic radii for Group 1A elements.

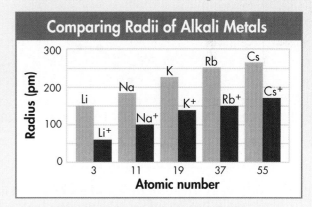

Comparing Radii of Alkali Metals

Radius (pm) vs *Atomic number*

- 3: Li, Li⁺
- 11: Na, Na⁺
- 19: K, K⁺
- 37: Rb, Rb⁺
- 55: Cs, Cs⁺

a. Describe and explain the trend in atomic radius within the group.

b. Explain the difference between the size of the atoms and the size of the ions.

62. Locate each of the following elements in the periodic table and decide whether its atoms are likely to form anions or cations.

a. sodium   **e.** iodine

b. fluorine   **f.** beryllium

c. calcium   **g.** oxygen

d. potassium   **h.** lithium

63. Predict Do you think there are more elements left to discover? If so, what is the lowest atomic number a new element could have? Explain.

64. Interpret Graphs The graphs show the relationship between the electronegativities and first ionization energies for Period 2 and Period 3 elements.

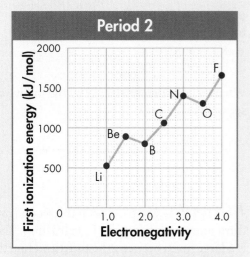

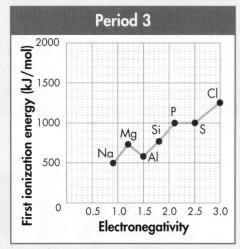

a. Based on data for these two periods, what is the general trend between these two values?

b. Use nuclear charge and shielding effect to explain this trend.

★65. Explain Give a reason for each of the following comparisons:

a. Calcium has a smaller second ionization energy than does potassium.

b. Lithium has a larger first ionization energy than does cesium.

c. Magnesium has a larger third ionization energy than does aluminum.

★66. Explain Why does it take more energy to remove a $4s$ electron from zinc than from calcium?

67. Sequence The following spheres represent Ca, Ca^{2+}, and Mg^{2+}. Which one is which? Explain your reasoning.

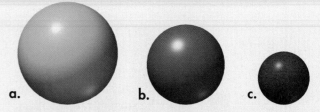

a. b. c.

★68. Apply Concepts Write the electron configurations of the following ions:

a. the liquid in Group 7A with a 1− charge
b. the metalloid in Period 3 with a 4+ charge
c. the gas in Group 6A with a 2− charge
d. the alkali earth metal in Period 3 with a 2+ charge

69. Interpret Diagrams Use the periodic table and Figure 6.13 to identify the following elements:

a. has its outermost electron in $7s^1$
b. contains only one electron in a d orbital

70. Make Generalizations Why is the first ionization energy of a nonmetal much higher than that of an alkali metal?

71. Infer The bar graph shows the densities for the first six elements in Period 4. The density increases across this period from potassium to chromium. Use trends in the periodic table to explain this behavior. *Hint*: What is the equation for determining density?

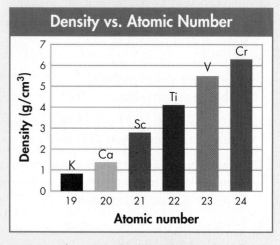

72. Explain Why are cations smaller and anions larger than the corresponding atoms?

73. **Analyze Data** Make a graph of atomic mass versus atomic number. Choose eleven points (atomic numbers 1, 10, 20, and so forth up to atomic number 100) to make your graph. Use the graph to describe the relationship between atomic mass and atomic number. Is there a 1:1 correlation between atomic mass and atomic number? Explain.

74. **Compare and Contrast** The Mg^{2+} and Na^+ ions each have ten electrons. Which ion would you expect to have the smaller radius? Why?

∗75. **Predict** Electron affinity is a measure of an atom's ability to gain electrons. Predict the trend for electron affinity across a period. Explain your answer.

76. **Explain** The ions S^{2-}, Cl^-, K^+, Ca^{2+}, and Sc^{3+} have the same total number of electrons as the noble gas argon. How would you expect the radii of these ions to vary? Would you expect to see the same variation in the series O^{2-}, F^-, Na^+, Mg^{2+}, and Al^{3+}, in which each ion has the same total number of electrons as the noble gas neon? Explain your answer.

77. **Graph** The ionization energies for the removal of the first six electrons in carbon are, starting with the first electron, 1086 kJ/mol, 2352 kJ/mol, 4619 kJ/mol, 6220 kJ/mol, 37,820 kJ/mol, and 47,260 kJ/mol.

    a. Use these data to construct a graph of ionization energy versus ionization number. *Note:* The ionization number indicates which electron is lost.
    b. Between which two ionization numbers does the ionization energy have the largest increase? Why is this behavior predictable?

∗78. **Infer** Atoms and ions with the same number of electrons are described as *isoelectronic*.

    a. Write the symbol for a cation and an anion that are isoelectronic with krypton.
    b. Is it possible for a cation to be isoelectronic with an anion in the same period? Explain.

79. **Predict** Estimate the atomic radius of praseodymium based on the following data for atomic radii of neighboring elements: La (187.9 pm), Ce (183.2 pm), Nd (182.1 pm), and Pm (181.1 pm). Compare your prediction to the value given in a chemistry handbook.

80. **Explain** Why does the size of an atom tend to increase from top to bottom within a group? Why does the size of an atom tend to decrease from left to right across a period?

81. **Connect to the BIGIDEA** The ion Zn^{2+} is important in several biological processes. One process depends on Zn^{2+} temporarily binding to a molecule in red blood cells. When Zn^{2+} is absent, Cd^{2+} can bind to the molecule. However, Cd^{2+} binds more strongly and adversely affects the process. The differences in ionic size is one important cause of the difference in biological activity. How would you expect Hg^{2+} to affect this process? Why?

CHEMYSTERY

Made in the USA

Several of the "unnatural" elements were in fact "made in the USA." For example, elements with atomic numbers 94 through 102 were first artificially prepared in California. Three of these elements have names to prove it—americium, berkelium, and californium. Elements such as these are labeled on the periodic table as "Not found in nature" in this book and as "Artificially prepared" in some others.

Most of the artificially prepared elements are actinides or transactinides. Each of these elements has an unstable nucleus. As a result, these elements undergo radioactive decay, which means their nuclei spontaneously break down into smaller parts in the attempt to gain stability.

82. **Infer** The elements with atomic numbers 99, 101, 104, and 107 were named to honor past influential scientists. Identify the scientist that each element is meant to honor.

83. **Connect to the BIGIDEA** Many smoke detectors use the artificially prepared element americium. For a challenge, write the electron configuration of americium.

84. Explain why science today depends less on chance discoveries than it did in the past.

*__85.__ Identify each process as a chemical change or a physical change.

    a. melting of iron   **c.** grinding corn

    b. lighting a match   **d.** souring of milk

86. Describe at least two methods to separate a mixture of small copper and iron beads.

87. In the United States, a typical can of cola holds 355 mL. How many 2.00-L bottles could be filled from a 24-can case of cola?

88. The volume of the liquid in the graduated cylinder is reported as 31.8 mL.

    a. How many significant figures are there in the measurement?

    b. In which digit is there uncertainty?

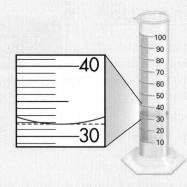

89. A cube of plastic 1.20×10^{-5} km on a side has a mass of 1.70 g. Show by calculation whether this plastic cube will sink or float in pure water.

*__90.__ Convert the measurements to meters. Express your answers in scientific notation.

    a. 2.24 nm   **c.** 7.4 pm

    b. 8.13 cm   **d.** 9.37 mm

91. An apprentice jeweler determines the density of a sample of pure gold to be 20.3 g/cm^3. The accepted value is 19.3 g/cm^3. What is the percent error of the jeweler's density measurement?

92. What is the mass of 7.7 L of gasoline at 20°C? Assume the density of gasoline to be 0.68 g/cm^3.

*__93.__ A black olive containing its seed has a mass of 4.5 g and a volume of 4.3 cm^3. Will the olive sink or float on water?

94. The distance from the sun to Earth is 1.50×10^8 km. The speed of light is 3.00×10^8 m/s. How many round trips between Earth and the sun could a beam of light make in one day?

95. The table shows how the volume of sulfur varies with mass. How does the density of sulfur vary with mass?

Mass of Sulfur vs. Volume of Sulfur	
Mass of sulfur (g)	Volume of sulfur (cm³)
23.5	11.4
60.8	29.2
115	55.5
168	81.1

96. Calculate the volume of acetone with the same mass as 15.0 mL of mercury. The density of mercury is 13.59 g/mL. The density of acetone is 0.792 g/mL.

97. A rectangular container has inside dimensions of 15.2 cm by 22.9 cm and is about 1 meter tall. Water is poured into the container to a height of 55.0 cm. When a jagged rock with a mass of 5.21 kg is placed in the container, it sinks to the bottom. The water level rises to 58.3 cm and completely covers the rock. What is the density of the rock?

*__98.__ How many neutrons does an atom of each isotope contain?

    a. $^{84}_{36}\text{Kr}$ **b.** $^{79}_{35}\text{Br}$ **c.** $^{190}_{76}\text{Os}$ **d.** $^{185}_{75}\text{Re}$

99. Name the element and calculate the number of requested subatomic particles in each isotope.

    a. neutrons in $^{109}_{47}\text{Ag}$ **c.** electrons in $^{96}_{42}\text{Mo}$

    b. protons in $^{118}_{50}\text{Sn}$ **d.** electrons in $^{45}_{21}\text{Sc}$

*__100.__ How many filled *p* orbitals do atoms of these elements contain?

    a. carbon   **c.** oxygen

    b. phosphorus   **d.** nitrogen

If You Have Trouble With . . .

Question	84	85	86	87	88	89	90	91	92	93	94	95	96	97	98	99	100
See Chapter	1	2	2	3	3	3	3	3	3	3	3	3	3	3	4	4	5

Standardized Test Prep

Select the choice that best answers each question or completes each statement.

1. Which of the following properties increases as you move across a period from left to right?

    I. electronegativity
    II. ionization energy
    III. atomic radius

    (A) I and II only   **(C)** II and III only
    (B) I and III only   **(D)** I, II, and III

2. List the symbols for sodium, sulfur, and cesium in order of increasing atomic radii.
    (A) Na, S, Cs   **(C)** S, Na, Cs
    (B) Cs, Na, S   **(D)** Cs, S, Na

3. The electron configuration for an element in the halogen group should always end with
    (A) ns^2np^6.   **(C)** ns^2np^4.
    (B) ns^2np^5.   **(D)** ns^2np^2.

Use the spheres to answer Questions 4 and 5.

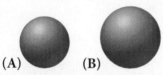

(A)   (B)

4. If the spheres represent a potassium atom and a potassium ion, which best represents the ion?

5. If the spheres represent an atom and an anion of the same element, which sphere represents the atom and which represents the anion?

Tips for Success

Interpreting Data Tables Tables can present a large amount of data in a small space. Before you try to answer questions based on a table, look at the table. Read the title, if there is one, and the column headings. Then read the questions. As you read each question, decide which data you will need to use to answer the question.

Use the data table to answer Questions 6–8.

Alkali metal	Atomic radius (pm)	First ionization energy (kJ/mol)	Electronegativity value
Li	152	520	1.0
Na	186	495.8	0.9
K	227	418.8	0.8
Rb	244	250	0.8
Cs	262	210	0.7

6. If you plot atomic radius versus first ionization energy, would the graph reveal a direct or inverse relationship?

7. If you plot atomic radius versus electronegativity, would the graph reveal a direct or inverse relationship?

8. If you plot first ionization energy versus electronegativity, would the graph reveal a direct or inverse relationship?

For each question there are two statements. Decide whether each statement is true or false. Then decide whether Statement II is a correct explanation for Statement I.

	Statement I		Statement II
9.	Electronegativity values are higher for metals than for nonmetals.	**BECAUSE**	Atoms of nonmetals are among the largest atoms.
10.	A calcium atom is larger than a calcium ion.	**BECAUSE**	Ions are always larger than the atoms from which they are formed.
11.	The element hydrogen is a metal.	**BECAUSE**	Hydrogen is on the left in the periodic table.
12.	Among all the elements in a period, the noble gas always has the smallest ionization energy.	**BECAUSE**	Within any period, atomic radii tend to decrease moving from right to left.

If You Have Trouble With . . .

Question	1	2	3	4	5	6	7	8	9	10	11	12
See Lesson	6.3	6.3	6.2	6.3	6.3	6.3	6.3	6.3	6.3	6.3	6.1	6.3

7

Ionic and Metallic Bonding

INSIDE:

- **7.1** Ions
- **7.2** Ionic Bonds and Ionic Compounds
- **7.3** Bonding in Metals

PearsonChem.com

Mexico's Cave of Crystals contains giant gypsum crystals. Gypsum crystals are composed of the ionic compound calcium sulfate ($CaSO_4$) and water.

BONDING AND INTERACTIONS

Essential Questions:

1. *How do ionic compounds form?*
2. *How does metallic bonding affect the properties of metals?*

CHEMYSTERY

It's Not Easy Being Green

While strolling through Central Park in New York City, you come across this statue of the composer Ludwig van Beethoven. It appears to be made of metal, but its surface is green in color and not very shiny. Is the statue's green complexion due to green paint, or something else?

After doing some research, you learn that the statue is made out of bronze, which is a mixture of metals. The statue was never painted. Instead, the exposed surface of the bronze underwent a chemical change, forming a green film over time. You wonder what the film is made of and how it formed. Are the properties of the film different from the bronze beneath it?

▶ Connect to the **BIGIDEA** As you read about ionic compounds and metals, think about why the statue changed color. Also, think about how the properties of the green film at the surface differ from the metal beneath it.

NATIONAL SCIENCE EDUCATION STANDARDS

A-1, B-2, B-4

7.1 Ions

Q: *What is fool's gold?* Pyrite (FeS_2) is often mistaken for gold—hence its nickname, "fool's gold." Pyrite is an example of a crystalline solid. In crystalline solids, the component particles of the substance are arranged in an orderly, repeating fashion. In this chapter, you will learn about crystalline solids, like pyrite, that are composed of ions that are bonded together.

Key Questions

How do you find the number of valence electrons in an atom of a representative element?

How are cations formed?

How are anions formed?

Vocabulary

- valence electron
- electron dot structure
- octet rule
- halide ion

Figure 7.1 Group 4A Elements
Silicon and germanium are Group 4A elements. **a.** Silicon is used in the manufacture of computer chips. **b.** Compounds of germanium are used to make optical fibers.

Valence Electrons

How do you find the number of valence electrons in an atom of a representative element?

Mendeleev used similarities in the properties of elements to organize his periodic table. Scientists later learned that all of the elements within each group of the periodic table react in a similar way because they have the same number of valence electrons. **Valence electrons** are the electrons in the highest occupied energy level of an element's atoms. The number of valence electrons largely determines the chemical properties of an element.

Determining the Number of Valence Electrons The number of valence electrons in an atom of an element is related to the element's group number in the periodic table. **To find the number of valence electrons in an atom of a representative element, simply look at its group number.** For example, atoms of the Group 1A elements (hydrogen, lithium, sodium, and so forth) all have one valence electron, corresponding to the 1 in 1A. Carbon and silicon atoms, in Group 4A, have four valence electrons. Figure 7.1 shows some applications of Group 4A elements. Nitrogen and phosphorus atoms, in Group 5A, have five valence electrons, and oxygen and sulfur atoms, in Group 6A, have six. The noble gases (Group 8A) are the only exceptions to the group-number rule: Atoms of helium have two valence electrons, and atoms of all of the other noble gases have eight valence electrons.

Table 7.1

Electron Dot Structures of Some Group A Elements

Period	Group							
	1A	**2A**	**3A**	**4A**	**5A**	**6A**	**7A**	**8A**
1	H·							He:
2	Li·	·Be·	·Ḃ·	·Ċ·	·Ṅ·	:Ö·	:Ḟ·	:Ṅe:
3	Na·	·Mg·	·Aİ·	·Sİ·	·Ṗ·	:Ṡ·	:Ċl·	:Är:
4	K·	·Ca·	·Ga·	·Ge·	·Äs·	:Se·	:Br·	:Kr:

Valence electrons are usually the only electrons involved in chemical bonds. Therefore, as a general rule, only the valence electrons are shown in electron dot structures. **Electron dot structures** are diagrams that show valence electrons in the atoms of an element as dots. Table 7.1 shows electron dot structures for atoms of some Group A elements. Notice that all of the elements within a given group (with the exception of helium) have the same number of electron dots in their structures.

The Octet Rule You learned in Chapter 6 that noble gases, such as neon and argon, are nonreactive in chemical reactions. That is, they are stable. In 1916, chemist Gilbert Lewis used this fact to explain why atoms form certain kinds of ions and molecules. He called his explanation the octet rule. The **octet rule** states that in forming compounds, atoms tend to achieve the electron configuration of a noble gas. An octet is a set of eight. Recall that atoms of each of the noble gases (except helium) have eight electrons in their highest occupied energy levels and the general electron configuration of ns^2np^6. The octet rule takes its name from this fact about noble gases.

Atoms of metals tend to lose their valence electrons, leaving a complete octet in the next-lowest energy level. Atoms of some nonmetals tend to gain electrons or to share electrons with another nonmetal atom or atoms to achieve a complete octet. Although exceptions occur, the octet rule applies to atoms in most compounds.

Formation of Cations

🔑 *How are cations formed?*

An atom is electrically neutral because it has equal numbers of protons and electrons. An ion forms when an atom or group of atoms loses or gains electrons. 🔑 **A positively charged ion, or a cation, is produced when an atom loses one or more valence electrons.** Note that for metals, the name of the cation is the same as the name of the element. For example, a sodium atom (Na) forms a sodium cation (Na^+). Likewise, a calcium atom (Ca) forms a calcium cation (Ca^{2+}). Although their names are the same, metals and their cations have many important chemical differences. Sodium metal, for example, reacts explosively with water. By contrast, sodium cations are quite nonreactive. As you may know, sodium cations are a component of table salt, a compound that is very stable in water.

READING SUPPORT

Build Vocabulary: *Word Origins* *Octet* comes from the Greek word *okto*, meaning "eight." There are eight electrons in the highest occupied energy level of the noble gases, except for helium. *How do you think the term* octet *might also be applied to music or poetry?*

Group 1A Cations The most common cations are those produced by the loss of valence electrons from metal atoms. Most of these atoms have one to three valence electrons, which are easily removed. Sodium (atomic number 11) is in Group 1A of the periodic table. Sodium atoms have a total of eleven electrons, including one valence electron. A sodium atom can lose an electron to become a positively charged sodium ion. Sodium atoms become sodium ions in a sodium vapor lamp, which is shown in Figure 7.2. The sodium ion has an electron configuration that is identical to the noble gas neon.

When forming a compound, a sodium atom loses its one valence electron and is left with an octet (eight electrons) in what is now its highest occupied energy level. The number of protons in the sodium nucleus is still eleven, so the loss of one unit of negative charge produces a cation with a charge of 1+. You can represent the loss of the electron, or ionization, of the sodium atom by writing the complete electron configuration of the atom and of the ion formed.

$$\text{Na} \quad 1s^2 2s^2 2p^6 3s^1 \xrightarrow{-e^-} \text{Na}^+ \quad 1s^2 \underbrace{2s^2 2p^6}_{\text{octet}}$$

Notice that the electron configuration of the sodium ion ($1s^2 2s^2 2p^6$) is the same as that of a neon atom.

$$\text{Ne} \quad 1s^2 \underbrace{2s^2 2p^6}_{\text{octet}}$$

The diagrams below help illustrate this point.

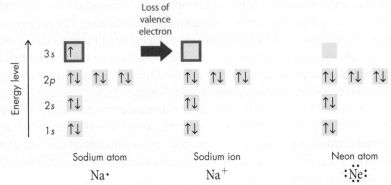

Both the sodium ion and the neon atom have eight electrons in their valence shells (highest occupied energy levels). Using electron dot structures, you can show the ionization more simply.

Na· $\xrightarrow[\text{ionization}]{\text{loss of one valence electron}}$ Na⁺ + e⁻

Sodium atom (electrically neutral, charge = 0)

Sodium ion (plus sign indicates one unit of positive charge)

Electron (minus sign indicates one unit of negative charge)

Figure 7.2 Sodium Vapor Lamp
The sodium atoms (Na) in a sodium vapor lamp ionize to form sodium cations (Na⁺).
Apply Concepts *How many electrons are in the highest occupied energy level of Na⁺?*

Group 2A Cations Magnesium (atomic number 12) belongs to Group 2A of the periodic table, so magnesium atoms have two valence electrons. A magnesium atom attains the electron configuration of a neon atom by losing both valence electrons and producing a magnesium cation with a charge of 2+.

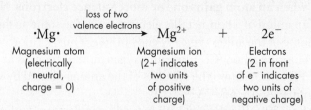

Magnesium atom (electrically neutral, charge = 0) → Magnesium ion (2+ indicates two units of positive charge) + Electrons (2 in front of e^- indicates two units of negative charge)

Figure 7.3 lists the symbols of the cations formed by metals in Groups 1A and 2A. Cations of Group 1A elements always have a charge of 1+. Cations of Group 2A elements always have a charge of 2+. This consistency can be explained in terms of the loss of valence electrons by metal atoms: The atoms lose the number of electrons necessary to attain the electron configuration of a noble gas.

Transition Metal Cations The charges of cations of the transition metals may vary. An atom of iron, for example, may lose two valence electrons, forming the Fe^{2+} cation, or three valence electrons, forming the Fe^{3+} cation.

Some ions formed by transition metals do not have noble-gas electron configurations ($ns^2 np^6$) and are therefore exceptions to the octet rule. Silver, with the electron configuration of $1s^2 2s^2 2p^6 3s^2 3p^6 3d^{10} 4s^2 4p^6 4d^{10} 5s^1$, is an example. To achieve the structure of krypton, which is the preceding noble gas, a silver atom would have to lose eleven electrons. To acquire the electron configuration of xenon, which is the following noble gas, a silver atom would have to gain seven electrons. Ions with charges of three or greater are uncommon. Thus silver does not achieve a noble-gas configuration. However, if a silver atom loses its $5s^1$ electron, forming a positive ion (Ag^+), the configuration that results ($4s^2 4p^6 4d^{10}$), with 18 electrons in the highest occupied energy level and all of the orbitals filled, is relatively favorable. Such a configuration is known as a pseudo noble-gas electron configuration. Other elements that behave similarly to silver are found at the right of the transition metal block of the periodic table. A copper atom loses its lone $4s$ electron to form a copper ion (Cu^+) with a pseudo noble-gas electron configuration as illustrated below.

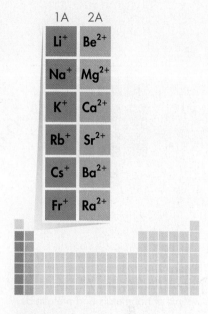

Figure 7.3
Group 1A and 2A Cations
Cations of Group 1A elements have a charge of 1+. Cations of Group 2A elements have a charge of 2+.

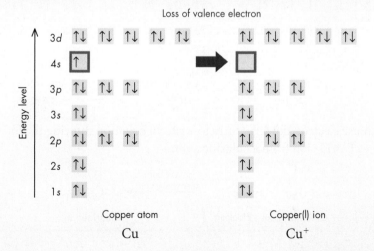

Loss of valence electron

Copper atom
Cu

Copper(I) ion
Cu^+

Cations of gold (Au^+), cadmium (Cd^{2+}), and mercury (Hg^{2+}) also have pseudo noble-gas electron configurations.

Formation of Anions

🔑 How are anions formed?

An anion is an atom or group of atoms with a negative charge. 🔑 **An anion is produced when an atom gains one or more valence electrons.** Note that the name of an anion of a nonmetallic element is *not* the same as the element name. The name of the anion typically ends in *-ide*. Thus, a chlorine atom (Cl) forms a chloride anion (Cl^-), and an oxygen atom (O) forms an oxide anion (O^{2-}). Figure 7.4 shows the symbols of the anions formed by some elements in Groups 5A, 6A, and 7A.

Atoms of nonmetallic elements attain noble-gas electron configurations more easily by gaining electrons than by losing them because these atoms have relatively full valence shells. For example, chlorine belongs to Group 7A (the halogen family). Atoms of chlorine have seven valence electrons. A gain of one electron gives a chlorine atom an octet and converts a chlorine atom into a chloride ion.

$$Cl \quad 1s^2 2s^2 2p^6 3s^2 3p^5 \xrightarrow{+e^-} Cl^- \quad 1s^2 2s^2 2p^6 \underbrace{3s^2 3p^6}_{octet}$$

The chloride ion has a single negative charge. Notice that the electron configuration of the chloride ion ($1s^2 2s^2 2p^6 3s^2 3p^6$) is the same as that of an argon atom.

$$Ar \quad 1s^2 2s^2 2p^6 \underbrace{3s^2 3p^6}_{octet}$$

Chlorine atoms, therefore, need one more valence electron to achieve the electron configuration of the nearest noble gas. The diagrams below illustrate how both the chloride ion and the argon atom have an octet of electrons in their highest occupied energy levels.

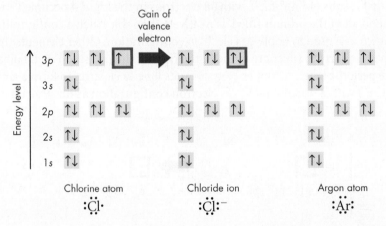

You can use electron dot structures to write an equation showing the formation of a chloride ion from a chlorine atom.

Figure 7.4
Group 5A, 6A, and 7A Anions
Atoms of nonmetals and metalloids form anions by gaining enough valence electrons to attain the electron configuration of the nearest noble gas.

Interpret Diagrams *To which group of the periodic table do the elements bromine and iodine belong?*

Q: *Fool's gold is composed of iron(II) cations (Fe^{2+}) and disulfide anions (S_2^{2-}). Write the electron configuration of the Fe^{2+} ion.*

The ions produced when atoms of chlorine and other halogens gain electrons are called **halide ions.** All halogen atoms have seven valence electrons and need to gain only one electron to achieve the electron configuration of a noble gas. Thus, all halide ions (F^-, Cl^-, Br^-, and I^-) have a charge of $1-$. The seawater in Figure 7.5 contains many different ions, but the anions are mostly chloride ions.

Oxygen is in Group 6A, and an oxygen atom has six valence electrons. An oxygen atom attains the electron configuration of neon by gaining two electrons, as shown in the diagrams below.

Gain of
two valence
electrons

Energy level						
2p	↑↓ ↑ ↑	→	↑↓ ↑↓ ↑↓		↑↓ ↑↓ ↑↓	
2s	↑↓		↑↓		↑↓	
1s	↑↓		↑↓		↑↓	

Oxygen atom   Oxide ion   Neon atom
:Ö·   :Ö:²⁻   :Ne:

The resulting oxide anion (O^{2-}) has a charge of $2-$. You can write the equation for the formation of oxide anions by using electron dot structures.

$$:\ddot{O}· + 2e^- \longrightarrow :\ddot{O}:^{2-}$$

Table 7.2 lists some common anions that you will be learning about in this book.

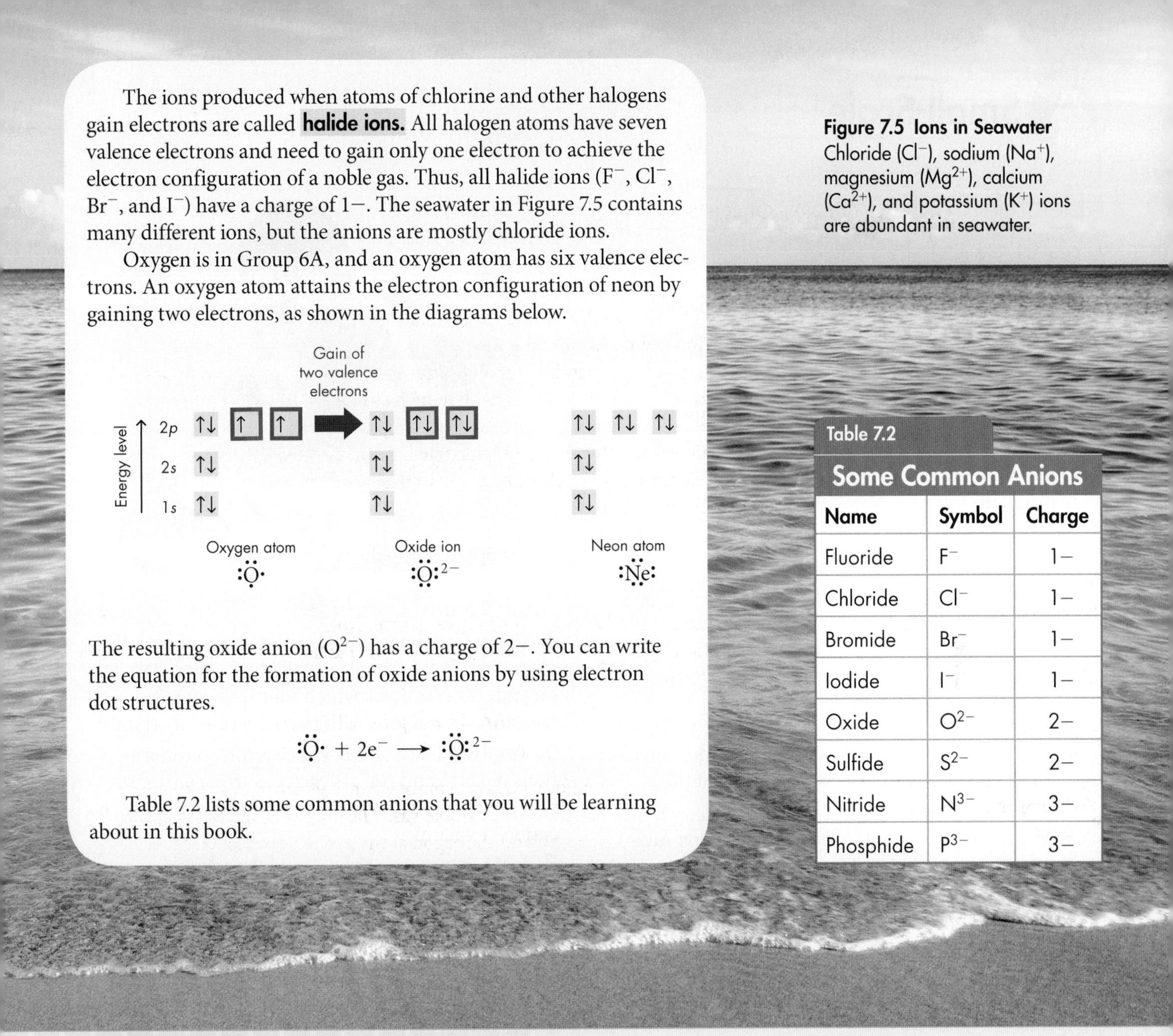

Figure 7.5 Ions in Seawater
Chloride (Cl^-), sodium (Na^+), magnesium (Mg^{2+}), calcium (Ca^{2+}), and potassium (K^+) ions are abundant in seawater.

Table 7.2

Some Common Anions

Name	Symbol	Charge
Fluoride	F^-	$1-$
Chloride	Cl^-	$1-$
Bromide	Br^-	$1-$
Iodide	I^-	$1-$
Oxide	O^{2-}	$2-$
Sulfide	S^{2-}	$2-$
Nitride	N^{3-}	$3-$
Phosphide	P^{3-}	$3-$

7.1 LessonCheck

1. **Explain** How can you determine the number of valence electrons in an atom of a representative element?

2. **Describe** How do cations form?

3. **Describe** How do anions form?

4. **Make Generalizations** Atoms of which elements tend to gain electrons? Atoms of which elements tend to lose electrons?

5. **Apply Concepts** How many valence electrons are in each atom?
   a. potassium
   c. magnesium
   b. carbon
   d. oxygen

6. **Use Models** Draw the electron dot structure for each element in Question 5.

7. **Apply Concepts** How many electrons will each element gain or lose in forming an ion?
   a. calcium
   c. aluminum
   b. fluorine
   d. oxygen

8. **Infer** Identify the charge of the ion formed when
   a. a potassium atom loses one electron.
   b. a zinc atom loses two electrons.
   c. a fluorine atom gains one electron.

9. **Describe** Write the electron configuration of Cd^{2+}.

Small-Scale Lab

Electron Configurations of Ions

Purpose
To relate the presence of color in an ionic solution as a characteristic of electron configurations

Materials
- reaction surface
- micropipettes or droppers
- chemicals shown in the grid below
- sodium hydroxide (NaOH) solution

Procedure

1. On separate sheets of paper, draw two grids similar to the one below. Make each square 2 cm on each side.

2. Place a reaction surface over one of the grids, and add one drop of each solution in the indicated places. Record the color of each solution on the other grid.

3. A precipitate is a solid that separates upon mixing solutions. Predict which of the metal cations will form colored precipitates upon the addition of NaOH. Add one drop of NaOH to find out. Record your results.

NaCl	MgSO$_4$	AlCl$_3$
FeCl$_3$	CaCl$_2$	NiSO$_4$
CuSO$_4$	ZnCl$_2$	AgNO$_3$

Analyze and Conclude

1. Draw Conclusions Transition-metal ions with partially filled *d* orbitals usually have color. Based on your observations, which solutions contain transition-metal ions with partially filled *d* orbitals?

2. Analyze Data Write the electron configurations of Cu^{2+} and Ag$^+$. Is each electron configuration consistent with the color you observed for each cation? Explain.

3. Infer What does the color of the solution containing Zn^{2+} ions suggest about its electron configuration? Write the electron configuration of Zn^{2+}.

4. Predict Which of the following transition-metal ions do you think have color: Cr^{3+}, Cd^{2+}, Hg^{2+}, V^{2+}? Explain your answers.

5. Draw Conclusions Do the colored precipitates all contain transition-metal ions with partially filled *d* orbitals?

You're the Chemist

1. Design an Experiment Predict which of the metal cations in this experiment will form colored precipitates upon the addition of sodium carbonate (Na$_2$CO$_3$). Design an experiment to find out.

2. Design an Experiment Design and carry out an experiment to find out which metal ions form precipitates with sodium phosphate (Na$_3$PO$_4$). What color are the precipitates?

7.2 Ionic Bonds and Ionic Compounds

CHEMISTRY & YOU

Q: *Where does table salt come from?* Sodium chloride, or table salt, has been used by people for centuries to add flavor to food and for preserving food. In some countries, salt is obtained by the evaporation of seawater. In other countries, salt is mined from rock deposits deep underground. In this lesson, you will learn how cations and anions combine to form stable compounds such as sodium chloride.

Key Questions

🔑 What is the electrical charge of an ionic compound?

🔑 What are three properties of ionic compounds?

Vocabulary

• ionic compound
• ionic bond
• chemical formula
• formula unit
• coordination number

Formation of Ionic Compounds

🔑 **What is the electrical charge of an ionic compound?**

Sodium chloride, or table salt, is an ionic compound consisting of sodium cations and chloride anions. An **ionic compound** is a compound composed of cations and anions. 🔑 **Although they are composed of ions, ionic compounds are electrically neutral.** The total positive charge of the cations equals the total negative charge of the anions.

Ionic Bonds Anions and cations have opposite charges and attract one another by means of electrostatic forces. The electrostatic forces that hold ions together in ionic compounds are called **ionic bonds.**

Sodium chloride provides a simple example of how ionic bonds are formed. Consider the reaction between a sodium atom and a chlorine atom. The sodium atom has a single valence electron that it can easily lose. (If the sodium atom loses its valence electron, it achieves the stable electron configuration of neon.) The chlorine atom has seven valence electrons and can easily gain one electron. (If the chlorine atom gains a valence electron, it achieves the stable electron configuration of argon.) When sodium and chlorine react to form a compound, the sodium atom transfers its one valence electron to the chlorine atom. Thus, sodium and chlorine atoms combine in a one-to-one ratio, and both ions have stable octets.

$$Na\cdot \qquad \cdot \ddot{\underset{..}{C}l}: \longrightarrow Na^+ \qquad :\ddot{\underset{..}{C}l}:^-$$

$$1s^22s^22p^6\underbrace{(3s^1)} \qquad 1s^22s^22p^63s^23p^5 \qquad 1s^2\underbrace{2s^22p^6}_{octet} \qquad 1s^22s^22p^6\underbrace{3s^23p^6}_{octet}$$

$$Ne \qquad\qquad Ar$$

$$1s^2\underbrace{2s^22p^6}_{octet} \qquad 1s^22s^22p^6\underbrace{3s^23p^6}_{octet}$$

Ionic and Metallic Bonding **201**

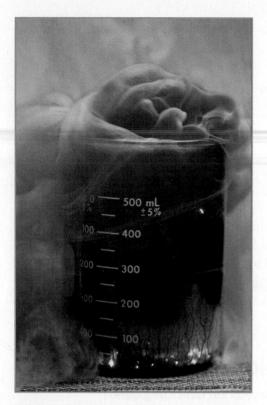

Figure 7.6 Formation of Aluminum Bromide
Aluminum metal and the nonmetal bromine react violently to form the ionic solid aluminum bromide.

Figure 7.6 shows the reaction of aluminum (Al) and bromine (Br_2) to form the ionic compound aluminum bromide ($AlBr_3$). Each aluminum atom has three valence electrons to lose. Each bromine atom has seven valence electrons and readily gains one additional electron. Therefore, when aluminum and bromine react, three bromine atoms combine with each aluminum atom.

Formula Units The ionic compound sodium chloride is composed of equal numbers of sodium cations (Na^+) and chloride anions (Cl^-). Chemists represent the composition of substances by writing chemical formulas. A **chemical formula** shows the numbers of atoms of each element in the smallest representative unit of a substance. For example, NaCl is the chemical formula for sodium chloride.

Note that the formula NaCl does not represent a single physical unit. As shown in Figure 7.7, the ions in solid sodium chloride are arranged in an orderly pattern. Ionic compounds do not exist as single discrete units, but as collections of positively and negatively charged ions arranged in repeating patterns. Therefore, the chemical formula of an ionic compound refers to a ratio known as a formula unit. A **formula unit** is the lowest whole-number ratio of ions in an ionic compound. For sodium chloride, the lowest whole-number ratio of the ions is 1:1 (one Na^+ ion to each Cl^- ion). Thus, the formula unit for sodium chloride is NaCl. Although ionic charges are used to derive the correct formula, they are not shown when you write the formula unit of the compound.

The ionic compound magnesium chloride contains magnesium cations (Mg^{2+}) and chloride anions (Cl^-). In magnesium chloride, the ratio of magnesium cations to chloride anions is 1:2 (one Mg^{2+} ion to two Cl^- ions). Therefore, the formula unit for magnesium chloride is $MgCl_2$. The compound has twice as many chloride anions (each with a 1− charge) as magnesium cations (each with a 2+ charge), so it is electrically neutral. In aluminum bromide, the ratio of aluminum cations to bromide anions is 1:3 (one Al^{3+} ion to three Br^- ions), so the formula unit is $AlBr_3$. Again, the compound is electrically neutral.

Figure 7.7 Formation of Sodium Chloride
Sodium cations and chloride anions form a repeating three-dimensional array in sodium chloride (NaCl).
Infer *How does the arrangement of ions in a sodium chloride crystal help explain why the compound is so stable?*

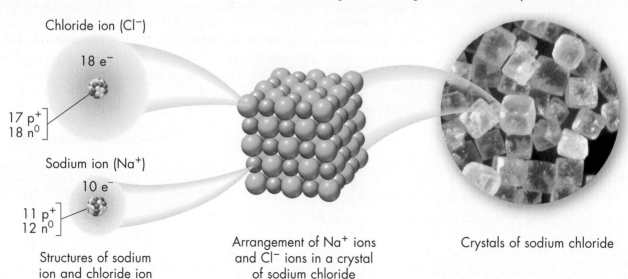

Chloride ion (Cl^-)

18 e^-

17 p^+
18 n^0

Sodium ion (Na^+)

10 e^-

11 p^+
12 n^0

Structures of sodium ion and chloride ion

Arrangement of Na^+ ions and Cl^- ions in a crystal of sodium chloride

Crystals of sodium chloride

Sample Problem 7.1

Predicting Formulas of Ionic Compounds

Use electron dot structures to predict the formulas of the ionic compounds formed from the following elements:
a. potassium and oxygen
b. magnesium and nitrogen

❶ **Analyze Identify the relevant concepts.** Atoms of metals lose valence electrons when forming an ionic compound. Atoms of nonmetals gain electrons. Enough atoms of each element must be used in the formula so that electrons lost equals electrons gained.

❷ **Solve Apply the concepts to this problem.**

Start with the atoms.	**a.** $K\cdot$ and $\cdot\ddot{O}\!:$
In order to have a completely filled valence shell, the oxygen atom must gain two electrons. These electrons come from two potassium atoms, each of which loses one electron.	$\begin{array}{c} K\cdot \\ \\ K\cdot \end{array} + \cdot\ddot{O}\!: \longrightarrow \begin{array}{c} K^{+} \\ \\ K^{+} \end{array} :\!\ddot{O}\!:^{2-}$
Express the electron dot structure as a formula.	The formula of the compound formed is K_2O (potassium oxide).
Start with the atoms.	**b.** $\dot{M}g$ and $\cdot\dot{N}\!:$
Each nitrogen atom needs three electrons to have an octet, but each magnesium atom can lose only two electrons. Three magnesium atoms are needed for every two nitrogen atoms.	$\begin{array}{c} \dot{M}g \\ \\ \dot{M}g \\ \\ \dot{M}g \end{array} + \begin{array}{c} \cdot\dot{N}\!: \\ \\ \cdot\dot{N}\!: \end{array} \longrightarrow \begin{array}{c} Mg^{2+} \\ \\ Mg^{2+} \\ \\ Mg^{2+} \end{array} \begin{array}{c} :\!\ddot{N}\!:^{3-} \\ \\ :\!\ddot{N}\!:^{3-} \end{array}$
Express the electron dot structure as a formula.	The formula of the compound formed is Mg_3N_2 (magnesium nitride).

Apply the octet rule to determine how many electrons each atom gains or loses.

10. Use electron dot structures to determine formulas of the ionic compounds formed when
   a. potassium reacts with iodine.
   b. aluminum reacts with oxygen.

11. What is the formula of the ionic compound composed of calcium cations and chloride anions?

Properties of Ionic Compounds

What are three properties of ionic compounds?

Figure 7.8 shows the striking beauty of the crystals of some ionic compounds. **Most ionic compounds are crystalline solids at room temperature.** The component ions in such crystals are arranged in repeating three-dimensional patterns. In solid sodium chloride, each sodium ion is surrounded by six chloride ions, and each chloride ion is surrounded by six sodium ions. In this arrangement, each ion is attracted strongly to each of its neighbors, and repulsions are minimized. The large attractive forces result in a very stable structure. This stability is reflected in the fact that NaCl has a melting point of about 800°C. **Ionic compounds generally have high melting points.**

Figure 7.8 Crystalline Solids
The beauty of crystalline solids, such as these, comes from the orderly arrangement of their component ions.

Go online to learn about properties of ionic compounds.

Fluorite (CaF_2)

Grossularite ($Ca_3Al_2(SiO_4)_3$)

Aragonite ($CaCO_3$)

Barite ($BaSO_4$)

Wulfenite ($PbMoO_4$)

Beryl ($Be_3Al_2(SiO_3)_6$)

Hematite (Fe_2O_3)

Cinnabar (HgS)

The **coordination number** of an ion is the number of ions of opposite charge that surround the ion in a crystal. Figure 7.9a shows the three-dimensional arrangement of ions in NaCl. The coordination number of Na^+ is 6 because each Na^+ ion is surrounded by six Cl^- ions. The coordination number of Cl^- is also 6 because each Cl^- ion is surrounded by six Na^+ ions. Cesium chloride (CsCl) has a formula unit that is similar to that of NaCl. As Figure 7.9b illustrates, both compounds have cubic crystals, but their internal crystal structures are different. Each Cs^+ ion is surrounded by eight Cl^- ions, and each Cl^- ion is surrounded by eight Cs^+ ions. Therefore, each anion and each cation in cesium chloride has a coordination number of 8.

Figure 7.10 shows the crystalline form of titanium dioxide (TiO_2), also known as rutile. In this compound, the coordination number for the cation (Ti^{4+}) is 6. Each Ti^{4+} ion is surrounded by six O^{2-} ions. The coordination number of the anion (O^{2-}) is 3. Each O^{2-} ion is surrounded by three Ti^{4+} ions.

See crystal structures of ionic compounds *online.*

KINETIC ART

Figure 7.9
Coordination Numbers
Sodium chloride and cesium chloride form cubic crystals.
a. In NaCl, each ion has a coordination number of 6.
b. In CsCl, each ion has a coordination number of 8.

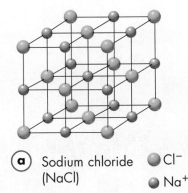

(a) Sodium chloride (NaCl)   ● Cl^- ● Na^+

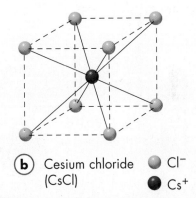

(b) Cesium chloride (CsCl)   ● Cl^- ● Cs^+

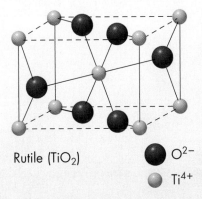

Figure 7.10 Rutile
Titanium dioxide, or rutile, forms tetragonal crystals. In TiO_2, each Ti^{4+} ion has a coordination number of 6, while each O^{2-} ion has a coordination number of 3.

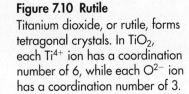

Rutile (TiO_2)   ● O^{2-} ● Ti^{4+}

Another characteristic property of ionic compounds relates to conductivity. 🔑 **Ionic compounds can conduct an electric current when melted or dissolved in water.** When sodium chloride is melted, the orderly crystal structure breaks down. As Figure 7.11a shows, if a voltage is applied across this molten mass, cations migrate freely to one electrode and anions migrate to the other. This movement of ions allows electric current to flow between the electrodes through an external wire. For a similar reason, ionic compounds also conduct electric current if they are dissolved in water. When dissolved, the ions are free to move about in the solution.

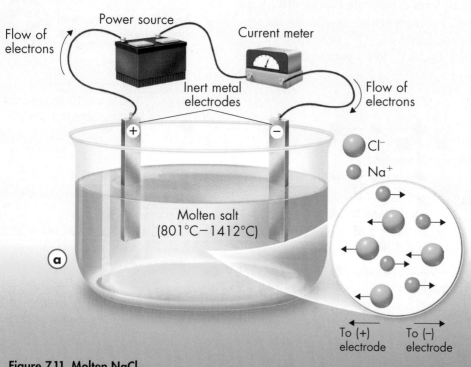

Flow of electrons

Power source

Current meter

Inert metal electrodes

Flow of electrons

+

−

Molten salt (801°C−1412°C)

Cl⁻

Na⁺

a

To (+) electrode

To (−) electrode

Figure 7.11 Molten NaCl
Sodium chloride melts at about 800°C. **a.** If a voltage is applied to molten NaCl, positive sodium ions move to the negative electrode, and negative chloride ions move to the positive electrode. **b.** This solar facility uses molten NaCl for its ability to absorb and hold a large quantity of heat, which is used to generate electricity.

b

Quick Lab

Purpose To show that ions in solution conduct an electric current

Materials

- 3 D-cell batteries
- masking tape
- 2 30-cm lengths of bell wire with ends scraped bare
- clear plastic cup
- distilled water
- tap water
- vinegar (acetic acid, $C_2H_4O_2$)
- table sugar (sucrose, $C_{12}H_{22}O_{11}$)
- table salt (sodium chloride, NaCl)
- baking soda (sodium hydrogen carbonate, $NaHCO_3$)

Solutions Containing Ions

Procedure

1. Tape the batteries together so the positive end of one touches the negative end of another. Tape the bare end of one wire to the positive terminal of the battery assembly and the bare end of the other wire to the negative terminal. **CAUTION** *Bare wire ends can be sharp and scratch skin. Handle with care.*

2. Half fill the cup with distilled water. Hold the bare ends of the wires close together in the water.

3. Look for the production of bubbles. They are a sign that the solution conducts electric current.

4. Repeat Steps 2 and 3 with tap water, vinegar, and concentrated solutions of table sugar, table salt, and baking soda.

Analyze and Conclude

1. Observe Which samples produced bubbles of gas? Which samples did not produce bubbles of gas?

2. Draw Conclusions Which samples conducted an electric current? What do these samples have in common?

3. Predict Would you expect the same results if you used only one battery? If you used six batteries? Explain your answers.

7.2 LessonCheck

12. Describe How can you describe the electrical charge of an ionic compound?

13. Identify What properties characterize ionic compounds?

14. Apply Concepts Write the correct chemical formula for the compounds formed from each pair of elements.
   a. potassium and sulfur
   b. calcium and oxygen
   c. sodium and oxygen
   d. aluminum and nitrogen

15. Describe Write formulas for each compound.
   a. barium chloride
   b. magnesium oxide
   c. lithium oxide
   d. calcium fluoride

16. Describe How can you describe the arrangement of sodium ions and chloride ions in a crystal of sodium chloride?

17. Relate Cause and Effect Why do ionic compounds conduct electric current when they are melted or dissolved in water?

18. Apply Concepts Read about restoring electrolytes on page R4 of the Elements Handbook. Write electron configurations for the two principal ions found in body fluids.

BIGIDEA BONDING AND INTERACTIONS

19. Which pairs of elements are likely to form ionic compounds? Explain your choices and write the formulas for the compounds that will form.
   a. Cl, Br   **c.** Li, Cl
   b. K, He   **d.** I, Na

Ionic Crystals

What ionic crystal is essential to human life, was found among the funeral offerings of ancient Egyptians, created and destroyed empires, and is now commonly used to season foods? If you said table salt, you'd be right! Table salt, or sodium chloride (NaCl) is an ionic compound composed of sodium cations (Na^+) and chloride anions (Cl^-).

Crystals of ionic compounds, such as sodium chloride, can be grown by a process called nucleation. During nucleation, the ionic compound that is to be crystallized is dissolved in a solvent, such as water. In the dissolution process, the positive and negative ions break away from each other. As the solvent is removed, the ions join together again to form a repeating three-dimensional pattern. Sodium chloride has a cubic crystal structure, but different ionic compounds form crystals with different shapes. Try the On Your Own activity at home and compare the shapes of two different ionic crystals.

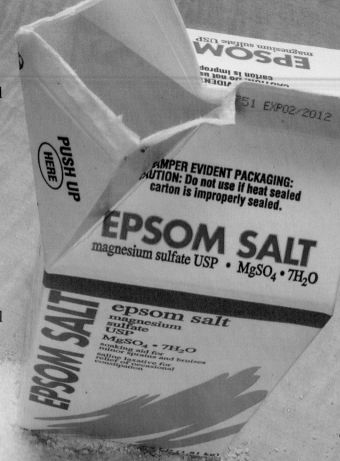

On Your Own

1. For this activity you will need **sea salt, Epsom salts, hot tap water, 2 pie plates, a measuring cup, and a stirring rod or spoon.** Epsom salts can be found in the medicine department of most grocery stores.

2. Mix together 1/4 cup of the sea salt and 1/4 cup of hot water in one of the pie plates. Stir to dissolve most of the salt. In the other pie plate, mix together 1/4 cup of the Epsom salts and 1/4 of hot water. Again, stir until most of the salt has dissolved.

3. Place both pie plates in the refrigerator for three hours. Once the crystals have formed, compare the shapes of the crystals made from the two substances. Record your observations.

Think About It

1. Compare and Contrast Describe the shapes of the crystals of sea salt and Epsom salts. How are they the same? How are they different?

2. Identify Epsom salts are magnesium sulfate ($MgSO_4$) crystals. A magnesium sulfate formula unit consists of a magnesium cation and a sulfate (SO_4^{2-}) anion. What is the charge on the magnesium cation?

3. Control Variables What factors do you think affect crystal growth? Identify two possible factors, then repeat the activity to test your hypotheses.

7.3 Bonding in Metals

CHEMISTRY & YOU

Q: *What are some properties that are unique to metals?* You have probably seen decorative fences, railings, or weather vanes made of a metal called wrought iron. Wrought iron is a very pure form of iron that contains trace amounts of carbon. It is a tough, malleable, ductile, and corrosion-resistant material that melts at a very high temperature. These properties derive from the way that metal ions form bonds with one another.

Metallic Bonds and Metallic Properties

🔑 *How can you model the valence electrons of metal atoms?*

Metals consist of closely packed cations and loosely held valence electrons rather than neutral atoms. 🔑 **The valence electrons of atoms in a pure metal can be modeled as a sea of electrons.** That is, the valence electrons are mobile and can drift freely from one part of the metal to another. **Metallic bonds** are the forces of attraction between the free-floating valence electrons and the positively charged metal ions. These bonds hold metals together.

Properties of Metals The sea-of-electrons model explains many physical properties of metals. Metals are good conductors of electric current because electrons can flow freely in the metal. As electrons enter one end of a bar of metal, an equal number of electrons leaves the other end. Metals are ductile—that is, they can be drawn into wires, as shown in Figure 7.12. Metals are also malleable, which means that they can be hammered or pressed into shapes.

Key Questions

🔑 **How can you model the valence electrons of metal atoms?**

🔑 **Why are alloys important?**

Vocabulary

- metallic bond
- alloy

Figure 7.12 Comparing Metals and Ionic Compounds
A metal rod can be forced through a narrow opening to produce wire. **a.** As this occurs, the metal changes shape but remains in one piece. **b.** If an ionic crystal were forced through the opening, it would shatter. **Interpret Diagrams** *What causes the ionic crystal to break apart?*

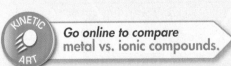
Go online to compare metal vs. ionic compounds.

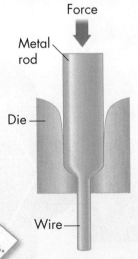

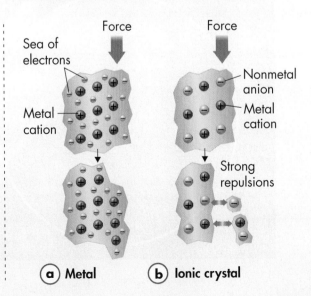

a Metal   **b** Ionic crystal

Both the ductility and malleability of metals can be explained in terms of the mobility of valence electrons. A sea of drifting valence electrons insulates the metal cations from one another. When a metal is subjected to pressure, the metal cations easily slide past one another like ball bearings immersed in oil. In contrast, if an ionic crystal is struck with a hammer, the blow tends to push the positive ions close together. The positive ions repel one another, and the crystal shatters.

CHEMISTRY & YOU

Q: *How are metals and ionic compounds different? How are they similar?*

Crystalline Structure of Metals The next time you visit a grocery store, take a look at how the apples or oranges are stacked. More than likely, they will have a close-packed arrangement, as shown in Figure 7.13. This arrangement helps save space while allowing as many oranges as possible to be stacked up high.

Similar close-packed arrangements can be found in the crystalline structures of metals. You may be surprised to learn that metals are crystalline. In fact, metals that contain just one kind of atom are among the simplest forms of all crystalline solids. Metal atoms are arranged in very compact and orderly patterns. For spheres of identical size, such as metal atoms, several closely packed arrangements are possible. Figure 7.14 on the following page shows three such arrangements: body-centered cubic, face-centered cubic, and hexagonal close-packed.

In a body-centered cubic structure, every atom (except those on the surface) has eight neighbors. The metallic elements sodium, potassium, iron, chromium, and tungsten crystallize in a body-centered cubic pattern. In a face-centered cubic arrangement, every atom has twelve neighbors. Among the metals that form a face-centered cubic structure are copper, silver, gold, aluminum, and lead. In a hexagonal close-packed arrangement, every atom also has twelve neighbors. However, because of its hexagonal shape, the pattern is different from the face-centered cubic arrangement. Metals that have a hexagonal close-packed crystal structure include magnesium, zinc, and cadmium.

Figure 7.13
Hexagonal Close Packing
These Thai oranges illustrate a pattern called a hexagonal close-packed arrangement. The same pattern is found in the crystal structures of some metals.

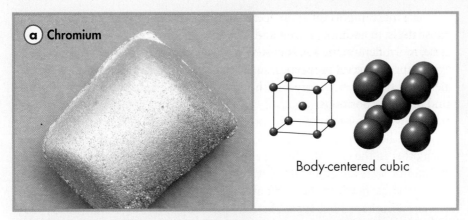

(a) Chromium

Body-centered cubic

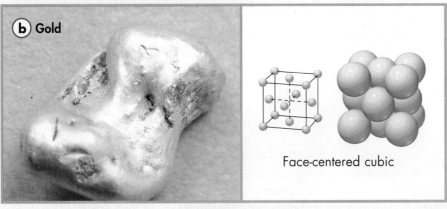

(b) Gold

Face-centered cubic

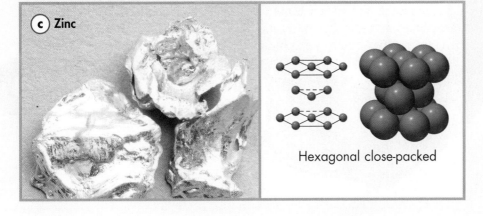

(c) Zinc

Hexagonal close-packed

Figure 7.14 Crystalline Structures of Metals
Metal atoms crystallize in characteristic patterns.
a. Chromium atoms have a body-centered cubic arrangement.
b. Gold atoms have a face-centered cubic arrangement.
c. Zinc atoms have a hexagonal close-packed arrangement.
Interpret Diagrams *Which of these arrangements is the most closely packed?*

Alloys

Why are alloys important?

Every day you use metallic items, such as utensils. However, very few of these objects are made out of a single kind of metal. Instead, most of the metals you encounter are alloys. **Alloys** are mixtures of two or more elements, at least one of which is a metal. Brass, for example, is an alloy of copper and zinc. **Alloys are important because their properties are often superior to those of their component elements.** Sterling silver (92.5 percent silver and 7.5 percent copper) is harder and more durable than pure silver, yet is still soft enough to be made into jewelry and tableware. Bronze is an alloy generally containing seven parts copper to one part tin. Bronze is harder than copper and is easier to cast into molds. Nonferrous (non-iron) alloys, such as bronze, copper-nickel, and aluminum alloys, are commonly used to make coins.

The most important alloys today are steels. The principal elements in most steels, in addition to iron and carbon, are boron, chromium, manganese, molybdenum, nickel, tungsten, and vanadium. As a result, steels have a wide range of useful properties, such as corrosion resistance, ductility, hardness, and toughness. Figure 7.15 shows some items made of common alloys and their compositions.

Alloys can form from their component atoms in different ways. If the atoms of the components in an alloy are about the same size, they can replace each other in the crystal. This type of alloy is called a substitutional alloy. If the atomic sizes are quite different, the smaller atoms can fit into the interstices (spaces) between the larger atoms. Such an alloy is called an interstitial alloy. In the various types of steel, for example, carbon atoms occupy the spaces between the iron atoms. Thus, steels are interstitial alloys.

Figure 7.15 Common Alloys
Alloys are composed of two or more elements. The compositions (by mass) of sterling silver, cast iron, and stainless steel are shown.

Stainless Steel
80.6% Fe
18.0% Cr
0.4% C
1.0% Ni

Sterling Silver
92.5% Ag
7.5% Cu

Cast Iron
96% Fe
4% C

7.3 LessonCheck

20. 🔑 **Describe** How do chemists model the valence electrons of metal atoms?

21. 🔑 **Explain** Why are alloys more useful than pure metals?

22. Explain What is meant by the terms *ductile* and *malleable*?

23. Relate Cause and Effect Why is it possible to bend metals but not ionic crystals?

24. Use Analogies How is the arrangement of fruit in a stack of oranges similar to the way some metal atoms are arranged in metallic crystals?

25. Describe Name two widely used alloys and describe some of their uses.

BIGIDEA BONDING AND INTERACTIONS

26. Describe how the sea-of-electrons model is used to explain the physical properties of metals.

7 **Study** Guide

BIGIDEA
BONDING AND INTERACTIONS

Atoms form positive ions (cations) by losing valence electrons and form negative ions (anions) by gaining valence electrons. The electrostatic forces between the oppositely charged ions hold the cations and anions together in an ionic compound. Ionic compounds generally have high melting points and can conduct an electric current in solution and in the molten state. Metals are made up of closely packed cations surrounded by a sea of electrons. The sea-of-electrons model explains why metals are good conductors of electric current and why they are ductile and malleable.

7.1 Ions

🔑 To find the number of valence electrons in an atom of a representative element, simply look at its group number.

🔑 A positively charged ion, or a cation, is produced when an atom loses one or more valence electrons.

🔑 An anion is produced when an atom gains one or more valence electrons.

- valence electron (194)
- electron dot structure (195)
- octet rule (195)
- halide ion (199)

7.2 Ionic Bonds and Ionic Compounds

🔑 Although they are composed of ions, ionic compounds are electrically neutral.

🔑 Most ionic compounds are crystalline solids at room temperature.

🔑 Ionic compounds generally have high melting points.

🔑 Ionic compounds can conduct an electric current when melted or dissolved in water.

- ionic compound (201)
- ionic bond (201)
- chemical formula (202)
- formula unit (202)
- coordination number (205)

7.3 Bonding in Metals

🔑 The valence electrons of atoms in a pure metal can be modeled as a sea of electrons.

🔑 Alloys are important because their properties are often superior to those of their component elements.

- metallic bond (209)
- alloy (211)

7 Assessment

Lesson by Lesson

7.1 Ions

27. What is a valence electron?

★28. To which group in the periodic table does each of the following elements belong? How many valence electrons do atoms of each element have?

   a. nitrogen   **d.** barium
   b. lithium   **e.** bromine
   c. phosphorus   **f.** carbon

29. Write electron dot structures for each of the following elements:

   a. Cl   **c.** Al
   b. S   **d.** Li

30. Describe two ways that an ion forms from an atom.

★31. How many electrons must an atom of each element lose to attain a noble-gas electron configuration?

   a. Ca   **c.** Li
   b. Al   **d.** Ba

32. Write the symbol for the ion formed when each of the following elements loses its valence electrons.

   a. aluminum   **d.** potassium
   b. lithium   **e.** calcium
   c. barium   **f.** strontium

33. Why do nonmetal atoms tend to form anions when they react to form compounds?

★34. How many electrons must be gained by each of the following atoms to achieve a stable electron configuration?

   a. N   **c.** Cl
   b. S   **d.** P

★35. What is the formula of the ions formed when atoms of the following elements gain or lose valence electrons and attain noble-gas configurations?

   a. sulfur   **c.** fluorine
   b. sodium   **d.** phosphorus

36. State the number of electrons either lost or gained in forming each ion.

   a. Br^- **e.** Ca^{2+}
   b. Na^+ **f.** Cu^+
   c. As^{3-} **g.** H^-
   d. Ba^{2+} **h.** Cu^{2+}

37. Name each ion in Problem 36. Identify each as an anion or a cation.

7.2 Ionic Bonds and Ionic Compounds

38. Define an ionic bond.

39. Explain why ionic compounds are electrically neutral.

★40. Which of the following pairs of atoms would you expect to combine chemically to form an ionic compound?

   a. Li and S   **d.** F and Cl
   b. O and S   **e.** I and K
   c. Al and O   **f.** H and N

41. Which of the following pairs of elements will not form ionic compounds?

   a. sulfur and oxygen
   b. sodium and calcium
   c. sodium and sulfur
   d. oxygen and chlorine

42. How can you represent the composition of an ionic compound?

★43. Identify the kinds of ions that form each ionic compound.

   a. calcium fluoride, CaF_2
   b. aluminum bromide, $AlBr_3$
   c. lithium oxide, Li_2O
   d. aluminum sulfide, Al_2S_3
   e. potassium nitride, K_3N

44. Write the formulas for the ions in the following compounds:

   a. KCl   **c.** $MgBr_2$
   b. BaS   **d.** Li_2O

45. Most ionic substances are brittle. Why?

46. Explain why molten $MgCl_2$ does conduct an electric current although crystalline $MgCl_2$ does not.

7.3 Bonding in Metals

★**47.** How can you describe the arrangement of atoms in metals?

48. Explain briefly why metals are good conductors of electric current.

★**49.** Name the three crystal arrangements of closely packed metal atoms. Give an example of a metal that crystallizes in each arrangement.

50. Name some alloys that you have used or seen today.

51. Explain why the properties of all steels are not identical.

Understand Concepts

52. Construct a table that shows the relationship among the group number, valence electrons lost or gained, and the formula of the cation or anion produced for the following metallic and nonmetallic elements: Na, Ca, Al, N, S, Br.

53. Write electron dot structures for the following elements.
- **a.** C
- **b.** Be
- **c.** O
- **d.** F
- **e.** Na
- **f.** P

54. Show the relationship between the electron dot structure of an element and the location of the element in the periodic table.

★**55.** In terms of electrons, why does a cation have a positive charge?

56. Why does an anion have a negative charge?

57. The spheres below represent the relative diameters of atoms or ions. Rearrange the sequences in (a) and (b) so the relative sizes of the particles correspond to the increasing size of the particles as shown in the illustration.

- **a.** oxygen atom, oxide ion, sulfur atom, sulfide ion
- **b.** sodium atom, sodium ion, potassium atom, potassium ion

★**58.** Write the name and symbol of the ion formed when
- **a.** a sulfur atom gains two electrons.
- **b.** an aluminum atom loses three electrons.
- **c.** a nitrogen atom gains three electrons.
- **d.** a calcium atom loses two electrons.

★**59.** Write electron configurations for the 2+ cations of these elements.
- **a.** Fe
- **b.** Co
- **c.** Ni

60. Write electron configurations for the 3+ cations of these elements.
- **a.** chromium
- **b.** manganese
- **c.** iron

61. Write the symbol for the ion formed when each element gains electrons and attains a noble-gas electron configuration.
- **a.** Br
- **b.** H
- **c.** As
- **d.** Se

★**62.** Write electron configurations for the following atoms and ions, and comment on the result.
- **a.** Ar
- **b.** Cl^-
- **c.** S^{2-}
- **d.** P^{3-}

63. Write electron configurations for the following atoms and ions and comment on the result.
- **a.** N^{3-}
- **b.** O^{2-}
- **c.** F^-
- **d.** Ne

64. Name the first four halogens. What group are they in, and how many valence electrons does an atom of each element have?

65. Write complete electron configurations for the following atoms and ions. For each group, comment on the results.
- **a.** Ar, K^+, Ca^{2+}
- **b.** Ne, Na^+, Mg^{2+}, Al^{3+}

66. If ionic compounds are composed of charged particles (ions), why isn't every ionic compound either positively or negatively charged?

★**67.** Which of the following compounds are most likely not ionic?
- **a.** H_2O
- **b.** Na_2O
- **c.** CO_2
- **d.** CaS
- **e.** SO_2
- **f.** NH_3

*68. Write the formulas for each ionic compound that can be made by combining each of pair of ions.
   a. Ba^{2+} and Br^-
   b. Al^{3+} and S^{2-}
   c. K^+ and N^{3-}

69. The atoms of the noble gas elements are stable. Explain.

70. What is the simplest formula for the compounds that can form when each of these ions combine with an oxide (O^{2-}) ion?
   a. Fe^{3+}
   b. Pb^{4+}
   c. Li^+
   d. Mg^{2+}

71. Can you predict the coordination number of an ion from the formula of an ionic compound? Explain.

*72. Metallic cobalt crystallizes in a hexagonal close-packed structure. How many neighbors will a cobalt atom have?

73. Explain how hexagonal close-packed, face-centered cubic, and body-centered cubic unit cells are different from one another.

Body-centered cubic   Face-centered cubic   Hexagonal close-packed

74. The properties of all samples of brass are not identical. Explain.

*75. For each alloy below, list the elements it contains.
   a. brass
   b. sterling silver
   c. bronze
   d. stainless steel

Think Critically

*76. **Make Generalizations** What is the relationship between the number of electrons in the valence shells in an electron configuration diagram for an atom and the number of dots in the corresponding electron dot structure?

77. **Relate Cause and Effect** Why are many elements more stable as ions than they are as atoms?

78. **Make Generalizations** Is it accurate to describe sodium chloride (NaCl) as consisting of individual particles, each made up of one Na^+ cation and one Cl^- anion? Explain your answer.

*79. **Infer** For each ionic formula, identify the A-group number to which element X belongs.
   a. CaX
   b. MgX_2
   c. X_3N
   d. Al_2X_3
   e. XF
   f. XS

80. **Compare** How do the motions of sodium ions and chloride ions in molten sodium chloride differ from the motions of these ions in sodium chloride crystals?

81. **Relate Cause and Effect** Two physical properties of metals are ductility and malleability. Explain these properties based on what you know about the valence electrons of metal atoms.

82. **Interpret Diagrams** How atoms and ions are arranged in crystals is not just dependent on size. The spheres in each atomic window below are identical in size. The windows have exactly the same area. In which window are the spheres more closely packed? Explain your reasoning.

a.
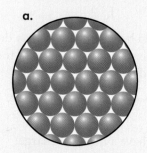

b.
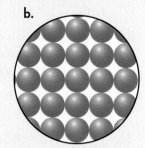

*83. **Compare and Contrast** Describe the similarities and differences between ionic compounds and metals in terms of their physical and chemical characteristics.

84. **Relate Cause and Effect** How does the octet rule explain the large increase in energy between the first and second ionization energies of Group 1A metals?

85. **Infer** An atom of the element M forms a stable ion in an ionic compound with chlorine having the formula MCl_2. In this compound, the ion of element M has a mass number of 66 and has 28 electrons.
   a. What is the identity of the element?
   b. How many neutrons does the ion have?

*86. **Apply Concepts** Classify each element in the following list. Will an atom of each element form a cation or an anion, or is the element chemically nonreactive? For the atoms that do form ions during a chemical reaction, write the number of electrons the atom will gain or lose.

   a. lithium
   b. sodium
   c. neon
   d. chlorine
   e. magnesium

87. **Infer** The chemically similar alkali metal chlorides NaCl and CsCl have different crystal structures, whereas the chemically different NaCl and MnS have the same crystal structures. Why? (*Hint:* Consider periodic and group trends among the properties of the elements.)

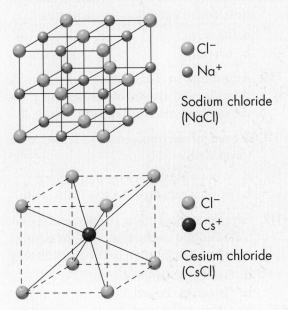

⚪ Cl⁻
🔵 Na⁺

Sodium chloride (NaCl)

⚪ Cl⁻
⚫ Cs⁺

Cesium chloride (CsCl)

88. **Calculate** Silver crystallizes in a face-centered cubic arrangement. A silver atom is at the edge of each lattice point (the corner of the unit cell). The length of the edge of the unit cell is 0.4086 nm. What is the atomic radius of silver?

*89. **Analyze Data** Consider two ionic compounds, NaCl and CaO.

   a. In which compound would you expect the electrostatic forces that hold the compound together to be the strongest? Explain.

   b. The melting point of NaCl is 801°C. The melting point of CaO is 2614°C. Does this data support your prediction? Why or why not?

Write About Science

90. **Compare** Describe the formation of a cation that is an exception to the octet rule. In your description, compare the electron configuration of the cation to the electron configurations of the nearest noble gases.

91. **Research** Go online and research X-ray diffraction crystallography. How are the samples prepared? How are the X-rays generated and detected? How is this technique used to study the structure of crystalline substances?

CHEMYSTERY

It's Not Easy Being Green

The statue of Ludwig van Beethoven in Central Park is made of bronze. Bronze is an alloy containing copper and tin.

When bronze is exposed to the elements, it reacts with water (H_2O), carbon dioxide (CO_2), and oxygen (O_2) in the air to produce a film of copper(II) carbonate ($CuCO_3$). Copper(II) carbonate is an ionic compound that is blue-green in color. A film of copper(II) carbonate on the Beethoven statue gives the statue its green color. The film also protects the metal against further corrosion.

*92. **Apply Concepts** A copper atom can lose one or two electrons to form a Cu^+ ion or a Cu^{2+} ion, respectively. The charge of the copper ion in $CuCO_3$ is 2+. Write the electron configuration of this cation.

93. **Form an Opinion** Why do you think bronze is often used to create statues?

94. **Connect to the BIGIDEA** How are the properties of the copper(II) carbonate film on the statue different from the properties of the bronze beneath the film? Explain how these properties are a result of the type of bonding present.

Cumulative Review

95. How is organic chemistry distinguished from inorganic chemistry?

96. What is the name given to a chemist who studies the composition of matter?

97. Explain two ways to meet modern society's need for energy.

∗98. Classify the following actions as chemical or physical changes.
  a. Cookies are baked.
  b. A firefly emits light.
  c. A figure is carved from wood.
  d. Caramel is made from sugar.

99. Which of the following substances are not homogeneous mixtures?
  a. gold ring
  b. spaghetti sauce
  c. cane sugar
  d. window glass
  e. river water
  f. bottled water

∗100. What physical state(s) can each of the following substances become as you raise its temperature?
  a. silver   **c.** ice
  b. gasoline   **d.** wax

101. Round each measurement to the number of significant figures indicated in parentheses.
  a. 56.55 g (3)   **c.** 1.8072 L (3)
  b. 0.004849 m (2)   **d.** 4.007×10^3 mg (2)

∗102. Which of the following linear measurements is the longest?
  a. 6×10^4 cm   **c.** 0.06 km
  b. 6×10^6 mm   **d.** 6×10^9 nm

103. Helium has a boiling point of 4 K. This is the lowest boiling point of any liquid. Express this temperature in degrees Celsius.

∗104. The density of silicon is 2.33 g/cm³. What is the volume of a piece of silicon that has a mass of 62.9 g?

105. Express the composition of each atom in shorthand form.
  a. zinc-64   **c.** hydrogen-3
  b. chlorine-37   **d.** calcium-40

106. An atom of carbon and an atom of element Z together have a mass of 6 amu less than double the mass of an atom of oxygen. If an atom of oxygen has a mass of 16 amu and the mass of an atom of carbon is 12 amu, what is the mass of an atom of element Z?

107. Determine the number of protons, electrons, and neutrons in each of the three isotopes of oxygen.

∗108. How many orbitals are in the following sublevels?
  a. 4s sublevel   **c.** 3s sublevel
  b. 2p sublevel   **d.** 4d sublevel

109. Give the symbol for each element and write the electron configuration for each atom.
  a. nitrogen   **c.** phosphorus
  b. beryllium   **d.** potassium

110. An atom of an element has 17 electrons. Give the name and symbol of the element and write the complete electron configuration.

∗111. A beam of electromagnetic radiation has a wavelength of 500 nm.
  a. What is this wavelength in meters?
  b. In what region of the spectrum is this?

∗112. Give the symbol of the element and the complete electron configuration of the element found at each location in the periodic table.
  a. Group 1A, Period 4
  b. Group 3A, Period 3
  c. Group 6A, Period 3
  d. Group 2A, Period 6

113. Which subatomic particle plays the most important role in chemistry?

114. Give the name and symbol of two elements that have properties similar to those of potassium.

If You Have Trouble With . . .

Question	95	96	97	98	99	100	101	102	103	104	105	106	107	108	109	110	111	112	113	114
See Chapter	1	1	1	2	2	2	3	3	3	3	4	4	4	5	5	5	5	6	6	6

Standardized Test Prep

Select the choice that best answers each question or completes each statement.

1. Which of these is not an ionic compound?
   (A) KF
   (B) SiO_2
   (C) Na_2SO_4
   (D) Na_2O

2. Which statements are correct when barium and oxygen react to form an ionic compound?

   I. Each barium atom loses 2 electrons and forms a cation.

   II. Oxygen atoms form oxide anions (O^{2-}).

   III. The ions are present in a one-to-one ratio in the compound.

   (A) I and II only
   (B) II and III only
   (C) I and III only
   (D) I, II, and III

The lettered choices below refer to Questions 3–6. A lettered choice may be used once, more than once, or not at all.
   (A) gains two electrons
   (B) loses two electrons
   (C) gains three electrons
   (D) loses one electron
   (E) gains one electron

Which choice describes what likely happens as each of the following elements forms an ion?

3. iodine

4. magnesium

5. cesium

6. phosphorus

7. How many valence electrons does arsenic have?
   (A) 5   (C) 3
   (B) 4   (D) 2

8. Which electron configuration represents a nitride ion?
   (A) $1s^2 2s^2 3s^2 4s^2$ (C) $1s^2 2s^2 2p^3$
   (B) $1s^2 2s^2 2p^6$ (D) $1s^2$

9. When a bromine atom gains an electron
   (A) a bromide ion is formed.
   (B) the ion formed has a 1− charge.
   (C) the ion formed is an anion.
   (D) all the above are correct.

Use the description and the graph to answer Questions 10–12.

Lattice energy is the energy required to change one mole (6.02×10^{23} formula units) of a crystalline, ionic solid to gaseous ions. The graph below shows the lattice energies for ionic compounds formed between selected alkali metals and halogens.

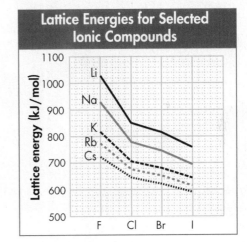

10. For a given alkali metal, what is the trend in lattice energy as the atomic radius of the halogen increases?

11. For a given halogen, what is the trend in lattice energy as the atomic radius of the alkali metal increases?

12. Complete this sentence: "As the atomic radius of either the halogen or the alkali metal increases, the lattice energy _____."

If You Have Trouble With . . .											
Question	1	2	3	4	5	6	7	8	9	10	11	12
See Lesson	7.2	7.2	7.1	7.1	7.1	7.1	7.1	7.1	7.1	7.2	7.2	7.2

8

Covalent Bonding

INSIDE:

PearsonChem.com

Water droplets result from attractions between water molecules.

BIGIDEA

BONDING AND INTERACTIONS

Essential Questions:

1. How is the bonding in molecular compounds different from the bonding in ionic compounds?

2. How do electrons affect the shape of a molecule?

3. What factors affect molecular properties?

CHEMYSTERY

What's That Alarm?

A family woke up in the middle of the night to the sound of a piercing alarm. The family thought it must be the fire alarm. They quickly evacuated the house and called 9-1-1. While they waited for the fire department to arrive, they didn't see smoke or any other signs of fire coming from the house.

The fire department inspected the home and told the family that a compound containing carbon and oxygen atoms caused the alarm. Carbon dioxide (CO_2) is made of carbon and oxygen, but the fire department confirmed that it wasn't carbon dioxide. Are other molecules besides carbon dioxide made of carbon and oxygen? What was this mystery substance, and why would it set off an alarm?

▶ Connect to the **BIG**IDEA As you read about covalent bonding, think about how there could be different molecules made of carbon and oxygen atoms.

NATIONAL SCIENCE EDUCATION STANDARDS

B-2, B-4

8.1 Molecular Compounds

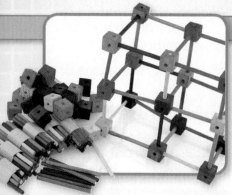

Q: *How are atoms joined together to make compounds with different structures?* This toy model is made from cubes joined together in units by sticks. Although the types of pieces are limited, you can make many different toy models depending on how many pieces you use and how they are arranged. In this lesson, you will learn how atoms are joined together to form units called molecules.

Key Questions

🔑 What information does a molecular formula provide?

🔑 What representative units define molecular compounds and ionic compounds?

Vocabulary

- covalent bond • molecule
- diatomic molecule
- molecular compound
- molecular formula

Figure 8.1
Comparing Gas Particles

Molecules and Molecular Compounds

🔑 **What information does a molecular formula provide?**

In nature, only the noble gas elements, such as helium and neon, exist as uncombined atoms. They are monatomic; that is they consist of single atoms, as shown in Figure 8.1. But not all elements are monatomic. For example, a key component of the air you breathe is oxygen gas, O_2. As you might guess from the chemical formula, O_2 represents two oxygen atoms that are bonded together.

In Chapter 7, you learned about ionic compounds, which are generally crystalline solids with high melting points. Other compounds, however, have very different properties. For example, water (H_2O) is a liquid at room temperature. Carbon dioxide (CO_2) and nitrous oxide (N_2O) are both gases at room temperature. The attractions that hold together the atoms in O_2, H_2O, CO_2, and N_2O cannot be explained by ionic bonding. These bonds do not involve the transfer of electrons.

Helium, which is less dense than air, is often used to inflate balloons.

Scuba divers breathe compressed air, a mixture that contains oxygen gas.

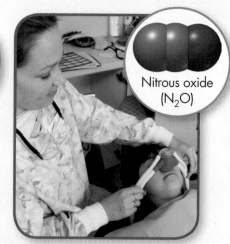

Nitrous oxide (also known as laughing gas) is sometimes used as a mild anesthetic in dental procedures.

Sharing Electrons Recall that ionic bonds form when the combining atoms give up or accept electrons. Another way that atoms can combine is by sharing electrons. Atoms that are held together by sharing electrons are joined by a **covalent bond.** In a covalent bond, a "tug of war" for electrons takes place between the atoms, bonding the atoms together. In Lesson 8.2, you will learn about the different types of covalent bonds.

In Figure 8.1, the representative units shown for oxygen and nitrous oxide are called molecules. A **molecule** is a neutral group of atoms joined together by covalent bonds. Oxygen gas consists of oxygen molecules; each oxygen molecule consists of two covalently bonded oxygen atoms. An oxygen molecule is an example of a **diatomic molecule**—a molecule that contains two atoms. Other elements found in nature in the form of diatomic molecules include hydrogen, nitrogen, and the halogens. Molecules can also be made of atoms of different elements. A compound composed of molecules is called a **molecular compound.** Water is an example of a molecular compound. The molecules in water are all the same; each water molecule is a tightly bound unit of two hydrogen atoms and one oxygen atom.

Representing Molecules A **molecular formula** is the chemical formula of a molecular compound. ▨ **A molecular formula shows how many atoms of each element a substance contains.** The molecular formula of water is H_2O. Notice that a subscript written after an element's symbol indicates the number of atoms of each element in the molecule. If there is only one atom, the subscript 1 is omitted. The molecular formula of carbon dioxide is CO_2. This formula represents a molecule containing one carbon atom and two oxygen atoms.

Butane, shown in Figure 8.2, is also a molecular compound. The molecular formula for butane is C_4H_{10}. According to this formula, one molecule of butane contains four carbon atoms and ten hydrogen atoms. A molecular formula reflects the actual number of atoms in each molecule. The subscripts are not necessarily lowest whole-number ratios. Note that molecular formulas also describe molecules consisting of atoms of one element. For example, an oxygen molecule consists of two oxygen atoms bonded together; its molecular formula is O_2.

A molecular formula does not tell you about a molecule's structure. In other words, it does not show either the arrangement of the various atoms in space or which atoms are covalently bonded to one another. A variety of diagrams and molecular models, some of them illustrated in Figure 8.3, can be used to show the arrangement of atoms in a molecule. Diagrams and models like these will be used throughout this textbook.

Figure 8.2 Butane
Butane (C_4H_{10}) is commonly used in lighters and household torches. The butane torch shown here is being used to caramelize sugar on a dessert.

Figure 8.3 Representations of an Ammonia Molecule
The formula NH_3 tells you the composition of an ammonia molecule, but it does not reveal the arrangement of the atoms. Molecular models and structural formulas specify the bonds between atoms and the arrangement of those atoms.

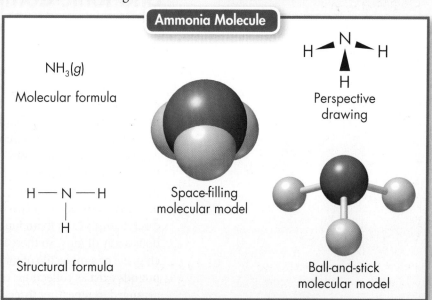

Ammonia Molecule

$NH_3(g)$
Molecular formula

Structural formula

Space-filling molecular model

Perspective drawing

Ball-and-stick molecular model

Figure 8.4
Molecular Formulas and Structures
The formula of a molecular compound indicates the numbers and kinds of atoms in each molecule of the compound.
Use Models *Which of these molecules has the greatest number of oxygen atoms?*

Hydrogen atom (H)

Oxygen atom (O)

Carbon atom (C)

Carbon dioxide (CO_2)
1 molecule of CO_2
contains
2 oxygen atoms
1 carbon atom

Water (H_2O)
1 molecule of H_2O
contains
2 hydrogen atoms
1 oxygen atom

Ethanol (C_2H_6O)
1 molecule of C_2H_6O
contains
6 hydrogen atoms
2 carbon atoms
1 oxygen atom

CHEMISTRY & YOU

Q: *Similar to how you can make different types of toy models, there are thousands of different types of molecular structures. How are atoms joined together to make compounds with different structures?*

Figure 8.4 shows the chemical formulas and structures of some other molecular compounds. The arrangement of the atoms within a molecule is called its molecular structure. Carbon dioxide, for example, is a gas produced by the complete burning of carbon. It is found in Earth's atmosphere and is dissolved in seawater. The molecular structure of carbon dioxide shows how the three atoms are arranged in a row. It also shows how the carbon atom in each molecule is in the middle between the two oxygen atoms. The molecular structure of water shows how the oxygen atom is in the middle between the hydrogen atoms. However, the atoms in water are not arranged in a row. Instead, the hydrogen atoms are mainly on one side of the water molecule. The molecular structure of ethanol (C_2H_6O) is more complicated. As you can see in the model, each carbon is bonded to four atoms, each hydrogen is bonded to one atom, and the one oxygen is bonded to two atoms.

Comparing Molecular and Ionic Compounds

🔑 *What representative units define molecular compounds and ionic compounds?*

You have now seen how formulas can be used to describe molecular compounds and ionic compounds. Each type of compound contains atoms of different elements that are combined chemically. However, the formulas describe different representative units. 🔑 **The representative unit of a molecular compound is a molecule. For an ionic compound, the representative unit is a formula unit.** Recall that a formula unit is the lowest whole-number ratio of ions in an ionic compound. It is important not to confuse formula units with molecules. A molecule is made up of two or more atoms that act as a unit. No such discrete units exist in an ionic compound, which consists of a continuous array of ions. So there is no such thing as a molecule of sodium chloride or a molecule of magnesium chloride. Instead, these compounds exist as collections of positively and negatively charged ions arranged in repeating three-dimensional patterns.

Molecular compounds tend to have relatively lower melting and boiling points than ionic compounds. Many molecular compounds are gases or liquids at room temperature. In contrast to ionic compounds, which are formed from a metal combined with a nonmetal, most molecular compounds are composed of atoms of two or more nonmetals. For example, one atom of carbon can combine with one atom of oxygen to produce one molecule of a compound known as carbon monoxide. Carbon monoxide is a poisonous gas produced by burning gasoline in internal combustion engines or in household gas appliances and furnaces. Figure 8.5 illustrates some differences between molecular and ionic compounds, using water and sodium chloride as examples.

Figure 8.5 Molecular and Ionic Compounds Water, which is a molecular compound, and sodium chloride, which is an ionic compound, are compared here.
Interpret Diagrams *How do molecular compounds differ from ionic compounds?*

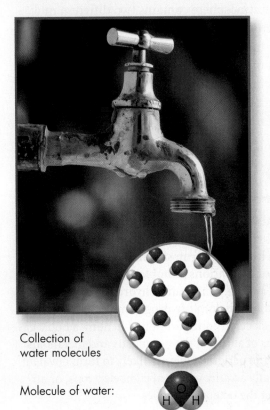

Collection of water molecules

Molecule of water:

Chemical formula: H_2O

Array of sodium ions and chloride ions

Formula unit of sodium chloride: Na^+ Cl^-

Chemical formula: NaCl

8.1 LessonCheck

1. **Identify** What information does a molecular formula provide?

2. **Compare** How is the representative unit of a molecular compound different from the representative unit of an ionic compound?

3. **Identify** What are the only elements that exist in nature as uncombined atoms? What term is used to describe such elements?

4. **Compare and Contrast** Describe how the molecule whose formula is NO is different from the molecule whose formula is N_2O.

5. **Apply Concepts** Give an example of a diatomic molecule found in Earth's atmosphere.

6. **Identify** What information does a molecular structure give?

8.2 The Nature of Covalent Bonding

Q: *What is the difference between the oxygen you breathe and the oxygen in ozone in the atmosphere?* Our atmosphere contains two different molecules that are both made of oxygen atoms. One is the oxygen that our cells need to survive. The other molecule containing only oxygen atoms is the ozone that protects us from the sun but also contributes to smog. The colors in this map indicate the concentrations of ozone in various parts of Earth's atmosphere. In this lesson, you will learn how oxygen atoms can join to form the oxygen you breathe and can also join to form ozone.

Key Questions

▸ What is the result of electron sharing in covalent bonds?

▸ How are coordinate covalent bonds different from other covalent bonds?

▸ What are some exceptions to the octet rule?

▸ How is the strength of a covalent bond related to its bond dissociation energy?

▸ How are resonance structures used?

Vocabulary

- single covalent bond
- structural formula
- unshared pair
- double covalent bond
- triple covalent bond
- coordinate covalent bond
- polyatomic ion
- bond dissociation energy
- resonance structure

The Octet Rule in Covalent Bonding

▸ **What is the result of electron sharing in covalent bonds?**

Recall that when ionic compounds form, electrons tend to be transferred so that each ion acquires a noble gas configuration. A similar rule applies for covalent bonds. ▸ **In covalent bonds, electron sharing usually occurs so that atoms attain the electron configurations of noble gases.** For example, a single hydrogen atom has one electron. But a pair of hydrogen atoms shares electrons to form a covalent bond in a diatomic hydrogen molecule. Each hydrogen atom, thus, attains the electron configuration of helium, a noble gas with two electrons. Combinations of atoms of the nonmetals and metalloids in Groups 4A, 5A, 6A, and 7A of the periodic table are likely to form covalent bonds. The combined atoms usually acquire a total of eight electrons, or an octet, by sharing electrons, so that the octet rule applies.

Single Covalent Bonds The hydrogen atoms in a hydrogen molecule are held together mainly by the attraction of the shared electrons to the positive nuclei. Two atoms held together by sharing one pair of electrons are joined by a **single covalent bond.** Hydrogen gas consists of diatomic molecules whose atoms share only one pair of electrons, forming a single covalent bond.

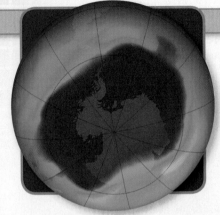

H·   +   ·H   ⟶   H:H   shared pair of electrons

Hydrogen atom   Hydrogen atom   Hydrogen molecule

shared pair of electrons { H ↑ / H ↓ }   1s

Hydrogen molecule

An electron dot structure such as H:H represents the shared pair of electrons of the covalent bond by two dots. The pair of shared electrons forming the covalent bond is also often represented as a dash, as in H—H for hydrogen. A **structural formula** represents the covalent bonds as dashes and shows the arrangement of covalently bonded atoms. In contrast, the molecular formula of hydrogen, H_2, indicates only the number of hydrogen atoms in each molecule.

The halogens also form single covalent bonds in their diatomic molecules. Fluorine is one example. Because a fluorine atom has seven valence electrons, it needs one more to attain the electron configuration of a noble gas. By sharing electrons and forming a single covalent bond, two fluorine atoms each achieve the electron configuration of neon.

See covalent bonding *animated online.*

KINETIC ART

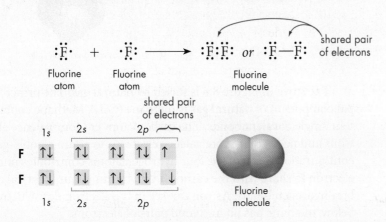

In the F_2 molecule, each fluorine atom contributes one electron to complete the octet. Notice that the two fluorine atoms share only one pair of valence electrons. A pair of valence electrons that is not shared between atoms is called an **unshared pair,** also known as a lone pair or a nonbonding pair. In F_2, each fluorine atom has three unshared pairs of electrons.

You can draw electron dot structures for molecules of compounds in much the same way that you draw them for molecules of diatomic elements. Water (H_2O) is a molecule containing three atoms with two single covalent bonds. Two hydrogen atoms share electrons with one oxygen atom. The hydrogen and oxygen atoms attain noble-gas configurations by sharing electrons. As you can see in the electron dot structures below, the oxygen atom in water has two unshared pairs of valence electrons.

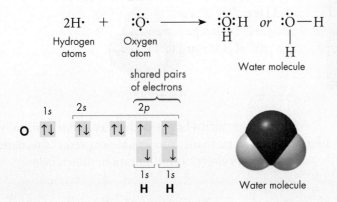

You can draw the electron dot structure for ammonia (NH_3), a suffocating gas, in a similar way. The ammonia molecule has one unshared pair of electrons.

$$3H\cdot \quad + \quad :\overset{\cdot}{N}\cdot \quad \longrightarrow \quad :\overset{H}{\underset{H}{N}}:H \quad or \quad :\overset{\displaystyle H}{\underset{\displaystyle H}{N}}-H$$

Hydrogen   Nitrogen   atoms   atom   Ammonia molecule

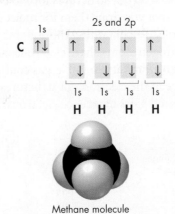

Ammonia molecule

The stove in Figure 8.6 is fueled by natural gas. The principal component of natural gas is methane (CH_4). Methane contains four single covalent bonds. The carbon atom has four valence electrons and needs four more valence electrons to attain a noble-gas configuration. Each of the four hydrogen atoms contributes one electron to share with the carbon atom, forming four identical carbon-hydrogen bonds. As you can see in the electron dot structure below, methane has no unshared pairs of electrons.

$$4H\cdot \quad + \quad \cdot\overset{\cdot}{C}\cdot \quad \longrightarrow \quad H:\overset{H}{\underset{H}{C}}:H \quad or \quad H-\overset{\displaystyle H}{\underset{\displaystyle H}{C}}-H$$

Hydrogen   Carbon   Methane molecule
atoms   atom

Methane molecule

When carbon forms bonds with other atoms, it usually forms four bonds, as in methane. You would not predict this pattern based on carbon's electron configuration, shown below.

Figure 8.6 Methane
Methane is the principal component of natural gas. Natural gas is commonly used as a fuel for household gas appliances such as gas stoves, water heaters, dryers, and furnaces.

If you tried to form covalent C—H bonds for methane by combining the two $2p$ electrons of the carbon with two $1s$ electrons of hydrogen atoms, you would incorrectly predict a molecule with the formula CH_2 (instead of CH_4). The formation of four bonds by carbon can be explained by the fact that one of carbon's $2s$ electrons is promoted to the vacant $2p$ orbital to form the following electron configuration:

$1s^2$ $2s$ and $2p$

This electron promotion requires only a small amount of energy. The promotion provides four electrons of carbon that are capable of forming covalent bonds with four hydrogen atoms. Methane, the carbon compound formed by electron sharing of carbon with four hydrogen atoms, is much more stable than CH_2. The stability of the resulting methane more than compensates for the small energy cost of the electron promotion. Therefore, formation of methane (CH_4) is more energetically favored than the formation of CH_2.

SampleProblem 8.1

Drawing an Electron Dot Structure

Hydrochloric acid (HCl (*aq*)) is prepared by dissolving gaseous hydrogen chloride (HCl (*g*)) in water. Hydrogen chloride is a diatomic molecule with a single covalent bond. Draw the electron dot structure for HCl.

❶ Analyze Identify the relevant concepts. In a single covalent bond, a hydrogen and a chlorine atom must share a pair of electrons. Each must contribute one electron to the bond. Then show the electron sharing in the compound they produce.

❷ Solve Apply concepts to the problem.

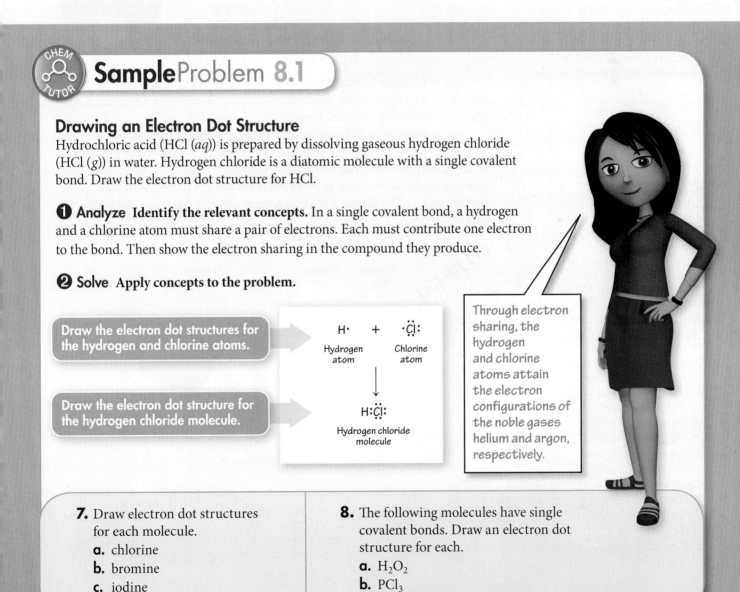

Draw the electron dot structures for the hydrogen and chlorine atoms.

Draw the electron dot structure for the hydrogen chloride molecule.

Through electron sharing, the hydrogen and chlorine atoms attain the electron configurations of the noble gases helium and argon, respectively.

7. Draw electron dot structures for each molecule.
 a. chlorine
 b. bromine
 c. iodine

8. The following molecules have single covalent bonds. Draw an electron dot structure for each.
 a. H_2O_2
 b. PCl_3

Double and Triple Covalent Bonds

Sometimes atoms bond by sharing more than one pair of electrons. **Atoms form double or triple covalent bonds if they can attain a noble gas structure by sharing two pairs or three pairs of electrons.** A **double covalent bond** is a bond that involves two shared pairs of electrons. Similarly, a bond formed by sharing three pairs of electrons is a **triple covalent bond.**

Carbon dioxide (CO_2) is used to carbonate many soft drinks like the one shown in Figure 8.7. The carbon dioxide molecule contains two oxygens, each of which shares two electrons with carbon to form a total of two carbon–oxygen double bonds.

Figure 8.7 Carbon Dioxide
Carbon dioxide gas is soluble in water and is used to carbonate many beverages. A carbon dioxide molecule has two carbon–oxygen double bonds.

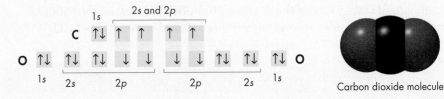

Carbon dioxide molecule

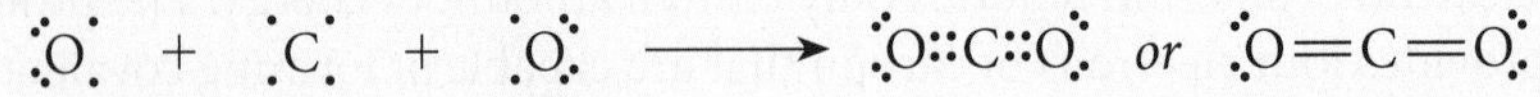

The two double bonds in the carbon dioxide molecule are identical to each other. Carbon dioxide is an example of a triatomic molecule, which is a molecule consisting of three atoms.

An example of an element whose molecules contain triple bonds is nitrogen (N_2), a major component of Earth's atmosphere, illustrated in Figure 8.8. A single nitrogen atom has five valence electrons. Each nitrogen atom in the nitrogen molecule must share three electrons to have the electron configuration of neon. In the nitrogen molecule, each nitrogen atom has one unshared pair of electrons.

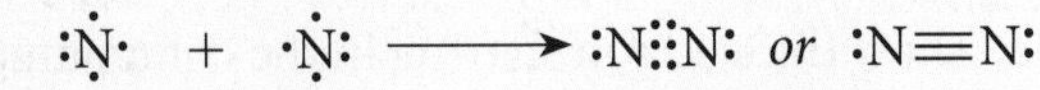

Nitrogen molecule

Figure 8.8 Oxygen and Nitrogen
Oxygen and nitrogen are the main components of Earth's atmosphere. The oxygen molecule is an exception to the octet rule. It has two unpaired electrons. Three pairs of electrons are shared in a nitrogen molecule.

You might think that an oxygen atom, with six valence electrons, would form a double bond by sharing two of its electrons with another oxygen atom.

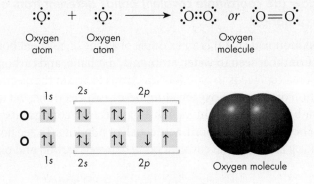

In such an arrangement, all the electrons within the molecule would be paired. Experimental evidence, however, indicates that two of the electrons in O_2 are still unpaired. Thus, the bonding in the oxygen molecule (O_2) does not obey the octet rule. You cannot draw an electron dot structure that adequately describes the bonding in the oxygen molecule.

Nitrogen and oxygen are both diatomic molecules. Table 8.1 lists the properties and uses of these elements and some others that exist as diatomic molecules.

Table 8.1

The Diatomic Elements

Name	Chemical formula	Electron dot structure	Properties and uses
Fluorine	F_2	:F̈—F̈:	Greenish-yellow reactive toxic gas. Compounds of fluorine, a halogen, are added to drinking water and toothpaste to promote healthy teeth.
Chlorine	Cl_2	:C̈l—C̈l:	Greenish-yellow reactive toxic gas. Chlorine is a halogen used in household bleaching agents.
Bromine	Br_2	:B̈r—B̈r:	Dense red-brown liquid with pungent odor. Compounds of bromine, a halogen, are used in the preparation of photographic emulsions.
Iodine	I_2	:Ï—Ï:	Dense gray-black solid that produces purple vapors; a halogen. A solution of iodine in alcohol (tincture of iodine) is used as an antiseptic.
Hydrogen	H_2	H—H	Colorless, odorless, tasteless gas. Hydrogen is the lightest known element.
Nitrogen	N_2	:N≡N:	Colorless, odorless, tasteless gas. Air is almost 80% nitrogen by volume.
Oxygen	O_2	Inadequate	Colorless, odorless, tasteless gas that is vital for life. Air is about 20% oxygen by volume.

Coordinate Covalent Bonds

How are coordinate covalent bonds different from other covalent bonds?

Carbon monoxide (CO) is an example of a type of covalent bonding different from that seen in water, ammonia, methane, and carbon dioxide. A carbon atom needs to gain four electrons to attain the electron configuration of neon. An oxygen atom needs two electrons. Yet it is possible for both atoms to achieve noble-gas electron configurations by a type of bonding called coordinate covalent bonding. To see how, begin by looking at the double covalent bond between carbon and oxygen.

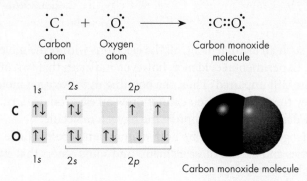

With the double bond in place, the oxygen has a stable configuration, but the carbon does not. As shown below, the dilemma is solved if the oxygen also donates one of its unshared pairs of electrons for bonding.

:C::O: ⟶ :C⦂⦂O:
Carbon monoxide
molecule

A covalent bond in which one atom contributes both bonding electrons is a **coordinate covalent bond.** In a structural formula, you can show coordinate covalent bonds as arrows that point from the atom donating the pair of electrons to the atom receiving them. The structural formula of carbon monoxide, with two covalent bonds and one coordinate covalent bond, is C≡O. **In a coordinate covalent bond, the shared electron pair comes from one of the bonding atoms.** Once formed, a coordinate covalent bond is like any other covalent bond.

The ammonium ion (NH_4^+), which is often found in fertilizers like the one in Figure 8.9, consists of atoms joined by covalent bonds, including a coordinate covalent bond. A **polyatomic ion,** such as NH_4^+, is a tightly bound group of atoms that has a positive or negative charge and behaves as a unit. The ammonium ion forms when a positively charged hydrogen ion (H^+) attaches to the unshared electron pair of an ammonia molecule (NH_3).

Figure 8.9 Ammonia Fertilizers
Most plants need nitrogen that is already combined in a compound rather than molecular nitrogen (N_2) to grow. The polyatomic ammonium ion (NH_4^+), present in ammonium hydroxide, also called aqua ammonia, is an important component of fertilizer for field crops, home gardens, and potted plants.

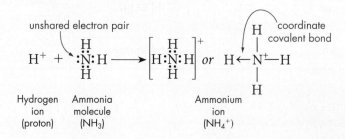

Most polyatomic cations and anions contain covalent and coordinate covalent bonds. Therefore, compounds containing polyatomic ions include both ionic and covalent bonding. As another example, draw the electron dot structure of the polyatomic ion SO_3^{2-}. First, draw the electron dot structures for the oxygen and sulfur atoms, and the two extra electrons indicated by the charge. Then, join two of the oxygens to sulfur by single covalent bonds.

$$:\ddot{O}: \; \cdot\ddot{S}: \; \cdot\ddot{O}: \;\; + \;\; \cdot\cdot \;\; \longrightarrow \;\; :\ddot{O}:\ddot{S}: \; \cdot\ddot{O}:$$
$$\cdot\ddot{O}: \qquad\qquad\qquad\qquad \cdot\ddot{O}:$$

Next, join the remaining oxygen by a coordinate covalent bond, with sulfur donating one of its unshared pairs to oxygen, and add the two extra electrons. Put brackets around the structure and indicate the 2− charge.

$$:\ddot{O}:\ddot{S}:\ddot{O}: \;\; + \;\; \cdot\cdot \;\; \longrightarrow \;\; \left[:\ddot{O}:\ddot{S}:\ddot{O}:\right]^{2-}$$
$$\cdot\ddot{O}: \qquad\qquad\qquad\qquad :\ddot{O}:$$

Each of the atoms now has eight valence electrons, satisfying the octet rule. Without the extra electrons, two of the oxygens would be electron-deficient.

Table 8.2 lists electron dot structures of some common compounds with covalent bonds.

> Remember, the charge of a negative polyatomic ion is equal to the number of electrons that are in addition to the valence electrons of the atoms present. Since a negatively charged polyatomic ion is part of an ionic compound, the positive charge of the cation of the compound balances the additional electrons.

Sample Problem 8.2

Drawing the Electron Dot Structure of a Polyatomic Ion

The H_3O^+ ion forms when a hydrogen ion is attracted to an unshared electron pair in a water molecule. Draw the electron dot structure of the hydronium ion.

① Analyze **Identify the relevant concepts.** Each atom must share electrons to satisfy the octet rule.

② Solve **Apply the concepts to the problem.**

> Remember to always include the charge when drawing electron dot structures of polyatomic ions.

Draw the electron dot structure of the water molecule and the hydrogen ion. Then, draw the electron dot structure of the hydronium ion. The oxygen must share a pair of electrons with the added hydrogen ion to form a coordinate covalent bond.

$$H^+ \;\; + \;\; :\ddot{O}:H \;\; \longrightarrow \;\; \left[H:\ddot{O}:H\right]^+ \;\; or \;\; \left[H\leftarrow\overset{\overset{\textstyle H}{|}}{O}-H\right]^+$$

Hydrogen ion (proton)   Water molecule (H_2O)   Hydronium ion (H_3O^+)

Check that all the atoms have the electrons they need and that the charge is correct.

The oxygen in the hydronium ion has eight valence electrons, and each hydrogen shares two valence electrons, satisfying the octet rule. The water molecule is neutral, and the hydrogen ion has a positive charge, giving the hydronium ion a charge of 1+.

9. Draw the electron dot structure of the hydroxide ion (OH^-).

10. Draw the electron dot structures for sulfate (SO_4^{2-}) and carbonate (CO_3^{2-}). Sulfur and carbon are the central atoms, respectively.

Table 8.2

Some Common Molecular Compounds

Name	Chemical formula	Structure	Properties and uses
Carbon monoxide	CO	:C≡O:	Colorless, highly toxic gas. It is a major air pollutant present in cigarette smoke and exhaust.
Carbon dioxide	CO_2	:O=C=O:	Colorless unreactive gas. This normal component of the atmosphere is exhaled in the breath of animals and is essential for plant growth.
Hydrogen peroxide	H_2O_2	H‒O‒O‒H	Colorless, unstable liquid when pure. It is used as rocket fuel. A 3% solution is used as a bleach and antiseptic.
Sulfur dioxide	SO_2	O=S‒O	Oxides of sulfur are produced in the combustion of petroleum products and coal. They are major air pollutants in industrial areas. Oxides of sulfur can lead to respiratory problems.
Sulfur trioxide	SO_3	O=S (‒O) (‒O)	
Nitric oxide*	NO	:O=N·	Oxides of nitrogen are major air pollutants produced by the combustion of fossil fuels in automobile engines. They irritate the eyes, throat, and lungs. Nitrogen dioxide, a dark-brown gas, readily converts to colorless dinitrogen tetroxide. Dinitrogen tetroxide is used as a rocket fuel.
Nitrogen dioxide*	NO_2	O=N‒O	
Dinitrogen tetroxide	N_2O_4	O=N‒N=O	
Nitrous oxide	N_2O	:O←N≡N:	Colorless, sweet-smelling gas. It is used as an anesthetic commonly called laughing gas.
Hydrogen cyanide	HCN	H‒C≡N:	Colorless, toxic gas with the smell of almonds.
Hydrogen fluoride	HF	H‒F:	Four hydrogen halides, all extremely soluble in water. Hydrogen chloride, a colorless gas with a pungent odor, readily dissolves in water to give a solution called hydrochloric acid.
Hydrogen chloride	HCl	H‒Cl:	
Hydrogen bromide	HBr	H‒Br:	
Hydrogen iodide	HI	H‒I:	

*Does not obey the octet rule

Exceptions to the Octet Rule

 What are some exceptions to the octet rule?

The octet rule provides guidance for drawing electron dot structures. For some molecules or ions, however, it is impossible to draw structures that satisfy the octet rule. **The octet rule cannot be satisfied in molecules whose total number of valence electrons is an odd number. There are also molecules in which an atom has less, or more, than a complete octet of valence electrons.** The nitrogen dioxide (NO_2) molecule, for example, contains a total of seventeen, an odd number, of valence electrons. Each oxygen contributes six electrons and the nitrogen contributes five. Two plausible electron dot structures can be drawn for the NO_2 molecule.

$$:\ddot{O}=\dot{N}-\ddot{O}:$$
$$:\ddot{O}-\dot{N}=\ddot{O}:$$

Nitrogen dioxide molecule

An unpaired electron is present in each of these structures, both of which fail to follow the octet rule. It is impossible to draw an electron dot structure for NO_2 that satisfies the octet rule for all atoms. Yet, NO_2 does exist as a stable molecule. In fact, it is produced naturally by lightning strikes of the sort shown in Figure 8.10.

A number of other molecules also have an odd number of electrons. In these molecules, as in NO_2, complete pairing of electrons is not possible. It is not possible to draw an electron dot structure that satisfies the octet rule. Examples of such molecules include chlorine dioxide (ClO_2) and nitric oxide (NO).

Several molecules with an even number of valence electrons, such as some compounds of boron, also fail to follow the octet rule. This outcome may occur because an atom acquires less than an octet of eight electrons. The boron atom in boron trifluoride (BF_3), for example, is deficient by two electrons and, therefore, is an exception to the octet rule. Boron trifluoride readily reacts with ammonia to make the compound $BF_3 \cdot NH_3$. In doing so, the boron atom accepts the unshared electron pair from ammonia and completes the octet.

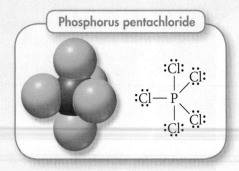

Phosphorus pentachloride

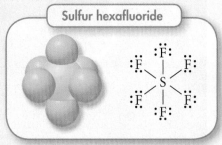

Sulfur hexafluoride

Figure 8.11
Exceptions to the Octet Rule
Phosphorus pentachloride and sulfur hexafluoride, are exceptions to the octet rule.

Interpret Diagrams
How many valence electrons does the sulfur in sulfur hexafluoride (SF₆) have for the structure shown in the figure?

A few atoms, especially phosphorus and sulfur, sometimes expand the octet to ten or twelve electrons. Consider phosphorus trichloride (PCl_3) and phosphorus pentachloride (PCl_5). Both are stable compounds in which all of the chlorine atoms are bonded to a single phosphorus atom. Covalent bonding in PCl_3 follows the octet rule because all the atoms have eight valence electrons. However, as shown in Figure 8.11, the electron dot structure for PCl_5 can be written so that phosphorus has ten valence electrons. The octet is also expanded in sulfur hexafluoride (SF_6). The electron dot structure for SF_6 can be written so that sulfur has twelve valence electrons.

Bond Dissociation Energies

🔑 **How is the strength of a covalent bond related to its bond dissociation energy?**

A large quantity of heat is released when hydrogen atoms combine to form hydrogen molecules. This release of heat suggests that the product is more stable than the reactants. The covalent bond in the hydrogen molecule (H_2) is so strong that it would take 435 kJ of energy to break apart all of the bonds in 1 mole (6.02×10^{23} bonds or about 2 grams) of H_2. (You will study the mole, abbreviated mol, in Chapter 12.) The energy required to break the bond between two covalently bonded atoms is the **bond dissociation energy.** The units for this energy are often given in kJ/mol, which is the energy needed to break one mole of bonds. For example, the bond dissociation energy for the H_2 molecule is 435 kJ/mol.

Table 8.3

Bond Dissociation Energies and Bond Lengths for Covalent Bonds

Bond	Bond dissociation energy (kJ/mol)	Bond length (pm)
H—H	435	74
C—H	393	109
C—O	356	143
C═O	736	121
C≡O	1074	113
C—C	347	154
C═C	657	133
C≡C	908	121
C—N	305	147
Cl—Cl	243	199
N—N	209	140
O—H	464	96
O—O	142	132

🔑 **A large bond dissociation energy corresponds to a strong covalent bond.** A typical carbon-carbon single bond has a bond dissociation energy of 347 kJ/mol. Typical carbon-carbon double and triple bonds have bond dissociation energies of 657 kJ/mol and 908 kJ/mol, respectively. Strong carbon-carbon bonds help explain the stability of carbon compounds. Compounds with only C—C and C—H single covalent bonds, such as methane, tend to be quite unreactive. They are unreactive partly because the dissociation energy for each of these bonds is high. Bond dissociation energies of some common bonds are shown in Table 8.3.

Resonance

🔑 **How are resonance structures used?**

Ozone in the upper atmosphere blocks harmful ultraviolet radiation from the sun. At lower elevations, as shown in Figure 8.12, it contributes to smog. The ozone molecule has two possible electron dot structures. Notice that the structure on the left can be converted to the one on the right by shifting electron pairs without changing the positions of the oxygen atoms.

$$:\ddot{\text{O}}:\ddot{\text{O}}::\ddot{\text{O}}: \longleftrightarrow :\ddot{\text{O}}::\ddot{\text{O}}:\ddot{\text{O}}:$$

As drawn, these electron dot structures suggest that the bonding in ozone consists of one single coordinate covalent bond and one double covalent bond. Because earlier chemists imagined that the electron pairs rapidly flip back and forth, or resonate, between the different electron dot structures, they used double-headed arrows to indicate that two or more structures are in resonance.

Double covalent bonds are usually shorter than single covalent bonds, so it was believed that the bond lengths in ozone were unequal. Experimental measurements show, however, that this is not the case. The two bonds in ozone are the same length. This result can be explained if you assume that the actual bonding in the ozone molecule is the average of the two electron dot structures. The electron pairs do not actually resonate back and forth. The actual bonding is a hybrid, or mixture, of the extremes represented by the resonance forms.

The two electron dot structures for ozone are examples of what are still referred to as resonance structures. **Resonance structures** are structures that occur when it is possible to draw two or more valid electron dot structures that have the same number of electron pairs for a molecule or ion. 🔑 **Chemists use resonance structures to envision the bonding in molecules that cannot be adequately described by a single structural formula.** Although no back-and-forth changes occur, double-headed arrows are used to connect resonance structures.

Learn more about oxygen in the air online.

CHEMISTRY & YOU

Q: *What is the difference between the oxygen you breathe and the oxygen in ozone in the atmosphere?*

Figure 8.12 Ozone Smog
Although ozone high above the ground forms a protective layer that absorbs ultraviolet radiation from the sun, at lower elevations ozone is a pollutant that contributes to smog. The smog shown here in Los Angeles, California, makes it difficult to see the city skyline.

Quick Lab

Purpose To compare and contrast the stretching of rubber bands and the dissociation energy of covalent bonds

Materials

- 1 170-g (6-oz) can of food
- 2 454-g (16-oz) cans of food
- 3 No. 25 rubber bands
- metric ruler
- coat hanger
- plastic grocery bag
- paper clip
- graph paper
- motion detector (optional)

Strengths of Covalent Bonds

Procedure

1. Bend the coat hanger to fit over the top of a door. The hook should hang down on one side of the door. Measure the length of the rubber bands (in cm). Hang a rubber band on the hook created by the coat hanger.

2. Place the 170-g can in the plastic bag. Use the paper clip to fasten the bag to the end of the rubber band. Lower the bag gently until it is suspended from the end of the rubber band. Measure and record the length of the stretched rubber band. Using different combinations of food cans, repeat this process three times with the following masses: 454 g, 624 g, and 908 g.

3. Repeat Step 2, first using two rubber bands to connect the hanger and the paper clip, and then using three.

4. Graph the length difference: (stretched rubber band) – (unstretched rubber band) on the y-axis versus mass (kg) on the x-axis for one, two, and three rubber bands. Draw the straight line that you estimate best fits the points for each set of data. (Your graph should have three separate lines.) The x-axis and y-axis intercepts of the lines should pass through zero, and the lines should extend past 1 kg on the x-axis. Determine the slope of each line in cm/kg.

Analyze and Conclude

1. Analyze Experimental Results Assuming the rubber bands are models for covalent bonds, what can you conclude about the relative strengths of single, double, and triple bonds?

2. Evaluate How does the behavior of the rubber bands differ from that of covalent bonds?

8.2 LessonCheck

11. Identify What electron configurations do atoms usually achieve by sharing electrons to form covalent bonds?

12. Compare How is a coordinate covalent bond different from other covalent bonds?

13. List List three ways in which the octet rule can sometimes fail to be obeyed.

14. Explain How is the strength of a covalent bond related to its bond dissociation energy?

15. Identify How are resonance structures used?

16. Explain How is an electron dot structure used to represent a covalent bond?

17. Infer When are two atoms likely to form a double bond between them? A triple bond?

18. Identify What kinds of information does a structural formula reveal about the compound it represents?

19. Compare Use the bond dissociation energies of H_2 and of a typical carbon–carbon bond to decide which bond is stronger. Explain your reasoning.

20. Use Models Draw electron dot structures for the following molecules, which have only single covalent bonds:

a. H_2S b. PH_3 c. ClF

Powder Coating

Have you ever admired a new car with its glossy, smooth paint? Car manufacturers use a special process to apply paint to a car. This process is called powder coating or electrostatic spray painting.

In powder coating, a custom-designed spray nozzle wired up to an electric power supply imparts a negative charge to the paint droplets as they exit the spray gun. The negatively charged droplets are attracted to the grounded, positively-charged, metal surface. Painting with attractive forces is very efficient, because almost all the paint is applied to the car body and very little is wasted.

Powder coating isn't just for cars. The process has many different applications, including the painting of motorcycles, outdoor furniture, exercise equipment, office furniture, and metal fencing.

An eye-catching paint finish isn't the only benefit of powder coating, however. This process is also environmentally friendly. Since the paint is actually attracted to its intended surface, the amount of wasted paint is much lower compared to traditional spray painting. Also, the amount of toxic volatile organic compounds (VOCs) released is minimal, if there are any at all.

APPLYING THE POWDER This worker is using an electrostatic spray gun to apply powder to the metal. Any powder that does not stick to the part can be collected and reused. Once the powder is applied, the part is baked in an oven to cure the paint.

GLOSSY FINISH Powder coating can produce a smooth, glossy paint finish.

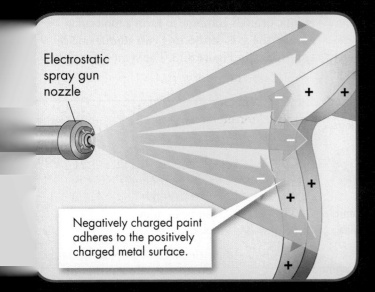

Electrostatic spray gun nozzle

Negatively charged paint adheres to the positively charged metal surface.

ATTRACTIVE PAINT The paint almost wraps around the metal, sticking to any available charged surface.

Take It Further

1. Analyze Benefits Powder coating is being used for more and more applications, partly because of its many benefits. Research other advantages of powder coating that are not mentioned here.

2. Infer Powder coating results in a smooth surface, usually without drips and runs. Given what you have learned about attractive forces, why do you think drips and runs are avoided during powder coating?

8.3 Bonding Theories

CHEMISTRY & YOU

Q: *How can you predict where an electron is most likely to be found in a molecule?* If you ever go hiking in a hilly area, you might see a topographic map like the one shown here. The lines on a topographic map show you where elevations change. In this lesson, you will learn how to interpret electron "maps" that show where you are most likely to find electrons.

Key Questions

How are atomic and molecular orbitals related?

What do scientists use the VSEPR theory for?

In what ways is orbital hybridization useful in describing molecules?

Vocabulary

• molecular orbital
• bonding orbital
• sigma bond
• pi bond
• tetrahedral angle
• VSEPR theory
• hybridization

Molecular Orbitals

How are atomic and molecular orbitals related?

The model you have been using for covalent bonding assumes the orbitals are those of the individual atoms. There is a quantum mechanical model of bonding, however, that describes the electrons in molecules using orbitals that exist only for groupings of atoms. When two atoms combine, this model assumes that their atomic orbitals overlap to produce **molecular orbitals,** or orbitals that apply to the entire molecule.

In some ways, atomic orbitals and molecular orbitals are similar. **Just as an atomic orbital belongs to a particular atom, a molecular orbital belongs to a molecule as a whole.** Each atomic orbital is filled if it contains two electrons. Similarly, two electrons are required to fill a molecular orbital. A molecular orbital that can be occupied by two electrons of a covalent bond is called a **bonding orbital.**

Sigma Bonds When two atomic orbitals combine to form a molecular orbital that is symmetrical around the axis connecting two atomic nuclei, a **sigma bond** is formed, as illustrated in Figure 8.13. The symbol for this bond is the Greek letter sigma (σ).

⊕ represents the nucleus.

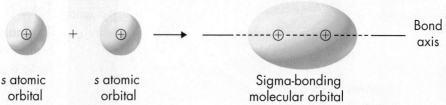

s atomic orbital   s atomic orbital   Sigma-bonding molecular orbital   Bond axis

Figure 8.13 s Orbital Sigma Bonds
Two s atomic orbitals can combine to form a molecular orbital, as in the case of hydrogen (H_2). In a bonding molecular orbital, the electron density between the nuclei is high.

⊕ represents the nucleus.

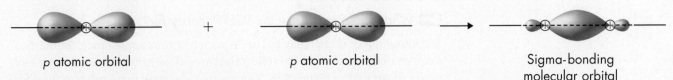

p atomic orbital   +   p atomic orbital   →   Sigma-bonding molecular orbital

Figure 8.14 p Orbital Sigma Bonds
Two p atomic orbitals can combine to form a sigma-bonding molecular orbital, as in the case of fluorine (F_2). Notice that the sigma bond is symmetrical around the bond axis connecting the nuclei.

In general, covalent bonding results from an imbalance between the attractions and repulsions of the nuclei and electrons involved. Because their charges have opposite signs, the nuclei and electrons attract each other. Conversely, nuclei repel other nuclei and electrons repel other electrons because their charges have the same sign. In a hydrogen molecule, the nuclei repel each other, as do the electrons. In a bonding molecular orbital of hydrogen, however, the attractions between the hydrogen nuclei and the electrons are stronger than the repulsions. The balance of all the interactions between the hydrogen atoms is thus tipped in favor of holding the atoms together. The result is a stable diatomic molecule of H_2.

Atomic p orbitals can also overlap to form molecular orbitals. A fluorine atom, for example, has a half-filled 2p orbital. When two fluorine atoms combine, as shown in Figure 8.14, the p orbitals overlap to produce a bonding molecular orbital. There is a high probability of finding a pair of electrons between the positively charged nuclei of the two fluorines. The fluorine nuclei are attracted to this region of high electron density. This attraction holds the atoms together in the fluorine molecule (F_2). The overlap of the 2p orbitals produces a bonding molecular orbital that is symmetrical when viewed around the F—F bond axis connecting the nuclei. Therefore, the F—F bond is a sigma bond.

Pi Bonds In the sigma bond of the fluorine molecule, the p atomic orbitals overlap end to end. In some molecules, however, orbitals can overlap side by side. As shown in Figure 8.15, the side-by-side overlap of atomic p orbitals produces what are called pi molecular orbitals. When a pi molecular orbital is filled with two electrons, a pi bond results. In a **pi bond** (symbolized by the Greek letter π), the bonding electrons are most likely to be found in sausage-shaped regions above and below the bond axis of the bonded atoms. Atomic orbitals in pi bonding overlap less than in sigma bonding. Therefore, pi bonds tend to be weaker than sigma bonds.

⊕ represents the nucleus.

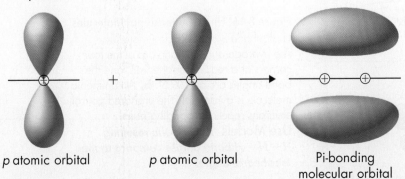

p atomic orbital   +   p atomic orbital   →   Pi-bonding molecular orbital

CHEMISTRY & YOU

Q: *Models and drawings are often used to help you visualize where something can be found. How can a drawing show you where an electron is most likely to be found?*

**Figure 8.15
p Orbital Pi Bonds**
The side-by-side overlap of two p atomic orbitals produces a pi-bonding molecular orbital. Together, the two sausage-shaped regions in which the bonding electron pair is most likely to be found constitute one pi-bonding molecular orbital.

Covalent Bonding **241**

VSEPR Theory

🗝 What do scientists use the VSEPR theory for?

A photograph or sketch may fail to do justice to your appearance. Similarly, electron dot structures fail to reflect the three-dimensional shapes of the molecules illustrated in Figure 8.16. The electron dot structure and structural formula of methane (CH_4), for example, show the molecule as if it were flat and merely two-dimensional.

$$H : \overset{\overset{\displaystyle H}{\displaystyle \cdot\cdot}}{\underset{\underset{\displaystyle H}{\displaystyle \cdot\cdot}}{C}} : H$$

Methane
(electron dot structure)

$$H - \overset{\displaystyle H}{\underset{\displaystyle H}{\overset{|}{\underset{|}{C}}}} - H$$

Methane
(structural formula)

READING SUPPORT

BUILD VOCABULARY: *Word Origins* *Tetrahedral* comes from the Greek *tetra-,* meaning "four," and *hedra,* meaning "face." *How do these word origins help you understand the shapes of molecules?*

In reality, methane molecules are three-dimensional. As Figure 8.16a shows, the hydrogens in a methane molecule are at the four corners of a geometric solid called a regular tetrahedron. In this arrangement, all of the H—C—H angles are 109.5°, the **tetrahedral angle.**

🗝 **In order to explain the three-dimensional shape of molecules, scientists use valence-shell electron-pair repulsion theory (VSEPR theory).** **VSEPR theory** states that the repulsion between electron pairs causes molecular shapes to adjust so that the valence-electron pairs stay as far apart as possible. The methane molecule has four bonding electron pairs and no unshared pairs. The bonding pairs are farthest apart when the angle between the central carbon and its attached hydrogens is 109.5°. This measurement is the H—C—H bond angle found experimentally.

Unshared pairs of electrons are also important in predicting the shapes of molecules. The nitrogen in ammonia (NH_3) is surrounded by four pairs of valence electrons, so you might predict the tetrahedral angle of 109.5° for the H—N—H bond angle. However, one of the valence-electron pairs shown in Figure 8.16b is an unshared pair. No bonding atom is vying for these unshared electrons. Thus, they are held closer to the nitrogen than are the bonding pairs. The unshared pair strongly repels the bonding pairs, pushing them together. The measured H—N—H bond angle is only 107°.

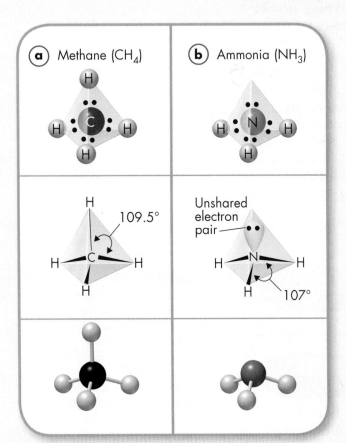

Figure 8.16 Three-Dimensional Molecules
a. Methane is a tetrahedral molecule. The hydrogens in methane are at the four corners of a regular tetrahedron, and the bond angles are all 109.5°. **b.** An ammonia molecule is pyramidal. The unshared pair of electrons repels the bonding pairs.
Use Models *How do the resulting H—N—H bond angles compare to the tetrahedral angle?*

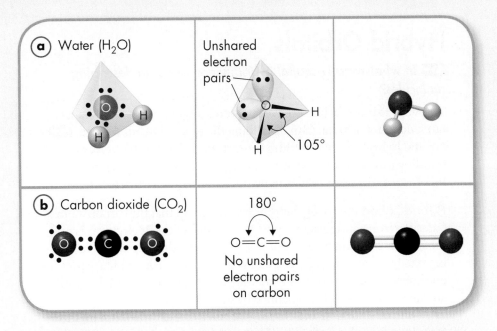

(a) Water (H₂O)

Unshared electron pairs

105°

(b) Carbon dioxide (CO₂)

180°

O=C=O

No unshared electron pairs on carbon

Figure 8.17
Planar and Linear Molecules
This comparison of water and carbon dioxide illustrates how unshared pairs of electrons can affect the shape of a molecule made of three atoms. **a.** The water molecule is bent because the two unshared pairs of electrons on oxygen repel the bonding electrons. **b.** In contrast, the carbon dioxide molecule is linear. The carbon atom has no unshared electron pairs.

In a water molecule, oxygen forms single covalent bonds with two hydrogen atoms. The two bonding pairs and the two unshared pairs of electrons form a tetrahedral arrangement around the central oxygen. Thus, the water molecule is planar (flat) but bent. With two unshared pairs repelling the bonding pairs, the H—O—H bond angle is compressed in comparison with the H—C—H bond angle in methane. The experimentally measured bond angle in water is about 105°, as shown in Figure 8.17a.

In contrast, the carbon in a carbon dioxide molecule has no unshared electron pairs. As illustrated in Figure 8.17b, the double bonds joining the oxygens to the carbon are farthest apart when the O=C=O bond angle is 180°. Thus, CO₂ is a linear molecule. Nine of the possible molecular shapes are shown in Figure 8.18.

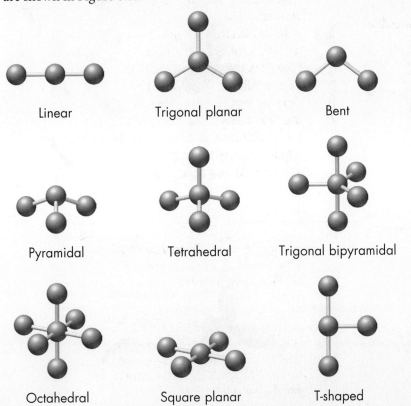

Linear

Trigonal planar

Bent

Pyramidal

Tetrahedral

Trigonal bipyramidal

Octahedral

Square planar

T-shaped

Figure 8.18
Molecular Shapes
Shown here are common molecular shapes.
Infer *What is the shape of an ammonium ion?*

Hybrid Orbitals

In what ways is orbital hybridization useful in describing molecules?

The VSEPR theory works well when accounting for molecular shapes, but it does not help much in describing the types of bonds formed. **Orbital hybridization provides information about both molecular bonding and molecular shape. In hybridization,** several atomic orbitals mix to form the same total number of equivalent hybrid orbitals.

Hybridization Involving Single Bonds Recall that the carbon atom's outer electron configuration is $2s^2 2p^2$, but one of the $2s$ electrons is promoted to a $2p$ orbital to give one $2s$ electron and three $2p$ electrons, allowing it to bond to four hydrogen atoms in methane. You might suspect that one bond would be different from the other three. In fact, all the bonds are identical. This fact is explained by orbital hybridization.

The one $2s$ orbital and three $2p$ orbitals of a carbon atom mix to form four sp^3 hybrid orbitals. These are at the tetrahedral angle of 109.5°. As you can see in Figure 8.19, the four sp^3 orbitals of carbon overlap with the $1s$ orbitals of the four hydrogen atoms. The sp^3 orbitals extend farther into space than either s or p orbitals, allowing a great deal of overlap with the hydrogen $1s$ orbitals. The eight available valence electrons fill the molecular orbitals to form four C—H sigma bonds. The extent of overlap results in unusually strong covalent bonds.

Figure 8.19 Methane Molecule
In methane, each of the four sp^3 hybrid orbitals of carbon overlaps with a $1s$ orbital of hydrogen.

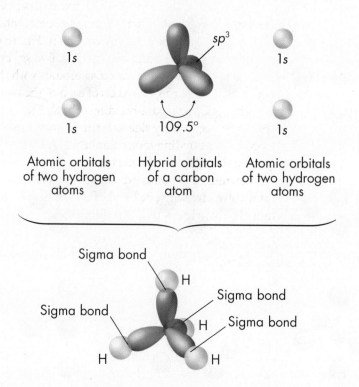

Atomic orbitals of two hydrogen atoms

Hybrid orbitals of a carbon atom

Atomic orbitals of two hydrogen atoms

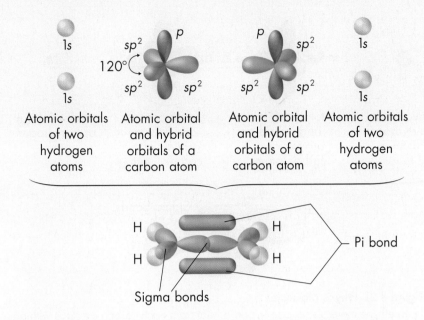

Figure 8.20 Ethene Molecule
In an ethene molecule, two sp^2 hybrid orbitals from each carbon overlap with a 1s orbital of hydrogen to form a sigma bond. The other sp^2 orbitals overlap to form a carbon-carbon sigma bond. The *p* atomic orbitals overlap to form a pi bond. **Infer** *What region of space does the pi bond occupy relative to the carbon atoms?*

Hybridization Involving Double Bonds Hybridization is also useful in describing double covalent bonds. Ethene is a relatively simple molecule that has one carbon–carbon double bond and four carbon–hydrogen single bonds.

Ethene

Experimental evidence indicates that the H—C—H bond angles in ethene are about 120°. In ethene, sp^2 hybrid orbitals form from the combination of one 2s and two 2p atomic orbitals of carbon. As you can see in Figure 8.20, each hybrid orbital is separated from the other two by 120°. Two sp^2 hybrid orbitals of each carbon form sigma-bonding molecular orbitals with the four available hydrogen 1s orbitals. The third sp^2 orbitals of each of the two carbons overlap to form a carbon-carbon sigma-bonding orbital. The nonhybridized 2p carbon orbitals overlap side by side to form a pi-bonding orbital. A total of twelve electrons fill six bonding molecular orbitals. Thus, five sigma bonds and one pi bond hold the ethene molecule together. Although they are drawn alike in structural formulas, pi bonds are weaker than sigma bonds. In chemical reactions that involve breaking one bond of a carbon-carbon double bond, the pi bond is more likely to break than the sigma bond.

Hybridization Involving Triple Bonds A third type of covalent bond is a triple bond, which is found in ethyne (C_2H_2), also called acetylene.

$$H—C≡C—H$$

As with other molecules, the hybrid orbital description of ethyne is guided by an understanding of the properties of the molecule. Ethyne is a linear molecule. The best hybrid orbital description is obtained if a 2s atomic orbital of carbon mixes with only one of the three 2p atomic orbitals. The result is two sp hybrid orbitals for each carbon.

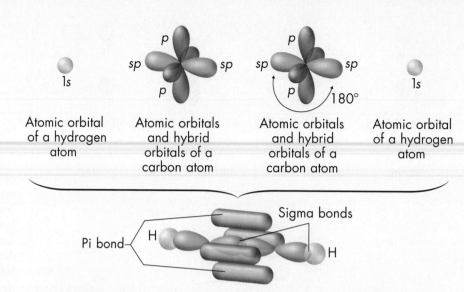

| Atomic orbital of a hydrogen atom | Atomic orbitals and hybrid orbitals of a carbon atom | Atomic orbitals and hybrid orbitals of a carbon atom | Atomic orbital of a hydrogen atom |

Figure 8.21 Ethyne Molecule
In an ethyne molecule, one *sp* hybrid orbital from each carbon overlaps with a 1*s* orbital of hydrogen to form a sigma bond. The other *sp* hybrid orbital of each carbon overlaps to form a carbon-carbon sigma bond. The two *p* atomic orbitals from each carbon also overlap.
Interpret Diagrams *How many pi bonds are formed in an ethyne molecule?*

The carbon-carbon sigma-bonding molecular orbital of the ethyne molecule shown in Figure 8.21 forms from the overlap of one *sp* orbital from each carbon. The other *sp* orbital of each carbon overlaps with the 1*s* orbital of each hydrogen, also forming sigma-bonding molecular orbitals. The remaining pair of *p* atomic orbitals on each carbon overlap side by side. They form two pi-bonding molecular orbitals that surround the central carbons. The ten available electrons completely fill five bonding molecular orbitals. The bonding of ethyne consists of three sigma bonds and two pi bonds.

8.3 LessonCheck

21. **Review** How are atomic and molecular orbitals related?

22. **Identify** What do scientists use VSEPR theory for?

23. **Describe** How is orbital hybridization useful in describing molecules?

24. **Classify** What shape would you expect a simple carbon-containing compound to have if the carbon atom has the following hybridizations?
a. sp^2 **b.** sp^3 **c.** sp

25. **Describe** What is a sigma bond? Describe, with the aid of a diagram, how the overlap of two half-filled 1*s* orbitals produces a sigma bond.

26. **Explain** Use VSEPR theory to predict bond angles in the following covalently bonded molecules. Explain your predictions.
a. methane   **b.** ammonia   **c.** water

27. **Identify** How many sigma and how many pi bonds are in an ethyne molecule (C_2H_2)?

28. **Classify** The BF_3 molecule is planar. The attachment of a fluoride ion to the boron in BF_3, through a coordinate covalent bond, creates the BF_4^- ion. What is the geometric shape of this ion?

8.4 Polar Bonds and Molecules

Q: *How does a snowflake get its shape?* Snow covers approximately 23 percent of Earth's surface. Each individual snowflake is formed from as many as 100 snow crystals. The size and shape of each crystal depends mainly on the air temperature and amount of water vapor in the air at the time the snow crystal forms. In this lesson, you will see how polar covalent bonds in water molecules influence the distinctive geometry of snowflakes.

Key Questions

🔑 How do electronegativity values determine the charge distribution in a polar bond?

🔑 How do the strengths of intermolecular attractions compare with the strengths of ionic and covalent bonds?

🔑 Why are the properties of covalent compounds so diverse?

Vocabulary

- nonpolar covalent bond
- polar covalent bond
- polar bond
- polar molecule
- dipole
- van der Waals forces
- dipole interaction
- dispersion force
- hydrogen bond
- network solid

Bond Polarity

🔑 How do electronegativity values determine the charge distribution in a polar bond?

Covalent bonds involve electron sharing between atoms. However, covalent bonds differ in terms of how the bonded atoms share the electrons. The character of the molecule depends on the kind and number of atoms joined together. These features, in turn, determine the molecular properties.

The bonding pairs of electrons in covalent bonds are pulled, as in the tug of war in Figure 8.22, between the nuclei of the atoms sharing the electrons. When the atoms in the bond pull equally (as occurs when identical atoms are bonded), the bonding electrons are shared equally, and each bond formed is a **nonpolar covalent bond.** Molecules of hydrogen (H_2), oxygen (O_2), and nitrogen (N_2) have nonpolar covalent bonds. Diatomic halogen molecules, such as Cl_2, are also nonpolar.

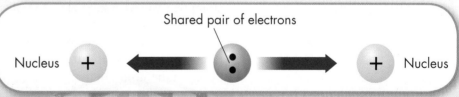

Shared pair of electrons

Nucleus + ← → + Nucleus

**Figure 8.22
Electron Tug of War**
The nuclei of atoms pull on the shared electrons, much as the knot in the rope is pulled toward opposing sides in a tug of war.

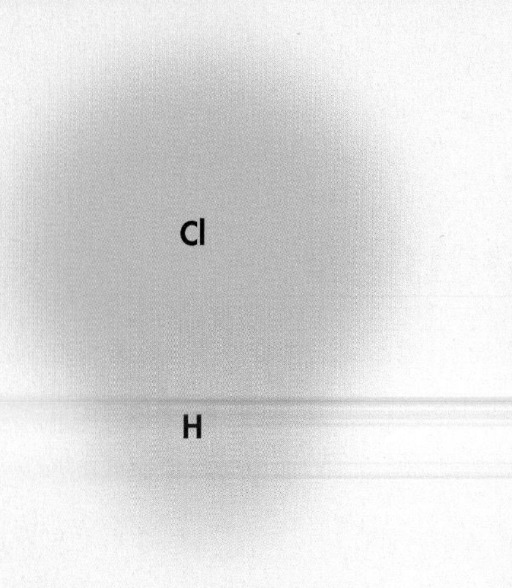

Cl

H

Figure 8.23 Electron Cloud Model of a Polar Bond
This electron-cloud picture of hydrogen chloride shows that the chlorine atom attracts the electron cloud more than the hydrogen atom does.
Infer *Which atom is more electronegative, a chlorine atom or a hydrogen atom?*

A **polar covalent bond,** known also as a **polar bond,** is a covalent bond between atoms in which the electrons are shared unequally. ⬦⬡ **The more-electronegative atom attracts electrons more strongly and gains a slightly negative charge. The less-electronegative atom has a slightly positive charge.** Refer back to Table 6.2 in Chapter 6 to see the electronegativities of some common elements. The higher the electronegativity value, the greater the ability of an atom to attract electrons to itself.

Describing Polar Covalent Bonds In the hydrogen chloride molecule (HCl), hydrogen has an electronegativity of 2.1 and chlorine has an electronegativity of 3.0. These values are significantly different, so the covalent bond in hydrogen chloride is polar. The chlorine atom, with its higher electronegativity, acquires a slightly negative charge. The hydrogen atom acquires a slightly positive charge. The lowercase Greek letter delta (δ) denotes that the atoms in the covalent bond acquire only partial charges, less than 1+ or 1−.

$$\overset{\delta+}{H}-\overset{\delta-}{Cl}$$

The minus sign in this notation shows that chlorine has acquired a slightly negative charge. The plus sign shows that hydrogen has acquired a slightly positive charge. These partial charges are shown as clouds of electron density as illustrated in Figure 8.23. The polar nature of the bond may also be represented by an arrow pointing to the more electronegative atom, as shown here:

$$\overset{\longmapsto}{H-Cl}$$

The O—H bonds in a water molecule are also polar. The highly electronegative oxygen partially pulls the bonding electrons away from hydrogen. The oxygen acquires a slightly negative charge. The hydrogen is left with a slightly positive charge.

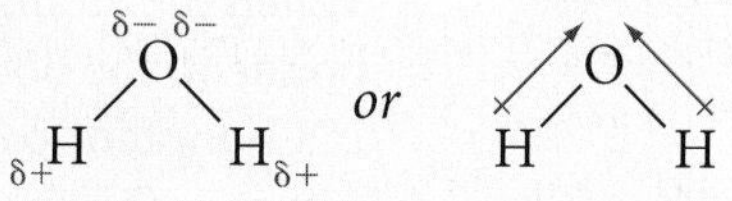

As shown in Table 8.4, the electronegativity difference between two atoms tells you what kind of bond is likely to form. There is no sharp boundary between ionic and covalent bonds. As the electronegativity difference between two atoms increases, the polarity of the bond increases. If the difference is more than 2.0, the electrons will likely be pulled away completely by one of the atoms. In that case, an ionic bond will form.

Table 8.4		
Electronegativity Differences and Bond Types		
Electronegativity difference range	**Most probable type of bond**	**Example**
0.0–0.4	Nonpolar covalent	H—H (0.0)
0.4–1.0	Moderately polar covalent	$\overset{\delta+}{H}-\overset{\delta-}{Cl}$ (0.9)
1.0–2.0	Very polar covalent	$\overset{\delta+}{H}-\overset{\delta-}{F}$ (1.9)
≥2.0	Ionic	Na$^+$Cl$^-$ (2.1)

SampleProblem 8.3

Identifying Bond Type

Which type of bond (nonpolar covalent, moderately polar covalent, very polar covalent, or ionic) will form between each of the following pairs of atoms?

a. N and H
b. F and F
c. Ca and Cl
d. Al and Cl

❶ **Analyze** Identify the relevant concepts. In each case, the pairs of atoms involved in the bonding pair are given. The types of bonds depend on the electronegativity differences between the bonding elements.

> The electronegativity difference between two atoms is expressed as the absolute value. So, you will never express the difference as a negative number.

❷ **Solve** Apply concepts to this problem.

- Identify the electronegativities of each atom using Table 6.2.
- Calculate the electronegativity difference between the two atoms.
- Based on the electronegativity difference, determine the bond type using Table 8.4.

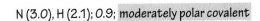

N (3.0), H (2.1); 0.9; *moderately polar covalent*

F (4.0), F (4.0); 0.0; *nonpolar covalent*

Ca (1.0), Cl (3.0); 2.0; ionic

Al (1.5), Cl (3.0); 1.5; *very polar covalent*

---

29. Identify the bonds between atoms of each pair of elements as nonpolar covalent, moderately polar covalent, very polar covalent, or ionic.

a. H and Br
b. K and Cl
c. C and O
d. Cl and F
e. Li and O
f. Br and Br

30. Place the following covalent bonds in order from least to most polar:

a. H—Cl
b. H—Br
c. H—S
d. H—C

Describing Polar Covalent Molecules The presence of a polar bond in a molecule often makes the entire molecule polar. In a **polar molecule,** one end of the molecule is slightly negative, and the other end is slightly positive. For example, in the hydrogen chloride molecule the partial charges on the hydrogen and chlorine atoms are electrically charged regions, or poles. A molecule that has two poles is called a dipolar molecule, or **dipole.** The hydrogen chloride molecule is a dipole. Look at Figure 8.24. When polar molecules are placed between oppositely charged plates, they tend to become oriented with respect to the positive and negative plates.

Figure 8.24
Polar Molecules in an Electric Field
When polar molecules, such as HCl, are placed in an electric field, the slightly negative ends of the molecules become oriented toward the positively charged plate, and the slightly positive ends of the molecules become oriented toward the negatively charged plate.
Predict *What would happen if, instead, carbon dioxide molecules were placed between the plates? Why?*

See Polar Molecules *animated online.*

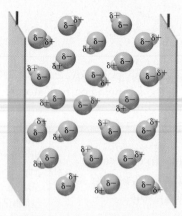

Negative plate   Positive plate

Electric field is absent.
Polar molecules orient randomly.

Electric field is on.
Polar molecules line up.

The effect of polar bonds on the polarity of an entire molecule depends on the shape of the molecule and the orientation of the polar bonds. A carbon dioxide molecule, for example, has two polar bonds and is linear.

$$O=C=O$$

Note that the carbon and oxygens lie along the same axis. Therefore, the bond polarities cancel because they are in opposite directions. Carbon dioxide is thus a nonpolar molecule, despite the presence of two polar bonds.

The water molecule also has two polar bonds. However, the water molecule is bent rather than linear. Therefore, the bond polarities do not cancel and a water molecule is polar.

Attractions Between Molecules

🔑 *How do the strengths of intermolecular attractions compare with ionic and covalent bonds?*

Molecules can be attracted to each other by a variety of different forces. 🔑 **Intermolecular attractions are weaker than either ionic or covalent bonds.** Nevertheless, you should not underestimate the importance of these forces. Among other things, these attractions are responsible for determining whether a molecular compound is a gas, a liquid, or a solid at a given temperature.

Van der Waals Forces The two weakest attractions between molecules are collectively called **van der Waals forces,** named after the Dutch chemist Johannes van der Waals (1837–1923). Van der Waals forces consist of dipole interactions and dispersion forces.

Dipole interactions occur when polar molecules are attracted to one another. The electrical attraction involved occurs between the oppositely charged regions of polar molecules, as shown in Figure 8.25. The slightly negative region of a polar molecule is weakly attracted to the slightly positive region of another polar molecule. Dipole interactions are similar to, but much weaker than, ionic bonds.

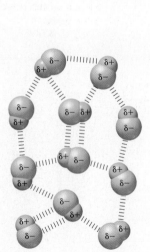

Figure 8.25 Dipole Interactions
Polar molecules are attracted to one another by dipole interactions, a type of van der Waals force.

Dispersion forces, the weakest of all molecular interactions, are caused by the motion of electrons. They
occur even between nonpolar molecules. When the
moving electrons happen to be momentarily more on
the side of a molecule closest to a neighboring molecule,
their electric force influences the neighboring molecule's electrons to be momentarily more on the opposite side. This shift causes an attraction between the two
molecules similar to, but much weaker than, the force
between permanently polar molecules. The strength of
dispersion forces generally increases as the number of
electrons in a molecule increases. The halogen diatomic
molecules, for example, attract each other mainly by means of dispersion
forces. Fluorine and chlorine have relatively few electrons and are gases at
ordinary room temperature and pressure because of their especially weak
dispersion forces. The larger number of electrons in bromine generates
larger dispersion forces. Bromine molecules therefore attract each other
sufficiently to make bromine a liquid at ordinary room temperature and
pressure. Iodine, with a still larger number of electrons, is a solid at ordinary room temperature and pressure.

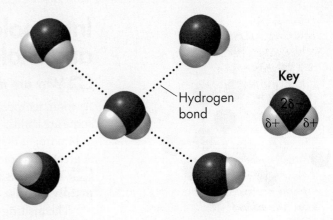
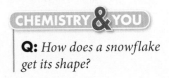

Key

Hydrogen Bonds   The dipole interactions in water produce an attraction between water molecules. Each O—H bond in the water molecule is
highly polar, and the oxygen acquires a slightly negative charge because
of its greater electronegativity. The hydrogens in water molecules acquire
a slightly positive charge. The positive region of one water molecule
attracts the negative region of another water molecule, as illustrated in
Figure 8.26. This attraction between the hydrogen of one water molecule
and the oxygen of another water molecule is strong compared to other
dipole interactions. This relatively strong attraction, which is also found
in hydrogen-containing molecules other than water, is called a hydrogen
bond. Figure 8.26 illustrates hydrogen bonding in water.

Hydrogen bonds are attractive forces in which a hydrogen covalently bonded to a very electronegative atom is also weakly bonded to an
unshared electron pair of another electronegative atom. This other atom
may be in the same molecule or in a nearby molecule. Hydrogen bonding
always involves hydrogen. It is the only chemically reactive element with
valence electrons that are not shielded from the nucleus by other electrons.

Remember that for a hydrogen bond to form, a covalent bond
must already exist between a hydrogen atom and a highly electronegative atom, such as oxygen, nitrogen, or fluorine. The
combination of this strongly polar bond and the lack of
shielding effect in a hydrogen atom is responsible for
the relative strength of hydrogen bonds. A hydrogen bond has about 5 percent of the strength of an
average covalent bond. Hydrogen bonds are the
strongest of the intermolecular forces. They
are extremely important in determining the
properties of water and biological molecules
such as proteins. Figure 8.27 shows how the
relatively strong attractive forces between
water molecules allows the water strider to
sit on the surface of the water.

Figure 8.26
Hydrogen Bonds in Water
The strong hydrogen bonding
between water molecules
accounts for many properties
of water, such as the fact that
water is a liquid rather than a
gas at room temperature.

CHEMISTRY & YOU

Q: *How does a snowflake
get its shape?*

Figure 8.27 Walking on Water
The strong attractions between
water molecules allow this water
strider to "walk" on water instead
of sinking into the water.

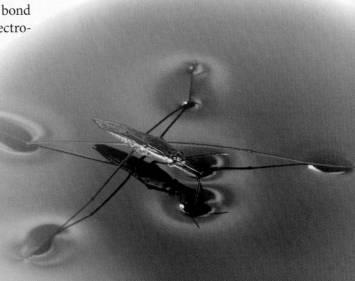

Intermolecular Attractions and Molecular Properties

Why are the properties of covalent compounds so diverse?

At room temperature, some compounds are gases, some are liquids, and some are solids. The physical properties of a compound depend on the type of bonding it displays—in particular, on whether it is ionic or covalent. A great range of physical properties occurs among covalent compounds. **The diversity of physical properties among covalent compounds is mainly because of widely varying intermolecular attractions.**

The melting and boiling points of most compounds composed of molecules are low compared with those of ionic compounds. In most solids formed from molecules, only the weak attractions between molecules need to be broken. However, a few solids that consist of molecules do not melt until the temperature reaches 1000°C or higher, or they decompose without melting at all. Most of these very stable substances are **network solids** (or network crystals), solids in which all of the atoms are covalently bonded to each other. Melting a network solid would require breaking covalent bonds throughout the solid.

Diamond is an example of a network solid. As shown in Figure 8.28, each carbon atom in a diamond is covalently bonded to four other carbons, interconnecting carbon atoms throughout the diamond. Cutting a diamond requires breaking a multitude of these bonds. Diamond does not melt; rather, it vaporizes to a gas at 3500°C and above.

Silicon carbide, with the formula SiC and a melting point of about 2700°C, is also a network solid. Silicon carbide is so hard that it is used in grindstones and as an abrasive. It is also used as a coating on materials that are exposed to high temperatures, as in Figure 8.29. The molecular structures of silicon carbide and diamond are similar to each other. You can think of samples of diamond, silicon carbide, and other network solids as single molecules.

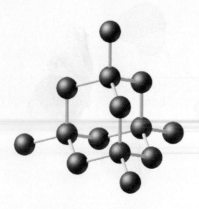

Figure 8.28 Diamond
Diamond is a network-solid form of carbon. Diamond has a three-dimensional structure, with each carbon at the center of a tetrahedron.

Figure 8.29 Silicon Carbide
Surfaces are coated with silicon carbide to make products that are non-adhesive and resistant to extreme temperature, abrasions, and corrosion.

Table 8.5 summarizes some of the characteristic differences between ionic and covalent (molecular) substances. Note that ionic compounds have higher melting points than molecular compounds. Ionic compounds also tend to be soluble in water.

Table 8.5

Characteristics of Ionic and Molecular Compounds

Characteristic	Ionic compound	Molecular compound
Representative unit	Formula unit	Molecule
Bond formation	Transfer of one or more electrons between atoms	Sharing of electron pairs between atoms
Type of elements	Metallic and nonmetallic	Nonmetallic
Physical state	Solid	Solid, liquid, or gas
Melting point	High (usually above 300°C)	Low (usually below 300°C)
Solubility in water	Usually high	High to low
Electrical conductivity of aqueous solution	Good conductor	Poor to nonconducting

 **8.4** LessonCheck

31. ☞ **Explain** How do electronegativity values determine the charge distribution in a polar covalent bond?

32. ☞ **Compare** How do the strengths of intermolecular attractions compare to the strengths of ionic bonds and covalent bonds?

33. ☞ **Explain** Why are the properties of covalent compounds so diverse?

34. Explain Explain this statement: Not every molecule with polar bonds is polar. Use CCl_4 as an example.

35. Draw Draw the electron dot structure for each molecule. Identify polar covalent bonds by assigning slightly positive (δ+) and slightly negative (δ−) symbols to the appropriate atoms.
  a. HOOH
  b. BrCl
  c. HBr
  d. H_2O

36. Compare How does a network solid differ from most other covalent compounds?

37. What happens when polar molecules are between oppositely charged metal plates?

BIGIDEA
BONDING AND INTERACTIONS

38. Explain how dipole interactions and dispersion forces are related. First, explain what produces the attractions between polar molecules. Then, explain what produces dispersion forces between molecules. Identify what is similar and what is different in the two mechanisms of intermolecular attraction.

Small-Scale Lab

Paper Chromatography of Food Dyes

Purpose

To use paper chromatography to separate and identify food dyes in various samples

Materials

- pencil
- ruler
- scissors
- toothpicks
- 4 different colors of food coloring
- plastic cup
- 0.1% NaCl solution
- chromatography paper

Procedure

Cut a 5 cm × 10 cm strip of chromatography paper and label it with a pencil, as shown below. Use a different toothpick to place a spot of each of the four food colors on the Xs on your chromatography paper. Allow the spots to dry for a few minutes. Fill the plastic cup so its bottom is just covered with the solvent (0.1% NaCl solution). Wrap the chromatography paper around a pencil. Remove the pencil and place the chromatography paper, color-spot side down, in the solvent. When the solvent reaches the top of the chromatography paper, remove the paper and allow it to dry.

Analysis

Using your experimental data, record the answers to the following questions below your data table.

1. If a food-color sample yields a single streak or spot, it is usually a pure compound. Which food colors consist of pure compounds?

2. Which food colors are mixtures of compounds?

3. Food colors often consist of a mixture of three colored dyes: Red No. 40, Yellow No. 5, and Blue No. 1. Read the label on the food-color package. Which dyes do your food-color samples contain?

Food Color Samples   Your name

0.1% NaCl solution

×   ×   ×   ×
Red   Yellow   Green   Blue

4. Identify each spot or streak on your chromatogram as Red No. 40, Yellow No. 5, or Blue No. 1.

5. Paper chromatography separates polar covalent compounds on the basis of their relative polarities. The dyes that are the most polar migrate the fastest and appear at the top of the paper. Which dye is the most polar? Which dye is the least polar?

You're the Chemist

The following small-scale activities allow you to develop your own procedures and analyze the results.

1. Design an Experiment Design and carry out an experiment to identify the dyes in various colored candies.

2. Design an Experiment Design and carry out an experiment to identify the dyes in various colored markers using the paper chromatography method.

3. Design an Experiment Design and carry out an experiment to identify the dyes in various colored powdered drinks using the paper chromatography method.

4. Analyze Data Use different solvents, such as 2-propanol (rubbing alcohol), vinegar, and ammonia, to separate food colors. Does the choice of solvent affect the results?

5. Analyze Data Explore the effect of different papers on your results. Try paper towels, notebook paper, and coffee filters. Report your results. Examine the relative positions of Blue No. 1 and Yellow No. 5. What do you observe?

8 Study Guide

BIGIDEA
BONDING AND INTERACTIONS

In molecular compounds, bonding occurs when atoms share electrons. In ionic compounds, bonding occurs when electrons are transferred between atoms. Shared electrons and the valence electrons that are not shared affect the shape of a molecular compound, as the valence electrons stay as far apart from each other as possible. The molecular properties of a molecule are affected by intermolecular attractions.

8.1 Molecular Compounds

🔑 A molecular formula shows how many atoms of each element a substance contains.

🔑 The representative unit of a molecular compound is a molecule. For an ionic compound, the representative unit is a formula unit.

- covalent bond (223)
- molecule (223)
- diatomic molecule (223)
- molecular compound (223)
- molecular formula (223)

8.2 The Nature of Covalent Bonding

🔑 In covalent bonds, electron sharing occurs so that atoms attain the configurations of noble gases.

🔑 In a coordinate covalent bond, the shared electron pair comes from a single atom.

🔑 The octet rule is not satisfied in molecules with an odd number of valence electrons and in molecules in which an atom has less, or more, than a complete octet of valence electrons.

🔑 A large bond dissociation energy corresponds to a strong covalent bond.

🔑 Chemists use resonance structures to envision the bonding in molecules that cannot be adequately described by a single structural formula.

- single covalent bond (226)
- structural formula (227)
- unshared pair (227)
- double covalent bond (230)
- triple covalent bond (230)
- coordinate covalent bond (232)
- polyatomic ion (232)
- bond dissociation energy (236)
- resonance structure (237)

8.3 Bonding Theories

🔑 Just as an atomic orbital belongs to a particular atom, a molecular orbital belongs to a molecule as a whole.

🔑 In order to explain the three-dimensional shape of molecules, scientists use the valence-shell electron-pair repulsion theory (VSEPR theory).

🔑 Orbital hybridization provides information about both molecular bonding and molecular shape.

- molecular orbital (240)
- bonding orbital (240)
- sigma bond (240)
- pi bond (241)
- tetrahedral angle (242)
- VSEPR theory (242)
- hybridization (244)

8.4 Polar Bonds and Molecules

🔑 When different atoms bond, the more-electronegative atom attracts electrons more strongly and acquires a slightly negative charge.

🔑 Intermolecular attractions are weaker than either an ionic or covalent bond.

🔑 The diversity of physical properties among covalent compounds is mainly because of widely varying intermolecular attractions.

- nonpolar covalent bond (247)
- polar covalent bond (248)
- polar bond (248)
- polar molecule (249)
- dipole (249)
- van der Waals forces (250)
- dipole interaction (250)
- dispersion force (251)
- hydrogen bond (251)
- network solid (252)

 **8 Assessment**

Lesson by Lesson

8.1 Molecular Compounds

39. The melting point of a compound is 1240°C. Is this compound most likely an ionic compound or a molecular compound?

40. Identify the number and kinds of atoms present in a molecule of each compound.

  a. ascorbic acid (vitamin C), $C_6H_8O_6$
  b. sucrose (table sugar), $C_{12}H_{22}O_{11}$
  c. trinitrotoluene (TNT), $C_7H_5N_3O_6$

41. Which of the following gases in Earth's atmosphere would you expect to find as molecules and which as individual atoms? Explain.

  a. nitrogen
  b. oxygen
  c. argon

42. Describe the differences between molecular formulas and structural formulas for molecular compounds.

43. Identify the phrases that generally apply to molecular compounds.

  a. contain metals and nonmetals
  b. are often gases or liquids
  c. have low melting points
  d. contain ionic bonds
  e. use covalent bonding

8.2 The Nature of Covalent Bonding

44. Explain why neon is monatomic but chlorine is diatomic.

45. Classify the following compounds as ionic or covalent:

  a. $MgCl_2$ **c.** H_2O
  b. Na_2S **d.** H_2S

46. Describe the difference between an ionic and a covalent bond.

47. How many electrons do two atoms in a double covalent bond share? How many in a triple covalent bond?

✱**48.** Characterize a coordinate covalent bond and give an example.

49. Draw plausible electron dot structures for the following substances. Each substance contains only single covalent bonds.

  a. I_2 **c.** H_2S
  b. OF_2 **d.** NI_3

✱**50.** Explain why compounds containing C—N and C—O single bonds can form coordinate covalent bonds with H^+ but compounds containing only C—H and C—C single bonds cannot.

51. Draw the electron dot structure of the polyatomic thiocyanate anion (SCN^-).

52. Draw the electron dot structure for the hydrogen carbonate ion (HCO_3^-). Carbon is the central atom, and hydrogen is attached to oxygen in this polyatomic anion.

53. Using electron dot structures, draw at least two resonance structures for the nitrite ion (NO_2^-). The oxygens in NO_2^- are attached to the nitrogen.

✱**54.** Which of these compounds contain elements that do not follow the octet rule? Explain.

  a. NF_3 **c.** SF_4
  b. PCl_2F_3 **d.** SCl_2

55. Explain what is meant by *bond dissociation energy*.

56. What is the relationship between the magnitude of a molecule's bond dissociation energy and its expected chemical reactivity?

57. How many electrons must the atoms of the elements below share with other atoms in covalent bonding to achieve an octet of electrons?

  a. S   **c.** N   **e.** I
  b. C   **d.** Br

✱**58.** Draw the electron dot structures for each of these molecules.

  a. NH_3 **c.** H_2O_2
  b. BrCl   **d.** SiH_4

8.3 Bonding Theories

59. What is a pi bond? Describe, with the aid of a diagram, how the overlap of two half-filled *p* atomic orbitals produces a pi bond.

*60. Use VSEPR theory to predict the shapes of the following compounds:

a. CO_2 c. SO_3 e. CO
b. $SiCl_4$ d. SCl_2 f. H_2Se

61. The molecule CO_2 has two carbon–oxygen double bonds. Describe the bonding in the CO_2 molecule, which involves hybridized orbitals for carbon and oxygen.

62. What type of bonding orbital is always formed between hydrogen and another atom in a covalent compound?

*63. What types of hybrid orbitals are involved in the bonding of the carbon atoms in the following molecules?

a. CH_4
b. $H_2C{=}CH_2$
c. $HC{\equiv}CH$
d. $N{\equiv}C-C{\equiv}N$

8.4 Polar Bonds and Molecules

64. How must the electronegativities of two atoms compare if a covalent bond between them is to be polar?

*65. The bonds between the following pairs of elements are covalent. Arrange them according to polarity, listing the most polar bond first.

a. H—Cl c. H—F e. H—H
b. H—C d. H—O f. S—Cl

66. What is a hydrogen bond?

67. Depict the hydrogen bonding between two ammonia molecules and between one ammonia molecule and one water molecule.

68. Why do compounds with strong intermolecular attractive forces have higher boiling points than compounds with weak intermolecular attractive forces?

*69. Use Table 8.3 to determine how many kilojoules are required to dissociate all the C—H bonds in 1 mol of methane (CH_4).

70. Which of these molecules is least likely to form a hydrogen bond with a water molecule?

a. NH_3 c. HF
b. CH_3Cl d. H_2O_2

Understand Concepts

*71. Devise a hybridization scheme for PCl_3 and predict the molecular shape based on this scheme.

72. The chlorine and oxygen atoms in thionyl chloride ($SOCl_2$) are bonded directly to the sulfur. Draw an acceptable electron dot structure for thionyl chloride.

73. Explain why each electron dot structure is incorrect. Replace each structure with one that is more acceptable.

a. $[:C::N:]^-$

b. $:\ddot{F}:P::\ddot{F}:$
$:\ddot{F}:$

74. Use VSEPR theory to predict the geometry of each of the following:

a. $SiCl_4$ c. CCl_4
b. CO_3^{2-} d. SCl_2

75. The following graph shows how the percent ionic character of a single bond varies according to the difference in electronegativity between the two elements forming the bond. Answer the following questions, using this graph and Table 6.2.

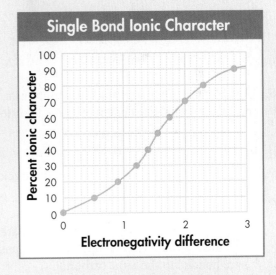

Single Bond Ionic Character

a. What is the relationship between the percent ionic character of single bonds and the electronegativity difference?
b. What electronegativity difference will result in a bond with a 50 percent ionic character?
c. Estimate the percent ionic character of the bonds formed between (1) lithium and oxygen, (2) nitrogen and oxygen, (3) magnesium and chlorine, and (4) nitrogen and fluorine.

76. Give the angles between the orbitals of each hybrid.

　　a. sp^3 hybrids
　　b. sp^2 hybrids
　　c. sp hybrids

77. What is the geometry around the central atom in each of these simple molecules?

a.

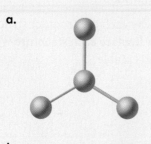

b.

c.

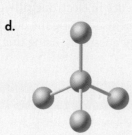

d.

*78. Which of the following molecules contains a central atom that does not obey the octet rule?

　　a. PBr_5　　　　**c.** PF_3
　　b. AlI_3　　　　**d.** $SiCl_4$

79. Vinegar contains the compound ethanoic acid, whose molecular formula is CH_3COOH.

　　a. Draw the electron dot structure of ethanoic acid. (*Hint:* The two carbon atoms are bonded to each other, and the two oxygens are bonded to the same carbon.)
　　b. Is the bonding between each of the oxygen atoms and the carbon the same?
　　c. Is the bonding between the carbon atom and each oxygen atom a polar or nonpolar bond?
　　d. Is ethanoic acid a polar molecule?

Think Critically

80. **Compare** Make a list of the elements in the compounds found in Table 8.2 on page 234. What do the elements that form covalent bonds have in common?

81. **Explain** Is there a clear difference between a very polar covalent bond and an ionic bond? Explain.

*82. **Explain** Ethyl alcohol (CH_3CH_2OH) and dimethyl ether (CH_3OCH_3) each have the same molecular formula, C_2H_6O. Ethyl alcohol has a much higher boiling point (78°C) than dimethyl ether (–25°C). Propose an explanation for this difference.

83. **Evaluate** Although the relative positions of the atoms are correct in each of these molecules, there are one or more incorrect bonds in each of the electron dot structures. Identify the incorrect bonds. Draw the correct electron dot structure for each molecule.

　　a. H=C=C=H
　　b. :F—O—H
　　c. :I⋮⋮⋮Cl:
　　d. H—N⋮⋮⋮N—H

*84. **Predict** What shape do you expect for a molecule with a central atom and the following pairings?

　　a. two bonding pairs of electrons and two nonbonding pairs of electrons
　　b. four bonding pairs and zero nonbonding pairs
　　c. three bonding pairs and one nonbonding pair

85. **Interpret Tables** Is this statement true or false? "As the electronegativity difference between covalently bonded atoms increases, the strength of the bond increases." Use the table below to justify your answer.

Bond	Electronegativity difference	Bond dissociation energy (kJ/mol)
C—C	2.5 – 2.5 = 0.0	347
C—H	2.5 – 2.1 = 0.4	393
C—N	3.0 – 2.5 = 0.5	305
C—O	3.5 – 2.5 = 1.0	356

86. **Explain** There are some compounds in which one atom has more electrons than the corresponding noble gas. Examples are PCl_5, SF_6, and IF_7. Draw the electron dot structures of P, S, and I atoms and of these compounds. Considering the outer shell configuration of P, S, and I, develop an orbital hybridization scheme to explain the existence of these compounds.

87. **Use Models** Draw the electron dot structure of formic acid, H_2CO_2. The carbon is the central atom, and all the atoms are attached to the carbon except for a hydrogen bonded to an oxygen.

88. **Predict** The electron structure and geometry of the methane molecule (CH_4) can be described by a variety of models, including electron dot structure, simple overlap of atomic orbitals, and orbital hybridization of carbon. Draw the electron dot structure of CH_4. Sketch two molecular orbital pictures of the CH_4 molecule. For your first sketch, assume that one of the paired $2s^2$ electrons of carbon has been promoted to the empty $2p$ orbital. Overlap each half-filled atomic orbital of carbon to a half-filled $2s$ orbital of hydrogen. What is the predicted geometry of the CH_4 molecule, using this simple overlap method? In your second sketch, assume hybridization of the $2s$ and $2p$ orbitals of carbon. Now what geometry would you predict for CH_4? Which picture is preferable based on the facts that all H—C—H bond angles in CH_4 are 109.5° and all C—H bond distances are identical?

89. **Use Models** Oxalic acid, $C_2H_2O_4$, is used in polishes and rust removers. Draw the electron dot structure for oxalic acid given that the two carbons are bonded together but neither of the hydrogen atoms is bonded to a carbon atom.

90. **Use Models** Draw as many resonance structures as you can for HN_3. (*Hint:* The three nitrogen atoms are bonded in a row, and the hydrogen atom is bonded to a nitrogen atom at the end of the row of nitrogens.)

*91. **Explain** Draw an electron dot structure for each molecule and explain why it fails to obey the octet rule.
  a. BeF_2 **c.** ClO_2 **e.** XeF_2
  b. SiF_6 **d.** BF_3

92. **Explain** Describe what a molecular compound is. Explain how a molecular formula is the chemical formula of a molecular compound.

93. **Research a Problem** Research how chemists know that an oxygen molecule has unpaired electrons. Write a brief report on what you find.

CHEMYSTERY

What's That Alarm?

The family realized that the alarm was caused by carbon monoxide (CO). In carbon monoxide, the carbon and oxygen atom are joined by a triple covalent bond. Although carbon monoxide and carbon dioxide are both made of carbon and oxygen atoms, they have very different properties.

Carbon monoxide is an odorless, tasteless gas. When it gets into the bloodstream, it causes the hemoglobin to convert to a form that is unable to transport oxygen. Symptoms of carbon monoxide poisoning include headaches, nausea, vomiting, and mental confusion. Exposure to high levels of carbon monoxide can result in death.

Fuel-burning appliances, such as water heaters, fireplaces, furnaces, and gas stoves, produce carbon monoxide. If the appliance is not functioning properly, it may release unsafe amounts of carbon monoxide. If a home contains one of these appliances, then the homeowners should install carbon monoxide detectors, since the gas cannot be detected by sight or smell.

94. **Use Models** Draw the electron dot structures of carbon monoxide and carbon dioxide. Describe the structural differences between these two molecules.

95. **Connect to the BIGIDEA** How does covalent bonding allow there to be different molecular compounds composed of the same kinds of atoms?

Cumulative Review

96. Name three indicators of chemical change.

* **97.** Make the following conversions:

   a. 66.5 mm to micrometers

   b. 4×10^{-2} g to centigrams

   c. 5.62 mg/mL to decigrams per liter

   d. 85 km/h to meters per second

98. How many significant figures are in each measurement?

   a. 0.00052 m   **c.** 5.050 mg

   b. 9.8×10^4 g   **d.** 8.700 mL

99. How many neutrons are in each atom?

   a. silicon-30   **c.** nitrogen-15

   b. magnesium-24   **d.** chromium-50

100. How do isotopes of an atom differ?

* **101.** In a neutral atom, the number of which two subatomic particles must always be equal?

102. How many electrons are in the $2p$ sublevel of an atom of each element?

   a. aluminum   **c.** fluorine

   b. carbon   **d.** lithium

103. What happens to the wavelength of light as the frequency increases?

104. What does the 5 in $3d^5$ represent?

105. Write correct electron configurations for atoms of the following elements:

   a. sodium   **c.** phosphorus

   b. sulfur   **d.** nitrogen

106. How does the ionic radius of a typical anion compare with the radius for the corresponding neutral atom?

107. What criteria did Mendeleev and Moseley use to arrange the elements on the periodic table?

108. Give the electron configuration of the element found at each location in the periodic table.

   a. Group 1A, period 4

   b. Group 3A, period 3

   c. Group 6A, period 3

   d. Group 2A, period 6

* **109.** Identify the larger atom of each pair.

   a. calcium and barium

   b. silicon and sulfur

   c. sodium and nitrogen

110. Which of these statements about the periodic table is correct?

   I. Elements are arranged in order of increasing atomic mass.

   II. A period is a horizontal row.

   III. Nonmetals are located on the right side of the table.

   a. I only

   b. I and II only

   c. I, II, and III

   d. I and III only

   e. II and III only

* **111.** Which of the following ions has the same number of electrons as a noble gas?

   a. Al^{3+}

   b. O^{2-}

   c. Br^-

   d. N^{3-}

112. Which element is likely to form an ionic compound with chlorine?

   a. iodine

   b. cesium

   c. helium

113. How many valence electrons does each atom have?

   a. argon

   b. aluminum

   c. selenium

   d. beryllium

114. Write the electron configuration of each ion.

   a. oxide ion

   b. magnesium ion

   c. nitride ion

   d. potassium ion

115. An alloy is composed of two or more elements. Is an alloy a compound? Explain your answer.

If You Have Trouble With . . .

Question	96	97	98	99	100	101	102	103	104	105	106	107	108	109	110	111	112	113	114	115
See Chapter	2	3	3	4	4	4	5	5	5	5	6	6	6	6	6	7	7	7	7	7

Standardized Test Prep

Select the choice that best answers each question or completes each statement.

1. A bond in which two atoms share a pair of electrons is not
   (A) a coordinate covalent bond.
   (B) a polar covalent bond.
   (C) an ionic bond.
   (D) a nonpolar covalent bond.

2. How many valence electrons are in a molecule of phosphoric acid, H_3PO_4?
   (A) 7   (C) 24
   (B) 16   (D) 32

3. Which of these molecules can form a hydrogen bond with a water molecule?
   (A) N_2 (C) O_2
   (B) NH_3 (D) CH_4

4. Which substance contains both covalent and ionic bonds?
   (A) NH_4NO_3 (C) LiF
   (B) CH_3OCH_3 (D) $CaCl_2$

5. Which of these bonds is most polar?
   (A) H—Cl   (C) H—F
   (B) H—Br   (D) H—I

Use the description and data table below to answer Questions 6–9.

The table relates molecular shape to the number of bonding and nonbonding electron pairs in molecules.

Bonding pairs	Non-bonding pairs	Arrangement of electron pairs	Molecular shape	Example
4	0	tetrahedral	tetrahedral	CH_4
3	1	tetrahedral	pyramidal	NCl_3
2	2	tetrahedral	bent	H_2S
1	3	tetrahedral	linear	HF

6. Draw the electron dot structure for each example molecule.

7. Explain why the arrangement of electron pairs is tetrahedral in each molecule.

8. H_2S has two hydrogen atoms bonded to a sulfur atom. Why isn't the molecule linear?

9. What is the arrangement of electron pairs in PBr_3? Predict the molecular shape of a PBr_3 molecule.

For Questions 10–11, identify the type of intermolecular bonding represented by the dotted lines in the drawings.

10. H_2O

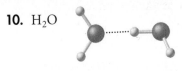

11. BrCl

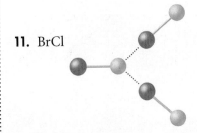

In Questions 12–14, a statement is followed by an explanation. Decide if each statement is true, and then decide if the explanation given is correct.

12. A carbon monoxide molecule has a triple covalent bond because carbon and oxygen atoms have an unequal number of valence electrons.

13. Xenon has a lower boiling point than neon because dispersion forces between xenon atoms are stronger than those between neon atoms.

14. The nitrate ion has three resonance structures because the nitrate ion has three single bonds.

If You Have Trouble With . . .														
Question	1	2	3	4	5	6	7	8	9	10	11	12	13	14
See Lesson	8.2	8.2	8.4	8.3	8.1	8.3	8.2	8.2	8.2	8.2	8.4	8.4	8.4	8.2

9

Chemical Names and Formulas

INSIDE:

PearsonChem.com

Many transition metals form brightly colored compounds that are used in making artists' paints.

- **ELECTRONS AND THE STRUCTURE OF ATOMS**
- **BONDING AND INTERACTIONS**

Essential Questions:

1. *How does the periodic table help you determine the names and formulas of ions and compounds?*

2. *What is the difference between an ionic and a molecular compound?*

CHEMYSTERY

Cucumber Blunder

Tara's friend, Ellie, raves about the delicious lime pickles that Tara's grandma makes. As a surprise, Tara decided to make a batch for Ellie. She got the recipe from her grandma. It called for "1 cup of lime for every 3 pounds of cucumbers."

When the pickles were ready, Tara proudly presented the gift to Ellie. She watched Ellie's face as she bit into a pickle. After the first bite, Ellie made an awful face. "What's wrong?" Tara asked. After a short pause, Ellie replied, "They taste . . . funny." Tara tried one and agreed; they tasted nothing like her grandma's pickles. What did Tara do wrong?

▶ Connect to the **BIGIDEA** As you read about naming compounds, think about what might have caused Tara's cucumber blunder.

NATIONAL SCIENCE EDUCATION STANDARDS

A-1, A-2, B-2, E-2, F-4, G-1, G-2, G-3

9.1 Naming Ions

CHEMISTRY & YOU

Q: *Do you speak "Chemistry"?* Try looking at the ingredient label on a household product—a bottle of shampoo, a tube of toothpaste, a box of detergent. Do the names of the ingredients make sense? To truly understand chemistry, you must learn its language. Part of learning the language of chemistry involves understanding how to name ionic compounds. For this you need to know how to name ions.

Key Questions

▬ How can you determine the charges of monatomic ions?

▬ How do polyatomic ions differ from monatomic ions? How are they similar?

Vocabulary

• monatomic ion

Monatomic Ions

▬ **How can you determine the charges of monatomic ions?**

Ionic compounds consist of a positive metal ion and a negative nonmetal ion combined in a proportion such that their charges add up to a net charge of zero. For example, the ionic compound sodium chloride (NaCl) consists of one sodium ion (Na^+) and one chloride ion (Cl^-). Probably you are already familiar with the name and formula of sodium chloride, which is common table salt. But it is important, in learning the language of chemistry, to be able to name and write the chemical formulas for all ionic compounds. The first step is to learn about the ions that form ionic compounds. Some ions, called **monatomic ions,** consist of a single atom with a positive or negative charge resulting from the loss or gain of one or more valence electrons, respectively.

Cations Recall that metallic elements tend to lose valence electrons. Lithium, sodium, and potassium in Group 1A lose one electron to form cations. All the Group 1A ions have a 1+ charge (Li^+, Na^+, K^+, Rb^+, Cs^+, and Fr^+). Magnesium and calcium are Group 2A metals. They tend to lose two electrons to form cations with a 2+ charge (Mg^{2+} and Ca^{2+}), as do all the other Group 2A metals. Aluminum is the only common Group 3A metal. As you might expect, aluminum tends to lose three electrons to form a 3+ cation (Al^{3+}). ▬ **When the metals in Groups 1A, 2A, and 3A lose electrons, they form cations with positive charges equal to their group number.** Figure 9.1 shows some of the elements whose ionic charges can be obtained from their positions in the periodic table.

The names of the cations of the Group 1A, Group 2A, and Group 3A metals are the same as the name of the metal, followed by the word *ion* or *cation*. Thus Na^+ is the sodium ion (or cation), Ca^{2+} is the calcium ion (or cation), and Al^{3+} is the aluminum ion (or cation).

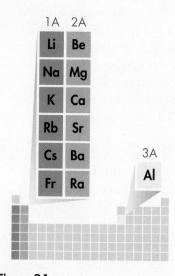

Figure 9.1
Elements That Form Cations
These representative elements form positive ions with charges equal to their group number.

Table 9.1

Ion Symbols for Some Group A Elements

1A	2A	3A	4A	5A	6A	7A	8A
Li^+	Be^{2+}			N^{3-}	O^{2-}	F^-	
Na^+	Mg^{2+}	Al^{3+}		P^{3-}	S^{2-}	Cl^-	
K^+	Ca^{2+}			As^{3-}	Se^{2-}	Br^-	
Rb^+	Sr^{2+}					I^-	
Cs^+	Ba^{2+}						

Anions Nonmetals tend to gain electrons to form anions, so the charge of a nonmetallic ion is negative. 🔑 **The charge of any ion of a Group A nonmetal is determined by subtracting 8 from the group number.** The elements in Group 7A form anions with a 1− charge (7 − 8 = −1). The name of an anion is not the same as the element's name. Anion names start with the stem of the element name and end in *-ide*. For example, two elements in Group 7A are fluorine and chlorine. The anions for these non-metals are the fluor*ide* ion (F^-) and chlor*ide* ion (Cl^-). Anions of nonmetals in Group 6A have a 2− charge (6 − 8 = −2). Group 6A elements, oxygen and sulfur, form the ox*ide* anion (O^{2-}) and the sulf*ide* anion (S^{2-}), respectively. The first three elements in Group 5A, nitrogen, phosphorus, and arsenic, can form anions with a 3− charge (5 − 8 = −3). These anions have the symbols N^{3-}, P^{3-}, and As^{3-} and are called, respectively, nitr*ide* ion, phosph*ide* ion, and arsen*ide* ion. Figure 9.2 shows some common Group A elements that form anions. Table 9.1 summarizes the ionic charges of representative elements that can be obtained from the periodic table. The majority of the elements in Groups 4A and 8A usually do not form ions.

Metals That Form More Than One Ion

The metals of Groups 1A, 2A, and 3A consistently form cations with charges of 1+, 2+, and 3+, respectively. Many of the transition metals (Groups 1B–8B) form more than one cation with different ionic charges. Some of these are shown in Figure 9.3. 🔑 **The charges of the cations of many transition metal ions must be deter-mined from the number of electrons lost.** For example, the tran-sition metal iron forms two common cations, Fe^{2+} (two electrons lost) and Fe^{3+} (three electrons lost). Cations of tin and lead, the two metals in Group 4A, can also have more than one common ionic charge.

Two methods are used to name these ions. The preferred method is called the Stock system. In the Stock system, you place a Roman numeral in parentheses after the name of the element to indicate the numerical value of the charge. For example, the cation Fe^{2+} is named iron(II) ion. Note that no space is left between the element name and the Roman numeral in parentheses. The name for Fe^{2+} is read "iron two ion." The Fe^{3+} ion is named iron(III) ion and is read "iron three ion."

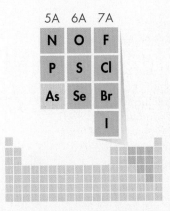

Figure 9.2 Elements That Form Anions
These representative elements form negative ions with charges equal to the group number of the element minus 8.

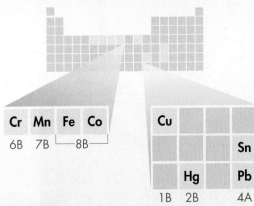

Figure 9.3
Elements That Form More Than One Ion
These metallic elements form more than one positive ion.
Identify *Which of these elements are transition metals?*

An older, less useful method for naming these cations uses a root word with different suffixes at the end of the word. The older, or classical, name of the element is used to form the root name for the element. For example, *ferrum* is Latin for iron, so *ferr-* is the root name for iron. The suffix *-ous* is used to name the cation with the lower of the two ionic charges. The suffix *-ic* is used with the higher of the two ionic charges. Using this system, Fe^{2+} is the ferrous ion, and Fe^{3+} is the ferric ion, as shown in Table 9.2. Notice that you can usually identify an element from what may be an unfamiliar classical name by looking for the element's symbol in the name. For example, *fe*rrous (Fe) is iron; *cu*prous (Cu) is copper; and *s*ta*n*nous (Sn) is tin. A major disadvantage of using classical names for ions is that they do not tell you the actual charge of the ion. A classical name tells you only that the cation has either the smaller (*-ous*) or the larger (*-ic*) charge of the pair of possible ions for that element.

CHEMISTRY & YOU

Q: *Suppose you were trying to teach someone how to name ions. Which rules about the "language of chemistry" would you emphasize?*

A few transition metals have only one ionic charge. The names of these cations do not have a Roman numeral. These exceptions include silver, with cations that have a 1+ charge (Ag^{+}), as well as cadmium and zinc, with cations that have a 2+ charge (Cd^{2+} and Zn^{2+}). As Figure 9.4 shows, some transition metal ions form colorful solutions.

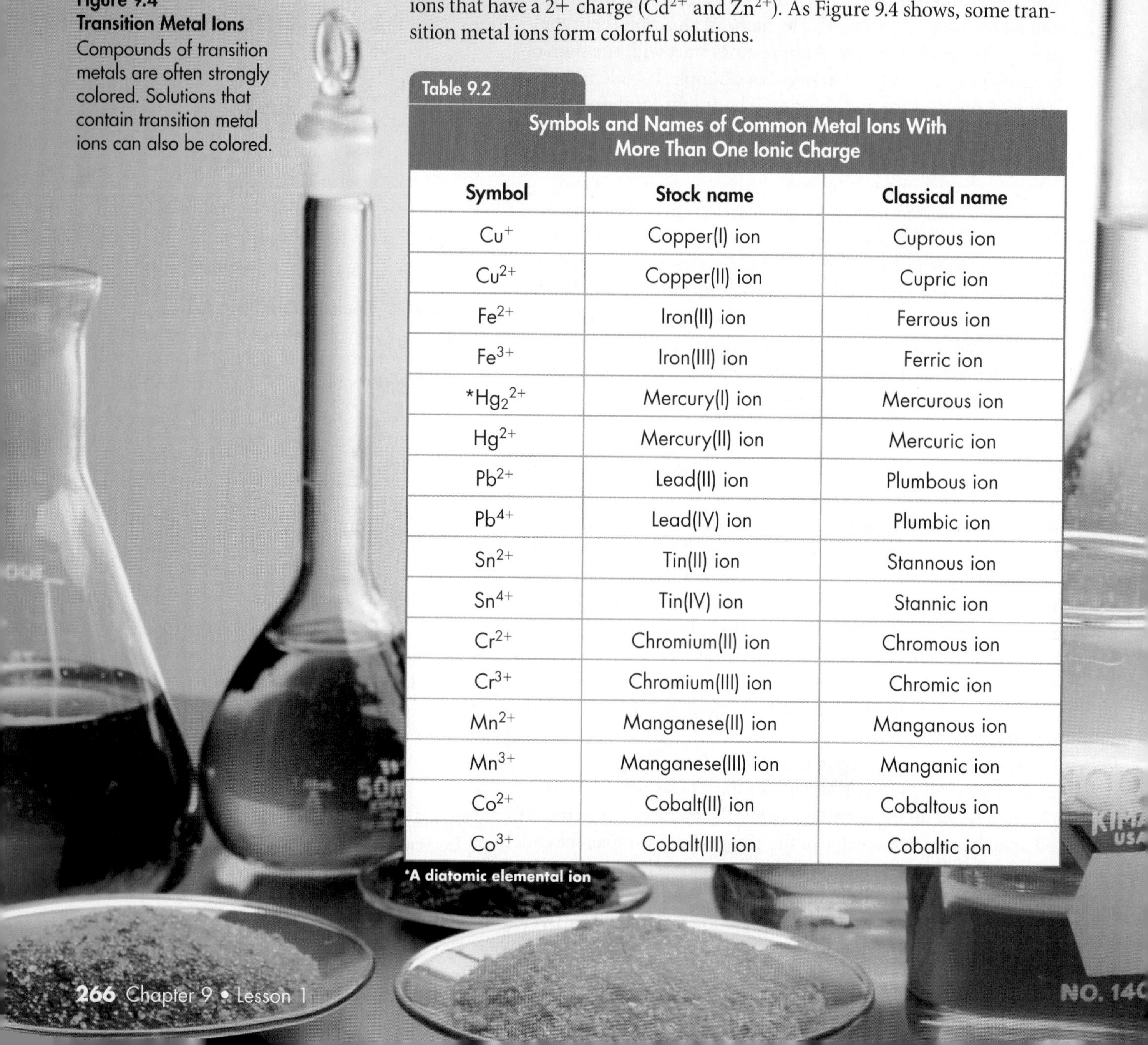

Figure 9.4
Transition Metal Ions
Compounds of transition metals are often strongly colored. Solutions that contain transition metal ions can also be colored.

Table 9.2

Symbols and Names of Common Metal Ions With More Than One Ionic Charge

Symbol	Stock name	Classical name
Cu^{+}	Copper(I) ion	Cuprous ion
Cu^{2+}	Copper(II) ion	Cupric ion
Fe^{2+}	Iron(II) ion	Ferrous ion
Fe^{3+}	Iron(III) ion	Ferric ion
*Hg_2^{2+}	Mercury(I) ion	Mercurous ion
Hg^{2+}	Mercury(II) ion	Mercuric ion
Pb^{2+}	Lead(II) ion	Plumbous ion
Pb^{4+}	Lead(IV) ion	Plumbic ion
Sn^{2+}	Tin(II) ion	Stannous ion
Sn^{4+}	Tin(IV) ion	Stannic ion
Cr^{2+}	Chromium(II) ion	Chromous ion
Cr^{3+}	Chromium(III) ion	Chromic ion
Mn^{2+}	Manganese(II) ion	Manganous ion
Mn^{3+}	Manganese(III) ion	Manganic ion
Co^{2+}	Cobalt(II) ion	Cobaltous ion
Co^{3+}	Cobalt(III) ion	Cobaltic ion

*A diatomic elemental ion

Naming Cations and Anions

Name the ion formed by each of the following elements:

a. potassium   **b.** lead, 4 electrons lost   **c.** sulfur

❶ Analyze   Identify the relevant concepts. You can use the periodic table to determine the charge of most Group A elements. Ions with positive charges are cations; ions with negative charges are anions. The names of nonmetallic anions end in *-ide*. Metallic cations take the name of the metal. Some metals, including transition metals, can form more than one cation. Use a Roman numeral in the Stock name or use the classical name with a suffix to name these metals.

❷ Solve   Apply the concepts to this problem.

	a. K	b. Pb	c. S
Write the symbol for the element.	a. K	b. Pb	c. S
Determine the charge of the ion formed by the element.	1+	4+	2−
Determine whether the ion is a cation or an anion.	K^+ is a cation.	Pb^{4+} is a cation.	S^{2-} is an anion.
Apply the appropriate rules for naming the ion. Use a Roman numeral if necessary.	Following the rules for naming metallic cations, K^+ is named potassium ion.	Following the rules for naming metals that can form more than one cation, Pb^{4+} is named lead(IV) or plumbic ion.	Following the rules for naming nonmetallic anions, S^{2-} is named sulfide ion.

1. Name the ions formed by the following elements:
   a. selenium
   b. barium
   c. phosphorus
   d. iodine

2. How many electrons were lost or gained to form these ions?
   a. Fe^{3+} **c.** Cu^+
   b. O^{2-} **d.** Sr^{2+}

A negative charge means electrons gained; a positive charge means electrons lost.

Ammonium ion
(NH_4^+)

Nitrate ion
(NO_3^-)

Sulfate ion
(SO_4^{2-})

Phosphate ion
(PO_4^{3-})

Figure 9.5 Polyatomic Ions
These molecular models show the arrangement of atoms in four common polyatomic ions.
Compare *How does the ammonium ion differ from the other three ions?*

Table 9.3		
Common Polyatomic Ions		
Charge	Formula	Name
1−	$H_2PO_4^-$	Dihydrogen phosphate
	$C_2H_3O_2^-$	Ethanoate
	HSO_3^-	Hydrogen sulfite
	HSO_4^-	Hydrogen sulfate
	HCO_3^-	Hydrogen carbonate
	NO_2^-	Nitrite
	NO_3^-	Nitrate
	CN^-	Cyanide
	OH^-	Hydroxide
	MnO_4^-	Permanganate
	ClO^-	Hypochlorite
	ClO_2^-	Chlorite
	ClO_3^-	Chlorate
	ClO_4^-	Perchlorate
2−	HPO_4^{2-}	Hydrogen phosphate
	$C_2O_4^{2-}$	Oxalate
	SO_3^{2-}	Sulfite
	SO_4^{2-}	Sulfate
	CO_3^{2-}	Carbonate
	CrO_4^{2-}	Chromate
	$Cr_2O_7^{2-}$	Dichromate
	SiO_3^{2-}	Silicate
3−	PO_3^{3-}	Phosphite
	PO_4^{3-}	Phosphate
1+	NH_4^+	Ammonium

Polyatomic Ions

🔑 *How do polyatomic ions differ from monatomic ions? How are they similar?*

Some ions, such as the sulfate ion, are called polyatomic ions. 🔑 **Unlike a monatomic ion, a polyatomic ion is composed of more than one atom. But like a monatomic ion, a polyatomic ion behaves as a unit and carries a charge.** The sulfate anion consists of one sulfur atom and four oxygen atoms. These five atoms together comprise a single anion with an overall 2− charge. The formula is written SO_4^{2-}. You can see the structure of the sulfate ion along with three other common polyatomic ions in Figure 9.5.

The names and formulas of some common polyatomic ions are shown in Table 9.3, grouped according to their charges. Note that the names of most polyatomic anions end in *-ite* or *-ate*. For example, notice the endings of the names of the hypochlor*ite* ion (ClO^-) and the hydrogen carbon*ate* ion (HCO_3^-). Also notice that three important ions have different endings—the cyan*ide* anion (CN^-), the hydrox*ide* anion (OH^-), and the ammon*ium* cation (NH_4^+).

Sometimes the same two or three elements combine in different ratios to form different polyatomic ions. Several examples appear in Table 9.3. Look for pairs of ions for which there is both an *-ite* and an *-ate* ending, for example, sulfite and sulfate. Examine the charge on each ion in the pair. Note the number of oxygen atoms and the endings on each name. You should be able to discern a pattern in the naming convention.

-ite	*-ate*
SO_3^{2-}, sulfite	SO_4^{2-}, sulfate
NO_2^-, nitrite	NO_3^-, nitrate
ClO_2^-, chlorite	ClO_3^-, chlorate

The charge on each polyatomic ion in a given pair is the same. The -*ite* ending indicates one less oxygen atom than the -*ate* ending. However, the ending does not tell you the actual number of oxygen atoms in the ion. For example, the nitrite ion has two oxygen atoms, and the sulfite ion has three oxygen atoms. All anions with names ending in -*ite* or -*ate* contain oxygen.

When the formula for a polyatomic ion begins with H (hydrogen), you can think of the H as representing a hydrogen ion (H^+) combined with another polyatomic ion. For example, HCO_3^- is a combination of H^+ and CO_3^{2-}. Note that the charge on the new ion is the algebraic sum of the ionic charges of the two component ions.

$$H^+ + CO_3^{2-} \longrightarrow HCO_3^-$$
carbonate   hydrogen carbonate

$$H^+ + PO_4^{3-} \longrightarrow HPO_4^{2-}$$
phosphate   hydrogen phosphate

$$H^+ + HPO_4^{2-} \longrightarrow H_2PO_4^-$$
hydrogen phosphate   dihydrogen phosphate

The hydrogen carbonate anion (HCO_3^-), the hydrogen phosphate anion (HPO_4^{2-}), and the dihydrogen phosphate anion ($H_2PO_4^-$) are essential components of living systems. In contrast, the cyanide ion (CN^-) is extremely poisonous to living systems because it blocks a cell's means of producing energy. Figure 9.6 shows two uses for compounds with hydrogen-containing polyatomic ions.

Figure 9.6 Hydrogen-Containing Polyatomic Ions
Polyatomic ions that contain hydrogen are part of several compounds that affect your daily life.

Antacid Sodium hydrogen carbonate, which contains the HCO_3^- ion, can relieve an upset stomach.

Blood The presence of dissolved HCO_3^-, HPO_4^{2-}, and $H_2PO_4^-$ ions in your blood is critical for your health.

9.1 LessonCheck

3. 🔑 **Explain** How can you determine the charges of metal cations? Of nonmetal anions? Of transition metal cations?

4. 🔑 **Review** What are the similarities and differences between polyatomic ions and monatomic ions?

5. **Identify** What are the charges on ions of Group 1A, Group 3A (aluminum), and Group 5A?

6. **Describe** Write the symbol for the ion of each element. Classify the ion as an anion or a cation, and name the ion.

   a. potassium
   b. oxygen
   c. bromine
   d. tin (2 electrons lost)
   e. beryllium
   f. cobalt (3 electrons lost)

7. **Describe** Write the symbol or formula (including charge) for each of the following ions:

   a. ammonium ion
   b. chromium(II) ion
   c. chromate ion
   d. nitrate ion

8. **Compare** How do the differences in the polyatomic ions PO_3^{3-} and PO_4^{3-} help you determine whether each ends in -*ite* or -*ate*?

BIGIDEA

ELECTRONS AND THE STRUCTURE OF ATOMS

9. How does the electron configuration of an ion of a Group 1A or Group 7A element compare to that of the nearest noble gas?

Algal Blooms

Have you ever seen a lake or river covered with what looks like green or blue-green paint? This "paint" is actually high concentrations of algae that have reproduced rapidly. This event is called an algal bloom. Freshwater algal blooms often occur when there is an excess of phosphate compounds, commonly called phosphates, in the water. Phosphates are nutrients that algae need to survive. However, when phosphate levels are too high, algae grow and reproduce at unusually rapid rates.

Although most algal blooms are not harmful, some release toxins that are dangerous to humans and animals. Even nontoxic algal blooms may cause problems. For example, they may deplete the amount of oxygen in water and block sunlight, which underwater plants need to live. In addition, algal blooms may alter the taste and odor of the water.

Phosphates are found in fertilizers, detergents, and other cleaning products. These products can enter waterways by direct dumping and runoff. To help reduce the occurrence of algae blooms, government agencies and industries have collaborated to provide detergents, soaps, and cleaning agents that are more environmentally friendly. Next time you go to the store, notice that many detergents have a "Phosphate Free" label.

CONTAMINATION Some blue-green algae such as this *Microcystis* species can produce toxins that may contaminate drinking water.

Take It Further

1. Identify Sodium phosphate is one example of a phosphate compound. It was once widely used in detergents. Write the formula for this compound.

2. Infer How might an algal bloom affect aquatic grasses?

3. Research a Problem There are several other factors that can contribute to an algal bloom. Research this topic and identify at least two other factors that contribute to algal blooms.

SUFFOCATION Algal blooms can result in the death of fish by consuming too much dissolved oxygen in the water.

9.2 Naming and Writing Formulas for Ionic Compounds

CHEMISTRY & YOU

Q: *What's the name of the secret ingredient?* If this ingredient isn't included in the recipe, the fruit can turn an ugly brown. Think about when you slice an apple at home. The slices don't look that tasty if you let them sit for too long because they begin to change color. But with the recipe and the secret ingredient, your apple slices could keep their color. Chemistry also uses recipes or formulas, but without any secrets. Once you know the rules, you can apply them and name any chemical compound. In this lesson, you will learn how to name ionic compounds.

Key Questions

🔑 How do you determine the formula and name of a binary ionic compound?

🔑 How do you determine the formula and name of a compound with a polyatomic ion?

Vocabulary

• binary compound

Binary Ionic Compounds

🔑 **How do you determine the formula and name of a binary ionic compound?**

In the days before the science of chemistry developed, the person who discovered a new compound often named it anything he or she wished. It was not uncommon for the name to describe some property of the substance or its source. For example, a common name for potassium carbonate (K_2CO_3) is *potash*. The name evolved because the compound was obtained by boiling wood ashes in iron pots. Baking soda ($NaHCO_3$) is another example. The common name, *baking soda,* describes its use in baking to make baked goods rise. Figure 9.7 shows a compound with the common name of cinnabar. Can you tell what elements are in cinnabar just from looking at the name? Unfortunately, such names do not tell you anything about the chemical composition of the compound.

The French chemist Antoine-Laurent Lavoisier (1743–1794) determined the composition of many compounds in his experiments to show how chemical compounds form. As more and more compounds were identified, Lavoisier recognized that it was becoming impossible to memorize all the unrelated names of the compounds. He worked with other chemists to develop a systematic method for naming chemical compounds. Their work is the basis for naming compounds today.

Figure 9.7 Cinnabar
The red substance that is deposited in this rock is commonly called cinnabar. Cinnabar (HgS) is comprised of mercury(II) ions and sulfide ions.

Figure 9.8 Steelworks
In the process for making steel, iron is extracted from hematite, an ore containing iron(III) oxide. **Apply Concepts** *What is the formula for iron(III) oxide?*

Writing Formulas for Binary Ionic Compounds

A **binary compound** is composed of two elements. Binary compounds can be ionic compounds or molecular compounds. If you know the name of a binary ionic compound, you can write the formula. **To write the formula of a binary ionic compound, first write the symbol of the cation and then the anion. Then add subscripts as needed to balance the charges.** The positive charge of the cation must balance the negative charge of the anion so that the net ionic charge of the formula is zero. The ionic compound potassium chloride is composed of potassium cations (K^+) and chloride anions (Cl^-), so potassium chloride is a binary ionic compound. The charge of each K^+ cation is balanced by the charge of each Cl^- anion. So, in potassium chloride, the potassium and chloride ions combine in a 1:1 ratio. Thus, the formula for potassium chloride is KCl. The net ionic charge of the formula unit is zero.

The binary ionic compound calcium bromide is composed of calcium cations (Ca^{2+}) and bromide anions (Br^-). The two ions do not have equal numerical charges. Thus, each calcium ion with its 2+ charge must combine with (or be balanced by) two bromide ions, each with a 1− charge. That means that the ions must combine in a 1:2 ratio, so the formula for calcium bromide is $CaBr_2$. The net ionic charge of the formula unit is zero.

Figure 9.8 shows one step in the process of making steel from iron ore. Hematite, a common ore of iron, contains iron(III) oxide. What is the formula for this compound? Recall that a Roman numeral in the name of an ion shows the charge of the metal ion. Thus, iron(III) oxide contains Fe^{3+} cations combined with oxide anions (O^{2-}). How can you balance a 3+ charge and a 2− charge? You must find the least common multiple of the charges, which is 6. Iron's three charges taken two times equals six ($3 \times 2 = 6$). Oxygen's two charges taken three times also equals six. Thus, two Fe^{3+} cations (a 6+ charge) will balance three O^{2-} anions (a 6− charge). The balanced formula, then, is Fe_2O_3.

Another approach to writing a balanced formula for a compound is to use the crisscross method. In this method, the numerical value of the charge of each ion is crossed over and becomes the subscript for the other ion. Notice that the signs of the charges are dropped.

$$Fe^{3+}_{} \quad O^{2-}$$
$$Fe_2O_3$$
$$2(3+) + 3(2-) = 0$$

The formula is correct because the overall charge of the formula is zero, and the subscripts are expressed in the lowest whole-number ratio.

If you use the crisscross method to write the formula for some compounds such as calcium sulfide (Ca^{2+} and S^{2-}), you will obtain the result Ca_2S_2. However, the 2:2 ratio of calcium and sulfide ions is not the lowest whole-number ratio. The correct formula for calcium sulfide is CaS.

$$Ca^{2+} \quad S^{2-}$$
$$Ca_2S_2 \text{ reduces to CaS}$$
$$1(2+) + 1(2-) = 0$$

Of course, if the magnitudes of the charges of the cation and anion are the same, as they are in this case, the ions combine in a 1:1 ratio, and the charges are balanced.

Sample Problem 9.2

Writing Formulas for Binary Ionic Compounds

Write formulas for the following binary ionic compounds.

a. copper(II) sulfide   **b.** potassium nitride

❶ Analyze Identify the relevant concepts. Binary ionic compounds are composed of a monatomic cation and a monatomic anion. The symbol for the cation appears first in the formula for the compound. The ionic charges in an ionic compound must balance, and the ions must be combined in the lowest whole-number ratio.

❷ Solve Apply the concepts to this problem.

Write the symbol and charge for each ion in the compound—the cation first, then the anion.	**a.** Cu^{2+} and S^{2-} **b.** K^+ and N^{3-}

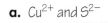
The crisscross method is used in the following solutions.

Balance the formula using appropriate subscripts. Make sure that the formula expresses the lowest whole-number ratio of ions.

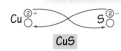
CuS

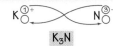
K_3N

Check that the charges of the two ions add up to zero.

$$1(2+) + 1(2-) = 0 \qquad 3(1+) + 1(3-) = 0$$

10. Write formulas for compounds formed from these pairs of ions.

a. Ba^{2+}, S^{2-} **c.** Ca^{2+}, N^{3-}
b. Li^+, O^{2-} **d.** Cu^{2+}, I^-

11. Write formulas for the following ionic compounds.

a. sodium iodide   **c.** potassium sulfide
b. stannous chloride   **d.** calcium iodide

Remember to add subscripts to make the compound neutral.

Figure 9.9 Tin Compounds
Tin(II) fluoride and tin(IV) oxide have different compositions and uses.
a. Tin(II) fluoride is added to some toothpastes to prevent cavities. **b.** Tin(IV) oxide is used in glazes for pottery.
Identify *What are the charges of the tin ions in the two compounds?*

(a)

(b)

See some everyday chemical names *online.*

CHEMISTRY & YOU

Q: *Many companies use sodium sulfite (Na₂SO₃) to keep dried fruit looking delicious. Is Na₂SO₃ a binary compound? Explain.*

Naming Binary Ionic Compounds If you know the formula for a binary ionic compound, you can write its name. First you must verify that the compound is composed of a monatomic metallic cation and a monatomic nonmetallic anion. 🔑 **To name any binary ionic compound, place the cation name first, followed by the anion name.** For example, the compound Cs_2O is composed of the metal cesium and the nonmetal oxygen. Both cesium and oxygen are Group A elements that have only one charge. The name of Cs_2O, then, is cesium oxide. Similarly, the name of NaBr is sodium bromide, and the name of SrF_2 is strontium fluoride.

But suppose you want to name the binary ionic compound CuO. Following the rule above, you would name this compound copper oxide. However, the name *copper oxide* is incomplete. Recall that copper commonly forms two cations: Cu^+ and Cu^{2+}. The names of these ions are copper(I) ion and copper(II) ion, respectively. How can you tell which of these cations forms the compound CuO? Working backward will help. The formula indicates that the copper cation and the oxide anion combine in a 1:1 ratio. You know that the oxide anion always has a 2− charge. Therefore, the charge of the copper cation must be 2+ in order to balance the 2− charge. The compound CuO must be copper(II) oxide. 🔑 **If the metallic element in a binary ionic compound has more than one common ionic charge, a Roman numeral must be included in the cation name.**

Table 9.2 lists the symbols and names of the common metals that form more than one cation. Recall that the charges of monatomic anions can be determined from the periodic table. Using these two sources, you can write the names of SnF_2 and SnS_2. Tin (Sn) forms cations with 2+ and 4+ charges. Fluorine is a Group 7A element, so the charge of the fluoride ion is 1−. In SnF_2, the ratio of cations to anions is 1:2. Therefore, the charge of the tin cation must be 2+ to balance the combined 2− charge of two fluoride ions. The name of SnF_2 is tin(II) fluoride or stannous fluoride. However, the name of SnO_2 is not tin(II) oxide. Oxygen is a Group 6A element, so its charge is 2−. The charge of the tin cation must be 4+ to balance the combined charges of two oxide anions. Thus, the name of SnO_2 is tin(IV) oxide or stannic oxide. Figure 9.9 shows examples of uses of stannous fluoride and stannic oxide.

Naming Binary Ionic Compounds

Name the following binary ionic compounds:

a. CoI_2 **b.** Li_2Se

❶ **Analyze** **Identify the relevant concepts.** Confirm that the compound is a binary ionic compound. To name the compound, name the ions in the order written in the formula—the cation name followed by the anion name. The name of a metal ion that has more than one common ionic charge must include a Roman numeral indicating the charge.

❷ **Solve** **Apply the concepts to this problem.**

Interpret the chemical formula in terms of component elements. If you find two elements, the compound is binary.	**a.** CoI_2 contains cobalt cations and iodide anions.
	b. Li_2Se contains lithium cations and selenide anions.
Determine whether the metal ion in the compound has more than one common ionic charge.	Cobalt forms two common cations: Co^{2+} and Co^{3+}.
	Lithium forms one cation: Li^+.
If the metal ion has more than one ionic charge, use the nonmetal anion to determine which cation is indicated by the formula.	Iodide ion is I^-. The formula CoI_2 specifies two iodide ions, which give a charge of 2–. So the cobalt ion must be Co^{2+} to balance the charge.
	This step is not needed for Li_2Se because the lithium ion has only one common charge.
Write the name of the cation, followed by the name of the anion. Include Roman numerals as needed.	cobalt(II) iodide
	lithium selenide

12. Name the following binary ionic compounds:

  a. ZnS   **c.** BaO
  b. KCl   **d.** $CuBr_2$

Check each answer by writing the formula using the ions from the name.

13. Write the names for these binary ionic compounds.

  a. CaO   **c.** FeS
  b. Cu_2Se **d.** AlF_3

Compounds With Polyatomic Ions

🔑 How do you determine the formula and name of a compound with a polyatomic ion?

The seashells shown in Figure 9.10 are made of calcium carbonate ($CaCO_3$). Calcium carbonate is obviously not a binary compound because it contains more than two elements. Remember that an -*ate* or -*ite* ending on the name of a compound indicates that the compound contains a polyatomic anion that includes oxygen. Calcium carbonate contains one monatomic ion (Ca^{2+}) and one polyatomic ion (CO_3^{2-}). Figure 9.10 also shows a typical automobile battery called a lead storage battery. The energy-producing reaction inside the battery uses the ionic compound lead(II) sulfate ($PbSO_4$), which consists of the monatomic ion Pb^{2+} and the polyatomic ion SO_4^{2-}.

Figure 9.10
Compounds With Polyatomic Ions
Some examples of ionic compounds that contain polyatomic ions are shown. **Explain** *Why is there a Roman numeral in the name lead(II) sulfate?*

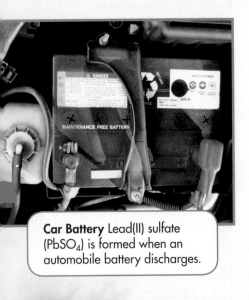

Car Battery Lead(II) sulfate ($PbSO_4$) is formed when an automobile battery discharges.

Writing Formulas for Compounds With Polyatomic Ions How would you write the formula for an ionic compound with a polyatomic ion? For starters, try following the same procedure you used for binary ionic compounds. 🔑 **To write the formula for a compound with a polyatomic ion, first write the symbol (or formula) for the cation followed by the symbol (or formula) for the anion. Then, add subscripts as needed to balance the charges.** For example, calcium nitrate is composed of a calcium cation (Ca^{2+}) and a polyatomic nitrate anion (NO_3^-). In calcium nitrate, two nitrate anions, each with a 1− charge, are needed to balance the 2+ charge of each calcium cation.

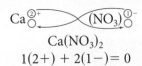

$$Ca(NO_3)_2$$
$$1(2+) + 2(1-) = 0$$

The charge is balanced and the ions are expressed in the lowest whole-number ratio, so the formula is correct. Parentheses are used around the nitrate ion in the formula because more than one nitrate anion is needed. The subscript 2 that follows the parentheses shows that the compound contains two nitrate anions. 🔑 **Whenever more than one polyatomic ion is needed to balance the charges in an ionic compound, use parentheses to set off the polyatomic ion in the formula.**

Go online to make and name some ionic *compounds.*

VIRTUAL LAB

Shells The shells of marine organisms are composed of calcium carbonate ($CaCO_3$).

Lithium carbonate is a compound that can be prescribed for patients who have mood disorders, such as manic-depressive disorder or bipolar disorder. The compound is composed of lithium cations (Li^+) and polyatomic carbonate anions (CO_3^{2-}). In the formula for lithium carbonate, two lithium cations, each with a 1+ charge, are needed to balance the 2− charge of one carbonate anion. Parentheses are not needed to set off the polyatomic carbonate anion.

$$Li \quad (CO_3)$$
$$Li_2CO_3$$
$$2(1+) + 1(2-) = 0$$

Strontium sulfate is another example of a compound in which only a single polyatomic ion (SO_4^{2-}) is needed to balance the cation (Sr^{2+}). So, no parentheses are needed when writing the formula: $SrSO_4$.

Sample Problem 9.4

Writing Formulas for Compounds With Polyatomic Ions

What are the formulas for these ionic compounds?

a. magnesium hydroxide
b. potassium sulfate

❶ Analyze Identify the relevant concepts. Write the symbol or formula for each ion in the order listed in the name. Use subscripts to balance the charges. The ions must be combined in the lowest whole-number ratio. If more than one polyatomic ion is needed to balance a formula, place the polyatomic ion formula in parentheses, followed by the appropriate subscript.

❷ Solve Apply the concepts to this problem.

Write the symbol or formula for each ion in the compound—the cation first, then the anion. Include the charge for each ion.	**a.** cation: Mg^{2+} **b.** cation: K^+ anion: OH^- anion: SO_4^{2-}
Balance the formula using appropriate subscripts. Make sure that the formula expresses the lowest whole-number ratio of ions.	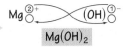 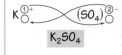
Check that the charges of the two ions add up to zero.	$1(2+) + 2(1-) = 0$ $2(1+) + 1(2-) = 0$

Remember: Only use parentheses if there is more than one polyatomic ion in the balanced formula.

14. Write formulas for compounds formed from these pairs of ions.
   a. NH_4^+, SO_3^{2-}
   b. calcium ion, phosphate ion

15. Write formulas for the following compounds:
   a. lithium hydrogen sulfate
   b. chromium(III) nitrite

Naming Compounds With Polyatomic Ions You have learned to write formulas for compounds containing polyatomic ions when you were given their names. Now, if you were given the formulas for these compounds, could you name them? When naming compounds containing polyatomic ions, you must first identify any polyatomic ions in the formula for the compound. If the polyatomic ion is unfamiliar, find its name in Table 9.3. 🔑 **To name a compound containing a polyatomic ion, state the cation name first and then the anion name. If the cation is a metallic element that has more than one common ionic charge, include a Roman numeral in the cation name.** Recall that the same rules apply when naming binary ionic compounds.

The compound NaClO is used as a disinfectant for swimming pools and as a bleach, as shown in Figure 9.11. The cation in this compound is sodium ion (Na^+). The other ion, ClO^-, is a polyatomic ion called hypochlorite ion. So, the name for NaClO is sodium hypochlorite.

Figure 9.11 Sodium Hypochlorite
The compound NaClO is often added to laundry water to bleach (brighten) white fabrics.

Sample Problem 9.5

Naming Compounds With Polyatomic Ions

Name the following ionic compounds:

a. $(NH_4)_2C_2O_4$ **b.** $Fe(ClO_3)_3$

❶ Analyze Identify the relevant concepts. Determine whether there is a polyatomic ion in the formula. To name the compound, list the names of the ions in the order written in the formula—the cation name followed by the anion name. The name of an ion that has more than one common ionic charge must include a Roman numeral indicating the charge.

❷ Solve Apply the concepts to this problem.

Identify any polyatomic ions.	**a.** NH_4^+ and $C_2O_4^{2-}$	**b.** ClO_3^-
Determine if any metal ions in the compound have more than one common ionic charge. If so, use the nonmetal anion to determine which cation is indicated by the formula.	This step is not needed because there is no metal ion in this compound.	Iron forms two common cations: Fe^{2+} and Fe^{3+}. Chlorate ion is ClO_3^-. Three chlorate ions give a charge of 3−. So the iron ion must be Fe^{3+} to balance the charge.
Write the name of the cation, then the name of the anion. Include Roman numerals as needed.	ammonium oxalate	iron(III) chlorate

16. Name the following ionic compounds:
     a. CaC_2O_4 **c.** $KMnO_4$
     b. $KClO$ **d.** Li_2SO_3

17. Write the names for these ionic compounds.
     a. $Al(OH)_3$ **c.** $Sn_3(PO_4)_2$
     b. $NaClO_3$ **d.** Na_2CrO_4

Quick Lab

Purpose To mix solutions containing cations and anions to make ionic compounds

Materials
- 9 small test tubes
- test tube rack
- paper, pencil, ruler
- 6 droppers
- solution A (Fe^{3+} ion)
- solution B (Ag^+ ion)
- solution C (Pb^{2+} ion)
- solution X (CO_3^{2-} ion)
- solution Y (OH^- ion)
- solution Z (PO_4^{3-} ion)

Making Ionic Compounds

Procedure

1. Label three test tubes A, three test tubes B, and three test tubes C.

2. Add 10 drops (approximately 0.5 mL) of solution A to the test tubes that are labeled A. Add 10 drops of solution B to the test tubes that are labeled B. Repeat this step with solution C.

3. Add 10 drops of solution X to one test tube of A, 10 drops to one test tube of B, and 10 drops to one test tube of C. Observe each test tube for the formation of a solid.

4. Make a 3-by-3 inch grid to record your observations. Label the rows A, B, and C. Label the columns X, Y, and Z. Describe any solid material you observe.

5. Repeat Step 3, adding 10 drops of solution Y to test tubes A, B, and C. Record your observations.

6. Repeat Step 3, adding 10 drops of solution Z to test tubes A, B, and C. Record your observations.

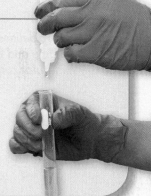

Analyze and Conclude

1. Infer Some ionic compounds are insoluble in water. What did you observe? How many of the compounds formed were insoluble?

2. Describe Write the formula for each ionic compound formed.

3. Describe Name each ionic compound formed.

4. Draw Conclusions Will mixing any cation with any anion always lead to the formation of an insoluble ionic compound? Explain your answer.

9.2 LessonCheck

18. Summarize Describe the procedures for writing the formulas and names of binary ionic compounds.

19. Review How do you write the formulas and the names of compounds with polyatomic ions?

20. Evaluate What are the advantages and disadvantages of common names?

21. Apply Concepts Write the formula for these binary ionic compounds.
- **a.** beryllium chloride
- **b.** cesium sulfide
- **c.** sodium iodide
- **d.** strontium oxide

22. Identify What condition must be met when writing a formula for an ionic compound?

23. Apply Concepts Write the formula for these compounds containing polyatomic ions.
- **a.** chromium(III) nitrite
- **b.** sodium perchlorate
- **c.** magnesium hydrogen carbonate
- **d.** calcium acetate

24. Explain When do you use parentheses in writing a chemical formula?

25. Describe Name the following ionic compounds:
- **a.** LiF
- **c.** $MnCO_3$
- **b.** SnS_2
- **d.** $Sr(H_2PO_4)_2$

26. Identify Which of the following formulas are incorrect? Explain your answer.
- **a.** $Mg_2(SO_4)_3$
- **c.** $BeCl_3$
- **b.** $AsRb_3$
- **d.** NaF

9.3 Naming and Writing Formulas for Molecular Compounds

Key Question

🔑 **What guidelines are used to write the name and formula of a binary molecular compound?**

Q: *How does a triathlon differ from a pentathlon? How does phosphorus trifluoride differ from phosphorus pentafluoride?*

CHEMISTRY & YOU

Q: *What numerical prefixes are used in chemistry?* You're already familiar with words containing numerical prefixes. For example, the word *triathlon* contains the prefix *tri-,* indicating the number 3. Athletes sometimes compete in multisport events—pentathlons, heptathlons, decathlons, and so on. The prefix of each tells you how may sports are in the event. Prefixes are used in chemistry, too. In this lesson, you will learn how prefixes in the name of a binary molecular compound tell you its composition.

Binary Molecular Compounds

🔑 **What guidelines are used to write the name and formula of a binary molecular compound?**

Recall that binary ionic compounds are composed of the ions of two elements, a metal and a nonmetal. Binary molecular compounds are also composed of two elements, but both elements are nonmetals and are not ions. These differences affect the naming of these compounds and the writing of their formulas. Binary molecular compounds are composed of molecules, not ions, so ionic charges cannot be used to write formulas or to name them.

When two nonmetallic elements combine, they often do so in more than one way. For example, the elements carbon and oxygen combine to form two gaseous compounds, CO and CO_2. How would you name a binary compound formed by the combination of carbon and oxygen atoms? It might seem satisfactory to call it carbon oxide. However, the two carbon oxides, CO and CO_2, are very different compounds. Sitting in a room with small amounts of CO_2 in the air would not present any problems. You exhale CO_2 as a product of your body chemistry, as shown in Figure 9.12. Thus, it is normally present in the air you breathe. On the other hand, if the same amount of CO were in the room, you could die of asphyxiation. The binary compound CO is a poisonous gas that interferes with your blood's ability to carry oxygen to body cells. Obviously, a naming system that distinguishes between these two compounds is needed.

Naming Binary Molecular Compounds Prefixes in the names of binary molecular compounds help distinguish compounds containing different numbers of atoms such as CO and CO_2. Table 9.4 lists the prefixes used to name binary molecular compounds. These prefixes tell how many atoms of an element are present in each molecule of the compound. According to the table, the prefix *mono-* would be used for the single oxygen atom in CO. The prefix *di-* would be used to indicate the presence of the two oxygen atoms in CO_2.

Use the prefixes listed in Table 9.4 along with the following guidelines to name a binary molecular compound. But before you apply these steps, you must confirm that the compound is a binary molecular compound. 🔑 **To name a binary molecular compound, use the following guidelines:**

1. **Write the names of the elements in the order listed in the formula.**

2. **Use prefixes appropriately to indicate the number of each kind of atom.** If just one atom of the first element is in the formula, omit the prefix *mono-* for that element. Also, the vowel at the end of a prefix is sometimes dropped when the name of the element begins with a vowel.

3. **End the name of the second element with the suffix *-ide*.**

Following these guidelines, CO is named carbon *mon*oxide and CO_2 is named carbon *di*oxide. What about the compound Cl_2O_8? This binary molecular compound consists of two chlorine atoms and eight oxygen atoms. The name is therefore *di*chlorine *oct*oxide.

Table 9.4	
Prefixes Used in Naming Binary Molecular Compounds	
Prefix	**Number**
mono-	1
di-	2
tri-	3
tetra-	4
penta-	5
hexa-	6
hepta-	7
octa-	8
nona-	9
deca-	10

Figure 9.12 Carbon Dioxide
When you exhale underwater, bubbles containing CO_2 rise to the surface of the water.

Sample Problem 9.6

Naming Binary Molecular Compounds

Name the following binary molecular compounds:

a. N_2O **b.** PCl_3

❶ Analyze **Identify the relevant concepts.** Confirm that the compound is a binary molecular compound—a compound composed of two nonmetals. To name the compound, name the elements in the order written in the formula. Use prefixes as necessary to indicate the number of each kind of atom. Use the suffix *-ide* on the name of the second element.

❷ Solve **Apply the concepts to this problem.**

Identify the elements in the compound and the number of atoms of each element in a molecule of the compound.	**a.** N_2O is composed of two nonmetals, nitrogen and oxygen. Each molecule of N_2O has: 2 nitrogen atoms; 1 oxygen atom.	**b.** PCl_3 is composed of two nonmetals, phosphorus and chlorine. Each molecule of PCl_3 has: 1 phosphorus atom; 3 chlorine atoms.

Write the names of the elements in the order they are written in the formula. Include prefixes to show how many atoms of each element. Use the suffix *-ide* with the name of the second element.

dinitrogen monoxide

phosphorus trichloride

The prefix *mono-* is not used with the first element indicated in the formula.

27. Name the following binary molecular compounds:
  a. OF_2 **c.** SO_3
  b. S_2F_{10} **d.** SF_6

Writing Formulas for Binary Molecular Compounds Suppose you know the name of a molecular compound and want to write the formula. 🔑 **To write the formula of a binary molecular compound, first use the prefixes in the name to tell you the subscript of each element in the formula. Then, write the correct symbols for the two elements with the appropriate subscripts.** An interesting example is tetraphosphorus trisulfide, which is used in some matches. The name *tetraphosphorus trisulfide* has the prefixes *tetra-* and *tri-*, so the subscripts of phosphorus and sulfur must be 4 and 3, respectively. Thus, the formula for tetraphosphorus trisulfide is P_4S_3.

Sample Problem 9.7

Writing Formulas for Binary Molecular Compounds

Write formulas for the following binary molecular compounds:
a. nitrogen trifluoride   **b.** disulfur dichloride

❶ Analyze Identify the relevant concepts. The prefixes in the name indicate the subscript of each element in the formula. Write the symbols for the two elements with the appropriate subscripts.

❷ Solve Apply the concepts to this problem.

Use the prefixes to determine how many atoms of each element are in the compound.	**a.** Each molecule of nitrogen trifluoride has: 1 nitrogen atom; 3 fluorine atoms.	**b.** Each molecule of disulfur dichloride has: 2 sulfur atoms; 2 chlorine atoms.
Construct the formula using the correct symbols and subscripts.	NF_3	S_2Cl_2

28. Write formulas for these binary molecular compounds.
   a. dinitrogen tetroxide   **c.** disulfur decafluoride
   b. xenon tetrafluoride   **d.** iodine heptafluoride

Note: The number 1 is never used as a subscript in a formula.

 ## 9.3 LessonCheck

29. 🔑 **Review** Explain how to write the name and formula of a binary molecular compound.

30. **Describe** Write the names of these molecular compounds.
   a. NCl_3 **c.** NI_3 **e.** N_2H_4
   b. BCl_3 **d.** SO_3 **f.** N_2O_3

31. **Apply Concepts** Write the formulas for these binary molecular compounds.
   a. phosphorus pentachloride
   b. iodine heptafluoride
   c. chlorine trifluoride
   d. iodine dioxide

32. **Describe** Write the formulas or names for these molecular compounds.
   a. CS_2 **c.** carbon tetrabromide
   b. Cl_2O_7 **d.** diphosphorus trioxide

33. **Evaluate** The name a student gives for the molecular compound $SiCl_4$ is monosilicon trichloride. Is this name correct? Explain your answer.

34. **Explain** Are the bonds between silicon and chlorine in silicon tetrachloride single bonds? Justify your answer by drawing an electron dot structure of silicon tetrachloride.

35. **Classify** Determine whether each of the following compounds is a molecular compound or an ionic compound. How can you tell?
   a. PBr_3 **c.** iron(III) oxide
   b. KBr **d.** carbon tetraiodide

BIGIDEA BONDING AND INTERACTIONS

36. What is the difference between an ionic compound and a molecular compound?

Sports Nutrition Advisor

Athletes have different nutrition requirements than the average person. As a result, many professional athletes hire nutrition advisors that specialize in athlete nutrition.

Sports nutrition advisors create individualized nutritional programs that ensure optimal body compositions, performance levels, and recovery rates in athletes. The program might include such things as how to maintain energy balance throughout the day, how to avoid dehydration or overhydration, or which vitamins and minerals to take to maintain proper body chemistry.

It is important that the advisors understand the "language of chemistry" to be able to decipher the ingredient labels on products. Registered advisors have taken courses in chemistry, biochemistry, anatomy, physiology, and statistics, in addition to several nutrition classes.

COMPETITIVE IN THE COLD
Winter athletes such as snowboarders must maintain their energy stores to train and compete at peak levels.

Take It Further

1. Infer How might understanding chemistry help a sports nutrition advisor develop a personalized meal plan for an athlete?

2. List Choose five nutritional consumer products—food or supplements—from your home. Read the ingredient labels on each product. Make a list of the compounds you understand and classify each as an ionic compound or a molecular compound.

9.4 Naming and Writing Formulas for Acids and Bases

Q: *What's the name of the acid responsible for the crisp taste in this drink?* There's a certain acid that gives many soft drinks their crisp, enjoyable taste. In this lesson, you will learn the names and formulas of some important acids, including one found in many soft drinks.

Names and Formulas of Acids

🔑 *How do you determine the name and formula of an acid?*

Acids are a group of ionic compounds with unique properties. As you will see in Chapter 19, acids can be defined in several ways. For now, it is enough to know that an **acid** is a compound that contains one or more hydrogen atoms and produces hydrogen ions when dissolved in water. Acids have many uses. For example, sulfuric acid is often used to etch circuit boards like the one shown in Figure 9.13.

When naming an acid, you can consider the acid to consist of an anion combined with as many hydrogen ions as needed to make the molecule electrically neutral. Therefore, the chemical formulas of acids are in the general form H_nX, where X is a monatomic or polyatomic anion and *n* is a subscript indicating the number of hydrogen ions that are combined with the anion.

Key Questions

🔑 **How do you determine the name and formula of an acid?**

🔑 **How do you determine the name and formula of a base?**

Vocabulary

- acid
- base

Figure 9.13 Sulfuric Acid
Circuit boards that are used in computers and other electronic devices have grooves (or circuits) that hold the wires for carrying signals. The circuits are often created using a mixture that contains sulfuric acid.

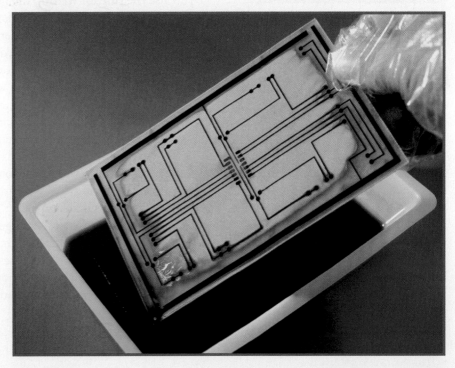

Table 9.5

Naming Common Acids			
Anion ending	**Example**	**Acid name**	**Example**
-ide	chloride, Cl^-	*hydro*-(stem)-*ic acid*	*hydro*chlor*ic acid*
-ite	sulfite, SO_3^-	(stem)-*ous acid*	sulfur*ous acid*
-ate	nitrate, NO_3^-	(stem)-*ic acid*	nitr*ic acid*

CHEMISTRY & YOU

Q: *An acid that provides the crisp taste in many soft drinks has the formula H_3PO_4. What's the name of this acid?*

Three rules can help you name an acid with the general formula H_nX dissolved in water. Read the rules and the examples carefully. Notice that the naming system depends on the name of the anion (X), in particular the suffix of the anion name. Each rule deals with an anion with a different suffix: *-ide*, *-ite*, and *-ate*.

1. **When the name of the anion ends in *-ide*, the acid name begins with the prefix *hydro-*. The stem of the anion has the suffix *-ic* and is followed by the word *acid*.** Therefore, HCl (X = chloride) is named *hydro*chlor*ic acid*.

2. **When the anion name ends in *-ite*, the acid name is the stem of the anion with the suffix *-ous*, followed by the word *acid*.** Thus, H_2SO_3 (X = sulfite) is named sulfur*ous acid*.

3. **When the anion name ends in *-ate*, the acid name is the stem of the anion with the suffix *-ic*, followed by the word *acid*.** Thus, HNO_3 (X = nitrate) is named nitr*ic acid*.

These three rules are summarized in Table 9.5. Use the table to help you write acid names until you become an expert.

Writing Formulas of Acids If you know the name of an acid, you can write its formula. **To write the formula for an acid, use the rule for writing the name of the acid in reverse. Then balance the ionic charges just as you would for any ionic compound.** For example, consider hydrobromic acid. Following Rule 1, hydrobromic acid (*hydro-* prefix and *-ic* suffix) must be a combination of hydrogen ion (H^+) and bromide ion (Br^-). So the formula of hydrobromic acid is HBr. How do you write the formula for phosphorous acid? Using Rule 2, hydrogen ion and phosphite ion (PO_3^{3-}) must be the components of phosphorous acid. You need three hydrogen ions to balance the 3− charge of the phosphite anion. Thus, the formula for phosphorous acid is H_3PO_3. Finally, what is the formula for sulfuric acid? According to Rule 3, sulfuric acid (*-ic* ending) must be a combination of hydrogen ion and sulfate ion (SO_4^{2-}). The formula for sulfuric acid is H_2SO_4 because two hydrogen ions are needed to balance the 2− charge of the sulfate anion.

Many industrial processes, including steel and fertilizer manufacturing, use acids. You should become familiar with the names and formulas of common acids such as those listed in Table 9.6.

Table 9.6

Common Acids	
Name	**Formula**
Hydrochloric acid	HCl
Sulfuric acid	H_2SO_4
Nitric acid	HNO_3
Ethanoic acid	$HC_2H_3O_2$
Phosphoric acid	H_3PO_4
Carbonic acid	H_2CO_3

Sample Problem 9.8

Naming Acids

Name the following compounds as acids:

a. HClO   **b.** HCN

❶ Analyze **Identify the relevant concepts.** The anion of the acid determines the acid name. (1) If the name of the anion ends in *-ide*, name the acid using the stem of the anion with the prefix *hydro-* and the suffix *-ic*, followed by the word *acid*. (2) If the anion name ends in *-ite*, name the acid using the stem of the anion with the suffix *-ous*, followed by the word *acid*. (3) If the anion name ends in *-ate*, name the acid using the stem of the anion with the suffix *-ic*, followed by the word *acid*.

❷ Solve **Apply the concepts to this problem.**

Identify the anion in the acid and the suffix of the anion name. →	**a.** ClO^- (hypochlor*ite*) **b.** CN^- (cyan*ide*)
Name the acid using the appropriate prefix (if any) and suffix. Finish with the word *acid*. →	hypochlorous acid (Rule 2) hydrocyanic acid (Rule 1)

37. Name the following compounds as acids:
  a. HF
  b. HNO_3
  c. H_2SO_3

38. Write formulas for the following acids:
  a. perchloric acid
  b. hydroiodic acid
  c. chlorous acid

Hint: For Problem 38, use the corresponding naming rule in reverse.

Names and Formulas of Bases

🔑 *How do you determine the name and formula of a base?*

A **base** is generally an ionic compound that produces hydroxide ions when dissolved in water. 🔑 **Bases are named in the same way as other ionic compounds—the name of the cation is followed by the name of the anion.** The common base sodium hydroxide is used in making cleaners, soap, and paper as shown in Figure 9.14. Sodium hydroxide (NaOH) is composed of sodium cations (Na^+) and hydroxide anions (OH^-).

🔑 **To write the formula for a base, first write the symbol for the metal cation followed by the formula for the hydroxide ion. Then, balance the ionic charges just as you would for any ionic compound.** For example, aluminum hydroxide consists of the aluminum cation (Al^{3+}) and the hydroxide anion (OH^-). You need three hydroxide ions to balance the 3+ charge of the aluminum cation. Thus, the formula for aluminum hydroxide is $Al(OH)_3$.

Figure 9.14 Use of Sodium Hydroxide
In the first step of papermaking, manufacturers use NaOH to break down recycled paper and wood to make pulp.

Naming Bases

Name the following bases:

a. KOH   **b.** $Fe(OH)_2$

❶ **Analyze** Identify the relevant concepts. Bases are named like other ionic compounds—the name of the cation is followed by the name of the anion.

❷ **Solve** Apply the concepts to this problem.

First identify the cation and the anion in the compound.

a. cation: K^+
anion: OH^-

b. cation: Fe^{2+}
anion: OH^-

Now write the name of the cation, followed by the name of the anion.

potassium hydroxide

iron(II) hydroxide

Remember: You need to include a Roman numeral if the metal ion can have different ionic charges.

39. Name the following bases:
 a. $Ba(OH)_2$
 b. $Ca(OH)_2$
 c. RbOH

40. Write formulas for the following bases:
 a. cesium hydroxide
 b. beryllium hydroxide
 c. manganese(III) hydroxide

9.4 LessonCheck

ONLINE PROBLEMS

41. 🔑 **Review** Explain how to determine the name and formula of an acid.

42. 🔑 **Review** How are the names and formulas determined for bases?

43. **Identify** Give the names of the following acids:
 a. HNO_2 **c.** HBr
 b. $HMnO_4$ **d.** H_2S

44. **Identify** Write the names of these bases.
 a. LiOH   **c.** $Mg(OH)_2$
 b. $Pb(OH)_2$ **d.** $Al(OH)_3$

45. **Classify** Identify each compound as an acid or a base. Then name each compound.
 a. NH_4OH **c.** $Fe(OH)_3$
 b. $HClO_3$ **d.** KOH

46. **Describe** Write the formulas for these ionic compounds.
 a. carbonic acid   **c.** iron(III) hydroxide
 b. sulfurous acid   **d.** zinc hydroxide

47. **Compare** What element generally appears in the formula of an acid? What ion generally appears in the formula of a base?

9.5 The Laws Governing How Compounds Form

CHEMISTRY & YOU

Q: *Did you know that sand from a beach can be used to make glass?* Sand contains the compound silicon dioxide, which is used in glass making. One molecule of silicon dioxide consists of one silicon atom and two oxygen atoms. In this lesson, you will learn why the ratio of silicon to oxygen atoms in silicon dioxide is always the same.

Key Questions

🔑 How is the law of definite proportions consistent with Dalton's atomic theory?

🔑 What general guidelines can help you write the name and formula of a chemical compound?

Vocabulary

• law of definite proportions
• law of multiple proportions

The Laws of Definite and Multiple Proportions

🔑 **How is the law of definite proportions consistent with Dalton's atomic theory?**

Consider the compound calcium carbonate ($CaCO_3$), which is commonly found in rocks. Whether you find the compound in a rock in Thailand or New Zealand, it is still calcium carbonate. This statement is true because the three elements—calcium, carbon, and oxygen—are combined in the same proportions in every molecule of $CaCO_3$. Two laws—the law of definite proportions and the law of multiple proportions—describe the proportions in which elements combine to form compounds. The rules for naming and writing formulas for compounds are possible because compounds obey these two rules.

Law of Definite Proportions A chemical formula tells you, by means of subscripts, the ratio of atoms of each element in the compound. Ratios of atoms can also be expressed as ratios of masses. For example, magnesium sulfide (MgS) is composed of magnesium cations and sulfide anions. If you could take 100.00 g of magnesium sulfide and break it down into its elements, you would obtain 43.13 g of magnesium and 56.87 g of sulfur. The Mg:S ratio of these masses is 43.13/56.87 or 0.758:1. This mass ratio does not change regardless of how the magnesium sulfide is formed or the size of the sample. Magnesium sulfide obeys the **law of definite proportions,** which states that in samples of any chemical compound, the masses of the elements are always in the same proportions. This law is consistent with Dalton's atomic theory. 🔑 **Dalton postulated that atoms combine in simple whole-number ratios. If the ratio of atoms of each element in a compound is fixed, then it follows that the ratio of their masses is also fixed.**

Law of Multiple Proportions In the early 1800s, Dalton and others studied pairs of compounds that contain the same elements but have different physical and chemical properties. Using the results from these studies, Dalton stated the **law of multiple proportions:** Whenever the same two elements form more than one compound, the different masses of one element that combine with the same mass of the other element are in the ratio of small whole numbers. Figure 9.15 shows two compounds—CuCl and CuCl₂—that demonstrate the law of multiple proportions.

Figure 9.15 CuCl and CuCl₂
a. Copper(I) chloride (CuCl) contains the elements copper and chlorine. This compound is green. **b.** Copper(II) chloride (CuCl₂) contains the same two elements as copper(I) chloride—copper and chlorine. But, this compound is blue.

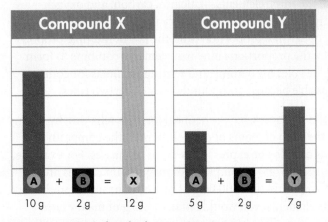

Figure 9.16 Law of Multiple Proportions
Two compounds, X and Y, contain equal masses of element B. The ratio of the masses of A in these compounds is 10:5 or 2:1 (a small whole-number ratio).
Compare *Would the ratio be different if samples of X and Y contained 3 g of B? Explain.*

See the law of multiple proportions *animated online.*

Two familiar compounds, water (H₂O) and hydrogen peroxide (H₂O₂), are formed by the same two elements. Although these compounds are formed by the elements hydrogen and oxygen, they have different physical and chemical properties. For example, water does not bleach fabric dyes, but hydrogen peroxide bleaches the dye in most fabrics. Each compound obeys the law of definite proportions. In every sample of hydrogen peroxide, 16.0 g of oxygen are present for each 1.0 g of hydrogen. The mass ratio of oxygen to hydrogen is always 16:1. In every sample of water, the mass ratio of oxygen to hydrogen is always 8:1. If a sample of hydrogen peroxide has the same mass of hydrogen as a sample of water, the ratio of the mass of oxygen in the two compounds is exactly 2:1.

$$\frac{16 \text{ g O (in H}_2\text{O}_2 \text{ sample that has 1 g H)}}{8 \text{ g O (in H}_2\text{O sample that has 1 g H)}} = \frac{16}{8} = \frac{2}{1} = 2:1$$

A simple example of the law of multiple proportions is shown in Figure 9.16.

Sample Problem 9.10

Calculating Mass Ratios

Carbon reacts with oxygen to form two compounds. Compound A contains 2.41 g of carbon for each 3.22 g of oxygen. Compound B contains 6.71 g of carbon for each 17.9 g of oxygen. What is the lowest whole-number mass ratio of carbon that combines with a given mass of oxygen?

❶ Analyze List the knowns and the unknown.
Apply the law of multiple proportions to the two compounds. For each compound, find the grams of carbon that combine with 1.00 g of oxygen. Then find the ratio of the masses of carbon in the two compounds. Confirm that the ratio is the lowest whole-number ratio.

> **KNOWNS**
> Compound A = 2.41 g C and 3.22 g O
> Compound B = 6.71 g C and 17.9 g O
>
> **UNKNOWN**
> Mass ratio of C per g O in the two compounds = ?

❷ Calculate Solve for the unknown.

First, calculate grams of carbon per gram of oxygen in compound A.

$$\frac{2.41 \text{ g C}}{3.22 \text{ g O}} = \frac{0.748 \text{ g C}}{1.00 \text{ g O}}$$

Then, calculate grams of carbon per gram of oxygen in compound B.

$$\frac{6.71 \text{ g C}}{17.9 \text{ g O}} = \frac{0.375 \text{ g C}}{1.00 \text{ g O}}$$

> To calculate the mass ratio, compare the masses of one element per one gram of the other element in each compound.

Calculate the mass ratio to compare the two compounds.

$$\frac{0.748 \text{ g C}}{0.375 \text{ g C}} = \frac{1.99}{1} \approx \frac{2}{1}$$

Express the mass ratio as the lowest whole-number ratio.

The mass ratio of carbon per gram of oxygen in the two compounds is 2:1.

❸ Evaluate Does this result make sense? The ratio is a low whole-number ratio, as expected. For a given mass of oxygen, compound A contains twice the mass of carbon as compound B.

48. Lead forms two compounds with oxygen. One contains 2.98 g of lead and 0.461 g of oxygen. The other contains 9.89 g of lead and 0.763 g of oxygen. For a given mass of oxygen, what is the lowest whole-number mass ratio of lead in the two compounds?

49. In the compound iron(III) oxide, also known as rust, the mass ratio of iron to oxygen is 7:3. A 33-g sample of a compound composed of iron and oxygen contains 10 g of oxygen. Is the sample iron(III) oxide? Explain.

> To answer Problem 49, first calculate the mass of iron in the sample.

Practicing Skills: Chemical Names and Formulas

What general guidelines can help you write the name and formula of a chemical compound?

In the average home, you can probably find hundreds of chemicals, including cleaning products, pharmaceuticals, and pesticides. You've probably noticed warning labels on products, which tell about their possible dangers. Most people would not know what to do if a child ingested one of these chemicals. A phone call to a poison control center can provide lifesaving information to victims of such poisonings. But a poison control center can be much more effective if the caller can supply some information about the name or formula of the substance.

Naming Chemical Compounds One of the skills you learned in this chapter is to name chemical compounds. If this is the first time you have tried to master this skill, you may feel a little overwhelmed. For example, you may find it difficult to know when you should or should not use prefixes and Roman numerals in a name. Or you may have trouble determining if a compound's name should end in *-ate, -ide,* or *-ite.*

Here are some guidelines to help you in naming a chemical compound from the chemical formula.

1. Follow the rules for naming acids when H is the first element in the formula.

2. If the compound is binary, generally the name ends with the suffix *-ide.* If the compound is a molecular binary compound, use prefixes to indicate the number of atoms.

3. When a polyatomic ion that includes oxygen is in the formula, the compound name generally ends in *-ite* or *-ate.*

4. If the compound contains a metallic cation that can have different ionic charges, use a Roman numeral to indicate the numerical value of the ionic charge in the compound.

The flowchart in Figure 9.18 provides you with a sequence of questions for naming a compound when you know its formula. Follow the arrows and answer the questions on the flowchart to write the correct name for a compound. The sequence of questions in the flowchart can help you name compounds you may have in your home as well as the compounds that are responsible for the beautiful colors in the petrified wood shown in Figure 9.17. Apply the general formula Q_xR_y to each compound. Q and R can be atoms, monatomic ions, or polyatomic ions. For example, to name HNO_3, let H = Q and NO_3 = R. Follow the first arrow down to the question "Q = H?" The answer is yes, so the arrow to the right tells you that the compound is an acid. You can then follow the rules for naming acids. HNO_3 is nitric acid.

To name the compound N_2O_3, let N = Q and O = R. The answer to the question "Q = H?" is no, so you follow the arrow down. Does the compound have more than two elements? The answer is no, so you follow the arrow to the left. The compound is binary, and its name ends in *-ide.* Is Q a metal? The answer is no, so you must use prefixes in the name for N_2O_3, which is *di*nitrogen *tri*oxide. Practice naming other compounds using the flowchart. Soon you won't need the flowchart anymore.

Figure 9.17 Petrified Wood
When wood ages, certain compounds from the sediment can replace the dead tissue in the wood. The process is called petrification. Some of these compounds are colored and provide the various colors in the petrified wood.

Figure 9.18 Naming Compounds
This flowchart will help you name compounds when given a chemical formula. Begin with the letters Q and R in the general formula Q_xR_y.
Interpret Diagrams *What is the correct name for Cr_2O_3?*

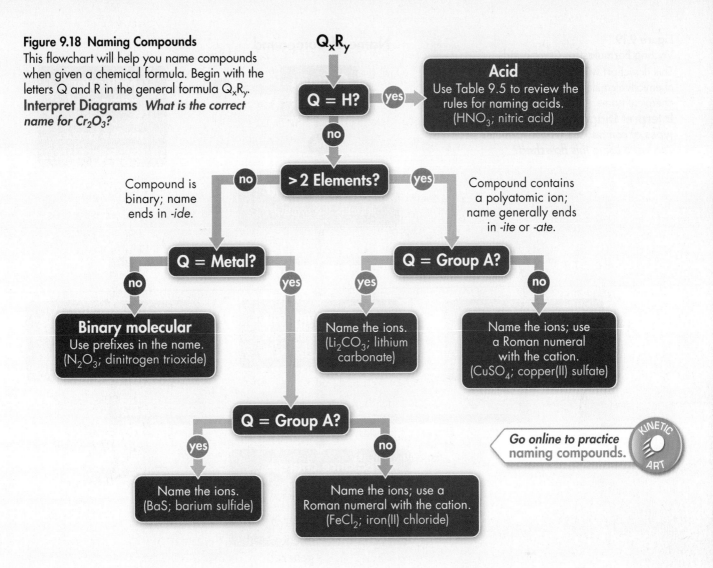

Writing Chemical Formulas In writing a chemical formula from a chemical name, it is helpful to remember the following guidelines:

1.  An *-ide* ending generally indicates a binary compound.

2. An *-ite* or *-ate* ending means a polyatomic ion that includes oxygen is in the formula.

3. Prefixes in a name generally indicate that the compound is molecular.

4. A Roman numeral after the name of a cation shows the ionic charge of the cation.

These guidelines and the questions in the flowchart in Figure 9.19 will help you write the formula for a compound when you know its name. For example, use the flowchart to write the formula for sodium chromate. The name does not contain prefixes, so the compound is ionic. The ions are sodium ion and chromate ion. Sodium is a Group A element, so use the periodic table or Table 9.1 to obtain its ionic charge (1+). Chromate ion is a polyatomic ion, so use Table 9.3 to obtain its charge (2−). Balance the charges to obtain the formula Na_2CrO_4. Use this flowchart to practice writing formulas until you don't need it anymore.

CHEMISTRY & YOU

Q: *Use the flowchart in Figure 9.19 to help you write the formula for silicon dioxide.*

Figure 9.19
Writing Formulas for Compounds
This flowchart will help you write a
chemical formula when given a
chemical name.
Interpret Diagrams *What are the two
types of compounds whose formulas you
can write using this flowchart?*

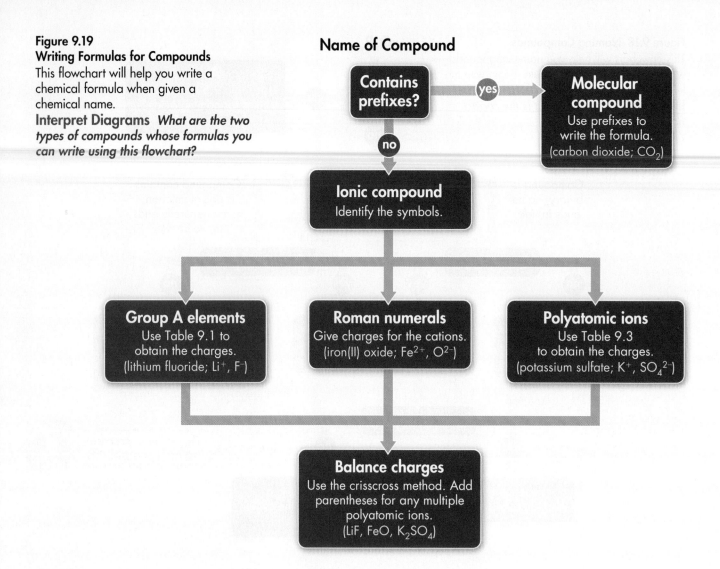

Name of Compound

Contains prefixes? — yes → **Molecular compound** Use prefixes to write the formula. (carbon dioxide; CO_2)

no ↓

Ionic compound Identify the symbols.

Group A elements Use Table 9.1 to obtain the charges. (lithium fluoride; Li^+, F^-)

Roman numerals Give charges for the cations. (iron(II) oxide; Fe^{2+}, O^{2-})

Polyatomic ions Use Table 9.3 to obtain the charges. (potassium sulfate; K^+, SO_4^{2-})

Balance charges Use the crisscross method. Add parentheses for any multiple polyatomic ions. (LiF, FeO, K_2SO_4)

9.5 LessonCheck

50. ⬚ **Review** How is the law of definite proportions consistent with Dalton's atomic theory?

51. ⬚ **List** What general guidelines can help you write the name and formula of a compound?

52. Compare Two compounds that contain copper and chlorine have the following masses:

Compound A: 32.10 g Cu and 17.90 g Cl
Compound B: 23.64 g Cu and 26.37 g Cl

Are the compounds the same? If not, what is the lowest whole-number mass ratio of copper that combines with a given mass of chlorine?

53. Identify Name the following compounds:
  a. $CaCO_3$ **b.** $PbCrO_4$ **c.** $SnCr_2O_7$

54. Describe Write the chemical formulas for each of the following compounds:
  a. tin(II) hydroxide   **c.** tetraiodide nonoxide
  b. barium fluoride   **b.** iron(III) oxalate

55. Evaluate Identify any incorrect names or formulas from the following choices. Explain your answer(s).
  a. calcium(II) oxide   **c.** $Na_2C_2O_4$
  b. aluminum oxide   **d.** $Mg(NH_4)_2$

BIGIDEA BONDING AND INTERACTIONS

56. Explain why the chemical composition of water (H_2O) is always the same.

Small-Scale Lab

Names and Formulas for Ionic Compounds

Purpose
To observe the formation of compounds and to write their names and formulas

Materials
- pencil
- paper
- ruler
- reaction surface
- chemicals shown in Figure A
- chemicals shown in Figure B

Procedure
On separate sheets of paper, draw two grids similar to Figure A. Make each square 2 cm on each side. Draw black X's on one of the grids. Use the other grid as a data table to record your observations. Place a reaction surface over the grid with black X's and add the chemicals as indicated in Figure A.

Analyze and Conclude
1. Observe Describe each precipitate (solid product) that forms. Use terms such as *milky, grainy, cloudy,* or *gelatinous*. Which mixture(s) did not form a precipitate?

2. Describe Write the formulas and names of the chemical compounds produced in the mixings.

You're the Chemist
1. Analyze Data Repeat the experiment, using the chemicals in Figure B. Identify the precipitates, write their formulas, and name them.

2. Explain In ionic equations, the precipitate is written to the right of an arrow, and the ions that produced it are written to the left. Write ionic equations for the precipitates formed from the reactions related to Figure B. For example, the first reaction in Figure B would be written as follows:

$$2Fe^{3+} + 3CO_3^{2-} \longrightarrow Fe_2(CO_3)_3$$

	$AgNO_3$ (Ag^+)	$Pb(NO_3)_2$ (Pb^{2+})	$CaCl_2$ (Ca^{2+})
Na_2CO_3 (CO_3^{2-})	a	e	i
Na_3PO_4 (PO_4^{3-})	b	f	j
NaOH (OH^-)	c	g	k
Na_2SO_4 (SO_4^{2-})	d	h	l

Figure A

	$FeCl_3$ (Fe^{3+})	$MgSO_4$ (Mg^{2+})	$CuSO_4$ (Cu^{2+})
Na_2CO_3 (CO_3^{2-})	a	e	i
Na_3PO_4 (PO_4^{3-})	b	f	j
NaOH (OH^-)	c	g	k
Na_2SO_4 (SO_4^{2-})	d	h	l

Figure B

9 Study Guide

BIGIDEAS THE STRUCTURE OF ATOMS; BONDING AND INTERACTIONS

An element's position in the periodic table supplies information on ion formation and bonding tendencies, which is used to write the names and formulas of ions and compounds. Ionic and molecular compounds differ in composition—ions form ionic compounds and molecules form molecular compounds.

9.1 Naming Ions

🔑 When metals in Groups 1A, 2A, and 3A lose electrons, they form cations with positive charges equal to their group number. The charge of any ion of a Group A nonmetal is determined by subtracting 8 from the group number. The charges of the cations of many transition metals must be determined from the number of electrons lost.

🔑 A polyatomic ion is composed of more than one atom that behaves as a unit and carries a charge.

• monatomic ion (264)

9.2 Naming and Writing Formulas for Ionic Compounds

🔑 To write the formula of a binary ionic compound, write the symbol of the cation and then the anion. Then balance the charges. The name of a binary ionic compound is the cation name followed by the anion name.

🔑 To write formulas for compounds with polyatomic ions, write the symbol for the cation followed by the symbol for the anion. Then balance the charges. To name a compound containing a polyatomic ion, state the cation name followed by the anion name.

• binary compound (272)

9.3 Naming and Writing Formulas for Molecular Compounds

🔑 To name a binary molecular compound, write the names of the elements in the order listed in the formula. Use prefixes to indicate the number of each atom. End the name of the second element with -ide.

🔑 To write the formula of a binary molecular compound, use the prefixes to determine the subscript of each element. Write the symbols for the elements with the subscripts.

9.4 Naming and Writing Formulas for Acids and Bases

🔑 If the anion name ends in -ide, the acid name begins with the prefix hydro-. The stem of the anion has the suffix -ic and is followed by the word acid. If the anion name ends in -ite, the acid name is the stem of the anion with the suffix -ous, followed by the word acid. If the anion name ends in -ate, the acid name is the stem of the anion with the suffix -ic, followed by the word acid. To write the formula for an acid, use the rule for writing the name of the acid in reverse.

🔑 Bases are named like other ionic compounds. To write the formula for a base, write the symbol for the metal cation followed by that of the hydroxide ion. Then, balance the ionic charges.

• acid (285)   • base (287)

9.5 The Laws Governing How Compounds Form

🔑 If the ratio of atoms of each element in a compound is fixed, then the ratio of their masses is also fixed.

🔑 Follow the rules for naming acids when H is the first element. If the compound is binary, generally the name ends with -ide. For a molecular binary compound, use prefixes to indicate the number of atoms. When a polyatomic ion with oxygen is in the formula, the compound name ends in -ite or -ate. If the compound contains a metallic cation that can have different ionic charges, use a Roman numeral to indicate the ionic charge.

🔑 An -ide ending usually indicates a binary compound. An -ite or -ate ending indicates a polyatomic ion with oxygen. Prefixes usually indicate a molecular compound. A Roman numeral after the name of a cation shows the ionic charge of the cation.

• law of definite proportions (289)
• law of multiple proportions (290)

Skills Tune-Up: Names and Formulas

Problem	❶ Analyze	❷ Solve
Write the name for the binary ionic compound CrI_2.	Name the ions in the order written in the formula. Use a Roman numeral if the metal cation in the compound can have more than one common ionic charge. Hint: Refer to Sample Problems 9.2–9.3 if you have trouble identifying binary ionic compounds.	CrI_2 contains chromium cations and iodide anions. Chromium forms two common cations: Cr^{2+} and Cr^{3+}. The compound CrI_2 is electrically neutral. Iodide ion is I^- and the formula CrI_2 specifies two iodide ions, which give a charge of 2−. So the chromium ion must be Cr^{2+}. The name of the compound is chromium(II) iodide.
Write the name for the binary molecular compound N_2O_5. Hint: Review Sample Problem 9.6 if you need help naming binary molecular compounds.	Name the elements in the order written in the formula. Use prefixes as necessary to indicate the number of each kind of atom. Use the suffix -ide on the name of the second element.	N_2O_5 is composed of two nitrogen atoms and five oxygen atoms. The name of the compound is dinitrogen pentoxide.
Write the formula for the ionic compound aluminum sulfate.	Write the symbol or formula for each ion in the order written in the name. Use subscripts to balance the charges. The ions must be combined in the lowest whole-number ratio. Use parentheses if more than one polyatomic ion is needed to balance a formula.	Aluminum sulfate contains Al^{3+} cations and SO_4^{2-} anions. $Al^{③+}$⟍⟋$(SO_4)^{②}$ The formula for aluminum sulfate is $Al_2(SO_4)_3$. Remember: Use parentheses when there is more than one polyatomic ion in the balanced formula.
Write the formula for the binary molecular compound selenium dioxide. Remember: The number 1 is never used as a subscript in a formula.	The prefixes in the name indicate the subscript of each element in the formula. Write the symbols for the two elements with the appropriate subscripts.	Selenium dioxide is composed of one selenium atom and two oxygen atoms. The formula for selenium dioxide is written as SeO_2.

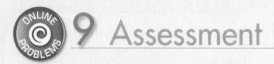 **9 Assessment**

Lesson by Lesson

9.1 Naming Ions

57. Give the expected charges on the ions of elements of these groups of the periodic table.

  a. Group 6A   **c.** Group 7A
  b. Group 1A   **d.** Group 3A

✴**58.** Give the expected charge of the cations of the following elements:

  a. Sr   **b.** Ca   **c.** Al   **d.** Cs

59. Name these ions, using Table 9.2, if necessary.

  a. Ba^{2+} **b.** I^- **c.** Ag^+ **d.** Hg^{2+}

60. Write the names and formulas of the two polyatomic anions in Table 9.3 with names that do not end in -ite or -ate.

61. Name the following ions:

  a. OH^- **b.** Pb^{4+} **c.** SO_4^{2-} **d.** O^{2-}

9.2 Naming and Writing Formulas for Ionic Compounds

62. What is the net charge of every ionic compound? Explain.

63. How are chemical formulas written for binary ionic compounds, given their names? How is the reverse done?

✴**64.** How do you determine the charge of a transition metal cation from the formula of an ionic compound containing that cation?

65. How are formulas written for ionic compounds with polyatomic ions, given their names? How is the reverse done?

66. Complete the table by writing correct formulas for the compounds formed by combining positive and negative ions. Then name each compound.

	NO_3^-	CO_3^{2-}	CN^-	PO_4^{3-}
NH_4^+	a.____	e.____	i.____	m.____
Sn^{4+}	b.____	f.____	j.____	n.____
Fe^{3+}	c.____	g.____	k.____	o.____
Mg^{2+}	d.____	h.____	l.____	p.____

67. Which of the following compounds are binary ionic compounds?

  a. KBr
  b. K_3PO_4
  c. sodium nitride
  d. calcium sulfate

68. When must parentheses be used in a formula for a compound?

9.3 Naming and Writing Formulas for Molecular Compounds

69. What are the components of a binary molecular compound?

✴**70.** What prefix indicates each of the following numbers of atoms in the formula of a binary molecular compound?

  a. 3   **b.** 1   **c.** 2   **d.** 6   **e.** 5   **f.** 4

71. How are formulas for binary molecular compounds written, given their names? How is the reverse performed, given their formulas?

72. Write the formula or name for the following compounds:

  a. P_2O_5
  b. CCl_4
  c. boron trichloride
  d. dinitrogen tetrahydride

9.4 Naming and Writing Formulas for Acids and Bases

73. Give the name or the formula for these acids.

  a. HCl   **c.** sulfuric acid
  b. HNO_3 **d.** acetic acid

74. Is every compound that contains hydrogen an acid? Explain.

75. Write formulas for these compounds.

  a. nitrous acid
  b. aluminum hydroxide
  c. hydroselenic acid
  d. strontium hydroxide
  e. phosphoric acid

✴**76.** Write names or formulas for these compounds.

  a. $Pb(OH)_2$ **c.** copper(II) hydroxide
  b. $Co(OH)_2$ **d.** iron(II) hydroxide

9.5 The Laws Governing How Compounds Form

77. What is the law of definite proportions?

78. Describe the law of multiple proportions.

★79. Nitrous oxide, laughing gas, is used as an anesthetic in dentistry. The mass ratio of nitrogen to oxygen is 7:4. A 68-g sample of a compound composed of nitrogen and oxygen contains 42 g of nitrogen. Is the sample nitrous oxide?

Understand Concepts

80. Write formulas for these compounds.

a. potassium permanganate
b. calcium hydrogen carbonate
c. dichlorine heptoxide
d. trisilicon tetranitride
e. sodium dihydrogen phosphate
f. phosphorus pentabromide

81. Write formulas for these compounds.

a. magnesium sulfide   **e.** potassium sulfite
b. sodium phosphite   **f.** calcium carbonate
c. barium hydroxide   **g.** sodium bromide
d. copper(II) nitrite   **h.** ferric sulfate

★82. Name these compounds.

a. $NaClO_3$ **d.** $HClO_4$ **g.** $KHSO_4$
b. Hg_2Br_2 **e.** SnO_2 **h.** $Ca(OH)_2$
c. K_2CrO_4 **f.** $Fe(C_2H_3O_2)_3$ **i.** BaS

83. Name each substance.

a. $LiClO_4$ **d.** CaO **g.** $SrSO_4$
b. Cl_2O **e.** $Ba_3(PO_4)_2$ **h.** $CuC_2H_3O_2$
c. HgF_2 **f.** I_2 **i.** $SiCl_4$

84. Name each compound.

a. $Mg(MnO_4)_2$ **d.** N_2H_4 **g.** PI_3
b. $Be(NO_3)_2$ **e.** $LiOH$ **h.** ZnO
c. K_2CO_3 **f.** BaF_2 **i.** H_3PO_3

85. Write formulas for these compounds.

a. calcium bromide   **e.** tin(IV) cyanide
b. silver chloride   **f.** lithium hydride
c. aluminum carbide   **g.** strontium acetate
d. nitrogen dioxide   **h.** sodium silicate

★86. A compound of general formula Q_xR_y contains no hydrogen, and Q and R are both elements. Neither Q nor R is a metal. Is Q_xR_y an acid, a binary ionic compound, or a binary molecular compound?

87. A compound of general formula Q_xR_y contains no hydrogen, Q is the alkali metal of lowest atomic mass, and R contains the elements oxygen and carbon in a 3:1 ratio. Write the name and the formula of the compound.

★88. Two compounds contain only tin and chlorine. The ratio of the masses of chlorine combined with 1.00 g of tin in the two compounds is 2:1. If one compound has the formula $SnCl_2$, what is the formula for the other compound?

89. Analysis of two compounds shows that they contain only lead and iodine in these amounts:

Compound I: 22.48 g Pb and 27.52 g I
Compound II: 5.80 g Pb and 14.20 g I

a. Determine the ratio of lead contained in the two compounds for every 1 g of iodine.
b. Use your ratio and your knowledge of ionic charges to write the formulas and the names of the two compounds.

90. The U.S. produces thousands of inorganic chemicals. Inorganic chemicals, for the most part, do not contain carbon. The table shows the amounts (in billions of kg) of the top ten inorganic chemicals produced in a recent year.

Chemical name	Amount produced (10^9 kg)
Sulfuric acid	39.4
Nitrogen	26.9
Oxygen	17.7
Ammonia	16.5
Lime	16.3
Phosphoric acid	11.2
Sodium hydroxide	11.0
Chlorine	10.3
Sodium carbonate	9.3
Nitric acid	6.8

a. What percentage of the total production of the top ten is lime (calcium oxide)?
b. Three diatomic gases are on the list. What are their names? What was the combined production of these gases in billions of kilograms?
c. The three acids make up what percentage of the total production of the top ten?
d. Write formulas for the top ten inorganic chemicals.

91. Compare and Contrast How does the information conveyed by a molecular formula differ from that given by a formula unit of a compound?

92. Make Generalizations Where on the periodic table will you find the two elements in a binary molecular compound?

93. Draw Conclusions Why is it important for chemists to have a system of writing chemical names and formulas?

94. Evaluate Criticize this statement: "The ionic charge of any metal can be determined from the position of the element in the periodic table."

95. Explain Summarize the rules that chemists use for naming ionic compounds. What is the purpose for each rule?

★96. Use Models Nitrogen and oxygen form a number of stable chemical compounds. In the models below, nitrogen is blue; oxygen is red. Write the molecular formula and name of each.

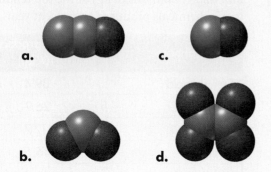

97. Evaluate and Revise Examine the following names for ionic compounds. Show, by writing all possible formulas for the compounds, that the names are incomplete. Then, write each complete name.

    a. copper sulfide   **c.** lead oxide
    b. iron sulfate   **d.** manganese fluoride

★98. Evaluate and Revise Explain what is wrong with each formula. Write the correct formula.

    a. $CsCl_2$ **c.** ZnO_2
    b. LiNe   **d.** Ba_2S_2

99. Infer Sodium aluminum sulfate is an active ingredient in baking powder. The molecular formula for this ionic compound contains two sulfate ions. Write the complete molecular formula for sodium aluminum sulfate.

★100. Classify Separate the following compounds into five categories: binary ionic compounds, binary molecular compounds, compounds with polyatomic ions, acids, and bases. Some compounds may fit in more than one category.

    a. CBr_4 **d.** MgS   **g.** Al_2O_3
    b. HCN   **e.** H_2SiO_3 **h.** Na_2HPO_4
    c. NH_4OH **f.** ClBr   **i.** $KMnO_4$

★101. Calculate A student heats 5.00 g of a white compound and obtains 3.60 g of a green compound and 1.40 g of a colorless gas. Another student heats a 9.00-g sample of the same compound and obtains 6.48 g of a green compound and 2.52 g of a colorless gas.

    a. Show by calculation that the white compound obeys the law of definite proportions.
    b. If a third student heats 14.0 g of the white compound, how many grams of colorless gas will be produced?

★102. Draw Conclusions What other law is illustrated (twice) by the experiment described in the previous question?

103. Apply Concepts Ionic compounds are present in items commonly found in your home. Write formulas for the ionic compounds found in the following common household products:

    a. antacid (calcium carbonate and magnesium hydroxide)
    b. toothpaste for sensitive teeth (sodium fluoride and potassium nitrate)
    c. sunscreen (titanium(IV) oxide and zinc oxide)
    d. pasta (ferrous sulfate)

104. Use Models In the models below, chlorine is green; phosphorus is orange; carbon is black; and sulfur is yellow. Write the formula and the name for each compound. Are these compounds ionic or molecular compounds?

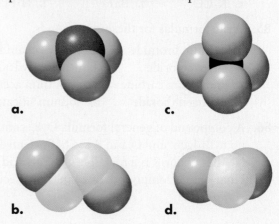

105. Organize Data *CRC Handbook of Chemistry and Physics* is a reference book that contains a wealth of information about elements and compounds. Two sections of this book that you might use are called "Physical Constants of Inorganic Compounds" and "Physical Constants of Organic Compounds." To familiarize yourself with this work, make a table with these headings: Name, Formula, Crystalline Form or Color, Density, Melting Point (°C), Boiling Point (°C), and Solubility in Water.

Name	Formula	Crystalline Form or Color	Density	MP (°C)	BP (°C)

Enter these substances in the body of the table: ammonium chloride, barium, barium sulfate, bromine, calcium carbonate, chlorine, copper(II) sulfate pentahydrate, iodine, iron(II) sulfate pentahydrate, mercury, potassium carbonate, and sulfur. Use the handbook to complete the table.

*106. Analyze Data Use the table you prepared for Problem 105 to answer the following questions:

a. You have two unlabeled bottles, each containing a white powder. One of the substances is calcium carbonate, and the other is potassium carbonate. How could you distinguish between these two compounds?

b. How would you distinguish between samples of copper(II) sulfate pentahydrate and iron(II) sulfate pentahydrate?

c. A bottle contains a mixture of ammonium chloride and barium sulfate. How could you separate these two compounds?

d. List the elements in the table in order of increasing density. Identify the elements as metals or nonmetals.

e. List the compounds in the table in order of decreasing density.

f. Calculate the mass of 47.0 cm³ of mercury.

g. Calculate the volume of 16.6 g of sulfur.

h. How would you distinguish among the Group 7A elements listed in the table?

107. Research a Problem Sodium ions (Na^+) and potassium ions (K^+) are needed for the human body to function. Deficiencies in these ions can have adverse effects on your health. Research where these ions are most likely to be found in the body and the roles they play. Write a brief essay describing your findings.

108. Explain Investigate the role of lithium carbonate in the successful treatment of bipolar disorder. Write a brief report that includes information on bipolar disorder and why lithium carbonate is used to treat it.

109. Connect to the BIGIDEA Choose five personal care products from your home. Read each ingredient label and identify all the compounds that you are able to decipher. Write a short paragraph in which you explain how learning to name chemical compounds has helped you decipher these ingredient labels.

CHEMYSTERY

Cucumber Blunder

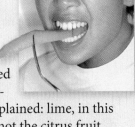

Tara called her grandmother to find out what she did wrong. She started to describe what she had done. When Tara mentioned squeezing limes, her grandmother interrupted and explained: lime, in this case, meant pickling lime, not the citrus fruit. "Pickling lime? I've never heard of that!" Tara exclaimed.

Her grandmother fetched a package of pickling lime from the cupboard to look at the ingredient label. She read aloud "food-grade calcium hydroxide." Her grandmother elaborated, "That's what makes the pickles crunchy like you like 'em."

110. Compare Lime is the common name for calcium hydroxide. What are the advantages and disadvantages of each name?

*111. Connect to the BIGIDEA Is calcium hydroxide an ionic or a molecular compound? Write the formula.

112. List five properties of the chair you are sitting on. Classify each as physical or chemical.

⋆113. How many significant figures are in the following measurements?

    a. 15.05 g   **d.** 300.0 cm^3

    b. 0.31 cm   **e.** $3.0 \times 10^5 \text{ kg}$

    c. 890 mL   **f.** 0.001 mm

114. Determine the sum of the following measurements to the correct number of significant figures.

$$1.55 \text{ cm} + 0.235 \text{ cm} + 3.4 \text{ cm}$$

115. Make the following conversions:

    a. 775 mL to microliters (μL)

    b. 65°C to K

    c. 8.32 mg Ag to centigrams of silver (cg Ag)

116. A student finds that 6.62 g of a substance occupies a volume of 12.3 cm^3. What is the density of the substance?

117. Compare neutrons and protons with respect to their charge, mass, and position in the atom.

⋆118. The diagrams show two models of the atom.

    a. Which model is more accurate?

    b. What do the positively charged particles represent?

    c. What do the negatively charged particles represent?

    d. What major subatomic particle is missing in both of these models?

(1) 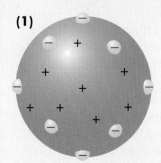   **(2)**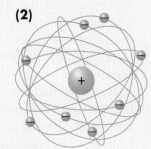

⋆119. What elements have these electron configurations?

    a. $1s^2 2s^2 2p^6$ **c.** $1s^2 2s^2 2p^1$

    b. $1s^2 2s^2 2p^2$ **d.** $1s^2$

120. Where are the metalloids found on the periodic table? Compare the properties of the metalloids to metals and nonmetals.

121. Arrange the following groups of elements in order of increasing ionization energy.

    a. potassium, cesium, lithium, sodium

    b. fluorine, boron, lithium, carbon, neon

122. From the positions of the elements in the periodic table, choose the element in each pair with the higher electronegativity.

    a. Cs and Li   **c.** S and Mg   **e.** Te and N

    b. Sr and I   **d.** O and Se   **f.** C and F

123. The ions of the elements of Groups 1A and 2A have smaller radii than their neutral atoms, whereas the ions of Group 7A have larger radii than their neutral atoms. Explain.

⋆124. How many valence electrons do atoms of the following elements have?

    a. lithium   **d.** calcium

    b. sulfur   **e.** bromine

    c. neon   **f.** phosphorus

125. Write the electron configuration for the element neon, then identify three ions that have the same electron configuration.

126. How many protons and electrons are in each ion?

    a. magnesium ion   **c.** strontium ion

    b. bromide ion   **d.** sulfide ion

⋆127. Which of these compounds would you expect to contain covalent bonds? Why?

    a. KCl   **b.** PBr_3 **c.** ClBr   **d.** NaI

128. Which of these substances would you expect to be polar?

    a. Cl_2 **c.** CO_2 **e.** CCl_4 **g.** CH_4

    b. CO   **d.** NH_3 **f.** H_2O

129. Draw electron dot structures for the substances in Question 128.

130. Explain what a hydrogen bond is and under what conditions a hydrogen bond will form.

131. Explain the difference between an ionic bond and a covalent bond. Use electron dot structures to illustrate your explanation.

If You Have Trouble With . . .

Question	112	113	114	115	116	117	118	119	120	121	122	123	124	125	126	127	128	129	130	131
See Chapter	2	3	3	3	3	4	5	5	6	6	6	6	7	7	7	8	8	8	8	8

Standardized Test Prep

Select the choice that best answers each question or completes each statement.

1. Identify the pair in which the formula does not match the name.
   - (A) sulfite, SO_3^{2-}
   - (B) nitrite, NO_3^{-}
   - (C) hydroxide, OH^{-}
   - (D) dichromate, $Cr_2O_7^{2-}$

2. Which of these compounds are ionic?
   - I. $CaSO_4$ II. N_2O_4 III. NH_4NO_3 IV. CaS
   - (A) I and II only
   - (B) II and III only
   - (C) III and IV only
   - (D) I, III, and IV only

3. What is the name of $AlCl_3$?
   - (A) aluminum trichloride
   - (B) aluminum(III) chloride
   - (C) aluminum chlorite
   - (D) aluminum chloride

4. The Roman numeral in manganese(IV) sulfide indicates the
   - (A) group number on the periodic table.
   - (B) positive charge on the manganese ion.
   - (C) number of manganese ions in the formula.
   - (D) number of sulfide ions needed in the formula.

Tips for Success

Eliminate Wrong Answers If you don't know which choice is correct, start by eliminating those you know are wrong. If you can rule out some choices, you'll increase your chances of choosing the correct answer.

5. Which of these statements does not describe every binary molecular compound?
   - (A) Molecules of binary molecular compounds are composed of two atoms.
   - (B) The names of binary molecular compounds contain prefixes.
   - (C) The names of binary molecular compounds end in the suffix *-ide*.
   - (D) Binary molecular compounds are composed of two nonmetals.

6. What is the formula of ammonium carbonate?
   - (A) NH_4CO_3
   - (B) $(NH_4)_2CO_3$
   - (C) NH_3CO_4
   - (D) NH_4CO_2

The lettered choices below refer to Questions 7–10.

   (A) QR   (B) QR_2 (C) Q_2R (D) Q_2R_3

Which formula shows the correct ratio of ions in the compound formed by each pair of elements?

	Element Q	Element R
7.	aluminum	sulfur
8.	potassium	oxygen
9.	lithium	chlorine
10.	strontium	bromine

Use the data table to answer Questions 11–12. The table gives formulas for some of the ionic compounds formed when cations (M, N, P) combine with anions (A, B, C, D).

Cation	Anion			
	A	B	C	D
M	MA_2	(1)	(2)	MD
N	(3)	N_2B	(4)	(5)
P	PA_3	(6)	PC	$P_2(D)_3$

11. Use the given formulas to determine the ionic charge of each cation and anion.

12. Write formulas for compounds (1) through (6).

Use the atomic windows to answer Question 13.

13. Classify the contents as elements only, compounds only, or elements and compounds.

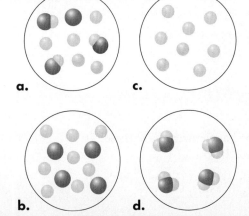

a.

b.

c.

d.

If You Have Trouble With . . .

Question	1	2	3	4	5	6	7	8	9	10	11	12	13
See Lesson	9.1	9.2	9.2	9.2	9.3	9.2	9.2	9.2	9.2	9.2	9.2	9.2	9.2

10
Chemical Quantities

INSIDE:

- **10.1** The Mole:
  A Measurement of Matter

- **10.2** Mole–Mass and
  Mole–Volume Relationships

- **10.3** Percent Composition
  and Chemical Formulas

PearsonChem.com

 CONCEPTS IN ACTION

 KINETIC ART

 VIRTUAL LAB

 MATH +/− TUTOR

 ONLINE PROBLEMS

 CHEM TUTOR

When you shop at the grocery store or farmers' market, you usually buy blueberries by the pint, not by the berry. Similarly, chemists use a unit called the mole to count atoms and molecules.

THE MOLE AND QUANTIFYING MATTER

Essential Questions:

1. *Why is the mole an important measurement in chemistry?*
2. *How can the molecular formula of a compound be determined experimentally?*

CHEMYSTERY

A Formula for Cheating

Anabolic steroids are compounds that are developed to increase muscle size and strength. Stories are often in the news about professional athletes, such as baseball players, cyclists, and track stars, who have used steroids to enhance their performance.

More than 100 different types of anabolic steroids have been developed, and each of these substances is illegal in the United States without a prescription. Steroids have also been banned by many sports organizations because of their dangerous side effects and because they give the user an unfair advantage. Therefore, athletes are often tested for steroid use. So, how can the presence of steroids in the body be detected?

▶ Connect to the **BIG**IDEA As you read about the mole and chemical quantities, think about how the molar mass and molecular formula of a compound can be determined and used to identify the presence of steroids in the body.

NATIONAL SCIENCE EDUCATION STANDARDS

A-1, A-2, B-2, E-2, G-1, G-3

10.1 The Mole: A Measurement of Matter

CHEMISTRY & YOU

Q: *How can you quantify the amount of sand in a sand sculpture?* Have you ever gone to the beach and created a castle or sculpture out of sand? You could measure the amount of sand in a sculpture by counting the grains of sand. Is there an easier way to measure the amount of sand? Chemists measure the amount of a substance using a unit called the mole.

Key Questions

🔑 How can you convert among the count, mass, and volume of something?

🔑 How do chemists count the number of atoms, molecules, or formula units in a substance?

🔑 How do you determine the molar mass of an element and of a compound?

Vocabulary

- mole
- Avogadro's number
- representative particle
- molar mass

Measuring Matter

🔑 How can you convert among the count, mass, and volume of something?

Chemistry is a quantitative science. In your study of chemistry, you will analyze the composition of samples of matter and perform chemical calculations that relate quantities of the reactants in a chemical reaction to quantities of the products. To solve these and other problems, you will have to be able to measure the amount of matter you have.

One way to measure matter is to count how many of something you have. For example, you can count the mp3s in your collection. Another way to measure matter is to determine its mass. You can buy apples by the kilogram or pound, as shown in Figure 10.1. You can also measure matter by volume. For instance, people buy gasoline by the liter or the gallon.

Some of the units used for measuring indicate a specific number of items. For example, a pair always means two. A pair of shoes is two shoes, and a pair of aces is two aces. Similarly, a dozen always means 12. A dozen eggs is 12 eggs, and a dozen pens is 12 pens.

Apples can be measured in three different ways. At a fruit stand, they are often sold by the count. In a supermarket, you usually buy apples by weight or mass. At an orchard, you can buy apples by volume. Each of these different ways to measure apples can be equated to a dozen apples.

By count: 1 dozen apples = 12 apples

For average-sized apples, the following approximations can be used.

By mass: 1 dozen apples = 2.0 kg apples

By volume: 1 dozen apples = 0.20 bushel apples

Figure 10.1 Measuring by Mass
The fruit on this scale has a mass of about 1.3 kg.

Knowing how the count, mass, and volume of an item relate to a common unit allows you to convert among these units. For example, based on the unit relationships given on the previous page, you could calculate the mass of a bushel of apples or the mass of 90 average-sized apples using conversion factors such as the following:

$$\frac{1 \text{ dozen apples}}{12 \text{ apples}} \qquad \frac{2.0 \text{ kg apples}}{1 \text{ dozen apples}} \qquad \frac{1 \text{ dozen apples}}{0.20 \text{ bushel apples}}$$

SampleProblem 10.1

Finding Mass From a Count

What is the mass of 90 average-sized apples if 1 dozen of the apples has a mass of 2.0 kg?

① Analyze **List the knowns and the unknown.** Use dimensional analysis to convert the number of apples to the mass of apples.

KNOWNS

number of apples = 90 apples
12 apples = 1 dozen apples
1 dozen apples = 2.0 kg apples

UNKNOWN

mass of 90 apples = ? kg

② Calculate **Solve for the unknown.**

First, identify the sequence of conversions needed to perform the calculation.	number of apples ⟶ dozens of apples ⟶ mass of apples
Write the conversion factor to convert from number of apples to dozens of apples.	$\dfrac{1 \text{ dozen apples}}{12 \text{ apples}}$
Write the conversion factor to convert from dozens of apples to mass of apples.	$\dfrac{2.0 \text{ kg apples}}{1 \text{ dozen apples}}$ The units apples and dozen apples cancel, so the answer has the unit kg.
Multiply the number of apples by these two conversion factors to get the answer in kilograms.	$90 \text{ apples} \times \dfrac{1 \text{ dozen apples}}{12 \text{ apples}} \times \dfrac{2.0 \text{ kg apples}}{1 \text{ dozen apples}} = \boxed{15 \text{ kg apples}}$

③ Evaluate **Does the result make sense?** A dozen apples has a mass of 2.0 kg, and 90 apples is less than 10 dozen apples, so the mass should be less than 20 kg of apples (10 dozen × 2.0 kg/dozen).

1. If 0.20 bushel is 1 dozen apples and a dozen apples has a mass of 2.0 kg, what is the mass of 0.50 bushel of apples?

In Problem 1, the desired conversion is bushels of apples ⟶ dozens of apples ⟶ mass of apples.

2. Assume 2.0 kg of apples is 1 dozen and that each apple has 8 seeds. How many apple seeds are in 14 kg of apples?

In Problem 2, the desired conversion is mass of apples ⟶ dozens of apples ⟶ number of apples ⟶ number of seeds.

What Is a Mole?

 **How do chemists count the number of atoms, molecules, or formula units in a substance?**

Counting objects as big as apples is a reasonable way to measure how much of the object you have. Picture trying to count the grains of sand in a sand sculpture. It would be an endless job. Recall that matter is composed of atoms, molecules, and ions. These particles are much, much smaller than grains of sand, and an extremely large number of them are in a small sample of a substance. Obviously, counting particles one by one is not practical. However, think about counting eggs. It's easier when the eggs are grouped into dozens, as shown in Figure 10.2. A dozen is a specified number (12) of things.

Counting With Moles Chemists also use a unit that is a specified number of particles. The unit is called the mole. A **mole** (mol) of a substance is 6.02×10^{23} representative particles of that substance and is the SI unit for measuring the amount of a substance. The number of representative particles in a mole, 6.02×10^{23}, is called **Avogadro's number.** It was named in honor of the Italian scientist Amedeo Avogadro di Quaregna (1776–1856), who helped clarify the difference between atoms and molecules.

The term **representative particle** refers to the species present in a substance, usually atoms, molecules, or formula units. The representative particle of most elements is the atom. Iron is composed of iron atoms. Helium is composed of helium atoms. Seven elements, however, normally exist as diatomic molecules (H_2, N_2, O_2, F_2, Cl_2, Br_2, and I_2). The representative particle of these elements and of all molecular compounds is the molecule. The molecular compounds water (H_2O) and sulfur dioxide (SO_2) are composed of H_2O and SO_2 molecules, respectively. For ionic compounds, such as calcium chloride, the representative particle is the formula unit $CaCl_2$.  **The mole allows chemists to count the number of representative particles in a substance.** A mole of any substance contains Avogadro's number of representative particles, or 6.02×10^{23} representative particles. Table 10.1 summarizes the relationship between representative particles and moles of substances.

Figure 10.2 Grouping Objects
Words other than *mole* are used to describe a number of something—for example, a *dozen* eggs is 12 eggs.

CHEMISTRY & YOU

Q: *What are the different ways you can measure the amount of sand in a sand sculpture?*

Table 10.1			
Representative Particles and Moles			
Substance	**Representative particle**	**Chemical formula**	**Representative particles in 1.00 mol**
Copper	Atom	Cu	6.02×10^{23}
Atomic nitrogen	Atom	N	6.02×10^{23}
Nitrogen gas	Molecule	N_2	6.02×10^{23}
Water	Molecule	H_2O	6.02×10^{23}
Sucrose	Molecule	$C_{12}H_{22}O_{11}$	6.02×10^{23}
Calcium ion	Ion	Ca^{2+}	6.02×10^{23}
Calcium fluoride	Formula unit	CaF_2	6.02×10^{23}

Converting Between Number of Particles and Moles The relationship, $1 \text{ mol} = 6.02 \times 10^{23}$ representative particles, is the basis for the following conversion factors that you can use to convert number of representative particles to moles and moles to number of representative particles.

$$\frac{1 \text{ mol}}{6.02 \times 10^{23} \text{ representative particles}} \quad \text{and} \quad \frac{6.02 \times 10^{23} \text{ representative particles}}{1 \text{ mol}}$$

SampleProblem 10.2

Converting Number of Atoms to Moles

Magnesium is a light metal used in the manufacture of aircraft, automobile wheels, and tools. How many moles of magnesium is 1.25×10^{23} atoms of magnesium?

❶ Analyze List the known and the unknown.
The desired conversion is atoms ⟶ moles.

KNOWN

number of atoms $= 1.25 \times 10^{23}$ atoms Mg

UNKNOWN

moles $= ?$ mol Mg

❷ Calculate Solve for the unknown.

First, state the relationship between moles and number of representative particles.	$1 \text{ mol Mg} = 6.02 \times 10^{23}$ atoms Mg
Write the conversion factors you get based on this relationship.	$\dfrac{1 \text{ mol Mg}}{6.02 \times 10^{23} \text{ atoms Mg}}$ and $\dfrac{6.02 \times 10^{23} \text{ atoms Mg}}{1 \text{ mol Mg}}$
Identify the conversion factor needed to convert from atoms to moles.	$\dfrac{1 \text{ mol Mg}}{6.02 \times 10^{23} \text{ atoms Mg}}$
Multiply the number of atoms of Mg by the conversion factor.	$1.25 \times 10^{23} \text{ atoms Mg} \times \dfrac{1 \text{ mol Mg}}{6.02 \times 10^{23} \text{ atoms Mg}}$ $= 0.208 \text{ mol Mg}$

❸ Evaluate Does the result make sense? The given number of atoms (1.25×10^{23}) is less than one fourth of Avogadro's number (6.02×10^{23}), so the answer should be less than one fourth (0.25) mol of atoms. The answer should have three significant figures.

> Bromine is a diatomic molecule, so the representative particle is Br_2.

3. How many moles is 2.80×10^{24} atoms of silicon?

4. How many moles is 2.17×10^{23} representative particles of bromine?

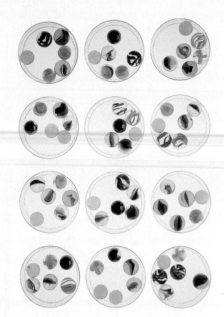

Figure 10.3 Counting Marbles
A dozen cups of marbles contain more than a dozen marbles. Similarly, a mole of molecules contains more than a mole of atoms.
Calculate *How many atoms are in one mole of molecules if each molecule consists of six atoms?*

Suppose you want to determine how many atoms are in a mole of a compound. To do this, you must know how many atoms are in a representative particle of the compound. This number is determined from the chemical formula. Figure 10.3 illustrates this idea with marbles (atoms) in cups (molecules). The number of marbles in a dozen cups is (6×12), or 72 marbles. In the formula for carbon dioxide (CO_2), the subscripts show that one molecule of carbon dioxide is composed of three atoms: one carbon atom and two oxygen atoms. A mole of carbon dioxide contains Avogadro's number of CO_2 molecules. Each molecule contains three atoms, so a mole of carbon dioxide contains three times Avogadro's number of atoms. A molecule of carbon monoxide (CO) consists of two atoms, so a mole of carbon monoxide contains two times Avogadro's number of atoms.

To find the number of atoms in a given number of moles of a compound, you must first determine the number of representative particles. To convert the number of moles of a compound to the number of representative particles (molecules or formula units), multiply the number of moles by 6.02×10^{23} representative particles/1 mol. Then, multiply the number of representative particles by the number of atoms in each molecule or formula unit.

The Size of a Mole Perhaps you are wondering just how large a mole is. The SI unit, the mole, is not related to the small burrowing animal of the same name, shown in Figure 10.4. However, this little animal can help you appreciate the size of the number 6.02×10^{23}. Assume that an average animal-mole is 15 cm long, 5 cm tall, and has a mass of 145 g. Based on this information, the mass of 6.02×10^{23} animal-moles is 8.73×10^{22} kg. That means that the mass of Avogadro's number of animal-moles is equal to more than 60 times the combined mass of Earth's oceans. If spread over the entire surface of Earth, Avogadro's number of animal-moles would form a layer more than 8 million animal-moles thick. What about the length of 6.02×10^{23} animal-moles? If lined up end-to-end, 6.02×10^{23} animal-moles would stretch from Earth to the nearest star, Alpha Centauri, more than two million times. Are you beginning to understand how enormous Avogadro's number is?

Figure 10.4 A Mole of Moles
An average animal-mole has a mass of 145 g. The mass of 6.02×10^{23} animal-moles is 8.73×10^{22} kg.

Sample Problem 10.3

Converting Moles to Number of Atoms

Propane is a gas used for cooking and heating. How many atoms are in 2.12 mol of propane (C_3H_8)?

❶ Analyze List the knowns and the unknown.
The desired conversion is moles $\longrightarrow$ molecules $\longrightarrow$ atoms.

> KNOWNS
>
> number of moles = 2.12 mol C_3H_8
> 1 mol C_3H_8 = 6.02×10^{23} molecules C_3H_8
> 1 molecule C_3H_8 = 11 atoms
> (3 carbon atoms and 8 hydrogen atoms)
>
> UNKNOWN
> number of atoms = ? atoms

❷ Calculate Solve for the unknown.

First, write the conversion factor to convert from moles to molecules.

$$\frac{6.02 \times 10^{23} \text{ molecules } C_3H_8}{1 \text{ mol } C_3H_8}$$

Remember to write the conversion factors so that the unit in the denominator cancels the unit in the numerator of the previous factor.

Write the conversion factor to convert from molecules to atoms.

$$\frac{11 \text{ atoms}}{1 \text{ molecule } C_3H_8}$$

Multiply the moles of C_3H_8 by the conversion factors.

$$2.12 \text{ mol } C_3H_8 \times \frac{6.02 \times 10^{23} \text{ molecules } C_3H_8}{1 \text{ mol } C_3H_8} \times \frac{11 \text{ atoms}}{1 \text{ molecule } C_3H_8}$$

$$= 1.40 \times 10^{25} \text{ atoms}$$

❸ Evaluate Does the result make sense? There are 11 atoms in each molecule of propane and more than 2 mol of propane, so the answer should be more than 20 times Avogadro's number of propane molecules. The answer has three significant figures based on the three significant figures in the given measurement.

> There are 3 atoms of carbon and 8 atoms of hydrogen in 1 molecule of propane.

5. How many atoms are in 1.14 mol of sulfur trioxide (SO_3)?

6. How many carbon atoms are in 2.12 mol of propane? How many hydrogen atoms are in 2.12 mol of propane?

Carbon Atoms		Hydrogen Atoms		Mass Ratio
Number	Mass (amu)	Number	Mass (amu)	$\dfrac{\text{Mass carbon}}{\text{Mass hydrogen}}$
•	12	◦	1	$\dfrac{12 \text{ amu}}{1 \text{ amu}} = \dfrac{12}{1}$
••	24 (2 × 12)	◦◦	2 (2 × 1)	$\dfrac{24 \text{ amu}}{2 \text{ amu}} = \dfrac{12}{1}$
••••• •••••	120 (10 × 12)	◦◦◦◦◦ ◦◦◦◦◦	10 (10 × 1)	$\dfrac{120 \text{ amu}}{10 \text{ amu}} = \dfrac{12}{1}$
(50 dots)	600 (50 × 12)	(50 circles)	50 (50 × 1)	$\dfrac{600 \text{ amu}}{50 \text{ amu}} = \dfrac{12}{1}$
Avogadro's number	$(6.02 \times 10^{23}) \times (12)$	Avogadro's number	$(6.02 \times 10^{23}) \times (1)$	$\dfrac{(6.02 \times 10^{23}) \times (12)}{(6.02 \times 10^{23}) \times (1)} = \dfrac{12}{1}$

Table 10.2 An average carbon atom is 12 times heavier than an average hydrogen atom.

a. Read Tables What is the mass of 50 carbon atoms? What is the mass of 50 hydrogen atoms?

b. Apply Concepts What is the ratio of the mass of 500 carbon atoms to the mass of 500 hydrogen atoms?

c. Infer Do 36.0 kg of carbon atoms and 3.0 kg of hydrogen atoms contain the same number of atoms? Explain.

Hint: To answer part c, determine the mass ratio of carbon to hydrogen.

Molar Mass

How do you determine the molar mass of an element and of a compound?

Remember that the atomic mass of an element (the mass of a single atom) is expressed in atomic mass units (amu). The atomic masses are relative values based on the mass of the most common isotope of carbon (carbon-12). Table 10.2 shows that an average carbon atom (C) with an atomic mass of 12.0 amu is 12 times heavier than an average hydrogen atom (H) with an atomic mass of 1.0 amu. Therefore, 100 carbon atoms are 12 times heavier than 100 hydrogen atoms. In fact, any number of carbon atoms is 12 times heavier than the same number of hydrogen atoms. So 12.0 g of carbon atoms and 1.0 g of hydrogen atoms must contain the same number of atoms.

If you look at the atomic masses of the elements in the periodic table, you will notice that they are not whole numbers. For example, the atomic mass of carbon is not exactly 12 times the mass of hydrogen. Recall from Chapter 4 that this is because atomic masses are weighted average masses of the isotopes of each element.

The Mass of a Mole of an Element Quantities measured in grams are convenient for working in the laboratory, so chemists have converted the relative scale of masses of the elements in amu to a relative scale of masses in grams. **The atomic mass of an element expressed in grams is the mass of a mole of the element.** The mass of a mole of an element is its **molar mass**. For carbon, the molar mass is 12.0 g. For atomic hydrogen, the molar mass is 1.0 g. Figure 10.5 shows one mole of carbon, sulfur, and iron. Compare the molar masses in the figure to the atomic masses in your periodic table. Notice that the molar masses are rounded off to one place after the decimal point. All the examples and problems in this text use molar masses that are rounded off in this way. If your teacher uses a different rounding rule for molar masses, your answers to problems may differ slightly from the answers given in the text.

If you were to compare 12.0 g of carbon atoms with 16.0 g of oxygen atoms, you would find they contain the same number of atoms. The molar masses of any two elements must contain the same number of atoms. How many atoms are contained in the molar mass of an element? You already know. The molar mass of any element contains 1 mol or 6.02×10^{23} atoms of that element.

The mole can now be further defined as the amount of substance that contains the same number of representative particles as the number of atoms in 12.0 g of carbon-12. You know that 12.0 g is the molar mass of carbon-12, so 12.0 g of carbon is 1 mol of carbon atoms. The same relationship applies to hydrogen: 1.0 g of hydrogen is 1 mol of hydrogen atoms. Similarly, 24.3 g is the molar mass of magnesium, so 1 mol of magnesium (or 6.02×10^{23} atoms of magnesium) has a mass of 24.3 g. Molar mass is the mass of 1 mol of atoms of any element.

READING SUPPORT
Build Comprehension:
Analogies You can buy small, medium, and large eggs. The size of the eggs doesn't affect how many eggs are in one dozen. Similarly, the size of the representative particles doesn't affect how many are in one mole. *Can you think of another analogy to show the relationship between moles and the size of representative particles?*

Figure 10.5 Molar Mass of an Element
One mole of carbon, sulfur, and iron are shown.
Apply Concepts *How many atoms of each element are present in each beaker?*

1 mol of sulfur atoms = 32.1 g

1 mol of carbon atoms = 12.0 g

1 mol of iron atoms = 55.8 g

1 mol of paradichlorobenzene (C$_6$H$_4$Cl$_2$)
molecules (moth crystals) = 147.0 g

1 mol of glucose (C$_6$H$_{12}$O$_6$)
molecules (blood sugar) = 180.0 g

1 mol of water (H$_2$O)
molecules = 18.0 g

**Figure 10.6 Molar Mass
of a Compound**
One mole is shown for each of
three molecular compounds.
Infer *How do you know that
each sample contains Avogadro's
number of molecules?*

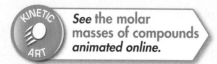

See the molar
masses of compounds
animated online.

The Mass of a Mole of a Compound To find the mass of a mole of a compound, you must know the formula of the compound. The formula of sulfur trioxide is SO$_3$. A molecule of SO$_3$ is composed of one atom of sulfur and three atoms of oxygen.

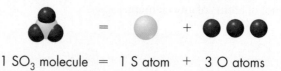

1 SO$_3$ molecule = 1 S atom + 3 O atoms

You can calculate the mass of a molecule of SO$_3$ by adding the atomic masses of the atoms making up the molecule. From the periodic table, the atomic mass of sulfur (S) is 32.1 amu. The mass of three atoms of oxygen is three times the atomic mass of a single oxygen atom (O): 3 × 16.0 amu = 48.0 amu. So, the molecular mass of SO$_3$ is 32.1 amu + 48.0 amu = 80.1 amu.

1 S atom + 3 O atoms = 1 SO$_3$ molecule
32.1 amu + 16.0 amu + 16.0 amu + 16.0 amu = 80.1 amu

Now substitute the unit grams for atomic mass units to find the molar mass of SO$_3$. The molar mass (g/mol) of any compound is the mass in grams of 1 mol of that compound. Thus, 1 mol of SO$_3$ has a mass of 80.1 g. This is the mass of 6.02 × 10^{23} molecules of SO$_3$.

🔑 **To calculate the molar mass of a compound, find the number of grams of each element in one mole of the compound. Then add the masses of the elements in the compound.** This method for calculating molar mass applies to any compound, molecular or ionic. The molar masses of paradichlorobenzene (C$_6$H$_4$Cl$_2$, 147.0 g), water (H$_2$O, 18.0 g), and glucose (C$_6$H$_{12}$O$_6$, 180.0 g) in Figure 10.6 were obtained in this way.

Sample Problem 10.4

Finding the Molar Mass of a Compound

The decomposition of hydrogen peroxide (H_2O_2) provides sufficient energy to launch a rocket. What is the molar mass of hydrogen peroxide?

KNOWNS

molecular formula = H_2O_2
mass of 1 mol H = 1.0 g H
mass of 1 mol O = 16.0 g O

UNKNOWN

molar mass = ? g/mol

❶ Analyze List the knowns and the unknown. Convert moles of atoms to grams by using conversion factors (g/mol) based on the molar mass of each element. The sum of the masses of the elements is the molar mass.

❷ Calculate Solve for the unknown.

Convert moles of hydrogen and oxygen to grams of hydrogen and oxygen.	$2 \text{ mol H} \times \dfrac{1.0 \text{ g H}}{1 \text{ mol H}} = 2.0 \text{ g H}$	One mole of H_2O_2 has 2 mol of H atoms and 2 mol of O atoms, so multiply the molar mass of each element by 2.

$$2 \text{ mol O} \times \dfrac{16.0 \text{ g O}}{1 \text{ mol O}} = 32.0 \text{ g O}$$

Add the results.

mass of 1 mol H_2O_2 = 2.0 g H + 32.0 g O = 34.0 g
molar mass of H_2O_2 = **34.0 g/mol**

❸ Evaluate Does the result make sense? The answer is the sum of two times the molar mass of hydrogen and oxygen (17.0 g/mol). The answer is expressed to the tenths place because the numbers being added are expressed to the tenths place.

One mole of PCl_3 has 1 mol of P atoms and 3 mol of Cl atoms.

7. Find the molar mass of PCl_3.

8. What is the mass of 1.00 mol of sodium hydrogen carbonate?

10.1 LessonCheck

9. Review What do you need to know to convert among the count, mass, and volume of something?

10. Describe How do chemists count the number of representative particles in a substance?

11. Explain How do you determine the molar mass of an element? How do you determine the molar mass of a compound?

12. Calculate If a dozen apples has a mass of 2.0 kg and 0.20 bushel is 1 dozen apples, how many bushels of apples are in 1.0 kg of apples?

13. Calculate How many moles is 1.50×10^{23} molecules of NH_3?

14. Calculate How many atoms are in 1.75 mol of $CHCl_3$?

15. Calculate What is the molar mass of $CaSO_4$?

How Big Is a Mole?

The mole is an especially useful tool to chemists, because it allows them to express the number of representative particles of a substance in grams. For example, a 1 mol sample of carbon, which contains Avogadro's number of carbon atoms (6.02×10^{23}), has a mass of 12.0 g.

The mole is a huge quantity. Written out, Avogadro's number is 602,000,000,000,000,000,000,000. However, it may be difficult for you to comprehend exactly how big a mole is. Here are some interesting ways to visualize the size of a mole.

TOO BIG TO COUNT If you were able to count at the rate of 1 million numbers per second, it would take almost 20 billion years to count to 6.02×10^{23}.

WORLDS OF ANTS Assume that ants live in anthills of 1 million ants each, and each hill has a surface area of 1 m².

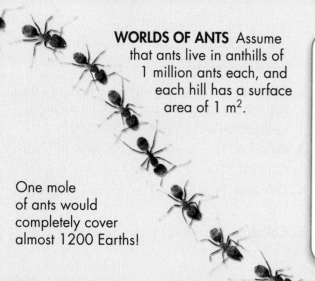

One mole of ants would completely cover almost 1200 Earths!

Take It Further

1. Calculate Show how to calculate the number of years it would take to count to Avogadro's number if you could count at the rate of 1 million numbers per second.

2. Use Models Develop your own concept to illustrate the size of Avogadro's number. Show your calculations.

3. Draw Conclusions At home, using a food scale, measure out a mole of table sugar (sucrose, $C_{12}H_{22}O_{11}$) or a mole of table salt (sodium chloride, NaCl). What does this measurement tell you about the size of atoms and molecules?

10.2 Mole–Mass and Mole–Volume Relationships

Q: *How can you calculate the moles of a substance in a given mass or volume?* Guess how many pennies are in the container and win a prize! You decide to enter the contest, and you win. You estimated the thickness and diameter of a penny to find its approximate volume. Then you estimated the dimensions of the container to obtain its volume. You did the arithmetic and made your guess. In a similar way, chemists use the relationships between the mole and quantities such as mass, volume, and number of particles to solve problems in chemistry.

The Mole–Mass Relationship

🔑 *How do you convert the mass of a substance to the number of moles of the substance?*

In the previous lesson, you learned that the molar mass of any substance is the mass in grams of one mole of that substance. This definition applies to all substances—elements, molecular compounds, and ionic compounds. In some situations, however, the term *molar mass* may be unclear. For example, suppose you were asked for the molar mass of oxygen. How you answer this question depends on what you assume to be the representative particle. If you assume the oxygen in the question is molecular oxygen (O_2), then the molar mass is 32.0 g/mol (2×16.0 g/mol). If you assume that the question is asking for the mass of a mole of oxygen atoms (O), then the answer is 16.0 g/mol. You can avoid confusion such as this by using the formula of the substance, in this case, O_2 or O.

Suppose you need a given number of moles of a substance for a laboratory experiment. How can you measure this amount? Suppose instead that you obtain a certain mass of a substance in a laboratory experiment. How many moles is this? 🔑 **Use the molar mass of an element or compound to convert between the mass of a substance and the moles of the substance.** The conversion factors for these calculations are based on the relationship: molar mass = 1 mol.

$$\frac{\text{molar mass}}{1 \text{ mol}} \quad \text{and} \quad \frac{1 \text{ mol}}{\text{molar mass}}$$

Key Questions

🔑 How do you convert the mass of a substance to the number of moles of the substance?

🔑 How do you convert the volume of a gas at STP to the number of moles of the gas?

Vocabulary

- Avogadro's hypothesis
- standard temperature and pressure (STP)
- molar volume

SampleProblem 10.5

Converting Moles to Mass

Items made out of aluminum, such as aircraft parts and cookware, are resistant to corrosion because the aluminum reacts with oxygen in the air to form a coating of aluminum oxide (Al_2O_3). This tough, resistant coating prevents any further corrosion. What is the mass, in grams, of 9.45 mol of aluminum oxide?

❶ Analyze List the known and the unknown. The mass of the compound is calculated from the known number of moles of the compound. The desired conversion is moles ⟶ mass.

> KNOWN
>
> number of moles = 9.45 mol Al_2O_3
>
> UNKNOWN
>
> mass = ? g Al_2O_3

❷ Calculate Solve for the unknown.

First, determine the mass of 1 mol of Al_2O_3.	$2 \text{ mol Al} \times \dfrac{27.0 \text{ g Al}}{1 \text{ mol Al}} = 54.0 \text{ g Al}$
	$3 \text{ mol O} \times \dfrac{16.0 \text{ g O}}{1 \text{ mol O}} = 48.0 \text{ g O}$

$1 \text{ mol } Al_2O_3 = 54.0 \text{ g Al} + 48.0 \text{ g O} = 102.0 \text{ g } Al_2O_3$

Identify the conversion factor relating moles of Al_2O_3 to grams of Al_2O_3.

$\dfrac{102.0 \text{ g } Al_2O_3}{1 \text{ mol } Al_2O_3}$

> Use the relationship:
> $1 \text{ mol } Al_2O_3 = 102.0 \text{ g } Al_2O_3$.

Multiply the given number of moles by the conversion factor.

$9.45 \text{ mol } Al_2O_3 \times \dfrac{102.0 \text{ g } Al_2O_3}{1 \text{ mol } Al_2O_3}$

$= 964 \text{ g } Al_2O_3$

❸ Evaluate Does the result make sense? The number of moles of Al_2O_3 is approximately 10, and each has a mass of approximately 100 g. The answer should be close to 1000 g. The answer has been rounded to the correct number of significant figures.

16. Find the mass, in grams, of 4.52×10^{-3} mol $C_{20}H_{42}$.

17. Calculate the mass, in grams, of 2.50 mol of iron(II) hydroxide.

> Start by determining the molar mass of each compound.

Converting Mass to Moles

When iron is exposed to air, it corrodes to form red-brown rust. Rust is iron(III) oxide (Fe_2O_3). How many moles of iron(III) oxide are contained in 92.2 g of pure Fe_2O_3?

❶ Analyze **List the known and the unknown.** The number of moles of the compound is calculated from the known mass of the compound. The conversion is mass ⟶ moles.

> KNOWN
>
> mass = 92.2 g Fe_2O_3
>
> UNKNOWN
>
> number of moles = ? mol Fe_2O_3

❷ Calculate **Solve for the unknown.**

First, determine the mass of 1 mol of Fe_2O_3.	⟹	$2 \text{ mol Fe} \times \dfrac{55.8 \text{ g Fe}}{1 \text{ mol Fe}} = 111.6 \text{ g Fe}$

$$3 \text{ mol O} \times \dfrac{16.0 \text{ g O}}{1 \text{ mol O}} = 48.0 \text{ g O}$$

$$1 \text{ mol } Fe_2O_3 = 111.6 \text{ g Fe} + 48.0 \text{ g O} = 159.6 \text{ g } Fe_2O_3$$

Identify the conversion factor relating grams of Fe_2O_3 to moles of Fe_2O_3.	⟹	$\dfrac{1 \text{ mol } Fe_2O_3}{159.6 \text{ g } Fe_2O_3}$	Note that the known unit (g) is in the denominator and the unknown unit (mol) is in the numerator.

Multiply the given mass by the conversion factor.	⟹	$92.2 \text{ g } Fe_2O_3 \times \dfrac{1 \text{ mol } Fe_2O_3}{159.6 \text{ g } Fe_2O_3}$ $= 0.578 \text{ mol } Fe_2O_3$

❸ Evaluate **Does the result make sense?** The given mass (about 90 g) is slightly larger than the mass of one-half mole of Fe_2O_3 (about 80 g), so the answer should be slightly larger than one-half (0.5) mol.

---

18. Find the number of moles in 3.70×10^{-1} g of boron.

19. Calculate the number of moles in 75.0 g of dinitrogen trioxide.

> Again, start by determining the molar mass of each substance.

The Mole–Volume Relationship

🔑 *How do you convert the volume of a gas at STP to the number of moles of the gas?*

Look back at Figure 10.6. Notice that the volumes of one mole of different solid and liquid substances are not the same. For example, the volumes of one mole of glucose (blood sugar) and one mole of paradichlorobenzene (moth crystals) are much larger than the volume of one mole of liquid water. What about the volumes of gases? Unlike liquids and solids, the volumes of moles of gases, measured under the same physical conditions, are much more predictable. Why is this?

Avogadro's Hypothesis In 1811, Amedeo Avogadro proposed a groundbreaking explanation. **Avogadro's hypothesis** states that equal volumes of gases at the same temperature and pressure contain equal numbers of particles. The particles that make up different gases are not the same size. However, the particles in all gases are so far apart that a collection of relatively large particles does not require much more space than the same number of relatively small particles. Whether the particles are large or small, large expanses of space exist between individual particles of gas, as shown in Figure 10.7.

The volume of a gas varies with a change in temperature or a change in pressure. Due to these variations with temperature and pressure, the volume of a gas is usually measured at a standard temperature and pressure. **Standard temperature and pressure (STP)** means a temperature of 0°C and a pressure of 101.3 kPa, or 1 atmosphere (atm). At STP, 1 mol, or 6.02×10^{23} representative particles, of any gas occupies a volume of 22.4 L. The quantity, 22.4 L, is called the **molar volume** of a gas.

Calculating the Volume and Moles of a Gas at STP The molar volume of a gas at STP is a useful quantity to chemists. 🔑 **The molar volume is used to convert between the number of moles of gas and the volume of the gas at STP.** The conversion factors for these calculations are based on the relationship 22.4 L = 1 mol at STP.

$$\frac{22.4\ \text{L}}{1\ \text{mol}} \quad \text{and} \quad \frac{1\ \text{mol}}{22.4\ \text{L}}$$

You can use these conversion factors to convert a known number of moles of gas to the volume of the gas at STP. Similarly, you can convert a known volume of gas at STP to the number of moles of the gas.

CHEMISTRY & YOU

Q: *How can you calculate the moles of a substance in a given mass? How can you calculate the moles of a gas in a given volume at STP?*

Figure 10.7 Volumes of Gases
In each container, the volume occupied by the gas molecules is small compared with the container's volume. **a.** The molecules in this container are small. **b.** This container can accommodate the same number of larger molecules.
Infer *If the containers contained liquid molecules, and the molecules in container* ***a*** *were smaller than the molecules in container* ***b***, *would both containers be able to accommodate the same number of molecules? Explain.*

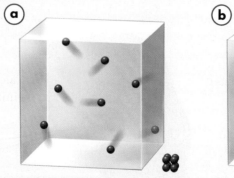

Calculating Gas Quantities at STP

Sulfur dioxide (SO_2) is a gas produced by burning coal. It is an air pollutant and one of the causes of acid rain. Determine the volume, in liters, of 0.60 mol SO_2 gas at STP.

❶ Analyze **List the knowns and the unknown.** Since SO_2 is a gas, the volume at STP can be calculated from the known number of moles.

KNOWNS

number of moles = 0.60 mol SO_2
1 mol SO_2 = 22.4 L SO_2 at STP

UNKNOWN

volume = ? L SO_2

❷ Calculate **Solve for the unknown.**

First, identify the conversion factor relating moles of SO_2 to volume of SO_2 at STP.

$$\frac{22.4\text{ L }SO_2}{1\text{ mol }SO_2}$$

The following relationship applies for gases at STP: 22.4 L = 1 mol.

Multiply the given number of moles by the conversion factor.

$$0.60\ \cancel{\text{mol }SO_2} \times \frac{22.4\text{ L }SO_2}{1\ \cancel{\text{mol }SO_2}}$$

$$= 13\text{ L }SO_2$$

❸ Evaluate **Does the result make sense?** One mole of any gas at STP has a volume of 22.4 L, so 0.60 mol should have a volume slightly larger than one half of a mole or 11.2 L. The answer should have two significant figures.

20. What is the volume of these gases at STP?
   a. 3.20×10^{-3} mol CO_2
   b. 3.70 mol N_2
   c. 0.960 mol CH_4

In Problem 20, convert from moles of gas to volume.

21. At STP, how many moles are in these volumes of gases?
   a. 67.2 L SO_2
   b. 0.880 L He
   c. 1.00×10^3 L C_2H_6

In Problem 21, convert from volume of gas to moles.

Calculating Molar Mass and Density A gas-filled balloon will either sink or float in the air depending on whether the density of the gas inside the balloon is greater or less than the density of the surrounding air. Different gases have different densities. Usually the density of a gas is measured in grams per liter (g/L) and at a specific temperature. The density of a gas at STP and the molar volume at STP (22.4 L/mol) can be used to calculate the molar mass of the gas. Similarly, the molar mass of a gas and the molar volume at STP can be used to calculate the density of a gas at STP.

You have now examined a mole in terms of particles, mass, and volume of gases at STP. Figure 10.8 summarizes these relationships and illustrates the importance of the mole.

Sample Problem 10.8

Calculating the Molar Mass of a Gas at STP

The density of a gaseous compound containing carbon and oxygen is found to be 1.964 g/L at STP. What is the molar mass of the compound?

KNOWNS
density = 1.964 g/L
1 mol of gas at STP = 22.4 L

UNKNOWN
molar mass = ? g/mol

❶ Analyze List the knowns and the unknown. The molar mass of the compound is calculated from the known density of the compound and the molar volume at STP.

❷ Calculate Solve for the unknown.

First, identify the conversion factor needed to convert density to molar mass.

$$\frac{22.4\text{ L}}{1\text{ mol}}$$

Use the density and molar volume at STP to calculate the molar mass.

$$\text{molar mass} = \frac{g}{\text{mol}} = \frac{g}{L} \times \frac{22.4\text{ L}}{1\text{ mol}}$$

Multiply the given density by the conversion factor.

$$\frac{1.964\text{ g}}{1\text{ L}} \times \frac{22.4\text{ L}}{1\text{ mol}}$$

$$= 44.0\text{ g/mol}$$

❸ Evaluate Does the result make sense? The ratio of the calculated mass (44.0 g) to the volume (22.4 L) is about 2, which is close to the known density. The answer should have three significant figures.

22. A gaseous compound composed of sulfur and oxygen has a density of 3.58 g/L at STP. What is the molar mass of this gas?

In Problem 22, use the density and molar volume of the gas at STP to calculate the molar mass.

23. What is the density of krypton gas at STP?

To do Problem 23, first find the molar mass of krypton. Use the molar mass and the molar volume at STP to calculate the density at STP.

Figure 10.8 Mole Roadmap
The mole is at the center of your chemical calculations. To convert from one unit to another, you must use the mole as an intermediate step. The form of the conversion factor depends on what you know and what you want to calculate.

Interpret Diagrams *How many conversion factors are needed to convert from the mass of a gas to the volume of a gas at STP?*

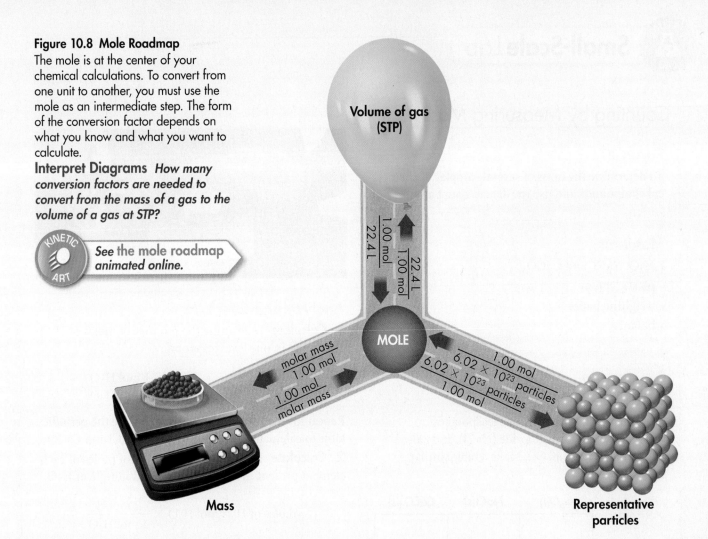

See the mole roadmap animated online.

Volume of gas (STP)

$\frac{1.00 \text{ mol}}{22.4 \text{ L}}$ $\frac{22.4 \text{ L}}{1.00 \text{ mol}}$

MOLE

$\frac{\text{molar mass}}{1.00 \text{ mol}}$ $\frac{1.00 \text{ mol}}{\text{molar mass}}$

$\frac{6.02 \times 10^{23} \text{ particles}}{1.00 \text{ mol}}$ $\frac{1.00 \text{ mol}}{6.02 \times 10^{23} \text{ particles}}$

Mass

Representative particles

ONLINE PROBLEMS

10.2 LessonCheck

24. Describe How do you convert between the mass and the number of moles of a substance?

25. Describe How do you convert between the volume of a gas at STP and the number of moles of the gas?

26. Calculate How many grams are in 5.66 mol of $CaCO_3$?

27. Calculate Find the number of moles in 508 g of ethanol (C_2H_6O).

28. Calculate What is the volume, in liters, of 1.50 mol Cl_2 at STP?

29. Apply Concepts Three balloons filled with three different gaseous compounds each have a volume of 22.4 L at STP. Do these balloons have the same mass or contain the same number of molecules? Explain.

30. Calculate The density of an elemental gas is 1.7824 g/L at STP. What is the molar mass of the element?

31. Analyze Data The densities of gases A, B, and C at STP are 1.25 g/L, 2.86 g/L, and 0.714 g/L, respectively. Calculate the molar mass of each substance. Identify each substance as ammonia (NH_3), sulfur dioxide (SO_2), chlorine (Cl_2), nitrogen (N_2), or methane (CH_4).

BIGIDEA
THE MOLE AND QUANTIFYING MATTER

32. A chemist collects 2.94 L of carbon monoxide (CO) gas at STP during an experiment. Explain how she can determine the mass of gas that she collected. Why is the mole important for this calculation?

Small-Scale Lab

Counting by Measuring Mass

Purpose

To determine the mass of several samples of chemical compounds and use the data to count atoms

Materials

- H_2O, NaCl, and $CaCO_3$
- plastic spoon
- weighing paper
- balance

Procedure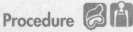

Measure the mass of one level teaspoon of water (H_2O), sodium chloride (NaCl), and calcium carbonate ($CaCO_3$). Make a table similar to the one below.

	$H_2O(l)$	$NaCl(s)$	$CaCO_3(s)$
Mass (g)			
Molar mass (g/mol)			
Moles of each compound			
Moles of each element			
Atoms of each element			

Analyze and Conclude

1. Calculate Determine the number of moles of H_2O contained in one level teaspoon.

$$\text{moles of } H_2O = g\, H_2O \times \frac{1\text{ mol } H_2O}{18.0\text{ g } H_2O}$$

Repeat for the remaining compounds. Use the periodic table to calculate the molar masses of NaCl and $CaCO_3$.

2. Calculate Determine the number of moles of each element present in the teaspoon-sized sample of H_2O.

$$\text{moles of } H = \text{mol } H_2O \times \frac{2\text{ mol } H}{1\text{ mol } H_2O}$$

Repeat for the other compounds in your table.

3. Calculate Determine the number of atoms of each element present in the teaspoon-sized sample of H_2O.

$$\text{atoms of } H = \text{mol } H \times \frac{6.02 \times 10^{23}\text{ atoms } H}{1\text{ mol } H}$$

Repeat for the other compounds in your table.

4. Analyze Data Which of the three teaspoon-sized samples contains the greatest number of moles of molecules or formula units?

5. Analyze Data Which of the three compounds contains the greatest number of atoms?

You're the Chemist

1. Design an Experiment Can you count by measuring volume? Design and carry out an experiment to do it.

2. Design an Experiment Design an experiment that will determine the number of atoms of calcium, carbon, and oxygen it takes to write your name on the chalkboard with a piece of chalk. Assume chalk is 100 percent calcium carbonate, $CaCO_3$.

10.3 Percent Composition and Chemical Formulas

CHEMISTRY & YOU

Q: *What does the percent composition of a compound tell you?* A tag sewn into the seam of a shirt usually tells you what fibers were used to make the cloth and the percent of each. It helps to know the percents of the components in the shirt because they affect how warm the shirt is, whether it will need to be ironed, and how it should be cleaned. Similarly, in chemistry it is important to know the percents of the elements in a compound.

Key Questions

🔑 How do you calculate the percent composition of a compound?

🔑 How can you calculate the empirical formula of a compound?

🔑 How does the molecular formula of a compound compare with the empirical formula?

Vocabulary

• percent composition
• empirical formula

Percent Composition of a Compound

🔑 *How do you calculate the percent composition of a compound?*

In lawn care, the relative amount, or the percent, of each nutrient in fertilizer is important. In spring, you may use a fertilizer that has a high percent of nitrogen to "green" the grass. In fall, you may want to use a fertilizer with a higher percent of potassium to strengthen the root system. Knowing the relative amounts of the components of a mixture or compound is often useful.

The relative amounts of the elements in a compound are expressed as the **percent composition** or the percent by mass of each element in the compound. As shown in Figure 10.9, the percent composition of potassium chromate, K_2CrO_4, is K = 40.3%, Cr = 26.8%, and O = 32.9%. These percents must total 100% (40.3% + 26.8% + 32.9% = 100%). The percent composition of a compound is always the same.

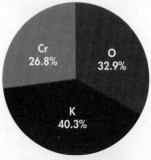

Potassium chromate, K_2CrO_4

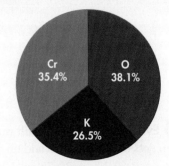

Potassium dichromate, $K_2Cr_2O_7$

Figure 10.9 Percent Composition
Potassium chromate (K_2CrO_4) is composed of 40.3% potassium, 26.8% chromium, and 32.9% oxygen.
Compare *How does this percent composition differ from the percent composition of potassium dichromate ($K_2Cr_2O_7$), a compound composed of the same three elements?*

Percent Composition From Mass Data If you know the relative masses of each element in a compound, you can calculate the percent composition of the compound. The percent by mass of an element in a compound is the number of grams of the element divided by the mass in grams of the compound, multiplied by 100%.

$$\% \text{ by mass of element} = \frac{\text{mass of element}}{\text{mass of compound}} \times 100\%$$

SampleProblem 10.9

Calculating Percent Composition From Mass Data

When a 13.60-g sample of a compound containing only magnesium and oxygen is decomposed, 5.40 g of oxygen is obtained. What is the percent composition of this compound?

❶ Analyze List the knowns and the unknowns. The percent by mass of an element in a compound is the mass of that element divided by the mass of the compound multiplied by 100%.

KNOWNS

mass of compound = 13.60 g
mass of oxygen = 5.40 g O
mass of magnesium = 13.60 g − 5.40 g O = 8.20 g Mg

UNKNOWNS

percent by mass of Mg = ?% Mg
percent by mass of O = ?% O

❷ Calculate Solve for the unknowns.

Determine the percent by mass of Mg in the compound.

$$\% \text{ Mg} = \frac{\text{mass of Mg}}{\text{mass of compound}} \times 100\% = \frac{8.20 \text{ g}}{13.60 \text{ g}} \times 100\%$$

$$= 60.3\% \text{ Mg}$$

Determine the percent by mass of O in the compound.

$$\% \text{ O} = \frac{\text{mass of O}}{\text{mass of compound}} \times 100\% = \frac{5.40 \text{ g}}{13.60 \text{ g}} \times 100\%$$

$$= 39.7\% \text{ O}$$

❸ Evaluate Does the result make sense? The percents of the elements add up to 100%.
60.3% + 39.7% = 100%

In Problem 34, calculate the percent by mass of mercury and oxygen in the compound.

33. A compound is formed when 9.03 g Mg combines completely with 3.48 g N. What is the percent composition of this compound?

34. When a 14.2-g sample of mercury(II) oxide is decomposed into its elements by heating, 13.2 g Hg is obtained. What is the percent composition of the compound?

Percent Composition From the Chemical Formula You can also calculate the percent composition of a compound using its chemical formula. The subscripts in the formula are used to calculate the mass of each element in a mole of that compound. Using the individual masses of the elements and the molar mass, you can calculate the percent by mass of each element.

Learn more about percent composition online.

$$\text{\% by mass of element} = \frac{\text{mass of element in 1 mol compound}}{\text{molar mass of compound}} \times 100\%$$

SampleProblem 10.10

Calculating Percent Composition From a Formula

Propane (C_3H_8), the fuel commonly used in gas grills, is one of the compounds obtained from petroleum. Calculate the percent composition of propane.

❶ Analyze **List the knowns and the unknowns.** Calculate the percent by mass of each element by dividing the mass of that element in one mole of the compound by the molar mass of the compound and multiplying by 100%.

KNOWNS

mass of C in 1 mol C_3H_8 = 3 mol × 12.0 g/mol = 36.0 g
mass of H in 1 mol C_3H_8 = 8 mol × 1.0 g/mol = 8.0 g
molar mass of C_3H_8 = 36.0 g/mol + 8.0 g/mol = 44.0 g/mol

UNKNOWNS

percent by mass of C = ?% C
percent by mass of H = ?% H

❷ Calculate **Solve for the unknowns.**

Determine the percent by mass of C in C_3H_8.

$$\% C = \frac{\text{mass of C in 1 mol } C_3H_8}{\text{molar mass of } C_3H_8} \times 100\% = \frac{36.0 \text{ g}}{44.0 \text{ g}} \times 100\%$$

$$= 81.8\% \text{ C}$$

Determine the percent by mass of H in C_3H_8.

$$\% H = \frac{\text{mass of H in 1 mol } C_3H_8}{\text{molar mass of } C_3H_8} \times 100\% = \frac{8.0 \text{ g}}{44.0 \text{ g}} \times 100\%$$

$$= 18\% \text{ H}$$

❸ Evaluate **Does the result make sense?** The percents of the elements add up to 100% when the answers are expressed to two significant figures (82% + 18% = 100%).

35. Calculate the percent by mass of nitrogen in these fertilizers.
   a. NH_3
   b. NH_4NO_3

36. Calculate the percent composition of these compounds.
   a. ethane (C_2H_6)
   b. sodium hydrogen sulfate ($NaHSO_4$)

Quick Lab

Purpose To measure the percent of water in a series of crystalline compounds called hydrates

Materials

- 3 medium-sized test tubes
- balance
- spatula
- hydrated compounds of copper(II) sulfate, calcium chloride, and sodium sulfate
- test tube holder
- gas burner

Percent Composition

Procedure

1. Label each test tube with the name of a compound. Measure and record the masses.

2. Add 2–3 g of each compound (a good-sized spatula full) to the appropriately labeled test tube. Measure and record the mass of each test tube and the compound.

3. Using a test tube holder, hold one of the tubes at a 45° angle and gently heat its contents over the burner, slowly passing it in and out of the flame. Note any change in the appearance of the solid compound.

4. As moisture begins to condense in the upper part of the test tube, gently heat the entire length of the tube. Continue heating until all of the moisture is driven from the tube. This process may take 2–3 minutes. Repeat Steps 3 and 4 for the other two tubes.

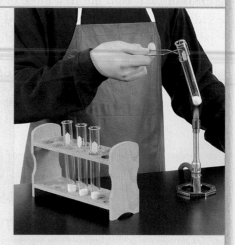

5. Allow each tube to cool. Then measure and record the mass of each test tube and the heated compound.

Analyze and Conclude

1. Organize Data Set up a data table so that you can subtract the mass of the empty tube from the mass of the compound and the test tube, both before and after heating.

2. Calculate Find the difference between the mass of each compound before and after heating. This difference represents the amount of water lost by the hydrated compound due to heating.

3. Calculate Determine the percent by mass of water lost by each compound.

4. Analyze Data Which compound lost the greatest percent by mass of water? Which compound lost the smallest percent by mass of water?

Q: *What information can you get from the percent composition of a compound?*

Percent Composition as a Conversion Factor You can use percent composition to calculate the number of grams of any element in a specific mass of a compound. To do this, multiply the mass of the compound by a conversion factor based on the percent composition of the element in the compound. In Sample Problem 10.10, you found that propane is 81.8 percent carbon and 18 percent hydrogen. That means that in a 100-g sample of propane, you would have 81.8 g of carbon and 18 g of hydrogen. You can use the following conversion factors to solve for the mass of carbon or hydrogen contained in a specific amount of propane.

$$\frac{81.8 \text{ g C}}{100 \text{ g C}_3\text{H}_8} \quad \text{and} \quad \frac{18 \text{ g H}}{100 \text{ g C}_3\text{H}_8}$$

Sample Problem 10.11

Calculating the Mass of an Element in a Compound Using Percent Composition

Calculate the mass of carbon and the mass of hydrogen in 82.0 g of propane (C_3H_8).

❶ Analyze List the known and the unknowns.

Use the conversion factors based on the percent composition of propane to make the following conversions: grams $C_3H_8 \longrightarrow$ grams C and grams $C_3H_8 \longrightarrow$ grams H.

KNOWN	UNKNOWNS
mass of C_3H_8 = 82.0 g	mass of carbon = ? g C
	mass of hydrogen = ? g H

❷ Calculate Solve for the unknowns.

To calculate the mass of C, first write the conversion factor to convert from mass of C_3H_8 to mass of C.

$$\frac{81.8 \, g \, C}{100 \, g \, C_3H_8}$$

From Sample Problem 10.10, the percent by mass of C in C_3H_8 is 81.8%.

Multiply the mass of C_3H_8 by the conversion factor.

$$82.0 \, g \, C_3H_8 \times \frac{81.8 \, g \, C}{100 \, g \, C_3H_8} = 67.1 \, g \, C$$

To calculate the mass of H, first write the conversion factor to convert from mass of C_3H_8 to mass of H.

$$\frac{18 \, g \, H}{100 \, g \, C_3H_8}$$

From Sample Problem 10.10, the percent by mass of H in C_3H_8 is 18%.

Multiply the mass of C_3H_8 by the conversion factor.

$$82.0 \, g \, C_3H_8 \times \frac{18 \, g \, H}{100 \, g \, C_3H_8} = 15 \, g \, H$$

❸ Evaluate Does the result make sense?

The sum of the two masses equals 82 g, the sample size, to two significant figures (67 g C + 15 g H = 82 g C_3H_8).

37. Calculate the grams of nitrogen in 125 g of each fertilizer.
   a. NH_3
   b. NH_4NO_3

In Problem 37, use the percent composition you calculated for each compound in Problem 35.

38. Calculate the mass of hydrogen in each of the following compounds:
   a. 350 g ethane (C_2H_6)
   b. 20.2 g sodium hydrogen sulfate ($NaHSO_4$)

In Problem 38, use the percent composition you calculated for each compound in Problem 36.

Figure 10.10 Interpreting Formulas
A formula can be interpreted on a microscopic level in terms of atoms or on a macroscopic level in terms of moles of atoms.

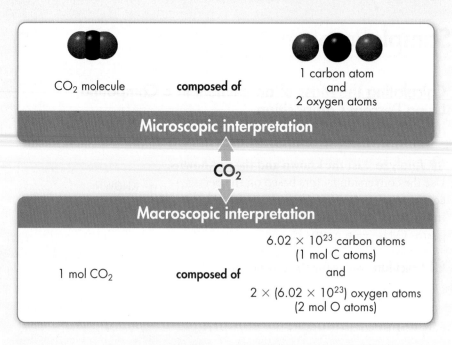

| CO_2 molecule | **composed of** | 1 carbon atom and 2 oxygen atoms |

Microscopic interpretation

CO_2

Macroscopic interpretation

| 1 mol CO_2 | **composed of** | 6.02×10^{23} carbon atoms (1 mol C atoms) and $2 \times (6.02 \times 10^{23})$ oxygen atoms (2 mol O atoms) |

Empirical Formulas

🔑 *How can you calculate the empirical formula of a compound?*

A useful formula for cooking rice is to use one cup of rice and two cups of water. If you needed twice the amount of cooked rice, you would need two cups of rice and four cups of water. The formulas for some compounds also show a basic ratio of elements. Multiplying that ratio by any factor can produce the formulas for other compounds.

The **empirical formula** of a compound gives the lowest whole-number ratio of the atoms or moles of the elements in a compound. Figure 10.10 shows that empirical formulas may be interpreted at the microscopic (atomic) or macroscopic (molar) level. An empirical formula may or may not be the same as a molecular formula. For example, the lowest ratio of hydrogen to oxygen in hydrogen peroxide is 1:1. Thus the empirical formula of hydrogen peroxide is HO. The molecular formula of hydrogen peroxide, H_2O_2, has twice the number of atoms as the empirical formula. Notice that the ratio of hydrogen to oxygen is still the same, 1:1. The molecular formula tells the actual number of each kind of atom present in a molecule of the compound. For carbon dioxide, the empirical and molecular formulas are the same—CO_2. Figure 10.11 shows two compounds of carbon and hydrogen having the same empirical formula (CH) but different molecular formulas.

🔑 **The percent composition of a compound can be used to calculate the empirical formula of that compound.** The percent composition tells the ratio of masses of the elements in a compound. The ratio of masses can be changed to a ratio of moles by using conversion factors based on the molar mass of each element. The mole ratio is then reduced to the lowest whole-number ratio to obtain the empirical formula of the compound.

Figure 10.11 Compounds With the Same Empirical Formula
Two different compounds can have the same empirical formula.
a. Ethyne (C_2H_2), also called acetylene, is a gas used in welders' torches. **b.** Styrene (C_8H_8) is used in making polystyrene.
Calculate *What is the empirical formula of ethyne and styrene?*

SampleProblem 10.12

Determining the Empirical Formula of a Compound

A compound is analyzed and found to contain 25.9% nitrogen and 74.1% oxygen. What is the empirical formula of the compound?

❶ Analyze **List the knowns and the unknown.** The percent composition gives the ratio of the mass of nitrogen atoms to the mass of oxygen atoms in the compound. Change the ratio of masses to a ratio of moles and reduce this ratio to the lowest whole-number ratio.

> **KNOWNS**
> percent by mass of N = 25.9% N
> percent by mass of O = 74.1% O
>
> **UNKNOWN**
> empirical formula = $N_?O_?$

❷ Calculate **Solve for the unknown.**

Convert the percent by mass of each element to moles.	$25.9 \, g\,N \times \dfrac{1 \, mol \, N}{14.0 \, g\,N} = 1.85 \, mol \, N$

$74.1 \, g\,O \times \dfrac{1 \, mol \, O}{16.0 \, g\,O} = 4.63 \, mol \, O$

The mole ratio of N to O is $N_{1.85}O_{4.63}$.

> *Percent means "parts per 100," so 100.0 g of the compound contains 25.9 g N and 74.1 g O.*

Divide each molar quantity by the smaller number of moles to get 1 mol for the element with the smaller number of moles.

$\dfrac{1.85 \, mol \, N}{1.85} = 1 \, mol \, N$

$\dfrac{4.63 \, mol \, O}{1.85} = 2.50 \, mol \, O$

The mole ratio of N to O is now $N_1O_{2.5}$.

Multiply each part of the ratio by the smallest whole number that will convert both subscripts to whole numbers.

$1 \, mol \, N \times 2 = 2 \, mol \, N$
$2.5 \, mol \, O \times 2 = 5 \, mol \, O$

The empirical formula is N_2O_5.

❸ Evaluate **Does the result make sense?** The subscripts are whole numbers, and the percent composition of this empirical formula equals the percents given in the original problem.

39. Calculate the empirical formula of each compound.
  a. 94.1% O, 5.9% H
  b. 67.6% Hg, 10.8% S, 21.6% O

> *Start by converting the percent by mass of each element to moles.*

40. 1,6-diaminohexane is used to make nylon. What is the empirical formula of this compound if its percent composition is 62.1% C, 13.8% H, and 24.1% N?

Comparison of Empirical and Molecular Formulas

Formula (name)	Classification of formula	Molar mass (g/mol)
CH	Empirical	13
C_2H_2 (ethyne)	Molecular	26 (2 × 13)
C_6H_6 (benzene)	Molecular	78 (6 × 13)
CH_2O (methanal)	Empirical and molecular	30
$C_2H_4O_2$ (ethanoic acid)	Molecular	60 (2 × 30)
$C_6H_{12}O_6$ (glucose)	Molecular	180 (6 × 30)

Table 10.3 Different compounds can have the same empirical formula.
a. Read Tables What is the molar mass of benzene, C_6H_6?
b. Interpret Tables Which compounds in the table have the empirical formula CH_2O?
c. Explain Why is the molar mass of glucose ($C_6H_{12}O_6$) equal to six times the molar mass of methanal (CH_2O)?

Hint: How is the formula $C_6H_{12}O_6$ related to the formula CH_2O?

Molecular Formulas

🔑 *How does the molecular formula of a compound compare with the empirical formula?*

Look at the compounds listed in Table 10.3. Ethyne and benzene have the same empirical formula—CH. Methanal, ethanoic acid, and glucose, shown in Figure 10.12, have the same empirical formula—CH_2O. Notice that the molar masses of the compounds in these two groups are simple whole-number multiples of the molar masses of the empirical formulas, CH and CH_2O. 🔑 **The molecular formula of a compound is either the same as its experimentally determined empirical formula, or it is a simple whole-number multiple of its empirical formula.**

Once you have determined the empirical formula of a compound, you can determine its molecular formula, if you know the compound's molar mass. A chemist often uses an instrument called a mass spectrometer to determine molar mass. The compound is broken into charged fragments (ions) that travel through a magnetic field. The magnetic field deflects the particles from their straight-line paths. The mass of the compound is determined from the amount of deflection experienced by the particles.

You can calculate the empirical formula mass (efm) of a compound from its empirical formula. This is simply the molar mass of the empirical formula. Then you can divide the experimentally determined molar mass by the empirical formula mass. This quotient gives the number of empirical formula units in a molecule of the compound and is the multiplier to convert the empirical formula to the molecular formula.

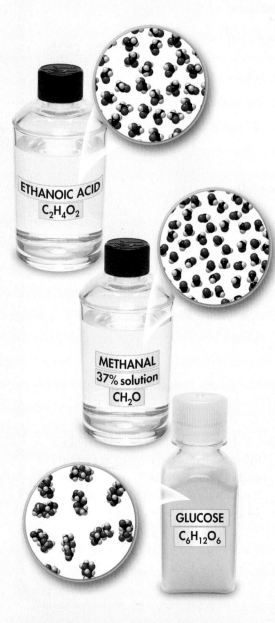

ETHANOIC ACID $C_2H_4O_2$

METHANAL 37% solution CH_2O

GLUCOSE $C_6H_{12}O_6$

Figure 10.12 Compounds With the Empirical Formula CH_2O
Methanal (formaldehyde), ethanoic acid (acetic acid), and glucose have the same empirical formula.
Apply Concepts *How could you easily obtain the molar mass of ethanoic acid using the molar mass of methanal?*

Finding the Molecular Formula of a Compound

Calculate the molecular formula of a compound whose molar mass is 60.0 g/mol and empirical formula is CH_4N.

❶ Analyze List the knowns and the unknown. Divide the molar mass by the empirical formula mass to obtain a whole number. Multiply the empirical formula subscripts by this value to get the molecular formula.

KNOWNS
empirical formula = CH_4N
molar mass = 60.0 g/mol

UNKNOWN
molecular formula = $C_?H_?N_?$

❷ Calculate Solve for the unknown.

First, calculate the empirical formula mass.

$$efm \text{ of } CH_4N = 12.0 \text{ g/mol} + 4(1.0 \text{ g/mol}) + 14.0 \text{ g/mol} = 30.0 \text{ g/mol}$$

Divide the molar mass by the empirical formula mass.

$$\frac{molar\ mass}{efm} = \frac{60.0 \text{ g/mol}}{30.0 \text{ g/mol}} = 2$$

Multiply the formula subscripts by this value.

$$(CH_4N) \times 2 = C_2H_8N_2$$

❸ Evaluate Does the result make sense? The molecular formula has the molar mass of the compound.

---

41. What is the molecular formula of a compound with the empirical formula CClN and a molar mass of 184.5 g/mol?

42. Find the molecular formula of ethylene glycol, which is used as antifreeze. The molar mass is 62.0 g/mol, and the empirical formula is CH_3O.

ⓒ 10.3 LessonCheck

43. 🔵 **Review** How do you calculate the percent by mass of an element in a compound?

44. 🔵 **Identify** What information can you use to calculate the empirical formula of a compound?

45. 🔵 **Explain** How is the molecular formula of a compound related to its empirical formula?

46. Calculate Determine the percent composition of the compound that forms when 222.6 g N combines completely with 77.4 g O.

47. Calculate Find the percent composition of calcium acetate, $Ca(C_2H_3O_2)_2$.

48. Calculate Using the results of Problem 47, calculate the grams of hydrogen in 124 g of $Ca(C_2H_3O_2)_2$.

BIGIDEA
THE MOLE AND QUANTIFYING MATTER

49. The compound methyl butanoate smells like apples. Its percent composition is 58.8% C, 9.8% H, and 31.4% O, and its molar mass is 102 g/mol. What is its empirical formula? What is its molecular formula?

Ion Mobility Spectrometry

In 2001, a terrorist boarded an airline flight with explosives inside his shoes. Since that time, Americans have had to remove their shoes during airport security checks. However, newer airport security devices, known as "puffer portals," allow airport security to scan for minute traces of explosives on a person's body and clothing, without the person having to remove any clothing or shoes.

The puffer portal looks like a standard airport metal detector. There are vents and nozzles on the walls and ceiling of the portal. When a passenger steps inside, the doors close, and the instrument sends sharp bursts of air to dislodge particles from his or her body, hair, and clothing. The air sample is then passed through a chemical analysis system called an ion mobility spectrometer (IMS). The IMS identifies compounds based on the amount of time it takes for ions to pass through an electrified field in a tube filled with a nonreactive gas (drift gas). This "drift time" is then compared to a database of drift times of different compounds. In this way, molecules of known explosive or narcotic materials can be detected and identified. If even a picogram of an explosive is detected, an alarm sounds.

PUFFING OUT EXPLOSIVES Bursts of air dislodge particles from a person's hair, body, and clothes. These particles are then directed to an ion mobility spectrometer (IMS).

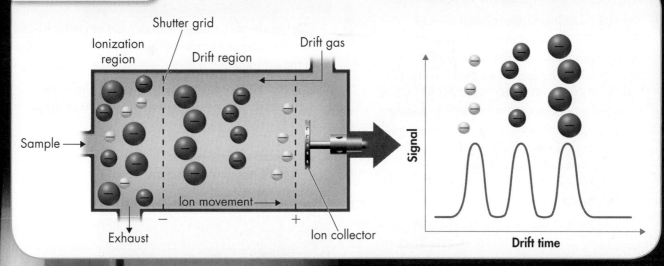

Ionization region · Shutter grid · Drift region · Drift gas · Sample · Ion movement · Exhaust · Ion collector · Signal · Drift time

IDENTIFYING IONS When the particles enter the IMS, they are ionized, or converted into ions. The ionized particles then travel through a tube containing an electric field, which causes the ions to separate according to their masses, sizes, and shapes. For example, smaller ions move faster and reach the end of the tube before larger ions.

Take It Further

1. Calculate Two common explosive compounds are trinitrotoluene (TNT) and cyclotrimethylenetrinitramine (RDX). The chemical formula of TNT is $C_7H_5N_3O_6$. The chemical formula of RDX is $C_3H_6N_6O_6$. Calculate the molar masses of these two compounds.

2. Analyze Data If TNT and RDX molecules are separated in an IMS solely based on mass, which compound would reach the ion collector first?

3. Predict What do you think would be some other uses for ion mobility spectrometers?

10 **Study** Guide

BIGIDEA
THE MOLE AND QUANTIFYING MATTER

The mole is an important measurement in chemistry. The mole allows you to convert among the amount of representative particles in a substance, the mass of a substance, and the volume of a gas at STP. The molecular formula of a compound can be determined by first finding the percent composition of the compound and determining the empirical formula. Using the empirical formula mass and the molar mass of the compound, the molecular formula can be determined.

10.1 The Mole: A Measurement of Matter

🔑 Knowing how the count, mass, and volume of an item relate to a common unit allows you to convert among these units.

🔑 The mole allows chemists to count the number of representative particles in a substance.

🔑 The atomic mass of an element expressed in grams is the mass of a mole of the element.

🔑 To calculate the molar mass of a compound, find the number of grams of each element in one mole of the compound. Then add the masses of the elements in the compound.

- mole (308)
- Avogadro's number (308)
- representative particle (308)
- molar mass (313)

10.2 Mole–Mass and Mole–Volume Relationships

🔑 Use the molar mass of an element or compound to convert between the mass of a substance and the moles of the substance.

🔑 The molar volume is used to convert between the number of moles of gas and the volume of the gas at STP.

- Avogadro's hypothesis (320)
- standard temperature and pressure (STP) (320)
- molar volume (320)

10.3 Percent Composition and Chemical Formulas

🔑 The percent by mass of an element in a compound is the number of grams of the element divided by the mass in grams of the compound, multiplied by 100%.

🔑 The percent composition of a compound can be used to calculate the empirical formula of that compound.

🔑 The molecular formula of a compound is either the same as its experimentally determined empirical formula, or it is a simple whole-number multiple of its empirical formula.

- percent composition (325)
- empirical formula (330)

Key Equations

$$\% \text{ by mass of element} = \frac{\text{mass of element}}{\text{mass of compound}} \times 100\%$$

$$\% \text{ by mass of element} = \frac{\text{mass of element in 1 mol compound}}{\text{molar mass of compound}} \times 100\%$$

Math Tune-Up: Mole Problems

Problem	❶ Analyze	❷ Calculate	❸ Evaluate
How many moles of lithium (Li) is 4.81×10^{24} atoms of lithium?	Knowns: number of atoms = 4.81×10^{24} atoms Li 1 mol Li = 6.02×10^{23} atoms Li Unknown: moles = ? mol Li The desired conversion is atoms $\longrightarrow$ moles.	Use the correct conversion factor to convert from atoms to moles. 4.81×10^{24} atoms Li $\times$ $\dfrac{1 \text{ mol Li}}{6.02 \times 10^{23} \text{ atoms Li}} = \boxed{7.99 \text{ mol Li}}$ **Hint:** Review Sample Problems 10.2 and 10.3 if you have trouble converting between number of representative particles and moles.	The given number of atoms is about 8 times Avogadro's number, so the answer should be around 8 mol of atoms.
Calculate the mass in grams of 0.160 mol H_2O_2.	Known: number of moles = 0.160 mol H_2O_2 Unknown: mass = ? g H_2O_2 The desired conversion is moles $\longrightarrow$ mass.	Determine the molar mass of H_2O_2 and use the correct conversion factor to convert from moles to grams. $1 \text{ mol } H_2O_2 = (2 \text{ mol})(1.0 \text{ g/mol}) +$ $(2 \text{ mol})(16.0 \text{ g/mol}) = 34.0 \text{ g } H_2O_2$ $0.160 \text{ mol } H_2O_2 \times \dfrac{34.0 \text{ g } H_2O_2}{1 \text{ mol } H_2O_2}$ $= \boxed{5.44 \text{ g } H_2O_2}$	The number of moles of H_2O_2 is about 0.2, and the molar mass is about 30 g/mol. The answer should be around 6 g.
What is the volume of 1.25 mol He at STP?	Knowns: number of moles = 1.25 mol He 1 mol He at STP = 22.4 L He Unknown: volume = ? L He The desired conversion is moles $\longrightarrow$ volume at STP.	Use the correct conversion factor to convert from moles to volume at STP. $1.25 \text{ mol He} \times \dfrac{22.4 \text{ L He}}{1 \text{ mol He}} = \boxed{28.0 \text{ L}}$ **Remember:** A mole of any gas at STP occupies a volume of 22.4 L.	One mole of gas at STP has a volume of 22.4 L, so 1.25 mol should have a volume larger than 22.4 L.
What is the percent composition of the compound formed when 29.0 g Ag combines completely with 4.30 g S?	Knowns: mass of Ag = 29.0 g Ag mass of S = 4.30 g S mass of compound = $29.0 \text{ g} + 4.30 \text{ g} = 33.3 \text{ g}$ Unknowns: percent by mass of Ag = ?% Ag percent by mass of S = ?% S Use the equation: % by mass of element = $\dfrac{\text{mass of element}}{\text{mass of compound}} \times 100\%$	Calculate the percent by mass of Ag and S in the compound. $\%\text{Ag} = \dfrac{29.0 \text{ g}}{33.3 \text{ g}} \times 100\%$ $\%\text{Ag} = 87.1\% \text{ Ag}$ $\%\text{S} = \dfrac{4.30 \text{ g}}{33.3 \text{ g}} \times 100\%$ $\%\text{S} = 12.9\% \text{ S}$ **Hint:** Review Sample Problems 10.9 and 10.10 if you have trouble calculating the percent composition of a compound.	The percents of the elements add up to 100%.

10 Assessment

Lesson by Lesson

10.1 The Mole: A Measurement of Matter

50. List three common ways that matter is measured. Give examples of each.

★ **51.** Name the representative particle (atom, molecule, or formula unit) of each substance.

   a. oxygen gas   **c.** sulfur dioxide
   b. sodium sulfide   **d.** potassium

★ **52.** How many hydrogen atoms are in a representative particle of each substance?

   a. $Al(OH)_3$ **c.** $(NH_4)_2HPO_4$
   b. $H_2C_2O_4$ **d.** $C_4H_{10}O$

53. Describe the relationship between Avogadro's number and one mole of any substance.

★ **54.** Find the number of moles in each substance.

   a. 2.41×10^{24} formula units of NaCl
   b. 9.03×10^{24} atoms of Hg
   c. 4.65×10^{24} molecules of NO_2

55. Which contains more molecules: 1.00 mol H_2O_2, 1.00 mol C_2H_6, or 1.00 mol CO?

56. Which contains more atoms: 1.00 mol H_2O_2, 1.00 mol C_2H_6, or 1.00 mol CO?

★ **57.** Find the number of representative particles in each substance.

   a. 3.00 mol Sn
   b. 0.400 mol KCl
   c. 7.50 mol SO_2
   d. 4.80×10^{-3} mol NaI

58. What is the molar mass of chlorine?

59. List the steps you would take to calculate the molar mass of any compound.

★ **60.** Calculate the molar mass of each substance.

   a. H_3PO_4 **d.** $(NH_4)_2SO_4$
   b. N_2O_3 **e.** $C_4H_9O_2$
   c. $CaCO_3$ **f.** Br_2

61. Calculate the mass of 1.00 mol of each of these substances.

   a. silicon dioxide (SiO_2)
   b. diatomic nitrogen (N_2)
   c. iron(III) hydroxide ($Fe(OH)_3$)
   d. copper (Cu)

10.2 Mole–Mass and Mole–Volume Relationships

62. Find the mass of each substance.

   a. 1.50 mol C_5H_{12} **d.** 7.00 mol H_2O_2
   b. 14.4 mol F_2 **e.** 5.60 mol NaOH
   c. 0.780 mol $Ca(CN)_2$ **f.** 3.21×10^{-2} mol Ni

★ **63.** Calculate the mass in grams of 0.250 mol of each of the following compounds:

   a. sucrose ($C_{12}H_{22}O_{11}$)
   b. sodium chloride (NaCl)
   c. potassium permanganate ($KMnO_4$)

★ **64.** Calculate the number of moles in 1.00×10^2 g of each of the compounds in Problem 63.

65. How many moles is each of the following?

   a. 15.5 g SiO_2 **d.** 5.96 g KOH
   b. 0.0688 g AgCl   **e.** 937 g $Ca(C_2H_3O_2)_2$
   c. 79.3 g Cl_2 **f.** 0.800 g Ca

66. What is the volume of one mole of any gas at STP?

★ **67.** Calculate the volume of each of the following gases at STP.

   a. 7.64 mol Ar
   b. 1.34 mol SO_2
   c. 0.442 mol C_2H_6
   d. 2.45×10^{-3} mol H_2S

★ **68.** A gas has a density of 0.902 g/L at STP. What is the molar mass of this gas?

69. What is the density of each of the following gases at STP?

   a. C_3H_8 **c.** Ne
   b. O_2 **d.** NO_2

70. Find each of the following quantities:

   a. the volume, in liters, of 835 g SO_3 at STP
   b. the mass, in grams, of a molecule of aspirin ($C_9H_8O_4$)
   c. the number of atoms in 5.78 mol NH_4NO_3

10.3 Percent Composition and Chemical Formulas

71. What is the percent composition of the compound formed when 2.70 g of aluminum combine with oxygen to form 5.10 g of aluminum oxide?

*72. Calculate the percent composition when 13.3 g Fe combine completely with 5.7 g O.

*73. Calculate the percent composition of each compound.

   a. H_2S **c.** $Mg(OH)_2$
   b. $(NH_4)_2C_2O_4$ **d.** Na_3PO_4

*74. Using your answers from Problem 73, calculate the number of grams of these elements.

   a. sulfur in 3.54 g H_2S
   b. nitrogen in 25.0 g $(NH_4)_2C_2O_4$
   c. magnesium in 97.4 g $Mg(OH)_2$
   d. phosphorus in 804 g Na_3PO_4

75. Which of the following compounds has the highest percent of iron by mass?

   a. $FeCl_2$ **c.** $Fe(OH)_2$
   b. $Fe(C_2H_3O_2)_3$ **d.** FeO

*76. What is an empirical formula? Which of the following molecular formulas are also empirical formulas?

   a. ribose $(C_5H_{10}O_5)$
   b. ethyl butyrate $(C_6H_{12}O_2)$
   c. chlorophyll $(C_{55}H_{72}MgN_4O_5)$
   d. DEET $(C_{12}H_{17}ON)$

77. Which of the following can be classified as an empirical formula?

   a. S_2Cl_2 **b.** $C_6H_{10}O_4$ **c.** Na_2SO_3

78. Which pair of molecules has the same empirical formula?

   a. $C_2H_4O_2$, $C_6H_{12}O_6$
   b. $NaCrO_4$, $Na_2Cr_2O_7$

*79. What is the molecular formula for each compound? Each compound's empirical formula and molar mass are given.

   a. CH_2O, 90 g/mol   **b.** HgCl, 472.2 g/mol

Understand Concepts

*80. Table sugar, or sucrose, has the chemical formula $C_{12}H_{22}O_{11}$.

   a. How many atoms are in 1.00 mol of sucrose?
   b. How many atoms of C are in 2.00 mol of sucrose?
   c. How many atoms of H are in 2.00 mol of sucrose?
   d. How many atoms of O are in 3.65 mol of sucrose?

81. How can you determine the molar mass of a gaseous compound if you do not know its molecular formula?

*82. A series of compounds has the empirical formula CH_2O. The graph shows the relationship between the molar mass of the compounds and the mass of carbon in each compound.

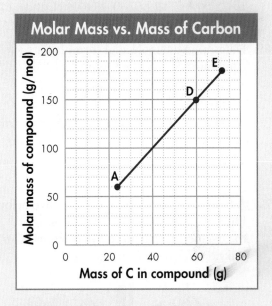

   a. What are the molecular formulas for the compounds represented by data points A, D, and E?
   b. Find the slope of the line. Is this value consistent with the empirical formula? Explain.
   c. Two other valid data points fall on the line between points A and D. What are the x, y values for these data points?

83. Explain what is wrong with each statement.

   a. One mole of any substance contains the same number of atoms.
   b. A mole and a molecule of a substance are identical in amount.
   c. One molar mass of CO_2 contains Avogadro's number of atoms.

84. Which of the following contains the largest number of atoms?

   a. 82.0 g Kr
   b. 0.842 mol C_2H_4
   c. 36.0 g N_2

*85. Calculate the grams of oxygen in 90.0 g of Cl_2O.

86. What is the total mass of a mixture of 3.50×10^{22} formula units Na_2SO_4, 0.500 mol H_2O, and 7.23 g AgCl?

★ **87.** The molecular formula of an antibacterial drug is $C_{17}H_{18}FN_3O_3$. How many fluorine atoms are in a 150-mg tablet of this drug?

88. Determine the empirical formulas of compounds with the following percent compositions:

   a. 42.9% C and 57.1% O
   b. 32.00% C, 42.66% O, 18.67% N, and 6.67% H
   c. 71.72% Cl, 16.16% O, and 12.12% C

★ **89.** Determine the molecular formula for each compound.

   a. 94.1% O and 5.9% H; molar mass = 34 g/mol
   b. 50.7% C, 4.2% H, and 45.1% O; molar mass = 142 g/mol
   c. 56.6% K, 8.7% C, and 34.7% O; molar mass = 138.2 g/mol

★ **90.** A fictitious "atomic balance" is shown below. Fifteen atoms of boron on the left side of the balance are balanced by six atoms of an unknown element E on the right side.

   a. What is the atomic mass of element E?
   b. What is the identity of element E?

★ **91.** A typical virus is 5×10^{-6} cm in diameter. If Avogadro's number of these virus particles were laid in a row, how many kilometers long would the line be?

92. Calculate the empirical formula for each compound.

   a. compound consisting of 0.40 mol Cu and 0.80 mol Br
   b. compound with 4 atoms of carbon for every 12 atoms of hydrogen

93. Muscle fatigue can result from the buildup of lactic acid. The percent composition of lactic acid is 40.0% C, 6.67% H, and 53.3% O. What is the molecular formula of lactic acid if its molar mass is 90.0 g/mol?

★ **94.** What mass of helium is needed to inflate a balloon to a volume of 5.50 L at STP?

95. How many water molecules are in a 1.00-L bottle of water? The density of water is 1.00 g/mL.

Think Critically

★ **96.** **Infer** What is the empirical formula of a compound that has three times as many hydrogen atoms as carbon atoms but only half as many oxygen atoms as carbon atoms?

97. **Apply Concepts** How are the empirical and molecular formulas of a compound related?

98. **Compare** Why does one mole of carbon have a smaller mass than one mole of sulfur? How are the atomic structures of these elements different?

99. **Analyze Data** One mole of any gas at STP equals 22.4 L of that gas. It is also true that different elements have different atomic volumes, or diameters. How can you reconcile these two statements?

★ **100.** **Interpret Graphs** The graph shows the percent composition of phenylalanine.

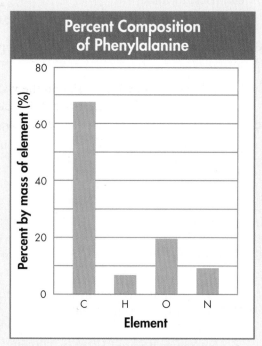

   a. What is the empirical formula for phenylalanine?
   b. If the molar mass of phenylalanine is 165.2 g/mol, what is its molecular formula?

*101. **Infer** Nitroglycerine contains 60% as many carbon atoms as hydrogen atoms, three times as many oxygen atoms as nitrogen atoms, and the same number of carbon and nitrogen atoms. The number of moles of nitroglycerine in 1.00 g is 0.00441. What is the molecular formula of nitroglycerine?

102. **Calculate** The density of nickel is 8.91 g/cm³. How large a cube, in cm³, would contain 2.00×10^{24} atoms of nickel?

*103. **Calculate** Dry air is about 20.95% oxygen by volume. Assuming STP, how many oxygen molecules are in a 75.0-g sample of air? The density of air is 1.19 g/L.

104. **Graph** The table below gives the molar mass and density of seven gases at STP.

Substance	Molar mass (g/mol)	Density (g/L)
Oxygen	32.0	1.43
Carbon dioxide	44.0	1.96
Ethane	30.0	1.34
Hydrogen	2.0	0.089
Sulfur dioxide	64.1	2.86
Ammonia	17.0	0.759
Fluorine	38.0	1.70

 a. Plot these data, with density on the x-axis.
 b. What is the slope of the straight-line plot?
 c. What is the molar mass of a gas at STP that has a density of 1.10 g/L?
 d. A mole of a gas at STP has a mass of 56.0 g. Use the graph to determine its density.

*105. **Calculate** Avogadro's number has been determined by about 20 different methods. In one approach, the spacing between ions in an ionic substance is determined by using a technique called X-ray diffraction. X-ray diffraction studies of sodium chloride have shown that the distance between adjacent Na^+ and Cl^- ions is 2.819×10^{-8} cm. The density of solid NaCl is 2.165 g/cm³. By calculating the molar mass to four significant figures, you can determine Avogadro's number. What value do you obtain?

106. **Use Models** In Chapter 3, you learned that the densities of solids and liquids are measured in g/cm³, but the densities of gases are measured in g/L. Draw atomic diagrams of a solid and of a gas that show why the two different units are practical.

107. **Connect to the BIGIDEA** Research the history of Avogadro's number. What elements other than carbon have been used to define a mole? Write a report that summarizes your findings.

CHEMYSTERY

A Formula for Cheating

Typically, steroids can be detected in an athlete's urine. A urine sample is collected and is first injected into an instrument that separates the chemical compounds in the urine.

The separated compounds are then analyzed using a mass spectrometer. The mass spectrometer provides information such as the molar mass of the compounds present in the urine sample and the molecular structure of these compounds. These structures can be compared against a database of known compounds to identify the presence of steroids in the sample.

*108. **Calculate** Analysis of an athlete's urine found the presence of a compound with a molar mass of 312 g/mol. How many moles of this compound are contained in 30.0 mg? How many molecules of the compound is this?

109. **Connect to the BIGIDEA** The compound found in the athlete's urine, the steroid THG, has a percent composition of 80.8% carbon, 8.97% hydrogen, and 10.3% oxygen. What is the empirical formula of THG? If the molar mass of THG is 312 g/mol, what is the molecular formula?

★110. Identify at least one chemical change and two physical changes that are occurring in the photo.

★111. Classify each of the following as a physical change or a chemical change.

  a. An aspirin tablet is crushed to a powder.
  b. A red rose turns brown.
  c. Grape juice turns to wine.
  d. Fingernail polish remover evaporates.
  e. A bean seed sprouts.
  f. A piece of copper is beaten into a thin sheet.

112. Which of these statements are true about every solution?

  a. Solutions are in the liquid state.
  b. Solutions are homogeneous.
  c. Solutions are mixtures.
  d. Solutions are composed of at least two compounds.

113. A student writes down the density of table sugar as 1.59 and the density of carbon dioxide as 1.83. Can these values be correct? Explain.

★114. A block of wood measuring 2.75 cm × 4.80 cm × 7.50 cm has a mass of 84.0 g. Will the block of wood sink or float in water?

★115. Convert each of the following:

  a. 4.72 g to mg
  b. 2.7×10^3 cm/s to km/h
  c. 4.4 mm to dm

★116. How many protons, electrons, and neutrons are in each isotope?

  a. zirconium-90   **c.** bromine-81
  b. palladium-108   **d.** antimony-123

★117. Write the complete electron configuration for each atom.

  a. fluorine   **b.** lithium   **c.** rubidium

118. Why do the elements magnesium and barium have similar chemical and physical properties?

★119. Which of the following are transition metals: Cr, Cd, Ca, Cu, Co, Cs, Ce?

120. How can the periodic table be used to infer the number of valence electrons in an atom?

121. How does a molecule differ from an atom?

122. Draw electron dot structures and predict the shapes of the following molecules:

  a. PH_3 **b.** CO   **c.** CS_2 **d.** CF_4

123. How are single, double, and triple bonds indicated in electron dot structures?

124. Give an example of each of the following:

  a. coordinate covalent bonding
  b. resonance structures
  c. exceptions to the octet rule

125. Explain how you can use electronegativity values to classify a bond as nonpolar covalent, polar covalent, or ionic.

★126. Identify any incorrect formulas among the following:

  a. H_2O_2 **d.** CaS_2
  b. $NaIO_4$ **e.** $CaHPO_4$
  c. SrO   **f.** BaOH

★127. Name these compounds.

  a. $Fe(OH)_3$ **c.** Na_2CO_3
  b. NH_4I **d.** CCl_4

★128. Write formulas for these compounds.

  a. potassium nitrate
  b. copper(II) oxide
  c. magnesium nitride
  d. silver fluoride

If You Have Trouble With . . .

Question	110	111	112	113	114	115	116	117	118	119	120	121	122	123	124	125	126	127	128
See Chapter	2	2	2	3	3	3	4	5	6	6	7	8	8	8	8	8	9	9	9

Standardized Test Prep

1. Choose the term that best completes the second relationship.
   a. dozen : eggs
      mole : _____
      (A) atoms   **(C)** size
      (B) 6.02×10^{23} **(D)** grams
   b. mole : Avogadro's number
      molar volume : _____
      (A) mole   **(C)** STP
      (B) water   **(D)** 22.4 L

Select the choice that best answers each question or completes each statement.

2. Calculate the molar mass of ammonium phosphate, $(NH_4)_3PO_4$.
   (A) 113.0 g/mol   **(C)** 149.0 g/mol
   (B) 121.0 g/mol   **(D)** 242.0 g/mol

3. Based on the structural formula below, what is the empirical formula for tartaric acid, a compound found in grape juice?

$$HO-CH-COOH$$
$$\quad\ \ |$$
$$HO-CH-COOH$$

   (A) $C_2H_3O_3$ **(C)** CHO
   (B) $C_4H_6O_6$ **(D)** $C_1H_{1.5}O_{1.5}$

4. How many hydrogen atoms are in six molecules of ethylene glycol, $C_2H_6O_2$?
   (A) 6   **(C)** $6 \times (6.02 \times 10^{23})$
   (B) 36   **(D)** $36 \times (6.02 \times 10^{23})$

5. Which of these compounds has the largest percent by mass of nitrogen?
   (A) N_2O **(D)** N_2O_3
   (B) NO **(E)** N_2O_4
   (C) NO_2

6. Which of these statements is true of a balloon filled with 1.00 mol $N_2(g)$ at STP?
   I. The balloon has a volume of 22.4 L.
   II. The contents of the balloon have a mass of 14.0 g.
   III. The balloon contains 6.02×10^{23} molecules.
   (A) I only   **(C)** I and III only
   (B) I and II only   **(D)** I, II, and III

7. Allicin, $C_6H_{10}S_2O$, is the compound that gives garlic its odor. A sample of allicin contains 3.0×10^{21} atoms of carbon. How many hydrogen atoms does this sample contain?
   (A) 10   **(C)** 1.8×10^{21}
   (B) 1.0×10^{21} **(D)** 5.0×10^{21}

The lettered choices below refer to Questions 8–11. A lettered choice may be used once, more than once, or not at all.

(A) CH **(B)** CH_2 **(C)** C_2H_5 **(D)** CH_3 **(E)** C_2H_3

Which of the formulas is the empirical formula for each of the following compounds?

8. C_8H_{12} 10. C_2H_6

9. C_6H_6 11. C_4H_{10}

For Questions 12–14, write the molecular formula for each compound whose structural formula is shown. Then calculate the compound's molar mass.

12.
$$\begin{array}{ccccc} & H & OH & H & \\ & | & | & | & \\ H- & C- & C- & C & -H \\ & | & | & | & \\ & H & H & H & \end{array}$$

13.
$$\begin{array}{ccc} & H & O \\ & | & || \\ H_2N- & C- & C-OH \\ & | & \\ & H & \end{array}$$

14.
$$\begin{array}{ccccc} & H & H & & O \\ & | & | & & || \\ H- & C- & C & -O- & C-H \\ & | & | & & \\ & H & H & & \end{array}$$

If You Have Trouble With . . .

Question	1	2	3	4	5	6	7	8	9	10	11	12	13	14
See Lesson	10.2	10.1	10.3	10.1	10.3	10.2	10.1	10.3	10.3	10.3	10.3	10.1	10.1	10.1

11

Chemical Reactions

INSIDE:

- **11.1** Describing Chemical Reactions
- **11.2** Types of Chemical Reactions
- **11.3** Reactions in Aqueous Solution

PearsonChem.com

Reef aquariums like this one use an aqueous solution of calcium hydroxide to provide calcium for marine animals such as snails and coral.

REACTIONS

Essential Questions:

1. *How do chemical reactions obey the law of conservation of mass?*

2. *How can you predict the products of a chemical reaction?*

CHEMYSTERY

Order in the Lab

"How does anybody find anything in this lab?" Maria muttered to herself. Her spice cabinet at home was in alphabetical order. If she wanted to find the cinnamon, it was right there between the bay leaves and cumin. She decided to help the teacher by rearranging the chemicals before class.

She found the sodium cyanide and put it next to the sodium sulfide. Then she picked up the sodium hydroxide and looked around until she found the sulfuric acid. Before Maria could put down the sodium hydroxide, her teacher walked in and called out "Maria, leave the chemicals alone! They're arranged the way they are for a reason."

Why did Maria's teacher stop her from rearranging the chemicals?

▶ Connect to the **BIG**IDEA As you read about chemical reactions, think about how you can predict the outcomes of chemical reactions.

NATIONAL SCIENCE EDUCATION STANDARDS

A-1, A-2, B-3, G-1

Q: *How is a chemical reaction going to change the way you drive?* You've probably heard about hydrogen fuel-cell cars. Fuel cells produce electricity through a chemical reaction without any of the combustion that you find in typical gasoline engines. In this lesson, you'll learn how to write and balance the equations that represent chemical reactions.

Key Questions

🔑 How do you write a skeleton equation?

🔑 What are the steps for writing and balancing a chemical equation?

Vocabulary

• chemical equation
• skeleton equation
• catalyst
• coefficient
• balanced equation

Introduction to Chemical Equations

🔑 **How do you write a skeleton equation?**

Every minute of the day chemical reactions take place—both inside you and around you. After a meal, a series of chemical reactions take place as your body digests food. Similarly, plants use sunlight to drive the photosynthetic processes needed to produce plant growth. Although the chemical reactions involved in photosynthesis and digestion are different, both chemical reactions are necessary to sustain life. All chemical reactions, whether simple or complex, involve changing substances.

In a chemical reaction, one or more reactants change into one or more products. Cooking food always involves a chemical reaction. In order to bake muffins, you begin with a recipe and ingredients, as shown in Figure 11.1. The recipe tells you which ingredients to mix together and how much of each to use. Chemical reactions take place when the ingredients or reactants are mixed together and heated in the oven. The product, in this case, is a batch of muffins. Chemists use a chemical equation—a quick, shorthand notation—to convey as much information as possible about what happens in a chemical reaction.

Figure 11.1
Reactants and Products
Reactants in the ingredients undergo chemical changes to form the product, the muffins.
Observing *What evidence shows that chemical changes have occurred?*

Figure 11.2 Examples of Reactions
Three common chemical reactions are shown below.

Iron turns to red-brown rust (iron(III) oxide) in the presence of oxygen.

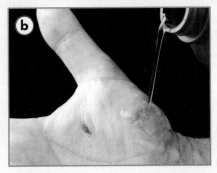

Water and oxygen form when hydrogen peroxide is poured on a cut.

The products of burning methane are carbon dioxide and water.

Word Equations How do you describe what happens in a chemical reaction? Recall from Chapter 2 the shorthand method for writing a description of a chemical reaction. In this method, the reactants were written on the left and the products on the right. An arrow separated them. You read the arrow as *yields, gives,* or *reacts to produce.*

$$\text{Reactants} \longrightarrow \text{products}$$

How could you describe the rusting of iron shown in Figure 11.2a? You could say: "Iron reacts with oxygen to produce iron(III) oxide (rust)." Although that is a perfectly good description, it's quicker to identify the reactants and product by means of a word equation.

$$\text{Iron} + \text{oxygen} \longrightarrow \text{iron(III) oxide}$$

In a word equation, write the names of the reactants to the left of the arrow, separated by plus signs; write the names of the products to the right of the arrow, also separated by plus signs. Notice that no plus sign is needed on the product side of this equation because iron(III) oxide is the only product.

Have you ever poured the antiseptic hydrogen peroxide on an open cut? Bubbles of oxygen gas form rapidly, as shown in Figure 11.2b. The production of a new substance, a gas, is evidence of a chemical change. Two new substances are produced in this reaction, oxygen gas and liquid water. You could describe this reaction by saying, "Hydrogen peroxide decomposes to form water and oxygen gas." But, you could also write a word equation.

$$\text{Hydrogen peroxide} \longrightarrow \text{water} + \text{oxygen}$$

When you light a burner on your stove, methane gas bursts into flames and produces the energy needed to heat your soup. Methane is the major component of natural gas, a common fuel for heating homes and cooking food. The burning of methane, as shown in Figure 11.2c, is a chemical reaction. How would you write the word equation for this reaction? Burning a substance typically requires oxygen, so methane and oxygen are the reactants. The products are water and carbon dioxide. Thus, the word equation is as follows:

$$\text{Methane} + \text{oxygen} \longrightarrow \text{carbon dioxide} + \text{water}$$

Figure 11.3
Speeding Up a Reaction
Hydrogen peroxide decomposes to form water and oxygen gas. **a.** Bubbles of oxygen appear slowly as decomposition proceeds. **b.** With the addition of the catalyst manganese(IV) oxide (MnO_2), decomposition speeds up. The white "smoke" is condensed water vapor.

Chemical Equations Word equations adequately describe chemical reactions, but they are cumbersome. It's easier to use the formulas for the reactants and products to write chemical equations. A **chemical equation** is a representation of a chemical reaction; the formulas of the reactants (on the left) are connected by an arrow with the formulas of the products (on the right). Here is a chemical equation for rusting:

$$Fe + O_2 \longrightarrow Fe_2O_3$$

Equations that show just the formulas of the reactants and products are called skeleton equations. A **skeleton equation** is a chemical equation that does not indicate the relative amounts of the reactants and products. The first step in writing a complete chemical equation is to write the skeleton equation. ⟶ **To write a skeleton equation, write the chemical formulas for the reactants to the left of the yields sign (arrow) and the formulas for the products to the right.**

To add more information to the equation, you can indicate the physical states of substances by putting a symbol after each formula. Use (*s*) for a solid, (*l*) for a liquid, (*g*) for a gas, and (*aq*) for a substance in aqueous solution (a substance dissolved in water). Here is the unbalanced equation for rusting with symbols for the physical states added:

$$Fe(s) + O_2(g) \longrightarrow Fe_2O_3(s)$$

In many chemical reactions, a catalyst is added to the reaction mixture. A **catalyst** is a substance that speeds up the reaction but is not used up in the reaction. A catalyst is neither a reactant nor a product, so its formula is written above the arrow in a chemical equation. For example, Figure 11.3 shows that the compound manganese(IV) oxide ($MnO_2(s)$) catalyzes the decomposition of an aqueous solution of hydrogen peroxide ($H_2O_2(aq)$) to produce water and oxygen.

$$H_2O_2(aq) \xrightarrow{\text{MnO}_2} H_2O(l) + O_2(g)$$

Many of the symbols commonly used in writing chemical equations are listed below.

Table 11.1

Symbols Used in Chemical Equations	
Symbol	**Explanation**
+	Separates two reactants or two products
⟶	"Yields," separates reactants from products
⇌	Used in place of ⟶ for reversible reactions
(s), (l), (g)	Designates a reactant or product in the solid state, liquid state, and gaseous state; placed after the formula
(aq)	Designates an aqueous solution; the substance is dissolved in water; placed after the formula
$\xrightarrow{\Delta}$ $\xrightarrow{\text{heat}}$	Indicates that heat is supplied to the reaction
$\xrightarrow{\text{Pt}}$	A formula written above or below the yield sign indicates its use as a catalyst (in this example, platinum).

Sample Problem 11.1

Writing a Skeleton Equation

Hydrochloric acid reacts with solid sodium hydrogen carbonate. The products formed are aqueous sodium chloride, water, and carbon dioxide gas. Write a skeleton equation for this chemical reaction.

❶ Analyze Identify the relevant concepts.

Write the correct formula for each substance in the reaction. Indicate the state of each substance. Separate the reactants from the products with an arrow. Use plus signs to separate the two reactants and each of the three products.

❷ Solve Apply concepts to this problem.

Start with the names of reactants and products. Include their physical states.	**Reactants** sodium hydrogen carbonate (solid) hydrochloric acid (aqueous) **Products** sodium chloride (aqueous) water (liquid) carbon dioxide (gas)
Write the correct formula for each reactant and each product.	**Reactants** $NaHCO_3(s)$ $HCl(aq)$ **Products** $NaCl(aq)$ $H_2O(l)$ $CO_2(g)$
Separate the reactants from the products with an arrow. Use plus signs to separate the reactants and the products.	$NaHCO_3(s) + HCl(aq) \longrightarrow NaCl(aq) + H_2O(l) + CO_2(g)$

1. Write a sentence that describes this chemical reaction:

$Na(s) + H_2O(l) \longrightarrow NaOH(aq) + H_2(g)$

2. Sulfur burns in oxygen to form sulfur dioxide. Write a skeleton equation for this chemical reaction.

Balancing Chemical Equations

🔑 *What are the steps for writing and balancing a chemical equation?*

How would you write a word equation for the manufacture of bicycles? Simplify your task by limiting yourself to four major components: frames, wheels, handlebars, and pedals. Your word equation for making a bicycle could read like this.

$$\underbrace{\text{Frame} + \text{wheel} + \text{handlebar} + \text{pedal}}_{\text{Reactants}} \longrightarrow \underbrace{\text{bicycle}}_{\text{Product}}$$

Your word equation shows the reactants (the kinds of parts) and the product (a bicycle).

But if you were responsible for ordering parts to make a bicycle, this word equation would be inadequate because it does not indicate the quantity of each part needed to make one bicycle.

A standard bicycle is composed of one frame (F), two wheels (W), one handlebar (H), and two pedals (P). The formula for a bicycle would be FW_2HP_2. The skeleton equation would be

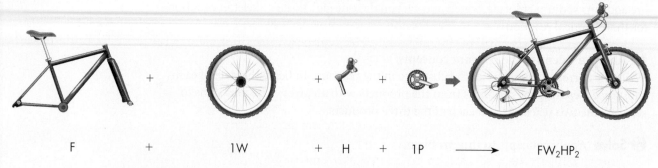

F   +   1W   +   H   +   1P   ⟶ FW_2HP_2

This equation is unbalanced. An unbalanced equation does not indicate the quantity of the reactants needed to make the product. A complete description of the reaction must include not only the kinds of parts involved but also the quantities of parts required.

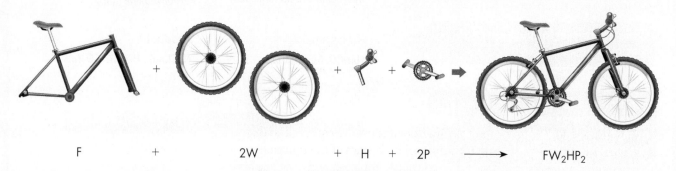

F   +   2W   +   H   +   2P   ⟶ FW_2HP_2

This equation for making a bicycle is balanced. It tells you that one frame, two wheels, one handlebar, and two pedals produce one bicycle. To balance the equation, the number 2 was placed before wheels and pedals. The number 1 is understood to be in front of *frame, handlebar,* and *bicycle.* These numbers are called **coefficients**—small whole numbers that are placed in front of the formulas in an equation in order to balance it. In this balanced equation, the number of each bicycle part on the reactant side is the same as the number of those parts on the product side. A chemical reaction is also described by a **balanced equation** in which each side of the equation has the same number of atoms of each element and mass is conserved.

Recall that John Dalton's atomic theory states that as reactants are converted to products, the bonds holding the atoms together are broken, and new bonds are formed. The atoms themselves are neither created nor destroyed; they are merely rearranged.

This part of Dalton's theory explains the law of conservation of mass: In any chemical change, mass is conserved. The atoms in the products are the same atoms that were in the reactants—they are just rearranged. Representing a chemical reaction by a balanced chemical equation is a two-step process. **To write a balanced chemical equation, first write the skeleton equation. Then use coefficients to balance the equation so that it obeys the law of conservation of mass.** In every balanced equation, each side of the equation has the same number of atoms of each element.

Sometimes, though, a skeleton equation may already be balanced. For example, carbon burns in the presence of oxygen to produce carbon dioxide.

C(s)   +   O$_2$(g)   →   CO$_2$(g)
Carbon   Oxygen   Carbon Dioxide

Reactants   **Product**
1 carbon atom, 2 oxygen atoms   1 carbon atom, 2 oxygen atoms

Q: *The reaction between oxygen and hydrogen in fuel cells produce the energy to power a car. What are the products of the reaction in a fuel cell that make the fuel-cell car a zero-emission car?*

This equation is balanced. One carbon atom and two oxygen atoms are on each side of the equation. You do not need to change the coefficients; they are all understood to be 1.

What about the equation for the reaction of hydrogen and oxygen gas? When hydrogen and oxygen are mixed, the product of the reaction is water. The skeleton equation is as follows:

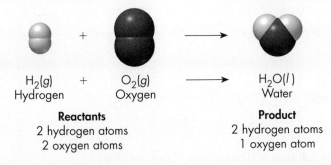

H$_2$(g)   +   O$_2$(g)   →   H$_2$O(l)
Hydrogen   Oxygen   Water

Reactants   **Product**
2 hydrogen atoms   2 hydrogen atoms
2 oxygen atoms   1 oxygen atom

The formulas for all the reactants and the product are correct, but this equation is not balanced. Count the atoms on both sides of the equation. Two oxygen atoms are on the reactant (left) side of the equation and only one oxygen atom is on the product (right) side. As written, the equation does not obey the law of conservation of mass, and so it does not describe quantitatively what really happens. What can you do to balance it?

To balance the equation for the reaction of hydrogen and oxygen, count the number of each kind of atom. Hydrogen is balanced, but oxygen is not. If you put the coefficient 2 in front of H$_2$O, the oxygen will be balanced. Now twice as many hydrogen atoms are in the product as are in the reactants. To correct this equation, put the coefficient 2 in front of H$_2$. Four hydrogen atoms and two oxygen atoms are on each side of the chemical equation. The equation is now balanced.

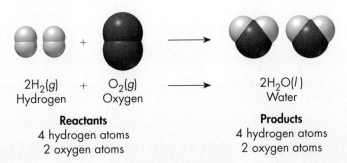

2H$_2$(g)   +   O$_2$(g)   →   2H$_2$O(l)
Hydrogen   Oxygen   Water

Reactants   **Products**
4 hydrogen atoms   4 hydrogen atoms
2 oxygen atoms   2 oxygen atoms

A few guidelines for writing and balancing equations are in the table on the next page.

See balancing equations *animated* online.

1. Determine the correct formulas for all the reactants and products.

2. Write the skeleton equation by placing the formulas for the reactants on the left and the formulas for the products on the right with a yields sign (⟶) in between. If two or more reactants or products are involved, separate their formulas with plus signs.

3. Determine the number of atoms of each element in the reactants and products. Count a polyatomic ion as a single unit if it appears unchanged on both sides of the equation.

4. Balance the elements one at a time by using coefficients. When no coefficient is written, it is assumed to be 1. Begin by balancing elements that appear only once on each side of the equation. Never balance an equation by changing the subscripts in a chemical formula. Each substance has only one correct formula.

5. Check each atom or polyatomic ion to be sure that the number is equal on both sides of the equation.

6. Make sure all the coefficients are in the lowest possible ratio.

SampleProblem 11.2

Balancing a Chemical Equation

Students suspended copper wire in an aqueous solution of silver nitrate. They noticed a deposit of silver crystals on the copper wire when the copper reacted with the silver nitrate. They recorded the equation for this reaction but didn't balance it. Balance their equation.

$$AgNO_3(aq) + Cu(s) \longrightarrow Cu(NO_3)_2(aq) + Ag(s)$$

❶ Analyze Identify the relevant concepts.

Apply the rules for balancing equations. Because the nitrate polyatomic ion appears as a reactant and a product, this ion can be balanced as a unit.

> Remember that a coefficient must always go in front of a compound's formula, not in the middle of it.

❷ Solve Apply concepts to this problem.

| Balance the nitrate ion. Put a coefficient 2 in front of $AgNO_3(aq)$. | ⟶ | $2AgNO_3(aq) + Cu(s) \longrightarrow Cu(NO_3)_2(aq) + Ag(s)$ |

| Balance the silver. Put a coefficient 2 in front of $Ag(s)$. | ⟶ | $2AgNO_3(aq) + Cu(s) \longrightarrow Cu(NO_3)_2(aq) + 2Ag(s)$ |

3. Balance the equation:
$$CO + Fe_2O_3 \longrightarrow Fe + CO_2$$

4. Write the balanced chemical equation for the reaction of carbon with oxygen to form carbon monoxide.

Balancing a Chemical Equation

Aluminum is a good choice for outdoor furniture because it reacts with oxygen in the air to form a thin protective coat of aluminum oxide. Balance the equation for this reaction.

$$Al(s) + O_2(g) \longrightarrow Al_2O_3(s)$$

❶ Analyze Identify the relevant concepts.

Apply the rules for balancing equations. Notice the odd number of oxygen atoms in the product.

❷ Solve Apply concepts to this problem.

First balance the aluminum by placing the coefficient 2 in front of Al(s).	$2Al(s) + O_2(g) \longrightarrow Al_2O_3(s)$
Multiply the formula with the odd number of oxygen atoms (on the right) by 2 to get an even number of oxygen atoms on the right.	$2Al(s) + O_2(g) \longrightarrow 2Al_2O_3(s)$
Balance the oxygens on the left by placing a 3 in front of O_2.	$2Al(s) + 3O_2(g) \longrightarrow 2Al_2O_3(s)$
Then rebalance the aluminum by changing the coefficient of Al(s) from 2 to 4.	$4Al(s) + 3O_2(g) \longrightarrow 2Al_2O_3(s)$

Any whole number coefficient placed in front of O_2 will always give an even number of oxygen atoms on the left.

5. Balance each equation.

a. $FeCl_3 + NaOH \longrightarrow Fe(OH)_3 + NaCl$

b. $CS_2 + Cl_2 \longrightarrow CCl_4 + S_2Cl_2$

c. $KI + Pb(NO_3)_2 \longrightarrow PbI_2 + KNO_3$

d. $C_2H_2 + O_2 \longrightarrow CO_2 + H_2O$

6. Write and balance these equations.

a. calcium hydroxide + sulfuric acid $\longrightarrow$ calcium sulfate + water

b. sodium + water $\longrightarrow$ sodium hydroxide + hydrogen

Suppose the equation for the formation of aluminum oxide was written this way:

$$8Al(s) + 6O_2(g) \longrightarrow 4Al_2O_3(s)$$

Each of the coefficients should be divided by 2 to get an equation with the lowest whole number ratio of coefficients.

Quick Lab

Materials

- aluminum foil, 20 cm × 20 cm
- large beaker or glass pan
- tarnished silver fork or spoon
- sodium hydrogen carbonate
- plastic tablespoon
- hot water

Removing Silver Tarnish

Procedure

1. Fill the beaker about three-quarters full of hot water and add 2 tablespoons of sodium hydrogen carbonate ($NaHCO_3$).

2. Crush the aluminum foil into a loose ball and place it in the beaker.

3. Write a brief description of the tarnished silver fork; then place it in the beaker so that it is touching the aluminum ball.

4. Allow the beaker to stand undisturbed for 30 minutes.

5. Remove the fork and aluminum ball and rinse them with water.

Analyze and Conclude

1. Observe Compare the silver fork with your observations before placing the fork in the water. What changes do you observe?

2. Explain Did a chemical reaction occur? How do you know?

3. Explain The tarnish on the silver fork is silver sulfide (Ag_2S). Silver becomes tarnished when it is exposed to air, egg yolk, or rubber bands. Each of these substances contains sulfur. Look carefully for a pale yellow precipitate of aluminum sulfide on the bottom of the beaker. Write the formula for aluminum sulfide.

4. Apply Concepts The unbalanced equation for the reaction is

$$Ag_2S(s) + Al(s) \longrightarrow Al_2S_3(s) + Ag(s)$$

Balance the equation.

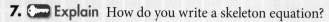

11.1 LessonCheck

7. 🔑 **Explain** How do you write a skeleton equation?

8. 🔑 **Summarize** Describe the steps in writing a balanced chemical equation.

9. Describe Write skeleton equations for these reactions.
   a. Heating copper(II) sulfide in the presence of diatomic oxygen produces pure copper and sulfur dioxide gas.
   b. When heated, baking soda (sodium hydrogen carbonate) decomposes to form the products sodium carbonate, carbon dioxide, and water.

10. Apply Concepts Balance the following equations:
   a. $SO_2(g) + O_2(g) \longrightarrow SO_3(g)$
   b. $Fe_2O_3(s) + H_2(g) \longrightarrow Fe(s) + H_2O(l)$
   c. $P(s) + O_2(g) \longrightarrow P_4O_{10}(s)$
   d. $Al(s) + N_2(g) \longrightarrow AlN(s)$

11. Apply Concepts Write and balance equations for the following reactions:
   a. Iron metal and chlorine gas react to form solid iron(III) chloride.
   b. Solid aluminum carbonate decomposes to form solid aluminum oxide and carbon dioxide gas.
   c. Solid magnesium reacts with aqueous silver nitrate to form solid silver and aqueous magnesium nitrate.

Kitchen Chemistry

Did you know that your kitchen is a good place to study chemistry? Food preparation generally involves a large number of chemical reactions. Compounds in raw food may combine, decompose, or oxidize to give the finished product. The acids in vinegars, lemon juice, or anything acidic used to marinate meat helps break down the connective tissue of the meat through chemical reactions. If raw food is heated, as in frying and baking, chemical reactions produce many complex compounds. When you eat the cooked food, your body performs another series of chemical reactions that allow the nutrients in the food to nourish your body.

In this lesson, you learned how to describe chemical reactions and write balanced chemical equations. Now you can use ordinary kitchen materials to create your own chemical reactions.

On Your Own

1. For this activity, you'll need a few **paper cups, baking soda, water, vinegar,** and **lemon juice.** You'll also need a **spoon** and an **eyedropper.**

2. Spoon a little bit of baking soda into four cups.

3. Using the eyedropper, add a few drops of water to the first cup. Watch what happens. Then record your observations in a chart similar to the one below.

4. Repeat the process for each substance in the chart.

What Did You See?

Substance	What's the Reaction?
Water	
Vinegar	
Lemon juice	
Your own choice	

Think About It

1. Draw Conclusions What clues tell you that a chemical reaction occurred?

2. Apply Concepts The skeleton equation for the reaction between baking soda and vinegar is:

$$NaHCO_3 + HC_2H_3O_2 \longrightarrow NaC_2H_3O_2 + H_2O + CO_2$$

Is this equation balanced? Explain.

3. Connect to the BIG IDEA How does the law of conservation of mass apply to this experiment?

Key Questions

🔑 **What are the five general types of reactions?**

Vocabulary

- combination reaction
- decomposition reaction
- single-replacement reaction
- activity series
- double-replacement reaction
- combustion reaction

Q: *What happens to the wax when you burn a candle?* You probably have noticed that you have less candle after burning than before, but you may not know that a candle will not burn unless oxygen is present. When you burn a candle, a chemical reaction called combustion takes place. In this lesson, you will learn that if you can recognize the type of reaction, you may be able to predict the products of the reaction.

Classifying Reactions

🔑 **What are the five general types of reactions?**

By classifying chemical reactions, you can more easily predict what products are likely to form. One classification system identifies five general types. 🔑 **The five general types of reactions include combination, decomposition, single-replacement, double-replacement, and combustion.** Not all chemical reactions fit uniquely into only one category. Occasionally, a reaction may fit equally well into two categories. Nevertheless, recognizing a reaction as a particular type is useful. Patterns of chemical behavior will become apparent and allow you to predict the products of reactions.

Combination Reactions The first type of reaction is the combination, or synthesis, reaction. A **combination reaction** is a chemical change in which two or more substances react to form a single new substance. As shown in Figure 11.4, magnesium metal and oxygen gas combine to form the compound magnesium oxide.

$$2Mg(s) + O_2(g) \longrightarrow 2MgO(s)$$

Notice that in this reaction, as in all combination reactions, the product is a single substance (MgO), which is a compound. The reactants in this combination reaction (Mg and O_2) are two elements, which is often the case. But two compounds may also combine to form a single substance.

When a Group A metal and a nonmetal react, the product is a binary ionic compound.

$$2K(s) + Cl_2(g) \longrightarrow 2KCl(s)$$

When two nonmetals react in a combination reaction, more than one product is often possible.

$$S(s) + O_2(g) \longrightarrow SO_2(g) \text{ sulfur dioxide}$$

$$2S(s) + 3O_2(g) \longrightarrow 2SO_3(g) \text{ sulfur trioxide}$$

More than one product may also result from the combination reaction of a transition metal and a nonmetal.

$$Fe(s) + S(s) \longrightarrow FeS(s) \text{ iron(II) sulfide}$$

$$2Fe(s) + 3S(s) \longrightarrow Fe_2S_3(s) \text{ iron(III) sulfide}$$

Some nonmetal oxides react with water to produce an acid, a compound that produces hydrogen ions in aqueous solution. You will learn about acids in Chapter 19.

$$SO_2(g) + H_2O(l) \longrightarrow H_2SO_3(aq) \text{ sulfurous acid}$$

Some metallic oxides react with water to give a base, or a compound containing hydroxide ions. Again in this case, you can use the ionic charges to derive the formula for the product.

$$CaO(s) + H_2O(l) \longrightarrow Ca(OH)_2(aq) \text{ calcium hydroxide}$$

Figure 11.4 Combination Reaction
When ignited, magnesium ribbon reacts with oxygen in the surrounding air to form magnesium oxide, a white solid. This reaction is a combination reaction.

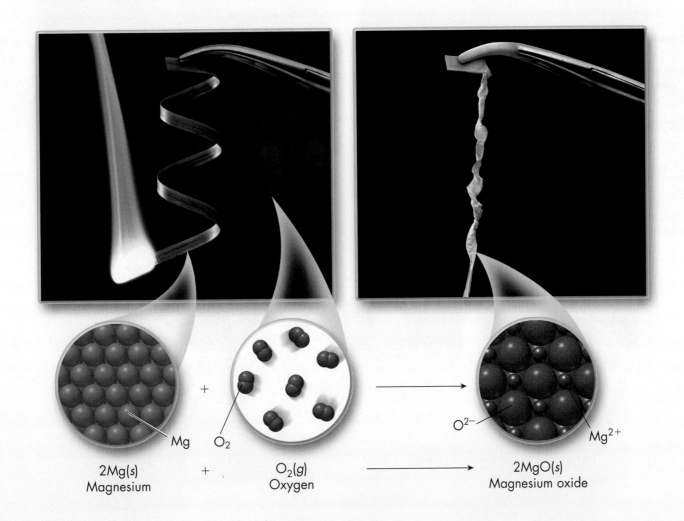

Mg $\quad$ O$_2$

O^{2-} $\quad$ Mg^{2+}

2Mg(s) $\quad + \quad$ O$_2$(g) $\quad \longrightarrow \quad$ 2MgO(s)
Magnesium $\qquad$ Oxygen $\qquad\qquad$ Magnesium oxide

Decomposition Reactions Some chemical reactions are the opposite of combination reactions. These kinds of reactions are classified as decomposition reactions. When mercury(II) oxide is heated, it decomposes or breaks down into two simpler substances, as shown in Figure 11.5.

$$2HgO(s) \longrightarrow 2Hg(l) + O_2(g)$$

A **decomposition reaction** is a chemical change in which a single compound breaks down into two or more simpler products. Decomposition reactions involve only one reactant and two or more products. The products can be any combination of elements and compounds. It is usually difficult to predict the products of decomposition reactions. However, when a simple binary compound such as HgO breaks down, you know that the products must be the constituent elements Hg and O_2. Most decomposition reactions require energy in the form of heat, light, or electricity.

Did you know that a decomposition reaction happens when an automobile air bag inflates? A device that can trigger the reaction is placed into the air bag along with sodium azide (NaN_3) pellets. When the device is triggered, the sodium azide pellets decompose and release nitrogen gas, which inflates the air bag quickly.

$$2NaN_3(s) \longrightarrow 2Na(s) + 3N_2(g)$$

Figure 11.5 Decomposition Reaction
When orange-colored mercury(II) oxide is heated, it decomposes into its constituent elements: liquid mercury and gaseous oxygen.
Compare and Contrast *How are the reactions pictured in Figures 11.4 and 11.5 similar? How are they different?*

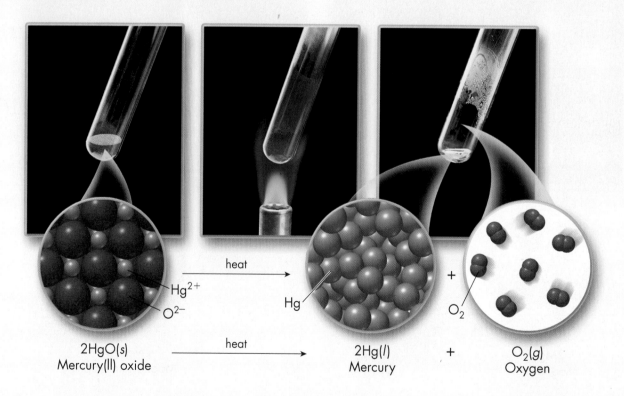

Hg^{2+}
O^{2-}
Hg
O_2

2HgO(s)   heat   2Hg(l)   + O_2(g)
Mercury(II) oxide   Mercury   Oxygen

Writing Equations for Combination and Decomposition Reactions

Write a balanced equation for each of the following reactions.

a. Combination of copper and sulfur:

$Cu(s) + S(s) \longrightarrow$ (two reactions possible)

b. Decomposition of water:

$H_2O(l) \xrightarrow{\text{electricity}}$

❶ Analyze **Identify the relevant concepts.** Two combination reactions are possible because copper is a transition metal and has more than one common ionic charge (Cu^+ and Cu^{2+}).

❷ Solve **Apply the concepts to this problem.**

Write the formula for the product(s) in each reaction.	**a.** Copper(I) sulfide $Cu_2S(s)$ Copper(II) sulfide $CuS(s)$ *Note that Cu_2S and CuS represent different products from different reactions.*	**b.** $H_2(g)$ $O_2(g)$
Write a skeleton equation for each reaction.	For Copper(I): $Cu(s) + S(s) \longrightarrow Cu_2S(s)$ For Copper(II): $Cu(s) + S(s) \longrightarrow CuS(s)$	$H_2O(l) \xrightarrow{\text{electricity}} H_2(g) + O_2(g)$ *The hydrogen is balanced but the oxygen is not. After balancing the oxygen, you must rebalance the hydrogen atoms.*
Apply the rules for balancing equations.	For Copper(I): $2Cu(s) + S(s) \longrightarrow Cu_2S(s)$ (balanced) For Copper(II): the skeleton equation is already balanced. $\boxed{Cu(s) + S(s) \longrightarrow CuS(s)}$ (balanced)	$2H_2O(l) \xrightarrow{\text{electricity}} H_2(g) + O_2(g)$ $\boxed{2H_2O(l) \xrightarrow{\text{electricity}} 2H_2(g) + O_2(g)}$

12. Write the formula for the binary compound that decomposes to the products H_2 and Br_2.

13. Complete and balance this decomposition reaction.

$HI \longrightarrow$

14. Write and balance the equation for the formation of magnesium nitride (Mg_3N_2) from its elements.

Single-Replacement Reactions Dropping a small piece of potassium into a beaker of water creates the vigorous reaction shown in Figure 11.6 The reaction produces hydrogen gas and a large quantity of heat. The released hydrogen gas can ignite explosively.

$$2K(s) + 2H_2O(l) \longrightarrow 2KOH(aq) + H_2(g)$$

Similar but less spectacular reactions can occur. For example, if you drop a piece of zinc into a solution of copper nitrate, this reaction occurs:

$$Zn(s) + Cu(NO_3)_2(aq) \longrightarrow Cu(s) + Zn(NO_3)_2(aq)$$

These equations describe two examples of single-replacement reactions. A **single-replacement reaction** is a chemical change in which one element replaces a second element in a compound. You can identify a single-replacement reaction by noting that both the reactants and the products consist of an element and a compound. In the equation above, zinc and copper change places. The reacting element Zn replaces copper in the reactant compound $Cu(NO_3)_2$. The products are the element Cu and the compound $Zn(NO_3)_2$.

Figure 11.6 Single-Replacement Reaction
The alkali metal potassium displaces hydrogen from water and forms a solution of potassium hydroxide in a single-replacement reaction. The heat of the reaction is often sufficient to ignite the hydrogen.
Inferring *Why are alkali metals stored under mineral oil or kerosene?*

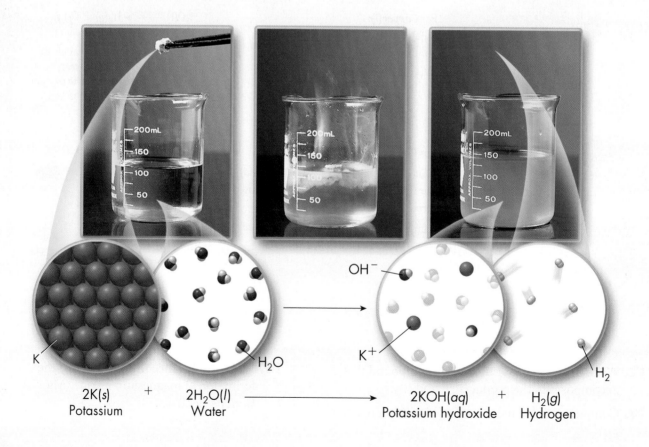

| 2K(s) | + | 2H₂O(l) | ⟶ | 2KOH(aq) | + | H₂(g) |
| Potassium | | Water | | Potassium hydroxide | | Hydrogen |

Sample Problem 11.5

Writing Equations for Single-Replacement Reactions

Write a balanced equation for the single-replacement reaction.

$$Cl_2(aq) + NaBr(aq) \longrightarrow$$

❶ Analyze Identify the relevant concepts. Chlorine is more reactive than bromine and displaces bromine from its compounds.

❷ Solve Apply concepts to this problem.

Write the skeleton equation.	$Cl_2(aq) + NaBr(aq) \longrightarrow NaCl(aq) + Br_2(aq)$
Apply the rules for balancing equations.	$Cl_2(aq) + 2NaBr(aq) \longrightarrow 2NaCl(aq) + Br_2(aq)$ (balanced)

Hint: You're starting with an unequal number of atoms:
- reactants
- 2 chlorine atoms
- 1 sodium atom
- 1 bromine atom
- products
- 1 chlorine atom
- 1 sodium atom
- 2 bromine atoms

15. Complete the equations for these single-replacement reactions in aqueous solution. Balance each equation. Write "no reaction" if a reaction does not occur.

a. $Fe(s) + Pb(NO_3)_2(aq) \longrightarrow$

b. $Cl_2(aq) + NaI(aq) \longrightarrow$

c. $Ca(s) + H_2O(l) \longrightarrow$

d. $Zn(s) + H_2SO_4(aq) \longrightarrow$

Hint: Look at Table 11.2. Zinc displaces hydrogen from an acid and takes its place.

Whether one metal will displace another metal from a compound depends upon the relative reactivities of the two metals. The **activity series** of metals, given in Table 11.2, lists metals in order of decreasing reactivity. A reactive metal will replace any metal listed below it in the activity series. Thus, iron will displace copper from a copper compound in solution, but iron does not similarly displace zinc or calcium.

A halogen can also replace another halogen from a compound. The activity of the halogens decreases as you go down Group 7A of the periodic table—fluorine, chlorine, bromine, and iodine. Bromine is more active than iodine, so this reaction occurs:

$$Br_2(aq) + 2NaI(aq) \longrightarrow 2NaBr(aq) + I_2(aq)$$

But bromine is less active than chlorine, so this reaction does not occur:

$$Br_2(aq) + NaCl(aq) \longrightarrow \text{No reaction}$$

Table 11.2

Activity Series of Metals

Name	Symbol
Lithium	Li
Potassium	K
Calcium	Ca
Sodium	Na
Magnesium	Mg
Aluminum	Al
Zinc	Zn
Iron	Fe
Lead	Pb
(Hydrogen)	(H)*
Copper	Cu
Mercury	Hg
Silver	Ag

Decreasing reactivity ↓

*Metals from Li to Na will replace H from acids and water; from Mg to Pb they will replace H from acids only.

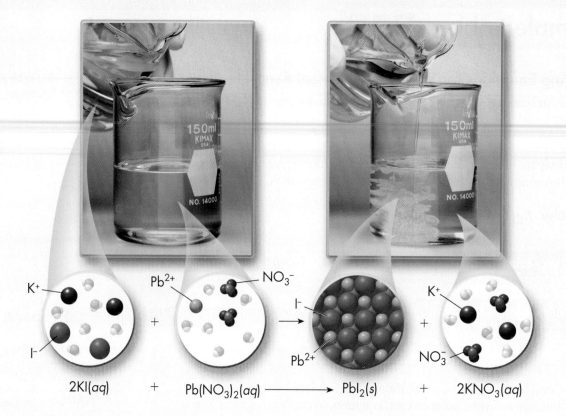

$$2KI(aq) \quad + \quad Pb(NO_3)_2(aq) \longrightarrow PbI_2(s) \quad + \quad 2KNO_3(aq)$$

Figure 11.7
Double-Replacement Reaction
Aqueous solutions of potassium iodide and lead(II) nitrate react in a double-replacement reaction to form the yellow precipitate lead(II) iodide.

Double-Replacement Reactions Sometimes, when two solutions of ionic compounds are mixed, nothing happens. At other times, the ions in the two solutions react. Figure 11.7 shows that mixing aqueous solutions of potassium iodide and lead(II) nitrate results in a chemical reaction in which a yellow precipitate of solid lead(II) iodide is formed. Potassium nitrate, the other product of the reaction, remains in solution. This reaction is an example of a **double-replacement reaction,** which is a chemical change involving an exchange of positive ions between two compounds. Double-replacement reactions are also referred to as double-displacement reactions. They generally take place in aqueous solution and often produce a precipitate, a gas, or a molecular compound such as water. For a double-replacement reaction to occur, one of the following is usually true:

1. One of the products is only slightly soluble and precipitates from solution. For example, the reaction of aqueous solutions of sodium sulfide and cadmium nitrate produces a yellow precipitate of cadmium sulfide.

$$Na_2S(aq) + Cd(NO_3)_2(aq) \longrightarrow CdS(s) + 2NaNO_3(aq)$$

2. One of the products is a gas. Poisonous hydrogen cyanide gas is produced when aqueous sodium cyanide, also a poison, is mixed with sulfuric acid.

$$2NaCN(aq) + H_2SO_4(aq) \longrightarrow 2HCN(g) + Na_2SO_4(aq)$$

3. One product is a molecular compound such as water. Combining solutions of calcium hydroxide and hydrochloric acid produces water.

$$Ca(OH)_2(aq) + 2HCl(aq) \longrightarrow CaCl_2(aq) + 2H_2O(l)$$

Writing Equations for Double-Replacement Reactions

A precipitate of barium carbonate is formed when an aqueous solution of barium chloride reacts with aqueous potassium carbonate. Write a balanced chemical equation for the double-replacement reaction.

$$K_2CO_3(aq) + BaCl_2(aq) \longrightarrow$$

❶ Analyze **Identify the relevant concepts.**
The driving force behind the reaction is the formation of a precipitate. Write correct formulas of the products using ionic charges. Then balance the equation.

❷ Solve **Apply concepts to this problem.**

| Write the skeleton equation. | $K_2CO_3(aq) + BaCl_2(aq) \longrightarrow KCl(aq) + BaCO_3(s)$ |

| Apply the rules for balancing equations. | $K_2CO_3(aq) + BaCl_2(aq) \longrightarrow 2KCl(aq) + BaCO_3(s)$ (balanced) |

16. Write the products of these double-replacement reactions. Then balance each equation.
  a. $NaOH(aq) + Fe(NO_3)_3(aq) \longrightarrow$ (Iron(III) hydroxide is a precipitate.)
  b. $Ba(NO_3)_2(aq) + H_3PO_4(aq) \longrightarrow$ (Barium phosphate is a precipitate.)
  c. $FeS(s) + HCl(aq) \longrightarrow$ (Hydrogen sulfide gas (H_2S) is formed.)

17. Write a balanced equation for each reaction.
  a. $KOH(aq) + H_3PO_4(aq) \longrightarrow$ (Water is formed.)
  b. $AgNO_3(aq) + NaCl(s) \longrightarrow$ (Silver chloride is a precipitate.)
  c. $Ca(OH)_2(aq) + H_3PO_4(aq) \longrightarrow$ (Water is formed.)
  d. $KI(aq) + Pb(NO_3)_2(aq) \longrightarrow$ (Lead(II) iodide is a precipitate.)
  e. $H_2SO_4(aq) + Al(OH)_3(aq) \longrightarrow$ (Water is formed.)

Hint: Use ionic charges to write the correct formula of the other product.

Combustion Reactions The flames of a campfire, candle, or a gas grill are evidence that a combustion reaction is taking place. A **combustion reaction** is a chemical change in which an element or a compound reacts with oxygen, often producing energy in the form of heat and light. A combustion reaction always involves oxygen as a reactant. Often the other reactant is a hydrocarbon, which is a compound composed of hydrogen and carbon. The complete combustion of a hydrocarbon produces carbon dioxide and water. But if the supply of oxygen is limited during a reaction, the combustion will not be complete. Elemental carbon (soot) and toxic carbon monoxide gas may be additional products.

Q: *Materials such as candle wax contain hydrogen and carbon. One type of wax has a formula of $C_{25}H_{52}$. The wax reacts with oxygen in the air. So, what happens to the wax as it burns?*

The complete combustion of a hydrocarbon releases a large amount of energy as heat. That's why hydrocarbons such as methane (CH_4), propane (C_3H_8), and butane (C_4H_{10}) are important fuels. The combustion reaction for methane is shown in Figure 11.8. Gasoline is a mixture of hydrocarbons that can be approximately represented by the formula C_8H_{18}. The complete combustion of gasoline in a car engine is shown by this equation.

$$2C_8H_{18}(l) + 25O_2(g) \longrightarrow 16CO_2(g) + 18H_2O(g)$$

The reactions between oxygen and some elements other than carbon are also examples of combustion reactions. For example, both magnesium and sulfur will burn in the presence of oxygen. As you look at these combustion equations, notice that the reactions could also be classified as combination reactions.

$$2Mg(s) + O_2(g) \longrightarrow 2MgO(s)$$

$$S(s) + O_2(g) \longrightarrow SO_2(g)$$

Figure 11.8 Combustion Reaction
Methane gas reacts with oxygen from the surrounding air in a combustion reaction to produce carbon dioxide and water.
Infer *What else is produced in this reaction?*

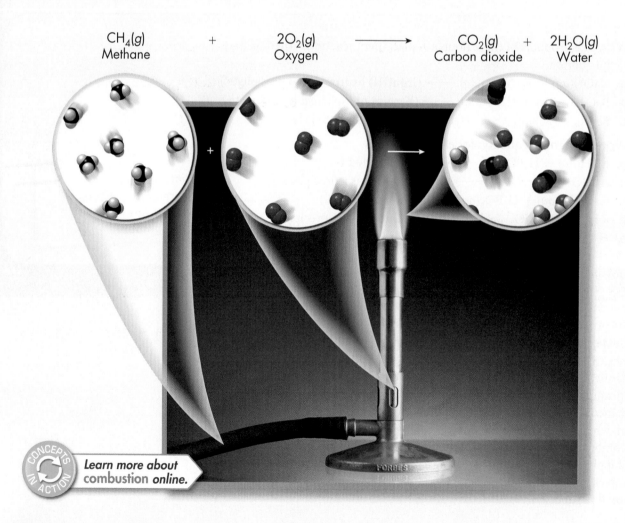

$CH_4(g)$
Methane
$+$
$2O_2(g)$
Oxygen
$CO_2(g)$
Carbon dioxide
$+$
$2H_2O(g)$
Water

CONCEPTS IN ACTION
Learn more about combustion *online.*

Writing Equations for Combustion Reactions

An alcohol lamp often uses ethanol as its fuel. Write a balanced equation for the complete combustion of ethanol.

$$C_2H_6O(l)$$

❶ Analyze Identify the relevant concepts.
Oxygen is the other reactant in a combustion reaction. The products are CO_2 and H_2O.

❷ Solve Apply concepts to this problem.

Write the skeleton equation. ➤ $C_2H_6O(l) + O_2(g) \longrightarrow CO_2(g) + H_2O(g)$

Apply the rules for balancing equations. ➤ $C_2H_6O(l) + 3O_2(g) \longrightarrow 2CO_2(g) + 3H_2O(g)$
(balanced)

18. Write a balanced equation for the complete combustion of each compound.
   a. formaldehyde ($CH_2O(g)$)
   b. heptane ($C_7H_{16}(l)$)
   c. benzene ($C_6H_6(l)$)

19. Write a balanced equation for the complete combustion of
   a. glucose ($C_6H_{12}O_6(s)$)
   b. acetone ($C_3H_6O(l)$)
   c. pentanol ($C_5H_{12}O(l)$)

Now that you have learned about some of the basic reaction types, you can predict the products of many reactions. The number of elements and/or compounds reacting is a good indicator of possible reaction type and, thus, possible products.

For example, in a combination reaction, two or more reactants (elements or compounds) combine to form a single product. In a decomposition reaction, a single compound is the reactant; two or more substances are the products. An element and a compound are the reactants in a single-replacement reaction. A different element and a new compound are the products. In a double-replacement reaction, two ionic compounds are the reactants; two new compounds are the products. The reactants in a combustion reaction are oxygen and usually a hydrocarbon. The products of most combustion reactions are carbon dioxide and water.

❶ Combination Reaction

General Equation: R + S ⟶ RS

Reactants: Generally two elements, or two compounds (where at least one compound is a molecular compound)

Probable Products: A single compound

Example: Burning magnesium in air

 See reactions *animated online.*

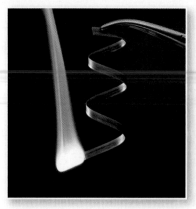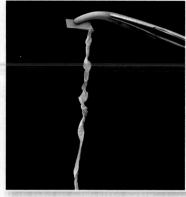

$$2Mg(s) + O_2(g) \longrightarrow 2MgO(s)$$

❷ Decomposition Reaction

General Equation: RS ⟶ R + S

Reactants: Generally a single binary compound or a compound with a polyatomic ion

Probable Products: Two elements (for a binary compound), or two or more elements and/or compounds (for a compound with a polyatomic ion)

Example: Heating mercury(II) oxide

$$2HgO(s) \longrightarrow 2Hg(l) + O_2(g)$$

❸ Single-Replacement Reaction

General Equation: T + RS ⟶ TS + R

Reactants: An element and a compound

In a single-replacement reaction, an element replaces another element from a compound in aqueous solution. For a single-replacement reaction to occur, the element that is replaced must be less active than the element that is doing the replacing.

Probable Products: A different element and a new compound

Example: Potassium in water

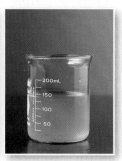

$$2K(s) + 2H_2O(l) \longrightarrow 2KOH(aq) + H_2(g)$$

④ Double-Replacement Reaction

General Equation: $R^+ S^- + T^+ U^- \longrightarrow R^+ U^- + T^+ S^-$

Reactants: Two ionic compounds

In a double-replacement reaction, two ionic compounds react by exchanging cations to form two different compounds.

Probable Products: Two new compounds Double-replacement reactions are driven by the formation of a precipitate, a gaseous product, or water.

Example: Reaction of aqueous solutions of potassium iodide and lead(II) nitrate.

$2KI(aq) + Pb(NO_3)_2(aq) \longrightarrow PbI_2(s) + 2KNO_3(aq)$

⑤ Combustion Reaction

General Equation: $C_x H_y + (x + y/4) O_2 \longrightarrow xCO_2 + (y/2)H_2O$

Reactants: Oxygen and a compound of C, H, (O) When oxygen reacts with an element or compound, combustion may occur.

Probable Products: CO_2 and H_2O With incomplete combustion, C and CO may also be products.

Example: The combustion of methane gas in air

$CH_4(g) + 2O_2(g) \longrightarrow CO_2(g) + 2H_2O(g)$

11.2 LessonCheck

20. ⊙ **Review** What are the five types of chemical reactions?

21. Apply Concepts Classify each reaction and balance the equations.
   a. $C_3H_6(g) + O_2(g) \longrightarrow CO_2(g) + H_2O(g)$
   b. $Al(OH)_3(s) \longrightarrow Al_2O_3(s) + H_2O(l)$
   c. $Li(s) + O_2(g) \longrightarrow Li_2O(s)$
   d. $Zn(s) + AgNO_3(aq) \longrightarrow Ag(s) + Zn(NO_3)_2(aq)$

22. Identify Which of the five general types of reaction would most likely occur, given each set of reactants? What are the probable products?
   a. an aqueous solution of two ionic compounds
   b. a single compound
   c. two elements
   d. oxygen and a compound of carbon and hydrogen

23. Apply Concepts Complete and balance an equation for each reaction.
   a. $CaI_2(aq) + Hg(NO_3)_2(aq) \longrightarrow$ (HgI_2 precipitates.)
   b. $Al(s) + Cl_2(g) \longrightarrow$
   c. $Ag(s) + HCl(aq) \longrightarrow$
   d. $C_2H_2(g) + O_2(g) \longrightarrow$

BIGIDEA REACTIONS

24. After wood burns, the ash weighs much less than the original wood. Explain why the law of conservation of mass is not violated in this situation.

The History of Dynamite

In 1846, Ascanio Sobrero added glycerol to a mixture of concentrated nitric and sulfuric acids. The resulting oily liquid, known as nitroglycerin, turned out to be such a powerful explosive that a small bottle could blow up a building. Unfortunately, it was also extremely unstable, and tended to explode after being handled roughly, or a temperature change.

Alfred Nobel (1833–1896), a Swedish chemist and industrialist, began experimenting with nitroglycerin, looking for a way to make it safe to use. In 1866, Nobel discovered that he could mix nitroglycerine with a fine sand called *kieselguhr* to turn the liquid into paste that could be shaped into rods. The rods were then packed into cylinders made of paper. He named these rods "dynamite."

BIG BLASTS Nobel began manufacturing the explosive, which was used to blast out dam sites, canal beds, mines, and the foundations for large buildings.

Originally, Nobel marketed dynamite as Nobel's Blasting Powder.

To safely ignite dynamite and control the timing of a detonation, Nobel also invented blasting caps, which create a small explosion that triggers the larger explosion in the dynamite itself.

Today, ammonium nitrate is used in place of nitroglycerin. This dynamite is stronger, safer, and cheaper than Nobel's original invention.

When he died in 1896, Alfred Nobel left a nine million dollar fortune to be used to fund different fields of study. The Nobel Prize is still awarded to people whose work helps humanity.

Take It Further

1. Classify The equation for the detonation of nitroglycerin is shown below. What kind of reaction is it?

$$4C_3H_5N_3O_9 \longrightarrow 12CO_2 + 10H_2O + 6N_2 + O_2$$

2. Research Fireworks are another kind of explosive. How are dynamite explosions different from fireworks explosions?

11.3 Reactions in Aqueous Solution

Key Questions

🔑 What does a net ionic equation show?

🔑 How can you predict the formation of a precipitate in a double-replacement reaction?

Vocabulary

• complete ionic equation
• spectator ion
• net ionic equation

CHEMISTRY & YOU

Q: *How did soda straws get into limestone caves?* These "soda straws" are really stalactites in a limestone cave. Soda straws grow on cave ceilings as thin-walled hollow tubes that result from chemical reactions involving water. In this lesson, you will learn to predict the formation of precipitates and write equations to describe the reactions that produce them.

Net Ionic Equations

🔑 **What does a net ionic equation show?**

Your world is water based. More than 70 percent of Earth's surface is covered by water, and about 66 percent of the adult human body is water. It is not surprising, then, that many important chemical reactions take place in water—that is, in aqueous solution. The reaction of aqueous solutions of silver nitrate with sodium chloride to form solid silver chloride and aqueous sodium nitrate is a double-replacement reaction. The reaction is shown in Figure 11.9.

$$AgNO_3(aq) + NaCl(aq) \longrightarrow AgCl(s) + NaNO_3(aq)$$

The equation above reflects the way you have been writing equations involving aqueous solutions of ionic compounds. However, the equation does not show that, like most ionic compounds, the reactants and one of the products dissociate, or separate, into cations and anions when they dissolve in water.

Figure 11.9 Precipitate in a Double Replacement Reaction
A precipitate of silver chloride forms when aqueous solutions of silver nitrate and sodium chloride are mixed.
Inferring *Which ions do not participate in the reaction?*

Figure 11.10 Silver Halide and Medical X-rays Small crystals of a silver halide, usually silver bromide, are embedded in the coating on film used to record medical X-rays. The crystals darken when exposed to X-rays that pass through the human body. Dense parts like bones absorb more X-rays; relatively few rays pass through these parts, which appear as light areas on the developed film. More rays pass through soft tissue, which shows up as darker areas on the developed film. Metals also strongly absorb X-rays.

Identify *How can you determine from this x-ray whether there is any metal in the foot?*

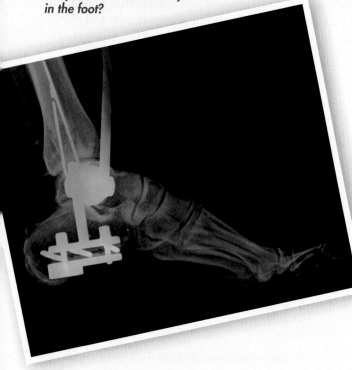

For example, when sodium chloride dissolves in water, it separates into sodium ions ($Na^+(aq)$) and chloride ions ($Cl^-(aq)$). Similarly, when dissolved in water, silver nitrate dissociates into silver ions ($Ag^+(aq)$) and nitrate ions ($NO_3^-(aq)$). You can use these ions to write a **complete ionic equation,** an equation that shows dissolved ionic compounds as dissociated free ions.

$$Ag^+(aq) + NO_3^-(aq) + Na^+(aq) + Cl^-(aq) \longrightarrow$$
$$AgCl(s) + Na^+(aq) + NO_3^-(aq)$$

Notice that the nitrate ion and the sodium ion appear unchanged on both sides of the equation. The equation can be simplified by eliminating these ions because they don't participate in the reaction.

$$Ag^+(aq) + \cancel{NO_3^-(aq)} + \cancel{Na^+(aq)} + Cl^-(aq) \longrightarrow$$
$$AgCl(s) + \cancel{Na^+(aq)} + \cancel{NO_3^-(aq)}$$

An ion that appears on both sides of an equation and is not directly involved in the reaction is called a **spectator ion.** When you rewrite an equation leaving out the spectator ions, you have the net ionic equation. The **net ionic equation** is an equation for a reaction in solution that shows only those particles that are directly involved in the chemical change.

$$Ag^+(aq) + Cl^-(aq) \longrightarrow AgCl(s)$$

In writing balanced net ionic equations, you must make sure that the ionic charge is balanced. For the previous reaction, the net ionic charge on each side of the equation is zero and is therefore balanced. But consider the skeleton equation for the reaction of lead with silver nitrate.

$$Pb(s) + AgNO_3(aq) \longrightarrow Ag(s) + Pb(NO_3)_2(aq)$$

The nitrate ion is the spectator ion in this reaction. The net ionic equation is as follows:

$$Pb(s) + Ag^+(aq) \longrightarrow Ag(s) + Pb^{2+}(aq) \text{ (unbalanced)}$$

Why is this equation unbalanced? Notice that a single unit of positive charge is on the reactant side of the equation. Two units of positive charge are on the product side. Placing the coefficient 2 in front of $Ag^+(aq)$ balances the charge. A coefficient of 2 in front of $Ag(s)$ rebalances the atoms.

$$Pb(s) + 2Ag^+(aq) \longrightarrow 2Ag(s) + Pb^{2+}(aq) \text{ (balanced)}$$

🔑 **A net ionic equation shows only those particles involved in the reaction and is balanced with respect to both mass and charge.** Of the five types of reactions identified in this chapter, both single- and double-replacement reactions can be written as net ionic equations.

Sample Problem 11.8

Writing and Balancing Net Ionic Equations

Aqueous solutions of iron(III) chloride and potassium hydroxide are mixed. A precipitate of iron(III) hydroxide forms. Identify the spectator ions and write a balanced net ionic equation for the reaction.

❶ Analyze Identify the relevant concepts. Write the complete ionic equation. Eliminate aqueous ions that appear in both the reactants and products. Then balance the equation with respect to both mass and charge.

❷ Solve Apply the concepts to this problem.

Write the complete ionic equation for the reaction, showing any soluble ionic compounds as individual ions.	$Fe^{3+}(aq) + 3Cl^-(aq) + 3K^+(aq) + 3OH^-(aq) \longrightarrow$ $Fe(OH)_3(s) + 3K^+(aq) + 3Cl^-(aq)$
Eliminate aqueous ions that appear as both reactants and products. The spectator ions are K^+ and Cl^-.	$Fe^{3+}(aq) + 3Cl^-(aq) + 3K^+(aq) + 3OH^-(aq) \longrightarrow$ $Fe(OH)_3(s) + 3K^+(aq) + 3Cl^-(aq)$
Balance the net ionic equation.	$Fe^{3+}(aq) + 3OH^-(aq) \longrightarrow Fe(OH)_3(s)$

25. Write the balanced net ionic equation for this reaction.

$$Ca^{2+}(aq) + OH^-(aq) + H^+(aq) + PO_4^{3-}(aq) \longrightarrow$$
$$Ca^{2+}(aq) + PO_4^{3-}(aq) + H_2O(l)$$

26. Write the complete ionic equation and net ionic equation for the reaction of aqueous calcium hydroxide with phosphoric acid. The products are calcium phosphate and water.

Predicting the Formation of a Precipitate

🔑 How can you predict the formation of a precipitate in a double-replacement reaction?

You have seen that mixing solutions of two ionic compounds can sometimes result in the formation of an insoluble salt called a precipitate. Some combinations of solutions produce precipitates, while others do not. Whether or not a precipitate forms depends upon the solubility of the new compounds that form. **🔑 By using the general rules for solubility of ionic compounds, you can predict the formation of a precipitate.** These general rules are shown in Table 11.3.

Table 11.3		
Solubility Rules for Ionic Compounds		
Compounds	**Solubility**	**Exceptions**
Salts of alkali metals and ammonia	Soluble	Some lithium compounds
Nitrate salts and chlorate salts	Soluble	Few exceptions
Sulfate salts	Soluble	Compounds of Pb, Ag, Hg, Ba, Sr, and Ca
Chloride salts	Soluble	Compounds of Ag and some compounds of Hg and Pb
Carbonates, phosphates, chromates, sulfides, and hydroxides	Most are insoluble	Compounds of the alkali metals and of ammonia

Learn how to identify ions in solution *online.*

CHEMISTRY & YOU

Q: *How did the soda straws, which are composed of calcium carbonate, get into the cave?*

Will a precipitate form when aqueous solutions of $Na_2CO_3(aq)$ and $Ba(NO_3)_2(aq)$ are mixed?

$$2Na^+(aq) + CO_3^{2-}(aq) + Ba^{2+}(aq) + 2NO_3^-(aq) \longrightarrow \text{?}$$

When these four ions are mixed, the cations could change partners. If they did, the two new compounds that would form are $NaNO_3$ and $BaCO_3$. These are the only new combinations of cation and anion possible. To find out if an exchange will occur, refer to Table 11.3, which gives guidelines for determining whether ion combinations are soluble. Recall that sodium is an alkali metal. Rows 1 and 2 tell you that sodium nitrate will not form a precipitate because alkali metal salts and nitrate salts are soluble. Row 5 indicates that carbonates in general are insoluble. Barium carbonate will precipitate. In this reaction, Na^+ and NO_3^- are spectator ions. The net ionic equation for this reaction is as follows:

$$Ba^{2+}(aq) + CO_3^{2-}(aq) \longrightarrow BaCO_3(s)$$

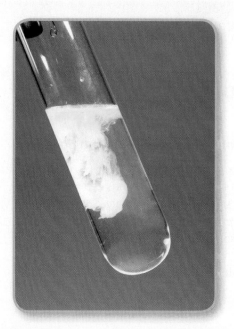

Figure 11.11
Formation of a Precipitate
A precipitate forms when aqueous solutions of sodium sulfate (Na_2SO_4) and barium nitrate ($Ba(NO_3)_2$) are mixed. The net ionic equation for this reaction is as follows:

$Ba^{2+}(aq) + SO_4^{2-}(aq) \longrightarrow BaSO_4(s)$

Apply Concepts *Which ions are present in the final solution but are not part of the net ionic equation?*

Writing and Balancing Net Ionic Equations

Aqueous potassium carbonate reacts with aqueous strontium nitrate. Identify the precipitate formed and write the net ionic equation for the reaction.

❶ **Analyze Identify the relevant concepts.** Write the reactants. Look at possible new pairings of cation and anion that give an insoluble substance. Eliminate the spectator ions.

❷ **Solve Apply the concepts to this problem.**

> Use the solubility rules in Table 11.3 to identify the precipitate formed.

Write the reactants, showing each as dissociated free ions.	$2K^+(aq) + CO_3^{2-}(aq) + Sr^{2+}(aq) + 2NO_3^-(aq) \longrightarrow ?$
Look at possible new pairings of cation and anion that give an insoluble substance.	Of the two possible combinations, KNO_3 is soluble and $SrCO_3$ is insoluble.
Eliminate the spectator ions and write the net ionic equation.	$CO_3^{2-}(aq) + Sr^{2+}(aq) \longrightarrow SrCO_3(s)$

27. Identify the precipitate formed when solutions of these compounds are mixed. Write the net ionic equation.

$$NH_4Cl(aq) + Pb(NO_3)_2(aq) \longrightarrow$$

28. Write a complete ionic equation and a net ionic equation for the reaction of aqueous solutions of iron(III) nitrate and sodium hydroxide.

11.3 LessonCheck

29. 🔑 **Review** What is a net ionic equation?

30. 🔑 **Explain** How can you predict the formation of a precipitate in a double-replacement reaction?

31. Apply Concepts Write a balanced net ionic equation for each reaction.

a. $Pb(NO_3)_2(aq) + H_2SO_4(aq) \longrightarrow$
$$PbSO_4(s) + HNO_3(aq)$$

b. $Pb(C_2H_3O_2)_2(aq) + HCl(aq) \longrightarrow$
$$PbCl_2(s) + HC_2H_3O_2(aq)$$

c. $Na_3PO_4(aq) + FeCl_3(aq) \longrightarrow$
$$NaCl(aq) + FePO_4(s)$$

d. $(NH_4)_2S(aq) + Co(NO_3)_2(aq) \longrightarrow$
$$CoS(s) + NH_4NO_3(aq)$$

32. Identify List the precipitate formed when solutions of these ionic compounds are mixed.

a. $H_2SO_4 + BaCl_2 \longrightarrow$
b. $Al_2(SO_4)_3 + NH_4OH \longrightarrow$
c. $AgNO_3 + H_2S \longrightarrow$
d. $CaCl_2 + Pb(NO_3)_2 \longrightarrow$
e. $Ca(NO_3)_2 + Na_2CO_3 \longrightarrow$

33. Apply Concepts Hard water contains calcium and magnesium ions. One way to soften water is to add sodium phosphate. Write complete and net ionic equations for the reaction of these two alkaline earth ions with aqueous sodium phosphate.

Small-Scale Lab

Precipitation Reactions: Formation of Solids

Purpose
To observe, identify, and write balanced equations for precipitation reactions

Materials
- pencil
- paper
- ruler
- reaction surface
- chemicals shown in the grid to the right

	AgNO$_3$ (Ag$^+$)	Pb(NO$_3$)$_2$ (Pb^{2+})	CaCl$_2$ (Ca^{2+})
Na$_2$CO$_3$ (CO$_3$$^{2-}$)	a	f	k
Na$_3$PO$_4$ (PO$_4$$^{3-}$)	b	g	l
NaOH (OH$^-$)	c	h	m
Na$_2$SO$_4$ (SO$_4$$^{2-}$)	d	i	n
NaCl (Cl$^-$)	e	j	o

Procedure
1. Copy the grid on two sheets of paper.
2. Make each square 2 cm on each side.
3. Draw large black Xs on one of the grids.
4. Place a reaction surface over the grid with black Xs and add the chemicals as shown. Use the other grid as a data table to record your observations for each solution.

Analyze
Using your experimental data, record your answers to the following in the space below your data table.

1. Explain Translate the following word equations into balanced chemical equations and explain how the equations represent what happens in grid spaces *a* and *g*.

   a. In grid space *a*, sodium carbonate reacts with silver nitrate to produce sodium nitrate and solid silver carbonate.

   b. In grid space *g*, sodium phosphate reacts with lead(II) nitrate to produce sodium nitrate and solid lead(II) phosphate.

2. Describe Write a word equation to represent what happens in grid space *m*.

3. Explain What happens in grid space *d*? Which other mixings gave similar results? Is it necessary to write an equation when no reaction occurs?

4. Describe Write balanced equations for the other precipitation reactions you observed.

5. Describe Write balanced net ionic equations for the other precipitation reactions you observed.

You're the Chemist
The following small-scale activities allow you to develop your own procedures and analyze the results.

1. Explain Mix a solution of potassium iodide (KI) with silver nitrate. Then mix potassium iodide solution with lead(II) nitrate. Describe your results. Write balanced equations and net ionic equations for each reaction.

2. Design an Experiment Table salt is mostly sodium chloride. Design and carry out an experiment to find out if table salt will form a precipitate with either lead(II) nitrate or silver nitrate. Interpret your results.

3. Design an Experiment Design and carry out an experiment to show that iodized table salt contains potassium iodide.

11 Study Guide

BIGIDEA REACTIONS

The law of conservation of mass states that mass is neither created nor destroyed. In order to show that mass is conserved during a reaction, a chemical equation must be balanced. You can predict the products of most chemical reactions by identifying the reaction type. To determine the reaction type, consider the number of reacting elements and compounds.

11.1 Describing Chemical Reactions

🔑 To write a skeleton equation, write the formulas for the reactants to the left of the yields sign and the formulas for the products to the right.

🔑 After writing the skeleton equation, use coefficients to balance the equation so that it obeys the law of conservation of mass.

- chemical equation (348)
- skeleton equation (348)
- catalyst (348)
- coefficient (350)
- balanced equation (350)

11.2 Types of Chemical Reactions

🔑 The five general types of reactions are combination, decomposition, single-replacement, double-replacement, and combustion.

🔑 The number of elements and/or compounds reacting is a good indicator of possible reaction type and, thus, possible products.

🔑 In a combination reaction, there is always a single product.

🔑 A decomposition reaction involves the breakdown of a single compound into two or more simpler substances.

🔑 In a single-replacement reaction, both the reactants and the products are an element and a compound.

🔑 A double-replacement reaction generally takes place between two ionic compounds in aqueous solution.

🔑 A combustion reaction always involves oxygen as a reactant.

- combination reaction (356)
- decomposition reaction (358)
- single-replacement reaction (360)
- activity series (361)
- double-replacement reaction (362)
- combustion reaction (363)

11.3 Reactions in Aqueous Solution

🔑 A net ionic equation shows only those particles involved in the reaction and is balanced with respect to mass and charge.

🔑 By using the general rules for solubility of ionic compounds, you can predict the formation of a precipitate.

- complete ionic equation (370)
- spectator ion (370)
- net ionic equation (370)

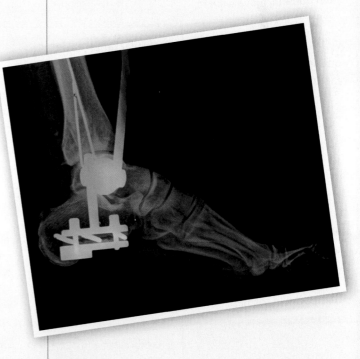

Skills Tune-Up: Balancing Chemical Equations

Problem	❶ Analyze	❷ Solve
Write the balanced equation for the following reaction: $C_2H_4 + O_2 \longrightarrow$	The reactants are a hydrocarbon and oxygen. The hydrocarbon tells you that the products must be CO_2 and H_2O. The oxygen tells you that this is a combustion reaction.	First write a skeleton equation. $C_2H_4 + O_2 \longrightarrow CO_2 + H_2O$ (unbalanced) Balance the C atoms and the H atoms first. $C_2H_4 + O_2 \longrightarrow 2CO_2 + 2H_2O$ (unbalanced) Balance the O atoms next. $C_2H_4 + 3O_2 \longrightarrow 2CO_2 + 2H_2O$ (balanced)
Write the balanced equation for the following reaction: $Al + Cu(NO_3)_2 \longrightarrow$	$Cu(NO_3)_2$ is an ionic compound, and Al is an element. This is a single-replacement reaction. Check Table 11.2 to be sure a reaction will take place.	First write a skeleton equation. $Al + Cu(NO_3)_2 \longrightarrow Al(NO_3)_3 + Cu$ (unbalanced) Balance the equation. $2Al + 3Cu(NO_3)_2 \longrightarrow 2Al(NO_3)_3 + 3Cu$ (balanced)

A subscript in a polyatomic ion moves with the ion. So the 3 in NO_3 stays with the ion. But the subscript 2 is there only to balance the charges. It's not part of the ion and doesn't move with it.

Write the balanced equation for the following reaction: $Na(OH)(aq) +$ $\quad Ba(NO_3)_2(aq) \longrightarrow$	Both reactants are ionic compounds, so this is a double-replacement reaction. In a double-replacement reaction, two compounds exchange positive ions. They often produce a gas, a precipitate, or another molecular compound such as water.	Write the reactants, showing each as dissociated free ions. $Na^+(aq) + OH^-(aq) +$ $Ba^{2+}(aq) + 2NO_3^-(aq) \longrightarrow$ Look at the possible new pairings of cation and anion that give an insoluble substance. Of the two possible combinations, $Na(NO)_3$ is soluble and $Ba(OH)_2$ is insoluble. Balance the equation. $2NaOH(aq) + Ba(NO_3)_2(aq) \longrightarrow$ $\qquad\qquad 2NaNO_3(aq) + Ba(OH)_2(s)$ (balanced)

Use the solubility rules in Table 11.3 to identify the precipitate formed.

Lesson by Lesson

11.1 Describing Chemical Reactions

34. Identify the reactants and products in each chemical reaction.

a. Hydrogen gas and sodium hydroxide are formed when sodium is dropped into water.

b. In photosynthesis, carbon dioxide and water react to form oxygen gas and glucose.

35. Write sentences that completely describe each of the chemical reactions shown in these skeleton equations.

a. $NH_3(g) + O_2(g) \xrightarrow{Pt} NO(g) + H_2O(g)$

b. $H_2SO_4(aq) + BaCl_2(aq) \longrightarrow$
$\qquad BaSO_4(s) + HCl(aq)$

c. $N_2O_3(g) + H_2O(l) \longrightarrow HNO_2(aq)$

36. The equation for the formation of water from its elements, $H_2(g) + O_2(g) \longrightarrow H_2O(l)$, can be "balanced" by changing the formula of the product to H_2O_2. Explain why this is incorrect.

⋆ 37. Balance the following equations:

a. $PbO_2(s) \longrightarrow PbO(s) + O_2(g)$

b. $Fe(OH)_3(s) \longrightarrow Fe_2O_3(s) + H_2O(s)$

c. $(NH_4)_2CO_3(s) \longrightarrow$
$\qquad NH_3(g) + H_2O(g) + CO_2(g)$

d. $CaCl_2(aq) + H_2SO_4(aq) \longrightarrow$
$\qquad CaSO_4(s) + HCl(aq)$

11.2 Types of Chemical Reactions

⋆38. Write balanced chemical equations for the following combination reactions:

a. $Mg(s) + O_2(g) \longrightarrow$

b. $P(s) + O_2(g) \longrightarrow$ diphosphorus pentoxide

c. $Ca(s) + S(s) \longrightarrow$

39. Write a balanced chemical equation for each decomposition reaction.

a. $Ag_2O(s) \xrightarrow{\Delta}$

b. ammonium nitrate $\xrightarrow{\Delta}$
$\qquad$ dinitrogen monoxide + water

40. Use the activity series of metals to write a balanced chemical equation for each single-replacement reaction.

a. $Au(s) + KNO_3(aq) \longrightarrow$

b. $Zn(s) + AgNO_3(aq) \longrightarrow$

c. $Al(s) + H_2SO_4(aq) \longrightarrow$

41. Write a balanced equation for each of the following double-replacement reactions:

a. $H_2C_2O_4(aq) + KOH(aq) \longrightarrow$

b. $CdBr_2(aq) + Na_2S(aq) \longrightarrow$
$\qquad$ (Cadmium sulfide is a precipitate.)

42. Write a balanced equation for the complete combustion of each compound.

a. butene (C_4H_8) **b.** propanal (C_3H_6O)

43. Balance each equation and identify its type.

a. $Hf(s) + N_2(g) \longrightarrow Hf_3N_4(s)$

b. $Mg(s) + H_2SO_4(aq) \longrightarrow MgSO_4(aq) + H_2(g)$

c. $C_2H_6(g) + O_2(g) \longrightarrow CO_2(g) + H_2O(g)$

d. $Pb(NO_3)_2(aq) + NaI(aq) \longrightarrow$
$\qquad PbI_2(s) + NaNO_3(aq)$

44. What is a distinguishing feature of every decomposition reaction?

11.3 Reactions in Aqueous Solution

45. What is a spectator ion?

⋆46. Write a balanced net ionic equation for the following reactions:

a. $HCl(aq) + Ca(OH)_2(aq) \longrightarrow$

b. $AgNO_3(aq) + AlCl_3(aq) \longrightarrow$
$\qquad$ (Silver chloride is a precipitate.)

47. Complete each equation and then write a net ionic equation.

a. $Al(s) + H_2SO_4(aq) \longrightarrow$

b. $HCl(aq) + Ba(OH)_2(aq) \longrightarrow$

c. $Au(s) + HCl(aq) \longrightarrow$

Understand Concepts

48. Write a balanced chemical equation for each reaction. Use the necessary symbols from Table 11.1 to describe the reaction completely.

a. Bubbling chlorine gas through a solution of potassium iodide gives elemental iodine and a solution of potassium chloride.

b. Bubbles of hydrogen gas and aqueous iron(III) chloride are produced when metallic iron is dropped into hydrochloric acid.

c. Solid tetraphosphorus decaoxide reacts with water to produce phosphoric acid.

49. Each equation is incorrect. Find the errors, then rewrite and balance each equation.

a. $Cl_2 + NaI \longrightarrow NaCl_2 + I$

b. $NH_3 \longrightarrow N + H_3$

c. $Na + O_2 \longrightarrow NaO_2$

50. Write balanced chemical equations for these double-replacement reactions that occur in aqueous solution.

a. Zinc sulfide is added to sulfuric acid.

b. Sodium hydroxide reacts with nitric acid.

c. Solutions of potassium fluoride and calcium nitrate are mixed.

★ 51. Write a balanced chemical equation for each combination reaction.

a. sodium oxide + water

b. hydrogen + bromine

c. dichlorine heptoxide + water

52. Write a balanced chemical equation for each single-replacement reaction that takes place in aqueous solution. Write "no reaction" if a reaction does not occur.

a. Steel wool (iron) is placed in sulfuric acid.

b. Mercury is poured into an aqueous solution of zinc nitrate.

c. Bromine reacts with aqueous barium iodide.

★53. Pieces of sodium and magnesium are dropped into separate water-filled test tubes (A and B). There is vigorous bubbling in Tube A but not in Tube B.

a. Which tube contains the sodium metal?

b. Write an equation for the reaction in the tube containing the sodium metal. What type of reaction is occurring in this tube?

54. Write a balanced equation for the complete combustion of each compound. Assume that the products are carbon dioxide and water.

a. octane (C_8H_{18})

b. glucose ($C_6H_{12}O_6$)

c. ethanoic acid ($HC_2H_3O_2$)

55. Write balanced chemical equations for these decomposition reactions.

a. Aluminum is obtained from aluminum oxide with the addition of a large amount of electrical energy.

b. Heating tin(IV) hydroxide gives tin(IV) oxide and water.

c. Silver carbonate decomposes into silver oxide and carbon dioxide when it is heated.

56. Write a balanced net ionic equation for each reaction. The product that is not ionized is given.

a. $H_2C_2O_4 + KOH \longrightarrow [H_2O]$

b. $Na_2S + HCl \longrightarrow [H_2S]$

c. $NaOH + Fe(NO_3)_3 \longrightarrow [Fe(OH_3)]$

★ 57. A yellow precipitate formed when aqueous solutions of sodium sulfide and cadmium nitrate were mixed in a beaker.

a. Write the formula of the yellow precipitate.

b. Identify the spectator ions in the solution.

c. Write the net ionic equation for the reaction.

Think Critically

58. **Interpret Photos** The photos show various types of reactions.

(1)    (2)

(3)    (4)

(1) Aluminum reacting with bromine

(2) The reaction of copper with aqueous silver nitrate

(3) Propane (C_3H_8) reacting with oxygen

(4) The reaction of lead(II) nitrate with potassium iodide

a. Identify each type of reaction.

b. Write the equation for each type of reaction.

59. Apply Concepts Write a balanced chemical equation for each reaction. Classify each by type.

    a. Sodium iodide reacts with phosphoric acid.
    b. Potassium oxide reacts with water.
    c. Heating sulfuric acid produces water, oxygen, and sulfur dioxide.
    d. Aluminum reacts with sulfuric acid.
    e. Pentane (C_5H_{12}) reacts with oxygen.

*60. Draw Conclusions When pale yellow chlorine gas is bubbled through a clear, colorless solution of sodium iodide, the solution turns brown.

    a. What type of reaction is taking place?
    b. Write the net ionic equation.

Enrichment

61. Interpret Graphs Alkanes are hydrocarbon molecules that have the general formula C_nH_{2n+2}. The graph shows the number of oxygen, carbon dioxide, and water molecules needed to balance the equations for the complete combustion of every alkane having from one to ten carbon atoms.

$$C_nH_{2n+2} + \underline{\quad} O_2 \longrightarrow \underline{\quad} CO_2 + \underline{\quad} H_2O$$

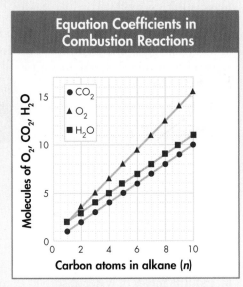

Equation Coefficients in Combustion Reactions

    a. Use the graph to write balanced equations for the combustion of C_5H_{12} and C_9H_{20}.
    b. Extrapolate the graph and write balanced equations for the combustion of $C_{12}H_{26}$ and $C_{17}H_{36}$.
    c. The coefficient for O_2 in the general equation is as follows:

$$n + \frac{n+1}{2}$$

What are the coefficients for CO_2 and H_2O?

*62. Apply Concepts Fill in the missing reactant, and then balance each equation.

    a. $K(s) + \underline{\quad} \longrightarrow KOH(aq) + H_2(g)$
    b. $C_2H_5OH(l) + \underline{\quad} \longrightarrow CO_2(g) + H_2O(g)$
    c. $Bi(NO_3)_3(aq) + \underline{\quad} \longrightarrow$
                               $Bi_2S_3(s) + HNO_3(aq)$
    d. $Al(s) + \underline{\quad} \longrightarrow AlBr_3(s)$

Write About Science

63. Explain Research organisms such as fireflies and jellyfish that use bioluminescence, including information on the discovery of green fluorescent protein (GFP). In a pamphlet or poster, explain how bioluminescence works and how each organism uses it.

64. Observe Make a list of five chemical reactions that happen in your kitchen. Describe and name each reaction on your list.

*65. Relate Cause and Effect Why is smoking not permitted near an oxygen source? What would happen if a match were struck in a room filled with oxygen?

CHEMYSTERY

Order in the Lab

Chemicals should not be stored in alphabetical order because some chemicals that will react if mixed could end up next to each other. For example, acids should not be stored near cyanides, sulfides and other chemicals that produce toxic gases when combined. Acids should also not be stored near bases or active metals. Reactions between acids and bases produce heat. Acids and active metals react to produce gases and heat. Acids and flammables should have separate, dedicated storage areas.

66. Connect to the BIGIDEA Should sulfuric acid be stored next to sodium hydroxide? Explain your answer. If they should not be stored next to each other, write a balanced chemical equation to support your answer.

67. When you take a glass of cold liquid outside on a warm, humid day, drops of liquid soon form on the outside of the glass.

  a. What is the liquid?
  b. Where did the liquid come from?
  c. Did a chemical or physical change occur?

68. Classify each of the following as an element, a compound, a homogeneous mixture, a heterogeneous mixture, or a substance. Some may fit in more than one category.

  a. salt water   **d.** salt and sand
  b. sodium chloride   **e.** gold
  c. air   **f.** water with ice

69. A block of ice measures 25.0 cm × 42.0 cm × 38.0 cm. What is the mass of the ice in kilograms? The density of ice is 0.917 g/cm³.

★70. List the number of protons, neutrons, and electrons in this isotope of titanium: $^{50}_{22}\text{Ti}$.

71. Write electron configurations for the following ions.

  a. Sr^{2+} **b.** S^{2-} **c.** Ga^{3+} **d.** Cu^+

72. Explain what is meant by *electronegativity*. How do electronegativity values change across a row of representative elements?

73. Are any of the following formulas for ionic compounds incorrect? If so, write the correct formulas.

  a. K_2Br **b.** Na_2S **c.** CaN_2 **d.** Al_2O_3

★74. Give the name or formula for the following compounds:

  a. potassium chromate
  b. sodium hydrogen sulfite
  c. $HMnO_4$
  d. $K_2C_2O_4$

75. Calculate the number of moles in each substance.

  a. 54.0 L of nitrogen dioxide (at STP)
  b. 1.68 g of magnesium ions
  c. 69.6 g of sodium hypochlorite
  d. 4.27×10^{24} molecules of carbon monoxide

76. The graph shows the percent composition of two different compounds formed by the elements iron, oxygen, and sulfur.

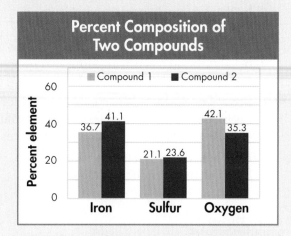

a. Using the data on the graphs, calculate the empirical formula of each compound.
b. Name each compound.

★77. Many coffees and colas contain the stimulant caffeine. The percent composition of caffeine is 49.5% C, 5.20% H, 16.5% O, and 28.9% N. What is the molecular formula of caffeine if its molar mass is 194.1 g/mol?

78. Calcium chloride ($CaCl_2$) is a white solid used as a drying agent. The maximum amount of water absorbed by different quantities of $CaCl_2$ is given in the table below.

$CaCl_2$ (g)	$CaCl_2$ (mol)	H_2O (g)	H_2O (mol)
17.3	a._____	5.62	e._____
48.8	b._____	15.8	f._____
124	c._____	40.3	g._____
337	d._____	109	h._____

a. Complete the table.
b. Plot the moles of water absorbed (*y*-axis) versus the moles of $CaCl_2$.
c. Based on your graph, how many molecules of water does each formula unit of $CaCl_2$ absorb?

If You Have Trouble With . . .											
Question	67	68	69	70	71	72	73	74	75	76	77	78
See Chapter	2	2	3	4	5	6	7	9	10	10	10	10

Standardized Test Prep

Select the choice that best answers each question or completes each statement.

1. When the equation $Fe_2O_3 + H_2 \longrightarrow Fe + H_2O$ is balanced using whole-number coefficients, what is the coefficient of H_2?

   (A) 6   (B) 3   (C) 2   (D) 1

2. Identify the spectator ion in this reaction.

   $Ba(OH)_2(aq) + H_2SO_4(aq) \longrightarrow BaSO_4(s) + H_2O(l)$

   (A) Ba^{2+}
   (B) SO_4^{2-}
   (C) OH^-
   (D) H^+
   (E) There is no spectator ion.

3. Magnesium ribbon reacts with an aqueous solution of copper(II) chloride in a single-replacement reaction. Which are the products of the balanced net ionic equation for the reaction?

   (A) $Mg^{2+}(aq) + 2Cl^-(aq) + Cu(s)$
   (B) $Mg^+(aq) + Cl^-(aq) + Cu^+(aq)$
   (C) $Mg^{2+}(aq) + Cu(s)$
   (D) $Cu(s) + 2Cl^-(aq)$

Use the following description and data table to answer Questions 4–6.

Dropper bottles labeled P, Q, and R contain one of three aqueous solutions: potassium carbonate, K_2CO_3; hydrochloric acid, HCl; and calcium nitrate, $Ca(NO_3)_2$. The table shows what happens when pairs of solutions are mixed.

Solution	P	Q	R
P	—	Precipitate	No reaction
Q	Precipitate	—	Gas forms.
R	No reaction	Gas forms.	—

4. Identify the contents of each dropper bottle.

5. Write the net ionic equation for the formation of the precipitate.

6. Write the complete ionic equation for the formation of the gas.

7. Which are the expected products of the decomposition reaction of potassium oxide, K_2O?

   (A) $K^+(s)$ and $O^{2-}(g)$
   (B) $K^+(s)$ and $O_2(g)$
   (C) $K(s)$ and $O_2^{2-}(g)$
   (D) $K(s)$ and $O_2(g)$

Use the diagram to answer Questions 8–11.

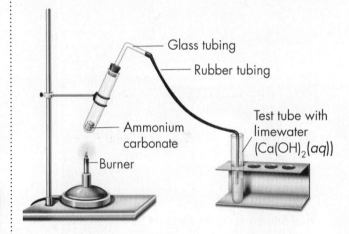

8. When ammonium carbonate is heated, water, ammonia, and carbon dioxide are produced. What type of chemical reaction is occurring?

9. Write formulas for the reaction products.

10. Write a balanced equation for the reaction. Include states for reactants and products.

11. Limewater is used to test for the presence of carbon dioxide gas. The products of the reaction of $Ca(OH)_2$ with CO_2 are calcium carbonate and water. Write a balanced equation for the reaction.

If You Have Trouble With . . .										
Question	1	2	3	4	5	6	7	8	9	10	11
See Lesson	11.2	11.3	11.2	11.3	11.3	11.3	11.2	11.2	11.1	11.2	11.2

12

Stoichiometry

INSIDE:

- **12.1** The Arithmetic of Equations
- **12.2** Chemical Calculations
- **12.3** Limiting Reagent and Percent Yield

PearsonChem.com

Like a chemical equation, a recipe tells you the amount of each ingredient (your reactants) needed to make your product, in this case, bread.

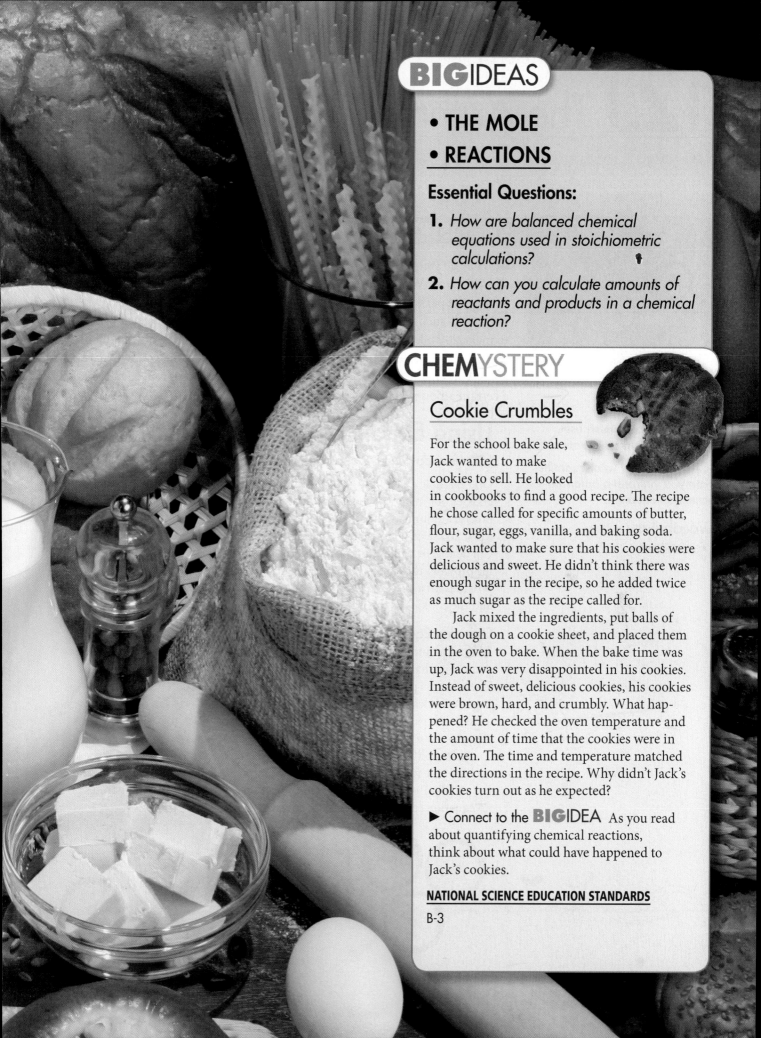

- **THE MOLE**
- **REACTIONS**

Essential Questions:

1. *How are balanced chemical equations used in stoichiometric calculations?*

2. *How can you calculate amounts of reactants and products in a chemical reaction?*

CHEMYSTERY

Cookie Crumbles

For the school bake sale, Jack wanted to make cookies to sell. He looked in cookbooks to find a good recipe. The recipe he chose called for specific amounts of butter, flour, sugar, eggs, vanilla, and baking soda. Jack wanted to make sure that his cookies were delicious and sweet. He didn't think there was enough sugar in the recipe, so he added twice as much sugar as the recipe called for.

Jack mixed the ingredients, put balls of the dough on a cookie sheet, and placed them in the oven to bake. When the bake time was up, Jack was very disappointed in his cookies. Instead of sweet, delicious cookies, his cookies were brown, hard, and crumbly. What happened? He checked the oven temperature and the amount of time that the cookies were in the oven. The time and temperature matched the directions in the recipe. Why didn't Jack's cookies turn out as he expected?

▶ **Connect to the BIGIDEA** As you read about quantifying chemical reactions, think about what could have happened to Jack's cookies.

NATIONAL SCIENCE EDUCATION STANDARDS

12.1 The Arithmetic of Equations

Q: *How do you figure out how much starting material you need to make a finished product?* Whenever you make something, you need to have the ingredients or the parts that make up the desired product. When making bikes, you need parts such as wheels, handlebars, pedals, and frames. If a factory needs to make 200 bikes, then the workers would need to calculate how many of each part they need to produce the 200 bikes. In this lesson, you will learn about how chemists determine how much of each reactant is needed to make a certain amount of product.

Key Questions

🔑 How do chemists use balanced chemical equations?

🔑 In terms of what quantities can you interpret a balanced chemical equation?

Vocabulary

• stoichiometry

Using Equations

🔑 **How do chemists use balanced chemical equations?**

One example of something that you might make is food. When you make cookies, for instance, you probably use a recipe. A cookie recipe tells you the precise amounts of ingredients to mix to make a certain number of cookies. If you need a larger number of cookies than the recipe provides for, you can double or triple the amounts of all the ingredients. In a way, a cookie recipe provides the same kind of information that a balanced chemical equation provides. In a cookie recipe, you can think of the ingredients as the reactants and the cookies as the products.

Everyday Equations The making of tricycles, like bikes and cookies, is a job that requires quantitative information to create the final product. Let's say you are in charge of manufacturing for the Travel Time Tricycle Company. The business plan for Travel Time requires the production of 640 custom-made tricycles each week. One of your responsibilities is to make sure there are enough parts available at the start of each workweek to make these tricycles. How can you determine the number of parts you need per week?

To simplify this discussion, assume that the major components of the tricycle are the frame (F), the seat (S), the wheels (W), the handlebars (H), and the pedals (P)—in other words, the reactants. The figure below illustrates how an equation can represent the manufacturing of a single tricycle.

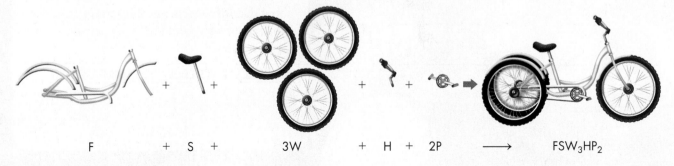

$$F \quad + \quad S \quad + \quad 3W \quad + \quad H \quad + \quad 2P \quad \longrightarrow \quad FSW_3HP_2$$

The finished tricycle, your product, has a "formula" of FSW_3HP_2. The balanced equation for making a single tricycle is

$$F + S + 3W + H + 2P \longrightarrow FSW_3HP_2$$

This balanced equation is a "recipe" to make a single tricycle: Making a tricycle requires assembling one frame, one seat, three wheels, one handlebar, and two pedals. Now look at Sample Problem 12.1. It shows you how to use the balanced equation to calculate the number of parts needed to manufacture a given number of tricycles.

SampleProblem 12.1

Using a Balanced Equation as a Recipe

In a five-day workweek, Travel Time is scheduled to make 640 tricycles. How many wheels should be in the plant on Monday morning to make these tricycles?

❶ Analyze List the knowns and the unknown.
Use the balanced equation to identify a conversion factor that will allow you to calculate the unknown. The conversion you need to make is from tricycles (FSW_3HP_2) to wheels (W).

KNOWNS

number of tricycles = 640 tricycles = 640 FSW_3HP_2
$F + S + 3W + H + 2P \longrightarrow FSW_3HP_2$

UNKNOWN

number of wheels = ? W

❷ Calculate Solve for the unknown.

Identify a conversion factor that relates wheels to tricycles. You can write two conversion factors relating wheels to tricycles.

$$\frac{3\ W}{1\ FSW_3HP_2} \quad and \quad \frac{1\ FSW_3HP_2}{3\ W}$$

The desired unit is W; so use the conversion factor on the left. Multiply the number of tricycles by the conversion factor.

$$640\ \cancel{FSW_3HP_2} \times \frac{3\ W}{1\ \cancel{FSW_3HP_2}} = \boxed{1920\ W}$$

When using conversion factors, remember to cancel like units when they are in both the numerator and denominator. This tells you that you are using the correct conversion factor.

❸ Evaluate Does the result make sense? If three wheels are required for each tricycle and more than 600 tricycles are being made, then a number of wheels in excess of 1800 is a logical answer. The unit of the known (FSW_3HP_2) cancels, and the answer has the correct unit (W).

1. Travel Time has decided to make 288 tricycles each day. How many tricycle seats, wheels, and pedals are needed for each day?

2. Write an equation that gives your own "recipe" for making a skateboard.

Q: *How can you determine the amount of each reactant you need to make a product?*

Learn more about stoichiometry online.

READING SUPPORT

Build Vocabulary: *Word Origins* *Stoichiometry* comes from the combination of the Greek words *stoikheioin*, meaning "element," and *metron*, meaning "to measure." Stoichiometry is the calculation of amounts of substances involved in chemical reactions. *What do you first need to know about a chemical reaction before doing stoichiometry calculations?*

Balanced Chemical Equations Nearly everything you use is manufactured from chemicals—soaps, shampoos and conditioners, CDs, cosmetics, medicines, and clothes. When manufacturing such items, the cost of making them cannot be greater than the price at which they are sold. Otherwise, the manufacturer will not make a profit. Therefore, the chemical processes used in manufacturing must be carried out economically. A situation like this is where balanced equations help.

A balanced chemical equation tells you what amounts of reactants to mix and what amount of a product to expect. **Chemists use balanced chemical equations as a basis to calculate how much reactant is needed or how much product will be formed in a reaction.** When you know the quantity of one substance in a reaction, you can calculate the quantity of any other substance consumed or created in the reaction. Quantity usually means the amount of a substance expressed in grams or moles. However, quantity could just as well be in liters, tons, or molecules.

The calculation of quantities in chemical reactions is a subject of chemistry called **stoichiometry.** Calculations using balanced equations are called stoichiometric calculations. For chemists, stoichiometry is a form of bookkeeping. For example, accountants can track income, expenditures, and profits for a small business by tallying each in dollars and cents. Chemists can track reactants and products in a reaction by stoichiometry. It allows chemists to tally the amounts of reactants and products using ratios of moles or representative particles derived from chemical equations.

Chemical Equations

In terms of what quantities can you interpret a balanced chemical equation?

In gardens such as the one shown in Figure 12.1, fertilizers are often used to improve the growth of flowers. Ammonia is widely used as a fertilizer. Ammonia is produced industrially by the reaction of nitrogen with hydrogen.

$$N_2(g) + 3H_2(g) \longrightarrow 2NH_3(g)$$

The balanced chemical equation tells you the relative amounts of reactants and product in the reaction. However, your interpretation of the equation depends on how you quantify the reactants and products. **A balanced chemical equation can be interpreted in terms of different quantities, including numbers of atoms, molecules, or moles; mass; and volume.** As you study stoichiometry, you will learn how to interpret a chemical equation in terms of any of these quantities.

Number of Atoms At the atomic level, a balanced equation indicates the number and types of atoms that are rearranged to make the product or products. Remember, both the number and types of atoms are not changed in a reaction. In the synthesis of ammonia, the reactants are composed of two atoms of nitrogen and six atoms of hydrogen. These eight atoms are recombined in the product.

2 atoms N + 6 atoms H $\longrightarrow$ 2 atoms N and 6 atoms H

8 atoms $\longrightarrow$ 8 atoms

Number of Molecules The balanced equation indicates that one molecule of nitrogen reacts with three molecules of hydrogen. Nitrogen and hydrogen will always react to form ammonia in a 1:3:2 ratio of molecules. If you could make 10 molecules of nitrogen react with 30 molecules of hydrogen, you would expect to get 20 molecules of ammonia. Of course, it is not practical to count such small numbers of molecules and allow them to react. You could, however, take Avogadro's number of nitrogen molecules and make them react with three times Avogadro's number of hydrogen molecules. This value would be the same 1:3 ratio of molecules of reactants. The reaction would form two times Avogadro's number of ammonia molecules.

$$1 \times \frac{6.02 \times 10^{23}}{\text{molecules N}_2} + 3 \times \frac{6.02 \times 10^{23}}{\text{molecules H}_2} \longrightarrow 2 \times \frac{6.02 \times 10^{23}}{\text{molecules NH}_3}$$

Moles You know that Avogrado's number of representative particles is equal to one mole of a substance. Therefore, since a balanced chemical equation tells you the number of representative particles, it also tells you the number of moles. The coefficients of a balanced chemical equation indicate the relative numbers of moles of reactants and products in a chemical reaction. These numbers are the most important pieces of information that a balanced chemical equation provides. Using this information, you can calculate the amounts of reactants and products. In the synthesis of ammonia, one mole of nitrogen molecules reacts with three moles of hydrogen molecules to form two moles of ammonia molecules. As you can see from this reaction, the total number of moles of reactants does not equal the total number of moles of product.

$$1 \text{ mol N}_2 + 3 \text{ mol H}_2 \longrightarrow 2 \text{ mol NH}_3$$

Mass A balanced chemical equation obeys the law of conservation of mass. This law states that mass can be neither created nor destroyed in an ordinary chemical or physical process. As you recall, the number and type of atoms does not change in a chemical reaction. Therefore, the total mass of the atoms in the reaction does not change. Using the mole relationship, you can relate mass to the number of atoms in the chemical equation. The mass of 1 mol of N_2 (28.0 g) plus the mass of 3 mol of H_2 (6.0 g) equals the mass of 2 mol of NH_3 (34.0 g). Although the number of moles of reactants does not equal the number of moles of product, the total number of grams of reactants does equal the total number of grams of product.

$$28.0 \text{ g N}_2 + (3 \times 2.0 \text{ g H}_2) \longrightarrow (2 \times 17.0 \text{ g NH}_3)$$
$$34.0 \text{ g} \longrightarrow 34.0 \text{ g}$$

Volume If you assume standard temperature and pressure, the equation also tells you about the volumes of gases. Recall that 1 mol of any gas at STP occupies a volume of 22.4 L. The equation indicates that 22.4 L of N_2 reacts with 67.2 L (3×22.4 L) of H_2. This reaction forms 44.8 L (2×22.4 L) of NH_3.

$$22.4 \text{ L N}_2 + 67.2 \text{ L H}_2 \longrightarrow 44.8 \text{ L NH}_3$$

Figure 12.1 Use of Ammonia
Gardeners use ammonium salts as fertilizer. The nitrogen in these salts is essential to plant growth.

SampleProblem 12.2

Interpreting a Balanced Chemical Equation

Hydrogen sulfide, which smells like rotten eggs, is found in volcanic gases. The balanced equation for the burning of hydrogen sulfide is

$$2H_2S(g) + 3O_2(g) \longrightarrow 2SO_2(g) + 2H_2O(g)$$

Interpret this equation in terms of
  a. numbers of representative particles and moles.
  b. masses of reactants and products.

❶ **Analyze** **Identify the relevant concepts.** The coefficients in the balanced equation give the relative number of representative particles and moles of reactants and products. A balanced chemical equation obeys the law of conservation of mass.

❷ **Solve** **Apply concepts to this situation.**

> Remember that atoms and molecules are both representative particles. In this equation, all the reactants and products are molecules; so all the representative particles are molecules.

Use the coefficients in the balanced equation to identify the number of representative particles and moles.

a. 2 molecules H_2S + 3 molecules $O_2 \longrightarrow$ 2 molecules SO_2 + 2 molecules H_2O
2 mol H_2S + 3 mol $O_2 \longrightarrow$ 2 mol SO_2 + 2 mol H_2O

Use the periodic table to calculate the molar mass of each reactant and product.

b. 1 mol H_2S = 34.1 g H_2S
1 mol O_2 = 32.0 g O_2
1 mol SO_2 = 64.1 g SO_2
1 mol H_2O = 18.0 g H_2O

Multiply the number of moles of each reactant and product by its molar mass.

2 mol H_2S + 3 mol $O_2 \longrightarrow$ 2 mol SO_2 + 2 mol H_2O.

$$\left(2 \text{ mol} \times 34.1 \frac{g}{mol}\right) + \left(3 \text{ mol} \times 32.0 \frac{g}{mol}\right) \longrightarrow$$

$$\left(2 \text{ mol} \times 64.1 \frac{g}{mol}\right) + \left(2 \text{ mol} \times 18.0 \frac{g}{mol}\right)$$

68.2 g H_2S + 96.0 g $O_2 \longrightarrow$ 128.2 g SO_2 + 36.0 g H_2O

$$164.2 \text{ g} = 164.2 \text{ g}$$

---

3. Interpret the equation for the formation of water from its elements in terms of numbers of molecules and moles, and volumes of gases at STP.

$$2H_2(g) + O_2(g) \longrightarrow 2H_2O(g)$$

4. Balance the following equation:

$$C_2H_4(g) + O_2(g) \longrightarrow CO_2(g) + H_2O(g)$$

Interpret the balanced equation in terms of relative numbers of moles, volumes of gas at STP, and masses of reactants and products.

Figure 12.2 summarizes the information derived from the balanced chemical equation for the formation of ammonia. As you can see, the mass of the reactants equals the mass of the products. In addition, the number of atoms of each type in the reactants equals the number of atoms of each type in the product. Mass and atoms are conserved in every chemical reaction. However, molecules, formula units, moles, and volumes are not necessarily conserved—although they may be. Consider, for example, the formation of hydrogen iodide.

$$H_2(g) + I_2(g) \longrightarrow 2HI(g)$$

In this reaction, molecules, moles, and volume are all conserved. But in the majority of chemical reactions, they are not.

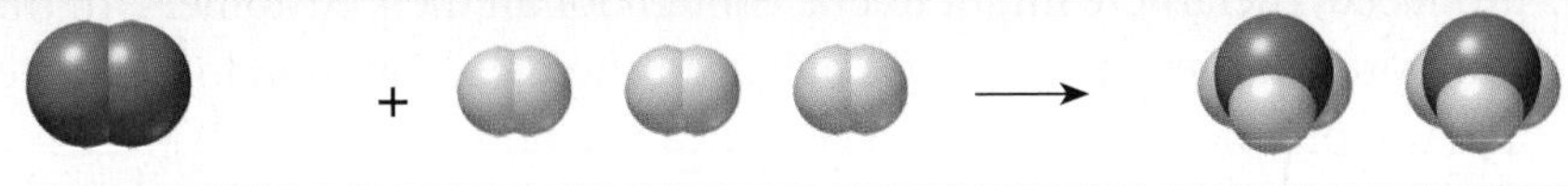

$N_2(g)$	+	$3H_2(g)$	$\longrightarrow$	$2NH_3(g)$
	+		$\longrightarrow$	
2 atoms N	+	6 atoms H	$\longrightarrow$	2 atoms N and 6 atoms H
1 molecule N_2	+	3 molecules H_2	$\longrightarrow$	2 molecules NH_3
10 molecules N_2	+	30 molecules H_2	$\longrightarrow$	20 molecules NH_3
$1 \times \begin{array}{c}6.02 \times 10^{23} \\ \text{molecules } N_2\end{array}$	+	$3 \times \begin{array}{c}6.02 \times 10^{23} \\ \text{molecules } H_2\end{array}$	$\longrightarrow$	$2 \times \begin{array}{c}6.02 \times 10^{23} \\ \text{molecules } NH_3\end{array}$
1 mol N_2	+	3 mol H_2	$\longrightarrow$	2 mol NH_3
28.0 g N_2	+	3×2.0 g H_2	$\longrightarrow$	2×17.0 g NH_3
		34.0 g reactants	$\longrightarrow$	34.0 g products
Assume STP 22.4 L	+	22.4 L 22.4 L 22.4 L	$\longrightarrow$	22.4 L 22.4 L
22.4 L N_2		67.2 L H_2		44.8 L NH_3

Figure 12.2 Interpreting a Balanced Chemical Equation
The balanced chemical equation for the formation of ammonia can be interpreted in several ways.
Predict *How many molecules of NH₃ could be made from 5 molecules of N₂ and 15 molecules of H₂?*

See balancing chemical equations animated online.

KINETIC ART

12.1 LessonCheck

ONLINE PROBLEMS

5. 🔑 **Explain** How do chemists use balanced equations?

6. 🔑 **Identify** Chemical reactions can be described in terms of what quantities?

7. Explain How is a balanced equation similar to a recipe?

8. Identify What quantities are always conserved in chemical reactions?

9. Apply Concepts Interpret the given equation in terms of relative numbers of representative particles, numbers of moles, and masses of reactants and products.

$$2K(s) + 2H_2O(l) \longrightarrow 2KOH(aq) + H_2(g)$$

10. Apply Concepts Balance this equation:

$$C_2H_5OH(l) + O_2(g) \longrightarrow CO_2(g) + H_2O(g)$$

Show that the balanced equation obeys the law of conservation of mass.

12.2 Chemical Calculations

CHEMISTRY & YOU

Q: *How do manufacturers know how to make enough of their desired product?* Chemical plants produce ammonia by combining nitrogen with hydrogen. If too much ammonia is produced, then it might be wasted. But if too little is produced, then there might not be enough for all their customers. In this lesson, you will learn how to use a balanced chemical equation to calculate the amount of product formed in a chemical reaction.

Key Questions

How are mole ratios used in chemical calculations?

What is the general procedure for solving a stoichiometric problem?

Vocabulary

- mole ratio

Writing and Using Mole Ratios

How are mole ratios used in chemical calculations?

As you learned in the previous lesson, a balanced chemical equation provides a great deal of quantitative information. It relates particles (atoms, molecules, formula units), moles of substances, and masses. A balanced chemical equation also is essential for all calculations involving amounts of reactants and products. For example, suppose you know the number of moles of one substance. The balanced chemical equation allows you to determine the number of moles of all other substances in the reaction.

Look again at the balanced equation for the production of ammonia.

$$N_2(g) + 3H_2(g) \longrightarrow 2NH_3(g)$$

The most important interpretation of this equation is that 1 mol of nitrogen reacts with 3 mol of hydrogen to form 2 mol of ammonia. Based on this interpretation, you can write ratios that relate moles of reactants to moles of product. A **mole ratio** is a conversion factor derived from the coefficients of a balanced chemical equation interpreted in terms of moles. **In chemical calculations, mole ratios are used to convert between a given number of moles of a reactant or product to moles of a different reactant or product.** Three mole ratios derived from the balanced equation above are

$$\frac{1 \text{ mol } N_2}{3 \text{ mol } H_2} \quad \frac{2 \text{ mol } NH_3}{1 \text{ mol } N_2} \quad \frac{3 \text{ mol } H_2}{2 \text{ mol } NH_3}$$

Mole-Mole Calculations In the mole ratio below, W is the unknown, wanted, quantity and G is the given quantity. The values of a and b are the coefficients from the balanced equation. Thus, a general solution for a mole-mole problem, such as Sample Problem 12.3, is given by

$$\underset{\text{Given}}{x \cancel{\text{ mol } G}} \times \underset{\text{Mole ratio}}{\frac{b \text{ mol } W}{a \cancel{\text{ mol } G}}} = \underset{\text{Calculated}}{\frac{xb}{a} \text{ mol } W}$$

Sample Problem 12.3

Calculating Moles of a Product

How many moles of NH_3 are produced when 0.60 mol of nitrogen reacts with hydrogen?

① Analyze List the known and the unknown. The conversion is mol $N_2 \longrightarrow$ mol NH_3. According to the balanced equation, 1 mol N_2 combines with 3 mol H_2 to produce 2 mol NH_3. To determine the number of moles of NH_3, the given quantity of N_2 is multiplied by the form of the mole ratio from the balanced equation that allows the given unit to cancel.

KNOWN

moles of nitrogen = 0.60 mol N_2

UNKNOWN

moles of ammonia = ? mol NH_3

② Calculate Solve for the unknown.

Write the mole ratio that will allow you to convert from moles N_2 to moles NH_3.	$\dfrac{2 \text{ mol } NH_3}{1 \text{ mol } N_2}$
Multiply the given quantity of N_2 by the mole ratio in order to find the moles of NH_3.	$0.60 \text{ mol } N_2 \times \dfrac{2 \text{ mol } NH_3}{1 \text{ mol } N_2} = 1.2 \text{ mol } NH_3$

③ Evaluate Does the result make sense? The ratio of 1.2 mol NH_3 to 0.60 mol N_2 is 2:1, as predicted by the balanced equation.

Remember that the mole ratio must have N_2 on the bottom so that the mol N_2 in the mol ratio will cancel with mol N_2 in the known.

11. This equation shows the formation of aluminum oxide, which is found on the surface of aluminum objects exposed to the air.

$$4Al(s) + 3O_2(g) \longrightarrow 2Al_2O_3(s)$$

a. Write the six mole ratios that can be derived from this equation.
b. How many moles of aluminum are needed to form 3.7 mol Al_2O_3?

12. According to the equation in Problem 11,
a. How many moles of oxygen are required to react completely with 14.8 mol Al?
b. How many moles of Al_2O_3 are formed when 0.78 mol O_2 reacts with aluminum?

Mass-Mass Calculations No laboratory balance can measure substances directly in moles. Instead, the amount of a substance is usually determined by measuring its mass in grams. From the mass of a reactant or product, the mass of any other reactant or product in a given chemical equation can be calculated. The mole interpretation of a balanced equation is the basis for this conversion. If the given sample is measured in grams, then the mass can be converted to moles by using the molar mass. Then the mole ratio from the balanced equation can be used to calculate the number of moles of the unknown. If it is the mass of the unknown that needs to be determined, the number of moles of the unknown can be multiplied by the molar mass. As in mole-mole calculations, the unknown can be either a reactant or a product.

Figure 12.3 Ammonia in Space
In this Hubble Space Telescope image, clouds of condensed ammonia are visible covering the surface of Saturn.

Steps for Solving a Mass-Mass Problem Mass-mass problems are solved in basically the same way as mole-mole problems. The steps for the mass-mass conversion of any given mass (G) to any wanted mass (W) are outlined below.

1. Change the mass of G to moles of G (mass $G \longrightarrow$ mol G) by using the molar mass of G.

$$\text{mass } G \times \frac{1 \text{ mol } G}{\text{molar mass } G} = \text{mol } G$$

2. Change the moles of G to moles of W (mol $G \longrightarrow$ mol W) by using the mole ratio from the balanced equation.

$$\text{mol } G \times \frac{b \text{ mol } W}{a \text{ mol } G} = \text{mol } W$$

3. Change the moles of W to grams of W (mol $W \longrightarrow$ mass W) by using the molar mass of W.

$$\text{mol } W \times \frac{\text{molar mass } W}{1 \text{ mol } W} = \text{mass } W$$

Figure 12.4 shows another way to represent the steps for doing mole-mass and mass-mole stoichiometric calculations. For a mole-mass problem, the first conversion (from mass to moles) is skipped. For a mass-mole problem, the last conversion (from moles to mass) is skipped. You can use parts of the three-step process shown in Figure 12.4 as they are appropriate to the problem you are solving.

Figure 12.4 Mass-Mass Conversion Steps
This general solution diagram indicates the steps necessary to solve a mass-mass stoichiometry problem: Convert mass to moles, use the mole ratio, and then convert moles to mass.
Infer *Is the given always a reactant?*

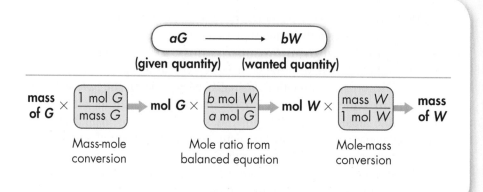

SampleProblem 12.4

Calculating the Mass of a Product

Ammonia (NH_3) clouds are present around some planets, as in Figure 12.3. Calculate the number of grams of NH_3 produced by the reaction of 5.40 g of hydrogen with an excess of nitrogen. The balanced equation is

$$N_2(g) + 3H_2(g) \longrightarrow 2NH_3(g)$$

❶ Analyze List the knowns and the unknown.
The mass of hydrogen will be used to find the mass of ammonia: $g\ H_2 \longrightarrow g\ NH_3$. The coefficients of the balanced equation show that 3 mol H_2 reacts with 1 mol N_2 to produce 2 mol NH_3. The following steps are necessary to determine the mass of ammonia:

$$g\ H_2 \longrightarrow mol\ H_2 \longrightarrow mol\ NH_3 \longrightarrow g\ NH_3$$

KNOWNS

mass of hydrogen = 5.40 g H_2
2 mol NH_3/3 mol H_2 (from balanced equation)
1 mol H_2 = 2.0 g H_2 (molar mass)
1 mol NH_3 = 17.0 g NH_3 (molar mass)

UNKNOWN

mass of ammonia = ? g NH_3

❷ Calculate Solve for the unknown.

Start with the given quantity, and convert from mass to moles.

$$5.40\ \cancel{g\ H_2} \times \frac{1\ mol\ H_2}{2.0\ \cancel{g\ H_2}}$$

Don't forget to cancel the units at each step.

Then convert from moles of reactant to moles of product by using the correct mole ratio.

$$5.40\ \cancel{g\ H_2} \times \frac{1\ \cancel{mol\ H_2}}{2.0\ \cancel{g\ H_2}} \times \frac{2\ mol\ NH_3}{3\ \cancel{mol\ H_2}}$$

$$g\ H_2 \longrightarrow mol\ H_2 \longrightarrow mol\ NH_3 \longrightarrow g\ NH_3$$

Finish by converting from moles to grams. Use the molar mass of NH_3.

$$5.40\ \cancel{g\ H_2} \times \frac{1\ \cancel{mol\ H_2}}{2.0\ \cancel{g\ H_2}} \times \frac{2\ \cancel{mol\ NH_3}}{3\ \cancel{mol\ H_2}} \times \frac{17.0\ g\ NH_3}{1\ \cancel{mol\ NH_3}} = 31\ g\ NH_3$$

| Given quantity | Change given unit to moles | Mole ratio | Change moles to grams |

❸ Evaluate Does the result make sense? Because there are three conversion factors involved in this solution, it is more difficult to estimate an answer. However, because the molar mass of NH_3 is substantially greater than the molar mass of H_2, the answer should have a larger mass than the given mass. The answer should have two significant figures.

---

13. Acetylene gas (C_2H_2) is produced by adding water to calcium carbide (CaC_2).

$$CaC_2(s) + 2H_2O(l) \longrightarrow C_2H_2(g) + Ca(OH)_2(aq)$$

How many grams of acetylene are produced by adding water to 5.00 g CaC_2?

14. Use the equation in Question 13 to determine how many moles of CaC_2 are needed to react completely with 49.0 g H_2O.

Other Stoichiometric Calculations

What is the general procedure for solving a stoichiometric problem?

As you already know, you can obtain mole ratios from a balanced chemical equation. From the mole ratios, you can calculate any measurement unit that is related to the mole. The given quantity can be expressed in numbers of representative particles, units of mass, or volumes of gases at STP. The problems can include mass-volume, particle-mass, and volume-volume calculations. For example, you can use stoichiometry to relate volumes of reactants and products in the reaction shown in Figure 12.5. **In a typical stoichiometric problem, the given quantity is first converted to moles. Then, the mole ratio from the balanced equation is used to calculate the number of moles of the wanted substance. Finally, the moles are converted to any other unit of measurement related to the unit mole, as the problem requires.**

Thus far, you have learned how to use the relationship between moles and mass (1 mol = molar mass) in solving mass-mass, mass-mole, and mole-mass stoichiometric problems. The mole-mass relationship gives you two conversion factors.

$$\frac{1 \text{ mol}}{\text{molar mass}} \text{ and } \frac{\text{molar mass}}{1 \text{ mol}}$$

Recall from Chapter 10 that the mole can be related to other quantities as well. For example, 1 mol = 6.02×10^{23} representative particles, and 1 mol of a gas = 22.4 L at STP. These two relationships provide four more conversion factors that you can use in stoichiometric calculations.

$$\frac{1 \text{ mol}}{6.02 \times 10^{23} \text{ particles}} \text{ and } \frac{6.02 \times 10^{23} \text{ particles}}{1 \text{ mol}}$$

$$\frac{1 \text{ mol}}{22.4 \text{ L}} \text{ and } \frac{22.4 \text{ L}}{1 \text{ mol}}$$

Figure 12.5 summarizes the steps for a typical stoichiometric problem. Notice that the units of the given quantity will not necessarily be the same as the units of the wanted quantity. For example, given the mass of *G*, you might be asked to calculate the volume of *W* at STP.

Figure 12.5
Solving Stoichiometric Problems
With your knowledge of conversion factors and this problem-solving approach, you can solve a variety of stoichiometric problems.
Identify *What conversion factor is used to convert moles to representative particles?*

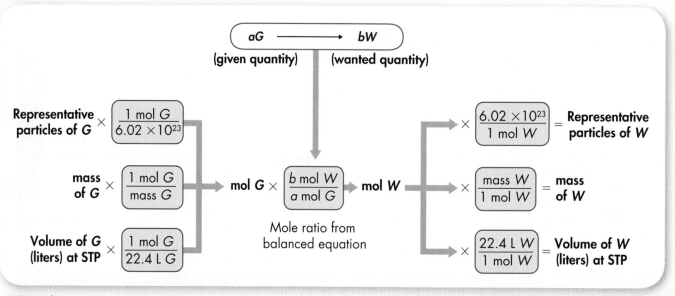

Calculating Molecules of a Product

How many molecules of oxygen are produced when 29.2 g of water is decomposed by electrolysis according to this balanced equation?

$$2H_2O(l) \xrightarrow{\text{electricity}} 2H_2(g) + O_2(g)$$

❶ Analyze **List the knowns and the unknown.** The following calculations need to be performed:

$$\text{g } H_2O \longrightarrow \text{mol } H_2O \longrightarrow \text{mol } O_2 \longrightarrow \text{molecules } O_2$$

The appropriate mole ratio relating mol O_2 to mol H_2O from the balanced equation is 1 mole O_2/2 mol H_2O.

KNOWNS

mass of water = 29.2 g H_2O
1 mol O_2/2 mol H_2O (from balanced equation)
1 mol H_2O = 18.0 g H_2O (molar mass)
1 mol O_2 = 6.02 × 10^{23} molecules O_2

UNKNOWN

molecules of oxygen = ? molecules O_2

❷ Calculate **Solve for the unknown.**

Start with the given quantity, and convert from mass to moles.

$$29.2 \text{ g } H_2O \times \frac{1 \text{ mol } H_2O}{18.0 \text{ g } H_2O}$$

Remember to start your calculations with the given quantity, even if the given quantity is a product in the reaction.

Then, convert from moles of reactant to moles of product.

$$29.2 \text{ g } H_2O \times \frac{1 \text{ mol } H_2O}{18.0 \text{ g } H_2O} \times \frac{1 \text{ mol } O_2}{2 \text{ mol } H_2O}$$

Finish by converting from moles to molecules.

$$29.2 \text{ g } H_2O \times \frac{1 \text{ mol } H_2O}{18.0 \text{ g } H_2O} \times \frac{1 \text{ mol } O_2}{2 \text{ mol } H_2O} \times \frac{6.02 \times 10^{23} \text{ molecules } O_2}{1 \text{ mol } O_2}$$

Given quantity　　Change to moles　　Mole ratio　　Change to molecules

$$= 4.88 \times 10^{23} \text{ molecules } O_2$$

❸ Evaluate **Does the result make sense?** The given mass of water should produce a little less than 1 mol of oxygen, or a little less than Avogadro's number of molecules. The answer should have three significant figures.

15. How many molecules of oxygen are produced by the decomposition of 6.54 g of potassium chlorate ($KClO_3$)?

$$2KClO_3(s) \longrightarrow 2KCl(s) + 3O_2(g)$$

16. The last step in the production of nitric acid is the reaction of nitrogen dioxide with water.

$$3NO_2(g) + H_2O(l) \longrightarrow 2HNO_3(aq) + NO(g)$$

How many grams of nitrogen dioxide must react with water to produce 5.00 × 10^{22} molecules of nitrogen monoxide?

Volume-Volume Stoichiometric Calculations

Nitrogen monoxide and oxygen gas combine to form the brown gas nitrogen dioxide, which contributes to photochemical smog. How many liters of nitrogen dioxide are produced when 34 L of oxygen react with an excess of nitrogen monoxide? Assume conditions are at STP.

$$2NO(g) + O_2(g) \longrightarrow 2NO_2(g)$$

❶ **Analyze** **List the knowns and the unknown.**
The following calculations need to be performed:

$$L\ O_2 \longrightarrow mol\ O_2 \longrightarrow mol\ NO_2 \longrightarrow L\ NO_2$$

For gaseous reactants and products at STP, 1 mol of a gas has a volume of 22.4 L.

KNOWNS

volume of oxygen = $34\ L\ O_2$
$2\ mol\ NO_2 / 1\ mol\ O_2$ (from balanced equation)
$1\ mol\ O_2 = 22.4\ L\ O_2$ (at STP)
$1\ mol\ NO_2 = 22.4\ L\ NO_2$ (at STP)

UNKNOWN

volume of nitrogen dioxide = $?\ L\ NO_2$

❷ **Calculate** **Solve for the unknown.**

Start with the given quantity, and convert from volume to moles by using the mole-volume ratio.

$$34\ L\ O_2 \times \frac{1\ mol\ O_2}{22.4\ L\ O_2}$$

Then, convert from moles of reactant to moles of product by using the correct mole ratio.

$$34\ L\ O_2 \times \frac{1\ mol\ O_2}{22.4\ L\ O_2} \times \frac{2\ mol\ NO_2}{1\ mol\ O_2}$$

Finish by converting from moles to liters. Use the mole-volume ratio.

$$34\ L\ O_2 \times \frac{1\ mol\ O_2}{22.4\ L\ O_2} \times \frac{2\ mol\ NO_2}{1\ mol\ O_2} \times \frac{22.4\ L\ NO_2}{1\ mol\ NO_2} = 68\ L\ NO_2$$

| Given quantity | Change to moles | Mole ratio | Change to liters |

❸ **Evaluate** **Does the result make sense?** Because 2 mol NO_2 are produced for each 1 mol O_2 that reacts, the volume of NO_2 should be twice the given volume of O_2. The answer should have two significant figures.

---

17. The equation for the combustion of carbon monoxide is

$$2CO(g) + O_2(g) \longrightarrow 2CO_2(g)$$

How many liters of oxygen are required to burn 3.86 L of carbon monoxide?

18. Phosphorus and hydrogen can be combined to form phosphine (PH_3).

$$P_4(s) + 6H_2(g) \longrightarrow 4PH_3(g)$$

How many liters of phosphine are formed when 0.42 L of hydrogen reacts with phosphorus?

Stoichiometric Safety

In a car collision, proper inflation of an air bag may save your life. Too much air in the bag could make the bag too hard, which could cause injury because the bag wouldn't effectively cushion the blow. Too little air in the bag could be insufficient to prevent a driver's impact with the steering wheel. Engineers use stoichiometry to determine the exact quantity of each reactant in the air bag's inflation system.

When a crash occurs, a series of reactions happen. Sodium azide (NaN_3) decomposes into sodium metal and nitrogen gas. The nitrogen gas causes the air bag to inflate, but the sodium can react explosively with water. So, air bags contain potassium nitrate (KNO_3) to react with the sodium. Silicon dioxide is also included in the air bag to react with the products of the second reaction. This final reaction produces a harmless substance.

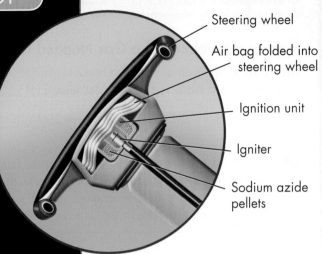

Steering wheel
Air bag folded into steering wheel
Ignition unit
Igniter
Sodium azide pellets

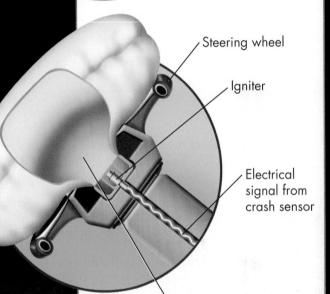

Steering wheel
Igniter
Electrical signal from crash sensor

Sodium azide pellets decomposing
$$2NaN_3(s) \longrightarrow 2Na(s) + 3N_2(g)$$
$$10Na(s) + 2KNO_3(s) \longrightarrow$$
$$K_2O(s) + 5Na_2O(s) + N_2(g)$$

CRASH TEST Air bag performance is tested using a crash test dummy. The production of nitrogen gas causes air bags to erupt from their storage site at speeds up to 200 miles per hour.

Take It Further

1. Draw Conclusions If a reaction in an air bag does not occur as intended, how might this affect the performance of an air bag?

2. Explain Research the regulations on automotive air bags, and explain why air bags are not safe for all passengers.

Sample Problem 12.7

Finding the Volume of a Gas Needed for a Reaction

Assuming STP, how many milliliters of oxygen are needed to produce 20.4 mL SO₃ according to this balanced equation?

$$2SO_2(g) + O_2(g) \longrightarrow 2SO_3(g)$$

❶ Analyze List the knowns and the unknown. For a reaction involving gaseous reactants or products, the coefficients also indicate relative amounts of each gas. So, you can use volume ratios in the same way you have used mole ratios.

> **KNOWNS**
> volume of sulfur trioxide = 20.4 mL
> 1 ml O₂/2 ml SO₃ (from balanced equation)
>
> **UNKNOWN**
> volume of oxygen = ? mL O₂

❷ Calculate Solve for the unknown.

> Multiply the given volume by the appropriate volume ratio.

$$20.4 \text{ mL } SO_3 \times \frac{1 \text{ mL } O_2}{2 \text{ mL } SO_3} = 10.2 \text{ mL } O_2$$

> The volume ratio can be written using milliliters as the units instead of liters.

❸ Evaluate Does the result make sense? Because the volume ratio is 2 volumes SO₃ to 1 volume O₂, the volume of O₂ should be half the volume of SO₃. The answer should have three significant figures.

Use the following chemical equation to answer Problems 19 and 20.

$$CS_2(l) + 3O_2(g) \longrightarrow CO_2(g) + 2SO_2(g)$$

19. Calculate the volume of sulfur dioxide, in milliliters, produced when 27.9 mL O₂ reacts with carbon disulfide.

20. How many deciliters of carbon dioxide are produced when 0.38 L SO₂ is formed?

12.2 LessonCheck

21. 🔧 **Explain** How are mole ratios used in chemical calculations?

22. 🔧 **Sequence** Outline the sequence of steps needed to solve a typical stoichiometric problem.

23. Calculate The combustion of acetylene gas is represented by this equation:

$$2C_2H_2(g) + 5O_2(g) \longrightarrow 4CO_2(g) + 2H_2O(g)$$

a. How many grams of CO₂ and grams of H₂O are produced when 52.0 g C₂H₂ burn in oxygen?

b. How many moles of H₂O are produced when 64.0 g C₂H₂ burn in oxygen?

24. Apply Concepts Write the 12 mole ratios that can be derived from the equation for the combustion of isopropyl alcohol.

$$2C_3H_7OH(l) + 9O_2(g) \longrightarrow 6CO_2(g) + 8H_2O(g)$$

BIGIDEA
THE MOLE AND QUANTIFYING MATTER

25. Use what you have learned about stoichiometric calculations to explain the following statement: Stoichiometric calculations are not possible without a balanced chemical equation.

Small-Scale Lab

Analysis of Baking Soda

(Probe or sensor version of this lab is available in the *Probeware Lab Manual*.)

Purpose

To determine the mass of sodium hydrogen carbonate in a sample of baking soda, using stoichiometry

Materials

- baking soda
- 3 plastic cups
- soda straw
- balance
- pipets of HCl, NaOH, and thymol blue

Procedure

A. Measure the mass of a clean, dry plastic cup.

B. Using the straw as a scoop, fill one end with baking soda to a depth of about 1 cm. Add the sample to the cup and measure its mass again.

C. Place two HCl pipets that are about 3/4 full into a clean cup and measure the mass of the system.

D. Transfer the contents of both HCl pipets to the cup containing baking soda. Swirl until the fizzing stops. Wait 5–10 minutes to be sure the reaction is complete. Measure the mass of the two empty HCl pipets in their cup again.

E. Add 5 drops of thymol blue to the plastic cup.

F. Place two full NaOH pipets in a clean cup and measure the mass of the system.

G. Add NaOH slowly to the baking soda/HCl mixture until the pink color just disappears. Measure the mass of the NaOH pipets in their cup again.

Analyze

Using your experimental data, record the answers to the following questions below your data table.

1. Evaluate Write a balanced equation for the reaction between baking soda ($NaHCO_3$) and HCl.

2. Calculate Calculate the mass in grams of the baking soda.

$$(\text{Step B} - \text{Step A})$$

3. Calculate Calculate the total mmol of $1M$ HCl. *Note:* Every gram of HCl contains 1 mmol.

$$(\text{Step C} - \text{Step D}) \times 1.00 \text{ mmol/g}$$

4. Calculate Calculate the total mmol of $0.5M$ NaOH. *Note:* Every gram of NaOH contains 0.5 mmol.

$$(\text{Step F} - \text{Step G}) \times 0.500 \text{ mmol/g}$$

5. Calculate Calculate the mmol of HCl that reacted with the baking soda. *Note:* The NaOH measures the amount of HCl that did not react.

$$(\text{Step 3} - \text{Step 4})$$

6. Calculate Calculate the mass of the baking soda from the reaction data.

$$(0.084 \text{ g/mmol} \times \text{Step 5})$$

7. Calculate Calculate the percent error of the experiment.

$$\frac{(\text{Step 2} - \text{Step 6})}{\text{Step 2}} \times 100\%$$

You're the Chemist

The following small-scale activities allow you to develop your own procedures and analyze the results.

1. Analyze Data For each calculation you did, substitute each quantity (number and unit) into the equation and cancel the units to explain why each step gives the quantity desired.

2. Design an Experiment Baking powder consists of a mixture of baking soda, sodium hydrogen carbonate, and a solid acid, usually calcium dihydrogen phosphate ($Ca(H_2PO_4)_2$). Design and carry out an experiment to determine the percentage of baking soda in baking powder.

12.3 Limiting Reagent and Percent Yield

CHEMISTRY & YOU

Q: *What determines how much product you can make?* If a carpenter had two tabletops and seven table legs, he would have difficulty building more than one functional four-legged table. The first table would require four of the legs, leaving just three legs for the second table. In this case, the number of table legs is limiting the construction of four-legged tables. In this lesson you will learn how the amount of product is limited in a chemical reaction.

Key Questions

🔑 How is the amount of product in a reaction affected by an insufficient quantity of any of the reactants?

🔑 What does the percent yield of a reaction measure?

Vocabulary

• limiting reagent
• excess reagent
• theoretical yield
• actual yield
• percent yield

Limiting and Excess Reagents

🔑 **How is the amount of product in a reaction affected by an insufficient quantity of any of the reactants?**

Many cooks follow a recipe when making a new dish. They know that sufficient quantities of all the ingredients must be available in order to follow the recipe. Suppose, for example, that you are preparing to make tacos like the ones in Figure 12.6. You would have more than enough meat, cheese, lettuce, tomatoes, sour cream, salsa, and seasoning on hand. However, you have only two taco shells. The quantity of taco shells you have will limit the number of tacos you can make. Thus, the taco shells are the limiting ingredient in this cooking venture. A chemist often faces a similar situation. 🔑 **In a chemical reaction, an insufficient quantity of any of the reactants will limit the amount of product that forms.**

Figure 12.6 Limiting Ingredients
The amount of product is determined by the quantity of the limiting reagent. In this example, the taco shells are the limiting reagent. No matter how much of the other ingredients you have, with two taco shells you can make only two tacos.

Chemical Equations

	$N_2(g)$	$+$ $3H_2(g)$	$\longrightarrow$	$2NH_3(g)$
Microscopic recipe:	1 molecule N_2	$+$ 3 molecules H_2	$\longrightarrow$	2 molecules NH_3
Macroscopic recipe:	1 mol N_2	$+$ 3 mol H_2	$\longrightarrow$	2 mol NH_3

Figure 12.7 Limiting Reagent
The "recipe" calls for three molecules of H_2 for every one molecule of N_2.

Experimental Conditions

	Reactants		Products
Before reaction	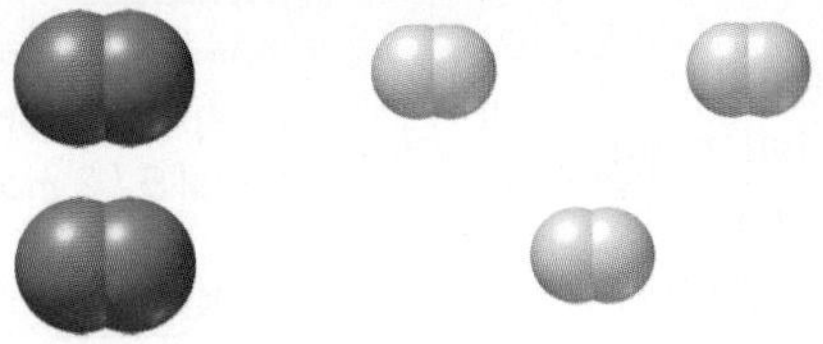 2 molecules N_2	3 molecules H_2	0 molecules NH_3
After reaction	 1 molecule N_2	0 molecules H_2	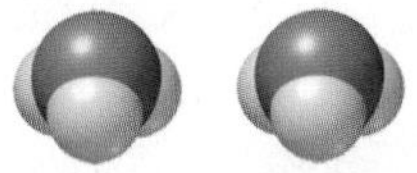 2 molecules NH_3

In this particular experiment, H_2 is the limiting reagent and N_2 is in excess.
Infer How would the amount of products formed change if you started with four molecules of N_2 and three molecules of H_2?

As you know, a balanced chemical equation is a chemist's recipe. You can interpret the recipe on a microscopic scale (interacting particles) or on a macroscopic scale (interacting moles). The coefficients used to write the balanced equation give both the ratio of representative particles and the mole ratio. Recall the equation for the preparation of ammonia:

$$N_2(g) + 3H_2(g) \longrightarrow 2NH_3(g)$$

When one molecule (mole) of N_2 reacts with three molecules (moles) of H_2, two molecules (moles) of NH_3 are produced. What would happen if two molecules (moles) of N_2 reacted with three molecules (moles) of H_2? Would more than two molecules (moles) of NH_3 be formed? Figure 12.7 shows both the particle and the mole interpretations of this problem.

Before the reaction takes place, nitrogen and hydrogen are present in a 2:3 molecule (mole) ratio. The reaction takes place according to the balanced equation. One molecule (mole) of N_2 reacts with three molecules (moles) of H_2 to produce two molecules (moles) of NH_3. At this point, all the hydrogen has been used up, and the reaction stops. One molecule (mole) of unreacted nitrogen is left in addition to the two molecules (moles) of NH_3 that have been produced by the reaction.

In this reaction, only the hydrogen is completely used up. This reactant is the **limiting reagent,** or the reactant that determines the amount of product that can be formed by a reaction. The reaction occurs only until the limiting reagent is used up. By contrast, the reactant that is not completely used up in a reaction is called the **excess reagent.** In this example, nitrogen is the excess reagent because some nitrogen remains unreacted.

Sometimes in stoichiometric problems, the given quantities of reactants are expressed in units other than moles. In such cases, the first step in the solution is to convert the quantity of each reactant to moles. Then the limiting reagent can be identified. The amount of product formed in a reaction can be determined from the given amount of limiting reagent.

See limiting reagents animated online.

Q: *What determines how much product you can make in a chemical reaction?*

SampleProblem 12.8

Determining the Limiting Reagent in a Reaction

Copper reacts with sulfur to form copper(I) sulfide according to the following balanced equation:

$$2Cu(s) + S(s) \longrightarrow Cu_2S(s)$$

What is the limiting reagent when 80.0 g Cu reacts with 25.0 g S?

❶ Analyze **List the knowns and the unknown.** The number of moles of each reactant must first be found. The balanced equation is used to calculate the number of moles of one reactant needed to react with the given amount of the other reactant.

KNOWNS

mass of copper = 80.0 g Cu
mass of sulfur = 25.0 g S
1 mol S / 2 mol Cu

UNKNOWN

limiting reagent = ?

❷ Calculate **Solve for the unknown.**

Start with one of the reactants and convert from mass to moles.

$$80.0 \, g \, Cu \times \frac{1 \, mol \, Cu}{63.5 \, g \, Cu} = 1.26 \, mol \, Cu$$

Then, convert the mass of the other reactant to moles.

$$25.0 \, g \, S \times \frac{1 \, mol \, S}{32.1 \, g \, S} = 0.779 \, mol \, S$$

Now convert moles of Cu to moles of S needed to react with 1.26 moles of Cu.

$$1.26 \, mol \, Cu \times \frac{1 \, mol \, S}{2 \, mol \, Cu} = 0.630 \, mol \, S$$

Given quantity   Mole ratio   Needed amount

It doesn't matter which reactant you use. If you used the actual number of moles of S to find the amount of copper needed, then you would still identify copper as the limiting reagent.

Compare the amount of sulfur needed with the given amount of sulfur.

0.630 mol S (amount needed to react) < 0.779 mol S (given amount)
Sulfur is in excess, so copper is the limiting reagent.

❸ Evaluate **Do the results make sense?** Since the ratio of the given mol Cu to mol S was less than the ratio (2:1) from the balanced equation, copper should be the limiting reagent.

---

26. The equation for the complete combustion of ethene (C_2H_4) is

$$C_2H_4(g) + 3O_2(g) \longrightarrow 2CO_2(g) + 2H_2O(g)$$

If 2.70 mol C_2H_4 reacts with 6.30 mol O_2, identify the limiting reagent.

27. Hydrogen gas can be produced by the reaction of magnesium metal with hydrochloric acid.

$$Mg(s) + 2HCl(aq) \longrightarrow MgCl_2(aq) + H_2(g)$$

Identify the limiting reagent when 6.00 g HCl reacts with 5.00 g Mg.

In Sample Problem 12.8, you may have noticed that even though the mass of copper used in the reaction is greater than the mass of sulfur, copper is the limiting reagent. The reactant that is present in the smaller amount by mass or volume is not necessarily the limiting reagent.

SampleProblem 12.9

Using a Limiting Reagent to Find the Quantity of a Product

What is the maximum number of grams of Cu_2S that can be formed when 80.0 g Cu reacts with 25.0 g S?

$$2Cu(s) + S(s) \longrightarrow Cu_2S(s)$$

❶ Analyze List the knowns and the unknown. The limiting reagent, which was determined in Sample Problem 12.8, is used to calculate the maximum amount of Cu_2S formed.

$$\text{mol Cu} \longrightarrow \text{mol } Cu_2S \longrightarrow \text{g } Cu_2S$$

KNOWNS

limiting reagent = 1.26 mol Cu (from sample problem 12.8)
1 mol Cu_2S = 159.1 g Cu_2S (molar mass)
1 mol Cu_2S / 2 mol Cu (from balanced equation)

UNKNOWN

yield = ? g Cu_2S

❷ Calculate Solve for the unknown.

Start with the moles of the limiting reagent and convert to moles of the product. Use the mole ratio from the balanced equation.

$$1.26 \,\cancel{\text{mol Cu}} \times \frac{1 \text{ mol } Cu_2S}{2 \,\cancel{\text{mol Cu}}}$$

Finish the calculation by converting from moles to mass of product.

$$1.26 \,\cancel{\text{mol Cu}} \times \frac{1 \,\cancel{\text{mol } Cu_2S}}{2 \,\cancel{\text{mol Cu}}} \times \frac{159.1 \text{ g } Cu_2S}{1 \,\cancel{\text{mol } Cu_2S}} = 1.00 \times 10^2 \text{ g } Cu_2S$$

❸ Evaluate Do the results make sense? Copper is the limiting reagent in this reaction. The maximum number of grams of Cu_2S produced should be more than the amount of copper that initially reacted because copper is combining with sulfur. However, the mass of Cu_2S produced should be less than the total mass of the reactants (105.0 g) because sulfur was in excess.

---

28. The equation below shows the incomplete combustion of ethene.

$$C_2H_4(g) + 2O_2(g) \longrightarrow 2CO(g) + 2H_2O(g)$$

If 2.70 mol C_2H_4 is reacted with 6.30 mol O_2,
a. identify the limiting reagent.
b. calculate the moles of water produced.

29. The heat from an acetylene torch is produced by burning acetylene (C_2H_2) in oxygen.

$$2C_2H_2(g) + 5O_2(g) \longrightarrow 4CO_2(g) + 2H_2O(g)$$

How many grams of water can be produced by the reaction of 2.40 mol C_2H_2 with 7.40 mol O_2?

Quick Lab

Purpose To illustrate the concept of a limiting reagent in a chemical reaction

Materials

- graduated cylinder
- balance
- 3 250-mL Erlenmeyer flasks
- 3 rubber balloons
- 4.2 g magnesium ribbon
- 300 mL 1.0*M* hydrochloric acid

Limiting Reagents

Procedure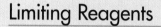

1. Add 100 mL of the hydrochloric acid solution to each flask.

2. Weigh out 0.6 g, 1.2 g, and 2.4 g of magnesium ribbon, and place each sample into its own balloon.

3. Stretch the end of each balloon over the mouth of each flask. Do not allow the magnesium ribbon in the balloon to fall into the flask.

4. Magnesium reacts with hydrochloric acid to form hydrogen gas. When you mix the magnesium with the hydrochloric acid in the next step, you will generate a certain volume of hydrogen gas. How do you think the volume of hydrogen produced in each flask will compare?

5. Lift up on each balloon and shake the magnesium into each flask. Observe the volume of gas produced until the reaction in each flask is completed. Record your observations.

Analyze and Conclude

1. Analyze Data How did the volumes of hydrogen gas produced, as measured by the size of the balloons, compare? Did the results agree with your prediction?

2. Apply Concepts Write a balanced equation for the reaction you observed.

3. Calculate The 100 mL of hydrochloric acid contained 0.10 mol HCl. Show by calculation why the balloon with 1.2 g Mg inflated to about twice the size of the balloon with 0.60 g Mg.

4. Calculate Show by calculation why the balloons with 1.2 g and 2.4 g Mg inflated to approximately the same volume. What was the limiting reagent when 2.4 g Mg was added to the acid?

Percent Yield

⬭ What does the percent yield of a reaction measure?

When a teacher gives an exam to the class, every student could get a grade of 100 percent. However, this outcome generally does not occur. Instead, the performance of the class is usually spread over a range of grades. Your exam grade, expressed as a percentage, is a ratio of two items. The first item is the number of questions you answered correctly. The second is the total number of questions. The grade compares how well you performed with how well you could have performed if you had answered all the questions correctly. Chemists perform similar calculations in the laboratory when the product from a chemical reaction is less than expected, based on the balanced chemical equation.

Figure 12.8 Batting Average
A batting average is actually a percent yield. A batting average is calculated by dividing the number of hits a batter has had (actual yield) by the number of at-bats (theoretical yield).

When a balanced chemical equation is used to calculate the amount of product that will form during a reaction, the calculated value represents the theoretical yield. The **theoretical yield** is the maximum amount of product that could be formed from given amounts of reactants. In contrast, the amount of product that actually forms when the reaction is carried out in the laboratory is called the **actual yield**. The **percent yield** is the ratio of the actual yield to the theoretical yield expressed as a percent.

$$\text{Percent yield} = \frac{\text{actual yield}}{\text{theoretical yield}} \times 100\%$$

Because the actual yield of a chemical reaction is often less than the theoretical yield, the percent yield is often less than 100 percent. 🔑 **The percent yield is a measure of the efficiency of a reaction carried out in the laboratory.** This yield is similar to an exam score measuring your efficiency of learning or a batting average measuring your efficiency of hitting a baseball, as in Figure 12.8.

Stoichiometry and conservation of mass dictate that yields of greater than 100 percent are not possible. However, errors and lack of knowledge in a process can cause a reaction to apear to have a yield that is more than 100 percent. For example, if air or water leaks into a system, then more product may be formed than expected.

Many factors can cause percent yields to be less than 100 percent. Reactions do not always go to completion; when a reaction is incomplete, less than the calculated amount of product is formed. Impure reactants and competing side reactions may cause unwanted products to form. Actual yield can also be lower than the theoretical yield due to a loss of product during filtration or in transferring between containers. Moreover, if reactants or products have not been carefully measured, a percent yield of 100 percent is unlikely.

An actual yield is an experimental value. Figure 12.9 shows a typical laboratory procedure for determining the actual yield of a product of a decomposition reaction. For reactions in which percent yields have been determined, you can calculate and, therefore, predict an actual yield if the reaction conditions remain the same.

Figure 12.9 Determining Percent Yield
Sodium hydrogen carbonate ($NaHCO_3$) will decompose when heated. **a.** The mass of $NaHCO_3$, the reactant, is measured. **b.** The reactant is heated. **c.** The mass of one of the products, sodium carbonate (Na_2CO_3), the actual yield, is measured. The percent yield is calculated once the actual yield is determined.
Predict *What are the other products of this reaction?*

SampleProblem 12.10

Calculating the Theoretical Yield of a Reaction

Calcium carbonate, which is found in seashells, is decomposed by heating. The balanced equation for this reaction is

$$CaCO_3(s) \xrightarrow{\Delta} CaO(s) + CO_2(g)$$

What is the theoretical yield of CaO if 24.8 g $CaCO_3$ is heated?

① Analyze List the knowns and the unknown. Calculate the theoretical yield using the mass of the reactant:

g $CaCO_3 \longrightarrow$ mol $CaCO_3 \longrightarrow$ mol CaO $\longrightarrow$ g CaO

> **KNOWNS**
>
> mass of calcium carbonate = 24.8 g $CaCO_3$
> 1 mol $CaCO_3$ = 1 mol CaO
>
> **UNKNOWN**
>
> theoretical yield = ? g CaO

② Calculate Solve for the unknown.

> **Start with the mass of the reactant and convert to moles of the reactant.**

$$24.8 \text{ g } CaCO_3 \times \frac{1 \text{ mol } CaCO_3}{100.1 \text{ g } CaCO_3}$$

> **Next, convert to moles of the product using the mole ratio.**

$$24.8 \text{ g } CaCO_3 \times \frac{1 \text{ mol } CaCO_3}{100.1 \text{ g } CaCO_3} \times \frac{1 \text{ mol CaO}}{1 \text{ mol } CaCO_3}$$

> **Finish by converting from moles to mass of the product.**

$$24.8 \text{ g } CaCO_3 \times \frac{1 \text{ mol } CaCO_3}{100.1 \text{ g } CaCO_3} \times \frac{1 \text{ mol CaO}}{1 \text{ mol } CaCO_3} \times \frac{56.1 \text{ g CaO}}{1 \text{ mol CaO}}$$

$$= 13.9 \text{ g CaO}$$

③ Evaluate Does the result make sense? The mole ratio of CaO to $CaCO_3$ is 1:1. The ratio of their masses in the reaction should be the same as the ratio of their molar masses, which is slightly greater than 1:2. The result of the calculations shows that the mass of CaO is slightly greater than half the mass of $CaCO_3$.

30. When 84.8 g of iron(III) oxide reacts with an excess of carbon monoxide, iron is produced.

$$Fe_2O_3(s) + 3CO(g) \longrightarrow 2Fe(s) + 3CO_2(g)$$

What is the theoretical yield of iron?

> If there is an excess of a reactant, then there is more than enough of that reactant and it will not limit the yield of the reaction.

31. When 5.00 g of copper reacts with excess silver nitrate, silver metal and copper(II) nitrate are produced. What is the theoretical yield of silver in this reaction?

Success Stats

You may not use the term "percent yield" outside of chemistry class, but there are many examples of percent yield in our lives. In chemical reactions, percent yield refers to the amount of product formed in a reaction compared to how much product was possible. In school, percent yield could refer to the graduation rate or a score on a test. In sports, percent yield could refer to the percent of shots that make it into a goal. The actual performance of a product compared to its advertised performance is also an example of percent yield.

Whether it's in the chemistry lab or anywhere else, percent yield is a way to measure how successfully something or someone has performed. The next time you calculate the percent yield of a chemical reaction, think about how this skill could be used in other situations outside of chemistry class.

85 PERCENT PERFORMANCE

Actual Yield: 153 minutes during which a drink stayed hot in thermos

Theoretical Yield: 180 minutes, as advertised by the thermos manufacturer

Take It Further

1. Calculate Sara's car is advertised to get 43 miles per gallon. Sara calculated her gas mileage over the last month and found that it was 39 miles per gallon. What is the percent yield of Sara's gas mileage.

2. Identify The percent yield of a reaction may be different each time the reaction occurs. Similarly, the performance of an athlete may vary. What are some factors that might affect percent yield?

38 PERCENT SHOT-CONVERSION RATE

Actual Yield: 8 goals scored

Theoretical Yield: 21 shots on goal

95 PERCENT GRADUATION RATE

Actual Yield: 305 students graduating

Theoretical Yield: 321 students in the senior class

SampleProblem 12.11

Calculating the Percent Yield of a Reaction

What is the percent yield if 13.1 g CaO is actually produced when 24.8 g $CaCO_3$ is heated?

$$CaCO_3(s) \xrightarrow{\Delta} CaO(s) + CO_2(g)$$

❶ Analyze **List the knowns and the unknown.** Use the equation for percent yield. The theoretical yield for this problem was calculated in Sample Problem 12.10.

KNOWNS
actual yield = 13.1 g CaO
theoretical yield = 13.9 g CaO (from Sample Problem 12.10)

UNKNOWN
percent yield = ? %

❷ Calculate **Solve for the unknown.**

$$percent\ yield = \frac{actual\ yield}{theoretical\ yield} \times 100\%$$

Substitute the values for actual yield and theoretical yield into the equation for percent yield.

$$percent\ yield = \frac{13.1\ \cancel{g\ CaO}}{13.9\ \cancel{g\ CaO}} \times 100\% = 94.2\%$$

❸ Evaluate **Does the result make sense?** In this example, the actual yield is slightly less than the theoretical yield. Therefore, the percent yield should be slightly less than 100 percent.

32. If 50.0 g of silicon dioxide is heated with an excess of carbon, 27.9 g of silicon carbide is produced.

$$SiO_2(s) + 3C(s) \xrightarrow{\Delta} SiC(s) + 2CO(g)$$

What is the percent yield of this reaction?

33. If 15.0 g of nitrogen reacts with 15.0 g of hydrogen, 10.5 g of ammonia is produced. What is the percent yield of this reaction?

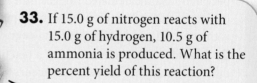

Calculate the theoretical yield first. Then you can calculate the percent yield.

12.3 LessonCheck

34. Relate Cause and Effect In a chemical reaction, how does an insufficient quantity of a reactant affect the amount of product formed?

35. Explain How can you gauge the efficiency of a reaction carried out in the laboratory?

36. Define What is a limiting reagent? An excess reagent?

37. Calculate How many grams of SO_3 are produced when 20.0 g FeS_2 reacts with 16.0 g O_2 according to this balanced equation?

$$4FeS_2(s) + 15O_2(g) \longrightarrow 2Fe_2O_3(s) + 8SO_3(g)$$

38. Calculate What is the percent yield if 4.65 g of copper is produced when 1.87 g of aluminum reacts with an excess of copper(II) sulfate?

$$2Al(s) + 3CuSO_4(aq) \longrightarrow Al_2(SO_4)_3(aq) + 3Cu(s)$$

12 Study Guide

BIGIDEAS
- THE MOLE AND QUANTIFYING MATTER
- REACTIONS

Balanced chemical equations are the basis for stoichiometric calculations. The coefficients of a balanced equation indicate the number of particles, moles, or volumes of gas in the reaction. Mole ratios from the balanced equation are used to calculate the amount of a reactant or product in a chemical reaction from a given amount of one of the reactants or products.

12.1 The Arithmetic of Equations

🔑 Chemists use balanced chemical equations as a basis to calculate how much reactant is needed or product is formed in a reaction.

🔑 A balanced chemical equation can be interpreted in terms of different quantities, including numbers of atoms, molecules, or moles; mass; and volume.

- stoichiometry (386)

12.2 Chemical Calculations

🔑 In chemical calculations, mole ratios are used to convert between a given number of moles of a reactant or product to moles of a different reactant or product.

🔑 In a typical stoichiometric problem, the given quantity is first converted to moles. Then, the mole ratio from the balanced equation is used to calculate the moles of the wanted substance. Finally, the moles are converted to any other unit of measurement related to the unit mole.

- mole ratio (390)

> ### Key Equation
>
> mole-mole relationship for $aG \rightarrow bW$:
>
> $$x \text{ mol } G \times \frac{b \text{ mol } W}{a \text{ mol } G} = \frac{xb}{a} \text{ mol } W$$

12.3 Limiting Reagent and Percent Yield

🔑 In a chemical reaction, an insufficient quantity of any of the reactants will limit the amount of product that forms.

🔑 The percent yield is a measure of the efficiency of a reaction performed in the laboratory.

- limiting reagent (401)
- excess reagent (401)
- theoretical yield (405)
- actual yield (405)
- percent yield (405)

> ### Key Equation
>
> $$\text{percent yield} = \frac{\text{actual yield}}{\text{theoretical yield}} \times 100\%$$

Math Tune-Up: Stoichiometry Problems

Problem

Iron metal (Fe) can be obtained from iron ore, Fe_2O_3.

$$Fe_2O_3(s) + 3CO(g) \longrightarrow 2Fe(s) + 3CO_2(g)$$

How much iron ore is needed to obtain 92.8 grams of iron metal?

Sodium hydroxide reacts with carbon dioxide according to the balanced equation below.

$$2NaOH(s) + CO_2(g) \longrightarrow Na_2CO_3(s) + H_2O(l)$$

What is the limiting reagent when 3.50 mol NaOH reacts with 2.00 mol CO_2?

❶ Analyze

Knowns:
mass of iron = 92.8 g Fe
1 mol Fe_2O_3 / 2 mol Fe (from balanced equation)
1 mol Fe = 55.8 g Fe (molar mass)
1 mol Fe_2O_3 = 159.6 g Fe_2O_3 (molar mass)

Unknown:
Mass of iron ore = ? g Fe_2O_3

Knowns:
moles of NaOH = 3.50 mol NaOH
moles of CO_2 = 2.00 mol CO_2

Unknown:
limiting reagent = ?

❷ Calculate

Perform the following steps:
g Fe ⟶ mol Fe ⟶ mol Fe_2O_3 ⟶ g Fe_2O_3

$$92.8 \text{ g Fe} \times \frac{1 \text{ mol Fe}}{55.8 \text{ g Fe}} \times \frac{1 \text{ mol Fe}_2O_3}{2 \text{ mol Fe}} \times \frac{159.6 \text{ g} \; 1 \text{ mol Fe}_2O_3}{1 \text{ mol Fe}_2O_3}$$

$$= \boxed{133.0 \text{ g Fe}_2O_3}$$

Hint: Review Sample Problem 12.4 if you have trouble with calculating the mass of a reactant.

Determine how many moles of CO_2 are needed to react with 3.50 mol NaOH.

$$3.50 \text{ mol NaOH} \times \frac{1 \text{ mol CO}_2}{2 \text{ mol NaOH}}$$

$$= \boxed{1.75 \text{ mol CO}_2}$$

Only 1.75 mol CO_2 are needed to react with 3.50 mol NaOH. Since there are 2.00 mol CO_2, there is excess CO_2. Therefore, NaOH is the limiting reagent.

❸ Evaluate

Since the molar mass of the iron ore is more than twice the molar mass of iron metal, it makes sense that the mass of the iron ore would be greater than the mass of the iron metal produced.

To check your work, you could start with the given amount of moles of CO_2 and solve for how many moles of NaOH are needed.

Hint: Review Sample Problem 12.8 if you have trouble identifying the limiting reagent.

Lesson by Lesson

12.1 The Arithmetic of Equations

39. Interpret each chemical equation in terms of interacting particles.

a. $2KClO_3(s) \longrightarrow 2KCl(s) + 3O_2(g)$
b. $4NH_3(g) + 6NO(g) \longrightarrow 5N_2(g) + 6H_2O(g)$
c. $4K(s) + O_2(g) \longrightarrow 2K_2O(s)$

40. Interpret each equation in Problem 39 in terms of interacting numbers of moles of reactants and products.

41. Calculate and compare the mass of the reactants with the mass of the products for each equation in Problem 39. Show that each balanced equation obeys the law of conservation of mass.

42. Balance the following equation:

$$C_5H_{12}(g) + O_2(g) \longrightarrow CO_2(g) + H_2O(g)$$

Interpret the balanced equation in terms of relative number of moles, volumes of gas at STP, and masses of reactants and products.

12.2 Chemical Calculations

43. Explain the term *mole ratio* in your own words. When would you use this term?

44. What ratio is used to carry out each conversion?

a. mol CH_4 to g CH_4
b. L $CH_4(g)$ to mol $CH_4(g)$ (at STP)
c. molecules CH_4 to mol CH_4

*45. Carbon disulfide is an important industrial solvent. It is prepared by the reaction of coke with sulfur dioxide.

$$5C(s) + 2SO_2(g) \longrightarrow CS_2(l) + 4CO(g)$$

a. How many moles of CS_2 form when 2.7 mol C reacts?
b. How many moles of carbon are needed to react with 5.44 mol SO_2?
c. How many moles of carbon monoxide form at the same time that 0.246 mol CS_2 forms?
d. How many mol SO_2 are required to make 118 mol CS_2?

*46. Methanol (CH_3OH) is used in the production of many chemicals. Methanol is made by reacting carbon monoxide and hydrogen at high temperature and pressure.

$$CO(g) + 2H_2(g) \longrightarrow CH_3OH(g)$$

a. How many moles of each reactant are needed to produce 3.60×10^2 g CH_3OH?
b. Calculate the number of grams of each reactant needed to produce 4.00 mol CH_3OH.
c. How many grams of hydrogen are necessary to react with 2.85 mol CO?

47. The reaction of fluorine with ammonia produces dinitrogen tetrafluoride and hydrogen fluoride.

$$5F_2(g) + 2NH_3(g) \longrightarrow N_2F_4(g) + 6HF(g)$$

a. If you have 66.6 g NH_3, how many grams of F_2 are required for a complete reaction?
b. How many grams of NH_3 are required to produce 4.65 g HF?
c. How many grams of N_2F_4 can be produced from 225 g F_2?

48. What information about a chemical reaction is derived from the coefficients in a balanced equation?

49. Rust is produced when iron reacts with oxygen.

$$4Fe(s) + 3O_2(g) \longrightarrow 2Fe_2O_3(s)$$

How many grams of Fe_2O_3 are produced when 12.0 g of iron rusts?

*50. Lithium nitride reacts with water to form ammonia and aqueous lithium hydroxide.

$$Li_3N(s) + 3H_2O(l) \longrightarrow NH_3(g) + 3LiOH(aq)$$

a. What mass of water is needed to react with 32.9 g Li_3N?
b. When the above reaction takes place, how many molecules of NH_3 are produced?
c. Calculate the number of grams of Li_3N that must be added to an excess of water to produce 15.0 L NH_3 (at STP).

12.3 Limiting Reagent and Percent Yield

51. What is the significance of the limiting reagent in a reaction? What happens to the amount of any reagent that is present in an excess?

52. How would you identify a limiting reagent in a chemical reaction?

*53. In a reaction chamber, 3.0 mol of aluminum is mixed with 5.3 mol Cl_2 and reacts. The following balanced chemical equation describes the reaction:

$$2Al(s) + 3Cl_2(g) \longrightarrow 2AlCl_3(s)$$

   a. Identify the limiting reagent for the reaction.
   b. Calculate the number of moles of product formed.
   c. Calculate the number of moles of excess reagent remaining after the reaction.

*54. Heating an ore of antimony (Sb_2S_3) in the presence of iron gives the element antimony and iron(II) sulfide.

$$Sb_2S_3(s) + 3Fe(s) \longrightarrow 2Sb(s) + 3FeS(s)$$

   When 15.0 g Sb_2S_3 reacts with an excess of Fe, 9.84 g Sb is produced. What is the percent yield of this reaction?

55. Phosphoric acid reacts with sodium hydroxide according to the equation:

$$H_3PO_4(aq) + 3NaOH(aq) \longrightarrow$$
$$Na_3PO_4(aq) + 3H_2O(l)$$

   If 1.75 mol H_3PO_4 is made to react with 5.00 mol NaOH, identify the limiting reagent.

Understand Concepts

56. Calcium carbonate reacts with phosphoric acid to produce calcium phosphate, carbon dioxide, and water.

$$3CaCO_3(s) + 2H_3PO_4(aq) \longrightarrow$$
$$Ca_3(PO_4)_2(aq) + 3CO_2(g) + 3H_2O(l)$$

   a. How many grams of phosphoric acid react with excess calcium carbonate to produce 3.74 g $Ca_3(PO_4)_2$?
   b. Calculate the number of grams of CO_2 formed when 0.773 g H_2O is produced.

*57. Nitric acid and zinc react to form zinc nitrate, ammonium nitrate, and water.

$$4Zn(s) + 10HNO_3(aq) \longrightarrow$$
$$4Zn(NO_3)_2(aq) + NH_4NO_3(aq) + 3H_2O(l)$$

   a. How many atoms of zinc react with 1.49 g HNO_3?
   b. Calculate the number of grams of zinc that must react with an excess of HNO_3 to form 29.1 g NH_4NO_3.

58. If 75.0 g of silderite ore ($FeCO_3$) is heated with an excess of oxygen, 45.0 g of ferric oxide (Fe_2O_3) is produced.

$$4FeCO_3(s) + O_2(g) \longrightarrow 2Fe_2O_3(s) + 4CO_2(g)$$

   What is the percent yield of this reaction?

59. In an experiment, varying masses of sodium metal are reacted with a fixed initial mass of chlorine gas. The following graph shows the amounts of sodium used and the amounts of sodium chloride formed.

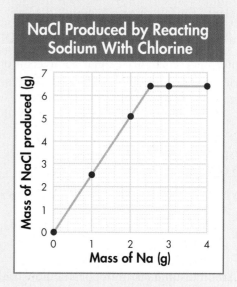

NaCl Produced by Reacting Sodium With Chlorine

   a. Explain the general shape of the graph.
   b. Estimate the amount of chlorine gas used in this experiment at the point where the curve becomes horizontal.

*60. Hydrazine (N_2H_4) is used as rocket fuel. It reacts with oxygen to form nitrogen and water.

$$N_2H_4(l) + O_2(g) \longrightarrow N_2(g) + 2H_2O(g)$$

   a. How many liters of N_2 (at STP) form when 1.0 kg N_2H_4 reacts with 1.2 kg O_2?
   b. How many grams of the excess reagent remain after the reaction?

61. When 50.0 g of silicon dioxide is heated with an excess of carbon, 32.2 g of silicon carbide is produced.

$$SiO_2(s) + 3C(s) \longrightarrow SiC(s) + 2CO(g)$$

  a. What is the percent yield of this reaction?
  b. How many grams of CO gas are made?

62. If the reaction below proceeds with a 96.8% yield, how many kilograms of $CaSO_4$ are formed when 5.24 kg SO_2 reacts with an excess of $CaCO_3$ and O_2?

$$2CaCO_3(s) + 2SO_2(g) + O_2(g) \longrightarrow$$
$$2CaSO_4(s) + 2CO_2(g)$$

63. Ammonium nitrate will decompose explosively at high temperatures to form nitrogen, oxygen, and water vapor.

$$2NH_4NO_3(s) \longrightarrow 2N_2(g) + 4H_2O(g) + O_2(g)$$

What is the total number of liters of gas formed when 228 g NH_4NO_3 is decomposed? (Assume STP.)

★64. Hydrogen gas can be made by reacting methane (CH_4) with high-temperature steam:

$$CH_4(g) + H_2O(g) \longrightarrow CO(g) + 3H_2(g)$$

How many hydrogen molecules are produced when 158 g of methane reacts with steam?

65. Suppose hydrogen gas and iodine vapor react to give gaseous hydrogen iodide.

  a. Write the balanced equation for the reaction.
  b. In the atomic window below, which reactant is the limiting reagent?
  c. How many molecules of the reagent in excess remain at the completion of the reaction?
  d. How many molecules of the limiting reagent need to be added to the atomic window so that all the reactants will react to form products?

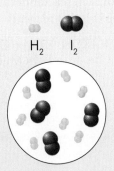

66. The following reaction occurs when an automobile battery is charged.

$$PbSO_4(s) + H_2O(l) \longrightarrow$$
$$PbO_2(s) + Pb(s) + H_2SO_4(aq)$$

  a. Balance the equation.
  b. How many grams of sulfuric acid are produced when 68.1 g of lead(II) sulfate react?

★67. Liquid sulfur difluoride reacts with fluorine gas to form gaseous sulfur hexafluoride.

  a. Write the balanced equation for the reaction.
  b. How many fluorine molecules are required to react with 5.00 mg of sulfur difluoride?
  c. What volume of fluorine gas at STP is required to react completely with 6.66 g of sulfur difluoride?

68. Ammonia (NH_3) reacts with oxygen (O_2) to produce nitrogen monoxide (NO) and water.

$$4NH_3(g) + 5O_2(g) \longrightarrow 4NO(g) + 6H_2O(l)$$

How many liters of NO are produced when 1.40 L of oxygen reacts with ammonia?

★69. The manufacture of compound F requires five separate chemical reactions. The initial reactant, compound A, is converted to compound B, compound B is converted to compound C, and so on. The diagram below summarizes the steps in the manufacture of compound F, including the percent yield for each step. Provide the missing quantities or missing percent yields. Assume that the reactant and product in each step react in a one-to-one mole ratio.

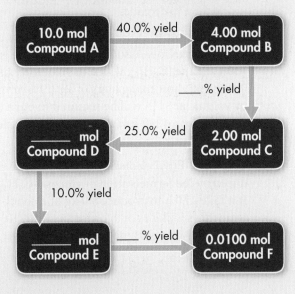

70. **Evaluate** Given a certain quantity of reactant, you calculate that a particular reaction should produce 55 g of a product. When you perform the reaction, you find that you have produced 63 g of product. What is your percent yield? What could have caused a percent yield greater than 100 percent?

71. **Explain** Would the law of conservation of mass hold in a net ionic equation? Explain.

★72. **Calculate** The element phosphorus is manufactured from a mixture of phosphate rock ($Ca_3(PO_4)_2$), sand (SiO_2), and coke (C) in an electric furnace. The chemistry is complex but is summarized by these two equations.

$$Ca_3(PO_4)_2 + SiO_2 \longrightarrow P_4O_{10} + CaSiO_3$$

$$P_4O_{10} + C \longrightarrow P_4 + CO$$

An excess of coke is reacted with 5.5×10^5 g of calcium phosphate and 2.3×10^5 g of sand.

a. Balance each of the equations.
b. What is the limiting reagent?
c. How many grams of phosphorus are produced?
d. How many grams of carbon are consumed?

73. **Calculate** Sulfuric acid reacts with calcium hydroxide to form calcium sulfate and water.

a. Write the balanced equation for the reaction.
b. Find the mass of unreacted starting material when 75.0 g sulfuric acid reacts with 55.0 g calcium hydroxide.

74. **Apply Concepts** A car gets 9.2 kilometers to a liter of gasoline. Assuming that gasoline is 100% octane (C_8H_{18}), which has a density of 0.69 g/cm^3, how many liters of air (21% oxygen by volume at STP) will be required to burn the gasoline for a 1250-km trip? Assume complete combustion.

★75. **Calculate** Ethyl alcohol (C_2H_5OH) can be produced by the fermentation of glucose ($C_6H_{12}O_6$). If it takes 5.0 h to produce 8.0 kg of alcohol, how many days will it take to consume 1.0×10^3 kg of glucose? (An enzyme is used as a catalyst.)

$$C_6H_{12}O_6 \xrightarrow{\text{enzyme}} 2C_2H_5OH + 2CO_2$$

76. **Calculate** A bicycle built for three has a frame, two wheels, six pedals, and three seats. The balanced equation for this bicycle is

$$F + 2W + 6P + 3S \longrightarrow FW_2P_6S_3$$

How many of each part are needed to make 29 bicycles built for three?

a. frames
b. wheels
c. pedals
d. seats

77. **Calculate** A 1004.0-g sample of $CaCO_3$ that is 95.0% pure gives 225 L CO_2 at STP when reacted with an excess of hydrochloric acid.

$$CaCO_3 + 2HCl \longrightarrow CaCl_2 + CO_2 + H_2O$$

What is the density (in g/L) of the CO_2?

★78. **Calculate** The white limestone cliffs of Dover, England, contain a large percentage of calcium carbonate ($CaCO_3$). A sample of limestone with a mass of 84.4 g reacts with an excess of hydrochloric acid to form calcium chloride.

$$CaCO_3 + 2HCl \longrightarrow CaCl_2 + H_2O + CO_2$$

The mass of calcium chloride formed is 81.8 g. What is the percentage of calcium carbonate in the limestone?

79. **Calculate** For the reaction below there are 100.0 g of each reactant available. Which reactant is the limiting reagent?

$$2MnO_2 + 4KOH + O_2 + Cl_2 \longrightarrow$$
$$2KMnO_4 + 2KCl + 2H_2O$$

80. Calculate The equation for one of the reactions in the process of reducing iron ore to the metal is

$$Fe_2O_3(s) + 3\ CO(g) \longrightarrow 2\ Fe(s) + 3\ CO_2(g)$$

a. What is the maximum mass of iron, in grams, that can be obtained from 454 g (1.00 lb) of iron(III) oxide?

b. What mass of CO is required to reduce the iron(III) oxide to iron metal?

81. Calculate Esters are a class of compounds that impart a characteristic odor to some fruits. The ester pentyl acetate, composed of carbon, hydrogen, and oxygen, has the odor of bananas. When 7.44 g of this compound undergoes complete combustion, 17.6 g CO_2 and 7.21 g H_2O are produced.

a. What is the empirical formula of pentyl acetate? (*Hint:* All the carbon ends up in the CO_2; all the hydrogen ends up in the H_2O.)

b. The molar mass of pentyl acetate is 130.0 g. What is the molecular formula of this compound?

c. Write the equation for the complete combustion of pentyl acetate.

d. Check your work by using your equation from part c to calculate the grams of CO_2 and H_2O produced by the complete combustion of 7.44 g of pentyl acetate.

*82. Calculate Nitric acid, HNO_3, is produced in a complex three-step process summarized by these unbalanced equations.

Step 1: $NH_3 + O_2 \longrightarrow NO + H_2O$

Step 2: $NO + O_2 \longrightarrow NO_2$

Step 3: $NO_2 + H_2O \longrightarrow HNO_3 + NO$

Notice that the nitric oxide, NO, produced in Step 3 is recycled into Step 2.

a. Balance each of the equations.

b. Assuming all the nitrogen from the ammonia will eventually be incorporated into the nitric acid, calculate the mass of nitric acid obtained from 88.0 g NH_3.

c. The concentrated nitric acid used in the lab is a 70.0% by mass solution of HNO_3 in water. Using your answer from part b, calculate the mass of ammonia needed to prepare 1.00 kg of concentrated nitric acid.

83. Calculate SO_3 can be produced in the following two-step process:

$$FeS_2 + O_2 \longrightarrow Fe_2O_3 + SO_2$$

$$SO_2 + O_2 \longrightarrow SO_3$$

Assuming that all the FeS_2 reacts, how many grams of SO_3 are produced when 20.0 g of the FeS_2 reacts with 16.0 g of O_2?

Write About Science

84. Explain Explain this statement: "Mass and atoms are conserved in every chemical reaction, but moles are not necessarily conserved."

85. Explain Review the "mole road map" at the end of Lesson 10.2. Explain how this road map ties into the summary of steps for stoichiometric problems shown in Figure 12.5.

CHEMYSTERY

Cookie Crumbles

Jack tried to make cookies that were extra sweet by adding more sugar than was in the recipe. What Jack didn't realize is that a recipe is like a balanced chemical equation. In order to get the desired product in the reaction of cooking, the reactants, or ingredients, must be combined in specific ratios. Jack changed the amount of sugar, but he didn't change any of the other ingredients. Therefore, he changed the ratios of the ingredients. Balanced chemical equations are important in cooking and in many other fields.

86. Infer If Jack's recipe calls for 2.5 cups of flour and 2 eggs, and Jack wants to scale up the recipe by 50 percent, then how much flour and eggs will he need?

87. Connect to the BIGIDEA How does Jack's baking experience illustrate the concept of a limiting reagent?

*88. How many electrons, protons, and neutrons are in an atom of each isotope?

   a. titanium-47
   b. tin-120
   c. oxygen-18
   d. magnesium-26

89. When comparing ultraviolet and visible electromagnetic radiation, which has

   a. a higher frequency?
   b. a higher energy?
   c. a shorter wavelength?

90. Identify the larger atom of each pair.

   a. sodium and chlorine
   b. arsenic and nitrogen
   c. fluorine and cesium

91. Write electron dot formulas for the following atoms:

   a. Cs   c. Ca
   b. Br   d. P

92. Which of these elements form ions with a 2+ charge?

   a. potassium
   b. sulfur
   c. barium
   d. magnesium

93. Distinguish among single, double, and triple covalent bonds.

94. Can a compound have both ionic and covalent bonds? Explain your answer.

95. How do you distinguish between a cation and an anion?

96. Name these ions.

   a. PO_4^{3-} c. Se^{2-}
   b. Al^{3+} d. NH_4^+

97. Name each substance.

   a. SiO_2 c. H_2CO_3
   b. K_2SO_4 d. MgS

98. Write the formula for each compound.

   a. aluminum carbonate
   b. nitrogen dioxide
   c. potassium sulfide
   d. manganese(II) chromate
   e. sodium bromide

*99. How many grams of beryllium are in 147 g of the mineral beryl ($Be_3Al_2Si_6O_{18}$)?

100. What is the mass, in grams, of a molecule of benzene (C_6H_6)?

*101. What is the molecular formula of oxalic acid, molar mass 90 g/mol? Its percent composition is 26.7% C, 2.2% H, and 71.1% O.

102. How many moles is each of the following?

   a. 47.8 g KNO_3
   b. 2.22 L SO_2 (at STP)
   c. 2.25×10^{22} molecules PCl_3

103. Write a balanced chemical equation for each reaction.

   a. When heated, lead(II) nitrate decomposes to form lead(II) oxide, nitrogen dioxide, and molecular oxygen.
   b. The complete combustion of isopropyl alcohol (C_3H_7OH) produces carbon dioxide and water vapor.
   c. When a mixture of aluminum and iron(II) oxide is heated, metallic iron and aluminum oxide are produced.

104. Balance each equation.

   a. $Ba(NO_3)_2(aq) + Na_2SO_4(aq) \longrightarrow$
                  $BaSO_4(s) + NaNO_3(aq)$
   b. $AlCl_3(aq) + AgNO_3(aq) \longrightarrow$
                  $AgCl(s) + Al(NO_3)_3(aq)$
   c. $H_2SO_4(aq) + Mg(OH)_2(aq) \longrightarrow$
                  $MgSO_4(aq) + H_2O(l)$

105. Write a net ionic equation for each reaction in Problem 104.

106. Identify the spectator ions in each reaction in Problem 104.

107. Write a balanced chemical equation for the complete combustion of ribose, $C_5H_{10}O_5$.

If You Have Trouble With . . .

Question	88	89	90	91	92	93	94	95	96	97	98	99	100	101	102	103	104	105	106	107
See Chapter	4	5	6	7	7	8	8	9	9	9	9	10	10	10	10	11	11	11	11	11

Standardized Test Prep

Tips for Success

Anticipate the answer. Use what you know to predict what you think the answer should be. Then look to see if your answer, or one much like it, is given as an option.

Select the choice that best answers each question or completes each statement.

1. Nitric acid is formed by the reaction of nitrogen dioxide with water.

$$3NO_2(g) + H_2O(l) \longrightarrow NO(g) + 2HNO_3(aq)$$

How many moles of water are needed to react with 8.4 mol NO_2?

(A) 2.8 mol   (C) 8.4 mol
(B) 3.0 mol   (D) 25 mol

2. Phosphorus trifluoride is formed from its elements.

$$P_4(s) + 6F_2(g) \longrightarrow 4PF_3(g)$$

How many grams of fluorine are needed to react with 6.20 g of phosphorus?

(A) 2.85 g   (C) 11.4 g
(B) 5.70 g   (D) 37.2 g

3. Magnesium nitride is formed in the reaction of magnesium metal with nitrogen gas.

$$3Mg(s) + N_2(g) \longrightarrow Mg_3N_2(s)$$

The reaction of 4.0 mol of nitrogen with 6.0 mol of magnesium produces

(A) 2.0 mol of Mg_3N_2 and no excess N_2.
(B) 2.0 mol of Mg_3N_2 and 2.0 mol of excess N_2.
(C) 4.0 mol of Mg_3N_2 and 1.0 mol of excess Mg.
(D) 6.0 mol of Mg_3N_2 and 3.0 mol of excess N_2.

Use the reaction below to answer Questions 4 and 5.

4. Write a balanced equation for the reaction between element T and element Q.

5. Based on the atomic windows below, identify the limiting reagent.

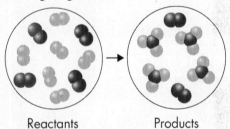

Reactants   Products

For each question, there are two statements. Decide whether each statement is true or false. Then decide whether Statement II is a correct explanation for Statement I.

	Statement I		Statement II
6.	Every stoichiometry calculation uses a balanced equation.	BECAUSE	Every chemical reaction obeys the law of conservation of mass.
7.	A percent yield is always greater than 0% and less than 100%.	BECAUSE	The actual yield in a reaction is never more than the theoretical yield.
8.	The amount of the limiting reagent left after a reaction is zero.	BECAUSE	The limiting reagent is completely used up in a reaction.
9.	The coefficients in a balanced equation represent the relative masses of the reactants and products.	BECAUSE	The mass of the reactants must equal the mass of the products in a chemical reaction.
10.	A mole ratio is always written with the larger number in the numerator.	BECAUSE	A mole ratio will always be greater than 1.

If You Have Trouble With . . .

Question	1	2	3	4	5	6	7	8	9	10
See Lesson	12.2	12.2	12.3	12.1	12.3	12.1	12.3	12.3	12.1	12.2

13

States of Matter

INSIDE:

- **13.1** The Nature of Gases
- **13.2** The Nature of Liquids
- **13.3** The Nature of Solids
- **13.4** Changes of State

PearsonChem.com

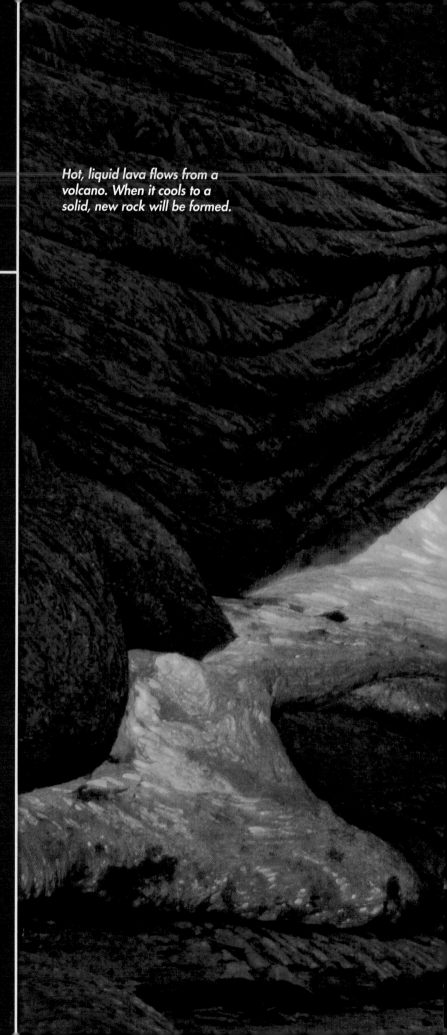

Hot, liquid lava flows from a volcano. When it cools to a solid, new rock will be formed.

BIGIDEA

KINETIC THEORY

Essential Questions:

1. *What factors determine the physical state of a substance?*

2. *What are the characteristics that distinguish gases, liquids, and solids?*

3. *How do substances change from one state to another?*

CHEMYSTERY

Foggy Car Windows

It's a cold, rainy day in September, and you and a friend are heading out to a movie. When you first get into your mom's car, you can clearly see nearby trees swaying in the wind. But shortly after your mom starts the car, the glass fogs up, making it almost impossible to see outside. Your mom sighs, and turns on the heat, which only makes the foggy windows worse. Then she turns on the air conditioner, and the fog is gone in seconds. Why do car windows fog up when it is cold or raining outside? Why does the fog go away when you turn on the air conditioner?

▶ **Connect to the BIGIDEA** As you read about states of matter, think about what might cause car windows to fog.

NATIONAL SCIENCE EDUCATION STANDARDS

A-1, A-2, B-2, B4, B-5, E-1, E-2

13.1 The Nature of Gases

Q: *What factors most strongly affect the weather?* The atmosphere is a gas, and the factors that determine the behavior of gases—temperature and pressure—affect the weather in the atmosphere. That is why weather maps show temperature readings and areas of high and low pressure. In this lesson, you will learn how temperature and pressure affect the particles of a gas.

Key Questions

What are the three assumptions of the kinetic theory as it applies to gases?

How does kinetic theory explain gas pressure?

What is the relationship between the temperature in kelvins and the average kinetic energy of particles?

Vocabulary

- kinetic energy
- kinetic theory
- gas pressure
- vacuum
- atmospheric pressure
- barometer
- pascal (Pa)
- standard atmosphere (atm)

Kinetic Theory and a Model for Gases

What are the three assumptions of the kinetic theory as it applies to gases?

The word *kinetic* refers to motion. The energy an object has because of its motion is called **kinetic energy.** According to the **kinetic theory,** all matter consists of tiny particles that are in constant motion. The particles in a gas are usually molecules or atoms. The kinetic theory as it applies to gases includes the following fundamental assumptions about gases.

The particles in a gas are considered to be small, hard spheres with an insignificant volume. Within a gas, the particles are relatively far apart compared with the distance between particles in a liquid or solid. Between the particles, there is empty space. No attractive or repulsive forces exist between the particles.

The motion of the particles in a gas is rapid, constant, and random. As a result, gases fill their containers regardless of the shape and volume of the containers. An uncontained gas can spread out into space without limit. The particles travel in straight-line paths until they collide with another particle, or another object, such as the wall of their container. The particles change direction only when they rebound from collisions with one another or with other objects.

Measurements indicate that the average speed of oxygen molecules in air at 20°C is an amazing 1700 km/h! At these high speeds, the odor from a hot cheese pizza in Washington, D.C., should reach Mexico City in about 115 minutes. That does not happen, however, because the molecules responsible for the odor are constantly striking molecules in air and rebounding in other directions. Their path of uninterrupted travel in a straight line is very short. The aimless path the molecules take is called a random walk.

All collisions between particles in a gas are perfectly elastic. During an elastic collision, kinetic energy is transferred without loss from one particle to another, and the total kinetic energy remains constant. The diagrams in Figure 13.1 illustrate the assumptions of kinetic theory as applied to gases.

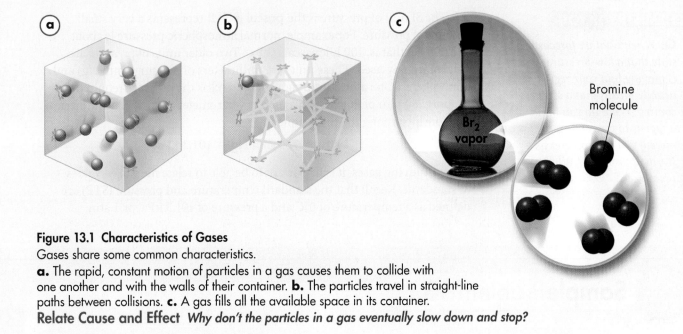

Figure 13.1 Characteristics of Gases
Gases share some common characteristics.
a. The rapid, constant motion of particles in a gas causes them to collide with one another and with the walls of their container. **b.** The particles travel in straight-line paths between collisions. **c.** A gas fills all the available space in its container.
Relate Cause and Effect *Why don't the particles in a gas eventually slow down and stop?*

Gas Pressure

⚷ How does kinetic theory explain gas pressure?

A balloon filled with helium or hot air maintains its shape because of the pressure of the gas within it. **Gas pressure** results from the force exerted by a gas per unit surface area of an object. What causes this force? Moving bodies exert a force when they collide with other bodies. Although a single particle in a gas is a moving body, the force it exerts is extremely small. Yet it is not hard to imagine that simultaneous collisions involving many particles would produce a measurable force on an object. ⚷ **Gas pressure is the result of billions of rapidly moving particles in a gas simultaneously colliding with an object.** If no particles are present, no collisions can occur. Consequently, there is no pressure. An empty space with no particles and no pressure is called a **vacuum.**

You are already familiar with a gas pressure caused by a mixture of gases—air. Air exerts pressure on Earth because gravity holds the particles in air within Earth's atmosphere. The collisions of atoms and molecules in air with objects results in **atmospheric pressure.** Atmospheric pressure decreases as you climb a mountain because the density of Earth's atmosphere decreases as the elevation increases.

A **barometer** is a device that is used to measure atmospheric pressure. Figure 13.2 shows an early type of mercury barometer. The height of the mercury column in the tube depends on the pressure exerted by particles in air colliding with the surface of the mercury in the dish. Atmospheric pressure depends on weather and on altitude. In fair weather at sea level, the atmospheric pressure is sufficient to support a mercury column 760 mm high.

Figure 13.2 Atmospheric Pressure
At sea level, air exerts enough pressure to support a 760-mm column of mercury. On top of Mount Everest, at 9000 m, the air exerts only enough pressure to support a 253-mm column of mercury.

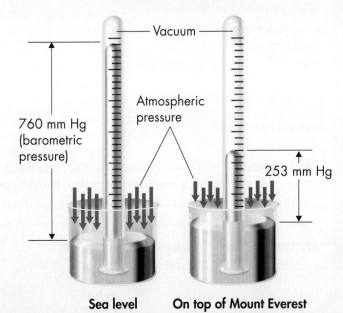

The SI unit of pressure is the **pascal (Pa).** It represents a very small amount of pressure. For example, normal atmospheric pressure is about 100,000 Pa, that is, 100 kilopascals (kPa). Two older units of pressure are still commonly used. These units are millimeters of mercury (mm Hg) and atmospheres. One **standard atmosphere (atm)** is the pressure required to support 760 mm of mercury in a mercury barometer at 25°C. The numerical relationship among the three units is

$$1 \text{ atm} = 760 \text{ mm Hg} = 101.3 \text{ kPa}$$

When studying gases, it is important to be able to relate measured values to standards. Recall that the standard temperature and pressure (STP) are defined as a temperature of 0°C and a pressure of 101.3 kPa, or 1 atm.

Sample Problem 13.1

Converting Between Units of Pressure

A pressure gauge records a pressure of 450 kPa. Convert this measurement to
a. atmospheres.   **b.** millimeters of mercury.

KNOWNS	UNKNOWNS
pressure = 450 kPa	pressure = ? atm
1 atm = 101.3 kPa	
1 atm = 760 mm Hg	pressure = ? mm Hg

❶ Analyze **List the knowns and the unknowns.** The given pressure is converted into the desired unit by multiplying by the proper conversion factor.

❷ Calculate **Solve for the unknowns.**

Identify the appropriate conversion factor to convert kPa to atm.

a. $\dfrac{1 \text{ atm}}{101.3 \text{ kPa}}$

Multiply the given pressure by the conversion factor.

$450 \text{ kPa} \times \dfrac{1 \text{ atm}}{101.3 \text{ kPa}} = 4.4 \text{ atm}$

Identify the appropriate conversion factor to convert kPa to mm Hg.

b. $\dfrac{760 \text{ mm Hg}}{101.3 \text{ kPa}}$

Multiply the given pressure by the conversion factor.

$450 \text{ kPa} \times \dfrac{760 \text{ mm Hg}}{101.3 \text{ kPa}} = 3400 \text{ mm Hg} = 3.4 \times 10^3 \text{ mm Hg}$

❸ Evaluate **Do the results make sense?** Because the first conversion factor is much less than 1 and the second is much greater than 1, it makes sense that the values expressed in atm and mm Hg are respectively smaller and larger than the value expressed in kPa.

1. What pressure, in kilopascals and in atmospheres, does a gas exert at 385 mm Hg?

2. The pressure at the top of Mount Everest is 33.7 kPa. Is that pressure greater or less than 0.25 atm?

Kinetic Energy and Temperature

🔑 *What is the relationship between the temperature in kelvins and the average kinetic energy of particles?*

As a substance is heated, its particles absorb energy, some of which is stored within the particles. This stored portion of the energy, or potential energy, does not raise the temperature of the substance. The remaining absorbed energy does speed up the particles—that is, increases their kinetic energy. This increase in kinetic energy results in an increase in temperature.

Average Kinetic Energy The particles in any collection of atoms or molecules at a given temperature have a wide range of kinetic energies. Most of the particles have kinetic energies somewhere in the middle of this range. Therefore, we use average kinetic energy when discussing the kinetic energy of a collection of particles in a substance. At any given temperature, the particles of all substances, regardless of physical state, have the same average kinetic energy. For example, the ions in table salt, the molecules in water, and the atoms in helium all have the same average kinetic energy at room temperature, even though the three substances are in different physical states.

Figure 13.3 shows the distribution of kinetic energies of water molecules at two different temperatures. The green curve shows the distribution of kinetic energy among the water molecules in cold water. The purple curve shows the distribution of kinetic energy among the water molecules in hot water. In both cases, most of the molecules have intermediate kinetic energies, which are close to the average value. Notice that molecules at the higher temperature have a wider range of kinetic energies.

The average kinetic energy of the particles in a substance is directly related to the substance's temperature. An increase in the average kinetic energy of the particles causes the temperature of a substance to rise. As a substance cools, the particles tend to move more slowly, and their average kinetic energy decreases.

READING SUPPORT

Build Vocabulary:
Word Origins Kinetic comes from the greek word *kinetos,* meaning "to move." Kinetic energy is the energy an object has because of its motion. *Some sculptures are kinetic. What characteristic do they share?*

Interpret Graphs

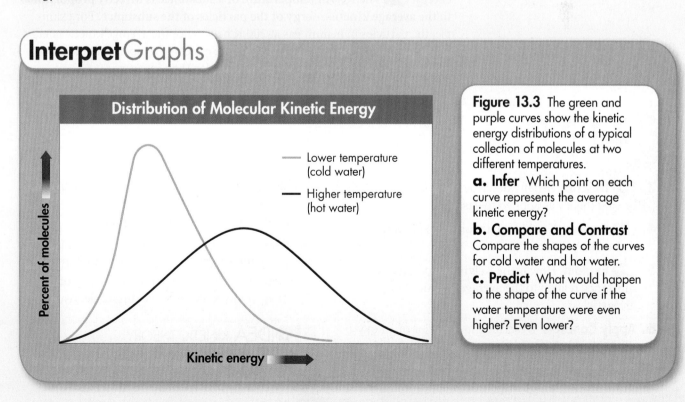

Distribution of Molecular Kinetic Energy

Lower temperature (cold water)

Higher temperature (hot water)

Percent of molecules

Kinetic energy

Figure 13.3 The green and purple curves show the kinetic energy distributions of a typical collection of molecules at two different temperatures.
a. Infer Which point on each curve represents the average kinetic energy?
b. Compare and Contrast Compare the shapes of the curves for cold water and hot water.
c. Predict What would happen to the shape of the curve if the water temperature were even higher? Even lower?

Figure 13.4
The Coldest Place in the Universe
The boomerang nebula is the coldest known region of space. A nebula is a large cloud of gas and dust spread out in an immense volume. Gases are moving rapidly away from a dying star at the center of this nebula. The rapid expansion of these gases is the reason why this nebula is so cold.

You could reasonably expect the particles of all substances to stop moving at some very low temperature. The particles would have no kinetic energy at that temperature because they would have no motion. Absolute zero (0 K, or −273.15°C) is the temperature at which the motion of particles theoretically ceases. No temperature can be lower than absolute zero. Absolute zero has never been produced in the laboratory. However, a near-zero temperature of about 0.000 000 000 1 K (0.1×10^{-9} K), which is 0.1 nanokelvin, has been achieved. The coldest temperatures recorded outside of the laboratory are from space. In 1995, astronomers used a radio telescope to measure the temperature of the boomerang nebula shown in Figure 13.4. At a temperature of about 1 K, it is the coldest known region of space.

Average Kinetic Energy and Kelvin Temperature The Kelvin temperature scale reflects the relationship between temperature and average kinetic energy. ⊙ **The Kelvin temperature of a substance is directly proportional to the average kinetic energy of the particles of the substance.** For example, the particles in helium gas at 200 K have twice the average kinetic energy as the particles in helium gas at 100 K. The effects of temperature on particle motion in liquids and solids are more complex than in gases.

13.1 LessonCheck

3. ⊙ **Describe** Briefly describe the assumptions of kinetic theory as applied to gases.

4. ⊙ **Explain** Use kinetic theory to explain what causes gas pressure.

5. ⊙ **Explain** How is the Kelvin temperature of a substance related to the average kinetic energy of its particles?

6. Apply Concepts Describe the behavior of an oxygen molecule in a sealed container of air. Include what happens when the molecule collides with another molecule or the container walls.

7. Calculate Convert the following pressures to kilopascals.
a. 0.95 atm   **b.** 45 mm Hg

8. Predict A cylinder of oxygen gas is cooled from 300 K (27°C) to 150 K (−123°C). By what factor does the average kinetic energy of the oxygen molecules in the cylinder decrease?

BIGIDEA KINETIC THEORY

9. Why does a gas take the shape and volume of its container?

13.2 The Nature of Liquids

Q: *How hot should water be when you make coffee?* Ground coffee beans contain many different oils, which contribute to the flavor and aroma of the brew. If the water used for brewing the coffee is too hot, some of these oils vaporize and escape into the air, leaving the coffee less rich and flavorful. For this reason, you should let boiling water cool a little before using it to brew your coffee. In this section, you will learn why different liquids have different boiling points.

Key Questions

🔑 **What factors determine the physical properties of a liquid?**

🔑 **What is the relationship between evaporation and kinetic energy?**

🔑 **When can a dynamic equilibrium exist between a liquid and its vapor?**

🔑 **Under what conditions does boiling occur?**

Vocabulary

- vaporization
- evaporation
- vapor pressure
- boiling point
- normal boiling point

A Model for Liquids

🔑 **What factors determine the physical properties of a liquid?**

According to the kinetic theory, both the particles in gases and the particles in liquids have kinetic energy. This energy allows the particles in gases and liquids to flow past one another, as shown in Figure 13.5. Substances that can flow are referred to as fluids. The ability of gases and liquids to flow allows them to conform to the shape of their containers.

Gases and liquids have a key difference between them. According to the kinetic theory, there are no attractions between the particles in a gas. However, the particles in a liquid are attracted to each other. These intermolecular attractions keep the particles in a liquid close together, which is why liquids have a definite volume. 🔑 **The interplay between the disruptive motions of particles in a liquid and the attractions among the particles determines the physical properties of liquids.**

Intermolecular attractions reduce the amount of space between the particles in a liquid. Thus liquids are much more dense than gases. Increasing the pressure on a liquid has hardly any effect on its volume. The same is true for solids. Therefore, liquids and solids are known as condensed states of matter.

Figure 13.5
Comparing Liquids and Gases
Both liquids and gases can flow. The liquid on the left is colored water. The gas on the right is bromine vapor. If a gas is denser than air, it can be poured from one container into another. These pictures were taken in a fume hood because bromine is both toxic and corrosive.
Predict *Over time, what will happen to the gas in the uncovered beaker? Explain.*

See **evaporation** animated online.

Figure 13.6 Open vs. Closed Systems
The process of evaporation has a different outcome in an open system, such as a lake or an open container, than in a closed system, such as a terrarium or a sealed container.
a. In an open system, molecules that evaporate can escape from the system.
b. In a closed system, the molecules cannot escape. They collect as a vapor above the liquid. Some molecules condense back into a liquid.
Predict *Does the water level change over time in either the open container or the sealed container? Why?*

Evaporation

What is the relationship between evaporation and kinetic energy?

As you probably know, water in an open container, like the one in Figure 13.6a, eventually escapes into the air as water vapor. The conversion of a liquid to a gas or vapor is called **vaporization.** When this conversion occurs at the surface of a liquid that is not boiling, the process is called **evaporation.** Most of the molecules in a liquid don't have enough kinetic energy to overcome the attractive forces and escape into the gaseous state. **During evaporation, only those molecules with a certain minimum kinetic energy can escape from the surface of the liquid.** Even some of the particles that do escape collide with molecules in the air and rebound back into the liquid.

You may have noticed that a liquid evaporates faster when heated. This occurs because heating the liquid increases the average kinetic energy of its particles. The added energy enables more particles to overcome the attractive forces keeping them in the liquid state. As evaporation occurs, the particles with the highest kinetic energy tend to escape first. The particles left in the liquid have a lower average kinetic energy than the particles that have escaped. The process is similar to removing the fastest runner from a race. The remaining runners have a lower average speed. As evaporation takes place, the liquid's temperature decreases. Therefore, evaporation is a cooling process.

You can observe the effects of evaporative cooling on hot days. When you perspire, water molecules in your perspiration absorb heat from your body and evaporate from the skin's surface. This evaporation leaves the remaining perspiration cooler. The perspiration that remains cools you further by absorbing more body heat.

Vapor Pressure (in kPa) of Three Substances at Different Temperatures						
Substance	0°C	20°C	40°C	60°C	80°C	100°C
Water	0.61	2.33	7.37	19.92	47.34	101.33
Ethanol	1.63	5.85	18.04	47.02	108.34	225.75
Diethyl ether	24.70	58.96	122.80	230.65	399.11	647.87

Table 13.1 The table compares vapor pressure values for water, ethanol, and diethyl ether at six temperatures.
a. Infer At a given temperature, ethanol has a higher vapor pressure than water. What does that say about the relative strength of attraction between particles of each substance?
b. Draw Conclusions How does an increase in temperature affect a compound's ability to evaporate?

Vapor Pressure

🔑 **When can a dynamic equilibrium exist between a liquid and its vapor?**

The evaporation of a liquid in a closed system differs from evaporation in an open system. No particles of liquid can escape into the outside air from the sealed container in Figure 13.6b. When a partially filled container of liquid is sealed, some of the particles at the surface of the liquid vaporize. These particles collide with the walls of the sealed container, producing pressure. A measure of the force exerted by a gas above a liquid is called **vapor pressure**. Over time, the number of particles entering the vapor increases and some of the particles condense and return to the liquid state. The following equation summarizes the process.

$$\text{Liquid} \underset{\longleftarrow \text{condensation}}{\overset{\text{evaporation} \longrightarrow}{\rightleftharpoons}} \text{Vapor (gas)}$$

Eventually, the number of particles condensing will equal the number of particles vaporizing. The vapor pressure will then remain constant. 🔑 **In a system at constant vapor pressure, a dynamic equilibrium exists between the vapor and the liquid. The system is in equilibrium because the rate of evaporation of liquid equals the rate of condensation of vapor.**

At equilibrium, the particles in the system continue to evaporate and condense, but no net change occurs in the number of particles in the liquid or vapor. The sealed terrarium in Figure 13.6b is an example of a closed system at equilibrium. The moisture on the inner walls of the terrarium is a sign that equilibrium has been established. Particles that once evaporated are condensing, but other particles are evaporating to take their place.

Vapor Pressure and Temperature Change An increase in the temperature of a contained liquid increases the vapor pressure. This happens because the particles in the warmed liquid have increased kinetic energy. As a result, more of the particles will reach the minimum kinetic energy necessary to escape the surface of the liquid. The particles escape the liquid and collide with the walls of the container at a greater frequency. Table 13.1 gives the vapor pressures of some common liquids at various temperatures. The vapor pressure data indicates how volatile a given liquid is, or how easily it evaporates. Of the three liquids shown, diethyl ether is the most volatile and water is the least volatile.

CHEMISTRY & YOU

Q: *To make the best tasting coffee, many people grind the coffee beans just prior to brewing the coffee. Also, they are careful not to grind the coffee beans too much. Explain how both of these methods help prevent the natural oils in coffee beans from vaporizing.*

Vapor Pressure Measurements The vapor pressure of a liquid can be determined with a device called a manometer. Figure 13.7 shows how a simple manometer works. One end of a U-shaped glass tube containing mercury is attached to a closed container. The other end of the tube is open to the atmosphere. When there is only air in the container, the pressure is the same on both sides of the tube and the mercury level is the same in each arm of the tube. When a liquid is added to the container, the pressure in the container increases due to the vapor pressure of the liquid. The vapor pressure of the liquid pushes the mercury down on the container side of the U-tube. The levels of mercury in the U-tube are no longer the same. You can determine the vapor pressure in mm of Hg by measuring the difference between the two levels of mercury. As the vapor pressure increases, so does the difference between the two levels.

Boiling Point

🔑 Under what conditions does boiling occur?

The rate of evaporation of a liquid from an open container increases as the liquid is heated. Heating allows a greater number of particles at the liquid's surface to overcome the attractive forces that keep them in the liquid state. The remaining particles in the liquid move faster and faster as they absorb the added energy. Thus, the average kinetic energy of the particles in the liquid increases and the temperature of the liquid rises. 🔑 **When a liquid is heated to a temperature at which particles throughout the liquid have enough kinetic energy to vaporize, the liquid begins to boil.** Bubbles of vapor form throughout the liquid, rise to the surface, and escape into the air. The **boiling point** (bp) is the temperature at which the vapor pressure of the liquid is just equal to the external pressure on the liquid.

Figure 13.7 Manometer
The vapor pressure of a contained liquid can be measured in a manometer. The vapor pressure is equal to the difference in height of the mercury in the two arms of the U-tube.
Calculate *What is the difference in vapor pressure between ethanol at 0°C and ethanol at 20°C?*

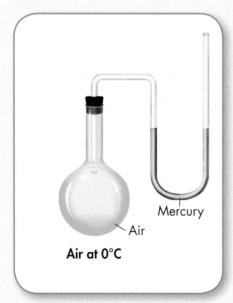

Air at 0°C

Mercury

Air

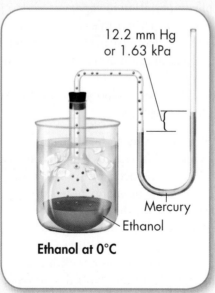

12.2 mm Hg or 1.63 kPa

Mercury

Ethanol

Ethanol at 0°C

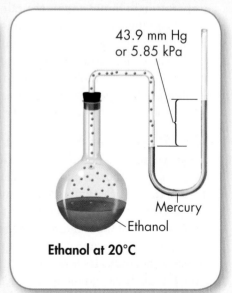

43.9 mm Hg or 5.85 kPa

Mercury

Ethanol

Ethanol at 20°C

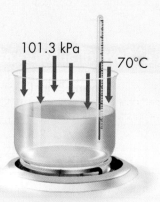

Sea Level
Atmospheric pressure at the surface of water at 70°C is greater than its vapor pressure. Bubbles of vapor cannot form in the water, and it does not boil.

Sea Level
At the boiling point, the vapor pressure is equal to atmospheric pressure. Bubbles of vapor form in the water, and it boils.

Atop Mount Everest
At higher altitudes, the atmospheric pressure is lower than it is at sea level. Thus the water boils at a lower temperature.

Boiling Point and Pressure Changes Because a liquid boils when its vapor pressure is equal to the external pressure, liquids don't always boil at the same temperature. Figure 13.8 shows how a change in altitude affects the boiling point of water. Because atmospheric pressure is lower at higher altitudes, boiling points decrease at higher altitudes. For example, in Denver, which is 1600 m above sea level, the average atmospheric pressure is 85.3 kPa. So water boils at about 95°C. In a pressure cooker, the vapor cannot escape and the vapor pressure increases. So water boils at a temperature above 100°C and food can cook more quickly.

Look at the vapor pressure versus temperature graph in Figure 13.9. You can use the graph to show how the boiling point of a liquid is related to vapor pressure. At a lower external pressure, the boiling point decreases. The particles in the liquid need less kinetic energy to escape from the liquid. At a higher external pressure, the boiling point increases. The particles in the liquid need more kinetic energy to escape from the liquid.

Figure 13.8
Boiling Point and Altitude
A liquid boils when the vapor pressure of particles within the liquid equals the atmospheric pressure. The boiling point varies with altitude.

Interpret Graphs

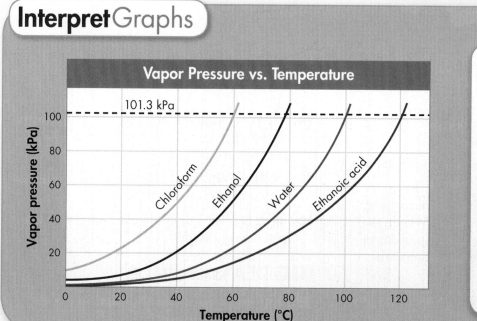

Figure 13.9 On the graph, the intersection of a curve with the 101.3-kPa line indicates the boiling point of that substance at standard pressure.
a. Read Graphs What is the boiling point of chloroform at 101.3 kPa?
b. Read Graphs What is the vapor pressure of ethanol at 40°C?
c. Predict What would atmospheric pressure need to be for ethanoic acid to boil at 80°C?

Table 13.2

Normal Boiling Points of Several Substances

Substance	Boiling Point (°C)
Carbon disulfide (CS_2)	46.0
Chloroform ($CHCl_3$)	61.7
Methanol (CH_4O)	64.7
Carbon tetrachloride (CCl_4)	76.8
Ethanol (C_2H_6O)	78.5
Water (H_2O)	100.0

Figure 13.10 Boiling Water
You should be careful when working with boiling water as you could get a burn from either the water or the invisible water vapor, or steam, in the air just above the water.

Boiling is a cooling process, similar to evaporation. During boiling, the particles with the highest kinetic energy escape first when the liquid is at the boiling point. Turning off the source of external heat drops the liquid's temperature below its boiling point. Supplying more heat allows more particles to acquire enough kinetic energy to escape. However, the temperature of the boiling liquid never rises above its boiling point. If heat is supplied at a greater rate, the liquid only boils faster. The vapor produced is at the same temperature as that of the boiling liquid. Although the vapor has the same average kinetic energy as the liquid, its potential energy (or stored energy) is much higher. Thus, a burn from steam is more severe than one from an equal mass of boiling water, even though they are both at the same temperature. This is one of the reasons why you need to be careful when straining boiling water from pasta or vegetables, as shown in Figure 13.10.

Normal Boiling Point A liquid can have various boiling points depending on pressure. The **normal boiling point** is defined as the boiling point of a liquid at a pressure of 101.3 kPa. Table 13.2 lists the normal boiling points of six molecular compounds.

13.2 LessonCheck

10. Identify What factors help determine the physical properties of liquids?

11. Explain In terms of kinetic energy, explain how a molecule in a liquid evaporates.

12. Describe A liquid is in a closed container and has a constant vapor pressure. What is the relationship between the rate of evaporation of the liquid and the rate of condensation of the vapor in the container?

13. Relate Cause and Effect What conditions must exist for a liquid to boil?

14. Interpret Graphs Use Figure 13.9 to determine the boiling point of ethanoic acid at 27 kPa and chloroform at 80 kPa.

15. Explain Why does the boiling point of a liquid vary with atmospheric pressure?

16. Infer Explain how evaporation lowers the temperature of a liquid.

BIGIDEA KINETIC THEORY

17. Why does a liquid take the shape but not the volume of its container?

13.3 The Nature of Solids

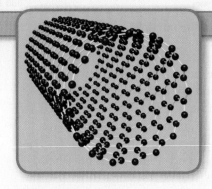

CHEMISTRY & YOU

Q: *What is the strongest material in the world?* It's not steel or any synthetic plastic, but a form of pure carbon known as fullerene nanotubes. These cylindrical structures, formed from carbon atoms linked together in hexagonal patterns, are over 300 times stronger than steel. They can be made with a diameter of only a few nanometers (hence the name) but several millimeters in length. Researchers in many different fields are finding new applications and possibilities for these structures, part of the new area of research known as nanotechnology. You will find out about fullerenes in this section.

Key Questions

🔑 How are the structure and properties of solids related?

🔑 What determines the shape of a crystal?

Vocabulary

- melting point
- freezing point
- crystal
- unit cell
- allotropes
- amorphous solid
- glass

A Model for Solids

🔑 **How are the structure and properties of solids related?**

The particles in liquids are relatively free to move. The particles in solids, however, are not. 🔑 **The general properties of solids reflect the orderly arrangement of their particles and the fixed locations of their particles.** In most solids, the atoms, ions, or molecules are packed tightly together. These solids are dense and not easy to compress. Because the particles in solids tend to vibrate about fixed points, solids do not flow.

When you heat a solid, its particles vibrate more rapidly as their kinetic energy increases. The organization of particles within the solid breaks down, and eventually the solid melts. The **melting point** (mp) is the temperature at which a solid changes into a liquid. At this temperature, the disruptive vibrations of the particles are strong enough to overcome the attractions that hold them in fixed positions. The **freezing point** (fp) is the temperature at which a liquid changes into a solid. The melting and freezing points of a substance are at the same temperature. At that temperature, the liquid and solid phases are in equilibrium.

$$\text{Solid} \underset{\longleftarrow \text{freezing}}{\overset{\text{melting} \longrightarrow}{\rightleftharpoons}} \text{Liquid}$$

In general, ionic solids have high melting points because relatively strong forces hold them together. Sodium chloride, an ionic compound, has a rather high melting point of 801°C. By contrast, molecular solids have relatively low melting points. For example, hydrogen chloride, a molecular compound, melts at −112° C. Not all solids melt, however. Wood and cane sugar, for example, decompose when heated.

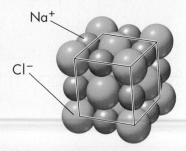

Figure 13.11 Ionic Crystal
In sodium chloride (NaCl), sodium ions (Na⁺) and chloride ions (Cl⁻) are closely packed in a regular array. The ions vibrate about fixed points on the crystal.

Crystal Structure and Unit Cells

🔑 What determines the shape of a crystal?

Most solid substances are crystalline. In a **crystal,** the particles are arranged in an orderly, repeating, three-dimensional pattern called a crystal lattice. Figure 13.11 shows part of the crystal lattice in sodium chloride. 🔑 **The shape of a crystal reflects the arrangement of the particles within the solid.**

Crystal Systems A crystal has sides, or faces. The angles at which the faces of a crystal intersect are always the same for a given substance and are characteristic of that substance. Crystals are classified into seven groups, or crystal systems, which have the characteristic shapes shown in Figure 13.12. The edges are labeled a, b, and c. The angles are labeled α, β, and γ. The seven crystal systems differ in terms of the angles between the faces and in the number of edges of equal length on each face.

The shape of a crystal depends on the arrangement of the particles within it. The smallest group of particles within a crystal that retains the geometric shape of the crystal is known as a **unit cell.** A crystal lattice is a repeating array of any one of fourteen kinds of unit cells. Each crystal system can be composed of from one to four types of unit cells. Figure 13.13 shows the three kinds of unit cells that can make up a cubic crystal system.

Figure 13.12 Crystal Systems
Crystals are classified into seven crystal systems.
Classify *In which of the systems are all three angles equal to 90°?*

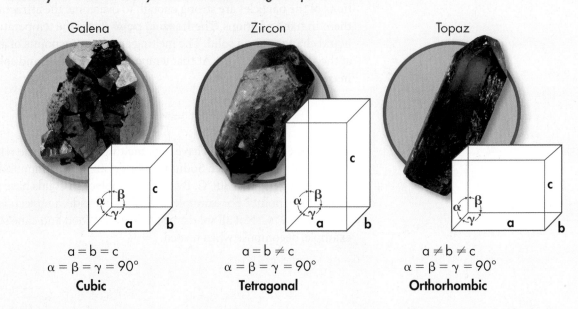

Galena

$a = b = c$
$\alpha = \beta = \gamma = 90°$
Cubic

Zircon

$a = b \neq c$
$\alpha = \beta = \gamma = 90°$
Tetragonal

Topaz

$a \neq b \neq c$
$\alpha = \beta = \gamma = 90°$
Orthorhombic

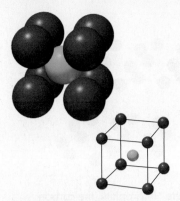

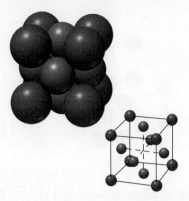

Simple Cubic In a simple cubic unit cell, the atoms or ions are arranged at the corners of an imaginary cube.

Body-Centered In a body-centered cubic unit cell, the atoms or ions are at the corners and in the center of an imaginary cube.

Face-Centered In a face-centered cubic unit cell, there are atoms or ions at the corners and in the center of each face of the imaginary cube.

Allotropes Some solid substances can exist in more than one form. A good example is the element carbon. Diamond is one crystalline form of carbon. It forms when carbon crystallizes under tremendous pressure (thousands of atmospheres). A different crystalline form of carbon is graphite. The lead in a pencil is not the element lead; it is graphite. In graphite, the carbon atoms are packed in sheets rather than in the extended three-dimensional array that is characteristic of diamond.

In 1985, a third crystalline form of carbon was discovered in ordinary soot. This form of carbon is called buckminsterfullerene. The carbon atoms in buckminsterfullerene are bonded together in groups of 60 atoms to form a hollow sphere, or cage, known as a buckyball. The atoms are arranged in a pattern of hexagons and pentagons on the surface of the cage, similar to the pattern on the surface of a soccer ball. Since 1985, other molecules of carbon with hollow cages have been discovered. The one with 70 carbon atoms is shaped like a football. As a group, these forms of carbon are called fullerenes.

Figure 13.13 Unit Cells
The unit cell in a cubic crystal system may be simple cubic, body-centered cubic, or face-centered cubic. In the space-filling models and line drawings, the spheres represent atoms or ions.

Learn more about crystal structures of solids *online.*

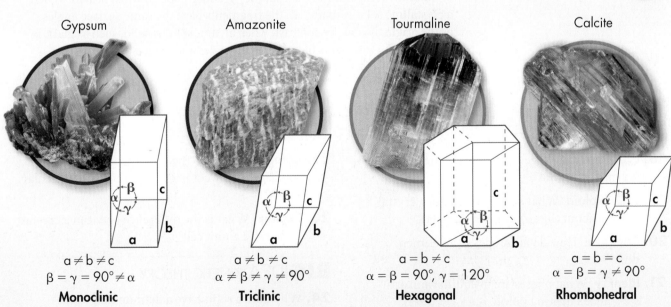

Gypsum

Amazonite

Tourmaline

Calcite

$a \neq b \neq c$
$\beta = \gamma = 90° \neq \alpha$
Monoclinic

$a \neq b \neq c$
$\alpha \neq \beta \neq \gamma \neq 90°$
Triclinic

$a = b \neq c$
$\alpha = \beta = 90°, \gamma = 120°$
Hexagonal

$a = b = c$
$\alpha = \beta = \gamma \neq 90°$
Rhombohedral

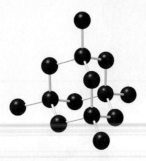 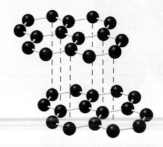 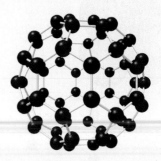

Diamond In diamond, each carbon atom in the interior of the diamond is strongly bonded to four others. The array is rigid and compact.

Graphite In graphite, the carbon atoms are linked in widely spaced layers of hexagonal (six-sided) arrays.

Fullerene In buckminsterfullerene, 60 carbon atoms form a hollow sphere. The carbons are arranged in pentagons and hexagons.

Figure 13.14 Allotropes of Carbon
Diamond, graphite, and fullerenes are allotropes of carbon.
Compare *Based on the arrangements of their atoms, explain why the properties of fullerenes are closer to those of diamond than of graphite.*

The physical properties of diamond, graphite, and fullerenes are quite different. Diamond has a high density and is very hard. Graphite has a relatively low density and is soft and slippery. The hollow cages in fullerenes give them great strength and rigidity. Diamond, graphite, and fullerenes are crystalline allotropes of carbon. **Allotropes** are two or more different molecular forms of the same element in the same physical state. Although allotropes are composed of atoms of the same element, they have different properties because their structures are different. Figure 13.14 compares the structures of carbon allotropes. Only a few elements have allotropes. In addition to carbon, these elements include phosphorus, sulfur, oxygen, boron, and antimony.

Non-Crystalline Solids Not all solids are crystalline in form; some solids are amorphous. An **amorphous solid** lacks an ordered internal structure. Rubber, plastic, and asphalt are amorphous solids. Their atoms are randomly arranged. Other examples of amorphous solids are glasses. A **glass** is a transparent fusion product of inorganic substances that have cooled to a rigid state without crystallizing. Glasses are sometimes called supercooled liquids. The irregular internal structures of glasses are intermediate between those of a crystalline solid and those of a free-flowing liquid. Glasses do not melt at a definite temperature. Instead, they gradually soften when heated. When a crystalline solid is shattered, the fragments have the same surface angles as the original solid. By contrast, when an amorphous solid, such as glass, is shattered, the fragments have irregular angles and jagged edges.

CHEMISTRY & YOU

Q: *What structural properties make fullerene nanotubes the strongest material in the world? Refer to Figure 13.14 in your answer.*

13.3 LessonCheck

18. Describe In general, how are the particles arranged in solids?

19. Explain What does the shape of a crystal tell you about the structure of a crystal?

20. Compare How do allotropes of an element differ?

21. Identify What phases are in equilibrium at a substance's melting point?

22. Compare How do the melting points of ionic solids generally compare with those of molecular solids?

23. Explain What is the difference between a crystal lattice and a unit cell?

BIGIDEA KINETIC THEORY

24. Why does a solid have a definite shape and a definite volume?

Small-Scale Lab

The Behavior of Liquids and Solids

Purpose
To explore and explain some behaviors of liquids and solids

Materials
- plastic Petri dish
- water
- ice
- rubbing alcohol
- graph paper, 1-cm
- calcium chloride

Procedure

1. In your notebook, make a copy of the table shown below. Add a column for your observations. In the experiments, you will place substances labeled A and B inside the Petri dish and substances labeled C on top of the dish.

2. For Experiment 1, place one drop of water in the Petri dish. Replace the cover and place a small piece of ice on top of the cover.

3. After a few minutes, observe the interior surface of the Petri dish cover and the contents of the dish. Record your observations. Clean and dry the Petri dish and its cover.

4. Repeat Steps 2 and 3 for Experiments 2–5, using the materials listed in the table. For Experiment 4, place the Petri dish on the graph paper so that you can place the water and the calcium chloride about 3 cm apart.

Experiment	Substance A	Substance B	Substance C
1	drop of water	–	ice cube
2	drop of water	–	drop of water
3	drop of rubbing alcohol	–	drop of water
4	drop of water	piece of $CaCl_2$	–
5	–	several pieces of $CaCl_2$	ice cube

Analyze and Conclude

1. Draw Conclusions Explain your observations in Experiment 1 in terms of the behavior of liquids.

2. Explain Why is ice not needed for cloud formation in Experiment 2?

3. Compare What differences do you observe about the behavior of rubbing alcohol in Experiment 3 and the behavior of water in the previous experiments? Explain.

4. Predict What happens to solid calcium chloride in a humid environment?

5. Draw Conclusions Propose an explanation for no cloud formation in Experiment 5.

You're the Chemist

1. Analyze Data Place a drop of water and a drop of rubbing alcohol about 3 cm apart in a Petri dish. Cover the dish and place it on a piece of graph paper. Be careful not to mix the contents. Observe what happens to the size of the water drops over time. Provide an explanation for what you observe.

2. Observe Add a drop of bromothymol blue (BTB) to a drop of vinegar. What happens?

3. Design an Experiment Vinegar is a solution of water and ethanoic acid, $C_2H_4O_2$. Design and carry out an experiment using what you learned from the previous exercise to see if ethanoic acid will evaporate from a drop of vinegar.

4. Design an Experiment Design and carry out an experiment to see if ammonia will evaporate from a drop of aqueous ammonia.

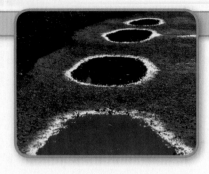

CHEMISTRY & YOU

Q: *Where does rain water go when a puddle dries up?* Water cycles through much of the matter on Earth. It falls as liquid rain or solid snow, collects in rivers, oceans, or glaciers and returns to the air as a gas through evaporation. All living organisms use water and release it back into the air. Other elements, such as carbon and nitrogen, also cycle through Earth as solids, liquids, or gases. In this section, you will learn what conditions can control the state of a substance.

Key Questions

🔑 When can sublimation occur?

🔑 How are the conditions at which phases are in equilibrium represented on a phase diagram?

Vocabulary

- sublimation
- phase diagram
- triple point

Sublimation

🔑 **When can sublimation occur?**

If you hang wet laundry on a clothesline on a very cold day, the water in the clothes quickly freezes to ice. Eventually, however, if the day is sunny, the clothes become dry although the ice never thaws. The ice changes directly to water vapor without melting and passing through the liquid state. The change of a substance from a solid to a vapor without passing through the liquid state is called **sublimation.** Sublimation can occur because solids, like liquids, have a vapor pressure. 🔑 **Sublimation occurs in solids with vapor pressures that exceed atmospheric pressure at or near room temperature.**

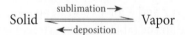

$$\text{Solid} \underset{\longleftarrow \text{deposition}}{\overset{\text{sublimation} \longrightarrow}{\rightleftharpoons}} \text{Vapor}$$

Iodine is another example of a substance that undergoes sublimation. This violet-black solid ordinarily changes into a purple vapor without passing through a liquid state. Notice in Figure 13.15 how dark crystals of iodine deposit on the outside of a test tube placed inside another test tube. The outer test tube contains solid iodine that is being gently heated. The inner test tube contains liquid water and ice. The iodine crystals at the bottom of the outer test tube change directly to iodine vapor. When the vapor reaches the cool surface of the inner test tube, it goes directly from the gaseous to the solid state.

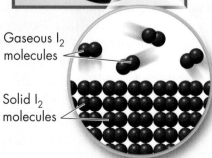

Gaseous I₂ molecules

Solid I₂ molecules

Figure 13.15 Sublimation
When solid iodine is heated, the crystals sublime, going directly from the solid to the gaseous state. When the vapor cools, it goes directly from the gaseous to the solid state.

Sublimation has many useful applications. If freshly brewed coffee is frozen and the water vapor is removed with a vacuum pump (a sublimation process), the result is freeze-dried coffee. The solid carbon dioxide (dry ice) shown in Figure 13.16 is often used as a coolant for goods, such as ice cream, that must remain frozen during shipment. Dry ice has a low temperature of $-78°C$. Because it sublimes, it does not produce a liquid, as ordinary ice does when it melts. Solid air fresheners contain a variety of substances that sublime at room temperature. Sublimation is also useful for separating substances. Organic chemists use sublimation to separate mixtures and to purify compounds.

Figure 13.16 Dry Ice Solid carbon dioxide, or dry ice, sublimes at normal atmospheric pressures. As it changes state, dry ice absorbs heat, keeping materials nearby cool and dry.
Interpret Photos *Why does fog form in the air around the dry ice?*

Quick Lab

Purpose
To observe the sublimation of air freshener

Materials
- small pieces of solid air freshener
- small shallow container
- 2 clear 8-oz plastic cups
- hot tap water
- ice
- 3 thick cardboard strips

Sublimation

Procedure

1. Place a few pieces of air freshener in one of the cups. **CAUTION** *Work in a well-ventilated room.*

2. Bend the cardboard strips and place them over the rim of the cup that has the air freshener pieces.

3. Place the second cup inside the first. The base of the second cup should not touch the air freshener. Adjust the cardboard as necessary. This assembly is your sublimator.

4. Fill the top cup with ice. Do not get any ice or water in the bottom cup.

5. Fill the shallow container about one-third full with hot tap water.

Ice

Shallow container with hot water

Air freshener

6. Carefully place your sublimator in the hot water. Observe what happens.

Analyze and Conclude

1. Define What is sublimation?

2. Predict What do you think would happen if the water in the shallow container were at room temperature? If it were boiling?

3. Explain Why is it possible to separate the substances in some mixtures by sublimation?

Phase Diagrams

🔹 **How are the conditions at which phases are in equilibrium represented on a phase diagram?**

The relationships among the solid, liquid, and vapor states (or phases) of a substance in a sealed container can be represented in a single graph. The graph is called a phase diagram. A **phase diagram** gives the conditions of temperature and pressure at which a substance exists as solid, liquid, or gas (vapor). 🔹 **The conditions of pressure and temperature at which two phases exist in equilibrium are indicated on a phase diagram by a line separating the two regions representing the phases.**

Figure 13.18 shows the phase diagram for water. In each of the colored regions of the phase diagram, water is in a single phase. The curving line that separates water's vapor phase from its liquid phase describes the equilibrium conditions for liquid and vapor. Under these conditions, water can change its state from liquid to vapor or from vapor to liquid. The same line also illustrates how the vapor pressure of water varies with temperature. The other two lines describe the conditions for equilibrium between liquid water and ice and between water vapor and ice. The point on the diagram at which all three lines meet is called the triple point. The **triple point** describes the only set of conditions at which all three phases can exist in equilibrium with one another. For water, the triple point is a temperature of 0.016°C and a pressure of 0.61 kPa (0.0060 atm). Figure 13.17 shows water at its triple point.

Figure 13.17 Triple Point
This flask is at the triple point, where ice, liquid water, and water vapor exist in equilibrium. Freezing, melting, boiling, and condensation are all occuring at the same time in the flask.

InterpretGraphs

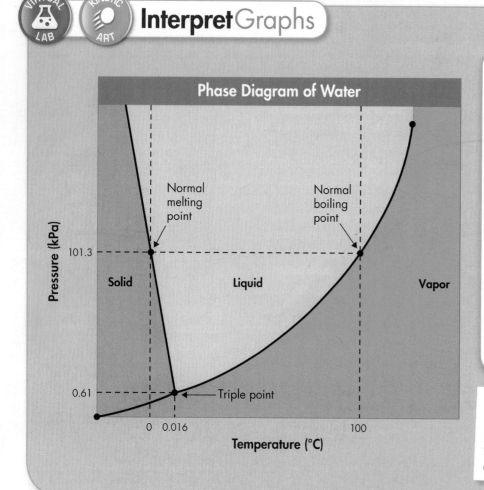

Figure 13.18 The phase diagram of water shows the relationship among pressure, temperature, and the physical states of water. Note that the scale on the axes is not linear.

a. Read Graphs At the triple point of water, what are the values of temperature and pressure?

b. Identify What states of matter are present at the triple point of water?

c. Analyze Assuming standard pressure, at what temperature is there an equilibrium between water vapor and liquid water? Between liquid water and ice?

Hint: Each line represents the set of possible temperature-pressure values at which the phases are in dynamic equilibrium.

By referring to Figure 13.18, you can determine what happens if you melt ice or boil water at pressures less than 101.3 kPa. A decrease in pressure lowers the boiling point and raises the melting point. An increase in pressure will raise the boiling point and lower the melting point.

Look at Figure 13.18. Follow the equilibrium line between liquid water and water vapor to the triple point. Below the triple point, the vapor and liquid cannot exist in equilibrium. Increasing the pressure won't change the vapor to a liquid. The solid and the vapor are in equilibrium at temperatures below 0.016°C. With an increase in pressure, the vapor begins to behave more like a solid. For example, it is no longer easily compressed.

Figure 13.18 also illustrates how an increase in pressure affects the melting point of ice. For years, the accepted hypothesis for how ice skaters move along the ice was the following. The blades of the skates exert pressure, which lowers the melting point of the ice. The ice melts and a film of water forms under the blades of the skates. This film acts as a lubricant, enabling the skaters to glide gracefully over the ice as shown in Figure 13.19. This hypothesis fails to explain why skiers also glide along very nicely on another solid form of water—snow. Wide skis exert much less pressure per unit area of snow than narrow skate blades exert on ice. Recent research shows that the surface of ice has a slippery, water-like surface layer that exists well below ice's melting point. Even ice that is at −129°C has this layer. A new hypothesis proposes that the liquid-like surface layer provides the lubrication needed for smooth skating and skiing.

 CHEMISTRY & YOU

Q: *Describe how water might move from Earth's surface to Earth's atmosphere and back again as part of the water cycle. Be sure to include any phase changes that occur in your description.*

Figure 13.19 Water on Ice
The surface of ice has a thin layer of water above it.
Apply Concepts *Research shows that the colder the ice is, the thinner the layer of water above the ice is. In which sports—ice hockey, speed skating or figure skating—do you think that it would benefit the athletes more to keep the ice colder?*

13.4 LessonCheck

ONLINE PROBLEMS

25. 🔑 **Identify** What properties must a solid have to undergo sublimation?

26. 🔑 **Explain** What do the curved lines on a phase diagram represent?

27. Apply Concepts Describe one practical use of sublimation.

28. Interpret Graphs Using Figure 13.18, estimate the boiling point of water at a pressure of 50 kPa.

29. Explain What does the triple point on a phase diagram describe?

30. Classify Would you expect a substance that sublimates at or near room temperature to be a molecular substance or an ionic substance? Use what you learned about bonding in Chapters 7 and 8 to answer the question.

Plasma Waste Converter

You are very familiar with solids, liquids, and gases, but did you know that there's a fourth state of matter called plasma? A plasma is a gaseous mixture of freely moving positive ions and electrons. Plasmas exist naturally in the sun and other stars, and in lightning. Plasmas can also be artificially created and used in a variety of technologies. One new application of plasma technology is plasma waste converters, which treat most waste material, including many hazardous wastes.

Plasma waste converters produce plasmas with temperatures as high as 7,000°C. The energy within the plasma breaks the waste material's molecular bonds so that the material separates into its elemental components. The end products are a hydrogen-rich gas known as syngas and a solid known as slag.

Plasma waste converters have many benefits over traditional waste treatments. They do not require the use of dumps or landfills, and they emit much less greenhouse gases and other pollutants than incinerators. Despite these benefits there are currently only two plasma waste treatment plants that process municipal solid waste. This is mostly due to the cost since each plant must be custom-built. Standardizing production should result in the construction of more plants.

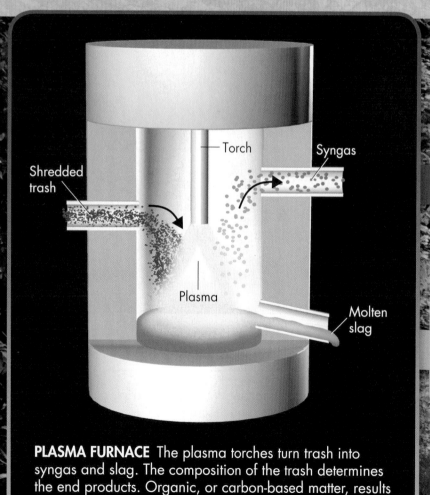

SYNGAS
The gases pass from the furnace into a chamber where any remaining organic matter or hazardous wastes are removed. The gases can then be used as a fuel source or to make electricity.

SLAG
Any hazardous materials in the molten slag are inert and will not dissolve out of the slag. The slag takes different forms depending on how it is cooled.

PLASMA FURNACE The plasma torches turn trash into syngas and slag. The composition of the trash determines the end products. Organic, or carbon-based matter, results in syngas while inorganic matter results in slag. The furnace is airtight, so that none of the syngas can escape.

FROM THE FURNACE TO THE GRID

The extremely hot syngas can heat water to produce steam that turns turbines producing electricity. Some of this electricity is used to power the plant while the rest of it is sold to the power grid.

FILL 'ER UP

The hydrogen-rich syngas can be used as a fuel source in fuel cell-powered vehicles.

SELLABLE SLAG

Air-cooled slag forms black, glassy rocks. These rocks can be sold and used to make concrete or asphalt.

Take It Further

1. Infer Describe how a gas might become a plasma.

2. Compare and Contrast Is it misleading to refer to a plasma waste converter as a plasma incinerator? Research how incinerators work and compare them to how plasma waste converters work.

3. Evaluate the Impact on Society How might the use of plasma waste converters change society?

13 Study Guide

BIGIDEA KINETIC THEORY

The state of a substance is determined by conditions of pressure and temperature. Low pressures and high temperatures favor gases, in which particles move randomly in constant, high-speed motion. At higher pressures and lower temperatures, the particles slow down and exert attractive forces on one another, producing a liquid. At still higher pressures and lower temperatures, the particles become fixed in orderly arrangements, producing solids. A substance changes state when there is a change in the balance between the random motion of its particles and the attractions among those particles.

13.1 The Nature of Gases

🔑 Particles in a gas are considered to be small, hard spheres with an insignificant volume. The motion of the particles in a gas is rapid, constant, and random. All collisions between particles in a gas are perfectly elastic.

🔑 Gas pressure is the result of billions of rapidly moving particles in a gas simultaneously colliding with an object.

🔑 The Kelvin temperature of a substance is directly proportional to the average kinetic energy of the particles of the substance.

- kinetic energy (420)
- kinetic theory (420)
- gas pressure (421)
- vacuum (421)
- atmospheric pressure (421)
- barometer (421)
- pascal (Pa) (422)
- standard atmosphere (atm) (422)

13.2 The Nature of Liquids

🔑 The interplay between the disruptive motions of particles in a liquid and the attractions among the particles determines the physical properties of liquids.

🔑 During evaporation, only those molecules with a certain minimum kinetic energy can escape from the surface of the liquid.

🔑 In a system at constant vapor pressure, a dynamic equilibrium exists between the vapor and the liquid. The rates of evaporation and condensation are equal.

🔑 At a temperature at which particles throughout a liquid have enough kinetic energy to vaporize, the liquid begins to boil.

- vaporization (426)
- evaporation (426)
- vapor pressure (427)
- boiling point (428)
- normal boiling point (430)

13.3 The Nature of Solids

🔑 The general properties of solids reflect the orderly arrangement and the fixed locations of their particles.

🔑 The shape of a crystal reflects the arrangement of the particles within the solid.

- melting point (431)
- freezing point (431)
- crystal (432)
- unit cell (432)
- allotropes (434)
- amorphous solid (434)
- glass (434)

13.4 Changes of State

🔑 Sublimation occurs in solids with vapor pressures that exceed atmospheric pressure at or near room temperature.

🔑 The conditions of pressure and temperature at which two phases exist in equilibrium are indicated on a phase diagram by a line separating the two regions representing the phases.

- sublimation (436)
- phase diagram (438)
- triple point (438)

13 Assessment

★ Solutions appear in Appendix E

Lesson by Lesson

13.1 The Nature of Gases

★**31.** What is meant by an elastic collision?

32. Which of these statements are characteristic of matter in the gaseous state?

   a. Gases fill their containers completely.
   b. Gases exert pressure.
   c. Gases have mass.
   d. The pressure of a gas is independent of the temperature.
   e. Gases are compressible.

33. List the various units used to measure pressure, and identify the SI unit.

34. Change 1656 kPa to atm.

★**35.** Change 190 mm Hg to kPa and atm.

36. Explain the relationship between the Kelvin temperature of a substance and the kinetic energy of its particles.

37. How is the average kinetic energy of water molecules affected when you pour hot water into cups at the same temperature as the water?

38. What does the abbreviation STP represent?

39. What is significant about the temperature absolute zero?

★**40.** By what factor does the average kinetic energy of the molecules of gas in an aerosol container increase when the temperature is raised from 27°C (300 K) to 627°C (900 K)?

13.2 The Nature of Liquids

41. Explain why liquids and gases differ in density and the ability to be compressed.

42. Compare evaporation of a liquid in a closed container with that of liquid in an open container.

★**43.** Describe what is happening at the molecular level when a dynamic equilibrium occurs.

44. Explain why increasing the temperature of a liquid increases its rate of evaporation.

45. Would you expect a dynamic equilibrium in a liquid in an open container? Explain.

46. Describe the effect that increasing temperature has on the vapor pressure of a liquid.

47. Distinguish between the boiling point and the normal boiling point of a liquid.

48. Use the graph to answer each question.

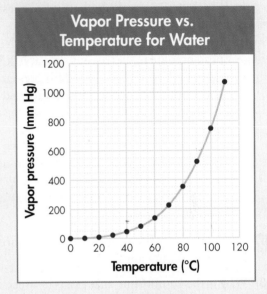

Vapor Pressure vs. Temperature for Water

   a. What is the vapor pressure of water at 40°C?
   b. At what temperature is the vapor pressure of water 600 mm Hg?
   c. What is the significance of the vapor pressure of water at 100°C?

★**49.** Explain how boiling is a cooling process.

13.3 The Nature of Solids

50. Name at least one physical property that would permit you to distinguish a molecular solid from an ionic solid.

51. Describe what happens when a solid is heated to its melting point.

★**52.** Explain why molecular solids usually have lower melting points than ionic solids.

13.4 Changes of State

★**53.** When you remove the lid from a food container that has been left in a freezer for several months, you discover a large collection of ice crystals on the underside of the lid. Explain what has happened.

54. Explain why a liquid stays at a constant temperature while it is boiling.

*55. What happens to the average kinetic energy of the water molecules in your body when you have a fever?

56. Refer back to Figure 13.9 to answer the following questions.

   a. What is the normal boiling point of ethanoic acid?

   b. Which liquid has the highest vapor pressure at 40°C?

   c. At standard atmospheric pressure, which of the substances are in the gaseous state at 70°C?

   d. Water boils at 100°C at standard pressure. How would the pressure on ethanol and on ethanoic acid have to change for these liquids to boil at 100°C?

   e. Mount McKinley in Alaska is the tallest peak in North America at 6194 m. The atmospheric pressure at its peak is 44 kPa. What is the boiling point of water at the peak of Mount McKinley?

57. Describe the evaporation process, vapor pressure, and boiling point.

58. Why is the equilibrium that exists between a liquid and its vapor in a closed container called a dynamic equilibrium?

59. The table gives the vapor pressure of isopropyl alcohol at various temperatures. Graph the data. Use a smooth curve to connect the data points.

Temperature (°C)	Vapor pressure (kPa)
0	1.11
25	6.02
50	23.9
75	75.3
100	198
125	452

   a. What is the estimated normal boiling point of isopropyl alcohol?

   b. What is the boiling point of isopropyl alcohol when the external pressure is increased to twice standard pressure?

*60. In a series of liquids, as the intermolecular forces of attraction strengthen, would you expect the vapor pressure to increase or decrease? Explain.

61. Predict the physical state of each substance at the specified temperature. Use the melting point and boiling point data from the table below.

   a. phenol at 99°C

   b. ammonia at −25°C

   c. methanol in an ice-water bath

   d. methanol in a boiling-water bath

   e. ammonia at −100°C

   f. phenol at 25°C

Substance	Melting Point (°C)	Boiling Point (°C)
ammonia	−77.7	−33.4
methanol	−97.7	64.7
water	0	100
phenol	40.9	181.9

62. Why is atmospheric pressure much lower on the top of a mountain than it is at sea level?

*63. A fully inflated raft is left outside overnight. The next morning the raft is not fully inflated. As the air temperature rises during the day, the raft expands to the size it was the night before. Assuming that the amount of air inside the raft did not change, use kinetic theory to explain why the size of the raft changes.

Think Critically

64. **Relate Cause and Effect** What role does atmospheric pressure play when someone is drinking a liquid through a straw?

*65. **Analyze Data** Your lab partner measures the boiling point of water in an open beaker as 108.2°C. You know that water can be made to boil at this temperature, but you still ask your partner to repeat the measurement. Explain.

66. **Infer** What everyday evidence suggests that all matter is in constant motion?

67. **Explain** Is the average kinetic energy of the particles in a block of ice at 0°C the same as or different from the average kinetic energy of the particles in a gas-filled weather balloon at 0°C? Explain.

68. **Infer** Can objects that are large enough for you to see collide elastically? Explain.

69. **Apply Concepts** How does perspiration help cool your body on a hot day?

70. Relate Cause and Effect Why do different liquids have different normal boiling points?

71. Explain A liquid-vapor equilibrium exists in a container. Explain why the equilibrium vapor pressure in the container is not affected when the volume of the container is changed.

★72. Analyze Data A teacher wants to demonstrate that unheated water can boil at room temperature in a beaker within a bell jar connected to a vacuum pump. However, the vacuum pump is faulty and can reduce pressures only to 15 kPa. Can the teacher use this pump to perform the demonstration successfully? Explain your answer.

73. Compare You have two sealed jars of water at the same temperature. In the first jar, there is a large amount of water. In the second jar, there is a small amount of water. Explain how the vapor pressure can be the same in both jars.

74. Draw Conclusions Why are pressure cookers recommended for cooking at high altitude?

75. Propose a Solution A mixture of gases contains oxygen, nitrogen, and water vapor. What physical process could you use to remove the water vapor from the sample?

Enrichment

★76. Apply Concepts Relative humidity is defined by the following equation

$$\text{Relative humidity} = \frac{(a)}{(b)} \times 100\%$$

where (a) is the pressure of water vapor in the air and (b) is the equilibrium vapor pressure of water in the air at the same temperature. Can the relative humidity exceed 100%? Explain.

77. Use Models The ions in sodium chloride are arranged in a face-centered cubic pattern. Draw a layer of ions in a sodium chloride crystal.

78. Use Models Using Figure 13.12, identify the crystal systems described below.
   a. three unequal edges meet at right angles
   b. three equal edges with three equal angles that are not right angles
   c. two equal edges and one unequal edge meet at right angles
   d. three unequal edges do not meet at right angles
   e. three equal edges meet at right angles

★79. Use Models Use this drawing to answer the questions.

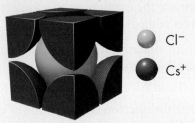

   a. What type of unit cell is in a lattice of cesium chloride?
   b. What is the coordination number of Cs^+? (*Hint:* Refer back to Section 7.2 for the definition of coordination number.)
   c. Based on the diagram, what is the formula of cesium chloride? Explain your answer.

80. Predict The solid-liquid equilibrium line in the phase diagram of a given substance slants to the right. How is the substance's freezing point affected by increased pressure?

CHEMYSTERY

Foggy Car Windows

Car windows fog up because of condensation. When warm, moist air comes into contact with a cold surface, the water vapor in the air condenses into liquid drops on the cold surface. When it's cold outside, your body and breath warm the air inside the car. This warm, moist air comes in contact with the cold surface of the car window, causing it to fog up. Using a car heater increases the amount of moisture in the air, since warm air can hold more water vapor than cold air. The amount of moisture in the air will also be higher on a rainy day because some of the water on the passengers evaporates. An air conditioner cools and removes moisture from the air.

81. Explain Describe why opening a window can also help defog a car windshield.

82. Connect to the BIGIDEA How does the average motion of the water molecules change as water vapor condenses on a car window? Why does the motion change?

83. How are the frequency and wavelength of light waves related?

84. Which atom in each pair has the larger atomic radius?

   a. O and S   **b.** K and Br

*85. Write the electron configuration of each ion.

   a. Ca^{2+} **b.** S^{2-} **c.** Li^+

86. How many unshared pairs of electrons are in each molecule?

   a. H_2O **b.** CO

87. List the intermolecular attractions between molecules in order of increasing strength.

   a. dispersion forces
   b. hydrogen bonds
   c. dipole interactions

88. Write a correct formula for each compound.

   a. copper(I) sulfite   **b.** nitrous acid

89. Identify the binary molecular compound in each pair of substances.

   a. NaCl or CO   **b.** PBr_3 or LiOH

90. Write formulas for these ions.

   a. iron(III) ion   **b.** cadmium ion

91. Calculate the percent by mass of the metal in each compound.

   a. Fe_2S_3 **b.** $Al(OH)_3$

92. How many moles are there in each sample?

   a. 888 g of sulfur dioxide
   b. 2.84×10^{22} molecules of ammonia

*93. Perchloric acid forms by the reaction of water with dichlorine heptoxide.

$$Cl_2O_7 + H_2O \longrightarrow 2HClO_4$$

   a. How many grams of Cl_2O_7 react with an excess of H_2O to form 56.2 g of $HClO_4$?
   b. How many mL of water are needed to form 3.40 mol $HClO_4$?

94. How many moles are there in each sample?

   a. 8.6 L CO_2 (at STP)   **b.** 63.4 g NH_3

*95. When hydrogen sulfide gas is bubbled into a solution of cadmium nitrate in water, the products are nitric acid and a precipitate of cadmium sulfide. Write a balanced equation for the reaction. Include physical states for all reactants and products. (Hydrogen sulfide gas is soluble in water.)

96. Balance these equations.

   a. $V_2O_5 + H_2 \longrightarrow V_2O_3 + H_2O$
   b. $(NH_4)_2Cr_2O_7 \longrightarrow Cr_2O_3 + N_2 + H_2O$

97. List the metal that ranks higher in the activity series of metals.

   a. magnesium or mercury
   b. potassium or lithium

98. Classify each reaction as a combination, decomposition, single-replacement, double-replacement, or combustion.

   a. $2Li(s) + Br_2(l) \longrightarrow 2LiBr(s)$
   b. $2C_2H_6(g) + 7O_2(g) \longrightarrow$
$$4CO_2(g) + 6H_2O(g)$$

*99. The complete decomposition of sucrose (table sugar) caused by strong heating may be represented by this equation.

$$C_{12}H_{22}O_{11}(s) \longrightarrow 11H_2O(l) + 12C(s)$$

For the decomposition of 1.00 mol of sucrose:

   a. How many grams of H_2O are produced?
   b. What is the total number of moles of products produced?
   c. How many grams of C are produced?

*100. Hydrogen reacts with ethene (C_2H_4) to form ethane (C_2H_6).

$$C_2H_4 + H_2 \longrightarrow C_2H_6$$

What is the limiting reagent when 40.0 g C_2H_4 reacts with 3.0 g H_2?

101. Iron(II) sulfide is produced when iron is heated with sulfur.

$$Fe(s) + S(s) \xrightarrow{\Delta} FeS(s)$$

What is the theoretical yield of FeS if 25.0 g Fe is heated with 32.0 g S?

102. What is the percent yield in Question 101 if 16.5 g of FeS is produced?

If You Have Trouble With . . .

Question	83	84	85	86	87	88	89	90	91	92	93	94	95	96	97	98	99	100	101	102
See Chapter	5	6	7	8	8	9	9	9	10	10	10	10	11	11	11	11	12	12	12	12

Standardized Test Prep

Use the graph to answer Questions 1 and 2.

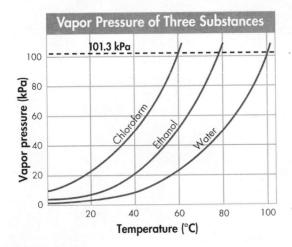

1. What is the normal boiling point of ethanol?

2. Can chloroform be heated to 90°C in an open container?

3. Which sequence has the states of CH_3OH correctly ordered in terms of increasing average kinetic energy?
   (A) $CH_3OH(s)$, $CH_3OH(g)$, $CH_3OH(l)$
   (B) $CH_3OH(g)$, $CH_3OH(l)$, $CH_3OH(s)$
   (C) $CH_3OH(l)$, $CH_3OH(g)$, $CH_3OH(s)$
   (D) $CH_3OH(s)$, $CH_3OH(l)$, $CH_3OH(g)$

Use the drawing to answer Questions 4–6. The same liquid is in each flask.

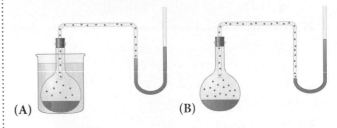

(A)   (B)

4. In which flask is the vapor pressure lower? Give a reason for your answer.

5. In which flask is the liquid at the higher temperature? Explain your answer.

6. How can the vapor pressure in each flask be determined?

For each question below, there are two statements. Decide whether each statement is true or false. Then decide whether Statement II is a correct explanation for Statement I.

Statement I		Statement II
7. In an open container, the rate of evaporation of a liquid always equals the rate of condensation.	BECAUSE	A dynamic equilibrium exists between the liquid and its vapor in an open container.
8. Water boils at a temperature below 100°C on top of a mountain.	BECAUSE	Atmospheric pressure decreases with an increase in altitude.
9. The temperature of a substance always increases as heat is added to the substance.	BECAUSE	The average kinetic energy of the particles in a substance increases with an increase in temperature.
10. Solids have a fixed volume.	BECAUSE	Particles in a solid cannot move.
11. Gases are more compressible than liquids.	BECAUSE	There is more space between particles in a gas than between particles in a liquid.

If You Have Trouble With . . .

Question	1	2	3	4	5	6	7	8	9	10	11
See Lesson	13.2	13.2	13.4	13.2	13.2	13.2	13.2	13.2	13.1	13.3	13.1

14

The Behavior of Gases

INSIDE:

- **14.1** Properties of Gases
- **14.2** The Gas Laws
- **14.3** Ideal Gases
- **14.4** Gases: Mixtures and Movements

PearsonChem.com

Aviators known as cluster balloonists rise above the clouds by harnessing themselves to balloons filled with helium gas.

KINETIC THEORY

Essential Questions:

1. *How do gases respond to changes in pressure, volume, and temperature?*
2. *Why is the ideal gas law useful even though ideal gases do not exist?*

CHEMYSTERY

Under Pressure

Just after 2 P.M., Becki completes her eighth scuba dive over a four-day period off the coast of Belize. After the dive, she feels fine.

A few hours later at dinner, Becki feels tired. She thinks that her fatigue is probably due to the many hours she had spent swimming during her vacation. But she also begins to feel itchy and notices a blotchy rash on her skin. Did she get stung by a sea creature during her last dive? Becki decides to go back to her hotel room to get some rest. As she is walking, she begins to feel severe pains in the joints of her arms and legs and feels achy all over her body. Becki feels like she is coming down with the flu, but she realizes that her symptoms are related to her dives. What is wrong with Becki?

▶ Connect to the **BIGIDEA** As you read about the behavior of gases, think about what may have caused Becki's symptoms.

NATIONAL SCIENCE EDUCATION STANDARDS:

A-1, A-2, B-2, B-5, E-2, F-1

14.1 Properties of Gases

Key Questions

🔑 Why are gases easier to compress than solids or liquids?

🔑 What are the three factors that affect gas pressure?

Vocabulary

• compressibility

Q: *Why is there a recommended pressure range for the air inside a soccer ball?* In organized soccer, there are rules about the equipment used in a game. For example, in international competitions, the ball's mass must not be more than 450 grams and not less than 410 grams. The pressure of the air inside the ball must be no lower than 0.6 atmospheres and no higher than 1.1 atmospheres at sea level.

In this lesson, you will study variables that affect the pressure of a gas. As you will discover, gas pressure is useful in a number of different objects, including auto air bags, inflatable rafts, aerosol sprays, and, yes, soccer balls.

Compressibility

🔑 Why are gases easier to compress than solids or liquids?

Recall from Chapter 13 that a gas can expand to fill its container, unlike a solid or liquid. The reverse is also true. Gases are easily compressed, or squeezed into a smaller volume. **Compressibility** is a measure of how much the volume of matter decreases under pressure.

The compressibility of a gas plays an important role in auto safety. When a car comes to a sudden stop, the people in the car will continue to move forward unless they are restrained. The driver and any passengers are more likely to survive a collision if they are wearing seat belts to restrict their forward movement. Cars also contain air bags as a second line of defense. A sudden reduction in speed triggers a chemical reaction inside an air bag. One product of the reaction is nitrogen gas, which causes the bag to inflate. An inflated air bag keeps the driver from colliding with the steering wheel. On the front passenger side of the car, an inflated air bag keeps a passenger from colliding with the dashboard or windshield.

Why does a collision with an inflated air bag cause much less damage than a collision with a steering wheel or dashboard? When a person collides with an inflated air bag, as shown in Figure 14.1, the impact forces the molecules of nitrogen gas in the bag closer together. The compression of the gas absorbs the energy of the impact.

Figure 14.1 Compression of a Gas
Because gases can be compressed, the air bag absorbs some of the energy from the impact of a collision. Air bags work best when combined with seat belts.
Describe *What happens to the gas molecules inside an air bag when a driver collides with the bag?*

Kinetic theory can explain why gases are compressed more easily than liquids or solids. **Gases are easily compressed because of the space between the particles in a gas.** Remember that the volume of the particles in a gas is small compared to the overall volume of the gas. So the distance between particles in a gas is much greater than the distance between particles in a liquid or solid. Under increased pressure, the particles in a gas are forced closer together, or compressed.

Figure 14.2 is a model of identical air samples in two different containers. Only oxygen and nitrogen—the two main gases in air—are represented. Each container has 8 nitrogen molecules and 2 oxygen molecules. In the larger container, the molecules are farther apart. In the smaller container, the air sample is compressed, and the molecules are closer together. Note that at STP, the distance between particles in an enclosed gas is about 10 times the diameter of a particle. However, it isn't practical to represent the actual distances between particles in all the molecular drawings of gases in this book. In order for the drawings to fit easily on a page, the particles are drawn closer together.

Figure 14.2 Modeling Air at Two Different Pressures
Air is primarily a mixture of two gases, nitrogen (N_2) and oxygen (O_2). A sample of air contains about 4 nitrogen molecules for every oxygen molecule.

Factors Affecting Gas Pressure

What are the three factors that affect gas pressure?

Kinetic theory can help explain other properties of gases, such as their ability to expand and take the shape and volume of their containers. Recall these assumptions about the particles in a gas. The particles move along straight-line paths until they collide with other particles or the walls of their container. The motion of the particles is constant and random. Because kinetic theory assumes there are no significant forces of attraction or repulsion among particles in a gas, particles in a gas can move freely.

Four variables are generally used to describe a gas. The variables and their common units are pressure (P) in kilopascals, volume (V) in liters, temperature (T) in kelvins, and the number of moles (n). **The amount of gas, the volume, and the temperature are factors that affect gas pressure.**

Learn more about gas properties online

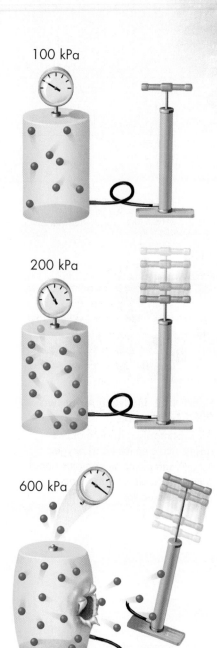

100 kPa

200 kPa

600 kPa

Figure 14.4 Gas in a Rigid Container When a gas is pumped into a closed rigid container, the pressure increases as more particles are added. If the number of particles is doubled, the pressure will double.

Figure 14.3 Gas in a Flexible Container
The volume of an air-filled raft is much larger than its volume before it was inflated. Using a pump to force air into a raft increases the pressure of the air inside the raft.
Compare *How does an underinflated raft compare with a fully inflated raft? Why do you think an underinflated raft might be dangerous to ride in?*

Amount of Gas An air-filled raft blasts through a narrow opening between rocks and plummets over a short waterfall into churning white water below. The raft bends and twists, absorbing some of the pounding energy of the river. The strength and flexibility of the raft rely on the pressure of the gas inside the raft. The raft must be made of a material that is strong enough to withstand the pressure of the air inside the raft. The material must also keep air from leaking out of the raft. The volume of the inflated raft in Figure 14.3 is dramatically larger than the volume of the raft before it is inflated. As air is added, the raft expands to its intended volume. The pressure of the air inside the raft keeps the raft inflated.

You can use kinetic theory to predict and explain how gases will respond to a change of conditions. If you inflate an air raft, for example, the pressure inside the raft will increase. Collisions of gas particles with the inside walls of the raft result in the pressure that is exerted by the enclosed gas. By adding gas, you increase the number of particles. Increasing the number of particles increases the number of collisions, which explains why the gas pressure increases.

Figure 14.4 shows what happens when gas is added to an enclosed, rigid container. Because the container is rigid, the volume of the gas is constant. Assume also that the temperature of the gas does not change. Under these conditions, doubling the number of particles of gas doubles the pressure. Tripling the number of particles triples the pressure, and so on. With a powerful pump and a strong container, you can generate very high pressures by adding more and more gas. However, once the pressure exceeds the strength of the container, the container will burst. Removing gas from a rigid container has the opposite effect. As the amount of gas is reduced, the pressure inside the container is reduced. If the number of particles in the container were cut in half, the pressure would drop by half.

If the pressure of the gas in a sealed container is lower than the outside air pressure, air will rush into the container when the container is opened. This movement causes the whoosh you hear when you open a vacuum-packed container. When the pressure of a gas in a sealed container is higher than the outside air pressure, the gas will flow out of the container when the container is unsealed.

The operation of an aerosol can depends on the movement of a gas from a region of high pressure to a region of lower pressure. Aerosol cans may contain whipped cream, hair mousse, or spray paint. Figure 14.5 shows how a can of spray paint works. The can contains a gas stored at high pressure. The air outside the can is at a lower pressure. Pushing the spray button creates an opening between the inside of the can and the air outside. The gas flows through the opening to the lower pressure region outside. The movement of the gas propels, or forces, the paint out of the can. As the gas is depleted, the pressure inside the can decreases until the gas can no longer propel paint from the can.

Volume You can raise the pressure exerted by a contained gas by reducing its volume. The more the gas is compressed, the more pressure the gas exerts inside the container. When gas is in a cylinder, as in an automobile engine, a piston can be used to reduce its volume. The snug-fitting piston keeps gas from escaping as the cylinder moves down and up.

Figure 14.6 shows a cylinder of gas under two different conditions. When the cylinder has a volume of 1 L, the gas exerts a pressure of 100 kPa. When the volume is halved to 0.5 L, the pressure is doubled to 200 kPa. Increasing the volume of the contained gas has the opposite effect. If the volume is doubled, the particles can expand into a volume that is twice the original volume. With the same number of particles in twice the volume, the pressure of the gas is cut in half.

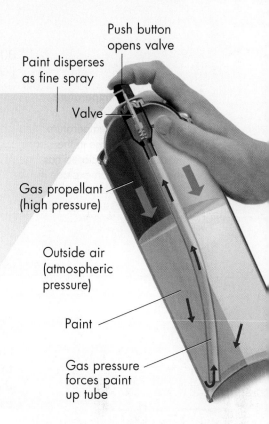

Figure 14.5 Aerosol Can
The pressure of the gas inside a new can of spray paint is greater than the air pressure outside the can. When gas rushes though an opening in the top of the can, it propels, or forces, paint out of the can. As the can is used, the pressure of the propellant decreases.
Relate Cause and Effect *What happens when the pressure of the propellant equals the air pressure outside the can?*

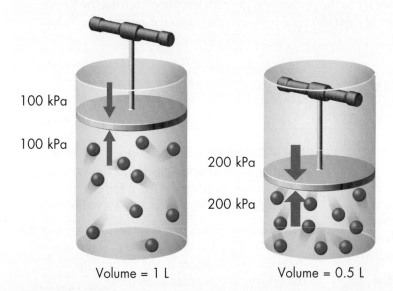

Figure 14.6 Pressure and Volume
A piston can be used to force a gas in a cylinder into a smaller volume. When the volume is decreased, the pressure the gas exerts is increased.
Interpret Diagrams *What happens to the gas pressure when the volume is reduced from 1 L to 0.5 L?*

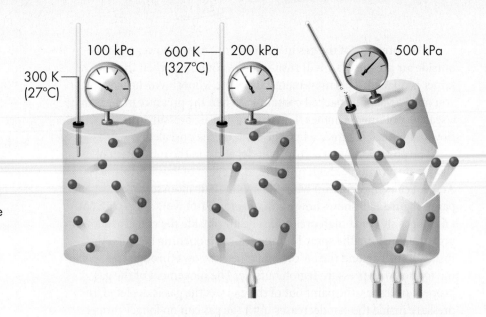

Figure 14.7 Temperature and Pressure
An increase in temperature causes an increase in the pressure of an enclosed gas. The container can explode if there is too great an increase in the gas pressure.

300 K (27°C) 100 kPa 600 K (327°C) 200 kPa 500 kPa

Temperature A sealed bag of potato chips bulges at the seams when placed in a sunny location. The bag bulges because an increase in the temperature of an enclosed gas causes an increase in its pressure. You can use kinetic theory to explain what happens. As a gas is heated, the temperature increases and the average kinetic energy of the particles in the gas increases. Faster-moving particles strike the walls of their container with more energy.

Look at Figure 14.7. The volume of the container and the amount of gas is constant. When the Kelvin temperature of the enclosed gas doubles from 300 K to 600 K, the pressure of the enclosed gas doubles from 100 kPa to 200 kPa. A gas in a sealed container may generate enormous pressure when heated. For that reason, an aerosol can, even an "empty" one, may explode if thrown onto a fire.

By contrast, as the temperature of an enclosed gas decreases, the pressure decreases. The particles, on average, move more slowly and have less kinetic energy. They strike the container walls with less force. Halving the Kelvin temperature of a gas in a rigid container decreases the gas pressure by half.

Q: *Which do you think would travel farther if kicked with the same amount of force: a properly inflated soccer ball or an under-inflated soccer ball? What might happen to an overinflated soccer ball if you kicked it too hard?*

⊙ 14.1 LessonCheck

1. ⊶ **Review** Why is a gas easy to compress?

2. ⊶ **Identify** List three factors that can affect gas pressure.

3. Compare and Contrast Why does a collision with an air bag cause less damage than a collision with a steering wheel?

4. Explain How does a decrease in temperature affect the pressure of a contained gas?

5. Apply Concepts If the temperature is constant, what change in volume would cause the pressure of an enclosed gas to be reduced to one quarter of its original value?

6. Apply Concepts Assuming the gas in a container remains at a constant temperature, how could you increase the gas pressure in the container a hundredfold?

7. Summarize Write a paragraph explaining how a pressurized garden sprayer works. Make sure to describe what happens to the air pressure inside the sprayer as it is pumped by hand.

BIGIDEA KINETIC THEORY

8. Use the kinetic theory of gases to explain why a gas can be easily squeezed into a smaller volume.

Atmospheric Chemist

Earth's atmosphere is a mixture of many gases, including oxygen, nitrogen, water vapor, carbon dioxide, methane, and ozone. Each one has an impact on life on Earth. The study of the chemical composition of the atmosphere is called atmospheric chemistry. Atmospheric chemists analyze the concentrations of atmospheric gases and determine how these gases chemically interact.

An important part of atmospheric research involves developing models that can predict the effects of fossil fuel emissions and other pollutants on air quality, climate, and the biosphere. Some atmospheric chemists study volcanic plumes, which are mixtures of hot gases and dust given off by volcanoes. Atmospheric chemistry is not limited to Earth's atmosphere. With the aid of telescopes, atmospheric chemists can study the composition of atmospheres of distant planets.

Atmospheric research is often a collaboration among scientists from different disciplines, including chemistry, physics, climatology, and oceanography. Atmospheric chemists typically have a bachelor's degree in chemistry or atmospheric science. Many also have a graduate degree in a specific field of research.

TOOLS AND TECHNOLOGY An atmospheric chemist adjusts a device used to analyze the motion and composition of air in the atmosphere.

AIR QUALITY Smog is a form of air pollution caused by tailpipe and smokestack emissions. The work of atmospheric chemists can help communities better understand how human activity impacts local air quality.

Take It Further

1. Infer What kinds of data do you think atmospheric chemists collect to study gases in the atmosphere?

2. Research a Problem Ozone (O_3) is one of many gases that atmospheric chemists study. Research the ozone layer and describe how atmospheric ozone levels have changed over time.

14.2 The Gas Laws

Q: *How do you fill up a hot air balloon?* A hot air balloon works on the principle that warm air is less dense than cooler air. To make a hot air balloon rise, the pilot heats the air inside the balloon. To make the balloon descend, the pilot releases hot air through a vent in the top of the balloon. In this section, you'll study the laws that allow you to predict gas behavior.

Boyle's Law

🔑 How are the pressure and volume of a gas related?

Kinetic theory tells you that there is empty space between the particles in a gas. Imagine how an increase in pressure would affect the volume of a contained gas. **🔑 If the temperature is constant, as the pressure of a gas increases, the volume decreases.** In turn, as the pressure decreases, the volume increases. Robert Boyle was the first person to study this pressure-volume relationship in a systematic way. In 1662, Boyle proposed a law to describe the relationship. **Boyle's law** states that for a given mass of gas at constant temperature, the volume of the gas varies inversely with pressure.

Look at Figure 14.8. A gas with a volume of 1.0 L (V_1) is at a pressure of 100 kPa (P_1). As the volume increases to 2.0 L (V_2), the pressure decreases to 50 kPa (P_2). The product $P_1 \times V_1$ (100 kPa × 1.0 L = 100 kPa·L) is the same as the product $P_2 \times V_2$ (50 kPa × 2.0 L = 100 kPa·L). As the volume decreases to 0.5 L (V_3), the pressure increases to 200 kPa (P_3). Again, the product of the pressure and the volume equals 100 kPa·L.

Key Question

🔑 How are the pressure, volume, and temperature of a gas related?

Vocabulary

- Boyle's law
- Charles's law
- Gay-Lussac's law
- combined gas law

Interpret Graphs

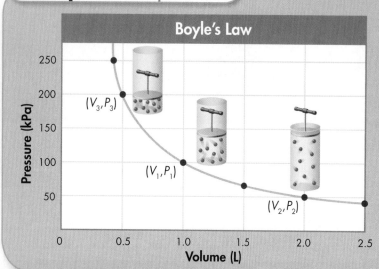

Figure 14.8 The pressure of a gas changes as the volume changes.

a. Read Graphs When the volume is 2.0 L, what is the pressure?

b. Predict What would the pressure be if the volume were increased to 3.0 L?

c. Draw Conclusions Based on the shape of the graph, describe the general pressure-volume relationship.

In an inverse relationship, the product of the two variable quantities is constant. So the product of pressure and volume at any two sets of pressure and volume conditions is always constant at a given temperature. The mathematical expression of Boyle's law is as follows.

$$P_1 \times V_1 = P_2 \times V_2$$

The graph of an inverse relationship is always a curve, as in Figure 14.8.

SampleProblem 14.1

Using Boyle's Law

A balloon contains 30.0 L of helium gas at 103 kPa. What is the volume of the helium when the balloon rises to an altitude where the pressure is only 25.0 kPa? (Assume that the temperature remains constant.)

❶ Analyze List the knowns and the unknown.
Use Boyle's law ($P_1 \times V_1 = P_2 \times V_2$) to calculate the unknown volume (V_2).

KNOWNS	UNKNOWN
P_1 = 103 kPa	V_2 = ? L
V_1 = 30.0 L	
P_2 = 25.0 kPa	

❷ Calculate Solve for the unknown.

Start with Boyle's law.

$$P_1 \times V_1 = P_2 \times V_2$$

Rearrange the equation to isolate V_2.

$$V_2 = \frac{P_1 \times V_1}{P_2}$$

Isolate V_2 by dividing both sides by P_2:

$$\frac{P_1 \times V_1}{P_2} = \frac{\cancel{P_2} \times V_2}{\cancel{P_2}}$$

Substitute the known values for P_1, V_1, and P_2 into the equation and solve.

$$V_2 = \frac{103 \,\cancel{kPa} \times 30.0 \,L}{25.0 \,\cancel{kPa}}$$

$$= 1.24 \times 10^2 \,L$$

❸ Evaluate Does the result make sense? A decrease in pressure at constant temperature must correspond to a proportional increase in volume. The calculated result agrees with both kinetic theory and the pressure-volume relationship. The units have canceled correctly.

9. Nitrous oxide (N_2O) is used as an anesthetic. The pressure on 2.50 L of N_2O changes from 105 kPa to 40.5 kPa. If the temperature does not change, what will the new volume be?

10. A gas with a volume of 4.00 L at a pressure of 205 kPa is allowed to expand to a volume of 12.0 L. What is the pressure in the container if the temperature remains constant?

Solve Problem 10 by rearranging Boyle's law to isolate P_2.

Figure 14.9 Cooling Balloons in Liquid Nitrogen
When the gas in a balloon is cooled at constant pressure, the volume of the gas decreases.
Predict *What would happen if you removed the balloons from the beaker and allowed them to warm back up to room temperature?*

Charles's Law

How are the temperature and volume of a gas related?

Figure 14.9 shows inflated balloons being dipped into a beaker of liquid nitrogen. For each balloon, the amount of air and the pressure are constant. As the air inside rapidly cools, the balloon shrinks. In fact, the gas volume decreases so much that all the cooled balloons can easily fit inside the beaker.

In 1787, the French physicist Jacques Charles studied the effect of temperature on the volume of a gas at constant pressure. When he graphed his data, Charles observed that a graph of gas volume versus temperature (in °C) is a straight line for any gas. **As the temperature of an enclosed gas increases, the volume increases if the pressure is constant.** When Charles extrapolated, or extended, the line to zero volume ($V = 0$), the line always intersected the temperature axis at $-273.15°C$. This value is equal to 0 on the Kelvin temperature scale. The observations that Charles made are summarized in Charles's law. **Charles's law** states that the volume of a fixed mass of gas is directly proportional to its Kelvin temperature if the pressure is kept constant. Look at the graph in Figure 14.10. When the temperature is 300 K, the volume is 1.0 L. When the temperature is 900 K, the volume is 3.0 L. In both cases, the ratio of V to T is 0.0033.

Interpret Graphs

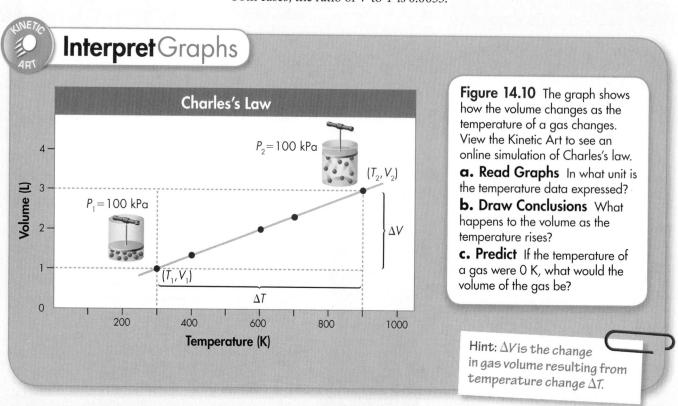

Charles's Law

$P_2 = 100$ kPa

(T_2, V_2)

$P_1 = 100$ kPa

(T_1, V_1)

ΔV

ΔT

Volume (L)

Temperature (K)

Figure 14.10 The graph shows how the volume changes as the temperature of a gas changes. View the Kinetic Art to see an online simulation of Charles's law.
a. Read Graphs In what unit is the temperature data expressed?
b. Draw Conclusions What happens to the volume as the temperature rises?
c. Predict If the temperature of a gas were 0 K, what would the volume of the gas be?

Hint: ΔV is the change in gas volume resulting from temperature change ΔT.

The ratio V_1/T_1 is equal to the ratio V_2/T_2. Because this ratio is constant at all conditions of temperature and volume, when the pressure is constant, you can write Charles's law as follows.

$$\frac{V_1}{T_1} = \frac{V_2}{T_2}$$

The ratio of the variables is always a constant in a direct relationship, and the graph is always a straight line. It is not a direct relationship if the temperatures are expressed in degrees Celsius. So when you solve gas law problems, the temperature must always be expressed in kelvins.

Q: *A hot air balloon contains a propane burner onboard to heat the air inside the balloon. What happens to the volume of the balloon as the air is heated?*

SampleProblem 14.2

Using Charles's Law

A balloon inflated in a room at 24°C has a volume of 4.00 L. The balloon is then heated to a temperature of 58°C. What is the new volume if the pressure remains constant?

❶ Analyze **List the knowns and the unknown.**
Use Charles's law ($V_1/T_1 = V_2/T_2$) to calculate the unknown volume (V_2).

❷ Calculate **Solve for the unknown.**

KNOWNS	UNKNOWN
$V_1 = 4.00$ L	$V_2 = ?$ L
$T_1 = 24°C$	
$T_2 = 58°C$	

Because you will use a gas law, start by expressing the temperatures in kelvins.

$T_1 = 24°C + 273 = 297$ K
$T_2 = 58°C + 273 = 331$ K

Write the equation for Charles's law.

$$\frac{V_1}{T_1} = \frac{V_2}{T_2}$$

Isolate V_2 by multiplying both sides by T_2:

$$T_2 \times \frac{V_1}{T_1} = \frac{V_2}{T_2} \times T_2$$

Rearrange the equation to isolate V_2.

$$V_2 = \frac{V_1 \times T_2}{T_1}$$

Substitute the known values for T_1, V_1, and T_2 into the equation and solve.

$$V_2 = \frac{4.00 \text{ L} \times 331 \text{ K}}{297 \text{ K}} = 4.46 \text{ L}$$

❸ Evaluate **Does the result make sense?** The volume increases as the temperature increases. This result agrees with both the kinetic theory and Charles's law.

11. If a sample of gas occupies 6.80 L at 325°C, what will its volume be at 25°C if the pressure does not change?

12. Exactly 5.00 L of air at −50.0°C is warmed to 100.0°C. What is the new volume if the pressure remains constant?

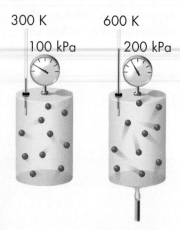

300 K
100 kPa

600 K
200 kPa

Figure 14.11 Gay-Lussac's Law
When a gas is heated at constant volume, the pressure increases.
Interpret Diagrams *How can you tell from the drawings that there is a fixed amount of gas in the cylinders?*

Gay-Lussac's Law

How are the pressure and temperature of a gas related?

When tires are not inflated to the recommended pressure, fuel efficiency and traction decrease. Treads can wear down faster. Most importantly, improper inflation can lead to tire failure. A driver should not check tire pressure after driving a long distance because the air in a tire heats up during a drive. **As the temperature of an enclosed gas increases, the pressure increases if the volume is constant.**

Joseph Gay-Lussac (1778–1850), a French chemist, discovered the relationship between the pressure and temperature of a gas in 1802. The gas law that describes the relationship bears his name. **Gay-Lussac's law** states that the pressure of a gas is directly proportional to the Kelvin temperature if the volume remains constant. Look at Figure 14.11. When the temperature is 300 K, the pressure is 100 kPa. When the temperature is doubled to 600 K, the pressure doubles to 200 kPa. Because Gay-Lussac's law involves direct proportions, the ratios P_1/T_1 and P_2/T_2 are equal at constant volume. You can write Gay-Lussac's law as follows:

$$\frac{P_1}{T_1} = \frac{P_2}{T_2}$$

Gay-Lussac's law can be applied to reduce the time it takes to cook food. One cooking method involves placing food above a layer of water and heating the water. The water vapor, or steam, that is produced cooks the food. Steam that escapes from the pot is at a temperature of about 100°C when the pressure is near one atmosphere. In a pressure cooker, like the one shown in Figure 14.12, steam is trapped inside the cooker. The temperature of the steam reaches about 120°C. The food cooks faster at this higher temperature, but the pressure rises, which increases the risk of an explosion. A pressure cooker has a valve that allows some vapor to escape when the pressure exceeds the set value.

Figure 14.12 Pressure Cooker
A pressure cooker is a gas-tight container in which pressurized steam is used to cook food. With the lid locked, the volume of steam and the number of water molecules are constant. So any increase in temperature causes an increase in pressure.

SampleProblem 14.3

Using Gay-Lussac's Law

Aerosol cans carry labels warning not to incinerate (burn) the cans or store them above a certain temperature. This problem will show why it is dangerous to dispose of aerosol cans in a fire. The gas in a used aerosol can is at a pressure of 103 kPa at 25°C. If the can is thrown onto a fire, what will the pressure be when the temperature reaches 928°C?

❶ Analyze List the knowns and the unknown. Use Gay-Lussac's law ($P_1/T_1 = P_2/T_2$) to calculate the unknown pressure (P_2). Remember, because this problem involves temperatures and a gas law, the temperatures must be expressed in kelvins.

KNOWNS	UNKNOWN
$P_1 = 103 \text{ kPa}$	$P_2 = ? \text{ kPa}$
$T_1 = 25°C$	
$T_2 = 928°C$	

❷ Calculate Solve for the unknown.

Start by converting the two known temperatures from degrees Celsius to kelvins.

$$T_1 = 25°C + 273 = 298 \text{ K}$$
$$T_2 = 928°C + 273 = 1201 \text{ K}$$

Write the equation for Gay-Lussac's law.

$$\frac{P_1}{T_1} = \frac{P_2}{T_2}$$

Isolate P_2 by multiplying both sides by T_2:

$$T_2 \times \frac{P_1}{T_1} = \frac{P_2}{T_2} \times T_2$$

Rearrange the equation to isolate P_2.

$$P_2 = \frac{P_1 \times T_2}{T_1}$$

Substitute the known values for P_1, T_2, and T_1 into the equation and solve.

$$P_2 = \frac{103 \text{ kPa} \times 1201 \text{ K}}{298 \text{ K}}$$

$$= 415 \text{ kPa}$$

$$= 4.15 \times 10^2 \text{ kPa}$$

❸ Evaluate Does the result make sense? From the kinetic theory, one would expect the increase in temperature of a gas to produce an increase in pressure if the volume remains constant. The calculated value does show such an increase.

13. The pressure in a sealed plastic container is 108 kPa at 41°C. What is the pressure when the temperature drops to 22°C? Assume that the volume has not changed.

14. The pressure in a car tire is 198 kPa at 27°C. After a long drive, the pressure is 225 kPa. What is the temperature of the air in the tire? Assume that the volume is constant.

To solve Problem 14, rearrange Gay-Lussac's law to isolate T_2.

The Combined Gas Law

🔑 *How are the pressure, volume, and temperature of a gas related?*

There is a single expression, called the **combined gas law**, that combines Boyle's law, Charles's law, and Gay-Lussac's law.

$$\frac{P_1 \times V_1}{T_1} = \frac{P_2 \times V_2}{T_2}$$

🔑 **When only the amount of gas is constant, the combined gas law describes the relationship among pressure, volume, and temperature.**

Sample Problem 14.4

Using the Combined Gas Law

The volume of a gas-filled balloon is 30.0 L at 313 K and 153 kPa pressure. What would the volume be at standard temperature and pressure (STP)?

❶ Analyze List the knowns and the unknown. Use the combined gas law ($P_1V_1/T_1 = P_2V_2/T_2$) to calculate the unknown volume (V_2).

KNOWNS	UNKNOWN
$V_1 = 30.0\,\text{L}$	$V_2 = ?\,\text{L}$
$T_1 = 313\,\text{K}$	
$P_1 = 153\,\text{kPa}$	
$T_2 = 273\,\text{K}$ (standard temperature)	
$P_2 = 101.3\,\text{kPa}$ (standard pressure)	

❷ Calculate Solve for the unknown.

State the combined gas law.

$$\frac{P_1 \times V_1}{T_1} = \frac{P_2 \times V_2}{T_2}$$

Isolate V_2 by multiplying both sides by T_2 and dividing both sides by P_2:

$$\frac{T_2}{P_2} \times \frac{P_1 \times V_1}{T_1} = \frac{\cancel{P_2} \times V_2}{\cancel{T_2}} \times \frac{\cancel{T_2}}{\cancel{P_2}}$$

Rearrange the equation to isolate V_2.

$$V_2 = \frac{P_1 \times V_1 \times T_2}{P_2 \times T_1}$$

Substitute the known quantities into the equation and solve.

$$V_2 = \frac{153\,\cancel{\text{kPa}} \times 30.0\,\text{L} \times 273\,\cancel{\text{K}}}{101.3\,\cancel{\text{kPa}} \times 313\,\cancel{\text{K}}} = \boxed{39.5\,\text{L}}$$

❸ Evaluate Does the result make sense? A decrease in temperature and a decrease in pressure have opposite effects on the volume. To evaluate the increase in volume, multiply V_1 (30.0 L) by the ratio of P_1 to P_2 (1.51) and the ratio of T_2 to T_1 (0.872). The result is 39.5 L.

15. A gas at 155 kPa and 25°C has an initial volume of 1.00 L. The pressure of the gas increases to 605 kPa as the temperature is raised to 125°C. What is the new volume?

16. A 5.00-L air sample has a pressure of 107 kPa at a temperature of −50.0°C. If the temperature is raised to 102°C and the volume expands to 7.00 L, what will the new pressure be?

Weather balloons, like the one in Figure 14.13, carry a package of data-gathering instruments up into the atmosphere. At an altitude of about 27,000 meters, the balloon bursts. The combined gas law can help to explain this situation. Both outside temperature and pressure drop as the balloon rises. These changes have opposite effects on the volume of the weather balloon. A drop in temperature causes the volume of an enclosed gas to decrease. A drop in outside pressure causes the volume to increase. Given that the balloon bursts, the drop in pressure must affect the volume more than the drop in temperature does.

The combined gas law can also help you solve gas problems when only two variables are changing. It may seem challenging to remember four different expressions for the gas laws. But you actually only need to remember one expression—the combined gas law. You can derive the other laws from the combined gas law by holding one variable constant.

To illustrate, suppose you hold the temperature constant $(T_1 = T_2)$. Rearrange the combined gas law so that the two temperature terms are on the same side of the equation. Because $T_1 = T_2$, the ratio of T_1 to T_2 is equal to one. Multiplying by 1 does not change a value in an equation. So when the temperature is constant, you can delete the temperature ratio from the rearranged combined gas law. What you are left with is the equation for Boyle's law.

$$P_1 \times V_1 = P_2 \times V_2 \times \frac{T_1}{T_2}$$

$$P_1 \times V_1 = P_2 \times V_2$$

A similar process yields Charles's law when pressure remains constant and Gay-Lussac's law when volume remains constant.

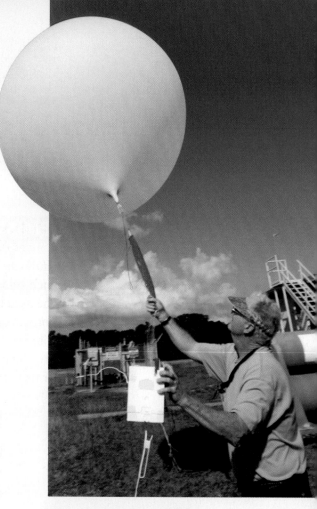

Figure 14.13 Weather Balloon
Meteorologists use weather balloons to gather data about Earth's atmosphere.
Infer *Why is helium more likely to be used in weather balloons than air?*

14.2 LessonCheck

17. 🔑 **Review** How are the pressure and volume of a gas related at constant temperature?

18. 🔑 **Review** If pressure is constant, how does a change in temperature affect the volume of a gas?

19. 🔑 **Review** What is the relationship between the temperature and pressure of a contained gas at constant volume?

20. 🔑 **Describe** In what situations is the combined gas law useful?

21. **Define** Write the mathematical equation for Boyle's law and explain the symbols.

22. **Calculate** A given mass of air has a volume of 6.00 L at 101 kPa. What volume will it occupy at 25.0 kPa if the temperature does not change?

23. **Explain** How can Charles's law be derived from the combined gas law?

24. **Apply Concepts** The volume of a weather balloon increases as the balloon rises in the atmosphere. Why doesn't the drop in temperature at higher altitudes cause the volume to decrease?

BIGIDEA KINETIC THEORY

25. Why do you think scientists cannot collect temperature and volume data for an enclosed gas at temperatures near absolute zero?

14.3 Ideal Gases

Q: *How can you make fog indoors?* Carbon dioxide freezes at $-78.5°C$, which is much colder than the ice in your freezer. Solid carbon dioxide, or dry ice, can be used to make stage fog. Dry ice doesn't melt—it sublimes. As solid carbon dioxide changes to gas, water vapor in the air condenses and forms a white fog. Dry ice can exist because gases don't obey the assumptions of kinetic theory at all conditions. In this section, you will learn how real gases differ from the ideal gases on which the gas laws are based.

Key Questions

🔑 How can you calculate the amount of a contained gas when the pressure, volume, and temperature are specified?

🔑 Under what conditions are real gases most likely to differ from ideal gases?

Vocabulary

• ideal gas constant
• ideal gas law

Ideal Gas Law

🔑 **How can you calculate the amount of a contained gas when the pressure, volume, and temperature are specified?**

Up to this point, you have worked with three variables that describe a gas: pressure, volume, and temperature. There is a fourth variable still to be considered: the amount of gas in the system, expressed in terms of the number of moles.

Suppose you want to calculate the number of moles (n) of a gas in a fixed volume at a known temperature and pressure. By modifying the combined gas law, you can solve for n. First, you must recognize that the volume occupied by a gas at a specified temperature and pressure depends on the number of particles. The number of moles of gas is directly proportional to the number of particles. So moles must be directly proportional to volume as well. You can now introduce moles into the combined gas law by dividing each side of the equation by n.

$$\frac{P_1 \times V_1}{T_1 \times n_1} = \frac{P_2 \times V_2}{T_2 \times n_2}$$

This equation shows that $(P \times V)/(T \times n)$ is a constant. This constant holds for what are called ideal gases—gases that conform to the gas laws.

If you know the values for P, V, T, and n for one set of conditions, you can calculate a value for the constant. Recall that 1 mol of every gas occupies 22.4 L at STP (101.3 kPa and 273 K). You can use these values to find the value of the constant, which has the symbol R and is called the ideal gas constant. Insert the values of P, V, T, and n into $(P \times V)/(T \times n)$.

$$R = \frac{P \times V}{T \times n} = \frac{101.3 \text{ kPa} \times 22.4 \text{ L}}{273 \text{ K} \times 1 \text{ mol}} = 8.31 \text{ (L} \cdot \text{kPa)} / (\text{K} \cdot \text{mol})$$

The **ideal gas constant** (*R*) has the value 8.31 (L·kPa)/(K·mol). The gas law that includes all four variables—*P*, *V*, *T*, and *n*—is called the **ideal gas law.** It is usually written as follows.

$$P \times V = n \times R \times T \text{ or } PV = nRT$$

🔑 **When the pressure, volume, and temperature of a contained gas are known, you can use the ideal gas law to calculate the number of moles of the gas.** The amount of helium in a balloon, the amount of air in a scuba tank or a bicycle tire—each of these quantities can be calculated using the ideal gas law as long as you know the values for *P*, *V*, and *T* in each case.

SampleProblem 14.5

Using the Ideal Gas Law

At 34°C, the pressure inside a nitrogen-filled tennis ball with a volume of 0.148 L is 212 kPa. How many moles of nitrogen gas are in the tennis ball?

❶ Analyze List the knowns and the unknown.
Use the ideal gas law ($P \times V = n \times R \times T$) to calculate the number of moles (*n*).

KNOWNS	UNKNOWN
P = 212 kPa	*n* = ? mol N_2
V = 0.148 L	
T = 34°C	
R = 8.31 (L·kPa) / (K·mol)	

❷ Calculate Solve for the unknown.

Convert degrees Celsius to kelvins.
$$T = 34°C + 273 = 307 \text{ K}$$

State the ideal gas law.
$$P \times V = n \times R \times T$$

Isolate *n* by dividing both sides by (*R* × *T*):
$$\frac{P \times V}{R \times T} = \frac{n \times \cancel{R} \times \cancel{T}}{\cancel{R} \times \cancel{T}}$$

Rearrange the equation to isolate *n*.
$$n = \frac{P \times V}{R \times T}$$

Substitute the known values for *P*, *V*, *R*, and *T* into the equation and solve.
$$n = \frac{P \times V}{R \times T} = \frac{212 \text{ k\cancel{Pa}} \times 0.148 \cancel{L}}{8.31 \text{ (}\cancel{L}\cdot\cancel{kPa}\text{) / (}\cancel{K}\cdot\text{mol)} \times 307 \cancel{K}} = 0.0123 \text{ mol } N_2$$

$$= 1.23 \times 10^{-2} \text{ mol } N_2$$

❸ Evaluate Does the result make sense? A tennis ball has a small volume and is not under great pressure. It is reasonable that the ball contains a small amount of nitrogen.

26. When the temperature of a rigid hollow sphere containing 685 L of helium gas is held to 621 K, the pressure of the gas is 1.89×10^3 kPa. How many moles of helium does the sphere contain?

27. What pressure will be exerted by 0.450 mol of a gas at 25°C if it is contained in a 0.650-L vessel?

Solve Problem 27 by rearranging the ideal gas law to isolate *P*.

SampleProblem 14.6

Using the Ideal Gas Law

A deep underground cavern contains 2.24×10^6 L of methane gas (CH_4) at a pressure of 1.50×10^3 kPa and a temperature of 315 K. How many kilograms of CH_4 does the cavern contain?

❶ Analyze List the knowns and the unknown.
Calculate the number of moles (n) using the ideal gas law. Use the molar mass of methane to convert moles to grams. Then convert grams to kilograms.

KNOWNS	UNKNOWN
$P = 1.50 \times 10^3$ kPa	$m = ?$ kg CH_4
$V = 2.24 \times 10^6$ L	
$T = 315$ K	
$R = 8.31$ (L·kPa) / (K·mol)	
molar mass$_{CH_4}$ = 16.0g	

❷ Calculate Solve for the unknown.

State the ideal gas law.

$$P \times V = n \times R \times T$$

Rearrange the equation to isolate n.

$$n = \frac{P \times V}{R \times T}$$

Substitute the known quantities into the equation to find the number of moles of methane.

$$n = \frac{(1.50 \times 10^3 \text{ kPa}) \times (2.24 \times 10^6 \text{ L})}{8.31 \frac{\text{L} \cdot \text{kPa}}{\text{K} \cdot \text{mol}} \times 315 \text{ K}} = 1.28 \times 10^6 \text{ mol } CH_4$$

Do a mole-mass conversion.

$$1.28 \times 10^6 \text{ mol } CH_4 \times \frac{16.0 \text{ g } CH_4}{1 \text{ mol } CH_4} = 20.5 \times 10^6 \text{ g } CH_4$$
$$= 2.05 \times 10^7 \text{ g } CH_4$$

Convert from grams to kilograms.

$$2.05 \times 10^7 \text{ g } CH_4 \times \frac{1 \text{ kg}}{10^3 \text{ g}} = 2.05 \times 10^4 \text{ kg } CH_4$$

❸ Evaluate Does the result make sense? Although the methane is compressed, its volume is still very large. So it is reasonable that the cavern contains a large mass of methane.

28. A child's lungs can hold 2.20 L. How many grams of air do her lungs hold at a pressure of 102 kPa and a body temperature of 37°C? Use a molar mass of 29 g for air, which is about 20% O_2 (32 g/mol) and 80% N_2 (28 g/mol).

29. What volume will 12.0 g of oxygen gas (O_2) occupy at 25°C and a pressure of 52.7 kPa?

In Problems 28 and 29, make sure to express the temperature in kelvins before substituting for T in the ideal gas law equation.

Ideal Gases and Real Gases

Under what conditions are real gases most likely to differ from ideal gases?

An ideal gas is one that follows the gas laws at all conditions of pressure and temperature. Such a gas would have to conform precisely to the assumptions of kinetic theory. Its particles could have no volume, and there could be no attraction between particles in the gas. As you probably suspect, there is no gas for which these assumptions are true. So an ideal gas does not exist. Nevertheless, at many conditions of temperature and pressure, a real gas behaves very much like an ideal gas.

The particles in a real gas do have volume, and there are attractions between the particles. Because of these attractions, a gas can condense, or even solidify, when it is compressed or cooled. For example, if water vapor is cooled below 100°C at standard atmospheric pressure, it condenses to a liquid. The behavior of other real gases is similar, although lower temperatures and greater pressures may be required. Such conditions are required to produce the liquid nitrogen in Figure 14.14. **Real gases differ most from an ideal gas at low temperatures and high pressures.**

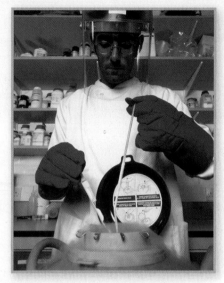

Figure 14.14 Liquid Nitrogen
A lab technician places a cell sample into an insulated tank containing liquid nitrogen. Nitrogen boils at −196°C.

Quick Lab

Purpose To measure the amount of carbon dioxide gas given off when antacid tablets dissolve in water

Materials
- 6 effervescent antacid tablets
- 3 rubber balloons (spherical)
- plastic medicine dropper
- water
- clock or watch
- metric tape measure
- graph paper
- water
- pressure sensor (optional)

Carbon Dioxide From Antacid Tablets

Procedure

1. Break six antacid tablets into small pieces. Keep the pieces from each tablet in a separate pile. Put the pieces from one tablet into the first balloon. Put the pieces from two tablets into a second balloon. Put the pieces from three tablets into a third balloon. **CAUTION** *If you are allergic to latex, do not handle the balloons.*

2. After you use the medicine dropper to squirt about 5 mL of cold water into each balloon, immediately tie off each balloon.

3. Shake the balloons to mix the contents. Allow the contents to warm to room temperature.

4. Measure and record the circumference of each balloon several times during the next 20 minutes.

5. Use the maximum circumference of each balloon to calculate its volume. (*Hint:* For the volume of a sphere, use $V = \frac{4}{3}\pi r^3$ and $r = $ circumference$/2\pi$.)

Analyze and Conclude

1. Graph Make a graph of volume versus number of tablets. Use your graph to describe the relationship between the number of tablets used and the volume of the balloon.

2. Calculate Assume that the balloon is filled with carbon dioxide gas at 20°C and standard pressure. Calculate the mass and the number of moles of CO_2 in each balloon at maximum inflation.

3. Analyze Data If a typical antacid tablet contains 2.0 g of sodium hydrogen carbonate, how many moles of CO_2 should one tablet yield? Compare this theoretical value with your results.

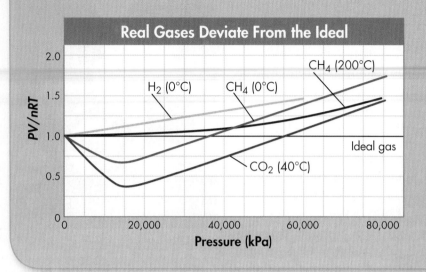

Real Gases Deviate From the Ideal

CH₄ (200°C)

H₂ (0°C)   CH₄ (0°C)

Ideal gas

CO₂ (40°C)

Pressure (kPa)

PV/nRT

Figure 14.15 This graph shows how real gases deviate from the ideal gas law at high pressures.
a. Read Graphs What are the values of (*PV/nRT*) for an ideal gas at 20,000 and 60,000 kPa?
b. Identify What variable is responsible for the differences between the two methane (CH₄) curves?
c. Make Generalizations How does an increase in pressure affect the value of (*PV/nRT*) for real gases?

Q: *Certain types of fog machines use dry ice and water to create stage fog. Chunks of dry ice are added to hot water, which causes the dry ice to sublime. The cold carbon dioxide gas causes water vapor in the surrounding air to condense into small droplets, resulting in a smoky fog. What phase changes occur when stage fog is made?*

Figure 14.15 shows how the value of the ratio (*PV/nRT*) changes as pressure increases. For an ideal gas, the result is a horizontal line because the ratio is always equal to 1. For real gases at high pressure, the ratio may deviate, or depart, from the ideal. When the ratio is greater than 1, the curve rises above the ideal gas line. When the ratio is less than 1, the curve drops below the line. The deviations can be explained by two factors. As attractive forces reduce the distance between particles, a gas occupies less volume than expected, causing the ratio to be less than 1. But the actual volume of the molecules causes the ratio to be greater than 1.

In portions of the curves below the line, intermolecular attractions dominate. In portions of the curves above the line, molecular volume dominates. Look at the curves for methane (CH₄) at 0°C and at 200°C. At 200°C, the molecules have more kinetic energy to overcome intermolecular attractions. So the curve for CH₄ at 200°C never drops below the line.

14.3 LessonCheck

30. **Review** How can you determine the number of moles of a contained gas when the pressure, volume, and temperature are known values?

31. **Identify** Under what conditions do real gases deviate most from ideal behavior?

32. Calculate Determine the volume occupied by 0.582 mol of a gas at 15°C if the pressure is 81.8 kPa.

33. Calculate You fill a rigid steel cylinder that has a volume of 20.0 L with nitrogen gas to a final pressure of 2.00×10^4 kPa at 28°C. How many kilograms of N_2 does the cylinder contain?

34. Compare What is the difference between a real gas and an ideal gas?

35. Analyze Data At standard pressure, ammonia condenses at −33.3°C but nitrogen does not condense until −195.79°C. Use what you know about bond polarity to explain this difference.

BIG IDEA KINETIC THEORY

36. Use the kinetic theory of gases to explain this statement: No gas exhibits ideal behavior at all temperatures and pressures.

14.4 Gases: Mixtures and Movements

Q: *Why do balloons filled with helium deflate faster than balloons filled with air?* You have probably seen party balloons inflated with air or helium. The surface of a latex balloon has tiny pores through which gas particles can pass, causing the balloon to deflate over time. The rate at which the balloon deflates depends on the gas it contains.

Key Questions

⬤ How is the total pressure of a gas mixture related to the partial pressures of the component gases?

⬤ How does the molar mass of a gas affect the rate at which the gas diffuses or effuses?

Vocabulary

- partial pressure
- Dalton's law of partial pressures
- diffusion • effusion
- Graham's law of effusion

Dalton's Law

⬤ **How is the total pressure of a gas mixture related to the partial pressures of the component gases?**

Gas pressure results from collisions of particles in a gas with an object. If the number of particles increases in a given volume, more collisions occur. If the average kinetic energy of the particles increases, more collisions occur. In both cases, the pressure increases. Gas pressure depends only on the number of particles in a given volume and on their average kinetic energy. Particles in a mixture of gases at the same temperature have the same average kinetic energy. So the kind of particle is not important.

Table 14.1 shows the composition of dry air, or air that does not contain any water vapor. The contribution each gas in a mixture makes to the total pressure is called the **partial pressure** exerted by that gas. In dry air, the partial pressure of nitrogen is 79.11 kPa. ⬤ **In a mixture of gases, the total pressure is the sum of the partial pressures of the gases.**

Interpret Data

Composition of Dry Air		
Component	Volume (%)	Partial pressure (kPa)
Nitrogen	78.08	79.11
Oxygen	20.95	21.22
Carbon dioxide	0.04	0.04
Argon and others	0.93	0.95
Total	**100.00**	**101.32**

Table 14.1 The total pressure of dry air is the sum of the partial pressures of its component gases.
a. Read Tables What is the partial pressure of oxygen in dry air?
b. Predict As altitude increases, atmospheric pressure decreases. What do you think happens to the partial pressure of oxygen in the air as altitude increases?

See Dalton's Law
animated online.

The data in Table 14.1 illustrate a law proposed by the chemist John Dalton. **Dalton's law of partial pressures** states that, at constant volume and temperature, the total pressure exerted by a mixture of gases is equal to the sum of the partial pressures of the component gases. You can express Dalton's law mathematically as follows:

$$P_{total} = P_1 + P_2 + P_3 + \ldots$$

Dalton's law holds true because each component gas exerts its own pressure independent of the pressure exerted by the other gases. Look at Figure 14.16a. The container is filled with heliox, a helium-oxygen gas mixture used in deep-sea scuba diving. The helium component of this mixture is shown in Figure 14.16b at the same volume and temperature. The oxygen component is shown in Figure 14.16c, also at the same volume and temperature. Each gas in the mixture exerts the pressure it exerted before the gases were mixed to make heliox. So the pressure in the container of heliox (500 kPa) is the sum of the pressures in the containers of helium and oxygen (400 kPa + 100 kPa).

If the percent composition of a mixture of gases does not change, the fraction of the pressure exerted by a gas does not change as the total pressure changes. This fact is important for people who must operate at high altitudes. For example, at the top of Mount Everest, the total atmospheric pressure is 33.73 kPa. This pressure is about one third of its value at sea level. The partial pressure of oxygen is also reduced by one third, to 7.06 kPa. But in order to support respiration in humans, the partial pressure of oxygen must be 10.67 kPa or higher. So climbers of Mount Everest need an oxygen mask and a cylinder of compressed oxygen to survive the ascent.

Figure 14.16 Dalton's Law
Heliox is a mixture of helium and oxygen gas. The pressure exerted by the helium in the mixture is independent of the pressure exerted by the oxygen. **Compare** *How does the ratio of helium atoms to oxygen molecules in heliox compare to the ratio of the partial pressures?*

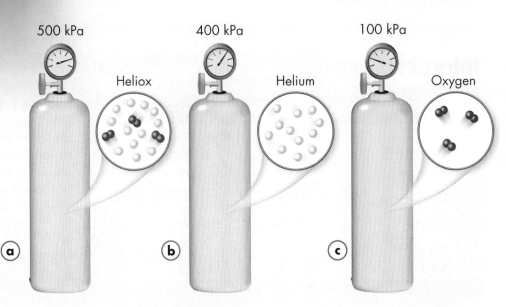

500 kPa Heliox (a)

400 kPa Helium (b)

100 kPa Oxygen (c)

SampleProblem 14.7

Using Dalton's Law of Partial Pressures

Air contains oxygen, nitrogen, carbon dioxide, and trace amounts of other gases. What is the partial pressure of oxygen (P_{O_2}) at 101.30 kPa of total pressure if the partial pressures of nitrogen, carbon dioxide, and other gases are 79.10 kPa, 0.040 kPa, and 0.94 kPa, respectively?

❶ Analyze List the knowns and the unknown.
Use the equation for Dalton's law of partial pressures ($P_{total} = P_{O_2} + P_{N_2} + P_{CO_2} + P_{others}$) to calculate the unknown value (P_{O_2}).

KNOWNS	UNKNOWN
P_{N_2} = 79.10 kPa	P_{O_2} = ? kPa
P_{CO_2} = 0.040 kPa	
P_{others} = 0.94 kPa	
P_{total} = 101.30 kPa	

❷ Calculate Solve for the unknown.

> Isolate P_{O_2} by subtracting the sum ($P_{N_2} + P_{CO_2} + P_{others}$) from both sides.

Start with Dalton's law of partial pressures.

$$P_{total} = P_{O_2} + P_{N_2} + P_{CO_2} + P_{others}$$

Rearrange Dalton's law to isolate P_{O_2}.

$$P_{O_2} = P_{total} - (P_{N_2} + P_{CO_2} + P_{others})$$

Substitute the values for P_{total} and the known partial pressures.

$$= 101.30 \text{ kPa} - (79.10 \text{ kPa} + 0.040 \text{ kPa} + 0.94 \text{ kPa})$$

$$= 21.22 \text{ kPa}$$

❸ Evaluate Does this result make sense? The partial pressure of oxygen must be smaller than that of nitrogen because P_{total} is only 101.30 kPa. The other partial pressures are small, so the calculated answer of 21.22 kPa seems reasonable.

37. A gas mixture containing oxygen, nitrogen, and carbon dioxide has a total pressure of 32.9 kPa. If P_{O_2} = 6.6 kPa and P_{N_2} = 23.0 kPa, what is P_{CO_2}?

38. Determine the total pressure of a gas mixture that contains oxygen, nitrogen, and helium. The partial pressures are P_{O_2} = 20.0 kPa, P_{N_2} = 46.7 kPa, and P_{He} = 26.7 kPa.

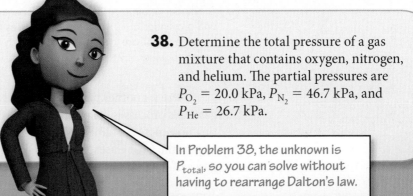

> In Problem 38, the unknown is P_{total}, so you can solve without having to rearrange Dalton's law.

Graham's Law

🔑 *How does the molar mass of a gas affect the rate at which the gas diffuses or effuses?*

READING SUPPORT

Build Vocabulary: Prefixes
Diffusion and *effusion* come from the Latin *fundere* meaning "to pour." They differ only in their prefixes. The prefix *dif-* means "apart." The prefix *ex-* means "out." *How do these prefixes help to contrast what happens to a gas during diffusion and effusion?*

Suppose you open a perfume bottle in one corner of a room. At some point, a person standing in the opposite corner will be able to smell the perfume. Molecules in the perfume evaporate and diffuse, or spread out, through the air in the room. **Diffusion** is the tendency of molecules to move toward areas of lower concentration until the concentration is uniform throughout.

The photo sequence in Figure 14.17 illustrates the diffusion process for bromine vapor. In Figure 14.17a, a glass cylinder containing air is inverted and sealed onto a cylinder containing bromine vapor. Figure 14.17b shows the bromine vapor diffusing through the air. The bromine vapor in the bottom cylinder has started to move upward into the top cylinder, where there is a lower concentration of bromine. In Figure 14.17c, the bromine has diffused to the top of the column formed by the combined cylinders. The concentration of bromine is now the same throughout the column.

Figure 14.17 Diffusion
The diffusion of one substance through another is a relatively slow process. **Describe** *How does the concentration of bromine in the bottom part of the column change during this sequence?*

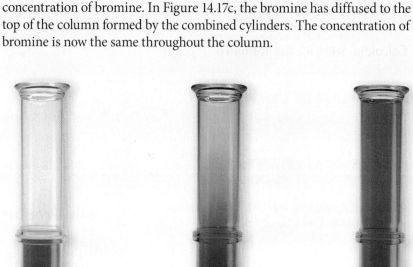

(**a**) A cylinder of air and a cylinder of bromine vapor are sealed together.

(**b**) Bromine vapor diffuses upward through the air.

(**c**) After several hours, bromine vapors reach the top of the column.

There is another process that involves the movement of molecules in a gas. This process is called effusion. During **effusion,** a gas escapes through a tiny hole in its container. With effusion and diffusion, the type of particle is important. 🔑 **Gases of lower molar mass diffuse and effuse faster than gases of higher molar mass.**

Thomas Graham's Contribution The Scottish chemist Thomas Graham studied rates of effusion during the 1840s. From his observations, he proposed a law. **Graham's law of effusion** states that the rate of effusion of a gas is inversely proportional to the square root of the gas's molar mass. This law can also be applied to the diffusion of gases.

Figure 14.18 Blimps
The cigar-shaped part of a blimp, called an envelope, is a sealed container of helium gas. **Infer** *What properties do you think are desirable for the materials used to make the envelope of a blimp?*

Graham's law makes sense if you know how the mass, velocity, and kinetic energy of a moving object are related. The expression that relates the mass (m) and the velocity (v) of an object to its kinetic energy (KE) is $\frac{1}{2}mv^2$. For the kinetic energy to be constant, any increase in mass must be balanced by a decrease in velocity. For example, a ball with a mass of 2 g must travel at 5 m/s to have the same kinetic energy as a ball with a mass of 1 g traveling at 7 m/s. There is an important principle here. If two objects with different masses have the same kinetic energy, the lighter object must move faster.

Comparing Effusion Rates The blimp shown in Figure 14.18 is inflated with helium, which is less dense than air. One of the challenges in maintaining blimps is to keep the helium from seeping out. You may have noticed that party balloons filled with either helium or air gradually deflate over time. Both helium atoms and the molecules in air can pass through the tiny pores in a latex balloon. But a helium-filled balloon will deflate faster than an air-filled balloon. Kinetic theory can explain the difference.

Suppose you have two balloons, one filled with helium and the other filled with air. If the balloons are at the same temperature, the particles in each balloon have the same average kinetic energy. But helium atoms are less massive than oxygen or nitrogen molecules. So the molecules in air move more slowly than helium atoms with the same kinetic energy. Because the rate of effusion is related only to a particle's speed, Graham's law can be written as follows for two gases, A and B.

$$\frac{\text{Rate}_A}{\text{Rate}_B} = \sqrt{\frac{\text{molar mass}_B}{\text{molar mass}_A}}$$

In other words, the rates of effusion of two gases are inversely proportional to the square roots of their molar masses. Sample Problem 14.8 on the following page compares the effusion rates of helium and nitrogen.

CHEMISTRY & YOU

Q: *Why do balloons filled with helium deflate faster than balloons filled with air? Use Graham's law of effusion to explain your answer.*

Sample Problem 14.8

Comparing Effusion Rates

How much faster does helium (He) effuse than nitrogen (N_2) at the same temperature?

❶ Analyze **List the knowns and the unknown.**
Use Graham's law and the molar masses of the two gases to calculate the ratio of effusion rates.

❷ Calculate **Solve for the unknown.** Helium effuses nearly three times faster than nitrogen at the same temperature.

KNOWNS
molar mass$_{He}$ = 4.0 g
molar mass$_{N_2}$ = 28.0 g

UNKNOWN
ratio of effusion rates = ?

Start with the equation for Graham's law of effusion.	$\dfrac{Rate_{He}}{Rate_{N_2}} = \dfrac{\sqrt{molar\ mass_{N_2}}}{\sqrt{molar\ mass_{He}}}$
Substitute the molar masses of nitrogen and helium into the equation.	$\dfrac{Rate_{He}}{Rate_{N_2}} = \sqrt{\dfrac{28.0\ g}{4.0\ g}} = \sqrt{7.0} = 2.7$

❸ Evaluate **Does the result make sense?** Helium atoms are less massive than nitrogen molecules, so it makes sense that helium effuses faster than nitrogen.

39. Calculate the ratio of the velocity of hydrogen molecules to the velocity of carbon dioxide molecules at the same temperature.

> Use what you know about chemical formulas and the mole to write the molar mass of each gas.

14.4 LessonCheck

40. 🔑 **Review** In a mixture of gases, how is the total pressure determined?

41. 🔑 **Review** What is the effect of molar mass on rates of diffusion and effusion?

42. Explain How is the partial pressure of a gas in a mixture calculated?

43. Calculate The pressure in an automobile tire filled with air is 245.0 kPa. If P_{O_2} = 51.3 kPa, P_{CO_2} = 0.10 kPa, and P_{others} = 2.3 kPa, what is P_{N_2}?

44. Compare What distinguishes effusion from diffusion? How are these processes similar?

45. Relate Cause and Effect Explain why the rates of diffusion of nitrogen gas and carbon monoxide are almost identical at the same temperature.

46. Analyze Data Both Table 14.1 on page 469 and the Elements in the Atmosphere table on page R1 list data on the composition of air. Look at the data included in each table. Identify two ways in which the tables are similar. Describe at least three differences.

Small-Scale Lab

Diffusion

(Probe or sensor version of this lab is available in the *Probeware Lab Manual*.)

Purpose

To infer diffusion of a gas by observing color changes during chemical reactions

Materials

- clear plastic cup or petri dish
- reaction surface
- dropper bottles containing bromothymol blue, hydrochloric acid, and sodium hydrogen sulfite
- ruler
- cotton swab
- NaOH, NH$_4$Cl (optional)

Procedure

1. Use the plastic cup or petri dish to draw the large circle shown below on a sheet of paper.

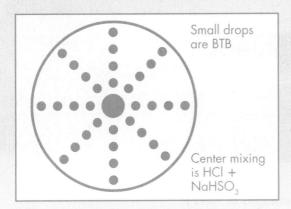

Small drops are BTB

Center mixing is HCl + NaHSO$_3$

2. Place a reaction surface over the grid and add small drops of bromothymol blue (BTB) in the pattern shown by the small circles. Make sure the drops do not touch one another.

3. Mix one drop each of hydrochloric acid (HCl) and sodium hydrogen sulfite (NaHSO$_3$) in the center of the pattern.

4. Place the cup or petri dish over the grid and observe what happens.

5. If you plan to do Activity 1 in the You're the Chemist section, don't dispose of your materials yet.

Analyze

1. Observe Describe in detail the changes you observed in the drops of BTB over time. Draw pictures to illustrate the changes.

2. Describe Draw a series of pictures showing how one of the BTB drops might look over time if you could view the drop from the side.

3. Explain The BTB changed even though you added nothing to it. If the mixture in the center circle produced a gas, would this explain the change in the drops of BTB? Use kinetic theory to explain your answer.

4. Describe Translate the following word equation into a balanced chemical equation: Sodium hydrogen sulfite reacts with hydrochloric acid to produce sulfur dioxide gas, water, and sodium chloride.

You're the Chemist

The following activities allow you to develop your own procedures and analyze the results.

1. Analyze Data Carefully absorb the center mixture of the original experiment onto a cotton swab and replace it with one drop of NaOH and one drop of NH$_4$Cl. Describe what happens and explain in terms of kinetic theory. Ammonium chloride reacts with sodium hydroxide to produce ammonia gas, water, and sodium chloride. Write and balance a chemical equation to describe this reaction.

2. Design an Experiment Design an experiment to observe the effect of the size of the BTB drops on the rate at which they change. Explain your results in terms of kinetic theory.

Natural Gas Vehicles

Most of the cars you see on the road run on gasoline, better known as gas—although the fuel itself is a liquid, not a gas. But in some U.S. cities, as well as parts of South America and Asia, vehicles that run on gaseous fuel are becoming increasingly common.

A natural gas vehicle, or NGV, runs on compressed natural gas (CNG), which is natural gas that has been compressed to less than 1 percent of its volume at standard pressure. The fuel is stored in a pressurized cylinder. Like other vehicles that burn fossil fuels, NGVs emit CO_2. However, natural gas burns cleaner than gasoline or diesel fuel. Many gasoline-powered cars can be retrofitted with NGV technology so that the driver can choose to run the car on either gasoline or CNG.

Pros & Cons

Advantages of NGVs

✔ **Less pollution** NGVs produce much less carbon monoxide, nitrogen oxides, and toxins than gasoline-powered vehicles.

✔ **Less maintenance** Because natural gas burns cleaner than gasoline, the engines of NGVs require less servicing than those of gasoline-powered vehicles.

✔ **Cheaper fuel** Natural gas costs less than gasoline.

✔ **Safety** The fuel tanks in NGVs are stronger and safer than gasoline storage tanks.

Disadvantages of NGVs

✘ **More expensive** NGVs tend to cost more than comparable gasoline-powered cars.

✘ **Less roomy** Due to the CNG tank, NGVs have less trunk space.

✘ **Limited travel range** On a single tank of gas, NGVs can travel only about 60 percent as far as gasoline-powered cars before needing more fuel.

✘ **Hard to refuel** CNG refueling stations are currently few and far between.

✘ **Still fossil-fueled** Like oil, natural gas is a nonrenewable resource.

ON THE ROAD Most of the NGVs found in the United States are buses. But don't be surprised if you start to see passenger cars sporting the "NGV" logo.

FILL 'ER UP Any building with a natural gas line can be equipped with a pressurized fueling device that delivers CNG. But NGV drivers must be patient—an empty CNG tank takes much longer to fill than an empty gasoline tank.

A REAL GAS IN THE GAS TANK A mid-sized NGV sedan has a fuel tank in the back with a volume of 8 gallons, or 30 L. At ambient temperatures, the pressure inside a full tank of CNG is about 3600 pounds per square inch (psi), or 25,000 kPa.

Take It Further

1. Calculate The natural gas in a 30-L NGV fuel tank has a pressure of 2.05×10^4 kPa at a temperature of 297 K. How many kilograms of fuel are in the tank? (Use a molar mass of 19 g/mol for natural gas.)

2. Calculate Natural gas is 89% methane (CH_4), 5% ethane (C_2H_6), 5% butane (C_4H_{10}), and 1% propane (C_3H_8). Use the data from Question 1 to determine the partial pressures of each component gas in the fuel tank.

14 **Study** Guide

BIGIDEA KINETIC THEORY

Ideal gases conform to the assumptions of kinetic theory. The behavior of ideal gases can be predicted by the gas laws. With the ideal gas law, the number of moles of a gas in a fixed volume at a known temperature and pressure can be calculated. Although an ideal gas does not exist, real gases behave ideally under a variety of temperature and pressure conditions.

14.1 Properties of Gases

🔑 Gases are easily compressed because of the space between the particles in a gas.

🔑 The amount of gas (n), volume (V), and temperature (T) are factors that affect gas pressure (P).

• compressibility (450)

14.2 The Gas Laws

🔑 If the temperature is constant, as the pressure of a gas increases, the volume decreases.

🔑 As the temperature of an enclosed gas increases, the volume increases if the pressure is constant.

🔑 As the temperature of an enclosed gas increases, the pressure increases if the volume is constant.

🔑 When only the amount of gas is constant, the combined gas law describes the relationship among pressure, volume, and temperature.

• Boyle's law (456)   • Gay-Lussac's law (460)
• Charles's law (458)   • combined gas law (462)

> **Key Equations**
>
> Boyle's law: Gay-Lussac's law:
> $$P_1 \times V_1 = P_2 \times V_2$$ $$\frac{P_1}{T_1} = \frac{P_2}{T_2}$$
>
> Charles's law: combined gas law:
> $$\frac{V_1}{T_1} = \frac{V_2}{T_2}$$ $$\frac{P_1 \times V_1}{T_1} = \frac{P_2 \times V_2}{T_2}$$

14.3 Ideal Gases

🔑 When the pressure, volume, and temperature of a contained gas are known, you can use the ideal gas law to calculate the number of moles of the gas.

🔑 Real gases differ most from an ideal gas at low temperatures and high pressures.

• ideal gas constant (465)   • ideal gas law (465)

> **Key Equation**
>
> ideal gas law:
> $$P \times V = n \times R \times T \text{ or } PV = nRT$$

14.4 Gases: Mixtures and Movements

🔑 In a mixture of gases, the total pressure is the sum of the partial pressures of the gases.

🔑 Gases of lower molar mass diffuse and effuse faster than gases of higher molar mass.

• partial pressure (469)   • effusion (472)
• Dalton's law of partial   • Graham's law of
  pressure (470)   effusion (472)
• diffusion (472)

> **Key Equations**
>
> Dalton's law: $P_{\text{total}} = P_1 + P_2 + P_3 + \dots$
>
> Graham's law: $\dfrac{\text{Rate}_A}{\text{Rate}_B} = \sqrt{\dfrac{\text{molar mass}_B}{\text{molar mass}_A}}$

Math Tune-Up: Gas Law Problems

Problem	❶ Analyze	❷ Calculate	❸ Evaluate
A 2.50-L sample of nitrogen gas at a temperature of 308 K has a pressure of 1.15 atm. What is the new volume of the gas if the pressure is increased to 1.80 atm and the temperature is decreased to 286 K?	Knowns: P_1 = 1.15 atm V_1 = 2.50 L T_1 = 308 K P_2 = 1.80 atm T_2 = 286 K Unknown: V_2 = ? Use the combined gas law: $$\frac{P_1 \times V_1}{T_1} = \frac{P_2 \times V_2}{T_2}$$	Solve for V_2 and calculate: $$V_2 = \frac{P_1 V_1 T_2}{P_2 T_1}$$ $$V_2 = \frac{(1.15 \text{ atm})(2.50 \text{ L})(286 \text{ K})}{(1.80 \text{ atm})(308 \text{ K})}$$ V_2 = 1.48 L	An increase in pressure causes the volume of a gas to decrease. Likewise, a decrease in temperature causes the volume of a gas to decrease. So, V_2 should be smaller than V_1. The answer makes sense.

Hint: Review Sample Problem 14.4 if you have trouble with the combined gas law.

How many moles of helium gas fill a 6.45-L balloon at a pressure of 105 kPa and a temperature of 278 K?	Knowns: P = 105 kPa V = 6.45 L T = 278 K R = 8.31 L·kPa/K·mol Unknown: n = ? Use the ideal gas law: $PV = nRT$	Solve for n and calculate: $$n = \frac{PV}{RT}$$ $$n = \frac{(105 \text{ kPa})(6.45 \text{ L})}{\left(8.31 \frac{\text{L·kPa}}{\text{K·mol}}\right)(278 \text{ K})}$$ n = 0.293 mol	The gas is not at high pressure, nor is the volume large. So the number of moles in the balloon should be small. The answer is reasonable, and the units have canceled correctly.

A gas mixture containing argon, krypton, and helium has a total pressure of 376 kPa. If the partial pressures of argon and krypton are 92 kPa and 144 kPa, respectively, what is the partial pressure of helium?	Knowns: P_{total} = 376 kPa P_{Ar} = 92 kPa P_{Kr} = 144 kPa Unknown: P_{He} = ? Dalton's law of partial pressures applies: $P_{\text{total}} = P_{\text{Ar}} + P_{\text{He}} + P_{\text{Kr}}$	Solve for P_{He} and calculate: $P_{\text{He}} = P_{\text{total}} - (P_{\text{Ar}} + P_{\text{Kr}})$ P_{He} = 376 kPa − (92 kPa + 144 kPa) P_{He} = 140 kPa $P_{\text{He}} = 1.40 \times 10^2$ kPa	The partial pressure of helium must be less than half the total pressure. The answer is reasonable.

Dalton's law: The total pressure exerted by a mixture of gases (P_{total}) is equal to the sum of the partial pressures of the component gases.

14 Assessment

★ Solutions appear in Appendix E

Lesson by Lesson

14.1 Properties of Gases

47. What happens to the particles in a gas when the gas is compressed?

48. Explain why heating a contained gas that is held at a constant volume increases its pressure.

49. Describe what happens to the volume of a balloon when it is taken outside on a cold winter day. Explain why the observed change happens.

50. A metal cylinder contains 1 mol of nitrogen gas. What will happen to the pressure if another mole of gas is added to the cylinder, but the temperature and volume do not change?

51. If a gas is compressed from 4 L to 1 L and the temperature remains constant, what happens to the pressure?

52. Use the drawing to help explain why gas pressure decreases when gas is removed from a container with a fixed volume.

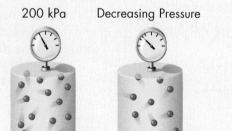

200 kPa   Decreasing Pressure

14.2 The Gas Laws

53. Write the mathematical equation for Charles's law and explain the symbols.

★54. The gas in a closed container has a pressure of 3.00×10^2 kPa at 30°C (303 K). What will the pressure be if the temperature is lowered to −172°C (101 K)?

55. Calculate the volume of a gas (in L) at a pressure of 1.00×10^2 kPa if its volume at 1.20×10^2 kPa is 1.50×10^3 mL.

56. A gas with a volume of 4.0 L at 90.0 kPa expands until the pressure drops to 20.0 kPa. What is its new volume if the temperature doesn't change?

★57. A gas with a volume of 3.00×10^2 mL at 150.0°C is heated until its volume expands to 6.00×10^2 mL. What is the new temperature of the gas if the pressure remains constant during the heating process?

★58. A gas with a volume of 15 L at 327°C is cooled at constant pressure until the volume reaches 5 L. What is the new temperature of the gas?

59. Write the mathematical expression for the combined gas law.

60. A sealed cylinder of gas contains nitrogen gas at 1.00×10^3 kPa pressure and a temperature of 20°C. When the cylinder is left in the sun, the temperature of the gas increases to 50°C. What is the new pressure in the cylinder?

★61. A sample of nitrogen gas has a pressure of 6.58 kPa at 539 K. If the volume does not change, what will the pressure be at 211 K?

62. Show how Gay-Lussac's law can be derived from the combined gas law.

14.3 Ideal Gases

63. Describe an ideal gas.

64. Explain why it is impossible for an ideal gas to exist.

★65. What is the volume occupied by 1.24 mol of a gas at 35°C if the pressure is 96.2 kPa?

66. What volume will 12.0 g of oxygen gas (O_2) occupy at 25°C and a pressure of 52.7 kPa?

★67. If 4.50 g of methane gas (CH_4) is in a 2.00-L container at 35°C, what is the pressure in the container?

68. What pressure is exerted by 0.450 mol of a gas at 25°C if the gas is in a 0.650-L container?

★69. A helium-filled weather balloon has a volume of 2.4×10^2 L at 99 kPa pressure and a temperature of 0°C. What is the mass of the helium in the balloon?

14.4 Gases: Mixtures and Movements

70. In your own words, state Dalton's law of partial pressure.

71. Which gas effuses faster: hydrogen or chlorine? How much faster?

72. Which gas effuses faster at the same temperature: molecular oxygen or atomic argon?

✻73. Calculate the ratio of the velocity of helium atoms to the velocity of neon atoms at the same temperature.

74. Calculate the ratio of the velocity of helium atoms to the velocity of fluorine molecules at the same temperature.

Understand Concepts

75. How does kinetic theory explain the compressibility of gases?

76. A teacher adds enough water to cover the bottom of an empty metal can with a screw cap. Using a stove, the teacher heats the can with the cap off until the water boils, and then screws on the cap tightly. When the sealed can is dunked in cold water, the sides of the can immediately collapse inward as though crushed in a trash compactor.

    a. Use kinetic theory to explain why the can collapsed inward.
    b. If the experiment were done with a dry can, would the results be similar? Explain.

77. Explain how the compressed gas in an aerosol can forces paint out of the can. Make sure to describe how the gas pressure inside the can changes as the paint is sprayed. (Refer to Figure 14.5 in Lesson 14.1.)

78. Why do aerosol containers display the warning, "Do not incinerate"?

79. The manufacturer of an aerosol deodorant packaged in a 150-mL container plans to produce a container of the same size that will hold twice as much gas. How will the pressure of the gas in the new product compare with that of the gas in the original container?

80. Why must Kelvin temperatures be used in calculations that involve gases?

81. Explain how using a pressure cooker reduces the time required to cook food.

82. The ratio of two variables is always a constant. What can you conclude about the relationship between the two variables?

✻83. A 3.50-L gas sample at 20°C and a pressure of 86.7 kPa expands to a volume of 8.00 L. The final pressure of the gas is 56.7 kPa. What is the final temperature of the gas in degrees Celsius?

84. Explain the reasons why real gases deviate from ideal behavior.

85. How would the number of particles of two gases compare if their partial pressures in a container were identical?

86. Why does a balloon filled with helium deflate more quickly than a balloon filled with air?

✻87. A certain gas effuses four times as fast as oxygen (O_2). What is the molar mass of the gas?

✻88. During an effusion experiment, a certain number of moles of an unknown gas passed through a tiny hole in 75 seconds. Under the same conditions, the same number of moles of oxygen gas passed through the hole in 30 seconds. What is the molar mass of the unknown gas?

89. The photograph shows a tube with cotton balls at each end. The cotton ball at the left was soaked with hydrochloric acid. The cotton ball on the right was soaked with a solution of ammonia. When these compounds react, they form a white solid, ammonium chloride. Based on the location of the ammonium chloride in the tube, which gas diffuses at a faster rate, hydrogen chloride or ammonia? Explain.

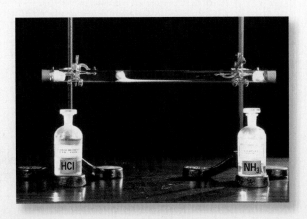

90. Infer Figure 14.14 in Lesson 14.3 shows an insulated tank used to store liquid nitrogen. How does the vacuum between the walls of the tank prevent heat transfer?

91. Infer Gases will diffuse from a region of higher concentration to a region of lower concentration. Why don't the gases in Earth's atmosphere escape into the near-vacuum of space?

92. Apply Concepts What real gas comes closest to having the characteristics of an ideal gas? Explain your answer.

93. Predict Death Valley in California is at 86 m below sea level. Will the partial pressure of oxygen in Death Valley be the same, lower, or higher than the partial pressure of oxygen at sea level? Give a reason for your answer.

★94. Calculate The following reaction takes place in a sealed 40.0-L container at a temperature of 120°C:

$$4NH_3(g) + 5O_2(g) \longrightarrow 4NO(g) + 6H_2O(g)$$

   a. When 34.0 g of NH_3 reacts with 96.0 g of O_2, what is the partial pressure of NO in the sealed container?

   b. What is the total pressure in the container?

95. Interpret Graphs The graph shows the direct relationship between volume and temperature for three different gas samples. Offer at least one explanation for why the graphs are not identical for the three samples. (*Hint:* What variables other than temperature and volume can be used to describe a gas?)

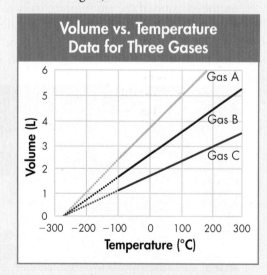

Volume vs. Temperature Data for Three Gases

★96. Analyze Data A student collected the following data for a fixed volume of gas.

Temperature (°C)	Pressure (mm Hg)
10	726
20	750
40	800
70	880
100	960

   a. Graph the data, using pressure as the dependent variable.

   b. What is the pressure of the gas at 0°C?

   c. Is the relationship between the variables directly or inversely proportional?

   d. How does the pressure of the gas change with each degree Celsius change in the temperature?

   e. Write an equation relating the pressure and temperature of the gas.

   f. Which gas law is illustrated by the data? Select two data points on your graph to confirm your answer.

97. Interpret Graphs The graph shows how the ratio (*PV/nRT*) changes with increasing pressure for methane (CH_4) at 0°C and 200°C.

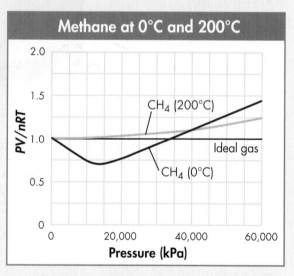

Methane at 0°C and 200°C

   a. At lower pressures, which gas behaves more like an ideal gas: methane at 0°C or methane at 200°C.

   b. The curve for methane at 0°C shows that the ratio *PV/nRT* is less than 1 at lower pressures and greater than 1 at higher pressures. What characteristics of real gases can explain these deviations?

98. Analyze Data Oxygen is produced in the laboratory by heating potassium nitrate (KNO_3). The data table below gives the volume of oxygen produced at STP from different quantities of KNO_3. Use the data to determine the mole ratio by which KNO_3 and O_2 react.

Mass of KNO_3 (g)	Volume of O_2 (cL)
0.84	9.3
1.36	15.1
2.77	30.7
4.82	53.5
6.96	77.3

✱99. Calculate A mixture of ethyne gas (C_2H_2) and methane gas (CH_4) occupied a certain volume at a total pressure of 16.8 kPa. When the sample burned, the products were CO_2 gas and H_2O vapor. The CO_2 was collected and its pressure found to be 25.2 kPa in the same volume and at the same temperature as the original mixture. What percentage of the original mixture was methane?

✱100. Calculate A 0.10-L container holds 3.0×10^{20} molecules of H_2 at 100 kPa and 0°C.

a. If the volume of a hydrogen molecule is 6.7×10^{-24} mL, what percentage of the volume of the gas is occupied by its molecules?

b. If the pressure is increased to 100,000 kPa, the volume of the gas is 1×10^{-4} L. What fraction of the total volume do the hydrogen molecules now occupy?

101. Draw Conclusions Many gases that have small molecules, such as N_2 and O_2, have the expected molar volume of 22.41 L at STP. However, other gases behave in a very non-ideal manner, even if extreme pressures and temperatures are not involved. The molar volumes of CH_4, CO_2, and NH_3 at STP are 22.37 L, 22.26 L, and 22.06 L, respectively. Explain the reasons for these large departures from the ideal.

102. Explain Why does a tennis ball bounce higher in the summer than it does in the winter? Use what you know about gas behavior to explain your answer.

103. Research a Problem Cars that run on natural gas or hydrogen require different fuel tanks and different refueling stations than cars that run on gasoline, which is a liquid at STP. How would you design a fuel tank for storing a gas? How would you design a gas pump that pumped a gas instead of a liquid? Research a kind of vehicle that runs on gaseous fuel and explain how these questions have been addressed.

CHEMYSTERY

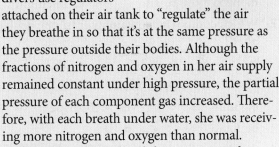

Under Pressure

Becki realized that she had decompression sickness, also known as the bends. Recreational divers use regulators attached on their air tank to "regulate" the air they breathe in so that it's at the same pressure as the pressure outside their bodies. Although the fractions of nitrogen and oxygen in her air supply remained constant under high pressure, the partial pressure of each component gas increased. Therefore, with each breath under water, she was receiving more nitrogen and oxygen than normal.

As Becki ascended and the pressure on her body decreased, the excess nitrogen formed bubbles in her blood and tissues, causing pain and other symptoms. Serious cases of the bends require treatment in a high-pressure chamber. The pressure is reduced gradually so that the excess nitrogen can leave the body harmlessly.

104. Infer How could Becki have prevented getting the bends?

105. Connect to the BIGIDEA What would have happened if Becki held her breath while ascending from a dive? Use the gas laws to explain.

106. What is the mathematical relationship between the Kelvin and Celsius temperature scales?

＊**107.** A metal sample has a mass of 9.92 g and measures 4.50 cm × 1.30 cm × 1.60 mm. What is the density of the metal?

108. How many electrons, protons, and neutrons are there in an atom of lead-206?

109. Which element has the following electron configuration?

1s	2s	2p	3s	3p	4s	3d
↑↓	↑↓	↑↓	↑↓	↑↓	↑↓	↑↓
		↑↓		↑↓		↑↓
		↑↓		↑↓		↑↓
						↑
						↑

110. Which of these elements are metals?
 a. arsenic **b.** tungsten **c.** xenon

111. Which element is most likely to form a compound with strontium?
 a. neon **b.** tin **c.** selenium

112. Which compound contains at least one double bond?
 a. H_2Se **b.** SO_2 **c.** PCl_3

＊**113.** Name each compound.
 a. $SnBr_2$ **c.** $Mg(OH)_2$
 b. $BaSO_4$ **d.** IF_5

114. An atom of lead has a mass 17.16 times greater than the mass of an atom of carbon-12. What is the molar mass of this isotope of lead?

＊**115.** Calculate the molar mass of each substance.
 a. $Ca(CH_3CO_2)_2$ **c.** $C_{12}H_{22}O_{11}$
 b. H_3PO_4 **d.** $Pb(NO_3)_2$

116. What is the significance of the volume 22.4 L?

＊**117.** Calculate the molecular formula of each of the following compounds.
 a. The empirical formula is C_2H_4O, and the molar mass is 88 g.
 b. The empirical formula is CH, and the molar mass is 104 g.
 c. The molar mass is 90 g. The percent composition is 26.7% C, 71.1% O, and 2.2% H.

118. Calculate the percent composition of 2-propanol (C_3H_7OH).

119. What type of reaction is each of the following?
 a. Calcium reacts with water to form calcium hydroxide and hydrogen gas.
 b. Mercury and oxygen are prepared by heating mercury(II) oxide.

120. Write balanced equations for the following chemical reactions.
 a. Tetraphosphorus decoxide reacts with water to form phosphoric acid.
 b. Aluminum hydroxide and hydrogen sulfide form when aluminum sulfide reacts with water.

＊**121.** Aluminum oxide is formed from its elements.

$$Al(s) + O_2(g) \longrightarrow Al_2O_3(s)$$

 a. Balance the equation.
 b. How many grams of each reactant are needed to form 583 g $Al_2O_3(s)$?

122. Explain why a gas expands until it takes the shape and volume of its container.

123. Use the drawings to explain how gas pressure is produced.

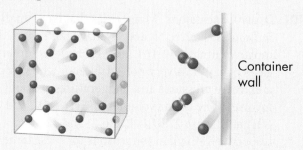

Container wall

Standardized Test Prep

Select the choice that best answers each question or completes each statement.

1. A gas in a balloon at constant pressure has a volume of 120.0 mL at −123°C. What is its volume at 27.0°C?
   (A) 60.0 mL   (C) 26.5 mL
   (B) 240.0 mL   (D) 546 mL

2. If the Kelvin temperature of a gas is tripled and the volume is doubled, the new pressure will be
   (A) 1/6 the original pressure.
   (B) 2/3 the original pressure.
   (C) 3/2 the original pressure.
   (D) 5 times the original pressure.

3. Which of these gases effuses fastest?
   (A) Cl_2 (C) NH_3
   (B) NO_2 (D) N_2

4. All the oxygen gas from a 10.0-L container at a pressure of 202 kPa is added to a 20.0-L container of hydrogen at a pressure of 505 kPa. After the transfer, what are the partial pressures of oxygen and hydrogen?
   (A) Oxygen is 101 kPa; hydrogen is 505 kPa.
   (B) Oxygen is 202 kPa; hydrogen is 505 kPa.
   (C) Oxygen is 101 kPa; hydrogen is 253 kPa.
   (D) Oxygen is 202 kPa; hydrogen is 253 kPa.

5. Which of the following changes would increase the pressure of a gas in a closed container?
       I. Part of the gas is removed.
       II. The container size is decreased.
       III. Temperature is increased.

   (A) I and II only
   (B) II and III only
   (C) I and III only
   (D) I, II, and III

6. A real gas behaves most nearly like an ideal gas
   (A) at high pressure and low temperature.
   (B) at low pressure and high temperature.
   (C) at low pressure and low temperature.
   (D) at high pressure and high temperature.

Use the graphs to answer Questions 7–10. A graph may be used once, more than once, or not at all.

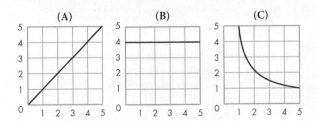

Which graph shows each of the following?

7. directly proportional relationship

8. graph with slope = 0

9. inversely proportional relationship

10. graph with a constant slope

Use the drawing to answer Questions 11 and 12.

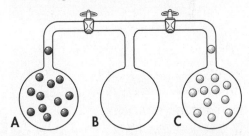

11. Bulb A and bulb C contain different gases. Bulb B contains no gas. If the valves between the bulbs are opened, how will the particles of gas be distributed when the system reaches equilibrium? Assume none of the particles are in the tubes that connect the bulbs.

> **Tips for Success**
>
> **Constructing a Diagram** If you are asked to draw a diagram, sketch lightly at first (so you can erase easily), or do a sketch on a separate piece of paper. Once you are sure of your answer, draw the final diagram.

12. Make a three-bulb drawing with 6 blue spheres in bulb A, 9 green spheres in bulb B, and 12 red spheres in bulb C. Then draw the setup to represent the distribution of gases after the valves are opened and the system reaches equilibrium.

If You Have Trouble With . . .

Question	1	2	3	4	5	6	7	8	9	10	11	12
See Lesson	14.2	14.2	14.4	14.3	14.1	14.3	14.2	14.2	14.2	14.2	14.4	14.4

15

Water and Aqueous Systems

INSIDE:

- **15.1** Water and Its Properties
- **15.2** Homogeneous Aqueous Systems
- **15.3** Heterogeneous Aqueous Systems

PearsonChem.com

Water has many unique properties. In this chapter, you will learn about the interactions between water molecules.

BONDING AND INTERACTIONS

Essential Questions:

1. *How do the interactions between water molecules account for the unique properties of water?*

2. *How do aqueous solutions form?*

CHEMYSTERY

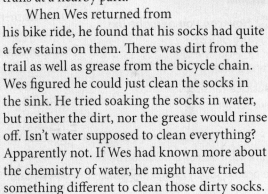

Coming Clean

On a beautiful Saturday afternoon, Wes decided to take his bicycle out for a ride. He set off on a long ride through the trails at a nearby park.

When Wes returned from his bike ride, he found that his socks had quite a few stains on them. There was dirt from the trail as well as grease from the bicycle chain. Wes figured he could just clean the socks in the sink. He tried soaking the socks in water, but neither the dirt, nor the grease would rinse off. Isn't water supposed to clean everything? Apparently not. If Wes had known more about the chemistry of water, he might have tried something different to clean those dirty socks.

▶ **Connect to the BIGIDEA** As you read about water and aqueous systems, think about how Wes could remove the dirt and grease from his socks.

NATIONAL SCIENCE EDUCATION STANDARDS

A1, B-2, E-2, F-3, F-4, F-6

15.1 Water and Its Properties

Q: *What properties of water make it essential to life on Earth?* When the *Apollo 8* astronauts first saw their home planet from a distance of thousands of kilometers, they called it the big blue marble. Water covers about three quarters of Earth's surface. In addition to making up Earth's oceans, water forms the polar ice caps and cycles through the atmosphere. All known life forms, including the penguin in Figure 15.1, are made mostly of water.

Key Questions

▭ What factor causes the high surface tension, low vapor pressure, and high boiling point of water?

▭ How can you describe the structure of ice?

Vocabulary

- surface tension
- surfactant

Figure 15.1 Water Is Vital to Life
The oceans supply penguins with an abundant supply of food.

Water in the Liquid State

▭ *What factor causes the high surface tension, low vapor pressure, and high boiling point of water?*

You couldn't live without water, nor could all the plants and animals that share space on the "big blue marble." Besides the water visible on Earth's surface, immense reserves of water exist deep underground. Water in the form of ice and snow dominates the polar regions of Earth. Water vapor from the evaporation of surface water and from steam spouted from geysers and volcanoes is always present in Earth's atmosphere.

Recall that water, H_2O, is a simple molecule consisting of three atoms. The oxygen atom forms a covalent bond with each of the hydrogen atoms. Oxygen has a greater electronegativity than hydrogen, so the oxygen atom attracts the electron pair of the covalent O—H bond to a greater extent than the hydrogen atom. Thus, the O—H bond is highly polar. As a result, the oxygen atom acquires a partial negative charge ($\delta-$). The less electronegative hydrogen atoms acquire partial positive charges ($\delta+$).

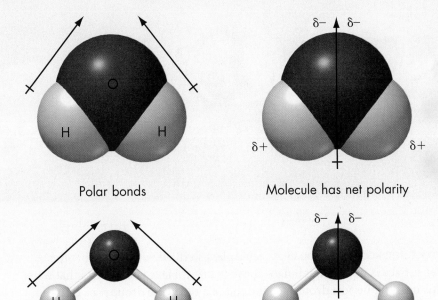

Polar bonds

Molecule has net polarity

Figure 15.2 Polarity of H₂O
In a water molecule, the bond polarities are equal, but the two poles do not cancel each other because a water molecule is bent. The molecule as a whole is polar.
Apply Concepts *Which element in water has the higher electronegativity?*

How do the polarities of the two O—H bonds affect the polarity of the molecule? The shape of the molecule is the determining factor. The bond angle of the water molecule is approximately 105°, which gives the molecule a bent shape. The two O—H bond polarities do not cancel, so the water molecule as a whole is polar. The net polarity of the water molecule is illustrated in Figure 15.2.

In general, polar molecules are attracted to one another by dipole interactions. The negative end of one molecule attracts the positive end of another molecule. However, in water, this attraction results in hydrogen bonding, as illustrated in Figure 15.3. Recall that hydrogen bonds are attractive forces that arise when a hydrogen atom is covalently bonded to a very electronegative atom and also weakly bonded to an unshared electron pair of another electronegative atom. Hydrogen bonds are not as strong as covalent bonds, but they are stronger than other intermolecular forces. **Many unique and important properties of water—including its high surface tension, low vapor pressure, and high boiling point—result from hydrogen bonding.**

Figure 15.3 Hydrogen Bonding in Water
The polarity of the water molecule results in hydrogen bonding. **a.** The oxygen atom has a partial negative charge. Each hydrogen atom has a partial positive charge. **b.** Hydrogen bonds form between the hydrogen atom of one water molecule and the oxygen atom of an adjacent water molecule.
Infer *To form a hydrogen bond, what must be true about hydrogen and the element to which it is hydrogen bonded?*

See hydrogen bonding *animated online.*

KINETIC ART

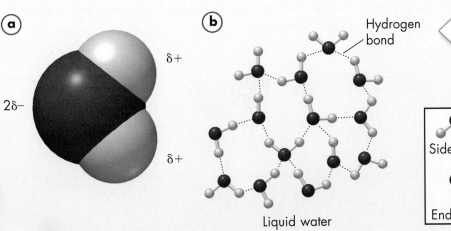

Liquid water

Side view

End view

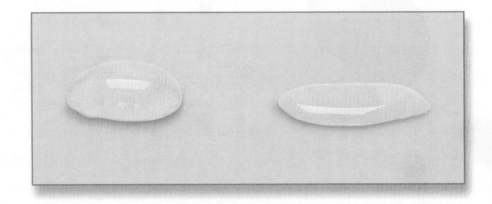

Figure 15.4
Surface Tension of Water
Water forms nearly spherical drops on a leaf. Water molecules at the surface of the water drop cannot form hydrogen bonds with molecules in the air, so they are drawn into the body of the liquid.

Air

Drop of water

Surface Tension Have you ever seen a glass so filled with water that the water surface is not flat but bulges above the rim? Have you noticed that water forms nearly spherical droplets at the end of a medicine dropper or on a leaf, as shown in Figure 15.4? The surface of water acts like a skin. This property of water's surface is explained by the ability of water molecules to form hydrogen bonds. The water molecules within the body of the liquid form hydrogen bonds with other molecules that surround them on all sides. The attractive forces on each of these molecules are balanced. However, water molecules at the surface of the liquid experience an unbalanced attraction. You can see in Figure 15.4 that the water molecules are hydrogen bonded on only the inside of the drop. As a result, water molecules at the surface tend to be drawn inward. The inward force, or pull, that tends to minimize the surface area of a liquid is called **surface tension.**

All liquids have a surface tension, but water's surface tension is higher than most. This is why, on some surfaces, water tends to bead up rather than spread out. The surface tension of water tends to hold a drop of liquid in a spherical shape. For example, you may notice that water tends to form beads on the surface of a newly waxed car. The wax molecules are nonpolar, so there is little or no attraction between the wax molecules and the polar water molecules. The drops are not perfect spheres because the force of gravity tends to pull them down, causing them to flatten.

It is possible to decrease the surface tension of water by adding a surfactant. A **surfactant** is any substance that interferes with the hydrogen bonding between water molecules and thereby reduces surface tension. Soaps and detergents are surfactants. Adding a detergent to beads of water on a greasy surface reduces surface tension, causing the beads of water to collapse and spread out, as shown in Figure 15.5.

Figure 15.5 Effect of a Surfactant
Water drops bead up on some surfaces. When detergent, a surfactant, is added to water, the drop spreads out.
Compare *Which liquid drop has a higher surface tension?*

Vapor Pressure Hydrogen bonding between water molecules also explains water's unusually low vapor pressure. Remember that the vapor pressure of a liquid is the result of molecules escaping from the surface of the liquid and entering the vapor phase. An extensive network of hydrogen bonds holds the molecules in liquid water to one another. These hydrogen bonds must be broken before water changes from the liquid to the vapor state, so the tendency of these molecules to escape is low and evaporation is slow. Imagine what would happen if it were not. All the lakes and oceans, with their large surface areas, would rapidly evaporate!

Boiling Point Molecular compounds of low molar mass are usually gases or liquids with low boiling points at normal atmospheric pressure. Ammonia (NH_3), a molecular compound, has a molar mass of 17.0 g/mol and boils at about $-33°C$. Water has a molar mass of 18.0 g/mol, but it has a boiling point of 100°C. The difference between the boiling points of these two compounds is due to hydrogen bonding, which is more extensive in water than in ammonia. It takes much more heat to disrupt the attractions between water molecules than those between ammonia molecules. If the hydrogen bonding in water were as weak as it is in ammonia, water would be a gas at the usual temperatures found on Earth.

READING SUPPORT
Build Reading Skills:
Inference If water molecules did not form hydrogen bonds with each other, water would have a much lower boiling point. *What do you think this would mean for life as we know it?*

Quick Lab

Purpose To observe an unusual surface property of water that results from hydrogen bonding

Materials

- shallow dish or petri dish
- water
- paper clip
- rubber band, approximately 5 cm in diameter
- micropipets or droppers (2)
- vegetable oil
- liquid dish detergent

Surface Tension

Procedure

1. Thoroughly clean and dry the dish.

2. Fill the dish almost full with water. Dry your hands.

3. Being careful not to break the surface, gently place the paper clip on the water. Observe what happens.

4. Repeat Steps 1 and 2.

5. Gently place the open rubber band on the water.

6. Slowly add the vegetable oil drop by drop onto the water encircled by the rubber band until that water is covered with a layer of oil. Observe for 15 seconds.

7. Allow one drop of dish detergent to fall onto the center of the oil layer. Observe the system for 15 seconds.

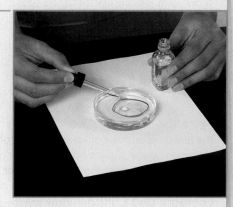

Analyze and Conclude

1. Observe What happened to the paper clip in Step 3? Why?

2. Predict If a paper clip becomes wet, does it float? Explain your answer.

3. Observe What shape did the rubber band take when the water inside it was covered with oil? Why did it take the observed shape?

4. Describe What happened when a drop of dish detergent was placed onto the layer of oil?

Water in the Solid State

How can you describe the structure of ice?

You have seen that water in the liquid state exhibits some unique properties. The same is true for water in the solid state. For example, ice cubes float in your glass of iced tea because solid water has a lower density than liquid water. This situation is not usual for liquids. As a typical liquid cools, it begins to contract and its density increases gradually. The density increases because the molecules of the liquid move closer together so that a given volume of the liquid contains more molecules and thus more mass. If the cooling continues, the liquid eventually solidifies with a density greater than the density of the liquid. A typical solid sinks in its own liquid because the density of the solid is greater than that of the corresponding liquid.

As water begins to cool, it behaves initially like a typical liquid. It contracts slightly and its density gradually increases, as shown in Table 15.1. Notice that at 4°C, the density of water is at its maximum of 1.0000 g/cm^3. When the temperature of the water falls below 4°C, the density of water actually starts to decrease. Below 4°C, water no longer behaves like a typical liquid. Ice, which forms at 0°C, has about a 10 percent lower density than liquid water at 0°C. You may have noticed that ice begins to form at the surface of a pond when the temperature reaches 0°C, but the ice does not sink. It floats at the surface, making ice skating and ice fishing possible. Ice is one of only a few solids that floats in its own liquid.

Why is ice less dense than liquid water? As you can see in Figure 15.6, hydrogen bonds hold the water molecules in place in the solid phase. **The structure of ice is a regular open framework of water molecules in a hexagonal arrangement.** When ice melts, the framework collapses. Looking back at Figure 15.3, you can see that the water molecules pack closer together in liquid water, making it more dense than ice.

Table 15.1	
Density of Liquid Water and Ice	
Temperature (°C)	**Density (g/cm^3)**
100 (liquid water)	0.9584
50	0.9881
25	0.9971
10	0.9997
4	1.0000
0 (liquid water)	0.9998
0 (ice)	0.9168

Figure 15.6 Structure of Ice
The unique properties of ice are a result of hydrogen bonding. **a.** Extensive hydrogen bonding in ice holds the water molecules farther apart in a more ordered arrangement than in liquid water. **b.** The hexagonal symmetry of a snowflake reflects the structure of the ice crystal.
Compare and Contrast *How are the structures of liquid water (shown in Figure 15.3) and ice similar? How are they different?*

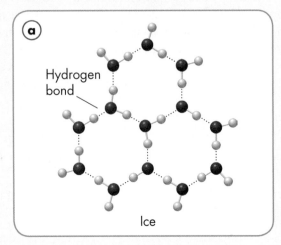

Hydrogen bond

Ice

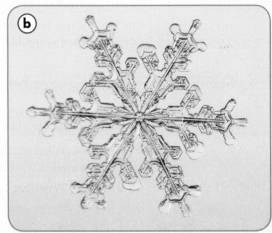

The fact that ice floats has important consequences for organisms. A layer of ice on the top of a body of water, such as the one shown in Figure 15.7, acts as an insulator for the water beneath, preventing the water from freezing solid except under extreme conditions. The liquid water at the bottom of an otherwise frozen body of water is warmer than 0°C, so fish and other aquatic life are better able to survive. If ice were denser than liquid water, bodies of water would tend to freeze solid during the winter months, destroying many types of organisms.

Ice melts at 0°C, which is a high melting temperature for a molecule with such a low molar mass. A considerable amount of energy is required to return water molecules in the solid state to the liquid state. The heat absorbed when 1 g of water at 0°C changes from a solid to a liquid is 334 J. This heat is the same amount of energy that is needed to raise the temperature of 1 g of liquid water from 0°C to 80°C.

Q: *What properties of water that result from hydrogen bonding make it essential to life on Earth?*

Figure 15.7 Ice Floats in Liquid Water
Many organisms that live in water would not survive if ice were more dense than liquid water.

 **15.1** LessonCheck

1. ☞ **Review** What causes the high surface tension, low vapor pressure, and high boiling point of water?

2. ☞ **Describe** How are water molecules arranged in ice?

3. **Explain** Why does water form spherical drops on some surfaces?

4. **Relate Cause and Effect** What effect does a surfactant have on the surface tension of water?

5. **Infer** Water (H_2O) and methane (CH_4) have similar molar masses. Methane changes from a liquid to a gas at −161°C. Water becomes a gas at 100°C. What could account for the difference?

6. **Apply Concepts** What causes water pipes to break in freezing weather?

BIGIDEA BONDING AND INTERACTIONS

7. Describe how hydrogen bonding accounts for the properties of water.

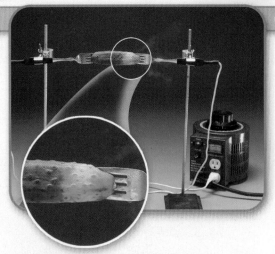

Q: *How can you make a pickle glow?* Is it possible to read by the light of a glowing pickle? Although it sounds absurd, an ordinary dill pickle from the deli can be a source of light! Metal forks are inserted into the ends of the pickle and connected to a source of alternating electric current. After a time, during which the pickle becomes hot and produces steam, the pickle begins to glow. The mechanism by which the light is generated is not fully understood, but it is clear that conduction of electric current by the pickle is an important factor.

Key Questions

 What types of substances dissolve most readily in water?

 Why are all ionic compounds electrolytes?

 Why do hydrates easily lose and regain water?

Vocabulary

• aqueous solution • solvent
• solute • solvation
• electrolyte • nonelectrolyte
• strong electrolyte
• weak electrolyte
• water of hydration • hydrate
• anhydrous • effloresce
• hygroscopic • desiccant
• deliquescent

Solutions

 What types of substances dissolve most readily in water?

Water dissolves so many of the substances that it comes in contact with that you won't find chemically pure water in nature. Even the tap water you drink is a solution that contains varying amounts of dissolved minerals and gases. An **aqueous solution** is water that contains dissolved substances.

Solvents and Solutes In a solution, the dissolving medium is the **solvent.** The dissolved particles in a solution are the **solute.** A solvent dissolves the solute, and the solute becomes dispersed in the solvent. Solvents and solutes may be gases, liquids, or solids.

Recall that solutions are homogeneous mixtures. They are also stable mixtures. For example, sodium chloride (NaCl) does not settle out when its solutions are allowed to stand, provided other conditions, such as temperature, remain constant. Solute particles can be atoms, ions, or molecules, and their average diameters are usually less than 1 nm (10^{-9} m). Therefore, if you filter a solution through filter paper, both the solute and the solvent pass through the filter.

 Substances that dissolve most readily in water include ionic compounds and polar covalent compounds. Nonpolar covalent compounds, such as methane, and compounds found in oil, grease, and gasoline, do not dissolve in water. However, oil and grease will dissolve in gasoline. To understand this difference, you must know more about the structures of the solvent and the solute and what attractions exist between them.

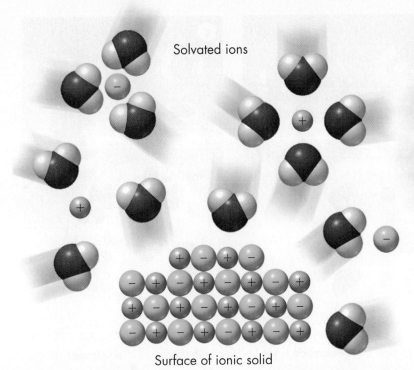

Solvated ions

Surface of ionic solid

Figure 15.8 Solvation of an Ionic Solid
When an ionic solid dissolves, the ions become solvated, or surrounded by solvent molecules.
Infer *Why do the water molecules orient themselves differently around the anions and the cations?*

See solvation animated online.

KINETIC ART

The Solution Process Water molecules are in continuous motion because they have kinetic energy. When a crystal of sodium chloride is placed in water, the water molecules collide with the crystal. Remember that a water molecule is polar, with a partial negative charge on the oxygen atom and partial positive charges on the hydrogen atoms. The polar solvent molecules (H_2O) attract the solute ions (Na^+, Cl^-). As individual solute ions break away from the crystal, the negatively and positively charged ions become surrounded by solvent molecules and the ionic crystal dissolves. The process by which the positive and negative ions of an ionic solid become surrounded by solvent molecules is called **solvation.** Figure 15.8 shows a model of the solvation of an ionic solid such as sodium chloride.

In some ionic compounds, the attractions among the ions in the crystals are stronger than the attractions exerted by water. These compounds cannot be solvated to any significant extent and are therefore nearly insoluble. Barium sulfate ($BaSO_4$) and calcium carbonate ($CaCO_3$) are examples of nearly insoluble ionic compounds.

Figure 15.9 shows that oil and water do not mix. What about oil in gasoline? Both oil and gasoline are composed of nonpolar molecules. The attractive forces that hold two molecules in oil together are similar in magnitude to the forces that hold two molecules in gasoline together. Molecules in oil can easily separate and replace molecules in gasoline to form a solution. As a rule, polar solvents such as water dissolve ionic compounds and polar compounds; nonpolar solvents such as gasoline dissolve nonpolar compounds. This relationship can be summed up in the expression "like dissolves like."

Figure 15.9 Oil and Water
Oil and water do not mix. Oil is less dense than water, so it floats on top. The colors result from the bending of light rays by the thin film of oil.

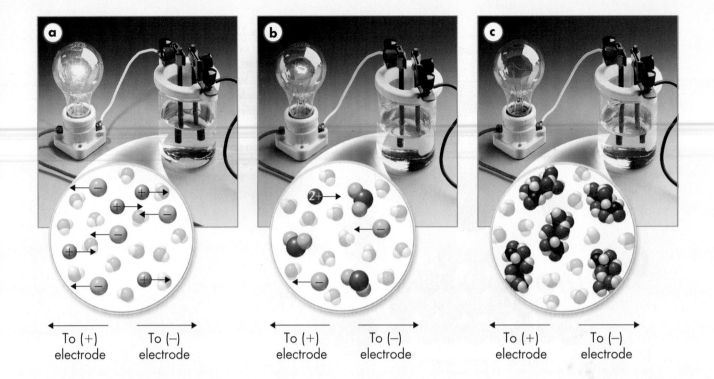

| To (+) electrode | To (−) electrode | To (+) electrode | To (−) electrode | To (+) electrode | To (−) electrode |

Figure 15.10 Conductivity of Solutions

A solution conducts an electric current if it contains ions. **a.** Sodium chloride, a strong electrolyte, is nearly 100 percent dissociated into ions in water. **b.** Mercury(II) chloride, a weak electrolyte, is only partially dissociated in water. **c.** Glucose, a nonelectrolyte, does not dissociate in water.

Predict *Silver chloride dissolves only slightly in water. If the electrodes were immersed in a solution of silver chloride, would the bulb glow brightly, dimly, or not at all?*

Electrolytes and Nonelectrolytes

Why are all ionic compounds electrolytes?

Remember the glowing pickle? The pickle contained an electrolyte. An **electrolyte** is a compound that conducts an electric current when it is in an aqueous solution or in the molten state. Conduction of an electric current requires ions that are mobile and, thus, able to carry charges through a liquid. **All ionic compounds are electrolytes because they dissociate into ions.** Sodium chloride, copper(II) sulfate, and sodium hydroxide are typical water-soluble electrolytes. Barium sulfate is an ionic compound that cannot conduct an electric current in aqueous solution because it is insoluble, but it can conduct in the molten state.

The experimental setup in Figure 15.10 can be used to determine whether a solution contains an electrolyte. In order for the bulb to light, an electric current must flow between the two electrodes that are immersed in the solution. If ions are present in the solution, they carry electrical charge from one electrode to the other, completing the electrical circuit.

A **nonelectrolyte** is a compound that does not conduct an electric current in either an aqueous solution or the molten state. Many molecular compounds are nonelectrolytes because they are not composed of ions. Most compounds of carbon, such as table sugar (sucrose) and the alcohol in rubbing alcohol (2-propanol), are nonelectrolytes.

Some polar molecular compounds are nonelectrolytes in the pure state but become electrolytes when they dissolve in water. This change occurs because such compounds ionize in solution. For example, neither ammonia ($NH_3(g)$) nor hydrogen chloride ($HCl(g)$) is an electrolyte in the pure state. Yet an aqueous solution of ammonia conducts an electric current because ammonium ions (NH_4^+) and hydroxide ions (OH^-) form when ammonia dissolves in water.

$$NH_3(g) + H_2O(l) \longrightarrow NH_4^+(aq) + OH^-(aq)$$

Similarly, in an aqueous solution, hydrogen chloride produces hydronium ions (H_3O^+) and chloride ions (Cl^-). An aqueous solution of hydrogen chloride conducts an electric current and is therefore an electrolyte.

$$HCl(g) + H_2O(l) \longrightarrow H_3O^+(aq) + Cl^-(aq)$$

Not all electrolytes conduct an electric current to the same degree. In Figure 15.10, the bulb glows brightly when the electrodes are immersed in a sodium chloride solution. The bright glow shows that sodium chloride is a strong electrolyte because nearly all the dissolved sodium chloride exists as separate Na^+ and Cl^- ions. In a solution that contains a **strong electrolyte,** all or nearly all of the solute exists as ions. The ions move in solution and conduct an electric current. Most soluble salts, inorganic acids, and inorganic bases are strong electrolytes.

The bulb glows dimly when the electrodes are immersed in a mercury(II) chloride solution because mercury(II) chloride is a weak electrolyte. A **weak electrolyte** conducts an electric current poorly because only a fraction of the solute in the solution exists as ions. Organic acids and bases are also examples of weak electrolytes. In a solution of glucose, the bulb does not glow. Glucose ($C_6H_{12}O_6$) is a molecular compound. It does not form ions, so it is a nonelectrolyte.

Electrolytes are essential to all metabolic processes. Your cells use electrolytes, such as sodium and potassium ions, to carry electrical impulses internally and to other cells. These impulses are crucial to nerve and muscle function. The kidneys help to maintain balanced electrolyte concentrations in the blood. However, an electrolyte imbalance can occur if you become dehydrated. For example, when you exercise, you can lose water and electrolytes from your body through perspiration. The athlete in Figure 15.11 understands that it is important to replenish these electrolytes by eating salty foods or by drinking sports drinks.

CHEMISTRY & YOU

Q: *Pickles contain table salt. Why can electric current flow through a pickle, causing it to glow?*

Figure 15.11 Sports Drinks
It is important to replenish electrolytes when exercising or sweating. Sports drinks often contain sodium and potassium.

Nutrition Facts
Serving Size 8 fl oz (240 mL)
Servings Per Container 4

Amount Per Serving

Calories 25

	% Daily Value*
Total Fat 0g	0%
Sodium 110mg	5%
Potassium 30mg	1%
Total Carbohydrate 7g	2%
Sugars 7g	
Protein 0g	

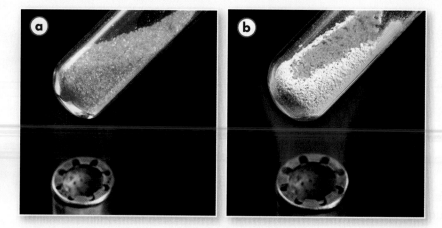

Figure 15.12 Heating a Hydrate
Water can be driven from a hydrate by heating it. **a.** Heating of a sample of blue $CuSO_4 \cdot 5H_2O$ begins. **b.** After a time, much of the blue hydrate has been converted to white anhydrous $CuSO_4$.

Hydrates

Why do hydrates easily lose and regain water?

When an aqueous solution of copper(II) sulfate is allowed to evaporate, deep-blue crystals of copper(II) sulfate pentahydrate are deposited. The chemical formula for this compound is $CuSO_4 \cdot 5H_2O$. Water molecules are an integral part of the crystal structure of copper(II) sulfate pentahydrate and many other substances. The water contained in a crystal is called the **water of hydration** or water of crystallization. A compound that contains water of hydration is called a **hydrate.** In writing the formula of a hydrate, use a dot to connect the formula of the compound and the number of water molecules per formula unit. Crystals of copper(II) sulfate pentahydrate always contain five molecules of water for each copper and sulfate ion pair. The deep-blue crystals are dry to the touch. They are unchanged in composition or appearance in normally moist air. However, when the crystals are heated above 100°C, they lose their water of hydration. **The forces holding the water molecules in hydrates are not very strong, so the water is easily lost and regained.** Figure 15.12 shows how the blue crystals of $CuSO_4 \cdot 5H_2O$ crumble to a white anhydrous powder that has the formula $CuSO_4$. A substance that is **anhydrous** does not contain water. If anhydrous copper(II) sulfate is treated with water, the blue pentahydrate is regenerated.

$$CuSO_4 \cdot 5H_2O(s) \underset{-\text{heat}}{\overset{+\text{heat}}{\rightleftharpoons}} CuSO_4(s) + 5H_2O(g)$$

Another compound that changes color in the presence of moisture is cobalt(II) chloride. A piece of filter paper that has been dipped in an aqueous solution of cobalt(II) chloride and then dried is blue in color (anhydrous $CoCl_2$). As you can see in Figure 15.13, when the paper is exposed to moist air, it turns pink because of the formation of the hydrate cobalt(II) chloride hexahydrate ($CoCl_2 \cdot 6H_2O$). The blue paper could be used to test for the presence of water.

Some familiar hydrates are listed in Table 15.2. Each one contains a fixed quantity of water and has a definite composition. To determine what percent by mass of a hydrate is water, first determine the mass of water in one mole of hydrate. Then determine the molar mass of the hydrate. The percent by mass of water can be calculated using the following equation:

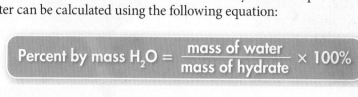

Percent by mass $H_2O = \dfrac{\text{mass of water}}{\text{mass of hydrate}} \times 100\%$

Figure 15.13 Exposing a Hydrate to Moist Air
Paper dipped in an aqueous cobalt(II) chloride solution and then dried is blue. In the presence of moisture, the paper turns pink. **Infer** *How could you change the pink paper back to blue?*

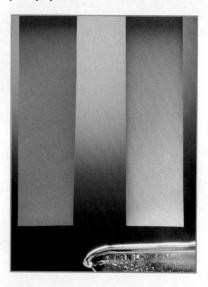

Table 15.2

Some Common Hydrates

Formula	Chemical name	Common name
$MgSO_4 \cdot 7H_2O$	Magnesium sulfate heptahydrate	Epsom salt
$Ba(OH)_2 \cdot 8H_2O$	Barium hydroxide octahydrate	
$CaCl_2 \cdot 2H_2O$	Calcium chloride dihydrate	
$CuSO_4 \cdot 5H_2O$	Copper(II) sulfate pentahydrate	Blue vitriol
$Na_2SO_4 \cdot 10H_2O$	Sodium sulfate decahydrate	Glauber's salt
$KAl(SO_4)_2 \cdot 12H_2O$	Potassium aluminum sulfate dodecahydrate	Alum
$Na_2B_4O_7 \cdot 10H_2O$	Sodium tetraborate decahydrate	Borax
$FeSO_4 \cdot 7H_2O$	Iron(II) sulfate heptahydrate	Green vitriol
$H_2SO_4 \cdot H_2O$	Sulfuric acid monohydrate (mp 8.6°C)	

Efflorescent Hydrates The water molecules in hydrates are held by weak forces, so hydrates often have an appreciable vapor pressure. If a hydrate has a vapor pressure higher than the pressure of water vapor in the air, the hydrate will lose its water of hydration or **effloresce.** For example, copper(II) sulfate pentahydrate has a vapor pressure of about 1.0 kPa at room temperature. The average pressure of water vapor at room temperature is about 1.3 kPa. Copper(II) sulfate pentahydrate is stable until the humidity decreases. When the vapor pressure drops below 1.0 kPa, the hydrate effloresces. Washing soda, or sodium carbonate decahydrate ($Na_2CO_3 \cdot 10H_2O$), is efflorescent. As the crystals lose water of hydration, they effloresce and become coated with a white powder of anhydrous sodium carbonate (Na_2CO_3).

Hygroscopic Hydrates Hydrated ionic compounds that have a low vapor pressure remove water from moist air to form higher hydrates. These hydrates and other compounds that remove moisture from air are called **hygroscopic.** For example, calcium chloride monohydrate spontaneously absorbs a second molecule of water when exposed to moist air.

$$CaCl_2 \cdot H_2O(s) \xrightarrow{\text{moist air}} CaCl_2 \cdot 2H_2O(s)$$

Calcium chloride is used as a desiccant in the laboratory. A **desiccant** is a substance used to absorb moisture from the air and create a dry atmosphere. Anhydrous calcium chloride can be placed in the bottom of a tightly sealed container called a desiccator, which is shown in Figure 15.14. Substances that must be kept dry are stored inside. A solid desiccant such as calcium sulfate ($CaSO_4$) can also be added to a liquid solvent, such as ethanol, to keep it dry. The calcium sulfate does not dissolve appreciably in the solvent but absorbs water from the ethanol. When a desiccant has absorbed all the water it can hold, the compound can be returned to its anhydrous state by heating.

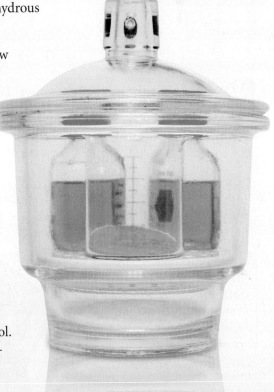

Figure 15.14 Desiccator
A desiccator may contain calcium chloride. Substances that must be kept dry are stored inside.

Sample Problem 15.1

Finding the Percent by Mass of Water in a Hydrate

Calculate the percent by mass of water in washing soda, sodium carbonate decahydrate ($Na_2CO_3 \cdot 10H_2O$).

❶ **Analyze** **List the known and the unknown.** To determine the percent by mass, divide the mass of water in the one mole of the hydrate by the molar mass of the hydrate and multiply by 100 percent.

KNOWN

formula of hydrate = $Na_2CO_3 \cdot 10H_2O$

UNKNOWN

percent by mass H_2O = ?%

❷ **Calculate** **Solve for the unknown.**

> For every 1 mol of $Na_2CO_3 \cdot 10H_2O$, there are 10 mol of H_2O.

| Determine the mass of 10 mol of water. | $\text{mass of 10 mol } H_2O = 10 [(2 \times 1.0 \text{ g}) + 16.0 \text{ g}] = 180.0 \text{ g}$ |

| Determine the mass of 1 mol of the hydrated compound. | $\text{mass of 1 mol } Na_2CO_3 \cdot 10H_2O = (2 \times 23.0 \text{ g}) + 12.0 \text{ g} + (3 \times 16.0 \text{ g}) + 180.0 \text{ g}$ $= 286.0 \text{ g}$ |

| Calculate the percent by mass of water in the hydrate. | $\text{percent by mass } H_2O = \dfrac{\text{mass of water}}{\text{mass of hydrate}} \times 100\%$ $= \dfrac{180.0 \text{ g}}{286.0 \text{ g}} \times 100\% = 62.94\%$ |

❸ **Evaluate** **Does the result make sense?** The mass of the water accounts for more than half the molar mass of the compound, so a percentage greater than 50 percent is expected.

8. What is the percent by mass of water in $CuSO_4 \cdot 5H_2O$?

> In Problem 8, start by determining the mass of 5 mol of water and 1 mol of the hydrate.

9. If you need 5.00 g of anhydrous Na_2CO_3 for your reaction, how many grams of $Na_2CO_3 \cdot 10H_2O$ could you use instead?

> You know from the Sample Problem above that 62.94% of the hydrate is water, so 37.06 g out of every 100 g of the hydrate is Na_2CO_3.

Deliquescent Compounds Have you ever noticed the small packets of silica gel that are often packaged with electronic equipment and leather goods? Although the structure of silica gel is not the same as a hydrated salt, it is a hygroscopic substance used to absorb moisture from the surrounding air to prevent damage to sensitive equipment and materials. Some compounds are so hygroscopic that they become wet when exposed to normally moist air. These compounds are **deliquescent**, which means that they remove sufficient water from the air to dissolve completely and form solutions. Figure 15.15 shows that pellets of sodium hydroxide are deliquescent. For this reason, containers of sodium hydroxide and other deliquescent chemicals should always be tightly stoppered and the chemicals should never come in contact with your skin. The solution formed by a deliquescent substance has a lower vapor pressure than that of the water in the air.

Figure 15.15 Sodium Hydroxide Deliquescent substances, such as sodium hydroxide, can remove water from the air. **a.** Sodium hydroxide pellets absorb moisture from the air. **b.** Eventually a solution is formed. **Classify** *What is the solvent? What is the solute?*

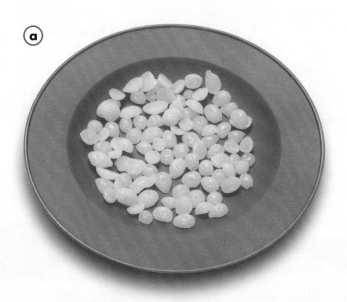
(a)

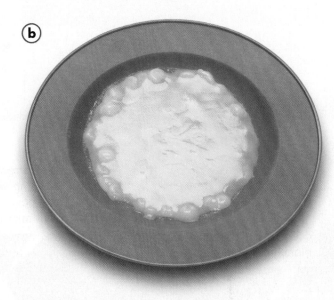
(b)

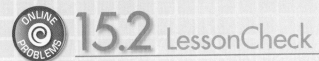

15.2 LessonCheck

10. Identify What types of substances dissolve most readily in water?

11. Review What property of all ionic compounds make them electrolytes?

12. Explain Why do hydrates easily lose water when heated and regain water when exposed to moisture?

13. Classify Identify the solvent and the solute in vinegar, a dilute aqueous solution of acetic acid.

14. Calculate What is the percent by mass of water in iron(II) sulfate heptahydrate ($FeSO_4 \cdot 7H_2O$)?

15. Compare Is the percent by mass of copper in $CuSO_4 \cdot 5H_2O$ the same as in $CuSO_4$? Explain.

16. Compare and Contrast Distinguish between efflorescent and hygroscopic substances.

BIGIDEA BONDING AND INTERACTIONS

17. Which of the following substances dissolve to a significant extent in water? Explain your answer in terms of the interactions between the solvent and solute.
   a. CH_4
   b. KCl
   c. I_2
   d. $MgSO_4$
   e. sucrose ($C_{12}H_{22}O_{11}$)
   f. $NaHCO_3$

Reverse Osmosis Desalination

Ninety-seven percent of the world's water is saltwater. Unfortunately, humans cannot drink saltwater. However, a process called reverse osmosis desalination can turn saltwater into drinkable water.

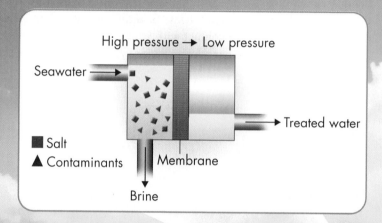

1 Seawater supply
Seawater moves from the ocean to the desalination plant through large pipes.

2 Pretreatment system
Incoming water is treated and filtered to remove debris, sediment, and other microscopic particles.

3 Reverse osmosis process During a process called reverse osmosis, high pressure is used to force the seawater through semi-permeable membranes. These membranes only allow water to pass through, leaving salts and contaminants behind in a concentrated seawater solution, called brine. The brine is then released back into the ocean.

Advantages of Reverse Osmosis Desalination

✔ **Expands drinking water resources** Some areas of the world do not have abundant sources of drinking water. Reverse osmosis desalination provides drinking water in cases of drought, water shortages, or national disasters.

✔ **Low environmental impact** The conversion of saltwater to drinking water via reverse osmosis desalination uses minimal chemicals.

✔ **Low start-up costs** The cost to install a reverse osmosis desalination facility is relatively low.

Disadvantages of Reverse Osmosis Desalination

✘ **High energy consumption** The cost of running a reverse osmosis desalination plant is high compared to other methods for obtaining drinking water.

✘ **Low efficiency** The volume of drinking water produced is low compared to the volume of seawater treated.

✘ **Potentially harmful to sea life** The process of removing seawater and returning brine to the ocean can disturb marine environments.

❺ Drinking water storage The treated drinking water is transferred to a tank and stored until needed.

❻ Drinking water supply The tap water you drink may have originally come from the sea!

❹ Post treatment system The treated water goes through more filters. In addition, chemical disinfectants are usually added.

Take It Further

1. Classify Would you consider seawater to be a homogeneous aqueous system or a heterogeneous aqueous system? Explain.

2. Infer Brine is more dense than seawater. How might the release of brine back into the ocean affect the marine environment?

Q: *Why are some sunsets red?* Have you ever wondered what causes the red glow of the evening sky? The atmosphere contains particles of water and dust. As sunlight passes through the particles, it is scattered. However, not all wavelengths are scattered to the same extent. The shorter wavelengths of visible light (blue and green) are scattered more than the longer wavelengths (red and orange). At sunrise and sunset, the longer wavelengths are more visible because the sun's light travels through more of Earth's atmosphere.

Key Questions

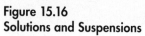 What is the difference between a suspension and a solution?

What distinguishes a colloid from a suspension and a solution?

Vocabulary

- suspension
- colloid
- Tyndall effect
- Brownian motion
- emulsion

Suspensions

What is the difference between a suspension and a solution?

So far in this chapter, you have learned about aqueous solutions, which are homogeneous mixtures. In contrast, heterogeneous mixtures are not solutions. If you shake a container containing a piece of clay with water, the clay breaks into fine particles. The water becomes cloudy because the clay particles are suspended in the water. If you stop shaking, the particles settle out. A **suspension** is a mixture from which particles settle out upon standing. **A suspension differs from a solution because the particles of a suspension are much larger and do not stay suspended indefinitely.** The particles in a typical suspension have an average diameter greater than 1000 nm. By contrast, the particle size in a solution is usually about 1 nm.

Suspensions are heterogeneous because at least two substances can be clearly identified. In the example of clay particles mixed with water, you can clearly see the dispersed phase (clay) in the dispersion medium (water). Figure 15.16 shows how the difference between a solution and suspension is easily seen when each type of mixture is filtered.

Figure 15.16
Solutions and Suspensions
A solution is a homogeneous mixture. A suspension is a heterogeneous mixture. **a.** The small size of the solute particles in a solution allows them to pass through filter paper. **b.** The suspended particles of a suspension can be removed by filtration.

Colloids

What distinguishes a colloid from a suspension and a solution?

Gelatin is an example of a type of mixture called a colloid. A **colloid** is a heterogeneous mixture containing particles that range in size from 1 nm to 1000 nm. The particles are spread, or dispersed, throughout the dispersion medium, which can be a solid, liquid, or a gas. The first substances to be identified as colloids were glues. Other colloids include such mixtures as paint, aerosol sprays, and smoke. Table 15.3 lists some common colloidal systems and gives examples of familiar colloids.

How do the properties of colloids differ from those of suspensions and solutions? Many colloids are cloudy or milky in appearance, like suspensions, when they are concentrated. Colloids may look clear or almost clear, like solutions, when they are dilute. The important difference between colloids and solutions and suspensions is in the size of the particles. **Colloids have particles smaller than those in suspensions and larger than those in solutions.** These intermediate-sized particles cannot be retained by filter paper as are the larger particles of a suspension, and they do not settle out with time. Colloids can be distinguished by a phenomenon called the Tyndall effect and by the observation of Brownian motion. They are also subject to coagulation or clumping together, and they can be emulsified or made stable.

Table 15.3

Some Colloidal Systems			
System			
Dispersed phase	**Dispersion medium**	**Type**	**Example**
Gas	Liquid	Foam	Whipped cream
Gas	Solid	Foam	Marshmallow
Liquid	Liquid	Emulsion	Milk, mayonnaise
Liquid	Gas	Aerosol	Fog, aerosol
Solid	Gas	Smoke	Dust in air
Solid	Liquid	Sols, gels	Egg white, jelly, paint, blood, starch in water, gelatin

Flashlight  Solution Colloid Suspension

Figure 15.17 Scattering of Light
The path of light is visible only when the light is scattered by particles. **a.** Fog or mist is a colloid and thus exhibits the Tyndall effect. **b.** Solutions do not scatter light. Particles in colloids and suspensions reflect or scatter light in all directions.
Explain *Why is it easier to see the light beam of an automobile on a foggy night than on a clear night?*

CHEMISTRY & YOU

Q: *What would be the ideal conditions to see a red sunset?*

The Tyndall Effect Ordinarily you cannot see a beam of sunlight unless the light passes through particles of water (mist) or dust in the air. These particles scatter the sunlight. Similarly, a beam of light is visible as it passes through a colloid. The scattering of visible light by colloidal particles is called the **Tyndall effect.** Suspensions also exhibit the Tyndall effect. Solutions do not exhibit the Tyndall effect. The particles in solutions are too small to scatter light. Figure 15.17 shows how the Tyndall effect can differentiate solutions from colloids and suspensions.

Brownian Motion Flashes of light, or scintillations, are seen when colloids are studied under a microscope. Colloids scintillate because the particles reflecting and scattering the light move erratically. The chaotic movement of colloidal particles, which was first observed by the Scottish botanist Robert Brown (1773–1858), is called **Brownian motion.** Brownian motion is caused by collisions of the molecules of the dispersion medium with the small, dispersed colloidal particles. These collisions help prevent the colloidal particles from settling.

Coagulation Colloidal particles also tend to stay suspended because they become charged by adsorbing ions from the dispersing medium onto their surface. *Adsorption* means to adhere to a surface. Some colloidal particles become positively charged by adsorbing positively charged ions. Other colloidal particles become negatively charged by adsorbing negatively charged ions. All the colloidal particles in a particular colloidal system will have the same charge, although the colloidal system is neutral. The repulsion between the like-charged particles prevents the particles from forming heavier aggregates that would have a greater tendency to settle out. Thus, a colloidal system can be destroyed or coagulated by the addition of electrolytes. The added ions neutralize the charged colloidal particles. The particles can clump together to form heavier aggregates and settle out from the dispersion.

Emulsions Mayonnaise is an example of a colloidal system called an emulsion. An **emulsion** is a colloidal dispersion of a liquid in a liquid. An emulsifying agent is essential for the formation of an emulsion and for maintaining the emulsion's stability. For example, oils and greases are not soluble in water. However, oils and greases readily form a colloidal dispersion if soap or detergent is added to the water. Soaps and detergents are emulsifying agents. One end of a large soap or detergent molecule is polar and is attracted to water molecules. The other end of the soap or detergent molecule is nonpolar and is soluble in oil or grease. Soaps and other emulsifying agents thus allow the formation of colloidal dispersions between liquids that do not ordinarily mix. Mayonnaise is a heterogeneous mixture of oil and vinegar. Such a mixture would quickly separate without the presence of egg yolk, which is the emulsifying agent. Other foods such as milk, margarine, and butter are also emulsions. Cosmetics, shampoos, and lotions are formulated with emulsifiers to maintain consistent quality. Table 15.4 summarizes the properties of solutions, colloids, and suspensions.

Go online to learn more about emulsions.

Table 15.4

Properties of Solutions, Colloids, and Suspensions

Property	System		
	Solution	Colloid	Suspension
Particle type	Ions, atoms, small molecules	Large molecules or particles	Large particles or aggregates
Particle size	0.1–1 nm	1–1000 nm	1000 nm and larger
Effect of light	No scattering	Exhibits Tyndall effect	Exhibits Tyndall effect
Effect of gravity	Stable, does not separate	Stable, does not separate	Unstable, sediment forms
Filtration	Particles not retained on filter	Particles not retained on filter	Particles retained on filter
Uniformity	Homogeneous	Heterogeneous	Heterogeneous

15.3 LessonCheck

18. **Describe** How does a suspension differ from a solution?

19. **Explain** What distinguishes a colloid from a suspension and a solution?

20. **Apply Concepts** How can you determine through observation that a mixture is a suspension?

21. **Explain** Could you separate a colloid by filtering? Explain.

22. **Infer** How can the Tyndall effect be used to distinguish between a colloid and a solution?

23. **Relate Cause and Effect** Can the presence of Brownian motion distinguish between a solution and a colloid? Explain.

Small-Scale Lab

Electrolytes

Purpose

To classify compounds as electrolytes by testing their conductivity in aqueous solution

Materials

- reaction surface
- chemicals shown in the grid below
- conductivity tester
- micropipet or dropper
- water

Procedure

1. On separate sheets of paper, draw two grids similar to the one below. Make each square 2 cm on each side.

2. Place a reaction surface over one of the grids and place a few grains of each solid in the indicated places.

3. Test each solid for conductivity.

4. Add 1 drop of water to each solid and test the wet mixture for conductivity. Be sure to clean and dry the conductivity leads between each test.

NaCl(s)	MgSO₄(s)
Na₂CO₃(s)	Table sugar $C_{12}H_{22}O_{11}$
NaHCO₃(s)	Cornstarch $(C_6H_{10}O_5)n$
KCl(s)	KI(s)

Analyze and Conclude

1. Infer Which compounds in your table are electrolytes? Which are not electrolytes?

2. Observe Do any of these electrolytes conduct electric current in the solid form? Explain.

3. Classify Identify each compound in the grid as ionic or covalent.

4. Draw Conclusions For a compound to be an electrolyte, what must happen when it dissolves in water?

You're the Chemist

1. Analyze Data When an ionic solid dissolves in water, water molecules attract the ions, causing them to come apart, or dissociate. The resulting dissolved ions are electrically charged particles that allow the solution to conduct electric current. The following chemical equations represent this phenomenon.

$$NaCl(s) \xrightarrow{H_2O} Na^+(aq) + Cl^-(aq)$$

$$Na_2CO_3(s) \xrightarrow{H_2O} 2Na^+(aq) + CO_3^{2-}(aq)$$

Write a similar chemical equation for each electrolyte you tested. Draw diagrams to explain how the ions conduct electric current.

2. Design an Experiment Obtain the following aqueous solutions: HCl, H_2SO_4, HNO_3, $C_2H_4O_2$, NH_3, NaOH, rubbing alcohol, and distilled water. Design and carry out an experiment to test their conductivities. Use your data to classify each substance as a strong electrolyte, weak electrolyte, or nonelectrolyte.

3. Design an Experiment Test various liquids for conductivity. Try soft drinks, orange juice, pickle juice, and coffee. Which liquids are electrolytes?

15 Study Guide

BIGIDEA
BONDING AND INTERACTIONS

Water molecules are held together through hydrogen bonds. The hydrogen bonding interactions between water molecules accounts for the unique properties of water including its high surface tension, low vapor pressure, and high boiling point. Hydrogen bonding also accounts for the fact that ice is less dense than liquid water. Ionic compounds and polar covalent compounds dissolve most readily in water to form aqueous solutions. Ionic compounds dissolve in water when the polar water molecules attract the ions of the solute, causing the individual solute ions to break away from the ionic crystal.

15.1 Water and Its Properties

🔑 Many unique and important properties of water—including its high surface tension, low vapor pressure, and high boiling point—result from hydrogen bonding.

🔑 The structure of ice is a regular open framework of water molecules in a hexagonal arrangement.

- surface tension (490)
- surfactant (490)

15.2 Homogeneous Aqueous Systems

🔑 Substances that dissolve most readily in water include ionic compounds and polar covalent compounds.

🔑 All ionic compounds are electrolytes because they dissociate into ions.

🔑 The forces holding the water molecules in hydrates are not very strong, so the water is easily lost and regained.

- aqueous solution (494)
- solvent (494)
- solute (494)
- solvation (495)
- electrolyte (496)
- nonelectrolyte (496)
- strong electrolyte (497)
- weak electrolyte (497)
- water of hydration (498)
- hydrate (498)
- anhydrous (498)
- effloresce (499)
- hygroscopic (499)
- desiccant (499)
- deliquescent (501)

Key Equation

$$\text{Percent by mass } H_2O = \frac{\text{mass of water}}{\text{mass of hydrate}} \times 100\%$$

15.3 Heterogeneous Aqueous Systems

🔑 A suspension differs from a solution because the particles of a suspension are much larger and do not stay suspended indefinitely.

🔑 Colloids have particles smaller than those in suspensions and larger than those in solutions.

- suspension (504)
- colloid (505)
- Tyndall effect (506)
- Brownian motion (506)
- emulsion (507)

Lesson by Lesson

15.1 Water and Its Properties

24. Explain why water molecules are polar.

★**25.** Why do the particles at the surface of a liquid behave differently from those in the bulk of the liquid?

26. Why does water have a high surface tension?

27. Describe some observable effects that are produced by the surface tension of a liquid.

★**28.** What is a surfactant? Explain how it works.

29. How can the unusually low vapor pressure of water be explained?

30. Explain why water has a relatively high boiling point.

★**31.** Explain why bodies of water with large surface areas such as lakes and oceans do not evaporate rapidly.

32. What characteristic of ice distinguishes it from most other solid substances?

33. Explain the role of hydrogen bonds in ice.

34. How does the structure of ice differ from the structure of water?

★**35.** What would be some of the consequences if ice were denser than water?

15.2 Homogeneous Aqueous Systems

36. Distinguish between a solution in general and an aqueous solution.

37. In the formation of a solution, how does the solvent differ from the solute?

★**38.** Identify the solvent and the solute in a solution of table sugar in water.

★**39.** Suppose an aqueous solution contains both table sugar and table salt. Can you separate either of these solutes from the water by filtration? Explain your reasoning.

★**40.** Describe the process of solvation.

41. Why is water an excellent solvent for most ionic and polar covalent compounds but not for non-polar compounds?

42. Explain why gasoline does not dissolve in water.

★**43.** Which of the following substances dissolve appreciably in water? Give reasons for your choices.
  a. HCl   **d.** C_2H_6
  b. K_2SO_4 **e.** NH_3
  c. NaI   **f.** $CaCO_3$

44. What particles must be present in a solution if it is to conduct an electric current?

★**45.** Why does molten sodium chloride conduct an electric current?

46. What is the main distinction between an aqueous solution of a strong electrolyte and an aqueous solution of a weak electrolyte?

47. What is meant by a substance's water of hydration?

★**48.** Write formulas for these hydrates.
  a. sodium sulfate decahydrate
  b. calcium chloride dihydrate
  c. barium hydroxide octahydrate

★**49.** Name each hydrate.
  a. $SnCl_4 \cdot 5H_2O$
  b. $FeSO_4 \cdot 7H_2O$
  c. $BaBr_2 \cdot 4H_2O$
  d. $FePO_4 \cdot 4H_2O$

★**50.** Epsom salt ($MgSO_4 \cdot 7H_2O$) changes to the monohydrate form at 150°C. Write an equation for this change.

51. Some hydrates are efflorescent. Explain what that means. Under what conditions will a hydrate effloresce?

★**52.** Explain why a hygroscopic substance can be used as a desiccant.

53. Why is it important to keep some hygroscopic substances in tightly sealed containers?

15.3 Heterogeneous Aqueous Systems

★**54.** Arrange colloids, suspensions, and solutions in order of increasing particle size.

★**55.** How could you distinguish through observation among a solution, a colloid, and a suspension?

56. What is the Tyndall effect?

57. Why don't solutions demonstrate the Tyndall effect?

58. What causes Brownian motion?

★59. What are two circumstances that help keep colloidal particles in suspension?

60. How can a colloid be destroyed?

61. What makes a colloidal dispersion stable?

Understand Concepts

★62. From your knowledge of intermolecular forces, arrange these liquids in order of increasing surface tension: water (H_2O), hexane (C_6H_{14}), ethanol (C_2H_6O).

★63. The graph below shows the density of water over the temperature range 0°C to 20°C.

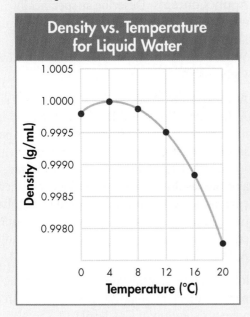

a. What is the maximum density of water?
b. At what temperature does the maximum density of water occur?
c. Would it be meaningful to expand the smooth curve of the graph to the left to temperatures below 0°C?

64. Explain why ions become solvated in aqueous solution.

★65. Methanol (CH_4O) and hydrobromic acid (HBr) are both molecular compounds. However, an aqueous solution of methanol does not conduct an electric current, but an aqueous solution of hydrobromic acid does. Account for this difference.

★66. Explain which properties of water are responsible for these occurrences.

a. Water in tiny cracks in rocks helps break up the rocks when it freezes.
b. Water beads up on a newly waxed car.
c. A longer time is needed for a teaspoon of water to evaporate than a teaspoon of alcohol.

67. Water has its maximum density at 4°C. Discuss the consequences of this fact.

★68. Water is a polar solvent; gasoline is a nonpolar solvent. Decide which compounds are more likely to dissolve in water and which are more likely to dissolve in gasoline.

a. CCl_4 **c.** Na_2SO_4
b. CH_4 **d.** KCl

★69. You have a solution containing either table sugar or table salt dissolved in water.

a. Can you tell which it is by visual inspection? Explain.
b. Give two ways by which you could easily tell which it is.

70. Explain why ethanol (C_2H_6O) will dissolve in both gasoline and water.

71. Are all liquids soluble in each other? Explain.

★72. Write equations to show how these substances ionize or dissociate in water.

a. NH_4Cl **c.** $Cu(NO_3)_2$
b. CH_3COOH **d.** $HgCl_2$

★73. Name these hydrates and determine the percent by mass of water in each.

a. $Na_2CO_3 \cdot H_2O$
b. $MgSO_4 \cdot 7H_2O$

74. Calculate the percent by mass of water in calcium chloride hexahydrate ($CaCl_2 \cdot 6H_2O$).

★75. Barium hydroxide forms an octahydrate.

a. Write the equation for the formation of this hydrate from the anhydrous salt.
b. Calculate the percent by mass of water in barium hydroxide octahydrate.

★76. How many grams of copper(II) sulfate pentahydrate would you need to measure in order to have 10.0 g of anhydrous copper(II) sulfate?

77. Explain the structural difference between ice and liquid water that accounts for the lower density of ice.

★78. Match each term with the following descriptions. A description may apply to more than one term.

  a. solution **b.** colloid **c.** suspension

  (1) does not settle out on standing
  (2) heterogeneous mixture
  (3) particle size less than 1 nm
  (4) particles can be filtered out
  (5) demonstrates the Tyndall effect
  (6) particles are invisible to the unaided eye
  (7) homogenized milk
  (8) saltwater
  (9) jelly

79. A student standing in front of a murky aquarium sees a sharply focused flashlight beam shining through the aquarium as only a broad, diffuse light. What phenomenon is the student observing?

★80. The diagrams below represent aqueous solutions of three different substances. Identify each substance as a strong electrolyte, weak electrolyte, or nonelectrolyte.

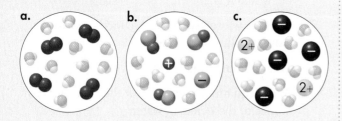

Think Critically

★81. **Predict** Describe what might happen if you put a sealed glass container full of water into a freezer.

82. **Use Models** Make a drawing to show how one molecule of water can be connected to as many as four other molecules of water by hydrogen bonds. Write an explanation of your drawing.

★83. **Relate Cause and Effect** A water strider is an insect with elongated legs that can easily walk on the surface of water. What would you expect to happen to the insect if a small amount of a surfactant were added to the water? Explain the reasoning behind your answer.

84. **Predict** Describe what would happen to a pond at 0°C if the density of ice were greater than the density of water. Do you think the pond would freeze more quickly? Explain.

★85. **Infer** When ethanol (C_2H_6O) dissolves in water, the volume of the final solution is less than the separate volumes of the water and alcohol added together. Can you explain this result? Do you think that it might be possible to mix two different liquids and get a mixture volume that is larger than the sum of the volumes of the two components? Explain.

★86. **Draw Conclusions** When the humidity is low and the temperature high, humans must take in large quantities of water or face serious dehydration. Why do you think water is so important for the proper functioning of your body?

87. **Apply Concepts** Describe as specifically as possible what would happen if a nonpolar molecular liquid were added to water. What would form if you shook this mixture vigorously?

88. **Analyze Data** You are given three white solids: A, B, and C. You know that one of the solids must be fructose ($C_6H_{12}O_6$), one must be potassium nitrate (KNO_3), and one must be barium sulfate ($BaSO_4$). Solid A dissolves in water and the resulting solution conducts an electric current. Solid B is insoluble. Solid C dissolves in water and the resulting solution does not conduct an electric current. Identify the solids A, B, and C.

★89. **Infer** Cobalt(II) chloride test paper is blue. This paper is made by soaking strips of paper in an aqueous solution of $CoCl_2 \cdot 6H_2O$. The paper strips are then dried in an oven.

$$CoCl_2 \cdot 6H_2O \xrightarrow{\text{heat}} CoCl_2 + 6H_2O$$
$$\text{pink} \qquad\qquad\qquad \text{blue}$$

  a. When cobalt(II) chloride hexahydrate is dissolved in water, what is the color of the solution?
  b. What is the color of wet cobalt(II) chloride paper?
  c. What is the color of dry cobalt(II) chloride paper?
  d. What is the percent by mass of water in the hexahydrate?
  e. What does cobalt(II) chloride test paper test for?

90. Compare How do the volumes of the following compare?

    a. 1 g of ice at 0°C and 1 g of liquid water at 0°C

    b. 1 g of liquid water at 100°C and 1 g of steam at 100°C

★91. Relate Cause and Effect When spring comes, ice melting at the surface of a pond begins a beneficial process that stirs up the water of the pond. Explain why the pond water begins to mix when the ice melts. (*Hint:* Consider the changes in density.)

★92. Infer A problem for firefighters is that much of the water they spray on a fire doesn't soak in but runs off carrying debris and pollution into the environment. Explain how the addition of a surfactant to water used to fight fires could help put out the fire more rapidly and protect the environment.

★93. Relate Cause and Effect After a winter of alternate periods of freezing and thawing, some roads have broken pavement and potholes. Using what you know of the properties of water, explain why potholes form.

94. Interpret Diagrams Detergents consist of molecules with a polar or charged head and a long, oil-like tail. In water, detergent molecules can aggregate into organized structures called micelles. As shown below, the polar heads face the water molecules and the oily chains are inside the micelle. Suggest an explanation for the formation of micelles.

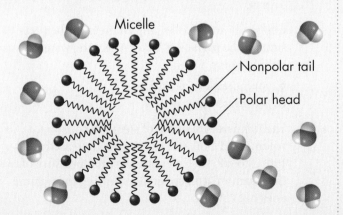

Micelle

Nonpolar tail

Polar head

95. Explain Research the importance of electrolytes in the body. Write a paragraph explaining why the concentration of these ions may decline and how they can be restored.

96. Research Clothes dryer sheets are often added to tumble dryers to prevent clothes from wrinkling. Do research to learn what compounds are used in dryer sheets and how they work. Write a brief report of your findings.

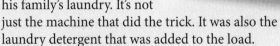
CHEMYSTERY

Coming Clean

Wes's dirty socks finally did become clean, but only after being thrown into the washing machine with a load of his family's laundry. It's not just the machine that did the trick. It was also the laundry detergent that was added to the load.

Water alone cannot remove many common stains. The particles of dirt and grease on Wes's socks were trapped in the cloth fibers and could not be dissolved by water. Also, because of its high surface tension, the water could not penetrate the fibers. Laundry detergents typically contain one or more surfactants. The surfactants reduce the surface tension of water, so that it can effectively wet and penetrate the fibers. The surfactants also act as emulsifiers. One end of the surfactant molecule is nonpolar and can dissolve the molecules in dirt and grease. The other end of the surfactant molecule is polar and can dissolve in water. Agitation provided by the washing machine helps pull the stain free from the cloth fibers.

★ 97. Infer What happens to the molecules in the dirt and grease once they are lifted from the cloth fibers?

98. Connect to the BIGIDEA Explain how detergents remove stains from clothing by describing the interactions among the molecules in the detergent, the molecules in the stain, and the water molecules.

99. A cylindrical vessel, 28.0 cm in height and 3.00 cm in diameter, is filled with water at 50°C. The density of water is 0.988 g/cm³ at this temperature. Express the mass of water in the vessel in the following units.

  a. grams   **b.** milligrams   **c.** kilograms

∗**100.** How many significant figures are in each measurement?

  a. 56.003 g
  b. 750 mL
  c. 0.0056 cm
  d. 0.4005 dg

101. Write the correct electron configuration for the oxide ion. Which noble gas has the same electron configuration?

∗**102.** When a proton is attracted to the unshared electron pair of a water molecule, the polyatomic hydronium ion (H_3O^+) is formed. Draw electron dot structures to show the formation of this ion.

103. The balloons contain 1 mol of He, CH_4, and O_2 at STP.

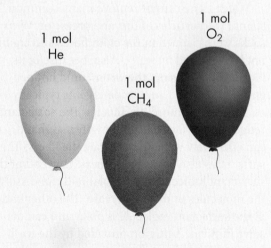

1 mol
O₂

1 mol
He

1 mol
CH₄

  a. What is the volume of each balloon?
  b. What is the mass of the gas in each balloon?
  c. Calculate the density of the gas in each balloon.
  d. The density of air at room temperature is about 1.2 g/mL. Predict whether each balloon will rise or sink when released.

∗**104.** Balance the following equations.

  a. $CO_2(g) + H_2O(l) \longrightarrow C_6H_{12}O_6(s) + O_2(g)$
  b. $Na(s) + H_2O(l) \longrightarrow$
  $$Na^+(aq) + OH^-(aq) + H_2(g)$$

105. How many grams each of hydrogen gas and oxygen gas are required to produce 4.50 mol of water?

∗**106.** The decomposition of hydrogen peroxide is given by this equation.

$$2H_2O_2(l) \longrightarrow 2H_2O(l) + O_2(g)$$

Calculate the mass of water and the volume of oxygen at STP formed when 2.00×10^{-3} mol of hydrogen peroxide is decomposed.

∗**107.** Acetaldehyde (C_2H_4O) is produced commercially by the reaction of acetylene (C_2H_2) with water, as shown by this equation.

$$C_2H_2(g) + H_2O(l) \longrightarrow C_2H_4O(l)$$

How many grams of C_2H_4O can be produced from 2.60×10^2 g H_2O, assuming sufficient C_2H_2 is present?

108. Hydrogen reacts with oxygen to form water.

$$2H_2(g) + O_2(g) \longrightarrow 2H_2O(l)$$

  a. How many moles of oxygen are required to produce 10.8 g H_2O?
  b. How many liters of oxygen is this at STP?

∗**109.** A mixture of 40 cm³ of oxygen gas and 60 cm³ of hydrogen gas at STP is ignited.

  a. Which gas is the limiting reagent?
  b. What is the mass of water produced?
  c. Which gas remains after reaction?
  d. What is the volume, at STP, of the remaining gas?

110. Explain how the following changes in the pressure on the surface of water affect the water's boiling point.

  a. an increase in pressure
  b. a decrease in pressure

∗**111.** The temperature of 1 L of steam at constant volume and 1.00 atm pressure is increased from 100°C to 200°C. Calculate the final pressure of the steam in atmospheres, assuming the volume does not change.

If You Have Trouble With . . .

Question	99	100	101	102	103	104	105	106	107	108	109	110	111
See Chapter	3	3	7	8	10	11	12	12	12	12	12	13	14

Standardized Test Prep

Select the choice that best answers each question or completes each statement.

1. When a sugar cube completely dissolves in a glass of water, it forms
   (A) a colloid.   (C) an emulsion.
   (B) a suspension.   (D) a solution.

2. How many water molecules are tied up per formula unit of a compound that is an octahydrate?
   (A) nine   (B) eight   (C) seven   (D) six

3. Which property is characteristic of water?
   (A) relatively high surface tension
   (B) relatively high vapor pressure
   (C) relatively low solvent ability
   (D) relatively low polarity

Use the atomic windows to answer Question 4.

4. Atomic window (A) represents solute particles in a given volume of solution. Which window represents the solute particles in the same volume of solution when the amount of solvent is doubled?

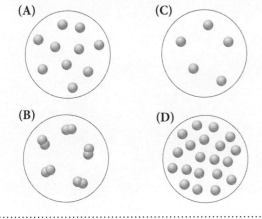

(A)   (C)
(B)   (D)

Use the description and the data table to answer Questions 5–7.

A student measured the conductivity of six aqueous solutions. Each solution had equal concentrations of solute. The magnitude of the conductivity value is proportional to the number of ions in the solution. The SI conductivity unit is the microsiemens/cm (μS/cm). The table gives the student's results.

Solution	Conductivity (μS/cm)
Potassium chloride, KCl	2050
Aluminum chloride, $AlCl_3$	4500
Calcium chloride, $CaCl_2$	3540
Sodium hydroxide, NaOH	2180
Ethanol, C_2H_6O	0
Magnesium bromide, $MgBr_2$	3490

5. Why does the ethanol solution have zero conductivity?

6. Explain why two pairs of conducting solutions have similar conductivities.

7. The $AlCl_3$ solution has a conductivity that is about twice that of the KCl solution. Explain.

For each question there are two statements. Decide whether each statement is true or false. Then decide whether Statement II is a correct explanation for Statement I.

Statement I		Statement II
8. Water has a relatively high surface tension.	BECAUSE	Water molecules form strong hydrogen bonds with other water molecules.
9. Particles in a colloid settle out faster than particles in a solution.	BECAUSE	Particles in a colloid are larger than particles in a solution.
10. Water molecules are polar.	BECAUSE	The bond between hydrogen and oxygen atoms in a water molecule is polar.

If You Have Trouble With . . .

Question	1	2	3	4	5	6	7	8	9	10
See Lesson	15.3	15.2	15.1	15.2	15.2	15.2	15.2	15.1	15.3	15.1

16

Solutions

INSIDE:

- **16.1** Properties of Solutions
- **16.2** Concentrations of Solutions
- **16.3** Colligative Properties of Solutions
- **16.4** Calculations Involving Colligative Properties

PearsonChem.com

River water contains many dissolved ions, including sodium, calcium, magnesium, chloride, and sulfate ions.

BIGIDEA

THE MOLE AND QUANTIFYING MATTER

Essential Questions:

1. *What properties are used to describe the nature of solutions?*

2. *In what ways can you quantify the concentration of a solution?*

CHEMYSTERY

That Sinking Feeling

It was there one minute and gone the next—a stretch of road that looked like it had been swallowed up by the ground beneath it. The pavement had fallen into a sinkhole caused by moving groundwater. Groundwater consists of rain and melted snow that has soaked into the ground. Over time, groundwater can dissolve huge amounts of rock, gradually forming beautiful limestone caves, as well as destructive sinkholes. One recorded sinkhole swallowed a house, several other buildings, five cars, and a swimming pool!

What factors do you think contribute to the formation of sinkholes? How do you think sinkhole accidents can be prevented?

▶ Connect to the **BIG**IDEA As you read about solutions, try to identify the factors that cause sinkholes to form.

NATIONAL SCIENCE EDUCATION STANDARDS

A-1, A-2, B-5, E-2, F-4, F-6

16.1 Properties of Solutions

CHEMISTRY & YOU

Q: *How can you grow a tree made out of crystals?* You're already familiar with the concept of liquids freezing. But what about crystals growing from a solution? The crystallization of a solute from solution is a physical change that is different from freezing. The crystal tree shown here began its "life" as an ordinary aqueous solution. The tree trunk, made of absorbent paper, soaks up the liquid. As water evaporates from the solution, the solutes crystallize onto the paper, forming delicate "leaves." Not all solutions will crystallize as this one did. The rate of crystallization depends on the nature of the solute and solvent, as well as on the temperature and humidity of the surroundings.

Key Questions

 What factors affect how fast a substance dissolves?

 How can you describe the equilibrium in a saturated solution?

 What factors affect the solubility of a substance?

Vocabulary

- saturated solution
- solubility
- unsaturated solution
- miscible
- immiscible
- supersaturated solution
- Henry's law

Solution Formation

 What factors affect how fast a substance dissolves?

Have you noticed, when making tea, that granulated sugar dissolves faster than sugar cubes, and that both granulated sugar and sugar cubes dissolve faster in hot tea or when you stir the tea? Figure 16.1 illustrates these observations. You will be able to explain these observations once you have gained an understanding of the properties of solutions.

Recall that solutions are homogeneous mixtures that may be solid, liquid, or gaseous. The compositions of the solvent and the solute determine whether or not a substance will dissolve. **Factors that affect how fast a substance dissolves include agitation, temperature, and the particle size of the solute.** Each of these factors involves the contact of the solute with the solvent.

Figure 16.1 Dissolving Sugar
Stirring and heating increase the rate at which a solute dissolves. **a.** A cube of sugar in cold tea dissolves slowly. **b.** Granulated sugar dissolves in cold water more quickly than a sugar cube, especially with stirring. **c.** Granulated sugar dissolves very quickly in hot tea.

Agitation If a teaspoon of granulated sugar (sucrose) is placed in a glass of tea, the crystals dissolve slowly. If the contents of the glass are stirred, however, the crystals dissolve more quickly. The dissolving process occurs at the surface of the sugar crystals. Stirring speeds up the process because fresh solvent (the water in tea) is continually brought into contact with the surface of the solute (sugar). It's important to realize, however, that agitation (stirring or shaking) affects only the rate at which a solid solute dissolves. It does not influence the amount of solute that will dissolve. An insoluble substance remains undissolved regardless of how vigorously or for how long the solvent/solute system is agitated.

Temperature Temperature also influences the rate at which a solute dissolves. Sugar dissolves much more rapidly in hot tea than in iced tea. At higher temperatures, the kinetic energy of water molecules is greater than at lower temperatures, so the molecules move faster. The more rapid motion of the solvent molecules leads to an increase in the frequency and the force of the collisions between water molecules and the surfaces of the sugar crystals.

Particle Size of the Solute The rate at which a solute dissolves also depends upon the size of the solute particles. A spoonful of granulated sugar dissolves more quickly than a sugar cube because the smaller particles in granulated sugar expose a much greater surface area to the colliding water molecules. Remember, the dissolving process is a surface phenomenon. The more surface area of the solute that is exposed, the faster the rate of dissolving.

Quick Lab

Purpose To classify mixtures as solutions or colloids using the Tyndall effect

Materials
- sodium hydrogen carbonate
- cornstarch
- stirring rod
- distilled water (or tap water)
- flashlight
- masking tape
- 3 jars with parallel sides
- teaspoon
- cup

Solutions and Colloids

Procedure

1. In a cup, make a paste: Mix one-half teaspoon of cornstarch with 4 teaspoons of water.

2. Fill one jar with water. Add one-half teaspoon of sodium hydrogen carbonate to a second jar and fill with water. Stir to mix. Add the cornstarch paste to the third jar and fill with water. Stir to mix.

3. Turn out the lights in the room. Shine the beam of light from the flashlight at each of the jars and record your observations.

Analyze and Conclude

1. Observe In which of the jars in the experiment was it possible to see the path of the beam of light?

2. Infer What made the light beam visible?

3. Explain If a system that made the light beam visible were filtered, would the light beam be visible in the filtrate? Explain your answer.

4. Predict What would you observe if you were to replace the sodium hydrogen carbonate with sucrose (cane sugar) or sodium chloride (table salt)? If you were to replace the cornstarch with flour or diluted milk?

Figure 16.2 Saturated Solution
In a saturated solution, a state of dynamic equilibrium exists between the solution and the excess solute. The rate of solvation (dissolving) equals the rate of crystallization, so the total amount of dissolved solute remains constant.
Predict *What would happen if you added more solute to this saturated solution?*

See a **saturated solution** animated online.

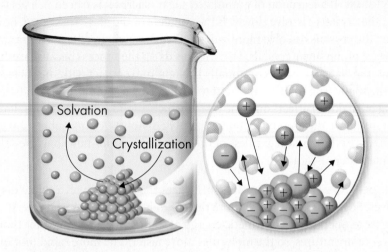

Solvation

Crystallization

Figure 16.3 Hot Spring
The water in this hot spring in Yellowstone National Park is saturated with minerals. As the water cools near the edges of the spring, some of the minerals crystallize because they are less soluble at the lower temperature.

Solubility

🔑 *How can you describe the equilibrium in a saturated solution?*

If you add 36.0 g of sodium chloride to 100 g of water at 25°C, all of the 36.0 g of salt dissolves. But if you add one more gram of salt and stir, no matter how vigorously or for how long, only 0.2 g of the last portion will dissolve. Why does the remaining 0.8 g of salt remain undissolved? According to the kinetic theory, water molecules are in continuous motion. Therefore, they should continue to bombard the excess solid, solvating and removing the ions. As ions are solvated, they dissolve in the water. Based on this information, you might expect all of the sodium chloride to dissolve eventually. That does not happen, however, because an exchange process is occurring. New particles from the solid are solvated and enter into solution, as shown in Figure 16.2. At the same time, an equal number of already-dissolved particles crystallize. These particles come out of solution and are deposited as a solid. The mass of undissolved crystals remains constant.

What is happening in Figure 16.2? Particles move from the solid into the solution. Some dissolved particles move from the solution back to the solid. Because these two processes occur at the same rate, no net change occurs in the overall system. Such a solution is said to be saturated. A **saturated solution** contains the maximum amount of solute for a given quantity of solvent at a constant temperature and pressure. 🔑 **In a saturated solution, a state of dynamic equilibrium exists between the solution and any undissolved solute, provided that the temperature remains constant.** At 25°C, 36.2 g of sodium chloride dissolved in 100 g of water forms a saturated solution. If additional solute is added to this solution, it will not dissolve.

The **solubility** of a substance is the amount of solute that dissolves in a given quantity of a solvent at a specified temperature and pressure to produce a saturated solution. Solubility is often expressed in grams of solute per 100 g of solvent (g/100 g H$_2$O). Sometimes the solubility of a gas is expressed in grams per liter of solution (g/L). A solution that contains less solute than a saturated solution at a given temperature and pressure is an **unsaturated solution.** If additional solute is added to an unsaturated solution, the solute will dissolve until the solution is saturated.

Some liquids—for example, water and ethanol—are infinitely soluble in each other. Any amount of ethanol will dissolve in a given volume of water, and vice versa. Similarly, ethylene glycol and water mix in all proportions. Pairs of liquids such as these are said to be completely miscible. Two liquids are **miscible** if they dissolve in each other in all proportions. In such a solution, the liquid that is present in the larger amount is usually considered the solvent. Liquids that are slightly soluble in each other—for example, water and diethyl ether—are partially miscible. Liquids that are insoluble in one another are **immiscible.** As you can see in Figure 16.4, oil and water are examples of immiscible liquids.

Factors Affecting Solubility

🔑 **What factors affect the solubility of a substance?**

You have read that solubility is defined as the mass of solute that dissolves in a given mass of a solvent at a specified temperature. 🔑 **Temperature affects the solubility of solid, liquid, and gaseous solutes in a solvent; both temperature and pressure affect the solubility of gaseous solutes.**

Temperature The solubility of most solid substances increases as the temperature of the solvent increases. For sodium chloride (NaCl), the increase in solubility is small—from 36.2 g per 100 g of water at 25°C to 39.2 g per 100 g of water at 100°C. Figure 16.5 shows how the solubility of several substances varies with temperature.

For a few substances, solubility decreases with temperature. For example, the solubility of ytterbium sulfate ($Yb_2(SO_4)_3$) in water drops from 44.2 g per 100 g of water at 0°C to 5.8 g per 100 g of water at 90°C. Table 16.1 on the next page lists the solubilities of some common substances in water at various temperatures.

Figure 16.4 Oil and Water
Vegetable oil is not soluble in water. Liquids that are insoluble in one another are immiscible.

InterpretGraphs

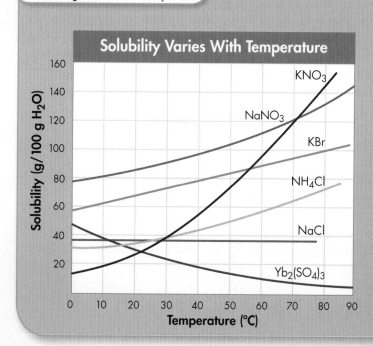

Solubility Varies With Temperature

(graph: Solubility (g/100 g H₂O) vs Temperature (°C), showing curves for KNO₃, NaNO₃, KBr, NH₄Cl, NaCl, and Yb₂(SO₄)₃)

Figure 16.5 Changing the temperature usually affects the solubility of a substance.
a. Read Graphs What happens to the solubility of KNO_3 as the temperature increases?
b. Identify Which substance exhibits the least change in solubility as temperature increases?
c. Predict Suppose you added some solid NaCl to a saturated solution of NaCl at 20°C and warmed the mixture to 40°C. What would happen to the added NaCl?
d. Infer The mineral deposits around the hot spring in Figure 16.3 include NaCl and KCl. How do you think the solubility of KCl changes as the temperature decreases? Explain your answer.

Table 16.1

Solubilities of Substances in Water at Various Temperatures

Substance		Solubility (g/100 g H$_2$O)			
Name	Formula	0°C	20°C	50°C	100°C
Barium hydroxide	Ba(OH)$_2$	1.67	31.89	—	—
Barium sulfate	BaSO$_4$	0.00019	0.00025	0.00034	—
Calcium hydroxide	Ca(OH)$_2$	0.189	0.173	—	0.07
Lead(II) chloride	PbCl$_2$	0.60	0.99	1.70	—
Lithium carbonate	Li$_2$CO$_3$	1.5	1.3	1.1	0.70
Potassium chlorate	KClO$_3$	4.0	7.4	19.3	56.0
Potassium chloride	KCl	27.6	34.0	42.6	57.6
Sodium chloride	NaCl	35.7	36.0	37.0	39.2
Sodium nitrate	NaNO$_3$	74	88.0	114.0	182
Aluminum chloride	AlCl$_3$	30.84	31.03	31.60	33.32
Silver nitrate	AgNO$_3$	122	222.0	455.0	733
Lithium bromide	LiBr	143.0	166	203	266.0
Sucrose (table sugar)	C$_{12}$H$_{22}$O$_{11}$	179	230.9	260.4	487
Hydrogen*	H$_2$	0.00019	0.00016	0.00013	0.0
Oxygen*	O$_2$	0.0070	0.0043	0.0026	0.0
Carbon dioxide*	CO$_2$	0.335	0.169	0.076	0.0

*Gas at 101 kPa (1 atm) total pressure

Q: *How do you think crystal growing kits work? Use what you know about solubility and saturated solutions to explain your answer.*

Suppose you make a saturated solution of sodium ethanoate (sodium acetate) at 30°C and let the solution stand undisturbed as it cools to 25°C. Because the solubility of this compound is greater at 30°C than at 25°C, you expect that solid sodium ethanoate will crystallize from the solution as the temperature drops. But no crystals form. You have made a supersaturated solution. A **supersaturated solution** contains more solute than it can theoretically hold at a given temperature. The crystallization of a supersaturated solution can be initiated if a very small crystal, called a seed crystal, of the solute is added. The rate at which excess solute deposits upon the surface of a seed crystal can be very rapid, as shown in Figure 16.6. Crystallization can also occur if the inside of the container is scratched.

Another example of crystallization in a supersaturated solution is the production of rock candy. A solution is supersaturated with sugar. Seed crystals cause the sugar to crystallize out of solution onto a string for you to enjoy.

The effect of temperature on the solubility of gases in liquid solvents is opposite that of solids. The solubilities of most gases are greater in cold water than in hot. For example, Table 16.1 shows that the most important component of air for living beings—oxygen— becomes less soluble in water as the temperature of the solution rises. This fact has some important consequences. When an industrial plant takes water from a lake to use for cooling and then dumps the resulting heated water back into the lake, the temperature of the entire lake increases. Such a change in temperature is known as thermal pollution. Aquatic animal and plant life can be severely affected because the increase in temperature lowers the concentration of dissolved oxygen in the lake water.

Pressure Changes in pressure have little effect on the solubility of solids and liquids, but pressure strongly influences the solubility of gases. Gas solubility increases as the partial pressure of the gas above the solution increases. Carbonated beverages are a good example. These drinks contain large amounts of carbon dioxide (CO_2) dissolved in water. Dissolved CO_2 makes the liquid fizz and your mouth tingle. The drinks are bottled under a high pressure of CO_2 gas, which forces large amounts of the gas into solution. When a carbonated-beverage container is opened, the partial pressure of CO_2 above the liquid decreases. Immediately, bubbles of CO_2 form in the liquid and escape from the open bottle, as shown in Figure 16.7. As a result, the concentration of dissolved CO_2 decreases. If the bottle is left open, the drink becomes "flat" as the solution loses most of its CO_2.

How is the partial pressure of carbon dioxide gas related to the solubility of CO_2 in a carbonated beverage? The relationship is described by **Henry's law,** which states that at a given temperature, the solubility (S) of a gas in a liquid is directly proportional to the pressure (P) of the gas above the liquid. In other words, as the pressure of the gas above the liquid increases, the solubility of the gas increases. Similarly, as the pressure of the gas decreases, the solubility of the gas decreases. You can write the relationship in the form of an equation.

$$\frac{S_1}{P_1} = \frac{S_2}{P_2}$$

S_1 is the solubility of a gas at one pressure, P_1; S_2 is the solubility at another pressure, P_2.

Figure 16.6 Supersaturated Solution
A supersaturated solution of sodium ethanoate ($NaC_2H_3O_2(aq)$) crystallizes rapidly when disturbed.
a. The solution is clear before a seed crystal is added. **b.** Crystals begin to form in the solution immediately after the addition of a seed crystal. **c–d.** The excess solute crystallizes rapidly.
Infer *When the crystallization has ceased, will the solution be saturated or unsaturated?*

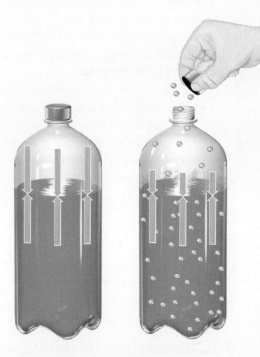

Figure 16.7 CO$_2$ in Solution
When a carbonated-beverage bottle is sealed, the pressure of CO_2 above the liquid is high, and the concentration of CO_2 in the liquid is also high. When the cap is removed, the pressure of CO_2 gas above the liquid decreases, and carbon dioxide bubbles out of the liquid.

SampleProblem 16.1

Using Henry's Law

If the solubility of a gas in water is 0.77 g/L at 3.5 atm of pressure, what is its solubility (in g/L) at 1.0 atm of pressure? (The temperature is held constant at 25°C.)

❶ Analyze List the knowns and the unknown. Use Henry's law to solve for the unknown solubility.

❷ Calculate Solve for the unknown.

KNOWNS	UNKNOWN
P_1 = 3.5 atm	S_2 = ? g/L
S_1 = 0.77 g/L	
P_2 = 1.0 atm	

State the equation for Henry's law.

$$\frac{S_1}{P_1} = \frac{S_2}{P_2}$$

Isolate S_2 by multiplying both sides by P_2:

$$P_2 \times \frac{S_1}{P_1} = \frac{S_2}{\cancel{P_2}} \times \cancel{P_2}$$

Solve Henry's law for S_2. Substitute the known values and calculate.

$$S_2 = \frac{S_1 \times P_2}{P_1} = \frac{0.77 \text{ g/L} \times 1.0 \cancel{\text{ atm}}}{3.5 \cancel{\text{ atm}}} = \boxed{0.22 \text{ g/L}}$$

❸ Evaluate Does the result make sense? The new pressure is approximately one third of the original pressure, so the new solubility should be approximately one third of the original. The answer is correctly expressed to two significant figures.

In Problem 1, you're solving Henry's law for an unknown solubility. In Problem 2, you're solving for an unknown pressure.

1. The solubility of a gas in water is 0.16 g/L at 104 kPa. What is the solubility when the pressure of the gas is increased to 288 kPa? Assume the temperature remains constant.

2. A gas has a solubility in water at 0°C of 3.6 g/L at a pressure of 1.0 atm. What pressure is needed to produce an aqueous solution containing 9.5 g/L of the same gas at 0°C?

16.1 LessonCheck

ONLINE PROBLEMS

3. ⚙ Review What determines how fast a substance will dissolve?

4. ⚙ Describe How can you describe the state of equilibrium in a saturated solution that contains undissolved solute?

5. ⚙ Describe What condition(s) determine the solubilities of solid, liquid, and gaseous solutes in a solvent?

6. Identify Name a unit used to express solubility.

7. Describe What determines whether or not a substance will dissolve?

8. Explain What would you do to change
  a. a saturated solid/liquid solution to an unsaturated solution?
  b. a saturated gas/liquid solution to an unsaturated solution?

9. Calculate The solubility of a gas is 0.58 g/L at a pressure of 104 kPa. What is its solubility if the pressure increases to 250 kPa at the same temperature?

16.2 Concentrations of Solutions

Q: *How can you describe the concentration of a solution?* Clean drinking water is important for all communities. What constitutes clean water? Your federal and state governments set standards limiting the amount of contaminants allowed in drinking water. These contaminants include metals, pesticides, and bacteria. Water must be tested continually to ensure that the concentrations of these contaminants do not exceed established limits.

Molarity

How do you calculate the molarity of a solution?

You have learned that a substance can dissolve to some extent in a particular solvent to form a solution. This lesson focuses on ways to express the actual extent of dissolving. The **concentration** of a solution is a measure of the amount of solute that is dissolved in a given quantity of solvent. A solution that contains a relatively small amount of solute is a **dilute solution.** By contrast, a **concentrated solution** contains a large amount of solute. An aqueous solution of sodium chloride containing 1 g NaCl per 100 g H_2O might be described as dilute when compared with a sodium chloride solution containing 30 g NaCl per 100 g H_2O. But the same solution might be described as concentrated when compared with a solution containing only 0.01 g NaCl per 100 g H_2O. You can see that the terms *concentrated* and *dilute* are only qualitative descriptions of the amount of a solute in solution.

How can concentration be expressed quantitatively? In chemistry, the most important unit of concentration is molarity. **Molarity (M)** is the number of moles of solute dissolved in one liter of solution. Molarity is also known as molar concentration. When the symbol *M* is accompanied by a numerical value, it is read as "molar." Figure 16.8 illustrates the procedure for making a 0.5*M*, or 0.5-molar, solution. Note that the volume involved is the total volume of the resulting solution, not the volume of the solvent alone.

Key Questions

How do you calculate the molarity of a solution?

What effect does dilution have on the amount of solute?

How do percent by volume and percent by mass differ?

Vocabulary

• concentration
• dilute solution
• concentrated solution
• molarity (*M*)

Figure 16.8 How to Make a 0.5M Solution
a. Add 0.5 mol of solute to a 1-L volumetric flask that is half filled with distilled water.
b. Swirl the flask carefully to dissolve the solute.
c. Fill the flask with water exactly to the 1-L mark.

To calculate the molarity of a solution, divide the number of moles of solute by the volume of the solution in liters.

$$\text{Molarity } (M) = \frac{\text{moles of solute}}{\text{liters of solution}}$$

For example, suppose 2 mol of glucose are dissolved in 5 L of solution. You would calculate the molarity of the solution as follows:

$$\frac{2 \text{ mol glucose}}{5 \text{ L solution}} = 0.4 \text{ mol/L} = 0.4M$$

If the amount of solute in a solution is expressed in mass units instead of moles, you can calculate molarity by using the appropriate conversion factors, as shown in Sample Problem 16.2.

SampleProblem 16.2

Calculating Molarity

Intravenous (IV) saline solutions are often administered to patients in the hospital. One saline solution contains 0.90 g NaCl in exactly 100 mL of solution. What is the molarity of the solution?

❶ Analyze List the knowns and the unknown.
Convert the concentration from g/100 mL to mol/L. The sequence is g/100 mL ⟶ mol/100 mL ⟶ mol/L.

KNOWNS

solution concentration = 0.90 g NaCl /100 mL
molar mass of NaCl = 58.5 g/mol

UNKNOWN

solution concentration = ?M

❷ Calculate Solve for the unknown.

Use the molar mass to convert g NaCl/100 mL to mol NaCl/100 mL. Then convert the volume units so that your answer is expressed in mol/L.

$$\frac{\text{Solution}}{\text{Concentration}} = \frac{0.90 \text{ g NaCl}}{100 \text{ mL}} \times \frac{1 \text{ mol NaCl}}{58.5 \text{ g NaCl}} \times \frac{1000 \text{ mL}}{1 \text{ L}}$$

$$= 0.15 \text{ mol/L}$$

$$= 0.15M$$

The relationship 1 L = 1000 mL gives you the conversion factor 1000 mL/1 L.

❸ Evaluate Does the result make sense? The answer should be less than 1M because a concentration of 0.90 g/100 mL is the same as 9.0 g/1000 mL (9.0 g/1 L), and 9.0 g is less than 1 mol of NaCl. The answer is correctly expressed to two significant figures.

10. A solution has a volume of 2.0 L and contains 36.0 g of glucose ($C_6H_{12}O_6$). If the molar mass of glucose is 180 g/mol, what is the molarity of the solution?

11. A solution has a volume of 250 mL and contains 0.70 mol NaCl. What is its molarity?

In some cases, you may need to determine the number of moles of solute dissolved in a given volume of solution. You can do this if the molarity of the solution is known. For example, how many moles are in 2.00 L of 2.5M lithium chloride (LiCl)? First, rearrange the formula for molarity to solve for the number of moles. Then, substitute the known values for molarity and volume.

$$\text{Molarity } (M) = \frac{\text{moles of solute}}{\text{liters of solution } (V)}$$

$$\text{Moles of solute} = \text{molarity } (M) \times \text{liters of solution } (V)$$

$$= 2.5M \times 2.00 \text{ L} = \left(\frac{2.5 \text{ mol}}{1 \text{ L}}\right) \times 2.00 \text{ L}$$

$$= 5.0 \text{ mol}$$

Thus, 2.00 L of 2.5M lithium chloride solution contains 5.0 mol of LiCl.

Sample Problem 16.3

Calculating the Moles of Solute in a Solution

Household laundry bleach is a dilute aqueous solution of sodium hypochlorite (NaClO). How many moles of solute are present in 1.5 L of 0.70M NaClO?

❶ **Analyze List the knowns and the unknown.** The conversion is volume of solution ⟶ moles of solute. Molarity has the units mol/L, so you can use it as a conversion factor between moles of solute and volume of solution.

KNOWNS
volume of solution = 1.5 L
solution concentration = 0.70 M NaClO

UNKNOWN
moles solute = ? mol

❷ **Calculate Solve for the unknown.**

Multiply the given volume by the molarity expressed in mol/L.

$$1.5 \text{ L} \times \frac{0.70 \text{ mol NaClO}}{1 \text{ L}} = 1.1 \text{ mol NaClO}$$

❸ **Evaluate Does the result make sense?** The answer should be greater than 1 mol but less than 1.5 mol, because the solution concentration is less than 0.75 mol/L and the volume is less than 2 L. The answer is correctly expressed to two significant figures.

12. How many moles of ammonium nitrate are in 335 mL of 0.425M NH$_4$NO$_3$?

13. How many moles of solute are in 250 mL of 2.0M CaCl$_2$? How many grams of CaCl$_2$ is this?

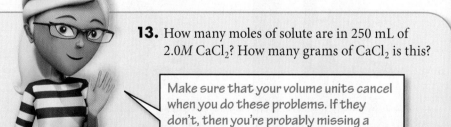

Make sure that your volume units cancel when you do these problems. If they don't, then you're probably missing a conversion factor in your calculations.

Figure 16.9 Dilution
Adding solvent to a concentrated solution lowers the concentration, but the total number of moles of solute present remains the same.

Solute particle

Solvent particle

Making Dilutions

What effect does dilution have on the amount of solute?

Both of the solutions in Figure 16.9 contain the same amount of solute. You can tell by the color of solution (a) that it is more concentrated than the solution (b); that is, solution (a) has the greater molarity. The more dilute solution (b) was made from solution (a) by adding more solvent. **Diluting a solution reduces the number of moles of solute per unit volume, but the total number of moles of solute in solution does not change.** You can also express this concept by writing an equation.

Moles of solute before dilution = moles of solute after dilution

Now recall the definition of molarity and how it can be rearranged to solve for moles of solute.

$$\text{Molarity } (M) = \frac{\text{moles of solute}}{\text{liters of solution } (V)}$$

Moles of solute = molarity (M) × liters of solution (V)

Figure 16.10 Making a Dilution
The student is preparing 100 mL of 0.40M $MgSO_4$ from a stock solution of 2.0M $MgSO_4$. **a.** She measures 20 mL of the stock solution with a 20-mL pipette. **b.** She transfers the 20 mL to a 100-mL volumetric flask. **c.** She carefully adds water to the mark to make 100 mL of solution.
Compare *How many moles of MgSO₄ are in 20 mL of the stock solution? In 100 mL of the dilute solution?*

The total number of moles of solute remains unchanged upon dilution, so you can now write this equation:

$$\text{Moles of solute} = M_1 \times V_1 = M_2 \times V_2$$

M_1 and V_1 are the molarity and volume of the initial solution, and M_2 and V_2 are the molarity and volume of the diluted solution. Volumes can be in liters or milliliters, as long as the same units are used for both V_1 and V_2. Figure 16.10 illustrates the procedure used for making a dilution in the lab.

Sample Problem 16.4

Preparing a Dilute Solution

How many milliliters of aqueous 2.00M $MgSO_4$ solution must be diluted with water to prepare 100.0 mL of aqueous 0.400M $MgSO_4$?

❶ **Analyze** **List the knowns and the unknown.** Use the equation $M_1 \times V_1 = M_2 \times V_2$ to solve for the unknown initial volume of solution (V_1) that is diluted with water.

KNOWNS

M_1 = 2.00M $MgSO_4$
M_2 = 0.400M $MgSO_4$
V_2 = 100.0 mL of 0.400M $MgSO_4$

UNKNOWN

V_1 = ? mL of 2.00M $MgSO_4$

❷ **Calculate** **Solve for the unknown.**

Solve for V_1 and substitute the known values into the equation.

$$V_1 = \frac{M_2 \times V_2}{M_1} = \frac{0.400M \times 100.0 \text{ mL}}{2.00M} = 20.0 \text{ mL}$$

Thus 20.0 mL of the initial solution must be diluted by adding enough water to increase the volume to 100.0 mL.

❸ **Evaluate** **Does the result make sense?** The initial concentration is five times larger than the dilute concentration. Because the number of moles of solute does not change, the initial volume of solution should be one fifth the final volume of the diluted solution.

---

14. How many milliliters of a solution of 4.00M KI are needed to prepare 250.0 mL of 0.760M KI?

15. How could you prepare 250 mL of 0.20M NaCl using only a solution of 1.0M NaCl and water?

What kind of volume-measuring device would you use to make the dilution in Sample Problem 16.4? The dilution requires a molarity with three significant figures, so you would need to measure 20.0 mL of the 2.00M $MgSO_4$ solution with a 20-mL volumetric pipette or a burette. (A graduated cylinder would not provide enough precision.) You would transfer the solution to a 100-mL volumetric flask and add distilled water to the flask exactly up to the etched line. The contents would then be 100.0 mL of 0.400M $MgSO_4$.

Percent Solutions

🔑 **How do percent by volume and percent by mass differ?**

If both the solute and the solvent are liquids, a convenient way to make a solution is to measure the volumes of the solute and the solution. The concentration of the solute is then expressed as a percent of the solution by volume.
🔑 **Percent by volume of a solution is the ratio of the volume of solute to the volume of solution.** For example, isopropyl alcohol (2-propanol) is sold as a 91 percent solution by volume. You could prepare such a solution by diluting 91 mL of pure isopropyl alcohol with enough water to make 100 mL of solution. The concentration is written as 91 percent by volume, 91 percent (volume/volume), or 91% (v/v).

$$\text{Percent by volume (\%(v/v))} = \frac{\text{volume of solute}}{\text{volume of solution}} \times 100\%$$

Calculating Percent by Volume

What is the percent by volume of ethanol (C_2H_6O, or ethyl alcohol) in the final solution when 85 mL of ethanol is diluted to a volume of 250 mL with water?

❶ Analyze List the knowns and the unknown. Use the known values for the volume of solute and volume of solution to calculate percent by volume.

KNOWNS

volume of solute = 85 mL ethanol
volume of solution = 250 mL

UNKNOWN

Percent by volume = ? % ethanol (v/v)

❷ Calculate Solve for the unknown.

State the equation for percent by volume.	$\text{Percent by volume (\% (v/v))} = \dfrac{\text{volume of solute}}{\text{volume of solution}} \times 100\%$
Substitute the known values into the equation and solve.	$\% \text{ (v/v)} = \dfrac{85 \text{ mL ethanol}}{250 \text{ mL}} \times 100\%$
	$= 34\% \text{ ethanol (v/v)}$

❸ Evaluate Does the result make sense? The volume of the solute is about one third the volume of the solution, so the answer is reasonable. The answer is correctly expressed to two significant figures.

16. If 10 mL of propanone (C_3H_6O, or acetone) is diluted with water to a total solution volume of 200 mL, what is the percent by volume of propanone in the solution?

17. A bottle of the antiseptic hydrogen peroxide (H_2O_2) is labeled 3.0% (v/v). How many mL H_2O_2 are in a 400.0-mL bottle of this solution?

Another way to express the concentration of a solution is as a percent by mass, or percent (mass/mass). 🔑 **Percent by mass of a solution is the ratio of the mass of the solute to the mass of the solution.**

$$\text{Percent by mass (\%(m/m))} = \frac{\text{mass of solute}}{\text{mass of solution}} \times 100\%$$

CHEMISTRY & YOU

Q: *What are three ways to calculate the concentration of a solution?*

You can also define percent by mass as the number of grams of solute per 100 g of solution. Percent by mass is sometimes a convenient measure of concentration when the solute is a solid. For example, a solution containing 7 g of sodium chloride in 100 grams of solution has a concentration of 7 percent by mass—also written as 7 percent (mass/mass) or 7% (m/m).

You have probably seen information on food labels expressed as a percent composition. For example, the label on a fruit-flavored drink often indicates the "percent juice" contained in the product. Such information can be misleading unless the units are given. When you describe percent solutions, be sure to specify whether the concentration is % (v/v) or % (m/m).

SampleProblem 16.6

Using Percent by Mass as a Conversion Factor

How many grams of glucose ($C_6H_{12}O_6$) are needed to make 2000 g of a 2.8% glucose (m/m) solution?

❶ Analyze List the knowns and the unknown. The conversion is mass of solution ⟶ mass of solute. In a 2.8% $C_6H_{12}O_6$ (m/m) solution, each 100 g of solution contains 2.8 g of glucose. Used as a conversion factor, the concentration allows you to convert g of solution to g of $C_6H_{12}O_6$.

KNOWNS

mass of solution = 2000 g
percent by mass = 2.8% $C_6H_{12}O_6$ (m/m)

UNKNOWN

mass of solute = ? g $C_6H_{12}O_6$

❷ Calculate Solve for the unknown.

Write the percent by mass as a conversion factor with g $C_6H_{12}O_6$ in the numerator.	$\dfrac{2.8\ g\ C_6H_{12}O_6}{100\ g\ solution}$
Multiply the mass of the solution by the conversion factor.	$2000\ g\ solution \times \dfrac{2.8\ g\ C_6H_{12}O_6}{100\ g\ solution} = 56\ g\ C_6H_{12}O_6$

❸ Evaluate Does the result make sense? The prepared mass of the solution is 20×100 g. Since a 100-g sample of 2.8% (m/m) solution contains 2.8 g of solute, you need 20×2.8 g = 56 g of solute. To make the solution, mix 56 g of $C_6H_{12}O_6$ with 1944 g of solvent. (56 g of solute + 1944 g of solvent = 2000 g of solution)

18. Calculate the grams of solute required to make 250 g of 0.10% $MgSO_4$ (m/m).

> You can solve this problem by using either dimensional analysis or algebra.

16.2 LessonCheck

19. ⬤ **Review** How do you calculate the molarity of a solution?

20. ⬤ **Compare** How does the number of moles of solute before a dilution compare with the number of moles of solute after the dilution?

21. ⬤ **Identify** What are two ways of expressing the concentration of a solution as a percent?

22. Calculate What is the molarity of a solution containing 400 g $CuSO_4$ in 4.00 L of solution?

23. Calculate How many milliliters of a stock solution of 2.00M KNO_3 would you need to prepare 100.0 mL of 0.150M KNO_3?

24. Calculate How many moles of solute are present in 50.0 mL of 0.20M KNO_3?

25. Calculate What is the concentration, in percent (v/v), of a solution containing 50 mL of diethyl ether ($C_4H_{10}O$) in 2.5 L of solution?

26. Calculate What mass of K_2SO_4 would you need to prepare 1500 g of 5.0% K_2SO_4 (m/m) solution?

BIGIDEA

THE MOLE AND QUANTIFYING MATTER

27. What information would you need in order to convert molarity to percent by volume?

Art of the Pickle

Every culture has its own version of the pickle, and the art of making pickles dates back to ancient history. The earliest known pickles were produced more than 4000 years ago using cucumbers native to India. In Korea, kimchi (pickled cabbage) has been produced for more than 3000 years. Ancient Egyptians and Greeks wrote about the nutritive value and healing power of pickles.

Nowadays, you can often count on the savory taste of a pickle when you order food at a restaurant or from a street vendor. Pickles come in many varieties. You might already know the taste of the dill pickles that accompany sandwiches, or the relish found at a hot dog stand. Other kinds of pickles include Japanese pickled ginger (often served with sushi), European pickled herring, and the hot pickled peppers found in some Mexican salsas.

Pickling is a way of preserving food using a solution of salt, acid (usually vinegar), spices, and/or sugar. Soaking vegetables and meats in the pickling solution prevents the growth of harmful bacteria and imparts a tangy, savory flavor to the food.

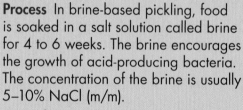

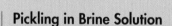

Main Types of Pickling

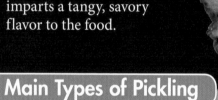

Pickling in Acid Solution

Process This type of pickling typically involves immersing and/or cooking vegetables for a few hours or days in a solution containing vinegar and spices. Vinegar is a 5% (v/v) aqueous solution of acetic acid ($C_2H_4O_2$).

Examples Acid solutions are used to prepare pickled ginger (above), pickled beets, bread-and-butter pickles, pickled herring, and hot dog relish.

Pickling in Brine Solution

Process In brine-based pickling, food is soaked in a salt solution called brine for 4 to 6 weeks. The brine encourages the growth of acid-producing bacteria. The concentration of the brine is usually 5–10% NaCl (m/m).

Examples Common brine pickles include dill cucumber pickles, sauerkraut (pickled fermented cabbage), Middle Eastern pickled turnips, and Indian mango pickles and chutneys.

SALTY SOLUTIONS As pickles soak, the salt in the solution encourages the growth of acid-producing bacteria, which prevent the growth of bacteria that cause spoilage. The salt concentration needs to be as exact as possible. If it's too high, the acid producers can't flourish; if it's too low, then not enough acid producers will grow, and your pickles may spoil.

Take It Further

1. Calculate A pickle recipe calls for 1.5 cups of pickling salt (NaCl) to be mixed with 1 gallon of water. If 1 cup of pickling salt has a mass of 220 grams, what is the percent by mass of NaCl in the pickling solution? (1 gal = 3785 cm³)

2. Evaluate Is enough information given in the previous question to calculate the percent by volume of NaCl in the pickling solution? Explain your answer.

3. Calculate How many grams of pickling salt would you need to prepare 3500 g of 5.0% NaCl (m/m) solution for a batch of cucumber pickles?

16.3 Colligative Properties of Solutions

Q: *Why do you need salt to make ice cream?* Here's a hint—it's *not* because ice cream is supposed to taste salty. Temperatures below 0°C are needed to make ice cream. Ice-cream makers know that if you add rock salt to ice, the mixture freezes at a few degrees below 0°C. In this lesson, you will discover how a solute can change the freezing point of a solution.

Key Question

🔑 **What are three colligative properties of solutions?**

Vocabulary

- colligative property
- freezing-point depression
- boiling-point elevation

See **vapor pressure** animated online.

Describing Colligative Properties

🔑 *What are three colligative properties of solutions?*

You already know that the physical properties of a solution differ from those of the pure solvent used to make the solution. After all, tea is not the same as pure water. But it might surprise you to learn that some of these differences in properties have little to do with the specific identity of the solute. Instead, they depend upon the mere presence of solute particles in the solution.

A **colligative property** is a property of solutions that depends only upon the number of solute particles, not upon their identity. 🔑 **Three important colligative properties of solutions are vapor-pressure lowering, freezing-point depression, and boiling-point elevation.**

Vapor-Pressure Lowering Recall that vapor pressure is the pressure exerted by a vapor that is in dynamic equilibrium with its liquid in a closed system. A solution that contains a solute that is nonvolatile (not easily vaporized) always has a lower vapor pressure than the pure solvent, as shown in Figure 16.11. Glucose, a molecular compound, and sodium chloride, an ionic compound, are examples of nonvolatile solutes. When glucose or sodium chloride is dissolved in a solvent, the vapor pressure of the solution is lower than the vapor pressure of the pure solvent. Why is this true?

Figure 16.11 Vapor Pressure The vapor pressure of a solution of a nonvolatile solute is less than the vapor pressure of a pure solvent. **a.** Equilibrium is established between the liquid and vapor in a pure solvent. **b.** In a solution, solute particles reduce the number of solvent particles able to escape the liquid. Equilibrium is established at a lower vapor pressure.

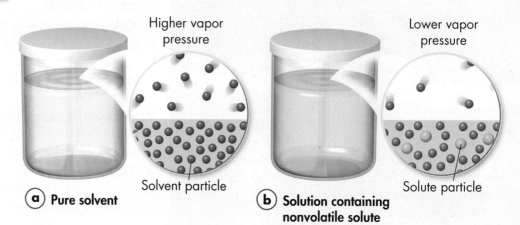

Higher vapor pressure

Solvent particle

a **Pure solvent**

Lower vapor pressure

Solute particle

b **Solution containing nonvolatile solute**

Figure 16.12 Molecular vs. Ionic Solutes

Particle concentrations differ for dissolved molecular and ionic compounds in water.
Compare *Which solution has the lowest vapor pressure? The highest?*

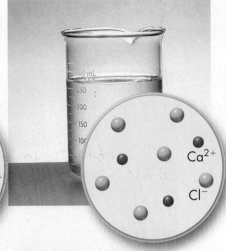

Glucose in Solution
Three moles of glucose dissolved in water produce 3 mol of particles because glucose does not dissociate.

Sodium Chloride in Solution
Three moles of sodium chloride dissolved in water produce 6 mol of particles because each formula unit of NaCl dissociates into two ions.

Calcium Chloride in Solution
Three moles of calcium chloride dissolved in water produce 9 mol of particles because each formula unit of $CaCl_2$ dissociates into three ions.

In an aqueous solution of sodium chloride, sodium ions and chloride ions are dispersed throughout the liquid water. Both within the liquid and at the surface, the ions are surrounded by layers of associated water molecules, or shells of water of solvation. The formation of these shells of water of solvation reduces the number of solvent molecules that have enough kinetic energy to escape as vapor. Thus, the solution has a lower vapor pressure than the pure solvent (water) would have at the same temperature.

Ionic solutes that dissociate, such as sodium chloride and calcium chloride, have greater effects on the vapor pressure than does a nondissociating solute such as glucose. Recall that each formula unit of the sodium chloride (NaCl) produces two particles in solution, a sodium ion and a chloride ion.

$$NaCl(s) \xrightarrow{\text{H}_2\text{O}} Na^+(aq) + Cl^-(aq)$$

Each formula unit of calcium chloride ($CaCl_2$) produces three particles, a calcium ion and two chloride ions.

$$CaCl_2(s) \xrightarrow{\text{H}_2\text{O}} Ca^{2+}(aq) + 2Cl^-(aq)$$

When glucose dissolves, the molecules do not dissociate.

$$C_6H_{12}O_6(s) \xrightarrow{\text{H}_2\text{O}} C_6H_{12}O_6(aq)$$

Figure 16.12 compares the number of particles in three solutions of the same concentration. The decrease in a solution's vapor pressure is proportional to the number of particles the solute makes in solution. For example, the vapor-pressure lowering caused by 0.1 mol of sodium chloride in 1000 g of water is twice that caused by 0.1 mol of glucose in the same quantity of water. In the same way, 0.1 mol of $CaCl_2$ in 1000 g of water produces three times the vapor-pressure lowering as 0.1 mol of glucose in the same quantity of water.

Build Study Skills: *Concept Map*
As you read, construct a concept map that organizes the major ideas of this lesson. *What factor determines the magnitude of colligative properties of solutions?*

Learn more about
freezing-point
depression *online*.

Freezing-Point Depression When a substance freezes, the particles of the solid take on an orderly pattern. The presence of a solute in water disrupts the formation of this pattern because of the shells of water of solvation. As a result, more kinetic energy must be withdrawn from a solution than from the pure solvent to cause the solution to solidify. The freezing point of a solution is lower than the freezing point of the pure solvent. The difference in temperature between the freezing point of a solution and the freezing point of the pure solvent is called the **freezing-point depression.**

Freezing-point depression is another colligative property. The magnitude of the freezing-point depression is proportional to the number of solute particles dissolved in the solvent and does not depend upon their identity. The addition of 1 mol of solute particles to 1000 g of water lowers the freezing point by 1.86°C. For example, if you add 1 mol (180 g) of glucose to 1000 g of water, the solution freezes at −1.86°C. However, if you add 1 mol (58.5 g) of sodium chloride to 1000 g of water, the solution freezes at −3.72°C, double the change for glucose. This difference occurs because 1 mol NaCl produces 2 mol of particles and, thus, doubles the freezing-point depression.

The freezing-point depression of aqueous solutions plays an important role in helping to keep travelers safe in cold, icy weather. The truck in Figure 16.13 spreads a layer of salt on the icy road to make the ice melt. The melted ice forms a solution with a lower freezing point than that of pure water. Similarly, ethylene glycol ($C_2H_6O_2$, antifreeze) is added to the water in automobile cooling systems to depress the freezing point of the water below 0°C. Automobiles can thus withstand subfreezing temperatures without freezing up.

Figure 16.13 De-icing Measures
Roads can be free of ice even at temperatures below 0°C if salt is applied. A common de-icer used on aircraft is a mixture of water and propylene glycol.
Infer *Why do you think $CaCl_2$ is a more effective road de-icer than NaCl?*

Figure 16.14 Antifreeze
The fluid circulating through a car's cooling system is a solution of water and ethylene glycol, or antifreeze. The resulting mixture freezes below 0°C and boils above 100°C.

Boiling-Point Elevation The boiling point of a substance is the temperature at which the vapor pressure of the liquid phase equals atmospheric pressure. As you just learned, adding a nonvolatile solute to a liquid solvent decreases the vapor pressure of the solvent. Because of the decrease in vapor pressure, additional kinetic energy must be added to raise the vapor pressure of the liquid phase of the solution to atmospheric pressure and initiate boiling. Thus, the boiling point of a solution is higher than the boiling point of the pure solvent. The difference in temperature between the boiling point of a solution and the boiling point of the pure solvent is the **boiling-point elevation.**

Figure 16.14 shows antifreeze being poured into a car's coolant tank. The antifreeze doesn't just lower the freezing point of the water in the cooling system. It also elevates the boiling point, which helps protect the engine from overheating in the summer.

Boiling-point elevation is a colligative property; it depends on the concentration of particles, not on their identity. Therefore, you can think about boiling-point elevation in terms of particles. It takes additional kinetic energy for the solvent particles to overcome the attractive forces that keep them in the liquid. Thus, the presence of a solute elevates the boiling point of the solvent. The magnitude of the boiling-point elevation is proportional to the number of solute particles dissolved in the solvent. The boiling point of water increases by 0.512°C for every mole of particles that the solute forms when dissolved in 1000 g of water.

Q: *Solutes other than NaCl could be used to produce the same freezing-point depression in an ice-cream machine. What factors do you think make NaCl a good choice?*

16.3 LessonCheck

28. 🗝 **Identify** Name three colligative properties of solutions.

29. Explain Why does a solution have a lower vapor pressure than the pure solvent of that solution?

30. Explain Why does a solution have a depressed freezing point and an elevated boiling point compared with the pure solvent?

31. Compare Would a dilute or a concentrated sodium fluoride solution have a higher boiling point? Explain.

32. Compare An equal number of moles of KI and MgI_2 are dissolved in equal volumes of water. Which solution has the higher
a. boiling point?
b. vapor pressure?
c. freezing point?

33. Apply Concepts Review what you learned in Lesson 13.2 about the relationship between the vapor pressure of liquids and their boiling points. Explain why only nonvolatile solutes cause the elevation of the solvent's boiling point.

16.4 Calculations Involving Colligative Properties

Q: *How hot is a pot of boiling pasta?* Cooking instructions for a wide variety of foods, from dried pasta to fresh vegetables, often call for the addition of a small amount of salt to the cooking water. Most people like the flavor of food cooked with salt.

But adding salt can have another effect on the cooking process. Recall that dissolved salt elevates the boiling point of water. Suppose you added a teaspoon of salt to two liters of water. A teaspoon of salt has a mass of about 20 g. Would the resulting boiling-point increase be enough to shorten the time required for cooking? In this lesson, you will learn how to calculate the amount the boiling point of the cooking water would rise.

Key Questions

▸ What are two ways of expressing the ratio of solute to solvent in a solution?

▸ How are freezing-point depression and boiling-point elevation related to molality?

Vocabulary

- molality (*m*)
- mole fraction
- molal freezing-point depression constant (K_f)
- molal boiling-point elevation constant (K_b)

Molality and Mole Fraction

▸ **What are two ways of expressing the ratio of solute to solvent in a solution?**

Recall that colligative properties of solutions depend only on the number of solute particles dissolved in a given amount of solvent. ▸ **Chemists use two ways to express the ratio of solute particles to solvent particles: in molality and in mole fractions.**

Molality (*m*) is the number of moles of solute dissolved in 1 kilogram (1000 grams) of solvent. Molality is also known as molal concentration.

$$\text{Molality } (m) = \frac{\text{moles of solute}}{\text{kilogram of solvent}}$$

Note that molality is not the same as molarity. Molality refers to moles of solute per kilogram of solvent rather than moles of solute per liter of solution. In the case of water as the solvent, 1 kg or 1000 g equals a volume of 1000 mL, or 1 L.

You can prepare a solution that is 1.00 molal (1*m*) in glucose, for example, by adding 1.00 mol (180 g) of glucose to 1000 g of water. A 0.500 molal (0.500*m*) sodium chloride solution is prepared by dissolving 0.500 mol (29.3 g) of NaCl in 1.000 kg (1000 g) of water.

Using Molality

How many grams of potassium iodide must be dissolved in 500.0 g of water to produce a 0.060 molal KI solution?

1 Analyze List the knowns and the unknown.

According to the definition of molality, the final solution must contain 0.060 mol KI per 1000 g H_2O. Use the molality as a conversion factor to convert from mass of the solvent (H_2O) to moles of the solute (KI). Then use the molar mass of KI to convert from mol KI to g KI. The steps are as follows: mass of $H_2O \longrightarrow$ mol KI $\longrightarrow$ g KI.

KNOWNS

mass of water = $500.0\,g$ = $0.5000\,kg$
solution concentration = $0.060m$
molar mass of KI = $166.0\,g/mol$

UNKNOWN

mass of solute = ? g KI

2 Calculate Solve for the unknown.

Identify the conversion factor based on 0.060*m* that allows you to convert from g H_2O to mol KI.	$\dfrac{0.060\ \text{mol KI}}{1.000\ \text{kg } H_2O}$
Identify the conversion factor based on the molar mass of KI that allows you to convert from mol KI to g KI.	$\dfrac{166.0\ \text{g KI}}{1\ \text{mol KI}}$
Multiply the known solvent volume by the conversion factors.	$0.5000\ \text{kg } H_2O \times \dfrac{0.060\ \text{mol KI}}{1.000\ \text{kg } H_2O} \times \dfrac{166.0\ \text{g KI}}{1\ \text{mol KI}} = 5.0\ \text{g KI}$

To make the 0.060-molal KI solution, you would dissolve 5.0 g of KI in 500.0 g of water.

3 Evaluate Does this result make sense? A 1-molal KI solution is one molar mass of KI (166.0 g) dissolved in 1000 g of water. The desired molal concentration (0.060*m*) is about $\frac{1}{20}$ of that value, so the mass of KI should be much less than the molar mass. The answer is correctly expressed to two significant figures.

34. How many grams of sodium fluoride are needed to prepare a 0.400*m* NaF solution that contains 750 g of water?

35. Calculate the molality of a solution prepared by dissolving 10.0 g NaCl in 600 g of water.

Remember: Molality equals moles of solute dissolved per kilogram of solvent.

The concentration of a solution also can be expressed as a mole fraction. The **mole fraction** of a solute in a solution is the ratio of the moles of that solute to the total number of moles of solvent and solute. In a solution containing n_A mol of solute A and n_B mol of solvent B, the mole fraction of solute A (X_A) and the mole fraction of solvent B (X_B) can be expressed as follows:

$$X_A = \frac{n_A}{n_A + n_B} \qquad X_B = \frac{n_B}{n_A + n_B}$$

Note that mole fraction is a dimensionless quantity. The sum of the mole fractions of all the components in a solution equals unity, or one.

Figure 16.15 below and Sample Problem 16.8 on the next page illustrate how to calculate the mole fractions of the solute and solvent for a solution of ethylene glycol (EG) in water.

Figure 16.15 Mole Fraction

Ethylene glycol (EG) is added to water as antifreeze in the proportions shown. A mole fraction is the ratio of the number of moles of one substance to the total number of moles of all substances in the solution.

Infer *What is the sum of all mole fractions in a solution?*

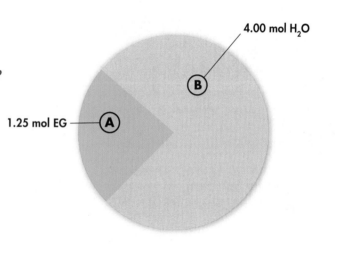

4.00 mol H_2O

1.25 mol EG

Total moles = Ⓐ + Ⓑ = 5.25 mol

Mole fraction EG $= \dfrac{Ⓐ}{Ⓐ+Ⓑ} = \dfrac{1.25}{5.25}$

Mole fraction $H_2O = \dfrac{Ⓑ}{Ⓐ+Ⓑ} = \dfrac{4.00}{5.25}$

Freezing-Point Depression and Boiling-Point Elevation

🔑 *How are freezing-point depression and boiling-point elevation related to molality?*

Depressions of freezing points and elevations of boiling points are usually quite small. For example, if you add a teaspoon of salt to a pot of water and boil the resulting solution, you will have a hard time detecting any change in the boiling point using a cooking thermometer. It turns out that the elevation is just a small fraction of a degree Celsius. To measure colligative properties accurately, you would need a thermometer that can measure temperatures to the nearest 0.001°C.

Another way to determine the magnitudes of colligative properties is by calculating them. You can do this if you know the molality of the solution and some reference data about the solvent.

SampleProblem 16.8

Calculating Mole Fractions

Ethylene glycol (EG, or $C_2H_6O_2$) is added to automobile cooling systems to protect against cold weather. What is the mole fraction of each component in a solution containing 1.25 mol of ethylene glycol and 4.00 mol of water?

❶ Analyze List the knowns and the unknowns.
The given quantities of solute (EG) and solvent (water) are expressed in moles. Use the equations for mole fraction of a solute and mole fraction of a solvent to solve this problem. (The pie graph in Figure 16.15 gives you a visual representation of the mole fraction of each component.)

KNOWNS

moles of ethylene glycol (n_{EG}) = 1.25 mol EG
moles of water (n_{H_2O}) = 4.00 mol H_2O

UNKNOWNS

mole fraction EG (X_{EG}) = ?
mole fraction H_2O (X_{H_2O}) = ?

❷ Calculate Solve for the unknowns.

Write the equation for the mole fraction of ethylene glycol (X_{EG}) in the solution.

$$X_{EG} = \frac{n_{EG}}{n_{EG} + n_{H_2O}}$$

Note that the denominator for each mole fraction is the same: the total number of moles of solvent and solute in the solution.

Write the equation for the mole fraction of water (X_{H_2O}) in the solution.

$$X_{H_2O} = \frac{n_{H_2O}}{n_{EG} + n_{H_2O}}$$

Substitute the known values into each equation.

$$X_{EG} = \frac{n_{EG}}{n_{EG} + n_{H_2O}} = \frac{1.25 \text{ mol}}{1.25 \text{ mol} + 4.00 \text{ mol}} = 0.238$$

$$X_{H_2O} = \frac{n_{H_2O}}{n_{EG} + n_{H_2O}} = \frac{4.00 \text{ mol}}{1.25 \text{ mol} + 4.00 \text{ mol}} = 0.762$$

❸ Evaluate Does the result make sense? The sum of the mole fractions of all the components in the solution equals 1 ($X_{EG} + X_{H_2O} = 1.000$). Each answer is correctly expressed to three significant figures.

36. What is the mole fraction of each component in a solution made by mixing 300 g of ethanol (C_2H_6O) and 500 g of water?

37. A solution contains 50.0 g of carbon tetrachloride (CCl_4) and 50.0 g of chloroform ($CHCl_3$). Calculate the mole fraction of each component in the solution.

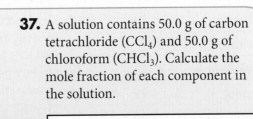

Remember: Mole fraction is a mole ratio, not a mass ratio. If the given quantities are masses, you must first convert each mass to moles using the molar mass of the substance.

Interpret Graphs

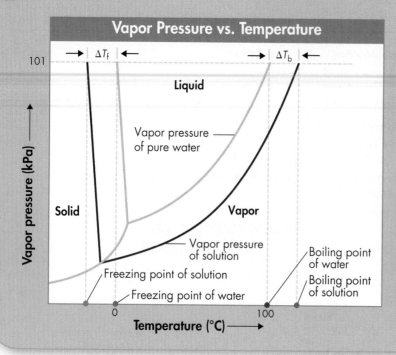

Vapor Pressure vs. Temperature

Figure 16.16 The graph shows the relationship between vapor pressure and temperature for pure water and aqueous solutions.

a. Read Graphs What is the freezing point of water? What is the boiling point?

b. Compare How do the freezing and boiling points of the solution compare to those of pure water?

c. Draw Conclusions Does adding a solute to water allow it to remain as a liquid over a longer or shorter temperature range? Explain.

The graph in Figure 16.16 shows that the freezing point of a solvent is lowered, and its boiling point is raised, by the addition of a nonvolatile solute. **The magnitudes of the freezing-point depression (ΔT_f) and the boiling-point elevation (ΔT_b) of a solution are directly proportional to the molal concentration (m), assuming the solute is molecular, not ionic.**

$$\Delta T_f \propto m$$
$$\Delta T_b \propto m$$

The change in the freezing temperature (T_f) is the difference between the freezing point of the solution and the freezing point of the pure solvent. Similarly, the change in the boiling temperature (T_b) is the difference between the boiling point of the solution and the boiling point of the pure solvent. The term m is the molal concentration of the solution.

With the addition of a constant, the proportionality between the freezing point depression (ΔT_f) and the molality m can be expressed as an equation.

$$\Delta T_f = K_f \times m$$

The constant, K_f, is the **molal freezing-point depression constant,** which is equal to the change in freezing point for a 1-molal solution of a nonvolatile molecular solute. The value of K_f depends upon the solvent. Its units are °C/m. Table 16.2 lists the K_f values for water and some other solvents.

Table 16.2

K_f and K_b Values for Some Common Solvents

Solvent	K_f (°C/m)	K_b (°C/m)
Acetic acid	3.90	3.07
Benzene	5.12	2.53
Camphor	37.7	5.95
Cyclohexane	20.2	2.79
Ethanol	1.99	1.19
Nitrobenzene	7.00	5.24
Phenol	7.40	3.56
Water	1.86	0.512

SampleProblem 16.9

Calculating the Freezing-Point Depression of a Solution

Antifreeze protects a car from freezing. It also protects it from overheating. Calculate the freezing-point depression of a solution containing exactly 100 g of ethylene glycol ($C_2H_6O_2$) antifreeze in 0.500 kg of water.

① Analyze List the knowns and the unknown.
Calculate the number of moles of $C_2H_6O_2$ and the molality of the solution. Then calculate the freezing-point depression using $\Delta T_f = K_f \times m$.

KNOWNS

mass of $C_2H_6O_2$ = 100 g
mass of water = 0.500 kg
K_f for H_2O = 1.86° C/m
molar mass of $C_2H_6O_2$ = 62.0 g/mol

UNKNOWN

ΔT_f = ?°C

② Calculate Solve for the unknown.

Use the molar mass of $C_2H_6O_2$ to convert the mass of solute to moles.

$$100 \, g \, C_2H_6O_2 \times \frac{1 \, mol \, C_2H_6O_2}{62.0 \, g \, C_2H_6O_2} = 1.61 \, mol \, C_2H_6O_2$$

Calculate the molality of the solution.

$$m = \frac{mol \, solute}{kg \, solvent} = \frac{1.61 \, mol}{0.500 \, kg} = 3.22m$$

Calculate the freezing-point depression.

$$\Delta T_f = K_f \times m = 1.86°C/m \times 3.22m = 5.99°C$$

The freezing point of the solution is
$0.00°C - 5.99°C = -5.99°C$.

③ Evaluate Does the result make sense? A 1-molal solution reduces the freezing temperature by 1.86°C, so a decrease of 5.99°C for an approximately 3-molal solution is reasonable.

38. What is the freezing-point depression of an aqueous solution of 10.0 g of glucose ($C_6H_{12}O_6$) in 50.0 g H_2O?

39. Calculate the freezing-point depression of a benzene solution containing 400 g of benzene and 200 g of the molecular compound acetone (C_3H_6O). K_f for benzene is 5.12°C/m.

As you might expect, the boiling-point elevation of a solution can also be expressed as an equation. In this case, the proportionality constant is K_b, the **molal boiling-point elevation constant,** which is equal to the change in boiling point for a 1-molal solution of a nonvolatile molecular solute.

$$\Delta T_b = K_b \times m$$

Table 16.2 lists the K_b values for some solvents. Like K_f, K_b has units of °C/m.
Sample Problem 16.9 above described how to determine ΔT_f if the solute is a molecular compound. But for ionic compounds, both ΔT_f and ΔT_b depend upon the number of ions produced by each formula unit. This number is used to calculate an effective molality, as you'll see in Sample Problem 16.10.

Q: *Does pasta cook at 100°C? After you read Sample Problem 16.10, calculate the boiling-point elevation for the solution described at the beginning of the lesson on page 538.*

Calculating the Boiling Point of a Solution

What is the boiling point of a 1.50*m* NaCl solution?

❶ Analyze List the knowns and the unknown. Each formula unit of NaCl dissociates into two particles, according to the equation NaCl(*s*) ⟶ Na$^+$(*aq*) + Cl$^-$(*aq*). Based on the total number of dissociated particles, the effective molality is 2 × 1.50*m* = 3.00*m*. Calculate the boiling-point elevation (using the equation $\Delta T_b = K_b \times m$), and then add it to 100°C.

KNOWNS
solution concentration = 1.50*m* NaCl
K_b for H_2O = 0.512° C/*m*

UNKNOWN
boiling point = ?°C

❷ Calculate Solve for the unknown.

Calculate the boiling-point elevation, making sure to use the molality of total dissociated particles in solution.	$\Delta T_b = K_b \times m = 0.512°C/m \times 3.00m = 1.54°C$
Calculate the boiling point of the solution.	$T_b = 100°C + 1.54°C = \boxed{101.54°C}$

❸ Evaluate Does the result make sense? The boiling point increases about 0.5°C for each mole of solute particles, so the total change is reasonable. Because the boiling point of water is defined as exactly 100°C, this value does not limit the number of significant figures in the solution of the problem.

40. What is the boiling point of a solution that contains 1.25 mol CaCl$_2$ in 1400 g of water?

41. What mass of NaCl would have to be dissolved in 1.000 kg of water to raise the boiling point by 2.00°C?

16.4 LessonCheck

42. 🔵 **List** What are two ways of expressing the ratio of solute particles to solvent particles?

43. 🔵 **Explain** How are freezing-point depression and boiling-point elevation related to molality?

44. Calculate How many grams of sodium bromide must be dissolved in 400.0 g of water to produce a 0.500 molal solution?

45. Calculate Calculate the mole fraction of each component in a solution of 2.50 mol ethanoic acid (C$_2$H$_4$O$_2$) in 10.00 mol of water.

46. Predict What is the freezing point of a solution of 12.0 g of CCl$_4$ dissolved in 750.0 g of benzene? The freezing point of benzene is 5.48°C; K_f is 5.12°C/*m*.

47. Make Generalizations Look at the table on page R1 of the Elements Handbook showing the distribution of elements in the oceans. What generalization can you make about the temperature at which ocean water will freeze? What effect does the presence of dissolved elements in the ocean have on the rate of evaporation of ocean water?

Small-Scale Lab

Making a Solution

Purpose
To make a solution and use carefully measured data to calculate the solution's concentration

Materials
- solid NaCl
- water
- 50-mL volumetric flask
- balance

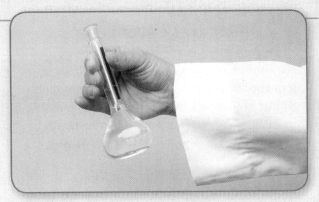

Procedure
Measure the mass of a clean, dry, volumetric flask. Add enough solid NaCl to fill approximately one tenth of the volume of the flask. Measure the mass of the flask again. Half fill the flask with water and shake it gently until all the NaCl dissolves. Fill the flask with water to the 50-mL mark and measure the mass again.

Analyze and Conclude
Answer the following questions based on your data.

1. Percent by mass tells how many grams of solute are present in 100 g of solution.

$$\% \text{ by mass} = \frac{\text{mass of solute}}{\text{mass of solute + solvent}} \times 100\%$$

a. Calculate the mass of the solute (NaCl).
b. Calculate the mass of the solvent (water).
c. Calculate the percent by mass of NaCl in the solution.

2. Mole fraction tells how many moles of solute are present for every 1 mol of total solution.

$$\text{Mole fraction} = \frac{\text{mol NaCl}}{\text{mol NaCl + mol } H_2O}$$

a. Calculate the moles of NaCl solute.
Molar mass of NaCl = 58.5 g/mol
b. Calculate the moles of water.
Molar mass of H_2O = 18.0 g/mol
c. Calculate the mole fraction of your solution.

3. Molality (m) tells how many moles of solute are present in 1 kg of solvent.

$$m = \frac{\text{mol NaCl}}{\text{kg } H_2O}$$

Calculate the molality of your solution.

4. Molarity (M) tells how many moles of solute are dissolved in 1 L of solution.

$$M = \frac{\text{mol NaCl}}{\text{L solution}}$$

a. Calculate the liters of solution.
b. Calculate the molarity of the NaCl solution.

5. Density tells how many grams of solution are present in 1 mL of solution.

$$\text{Density} = \frac{\text{g solution}}{\text{mL solution}}$$

Calculate the density of the solution.

You're the Chemist
The following small-scale activities allow you to develop your own procedures and analyze the results.

1. Analyze Data Measure the mass of an empty volumetric flask. Use a small-scale pipette to extract a sample of your NaCl solution and deliver it to the flask. Measure the mass of the flask again and fill it with water to the 50-mL line. Measure the mass of the flask again. Calculate the concentration of this dilute solution using the same units you used to calculate the concentration of the NaCl solution. Are the results you obtained reasonable?

2. Design an Experiment Design and carry out an experiment to make a solution of table sugar quantitatively. Calculate the concentration of the table sugar solution using the same units you used to calculate the concentration of the NaCl solution. Is the effective molality of the table sugar solution the same as the effective molality of a sodium chloride solution of the same concentration? Recall that effective molality is the concentration value used to calculate boiling-point elevation and freezing-point depression.

16 Study Guide

BIG IDEA
THE MOLE AND QUANTIFYING MATTER

Solubility, miscibility, concentration, and colligative properties are used to describe and characterize solutions. Solution concentration can be quantified in terms of molarity (moles of solute per liter of solution), molality (moles of solute per kilogram of solvent), percent by volume, and percent by mass.

Key Equations

$$\text{Molarity } (M) = \frac{\text{moles of solute}}{\text{liters of solution}}$$

$$M_1 \times V_1 = M_2 \times V_2$$

$$\text{Percent by volume} = \frac{\text{volume of solute}}{\text{volume of solution}} \times 100\%$$

$$\text{Percent by mass} = \frac{\text{mass of solute}}{\text{mass of solution}} \times 100\%$$

16.1 Properties of Solutions

🔑 Factors that determine how fast a substance dissolves are stirring, temperature, and surface area.

🔑 In a saturated solution, a state of dynamic equilibrium exists between the solution and any undissolved solute, provided that the temperature remains constant.

🔑 Temperature affects the solubility of solid, liquid, and gaseous solutes in a solvent; both temperature and pressure affect the solubility of gaseous solutes.

- saturated solution (520)
- solubility (520)
- unsaturated solution (520)
- miscible (521)
- immiscible (521)
- supersaturated solution (522)
- Henry's law (523)

Key Equation

$$\text{Henry's law: } \frac{S_1}{P_1} = \frac{S_2}{P_2}$$

16.2 Concentrations of Solutions

🔑 To calculate the molarity of a solution, divide the moles of solute by the volume of the solution in liters.

🔑 Diluting a solution reduces the number of moles of solute per unit volume, but the total number of moles of solute in solution does not change.

🔑 Percent by volume is the ratio of the volume of solute to the volume of solution. Percent by mass is the ratio of the mass of the solute to the mass of the solution.

- concentration (525)
- dilute solution (525)
- concentrated solution (525)
- molarity (M) (525)

16.3 Colligative Properties of Solutions

🔑 Colligative properties of solutions include vapor-pressure lowering, freezing-point depression, and boiling-point elevation.

- colligative property (534)
- freezing-point depression (536)
- boiling-point elevation (537)

16.4 Calculations Involving Colligative Properties

🔑 Chemists use two ways to express the ratio of solute to solvent: in molality and in mole fractions.

🔑 The magnitudes of freezing-point depression and boiling-point elevation are proportional to molality.

- molality (m) (538)
- mole fraction (540)
- molal freezing-point depression constant (K_f) (542)
- molal boiling-point elevation constant (K_b) (543)

Key Equations

$$\text{Molality } (m) = \frac{\text{moles of solute}}{\text{kilogram of solvent}}$$

$$\text{Mole fractions: } X_A = \frac{n_A}{n_A + n_B} \qquad X_B = \frac{n_B}{n_A + n_B}$$

$$\Delta T_f = K_f \times m$$

$$\Delta T_b = K_b \times m$$

Math Tune-Up: Solution Concentration Problems

Problem	❶ Analyze	❷ Calculate	❸ Evaluate
What volume of 12.00M sulfuric acid is required to prepare 1.00 L of 0.400M sulfuric acid?	**Knowns:** $M_1 = 12.00M$ H_2SO_4 $M_2 = 0.400M$ H_2SO_4 $V_2 = 1.00$ L of 0.400M H_2SO_4 **Unknown:** $V_1 = ?$ L of 12.00M H_2SO_4 Use the following equation to solve for the unknown initial volume of solution that is diluted: $M_1 \times V_1 = M_2 \times V_2$	Solve the equation for V_1 and substitute. $$V_1 = \frac{M_2 \times V_2}{M_1}$$ $$V_1 = \frac{0.400M \times 1.00 \text{ L}}{12.00M}$$ $V_1 = 0.0333$ L	The concentration of the initial solution (12.00M) is 30 times larger than the concentration of the diluted solution (0.400M). So, the volume of the solution to be diluted should be one thirtieth the final volume of the diluted solution.
Ethanol is mixed with gasoline to make a solution called gasohol. What is the percent by volume of ethanol in gasohol when 95 mL of ethanol is added to sufficient gasoline to make 1.0 L of gasohol?	**Knowns:** volume of ethanol = 95 mL volume of solution = 1.0 L **Unknown:** solution concentration = ? % (v/v) Use the equation for percent by volume: $$\% \text{ (v/v)} = \frac{\text{volume of solute}}{\text{volume of solution}} \times 100\%$$	Make sure the known volumes are expressed in the same units. Then calculate percent by volume of ethanol. $$\% \text{ (v/v)} = \frac{0.095 \text{ L}}{1.00 \text{ L}} \times 100\%$$ $$= 9.5\% \text{ (v/v)}$$	The volume of the solute is about one tenth the volume of the solution, so the answer is reasonable. The answer is correctly expressed to two significant figures.
Calculate the molality of a solution prepared by mixing 5.40 g LiBr with 444 g of water.	**Knowns:** mass of solute = 5.40 g mass of water = 444 g molar mass of LiBr = 86.8 g **Unknown:** solution concentration = ?m Use the equation for molal concentration: $$\text{Molality} = \frac{\text{mol of solute}}{\text{kg of solvent}}$$	Convert the mass of the solute to moles of solute. $5.40 \text{ g LiBr} \times \frac{1 \text{ mol LiBr}}{86.8 \text{ g LiBr}} =$ $\qquad$ 0.0622 mol LiBr Calculate molality. $$\text{Molality} = \frac{0.0622 \text{ mol LiBr}}{0.444 \text{ kg } H_2O}$$ $$= 0.140m$$	The answer has the correct units (mol of solute per kg of solvent) and is correctly expressed to three significant figures.

> **Remember:** Molality is mol of solute per kg of solvent. Make sure you have the correct mass units in the denominator.

16 Assessment

Lesson by Lesson

16.1 Properties of Solutions

48. Name and distinguish between the two components of a solution.

49. Explain why the dissolved component does not settle out of a solution.

50. Define the following terms: *solubility, saturated solution, unsaturated solution, miscible,* and *immiscible.*

51. If a saturated solution of sodium nitrate is cooled, what change might you observe?

52. Can a solution with undissolved solute be supersaturated? Explain.

53. What mass of $AgNO_3$ can be dissolved in 250 g of water at 20°C? Use Table 16.1.

54. What is the effect of pressure on the solubility of gases in liquids?

★55. The solubility of methane, the major component of natural gas, in water at 20°C and 1.00 atm pressure is 0.026 g/L. If the temperature remains constant, what will be the solubility of this gas at the following pressures?

　　a. 0.60 atm
　　b. 1.80 atm

16.2 Concentrations of Solutions

56. Knowing the molarity of a solution is more meaningful than knowing whether a solution is dilute or concentrated. Explain.

57. Define *molarity,* and then calculate the molarity of each solution.

　　a. 1.0 mol KCl in 750 mL of solution
　　b. 0.50 mol $MgCl_2$ in 1.5 L of solution

★58. How many milliliters of 0.500*M* KCl solution would you need to dilute to make 100.0 mL of 0.100*M* KCl?

★59. Calculate the molarity of a solution that contains 0.50 g of NaCl dissolved in 100 mL of solution.

60. Calculate the moles and grams of solute in each solution.

　　a. 1.0 L of 0.50*M* NaCl
　　b. 5.0×10^2 mL of 2.0*M* KNO_3
　　c. 250 mL of 0.10*M* $CaCl_2$
　　d. 2.0 L of 0.30*M* Na_2SO_4

★61. Calculate the grams of solute required to make the following solutions:

　　a. 2500 g of saline solution (0.90% NaCl (m/m))
　　b. 0.050 kg of 4.0% (m/m) $MgCl_2$

62. What is the percent by mass of sodium chloride in each of the following solutions?

　　a. 44 g NaCl dissolved in 756 g H_2O
　　b. 15 g NaCl dissolved in 485 g H_2O
　　c. 135 g NaCl dissolved in 765 g H_2O

★63. What is the concentration (in % (v/v)) of the following solutions?

　　a. 25 mL of ethanol (C_2H_6O) is diluted to a volume of 150 mL with water.
　　b. 175 mL of isopropyl alcohol (C_3H_8O) is diluted with water to a total volume of 275 mL.

16.3 Colligative Properties of Solutions

64. What are colligative properties? Identify three colligative properties and explain why each occurs.

65. Which has the higher boiling point:

　　a. seawater or distilled water?
　　b. 1.0*M* KNO_3 or 1.5*M* KNO_3?
　　c. 0.100*M* KCl or 0.100*M* $MgCl_2$?

66. Why does a 1*m* solution of calcium nitrate have a lower freezing point than a 1*m* solution of sodium nitrate?

67. Explain how a decrease in the vapor pressure of a solution results in an increase in its boiling point.

68. When the water inside a living cell freezes, the ice crystals damage the cell. The wood frog is a unique creature that can survive being frozen. In extremely cold conditions, the frog's liver produces large amounts of glucose ($C_6H_{12}O_6$), which becomes concentrated in the frog's cells. How does the glucose help prevent ice from forming in the frog's cells?

16.4 Calculations Involving Colligative Properties

69. Distinguish between a 1*M* solution and a 1*m* solution.

70. Describe how you would make an aqueous solution of methanol (CH_4O) in which the mole fraction of methanol is 0.40.

71. What is the boiling point of each solution?
    a. 0.50 mol glucose in 1000 g H_2O
    b. 1.50 mol NaCl in 1000 g H_2O

★72. What is the freezing point of each solution?
    a. 1.40 mol Na_2SO_4 in 1750 g H_2O
    b. 0.060 mol $MgSO_4$ in 100 g H_2O

73. Determine the freezing points of each 0.20*m* aqueous solution.
    a. K_2SO_4
    b. $CsNO_3$
    c. $Al(NO_3)_3$

Understand Concepts

74. Different numbers of moles of two different solutes, A and B, were added to identical quantities of water. The graph shows the freezing point of each of the solutions formed.

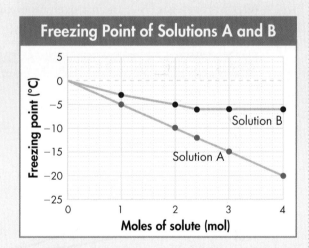

a. Explain the relative slopes of the two lines between 0 and 2 mol of solute added.
b. Why does the freezing point for solution B not continue to drop as amounts of solute B are added beyond 2.4 mol?

75. A mixture of ethylene glycol (EG) and water is used as antifreeze in automobile engines. The freezing point and density of the mixture vary with the percent by mass of (EG) in the mixture. On the following graph, point A represents 20% (EG) by mass; point B, 40%; and point C, 60%.

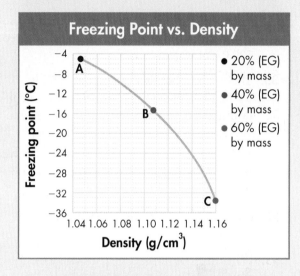

a. What is the density of the antifreeze mixture that freezes at −25°C?
b. What is the freezing point of a mixture that has a density of 1.06?
c. Estimate the freezing point of a mixture that is 30% by mass (EG).

★76. Calculate the freezing- and boiling-point changes for a solution containing 12.0 g of naphthalene ($C_{10}H_8$) in 50.0 g of benzene.

77. Describe how you would prepare an aqueous solution of acetone (C_3H_6O) in which the mole fraction of acetone is 0.25.

78. The solubility of sodium hydrogen carbonate ($NaHCO_3$) in water at 20°C is 9.6 g/100 g H_2O. What is the mole fraction of $NaHCO_3$ in a saturated solution? What is the molality of the solution?

79. A solution is labeled 0.150*m* NaCl. What are the mole fractions of the solute and solvent in this solution?

80. You are given a clear aqueous solution containing KNO_3. How would you determine experimentally if the solution is unsaturated, saturated, or supersaturated?

81. Plot a graph of solubility versus temperature for the three gases listed in Table 16.1.

82. Calculate the freezing point and the boiling point of a solution that contains 15.0 g of urea (CH_4N_2O) in 250 g of water. Urea is a covalently bonded compound.

83. Calculate the mole fractions in a solution that is 25.0 g of ethanol (C_2H_6O) and 40.0 g of water.

84. Estimate the freezing point of an aqueous solution of 20.0 g of glucose ($C_6H_{12}O_6$) dissolved in 500.0 g of water.

∗85. The solubility of KCl in water at 20°C is 34.0 g KCl/100 g H_2O. A warm solution containing 50.0 g KCl in 130 g H_2O is cooled to 20°C.

   a. How many grams of KCl remain dissolved?
   b. How many grams came out of solution?

86. How many moles of ions are present when 0.10 mol of each compound is dissolved in water?

   a. K_2SO_4
   b. $Fe(NO_3)_3$
   c. $Al_2(SO_4)_3$
   d. $NiSO_4$

Think Critically

∗87. Analyze Data A solution contains 26.5 g NaCl in 75.0 g H_2O at 20°C. Determine if the solution is unsaturated, saturated, or supersaturated. (The solubility of NaCl at 20°C is 36.0 g/100 g H_2O.)

88. Infer An aqueous solution freezes at −2.47°C. What is its boiling point?

89. Calculate Percent (mass/volume), or % (m/v), is the number of grams of solute per 100 mL of solution. Hydrogen peroxide is often sold commercially as a 3.0% (m/v) aqueous solution.

   a. If you buy a 250-mL bottle of 3.0% H_2O_2 (m/v), how many grams of hydrogen peroxide have you purchased?
   b. What is the molarity of this solution?

90. Calculate How many grams of $NaNO_3$ will precipitate if a saturated solution of $NaNO_3$ in 200 g H_2O at 50°C is cooled to 20°C?

∗91. Calculate What is the molar mass of a nondissociating compound if 5.76 g of the compound in 750 g of benzene gives a freezing-point depression of 0.460°C?

∗92. Calculate The molality of an aqueous solution of sugar ($C_{12}H_{22}O_{11}$) is 1.62m. Calculate the mole fractions of sugar and water.

93. Apply Concepts Why might calcium chloride spread on icy roads be more effective at melting ice than an equal amount of sodium chloride?

94. Calculate The following table lists the molar concentrations of the most abundant monatomic ions in seawater. Calculate the mass in grams of each ion contained in 5.00 L of seawater. The density of seawater is 1.024 g/mL.

Ion	Molarity (M)
Chloride	0.546
Sodium	0.470
Magnesium	0.053
Calcium	0.0103
Potassium	0.0102

95. Compare and Contrast Which will have a greater boiling point elevation: 3.00 g $Ca(NO_3)_2$ in 60.0 g of water or 6.00 g $Ca(NO_3)_2$ in 30.0 g of water?

96. Interpret Graphs The graph shows the effect of temperature on the solubilities of oxygen gas (O_2), nitrogen gas (N_2), and nitrogen monoxide (NO) in water.

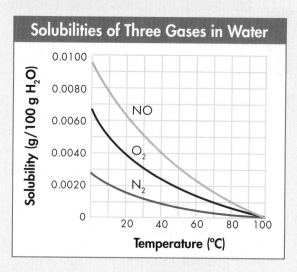

Solubilities of Three Gases in Water

   a. How does an increase in temperature affect the solubility in water of each gas?
   b. At what temperature do the gases become virtually insoluble?
   c. Use kinetic theory to explain the solubility behavior shown in the graph.

97. Calculate When an excess of zinc is added to 800 mL of a hydrochloric acid solution, the solution evolves 1.21 L of hydrogen gas measured over water at 21°C and 747.5 mm Hg. What was the molarity of the acid? The vapor pressure of water at 21°C is 18.6 mm Hg.

98. Calculate How many milliliters of 1.50M HNO_3 contain enough nitric acid to dissolve an old copper penny with a mass of 3.94 g?

$$3Cu + 8HNO_3 \longrightarrow 3Cu(NO_3)_2 + 2NO + 4H_2O$$

99. Graph One way to express the solubility of a compound is in terms of moles of compound that will dissolve in 1 kg of water. Solubility depends on temperature. Plot a graph of the solubility of potassium nitrate (KNO_3) from the following data:

Temperature (°C)	Solubility (mol/kg)
0	1.61
20	2.80
40	5.78
60	11.20
80	16.76
100	24.50

Using your graph, estimate

a. the solubility of KNO_3 at 76°C and at 33°C.

b. the temperature at which its solubility is 17.6 mol/kg of water.

c. the temperature at which the solubility is 4.24 mol/kg of water.

✳100. Calculate A 250-mL sample of Na_2SO_4 is reacted with an excess of $BaCl_2$. If 5.28 g $BaSO_4$ is precipitated, what is the molarity of the Na_2SO_4 solution?

101. Design an Experiment Suppose you have an unknown compound and want to identify it by means of its molar mass. Design an experiment that uses the concept of freezing-point depression to obtain the molar mass. What laboratory measurements would you need to make? What calculations would be needed?

102. Describe Find a recipe for rock candy online or in a cookbook. Write a short paragraph describing how the recipe applies key concepts that you have learned about solutions. Use the terms *solute*, *solvent*, *solubility*, *crystallization*, and *supersaturated solution* in your paragraph.

✳103. Sequence Write a stepwise procedure for preparing 100 mL of 0.50M KCl, starting with a stock solution that is 2.0M KCl.

CHEMYSTERY

That Sinking Feeling

Although you can't see it happening, the groundwater beneath your feet is very slowly dissolving away rocks and minerals below ground. Eventually, enough of these mineral solutes dissolve to hollow out underground cavities or caverns. A sinkhole occurs when the roof of an underground cavern depresses or collapses.

104. Explain Why do you think areas underlain by salt beds are prone to sinkholes?

105. Infer As you read earlier in this chapter, agitation can speed up the rate at which a solid dissolves in liquid. What forces might contribute to agitating groundwater as it dissolves minerals underground?

106. Connect to the BIGIDEA Limestone, which contains mostly calcium carbonate ($CaCO_3$), is insoluble in water. Yet areas underlain by limestone are prone to sinkholes. Read the article on limestone caves on page R9. How does the "dissolving" of limestone differ from solvation?

107. Convert each of the following mass measurements to its equivalent in kilograms.

   a. 347 g   **c.** 9.43 mg

   b. 73 mg   **d.** 877 mg

*108. Rubidium has two naturally occurring isotopes. Rubidium-85 (72.165%) has a mass of 84.912 amu. Rubidium-87 (27.835%) has a mass of 86.909 amu. Calculate the average atomic mass of rubidium.

109. What is the most significant difference between the Thomson model of the atom and the Rutherford model?

110. Name and give the symbol for the element in the following positions in the periodic table:

   a. Group 7B, Period 4   **c.** Group 1A, Period 7

   b. Group 3A, Period 5   **d.** Group 6A, Period 6

111. How many atoms of each element are present in four formula units of calcium permanganate?

112. Draw electron dot structures for the following atoms:

   a. I   **b.** Te   **c.** Sb   **d.** Sr

113. Terephthalic acid is an organic compound used in the synthesis of polyesters. Terephthalic acid contains 57.8 percent C, 3.64 percent H, and 38.5 percent O. The molar mass is approximately 166 g/mol. What is the molecular formula of terephthalic acid?

*114. The photograph shows one mole each of iron, copper, mercury, and sulfur.

   a. What is the mass of each element?

   b. How many atoms are in each sample?

   c. How many moles is 25.0 g of each element?

*115. What is the volume occupied by 1500 g of hydrogen gas (H_2) at STP?

116. Identify the type of chemical reaction.

   a. $H_2(g) + Cl_2(g) \longrightarrow 2HCl(g)$

   b. $2H_2O(l) \longrightarrow O_2(g) + 2H_2(g)$

   c. $2K(s) + 2H_2O(l) \longrightarrow 2KOH(aq) + H_2(g)$

   d. $C_2H_6O(l) + 3O_2(g) \longrightarrow 2CO_2(g) + 3H_2O(l)$

   e. $Cl_2(aq) + 2KBr(aq) \longrightarrow 2KCl(aq) + Br_2(aq)$

   f. $Pb(NO_3)_2(aq) + 2NaCl(aq) \longrightarrow$
                    $PbCl_2(s) + 2NaNO_3(aq)$

117. Write the net ionic equation for the following reaction:

$$2HI(aq) + Na_2S(aq) \longrightarrow H_2S(g) + 2NaI(aq)$$

118. Indicate by simple equations how the following substances ionize or dissociate in water:

   a. NH_4Cl **d.** $HC_2H_3O_2$

   b. $Cu(NO_3)_2$ **e.** Na_2SO_4

   c. HNO_3 **f.** $HgCl_2$

119. The equation for the combustion of methanol (CH_4O) is the following:

$$2CH_4O(l) + 3O_2(g) \longrightarrow 2CO_2(g) + 4H_2O(l)$$

What volume of oxygen, measured at STP, is required to completely burn 35.0 g of methanol?

*120. A cylinder of nitrogen gas at 25°C and 101.3 kPa is heated to 45°C. What is the new pressure of the gas?

121. Why does an ideal gas not exist?

122. What relationship exists between surface tension and intermolecular attractions in a liquid?

123. The solubility of hydrogen chloride gas in the polar solvent water is much greater than its solubility in the nonpolar solvent benzene. Why?

124. When soap is shaken with water, which is formed: a solution, a suspension, or a colloid? Explain.

If You Have Trouble With . . .

Question	107	108	109	110	111	112	113	114	115	116	117	118	119	120	121	122	123	124
See Chapter	3	4	5	6	7	7	10	10	10	11	11	11	12	14	14	15	15	15

Standardized Test Prep

Select the choice that best answers each question or completes each statement.

1. An aqueous solution is 65% (v/v) rubbing alcohol. How many milliliters of water are in a 95-mL sample of this solution?
   (A) 62 mL   (C) 33 mL
   (B) 1.5 mL   (D) 30 mL

2. When 2.0 mol of methanol is dissolved in 45 g of water, the mole fraction of methanol is
   (A) 0.44.   (C) 2.25.
   (B) 0.043.   (D) 0.55.

The lettered choices below refer to Questions 3–6. A lettered choice may be used once, more than once, or not at all.
   (A) moles/liter of solution
   (B) grams/mole
   (C) moles/kilogram of solvent
   (D) °C/molal
   (E) no units

Which of the above units is appropriate for each measurement?

3. molality

4. mole fraction

5. molar mass

6. molarity

Use the atomic windows to answer Questions 7–9. The windows show water and two aqueous solutions with different concentrations. Black spheres represent solute particles; gray spheres represent water.

     (A)   (B)   (C)

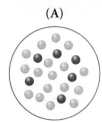 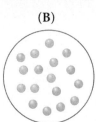 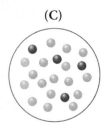

10. Which of these actions will cause more sugar to dissolve in a saturated sugar water solution?
    I. Add more sugar while stirring.
    II. Add more sugar and heat the solution.
    III. Grind the sugar to a powder; then add while stirring.
    (A) I only   (D) I and II only
    (B) II only   (E) II and III only
    (C) III only

Use the description and the data table to answer Questions 11–14.

A student measured the freezing points of three different aqueous solutions at five different concentrations. The data are shown below.

Molarity (M)	Freezing Point Depression (°C)		
	NaCl	CaCl₂	C₂H₆O
0.5	1.7	2.6	0.95
1.0	3.5	5.6	2.0
1.5	5.3	8.3	3.0
2.0	7.2	11.2	4.1
2.5	9.4	14.0	5.3

11. Graph the data for all three solutes on the same graph, using molarity as the independent variable.

12. Summarize the relationship between molarity and freezing-point depression.

13. Compare the slopes of the three lines and explain any difference.

14. If you collected similar data for KOH and added a fourth line to your graph, which existing line would the new line approximate?

If You Have Trouble With . . .														
Question	1	2	3	4	5	6	7	8	9	10	11	12	13	14
See Lesson	16.2	16.4	16.4	16.4	16.2	16.2	16.3	16.3	16.3	16.1	16.3	16.4	16.3	16.3

17

Thermochemistry

INSIDE:

- **17.1** The Flow of Energy
- **17.2** Measuring and Expressing Enthalpy Changes
- **17.3** Heat in Changes of State
- **17.4** Calculating Heats of Reaction

PearsonChem.com

This solar furnace in Font Romeu, France converts light from the sun into heat.

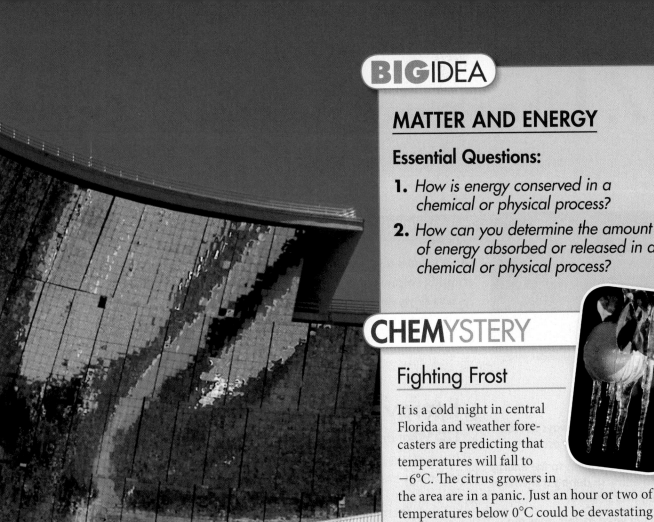

BIGIDEA

MATTER AND ENERGY

Essential Questions:

1. *How is energy conserved in a chemical or physical process?*
2. *How can you determine the amount of energy absorbed or released in a chemical or physical process?*

CHEMYSTERY

Fighting Frost

It is a cold night in central Florida and weather forecasters are predicting that temperatures will fall to −6°C. The citrus growers in the area are in a panic. Just an hour or two of temperatures below 0°C could be devastating to the citrus trees and fruit.

Citrus growers can use a number of methods to minimize the damage to their trees and fruit in the event of a frost or freeze. Some growers install heaters to protect their crops. Other farmers use wind machines or helicopters to mix the layers of warm and cold air in the atmosphere and raise the temperature at the surface. However, one of the most common methods of protecting citrus trees is to spray water on them. The freezing of the water protects the branches, leaves, and fruit.

▶ Connect to the **BIG**IDEA As you read about thermochemistry, think about how water freezing can protect citrus trees from frost.

NATIONAL SCIENCE EDUCATION STANDARDS

A-1, B-3, B-5, D-1, E-2, F-3, F-4, F-6

17.1 The Flow of Energy

Q: *Why does lava cool faster in water than in air?* Lava flowing out of an erupting volcano is very hot. Its temperature ranges from 550°C to 1400°C. As lava flows down the side of a volcano, it loses heat and begins to cool slowly. In some instances, the lava may flow into the ocean, where it cools more rapidly. In this lesson, you will learn about heat flow.

Key Questions

🔑 What are the ways in which energy changes can occur?

🔑 What happens to the energy of the universe during a chemical or physical process?

🔑 On what factors does the heat capacity of an object depend?

Vocabulary

- thermochemistry
- chemical potential energy
- heat • system
- surroundings
- law of conservation of energy
- endothermic process
- exothermic process
- heat capacity
- specific heat

Energy Transformations

🔑 **What are the ways in which energy changes can occur?**

Energy is the capacity for doing work or supplying heat. Unlike matter, energy has neither mass nor volume. Energy is detected only because of its effects. For example, a car moves because of the energy supplied by the fuel. **Thermochemistry** is the study of energy changes that occur during chemical reactions and changes in state. Every substance has a certain amount of energy stored inside it. The energy stored in the chemical bonds of a substance is called **chemical potential energy.** The kinds of atoms and the arrangement of the atoms in a substance determine the amount of energy stored in the substance.

During a chemical reaction, a substance is transformed into another substance with a different amount of chemical potential energy. When you buy gasoline, shown in Figure 17.1, you are actually buying the stored potential energy it contains. The controlled explosions of the gasoline in a car's engine transform the potential energy into useful work, which can be used to propel the car. At the same time, however, heat is also produced, making the car's engine extremely hot. 🔑 **Energy changes occur as either heat transfer or work, or a combination of both.**

Heat, represented by q, is energy that transfers from one object to another because of a temperature difference between the objects. One of the effects of adding heat to an object is an increase in its temperature. Heat flows spontaneously from a warmer object to a cooler object. If two objects remain in contact, heat will flow from the warmer object to the cooler object until the temperature of both objects is the same.

Figure 17.1 Chemical Potential Energy
Chemical potential energy is stored within the bonds of the molecules in gasoline.

Endothermic and Exothermic Processes

🔑 *What happens to the energy of the universe during a chemical or physical process?*

Chemical reactions and changes in physical state generally involve either the absorption or the release of heat. In studying energy changes, you can define a **system** as the part of the universe on which you focus your attention. Everything else in the universe makes up the **surroundings.** In thermochemical experiments, you can consider the region in the immediate vicinity of the system as the surroundings. Together, the system and its surroundings make up the universe.

A major goal of thermochemistry is to examine the flow of heat between the system and its surroundings. The **law of conservation of energy** states that in any chemical or physical process, energy is neither created nor destroyed. 🔑 **During any chemical or physical process, the energy of the universe remains unchanged.** If the energy of the system increases during that process, the energy of the surroundings must decrease by the same amount. Likewise, if the energy of the system decreases during that process, the energy of the surroundings must increase by the same amount.

Direction of Heat Flow In thermochemical calculations, the direction of heat flow is given from the point of view of the system. Heat is absorbed from the surroundings in an **endothermic process.** In an endothermic process, the system gains heat as the surroundings lose heat. In Figure 17.2a, the system (the body) gains heat from its surroundings (the fire). Heat flowing into a system from its surroundings is defined as positive; q has a positive value. An **exothermic process** is one that releases heat to its surroundings. In an exothermic process, the system loses heat as the surroundings gain heat. In Figure 17.2b, the system (the body) loses heat to the surroundings (the perspiration on the skin, and the air). Heat flowing out of a system into its surroundings is defined as negative; q has a negative value.

Learn about temperature and heat *online.*

Figure 17.2 Heat Flow
Heat flow is defined from the point of view of the system. **a.** In an endothermic process, heat flows into the system from the surroundings. **b.** In an exothermic process, heat flows from the system to the surroundings. In both cases, energy is conserved.
Apply Concepts *In which process does q have a negative value?*

Recognizing Endothermic and Exothermic Processes

On a sunny winter day, the snow on a rooftop begins to melt. As the melted water drips from the roof, it refreezes into icicles. Describe the direction of heat flow as the water freezes. Is this process endothermic or exothermic?

❶ **Analyze Identify the relevant concepts.** Heat flows from a warmer object to a cooler object. An endothermic process absorbs heat from the surroundings. An exothermic process releases heat to the surroundings.

❷ **Solve Apply the concepts to this problem.**

First, identify the system and the surroundings.	System: water Surroundings: air
Determine the direction of heat flow.	In order for water to freeze, its temperature must decrease. Heat flows out of the water and into the air.
Determine if the process is endothermic or exothermic.	Heat is released from the system to the surroundings. The process is exothermic.

1. A container of melted wax stands at room temperature. What is the direction of heat flow as the liquid wax solidifies? Is the process endothermic or exothermic?

First, identify the system and surroundings in each situation. Then, determine the direction of heat flow.

2. When barium hydroxide octahydrate, $Ba(OH)_2 \cdot 8H_2O$ is mixed in a beaker with ammonium thiocyanate, NH_4SCN, a reaction occurs. The beaker becomes very cold. Is the reaction endothermic or exothermic?

Units for Measuring Heat Flow Describing the amount of heat flow requires units different than those used to describe temperature. Heat flow is measured in two common units, the calorie and the joule. You have probably heard of someone exercising to "burn calories." During exercise, your body breaks down sugars and fats in a process that releases heat. Although there is not an actual fire burning the sugars and fats within your body, chemical reactions accomplish the same result. For example, in breaking down 10 g of sugar, your body releases the same amount of heat that would be released if 10 g of sugar were completely burned in a fire.

A calorie (cal) is defined as the quantity of heat needed to raise the temperature of 1 g of pure water 1°C. The word *calorie* is written with a small *c* except when referring to the energy contained in food. The dietary Calorie, written with a capital *C*, always refers to the energy in food. One dietary Calorie is equal to one kilocalorie, or 1000 calories.

$$1 \text{ Calorie} = 1 \text{ kilocalorie} = 1000 \text{ calories}$$

The joule (J) is the SI unit of energy. One joule of heat raises the temperature of 1 g of pure water 0.2390°C. You can convert between calories and joules using the following relationships:

$$1 \text{ J} = 0.2390 \text{ cal} \qquad 4.184 \text{ J} = 1 \text{ cal}$$

Heat Capacity and Specific Heat

On what factors does the heat capacity of an object depend?

The amount of heat needed to increase the temperature of an object exactly 1°C is the **heat capacity** of that object. **The heat capacity of an object depends on both its mass and its chemical composition.** The greater the mass of the object, the greater its heat capacity. One of the massive steel cables on the bridge in Figure 17.3, for example, requires much more heat to raise its temperature 1°C than a small steel nail does.

Different substances with the same mass may have different heat capacities. On a sunny day, a 20-kg puddle of water may be cool, while a nearby 20-kg iron sewer cover may be too hot to touch. This situation illustrates how different heat capacities affect the temperature of objects. Assuming that both the water and the iron absorb the same amount of radiant energy from the sun, the temperature of the water changes less than the temperature of the iron in the same amount of time because the specific heat capacity of water is larger than the specific heat capacity of iron.

The specific heat capacity, or simply the **specific heat,** of a substance is the amount of heat it takes to raise the temperature of 1 g of the substance 1°C. Table 17.1 gives specific heats for some common substances. Water has a very high specific heat compared with the other substances in the table. Metals generally have low specific heats. The same amount of heat affects the temperature of objects of the same mass with a high specific heat much less than the temperature of those with a low specific heat.

Figure 17.3 Heat Capacity
A massive steel cable has a higher heat capacity than a steel nail.
Compare *Which has a greater heat capacity: a cup of water or a drop of water?*

InterpretData

Specific Heats of Some Common Substances		
Substance	**Specific heat**	
	J/(g·°C)	cal/(g·°C)
Liquid water	4.18	1.00
Ethanol	2.4	0.58
Ice	2.1	0.50
Steam	1.9	0.45
Chloroform	0.96	0.23
Aluminum	0.90	0.21
Iron	0.46	0.11
Silver	0.24	0.057
Mercury	0.14	0.033

Table 17.1 The specific heat of a substance can be expressed in J/(g·°C) or cal/(g·°C).
a. Read Tables What is the specific heat of chloroform in cal/(g·°C)?
b. Compare Which metal in the table has the highest specific heat?
c. Calculate Show how to convert the specific heat of liquid water from J/(g·°C) to cal/(g·°C).

Hint: For part c, use the relationship 1 J = 0.2390 cal to write the appropriate conversion factor.

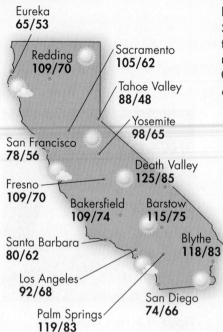

Eureka
65/53

Redding
109/70

Sacramento
105/62

Tahoe Valley
88/48

Yosemite
98/65

San Francisco
78/56

Death Valley
125/85

Fresno
109/70

Bakersfield
109/74

Barstow
115/75

Santa Barbara
80/62

Blythe
118/83

Los Angeles
92/68

San Diego
74/66

Palm Springs
119/83

Figure 17.4 Temperature Moderation
San Francisco is located on the Pacific coast. The high specific heat of the water in the ocean helps keep the temperature in San Francisco much more moderate than that of the towns and cities farther inland.
Compare *Describe how the ocean affects the temperature of coastal areas in the summer and in the winter.*

Specific Heat of Water Just as it takes a lot of heat to raise the temperature of water, water also releases a lot of heat as it cools. Water in lakes and oceans absorbs heat from the air on hot days and releases it back into the air on cool days. As illustrated in Figure 17.4, this property of water is responsible for moderate climates in coastal areas. Citrus farmers often spray their trees with water to protect the fruit from frost damage during icy weather. As the water freezes, it releases heat, which helps prevent the fruit from freezing. When a freshly baked apple pie, such as the one shown in Figure 17.5, comes out of the oven, both the filling and crust are at the same temperature. However, the filling, which is mostly water, has a higher specific heat than the crust. In order to cool down, the filling must give off a lot of heat. This release of heat is why you have to be careful not to burn your tongue when eating hot apple pie.

Calculating Specific Heat To calculate the specific heat (C) of a substance, you divide the heat input by the mass of the substance times the temperature change.

$$C = \frac{q}{m \times \Delta T} = \frac{\text{heat (J or cal)}}{\text{mass (g)} \times \text{change in temperature (°C)}}$$

In the equation above, q is heat and m is mass. The symbol ΔT (read "delta T") represents the change in temperature. ΔT is calculated from the equation $\Delta T = T_f - T_i$, where T_f is the final temperature and T_i is the initial temperature. As you can see from the equation and in Table 17.1 on the previous page, heat may be expressed in terms of joules or calories. Therefore, the units of specific heat are either J/(g·°C) or cal/(g·°C).

CHEMISTRY & YOU

Q: *Heat will flow from the lava to the surroundings until the lava and surroundings are at the same temperature. Air has a smaller specific heat than water. Why would lava then cool more quickly in water than in air?*

Figure 17.5 Cooling of Water
The filling of a hot apple pie is mostly water, so you are much more likely to burn your tongue on the hot filling than on the hot crust.

Calculating the Specific Heat of a Substance

The temperature of a 95.4-g piece of copper increases from 25.0°C to 48.0°C when the copper absorbs 849 J of heat. What is the specific heat of copper?

KNOWNS

$m_{Cu} = 95.4\ g$
$\Delta T = 48.0°C - 25.0°C = 23.0°C$
$q = 849\ J$

UNKNOWN

$C_{Cu} = ?\ J/(g·°C)$

①Analyze List the knowns and the unknown. Use the known values and the definition of specific heat.

②Calculate Solve for the unknown.

Start with the equation for specific heat.	$C_{Cu} = \dfrac{q}{m_{Cu} \times \Delta T}$
Substitute the known quantities into the equation to calculate the unknown value C_{Cu}.	$C_{Cu} = \dfrac{849\ J}{95.4\ g \times 23.0°C} = 0.387\ J/(g·°C)$

③Evaluate Does the result make sense? Remember that liquid water has a specific heat of 4.18 J/(g·°C). Metals have specific heats lower than water. Thus the calculated value of 0.387 J/(g·°C) seems reasonable.

3. When 435 J of heat is added to 3.4 g of olive oil at 21°C, the temperature increases to 85°C. What is the specific heat of the olive oil?

4. How much heat is required to raise the temperature of 250.0 g of mercury 52°C?

> You can find the specific heat of mercury on Table 17.1.

17.1 LessonCheck

5. ⚷ **Review** What are the ways that energy conversion can occur?

6. ⚷ **Describe** What happens to the energy of the universe during a physical or chemical process?

7. ⚷ **List** On what two factors does the heat capacity of an object depend?

8. Classify On a cold night you use an electric blanket to warm your body. Describe the direction of heat flow. Is this process endothermic or exothermic?

9. Calculate A chunk of silver has a heat capacity of 42.8 J/°C and a mass of 181 g. Calculate the specific heat of silver.

10. Calculate Using calories, calculate how much heat 32.0 g of water absorbs when it is heated from 25.0°C to 80.0°C. How many joules is this?

BIGIDEA MATTER AND ENERGY

11. How is the energy of the universe conserved during the combustion of gasoline in a car engine?

Q: *How can you measure the amount of heat released when a match burns?* When you strike a match, heat is released to the surroundings. In addition to describing the direction of heat flow, you may also want to determine the quantity of heat that is transferred. The concept of specific heat allows you to measure heat flow in chemical and physical processes.

Key Questions

How can you measure the change in enthalpy of a reaction?

How can you express the enthalpy change for a reaction in a chemical equation?

Vocabulary

- calorimetry
- calorimeter
- enthalpy
- thermochemical equation
- heat of reaction
- heat of combustion

Calorimetry

How can you measure the change in enthalpy of a reaction?

Heat that is absorbed or released during many chemical reactions can be measured by a technique called calorimetry. **Calorimetry** is the measurement of the heat flow into or out of a system for chemical and physical processes. In a calorimetry experiment involving an endothermic process, the heat absorbed by the system is equal to the heat released by its surroundings. In an exothermic process, the heat released by a system is equal to the heat absorbed by its surroundings. The insulated device used to measure the absorption or release of heat in chemical or physical processes is called a **calorimeter.**

Constant-Pressure Calorimeters Foam cups can be used as simple calorimeters because they do not let much heat in or out. The heat flows for many chemical reactions can be measured in a constant-pressure calorimeter similar to the one shown in Figure 17.6. Most chemical reactions and physical changes carried out in the laboratory are open to the atmosphere and, thus, occur at constant pressure. The **enthalpy** (*H*) of a system accounts for the heat flow of the system at constant pressure.

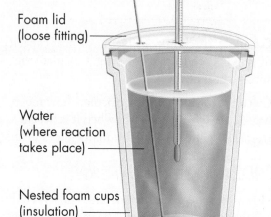

Stirrer

Thermometer

Foam lid (loose fitting)

Water (where reaction takes place)

Nested foam cups (insulation)

Figure 17.6 Constant-Pressure Calorimeter
In a simple constant-pressure calorimeter, a thermometer records the temperature change as chemicals react in water. The reacting substances constitute the system. The water constitutes the surroundings.
Relate Cause and Effect *What happens to the temperature of the water if heat is released by the reaction in the calorimeter?*

The heat absorbed or released by a reaction at constant pressure is the same as the change in enthalpy, symbolized as ΔH.  **The value of ΔH of a reaction can be determined by measuring the heat flow of the reaction at constant pressure.** In this textbook, the terms *heat* and *enthalpy change* are used interchangeably because the reactions presented occur at constant pressure. In other words, $q = \Delta H$.

To measure the enthalpy change for a reaction in aqueous solution in a foam cup calorimeter, dissolve the reacting chemicals (the system) in known volumes of water (the surroundings). Measure the initial temperature of each solution, and mix the solutions in the foam cup. After the reaction is complete, measure the final temperature of the mixed solutions. You can calculate the heat absorbed or released by the surroundings (q_{surr}) using the mass of the water, the specific heat of water, and the initial and final temperatures.

$$q_{surr} = m \times C \times \Delta T$$

In this expression, m is the mass of the water, C is the specific heat of water, and $\Delta T = T_f - T_i$. The heat absorbed by the surroundings is equal to, but has the opposite sign of, the heat released by the system. Conversely, the heat released by the surroundings is equal to, but has the opposite sign of, the heat absorbed by the system. Therefore, the enthalpy change for the reaction (ΔH) can be written as follows:

$$q_{sys} = \Delta H = -q_{surr} = -m \times C \times \Delta T$$

The sign of ΔH is positive for an endothermic reaction and negative for an exothermic reaction.

Constant-Volume Calorimeters Calorimetry experiments can also be performed at constant volume using a device called a bomb calorimeter. In a bomb calorimeter, which is shown in Figure 17.7, a sample of a compound is burned in a constant-volume chamber in the presence of oxygen at high pressure. The heat that is released warms the water surrounding the chamber. By measuring the temperature increase of the water, it is possible to calculate the quantity of heat released during the combustion reaction.

CHEMISTRY & YOU

Q: *What type of calorimeter would you use to measure the heat released when a match burns? Describe the experiment and how you would calculate the heat released.*

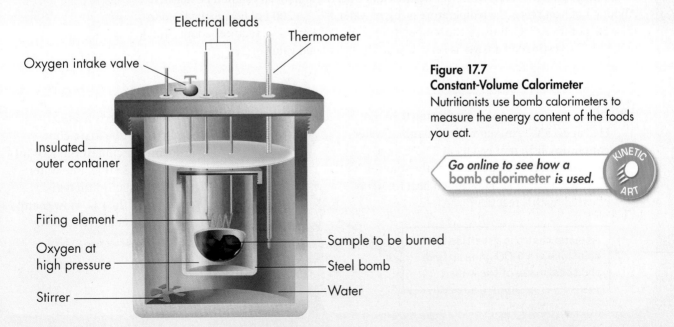

Electrical leads
Thermometer
Oxygen intake valve
Insulated outer container
Firing element
Oxygen at high pressure
Stirrer
Sample to be burned
Steel bomb
Water

Figure 17.7
Constant-Volume Calorimeter
Nutritionists use bomb calorimeters to measure the energy content of the foods you eat.

Go online to see how a bomb calorimeter is used.
KINETIC ART

SampleProblem 17.3

Enthalpy Change in a Calorimetry Experiment

When 25.0 mL of water containing 0.025 mol HCl at 25.0°C is added to 25.0 mL of water containing 0.025 mol NaOH at 25.0°C in a foam cup calorimeter, a reaction occurs. Calculate the enthalpy change (in kJ) during this reaction if the highest temperature observed is 32.0°C. Assume the densities of the solutions are 1.00 g/mL and that the volume of the final solution is equal to the sum of the volumes of the reacting solutions.

KNOWNS	UNKNOWN
$C_{water} = 4.18\ J/(g \cdot °C)$	$\Delta H = ?\ kJ$
$V_{final} = V_{HCl} + V_{NaOH}$	
$\quad = 25.0\ mL + 25.0\ mL = 50.0\ mL$	
$T_i = 25.0°C$	
$T_f = 32.0°C$	
$density_{solution} = 1.00\ g/mL$	

1 Analyze List the knowns and the unknown.
Use dimensional analysis to determine the mass of the water. You must also calculate ΔT. Use $\Delta H = - q_{surr} = -m \times C \times \Delta T$ to solve for ΔH.

2 Calculate Solve for the unknown.

First, calculate the total mass of the water.

$$m_{water} = 50.0\ mL \times \frac{1.00\ g}{1\ mL} = 50.0\ g$$

Now, calculate ΔT.

$$\Delta T = T_f - T_i = 32.0°C - 25.0°C = 7.0°C$$

Use the values for m_{water}, C_{water}, and ΔT to calculate ΔH.

$$\Delta H = -q_{surr} = -m_{water} \times C_{water} \times \Delta T$$
$$= -(50.0\ g)(4.18\ J/(g \cdot °C))(7.0°C)$$
$$= -1500\ J = -1.5\ kJ$$

Use the relationship 1 kJ = 1000 J to convert your answer from J to kJ.

3 Evaluate Does the result make sense? The temperature of the solution increases, which means that the reaction is exothermic, and thus the sign of ΔH should be negative. About 4 J of heat raises the temperature of 1 g of water 1°C, so 200 J of heat is required to raise 50 g of water 1°C. Raising the temperature of 50 g of water 7°C requires about 1400 J, or 1.4 kJ. This estimated answer is very close to the calculated value of ΔH.

---

12. When 50.0 mL of water containing 0.50 mol HCl at 22.5°C is mixed with 50.0 mL of water containing 0.50 mol NaOH at 22.5°C in a calorimeter, the temperature of the solution increases to 26.0°C. How much heat (in kJ) is released by this reaction?

Assume that the densities of the solutions are 1.00 g/mL to find the total mass of the water.

13. A small pebble is heated and placed in a foam cup calorimeter containing 25.0 mL of water at 25.0°C. The water reaches a maximum temperature of 26.4°C. How many joules of heat are released by the pebble?

Thermochemical Equations

How can you express the enthalpy change for a reaction in a chemical equation?

If you mix calcium oxide with water, the water in the mixture becomes warm. This exothermic reaction occurs when cement, which contains calcium oxide, is mixed with water to make concrete. When 1 mol of calcium oxide reacts with 1 mol of water, 1 mol of calcium hydroxide forms and 65.2 kJ of heat is released. **In a chemical equation, the enthalpy change for the reaction can be written as either a reactant or a product.** In the equation describing the exothermic reaction of calcium oxide and water, the enthalpy change can be considered a product.

$$CaO(s) + H_2O(l) \longrightarrow Ca(OH)_2(s) + 65.2 \text{ kJ}$$

This equation is presented visually in Figure 17.8. A chemical equation that includes the enthalpy change is called a **thermochemical equation.**

Heats of Reaction The **heat of reaction** is the enthalpy change for the chemical equation exactly as it is written. You will usually see heats of reaction reported as ΔH, which is equal to the heat flow at constant pressure. The physical state of the reactants and products must also be given. The standard conditions are that the reaction is carried out at 101.3 kPa (1 atm) and that the reactants and products are in their usual physical states at 25°C. The heat of reaction, or ΔH, in the above example is -65.2 kJ. Each mole of calcium oxide and water that reacts to form calcium hydroxide produces 65.2 kJ of heat.

$$CaO(s) + H_2O(l) \longrightarrow Ca(OH)_2(s) \qquad \Delta H = -65.2 \text{ kJ}$$

In this and other exothermic processes, the chemical potential energy of the reactants is higher than the chemical potential energy of the products.

READING SUPPORT

Build Comprehension:
Use Prior Knowledge
Thermochemical equations are just like other balanced equations. If heat is absorbed in the reaction, it is written as a reactant. If heat is released, it is written as a product. *Recall chemical reactions from Chapter 11. For the combustion of methane, on which side of the reaction arrow would you write the heat absorbed or released by the reaction?*

Figure 17.8 Exothermic Process
Calcium oxide is one of the components of cement. The reaction of calcium oxide and water is an exothermic process.

Enthalpy (H)

CaO(s) + H₂O(l)

$\Delta H = -65.2$ kJ

Ca(OH)₂(s)

Figure 17.9 Endothermic Process
Muffin batter often contains baking soda, also known as sodium bicarbonate. The decomposition of sodium bicarbonate is an endothermic process.

Other reactions absorb heat from the surroundings. For example, baking soda (sodium bicarbonate) decomposes when it is heated. The carbon dioxide released in the reaction causes muffins to rise while baking. This process is endothermic.

$$2NaHCO_3(s) + 85 \text{ kJ} \longrightarrow Na_2CO_3(s) + H_2O(l) + CO_2(g)$$

Remember that ΔH is positive for endothermic reactions. Therefore, you can write the reaction as follows:

$$2NaHCO_3(s) \longrightarrow Na_2CO_3(s) + H_2O(l) + CO_2(g) \qquad \Delta H = 85 \text{ kJ}$$

Figure 17.9 shows the enthalpy diagram for this reaction.

Chemistry problems involving enthalpy changes are similar to stoichiometry problems. The amount of heat released or absorbed during a reaction depends on the number of moles of the reactants involved. The decomposition of 2 mol of sodium bicarbonate, for example, requires 85 kJ of heat. Therefore, the decomposition of 4 mol of the same substance would require twice as much heat, or 170 kJ. In this and other endothermic processes, the chemical potential energy of the products is higher than the chemical potential energy of the reactants.

To see why the physical state of the reactants and products in a thermochemical reaction must be stated, compare the following two equations for the decomposition of 1 mol H_2O:

$$H_2O(l) \longrightarrow H_2(g) + \tfrac{1}{2}O_2(g) \qquad \Delta H = 285.8 \text{ kJ}$$
$$H_2O(g) \longrightarrow H_2(g) + \tfrac{1}{2}O_2(g) \qquad \underline{\Delta H = 241.8 \text{ kJ}}$$
$$\text{difference} = 44.0 \text{ kJ}$$

Although the two equations are very similar, the different physical states of H_2O result in different ΔH values. In one case, the reactant is a liquid; in the other case, the reactant is a gas. The vaporization of 1 mol of liquid water to water vapor at 25°C requires 44.0 kJ of heat.

$$H_2O(l) \longrightarrow H_2O(g) \qquad \Delta H = 44.0 \text{ kJ}$$

SampleProblem 17.4

Using the Heat of Reaction to Calculate Enthalpy Change

Calculate the amount of heat (in kJ) required to decompose 2.24 mol $NaHCO_3(s)$.

$$2NaHCO_3(s) + 85 \text{ kJ} \longrightarrow Na_2CO_3(s) + H_2O(l) + CO_2(g)$$

❶ **Analyze** List the knowns and the unknown.
Use the thermochemical equation above to write a conversion factor relating kilojoules of heat and moles of $NaHCO_3$. Then use the conversion factor to determine ΔH for 2.24 mol $NaHCO_3$.

KNOWNS
amount of $NaHCO_3(s)$ that decomposes = 2.24 mol
ΔH = 85 kJ for 2 mol $NaHCO_3$

UNKNOWN
ΔH = ? kJ for 2.24 mol $NaHCO_3$

❷ **Calculate** Solve for the unknown.

Write the conversion factor relating kJ of heat and moles of $NaHCO_3$.

$$\frac{85 \text{ kJ}}{2 \text{ mol } NaHCO_3(s)}$$

The thermochemical equation indicates that 85 kJ are needed to decompose 2 mol $NaHCO_3(s)$.

Using dimensional analysis, solve for ΔH.

$$\Delta H = 2.24 \text{ mol } NaHCO_3(s) \times \frac{85 \text{ kJ}}{2 \text{ mol } NaHCO_3(s)}$$
$$= 95 \text{ kJ}$$

❸ **Evaluate** Does the result make sense? The 85 kJ in the thermochemical equation refers to the decomposition of 2 mol $NaHCO_3(s)$. Therefore, the decomposition of 2.24 mol should absorb more heat than 85 kJ. The answer of 95 kJ is consistent with this estimate.

To do Problem 15, first convert from mass of CS_2 to moles of CS_2.

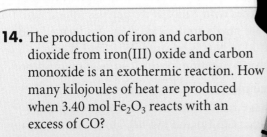

14. The production of iron and carbon dioxide from iron(III) oxide and carbon monoxide is an exothermic reaction. How many kilojoules of heat are produced when 3.40 mol Fe_2O_3 reacts with an excess of CO?

$$Fe_2O_3(s) + 3CO(g) \longrightarrow$$
$$2Fe(s) + 3CO_2(g) + 26.3 \text{ kJ}$$

15. When carbon disulfide is formed from its elements, heat is absorbed. Calculate the amount of heat (in kJ) absorbed when 5.66 g of carbon disulfide is formed.

$$C(s) + 2S(s) \longrightarrow CS_2(l)$$
$$\Delta H = 89.3 \text{ kJ}$$

Figure 17.10 Combustion
The combustion of natural gas is an exothermic reaction. As bonds in methane (the main component of natural gas) and oxygen are broken and bonds in carbon dioxide and water are formed, large amounts of energy are released.

Table 17.2

Heats of Combustion at 25°C		
Substance	Formula	ΔH (kJ/mol)
Hydrogen	$H_2(g)$	−286
Carbon	$C(s, graphite)$	−394
Methane	$CH_4(g)$	−890
Acetylene	$C_2H_2(g)$	−1300
Ethanol	$C_2H_6O(l)$	−1368
Propane	$C_3H_8(g)$	−2220
Glucose	$C_6H_{12}O_6(s)$	−2808
Octane	$C_8H_{18}(l)$	−5471
Sucrose	$C_{12}H_{22}O_{11}(s)$	−5645

Heats of Combustion Table 17.2 lists heats of combustion for some common substances. The **heat of combustion** is the heat of reaction for the complete burning of one mole of a substance. Figure 17.10 shows the combustion of natural gas, which is mostly methane. Small amounts of natural gas within crude oil are burned off at oil refineries. This is an exothermic reaction.

$$CH_4(g) + 2O_2(g) \longrightarrow CO_2(g) + 2H_2O(l) + 890 \text{ kJ}$$

You can also write this equation as follows:

$$CH_4(g) + 2O_2(g) \longrightarrow CO_2(g) + 2H_2O(l) \qquad \Delta H = -890 \text{ kJ}$$

Burning 1 mol of methane releases 890 kJ of heat. The heat of combustion (ΔH) for this reaction is −890 kJ per mole of methane burned.

Like other heats of reaction, heats of combustion are reported as the enthalpy changes when the reactions are carried out at 101.3 kPa of pressure and the reactants and products are in their physical states at 25°C.

17.2 LessonCheck

16. **Describe** How can you determine the value of ΔH of a reaction?

17. **Review** How are enthalpy changes expressed in chemical equations?

18. Calculate A lead mass is heated and placed in a foam cup calorimeter containing 40.0 mL of water at 17.0°C. The water reaches a temperature of 20.0°C. How many joules of heat were released by the lead?

19. Explain What does the term *heat of combustion* refer to?

20. Describe When 2 mol of solid magnesium (Mg) combines with 1 mol of oxygen gas (O_2), 2 mol of solid magnesium oxide (MgO) is formed and 1204 kJ of heat is released. Write the thermochemical equation for this combustion reaction.

21. Calculate Gasohol contains ethanol, $C_2H_6O(l)$. When ethanol burns, it reacts with $O_2(g)$ to produce $CO_2(g)$ and $H_2O(l)$. How much heat is released when 12.5 g of ethanol burns?

$$C_2H_6O(l) + 3O_2(g) \longrightarrow 2CO_2(g) + 3H_2O(l)$$
$$\Delta H = -1368 \text{ kJ}$$

17.3 Heat in Changes of State

Key Questions

 What is the relationship between molar heat of fusion and molar heat of solidification?

 What is the relationship between molar heat of vaporization and molar heat of condensation?

 What thermochemical changes can occur when a solution forms?

Vocabulary

- molar heat of fusion
- molar heat of solidification
- molar heat of vaporization
- molar heat of condensation
- molar heat of solution

CHEMISTRY & YOU

Q: *Why does sweating help cool you off?* An athlete can burn a lot of calories during a game. These calories are either used to do work or are released as heat. When your body heats up, you start to sweat. The evaporation of sweat is your body's way of cooling itself to a normal temperature.

Heats of Fusion and Solidification

 What is the relationship between molar heat of fusion and molar heat of solidification?

What happens if you place an ice cube on a table in a warm room? The ice cube is the system, and the table and air around it are the surroundings. The ice absorbs heat from its surroundings and begins to melt. The temperature of the ice and the liquid water produced remains at 0°C until all of the ice has melted.

Like ice cubes, all solids absorb heat as they melt to become liquids. The gain of heat causes a change of state instead of a change in temperature. Whenever a change of state occurs by a gain or loss of heat, the temperature of the substance undergoing the change remains constant. The heat absorbed by one mole of a solid substance as it melts to a liquid at a constant temperature is the **molar heat of fusion** (ΔH_{fus}). The **molar heat of solidification** (ΔH_{solid}) is the heat lost when one mole of a liquid substance solidifies at a constant temperature.  **The quantity of heat absorbed by a melting solid is exactly the same as the quantity of heat released when the liquid solidifies; that is, $\Delta H_{\text{fus}} = -\Delta H_{\text{solid}}$.**

The melting of 1 mol of ice at 0°C to 1 mol of liquid water at 0°C requires the absorption of 6.01 kJ of heat. This quantity of heat is the molar heat of fusion of water. Likewise, the conversion of 1 mol of liquid water at 0°C to 1 mol of ice at 0°C releases 6.01 kJ of heat. This quantity of heat is the molar heat of solidification of water.

$$H_2O(s) \longrightarrow H_2O(l) \qquad \Delta H_{\text{fus}} = 6.01 \text{ kJ/mol}$$

$$H_2O(l) \longrightarrow H_2O(s) \qquad \Delta H_{\text{solid}} = -6.01 \text{ kJ/mol}$$

SampleProblem 17.5

Using the Heat of Fusion in Phase-Change Calculations

How many grams of ice at 0°C will melt if 2.25 kJ of heat are added?

❶ Analyze **List the knowns and the unknown.** Find the number of moles of ice that can be melted by the addition of 2.25 kJ of heat. Convert moles of ice to grams of ice.

> **KNOWNS**
>
> Initial and final temperatures are $0°C$
>
> $\Delta H_{fus} = 6.01$ kJ/mol
>
> $\Delta H = 2.25$ kJ
>
> **UNKNOWN**
>
> $m_{ice} = ?$ g

❷ Calculate **Solve for the unknown.**

Start by expressing ΔH_{fus} as a conversion factor.	$\dfrac{1 \text{ mol } H_2O(s)}{6.01 \text{ kJ}}$ — Use the thermochemical equation $H_2O(s) + 6.01 \text{ kJ} \longrightarrow H_2O(l)$

Express the molar mass of ice as a conversion factor.

$$\frac{18.0 \text{ g } H_2O(s)}{1 \text{ mol } H_2O(s)}$$

Multiply the known enthalpy change by the conversion factors.

$$m_{ice} = 2.25 \text{ kJ} \times \frac{1 \text{ mol } H_2O(s)}{6.01 \text{ kJ}} \times \frac{18.0 \text{ g } H_2O(s)}{1 \text{ mol } H_2O(s)}$$

$$= 6.74 \text{ g } H_2O(s)$$

❸ Evaluate **Does the result make sense?** To melt 1 mol of ice, 6.01 kJ of energy is required. Only about one third of this amount of heat (roughly 2 kJ) is available, so only about one-third mol of ice, or 18.0 g/3 = 6 g, should melt. This estimate is close to the calculated answer.

22. How many grams of ice at 0°C could be melted by the addition of 0.400 kJ of heat?

23. How many kilojoules of heat are required to melt a 50.0-g popsicle at 0°C? Assume the popsicle has the same molar mass and heat of fusion as water.

> To do Problem 23, first convert from mass to moles. Then, express ΔH_{fus} as a conversion factor to convert from moles of ice to kJ of heat.

Purpose To estimate the heat of fusion of ice

Materials

- 100-ml graduated cylinder
- hot tap water
- foam cup
- thermometer
- ice

Heat of Fusion of Ice

Procedure

1. Fill the graduated cylinder with hot tap water and let stand for 1 minute. Pour the water into the sink.

2. Measure 70 mL of hot water. Pour the water into the foam cup. Measure the temperature of the water.

3. Add an ice cube to the cup of water. Gently swirl the cup. Measure the temperature of the water as soon as the ice cube has completely melted.

4. Pour the water into the graduated cylinder and measure the volume.

Analyze and Conclude

1. Calculate Determine the mass of the ice. (*Hint:* Use the increase in the volume of water and the density of water.) Convert this mass into moles.

2. Calculate Determine the heat transferred from the water to the ice using the mass of the hot water, the specific heat of liquid water, and the change in temperature.

3. Calculate Determine ΔH_{fus} of ice (kJ/mol) by dividing the heat transferred from the water by the moles of ice melted.

4. Perform Error Analysis Compare your experimental value of ΔH_{fus} of ice with the accepted value of 6.01 kJ/mol. Account for any error.

Heats of Vaporization and Condensation

What is the relationship between molar heat of vaporization and molar heat of condensation?

A liquid that absorbs heat at its boiling point becomes a vapor. The amount of heat required to vaporize one mole of a given liquid at a constant temperature is called its **molar heat of vaporization** (ΔH_{vap}). Table 17.3 lists the molar heats of vaporization for several substances at their normal boiling points.

The molar heat of vaporization of water is 40.7 kJ/mol. This means that it takes 40.7 kJ of energy to convert 1 mol of liquid water to 1 mol of water vapor at the normal boiling point of water (100°C at 101.3 kPa).

$$H_2O(l) \longrightarrow H_2O(g) \qquad \Delta H_{vap} = 40.7 \text{ kJ/mol}$$

Diethyl ether ($C_4H_{10}O$) has a boiling point of 34.6°C and a molar heat of vaporization (ΔH_{vap}) of 26.5 kJ/mol. If liquid diethyl ether is poured into a beaker on a warm, humid day, the ether will absorb heat from the beaker walls and evaporate rapidly. If the beaker loses enough heat, the water vapor in the air may condense and freeze on the beaker walls, forming a coating of frost on the outside of the beaker.

$$C_4H_{10}O(l) \longrightarrow C_4H_{10}O(g) \qquad \Delta H_{vap} = 26.5 \text{ kJ/mol}$$

Table 17.3		
Heats of Physical Change		
Substance	ΔH_{fus} (kJ/mol)	ΔH_{vap} (kJ/mol)
Ammonia (NH_3)	5.66	23.3
Ethanol (C_2H_6O)	4.93	38.6
Hydrogen (H_2)	0.12	0.90
Methanol (CH_4O)	3.22	35.2
Oxygen (O_2)	0.44	6.82
Water (H_2O)	6.01	40.7

Figure 17.11 Changes in State
Enthalpy changes accompany changes in state. Fusion and vaporization are endothermic processes. Solidification and condensation are exothermic processes.
Interpret Diagrams *Which arrows represent processes that release heat to the surroundings?*

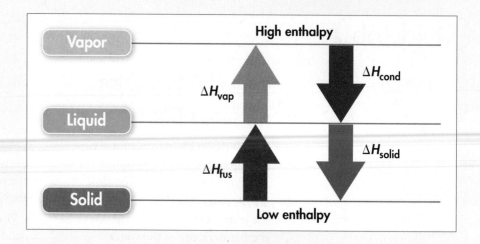

CHEMISTRY & YOU

Q: *Explain why the evaporation of sweat off your body helps to cool you off.*

Condensation is the exact opposite of vaporization. When a vapor condenses, heat is released. The **molar heat of condensation** (ΔH_{cond}) is the amount of heat released when one mole of a vapor condenses at its normal boiling point. 🔑 **The quantity of heat absorbed by a vaporizing liquid is exactly the same as the quantity of heat released when the vapor condenses; that is, $\Delta H_{vap} = -\Delta H_{cond}$.** Figure 17.11 shows the relationships between the molar heat of fusion and molar heat of solidification and between the molar heat of vaporization and molar heat of condensation.

Figure 17.12 summarizes the enthalpy changes that occur as ice is heated to a liquid and then to a vapor. You should be able to identify certain trends regarding the temperature during changes of state and the energy requirements that accompany these changes from the graph. The large values for ΔH_{vap} and ΔH_{cond} are the reason hot vapors such as steam can be very dangerous. You can receive a scalding burn from steam when the heat of condensation is released as the steam touches your skin.

$$H_2O(g) \longrightarrow H_2O(l) \qquad \Delta H_{cond} = -40.7 \text{ kJ/mol}$$

Interpret Graphs

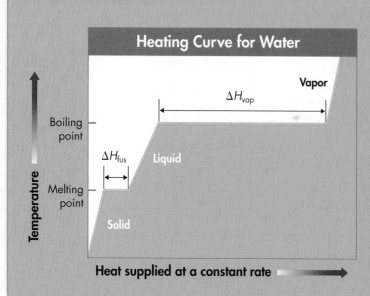

Figure 17.12 A heating curve graphically describes the enthalpy changes that take place during phase changes.

a. Identify In which region(s) of the graph is temperature constant?

b. Compare How does the amount of energy required to melt a given mass of ice compare to the energy required to vaporize the same mass of liquid water? Explain.

c. Apply Concepts Which region of the graph represents the coexistence of solid and liquid? Liquid and vapor?

Remember: The temperature of a substance remains constant during a change in state.

SampleProblem 17.6

Using the Heat of Vaporization in Phase-Change Calculations

How much heat (in kJ) is absorbed when 24.8 g $H_2O(l)$ at 100°C and 101.3 kPa is converted to $H_2O(g)$ at 100°C?

❶ Analyze List the knowns and the unknown. First, convert grams of water to moles of water. Then, find the amount of heat that is absorbed when the liquid water is converted to steam.

> **KNOWNS**
>
> Initial and final conditions are 100°C and 101.3 kPa
> mass of liquid water converted to steam = 24.8 g
> ΔH_{vap} = 40.7 kJ/mol
>
> **UNKNOWN**
>
> ΔH = ? kJ

❷ Calculate Solve for the unknown.

Start by expressing the molar mass of water as a conversion factor.

$$\frac{1 \text{ mol } H_2O(l)}{18.0 \text{ g } H_2O(l)}$$

Express ΔH_{vap} as a conversion factor.

$$\frac{40.7 \text{ kJ}}{1 \text{ mol } H_2O(l)}$$

> Use the thermochemical equation
> $H_2O(l) + 40.7 \text{ kJ} \longrightarrow H_2O(g)$

Multiply the mass of water in grams by the conversion factors.

$$\Delta H = 24.8 \text{ g } H_2O(l) \times \frac{1 \text{ mol } H_2O(l)}{18.0 \text{ g } H_2O(l)} \times \frac{40.7 \text{ kJ}}{1 \text{ mol } H_2O(l)}$$

$$= 56.1 \text{ kJ}$$

❸ Evaluate Does the result make sense? Knowing the molar mass of water is 18.0 g/mol, 24.8 g $H_2O(l)$ can be estimated to be somewhat less than 1.5 mol H_2O. The calculated enthalpy change should be a little less than 1.5 ~~mol~~ × 40 kJ/~~mol~~ = 60 kJ, and it is.

---

24. How much heat is absorbed when 63.7 g $H_2O(l)$ at 100°C and 101.3 kPa is converted to $H_2O(g)$ at 100°C? Express your answer in kJ.

25. How many kilojoules of heat are absorbed when 0.46 g of chloroethane (C_2H_5Cl, bp 12.3°C) vaporizes at its normal boiling point? The molar heat of vaporization of chloroethane is 24.7 kJ/mol.

> For Problem 25, start by writing the thermochemical equation for the vaporization of chloroethane.

Heat of Solution

What thermochemical changes can occur when a solution forms?

If you've ever used a hot pack or a cold pack, then you have felt the enthalpy changes that occur when a solute dissolves in a solvent. **During the formation of a solution, heat is either released or absorbed.** The enthalpy change caused by the dissolution of one mole of substance is the **molar heat of solution** (ΔH_{soln}). For example, when 1 mol of sodium hydroxide, $NaOH(s)$, is dissolved in water, the solution can become so hot that it steams. The heat from this process is released as the sodium ions and the hydroxide ions interact with the water. The temperature of the solution increases, releasing 44.5 kJ of heat as the molar heat of solution.

$$NaOH(s) \longrightarrow Na^+(aq) + OH^-(aq)$$
$$\Delta H_{soln} = -44.5 \text{ kJ/mol}$$

A practical application of an exothermic dissolution process is a hot pack. In a hot pack, calcium chloride, $CaCl_2(s)$, mixes with water, producing heat.

$$CaCl_2(s) \longrightarrow Ca^{2+}(aq) + 2Cl^-(aq)$$
$$\Delta H_{soln} = -82.8 \text{ kJ/mol}$$

The dissolution of ammonium nitrate, $NH_4NO_3(s)$, is an example of an endothermic process. When ammonium nitrate dissolves in water, the solution becomes so cold that frost may form on the outside of the container. The cold pack in Figure 17.13 contains solid ammonium nitrate crystals and water. Once the solute dissolves in the solvent, the pack becomes cold. In this case, the solution process absorbs energy from the surroundings.

$$NH_4NO_3(s) \longrightarrow NH_4^+(aq) + NO_3^-(aq)$$
$$\Delta H_{soln} = 25.7 \text{ kJ/mol}$$

Figure 17.13 Cold Pack
The cold pack shown has two sealed plastic bags, one inside the other. The outer bag contains ammonium nitrate crystals. The inner bag contains liquid water. When the pack is squeezed, the inner bag breaks, allowing the ammonium nitrate and water to mix.
Infer *How would you define the system and the surroundings in this process?*

Cold Therapy is no
Raynauds Syndrome, or Diabetes, withou
Supervise children during use.
...ion contacts eyes, skin or open wounds, flush
...wed, give one or two glasses of milk or water
...t poison control immediately. FOR EXTERNAL U
CONTENTS: Ammonium nitrate and water.

SampleProblem 17.7

Calculating the Enthalpy Change in Solution Formation

How much heat (in kJ) is released when 2.50 mol NaOH(s) is dissolved in water?

❶ Analyze **List the knowns and the unknown.** Use the heat of solution for the dissolution of NaOH(s) in water to solve for the amount of heat released (ΔH).

❷ Calculate **Solve for the unknown.**

> **KNOWNS**
> $\Delta H_{soln} = -44.5$ kJ/mol
> amount of NaOH(s) dissolved = 2.50 mol
>
> **UNKNOWN**
> $\Delta H = ?$ kJ

Start by expressing ΔH_{soln} as a conversion factor.

$$\frac{-44.5 \text{ kJ}}{1 \text{ mol NaOH}(s)}$$

Use the thermochemical equation
$$NaOH(s) \longrightarrow Na^+(aq) + OH^-(aq) + 44.5 \text{ kJ/mol}$$

Multiply the number of moles by the conversion factor.

$$\Delta H = 2.50 \text{ mol NaOH}(s) \times \frac{-44.5 \text{ kJ}}{1 \text{ mol NaOH}(s)} = -111 \text{ kJ}$$

❸ Evaluate **Does the result make sense?** ΔH is 2.5 times greater than ΔH_{soln}, as it should be. Also, ΔH should be negative, as the dissolution of NaOH(s) in water is exothermic.

26. How much heat (in kJ) is released when 0.677 mol NaOH(s) is dissolved in water?

27. How many moles of $NH_4NO_3(s)$ must be dissolved in water so that 88.0 kJ of heat is absorbed from the water?

ΔH_{soln} for the dissolution of $NH_4NO_3(s)$ in water is 25.7 kJ/mol.

17.3 LessonCheck

28. ⬤ **Describe** How does the molar heat of fusion of a substance compare to its molar heat of solidification?

29. ⬤ **Describe** How does the molar heat of vaporization of a substance compare to its molar heat of condensation?

30. ⬤ **Identify** What enthalpy changes occur when a solute dissolves in a solvent?

31. **Calculate** How much heat must be removed to freeze a tray of ice cubes at 0°C if the water has a mass of 225 g?

32. **Calculate** How many kilojoules of heat are required to vaporize 50.0 g of ethanol, C_2H_6O? The boiling point of ethanol is 78.3°C. Its molar heat of vaporization is 38.6 kJ/mol.

33. **Calculate** How many kilojoules of heat are released when 25.0 g of NaOH(s) is dissolved in water?

BIGIDEA MATTER AND ENERGY

34. Use what you know about hydrogen bonding to explain why water has such a large heat of vaporization.

Geothermal Energy

Deep within Earth lies a powerful source of clean, renewable energy—the heat of Earth's interior. This energy, known as geothermal energy, is contained in the molten rock (magma), hot water, and steam of Earth's subsurface. Underground pockets of hot steam or heated water can be harnessed to generate heat and electricity, which can then be used to heat, cool, and provide electrical power to buildings.

The three main ways to tap into Earth's geothermal energy supply is through direct heating systems, heat pumps, and power plants. Using direct geothermal energy involves piping hot water from hot springs on Earth's surface directly into a building's heat system. Geothermal heat pumps are systems that make use of the relatively constant temperatures near Earth's surface. In the winter, the temperature below Earth's surface is warmer than the temperature of the air. Heat pumps are used to move heat from the ground to the surface through a series of pipes containing fluid. In the summer, the temperature below Earth's surface is cooler than the temperature of the air. Therefore, heat pumps can also be used to cool buildings by drawing heat away from a building and transferring it to the ground outside. Geothermal power plants tap into hot water and steam buried deep beneath Earth's surface. Hot steam or water can then be piped or pumped under high pressures from geothermal reservoirs into generators in the power plants on the surface. These power plants provide electricity to homes and businesses.

Pros & Cons

Advantages of Using Geothermal Energy	Disadvantages of Using Geothermal Energy
✔ **Low operating costs** Once the initial cost of constructing a geothermal energy facility has been paid for, there are no additional fuel costs.	✗ **Large initial expense** The initial cost of drilling wells to reach geothermal reservoirs and installing geothermal power plants is millions of dollars.
✔ **Clean Energy** Direct geothermal heating systems, geothermal heat pumps, and geothermal power plants emit little or no greenhouse gases.	✗ **Large space requirements** Geothermal heat pumps and power plants require large expanses of land for pipes and wells.
✔ **Sustainable Energy Source** Unlike fossil fuels, heat from beneath Earth's surface is a renewable resource.	✗ **Disruptive to the environment** Deep drilling can cause small earthquakes and hot water and steam can bring contaminants to Earth's surface.

THE POWER OF STEAM This power plant in Iceland taps into a geothermal reservoir 2000 meters below the surface. The steam, which can reach 240°C, is used to generate electricity. The condensed steam (liquid water) is then directed to a lagoon, where people bathe in it for healing and wellness purposes.

NATURAL HEAT Geysers and hot springs on Earth's surface indicate the presence of subsurface heat sources. These monkeys are keeping warm in one of Japan's hot springs.

Take It Further

1. Classify Describe the direction of heat flow when a geothermal heat pump is used to heat a building. What is the system and what are the surroundings? Is this process endothermic or exothermic?

2. Calculate How much energy is absorbed or released when: 535 kg of steam at 154°C cools to 100°C, the steam condenses at 100°C, and the liquid water cools from 100°C to 37°C?

3. Compare and Contrast Compare geothermal energy to one or more other sources of energy. Assess the costs and benefits of each.

Q: *How much heat is released when a diamond changes into graphite?* Diamonds are gemstones composed of carbon. Over a time period of millions and millions of years, diamond will break down into graphite, which is another form of carbon. How then can you determine the enthalpy change for the reaction?

Key Question

🔑 How can you calculate the heat of reaction when it cannot be directly measured?

Vocabulary

- Hess's law of heat summation
- standard heat of formation

Hess's Law

🔑 **How can you calculate the heat of reaction when it cannot be directly measured?**

Sometimes it is hard to measure the enthalpy change for a reaction. The reaction might take place too slowly to measure the enthalpy change, or the reaction might be an intermediate step in a series of reactions. Fortunately, it is possible to determine a heat of reaction indirectly using Hess's law of heat summation. **Hess's law of heat summation** states that if you add two or more thermochemical equations to give a final equation, then you can also add the heats of reaction to give the final heat of reaction. 🔑 **Hess's law allows you to determine the heat of reaction indirectly by using the known heats of reaction of two or more thermochemical equations.**

Consider the conversion of diamond to graphite, discussed above.

$$C(s, \text{diamond}) \longrightarrow C(s, \text{graphite})$$

Although the enthalpy change for this reaction cannot be measured directly, you can use Hess's law to find the enthalpy change for the conversion of diamond to graphite by using the following combustion reactions and Figure 17.14:

a. $C(s, \text{graphite}) + O_2(g) \longrightarrow CO_2(g)$ $\Delta H = -393.5$ kJ
b. $C(s, \text{diamond}) + O_2(g) \longrightarrow CO_2(g)$ $\Delta H = -395.4$ kJ

Write equation **a** in reverse to give:

c. $CO_2(g) \longrightarrow C(s, \text{graphite}) + O_2(g)$ $\Delta H = 393.5$ kJ

When you write a reverse reaction, you must also change the sign of ΔH. If you add equations **b** and **c,** you get the equation for the conversion of diamond to graphite. The $CO_2(g)$ and $O_2(g)$ terms on both sides of the summed equations cancel. If you also add the values of ΔH for equations **b** and **c,** you get the heat of reaction for this conversion.

$C(s, \text{diamond}) + O_2(g) \longrightarrow \cancel{CO_2(g)}$	$\Delta H = -395.4$ kJ
$\cancel{CO_2(g)} \longrightarrow C(s, \text{graphite}) + \cancel{O_2(g)}$	$\Delta H = 393.5$ kJ
$C(s, \text{diamond}) \longrightarrow C(s, \text{graphite})$	$\Delta H = -1.9$ kJ

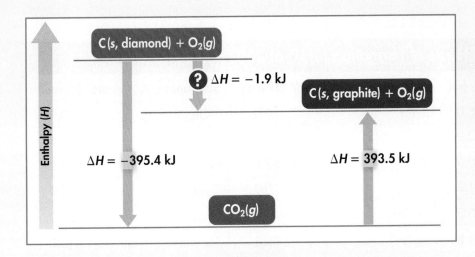

Figure 17.14 Conversion
of Diamond to Graphite
Hess's law is used to determine
the enthalpy change for the
conversion of diamond to
graphite.

Go online to see how
Hess's law is used.

Another case where Hess's law is useful is when reactions yield products in addition to the product of interest. Suppose you want to determine the enthalpy change for the formation of carbon monoxide from its elements. You can write the following equation for this reaction.

$$C(s, graphite) + \tfrac{1}{2}O_2(g) \longrightarrow CO(g) \qquad \Delta H = ?$$

Although it is easy to write the equation, carrying out the reaction in the laboratory as written is virtually impossible. Carbon dioxide is produced along with carbon monoxide. Therefore, any measured heat of reaction is related to the formation of both $CO(g)$ and $CO_2(g)$, and not $CO(g)$ alone. However, you can calculate the desired enthalpy change by using Hess's law and the following two reactions that can be carried out in the laboratory:

a. $C(s, graphite) + O_2(g) \longrightarrow CO_2(g) \qquad \Delta H = -393.5$ kJ
b. $CO(g) + \tfrac{1}{2}O_2(g) \longrightarrow CO_2(g) \qquad \Delta H = -283.0$ kJ

Writing the reverse of equation **b** yields equation **c.**

c. $CO_2(g) \longrightarrow CO(g) + \tfrac{1}{2}O_2(g) \qquad \Delta H = 283.0$ kJ

Adding equations **a** and **c** gives the expression for the formation of $CO(g)$ from its elements. The enthalpy diagram for this heat summation is shown in Figure 17.15. Notice that only $\tfrac{1}{2}O_2(g)$ cancels from each equation.

$$C(s, graphite) + O_2(g) \longrightarrow \cancel{CO_2(g)} \qquad \Delta H = -393.5 \text{ kJ}$$
$$\cancel{CO_2(g)} \longrightarrow CO(g) + \tfrac{1}{2}O_2(g) \qquad \Delta H = 283.0 \text{ kJ}$$
$$\overline{C(s, graphite) + \tfrac{1}{2}O_2(g) \longrightarrow CO(g) \qquad \Delta H = -110.5 \text{ kJ}}$$

CHEMISTRY & YOU

Q: *How can you determine
ΔH for the conversion of
diamond to graphite without
performing the reaction?*

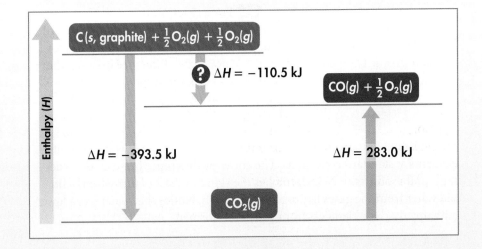

Figure 17.15 Formation of CO(*g*)
From Its Elements
Hess's law is used to determine the
enthalpy change for the formation
of CO(*g*) from its elements.
Interpret Diagrams *How
does the diagram represent
endothermic and exothermic
reactions differently?*

Table 17.4

Standard Heats of Formation (ΔH_f°) at 25°C and 101.3 kPa					
Substance	**ΔH_f° (kJ/mol)**	**Substance**	**ΔH_f° (kJ/mol)**	**Substance**	**ΔH_f° (kJ/mol)**
$Al_2O_3(s)$	−1676.0	$F_2(g)$	0.0	$NO(g)$	90.37
$Br_2(g)$	30.91	$Fe(s)$	0.0	$NO_2(g)$	33.85
$Br_2(l)$	0.0	$Fe_2O_3(s)$	−822.1	$NaCl(s)$	−411.2
$C(s, \text{diamond})$	1.9	$H_2(g)$	0.0	$O_2(g)$	0.0
$C(s, \text{graphite})$	0.0	$H_2O(g)$	−241.8	$O_3(g)$	142.0
$CH_4(g)$	−74.86	$H_2O(l)$	−285.8	$P(s, \text{white})$	0.0
$CO(g)$	−110.5	$H_2O_2(l)$	−187.8	$P(s, \text{red})$	−18.4
$CO_2(g)$	−393.5	$I_2(g)$	62.4	$S(s, \text{rhombic})$	0.0
$CaCO_3(s)$	−1207.0	$I_2(s)$	0.0	$S(s, \text{monoclinic})$	0.30
$CaO(s)$	−635.1	$N_2(g)$	0.0	$SO_2(g)$	−296.8
$Cl_2(g)$	0.0	$NH_3(g)$	−46.19	$SO_3(g)$	−395.7

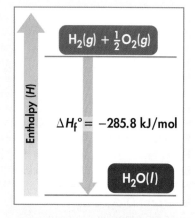

Figure 17.16 Standard Heat of Formation of Water
This enthalpy diagram shows the standard heat of formation of water.
Classify *Is the reaction endothermic or exothermic?*

Standard Heats of Formation

🔦 *How can you calculate the heat of reaction when it cannot be directly measured?*

Enthalpy changes generally depend on conditions of the process. To compare enthalpy changes, scientists specify a common set of conditions. These conditions, called the standard state, refer to the stable form of a substance at 25°C and 101.3 kPa. The **standard heat of formation** (ΔH_f°) of a compound is the change in enthalpy that accompanies the formation of one mole of a compound from its elements with all substances in their standard states. The ΔH_f° of a free element in its standard state is arbitrarily set at zero. Thus, $\Delta H_f^\circ = 0$ kJ/mol for the diatomic molecules $H_2(g)$, $N_2(g)$, $O_2(g)$, $F_2(g)$, $Cl_2(g)$, $Br_2(l)$, and $I_2(s)$. Similarly, $\Delta H_f^\circ = 0$ kJ/mol for the graphite form of carbon, $C(s, \text{graphite})$. Table 17.4 lists ΔH_f° values for some common substances.

Standard heats of formation provide an alternative to Hess's law in determining heats of reaction indirectly. 🔦 **For a reaction that occurs at standard conditions, you can calculate the heat of reaction by using standard heats of formation.** Such an enthalpy change is called the standard heat of reaction (ΔH°). The standard heat of reaction is the difference between the standard heats of formation of all the reactants and products.

$$\Delta H^\circ = \Delta H_f^\circ \text{ (products)} - \Delta H_f^\circ \text{ (reactants)}$$

Figure 17.16 is an enthalpy diagram for the formation of water from its elements at standard conditions. The enthalpy difference between the reactants and products, −285.8 kJ/mol, is the standard heat of formation of liquid water from the gases hydrogen and oxygen. Notice that water has a lower enthalpy than the elements from which it is formed.

Calculating the Standard Heat of Reaction

What is the standard heat of reaction ($\Delta H°$) for the reaction of $CO(g)$ with $O_2(g)$ to form $CO_2(g)$?

① Analyze List the knowns and the unknown. Balance the equation of the reaction of $CO(g)$ with $O_2(g)$ to form $CO_2(g)$. Then determine $\Delta H°$ using the standard heats of formation of the reactants and products.

② Calculate Solve for the unknown.

KNOWNS
(from Table 17.4)
$\Delta H_f°CO(g) = -110.5$ kJ/mol
$\Delta H_f°O_2(g) = 0$ kJ/mol (free element)
$\Delta H_f°CO_2(g) = -393.5$ kJ/mol

UNKNOWN
$\Delta H° = ?$ kJ

First, write the balanced equation.	$2CO(g) + O_2(g) \longrightarrow 2CO_2(g)$

Find and add $\Delta H_f°$ of all of the reactants.

$\Delta H_f°(\text{reactants}) = 2 \text{ mol } CO(g) \times \Delta H_f°CO(g) + 1 \text{ mol } O_2(g) \times \Delta H_f°O_2(g)$

$= 2 \text{ mol } CO(g) \times \dfrac{-110.5 \text{ kJ}}{1 \text{ mol } CO(g)} + 1 \text{ mol } O_2(g) \times \dfrac{0 \text{ kJ}}{1 \text{ mol } O_2(g)}$

$= -221.0$ kJ

> Remember to take into account the number of moles of each reactant and product.

Find $\Delta H_f°$ of the product in a similar way.

$\Delta H_f°(\text{products}) = 2 \text{ mol } CO_2(g) \times \Delta H_f°CO_2(g)$

$= 2 \text{ mol } CO_2(g) \times \dfrac{-393.5 \text{ kJ}}{1 \text{ mol } CO_2(g)}$

$= -787.0$ kJ

Calculate $\Delta H°$ for the reaction.

$\Delta H° = \Delta H_f°(\text{products}) - \Delta H_f°(\text{reactants})$

$= (-787.0 \text{ kJ}) - (-221.0 \text{ kJ})$

$= -566.0$ kJ

③ Evaluate Does the result make sense? The $\Delta H°$ is negative, so the reaction is exothermic. This outcome makes sense because combustion reactions always release heat.

35. Calculate $\Delta H°$ for the following reaction:

$$Br_2(g) \longrightarrow Br_2(l)$$

> Remember, $Br_2(l)$ is a free element.

36. What is the standard heat of reaction ($\Delta H°$) for the formation of $NO_2(g)$ from $NO(g)$ and $O_2(g)$?

> To do Problem 36, first write the balanced equation for the reaction.

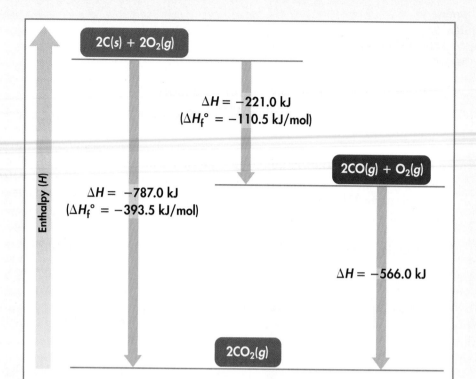

Figure 17.17 Reaction of Carbon Monoxide and Oxygen
Standard heats of formation are used to calculate the enthalpy change for the reaction of carbon monoxide and oxygen.
Explain *How does this diagram also demonstrate Hess's law?*

In the diagram:

$2C(s) + 2O_2(g)$

$\Delta H = -221.0$ kJ
$(\Delta H_f° = -110.5$ kJ/mol$)$

$2CO(g) + O_2(g)$

$\Delta H = -787.0$ kJ
$(\Delta H_f° = -393.5$ kJ/mol$)$

$\Delta H = -566.0$ kJ

$2CO_2(g)$

Enthalpy (H)

Figure 17.17 is an enthalpy diagram that shows how the standard heat of reaction was calculated in Sample Problem 17.8.

$$2CO(g) + O_2(g) \longrightarrow 2CO_2(g)$$

The standard heat of formation of the product, $CO_2(g)$, is -393.5 kJ/mol. The standard heats of formation of the reactants, $CO(g)$ and $O_2(g)$, are -110.5 kJ/mol and 0 kJ/mol, respectively. The diagram shows the difference between $\Delta H_f°$(product) and $\Delta H_f°$(reactants) after taking into account the number of moles of each.

17.4 LessonCheck

37. Describe What are two ways the heat of reaction can be determined when it cannot be directly measured?

38. Calculate What is the enthalpy change (ΔH) in kJ for the following reaction?

$$2Al(s) + Fe_2O_3(s) \longrightarrow 2Fe(s) + Al_2O_3(s)$$

Use the enthalpy changes for the combustion of aluminum and iron:

$2Al(s) + \frac{3}{2}O_2(g) \longrightarrow Al_2O_3(s)$ $\Delta H = -1676.0$ kJ
$2Fe(s) + \frac{3}{2}O_2(g) \longrightarrow Fe_2O_3(s)$ $\Delta H = -822.1$ kJ

39. Explain How can you calculate the standard heat of reaction?

40. Calculate What is the standard heat of reaction ($\Delta H°$) for the decomposition of hydrogen peroxide?

$$2H_2O_2(l) \longrightarrow 2H_2O(l) + O_2(g)$$

BIGIDEA MATTER AND ENERGY

41. Use Hess's law and two thermochemical equations on page R34 to calculate ΔH for the following reaction:

$$2H_2O(g) + CH_4(g) \longrightarrow CO_2(g) + 4H_2(g)$$

Small-Scale Lab

Heat of Combustion of a Candle

Probe or sensor version of this lab is available in the *Probeware Lab Manual*.

Purpose

To observe a burning candle and calculate the heat associated with the combustion reaction

Materials

- ruler • candle • aluminum foil
- balance • safety matches

Procedure

1. Measure and record the length of a candle in centimeters.

2. Place the candle on a small piece of aluminum foil and measure the mass of the foil-candle system.

3. Note the time as you light the candle. Let the candle burn for about five minutes. **CAUTION** *Keep clothing away from the flame.* While you wait, begin answering the Analyze and Conclude questions.

4. Extinguish the candle and record the time.

5. Measure the mass of the foil-candle system again. **DO NOT** try to measure the mass while the candle is burning.

Analyze and Conclude

1. Observe While the candle is burning, draw a picture of what you see.

2. Observe Examine the flame closely. Is it the wax or the wick that burns?

3. Infer If you said the wax, how does the wax burn without touching the flame? If you said the wick, what is the function of the wax?

4. Analyze Data If you could measure the temperature near the flame, you would find that the air is much hotter above the flame than it is beside it. Why?

5. Draw Conclusions How much length and mass did the candle lose? Are these data more consistent with the wax or the wick burning?

6. Infer Keeping in mind that *wick* is also a verb, explain how a candle works.

7. Describe The formula for candle wax can be approximated as $C_{20}H_{42}$. Write a balanced equation for the complete combustion of candle wax.

8. Calculate Determine the number of moles of candle wax burned in the experiment.

9. Calculate What is the heat of combustion of candle wax in kJ/mol? The standard heat of formation of candle wax ($C_{20}H_{42}$) is −2230 kJ/mol. The standard heats of formation of carbon dioxide gas and liquid water are −394 kJ/mol and −286 kJ/mol, respectively.

10. Calculate Determine the amount of heat (in kJ) released in your reaction. (*Hint:* Multiply the number of moles of candle wax burned in the experiment by the heat of combustion of candle wax.)

You're the Chemist

1. Design an Experiment Design an experiment to show that the candle wax does not burn with complete combustion.

2. Design an Experiment Design an experiment to show that water is a product of the combustion of a candle.

17 Study Guide

BIGIDEA MATTER AND ENERGY

During a chemical or physical process, the energy of the universe is conserved. If energy is absorbed by the system in a chemical or physical process, the same amount of energy is released by the surroundings. Conversely, if energy is released by the system, the same amount of energy is absorbed by the surroundings. The heat of reaction or process can be determined experimentally through calorimetry. The heat of reaction can also be calculated by using the known heats of reaction of two or more thermochemical equations or by using standard heats of formation.

17.1 The Flow of Energy

🔑 Energy changes occur as either heat transfer or work, or a combination of both.

🔑 During any chemical or physical process, the energy of the universe remains unchanged.

🔑 The heat capacity of an object depends on both its mass and its chemical composition.

- thermochemistry (556)
- chemical potential energy (556) • heat (556)
- system (557) • surroundings (557)
- law of conservation of energy (557)
- endothermic process (557)
- exothermic process (557)
- heat capacity (559) • specific heat (559)

Key Equation

$$C = \frac{q}{m \times \Delta T}$$

17.2 Measuring and Expressing Enthalpy Changes

🔑 The value of ΔH of a reaction can be determined by measuring the heat flow of the reaction at constant pressure.

🔑 In a chemical equation, the enthalpy change for the reaction can be written as either a reactant or a product.

- calorimetry (562)
- calorimeter (562)
- enthalpy (562)
- thermochemical equation (565)
- heat of reaction (565)
- heat of combustion (568)

Key Equation

$$q_{sys} = \Delta H = -q_{surr} = -m \times C \times \Delta T$$

17.3 Heat in Changes of State

🔑 The quantity of heat absorbed by a melting solid is exactly the same as the quantity of heat released when the liquid solidifies; that is, $\Delta H_{fus} = -\Delta H_{solid}$.

🔑 The quantity of heat absorbed by a vaporizing liquid is exactly the same as the quantity of heat released when the vapor condenses; that is, $\Delta H_{vap} = -\Delta H_{cond}$.

🔑 During the formation of a solution, heat is either released or absorbed.

- molar heat of fusion (569)
- molar heat of solidification (569)
- molar heat of vaporization (571)
- molar heat of condensation (572)
- molar heat of solution (574)

17.4 Calculating Heats of Reaction

🔑 Hess's law allows you to determine the heat of reaction indirectly by using the known heats of reaction of two or more thermochemical equations.

🔑 For a reaction that occurs at standard conditions, you can calculate the heat of reaction by using standard heats of formation.

- Hess's law of heat summation (578)
- standard heat of formation (580)

Key Equation

$$\Delta H° = \Delta H_f°(products) - \Delta H_f°(reactants)$$

Math Tune-Up: Calculating Enthalpy Changes

Problem	❶ Analyze	❷ Calculate	❸ Evaluate
When 75.0 mL of water containing 0.100 mol HCl at 21.0°C is added to 75.0 mL of water containing 0.100 mol NaOH at 21.0°C in a foam cup calorimeter, the temperature of the solution increases to 29.6°C. Calculate the enthalpy change (in kJ) during this reaction.	Knowns: $C_{water} = 4.18$ J/(g·°C) $V_{final} = V_{HCl} + V_{NaOH}$ $\quad = 75.0$ mL $+ 75.0$ mL $\quad = 150.0$ mL $\Delta T = T_f - T_i$ $\quad = 29.6°C - 21.0°C$ $\quad = 8.6°C$ $density_{solution} = 1.00$ g/mL Unknown: $\Delta H = ?$ kJ Use $\Delta H = -q_{surr}$ $\quad = -m \times C \times \Delta T$	Calculate the mass of water. $m_{water} = 150.0 \text{ mL} \times \dfrac{1.00 \text{ g}}{1 \text{ mL}}$ $\quad = 150.0$ g Use the values for m_{water}, C_{water}, and ΔT to calculate ΔH. $\Delta H = -(150.0 \text{ g})(4.18 \text{ J/(g·°C)})$ $\quad\quad \times (8.6°C)$ $\quad = -5400$ J $\Delta H = -5.4$ kJ	About 4 J of heat raises the temperature of 1 g of water 1°C, so 600 J of heat is required to raise the temperature of 150 g of water 1°C. To heat 150 g of water 9°C requires about 5400 J, or 5.4 kJ.

Note: For reactions in aqueous solutions, you can assume that the densities of the solutions are 1.00 g/mL.

Problem	❶ Analyze	❷ Calculate	❸ Evaluate
How much heat is absorbed when 54.9 g $H_2O(l)$ at 100°C and 101.3 kPa is converted to $H_2O(g)$ at 100°C?	Knowns: Initial and final conditions are 100°C and 101.3 kPa mass of liquid water converted to steam = 54.9 g $\Delta H_{vap} = 40.7$ kJ/mol Unknown: $\Delta H = ?$ kJ Refer to the thermochemical equation $H_2O(l) + 40.7$ kJ $\longrightarrow$ $H_2O(g)$	The required conversion factors come from the molar mass of water and ΔH_{vap}. $\dfrac{1 \text{ mol } H_2O(l)}{18.0 \text{ g } H_2O(l)}$ and $\dfrac{40.7 \text{ kJ}}{1 \text{ mol } H_2O(l)}$ Multiply the mass of water by the conversion factors. $\Delta H = 54.9 \text{ g } H_2O(l) \times \dfrac{1 \text{ mol } H_2O(l)}{18.0 \text{ g } H_2O(l)}$ $\quad\quad \times \dfrac{40.7 \text{ kJ}}{1 \text{ mol } H_2O(l)}$ $\Delta H = 124$ kJ	Knowing the molar mass of water is 18.0 g/mol, 54.9 g $H_2O(l)$ is about 3 mol H_2O. The calculated enthalpy change should be about 3 mol $\times$ 40 kJ/mol $= 120$ kJ, and it is.

Problem	❶ Analyze	❷ Calculate	❸ Evaluate
What is the standard heat of reaction ($\Delta H°$) for the reaction of $SO_2(g)$ with $O_2(g)$ to form $SO_3(g)$?	Knowns: (from Table 17.4) $\Delta H_f°SO_2(g) = -296.8$ kJ/mol $\Delta H_f°O_2(g) = 0$ kJ/mol $\Delta H_f°SO_3(g) = -395.7$ kJ/mol Unknown: $\Delta H° = ?$ kJ Use the standard heats of formation for the reactants and products to calculate $\Delta H°$. $\Delta H° = \Delta H_f°(\text{products}) -$ $\quad\quad \Delta H_f°(\text{reactants})$	Write the balanced equation. $2SO_2(g) + O_2(g) \longrightarrow 2SO_3(g)$ Find $\Delta H_f°$ of the reactants. $\Delta H_f°(\text{reactants}) = 2 \text{ mol } SO_2(g) \times$ $\dfrac{-296.8 \text{ kJ}}{1 \text{ mol } SO_2(g)} + 0 \text{ kJ} = -593.6$ kJ Find $\Delta H_f°$ of the product. $\Delta H_f°(\text{product}) = 2 \text{ mol } SO_3(g) \times$ $\dfrac{-395.7 \text{ kJ}}{1 \text{ mol } SO_3(g)} = -791.4$ kJ Calculate $\Delta H°$ for the reaction. $\Delta H° = (-791.4 \text{ kJ}) - (-593.6 \text{ kJ})$ $\Delta H° = -197.8$ kJ	The $\Delta H°$ is negative, so the reaction is exothermic. This makes sense because combustion reactions always release heat.

Remember: The $\Delta H_f°$ of a free element in its standard state is 0.

Lesson by Lesson

17.1 The Flow of Energy

42. Define *chemical potential energy.*

43. What always happens when two objects of different temperatures come in contact? Give an example from your own experience.

44. Why do you think it is important to define the system and the surroundings?

45. Explain in your own words the law of conservation of energy.

46. How do endothermic processes differ from exothermic processes?

★ 47. Two substances in a glass beaker chemically react, and the beaker becomes too hot to touch.
   a. Is the reaction endothermic or exothermic?
   b. If the two substances are defined as the system, what constitutes the surroundings?

★48. Classify these processes as endothermic or exothermic.
   a. condensing steam
   b. evaporating alcohol
   c. burning alcohol
   d. baking a potato

49. Describe the sign convention that is used when describing heat flow in a system.

50. What is the relationship between a calorie and a Calorie?

★ 51. Make the following conversions.
   a. 8.50×10^2 cal to Calories
   b. 444 cal to joules
   c. 1.8 kJ to joules
   d. 4.5×10^{-1} kJ to calories

52. What factors determine the heat capacity of an object?

★53. How much heat is required to raise the temperature of 400.0 g of silver 45°C?

17.2 Measuring and Expressing Enthalpy Changes

54. Calorimetry is based on what basic concepts?

55. What is the function of a calorimeter?

56. What is the property that describes heat change at constant pressure?

57. What device would you use to measure the heat released at constant volume?

58. What information is given in a thermochemical equation?

★ 59. The burning of magnesium is a highly exothermic reaction.

$$2Mg(s) + O_2(g) \longrightarrow 2MgO(s) + 1204 \text{ kJ}$$

How many kilojoules of heat are released when 0.75 mol of Mg burn in an excess of O_2?

60. Give the standard conditions for heat of combustion.

17.3 Heat in Changes of State

61. Explain why ice melts at 0°C without an increase of temperature, even though heat flows from the surroundings to the system (the ice).

★62. Calculate the quantity of heat gained or lost in the following changes:
   a. 3.50 mol of water freezes at 0°C
   b. 0.44 mol of steam condenses at 100°C
   c. 1.25 mol $NaOH(s)$ dissolves in water
   d. 0.15 mol $C_2H_6O(l)$ vaporizes at 78.3°C

63. Sodium ethanoate dissolves readily in water according to the following equation:

$$NaC_2H_3O_2(s) \longrightarrow NaC_2H_3O_2(aq)$$

$$\Delta H = -17.3 \text{ kJ/mol}$$

Would this process increase or decrease the temperature of the water?

17.4 Calculating Heats of Reaction

64. Explain Hess's law of heat summation.

★65. A considerable amount of heat is required for the decomposition of aluminum oxide.

$$2Al_2O_3(s) \longrightarrow 4Al(s) + 3O_2(g)$$

$$\Delta H = 3352 \text{ kJ}$$

   a. What is the enthalpy change for the formation of 1 mol of aluminum oxide from its elements?
   b. Is the reaction endothermic or exothermic?

*66. Calculate the enthalpy change for the formation of lead(IV) chloride by the reaction of lead(II) chloride with chlorine.

$$PbCl_2(s) + Cl_2(g) \longrightarrow PbCl_4(l)$$

$$\Delta H = ?$$

Use the following thermochemical equations:

$$Pb(s) + 2Cl_2(g) \longrightarrow PbCl_4(l)$$

$$\Delta H = -329.2 \text{ kJ}$$

$$Pb(s) + Cl_2(g) \longrightarrow PbCl_2(s)$$

$$\Delta H = -359.4 \text{ kJ}$$

67. What is the standard heat of formation of a compound?

68. What is the standard heat of formation of a free element in its standard state?

Understand Concepts

69. How many kilojoules of heat are absorbed when 1.00 L of water is heated from 18°C to 85°C?

*70. Equal masses of two substances absorb the same amount of heat. The temperature of substance A increases twice as much as the temperature of substance B. Which substance has the higher specific heat? Explain.

71. Identify each enthalpy change by name and classify each change as endothermic or exothermic.
 a. 1 mol $C_3H_8(l) \longrightarrow$ 1 mol $C_3H_8(g)$
 b. 1 mol $Hg(l) \longrightarrow$ 1 mol $Hg(s)$
 c. 1 mol $NH_3(g) \longrightarrow$ 1 mol $NH_3(l)$
 d. 1 mol $NaCl(s) + 3.88$ kJ $\longrightarrow$
 1 mol $NaCl(aq)$
 e. 1 mol $NaCl(s) \longrightarrow$ 1 mol $NaCl(l)$

72. Name at least three sources of error in experiments that use foam cups as calorimeters.

73. Calculate the enthalpy change in calories when 45.2 g of steam at 100°C condenses to water at the same temperature. What is the enthalpy change in joules?

*74. A 1.55-g piece of stainless steel absorbs 141 J of heat when its temperature increases by 178°C. What is the specific heat of the stainless steel?

75. With one exception, the standard heats of formation of $Na(s)$, $O_2(g)$, $Br_2(l)$, $CO(g)$, $Fe(s)$, and $He(g)$ are identical. What is the exception?

*76. Calculate the change in enthalpy (in kJ) for the following reactions using standard heats of formation (ΔH_f°):
 a. $CH_4(g) + \frac{3}{2}O_2(g) \longrightarrow CO(g) + 2H_2O(l)$
 b. $2CO(g) + O_2(g) \longrightarrow 2CO_2(g)$

77. The amounts of heat required to change different quantities of carbon tetrachloride, $CCl_4(l)$, into vapor are given in the table.

Mass of CCl₄	Heat	
(g)	(J)	(cal)
2.90	652	156
7.50	1689	404
17.0	3825	915
26.2	5894	1410
39.8	8945	2140
51.0	11453	2740

 a. Graph the data, using heat as the dependent variable.
 b. What is the slope of the line?
 c. The heat of vaporization of $CCl_4(l)$ is 53.8 cal/g. How does this value compare with the slope of the line?

*78. Find the enthalpy change for the formation of phosphorus pentachloride from its elements.

$$2P(s) + 5Cl_2(g) \longrightarrow 2PCl_5(s)$$

Use the following thermochemical equations:

$$PCl_5(s) \longrightarrow PCl_3(g) + Cl_2(g)$$

$$\Delta H = 156.5 \text{ kJ}$$

$$2P(s) + 3Cl_2(g) \longrightarrow 2PCl_3(g)$$

$$\Delta H = -574.0 \text{ kJ}$$

79. Use standard heats of formation (ΔH_f°) to calculate the change in enthalpy for these reactions.
 a. $2C(s, \text{graphite}) + O_2(g) \longrightarrow 2CO(g)$
 b. $2H_2O_2(l) \longrightarrow 2H_2O(l) + O_2(g)$
 c. $4NH_3(g) + 5O_2(g) \longrightarrow$
 $4NO(g) + 6H_2O(g)$
 d. $CaCO_3(s) \longrightarrow CaO(s) + CO_2(g)$

80. The molar heat of vaporization of ethanol, $C_2H_6O(l)$, is 38.6 kJ/mol. Calculate the heat required to vaporize 25.0 g of ethanol at its boiling point.

*81. An orange contains 106 Calories. What mass of water could this same amount of energy raise from 25.0°C to the boiling point?

82. The combustion of ethene (C_2H_4) is an exothermic reaction.

$$C_2H_4(g) + 3O_2(g) \longrightarrow 2CO_2(g) + 2H_2O(l)$$

$$\Delta H = -1.40 \times 10^3 \text{ kJ}$$

Calculate the amount of heat liberated when 4.79 g C_2H_4 reacts with excess oxygen.

83. Calculate the enthalpy change (ΔH) for the formation of nitrogen monoxide from its elements.

$$N_2(g) + O_2(g) \longrightarrow 2NO(g)$$

Use the following thermochemical equations:

$$4NH_3(g) + 3O_2(g) \longrightarrow 2N_2(g) + 6H_2O(l)$$

$$\Delta H = -1.53 \times 10^3 \text{ kJ}$$

$$4NH_3(g) + 5O_2(g) \longrightarrow 4NO(g) + 6H_2O(l)$$

$$\Delta H = -1.17 \times 10^3 \text{ kJ}$$

84. How much heat must be removed from a 45.0-g sample of liquid naphthalene ($C_{10}H_8$) at its freezing point to bring about solidification? The heat of fusion of naphthalene is 19.1 kJ/mol.

*85. If 3.20 kcal of heat is added to 1.00 kg of ice at 0°C, how much liquid water at 0°C is produced, and how much ice remains?

Think Critically

86. Relate Cause and Effect Your fingers quickly begin to feel cold when you touch an ice cube. What important thermochemical principle does this change illustrate?

87. Calculate You place a bottle containing 2.0 L of mineral water at 25°C into a refrigerator to cool to 7°C.

a. How many kJ of heat are lost by the water?
b. How many kJ of heat are absorbed by the refrigerator?
c. What assumptions did you make in your calculations?

88. Evaluate Consider the statement, "the more negative the value of $\Delta H_f°$, the more stable the compound." Is this statement true or false? Explain.

*89. Calculate When 1.000 mol of $N_2(g)$ reacts completely with 3.000 mol of $H_2(g)$, 2.000 mol of $NH_3(g)$ and 92.38 kJ of heat are produced.

$$N_2(g) + 3H_2(g) \longrightarrow 2NH_3(g) + 92.38 \text{ kJ}$$

Use this thermochemical equation to calculate ΔH for the following reactions:

a. $2N_2(g) + 6H_2(g) \longrightarrow 4NH_3(g)$
b. $\frac{3}{2}N_2(g) + \frac{9}{2}H_2(g) \longrightarrow 3NH_3(g)$
c. $\frac{1}{2}N_2(g) + \frac{3}{2}H_2(g) \longrightarrow NH_3(g)$

90. Explain Why is fusion an endothermic process, but freezing is an exothermic process?

*91. Calculate An ice cube with a mass of 40.0 g melts in water originally at 25.0°C.

a. How much heat does the ice cube absorb from the water when it melts? Report your answer in calories, kilocalories, and joules.
b. Calculate the number of grams of water that can be cooled to 0°C by the melting ice cube.

92. Evaluate and Revise Evaluate this statement: "The energy content of a substance is higher in the liquid phase than in the vapor phase at the same temperature." If the statement is incorrect, restate it so it is correct.

93. Apply Concepts Using the following equations,

$$Ca(s) + 2C(s) \longrightarrow CaC_2(s)$$

$$\Delta H = -62.8 \text{ kJ}$$

$$CO_2(g) \longrightarrow C(s) + O_2(g)$$

$$\Delta H = 393.5 \text{ kJ}$$

$$CaCO_3(s) + CO_2(g) \longrightarrow CaC_2(s) + \tfrac{5}{2}O_2(g)$$

$$\Delta H = 1538 \text{ kJ}$$

determine the heat of reaction (in kJ) for

$$Ca(s) + C(s) + \tfrac{3}{2}O_2(g) \longrightarrow CaCO_3(s)$$

*94. Calculate The sugar glucose ($C_6H_{12}O_6$) is an important nutrient for living organisms to meet their energy needs. The standard heat of formation ($\Delta H_f°$) of glucose is −1260 kJ/mol. Calculate how much heat (in kJ/mol) is released at standard conditions if 1 mol of glucose undergoes the following reaction:

$$C_6H_{12}O_6(s) + 6O_2(g) \longrightarrow$$
$$6CO_2(g) + 6H_2O(l)$$

95. Calculate Ethane, $C_2H_6(g)$, can be formed by the reaction of ethene, $C_2H_4(g)$, with hydrogen gas.

$$C_2H_4(g) + H_2(g) \longrightarrow C_2H_6(g)$$

Use the heats of combustion for the following reactions to calculate the heat change for the formation of ethane from ethene and hydrogen.

$$2H_2(g) + O_2(g) \longrightarrow 2H_2O(l)$$
$$\Delta H = -5.72 \times 10^2 \text{ kJ}$$

$$C_2H_4(g) + 3O_2(g) \longrightarrow 2CO_2(g) + 2H_2O(l)$$
$$\Delta H = -1.401 \times 10^3 \text{ kJ}$$

$$2C_2H_6(g) + 7O_2(g) \longrightarrow 4CO_2(g) + 6H_2O(l)$$
$$\Delta H = -3.100 \times 10^3 \text{ kJ}$$

96. Infer An ice cube at 0°C was dropped into 30.0 g of water in a cup at 45.0°C. At the instant that all of the ice was melted, the temperature of the water in the cup was 19.5°C. What was the mass of the ice cube?

⋆ 97. Calculate A 41.0-g piece of glass at 95°C is placed in 175 g of water at 21°C in an insulated container. They are allowed to come to the same temperature. What is the final temperature of the glass-water mixture? The specific heat of glass is 2.1 cal/(g·°C).

98. Interpret Graphs The molar heat of vaporization of water at various temperatures is given in the graph. Estimate the amount of heat required to convert 1 L of water to steam on the summit of Mount Everest (8850 m), where the boiling temperature of water is 70°C.

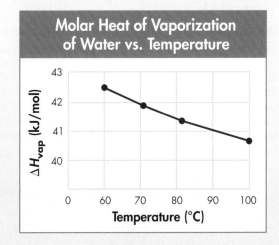

Molar Heat of Vaporization of Water vs. Temperature

Write About Science

99. Explain Use the concept of heat capacity to explain why on a sunny day, the concrete deck around an outdoor swimming pool becomes hot, while the water stays cool.

100. Compare Why is a burn from steam potentially far more serious than a burn from very hot water?

CHEMYSTERY

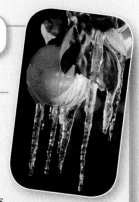

Fighting Frost

If the temperature of the branches, leaves, and fruit of a citrus tree falls below 0°C, severe damage can occur. When ice crystals form in the plant cells, water becomes unavailable to the plant tissues. This lack of fluids can kill a young tree. The fruit itself can also be damaged by frost. The juice vesicles inside the fruit rupture as ice crystals form within them. These ruptured vesicles cause the fruit to lose water and dry out. Upon an impending frost, if the fruit is not ready for harvest, citrus growers must find a way to protect their precious crops.

Spraying the trees with water throughout the duration of a frost is an effective way to prevent the trees and fruit from freezing. The water freezes directly on the branches, leaves, and fruit. Freezing is an exothermic process. As the water freezes, it releases heat and prevents the plant cells from reaching freezing temperatures.

101. Apply Concepts Identify the system and the surroundings when water freezes on a citrus fruit.

⋆102. Predict Evaporation of the water on a plant surface can occur under dry and windy conditions. How would this affect the citrus tree and fruit?

103. Connect to the BIGIDEA Explain, in terms of the law of conservation of energy, why the freezing of water on a citrus tree can cause the temperature of the tree to increase.

104. Explain the difference between an independent variable and a dependent variable.

105. Write the correct chemical symbol for each element.

    a. chromium
    b. copper
    c. carbon
    d. calcium
    e. cesium

∗106. Express the results of the following calculations with the correct number of significant figures.

    a. $6.723 \text{ m} \times 1.04 \text{ m}$
    b. $8.934 \text{ g} + 0.2005 \text{ g} + 1.55 \text{ g}$
    c. $864 \text{ m} \div 2.4 \text{ s}$
    d. $9.258°C - 4.82°C$

107. List three kinds of subatomic particles in an atom. Describe each kind in terms of charge, relative mass, and location with respect to the nucleus.

∗108. Calculate the wavelength of a radio wave with a frequency of $93.1 \times 10^6 \text{ s}^{-1}$.

109. List the following atoms in order of increasing atomic radius: phosphorus, germanium, arsenic.

110. How many chloride ions would be required to react with these cations to make an electrically neutral particle?

    a. strontium cation
    b. calcium cation
    c. aluminum cation
    d. lithium cation

111. How does a polar covalent bond differ from a nonpolar covalent bond? Which type of bond is found in molecular oxygen (O_2)? In carbon monoxide (CO)?

∗112. Write formulas for the following compounds:

    a. potassium nitride
    b. aluminum sulfide
    c. calcium nitrate
    d. calcium sulfate

∗113. How many hydrogen molecules are in 44.8 L $H_2(g)$ at STP?

114. Write the net ionic equation for the reaction of aqueous solutions of sodium chloride and silver acetate.

∗115. When lightning flashes, nitrogen and oxygen combine to form nitrogen monoxide. The nitrogen monoxide reacts with oxygen to form nitrogen dioxide. Write equations for these two reactions.

116. How many grams of oxygen are formed by the decomposition of 25.0 g of hydrogen peroxide?

$$2H_2O_2(l) \longrightarrow 2H_2O(l) + O_2(g)$$

117. What fraction of the average kinetic energy of hydrogen gas at 100 K does hydrogen gas have at 40 K?

∗118. A gas has a volume of 8.57 L at 273 K. What will be the volume at 355 K if its pressure does not change?

119. What property of water makes it impossible to find pure water in nature?

120. Do colloids, suspensions, or solutions contain the smallest particles? Which contain the largest particles?

If You Have Trouble With . . .

Question	104	105	106	107	108	109	110	111	112	113	114	115	116	117	118	119	120
See Chapter	1	2	3	4	5	6	7	8	9	10	11	11	12	13	14	15	15

Standardized Test Prep

Select the choice that best answers each question or completes each statement.

1. The ΔH_{fus} of ethanol (C_2H_6O) is 4.93 kJ/mol. How many kilojoules are required to melt 24.5 g of ethanol at its freezing point?
   - **(A)** 2.63 kJ
   - **(B)** 4.97 kJ
   - **(C)** 9.27 kJ
   - **(D)** 263 kJ

2. How much heat, in kilojoules, must be added to 178 g of liquid water to increase the temperature of the water by 5.0°C ?
   - **(A)** 890 kJ
   - **(B)** 36 kJ
   - **(C)** 3.7 kJ
   - **(D)** 0.093 kJ

3. The standard heat of formation of a free element in its standard state is always
   - **(A)** zero.
   - **(B)** positive.
   - **(C)** negative.
   - **(D)** higher for solids than for gases.

4. If ΔH for the reaction $2HgO(s) \longrightarrow 2Hg(l) + O_2(g)$ is 181.66 kJ, then ΔH for the reaction $Hg(l) + \frac{1}{2}O_2(g) \longrightarrow HgO(s)$ is
   - **(A)** 90.83 kJ.
   - **(B)** 181.66 kJ.
   - **(C)** −90.83 kJ.
   - **(D)** −181.66 kJ.

5. The specific heat capacity of ethanol is ten times larger than the specific heat capacity of silver. A hot bar of silver with a mass of 55 g is dropped into an equal mass of cool alcohol. If the temperature of the silver bar drops 45°C, the temperature of the alcohol
   - **(A)** increases 45°C.
   - **(B)** decreases 4.5°C.
   - **(C)** increases 4.5°C.
   - **(D)** decreases 45°C.

6. Hydrogen gas and fluorine gas react to form hydrogen fluoride, HF. Calculate the enthalpy change (in kJ) for the conversion of 15.0 g of $H_2(g)$ to $HF(g)$ at constant pressure.

$$H_2(g) + F_2(g) \longrightarrow 2HF(g)$$
$$\Delta H = -536 \text{ kJ}$$

Use the graph and table to answer Questions 7–10. Assume 1.00 mol of each substance.

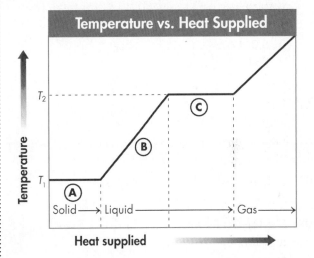

Substance	Freezing point (K)	ΔH_{fus} (kJ/mol)	Boiling point (K)	ΔH_{vap} (kJ/mol)
Ammonia	195.3	5.66	239.7	23.3
Benzene	278.7	9.87	353.3	30.8
Methanol	175.5	3.22	337.2	35.2
Neon	24.5	0.33	27.1	1.76

7. Calculate heat absorbed in region A for neon.

8. Calculate heat absorbed in region C for ammonia.

9. Calculate heat absorbed in regions B and C for methanol. [specific heat = 2.53 J/(g·°C)]

10. Calculate heat absorbed in regions A, B, and C for benzene. [specific heat = 1.74 J/(g·°C)]

If You Have Trouble With . . .

Question	1	2	3	4	5	6	7	8	9	10
See Lesson	17.3	17.1	17.4	17.4	17.1	17.2	17.3	17.3	17.3	17.3

18

Reaction Rates and Equilibrium

If the rate at which vehicles enter the city equals the rate at which vehicles exit the city, the number of vehicles in the city is constant. This situation represents a system in a state of balance. Similarly, chemical reactions can also reach a state of balance.

INSIDE:

PearsonChem.com

BIGIDEAS

- ## REACTIONS
- ## MATTER AND ENERGY

Essential Questions:

1. *How can the rate of a chemical reaction be controlled?*
2. *What is the role of energy in chemical reactions?*
3. *Why do some reactions occur naturally, and others do not?*

CHEMYSTERY

Explosive Sugar

At a sugar refinery, sugar is processed until it is pure enough to sell to consumers. Conveyor belts connect large storage silos to the packaging warehouse. In February 2008, workers at a refinery in Georgia heard a small explosion. The sound came from the location where the conveyor belts entered the warehouse.

Five minutes later, a much larger explosion occurred, which destroyed the warehouse. The fire spread to the storage silos. Thirteen workers died, and dozens more were injured. It took four days for 232 firefighters to put out the fire in the warehouse. The fire in the silos took a few days longer to extinguish.

How did the first small explosion lead to the second, more destructive explosion?

▶ Connect to the **BIG**IDEA As you read about reaction rates, think about what could cause an explosion at a sugar refinery.

NATIONAL SCIENCE EDUCATION STANDARDS

A-1, A-2, B-2, B-3, B-5, B-6, E-2, G-1

18.1 Rates of Reaction

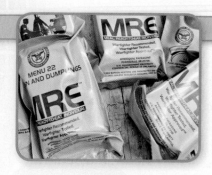

Q: *How can rusting be used to cook a meal?* Sometimes a soldier or hiker wants a hot meal but has no place to cook it. Normally, rusting takes place at such a slow rate that the heat released could not be used to cook a meal. However, there are products that use the rusting of an iron-magnesium alloy to heat packaged food. These products are known as Meals Ready to Eat, or MREs for short.

Key Questions

⚷ How is the rate of a chemical reaction expressed?

⚷ What four factors influence the rate of a chemical reaction?

Vocabulary

- rate
- collision theory
- activation energy
- activated complex
- inhibitor

Describing Reaction Rates

⚷ **How is the rate of a chemical reaction expressed?**

When you strike a match, it erupts into flame almost instantly and burns quickly. Other reactions occur more slowly. For example, millions of years were required for plants buried beneath Earth's surface to be converted to coal. These examples show that the speed of chemical reactions can vary from very fast to extremely slow.

The concept of speed is a familiar one. In a race, speed determines the winner. The swimmers in Figure 18.1 are competing in a 100-meter race. (The pool is 25 meters long, so they must swim four lengths of the pool to finish the race.) A world-class swimmer might finish the race in 54.5 seconds. His average speed can be calculated by using the following equation:

$$\text{Average speed (m/s)} = \frac{\text{Distance (m)}}{\text{Time (s)}}$$

The swimmer's average speed, which is expressed in meters per second, is 100 m/54.5 s = 1.83 m/s. A slower swimmer might take 60.0 seconds to cover the same distance. He swims at an average speed of 1.67 m/s. Both 1.83 m/s and 1.67 m/s express rates of travel.

Figure 18.1 Speed
Speed is a change in distance over a given interval of time. A swimmer's average speed can be expressed in units of m/s.

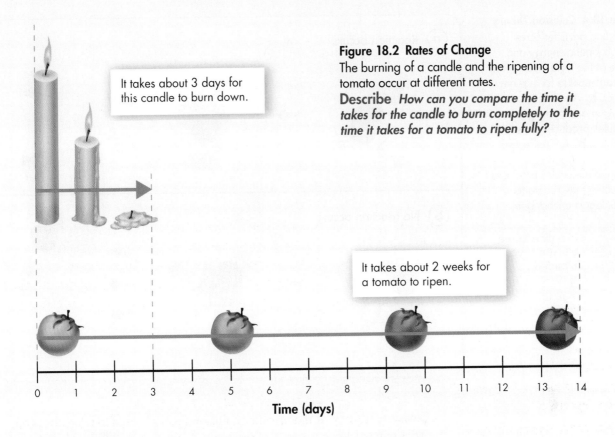

Figure 18.2 Rates of Change
The burning of a candle and the ripening of a tomato occur at different rates.
Describe *How can you compare the time it takes for the candle to burn completely to the time it takes for a tomato to ripen fully?*

It takes about 3 days for this candle to burn down.

It takes about 2 weeks for a tomato to ripen.

Time (days)

Rates of Change Speed is an example of a rate. A **rate** is a measure of how much something changes within a specified amount of time. The interval of time can range from less than a second to centuries. Figure 18.2 compares the rate of two changes—the burning of a candle and the ripening of a tomato.

🔑 **In chemistry, the rate of a chemical reaction, or the reaction rate, is usually expressed as the change in the amount of reactant or product per unit time.** The amount of a reactant is usually expressed in moles. For example, if one half of a 1-mole piece of iron turns to rust in one year, the rate at which iron rusts might be expressed as 0.5 mol/yr. This number is an average rate. Figure 18.3 illustrates the progress of a typical reaction. Over time, the amount of reactant decreases and the amount of product increases.

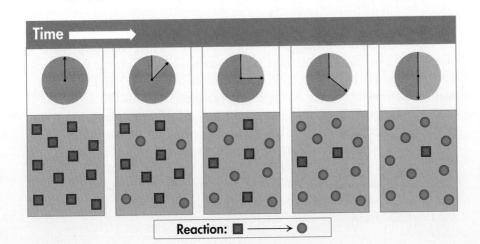

Reaction: ■ ⟶ ●

Figure 18.3 Reaction Progress
During a reaction, reactants are converted into products. The red squares represent the reactants. The blue circles represent the products. Assume that each box represents the same time interval.
Interpret Diagrams *Is the rate of conversion of reactant to product constant throughout the reaction? How can you tell?*

Figure 18.4 Collision Theory
If colliding particles have enough kinetic energy and collide at the right orientation, they can react to form a new product. **a.** An effective collision of oxygen and hydrogen molecules produces water molecules. **b.** An ineffective collision of oxygen and hydrogen molecules produces no reaction; the reactants bounce apart unchanged.

Go online to see collision theory animated.

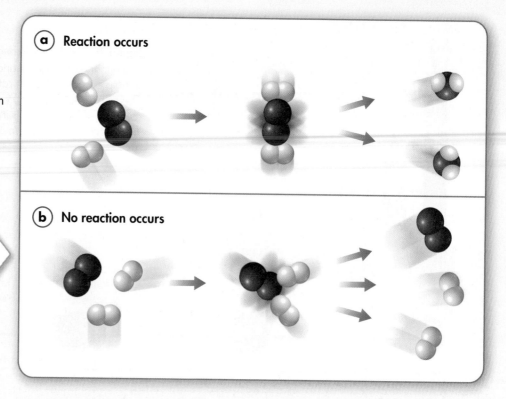

a Reaction occurs

b No reaction occurs

Collision Theory A model called collision theory is used to relate the properties of particles to the rates of reactions. According to **collision theory,** atoms, ions, and molecules can react to form products when they collide if the particles have enough kinetic energy. Particles that do not have enough energy to react bounce apart unchanged when they collide. Figure 18.4 shows what can happen when hydrogen and oxygen molecules collide.

You can use two balls of soft modeling clay to illustrate collision theory. If you throw the balls of clay together gently, they don't stick to one another. This situation is analogous to colliding particles of low energy that fail to react. If the same balls of clay are thrown together with great force, they will stick tightly to each other. This situation is analogous to the collision of two high-energy particles that results in the formation of a product.

You can also use modeling clay to illustrate another point about chemical reactions. Roll the clay into a rope and begin to shake one end more and more vigorously. At some point, the clay rope will break. Similarly, if enough energy is applied to a molecule, the bonds holding the molecule together can break, forming different products.

The minimum energy that colliding particles must have in order to react is called the **activation energy.** You can think of the activation energy for a reaction as a barrier that reactants must cross before products can form. Look at the diagrams in Figure 18.5. When two reactant particles collide, they may form an activated complex. An **activated complex** is an unstable arrangement of atoms that forms for a moment at the peak of the activation-energy barrier. The activated complex forms only if the colliding particles have enough energy and if the atoms are oriented properly. The lifetime of an activated complex is typically about 10^{-13} seconds. Its brief existence ends with the reformation of the reactants or with the formation of products. The two outcomes are equally likely. Thus, the activated complex is sometimes called the *transition state.*

Collision theory explains why some reactions are extremely slow at room temperature. For example, carbon and oxygen react when charcoal burns, but the reaction has a high activation energy. The O—O bonds and C—C bonds must be broken to form the activated complex. At room temperature, the collisions of oxygen and carbon molecules are not energetic enough to break the bonds. Thus, the reaction rate of carbon with oxygen at room temperature is essentially zero.

Interpret Graphs

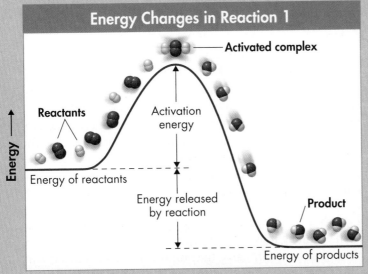

Energy Changes in Reaction 1

Activated complex
Reactants
Energy
Activation energy
Energy of reactants
Energy released by reaction
Product
Energy of products
Reaction progress ⟶

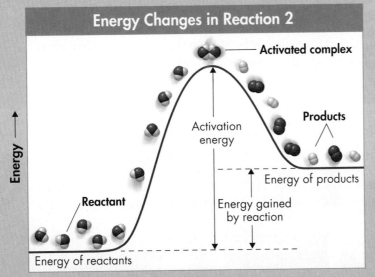

Energy Changes in Reaction 2

Activated complex
Energy
Activation energy
Products
Energy of products
Reactant
Energy gained by reaction
Energy of reactants
Reaction progress ⟶

Figure 18.5 The activation-energy barrier must be crossed before reactants are converted to products.

a. Read Graphs Is energy absorbed or released as a reaction progresses from the reactants to the activated complex?

b. Compare How are the graphs for reactions 1 and 2 different?

c. Classify Which reaction is endothermic and which is exothermic? How do you know?

d. Explain Why might a reaction that releases energy require some energy before the reaction will begin?

e. Draw Conclusions Once an activated complex forms, does it always proceed to form products?

Remember: An endothermic reaction absorbs heat, and an exothermic reaction releases heat.

Factors Affecting Reaction Rates

What four factors influence the rate of a chemical reaction?

Every chemical reaction proceeds at its own rate. Some reactions are naturally fast, and some are naturally slow under the same conditions. However, by varying the conditions, you can modify the rate of almost any reaction. **Factors that can affect the rate of a chemical reaction are temperature, concentration, particle size, and the use of a catalyst.** Collision theory helps explain why changing one or more of these factors may affect the rate of a chemical reaction.

Temperature Usually, raising the temperature speeds up a reaction. Lowering the temperature usually slows down a reaction. At higher temperatures, particles move faster. The frequency of collisions increases along with the percentage of particles that have enough kinetic energy to slip over the activation-energy barrier. Thus, an increase in temperature causes products to form faster.

A familiar example of the effect of temperature on reaction rate is the burning of charcoal. The reactants are carbon and oxygen. The product is carbon dioxide. At room temperature, a bag of charcoal in contact with air does not burn. However, when a starter flame touches the charcoal, carbon atoms and oxygen molecules collide with higher energy and greater frequency. Some collisions are at a high enough energy to form the product. The heat released by the reaction then supplies enough energy to get more carbon and oxygen over the activation-energy barrier. When the starter flame is removed, the reaction continues.

Concentration In a crowded room where people are moving about, you may find yourself bumping into people more frequently than if there were only a few people in the room. Similarly, the number of particles in a given volume affects the rate at which reactions occur. Cramming more particles into a fixed volume increases the concentration of reactants and, thus, the frequency of collision. Increased collision frequency leads to a higher reaction rate.

The lighted splint in Figure 18.6 glows in air and soon dies out because air is only 20 percent oxygen. But when the glowing splint is plunged into pure oxygen, it immediately bursts into flame. The increased concentration of oxygen greatly speeds up the combustion reaction.

Figure 18.6
Effect of Concentration on Reaction Rate
The rate of a reaction depends upon the concentrations of the reactants. **a.** In air, a lighted splint glows and soon goes out. **b.** When placed in a vial containing pure oxygen, the splint bursts into flame.
Infer *In areas where oxygen tanks are used, why do warning signs say "No smoking. No open flames"?*

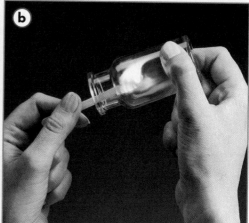

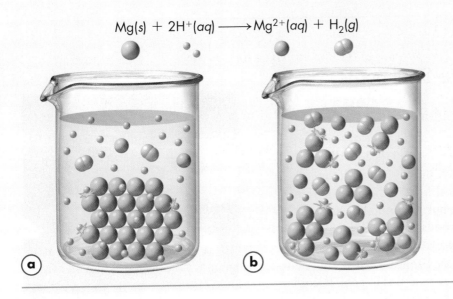

$$Mg(s) + 2H^+(aq) \longrightarrow Mg^{2+}(aq) + H_2(g)$$

(a)   **(b)**

Figure 18.7 Effect of Particle Size on Reaction Rate
When a piece of magnesium is placed in a dilute acid, hydrogen ions can collide with magnesium atoms.
a. Only atoms at the surface of the metal are available for reaction.
b. Dividing the metal into smaller pieces increases the surface area and the number of particle collisions.
Explain *How does increasing the number of collisions increase the reaction rate?*

Particle Size If you put a bundle of sticks on a fire, they burn quickly. A log with the same mass burns more slowly. The small pieces of wood have more surface area than the log, and surface area plays an important role in determining the rate of the combustion reaction. The same is true for other chemical reactions because collisions occur at the surface of particles.

The total surface area of a solid or liquid reactant affects the rate of a reaction. The smaller the particle size, the greater the surface area is for a given mass of particles. Figure 18.7 shows how a decrease in particle size affects the amount of a reactant exposed for reaction. When a piece of metal is divided into several smaller pieces, the total surface area increases. The result of an increase in surface area is an increase in the frequency of collisions and the reaction rate.

Another way to increase the surface area of solids is to dissolve them. In a solution, particles are separated and more accessible to other reactants. You can also increase the surface area of a solid by grinding it into a fine powder. Small dustlike particles, however, can be dangerous when suspended in air. As coal miners know, coal dust mixed with air is an explosive hazard because of the large surface area of the coal dust particles. The same risk exists in flour mills, grain elevators, and sugar refineries. The photograph in Figure 18.8 shows a sugar refinery in Georgia after such an explosion.

Figure 18.8 Dust Explosion
An explosion destroyed this sugar refinery. The tiny size of the reactant particles (sugar dust) caused the reaction of sugar with oxygen in the air to be explosive.

Quick Lab

Purpose To determine whether steel will burn

Materials
- #0000 steel wool pad
- tongs
- gas burner
- heat-resistant pad
- tweezers

Does Steel Burn?

Procedure

1. Roll a small piece of steel wool into a very tight, pea-sized ball.

2. Holding the ball with tongs, heat the steel wool in the blue-tip flame of the burner for no longer than 10 seconds. **CAUTION** *Observe all precautions for working with flames.*

3. Place the heated steel wool on the heat-resistant pad to cool. Record your observations.

4. Gently roll a second small piece of steel wool into a loose ball. Repeat Steps 2 and 3.

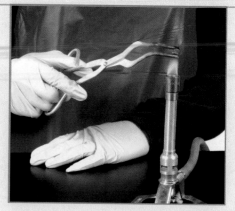

5. Use tweezers to pull a few individual fibers of steel wool from the pad. Hold one end of the loose fibers with the tongs. Repeat Steps 2 and 3.

Analyze and Conclude

1. Observe What differences did you observe when the tight ball, the loose ball, and the loose fibers were heated in the flame?

2. Relate Cause and Effect Give a reason for any differences you observed.

3. Describe Write the balanced equation for any chemical reaction you may have observed. Assume that the steel wool is composed mainly of iron.

4. Compare and Contrast How do your results differ from those observed in the rusting of an automobile body?

5. Apply Concepts Explain why steel wool is a hazard in shops where there are hot plates, open flames, or sparking motors.

CHEMISTRY & YOU

Q: *When salt water is added to the metal alloy in an MRE, the rate of the rusting reaction increases, and heat is produced rapidly. Which factor that can affect reaction rates is being applied in this situation?*

Catalysts Increasing the temperature is not always the best way to increase the rate of a reaction. A catalyst is often better. Recall that a catalyst is a substance that increases the rate of a reaction without being used up during the reaction. Catalysts permit reactions to proceed along a lower energy path. Figure 18.9 shows that the activation-energy barrier for the catalyzed reaction is lower than that of the uncatalyzed reaction. When the barrier is lower, a greater fraction of reactants have the energy to form products within a given time. For instance, the rate of the reaction of hydrogen and oxygen at room temperature is negligible. But with a small amount of platinum (Pt) as a catalyst, the reaction is rapid.

$$2H_2(g) + O_2(g) \xrightarrow{\text{Pt}} 2H_2O(l)$$

A catalyst is not consumed during a reaction. Therefore, it does not appear as a reactant in the chemical equation. Instead, the catalyst is often written above the yield arrow, as in the equation above.

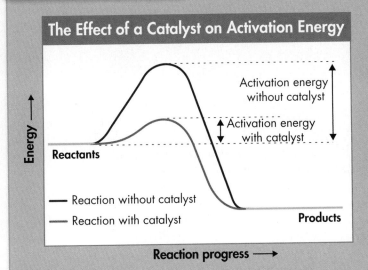

The Effect of a Catalyst on Activation Energy

Energy →

Activation energy without catalyst

Activation energy with catalyst

Reactants

—— Reaction without catalyst

—— Reaction with catalyst

Products

Reaction progress →

Figure 18.9 A catalyst lowers the activation-energy barrier for a reaction. With a lower barrier, more particles have enough energy for a successful collision.

a. Read Graphs How does using a catalyst change the amount of energy needed for products to form?

b. Make Generalizations Does the catalyst change the amount of energy released in the reaction?

c. Compare Along which of the two reaction paths are reactants converted more rapidly to products?

Hint: The reactant particles must have an energy equal to or greater than the activation energy to be converted to products.

Normal body temperature is only about 37°C. Your body needs to maintain this temperature to avoid damage to cells. At 37°C, reactions in the body would be too slow without catalysts. The catalysts that increase the rates of biological reactions are called enzymes. When you eat a meal containing protein, enzymes in your digestive tract help break down the protein molecules in a few hours. Without enzymes, the digestion of protein at 37°C would take many years!

An **inhibitor** is a substance that interferes with the action of a catalyst. Some inhibitors work by reacting with, or "poisoning," the catalyst itself. Thus, the inhibitor reduces the amount of catalyst available for a reaction. Reactions slow or even stop when a catalyst is poisoned.

18.1 LessonCheck

1. 🔲 **Explain** How can you express the rate of a chemical reaction?

2. 🔲 **Identify** List the four factors that can influence the rate of a chemical reaction.

3. **Describe** A thin, 0.2-mol sheet of zinc is completely converted to zinc oxide (ZnO) in one month. How would you express the rate of conversion of the zinc?

4. **Summarize** Does every collision between reacting particles lead to products? Explain.

5. **Relate Cause and Effect** Food stored in a refrigerator can stay fresh for long periods. Why does the same food stored at room temperature quickly spoil?

BIGIDEA MATTER AND ENERGY

6. Make a Venn diagram with two circles. Label one Matter and the other Energy. Choose a location in the diagram for each factor that can influence the rate of a reaction. Write a paragraph explaining your choices.

Catalytic Converters

Vehicles that run on fossil fuels are a major source of air pollution. One technology that significantly reduces air pollution caused by vehicles is called a catalytic converter. The device keeps pollutants from being released into the air by converting them into less-harmful emissions. A typical catalytic converter is capable of eliminating about 98 percent of a vehicle's pollution—unreacted hydrocarbons, carbon monoxide, and nitrogen oxides. Precious metals such as platinum, palladium, and rhodium are catalysts for the reactions that occur inside the converter.

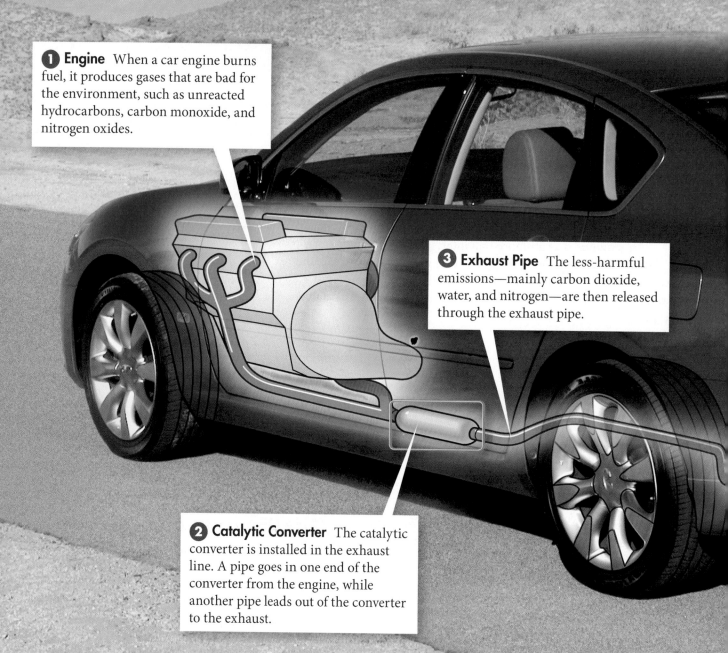

1 Engine When a car engine burns fuel, it produces gases that are bad for the environment, such as unreacted hydrocarbons, carbon monoxide, and nitrogen oxides.

3 Exhaust Pipe The less-harmful emissions—mainly carbon dioxide, water, and nitrogen—are then released through the exhaust pipe.

2 Catalytic Converter The catalytic converter is installed in the exhaust line. A pipe goes in one end of the converter from the engine, while another pipe leads out of the converter to the exhaust.

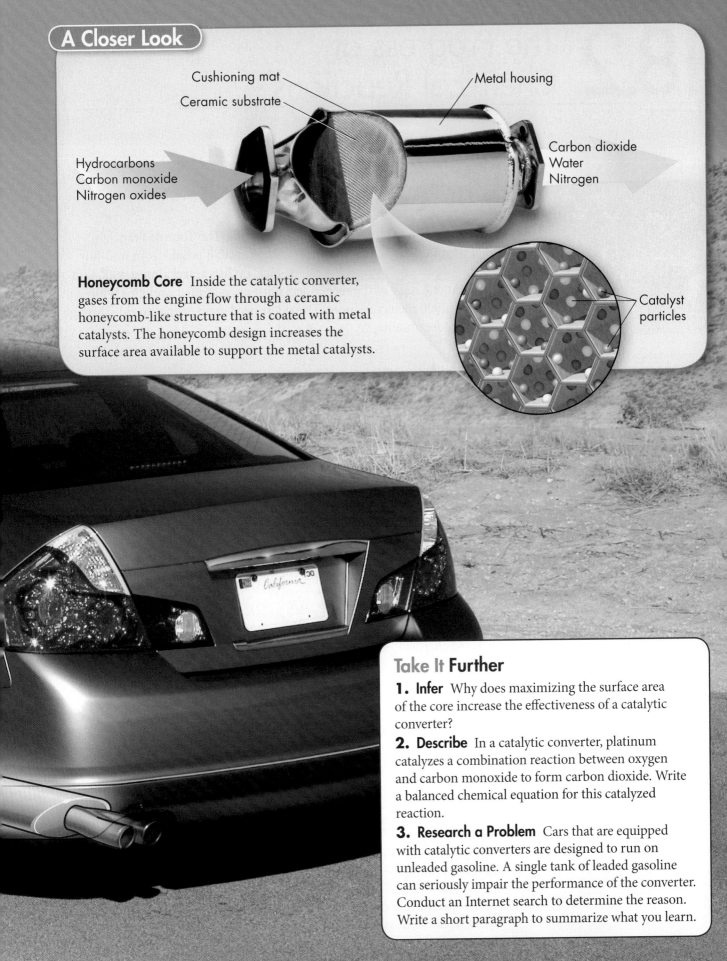

Cushioning mat

Ceramic substrate

Metal housing

Hydrocarbons
Carbon monoxide
Nitrogen oxides

Carbon dioxide
Water
Nitrogen

Honeycomb Core Inside the catalytic converter, gases from the engine flow through a ceramic honeycomb-like structure that is coated with metal catalysts. The honeycomb design increases the surface area available to support the metal catalysts.

Catalyst particles

Take It Further

1. Infer Why does maximizing the surface area of the core increase the effectiveness of a catalytic converter?

2. Describe In a catalytic converter, platinum catalyzes a combination reaction between oxygen and carbon monoxide to form carbon dioxide. Write a balanced chemical equation for this catalyzed reaction.

3. Research a Problem Cars that are equipped with catalytic converters are designed to run on unleaded gasoline. A single tank of leaded gasoline can seriously impair the performance of the converter. Conduct an Internet search to determine the reason. Write a short paragraph to summarize what you learn.

CHEMISTRY & YOU

Q: *How is a bicycle race like a chemical reaction?* The Tour de France is one of the most famous bicycle races in the world. It is held from mid-July to early August every year. During the race, cyclists travel almost 4000 kilometers. At one stage of the race, riders must cross steep mountains with heights of 1900 meters or more. The riders need extra energy to ride through these steep mountains.

Key Questions

🔑 What is the relationship between the value of the specific rate constant, k, and the speed of a chemical reaction?

🔑 How do most reactions progress from start to finish?

Vocabulary

• rate law
• specific rate constant
• first-order reaction
• elementary reaction
• reaction mechanism
• intermediate

Rate Laws

🔑 **What is the relationship between the value of the specific rate constant, k, and the speed of a chemical reaction?**

The rate of a reaction depends in part on the concentrations of the reactants. Suppose there were a reaction with only one reactant and one product. You could write a simple equation for this reaction.

$$A \longrightarrow B$$

The rate at which A forms B can be expressed as the change in A (ΔA) with time, where $[A_1]$ is the initial molar concentration of A at time t_1 and $[A_2]$ is the molar concentration of A at a later time, t_2.

$$\text{Rate} = \frac{\Delta A}{\Delta t} = \frac{[A_2] - [A_1]}{t_2 - t_1}$$

The rate of disappearance of A is proportional to the concentration of A.

$$\frac{\Delta A}{\Delta t} \propto [A]$$

The proportionality can be expressed as the concentration of A, [A], multiplied by a constant, k.

$$\text{Rate} = \frac{\Delta A}{\Delta t} = k \times [A]$$

This equation is a **rate law,** an expression for the rate of a reaction in terms of the concentration of reactants. The **specific rate constant** (k) for a reaction is a proportionality constant relating the concentrations of reactants to the rate of the reaction. The value of the specific rate constant depends on the conditions of the reaction and is determined through experiments. 🔑 **The value of the specific rate constant, k, in a rate law is large if the products form quickly; the value is small if the products form slowly.**

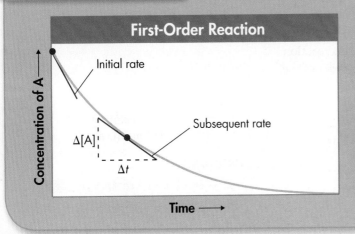

First-Order Reaction

Initial rate

Subsequent rate

$\Delta[A]$

Δt

Concentration of A ⟶

Time ⟶

Figure 18.10 The graph shows how the concentration of a reactant changes during a first-order reaction.

a. Identify What are the independent and dependent variables?

b. Describe What happens to the concentration of reactant A over time?

c. Compare The short red lines (tangents) illustrate the reaction rates at two different points in the reaction. Which rate is faster—the *initial rate* or the *subsequent rate*?

Hint: The slope of the tangent to the curve at any point is equal to the rate at that point.

First-Order Reactions The order of a reaction is the power to which the concentration of a reactant must be raised to match the experimental data on concentration and rate. In a **first-order reaction,** the rate is directly proportional to the concentration of only one reactant. Assume the reaction A ⟶ B is an example of a first-order reaction. The reaction rate is proportional to the concentration of A raised to the first power: $[A]^1 = [A]$.

The graph in Figure 18.10 shows the progress of a first-order reaction. Over time, the rate of reaction decreases because the concentration of the reactant is decreasing. For a first-order reaction, if [A] is reduced by one half, the reaction rate is reduced by one half. The rate $(\Delta A/\Delta t)$ at any point on the graph equals the slope of the tangent to the curve at that point.

Higher-Order Reactions In some reactions, two substances react to give products. One example is a double-replacement reaction. The general equation for a double-replacement reaction can be written as follows. The coefficients are represented by lowercase letters.

$$aA + bB \longrightarrow cC + dD$$

For the reaction of A with B, the rate of reaction is dependent on the concentrations of both A and B.

$$\text{Rate} = k[A]^x[B]^y$$

When each exponent in the rate law equals 1 (that is, $x = y = 1$), the reaction is said to be first order in A and first order in B. The overall order of a reaction is the sum of the exponents for the individual reactants. A reaction that is first order in A and first order in B is thus second order overall.

You might assume that the coefficients in a chemical equation and the exponents in the rate law for that reaction would always be the same. If your assumption were true, you could use the coefficients of the reactants to find the order of a reaction. For most reactions, however, the exponents in the rate law and the coefficients in the equation do not correspond. Most reactions are more complex than the reactions used in the examples. Thus, the actual order of a reaction must be determined by experiment.

Finding the Order of a Reaction From Experimental Data

Consider the reaction $aA \longrightarrow B$. The rate law for this reaction is Rate = $k[A]^x$. From the data in the table, find the order of the reaction with respect to A and the overall order of the reaction.

Trial	Initial concentration of A (mol/L)	Initial rate (mol/(L·s))
1	0.050	3.0×10^{-4}
2	0.10	12×10^{-4}
3	0.20	48×10^{-4}

KNOWNS

$[A]_1 = 0.050$ mol/L
$[A]_2 = 0.10$ mol/L
Rate$_1$ = 3.0×10^{-4} mol/(L·s)
Rate$_2$ = 12×10^{-4} mol/(L·s)

UNKNOWNS

Order of reaction with respect to A = ?

Overall order of the reaction = ?

❶ Analyze **List the knowns and the unknowns.** Use the first two trials to calculate the order and the third to evaluate your answer.

❷ Calculate **Solve for the unknowns.**

Start with the rate law for each initial concentration of A.	$\text{Rate}_1 = k[A_1]^x$ $\text{Rate}_2 = k[A_2]^x$	The rate law of the reaction and the specific rate constant, k, is the same for any initial concentration of A.
Divide the second expression by the first expression.	$\dfrac{\text{Rate}_2}{\text{Rate}_1} = \dfrac{\cancel{k}[A_2]^x}{\cancel{k}[A_1]^x} = \left(\dfrac{[A_2]}{[A_1]}\right)^x$	
Substitute the known quantities into the equation.	$\dfrac{12 \times 10^{-4} \text{ mol/(L·s)}}{3.0 \times 10^{-4} \text{ mol/(L·s)}} = \left(\dfrac{0.10 \text{ mol/L}}{0.050 \text{ mol/L}}\right)^x$ $4.0 = 2.0^x$	
Determine the value of x.	$x = 2$	

The reaction is second order in A.
Since A is the only reactant, the reaction must be second order overall.

❸ Evaluate **Does this result make sense?** If the reaction was first order in A, doubling the concentration would double the rate. However, Rate$_2$ is *four* times Rate$_1$. So the reaction is second order for A and second order overall because A is the only reactant. As a further check, look at what happens to the rate when the concentration doubles again from 0.10 mol/L to 0.20 mol/L.

To do Problem 8, isolate k, and then substitute the units for rate and concentration.

7. Suppose the initial rate for a first-order reaction is 0.5 mol/(L·s). What is the rate when half the reactant remains? When one fourth of the reactant remains?

8. Show that the unit of k for a first-order reaction is a reciprocal unit of time, such as a reciprocal second (s^{-1}). Begin with the expression Rate = $k[A]$.

Reaction Mechanisms

How do most reactions progress from start to finish?

Balanced equations are extremely useful. They tell you what reactants are present at the start of a reaction and what products are present at the end. What a balanced equation does not tell you is *how* the reaction occurred. For example, plants use photosynthesis to capture and store light energy. The process can be summarized by stating that carbon dioxide and water yield simple sugars and oxygen. However, the process of photosynthesis is not as simple as this summary implies.

One-Step and Multistep Reactions If you had enough data, you could graph all the energy changes that occur as reactants are converted to products in a chemical reaction. Such a graph is called a reaction progress curve, or reaction profile. For an elementary reaction, you would get a graph like the ones in Figure 18.5. An **elementary reaction** is a reaction in which reactants are converted to products in a single step. This type of reaction has only one activation-energy peak and one activated complex.

Most chemical reactions consist of two or more elementary reactions. The series of elementary reactions or steps that take place during the course of a complex reaction is called a **reaction mechanism.** Figure 18.11 shows a reaction progress curve for a complex chemical reaction. The graph has a peak for each activated complex and a valley for each intermediate.

An **intermediate** is a product of one step in a reaction mechanism and a reactant in the next step. An intermediate has a more stable structure and a longer lifetime than an activated complex. Yet, an intermediate is reactive enough to take part in the next step. Intermediates do not appear in the overall chemical equation for a reaction.

CHEMISTRY & YOU

Q: *In the mountain stage of the Tour de France, a rider encounters a series of peaks and valleys. In terms of energy, how does the trip through the mountains compare to what happens during a multistep reaction?*

Interpret Graphs

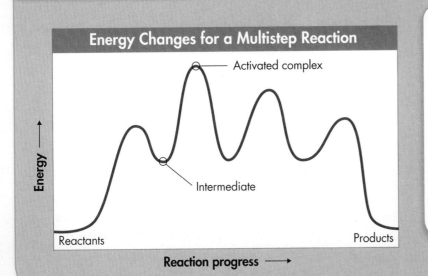

Energy Changes for a Multistep Reaction

Activated complex

Intermediate

Reactants

Products

Energy →

Reaction progress →

Figure 18.11 A reaction progress curve shows an activation-energy peak for each elementary reaction. Valleys indicate the formation of intermediates.

a. Read Graphs How many steps are in the reaction mechanism represented by this graph?

b. Read Graphs How many intermediates are formed as the reaction progresses?

c. Predict What effect might a catalyst have on the height of the peaks and depth of the valleys in this curve?

Hint: To answer part c, refer back to Figure 18.9.

Rate-Determining Steps In a multistep chemical reaction, the steps do not all progress at the same rate. One step will be slower than the others. The slowest step will determine, or limit, the rate of the overall reaction. As an analogy, think about shopping in a supermarket. First, you collect the items you want to buy. Then, you go through the checkout line and pay for your purchases. If you are buying many items, the first step is likely to take longer than the second. If you are buying only one or two items, getting through the checkout line may be the slower step.

Consider the reaction mechanism for the decomposition of nitrous oxide (N_2O). Experiments have shown that the mechanism consists of the two steps shown below.

$$\begin{aligned}
\text{Step 1:} \quad & N_2O(g) \longrightarrow N_2(g) + O(g) \quad \text{(slow)} \\
\text{Step 2:} \quad & N_2O(g) + O(g) \longrightarrow N_2(g) + O_2(g) \quad \text{(fast)} \\
\hline
\text{Overall:} \quad & 2N_2O(g) \longrightarrow 2N_2(g) + O_2(g)
\end{aligned}$$

In the first step, nitrous oxide decomposes into nitrogen gas and oxygen atoms. The oxygen atoms are an intermediate. They react with nitrous oxide in the second step to produce nitrogen molecules and oxygen molecules. The reaction in the second, faster step cannot occur until the first, slower step occurs. Therefore, the rate of the overall reaction depends on the rate of the first step. To increase the rate of the overall reaction, you would need to increase the rate of the first step. Thus, for the decomposition of nitrous oxide, the first step is called the *rate-determining step*.

When the equations for the two steps are summed, the oxygen atoms disappear. This example illustrates why you cannot use the overall chemical equation for a complex reaction to determine the reaction mechanism. Instead, the mechanism must be determined through experiments.

 **18.2** LessonCheck

9. Explain What does the size of the specific rate constant, k, indicate about the rate of a chemical reaction?

10. Summarize How do most chemical reactions progress from start to finish?

11. Describe How can you use a graph of reactant concentration versus time to determine the rate of a chemical reaction?

12. Draw Conclusions Consider the one-step reaction $aA \longrightarrow B$, with the following rate law: Rate $= k[A]^x$. When the initial concentration of A is increased from 0.35 mol/L to 0.70 mol/L, the initial rate increases from 1.6 mol/(L·s) to 3.2 mol/(L·s). What is the order of the reaction with respect to A? What is the overall order of the reaction?

13. Apply Concepts The rate law for the following reaction is first order in NO and O_3, and second order overall.

$$NO(g) + O_3(g) \longrightarrow NO_2(g) + O_2(g)$$

Write the rate law for this reaction.

14. Explain What is an elementary reaction, and how is it related to a reaction mechanism?

15. Classify Is an intermediate a reactant or a product? Explain.

16. Infer Look at the equation for the reaction of nitric oxide and oxygen. Do you think this is a single-step reaction or a multistep reaction? Use what you know about collision theory to explain your answer.

$$2NO(g) + O_2(g) \longrightarrow 2NO_2(g)$$

18.3 Reversible Reactions and Equilibrium

CHEMISTRY & YOU

Q: *How did chemists help farmers produce more food?* Fertilizers can increase the amount of a crop per unit of land. Most fertilizers contain ammonia or nitrogen compounds made from ammonia. For years, scientists tried and failed to develop an efficient way to produce ammonia from nitrogen and hydrogen. In the early 1900s, two German chemists, Fritz Haber and Karl Bosch, found the solution.

Key Questions

🔑 What happens at the molecular level in a chemical system at equilibrium?

🔑 What three stresses can cause a change in the equilibrium position of a chemical system?

🔑 What does the size of an equilibrium constant indicate about a system at equilibrium?

Vocabulary

- reversible reaction
- chemical equilibrium
- equilibrium position
- Le Châtelier's principle
- equilibrium constant

Reversible Reactions

🔑 What happens at the molecular level in a chemical system at equilibrium?

Based on the chemical equations you have seen, you may have inferred that chemical reactions always progress in one direction. This inference is not true. Some reactions are reversible. A **reversible reaction** is one in which the conversion of reactants to products and the conversion of products to reactants occur at the same time. Here's an example of a reversible reaction.

$$\text{Forward reaction: } 2SO_2(g) + O_2(g) \longrightarrow 2SO_3(g)$$

$$\text{Reverse reaction: } 2SO_2(g) + O_2(g) \longleftarrow 2SO_3(g)$$

In the first reaction, which is read from left to right, sulfur dioxide and oxygen produce sulfur trioxide. In the second reaction, which is read from right to left, sulfur trioxide decomposes into oxygen and sulfur dioxide. The first reaction is called the forward reaction. The second is called the reverse reaction. The two equations can be combined into one using a double arrow. The double arrow tells you that the reaction is reversible.

$$2SO_2(g) + O_2(g) \rightleftharpoons 2SO_3(g)$$

Sulfur   Oxygen   Sulfur
dioxide   trioxide

Figure 18.12 models what is happening at the molecular level.

Figure 18.12 Opposite Reactions Molecules of SO_2 and O_2 react to give SO_3. Molecules of SO_3 decompose to give SO_2 and O_2.

KINETIC ART
See reversible reactions animated online.

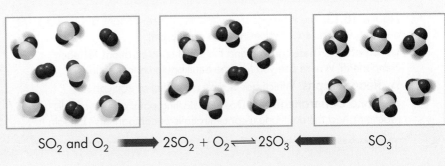

SO_2 and O_2 ➡ $2SO_2 + O_2 \rightleftharpoons 2SO_3$ ⬅ SO_3

Establishing Equilibrium What actually happens when sulfur dioxide and oxygen gases are mixed in a sealed container? The forward reaction begins at a given rate. Because no sulfur trioxide is present at the start, the initial rate of the reverse reaction is zero. As sulfur trioxide forms, however, the decomposition of sulfur trioxide begins. The rate of the reverse reaction is slow at first. Its rate increases as the concentration of sulfur trioxide increases. At the same time, the rate of the forward reaction decreases because sulfur dioxide and oxygen are being used up. Eventually, sulfur trioxide is decomposing as fast as sulfur dioxide and oxygen are combining. When the rates of the forward and reverse reactions are equal, the reaction has reached a state of balance called **chemical equilibrium.**

Look at the graphs in Figure 18.13. The graph on the left shows the progress of a reaction that starts with initial concentrations of SO_2 and O_2, but with zero SO_3. The graph on the right shows the progress of a reaction that begins with an initial concentration of SO_3 and zero concentrations for SO_2 and O_2. Notice that after a certain time, equilibrium is achieved and all the concentrations remain constant. The amount of SO_3 in the equilibrium mixture is the maximum amount that can be produced by this reaction under the conditions of the reaction.

Conditions at Equilibrium The unchanging amounts of SO_2, O_2, and SO_3 in the reaction mixture at equilibrium might cause you to think that both reactions have stopped. This is not the case. Chemical equilibrium is a dynamic state. ◁▭▷ **At chemical equilibrium, both the forward and reverse reactions continue, but because their rates are equal, no net change occurs in the concentrations of the reaction components.** Figure 18.14 provides an analogy for how an equilibrium is established and maintained.

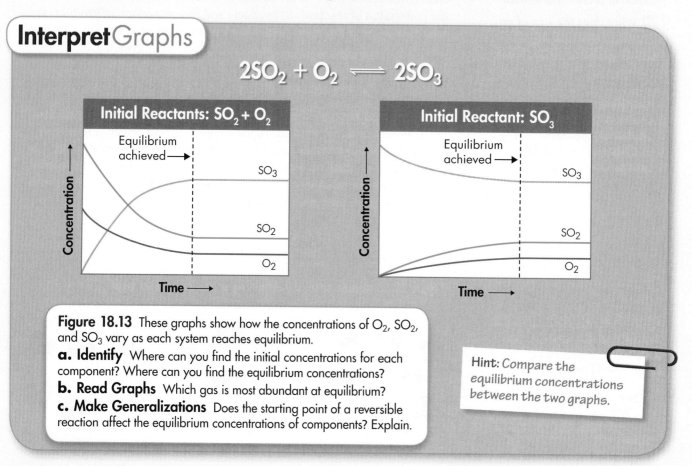

Interpret Graphs

$$2SO_2 + O_2 \rightleftharpoons 2SO_3$$

Initial Reactants: $SO_2 + O_2$

Equilibrium achieved →

Concentration →   Time →

SO_3 SO_2 O_2

Initial Reactant: SO_3

Equilibrium achieved →

Concentration →   Time →

SO_3 SO_2 O_2

Figure 18.13 These graphs show how the concentrations of O_2, SO_2, and SO_3 vary as each system reaches equilibrium.
a. Identify Where can you find the initial concentrations for each component? Where can you find the equilibrium concentrations?
b. Read Graphs Which gas is most abundant at equilibrium?
c. Make Generalizations Does the starting point of a reversible reaction affect the equilibrium concentrations of components? Explain.

Hint: Compare the equilibrium concentrations between the two graphs.

Figure 18.14 Equilibrium Positions
The up and down escalators in a store could represent a forward reaction and its reverse reaction. **a.** When the store opens, only the forward reaction occurs as shoppers head to the second floor. **b.** Equilibrium is reached when the rate at which shoppers move from the first floor to the second is equal to the rate at which shoppers move from the second floor to the first.
Use Analogies *Do the number of people on each floor have to be equal at equilibrium? Explain.*

Concentrations at Equilibrium Although the rates of the forward and reverse reactions are equal at equilibrium, the concentrations of the components usually are not. Look again at Figure 18.13. At equilibrium, the concentration of SO_3 is much greater than the concentrations of SO_2 and O_2. The relative concentrations of the reactants and products at equilibrium mark the **equilibrium position** of a reaction. This position tells you whether the forward or reverse reaction is more likely to happen. Suppose a single reactant, A, forms a single product, B. If the equilibrium mixture contains 1 percent A and 99 percent B, then the formation of B is said to be favored.

$$A \; \underset{}{\overset{}{\rightleftharpoons}} \; B$$
$$\text{1\%} \qquad \text{99\%}$$

If the mixture contains 99 percent A and 1 percent B at equilibrium, then the formation of A is favored.

$$A \; \underset{}{\overset{}{\rightleftharpoons}} \; B$$
$$\text{99\%} \qquad \text{1\%}$$

Notice that the equilibrium arrows are not of equal length. The longer of the two arrows indicates which reaction is favored and whether reactants or products will be more common at equilibrium.

In principle, almost all reactions are reversible to some extent under the right conditions. In practice, one set of components is often so favored at equilibrium that the other set cannot be detected. When no reactants can be detected, you can say that the reaction has gone to completion, or is irreversible. When no products can be detected, you can say that no reaction has taken place. Reversible reactions occupy a middle ground between the extremes of irreversibility and no reaction.

Factors Affecting Equilibrium: Le Châtelier's Principle

🔑 *What three stresses can cause a change in the equilibrium position of a chemical system?*

The balance that exists in a chemical system at equilibrium is a delicate one. It can be disrupted when one or more of the conditions of the reaction are changed. When the equilibrium of a system is disturbed, the system makes adjustments to restore the equilibrium. However, the equilibrium position of the restored equilibrium will not be the same as the original equilibrium position. That is, the amount of reactants may have increased or the amount of products may have increased. Such a change is called a shift in the equilibrium position.

The French chemist Henri Le Châtelier (1850–1936) studied how the equilibrium position shifts as a result of changing conditions. He proposed what has come to be called **Le Châtelier's principle**: If a stress is applied to a system in dynamic equilibrium, the system changes in a way that relieves the stress. 🔑 **Stresses that upset the equilibrium of a chemical system include changes in concentration of reactants or products, changes in temperature, and changes in pressure.**

In the examples of Le Châtelier's principle presented in this lesson, reactants will be to the left of the double arrow and products will be to the right. Blue arrows show the shifts when something is added to or removed from the system. The blue arrows always point in the direction of the shift in the equilibrium position—that is, toward the favored side.

Concentration Changing the amount, or concentration, of any reactant or product in a system at equilibrium disturbs the equilibrium. The system will adjust to minimize the effects of the change. Consider the decomposition of carbonic acid (H_2CO_3) in aqueous solution. The products are carbon dioxide and water. The system has reached equilibrium. The amount of carbonic acid is less than 1 percent.

$$H_2CO_3(aq) \underset{\substack{\text{Remove } CO_2 \\ \text{Direction of shift} \rightarrow}}{\overset{\substack{\text{Add } CO_2 \\ \leftarrow \text{Direction of shift}}}{\rightleftharpoons}} CO_2(aq) + H_2O(l)$$

$<1\%$ $>99\%$

Suppose carbon dioxide is added to the system. This increase in the concentration of CO_2 causes the rate of the reverse reaction to increase. As more reactant (H_2CO_3) is formed, the rate of the forward reaction also begins to increase. In time, the rates of the forward and reverse reactions again become equal. A new equilibrium is established with a higher concentration of reactant (H_2CO_3). Adding a product to a reaction at equilibrium pushes a reversible reaction in the direction of the reactants.

Suppose, on the other hand, carbon dioxide is removed. This decrease in the concentration of CO_2 causes the rate of the reverse reaction to decrease. As less reactant (H_2CO_3) is formed, the rate of the forward reaction also begins to decrease. In time, the rates of the forward and reverse reactions again become equal. The equilibrium is restored but at a different equilibrium position. Removing a product always pulls a reversible reaction in the direction of the products.

Farmers use the removal of a product to increase the yield of eggs laid by hens. Hens lay eggs and then proceed to hatch them. If the eggs are removed after they are laid, the hen will lay more eggs. Similarly as products are removed from a reaction mixture, the system attempts to restore equilibrium by producing more products. However, the reaction can never reestablish equilibrium because the products are constantly being removed. The reaction continues to produce products until the reactants are used up.

Your body provides another example of the effect of removing a product. Carbon dioxide is a product of the reactions that provide your body with energy. Carbon dioxide produced in the cells is carried through blood vessels to the lungs. Some of the carbon dioxide diffuses from the blood into the lungs and is exhaled into the air. An equilibrium between carbonic acid, carbon dioxide, and water exists in your blood.

The athletes in Figure 18.15 use more energy than a person at rest. During exercise, the concentration of CO_2 in the blood increases. This increase in CO_2 shifts the equilibrium in the direction of carbonic acid. The level of H_2CO_3 in the blood needs to remain fairly constant. Fortunately, the increase in the level of CO_2 also triggers an increase in the rate of breathing. With more breaths per minute, more CO_2 is removed through the lungs. The removal of CO_2 causes the equilibrium to shift toward the products, which reduces the amount of H_2CO_3.

The same principle applies to adding or removing reactants. When a reactant is added to a system at equilibrium, the reaction shifts in the direction of the formation of products. When a reactant is removed, the reaction shifts in the direction of formation of reactants.

Figure 18.15 Effect of Concentration on Equilibrium
Carbon dioxide is a product of reactions in cells. Rapid breathing during and after vigorous exercise helps reduce the level of CO_2 in the blood and, thus, helps control the level of H_2CO_3.
Predict *Is the concentration of CO_2 greater in inhaled air or in exhaled air? Explain.*

Temperature Increasing the temperature causes the equilibrium position of a reaction to shift in the direction that absorbs heat. In other words, it will shift in the direction that reduces the stress. For example, the reaction that occurs when ammonia (NH_3) is produced from N_2 and H_2 is exothermic.

$$\underset{\substack{\text{Remove heat (cool).}\\ \text{Direction of shift}\rightarrow}}{\overset{\substack{\text{Add heat.}\\ \leftarrow\text{Direction of shift}}}{N_2(g) + 3H_2(g) \rightleftharpoons}} 2NH_3(g) + \text{heat}$$

Heat can be considered to be a product, just like NH_3. Heating the reaction mixture at equilibrium pushes the equilibrium position to the left, which favors the reactants. As a result, the product yield decreases. Cooling, or removing heat, pulls the equilibrium position to the right, and the product yield increases.

Pressure Equilibrium systems in which some reactants and products are gases can be affected by a change in pressure. A shift will occur only if there are an unequal number of moles of gas on each side of the equation. The reaction in which ammonia forms is a useful example. Figure 18.16 shows how a change in pressure affects the system. The three gases are in a cylinder with a piston attached to a plunger. When the plunger is pushed down, the volume decreases and the pressure increases. You can predict which way the equilibrium position will shift by comparing the number of molecules of reactants and products. When two molecules of ammonia form, four molecules of reactants are used up (three of hydrogen and one of nitrogen). A shift toward ammonia (the product) will reduce the number of molecules. This shift will decrease the pressure but not to the original pressure.

Figure 18.16
Effect of Pressure on Equilibrium
Pressure affects a mixture of nitrogen, hydrogen, and ammonia.
a. The system is at equilibrium.
b. Equilibrium is disturbed by an increase in pressure. **c.** A new equilibrium position is established with fewer molecules.
Explain *How does the ideal gas law (PV = nRT) explain this shift in the equilibrium position?*

$$\underset{\substack{\text{Reduce pressure.}\\ \leftarrow\text{Direction of shift}}}{\overset{\substack{\text{Increase pressure.}\\ \text{Direction of shift}\rightarrow}}{N_2(g) + 3H_2(g) \rightleftharpoons}} 2NH_3(g)$$

A change in pressure can be used to favor the reactants in the ammonia reaction. Pulling up on the plunger in Figure 18.16 will increase the volume that the gases occupy. This increase in volume causes a decrease in pressure. Adding molecules to the container can help to restore the pressure. Thus, the decomposition of ammonia, which increases the number of molecules, is favored. A new equilibrium is established at a pressure that is higher than when the system was disturbed but not as high as the original pressure.

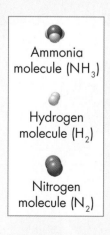

Ammonia molecule (NH_3)

Hydrogen molecule (H_2)

Nitrogen molecule (N_2)

a Initial equilibrium (11 gas molecules)

b Pressure increased, equilibrium disturbed

c New equilibrium (9 gas molecules)

Catalysts and Equilibrium Catalysts decrease the time it takes to establish equilibrium. However, they do not affect the amounts of reactants and products present at equilibrium. The energy path for a reverse reaction is the exact opposite of the energy path for the forward reaction. So adding a catalyst lowers the energy path by the same amount for both reactions.

SampleProblem 18.2

Applying Le Châtelier's Principle

What effect will each of the following changes have on the equilibrium position for this reversible reaction?

$$PCl_5(g) + heat \rightleftharpoons PCl_3(g) + Cl_2(g)$$

a. Cl_2 is added.
b. Pressure is increased.
c. Heat is removed.
d. PCl_3 is removed as it forms.

❶ **Analyze** Identify the relevant concepts. According to Le Châtelier's principle, the equilibrium position will shift in a direction that minimizes the imposed stress.

❷ **Solve** Apply the concepts to this problem.

| Start with the addition of Cl_2. | ➤ | **a.** Cl_2 is a product. Increasing the concentration of a product shifts the equilibrium to the left. |

| Analyze the effect of an increase in pressure. | ➤ | **b.** Reducing the number of gas molecules decreases the pressure. The equilibrium shifts to the left. |

| Analyze the effect of removing heat. | ➤ | **c.** The reverse reaction produces heat. The removal of heat causes the equilibrium to shift to the left. |

| Analyze the effect of removing PCl_3. | ➤ | **d.** PCl_3 is a product. Removal of a product as it forms causes the equilibrium to shift to the right. |

17. How is the equilibrium position of this reaction affected by the following changes?

$$2SO_2(g) + O_2(g) \rightleftharpoons 2SO_3(g) + heat$$

a. lowering the temperature
b. decreasing the pressure
c. removing oxygen
d. adding sulfur trioxide (SO_3)

18. How is the equilibrium position of this reaction affected by the following changes?

$$C(s) + H_2O(g) + heat \rightleftharpoons CO(g) + H_2(g)$$

a. lowering the temperature
b. increasing the pressure
c. removing hydrogen
d. adding water vapor

For a change in pressure, compare the number of gas molecules on both sides of the equation.

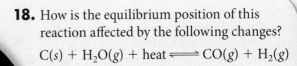

Equilibrium Constants

🔑 **What does the size of an equilibrium constant indicate about a system at equilibrium?**

Chemists express the equilibrium position as a numerical value. This value relates the amounts of reactants to products at equilibrium. Look at the following general reaction in which two reactants form two products. The coefficients *a*, *b*, *c*, and *d* represent the number of moles.

$$aA + bB \rightleftharpoons cC + dD$$

The **equilibrium constant** (K_{eq}) is the ratio of product concentrations to reactant concentrations at equilibrium. Each concentration is raised to a power equal to the number of moles of that substance in the balanced chemical equation. Here is the expression for the equilibrium constant for the general reaction stated above.

$$K_{eq} = \frac{[C]^c \times [D]^d}{[A]^a \times [B]^b}$$

The exponents in the equilibrium-constant expression are the coefficients in the balanced chemical equation. The concentrations of substances are in moles per liter (mol/L). The value of K_{eq} depends on the temperature of the reaction. If the temperature changes, the value of K_{eq} also changes.

🔑 **The size of the equilibrium constant indicates whether reactants or products are more common at equilibrium.** When K_{eq} has a large value, such as 3.1×10^{11}, the reaction mixture at equilibrium will consist mainly of product. When K_{eq} has a small value, such as 3.1×10^{-11}, the mixture at equilibrium will consist mainly of reactant. When K_{eq} has an intermediate value, such as 0.15 or 50, the mixture will have significant amounts of both reactant and product.

When the value of an equilibrium constant is calculated, the cancellation of units may or may not lead to a unit for the constant. As a result, chemists have agreed to report equilibrium constants without a stated unit. Sample Problem 18.3 shows how to calculate the equilibrium constant for the reaction illustrated in Figure 18.17.

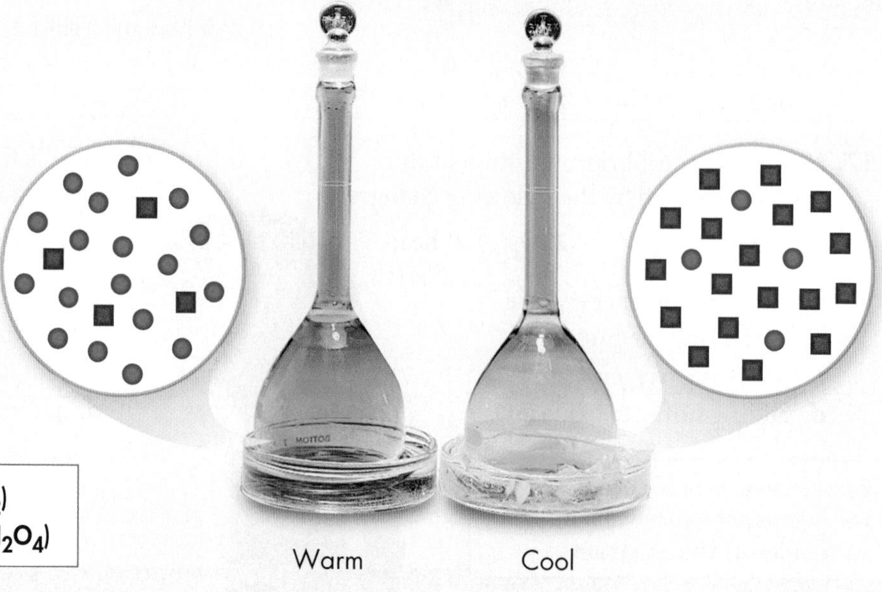

Figure 18.17
Favoring Reactants or Products
Dinitrogen tetroxide is a colorless gas. Nitrogen dioxide is a brown gas. The flask on the left is in a dish of hot water. The flask on the right is in ice.
Interpret Diagrams *How does an increase in temperature affect the equilibrium mixture of these gases?*

● Nitrogen dioxide (NO_2)
■ Dinitrogen tetroxide (N_2O_4)

Warm   Cool

Expressing and Calculating K_{eq}

The colorless gas dinitrogen tetroxide (N_2O_4) and the brown gas nitrogen dioxide (NO_2) exist in equilibrium with each other.

$$N_2O_4(g) \rightleftharpoons 2NO_2(g)$$

A liter of the gas mixture at equilibrium contains 0.0045 mol of N_2O_4 and 0.030 mol of NO_2 at 10°C. Write the expression for the equilibrium constant (K_{eq}) and calculate the value of the constant for the reaction.

❶ Analyze List the knowns and the unknowns.
Modify the general expression for the equilibrium constant and substitute the known concentrations to calculate K_{eq}.

KNOWNS	UNKNOWNS
$[N_2O_4]$ = 0.0045 mol/L	K_{eq} (algebraic expression) = ?
$[NO_2]$ = 0.030 mol/L	K_{eq} (numerical value) = ?

❷ Calculate Solve for the unknowns.

Start with the general expression for the equilibrium constant.

$$K_{eq} = \frac{[C]^c \times [D]^d}{[A]^a \times [B]^b}$$

Place the concentration of the product in the numerator and the concentration of the reactant in the denominator. Raise each concentration to the power equal to its coefficient in the chemical equation.

Write the equilibrium constant expression for this reaction.

$$K_{eq} = \frac{[NO_2]^2}{[N_2O_4]}$$

Substitute the concentrations that are known, and calculate K_{eq}.

$$K_{eq} = \frac{(0.030 \text{ mol/L})^2}{0.0045 \text{ mol/L}} = \frac{(0.030 \text{ mol/L} \times 0.030 \text{ mol/L})}{0.0045 \text{ mol/L}}$$

$$= 0.20 \text{ mol/L} = 0.20$$

You can ignore the unit mol/L; chemists report equilibrium constants without a stated unit.

❸ Evaluate Does the result make sense? Each concentration is raised to the correct power. The numerical value of the constant is correctly expressed to two significant figures. The value for the K_{eq} is appropriate for an equilibrium mixture that contains significant amounts of both gases.

Here's a hint for Problem 20: Calculate $1/K_{eq}$ for the forward reaction.

19. The reaction in which ammonia is formed is $N_2(g) + 3H_2(g) \rightleftharpoons 2NH_3(g)$. At equilibrium, a 1-L flask contains 0.15 mol H_2, 0.25 mol N_2, and 0.10 mol NH_3. Calculate K_{eq} for this reaction.

20. Using the equilibrium conditions described in Problem 19, Calculate K_{eq} for $2NH_3(g) \rightleftharpoons N_2(g) + 3H_2(g)$. How is the K_{eq} for a forward reaction related to the K_{eq} for a reverse reaction?

Finding the Equilibrium Constant

One mole of colorless hydrogen gas and one mole of violet iodine vapor are sealed in a 1-L flask and allowed to react at 450°C. At equilibrium, 1.56 mol of colorless hydrogen iodide is present, together with some of the reactant gases. Calculate K_{eq} for the reaction.

$$H_2(g) + I_2(g) \rightleftharpoons 2HI(g)$$

❶ Analyze List the knowns and the unknowns. Find the concentrations of the reactants at equilibrium. Then substitute the equilibrium concentrations in the expression for the equilibrium constant for this reaction.

KNOWNS	UNKNOWN
$[H_2]$ (initial) = 1.00 mol/L	K_{eq} = ?
$[I_2]$ (initial) = 1.00 mol/L	
[HI] (equilibrium) = 1.56 mol/L	

❷ Calculate Solve for the unknown.

First use the balanced equation to find out how much H_2 and I_2 are consumed in the reaction.

$$1.56 \text{ mol HI} \times \frac{1 \text{ mol } H_2}{2 \text{ mol HI}} = 0.780 \text{ mol } H_2$$

In this reaction, the number of mol I_2 used equals mol H_2 used.

Calculate how much H_2 and I_2 remain at equilibrium.

$$\text{mol } H_2 = \text{mol } I_2 = (1.00 \text{ mol} - 0.780 \text{ mol}) = 0.22 \text{ mol}$$

Write the expression for K_{eq}.

$$K_{eq} = \frac{[HI]^2}{[H_2] \times [I_2]}$$

Use the general expression for K_{eq} as a guide:

$$K_{eq} = \frac{[C]^c \times [D]^d}{[A]^a \times [B]^b}$$

Substitute the equilibrium concentrations of the reactants and products into the equation and solve for K_{eq}.

$$K_{eq} = \frac{(1.56 \text{mol/L})^2}{0.22 \text{ mol/L} \times 0.22 \text{ mol/L}} = \frac{1.56 \text{ mol/L} \times 1.56 \text{ mol/L}}{0.22 \text{ mol/L} \times 0.22 \text{ mol/L}} = 5.0 \times 10^1$$

❸ Evaluate Does the result make sense? Each concentration is raised to the correct power. The value of the constant reflects the presence of significant amounts of reactants and product in the equilibrium mixture.

In Problem 22, you must first find the equilibrium concentrations of H_2 and CO_2.

21. Suppose the following system reaches equilibrium:
$N_2(g) + O_2(g) \rightleftharpoons 2NO(g)$
Analysis of the equilibrium mixture in a 1-L flask gives the following results: 0.50 mol of N_2, 0.50 mol of O_2, and 0.020 mol of NO. Calculate K_{eq} for the reaction.

22. At 750°C, the following reaction reaches equilibrium in a 1-L flask:
$H_2(g) + CO_2(g) \rightleftharpoons H_2O(g) + CO(g)$
The reaction begins with 0.10 mol H_2 and 0.10 mol CO_2. At equilibrium, there is 0.047 mol H_2O and 0.047 mol CO. Calculate K_{eq} for the reaction.

SampleProblem 18.5

Finding Concentrations at Equilibrium

Bromine chloride (BrCl) decomposes to form bromine and chlorine.

$$2BrCl(g) \rightleftharpoons Br_2(g) + Cl_2(g)$$

At a certain temperature, the equilibrium constant for the reaction is 11.1. A sample of pure BrCl is placed in a 1-L container and allowed to decompose. At equilibrium, the reaction mixture contains 4.00 mol Cl_2. What are the equilibrium concentrations of Br_2 and BrCl?

❶ Analyze List the knowns and the unknowns.
Use the balanced equation, equilibrium constant, and the equilibrium constant expression to find the unknown concentrations. According to the balanced equation, when BrCl decomposes, equal numbers of moles of Br_2 and Cl_2 are formed.

KNOWNS

$[Cl_2]$ (equilibrium) = 4.00 mol/L
K_{eq} = 11.1

UNKNOWNS

$[Br_2]$ (equilibrium) = ? mol/L
$[BrCl]$ (equilibrium) = ? mol/L

❷ Calculate Solve for the unknowns.

The volume of the container is 1 L, so calculate $[Br_2]$ at equilibrium.

$$[Br_2] = \frac{4.00 \text{ mol}}{1 \text{ L}} = 4.00 \text{ mol/L}$$

Write the equilibrium expression for the reaction.

$$K_{eq} = \frac{[Br_2] \times [Cl_2]}{[BrCl]^2}$$

Rearrange the equation to solve for $[BrCl]^2$. Then substitute the known values for K_{eq}, $[Br_2]$, and $[Cl_2]$.

$$[BrCl]^2 = \frac{[Br_2] \times [Cl_2]}{K_{eq}} = \frac{4.00 \text{ mol/L} \times 4.00 \text{ mol/L}}{11.1}$$

$$= 1.44 \text{ mol}^2/L^2$$

Find [BrCl] by taking the square root of each side of the equation.

$$[BrCl] = \sqrt{1.44 \text{ mol}^2/L^2} = 1.20 \text{ mol/L}$$

Use your calculator to find the square root.

❸ Evaluate Does the result make sense? It makes sense that the equilibrium concentration of the reactant and the products are both present in significant amounts because K_{eq} has an intermediate value.

---

23. At a certain temperature, the equilibrium constant for the reaction in which nitrogen dioxide forms dinitrogen tetroxide is 5.6.

$$2NO_2(g) \rightleftharpoons N_2O_4(g)$$

In a 1-L container, the amount of N_2O_4 at equilibrium is 0.66 mol. What is the equilibrium concentration of NO_2?

24. Hydrogen iodide decomposes to form hydrogen and iodine.

$$2HI(g) \rightleftharpoons H_2(g) + I_2(g)$$

In a 1-L container at 450°C, the equilibrium mixture contains 0.50 mol of hydrogen. What are the equilibrium concentrations of hydrogen and hydrogen iodide? (K_{eq} = 0.020)

Chemical Engineer

You may think that surfing is about as far away from chemistry as you can get. But you'd be wrong! Surfboards, wet suits, and even the synthetic waxes used to help keep your feet on the board were created using products developed by chemical engineers.

Chemical engineers are primarily concerned with the large-scale manufacture of chemical products, such as plastics and other petroleum products, pharmaceuticals, and foods. Chemical engineers may also be involved in research, the design and development of processing plants, the evaluation of operating processes, and the extraction and processing of raw materials.

Take It Further

1. Infer What are some reasons why chemical engineers might need a wide range of science and engineering knowledge in their work?

2. Identify What are some products you use every day that could have been developed by a chemical engineer?

18.3 LessonCheck

25. 🔑 **Review** What happens to the amounts of reactants and products after a reaction has reached chemical equilibrium?

26. 🔑 **List** What are the three stresses that can upset the equilibrium of a chemical system?

27. 🔑 **Explain** What does the value of the equilibrium constant tell you about the amounts of reactants and products present at equilibrium?

28. Relate Cause and Effect Can a change in pressure shift the equilibrium position in every reversible reaction? Explain.

29. Describe How can you use a balanced chemical equation to write an equilibrium-constant expression?

30. Apply Concepts Which of the equilibrium constants indicates a reaction in which the amount of product is much larger than the amount of reactant at equilibrium? Explain.

a. $K_{eq} = 1 \times 10^8$
b. $K_{eq} = 3 \times 10^{-6}$

31. Calculate The equilibrium mixture for the reaction $2HI(g) \rightleftharpoons H_2(g) + I_2(g)$ contains 0.050 mol H_2. How many moles of I_2 and HI are present at equilibrium ($K_{eq} = 0.018$)?

BIGIDEA REACTIONS

32. Review the concept of percent yield from Lesson 12.3. How can understanding Le Châtelier's principle help chemists increase the percent yield of a reversible chemical reaction?

18.4 Solubility Equilibrium

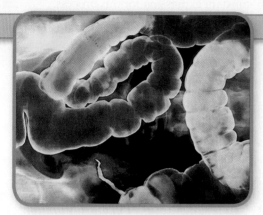

CHEMISTRY & YOU

Q: *How is it possible to ingest a poison without being harmed?* Chemical substances are needed to make organs other than bones visible on X-ray images. In one test, a patient drinks a thick liquid mixture that contains barium sulfate, which is a poison. Because barium sulfate can absorb X-rays, tissues coated with the liquid will appear as light areas in the X-ray images. This lesson will help you understand how a poison like barium sulfate can be safely used for this test.

Key Questions

🔑 What is the relationship between the solubility product constant and the solubility of a compound?

🔑 How can you predict whether precipitation will occur when two solutions are mixed?

Vocabulary

- solubility product constant
- common ion
- common ion effect

The Solubility Product Constant

🔑 **What is the relationship between the solubility product constant and the solubility of a compound?**

Most ionic compounds containing alkali metals are soluble in water. For example, more than 35 g of sodium chloride will dissolve in only 100 g of water. By contrast, some ionic compounds are insoluble in water. For example, compounds that contain phosphate, sulfite, or carbonate ions tend not to dissolve in water. Exceptions to this rule are compounds in which these ions are combined with ammonium ions or alkali metal ions. Table 18.1 provides some general rules for the solubility of ionic compounds in water.

Table 18.1

Solubility of Ionic Compounds in Water		
Compounds	**Solubility**	**Exceptions**
Salts of Group 1A metals and ammonia	Soluble	Some lithium compounds
Ethanoates, nitrates, chlorates, and perchlorates	Soluble	Few exceptions
Sulfates	Soluble	Compounds of Pb, Ag, Hg, Ba, Sr, and Ca
Chlorides, bromides, and iodides	Soluble	Compounds of Ag and some compounds of Hg and Pb
Sulfides and hydroxides	Most are insoluble	Alkali metal sulfides and hydroxides are soluble. Compounds of Ba, Sr, and Ca are slightly soluble.
Carbonates, phosphates, and sulfites	Insoluble	Compounds of the alkali metals and of ammonium ions

Figure 18.18 Silver Chloride

Some ionic compounds, such as silver chloride, are slightly soluble in water.

Predict *Would adding solid silver chloride to this test tube increase the concentrations of silver ions and chloride ions?*

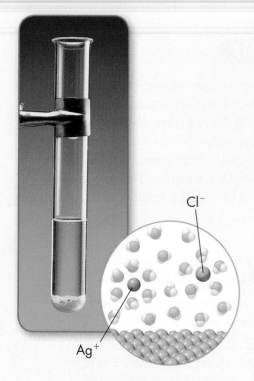

Cl^-

Ag^+

Most insoluble ionic compounds will actually dissolve to some extent in water. These compounds are said to be slightly soluble in water. Figure 18.18 models what happens when the "insoluble" compound silver chloride is mixed with water. A very small amount of silver chloride dissolves in the water. An equilibrium is established between the solid and the dissolved ions in the saturated solution.

$$AgCl(s) \rightleftharpoons Ag^+(aq) + Cl^-(aq)$$

You can write an equilibrium-constant expression for this process.

$$K_{eq} = \frac{[Ag^+] \times [Cl^-]}{[AgCl]}$$

The expression includes the dissolved ions, which are in solution, and the solid AgCl, which is not. To compare the solubility of salts, it is useful to have a constant that reflects only the concentrations of the dissolved ions. This constant is called the **solubility product constant** (K_{sp}), which is equal to the product of the concentrations of the ions each raised to a power equal to the coefficient of the ion in the dissociation equation.

$$K_{sp} = [A]^a \times [B]^b$$

The coefficients for the dissociation of silver chloride are each 1, so the K_{sp} expression for the dissociation is written as follows:

$$K_{sp} = [Ag^+] \times [Cl^-]$$

What does the size of the solubility product constant tell you about the solubility of a compound? **The smaller the value of the solubility product constant, the lower the solubility of the compound.** Table 18.2 lists the K_{sp} values for some ionic compounds that are slightly soluble in water.

Table 18.2

Solubility Product Constants (K_{sp}) at 25°C					
Ionic compound	K_{sp}	**Ionic compound**	K_{sp}	**Ionic compound**	K_{sp}
Halides		**Sulfates**		**Hydroxides**	
AgCl	1.8×10^{-10}	$PbSO_4$	6.3×10^{-7}	$Al(OH)_3$	3.0×10^{-34}
AgBr	5.0×10^{-13}	$BaSO_4$	1.1×10^{-10}	$Zn(OH)_2$	3.0×10^{-16}
AgI	8.3×10^{-17}	$CaSO_4$	2.4×10^{-5}	$Ca(OH)_2$	6.5×10^{-6}
$PbCl_2$	1.7×10^{-5}	**Sulfides**		$Mg(OH)_2$	7.1×10^{-12}
$PbBr_2$	2.1×10^{-6}	NiS	4.0×10^{-20}	$Fe(OH)_2$	7.9×10^{-16}
PbI_2	7.9×10^{-9}	CuS	8.0×10^{-37}	**Carbonates**	
PbF_2	3.6×10^{-8}	Ag_2S	8.0×10^{-51}	$CaCO_3$	4.5×10^{-9}
CaF_2	3.9×10^{-11}	ZnS	3.0×10^{-23}	$SrCO_3$	9.3×10^{-10}
Chromates		FeS	8.0×10^{-19}	$ZnCO_3$	1.0×10^{-10}
$PbCrO_4$	1.8×10^{-14}	CdS	1.0×10^{-27}	Ag_2CO_3	8.1×10^{-12}
Ag_2CrO_4	1.2×10^{-12}	PbS	3.0×10^{-28}	$BaCO_3$	5.0×10^{-9}

SampleProblem 18.6

Finding the Ion Concentrations in a Saturated Solution

What is the concentration of lead ions and chromate ions in a saturated solution of lead(II) chromate at 25°C? ($K_{sp} = 1.8 \times 10^{-14}$)

KNOWNS

$K_{sp} = 1.8 \times 10^{-14}$

$PbCrO_4(s) \rightleftharpoons Pb^{2+}(aq) + CrO_4^{2-}(aq)$

UNKNOWNS

$[Pb^{2+}] = ?\ M$

$[CrO_4^{2-}] = ?\ M$

❶ Analyze List the knowns and the unknowns. Write the expression for K_{sp}. Then modify it so that there is a single unknown.

❷ Calculate Solve for the unknowns.

Start with the general expression for the solubility product constant.	$K_{sp} = [A]^a \times [B]^b$

The exponent for each ion is 1.

Use the chemical equation to write the correct expression for K_{sp} for the reaction.	$K_{sp} = [Pb^{2+}] \times [CrO_4^{2-}] = 1.8 \times 10^{-14}$

At equilibrium, $[Pb^{2+}] = [CrO_4^{2-}]$

Substitute $[Pb^{2+}]$ for $[CrO_4^{2-}]$ in the expression to get an equation with one unknown.	$K_{sp} = [Pb^{2+}] \times [Pb^{2+}] = [Pb^{2+}]^2 = 1.8 \times 10^{-14}$

Solve for $[Pb^{2+}]$.	$[Pb^{2+}] = \sqrt{1.8 \times 10^{-14}}$ $[Pb^{2+}] = [CrO_4^{2-}] = 1.3 \times 10^{-7} M$

❸ Evaluate Does the result make sense? Calculate $[Pb^{2+}] \times [CrO_4^{2-}]$ to evaluate the answer. The result is 1.7×10^{-14}, which is close to the value for K_{sp}. The result varies slightly from the actual value because the answers were rounded to two significant figures.

33. Lead(II) sulfide (PbS) has a K_{sp} value of 3.0×10^{-28}. What is the concentration of lead(II) ions in a saturated solution of PbS at 25°C?

Start by writing the equation for the dissociation of the solid ionic compound.

34. What is the concentration of calcium ions in a saturated calcium carbonate solution at 25°C? Use the K_{sp} value for calcium carbonate from Table 18.2.

The Common Ion Effect

🔑 **How can you predict whether precipitation will occur when two solutions are mixed?**

In a saturated solution of lead(II) chromate, an equilibrium is established between the solid lead(II) chromate and its ions in solution.

$$PbCrO_4(s) \rightleftharpoons Pb^{2+}(aq) + CrO_4^{2-}(aq) \quad K_{sp} = 1.8 \times 10^{-14}$$

What would happen if you added some lead nitrate to this solution? Lead(II) nitrate, $Pb(NO_3)_2$, is soluble in water. So adding $Pb(NO_3)_2$ causes the concentration of lead ion to increase. The product of $[Pb^{2+}]$ and $[CrO_4^{2-}]$ would be greater than the K_{sp} for lead(II) chromate. The addition of lead ions is a stress on the equilibrium. Applying Le Châtelier's principle, the stress can be relieved if the reaction shifts to the left. Figure 18.19 shows the result. The excess lead ions combine with chromate ions in solution to form additional solid $PbCrO_4$. Lead(II) chromate continues to precipitate from the solution until the product of $[Pb^{2+}]$ and $[CrO_4^{2-}]$ once again equals 1.8×10^{-14}. The difference is that now the lead ions in solution come from two sources, $PbCrO_4$ and $Pb(NO_3)_2$.

K_{sp} for the original solution: $[Pb^{2+}][CrO_4^{2-}] = 1.8 \times 10^{-14}$

K_{sp} after addition of $Pb(NO_3)_2$: $\left[Pb^{2+}\right]_{[CrO_4^{2-}]} = 1.8 \times 10^{-14}$

In this example, the lead ion is a common ion. A **common ion** is an ion that is found in both ionic compounds in a solution. The lowering of the solubility of an ionic compound as a result of the addition of a common ion is called the **common ion effect.** Chemists can use an ionic compound with a common ion to cause a solid to precipitate from solution. For the common ion effect to work, the added compound must be more soluble than the compound that is already in solution. Adding lead(II) nitrate to a saturated solution of $PbCrO_4$ causes the solubility of $PbCrO_4$ to decrease. Adding sodium chromate, Na_2CrO_4, to the solution would produce the same effect. The chromate ion is common to both salts, and Na_2CrO_4 is much more soluble in water than is $PbCrO_4$.

CHEMISTRY & YOU

Q:: *The K_{sp} of $BaSO_4$ is 1.1×10^{-10}. How can patients ingest the toxic $BaSO_4$ without being harmed?*

Figure 18.19 Lead(II) Chromate
Lead(II) chromate, $PbCrO_4$, is slightly soluble in water. **a.** The yellow solid in the test tube is $PbCrO_4$. It cannot dissolve because the solution is saturated with Pb^{2+} and CrO_4^{2-} ions.
b. Adding some lead(II) nitrate, $Pb(NO_3)_2$, to the solution causes $PbCrO_4$ to precipitate from solution, which increases the amount of solid $PbCrO_4$.
Relate Cause and Effect *How does adding lead nitrate disturb the $PbCrO_4$ equilibrium?*

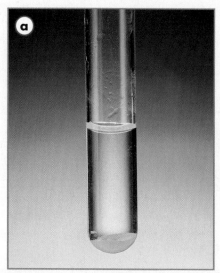

SampleProblem 18.7

Finding Equilibrium Ion Concentrations in the Presence of a Common Ion

Small amounts of silver bromide can be added to the lenses used for eyeglasses. The silver bromide causes the lenses to darken in the presence of large amounts of UV light. The K_{sp} of silver bromide is 5.0×10^{-13}. What is the concentration of bromide ion in a 1.00-L saturated solution of AgBr to which 0.020 mol of $AgNO_3$ is added?

❶ Analyze List the knowns and the unknown.
Use one unknown to express both $[Ag^+]$ and $[Br^-]$. Let x be the equilibrium concentration of bromide ion and $x + 0.020$ be the equilibrium concentration of silver ion.

KNOWNS	UNKNOWN
$K_{sp} = 5.0 \times 10^{-13}$	$[Br^-] = ?\ M$
moles of $AgNO_3$ added $= 0.020$ mol	
$AgBr(s) \rightleftharpoons Ag^+(aq) + Br^-(aq)$	

❷ Calculate Solve for the unknown.

Write the expression for K_{sp}.

$$K_{sp} = [Ag^+] \times [Br^-]$$

Substitute x for $[Br^-]$ in the solubility product expression.

$$K_{sp} = [Ag^+] \times x$$

Rearrange the equation to solve for x.

$$x = \frac{K_{sp}}{[Ag^+]}$$

> Based on the small value of K_{sp}, you can assume that x will be very small compared to 0.020. Thus, $[Ag^+] \approx 0.020\ M$.

Substitute the values for K_{sp} and $[Ag^+]$ in the expression and solve.

$$x = \frac{(5.0 \times 10^{-13})}{0.020}$$

$$[Br^-] = 2.5 \times 10^{-11}M$$

❸ Evaluate Does the result make sense? The concentration of Br^- in a saturated solution of AgBr is $7.0 \times 10^{-7}M$ (the square root of the K_{sp}). It makes sense that the addition of $AgNO_3$ would lower the concentration of Br^- because the presence of a common ion, Ag^+, causes AgBr to precipitate from solution.

35. What is the concentration of sulfide ion in a 1.0-L solution of iron(II) sulfide to which 0.04 mol of iron(II) nitrate is added? The K_{sp} of FeS is 8×10^{-19}.

36. The K_{sp} of $SrSO_4$ is 3.2×10^{-7}. What is the equilibrium concentration of sulfate ion in a 1.0-L solution of strontium sulfate to which 0.10 mol of $Sr(CH_3CO_2)_2$ is added?

> You can usually assume that the amount of the slightly soluble compound that dissociates is small compared to the amount of the common ion that is added.

Figure 18.20
Formation of a Precipitate
As solutions of barium nitrate and sodium sulfate are mixed, a precipitate of $BaSO_4$ is formed.
Explain *Why is barium sulfate the only compound that precipitates when the solutions are mixed?*

You can use the solubility product constant to predict whether a precipitate will form when two solutions are mixed. **A precipitate will form if the product of the concentrations of two ions in the mixture is greater than the K_{sp} value for the compound formed from the ions.** After the precipitate forms, the solution is saturated for that compound. If the product of the concentrations is less than the K_{sp} value, no precipitate will form and the solution is unsaturated.

Suppose you mix two solutions, 0.50 L of $0.002M$ $Ba(NO_3)_2$ and 0.50 L of $0.008M$ Na_2SO_4. The mixture will have a volume of one liter. The compound that might form a precipitate is barium sulfate ($BaSO_4$), which has a K_{sp} value of 1.1×10^{-10}. Precipitation will occur if the product of the concentrations of Ba^{2+} and SO_4^{2-} is greater than the K_{sp} value.

To predict whether a precipitate will form, you need to know the concentration of the ions after the solutions were mixed. During mixing, each solution is diluted with an equal volume of the other solution. So the concentrations of both Ba^{2+} and SO_4^{2-} will be half of their original concentrations. Therefore, in the combined solution, $[Ba^{2+}] = 0.001M$ and $[SO_4^{2-}] = 0.004M$. You can multiply these concentrations and compare the result with the K_{sp} value.

$$[Ba^{2+}] \times [SO_4^{2-}] = (0.001M) \times (0.004M) = 4 \times 10^{-6}$$

The calculated result is larger than the K_{sp} value for barium sulfate (1.1×10^{-10}). Therefore, $BaSO_4$ will precipitate from the solution. The process will continue until the product of the concentrations of the ions remaining in solution is equal to 1.1×10^{-10}. Figure 18.20 shows the mixing of the two solutions and the formation of the barium sulfate precipitate.

18.4 LessonCheck

37. Summarize What does the solubility product constant, K_{sp}, tell you about the solubility of a compound?

38. Identify What two values should you compare to predict whether a precipitate will form when two solutions are mixed?

39. Apply Concepts Write the solubility product expression for Ag_2CO_3.

40. Compare Which compound has the higher solubility: FeS ($K_{sp} = 8.0 \times 10^{-19}$) or CuS ($K_{sp} = 8.0 \times 10^{-37}$)?

41. Calculate What is the K_{sp} of nickel(II) sulfide if the equilibrium concentrations of Ni^{2+} and S^{2-} in a saturated solution of NiS are each $2 \times 10^{-10}M$?

42. Calculate What is the concentration of lead ions and sulfide ions in a saturated solution of lead sulfide (PbS) solution at 25°C? ($K_{sp} = 3.0 \times 10^{-28}$)

43. Calculate The K_{sp} value for barium sulfate is 1.1×10^{-10}. What is the sulfate-ion concentration of a 1.00 L saturated solution of $BaSO_4$ to which 0.015 mol of $Ba(NO_3)_2$ is added?

44. Predict Will a precipitate form when 500 mL of a $0.02M$ solution of $AgNO_3$ is mixed with 500 mL of a $0.001M$ solution of NaCl? Explain.

BIGIDEA REACTIONS

45. Explain how the common ion effect illustrates Le Châtelier's principle.

18.5 Free Energy and Entropy

CHEMISTRY & YOU

Q: *How can a fire start on its own?* Sometimes a fire can occur without an external source of ignition, such as a match or an electrical spark. The fuel might be a pile of oily rags or a stack of hay that has not been thoroughly dried. *Spontaneous combustion* is the term used to describe these fires. In this lesson, you will learn about the conditions that can cause such a fire.

Key Questions

🔑 What are two characteristics of spontaneous reactions?

🔑 What part does entropy play in a reaction?

🔑 What two factors determine whether a reaction is spontaneous?

🔑 How is the value of ΔG related to the spontaneity of a reaction?

Vocabulary

- free energy
- spontaneous reaction
- nonspontaneous reaction
- entropy
- law of disorder

Free Energy and Spontaneous Reactions

🔑 *What are two characteristics of spontaneous reactions?*

Some of the energy released in a chemical reaction can be harnessed to do work, such as pushing the pistons in an internal-combustion engine. The energy that is available to do work is called **free energy.** Just because energy is available to do work, however, does not mean that it can be used efficiently. For example, an internal-combustion engine in a car is only about 30 percent efficient. That is, only about 30 percent of the free energy released as gasoline burns is used to move the car. The remaining 70 percent is lost as friction and waste heat. No process can be made 100 percent efficient. Even in living things, which are among the most efficient users of free energy, processes are seldom more than 70 percent efficient.

Spontaneous Versus Nonspontaneous Reactions Energy can be obtained from a reaction only if the reaction actually occurs. In other words, you can write a balanced equation for a chemical reaction, but the reaction may not actually take place. For example, you can write an equation for the decomposition of carbon dioxide to carbon and oxygen.

$$CO_2(g) \longrightarrow C(s) + O_2(g)$$

This equation, which represents the reverse of combustion, is balanced. However, experience tells you that this reaction does not tend to occur. Carbon and oxygen react to form carbon dioxide, not the reverse. The world of balanced chemical equations is really divided into two groups. One group contains equations representing reactions that actually occur. The other contains equations representing reactions that do not tend to occur, or at least not efficiently.

Figure 18.21 Spontaneous Reaction

Fireworks displays are the result of highly favored spontaneous reactions. A large quantity of free energy is released.

Some chemical reactions are spontaneous. A **spontaneous reaction** occurs naturally and favors the formation of products at the stated conditions. Figure 18.21 shows an example of a spontaneous reaction. **Spontaneous reactions produce large amounts of products and release free energy.** A chemical reaction that does not favor the formation of products at the stated conditions is called a **nonspontaneous reaction.** Such reactions produce little, if any, product.

Reversible Reactions In nearly all reversible reactions, one reaction is favored over the other. Consider the decomposition of carbonic acid in water.

$$H_2CO_3(aq) \rightleftharpoons CO_2(g) + H_2O(l)$$
$$<1\% \qquad\qquad >99\%$$

In the forward reaction, carbonic acid is the reactant. Suppose you could start with pure carbonic acid in water and let the system come to equilibrium. More than 99 percent of the reactant would be converted to the products carbon dioxide and water. These products are highly favored at equilibrium. The natural tendency is for carbonic acid to decompose to carbon dioxide and water. Thus, the forward reaction is spontaneous and releases free energy. In the reverse reaction, carbon dioxide and water are the reactants, and carbonic acid is the product. Suppose you allow a solution of carbon dioxide in water to come to equilibrium. Less than 1 percent of the reactants will combine to form carbonic acid. The reactants show little natural tendency to go to products. Thus, the combination of carbon dioxide and water to form carbonic acid is a nonspontaneous reaction.

Figure 18.22 shows another example of a reversible reaction. When solutions of cadmium nitrate and sodium sulfide are mixed, the products are aqueous sodium nitrate and solid yellow cadmium sulfide. Cadmium sulfide is highly favored. Thus, the forward reaction is spontaneous. The reverse reaction, the production of cadmium nitrate and sodium sulfide from cadmium sulfide and sodium nitrate, is nonspontaneous.

$$Cd(NO_3)_2(aq) + Na_2S(aq) \rightleftharpoons CdS(s) + 2NaNO_3(aq)$$

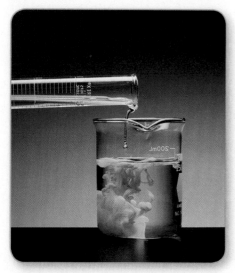

Figure 18.22 Reversible Reaction

A precipitate of cadmium sulfide forms spontaneously when solutions of sodium sulfide and cadmium nitrate are mixed. The reverse reaction is nonspontaneous.

Infer *Is free energy released in this reaction?*

Figure 18.23 Photosynthesis
Outside of plants, carbon dioxide and water do not normally combine to produce glucose ($C_6H_{12}O_6$) and oxygen. Photosynthesis, which is a series of reactions, does occur in plants.
Infer *What happens to the energy that is stored in glucose?*

$$6CO_2 \quad + \quad 6H_2O \xrightarrow{\text{light energy}} C_6H_{12}O_6 \quad + \quad 6O_2$$

The Rate of Spontaneous Reactions It is important to note that the terms *spontaneous* and *nonspontaneous* do not refer to the rate of a reaction. Some spontaneous reactions are so slow that they appear to be nonspontaneous. The reaction of table sugar and oxygen is an example of such a reaction.

$$C_{12}H_{22}O_{11} + 12O_2 \longrightarrow 12CO_2 + 11H_2O$$

Nothing appears to be happening in a bowl of sugar sitting on a table. You might assume that the reaction is nonspontaneous. In fact, the reaction is highly spontaneous, but at room temperature the reaction is so slow that it would take thousands of years for the reaction to reach completion. When you supply energy in the form of heat, the reaction is fast. Then it is obvious that the formation of carbon dioxide and water is highly favored.

Changing the conditions of a chemical reaction can affect more than the reaction rate. It can also affect whether a reaction will occur. A reaction that is nonspontaneous in one set of conditions may be spontaneous in other conditions. Consider the photosynthesis reaction, which is summarized in Figure 18.23. This multistep reaction takes place in plant leaves. This complex process could not happen without the energy supplied by sunlight. Other requirements include plant pigments, such as chlorophyll, that absorb the light energy.

Coupled Reactions Sometimes a nonspontaneous reaction can be made to occur if it is coupled to a spontaneous reaction. One reaction releases energy that is used by the other reaction. Coupled reactions are common in the complex biological processes that take place in living organisms. Within cells, a series of spontaneous reactions release the energy stored in glucose. Molecules in cells capture and transfer the free energy to nonspontaneous reactions, such as the formation of proteins. Chapter 24 describes these processes.

Q: *Decomposition reactions that occur inside a pile of oily rags or a damp stack of hay cause heat to build up. If the heat cannot escape, the temperature within the pile or stack will rise. How can a rise in temperature cause a fire to start on its own? Hint: Think about the reaction of table sugar and oxygen.*

Figure 18.24 Order and Disorder
A dog walker with several dogs could represent relative order and disorder. **a.** All of the dogs are on leashes and are strolling orderly along the path. **b.** The dogs are no longer wearing leashes and are running freely. This situation represents disorder.

Learn more about entropy online.

Entropy

🔑 What part does entropy play in a reaction?

Recall that changes in the heat content, or enthalpy, of a system occur with most chemical and physical processes. These changes help determine whether a process is spontaneous. For example, the combustion of carbon (graphite) is exothermic. The reaction releases 393.5 kJ for each mole of carbon burned. The reaction is spontaneous.

$$C(s, \text{graphite}) + O_2(g) \longrightarrow CO_2(g) + 393.5 \text{ kJ/mol}$$

You might expect that only exothermic reactions are spontaneous. Some processes, however, are spontaneous even though they absorb heat. Consider what happens as ice melts. As it changes from a solid to a liquid, 1 mol of ice at 25°C absorbs 6.0 kJ of heat from its surroundings. The liquid water has a higher energy than the solid ice.

$$H_2O(s) + 6.0 \text{ kJ/mol} \longrightarrow H_2O(l)$$

If you consider only enthalpy changes, it is difficult to explain why the ice melts. In spontaneous processes, the rule seems to be that the direction of energy change is from higher energy to lower energy. Yet the ice does melt. Some factor other than the enthalpy change must help determine whether a physical or chemical process is spontaneous.

The other factor is related to order. You are probably familiar with everyday ideas about order and disorder. For example, a handful of marbles is relatively ordered in the sense that all the marbles are collected in one place. If the marbles are dropped, it is not probable that they will end up in the same neat arrangement. Instead, the marbles scatter on the ground. They become disordered. Scattered marbles have a higher entropy than a handful of marbles. **Entropy** is a measure of the disorder of a system. Figure 18.24 provides another comparison of relative order and disorder.

The **law of disorder** states that the natural tendency is for systems to move in the direction of increasing disorder or randomness. You are probably familiar with this tendency. For example, you start the school year with an empty locker that you gradually fill with items. For a few weeks, it is easy to find items in your locker. Over time, your locker may tend to become more disordered unless you put energy (work) into maintaining the order.

The law of disorder also applies at the level of atoms and molecules. So entropy can affect the direction of a reaction. 🔑 **Reactions in which entropy increases as reactants form products tend to be favored.** Figure 18.25 provides some general rules to help you predict the effect of entropy on a reaction.

Figure 18.25 Entropy
Here are four examples of changes that can increase the entropy of a system.

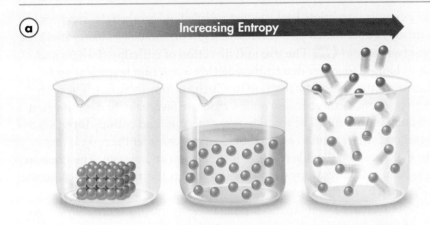

(a) For a given substance, the entropy of the gas is greater than the entropy of the liquid or the solid. Similarly, the entropy of the liquid is greater than that of the solid. Thus, entropy increases in reactions in which solid reactants form liquid or gaseous products. Entropy also increases when liquid reactants form gaseous products.

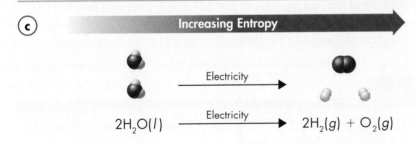

(b) Entropy increases when a substance is divided into parts. For instance, entropy increases when an ionic compound, such as sodium chloride, dissolves in water. The sodium ions and chloride ions are less ordered in solution than they are in the solid crystal.

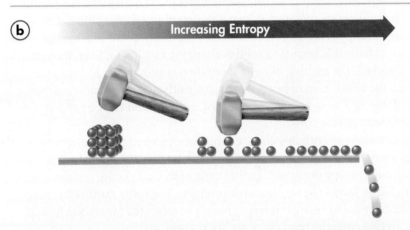

$$2H_2O(l) \xrightarrow{\text{Electricity}} 2H_2(g) + O_2(g)$$

(c) Entropy tends to increase in chemical reactions in which the total number of product molecules is greater than the total number of reactant molecules.

(d) Entropy tends to increase when the temperature increases. As the temperature rises, the molecules move faster and faster, which increases the disorder.

Enthalpy and Entropy

🔑 *What two factors determine whether a reaction is spontaneous?*

In every chemical reaction, heat is either released or absorbed. In every reaction, entropy either increases or decreases. How do these two factors affect the course of a reaction? 🔑 **The size and direction of enthalpy changes and entropy changes together determine whether a reaction is spontaneous.**

Consider an exothermic reaction in which entropy increases. The reaction will be spontaneous because both factors are favorable. The combustion of carbon is an example. The reaction is exothermic, and entropy increases as solid carbon forms gaseous carbon dioxide. Now consider the reverse reaction in which carbon dioxide reacts to form carbon and oxygen. The reaction absorbs heat, and the entropy decreases as a solid is formed from gases. So the reaction must be nonspontaneous.

A reaction can be spontaneous if a decrease in entropy is offset by a large release of heat. A reaction can also be spontaneous if an increase in enthalpy is offset by an increase in entropy. Recall the example of ice melting. The change in enthalpy is not favorable because heat is absorbed. The change in entropy is favorable because a solid is changing to a liquid. Even though heat is absorbed, the melting of ice is spontaneous above 0°C. At such temperatures, the absorption of heat is sufficiently offset by a favorable entropy change. Table 18.3 summarizes the effect of enthalpy and entropy changes on the spontaneity of reactions.

You can also use enthalpy changes and entropy changes to determine whether a reaction is nonspontaneous. Consider a reaction when heat is absorbed and entropy decreases. In that case, both changes are unfavorable. Neither change favors the formation of products. For some exothermic reactions, the decrease in entropy is large enough to offset the favorable enthalpy change. In that case, the reaction is not spontaneous. Finally, a reaction that absorbs heat could have an increase in entropy that is too small to offset the unfavorable enthalpy change. Figure 18.26 uses visuals to show the results of six possible combinations of an enthalpy change and an entropy change.

Table 18.3

How Enthalpy Changes and Entropy Changes Affect Reaction Spontaneity

Enthalpy change	Entropy change	Is the reaction spontaneous?
Decreases (exothermic)	Increases (more disorder in products than in reactants)	Yes
Increases (endothermic)	Increases	Only if unfavorable enthalpy change is offset by favorable entropy change
Decreases (exothermic)	Decreases (less disorder in products than in reactants)	Only if unfavorable entropy change is offset by favorable enthalpy change
Increases (endothermic)	Decreases	No

Figure 18.26 Enthalpy and Entropy
The combination of the enthalpy change and the change in entropy for a reaction determines whether or not the reaction is spontaneous.
Summarize *Explain why a spontaneous reaction can occur when one factor is unfavorable but not when both factors are unfavorable.*

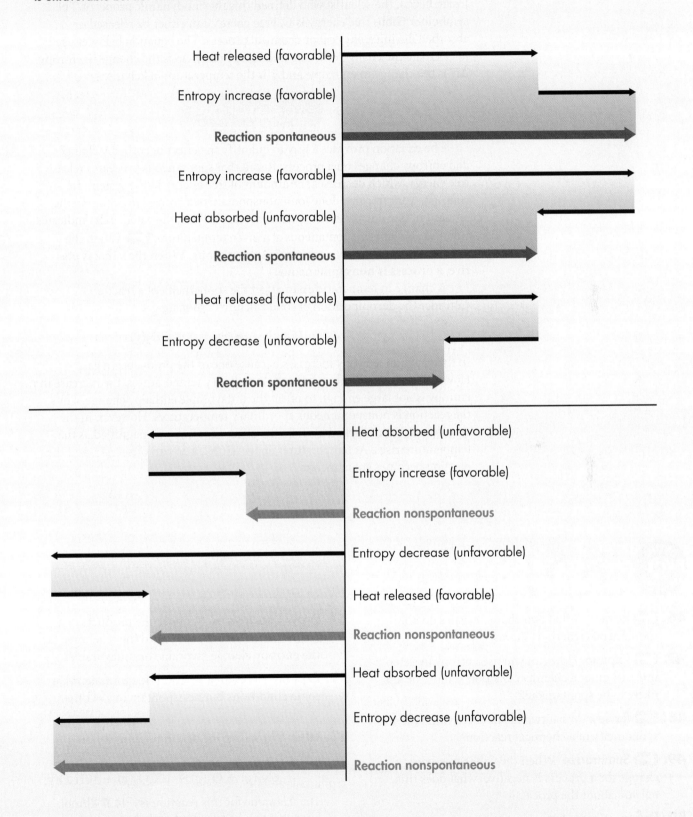

Free Energy Change

How is the value of ΔG related to the spontaneity of a reaction?

Free energy is often expressed as Gibbs free energy. This term is named for Josiah Gibbs, the scientist who defined this thermodynamic property. The symbol for Gibbs free energy is G. Free energy can either be released or absorbed during a physical or chemical process. The equation below is used to calculate the change in Gibbs free energy (ΔG). ΔS is the change in entropy, ΔH is the change in enthalpy, and T is the temperature in kelvins.

$$\Delta G = \Delta H - T\Delta S$$

The equation provides a way to quantify the effect of enthalpy changes and entropy changes on a process. Recall that spontaneous processes release free energy, which decreases the amount of free energy in the system. In contrast, work must be done for a nonspontaneous process to occur. So the amount of free energy in the system increases. Thus, the value of ΔG indicates whether a process is spontaneous at a given temperature. **When the value of ΔG is negative, a process is spontaneous. When the value is positive, a process is nonspontaneous.**

A change in temperature can affect the spontaneity of a reaction. Consider the decomposition of solid calcium carbonate.

$$CaCO_3(s) + 178 \text{ kJ} \longrightarrow CaO(s) + CO_2(g)$$

In this reaction, entropy increases because one of the products is a gas. However, the reaction absorbs heat. At ordinary temperatures, the increase in entropy is not large enough to offset the unfavorable enthalpy change. Thus, the reaction is nonspontaneous at ordinary temperatures. However, in the equation, ΔS is multiplied by T. So the effect of entropy is magnified as the temperature rises. At temperatures above 850°C, $T\Delta S$ can offset ΔH, and the reaction becomes spontaneous.

ONLINE PROBLEMS 18.5 LessonCheck

46. Review What two characteristics do all spontaneous reactions share?

47. Explain How can you use entropy to determine whether a chemical reaction is more or less likely to be spontaneous?

48. Review What two factors determine the spontaneity of a chemical reaction?

49. Summarize When the Gibbs free-energy change for a process is negative, what does this tell you about the process?

50. Define What is free energy?

51. Draw Conclusions Suppose the products of a reaction are more ordered than the reactants. Is the entropy change favorable or unfavorable?

52. Explain How can a reaction be spontaneous at some conditions but nonspontaneous at other conditions?

53. Infer Nitroglycerine decomposes as follows:

$$4C_3H_5(NO_3)_3(l) \longrightarrow$$
$$6N_2(g) + O_2(g) + 12CO_2(g) + 10H_2O(g)$$

The ΔH value for this reaction is -1427 kJ/mol. Use what you know about enthalpy and entropy to explain why this reaction is so explosive.

Small-Scale Lab

Enthalpy and Entropy

Purpose

To observe and measure energy changes during the formation of a solution and to describe and explain these changes in terms of enthalpy and entropy

Materials

- alcohol thermometer
- four 1-oz plastic cups
- plastic spoon
- sodium chloride
- ammonium chloride
- calcium chloride
- water
- crushed ice
- stirring rod

Procedure

1. Make a data table like the one below on a separate sheet of paper.

2. Place two level spoonfuls of water in one plastic cup. Measure and record the water temperature (T_1).

3. Dry the spoon. Then, add one level spoonful of NaCl to the cup. Stir gently with the thermometer.

4. Record the highest or lowest temperature that results (T_2).

5. Rinse the thermometer and spoon.

6. Repeat Steps 2–5, using NH_4Cl and $CaCl_2$.

Mixture	T_1	T_2	ΔT
$NaCl(s) + H_2O(l)$			
$NH_4Cl(s) + H_2O(l)$			
$CaCl_2(s) + H_2O(l)$			

Analyze and Conclude

1. Calculate Determine ΔT for each mixture using the following equation: $\Delta T = T_2 - T_1$

2. Observe An exothermic process releases heat. An endothermic process absorbs heat. In which mixture was the process of dissolving endothermic? In which mixture was the process exothermic? In which mixture, was heat neither released nor absorbed? Which solution(s) had little or no change in temperature?

3. Describe This is the equation for the dissociation of NaCl in water:

$$NaCl(s) \longrightarrow Na^+(aq) + Cl^-(aq)$$

Write similar ionic equations to show how NH_4Cl and $CaCl_2$ dissociate in water. Include heat as a reactant or a product in each equation.

4. Draw Conclusions When a solid dissolves in water, does entropy increase or decrease? Explain your reasoning.

5. Relate Cause and Effect Both the entropy change and the enthalpy change were favorable for a spontaneous change in which mixture? In which mixture was one change favorable and the other unfavorable for a spontaneous change? Explain why the change still happened?

You're the Chemist

1. Analyze Data Mix a tablespoon of crushed ice with a tablespoon of NaCl. Stir gently with a stirring rod. Then measure and record the lowest temperature reached. Compare the temperature change for this mixture with the results for the mixture of NaCl and liquid water.

2. Analyze Data Explain what you observed in the first activity. *Hint:* Is the process of melting ice exothermic or endothermic?

3. Design an Experiment Will the results be the same when an ionic compound other than NaCl is mixed with crushed ice? Try doing Activity 1 with NH_4Cl and $CaCl_2$.

18 **Study** Guide

BIGIDEAS
REACTIONS, MATTER AND ENERGY

The rate of a chemical reaction can be controlled by adjusting temperature, concentration, or particle size. Adding a catalyst speeds up a reaction by lowering the activation energy. Energy is released in some reactions and absorbed in others. Changes in enthalpy and entropy can be used to explain why some reactions occur naturally and others do not.

18.1 Rates of Reaction

🔑 In chemistry, the rate of a chemical reaction, or the reaction rate, is usually expressed as the change in the amount of reactant or product per unit time.

🔑 Factors that can affect the rate of a chemical reaction are temperature, concentration, particle size, and the use of a catalyst.

- rate (595)
- collision theory (596)
- activation energy (596)
- activated complex (596)
- inhibitor (601)

18.2 The Progress of Chemical Reactions

🔑 The value of the specific rate constant, k, in a rate law is large if products form quickly; the value is small if the products form slowly.

🔑 Most chemical reactions consist of two or more elementary reactions.

- rate law (604)
- specific rate constant (604)
- first-order reaction (605)
- elementary reaction (607)
- reaction mechanism (607)
- intermediate (607)

18.3 Reversible Reactions and Equilibrium

🔑 At chemical equilibrium, both the forward and reverse reactions continue, but because their rates are equal, no net change occurs in the concentrations of the reaction components.

🔑 Stresses that upset the equilibrium of a chemical system include changes in concentration of reactants or products, changes in temperature, and changes in pressure.

🔑 The size of the equilibrium constant indicates whether reactants or products are more common at equilibrium.

- reversible reaction (609)
- chemical equilibrium (610)
- equilibrium position (611)
- Le Châtelier's principle (612)
- equilibrium constant (616)

18.4 Solubility Equilibrium

🔑 The smaller the value of the solubility product constant, the lower the solubility of the compound.

🔑 A precipitate will form if the product of the concentrations of two ions in the mixture is greater than the K_{sp} value of the compound formed from the ions.

- solubility product constant (622)
- common ion (624)
- common ion effect (624)

18.5 Free Energy and Entropy

🔑 Spontaneous reactions produce large amounts of products and release free energy.

🔑 Reactions in which entropy increases as reactants form products tend to be favored.

🔑 The size and direction of enthalpy changes and entropy changes together determine whether a reaction is spontaneous.

🔑 When the value of ΔG is negative, a process is spontaneous. When the value is positive, a process is nonspontaneous.

- free energy (627)
- spontaneous reaction (628)
- nonspontaneous reaction (628)
- entropy (630)
- law of disorder (630)

Key Equations

$$\text{Rate} = \frac{\Delta A}{\Delta t} = k \times [\text{A}] \qquad \text{Rate} = k[\text{A}]^x[\text{B}]^y$$

$$K_{eq} = \frac{[\text{C}]^c \times [\text{D}]^d}{[\text{A}]^a \times [\text{B}]^b}$$

$$K_{sp} = [\text{A}]^a \times [\text{B}]^b$$

$$\Delta G = \Delta H - T\Delta S$$

Math Tune-Up: Equilibrium Problems

Problem	**❶ Analyze**	**❷ Calculate**	**❸ Evaluate**
Gaseous sulfur dioxide reacts with oxygen in a 1.0-L container at 600°C to form gaseous sulfur trioxide. $2SO_2(g) + O_2(g) \rightleftharpoons 2SO_3(g)$ At equilibrium, a mixture of these gases contains 1.5 mol SO_2, 1.2 mol O_2, and 3.4 mol SO_3. What is the equilibrium constant for this reaction?	Knowns: $[SO_2] = 1.5$ mol/L $[O_2] = 1.2$ mol/L $[SO_3] = 3.4$ mol/L Unknown: $K_{eq} = ?$ Use the expression for K_{eq}: $K_{eq} = \dfrac{[C]^c \times [D]^d}{[A]^a \times [B]^b}$	Write the expression for K_{eq} for this equation and substitute the equilibrium concentrations in the expression. $K_{eq} = \dfrac{[SO_3]^2}{[SO_2]^2 \times [O_2]}$ $= \dfrac{(3.4 \text{ mol/L})^2}{(1.5 \text{ mol/L})^2 \times (1.2 \text{ mol/L})}$ $K_{eq} = 4.3$	Each concentration is raised to the correct power. The value for K_{eq} is appropriate for an equilibrium mixture that contains a larger number of moles of products than of reactants.
What is the concentration of silver ions and chloride ions in a saturated solution of silver chloride at 25°C? ($K_{sp} = 1.8 \times 10^{-10}$)	Knowns: $K_{sp} = 1.8 \times 10^{-10}$ $AgCl(s) \rightleftharpoons$ $\quad Ag^+(aq) + Cl^-(aq)$ Unknowns: $[Ag^+] = ?M$ $[Cl^-] = ?M$ Use the expression for K_{sp}: $K_{sp} = [A]^a \times [B]^b$	Write the expression for K_{sp}, modify it so there is a single unknown, and solve for that unknown. $K_{sp} = [Ag^+] \times [Cl^-]$ $1.8 \times 10^{-10} = [Ag^+]^2$ $[Ag^+] = \sqrt{1.8 \times 10^{-10}}$ $[Ag^+] = 1.3 \times 10^{-5}M$ $[Cl^-] = 1.3 \times 10^{-5}M$	If you multiply $[Ag^+] \times [Cl^-]$, the result is 1.7×10^{-10}, which is close to the value of K_{sp}. The value is not exactly the same because the answers are rounded to two significant figures. **Hint:** At equilibrium, $[Ag^+] = [Cl^-]$.
Predict whether a precipitate will form when 0.50 L of 0.001M $Ca(NO_3)_2$ is mixed with 0.50 L of 0.0008M Na_2CO_3 to form one liter of solution. The K_{sp} of $CaCO_3$ is 4.5×10^{-9}.	Knowns: 0.50 L of 0.001M $Ca(NO_3)_2$ 0.50 L of 0.0008M Na_2CO_3 K_{sp} of $CaCO_3 = 4.5 \times 10^{-9}$ Unknown: $[Ca^{2+}] \times [CO_3^{2-}] > K_{sp}?$ Precipitation will occur if the product of the concentrations of the two ions exceeds the K_{sp} value of $CaCO_3$.	Divide the initial concentrations in half because the volume of the solution has doubled. Multiply the concentrations together as a trial product and compare with K_{sp}. $[Ca^{2+}]$ (final) $= 0.0005M$ $[CO_3^{2-}]$ (final) $= 0.0004M$ $[Ca^{2+}] \times [CO_3^{2-}] =$ $(0.0005M) \times (0.0004M) =$ 2×10^{-7} $2 \times 10^{-7} > K_{sp}$, so a precipitate will form.	A precipitate will form in this case because 2.0×10^{-7} is greater than 4.5×10^{-9}. **Remember:** Equilibrium constants are not reported with units.

Lesson by Lesson

18.1 Rates of Reaction

*54. According to collision theory, what are two things that can happen when atoms, ions, or molecules collide?

55. What is activation energy?

56. Which of these statements is true?

   a. Chemical reactions tend to slow down when the temperature rises.

   b. Once a chemical reaction starts, the reacting particles no longer have to collide for products to form.

   c. Increasing the total surface area of solid or liquid reactants increases the rate of the reaction.

57. When the gas to a stove is turned on, the gas does not burn until it is lit by a flame. Explain this observation in terms of the effect of temperature on reaction rate.

*58. Explain how a catalyst is able to change the rate of a reaction.

18.2 The Progress of Chemical Reactions

59. What is a rate law?

60. How is a first-order reaction different from higher-order reactions?

*61. Sketch a reaction progress curve for the overall reaction with the following mechanism:

$$2NO(g) \longrightarrow N_2O_2(g) \text{ (fast)}$$

$$N_2O_2(g) + O_2(g) \longrightarrow 2NO_2(g) \text{ (slow)}$$

What is the intermediate in this reaction?

62. Write the balanced equation for the overall reaction described in Question 61.

18.3 Reversible Reactions and Equilibrium

63. In your own words, define a reversible reaction.

64. Compare the rates of the forward and reverse reactions when a chemical equilibrium has been established.

65. What is Le Châtelier's principle?

*66. Write the expression for the equilibrium constant for each reaction.

   a. $4H_2(g) + CS_2(g) \rightleftharpoons CH_4(g) + 2H_2S(g)$

   b. $PCl_5(g) \rightleftharpoons PCl_3(g) + Cl_2(g)$

67. For each reaction, decide whether products or reactants will be more common at equilibrium.

   a. $H_2(g) + F_2(g) \rightleftharpoons 2HF(g); K_{eq} = 1 \times 10^{13}$

   b. $SO_2(g) + NO_2(g) \rightleftharpoons$
   $$NO(g) + SO_3(g); K_{eq} = 1 \times 10^2$$

   c. $2H_2O(g) \rightleftharpoons$
   $$2H_2(g) + O_2(g); K_{eq} = 6 \times 10^{-28}$$

68. For which reaction will a change in pressure affect the equilibrium position? How will the position change, and why?

   a. $H_2(g) + F_2(g) \longrightarrow 2HF(g)$

   b. $SO_2(g) + NO_2(g) \longrightarrow NO(g) + SO_3(g)$

   c. $2H_2O(g) \longrightarrow 2H_2(g) + O_2(g)$

18.4 Solubility Equilibrium

69. What does the solubility product constant (K_{sp}) represent?

70. Write the expression for K_{sp} for each of the following compounds:

   a. NiS   b. $BaCO_3$

*71. Use Table 18.2 to rank these compounds from most soluble to least soluble.

   a. CuS   b. $BaSO_4$ c. $SrCO_3$ d. AgI

72. What happens when a common ion is added to a saturated solution of an ionic compound?

18.5 Free Energy and Entropy

73. Explain what it means to say that a process is 50 percent efficient.

74. Compare the amount of product at equilibrium in a spontaneous reaction to the amount of product at equilibrium in a nonspontaneous reaction.

75. State the law of disorder in your own words.

76. Which system in each example below has the lower entropy?

   a. 50 mL of liquid water or 50 mL of ice

   b. 10 g of sodium chloride crystals or a solution containing 10 g of sodium chloride

77. Does entropy increase or decrease in each of the following reactions:

a. $CaCO_3(s) \longrightarrow CaO(s) + CO_2(g)$
b. $NH_3(g) + HCl(g) \longrightarrow NH_4Cl(s)$

78. Is it true that all spontaneous processes are exothermic? Explain your answer.

79. Explain why steam condenses to liquid water at normal atmospheric pressure even though the entropy change is unfavorable. *Hint:* Is condensation exothermic or endothermic?

80. How can a change in Gibbs free energy be used to predict whether a reaction will be spontaneous?

Understand Concepts

81. Which of the following statements are always true for a reaction that is spontaneous?

a. The reaction is exothermic.
b. Entropy is increased in the reaction.
c. Free energy is released in the reaction.

82. Use Le Châtelier's principle to explain why carbonated drinks go flat when their containers are left open.

83. Consider the decomposition of N_2O_5 in carbon tetrachloride (CCl_4) at 45°C.

$$2N_2O_5(soln) \longrightarrow 4NO_2(g) + O_2(g)$$

The reaction is first order in N_2O_5, with the specific rate constant $6.08 \times 10^{-4}\,s^{-1}$. Calculate the reaction rate at these conditions.

a. $[N_2O_5] = 0.200\ mol/L$
b. $[N_2O_5] = 0.319\ mol/L$

84. Consider the following reversible reaction:

$$2NO_2(g) \rightleftharpoons N_2O_4(g)$$

What will happen to the reaction rate if the concentration of NO_2 is changed from 0.020 mol/L to 0.030 mol/L? What will happen to the equilibrium position?

85. For the reaction $A + B \rightleftharpoons C$, the activation energy of the forward reaction is 5 kJ, and the total energy change is −20 kJ. What is the activation energy of the reverse reaction?

86. Sketch a reaction progress curve for a reaction that has an activation energy of 22 kJ and a total energy change of −103 kJ.

87. A large box is divided into two compartments with a door between them. In (a), equal quantities of two different monatomic gases are placed in the two compartments. In (b), the door between the compartments is opened, and the gases start to mix. Why would it be highly unlikely for the system in (b) to progress to the system in (c)?

a.   b.   c.

88. Would you expect the entropy to increase in each of the following reactions? Explain your reasoning.

a. $C(s) + O_2(g) \longrightarrow CO_2(g)$
b. $2Al_2O_3(s) \longrightarrow 4Al(s) + 3O_2(g)$
c. $2N(g) \longrightarrow N_2(g)$
d. $N_2(g) \longrightarrow 2N(g)$

89. What would be the effect on the equilibrium position if the volume is decreased in the following reaction?

$$4HCl(g) + O_2(g) \rightleftharpoons 2Cl_2(g) + 2H_2O(g)$$

90. Write the equilibrium-constant expression for this reaction.

$$2SO_2(g) + O_2(g) \rightleftharpoons 2SO_3(g)$$

91. A mixture at equilibrium at 827°C contains 0.552 mol CO_2, 0.552 mol H_2, 0.448 mol CO, and 0.448 mol H_2O. The balanced equation is shown below.

$$CO_2(g) + H_2(g) \rightleftharpoons CO(g) + H_2O(g)$$

What is the value of K_{eq}?

92. What must be true about the concentration of two ions if precipitation occurs when solutions of the two ions are mixed?

93. What is the concentration of carbonate ions in a saturated solution of $SrCO_3$? ($K_{sp} = 9.3 \times 10^{-10}$)

94. Predict what will happen to the rate of a slow reversible reaction if a catalyst is added. What will happen to the equilibrium position?

95. Make a list of five things you did today that resulted in an increase in entropy.

96. What is the equilibrium concentration of barium ion in a 1.0-L saturated solution of barium carbonate to which 0.25 mol K_2CO_3 is added?

* 97. Suppose equilibrium is established for the following reaction at 425 K:

$$Fe_3O_4(s) + 4H_2(g) \rightleftharpoons 3Fe(s) + 4H_2O(g)$$

How would the equilibrium concentration of H_2O be affected by these actions?

a. adding more H_2 to the mixture
b. increasing the pressure
c. removing $H_2(g)$
d. adding a catalyst

98. A student prepares a solution by combining 0.025 mol $CaCl_2$ and 0.015 mol $Pb(NO_3)_2$ and adding water to make 1.0 L of solution. Will a precipitate of $PbCl_2$ form in this solution?

Think Critically

99. **Relate Cause and Effect** An increase in temperature raises the energy of the collisions between reactant molecules. An increase in the concentration of reactants increases the number of collisions. What is the effect of a catalyst on the collisions between molecules?

* 100. **Draw Conclusions** The mechanism for the decomposition of hydrogen peroxide is thought to be as follows:

$$H_2O_2(aq) + I^-(aq) \longrightarrow$$
$$H_2O(l) + IO^-(aq) \text{ (slow)}$$

$$IO^-(aq) + H_2O_2(aq) \longrightarrow$$
$$H_2O(l) + O_2(g) + I^-(aq) \text{ (fast)}$$

a. What is the intermediate?
b. What is the minimum number of activated complexes needed to describe the reaction?
c. Which of the two reactions has the smaller specific rate constant?
d. Write the overall balanced chemical equation for the reaction.
e. Does I^- qualify as a catalyst? Explain.

101. **Relate Cause and Effect** The freezing of liquid water at 0°C can be represented as follows.

$$H_2O(l) \rightleftharpoons H_2O(s)$$

The density of the liquid water is 1.00 g/cm³. The density of the ice is 0.92 g/cm³. Explain why applying pressure causes ice to melt.

102. **Apply Concepts** Explain what is happening in each of the following situations.

a. A campfire is "fanned" to help get it going.
b. Ice cubes melt faster than a block of ice with the same mass.
c. A pinch of powdered manganese dioxide causes hydrogen peroxide to explode even though the manganese dioxide is not changed.

*103. **Analyze Data** Ammonium ions and nitrite ions react in water to form nitrogen gas.

$$NO_2^-(aq) + NH_4^+(aq) \longrightarrow N_2(g) + 2H_2O(l)$$

From the following data, decide the order of the reaction with respect to NH_4^+ and NO_2^- and the overall order of the reaction.

Initial $[NO_2^-]$ (mol/L)	Initial $[NH_4^+]$ (mol/L)	Initial rate (mol/(L·s))
0.0100	0.200	5.4×10^{-7}
0.0200	0.200	10.8×10^{-7}
0.0400	0.200	21.5×10^{-7}
0.0600	0.200	32.3×10^{-7}
0.200	0.0202	10.8×10^{-7}
0.200	0.0404	21.6×10^{-7}
0.200	0.0606	32.4×10^{-7}
0.200	0.0808	43.3×10^{-7}

104. **Use Analogies** A speed bump is a raised ridge that runs across the surface of a street, a parking lot, or driveway. What is the purpose of a speed bump, and how is it similar to activation energy?

*105. **Apply Concepts** In the reversible reaction for the formation of ammonia, the enthalpy change and the entropy change both favor the reverse reaction.

$$N_2(g) + 3H_2(g) \rightleftharpoons 2NH_3(g) + heat$$

You are the chemical engineer in charge of the large-scale production of ammonia. What are three things you can do to increase the percent yield of your product?

106. **Compare and Contrast** When you calculate the K_{eq} for a reaction, you use the coefficient from the balanced equation. Why are the coefficients not used to find the order of a reaction?

107. **Infer** Jars of jam are stored on grocery shelves at room temperature. Why does the instruction "Refrigerate after opening" appear on the label?

108. Graph The following data were collected for the decomposition of compound AB into its elements. The reaction is first order in AB. Answer the following questions.

[AB] (mol/L)	Time (s)
0.300	0
0.246	50
0.201	100
0.165	150
0.135	200
0.111	250
0.090	300
0.075	350

a. Make a graph of concentration (y-axis) versus time (x-axis).

b. Determine the rate of the reaction at $t = 100$ seconds and $t = 250$ seconds.

★109. Interpret Graphs When table sugar, or sucrose, is dissolved in an acid, the sucrose slowly decomposes into two simpler sugars: fructose and glucose. Use the graph to answer the following questions:

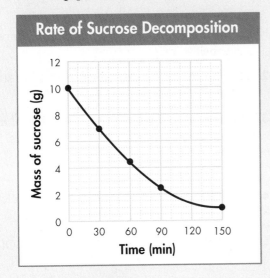

Rate of Sucrose Decomposition

(Graph: y-axis "Mass of sucrose (g)" from 0 to 12; x-axis "Time (min)" from 0 to 150)

a. How many grams of sucrose decompose in the first 30 minutes?

b. How many grams of sucrose decompose in the interval between 90 minutes and 120 minutes?

c. In general, what happens to the rate of decomposition with time?

110. Explain Compost is a mixture that gardeners add to soil to improve the soil. Many gardeners make their own compost by recycling yard and kitchen waste. What types of reactions take place in a compost pile? Why is it important that the compost pile be turned regularly?

111. Connect to the BIGIDEA A discussion of reaction rates often focuses on ways to speed up reactions. However, sometimes it is important to know how to slow down a reaction, such as combustion. Use Le Châtelier's principle to explain why some of the methods that are used to fight fires work.

CHEMYSTERY

Explosive Sugar

The U.S. Chemical Safety Board (CSB) investigates chemical accidents in the workplace. The agency uses what it learns to recommend ways to improve safety. In 2009, the CSB issued a report on the explosion at the sugar refinery in Georgia.

A year before the blast, a steel cover was added to the conveyor belt where the first explosion took place. The cover was added to keep the sugar clean. But the cover also allowed dangerous concentrations of sugar dust to build up around the belt. It was difficult for the CSB to pinpoint the exact cause of the first explosion because of the amount of damage. However, they suspected that an overheated part of the belt ignited the dust.

Vibrations from the small explosion shook loose sugar dust that had collected on many surfaces in the warehouse. Suddenly the air inside the warehouse was filled with tiny particles of sugar.

112. Relate Cause and Effect Explain how the first explosion increased the likelihood that a second, more violent explosion would occur?

113. Connect to the BIGIDEA Suppose you worked for the CSB. What recommendations would you make to prevent similar fires in the future?

114. Write electron configurations and draw electron dot structures for the following elements:
  a. Ge **c.** O **e.** Cl
  b. Ca **d.** Ar **f.** P

∗115. Why is it wrong to say that solid potassium chloride is composed of KCl molecules?

116. Name each ion and then identify it as an anion or a cation.
  a. F^- **c.** P^{3-} **e.** Na^+ **g.** O^{2-}
  b. Cu^{2+} **d.** H^+ **f.** I^- **h.** Mg^{2+}

∗117. Name the following compounds and give the charge on the anion for each.
  a. $NaClO_4$ **c.** $Ca_3(PO_4)_2$ **e.** Na_2SO_4
  b. $KMnO_4$ **d.** $MgCO_3$ **f.** $K_2Cr_2O_7$

118. Which atoms from the following list would you expect to form positive ions, and which would you expect to form negative ions?
  a. Cl **c.** P **e.** Cu **g.** K
  b. Ca **d.** Se **f.** Sn **h.** Fe

119. Find the mass in grams of each quantity.
  a. 4.50 mol Fe
  b. 36.8 L CO (at STP)
  c. 1 molecule of glucose, $C_6H_{12}O_6$
  d. 0.0642 mol ammonium phosphate

120. Aqueous silver nitrate reacts with aqueous potassium iodide to form the precipitate silver iodide.
  a. Write the complete ionic equation.
  b. What are the spectator ions?
  c. Write the net ionic equation.

∗121. When heated, potassium chlorate decomposes into potassium chloride and oxygen gas.
  a. Write the balanced equation for this chemical reaction.
  b. How many grams of oxygen are formed when 4.88 g $KClO_3$ decompose?

122. Give the names and abbreviations of three units of pressure.

123. Is the boiling point of a liquid substance a constant? Explain.

124. What happens to the pressure of a contained gas in each instance?
  a. More gas particles are added.
  b. The temperature of the gas is decreased.
  c. The volume of the container is reduced.

125. What volume will 24.5 g of carbon dioxide gas occupy at 55°C and a pressure of 88.8 kPa?

126. Which of these compounds should readily dissolve in water?
  a. KI(s) **c.** $NH_4Cl(s)$
  b. $C_2H_6(g)$ **d.** $Na_3PO_4(s)$

127. Calculate the percent by mass of water in barium bromide tetrahydrate.

128. For which of these substances would the solubility in water be most likely to decrease with an increase in temperature?
  a. $NH_4NO_3(s)$ **c.** KI(s)
  b. $NH_3(g)$ **d.** NaCl(s)

∗129. How many moles of solute are in 2.40 L of 0.66M KCl?

130. How many liters of a stock solution of 6.00M HCl would you need to prepare 15.0 L of 0.500M HCl?

131. A small amount of ethanol (C_2H_5OH) is dissolved in a large beaker of water.
  a. Identify the solute and the solvent.
  b. Is the freezing point of the solution above or below 0°C?

132. How much heat is released when 12.4 g of steam at 100°C condenses to water at 100°C?

∗133. When solid sodium hydroxide is dissolved in water, the temperature of the solution rises. Is this an exothermic or endothermic process? Explain your answer.

134. The following is the equation for the complete combustion of ethene:

$$C_2H_4(g) + 3O_2(g) \longrightarrow 2CO_2(g) + 2H_2O(g)$$
$$\Delta H = -1411 \text{ kJ}$$

How many kilojoules of heat are released when 32.8 g of ethene are burned?

If You Have Trouble With . . .

Question	114	115	116	117	118	119	120	121	122	123	124	125	126	127	128	129	130	131	132	133	134
See Chapter	5	7	9	9	9	10	11	12	13	13	14	14	15	15	16	16	16	16	17	17	17

Standardized Test Prep

Select the choice that best answers each question or completes each statement.

1. Which reaction is represented by the following expression for an equilibrium constant?

$$K_{eq} = \frac{[CO]^2 \times [O_2]}{[CO_2]^2}$$

   (A) $2CO_2 \rightleftharpoons O_2 + 2CO$
   (B) $CO_2^2 \rightleftharpoons O_2 + 2CO^2$
   (C) $O_2 + 2CO \rightleftharpoons 2CO_2$
   (D) $O_2 + CO_2 \rightleftharpoons CO_2^2$

2. At 25°C, zinc sulfide has a K_{sp} of 3.0×10^{-23}, zinc carbonate has a K_{sp} of 1.0×10^{-10}, and silver iodide has a K_{sp} of 8.3×10^{-17}. Order these salts from most soluble to least soluble.
   (A) zinc carbonate, zinc sulfide, silver iodide
   (B) silver iodide, zinc carbonate, zinc sulfide
   (C) zinc carbonate, silver iodide, zinc sulfide
   (D) zinc sulfide, silver iodide, zinc carbonate

Tips for Success

Multiple Parts Sometimes two phrases in a true/false question are connected with a word such as *because*, *therefore*, or *so*. These words imply a cause-and-effect relationship between the two phrases. Be aware that the overall statement can be false even if each phrase is true on its own.

Use the table to answer Questions 3 and 4.

ΔS	ΔH	ΔG	Spontaneous
+	−	(a)	Yes
+	(b)	+ or −	At high T
(c)	+	+	No
−	−	(d)	At low T

3. The value of ΔG depends on the enthalpy (ΔH) and entropy (ΔS) terms for a reaction. The value of ΔG also varies as a function of temperature. Use the data in the table to identify the missing entries (a), (b), (c), and (d).

4. Which of these reactions would you expect to be spontaneous at relatively low temperatures? At relatively high temperatures?
   (A) $H_2O(l) \longrightarrow H_2O(g)$
   (B) $H_2O(g) \longrightarrow H_2O(l)$
   (C) $H_2O(s) \longrightarrow H_2O(l)$

5. The atomic windows below represent different degrees of entropy. Arrange the windows in order of increasing entropy.

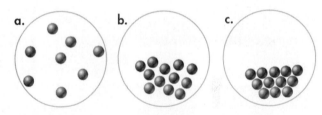

For each question below there are two statements. Decide whether each statement is true or false. Then decide whether Statement II is a correct explanation for Statement I.

Statement I		Statement II
6. A catalyst lowers the activation energy for a chemical reaction.	BECAUSE	A catalyst makes a reaction more exothermic.
7. The entropy of ice is greater than the entropy of steam.	BECAUSE	The density of ice is greater than the density of steam.
8. The rate of a chemical reaction is affected by a change in temperature.	BECAUSE	The kinetic energy of particles is related to the temperature.
9. A large value for an equilibrium constant indicates that products are favored at equilibrium.	BECAUSE	The ratio of products to reactants at equilibrium is always > 1.

If You Have Trouble With . . .

Question	1	2	3	4	5	6	7	8	9
See Lesson	18.3	18.4	18.5	18.5	18.5	18.1	18.5	18.1	18.3

19

Acids, Bases, and Salts

INSIDE:

- **19.1** Acid-Base Theories
- **19.2** Hydrogen Ions and Acidity
- **19.3** Strengths of Acids and Bases
- **19.4** Neutralization Reactions
- **19.5** Salts in Solution

PearsonChem.com

Artists often use hydrofluoric acid to etch designs on glass.

REACTIONS

Essential Questions:

1. *What are the different ways chemists define acids and bases?*
2. *What does the pH of a solution mean?*
3. *How do chemists use acid-base reactions?*

CHEMYSTERY

Paper Trail

The invention of the printing press in 1440 increased the number of books that could be printed and the need for paper on which to print these books. The main ingredient in paper was cotton, which is almost pure cellulose. This type of paper is referred to as rag-based paper. When books printed on high-quality rag-based paper are stored correctly, they can last for hundreds of years.

By 1880, the demand for paper was so great that printers switched from rag-based paper to wood-based paper. Over time, the wood-based paper tended to yellow and crack. Sometimes the paper was so brittle that it crumbled when touched.

Why did a change in the content of paper cause such a dramatic change in the properties of the paper?

▶ Connect to the **BIGIDEA** As you read about acids and bases, think about what could cause paper to crumble.

NATIONAL SCIENCE EDUCATION STANDARDS

A-1, A-2, B-3, G-1, G-2, G-3

19.1 Acid-Base Theories

Q: *Why are high levels of ammonia harmful to you?* Bracken Cave, near San Antonio, Texas, is home to millions of Mexican free-tailed bats. Nitrogen compounds in bat urine can decompose and release ammonia into the air. Visitors to the cave must wear protective goggles and respirators. They need this protection because of what happens when ammonia reacts with water. Ammonia is an example of a base. In this lesson, you will learn about some of the properties of acids and bases.

Key Questions

🔑 How did Arrhenius define an acid and a base?

🔑 What distinguishes an acid from a base in the Brønsted-Lowry theory?

🔑 How did Lewis define an acid and a base?

Vocabulary

- hydronium ion (H_3O^+)
- conjugate acid
- conjugate base
- conjugate acid-base pair
- amphoteric
- Lewis acid
- Lewis base

Arrhenius Acids and Bases

🔑 How did Arrhenius define an acid and a base?

Acids and bases have distinctive properties. Many of the foods you eat, including those shown in Figure 19.1a, contain acids. Acids give foods a tart or sour taste. Lemons, which taste sour enough to make your mouth pucker, contain citric acid. Aqueous solutions of acids are strong or weak electrolytes. Recall that an electrolyte can conduct electricity. The electrolyte in a car battery is an acid. Acids cause certain chemical dyes, called indicators, to change color. Many metals, such as zinc and magnesium, react with aqueous solutions of acids to produce hydrogen gas.

The soap in Figure 19.1b is a familiar material that has the properties of a base. If you have accidentally tasted soap, you know that it has a bitter taste. This bitter taste is a general property of bases, but one that is dangerous to test. The slippery feel of soap is another property of bases. Like acids, bases will cause an indicator to change color. Bases also form aqueous solutions that are strong or weak electrolytes.

Chemists had known the properties of acids and bases for many years. Yet they were not able to propose a theory to explain this behavior. Then, in 1887, the Swedish chemist Svante Arrhenius proposed a new way of defining and thinking about acids and bases. 🔑 **According to Arrhenius, acids are hydrogen-containing compounds that ionize to yield hydrogen ions (H^+) in aqueous solution. Bases are compounds that ionize to yield hydroxide ions (OH^-) in aqueous solution.**

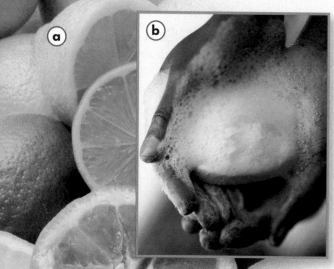

Figure 19.1 Acids and Bases
Many items contain acids or bases, or produce acids and bases when dissolved in water. **a.** Citrus fruits contain citric acid ($HC_6H_7O_7$). **b.** Many soaps are made using the common base sodium hydroxide (NaOH).

Arrhenius Acids   Table 19.1 lists six common acids. They vary in the number of hydrogens they contain that can form hydrogen ions. A hydrogen atom that can form a hydrogen ion is described as *ionizable*. Nitric acid (HNO_3) has one ionizable hydrogen, so nitric acid is classified as a *monoprotic* acid. The prefix *mono-* means "one," and the stem *protic* reflects the fact that a hydrogen ion is a proton. Acids that contain two ionizable hydrogens, such as sulfuric acid (H_2SO_4), are called *diprotic* acids. Acids that contain three ionizable hydrogens, such as phosphoric acid (H_3PO_4), are called *triprotic* acids.

Not all compounds that contain hydrogen are acids. Also, some hydrogens in an acid may not form hydrogen ions. Only a hydrogen that is bonded to a very electronegative element can be released as an ion. Recall that such bonds are highly polar. When a compound that contains such bonds dissolves in water, it releases hydrogen ions. An example is the hydrogen chloride molecule, shown below.

$$\overset{\delta+}{H}-\overset{\delta-}{Cl}(g) \xrightarrow{H_2O} H^+(aq) + Cl^-(aq)$$

Hydrogen   Hydrogen   Chloride
chloride   ion   ion
(hydrochloric acid)

However, in an aqueous solution, hydrogen ions are not present. Instead, the hydrogen ions are joined to water molecules as hydronium ions. A **hydronium ion (H_3O^+)** is the ion that forms when a water molecule gains a hydrogen ion. As seen in Figure 19.2, hydrogen chloride ionizes to form an aqueous solution of hydronium ions and chloride ions.

HCl   + H_2O → H_3O^+ + Cl^-
Hydrogen chloride   Water   Hydronium ion   Chloride ion

In contrast to hydrogen chloride, methane (CH_4) is an example of a hydrogen-containing compound that is not an acid. The four hydrogen atoms in methane are attached to the central carbon atom by weakly polar C—H bonds. Thus, methane has no ionizable hydrogens and is not an acid. Ethanoic acid (CH_3COOH), which is commonly called acetic acid, is an example of a molecule that contains both hydrogens that do not ionize and a hydrogen that does ionize. Although its molecules contain four hydrogens, ethanoic acid is a monoprotic acid. The structural formula shows why.

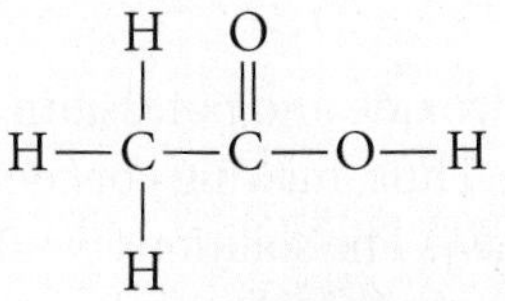

$$H-\underset{\underset{H}{|}}{\overset{\overset{H}{|}}{C}}-\overset{\overset{O}{\|}}{C}-O-H$$

Ethanoic acid
(CH_3COOH)

The three hydrogens attached to a carbon atom are in weakly polar bonds. They do not ionize. Only the hydrogen bonded to the highly electronegative oxygen can be ionized. For complex acids, you need to look at the structural formula to recognize which hydrogens can be ionized.

Table 19.1	
Some Common Acids	
Name	**Formula**
Hydrochloric acid	HCl
Nitric acid	HNO_3
Sulfuric acid	H_2SO_4
Phosphoric acid	H_3PO_4
Ethanoic acid	CH_3COOH
Carbonic acid	H_2CO_3

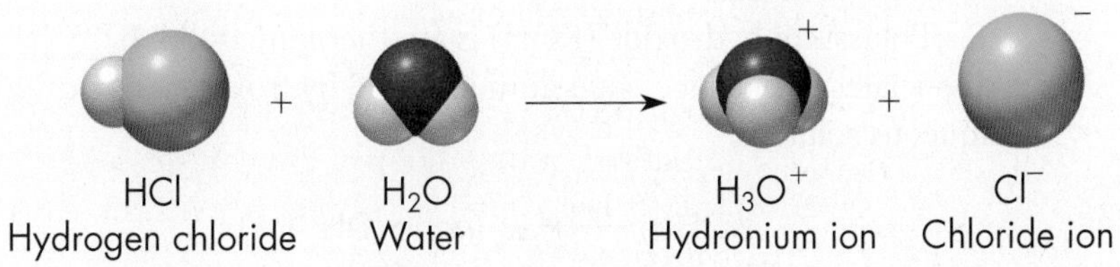

Figure 19.2 Hydrochloric Acid
Hydrochloric acid is actually an aqueous solution of hydrogen chloride. Hydrogen chloride forms hydronium ions, making this compound an acid.
Explain *Why does hydrogen chloride release a hydrogen ion when dissolved in water?*

See acid dissociation *animated online.*

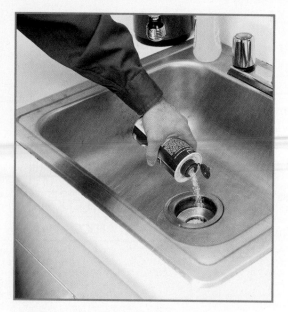

Figure 19.3 Clogged Drains
Sometimes water backs up in a sink because the drain is clogged. A plumber can take apart the pipes to remove a clog, or a drain cleaner containing sodium hydroxide can be used to eat away the clog.

Q: *Visitors to Bracken Cave wear protective gear to keep ammonia gas out of their eyes and respiratory tracts. Think about the properties of bases. Why are high levels of ammonia harmful?*

Table 19.2		
Some Common Bases		
Name	**Formula**	**Solubility in water**
Sodium hydroxide	NaOH	High
Potassium hydroxide	KOH	High
Calcium hydroxide	$Ca(OH)_2$	Very low
Magnesium hydroxide	$Mg(OH)_2$	Very low

Arrhenius Bases Table 19.2 lists four common bases. You may be familiar with the base sodium hydroxide (NaOH), which is also known as lye. Sodium hydroxide is an ionic solid. It dissociates into sodium ions and hydroxide ions in aqueous solution.

$$NaOH(s) \xrightarrow{H_2O} Na^+(aq) + OH^-(aq)$$

Sodium hydroxide   Sodium ion   Hydroxide ion

Sodium hydroxide is extremely caustic. A caustic substance can burn or eat away materials with which it comes in contact. This property is the reason that sodium hydroxide is a major component of products that are used to clean clogged drains. Figure 19.3 shows a drain cleaner that contains sodium hydroxide.

Potassium hydroxide (KOH) is another ionic solid. It dissociates to produce potassium ions and hydroxide ions in aqueous solution.

$$KOH(s) \xrightarrow{H_2O} K^+(aq) + OH^-(aq)$$

Potassium hydroxide   Potassium ion   Hydroxide ion

Sodium and potassium are Group 1A elements. Elements in Group 1A, the alkali metals, react violently with water. The products of these reactions are aqueous solutions of a hydroxide and hydrogen gas. The following equation summarizes the reaction of sodium with water.

$$2Na(s) + 2H_2O(l) \longrightarrow 2NaOH(aq) + H_2(g)$$

Sodium metal   Water   Sodium hydroxide   Hydrogen

Sodium hydroxide and potassium hydroxide are very soluble in water. Thus, making concentrated solutions of these compounds is easy. The solutions would have the typically bitter taste and slippery feel of a base. However, these are not properties that you would want to confirm. The solutions are extremely caustic to the skin. They can cause deep, painful, slow-healing wounds if not immediately washed off.

Calcium hydroxide, $Ca(OH)_2$, and magnesium hydroxide, $Mg(OH)_2$, are compounds of Group 2A metals. These compounds are not very soluble in water. Their solutions are always very dilute, even when saturated. A saturated solution of calcium hydroxide has only 0.165 g $Ca(OH)_2$ per 100 g of water. Magnesium hydroxide is even less soluble than calcium hydroxide. A saturated solution has only 0.0009 g $Mg(OH)_2$ per 100 g of water. Figure 19.4 shows a suspension of magnesium hydroxide in water. Some people use this suspension as an antacid and as a mild laxative.

Brønsted-Lowry Acids and Bases

What distinguishes an acid from a base in the Brønsted-Lowry theory?

The Arrhenius definition of acids and bases is not a very broad one. It excludes some substances that have acidic or basic properties, on their own or in solution. For example, sodium carbonate (Na_2CO_3) and ammonia (NH_3) act as bases when they form aqueous solutions. Yet neither of these compounds is a hydroxide-containing compound, so neither compound would be classified as a base by the Arrhenius definition.

In 1923, the Danish chemist Johannes Brønsted and the English chemist Thomas Lowry were working independently. Each chemist proposed the same definition of acids and bases. **According to the Brønsted-Lowry theory, an acid is a hydrogen-ion donor and a base is a hydrogen-ion acceptor.** This theory includes all the acids and bases that Arrhenius defined. It also includes some compounds that Arrhenius did not classify as bases.

You can use the Brønsted-Lowry theory to understand why ammonia is a base. Ammonia gas is very soluble in water. When ammonia dissolves in water, hydrogen ions are transferred from water to ammonia to form ammonium ions and hydroxide ions.

$$NH_3(aq) + H_2O(l) \rightleftharpoons NH_4^+(aq) + OH^-(aq)$$

Figure 19.5 illustrates how each water molecule donates a hydrogen ion to ammonia. Ammonia is a Brønsted-Lowry base because it accepts hydrogen ions. Water is a Brønsted-Lowry acid because it donates hydrogen ions.

Figure 19.4 Milk of Magnesia
This product is a suspension of magnesium hydroxide in water. Most bases are too caustic to be swallowed. But, the low solubility of magnesium hydroxide makes the suspension safe to consume.

See ammonia in water animated online.

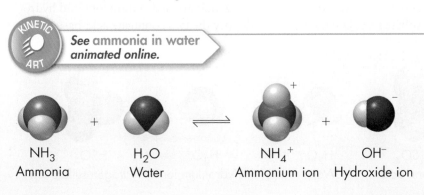

NH_3	H_2O		NH_4^+	OH^-
Ammonia	Water		Ammonium ion	Hydroxide ion

**Figure 19.5
Ammonia in Water**
When ammonia and water react, water molecules donate hydrogen ions to ammonia molecules. The reaction produces ammonium ions and hydroxide ions.
Explain *Why is ammonia not classified as an Arrhenius base?*

Conjugate Acids and Bases All gases become less soluble in water as the temperature rises. Thus, when the temperature of an aqueous solution of ammonia is increased, ammonia gas is released. This release acts as a stress on the system. In response to this stress, NH_4^+ reacts with OH^- to form more NH_3 and H_2O. In the reverse reaction, ammonium ions donate hydrogen ions to hydroxide ions. Thus, NH_4^+ (the donor) acts as a Brønsted-Lowry acid, and OH^- (the acceptor) acts as a Brønsted-Lowry base. In essence, the reversible reaction of ammonia and water has two acids and two bases.

$$NH_3(aq) + H_2O(l) \rightleftharpoons NH_4^+(aq) + OH^-(aq)$$

Base   Acid   Conjugate acid   Conjugate base

In the equation, the products of the forward reaction are distinguished from the reactants by the use of the adjective *conjugate*. This term comes from a Latin word meaning "to join together." A **conjugate acid** is the ion or molecule formed when a base gains a hydrogen ion. In the reaction above, NH_4^+ is the conjugate acid of the base NH_3. A **conjugate base** is the ion or molecule that remains after an acid loses a hydrogen ion. In the reaction above, OH^- is the conjugate base of the acid H_2O.

Conjugate acids are always paired with a base, and conjugate bases are always paired with an acid. A **conjugate acid-base pair** consists of two ions or molecules related by the loss or gain of one hydrogen ion. The ammonia molecule and the ammonium ion are a conjugate acid-base pair. The water molecule and the hydroxide ion are also a conjugate acid-base pair.

$$NH_3(aq) + H_2O(l) \rightleftharpoons NH_4^+(aq) + OH^-(aq)$$

Base   Acid   Conjugate acid   Conjugate base

The dissociation of hydrogen chloride in water provides another example of conjugate acids and bases.

$$HCl(g) + H_2O(l) \rightleftharpoons H_3O^+(aq) + Cl^-(aq)$$

Acid   Base   Conjugate acid   Conjugate base

In this reaction, hydrogen chloride is the hydrogen-ion donor. Thus, it is by definition a Brønsted-Lowry acid. Water is the hydrogen-ion acceptor and a Brønsted-Lowry base. The chloride ion is the conjugate base of the acid HCl. The hydronium ion is the conjugate acid of the base water.

Figure 19.6 shows the reaction that takes place when sulfuric acid dissolves in water. The products of this reaction are hydronium ions and hydrogen sulfate ions. Use the figure to identify the two conjugate acid-base pairs.

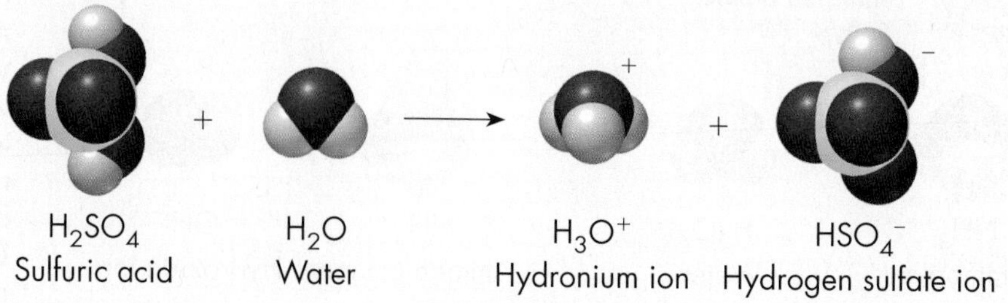

Figure 19.6 Sulfuric Acid
When sulfuric acid and water react, they form hydronium ions and hydrogen sulfate ions.
Identify *Which product is the conjugate acid, and which is the conjugate base?*

H_2SO_4 H_2O H_3O^+ HSO_4^-
Sulfuric acid   Water   Hydronium ion   Hydrogen sulfate ion

Amphoteric Substances Look at Table 19.3. Note that water appears in both the list of acids and the list of bases. Sometimes water accepts a hydrogen ion. At other times, it donates a hydrogen ion. How water behaves depends on the other reactant. A substance that can act as either an acid or a base is said to be **amphoteric.** Water is amphoteric. In the reaction with hydrochloric acid, water accepts a proton and is therefore a base. In the reaction with ammonia, water donates a proton and is therefore an acid. Look for two other substances in Table 19.3 that are amphoteric.

Lewis Acids and Bases

🔑 How did Lewis define an acid and a base?

The work that Gilbert Lewis (1875–1946) did on bonding led to a new concept of acids and bases. **🔑 According to Lewis, an acid accepts a pair of electrons and a base donates a pair of electrons during a reaction.** This definition is more general than those offered by Arrhenius or by Brønsted and Lowry. A **Lewis acid** is a substance that can accept a pair of electrons to form a covalent bond. Similarly, a **Lewis base** is a substance that can donate a pair of electrons to form a covalent bond.

The Lewis definitions include all the Brønsted-Lowry acids and bases. Consider the reaction of H^+ and OH^-. The hydrogen ion donates itself to the hydroxide ion. Therefore, H^+ is a Brønsted-Lowry acid and OH^- is a Brønsted-Lowry base. The hydroxide ion can bond to the hydrogen ion because it has an unshared pair of electrons. Thus, OH^- is also a Lewis base, and H^+, which accepts the pair of electrons, is a Lewis acid.

$$H^+ + \ ^-\!\ddot{\underset{..}{O}}\!-\!H \longrightarrow \overset{..}{\underset{..}{O}}$$

Lewis acid   Lewis base   H   H

A second example of a reaction between a Lewis acid and a Lewis base is what happens when ammonia dissolves in water. Hydrogen ions from the dissociation of water are the electron-pair acceptor and the Lewis acid. Ammonia is the electron-pair donor and the Lewis base.

Table 19.4 compares the definitions of acids and bases. The Lewis definition is the broadest. It extends to compounds that the Brønsted-Lowry theory does not classify as acids and bases. Sample Problem 19.1 provides some examples of those compounds.

Table 19.3

Some Conjugate Acid-Base Pairs

Acid	Base
HCl	Cl^-
H_2SO_4	HSO_4^-
H_3O^+	H_2O
HSO_4^-	SO_4^{2-}
CH_3COOH	CH_3COO^-
H_2CO_3	HCO_3^-
HCO_3^-	CO_3^{2-}
NH_4^+	NH_3
H_2O	OH^-

Table 19.4

Acid-Base Definitions

Type	Acid	Base
Arrhenius	H^+ producer	OH^- producer
Brønsted-Lowry	H^+ donor	H^+ acceptor
Lewis	electron-pair acceptor	electron-pair donor

Identifying Lewis Acids and Bases

Identify the Lewis acid and the Lewis base in this reaction between ammonia and boron trifluoride.

$$NH_3 + BF_3 \longrightarrow NH_3BF_3$$

❶ Analyze **Identify the relevant concepts.** When a Lewis acid reacts with a Lewis base, the base donates a pair of electrons and the acid accepts the donated pair.

❷ Solve **Apply the concepts to this problem.**

> Draw electron dot structures to identify which reactant has an unshared pair of electrons.

> Identify the reactant with the unshared pair of electrons and the reactant that can accept the pair of electrons.

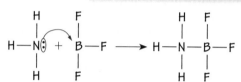

Ammonia has an unshared pair of electrons to donate. The boron atom can accept the donated electrons.

> Classify the reactants based on their behavior.

Lewis bases donate a pair of electrons, so ammonia is the Lewis base. Lewis acids accept a pair of electrons, so boron trifluoride is the Lewis acid.

1. Identify the Lewis acid and Lewis base in each reaction.
 a. $H^+ + H_2O \longrightarrow H_3O^+$
 b. $AlCl_3 + Cl^- \longrightarrow AlCl_4^-$

2. Predict whether PCl_3 would be a Lewis acid or a Lewis base in typical chemical reactions. Explain your prediction.

19.1 LessonCheck

3. **Review** What is the Arrhenius definition of an acid and a base?

4. **Describe** How are acids and bases defined by the Brønsted-Lowry theory?

5. **Explain** How did Lewis broaden the definition of acids and bases?

6. Compare and Contrast How are the properties of acids and bases similar? How are they different?

7. Classify Determine whether the following acids are monoprotic, diprotic, or triprotic:
 a. H_2CO_3 **b.** H_3PO_4 **c.** HCl   **d.** H_2SO_4

8. Apply Concepts Write a chemical equation for the ionization of HNO_3 in water and for the reaction of CO_3^{2-} with water. Identify the hydrogen-ion donor and the hydrogen-ion acceptor in each equation. Then, label each conjugate acid-base pair in the two equations.

BIGIDEA REACTIONS

9. Some household drain cleaners contain both sodium hydroxide and small particles of aluminum or zinc. Research how adding these metals can increase the effectiveness of the product.

19.2 Hydrogen Ions and Acidity

Q: *What factors do you need to control so a fish has healthy water to live in?* Goldfish can live for 20 years or more in an aquarium if the conditions are right. The water in the aquarium must be cleaned regularly. You must also control the temperature of the water. In this lesson, you will study another factor that affects the ability of fish to survive.

Key Questions

🔑 How are [H⁺] and [OH⁻] related in an aqueous solution?

🔑 How is pH used to classify a solution as neutral, acidic, or basic?

🔑 What are two methods that are used to measure pH?

Vocabulary

- self-ionization
- neutral solution
- ion-product constant for water (K_w)
- acidic solution
- basic solution
- pH

Hydrogen Ions From Water

🔑 **How are [H⁺] and [OH⁻] related in an aqueous solution?**

Water molecules are highly polar and are in constant motion, even at room temperature. On occasion, the collisions between water molecules are energetic enough for a reaction to occur. When this happens, a hydrogen ion is transferred from one water molecule to another, as illustrated below. A water molecule that gains a hydrogen ion becomes a hydronium ion (H_3O^+). A water molecule that loses a hydrogen ion becomes a hydroxide ion (OH^-).

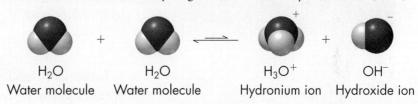

H_2O	+	H_2O	⇌	H_3O^+	+	OH^-
Water molecule		Water molecule		Hydronium ion		Hydroxide ion

Self-Ionization of Water The reaction in which water molecules produce ions is called the **self-ionization** of water. This reaction can be written as a simple dissociation.

$$H_2O(l) \rightleftharpoons H^+(aq) + OH^-(aq)$$
Hydrogen ion   Hydroxide ion

In water or in an aqueous solution, hydrogen ions are always joined to water molecules as hydronium ions. Yet chemists may still refer to these ions as hydrogen ions or even protons. In this textbook, either H^+ or H_3O^+ is used to represent hydrogen ions in aqueous solution.

The self-ionization of water occurs to a very small extent. In pure water at 25°C, the concentration of hydrogen ions is only $1 \times 10^{-7} M$. The concentration of OH^- is also $1 \times 10^{-7} M$ because the numbers of H^+ and OH^- ions are equal in pure water. Any aqueous solution in which [H⁺] and [OH⁻] are equal is a **neutral solution.**

Ion-Product Constant for Water The ionization of water is a reversible reaction, so Le Châtelier's principle applies. Adding either hydrogen ions or hydroxide ions to an aqueous solution is a stress to the system. In response, the equilibrium will shift toward the formation of water. The concentration of the other ion will decrease. In any aqueous solution, when $[H^+]$ increases, $[OH^-]$ decreases. Likewise, when $[H^+]$ decreases, $[OH^-]$ increases.

$$H^+(aq) + OH^-(aq) \rightleftharpoons H_2O(l)$$

For aqueous solutions, the product of the hydrogen-ion concentration and the hydroxide-ion concentration equals 1.0×10^{-14}.

$$[H^+] \times [OH^-] = 1.0 \times 10^{-14}$$

This equation is true for all dilute aqueous solutions at 25°C. When substances are added to water, the concentrations of H^+ and OH^- may change. However, the product of $[H^+]$ and $[OH^-]$ does not change. The product of the concentrations of the hydrogen ions and hydroxide ions in water is called the **ion-product constant for water (K_w).**

$$K_w = [H^+] \times [OH^-] = 1.0 \times 10^{-14}$$

Acidic Solutions Not all solutions are neutral. When some substances dissolve in water, they release hydrogen ions. For example, when hydrogen chloride dissolves in water, it forms hydrochloric acid.

$$HCl(aq) \longrightarrow H^+(aq) + Cl^-(aq)$$

In hydrochloric acid, the hydrogen-ion concentration is greater than the hydroxide-ion concentration. (The hydroxide ions come from the self-ionization of water.) A solution in which $[H^+]$ is greater than $[OH^-]$ is an **acidic solution.** In acidic solutions, the $[H^+]$ is greater than $1 \times 10^{-7}M$. Figure 19.7 shows a guitar that was artificially aged by using hydrochloric acid.

Basic Solutions When sodium hydroxide dissolves in water, it forms hydroxide ions in solution.

$$NaOH(aq) \longrightarrow Na^+(aq) + OH^-(aq)$$

In such a solution, the hydrogen-ion concentration is less than the hydroxide-ion concentration. Remember, the hydrogen ions are present from the self-ionization of water. A **basic solution** is one in which $[H^+]$ is less than $[OH^-]$. The $[H^+]$ of a basic solution is less than $1 \times 10^{-7}M$. Basic solutions are also known as alkaline solutions.

Figure 19.7 Aged by Acid
Sometimes guitar players want a new guitar to look like it is old or "vintage." The guitarist can remove the shiny new metal parts of the guitar and expose them to hydrochloric acid. The acid will make the metal parts look dull. Both of the guitars in the photo below are new, but the bottom one has been aged with acid.

SampleProblem 19.2

Using the Ion-Product Constant for Water

If the $[H^+]$ in a solution is $1.0 \times 10^{-5}M$, is the solution acidic, basic, or neutral? What is the $[OH^-]$ of this solution?

① Analyze List the knowns and the unknowns. Use the expression for the ion-product constant for water and the known concentration of hydrogen ions to find the concentration of hydroxide ions.

② Calculate Solve for the unknowns.

Use $[H^+]$ to determine whether the solution is acidic, basic, or neutral.	$[H^+]$ is $1.0 \times 10^{-5}M$, which is greater than $1.0 \times 10^{-7}M$. Thus, the solution is acidic.
Rearrange the expression for the ion-product constant to solve for $[OH^-]$.	$K_w = [H^+] \times [OH^-]$ $[OH^-] = \dfrac{K_w}{[H^+]}$
Substitute the known values of $[H^+]$ and K_w. Then, solve for $[OH^-]$.	$[OH^-] = \dfrac{1.0 \times 10^{-14}}{1.0 \times 10^{-5}}$ $= 1.0 \times 10^{-9}M$

When you divide numbers written in scientific notation, subtract the exponent in the denominator from the exponent in the numerator.

③ Evaluate Does the result make sense? If $[H^+]$ is greater than $1.0 \times 10^{-7}M$, then $[OH^-]$ must be less than $1.0 \times 10^{-7}M$. $1 \times 10^{-9}M$ is less than $1 \times 10^{-7}M$. To check your calculation, multiply the values for $[H^+]$ and $[OH^-]$ to make sure the result equals 1×10^{-14}.

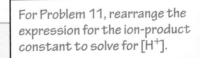

For Problem 11, rearrange the expression for the ion-product constant to solve for $[H^+]$.

10. Classify each solution as acidic, basic, or neutral.
   a. $[H^+] = 6.0 \times 10^{-10}M$
   b. $[OH^-] = 3.0 \times 10^{-2}M$
   c. $[H^+] = 2.0 \times 10^{-7}M$
   d. $[OH^-] = 1.0 \times 10^{-7}M$

11. If the hydroxide-ion concentration of an aqueous solution is $1 \times 10^{-3}M$, what is the $[H^+]$ in the solution? Is the solution acidic, basic, or neutral?

The pH Concept

🔑 **How is pH used to classify a solution as neutral, acidic, or basic?**

Expressing hydrogen-ion concentration in molarity is not practical. A more widely used system for expressing [H^+] is the pH scale, proposed in 1909 by the Danish scientist Søren Sørensen. The pH scale ranges from 0 to 14.

Hydrogen Ions and pH The **pH** of a solution is the negative logarithm of the hydrogen-ion concentration. The pH may be represented mathematically using the following equation:

$$pH = -\log[H^+]$$

In pure water or a neutral solution, the [H^+] = $1 \times 10^{-7}M$, and the pH is 7.

$$pH = -\log(1 \times 10^{-7})$$
$$= -(\log 1 + \log 10^{-7})$$
$$= -(0.0 + (-7.0)) = 7.0$$

If the [H^+] of a solution is greater than $1 \times 10^{-7}M$, the pH is less than 7.0. If the [H^+] of the solution is less than $1 \times 10^{-7}M$, the pH is greater than 7.0. 🔑 **A solution with a pH less than 7.0 is acidic. A solution with a pH of 7.0 is neutral. A solution with a pH greater than 7.0 is basic.** Table 19.5 summarizes the relationship among [H^+], [OH^-], and pH. It also indicates the pH values of some common aqueous systems, including milk and blood.

CHEMISTRY & YOU

Q: *In an aquarium, the pH of water is another factor that affects the ability of fish to survive. Most freshwater fish need a slightly acidic or neutral pH. For a saltwater tank, the ideal pH is slightly basic. What might explain this difference in the ideal pH range?*

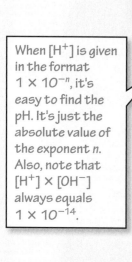

When [H^+] is given in the format 1×10^{-n}, it's easy to find the pH. It's just the absolute value of the exponent *n*. Also, note that [H^+] × [OH^-] always equals 1×10^{-14}.

Table 19.5

Relationships Among [H^+], [OH^-], and pH

	[H^+] (mol/L)	[OH^-] (mol/L)	pH	
Increasing acidity	1×10^{0}	1×10^{-14}	0.0	1M HCl
	1×10^{-1}	1×10^{-13}	1.0	0.1M HCl
	1×10^{-2}	1×10^{-12}	2.0	Gastric juice
	1×10^{-3}	1×10^{-11}	3.0	Lemon juice
	1×10^{-4}	1×10^{-10}	4.0	Tomato juice
	1×10^{-5}	1×10^{-9}	5.0	Black coffee
	1×10^{-6}	1×10^{-8}	6.0	Milk
Neutral	1×10^{-7}	1×10^{-7}	7.0	Pure water / Blood
Increasing basicity	1×10^{-8}	1×10^{-6}	8.0	Seawater
	1×10^{-9}	1×10^{-5}	9.0	
	1×10^{-10}	1×10^{-4}	10.0	Milk of magnesia
	1×10^{-11}	1×10^{-3}	11.0	Household ammonia
	1×10^{-12}	1×10^{-2}	12.0	
	1×10^{-13}	1×10^{-1}	13.0	0.1M NaOH
	1×10^{-14}	1×10^{0}	14.0	1M NaOH

Calculating pH From [H⁺] Expressing $[H^+]$ in scientific notation can make it easier to calculate pH. For example, you would rewrite $0.0010M$ as $1.0 \times 10^{-3}M$. The coefficient 1.0 has two significant figures. The pH for a solution with this concentration is 3.00. The two numbers to the right of the decimal point represent the two significant figures in the concentration.

It is easy to find the pH for solutions when the coefficient is 1.0. The pH of the solution equals the exponent, with the sign changed from minus to plus. For example, a solution with $[H^+] = 1 \times 10^{-2}M$ has a pH of 2.0. When the coefficient is a number other than 1, you will need to use a calculator with a log function key to calculate pH.

SampleProblem 19.3

Calculating pH From [H⁺]

What is the pH of a solution with a hydrogen-ion concentration of $4.2 \times 10^{-10}M$?

❶ Analyze List the known and the unknown. To find the pH from the hydrogen-ion concentration, you use the equation $pH = -\log[H^+]$.

KNOWN	UNKNOWN
$[H^+] = 4.2 \times 10^{-10}M$	pH = ?

❷ Calculate Solve for the unknown.

Start with the equation for finding pH from [H⁺].

$$pH = -\log[H^+]$$

Substitute the known [H⁺] and use the log function on your calculator to calculate the pH.

$$pH = -\log(4.2 \times 10^{-10})$$
$$= -(-9.37675)$$
$$= 9.37675$$
$$= 9.38$$

Round the pH to two decimal places because the hydrogen-ion concentration has two significant figures.

❸ Evaluate Does the result make sense? The value of the hydrogen-ion concentration is between $1 \times 10^{-9}M$ and $1 \times 10^{-10}M$. So, the calculated pH should be between 9 and 10, which it is.

12. Find the pH of each solution.
 a. $[H^+] = 0.045M$
 b. $[H^+] = 8.7 \times 10^{-6}M$
 c. $[H^+] = 0.0015M$
 d. $[H^+] = 1.2 \times 10^{-3}M$

13. What are the pH values of the following solutions, based on their hydrogen-ion concentrations?
 a. $[H^+] = 1.0 \times 10^{-12}M$
 b. $[H^+] = 1 \times 10^{-4}M$

Calculating [H⁺] From pH You can calculate the hydrogen-ion concentration of a solution if you know the pH. If the pH is an integer, it is easy to find the value of $[H^+]$. For a pH of 9.0, $[H^+] = 1 \times 10^{-9}M$. For a pH of 4.0, $[H^+]$ is $1 \times 10^{-4}M$.

However, most pH values are not whole numbers. For example, milk of magnesia has a pH of 10.50. The $[H^+]$ must be less than $1 \times 10^{-10}M$ (pH 10.0) but greater than $1 \times 10^{-11}M$ (pH 11.0). The hydrogen-ion concentration is $3.2 \times 10^{-11}M$. When the pH value is not a whole number, you will need a calculator with an antilog (10^x) function to get an accurate value for the hydrogen-ion concentration.

Sample Problem 19.4

Calculating [H⁺] From pH

The pH of an unknown solution is 6.35. What is the hydrogen-ion concentration of the solution?

KNOWN
pH = 6.35

UNKNOWN
$[H^+] = ?M$

❶ Analyze List the known and the unknown. You will use the antilog function of your calculator to find the concentration.

❷ Calculate Solve for the unknown.

First, simply swap the sides of the equation for finding pH and substitute the known value.

$$pH = -\log [H^+]$$
$$-\log [H^+] = pH$$
$$-\log [H^+] = 6.35$$

Change the signs on both sides of the equation and then solve for the unknown.

$$\log [H^+] = -6.35$$
$$[H^+] = \text{antilog} (-6.35)$$

Use the antilog (10^x) function on your calculator to find [H⁺]. Report the answer in scientific notation.

$$[H^+] = 4.5 \times 10^{-7}M$$

On most calculators, use the 2nd or the INV key followed by log to get the antilog.

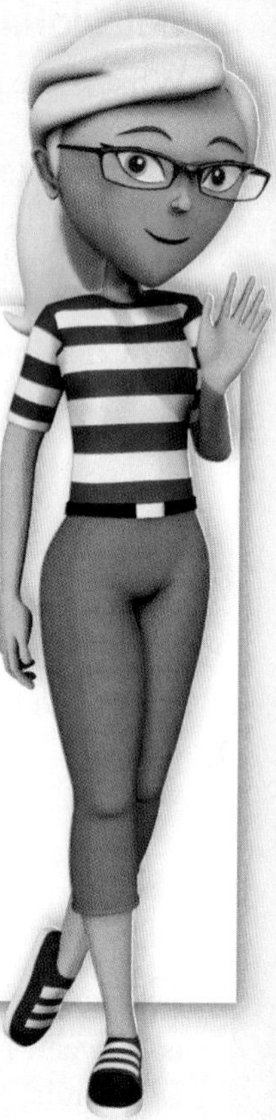

❸ Evaluate Does the result make sense? The pH is between 6 and 7. So, the hydrogen ion concentration must be between $1 \times 10^{-6}M$ and $1 \times 10^{-7}M$. The answer is rounded to two significant figures because the pH was measured to two decimal places.

---

14. Calculate [H⁺] for each solution.
   a. pH = 5.00
   b. pH = 12.83

15. What are the hydrogen-ion concentrations for solutions with the following pH values?
   a. 4.00
   b. 11.55

Calculating pH From [OH⁻] If you know the $[OH^-]$ of a solution, you can find its pH. Recall that the ion-product constant for water defines the relationship between $[H^+]$ and $[OH^-]$. Therefore, you can use the ion-product constant for water to determine $[H^+]$ for a known $[OH^-]$. Then, you use $[H^+]$ to calculate the pH. For practice, try doing Sample Problem 19.5.

SampleProblem 19.5

Calculating pH From [OH⁻]

What is the pH of a solution if $[OH^-] = 4.0 \times 10^{-11} M$?

❶ Analyze **List the knowns and the unknown.**
To find $[H^+]$, divide K_w by the known $[OH^-]$. Then, calculate pH as you did in Sample Problem 19.3.

KNOWNS	UNKNOWN
$[OH^-] = 4.0 \times 10^{-11} M$	pH = ?
$K_w = 1.0 \times 10^{-14}$	

❷ Calculate **Solve for the unknown.**

Start with the ion-product constant to find $[H^+]$. Rearrange the equation to solve for $[H^+]$.

$$K_w = [OH^-] \times [H^+]$$

$$[H^+] = \frac{K_w}{[OH^-]}$$

Substitute the values for K_w and $[OH^-]$ to find $[H^+]$.

$$[H^+] = \frac{1.0 \times 10^{-14}}{4.0 \times 10^{-11}} = 0.25 \times 10^{-3} M$$

$$= 2.5 \times 10^{-4} M$$

Next, use the equation for finding pH. Substitute the value for $[H^+]$ that you just calculated.

$$pH = -\log [H^+]$$
$$= -\log (2.5 \times 10^{-4})$$

Use a calculator to find the log.

$$= -(-3.60205)$$

$$= 3.60$$

> Round the pH to two decimal places because the $[OH^-]$ has two significant figures.

❸ Evaluate **Does the result make sense?** A solution in which $[OH^-]$ is less than $1 \times 10^{-7} M$ is acidic because $[H^+]$ is greater than $1 \times 10^{-7} M$. The hydrogen-ion concentration is between $1 \times 10^{-3} M$ and $1 \times 10^{-4} M$. Thus, the pH should be between 3 and 4.

---

16. Calculate the pH of each solution.
   a. $[OH^-] = 4.3 \times 10^{-5} M$
   b. $[OH^-] = 4.5 \times 10^{-11} M$

17. Calculate the pH of each solution.
   a. $[OH^-] = 5.0 \times 10^{-9} M$
   b. $[OH^-] = 8.3 \times 10^{-4} M$

Measuring pH

What are two methods that are used to measure pH?

In many situations, knowing the pH is useful. A custodian might need to maintain the correct acid-base balance in a swimming pool. A gardener may want to know if a certain plant will thrive in a yard. A doctor might be trying to diagnose a medical condition. **Either acid-base indicators or pH meters can be used to measure pH.**

Acid-Base Indicators An indicator is often used for initial pH measurements and for samples with small volumes. An indicator (HIn) is an acid or a base that dissociates in a known pH range. Indicators work because their acid form and base form have different colors in solution. The following general equation represents the dissociation of an acid-base indicator (HIn).

$$\text{HIn}(aq) \rightleftharpoons \text{H}^+(aq) + \text{In}^-(aq)$$
Acid form   Base form

The acid form of the indicator (HIn) is dominant at low pH and high [H$^+$]. The base form (In$^-$) is dominant at high pH and high [OH$^-$].

The change from dominating acid form to dominating base form occurs within a narrow range of about two pH units. Within this range, the color of the solution is a mixture of the colors of the acid and the base forms. If you know the pH range over which this color change occurs, you can make a rough estimate of the pH of a solution. At all pH values below this range, you would see only the color of the acid form. At all pH values above this range, you would see only the color of the base form.

For a more precise estimate of the solution's pH, you could repeat the test with indicators that have different pH ranges for their color change. Many indicators are needed to span the entire pH spectrum. Figure 19.8 shows the pH ranges of some common acid-base indicators.

Interpret Graphs

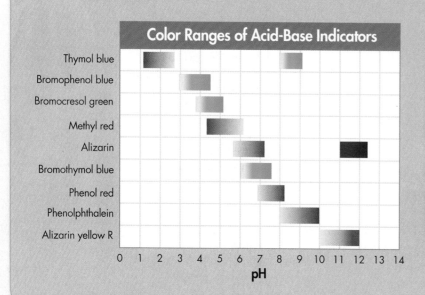

Color Ranges of Acid-Base Indicators

Thymol blue
Bromophenol blue
Bromocresol green
Methyl red
Alizarin
Bromothymol blue
Phenol red
Phenolphthalein
Alizarin yellow R

pH: 0 1 2 3 4 5 6 7 8 9 10 11 12 13 14

Figure 19.8 Each indicator is useful for a specific range of pH values.
a. Identify At a pH of 12, which indicator would be yellow?
b. Apply Concepts Which indicator could you use to show that the pH of a solution has changed from 3 to 5?
c. Make Generalizations What do you notice about the range over which each indicator changes color?

Figure 19.9 Effects of Soil Acidity
Soil pH can affect how plants develop. **a.** In acidic soils, hydrangeas produce blue flowers. **b.** In basic soils, hydrangeas produce pink flowers.

Indicators have certain properties that limit their usefulness. The pH values of indicators are usually given for 25°C. At other temperatures, an indicator may change color at a different pH. If the solution being tested is not colorless, the color of the indicator may be misleading. Dissolved salts in a solution may affect an indicator's dissociation. Using indicator strips can help overcome these problems. An indicator strip is a piece of paper or plastic that has been soaked in an indicator, and then dried. The paper is dipped into an unknown solution. The color that results is compared with a color chart to measure the pH. Some indicator paper has absorbed multiple indicators. The colors that result will cover a wide range of pH values. Before planting the shrub shown in Figure 19.9, you might want to test the pH of your soil.

Figure 19.10 pH Meter
A pH meter provides a quick and accurate way to measure the pH of a system.

pH Meters Your chemistry laboratory probably has a pH meter. A pH meter is used to make rapid, continuous measurements of pH. The measurements of pH obtained with a pH meter are typically accurate to within 0.01 pH unit of the true pH. If the pH meter is connected to a computer or chart recorder, the user will have a record of the pH changes.

A pH meter can be easier to use than liquid indicators or indicator strips. As shown in Figure 19.10, the pH reading is visible in a display window on the meter. Hospitals use pH meters to find small but meaningful changes in the pH of blood and other body fluids. Sewage, industrial wastes, and soil pH are also easily monitored with a pH meter. The color and cloudiness of the solution do not affect the accuracy of the pH value obtained.

Quick Lab

Purpose To measure the pH of household materials using a natural indicator

Materials

- red cabbage leaves
- 1-cup measure
- hot water
- 2 jars
- spoon
- cheesecloth
- 3 sheets of plain white paper
- transparent tape
- metric ruler
- pencil
- 10 small clear plastic cups
- permanent marker
- white vinegar (CH$_3$COOH)
- baking soda (NaHCO$_3$)
- spatula
- household ammonia
- dropper
- assorted household materials

Indicators From Natural Sources

Procedure

1. Put one-half cup of finely chopped red cabbage leaves in a jar and add one-half cup of hot water. Stir and crush the leaves with a spoon. Continue this process until the water has a distinct color.

2. Strain the mixture through a piece of clean cheesecloth into a clean jar. The liquid that collects in the jar is your indicator.

3. Tape three sheets of paper end to end. Draw a line along the center of the taped sheets. Label the line at 5-cm intervals with the numbers 1 to 14. This labeled line is your pH scale.

4. Use the permanent marker to label three cups vinegar, baking soda, and ammonia. Pour indicator into each cup to a depth of about 1 cm.

5. Add several drops of vinegar to the first cup. Use a spatula to add a pinch of baking soda to the second cup. Add several drops of ammonia to the third cup. The pH values for the solutions of vinegar, baking soda, and household ammonia are about 3, 9, and 11, respectively. Record the colors you observe at the correct locations on your pH scale.

6. Repeat the procedure for household items such as table salt, milk, lemon juice, laundry detergent, milk of magnesia, toothpaste, shampoo, and carbonated beverages.

Analyze and Conclude

1. Observe What color is the indicator in acidic, neutral, and basic solutions?

2. Relate Cause and Effect What caused the color of the indicator to change when a material was added to a cup?

3. Classify Divide the household materials you tested into three groups—acidic, basic, and neutral.

4. Analyze Data Which group contains items used for cleaning? Which group contains items used for personal hygiene?

19.2 LessonCheck

18. Review How are the concentrations of hydrogen ions and hydroxide ions related in an aqueous solution?

19. Identify What is the range of pH values in the following solutions?
   a. basic   **b.** acidic   **c.** neutral

20. List What methods can you use to measure the pH of a solution?

21. Relate Cause and Effect What happens to the [H$^+$] as the pH of a solution increases?

22. Calculate Determine the pH of each solution.
   a. [H$^+$] = $1 \times 10^{-6}M$
   b. [H$^+$] = 0.00010M
   c. [OH$^-$] = $1 \times 10^{-2}M$
   d. [OH$^-$] = $1 \times 10^{-11}M$

23. Compare In terms of ion concentrations, how do basic solutions differ from acidic solutions?

24. Calculate Find the hydroxide-ion concentrations for solutions with the following pH values:
   a. 6.00   **b.** 9.00   **c.** 12.00

Agronomist

Do you like the idea of working with plants but find chemistry more interesting than biology? If so, you might want to consider a career in agronomy. Agronomy is a branch of agriculture that deals with the interactions between plants, soils, and the environment. Agronomists use their knowledge of chemistry to help produce healthy crops and increase yields, while preserving the environment.

The opportunities for agronomists extend beyond laboratories and greenhouses. Agronomists also work for business firms, government agencies, conservation groups, philanthropic organizations, and universities. Agronomists can also use their knowledge of water and land management to address such issues as urban area beautification and highway landscaping.

SOIL ACIDITY The pH of the soil is among the most important factors in crop production. Agronomists can help farmers obtain the right soil pH for a specific crop.

FIELD CHEMISTRY Many agronomists have the opportunity to work with local communities. This agronomist is advising a Kenyan farming group on how to improve their crops using science.

Take It Further

1. **Apply Concepts** The ideal soil pH for corn is around 6.0. If $[H^+]$ equals $2.14 \times 10^{-5} M$, is the soil too acidic or too basic for growing corn?

2. **Infer** What are two nonfood items that an agronomist might help produce?

19.3 Strengths of Acids and Bases

Q: *What makes one acid safer than another?* Lemon juice, which contains citric acid, has a pH of about 2.3. Yet, you consume lemon juice. When you cut a lemon, you usually don't wear gloves or safety goggles. But some acids do require such precautions. This lesson will explain the difference between a "weak" acid such as citric acid and a "strong" acid such as sulfuric acid.

Strong and Weak Acids and Bases

How are acids and bases classified as either strong or weak?

Table 19.6 compares the strengths of some acids and bases. **Acids and bases are classified as strong or weak based on the degree to which they ionize in water.** Hydrochloric acid and sulfuric acid are examples of strong acids. In general, a **strong acid** is completely ionized in aqueous solution.

$$HCl(g) + H_2O(l) \longrightarrow H_3O^+(aq) + Cl^-(aq)$$
$$100\%$$

A **weak acid** ionizes only slightly in aqueous solution. The ionization of ethanoic acid (CH_3COOH), a typical weak acid, is not complete.

$$CH_3COOH(aq) + H_2O(l) \rightleftharpoons H_3O^+(aq) + CH_3COO^-(aq)$$
$$< 1\%$$

Key Question

How are acids and bases classified as either strong or weak?

Vocabulary

- strong acid
- weak acid
- acid dissociation constant (K_a)
- strong base
- weak base
- base dissociation constant (K_b)

Table 19.6

Relative Strengths of Common Acids and Bases		
Substance	**Formula**	**Relative strength**
Hydrochloric acid	HCl ⎫	
Nitric acid	HNO₃ ⎬ Strong acids	
Sulfuric acid	H₂SO₄ ⎭	
Phosphoric acid	H₃PO₄	
Ethanoic acid	CH₃COOH	Increasing strength of acid
Carbonic acid	H₂CO₃	
Hypochlorous acid	HClO	
		Neutral solution
Ammonia	NH₃	
Sodium silicate	Na₂SiO₃	Increasing strength of base
Calcium hydroxide	Ca(OH)₂ ⎫	
Sodium hydroxide	NaOH ⎬ Strong bases	
Potassium hydroxide	KOH ⎭	

InterpretGraphs

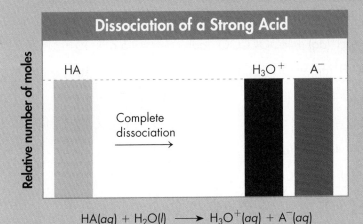

Dissociation of a Strong Acid

Relative number of moles

HA H_3O^+ A^-

Complete dissociation →

$$HA(aq) + H_2O(l) \longrightarrow H_3O^+(aq) + A^-(aq)$$

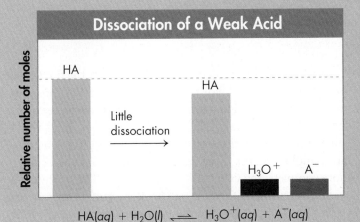

Dissociation of a Weak Acid

Relative number of moles

HA

HA

Little dissociation →

H_3O^+ A^-

$$HA(aq) + H_2O(l) \rightleftharpoons H_3O^+(aq) + A^-(aq)$$

Figure 19.11 Dissociation of an acid (HA) in water yields H_3O^+ and an anion, A^-. The bar graphs compare the extent of dissociation of a strong acid and a weak acid.

a. Explain Why is there only one bar for HA in the graph for the strong acid, but two bars for HA in the graph for the weak acid?

b. Apply Concepts In the graph for the strong acid, why do the bars for H_3O^+ and A^- have the same height as the bar for HA?

c. Infer In the graph for the weak acid, why is the height of the bar for H_3O^+ equal to the distance from the top of the second HA bar to the dotted line?

Hint: The bars represent the relative amounts of the acid and the ions it forms in solution.

Acid Dissociation Constant Figure 19.11 compares the extent of dissociation of strong and weak acids. A strong acid, such as hydrochloric acid, completely dissociates in water. As a result, $[H_3O^+]$ is high in an aqueous solution of a strong acid. By contrast, weak acids remain largely undissociated. For example, in an aqueous solution of ethanoic acid, less than 1 percent of the molecules are ionized at any time.

You can use a balanced equation to write the equilibrium-constant expression for a reaction. The equilibrium-constant expression shown below is for ethanoic acid.

$$K_{eq} = \frac{[H_3O^+] \times [CH_3COO^-]}{[CH_3COOH] \times [H_2O]}$$

For dilute aqueous solutions, the concentration of water is a constant. This constant can be combined with K_{eq} to give an acid dissociation constant. An **acid dissociation constant (K_a)** is the ratio of the concentration of the dissociated form of an acid to the concentration of the undissociated form. The dissociated form includes both the H_3O^+ and the anion.

$$K_{eq} \times [H_2O] = K_a = \frac{[H_3O^+] \times [CH_3COO^-]}{[CH_3COOH]}$$

Table 19.7

Dissociation Constants of Weak Acids		
Acid	**Chemical equation for dissociation**	**K_a (25°C)**
Oxalic acid	$HOOCCOOH(aq) \rightleftharpoons H^+(aq) + HOOCCOO^-(aq)$	5.6×10^{-2}
	$HOOCCOO^-(aq) \rightleftharpoons H^+(aq) + OOCCOO^{2-}(aq)$	5.1×10^{-5}
Phosphoric acid	$H_3PO_4(aq) \rightleftharpoons H^+(aq) + H_2PO_4^-(aq)$	7.5×10^{-3}
	$H_2PO_4^-(aq) \rightleftharpoons H^+(aq) + HPO_4^{2-}(aq)$	6.2×10^{-8}
	$HPO_4^{2-}(aq) \rightleftharpoons H^+(aq) + PO_4^{3-}(aq)$	4.8×10^{-13}
Methanoic acid	$HCOOH(aq) \rightleftharpoons H^+(aq) + HCOO^-(aq)$	1.8×10^{-4}
Benzoic acid	$C_6H_5COOH(aq) \rightleftharpoons H^+(aq) + C_6H_5COO^-(aq)$	6.3×10^{-5}
Ethanoic acid	$CH_3COOH(aq) \rightleftharpoons H^+(aq) + CH_3COO^-(aq)$	1.8×10^{-5}
Carbonic acid	$H_2CO_3(aq) \rightleftharpoons H^+(aq) + HCO_3^-(aq)$	4.3×10^{-7}
	$HCO_3^-(aq) \rightleftharpoons H^+(aq) + CO_3^{2-}(aq)$	4.8×10^{-11}

The acid dissociation constant (K_a) reflects the fraction of an acid that is ionized. For this reason, dissociation constants are sometimes called ionization constants. If the degree of dissociation or ionization of the acid in a solution is small, the value of the dissociation constant will be small. Weak acids have small K_a values. If the degree of ionization of an acid is more complete, the value of K_a will be larger. The stronger an acid is, the larger its K_a value will be. For example, nitrous acid (HNO_2) has a K_a of 4.4×10^{-4}, but ethanoic acid (CH_3COOH) has a K_a of 1.8×10^{-5}. This means that nitrous acid is more ionized in solution than ethanoic acid. Therefore, nitrous acid is a stronger acid than ethanoic acid.

Table 19.7 shows the ionization equations and dissociation constants of a few weak acids. Some of the acids have more than one dissociation constant because they have more than one ionizable hydrogen. Oxalic acid, for example, is a diprotic acid. It loses two hydrogens, one at a time. Therefore, it has two dissociation constants. Oxalic acid is found naturally in certain herbs and vegetables, such as those pictured in Figure 19.12.

The acids in Table 19.7 are ranked by the value of the first dissociation constant. Observe what happens to the K_a with each ionization. The K_a decreases from the first ionization to the second. It decreases again from the second ionization to the third.

Figure 19.12 Oxalic Acid
Chives and parsley have relatively high amounts of oxalic acid compared to other fruits and vegetables.

Calculating Dissociation Constants To calculate the acid dissociation constant (K_a) of a weak acid, you need to know the initial molar concentration of the acid and the [H^+] (or alternatively, the pH) of the solution at equilibrium. You can use these data to find the equilibrium concentrations of the acid and the ions. These values are then substituted into the expression for K_a.

In general, you can find the K_a of an acid in water by substituting the equilibrium concentrations of the acid, [HA], the anion from the dissociation of the acid, [A^-], and the hydrogen ion, [H^+], into the equation below.

$$K_a = \frac{[H^+][A^-]}{[HA]}$$

SampleProblem 19.6

Calculating a Dissociation Constant

In a $0.1000M$ solution of ethanoic acid, [H^+] = $1.34 \times 10^{-3}M$. Calculate K_a of this acid. Refer to Table 19.7 for the ionization equation for ethanoic acid.

❶ **Analyze** List the knowns and the unknown.

KNOWNS	UNKNOWN
[ethanoic acid] = $0.1000M$	K_a = ?
[H^+] = $1.34 \times 10^{-3}M$	

❷ **Calculate** Solve for the unknown.

Start by determining the equilibrium concentration of the ions.

[H^+] = [CH_3COO^-] = $1.34 \times 10^{-3}M$

Each molecule of CH_3COOH that ionizes gives an H^+ ion and a CH_3COO^- ion.

Then determine the equilibrium concentrations of each component.

$(0.1000 - 0.00134)M = 0.0987M$

Concentration	[CH_3COOH]	[H^+]	[CH_3COO^-]
Initial	0.1000	0	0
Change	-1.34×10^{-3}	1.34×10^{-3}	1.34×10^{-3}
Equilibrium	0.0987	1.34×10^{-3}	1.34×10^{-3}

Substitute the equilibrium values into the expression for K_a.

$$K_a = \frac{[H^+] \times [CH_3COO^-]}{[CH_3COOH]} = \frac{(1.34 \times 10^{-3}) \times (1.34 \times 10^{-3})}{0.0987}$$

$$= 1.82 \times 10^{-5}$$

❸ **Evaluate** Does the result make sense? The calculated value of K_a is consistent with that of a weak acid.

25. In a $0.1000M$ solution of methanoic acid, [H^+] = $4.2 \times 10^{-3}M$. Calculate the K_a of this acid.

26. In a $0.2000M$ solution of a monoprotic weak acid, [H^+] = $9.86 \times 10^{-4}M$. What is the K_a for this acid?

Figure 19.13 Use of Ammonia
Window cleaners often use a solution of ammonia in water to clean glass.
Explain *Why is this solution relatively safe to use?*

Base Dissociation Constant Just as there are strong acids and weak acids, there are strong bases and weak bases. A **strong base** dissociates completely into metal ions and hydroxide ions in aqueous solution. Some strong bases, such as calcium hydroxide and magnesium hydroxide, are not very soluble in water. The small amounts of these bases that dissolve in water dissociate completely.

A **weak base** reacts with water to form the conjugate acid of the base and hydroxide ions. For a weak base, the amount of dissociation is relatively small. Ammonia is an example of a weak base. One use for an aqueous solution of ammonia is shown in Figure 19.13.

$$NH_3(aq) + H_2O(l) \rightleftharpoons NH_4^+(aq) + OH^-(aq)$$

Ammonia   Water   Ammonium ion   Hydroxide ion

When equilibrium is established, only about 1 percent of the ammonia is present as NH_4^+. This ion is the conjugate acid of NH_3. The concentrations of NH_4^+ and OH^- are low and equal. The equilibrium-constant expression for the dissociation of ammonia in water is as follows:

$$K_{eq} = \frac{[NH_4^+] \times [OH^-]}{[NH_3] \times [H_2O]}$$

Recall that the concentration of water is constant in dilute solutions. This constant can be combined with the K_{eq} for ammonia to give a base dissociation constant (K_b) for ammonia.

$$K_{eq} \times [H_2O] = K_b = \frac{[NH_4^+] \times [OH^-]}{[NH_3]}$$

In general, the **base dissociation constant (K_b)** is the ratio of the concentration of the conjugate acid times the concentration of the hydroxide ion to the concentration of the base. The general form of the expression for the base dissociation constant is shown below.

$$K_b = \frac{[\text{conjugate acid}] \times [OH^-]}{[\text{base}]}$$

You can use this equation to calculate the K_b of a weak base. You need to know the initial concentration of the base and the concentration of hydroxide ions at equilibrium. If you know the pH, you can calculate $[H^+]$ and the corresponding $[OH^-]$.

The magnitude of K_b indicates the ability of a weak base to compete with the very strong base OH^- for hydrogen ions. Because bases such as ammonia are weak relative to the hydroxide ion, the K_b for such a base is usually small. The K_b for ammonia is 1.8×10^{-5}. The smaller the value of K_b, the weaker the base.

Table 19.8

Comparing Concentration and Strength of Acids			
	Concentration		
Acidic solution	Quantitative [or Molar]	Relative	Strength
Hydrochloric acid	12M HCl	Concentrated	Strong
Gastric juice	0.08M HCl	Dilute	Strong
Ethanoic acid	17M CH₃COOH	Concentrated	Weak
Vinegar	0.2M CH₃COOH	Dilute	Weak

CHEMISTRY & YOU

Q: *Despite its relatively low pH, lemon juice is safe to consume because citric acid is a weak acid. Citric acid has three K_a values. What does this information tell you about citric acid?*

Concentration Versus Strength Sometimes people confuse the concepts of concentration and strength. The words *concentrated* and *dilute* indicate how much of an acid or base is dissolved in solution. These terms refer to the number of moles of the acid or base in a given volume. The words *strong* and *weak* refer to the extent of ionization or dissociation of an acid or base.

Table 19.8 shows four possible combinations of concentration and strength for acids. Hydrochloric acid, HCl(*aq*), is a strong acid because it completely dissociates into ions. The gastric juice in your stomach is a dilute solution of HCl. The relatively small number of HCl molecules in a given volume of gastric juice are all dissociated into ions. To summarize, even when concentrated hydrochloric acid is diluted with water, it is still a strong acid. Conversely, ethanoic acid (acetic acid) is a weak acid because it ionizes only slightly in solution. Vinegar is a dilute solution of ethanoic acid. Even at a high concentration, ethanoic acid is still a weak acid.

The same concepts apply to bases. A solution of ammonia can be either dilute or concentrated. However, in any solution of ammonia, the relative amount of ionization will be small. Thus, ammonia is a weak base at any concentration. Likewise, sodium hydroxide is a strong base at any concentration.

 ## 19.3 LessonCheck

27. 🔒 **Review** What factor determines whether an acid or base is strong or weak?

28. Compare How do acid dissociation constants vary between strong acids and weak acids?

29. Draw Conclusions Which of the acids in Table 19.6 would you expect to have the lowest dissociation constant?

30. Describe How do you determine the K_a of a weak acid or the K_b of a weak base?

31. Predict Acid HX has a very small K_a. How will the relative amounts of H^+ and HX compare at equilibrium?

32. Calculate A 0.500M solution of an acid has a hydronium-ion concentration of $5.77 \times 10^{-6}M$. Calculate the K_a of this acid.

33. Describe Write a chemical equation for the dissociation of each of the following acids and bases in water.
   a. nitric acid
   b. ethanoic acid
   c. ammonia
   d. magnesium hydroxide

34. Classify A 15M solution of an acid has a K_a of 7.5×10^{-3}. Explain how you would classify this solution in terms of concentration and strength.

Small-Scale Lab

Dissociation Constants of Weak Acids

Purpose
To measure dissociation constants of weak acids

Materials
- paper, pencil, and ruler
- reaction surface
- 12 solutions with different pH values
- bromocresol green
- solutions of other acid-base indicators

Procedure

1. On two separate sheets of paper, draw two grids similar to the one below. Make each square 2 cm on each side.

2. Place a reaction surface over one of the grids and place one drop of bromocresol green in each square.

3. Add one drop of the solution with a pH of 1 to the square labeled 1. Add one drop of the solution with a pH of 2 to the square labeled 2. Continue adding drops in this manner until you have added a drop to each square.

4. Use the second grid as a data table to record your observations for each square.

pH

1	2	3
4	5	6
7	8	9
10	11	12

Analyze and Conclude

1. Observe What colors are the solutions with the lowest pH and the highest pH?

2. Observe At which pH does the bromocresol green change from one color to the other?

3. Infer Acid-base indicators, such as bromocresol green, are usually weak acids. Because bromocresol green has a fairly complex formula, it is convenient to represent its formula as HBCG. HBCG dissociates in water according to the following equation. HBCG and BCG^- are a conjugate acid-base pair.

$$HBCG(aq) + H_2O(l) \rightleftharpoons BCG^-(aq) + H_3O^+(aq)$$
(yellow)   (blue)

The K_a expression is

$$K_a = \frac{[BCG^-] \times [H_3O^+]}{[HBCG]}$$

When $[BCG^-] = [HBCG]$, $K_a = [H_3O^+]$.

What color is the conjugate base of HBCG? What color is the conjugate acid of BCG^-?

4. Draw Conclusions At what pH is there an equal amount of the conjugate acid and conjugate base? How can you tell?

5. Calculate What is the K_a for the solution described in Question 4?

You're the Chemist

1. Design an Experiment Design and carry out an experiment to measure the dissociation constants of some other acid-base indicators. Record the color of each conjugate acid and conjugate base. Calculate the K_a for each acid.

2. Explain How can you measure the dissociation constant of an acid-base indicator? Describe what to do and how to interpret the results.

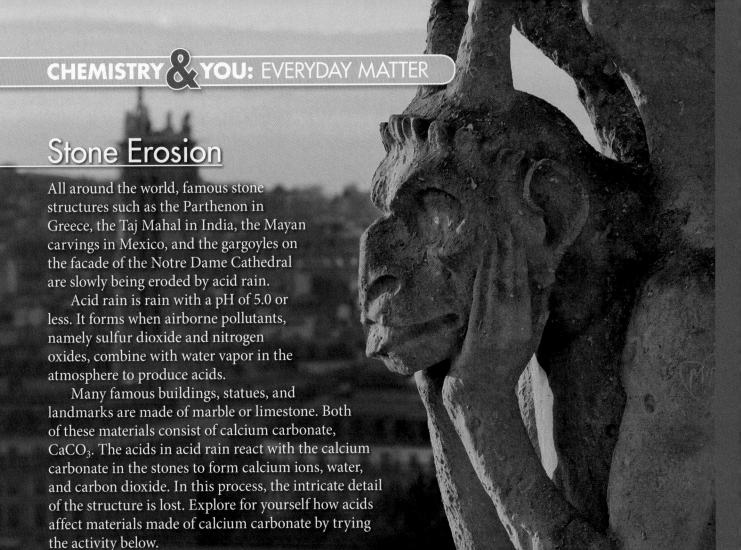

Stone Erosion

All around the world, famous stone structures such as the Parthenon in Greece, the Taj Mahal in India, the Mayan carvings in Mexico, and the gargoyles on the facade of the Notre Dame Cathedral are slowly being eroded by acid rain.

Acid rain is rain with a pH of 5.0 or less. It forms when airborne pollutants, namely sulfur dioxide and nitrogen oxides, combine with water vapor in the atmosphere to produce acids.

Many famous buildings, statues, and landmarks are made of marble or limestone. Both of these materials consist of calcium carbonate, $CaCO_3$. The acids in acid rain react with the calcium carbonate in the stones to form calcium ions, water, and carbon dioxide. In this process, the intricate detail of the structure is lost. Explore for yourself how acids affect materials made of calcium carbonate by trying the activity below.

On Your Own

1. For this activity you will need **2 bowls, 2 same-size pieces of chalk made of calcium carbonate, white vinegar, tap water, masking tape, a permanent marker,** and **a paper towel.** Put vinegar in the first bowl. Label the bowl with a piece of masking tape and a marker. Put the same amount of water in the second bowl and label it. *Optional*: If you'd like, you can scratch a design (with a needle, nail, or thumb tack) into each piece of chalk before going to Step 2.

2. Place a piece of chalk in each bowl. Observe what happens to the chalk.

3. After about 5 minutes, remove the chalk pieces from the bowls and place the pieces on a paper towel. Compare the pieces of chalk.

Think About It

1. Compare How did the vinegar affect the chalk compared to the water?

2. Infer What causes the bubbles you see when the chalk is placed in vinegar?

3. Describe Write a balanced equation to explain what happens to the chalk when it is placed in vinegar. *Note*: Let $H^+(aq)$ represent the acid.

4. Draw Conclusions Why does acid rain result in a loss of detail in the gargoyle above? What would be the effect of acid rain on a statue over a long period of time?

19.4 Neutralization Reactions

Q: *What could cause leaves to turn yellow during the growing season?* You may have noticed yellow leaves like these during a season when the leaves should still be green. This condition is called *chlorosis* because the plant lacks a pigment called chlorophyll. To produce chlorophyll, plants need to absorb nutrients, such as iron, from the soil. Sometimes there is plenty of iron, but it is not taken up by the roots of the plant because the pH of the soil is too high.

Key Questions

🔑 What products form when an acid and a base react?

🔑 At what point in a titration does neutralization occur?

Vocabulary

- neutralization reaction
- titration
- standard solution
- equivalence point
- end point

Acid-Base Reactions

🔑 **What products form when an acid and a base react?**

Suppose you mix a solution of a strong acid, such as HCl, with a solution of a strong base, such as NaOH. The products are sodium chloride and water.

$$HCl(aq) + NaOH(aq) \longrightarrow NaCl(aq) + H_2O(l)$$

🔑 **In general, acids and bases react to produce a salt and water.** The complete reaction of a strong acid and a strong base produces a neutral solution. Thus, this type of reaction is called a **neutralization reaction.**

When you hear the word *salt,* you may think of the substance that is used to flavor food. Table salt (NaCl) is only one example of a salt. Salts are ionic compounds consisting of an anion from an acid and a cation from a base.

A reaction between an acid and base will go to completion when the solutions contain equal numbers of hydrogen ions and hydroxide ions. The balanced equation provides the correct ratio of acid to base. For hydrochloric acid and sodium hydroxide, the mole ratio is 1:1.

$$HCl(aq) + NaOH(aq) \longrightarrow NaCl(aq) + H_2O(l)$$
$$\text{1 mol} \qquad \text{1 mol} \qquad \text{1 mol} \qquad \text{1 mol}$$

For sulfuric acid and sodium hydroxide, the ratio is 1:2. Two moles of the base are required to neutralize one mole of the acid.

$$H_2SO_4(aq) + 2NaOH(aq) \longrightarrow Na_2SO_4(aq) + 2H_2O(l)$$
$$\text{1 mol} \qquad \text{2 mol} \qquad \text{1 mol} \qquad \text{2 mol}$$

Similarly, hydrochloric acid and calcium hydroxide react in a 2:1 ratio.

$$2HCl(aq) + Ca(OH)_2(aq) \longrightarrow CaCl_2(aq) + 2H_2O(l)$$
$$\text{2 mol} \qquad \text{1 mol} \qquad \text{1 mol} \qquad \text{2 mol}$$

Learn more about acid-base reactions online.

Finding the Moles Needed for Neutralization

The term *neutralization* is used to describe both the reaction and the point at which a neutralization reaction is complete. How many moles of sulfuric acid are required to neutralize 0.50 mol of sodium hydroxide? The equation for the reaction is

$$H_2SO_4(aq) + 2NaOH(aq) \longrightarrow Na_2SO_4(aq) + 2H_2O(l)$$

❶ Analyze **List the knowns and the unknown.**
To determine the number of moles of acid, you need to know the number of moles of base and the mole ratio of acid to base.

KNOWNS	UNKNOWN
mol NaOH = 0.50 mol	mol H_2SO_4 = ? mol
1 mol H_2SO_4/2 mol NaOH	
(from balanced equation)	

❷ Calculate **Solve for the unknown.**

Use the mole ratio of acid to base to determine the number of moles of acid.

$$0.50 \; \text{mol NaOH} \times \frac{1 \; \text{mol } H_2SO_4}{2 \; \text{mol NaOH}} = 0.25 \; \text{mol } H_2SO_4$$

❸ Evaluate **Does the result make sense?** Because the mole ratio of H_2SO_4 to NaOH is 1:2, the number of moles of H_2SO_4 should be half the number of moles of NaOH.

35. How many moles of potassium hydroxide are needed to neutralize 1.56 mol of phosphoric acid?

To solve each problem, begin by writing a balanced equation.

36. How many moles of sodium hydroxide are required to neutralize 0.20 mol of nitric acid?

Titration

🔑 **At what point in a titration does neutralization occur?**

You can use a neutralization reaction to determine the concentration of an acid or base. The process of adding a measured amount of a solution of known concentration to a solution of unknown concentration is called a **titration**. The steps in an acid-base titration are as follows.

1. A measured volume of an acid solution of unknown concentration is added to a flask.

2. Several drops of an indicator are added to the solution while the flask is gently swirled.

3. Measured volumes of a base of known concentration are mixed into the acid until the indicator just barely changes color.

Figure 19.14 Titration
The photographs show steps in an acid-base titration.
a. A flask with a known volume of acid (and some phenolphthalein indicator) is placed beneath a buret that is filled with a base of known concentration.
b. Base is slowly added from the buret to the acid while the flask is gently swirled. **c.** A change in the color of the solution is the signal that neutralization has occurred.

CHEMISTRY & YOU

Q: *Iron compounds need to dissociate before the iron can be absorbed by plants. However, these compounds become less soluble as the pH rises. For most plants, a pH between 5.0 and 6.5 will provide enough usable iron. How could you change the pH of soil?*

The solution of known concentration is the **standard solution.** The steps in the titration of an acid of unknown concentration with a standard base are shown in Figure 19.14. You can use a similar procedure to find the concentration of a base using a standard acid.

🗝 **Neutralization occurs when the number of moles of hydrogen ions is equal to the number of moles of hydroxide ions.** Two things that are equal in value are said to be *equivalent*. Thus, the point at which neutralization occurs is called the **equivalence point.** The indicator that is chosen for a titration must change color at or near the pH of the equivalence point. The point at which the indicator changes color is the **end point** of the titration.

Figure 19.15 shows how the pH of a solution changes during the titration of a strong acid (HCl) with a strong base (NaOH). The initial acid solution has a low pH (about 1). As NaOH is added, the pH increases because some of the acid reacts with the base. The equivalence point for this reaction occurs at a pH of 7. As the titration nears the equivalence point, the pH rises dramatically because hydrogen ions are being used up. Extending the titration beyond the point of neutralization produces a further increase of pH. If the titration of HCl and NaOH could be stopped right at the equivalence point, the solution in the beaker would consist of only H_2O and NaCl, plus a small amount of indicator.

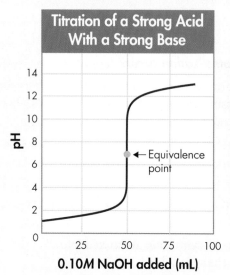

Titration of a Strong Acid With a Strong Base

← Equivalence point

pH

0.10M NaOH added (mL)

Figure 19.15 Titration Curve
In this titration, 0.10M NaOH is slowly added to 50.0 mL of 0.10M HCl. The pH of the solution is measured and recorded periodically to construct a titration curve. The equivalence point is located at the midpoint of the vertical part of the curve. Neutralization occurs when 50.0 mL of NaOH have been added to the flask.
Compare *How are [H⁺] and [OH⁻] related at the equivalence point?*

SampleProblem 19.8

Determining Concentration by Titration

A 25-mL solution of H_2SO_4 is neutralized by 18 mL of 1.0M NaOH. What is the concentration of the H_2SO_4 solution? The equation for the reaction is

$$H_2SO_4(aq) + 2NaOH(aq) \longrightarrow Na_2SO_4(aq) + 2H_2O(l)$$

KNOWNS

[NaOH] = 1.0M
V_{NaOH} = 18 mL = 0.018 L
$V_{H_2SO_4}$ = 25 mL = 0.025 L

UNKNOWN

[H_2SO_4] = ?M

❶ **Analyze** List the knowns and the unknown. The conversion steps are as follows: L NaOH $\longrightarrow$ mol NaOH $\longrightarrow$ mol H_2SO_4 $\longrightarrow$ M H_2SO_4.

❷ **Calculate** Solve for the unknown.

Convert volumes to liters because molarity is in moles per liter.

Use the molarity to convert the volume of base to moles of base.	$0.018 \text{ L NaOH} \times \dfrac{1.0 \text{ mol NaOH}}{1 \text{ L NaOH}} = 0.018 \text{ mol NaOH}$
Use the mole ratio to find the moles of acid.	$0.018 \text{ mol NaOH} \times \dfrac{1 \text{ mol } H_2SO_4}{2 \text{ mol NaOH}} = 0.0090 \text{ mol } H_2SO_4$
Calculate the molarity by dividing moles of acid by liters of solution.	$\text{molarity} = \dfrac{\text{mol of solute}}{\text{L of solution}} = \dfrac{0.0090 \text{ mol}}{0.025 \text{ L}} = 0.36M \, H_2SO_4$

❸ **Evaluate** Does the result make sense? If the acid had the same molarity as the base (1.0M), 50 mL of base would neutralize 25 mL of acid. Because the volume of base is much less than 50 mL, the molarity of the acid must be much less than 1.0M.

37. How many milliliters of 0.45M HCl will neutralize 25.0 mL of 1.00M KOH?

38. What is the molarity of a solution of H_3PO_4 if 15.0 mL is neutralized by 38.5 mL of 0.150M NaOH?

 19.4 LessonCheck

39. 🔑 **Review** What are the products of a reaction between an acid and a base?

40. 🔑 **Explain** Why is the point in the titration when neutralization occurs called the equivalence point?

41. Calculate How many moles of HCl are required to neutralize aqueous solutions of these bases?
 a. 0.03 mol KOH
 b. 2 mol NH_3
 c. 0.1 mol $Ca(OH)_2$

42. Describe Write complete balanced equations for the following acid-base reactions:
 a. $H_2SO_4(aq) + KOH(aq) \longrightarrow$
 b. $H_3PO_4(aq) + Ca(OH)_2(aq) \longrightarrow$
 c. $HNO_3(aq) + Mg(OH)_2(aq) \longrightarrow$

BIGIDEA REACTIONS

43. Review the information on types of chemical reactions in Chapter 11. Which types of reactions are neutralization reactions? Explain your answer.

19.5 Salts in Solution

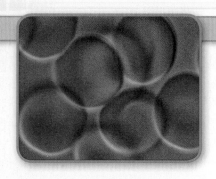

CHEMISTRY & YOU

Q: *How is the pH of blood controlled in the human body?* Chemical reactions in cells are very sensitive to slight changes in pH. For example, the pH of human blood needs to be kept close to 7.4. A person cannot survive for more than a few minutes if the pH of blood drops below 6.8 or rises above 7.8. This lesson will explain the process that prevents such a life-threatening event.

Key Questions

🔑 When is the solution of a salt acidic or basic?

🔑 What are the components of a buffer?

Vocabulary

• salt hydrolysis
• buffer
• buffer capacity

Salt Hydrolysis

🔑 **When is the solution of a salt acidic or basic?**

Recall that a salt is one of the products of a neutralization reaction. A salt consists of an anion from an acid and a cation from a base. The solutions of many salts are neutral. Salts that form neutral solutions include sodium chloride and potassium sulfate. Some salts form acidic or basic solutions, as shown in Figure 19.16. The indicator used for Figure 19.16 is called universal indicator because it can be used for a wide range of pH values.

Figure 19.17 shows two titration curves. One curve is for the addition of sodium hydroxide, a strong base, to ethanoic acid, a weak acid. An aqueous solution of sodium ethanoate exists at the equivalence point.

$$CH_3COOH(aq) + NaOH(aq) \longrightarrow CH_3COONa(aq) + H_2O(l)$$

Ethanoic acid   Sodium   Sodium   Water
              hydroxide   ethanoate

The second titration curve is for the reaction between hydrochloric acid, which is a strong acid, and sodium hydroxide. This second curve should look familiar. It first appeared in Lesson 19.4 in the section on titrations.

Figure 19.16
The pH of Salt Solutions
Universal indicator was added to 0.10M aqueous salt solutions. Based on the indicator color, the solutions can be classified as follows: **a.** Ammonium chloride, NH₄Cl(aq), is acidic (pH of about 5.3). **b.** Sodium chloride, NaCl(aq), is neutral (pH of 7). **c.** Sodium ethanoate, CH₃COONa(aq), is basic (pH of about 8.7).

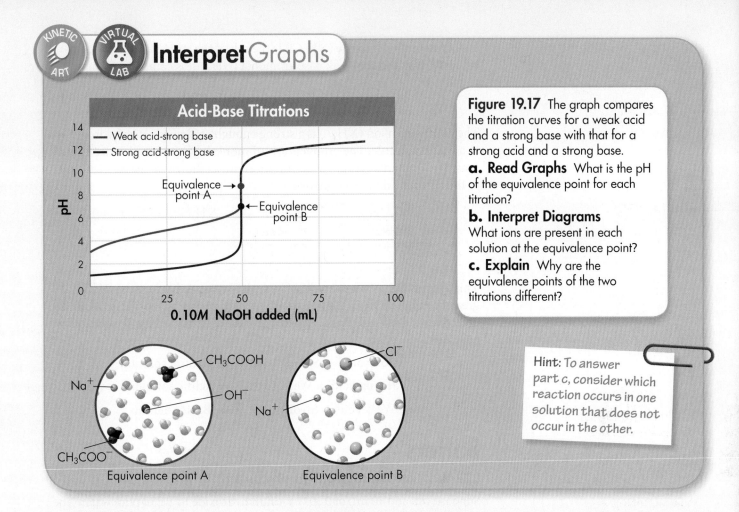

Figure 19.17 The graph compares the titration curves for a weak acid and a strong base with that for a strong acid and a strong base.

a. Read Graphs What is the pH of the equivalence point for each titration?

b. Interpret Diagrams What ions are present in each solution at the equivalence point?

c. Explain Why are the equivalence points of the two titrations different?

Hint: To answer part c, consider which reaction occurs in one solution that does not occur in the other.

The pH at the equivalence point for the weak acid-strong base titration is basic. For a strong acid-strong base titration, the pH at the equivalence point is neutral. This difference in pH exists because hydrolysis occurs with some salts in solution. In **salt hydrolysis,** the cations or anions of a dissociated salt remove hydrogen ions from, or donate hydrogen ions to, water. **Salts that produce acidic solutions have positive ions that release hydrogen ions to water. Salts that produce basic solutions have negative ions that attract hydrogen ions from water**.

Sodium ethanoate (CH_3COONa) is the salt of a weak acid and a strong base. In solution, the salt is completely ionized.

$$CH_3COONa(aq) \longrightarrow CH_3COO^-(aq) + Na^+(aq)$$

Sodium ethanoate   Ethanoate ion   Sodium ion

The ethanoate ion is a Brønsted-Lowry base, which means it is a hydrogen-ion acceptor. It reacts with water to form ethanoic acid and hydroxide ions. At equilibrium, the reactants are favored.

$$CH_3COO^-(aq) + H_2O(l) \rightleftharpoons CH_3COOH(aq) + OH^-(aq)$$

H$^+$ acceptor,   H$^+$ donor,   (makes the
Brønsted-Lowry base   Brønsted-Lowry acid   solution basic)

This process is called hydrolysis because a hydrogen ion is split off a water molecule. The suffix *-lysis* comes from a Greek word meaning to "separate" or "loosen." In the solution, the hydroxide-ion concentration is greater than the hydrogen-ion concentration. Thus, the solution is basic.

Ammonium chloride (NH$_4$Cl) is the salt of the strong acid hydrochloric acid (HCl) and the weak base ammonia (NH$_3$). It is completely ionized in solution.

$$NH_4Cl(aq) \longrightarrow NH_4^+(aq) + Cl^-(aq)$$

The ammonium ion (NH$_4^+$) is a strong enough acid to donate a hydrogen ion to a water molecule. The products are ammonia molecules and hydronium ions. The reactants are favored at equilibrium, as shown by the relative sizes of the forward and reverse arrows.

$$\underset{\substack{\text{H}^+ \text{ donor,} \\ \text{Br\o nsted-Lowry acid}}}{NH_4^+(aq)} + \underset{\substack{\text{H}^+ \text{ acceptor,} \\ \text{Br\o nsted-Lowry base}}}{H_2O(l)} \rightleftharpoons NH_3(aq) + \underset{\substack{\text{(makes the} \\ \text{solution acidic)}}}{H_3O^+(aq)}$$

This process is another example of hydrolysis. At equilibrium the [H$_3$O$^+$] is greater than the [OH$^-$]. Thus, a solution of ammonium chloride is acidic. To determine if a salt will form an acidic or basic solution, remember the following rules:

Strong acid + **Strong base** $\longrightarrow$ Neutral solution

Strong acid + Weak base $\longrightarrow$ **Acidic** solution

Weak acid + **Strong base** $\longrightarrow$ **Basic** solution

Buffers

What are the components of a buffer?

Suppose you add 10 mL of 0.10M sodium hydroxide to 1 L of pure water. The pH will increase about 4 pH units—from 7.0 to about 11.0. This change is a relatively large increase in pH. Now consider a solution containing 0.20M each of ethanoic acid and sodium ethanoate. This solution has a pH of 4.76. If you add 10 mL of 0.10M sodium hydroxide to 1 L of this solution, the pH increases 0.01 pH units—from 4.76 to 4.77. This is a relatively small change in pH. If 10 mL of acid had been added instead of the base, the amount of change in pH would also have been small.

The solution of ethanoic acid and sodium ethanoate is an example of a buffer. A **buffer** is a solution in which the pH remains fairly constant when small amounts of acid or base are added. **A buffer is a solution of a weak acid and one of its salts or a solution of a weak base and one of its salts.** Figure 19.18 compares what happens when 1.0 mL of 0.01M HCl solution is added to an unbuffered solution and to a solution with a buffer.

Figure 19.18 Effect of a Buffer
In a buffer solution, the pH does not shift dramatically. **a.** The indicator shows that both solutions are basic (pH of about 8). **b.** HCl is added to each solution. The indicator shows no visible pH change in the buffered solution. The color change in the unbuffered solution indicates a change in pH from 8 to about 3.
Predict How would the original solutions respond if NaOH were added?

buffered   unbuffered

buffered   unbuffered

How Buffers Work A buffer solution is better able to resist drastic changes in pH than is pure water. The reason is fairly simple. A buffer solution contains one component that can react with hydrogen ions (a hydrogen-ion acceptor) and another component that can react with hydroxide ions (a hydrogen-ion donor). These components act as reservoirs of neutralizing power that can be tapped when either hydrogen ions or hydroxide ions are added to the solution.

The ethanoic acid–ethanoate ion buffer can be used to show how a buffer works. When an acid is added to the buffer, the ethanoate ions (CH_3COO^-) act as a hydrogen-ion "sponge." As the ethanoate ions react with the hydrogen ions, they form ethanoic acid. This weak acid does not ionize extensively in water, so the change in pH is very slight.

$$CH_3COO^-(aq) + H^+(aq) \rightleftharpoons CH_3COOH(aq)$$

Ethanoate ion   Hydrogen ion   Ethanoic acid

When hydroxide ions are added to the buffer, the ethanoic acid and the hydroxide ions react to produce water and the ethanoate ion.

$$CH_3COOH(aq) + OH^-(aq) \rightleftharpoons CH_3COO^-(aq) + H_2O(l)$$

Ethanoic acid   Hydroxide ion   Ethanoate ion   Water

The ethanoate ion is not a strong enough base to accept hydrogen ions from water to a great extent. Therefore, the reverse reaction is minimal and the change in pH is very slight.

The Capacity of a Buffer Buffer solutions have their limits. As acid is added to an ethanoate buffer, eventually no more ethanoate ions will be present to accept the hydrogen ions. At that point, the buffer can no longer control the pH. The ethanoate buffer also becomes ineffective when too much base is added. In that case, no more ethanoic acid molecules are present to donate hydrogen ions. Adding too much acid or base will exceed the buffer capacity of a solution. The **buffer capacity** is the amount of acid or base that can be added to a buffer solution before a significant change in pH occurs.

Table 19.9 lists some common buffer systems. Two of these buffer systems help maintain optimal human blood pH. One is the carbonic acid–hydrogen carbonate buffer system. The other is the dihydrogen phosphate–hydrogen phosphate buffer system.

Table 19.9

Important Buffer Systems		
Buffer name	**Formulas**	**Buffer pH***
Ethanoic acid–ethanoate ion	CH_3COOH / CH_3COO^-	4.76
Dihydrogen phosphate ion–hydrogen phosphate ion	$H_2PO_4^- / HPO_4^{2-}$	7.20
Carbonic acid–hydrogen carbonate ion (solution saturated with CO_2)	H_2CO_3 / HCO_3^-	6.46
Ammonium ion–ammonia	NH_4^+ / NH_3	9.25

*Components have concentrations of 0.1M.

Describing Buffer Systems

Write balanced chemical equations to show how the carbonic acid–hydrogen carbonate buffer can "mop up" added hydroxide ions and hydrogen ions.

❶ **Analyze** Identify the relevant concepts. A buffer contains two components: a hydrogen-ion acceptor (which can react with H^+) and a hydrogen-ion donor (which can react with OH^-).

❷ **Solve** Apply the concepts to this problem.

Identify the hydrogen-ion acceptor and the hydrogen-ion donor.	H_2CO_3, a weak acid, can release hydrogen ions. HCO_3^- is the conjugate base, which can accept hydrogen ions.
Write the equation for the reaction that occurs when a base is added to the buffer.	When a base is added, the hydroxide ions react with H_2CO_3. $$H_2CO_3(aq) + (OH^-)(aq) \rightleftharpoons HCO_3^-(aq) + H_2O(l)$$
Write the equation for the reaction that occurs when an acid is added to the buffer.	When an acid is added, the hydrogen ions react with HCO_3^-. $$HCO_3^-(aq) + (H^+)(aq) \rightleftharpoons H_2CO_3(aq)$$

44. Write equations to show what happens in the following situations:
  a. Acid is added to a solution that contains HPO_4^{2-} ions.
  b. Base is added to a solution that contains $H_2PO_4^-$ ions.

45. A buffer consists of methanoic acid (HCOOH) and methanoate ion ($HCOO^-$). Write an equation to show what happens when an acid is added to this buffer.

19.5 LessonCheck

46. 🔑 **Review** What type of salt produces an acidic solution? What type of salt produces a basic solution?

47. 🔑 **Describe** What types of substances can be combined to make a buffer solution?

48. **Classify** Which of these salts would hydrolyze to produce an acidic aqueous solution, and why?
  a. $KC_2H_3O_2$
  b. LiCl
  c. $NaHCO_3$
  d. $(NH_4)_2SO_4$

49. **Identify** Which of the following pairs can form a buffer solution? Explain.
  a. NH_3 and HCO_3^-
  b. C_6H_5COOH and $C_6H_5COO^-$

50. **Describe** Write a balanced chemical equation to show what happens when an acid is added to an ammonium ion–ammonia buffer. Write an equation to show what happens when a base is added.

51. **Relate Cause and Effect** Use Le Châtelier's principle to explain how a buffer system maintains the pH of a solution.

Ocean Buffers

As atmospheric carbon dioxide (CO_2) levels rise due to increased burning of fossil fuels, global warming is not the only potential environmental problem that Earth faces. Additionally, ocean water becomes more acidic, which can disrupt the ocean ecosystem.

The oceans naturally absorb CO_2 from the atmosphere. Some of the absorbed CO_2 is converted to carbonic acid (H_2CO_3), which can lower the pH of ocean water. Fortunately, the oceans have an excellent natural buffer system that helps maintain the optimal pH for supporting ocean life—about 8.2. The ocean's buffer system is largely based on the hydrogen carbonate–carbonate ion buffer system. However, the buffer capacity of the buffers in ocean water is limited, and current human activities are pushing these limits.

Try the following activity at home to gain a better understanding of the effects of CO_2 and sea salt on the pH of ocean water.

On Your Own

1. For this activity, you will need the following materials: **4 drinking glasses, masking tape, a permanent marker, distilled water, carbonated water, sea salt, a measuring cup, ¼ teaspoon measuring spoon,** and **4 pH test strips.** (You can ask your teacher for pH test strips if you do not have them at home.) Use the masking tape and marker to label the glasses 1, 2, 3, and 4.

2. Add ½ cup of distilled water to glasses 1 and 2. Add ½ cup of carbonated water to glasses 3 and 4.

3. Add ¾ teaspoon of sea salt to containers 2 and 4. Stir until the salt is dissolved. (This ratio of sea salt to water is similar to that found in the ocean.)

4. Measure the pH of each solution and record it in a table similar to the one shown to the right.

What Did You Find?

Glass	1	2	3	4
Contents				
pH				

Think About It

1. Compare Determine whether each solution is acidic, basic, or neutral. How do the four solutions differ?

2. Explain How does a solution containing hydrogen carbonate ions (HCO_3^-) and carbonate ions (CO_3^{2-}) act as a buffer? Use chemical equations to support your explanation.

3. Draw Conclusions What does this experiment demonstrate about the effects of dissolved CO_2 (in the carbonated water) and sea salt on the pH of ocean water?

19 Study Guide

BIGIDEA REACTIONS

Chemists define acids and bases according to the ions they yield in aqueous solution. Chemists also define acids and bases based on whether they accept or donate hydrogen ions, and whether they are electron-pair donors or acceptors. The pH of a solution reflects the hydrogen-ion concentration. Chemists use acid-base reactions to determine the concentration of an acid or a base in solution.

19.1 Acid-Base Theories

🔑 According to Arrhenius, acids are hydrogen-containing compounds that ionize to yield hydrogen ions in aqueous solution. Bases are compounds that ionize to yield hydroxide ions in aqueous solution.

🔑 According to the Brønsted-Lowry theory, an acid is a hydrogen-ion donor and a base is a hydrogen-ion acceptor.

🔑 According to Lewis, an acid accepts a pair of electrons and a base donates a pair of electrons.

- hydronium ion (H_3O^+) (647)
- conjugate acid (650)
- conjugate base (650)
- conjugate acid-base pair (650)
- amphoteric (651)
- Lewis acid (651)
- Lewis base (651)

19.2 Hydrogen Ions and Acidity

🔑 For aqueous solutions, the product of the hydrogen-ion concentration and the hydroxide-ion concentration equals 1×10^{-14}.

🔑 A solution with a pH less than 7.0 is acidic. A solution with a pH of 7 is neutral. A solution with a pH greater than 7.0 is basic.

🔑 Either acid-base indicators or pH meters can be used to measure pH.

- self-ionization (653)
- neutral solution (653)
- ion-product constant for water (K_w) (654)
- acidic solution (654)
- basic solution (654)
- pH (656)

Key Equations

$$K_w = [H^+] \times [OH^-] = 1.0 \times 10^{-14}$$

$$pH = -\log[H^+]$$

19.3 Strengths of Acids and Bases

🔑 Acids and bases are classified as strong or weak based on the degree to which they ionize in water.

- strong acid (664)
- weak acid (664)
- acid dissociation constant (K_a) (665)
- strong base (668)
- weak base (668)
- base dissociation constant (K_b) (668)

Key Equation

$$K_a = \frac{[H^+][A^-]}{[HA]}$$

19.4 Neutralization Reactions

🔑 In general, acids and bases react to produce a salt and water.

🔑 Neutralization occurs when the number of moles of hydrogen ions is equal to the number of moles of hydroxide ions.

- neutralization reaction (672)
- titration (673)
- standard solution (674)
- equivalence point (674)
- end point (674)

19.5 Salts in Solution

🔑 Salts that produce acidic solutions have positive ions that release hydrogen ions to water. Salts that produce basic solutions have negative ions that attract hydrogen ions from water.

🔑 A buffer is a solution of a weak acid and one of its salts or a weak base and one of its salts.

- salt hydrolysis (677)
- buffer (678)
- buffer capacity (679)

Math Tune-Up: Acid-Base Problems

Problem	❶ Analyze	❷ Calculate	❸ Evaluate
The pH of an unknown solution is 3.70. What is the hydrogen-ion concentration?	Known: pH = 3.70 Unknown: $[H^+] = ?M$ Use the following equation: $pH = -\log[H^+]$	Rearrange the expression for pH and substitute the known pH value to solve for the unknown: $-\log[H^+] = pH$ $-\log[H^+] = 3.70$ $\log[H^+] = -3.70$ The antilog of -3.70 is 2.0×10^{-4}. Thus, $[H^+] = 2.0 \times 10^{-4}M$. **Note:** To determine the antilog on most calculators, press the 2nd or INV key then the log key.	The pH is between 3 and 4. So, the hydrogen ion concentration must be between $1 \times 10^{-3}M$ and $1 \times 10^{-4}M$.
In a $0.500M$ solution of a weak acid (HA), the $[H^+]$ is 4.02×10^{-3} at equilibrium. Find the K_a for this acid. The acid dissociates as follows: $HA \rightleftharpoons H^+ + A^-$	Knowns: $[HA] = 0.500M$ $[H^+] = 4.02 \times 10^{-3}$ Unknown: $K_a = ?$ Use the general expression for K_a: $K_a = \dfrac{[H^+] \times [A^-]}{[HA]}$ **Hint:** Review Sample Problem 19.6 for help on finding equilibrium concentrations.	At equilibrium, $[H^+]$ is equal to $[A^-]$: $[H^+] = [A^-] = 4.02 \times 10^{-3}$ Calculate [HA] at equilibrium: $0.500M - 0.00402M = 0.496M$ Substitute the equilibrium concentrations into the equation for K_a and solve: $K_a = \dfrac{(4.02 \times 10^{-3}) \times (4.02 \times 10^{-3})}{0.496}$ $K_a = 3.26 \times 10^{-5}$	The value of K_a is consistent with that of a weak acid.
How many moles of KOH are needed to neutralize 0.25 mol of H_2SO_4? The equation for the reaction is $2KOH(aq) + H_2SO_4(aq) \longrightarrow$ $\quad K_2SO_4(aq) + 2H_2O(l)$	Known: mol $H_2SO_4 = 0.25$ mol Unknown: mol KOH = ? mol	Use the mole ratio of base to acid (2 mol KOH to 1 mol H_2SO_4) to determine the number of moles of base: $0.25 \text{ mol } H_2SO_4 \times \dfrac{2 \text{ mol KOH}}{1 \text{ mol } H_2SO_4}$ $\qquad = 0.50 \text{ mol KOH}$	The mole ratio of KOH to H_2SO_4 is 2:1. So, the number of moles of KOH should be twice the number of moles of H_2SO_4.

19 Assessment

* Solutions appear in Appendix E

Lesson by Lesson

19.1 Acid-Base Theories

*52. How did Arrhenius describe acids and bases?

53. Classify each compound as an Arrhenius acid or an Arrhenius base.
   a. $Ca(OH)_2$ **c.** HNO_3 **e.** HBr
   b. C_2H_5COOH **d.** KOH   **f.** H_2SO_4

54. Write an equation for the dissociation of each compound in water.
   a. KOH   **b.** $Mg(OH)_2$

*55. Write balanced equations for the reaction of each metal with water.
   a. lithium   **b.** barium

56. Identify each reactant in the following equations as a hydrogen-ion donor (acid) or a hydrogen-ion acceptor (base). All the reactions take place in aqueous solution.
   a. $HNO_3 + H_2O \longrightarrow H_3O^+ + NO_3^-$
   b. $CH_3COOH + H_2O \rightleftharpoons H_3O^+ + CH_3COO^-$
   c. $NH_3 + H_2O \rightleftharpoons NH_4^+ + OH^-$
   d. $H_2O + CH_3COO^- \rightleftharpoons CH_3COOH + OH^-$

57. Label the conjugate acid-base pairs for each equation in Question 56.

58. What is a Lewis acid? What is a Lewis base?

19.2 Hydrogen Ions and Acidity

59. Write an equation showing the self-ionization of water.

60. What are the concentrations of H^+ and OH^- in pure water at 25°C?

61. How is the pH of a solution calculated?

62. Why is the pH of pure water at 25°C equal to 7.0?

*63. Calculate the pH for the following solutions and indicate whether each solution is acidic or basic.
   a. $[OH^-] = 1 \times 10^{-2} M$ **b.** $[H^+] = 1 \times 10^{-2} M$

64. What are the hydroxide-ion concentrations for solutions with the following pH values?
   a. 4.00   **b.** 8.00   **c.** 12.00

65. Calculate the pH or $[H^+]$ for each solution.
   a. $[H^+] = 2.4 \times 10^{-6} M$ **b.** pH = 13.20

19.3 Strengths of Acids and Bases

*66. Identify each compound as a strong or weak acid or base.
   a. NaOH   **b.** NH_3 **c.** H_2SO_4 **d.** HCl

67. Would a strong acid have a large or a small K_a? Explain your answer.

68. Why are $Mg(OH)_2$ and $Ca(OH)_2$ classified as strong bases even though their saturated solutions are only mildly basic?

69. Write the expression for K_a for each acid. Assume only one hydrogen is ionized.
   a. HF   **b.** H_2CO_3

19.4 Neutralization Reactions

70. Write a general word equation for a neutralization reaction.

71. Identify the products and write balanced equations for each neutralization reaction.
   a. $HNO_3(aq) + KOH(aq) \longrightarrow$
   b. $HCl(aq) + Ca(OH)_2(aq) \longrightarrow$
   c. $H_2SO_4(aq) + NaOH(aq) \longrightarrow$

72. How is it possible to recognize the end point of a titration?

*73. What is the molarity of sodium hydroxide if 20.0 mL of the solution is neutralized by each of the following 1.00M solutions?
   a. 28.0 mL of HCl
   b. 17.4 mL of H_3PO_4

19.5 Salts in Solution

74. What kinds of salts hydrolyze water?

*75. Write an equation showing why an aqueous solution of sodium hydrogen carbonate is basic.

76. Explain why solutions of salts that hydrolyze water do not have a pH of 7.

77. Predict whether an aqueous solution of each salt will be acidic, basic, or neutral.
   a. $NaHCO_3$ **d.** Na_2CO_3
   b. NH_4NO_3 **e.** Na_2SO_4
   c. KCl   **f.** NH_4Cl

78. Explain why a buffered solution cannot absorb an unlimited amount of acid or base.

79. Explain how the Lewis theory is a more general classification system than either the Arrhenius descriptions or the Brønsted-Lowry theory.

80. Is it possible to have a concentrated weak acid? Explain.

⋆81. Write equations showing that the hydrogen phosphate ion (HPO_4^{2-}) is amphoteric.

82. The pH of a $0.5000M$ HNO_2 solution is 1.83. What is the K_a of this acid?

83. How do the $[H^+]$ and the $[OH^-]$ compare in each type of solution?

  a. neutral solution
  b. basic solution
  c. acidic solution

84. Write the formula and name of the conjugate base of each Brønsted-Lowry acid.

  a. HCO_3^- **b.** NH_4^+ **c.** HI **d.** H_2SO_3

⋆85. Write the formula and name of the conjugate acid of each Brønsted-Lowry base.

  a. ClO_2^- **b.** H_2O **c.** $H_2PO_4^-$ **d.** NH_3

86. Calculate the $[OH^-]$ or pH of each solution.

  a. pH = 4.60   **c.** $[OH^-] = 1.8 \times 10^{-2}M$
  b. pH = 9.30   **d.** $[OH^-] = 7.3 \times 10^{-9}M$

87. Write the three equations for the stepwise ionization of phosphoric acid.

88. Use the Brønsted-Lowry and Lewis definitions of acids and bases to identify each reactant as an acid or a base.

  a. $KOH(aq) + HBr(aq) \longrightarrow KBr(aq) + H_2O(l)$
  b. $HCl(aq) + H_2O(l) \longrightarrow Cl^-(aq) + H_3O^+(aq)$

89. Write the formula for the conjugate base of each of the following acids:

  a. H_2SO_4 **b.** CH_3COOH **c.** H_2O

90. Use the phosphate buffer ($H_2PO_4^-/HPO_4^{2-}$) to illustrate how a buffer system works. Use equations to show how the pH of a solution can be kept almost constant when small amounts of acid or base are added.

⋆91. Write an equation for the reaction of each antacid with hydrochloric acid.

  a. magnesium hydroxide
  b. calcium carbonate
  c. aluminum hydroxide

92. How would the addition of each substance affect the equilibrium between hypochlorous acid and the hypochlorite ion?

$$HOCl(aq) + OH^-(aq) \rightleftharpoons OCl^-(aq) + H_2O(l)$$

  a. HCl   **b.** NaOH

93. The following data were collected from a titration of 50.00 mL of ethanoic acid (CH_3COOH) of unknown concentration with $0.100M$ NaOH. Plot these data to obtain a titration curve. Place pH on the y-axis.

Volume of NaOH (mL)	pH	Volume of NaOH (mL)	pH
0	3.18	50.00	8.73
10.00	4.15	50.01	8.89
25.00	4.76	51.00	11.00
40.00	5.36	60.00	11.96
49.00	6.45	75.00	12.30
49.99	8.55	100.00	12.52

  a. What is the pH at the end point of this titration?
  b. Use Figure 19.8 to identify one or more acid-base indicators that could be used to determine the end point in this titration.

94. Write an equation to show that an aqueous solution of sodium ethanoate will be basic.

⋆95. Arrange the following solutions in order of decreasing acidity:

  a. $0.1M$ NaOH   **c.** $0.1M$ NH_4Cl
  b. $0.1M$ HCl   **d.** $0.1M$ CH_3COONa

96. Vapors of the strong acid $HCl(aq)$ and the weak base $NH_3(aq)$ combine to form a white salt.

  a. What is the name and formula of the salt?
  b. What kind of solution will this salt form when it dissolves in water?

97. Compare Arrhenius, Brønsted-Lowry, and Lewis all offered explanations for the behavior of acids and bases.

   a. Which explanation is easiest for you to understand?

   b. How is it possible for all three explanations to be accepted by chemists?

98. Predict The solubility of carbon dioxide in water depends on four different reversible reactions.

$$CO_2(g) \rightleftharpoons CO_2(aq)$$
$$CO_2(aq) + H_2O(l) \rightleftharpoons H_2CO_3(aq)$$
$$H_2CO_3(aq) \rightleftharpoons H^+(aq) + HCO_3^-(aq)$$
$$HCO_3^-(aq) \rightleftharpoons H^+(aq) + CO_3^{2-}(aq)$$

If seawater is slightly alkaline, would you expect the concentration of dissolved CO_2 to be higher or lower than in pure water? Explain your answer.

99. Evaluate Critique the accuracy of each of these statements.

   a. Indicators such as methyl red provide accurate and precise measurements of pH.

   b. According to the Arrhenius definition of acids and bases, ammonia qualifies as a base.

   c. The strength of an acid or base changes as its concentration changes.

*100. Relate Cause and Effect Use the cyanate buffer HOCN/OCN⁻ to explain how a buffer system works. Use equations to show how the pH of a solution can be kept almost constant when small amounts of acid or base are added.

*101. Identify Which quantity might correspond to the y-axis on this graph: $[H^+]$, pH, or $[OH^-]$? Explain your answer.

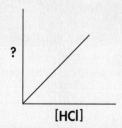

102. Calculate The sugar substitute saccharin ($HNC_7H_4SO_3$) has one acidic hydrogen. A $1.000M$ aqueous solution of saccharin has a pH of 1.71. Calculate the K_a of saccharin.

103. Interpret Graphs The graph shows the number of millimoles (mmol) of water formed as drops of $1.0M$ HCl are added to a 25.0-mL sample of NaOH of unknown concentration.

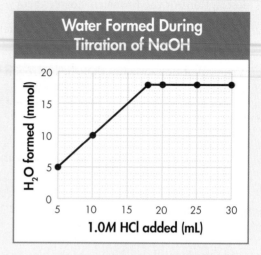

   a. Write an equation for the reaction.

   b. Estimate the concentration of the NaOH.

104. Calculate Suppose you slowly add $0.1M$ NaOH to 50.0 mL of $0.1M$ HCl. What volume of NaOH must you add before neutralization will occur? Explain your reasoning.

105. Predict Will the resulting solutions be neutral, acidic, or basic at the equivalence point for each of the following titrations? Explain.

   a. HCl titrated with NaOH

   b. NaOH titrated with HCl

   c. CH_3COOH titrated with NaOH

   d. NH_3 titrated with HCl

   e. CH_3COOH titrated with NH_3

*106. Use Models You can use the following expression to find the pH of a solution:

$$pH = -\log[H^+]$$

What expression could you use to find the analogous quantity, the pOH of a solution?

107. Apply Concepts Milk, an aqueous emulsion, has a pH of about 6.7. Calculate the pOH of milk using the equation you derived in Question 106. If the equation you derived is correct, the sum of the values for pH and pOH will equal 14.

108. Apply Concepts Use the expression for K_w to demonstrate the following relationship:

$$pH + pOH = 14$$

109. **Calculate** What is the pH of a 0.010M solution of NaCN ($K_b = 2.1 \times 10^{-5}$)?

⋆110. **Make Generalizations** Show that for any conjugate acid-base pair, $K_a \times K_b = K_w$.

111. **Interpret Data** The K_w of water varies with temperature, as shown in the table.

Temperature (°C)	K_w	pH
0	1.137×10^{-15}	a. _____
10	2.917×10^{-15}	b. _____
20	6.807×10^{-15}	c. _____
30	1.469×10^{-14}	d. _____
40	2.917×10^{-14}	e. _____
50	5.470×10^{-14}	f. _____

a. Calculate the pH of water for each temperature in the table.

b. Use the data to prepare a graph of pH versus temperature. Use the graph to estimate the pH of water at 5°C.

c. At what temperature is the pH of water approximately 6.85?

112. **Calculate** What is the molarity of an H_2SO_4 solution if 80.0 mL of the solution reacts with 0.424 g Na_2CO_3?

$$H_2SO_4(aq) + Na_2CO_3(aq) \longrightarrow$$
$$H_2O(l) + CO_2(aq) + Na_2SO_4(aq)$$

⋆113. **Apply Concepts** The hydrogen carbonate ion–carbonic acid buffer system is an important buffer system in the blood. This system is represented by the following equations:

$$H_2O(l) + CO_2(g) \rightleftharpoons H_2CO_3(aq)$$
$$H_2CO_3(aq) \rightleftharpoons H^+(aq) + HCO_3^-(aq)$$

Reactions in cells produce carbon dioxide. Excess carbon dioxide is released through the lungs. How could rapid breathing lead to an abnormally high blood pH (alkalosis)? How could slow breathing lead to an abnormally low blood pH (acidosis)?

114. **Calculate** Household bleach is a solution of sodium hypochlorite. What is the $[OH^-]$ in an aqueous solution that is 5.0% NaClO by mass? What is the pH of the solution? (The density of the solution is 1.0 g/mL, and $K_a = 3.5 \times 10^{-8}$.)

115. **Research** The main cause of tooth decay is the weak acid lactic acid (C_2H_5OCOOH). Lactic acid forms when bacteria, such as *Streptococcus mutans,* feed on sugar. In the mouth, sugars are present in the sticky plaque on tooth surfaces. Starting with the information on page R30, research current efforts to fight tooth decay. Write a report summarizing your findings.

116. **Connect to the BIGIDEA** Hypochlorite salts are used to disinfect swimming pools. On page R30 in the Elements Handbook, read about what happens when chlorine compounds are added to pool water. Use hydrolysis reactions to explain how the pH of the water affects the concentration of hypochlorous acid (HOCl).

CHEMYSTERY

Paper Trail

The wood pulp used to make paper is a suspension of cellulose fibers in water. Wood chips can be ground into a pulp. This is the process used to make newsprint. For higher-quality paper, the pulp is treated chemically to remove parts of the wood other than cellulose.

The paper is often coated with a chemical such as aluminum sulfate to keep it from absorbing too much ink. The chemicals that were used for this purpose often left a residue of acid in the paper. Over time, the acid caused the cellulose fibers to decay.

117. **Infer** The process of treating the paper is called deacidification. The first step in a popular deacidification method is to immerse the paper in a dilute solution of calcium hydroxide. Write a chemical equation to describe what occurs in this deacidification step.

⋆118. **Connect to the BIGIDEA** What type of reaction is performed in the process of deacidification? Would you expect the pH of the paper to be raised or lowered in the process of deacidification?

119. Write the product of each of these combination reactions.

a. $K(s) + O_2(g) \longrightarrow$
b. $Ca(s) + S(s) \longrightarrow$
c. $F_2(g) + Al(s) \longrightarrow$

120. How many grams of oxygen are needed to completely burn 87.4 g of sulfur to form sulfur trioxide?

$$S(s) + O_2(g) \longrightarrow SO_3(g)$$

∗121. Which state of matter is not part of the process of sublimation?

122. State Dalton's law of partial pressures.

123. Which of these laws describes an inverse relationship?

a. Charles's law
b. Boyle's law
c. Gay-Lussac's law

124. Which has the largest particles, a solution, a colloid, or a suspension?

125. Which of these is not an electrolyte?

a. $NaCl(l)$ **c.** $SiO_2(s)$
b. $KNO_2(aq)$ **d.** $NaCl(aq)$

∗126. What type of bond is responsible for water's high surface tension?

127. How many grams of potassium chloride are in 45.0 mL of a 5.00% (by mass) solution?

128. How would you prepare 400.0 mL of a 0.680M KOH solution?

∗129. How many liters of 8.0M HCl are needed to prepare 1.50 L of 2.5M HCl?

130. Which of these is an endothermic process? Provide an explanation.

a. burning wax
b. evaporating water
c. melting wax
d. roasting a marshmallow

131. How many joules of heat are required to melt a 55.0-g ice cube at 0°C?

∗132. Make the following conversions:

a. 34.5 cal to joules
b. 250 Cal to kilojoules
c. 0.347 kJ to calories

133. The specific heat capacity of iron is 0.46 J/(g·°C). How many kilojoules of energy are needed to raise the temperature of a 432-g iron bar 14°C?

134. What must be true about the concentration of two ions if precipitation occurs when solutions of the two ions are mixed?

135. Write an equilibrium-constant expression for each equation.

a. $2CO_2(g) \rightleftharpoons 2CO(g) + O_2(g)$
b. $N_2(g) + 3H_2(g) \rightleftharpoons 2NH_3(g)$

136. What is the equilibrium concentration of barium ion in a 1.0-L saturated solution of $BaCO_3$ to which 0.25 mol K_2CO_3 has been added?

∗137. In each pair, which has the higher entropy?

a. $NaCl(s)$ or $NaCl(aq)$
b. $CO_2(s)$ or $CO_2(g)$
c. hot water or cold water

138. How would each change affect the position of equilibrium of this reaction?

$$2H_2(g) + O_2(g) \rightleftharpoons 2H_2O(g) + heat$$

a. increasing the pressure
b. adding a catalyst
c. increasing the concentration of $H_2(g)$
d. cooling the reaction mixture
e. removing water vapor from the container

139. For the reaction $A(g) + B(g) + C(g) \longrightarrow D(g)$, the following data were obtained at a constant temperature. From the data, determine the order of reaction with respect to A, B, and C, and the overall order of reaction.

Initial [A] (mol/L)	Initial [B] (mol/L)	Initial [C] (mol/L)	Initial rate (mol/(L·min))
0.0500	0.0500	0.0100	6.25×10^{-3}
0.1000	0.0500	0.0100	1.25×10^{-2}
0.1000	0.1000	0.0100	5.00×10^{-2}
0.0500	0.0500	0.0200	6.25×10^{-3}

If You Have Trouble With . . .

Question	119	120	121	122	123	124	125	126	127	128	129	130	131	132	133	134	135	136	137	138	139
See Chapter	11	12	13	14	14	15	15	15	16	16	16	17	17	17	17	18	18	18	18	18	18

Standardized Test Prep

Select the choice that best answers each question or completes each statement.

1. If an acid has a measured K_a of 3×10^{-6},
   (A) the acid is a strong acid.
   (B) an aqueous solution of the acid would have a pH < 7.
   (C) the acid is a strong electrolyte.
   (D) All of the above are correct.

2. The pH of a sample of orange juice is 3.5. A sample of tomato juice has a pH of 4.5. Compared to the $[H^+]$ of orange juice, the $[H^+]$ of tomato juice is
   (A) 1.0 times higher. (C) 10 times higher.
   (B) 10 times lower. (D) 1.0 times lower.

> ## Tips for Success
>
> **Eliminate Wrong Answers** If you don't know which choice is correct, eliminate those you know are wrong. If you can rule out some choices, you'll increase your chances of choosing the correct answer.

3. Which ion or molecule is the conjugate base of the ammonium ion, NH_4^+?
   (A) H_2O (B) OH^- (C) NH_3 (D) H_3O^+

4. How many moles of NaOH are required to neutralize 2.4 mol H_2SO_4?
   (A) 1.2 mol (B) 2.4 mol (C) 3.6 mol (D) 4.8 mol

5. A solution with a hydrogen-ion concentration of $2.3 \times 10^{-8}M$ has a pH between
   (A) 2 and 3. (B) 3 and 4. (C) 7 and 8. (D) 8 and 9.

6. The net ionic equation for the neutralization reaction between solutions of potassium hydroxide and hydrochloric acid is
   (A) $H^+(aq) + OH^-(aq) \longrightarrow H_2O(l)$
   (B) $KOH(aq) + HCl(aq) \longrightarrow H_2O(l) + KCl(aq)$
   (C) $K^+(aq) + Cl^-(aq) \longrightarrow KCl(aq)$
   (D) $K^+(aq) + OH^-(aq) + H^+(aq) + Cl^-(aq) \longrightarrow$
   $KCl(aq) + H_2O(l)$

7. Calculate the molarity of an HCl solution if 25.0 mL of the solution is neutralized by 15.5 mL of $0.800M$ NaOH.
   (A) $0.248M$ (B) $0.496M$ (C) $1.29M$ (D) $0.645M$

8. Which combination of compound and ion would not make a useful buffer solution?
   (A) ammonium ion and ammonia
   (B) hydrogen carbonate ion and carbonic acid
   (C) sulfate ion and sulfuric acid
   (D) ethanoate ion and ethanoic acid

The lettered choices below refer to Questions 9–11. In each formula, P is the cation, and Q is the anion.
   (A) PQ (B) P_2Q_3 (C) PQ_3 (D) P_3Q

Which of the choices is the general formula for the salt formed in each of the following neutralization reactions?

9. $H_3PO_4 + NaOH \longrightarrow$

10. $H_2SO_4 + Mg(OH)_2 \longrightarrow$

11. $HNO_3 + Al(OH)_3 \longrightarrow$

Use the drawings below to answer Questions 12 and 13. Water molecules have been omitted from the solution windows.

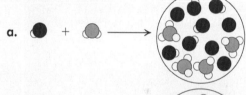
a.

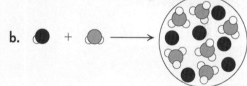
b.

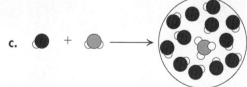
c.

- ● Undissociated acid
- ◯ Water
- ● Conjugate base
- ◯ Hydronium ion

12. Rank the acids in order of increasing strength.

13. How many of the acids are strong acids?

If You Have Trouble With . . .

Question	1	2	3	4	5	6	7	8	9	10	11	12	13
See Lesson	19.3	19.2	19.1	19.4	19.2	19.4	19.4	19.5	19.4	19.4	19.4	19.3	19.3

20

Oxidation-Reduction Reactions

INSIDE:

- **20.1** The Meaning of Oxidation and Reduction
- **20.2** Oxidation Numbers
- **20.3** Describing Redox Equations

PearsonChem.com

The color of the Statue of Liberty is the result of the copper in her outer shell reacting with water, carbon dioxide, and other compounds in the air.

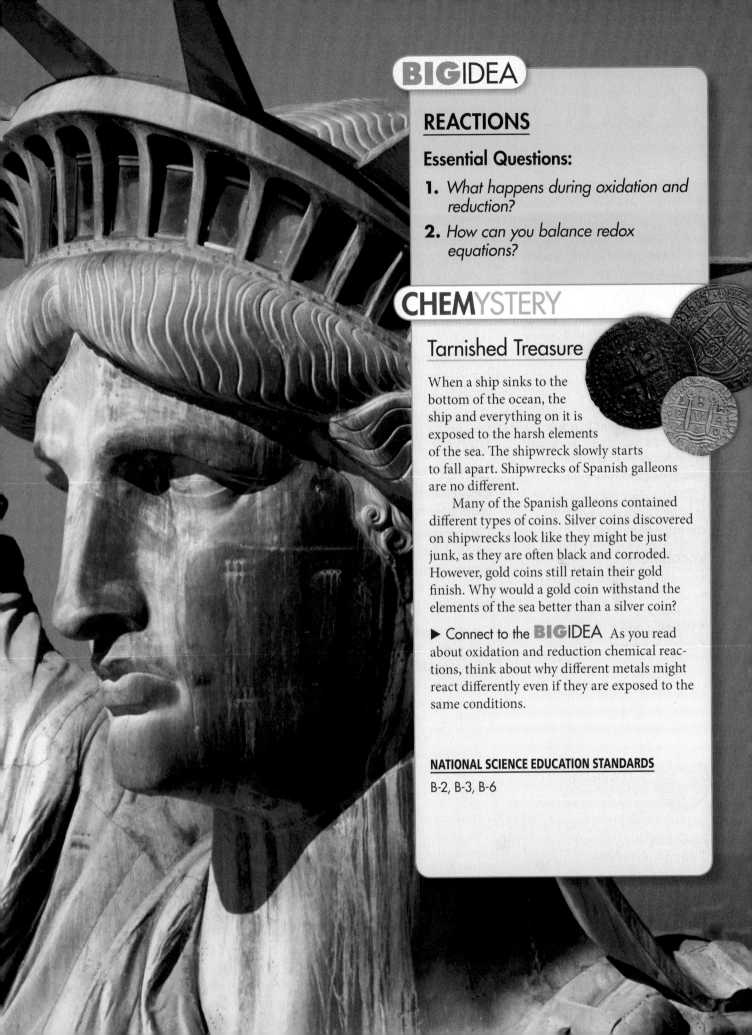

BIGIDEA

REACTIONS

Essential Questions:

1. *What happens during oxidation and reduction?*
2. *How can you balance redox equations?*

CHEMYSTERY

Tarnished Treasure

When a ship sinks to the bottom of the ocean, the ship and everything on it is exposed to the harsh elements of the sea. The shipwreck slowly starts to fall apart. Shipwrecks of Spanish galleons are no different.

Many of the Spanish galleons contained different types of coins. Silver coins discovered on shipwrecks look like they might be just junk, as they are often black and corroded. However, gold coins still retain their gold finish. Why would a gold coin withstand the elements of the sea better than a silver coin?

▶ **Connect to the BIGIDEA** As you read about oxidation and reduction chemical reactions, think about why different metals might react differently even if they are exposed to the same conditions.

NATIONAL SCIENCE EDUCATION STANDARDS

B-2, B-3, B-6

The Meaning of Oxidation and Reduction

Q: *Why do you need to wash the bottom of your car?* A clean car may look better than a dirty car, but looks aren't the only reason to wash your car. During winter in cold climates, salt is often spread on roads to lower the freezing point of water and thereby prevent the buildup of slippery ice. Salt may make driving safer, but the salt that clings to the metallic parts of cars can cause damage to your car. In this lesson, you will learn about oxidation-reduction reactions, including those that damage salty cars by causing them to corrode or rust relatively quickly.

Key Questions

🔑 What happens to a substance that undergoes oxidation? What happens to a substance that undergoes reduction?

🔑 How does the presence of salts and acids accelerate the corrosion of metals?

Vocabulary

• oxidation-reduction reactions
• oxidation
• reduction
• reducing agent
• oxidizing agent

What Are Oxidation and Reduction?

🔑 What happens to a substance that undergoes oxidation? What happens to a substance that undergoes reduction?

The combustion of gasoline in an automobile engine and the burning of wood in a fireplace are reactions that require oxygen as they release energy. The reactions that break down food in your body and release energy use oxygen from the air you breathe.

Oxygen and Redox Early chemists saw oxidation only as the combining of an element with oxygen to produce an oxide. The burning of a fuel is also an oxidation reaction that uses oxygen. For example, when methane (CH_4), the main component of natural gas, burns in air, it oxidizes and forms oxides of carbon and hydrogen, as shown in Figure 20.1. One oxide of carbon is carbon dioxide, CO_2.

See Oxidation animated online.

**Figure 20.1
Oxidation of Methane**
In a Bunsen burner, oxygen from the air is mixed with methane from the gas line. The methane is oxidized, and carbon dioxide and water are produced.

$$CH_4(g) \quad + \quad 2O_2(g) \quad \longrightarrow \quad CO_2(g) \quad + \quad 2H_2O(g)$$

Not all oxidation processes that use oxygen involve burning. For example, when elemental iron turns to rust as in Figure 20.2, it slowly oxidizes to compounds such as iron(III) oxide (Fe_2O_3). Bleaching stains in fabrics is another example of oxidation that does not involve burning. Common liquid household bleach contains sodium hypochlorite (NaClO), a substance that releases oxygen, which oxidizes stains to a colorless form. Powder bleaches may contain calcium hypochlorite ($Ca(ClO)_2$), sodium perborate ($NaBO_3$), or sodium percarbonate ($2Na_2CO_3 \cdot 3H_2O_2$). Hydrogen peroxide (H_2O_2) also releases oxygen when it decomposes. It is both a bleach and a mild antiseptic that kills bacteria by oxidizing them.

A process called reduction is the opposite of oxidation. Originally, reduction meant the loss of oxygen from a compound. The reduction of iron ore to metallic iron involves the removal of oxygen from iron(III) oxide. The reduction is accomplished by heating the ore with carbon, usually in the form of coke. The equation for the reduction of iron ore is shown below.

$$2Fe_2O_3(s) + 3C(s) \longrightarrow 4Fe(s) + 3CO_2(g)$$

Iron(III) oxide   Carbon   Iron   Carbon dioxide

The reduction of iron also includes an oxidation process. As iron(III) oxide is reduced to iron by losing oxygen, carbon oxidizes to carbon dioxide by gaining oxygen. Oxidation and reduction always occur simultaneously. **A substance that undergoes oxidation gains oxygen. A substance that undergoes reduction loses oxygen.** No oxidation occurs without reduction, and no reduction occurs without oxidation. Reactions that involve the processes of oxidation and reduction are therefore called **oxidation-reduction reactions.** Oxidation-reduction reactions are also known as *redox reactions*.

Figure 20.2 Oxidation of Iron
When items made of iron are exposed to moist air, the Fe atoms react with O_2 molecules. The iron rusts; it is oxidized to compounds such as iron(III) oxide (Fe_2O_3).

4Fe(s)   + $3O_2(g)$ $\longrightarrow$ $2Fe_2O_3(s)$
Iron   Oxygen   Iron(III) oxide

Electron Shift in Redox Reactions The modern concepts of oxidation and reduction have been extended to include many reactions that do not even involve oxygen. You learned in Chapter 6 that, with the exception of fluorine, oxygen is the most electronegative element. As a result, when oxygen bonds with an atom of a different element (other than fluorine), electrons from that atom shift toward oxygen. Redox reactions are currently understood to involve any shift of electrons between reactants. **Oxidation** is now defined to mean complete or partial loss of electrons or gain of oxygen. **Reduction** is now defined to mean complete or partial gain of electrons or loss of oxygen.

Oxidation	Reduction
Loss of electrons	Gain of electrons
Gain of oxygen	Loss of oxygen

Redox Reactions That Form Ions During a reaction between a metal and a nonmetal, electrons are transferred from atoms of the metal to atoms of the nonmetal. For example, when magnesium metal is heated with the nonmetal sulfur, the ionic compound magnesium sulfide is produced as shown in Figure 20.3. Two electrons are transferred from a magnesium atom to a sulfur atom. The magnesium atoms are made more stable by the loss of electrons. The sulfur atoms become more stable due to the gain of electrons.

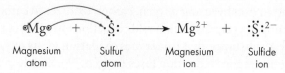

Magnesium	Sulfur	Magnesium	Sulfide
atom	atom	ion	ion

Because it loses electrons, the magnesium atom is said to be oxidized to a magnesium ion. Simultaneously, the sulfur atom gains two electrons and is reduced to a sulfide ion. The overall process is represented as the two component processes below.

Oxidation: $\cdot Mg \cdot \longrightarrow Mg^{2+} + 2e^-$ (loss of electrons)

Reduction: $\cdot \ddot{S} : + 2e^- \longrightarrow : \ddot{S} :^{2-}$ (gain of electrons)

Figure 20.3
Synthesis of an Ionic Compound
When magnesium and sulfur are heated together, they undergo an oxidation-reduction reaction to form magnesium sulfide.

Mg(s)   +   S(s) $\xrightarrow{\text{heat}}$ MgS(s)

A substance that undergoes oxidation loses electrons. A substance that undergoes reduction gains electrons. The substance that loses electrons is the **reducing agent.** By losing electrons to sulfur, magnesium reduces the sulfur. Magnesium is thus the reducing agent. The substance that accepts electrons is the **oxidizing agent.** By accepting electrons from magnesium, sulfur oxidizes the magnesium. Sulfur is the oxidizing agent. Another way to identify oxidizing and reducing agents is to remember that the species that is reduced is the oxidizing agent and the species oxidized is the reducing agent.

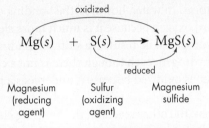

Magnesium (reducing agent)   Sulfur (oxidizing agent)   Magnesium sulfide

READING SUPPORT

Build Study Skills: *Use Mnemonics* To help you remember the definitions of *oxidation* and *reduction*, use the phrase "*LEO* the lion goes *GER*." LEO stands for Losing Electrons is Oxidation; GER stands for Gaining Electrons is Reduction.

CHEM TUTOR **Sample**Problem 20.1

Identifying Oxidized and Reduced Reactants

Silver nitrate reacts with copper to form copper nitrate and silver. From the equation below, determine what is oxidized and what is reduced. Identify the oxidizing agent and the reducing agent.

$$2AgNO_3(aq) + Cu(s) \longrightarrow Cu(NO_3)_2(aq) + 2Ag(s)$$

① Analyze **Identify the relevant concepts.** Identify the ions in the reaction and then trace how the electrons were transferred.

② Solve **Apply concepts to this situation.**

Rewrite the equation in ionic form so it will be easier to analyze the reaction.	$2Ag^+ + 2NO_3^- + Cu \longrightarrow Cu^{2+} + 2NO_3^- + 2Ag$

In this reaction, two electrons are lost from a copper atom (Cu) when it becomes a Cu^{2+} ion. These electrons are gained by two silver ions (Ag^+), which become neutral silver atoms.

The species that loses electrons is oxidized and is the reducing agent. The species that gains electrons is reduced and is the oxidizing agent.

Oxidation: $Cu \longrightarrow Cu^{2+} + 2e^-$ (loss of electrons)
Reduction: $2Ag^+ + 2e^- \longrightarrow 2Ag$ (gain of electrons)

The Cu is the reducing agent. The Ag^+ is the oxidizing agent.

---

1. Determine what is oxidized and what is reduced in each reaction. Identify the oxidizing agent and reducing agent in each case.

a. $2Na(s) + S(s) \longrightarrow Na_2S(s)$
b. $4Al(s) + 3O_2(g) \longrightarrow 2Al_2O_3(s)$

2. Identify these processes as either oxidation or reduction.

a. $Li \longrightarrow Li^+ + e^-$ **c.** $Zn^{2+} + 2e^- \longrightarrow Zn$
b. $2I^- \longrightarrow I_2 + 2e^-$ **d.** $Br_2 + 2e^- \longrightarrow 2Br^-$

Figure 20.4 Welding
This welder is using a torch fueled with a mixture of H_2 and O_2 called oxyhydrogen to cut and weld steel. When hydrogen burns in oxygen, the redox reaction generates temperatures of about 2600°C.
Infer *What is the product of this redox reaction?*

Redox With Covalent Compounds When a metal and a non-metal react and form ions, it is easy to identify complete transfers of electrons. But some reactions involve covalent compounds, that is, compounds in which complete electron transfer does not occur. One example is the reaction of hydrogen with oxygen.

$$2H_2(g) + O_2(g) \longrightarrow 2H_2O(l)$$

Consider what happens to the bonding electrons in the formation of a water molecule. In each reactant hydrogen molecule, the bonding electrons are shared equally between the hydrogen atoms. In water, however, the bonding electrons are pulled toward oxygen because it is much more electronegative than hydrogen. The result is a shift of bonding electrons away from hydrogen, even though there is not a complete transfer. Hydrogen is oxidized because it undergoes a partial loss of electrons.

In oxygen, the other reactant, the bonding electrons are shared equally between oxygen atoms in the reactant oxygen molecule. However, when oxygen bonds to hydrogen in the water molecule, there is a shift of electrons toward oxygen. Oxygen is thus reduced because it undergoes a partial gain of electrons.

$$\text{H—H} \qquad \text{O—O} \qquad \text{H—O}$$
electrons shared equally   electrons shared equally   shift of bonding electrons away from hydrogen and towards oxygen

In the reaction of hydrogen and oxygen to produce water, hydrogen is the reducing agent because it is oxidized. Oxygen is the oxidizing agent because it is reduced. This redox reaction is highly exothermic—that is, it releases a great deal of energy, as shown in Figure 20.4.

In some reactions involving covalent reactants or products, the partial electron shifts are less obvious. Some general guidelines are helpful. For example, for carbon compounds, the addition of oxygen or the removal of hydrogen is always oxidation. Table 20.1 below lists processes that constitute oxidation and reduction. The last entry in the table refers to oxidation numbers, which are introduced in Lesson 20.2.

Table 20.1

Processes Leading to Oxidation and Reduction	
Oxidation	**Reduction**
Complete loss of electrons (ionic reactions)	Complete gain of electrons (ionic reactions)
Shift of electrons *away* from an atom in a covalent bond	Shift of electrons *toward* an atom in a covalent bond
Gain of oxygen	Loss of oxygen
Loss of hydrogen by a covalent compound	Gain of hydrogen by a covalent compound
Increase in oxidation number	Decrease in oxidation number

Corrosion

How does the presence of salts and acids accelerate the corrosion of metals?

Billions of dollars are spent yearly to prevent and to repair damage caused by the corrosion of metals. Iron, a common construction metal often used in the form of the alloy steel, corrodes by being oxidized by oxygen to ions of iron. Water in the environment accelerates the rate of corrosion. Oxygen, the oxidizing agent, is reduced to oxide ions (in compounds such as Fe_2O_3) or to hydroxide ions. The following equations describe the corrosion of iron to iron hydroxides in moist conditions.

$$2Fe(s) + O_2(g) + 2H_2O(l) \longrightarrow 2Fe(OH)_2(s)$$

$$4Fe(OH)_2(s) + O_2(g) + 2H_2O(l) \longrightarrow 4Fe(OH)_3(s)$$

Corrosion occurs more rapidly in the presence of salts and acids. **The presence of salts and acids accelerates corrosion by producing conductive solutions that make electron transfer easier.** The corrosion of some metals can be a desirable feature, as Figure 20.5 shows.

Resistance to Corrosion Not all metals corrode easily. Gold and platinum are called noble metals because they are very resistant to losing their electrons by corrosion. Other metals lose electrons easily but are protected from extensive corrosion by the oxide coating formed on their surface. For example, aluminum oxidizes quickly in air to form a coating of very tightly packed aluminum oxide particles. This coating protects the aluminum object from further corrosion, as shown in Figure 20.6. Iron also forms a coating when it corrodes, but the coating of iron oxide that forms is not tightly packed. Water and air can penetrate the coating and attack the iron metal beneath it. The corrosion continues until the iron object becomes only a pile of rust.

See corrosion animated online.

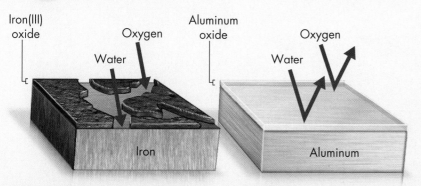

Figure 20.6 Comparing Oxides
Oxidation causes the complete corrosion of some metals. **a.** Iron reacts with water and oxygen to form iron(III) oxide, or rust. **b.** Aluminum, however, resists such corrosion because it forms a protective coating of aluminum oxide.
Apply Concepts *How does the aluminum oxide on aluminum differ from the iron(III) oxide formed on corroding iron?*

Figure 20.5 Corrosion
Oxidation-reduction reactions cause corrosion. The copper on this building reacted with water vapor, carbon dioxide, and other substances in the air to form a patina. This patina consists of a pale-green film of basic copper(II) carbonate. Patinas enhance the surface appearance of copper objects.

CHEMISTRY & YOU

Q: *If your car is exposed to salt on the roads in the winter, why is it important to wash the salt off your car?*

zinc block

Figure 20.7 Corrosion Control
Painting a surface, like this bridge, protects it from the effects of
the environment. **a.** Chromium metal also serves as a protective
coating and imparts an attractive, mirrorlike finish. Like aluminum,
chromium forms a corrosion-resistant oxide film on its surface.
b. Zinc blocks are attached to the steel (iron) hull of this ship. The
zinc blocks oxidize (corrode) instead of the iron, preventing the
hull from corroding.

Controlling Corrosion The corrosion of objects such as shovels or
knives is a common problem but not usually a serious one. In contrast,
the corrosion of a steel support pillar of a bridge or the steel hull of an
oil tanker is much more serious and costly. To prevent corrosion in such
cases, the metal surface may be coated with oil, paint, plastic, or another
metal, as shown in Figure 20.7. These coatings exclude air and water
from the surface, thus preventing corrosion. If the coating is scratched
or worn away, however, the exposed metal will begin to corrode.

In another method of corrosion control, one metal is "sacrificed,"
or allowed to corrode, to save a second metal. For example, to protect an iron object, a piece of magnesium (or another active metal) may
be placed in electrical contact with the iron. When oxygen and water
attack the iron object, the iron atoms lose electrons as the iron begins
to be oxidized. However, because magnesium is a better reducing agent
than iron, the magnesium immediately transfers electrons to the iron
atoms, preventing their oxidation.

Sacrificial zinc and magnesium blocks are sometimes attached to
piers and ship hulls to prevent corrosion damage in areas submerged
in water. Figure 20.7b shows zinc blocks attached to the steel hull of a
ship. The blocks corrode instead of the iron. Underground pipelines and
storage tanks may be connected to magnesium blocks for protection.
It is easier and cheaper to replace a block of magnesium or zinc than to
replace a bridge or a pipeline.

Learn more about
corrosion online.

CONCEPTS IN ACTION

Quick Lab

Purpose To test the effect of oxidizing agents on stains and dyes

Materials
- spot plate
- dropper
- water
- colorimeter (optional)

Oxidizing Agents
- liquid chlorine bleach (5% (m/v) sodium hypochlorite)
- powder bleach
- oxalic acid solution (1% (m/v))
- sodium thiosulfate solution (hypo) (0.2M $Na_2S_2O_3$)
- hydrogen peroxide (3% (v/v) H_2O_2)

Samples
- iodine solution (1% I_2 in 2% (m/v) KI)
- potassium permanganate solution (0.05M $KMnO_4$)
- grape juice
- rusty water
- piece of colored fabric
- colored flower petals
- grass stain on piece of white fabric

Bleach It! Oxidize the Color Away

Procedure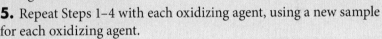

1. Place samples on a spot plate. Use 4 drops of each liquid or a small piece of each solid.

2. Describe the color and appearance of each sample in Step 1.

3. Add a few drops of the first oxidizing agent to each sample.

4. Describe any immediate change in appearance and any further change after 15 minutes.

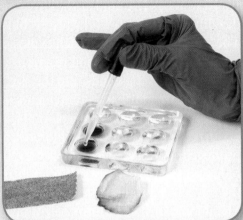

5. Repeat Steps 1–4 with each oxidizing agent, using a new sample for each oxidizing agent.

Analyze and Conclude

1. Organize Data Make a grid and record your observations.

2. Compare and Contrast Compare the oxidizing power of the oxidizing agents.

3. Explain How do you know that chemical changes have occurred?

20.1 LessonCheck

3. **Define** Define oxidation and reduction in terms of the gain or loss of oxygen.

4. **Define** Define oxidation and reduction in terms of the gain or loss of electrons.

5. **Explain** How does the presence of salts and acids accelerate the corrosion of metals?

6. Explain How do you identify the oxidizing agent and the reducing agent in a redox reaction?

7. Identify Which of the following would most likely be oxidizing agents and which would most likely be reducing agents? (*Hint:* Think in terms of tendencies to lose or gain electrons.)
 a. Cl_2 **b.** K **c.** Ag^+

8. Apply Concepts Use electron transfer or electron shift to identify what is oxidized and what is reduced in each reaction. Use the electronegativity values in Table 6.2 in Chapter 6, for covalent compounds.
 a. $2Na(s) + Br_2(l) \longrightarrow 2NaBr(s)$
 b. $H_2(g) + Cl_2(g) \longrightarrow 2HCl(g)$
 c. $2Li(s) + F_2(g) \longrightarrow 2LiF(s)$
 d. $S(s) + Cl_2(g) \longrightarrow SCl_2(g)$
 e. $N_2(g) + 2O_2(g) \longrightarrow 2NO_2(g)$
 f. $Mg(s) + Cu(NO_3)_2(aq) \longrightarrow Mg(NO_3)_2(aq) + Cu(s)$

9. Identify For each reaction in Problem 8, identify the reducing agent and the oxidizing agent.

Fireworks

It's New Year's Eve, and at the stroke of midnight, a dazzling array of fireworks begins bursting overhead. The sights and sounds of each explosion are the result of several oxidation-reduction reactions taking place within the firework as it ascends into the sky.

There are four basic components in any firework: oxidizers, reducing agents, colorants, and binders. Oxidizers, such as nitrates, chlorates, and perchlorates, produce the oxygen needed to let the firework burn. The reducing agents, usually sulfur and carbon, combine with the oxygen to produce the heat energy for the explosion. Metal ions, such as lithium, calcium, and sodium, create the bright colors you see. And the binders hold the materials together.

These four materials are formed into small lumps known as stars. The stars are placed in a cardboard or paper shell along with gunpowder (also called black powder) and two charges. When the first charge is lit, the gunpowder propels the firework into the air. Then the second charge causes additional gunpowder to propel the stars into the sky and ignite the oxidizers, which react with the reducing agents, causing the stars to explode in brilliant flashes of color.

RED, WHITE, AND BLUE Different metal salts and compounds are used to create the different colors in fireworks. Lithium and strontium are used for red, magnesium and aluminum are used for white, and copper is used for blue.

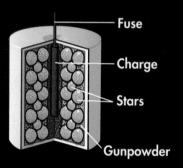

Fuse

Charge

Stars

Gunpowder

FIREWORK ANATOMY Aerial fireworks contain stars and gunpowder within a cardboard shell. The charge and fuse are used to ignite the firework. The arrangement of the stars determines the shape of the burst, while the size and shape of the star determine the size, shape, and speed of the burst.

Take It Further

1. Identify Potassium nitrate (KNO_3) was originally used in fireworks and gunpowder. The reaction for the production of KNO_3 is
$$4KCl + 4HNO_3 + O_2 \longrightarrow 4KNO_3 + 2Cl_2 + 2H_2O$$
Is this a redox reaction? If so, which substance is oxidized and which is reduced?

2. Describe The bright white light of some fireworks is produced when magnesium reacts with oxygen in the air to form magnesium oxide. Write a balanced equation for this reaction.

20.2 Oxidation Numbers

Q: *Why does a sparkler have such a bright light?* If you have ever seen or held a sparkler, then you know that sparklers give off very bright light. They are like handheld fireworks. Sparklers contain powdered metals. As the sparklers burn, a chemical reaction changes the metals. In this lesson, you will learn about how oxidation and reduction in reactions like these are defined in terms of a change in oxidation number.

Key Questions

⬤ What is the general rule for assigning oxidation numbers?

⬤ How are oxidation and reduction defined in terms of a change in oxidation number?

Vocabulary

• oxidation number

Assigning Oxidation Numbers

⬤ **What is the general rule for assigning oxidation numbers?**

An **oxidation number** is a positive or negative number assigned to an atom to indicate its degree of oxidation or reduction. ⬤ **As a general rule, a bonded atom's oxidation number is the charge that it would have if the electrons in the bond were assigned to the atom of the more electronegative element.** In the next lesson, you will learn that equations of complex redox reactions can be balanced by the use of oxidation-number changes. The set of rules on the next page should help you determine oxidation numbers.

In binary ionic compounds, such as NaCl and $CaCl_2$, the oxidation numbers of the atoms equal their ionic charges (Rule 1). The compound sodium chloride is composed of sodium ions (Na^{1+}) and chloride ions (Cl^{1-}). Thus the oxidation number of sodium is +1, and that of chlorine is −1. In $CaCl_2$, the oxidation number of calcium is +2, and that of chlorine is −1. Notice that the sign is put before the oxidation number.

Because water is a molecular compound, no ionic charges are associated with its atoms. However, oxygen is reduced in the formation of water. Oxygen is more electronegative than hydrogen. So, in water, the two shared electrons in the H—O bond are shifted toward oxygen and away from hydrogen. Picture the electrons contributed by the two hydrogen atoms as being completely transferred to the oxygen. The charges that would result from this transfer are the oxidation numbers of the bonded elements. The oxidation number of oxygen is −2, and the oxidation number of each hydrogen is +1 (Rules 2 and 3). Oxidation numbers are often written above the chemical symbols in a formula. For example, water can be represented as

$$\overset{+1\ -2}{H_2O}$$

Many elements can have several different oxidation numbers. Use rules 5 and 6 to determine the oxidation number of atoms of these elements, plus other elements not covered in the first four rules. All the substances shown in Figure 20.8 contain chromium, but chromium has a different oxidation number in its uncombined state and in each compound.

Rules for Assigning Oxidation Numbers

1. The oxidation number of a monatomic ion is equal in magnitude and sign to its ionic charge. For example, the oxidation number of the bromide ion (Br^{1-}) is −1; that of the Fe^{3+} ion is +3.

2. The oxidation number of hydrogen in a compound is +1, except in metal hydrides, such as NaH, where it is −1.

3. The oxidation number of oxygen in a compound is −2, except in peroxides, such as H_2O_2, where it is −1, and in compounds with the more electronegative fluorine, where it is positive.

4. The oxidation number of an atom in uncombined (elemental) form is 0. For example, the oxidation number of the potassium atoms in potassium metal (K) or of the nitrogen atoms in nitrogen gas (N_2) is 0.

5. For any neutral compound, the sum of the oxidation numbers of the atoms in the compound must equal 0.

6. For a polyatomic ion, the sum of the oxidation numbers must equal the ionic charge of the ion.

Figure 20.8
Chromium in its uncombined state is a dull silvery color. Orange potassium dichromate ($K_2Cr_2O_7$) and purple chromium(III) potassium sulfate ($CrK(SO_4)_2 \cdot 12H_2O$) are both compounds of chromium.
Infer *What is the oxidation number of chromium in each compound?*

SampleProblem 20.2

Assigning Oxidation Numbers to Atoms

What is the oxidation number of each kind of atom in the following ions and compounds?

a. SO_2

b. CO_3^{2-}

c. Na_2SO_4

d. $(NH_4)_2S$

❶ Analyze **Identify the relevant concepts.** Use the set of rules you just learned to assign and calculate oxidation numbers.

❷ Solve **Apply concepts to this situation.**

a. There are two oxygen atoms, and the oxidation number of each oxygen is -2 (Rule 3). The sum of the oxidation numbers for the neutral compound must be 0 (Rule 5). Therefore, the oxidation number of sulfur is $+4$, because $+4 + (2 \times (-2)) = 0$.

$$\underset{SO_2}{+4\,-2}$$

b. The oxidation number of oxygen is -2 (Rule 3).

$$\underset{CO_3^{2-}}{?\,-2}$$

The sum of the oxidation numbers of the carbon and oxygen atoms must equal the ionic charge, -2 (Rule 6). The oxidation number of carbon must be $+4$, because $+4 + (3 \times (-2)) = -2$.

$$\underset{CO_3^{2-}}{+4\,-2}$$

c. The oxidation number of each sodium ion, Na^+, is the same as its ionic charge, $+1$ (Rule 1). The oxidation number of oxygen is -2 (Rule 3).

$$\underset{Na_2SO_4}{+1\ ?\,-2}$$

For the sum of the oxidation numbers in the compound to be 0 (Rule 5), the oxidation number of sulfur must be $+6$, because $(2 \times (+1)) + (+6) + (4 \times (-2)) = 0$.

$$\underset{Na_2SO_4}{+1\,+6\,-2}$$

d. Ammonium ions, NH_4^+, have an ionic charge of $+1$, so the sum of the oxidation numbers of the atoms in the ammonium ion must be $+1$. The oxidation number of hydrogen is $+1$ in this ion. So, the oxidation number of nitrogen must be -3.

$$\underset{NH_4^+}{?\ +1}$$
$$? + 4(+1) = +1$$
$$-3 + 4(+1) = +1$$

Two ammonium ions have a total charge of $+2$. Since the compound $(NH_4)_2S$ is neutral, sulfur must have a balancing oxidation number of -2.

$$\underset{(NH_4)_2S}{-3\,+1\,-2}$$

❸ Evaluate **Do the results make sense?** The results are consistent with the rules for determining oxidation numbers. Also, addition of the oxidation numbers correctly gives the final overall charge for the ion and the three neutral compounds.

---

10. Determine the oxidation number of each element in the following:

a. S_2O_3

b. Na_2O_2

c. P_2O_5

d. NO_3^-

11. Determine the oxidation number of chlorine in each of the following substances:

a. $KClO_3$

b. Cl_2

c. $Ca(ClO_4)_2$

d. Cl_2O

Oxidation-Number Changes in Chemical Reactions

🔑 **How are oxidation and reduction defined in terms of a change in oxidation number?**

Figure 20.9 shows what happens when copper wire is placed in a solution of silver nitrate. In this reaction, the oxidation number of silver decreases from +1 to 0 as each silver ion (Ag^{1+}) gains an electron and is reduced to silver metal (Ag^0). Copper's oxidation number increases from 0 to +2 as each atom of copper metal (Cu^0) loses two electrons and is oxidized to a copper(II) ion (Cu^{2+}). Here is the equation with oxidation numbers added:

$$\overset{+1\ +5-2}{2AgNO_3(aq)} + \overset{0}{Cu(s)} \longrightarrow \overset{+2\ +5-2}{Cu(NO_3)_2(aq)} + \overset{0}{2Ag(s)}$$

Figure 20.9
Oxidation of Copper
Copper reacts with silver nitrate. **a.** A copper wire is placed in a silver nitrate solution. **b.** Crystals of silver coat the wire, and the solution slowly turns blue as a result of the formation of copper(II) nitrate.
Draw Conclusions *What change occurs in the oxidation number of silver? How does the oxidation number of copper change?*

Figure 20.10 illustrates a redox reaction that shows what occurs when a shiny iron nail is dipped into a solution of copper(II) sulfate.

You can define oxidation and reduction in terms of a change in oxidation number. 🔑 **An increase in the oxidation number of an atom or ion indicates oxidation. A decrease in the oxidation number of an atom or ion indicates reduction.**

Figure 20.10
Reduction of Copper
A redox reaction occurs between iron and copper. **a.** An iron nail is placed in a copper(II) sulfate solution. **b.** The iron reduces Cu^{2+} ions in solution and is simultaneously oxidized to Fe^{2+}. The iron becomes coated with metallic copper.

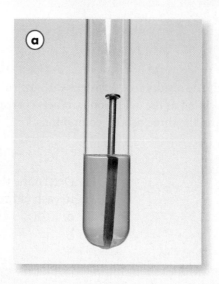
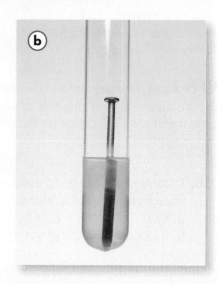

Sample Problem 20.3

Identifying Oxidized and Reduced Atoms

Use changes in oxidation number to identify which atoms are oxidized and which are reduced in the following reactions. Also identify the oxidizing agent and the reducing agent.

a. $Cl_2(g) + 2HBr(aq) \longrightarrow 2HCl(aq) + Br_2(l)$
b. $C(s) + O_2(g) \longrightarrow CO_2(g)$

❶ Analyze **Identify the relevant concepts.** An increase in oxidation number indicates oxidation. A decrease in oxidation number indicates reduction. The substance that is oxidized in a redox reaction is the reducing agent. The substance that is reduced is the oxidizing agent.

❷ Solve **Apply concepts to this situation.**

> The oxidation number of each chlorine in Cl_2 is 0 because of Rule 4.

a. Use the rules to assign oxidation numbers to each atom in the equation.

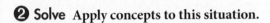
$$\overset{0}{Cl_2(g)} + \overset{+1\;-1}{2HBr(aq)} \longrightarrow \overset{+1\;-1}{2HCl(aq)} + \overset{0}{Br_2(l)}$$

Then, use the changes in oxidation numbers to identify which atoms are oxidized and which are reduced.

Finally, identify the oxidizing and reducing agent.

The element chlorine is reduced because its oxidation number decreases (0 to −1). The bromide ion from $HBr(aq)$ is oxidized because its oxidation number increases (−1 to 0). Chlorine is reduced, so Cl_2 is the oxidizing agent. The bromide ion from $HBr(aq)$ is oxidized, so Br^- is the reducing agent.

b. Use the rules to assign oxidation numbers to each atom in the equation.

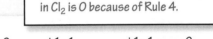
$$\overset{0}{C(s)} + \overset{0}{O_2(g)} \longrightarrow \overset{+4\;-2}{CO_2(g)}$$

Then, use the changes in oxidation numbers to identify which atoms are oxidized and which are reduced.

Finally, identify the oxidizing agent and reducing agent.

The element carbon is oxidized because its oxidation number increases (0 to +4). The element oxygen in reduced because its oxidation decreases (0 to −2). Carbon is oxidized, so C is the reducing agent. Oxygen is reduced, so O_2 is the oxidizing agent.

❸ Evaluate **Do the results make sense?** It makes sense that what is oxidized in a chemical reaction is the reducing agent because it loses electrons—it becomes the agent by which the atom that is reduced gains electrons. Conversely, it makes sense that what is reduced in a chemical reaction is the oxidizing agent because it gains electrons—it is the agent by which the atom that is oxidized loses electrons.

---

12. Use the changes in oxidation numbers to identify which atoms are oxidized and which are reduced in each reaction.
   a. $2H_2(g) + O_2(g) \longrightarrow 2H_2O(l)$
   b. $2KNO_3(s) \longrightarrow 2KNO_2(s) + O_2(g)$

13. Identify the oxidizing agent and the reducing agent in each equation in Problem 12.

Identifying Oxidized and Reduced Atoms

Use changes in oxidation number to identify which atoms are oxidized and which are reduced in the following reaction. Also identify the oxidizing agent and the reducing agent.

$$Zn(s) + 2MnO_2(s) + 2NH_4Cl(aq) \longrightarrow ZnCl_2(aq) + Mn_2O_3(s) + 2NH_3(g) + H_2O(l)$$

❶ Analyze Identify the relevant concepts.

❷ Solve Apply concepts to this situation.

Use the rules to assign oxidation numbers to each atom in the equation.	$$\overset{0}{Zn}(s) + 2\overset{+4\ -2}{MnO_2}(s)\ \overset{-3+1-1}{2NH_4Cl}(aq) \longrightarrow \overset{+2-1}{ZnCl_2}(aq) + \overset{+3\ -2}{Mn_2O_3}(s) + \overset{-3+1}{2NH_3}(g) + \overset{+1-2}{H_2O}(l)$$
Then, use the changes in oxidation numbers to identify which atoms are oxidized and which are reduced.	The element zinc is oxidized because its oxidation number increases (0 to +2). The manganese ion is reduced because its oxidation number decreases (+4 to +3).
Finally, identify the oxidizing and reducing agent.	Zinc is oxidized, so Zn is the reducing agent. Manganese (in MnO_2) is reduced, so Mn^{4+} is the oxidizing agent.

14. Identify which atoms are oxidized and which are reduced in each reaction.
  a. $NH_4NO_2(s) \longrightarrow N_2(g) + 2H_2O(g)$
  b. $PbO_2(aq) + 4HI(aq) \longrightarrow I_2(aq) + PbI_2(s) + 2H_2O(l)$

15. Identify the oxidizing agent and the reducing agent in each equation in Problem 14.

20.2 LessonCheck

16. 🔑 **Explain** What is the general rule for assigning oxidation numbers?

17. 🔑 **Explain** How is a change in oxidation number related to the process of oxidation and reduction?

18. Explain How is charge used to assign oxidation numbers to the elements in a polyatomic ion?

19. Identify Use the changes in oxidation numbers to identify which atoms are oxidized and which are reduced in each reaction.
  a. $2Na(s) + Cl_2(g) \longrightarrow 2NaCl(s)$
  b. $2HNO_3(aq) + 6HI(aq) \longrightarrow 2NO(g) + 3I_2(s) + 4H_2O(l)$
  c. $3H_2S(g) + 2HNO_3(aq) \longrightarrow 3S(s) + 2NO(g) + 4H_2O(l)$
  d. $2PbSO_4(s) + 2H_2O(l) \longrightarrow Pb(s) + PbO_2(s) + 2H_2SO_4(aq)$

20. Identify Identify the oxidizing agent and the reducing agent in each reaction in Problem 19.

20.3 Describing Redox Equations

Q: *Why does cut fruit turn brown?* If you have eaten an apple, then you have probably noticed that the flesh of the apple turns brown after you remove the skin. The apple is still safe to eat; it just doesn't look as appetizing. As you may have guessed, the browning is a chemical reaction. In this lesson, you will learn more about identifying certain types of chemical reactions and how to write and balance chemical equations for redox reactions.

Key Questions

🔑 What are the two classes of chemical reactions?

🔑 What are two different methods for balancing a redox equation?

Vocabulary

- oxidation-number-change method
- half-reaction
- half-reaction method

Identifying Redox Reactions

🔑 **What are the two classes of chemical reactions?**

In general, all chemical reactions can be assigned to one of two classes.

🔑 **One class of chemical reactions is oxidation-reduction (redox) reactions, in which electrons are transferred from one reacting species to another. The other class includes all other reactions, in which no electron transfer occurs.** Many single-replacement reactions, combination reactions, decomposition reactions, and combustion reactions are redox reactions. Two examples of redox reactions are shown in Figure 20.11. Figure 20.11a shows what happens when potassium metal reacts with water. Figure 20.11b shows the reaction of zinc with hydrochloric acid. Examples of reactions that are not redox reactions include double-replacement reactions and acid-base reactions.

Figure 20.11 Single-Replacement Redox Reactions
Single-replacement reactions are redox reactions. **a.** Potassium metal reacts violently with water to produce hydrogen gas (which ignites) and potassium hydroxide. **b.** Zinc metal reacts vigorously with hydrochloric acid to produce hydrogen gas and zinc chloride. **Apply Concepts** *Explain why each reaction is a redox reaction.*

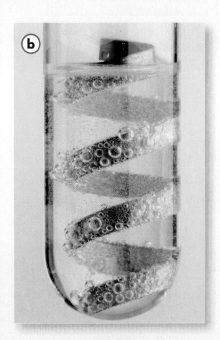

Figure 20.12 Redox in Lightning
When lightning bolts heat the air to extreme temperatures, the redox reaction that takes place between nitrogen and oxygen forms nitrogen monoxide.

During an electrical storm, as shown in Figure 20.12, oxygen molecules and nitrogen molecules in the air react to form nitrogen monoxide. This reaction is an example of a combination reaction. The equation for the reaction is shown below.

$$N_2(g) + O_2(g) \longrightarrow 2NO(g)$$

How can you tell if this is a redox reaction? If the oxidation number of an element in a reacting species changes, then that element has undergone either oxidation or reduction. Therefore, the reaction as a whole must be a redox reaction. In the example above, the oxidation number of nitrogen increases from 0 to +2, while the oxidation number of oxygen decreases from 0 to −2. Therefore, the reaction between nitrogen and oxygen to form nitrogen monoxide is a redox reaction.

Many reactions in which color changes occur are redox reactions. One example is the apple on the first page of this lesson. Another example is shown in Figure 20.13. Written in ionic form, the unbalanced equation for this reaction is

$$\underset{\substack{\text{Permanganate} \\ \text{ion (purple)}}}{MnO_4{}^-(aq)} + \underset{\substack{\text{Bromide ion} \\ \text{(colorless)}}}{Br^-(aq)} \longrightarrow \underset{\substack{\text{Manganese(II)} \\ \text{ion (colorless)}}}{Mn^{2+}(aq)} + \underset{\substack{\text{Bromine} \\ \text{(brown)}}}{Br_2(aq)}$$

CHEMISTRY & YOU

Q: *Some fruits, including apples, turn brown when you cut them. What do you think is happening on the surface of the fruit that causes it to turn brown?*

Figure 20.13 Color Clues
A color change can signal a redox reaction. When a colorless solution containing bromide ions (Br⁻) is added to a solution containing permanganate ions (MnO₄⁻), the distinctive purple color of the permanganate ion is replaced by the pale brown color of bromine.

Sample Problem 20.5

Identifying Redox Reactions

Use the change in oxidation number to identify whether each reaction is a redox reaction or a reaction of some other type. If a reaction is a redox reaction, identify the element reduced, the element oxidized, the reducing agent, and the oxidizing agent.

a. $Cl_2(g) + 2NaBr(aq) \longrightarrow 2NaCl(aq) + Br_2(aq)$

b. $2NaOH(aq) + H_2SO_4(aq) \longrightarrow Na_2SO_4(aq) + 2H_2O(l)$

❶ Analyze Identify the relevant concepts.

If changes in oxidation number occur, the reaction is a redox reaction. The element whose oxidation number increases is oxidized and is the reducing agent. The element whose oxidation number decreases is reduced and is the oxidizing agent.

❷ Solve Apply concepts to this situation.

a. Assign oxidation numbers.	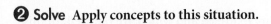 $\underset{0}{Cl_2}(g) + \underset{+1\ -1}{2NaBr}(aq) \longrightarrow \underset{+1\ -1}{2NaCl}(aq) + \underset{0}{Br_2}(aq)$
Interpret the change (or lack of change) in oxidation numbers to identify if the reaction is a redox reaction.	This is a redox reaction. The chlorine is reduced. The bromide ion is oxidized. Chlorine is the oxidizing agent; the bromide ion is the reducing agent.
b. Assign oxidation numbers.	 $\underset{+1\ -2\ +1}{2NaOH}(aq) + \underset{+1\ +6\ -2}{H_2SO_4}(aq) \longrightarrow \underset{+1\ +6\ -2}{Na_2SO_4}(aq) + \underset{+1\ -2}{2H_2O}(l)$
Interpret the change (or lack of change) in oxidation numbers to identify if the reaction is a redox reaction.	None of the elements change in oxidation number. This is not a redox reaction.

> This is an acid-base (neutralization) reaction.

21. Identify which of the following are redox reactions. If a reaction is a redox reaction, name the element oxidized and the element reduced.
  a. $Mg(s) + Br_2(l) \longrightarrow MgBr_2(s)$
  b. $H_2CO_3(aq) \longrightarrow H_2O(l) + CO_2(g)$

22. Identify which of the following are oxidation-reduction reactions. If a reaction is a redox reaction, name the element oxidized and the element reduced.
  a. $CaCO_3(s) + 2HCl(aq) \longrightarrow CaCl_2(aq) + H_2O(l) + CO_2(g)$
  b. $CuO(s) + H_2(g) \longrightarrow Cu(s) + H_2O(l)$

Balancing Redox Equations

🔑 *What are two different methods for balancing a redox equation?*

Many oxidation-reduction reactions are too complex to be balanced by trial and error. Fortunately, two systematic methods are available. 🔑 **Two different methods for balancing redox equations are the oxidation-number-change method and the half-reaction method.** These two methods are based on the fact that the total number of electrons gained in reduction must equal the total number of electrons lost in oxidation. One method uses oxidation-number changes, and the other uses half-reactions.

Using Oxidation-Number Changes You can use oxidation numbers to keep track of electron transfers. In the **oxidation-number-change method,** you balance a redox equation by comparing the increases and decreases in oxidation numbers. To use this method, start with the skeleton equation for the redox reaction. As an example, look at the process used to obtain metallic iron from iron ore in a blast furnace, shown in Figure 20.14.

$$Fe_2O_3(s) + CO(g) \longrightarrow Fe(s) + CO_2(g) \text{ (unbalanced)}$$

Step 1: Assign oxidation numbers to all the atoms in the equation. Write the numbers above the atoms.

$$\overset{+3\ -2}{Fe_2O_3}(s) + \overset{+2\ -2}{CO}(g) \longrightarrow \overset{0}{Fe}(s) + \overset{+4\ -2}{CO_2}(g)$$

The oxidation number is stated per atom. So although the total positive charge of Fe ions in Fe_2O_3 is 6+, the oxidation number of each Fe ion is +3.

Step 2: Identify which atoms are oxidized and which are reduced. In this reaction, iron decreases in oxidation number from +3 to 0, a change of −3. Therefore, iron is reduced. Carbon increases in oxidation number from +2 to +4, a change of +2. Thus, carbon is oxidized.

Step 3: Use one bracketing line to connect the atoms that undergo oxidation and another such line to connect those that undergo reduction. Write the oxidation-number change at the midpoint of each line.

$$\overset{+3\ -2}{Fe_2O_3}(s) + \overset{+2\ -2}{CO}(g) \longrightarrow \overset{0}{Fe}(s) + \overset{+4\ -2}{CO_2}(g)$$

+2 (oxidation)

−3 (reduction)

Remember that a change in oxidation number represents the number of electrons transferred. Each carbon atom in CO loses 2 electrons in oxidation, and each iron atom in Fe_2O_3 accepts 3 electrons in reduction. As the equation is written, the number of electrons transferred in oxidation does not equal the number of electrons transferred in reduction. Step 4 will make the oxidation-number changes equal.

Step 4: Make the total increase in oxidation number equal to the total decrease in oxidation number by using appropriate coefficients. In this example, the oxidation-number increase should be multiplied by 3 and the oxidation-number decrease should be multiplied by 2, which gives an increase of +6 and a decrease of −6. This equalization can be achieved in the equation by placing the coefficient 2 in front of Fe on the right side and the coefficient 3 in front of both CO and CO_2. The formula Fe_2O_3 does not need a coefficient because the formula already indicates 2 Fe.

$$Fe_2O_3(s) + 3CO(g) \longrightarrow 2Fe(s) + 3CO_2(g)$$

$3 \times (+2) = +6$

$2 \times (-3) = -6$

Step 5: Finally, make sure the equation is balanced for both atoms and charge. If necessary, finish balancing the equation by inspection.

$$Fe_2O_3(s) + 3CO(g) \longrightarrow 2Fe(s) + 3CO_2(g)$$

Figure 20.14
Reduction of Iron Ions
In a blast furnace like this one, air is blown through a combination of iron ore and coke. The carbon monoxide produced from the oxidation of coke reduces the Fe^{3+} ions to metallic iron.

SampleProblem 20.6

Balancing Redox Equations by Oxidation-Number Change

Balance this redox equation by using the oxidation-number-change method.

$$K_2Cr_2O_7(aq) + H_2O(l) + S(s) \longrightarrow KOH(aq) + Cr_2O_3(s) + SO_2(g)$$

❶ Analyze Identify the relevant concepts. You can balance redox equations by determining changes in oxidation numbers and applying the five steps.

❷ Solve Apply the concepts to this problem.

Step 1: Assign oxidation numbers.	$\overset{+1\,+6\,-2}{K_2Cr_2O_7}(aq) + \overset{+1\,-2}{H_2O}(l) + \overset{0}{S}(s) \longrightarrow \overset{+1\,-2\,+1}{KOH}(aq) + \overset{+3\,-2}{Cr_2O_3}(s) + \overset{+4\,-2}{SO_2}(g)$
Step 2: Identify the atoms that are oxidized and reduced.	Cr is reduced. S is oxidized.
Step 3: Connect the atoms that change in oxidation number. Indicate the signs and magnitudes of the changes.	$\overset{+6}{K_2Cr_2O_7}(aq) + H_2O(l) + \overset{0}{S}(s) \longrightarrow KOH(aq) + \overset{+3}{Cr_2O_3}(s) + \overset{+4}{SO_2}(g)$ −3 ... +4
Step 4: Balance the increase and decrease in oxidation numbers.	$2K_2Cr_2O_7(aq) + H_2O(l) + 3S(s) \longrightarrow KOH(aq) + 2Cr_2O_3(s) + 3SO_2(g)$ (4)(−3) = −12 ... (3)(+4) = +12

Four chromium atoms must be reduced (4 × (−3) = −12 decrease) for every three sulfur atoms that are oxidized (3 × (+4) = +12 increase). Put the coefficient 3 in front of S and SO$_2$, and the coefficient 2 in front of K$_2$Cr$_2$O$_7$ and Cr$_2$O$_3$.

Step 5: Check the equation and balance by inspection, if necessary.	$2K_2Cr_2O_7(aq) + 2H_2O(l) + 3S(s) \longrightarrow 4KOH(aq) + 2Cr_2O_3(s) + 3SO_2(g)$

The coefficient 4 in front of KOH balances potassium. The coefficient 2 in front of H$_2$O balances hydrogen and oxygen.

23. Balance each redox equation using the oxidation-number-change method.
  a. $KClO_3(s) \longrightarrow KCl(s) + O_2(g)$
  b. $HNO_2(aq) + HI(aq) \longrightarrow NO(g) + I_2(s) + H_2O(l)$

24. Balance each redox equation using the oxidation-number-change method.
  a. $Bi_2S_3(s) + HNO_3(aq) \longrightarrow Bi(NO_3)_3(aq) + NO(g) + S(s) + H_2O(l)$
  b. $SbCl_5(aq) + KI(aq) \longrightarrow SbCl_3(aq) + KCl(aq) + I_2(s)$

Figure 20.15
Sulfur Dioxide
Sulfur dioxide is often used to preserve dried fruits.

Table 20.2

Oxidation Numbers of Sulfur in Different Substances

Substance	Oxidation number
H_2SO_4	+6
SO_3	+6
H_2SO_3	+4
SO_2	+4
$Na_2S_2O_3$	+2
SCl_2	+2
S_2Cl_2	+1
S	0
H_2S	−2

Using Half-Reactions The second method for balancing redox equations involves the use of half-reactions. A **half-reaction** is an equation showing just the oxidation or just the reduction that takes place in a redox reaction. In the **half-reaction method,** you write and balance the oxidation and reduction half-reactions separately before combining them into a balanced redox equation. The procedure is different, but the outcome is the same as with the oxidation-number-change method.

Sulfur is an element that can have several different oxidation numbers, as you can see in Table 20.2. Sulfur dioxide can be used to preserve dried fruit like the fruit shown in Figure 20.15. The oxidation of sulfur by nitric acid in aqueous solution is one example of a redox reaction that can be balanced by following the steps of the half-reaction method, which is outlined below.

$$S(s) + HNO_3(aq) \longrightarrow SO_2(g) + NO(g) + H_2O(l) \text{ (unbalanced)}$$

Step 1: Write the unbalanced equation in ionic form. In this case, only HNO_3 is ionized. The products are covalent compounds.

$$S(s) + H^+(aq) + NO_3^-(aq) \longrightarrow SO_2(g) + NO(g) + H_2O(l)$$

Step 2: Write separate half-reactions for the oxidation and reduction processes. Sulfur is oxidized in this reaction because its oxidation number increases from 0 to +4. Nitrogen is reduced because its oxidation number decreases from +5 to +2.

$$\text{Oxidation half-reaction:} \quad \overset{0}{S}(s) \longrightarrow \overset{+4}{SO_2}(g)$$

$$\text{Reduction half-reaction:} \quad \overset{+5}{NO_3^-}(aq) \longrightarrow \overset{+2}{NO}(g)$$

Notice that H^+ ions and H_2O are not included in the half-reactions because they are neither oxidized nor reduced. However, they will be used in balancing the half-reactions.

Step 3: Balance the atoms in the half-reactions.
a. Balance the oxidation half-reaction. Sulfur is already balanced in the half-reaction, but oxygen is not. This reaction takes place in acid solution, so H_2O and $H^+(aq)$ are present and can be used to balance oxygen and hydrogen as needed. If the reaction takes place in basic solution, H_2O and OH^- are used to balance these species. Add two molecules of H_2O on the left to balance the oxygen in the half-reaction.

$$2H_2O(l) + S(s) \longrightarrow SO_2(g)$$

Oxygen is now balanced, but four hydrogen ions ($4H^+$) must be added to the right to balance the hydrogen on the left.

$$2H_2O(l) + S(s) \longrightarrow SO_2(g) + 4H^+(aq)$$

This half-reaction is now balanced in terms of atoms. Note that it is not balanced in terms of charge. The charges will be balanced in Step 4.

b. Balance the reduction half-reaction. Nitrogen is already balanced. Add two molecules of H_2O on the right to balance the oxygen.

$$NO_3^-(aq) \longrightarrow NO(g) + 2H_2O(l)$$

Oxygen is balanced, but four hydrogen ions ($4H^+$) must be added to the left to balance hydrogen.

$$4H^+(aq) + NO_3^-(aq) \longrightarrow NO(g) + 2H_2O(l)$$

This half-reaction is now balanced in terms of atoms.

Step 4: Add enough electrons to one side of each half-reaction to balance the charges. Note that neither half-reaction is balanced for charge. Four electrons are needed on the right side in the oxidation half-reaction.

Oxidation: $2H_2O(l) + S(s) \longrightarrow SO_2(g) + 4H^+(aq) + 4e^-$

Three electrons are needed on the left side in the reduction half-reaction.

Reduction: $4H^+(aq) + NO_3^-(aq) + 3e^- \longrightarrow NO(g) + 2H_2O(l)$

Each half-reaction is now balanced with respect to both atoms and charge.

Step 5: Multiply each half-reaction by an appropriate number to make the numbers of electrons equal in both. The number of electrons lost in oxidation must equal the number of electrons gained in reduction. In this case, the oxidation half-reaction is multiplied by 3 and the reduction half-reaction is multiplied by 4. Therefore, the number of electrons lost in oxidation and the number of electrons gained in reduction both equal 12.

Oxidation: $6H_2O(l) + 3S(s) \longrightarrow 3SO_2(g) + 12H^+(aq) + 12e^-$

Reduction: $16H^+(aq) + 4NO_3^-(aq) + 12e^- \longrightarrow 4NO(g) + 8H_2O(l)$

Step 6: Add the balanced half-reactions to show an overall equation.

$$6H_2O(l) + 3S(s) + 16H^+(aq) + 4NO_3^-(aq) + 12e^- \longrightarrow$$
$$3SO_2(g) + 12H^+(aq) + 12e^- + 4NO(g) + 8H_2O(l)$$

Then, subtract terms that appear on both sides of the equation.

$$3S(s) + 4H^+(aq) + 4NO_3^-(aq) \longrightarrow 3SO_2(g) + 4NO(g) + 2H_2O(l)$$

Step 7: Add the spectator ions and balance the equation. Recall that spectator ions are present but do not participate in or change during a reaction. Because none of the ions in the reactants appear in the products, there are no spectator ions in this particular example. The balanced equation is correct. However, it can be written to show the HNO_3 as not ionized.

$$3S(s) + 4HNO_3(aq) \longrightarrow 3SO_2(g) + 4NO(g) + 2H_2O(l)$$

The half-reaction method is very useful in balancing equations for reactions that take place in acidic or basic solutions.

SampleProblem 20.7

Balancing Redox Equations by Half-Reactions

Balance this redox equation using the half-reaction method.

$$KMnO_4(aq) + HCl(aq) \longrightarrow MnCl_2(aq) + Cl_2(g) + H_2O(l) + KCl(aq)$$

❶ Analyze Identify the relevant concepts. You can use the seven steps of the half-reaction method.

❷ Solve Apply the concepts to this problem.

Step 1: Write the equation in ionic form.	$K^+(aq) + MnO_4^-(aq) + H^+(aq) + Cl^-(aq) \longrightarrow$ $\qquad Mn^{2+}(aq) + 2Cl^-(aq) + Cl_2(g) + H_2O(l) + K^+(aq) + Cl^-(aq)$
Step 2: Write half-reactions. Determine the oxidation and reduction processes.	Oxidation half-reaction: $\overset{-1}{Cl^-} \longrightarrow \overset{0}{Cl_2}$ Reduction half-reaction: $\overset{+7}{MnO_4^-} \longrightarrow \overset{+2}{Mn^{2+}}$
Step 3: Balance the atoms in each half-reaction. The solution is acidic, so use H_2O and H^+ to balance the oxygen and hydrogen.	Oxidation: $2Cl^-(aq) \longrightarrow Cl_2(g)$ (atoms balanced) Reduction: $MnO_4^-(aq) + 8H^+(aq) \longrightarrow$ $\qquad\qquad Mn^{2+}(aq) + 4H_2O(l)$ (atoms balanced)
Step 4: Balance the charges by adding electrons.	Oxidation: $2Cl^-(aq) \longrightarrow Cl_2(g) + 2e^-$ (charges balanced) Reduction: $MnO_4^-(aq) + 8H^+(aq) + 5e^- \longrightarrow$ $\qquad\qquad Mn^{2+}(aq) + 4H_2O(l)$ (charges balanced)
Step 5: Make the numbers of electrons equal. Multiply the oxidation half-reaction by 5 and the reduction half-reaction by 2.	Oxidation: $10Cl^-(aq) \longrightarrow 5Cl_2(g) + 10e^-$ Reduction: $2MnO_4^-(aq) + 16H^+(aq) + 10e^- \longrightarrow 2Mn^{2+}(aq) + 8H_2O(l)$
Step 6: Add the half-reactions. Then, subtract the terms that appear on both sides.	$10Cl^-(aq) + 2MnO_4^-(aq) + 16H^+(aq) + \cancel{10e^-} \longrightarrow$ $\qquad\qquad 5Cl_2(g) + \cancel{10e^-} + 2Mn^{2+}(aq) + 8H_2O(l)$
Step 7: Add the spectator ions, making sure the charges and atoms are balanced.	$10Cl^- + 2MnO_4^- + 2K^+ + 16H^+ + 6Cl^- \longrightarrow$ $\qquad\qquad 5Cl_2 + 2Mn^{2+} + 4Cl^- + 8H_2O + 2K^+ + 2Cl^-$

Combine the spectator and nonspectator Cl^- on each side.	$16Cl^-(aq) + 2MnO_4^-(aq) + 2K^+(aq) + 16H^+(aq) \longrightarrow$ $5Cl_2(g) + 2Mn^{2+}(aq) + 6Cl^-(aq) + 8H_2O(l) + 2K^+(aq)$

Show the balanced equation for the substances given in the question (rather than for ions).	$2KMnO_4(aq) + 16HCl(aq) \longrightarrow 2MnCl_2(aq) + 5Cl_2(g) + 8H_2O(l) + 2KCl(aq)$

25. The following reaction takes place in an acidic solution. Balance the equation using the half-reaction method.
$$Sn^{2+}(aq) + Cr_2O_7^{2-}(aq) \longrightarrow Sn^{4+}(aq) + Cr^{3+}(aq)$$

26. The following reaction takes place in basic solution. Balance the equation using the half-reaction method.
$$Zn(s) + NO_3^-(aq) \longrightarrow NH_3(aq) + Zn(OH)_4^{2-}(aq)$$

For a solution that is basic, use H_2O and OH^- in Step 3 to balance the atoms.

  # 20.3 LessonCheck

27. 🔑 **Identify** What are the two classes of chemical reactions?

28. 🔑 **Compare** What are two different methods for balancing a redox equation?

29. Calculate Balance each redox equation, using the oxidation-number-change method.
   a. $ClO_3^-(aq) + I^-(aq) \longrightarrow Cl^-(aq) + I_2(aq)$ [acidic solution]
   b. $C_2O_4^{2-}(aq) + MnO_4^-(aq) \longrightarrow$ $Mn^{2+}(aq) + CO_2(g)$ [acidic solution]
   c. $Br_2(l) + SO_2(g) \longrightarrow Br^-(aq) + SO_4^{2-}(aq)$ [acidic solution]

30. Calculate Use the half-reaction method to write a balanced ionic equation for each reaction.
   a. $Zn(s) + As_2O_3(aq) \longrightarrow AsH_3(aq) + Zn^{2+}(aq)$ [basic solution]
   b. $NiO_2(s) + S_2O_3^{2-}(aq) \longrightarrow$ $Ni(OH)_2(s) + SO_3^{2-}(aq)$ [basic solution]

31. Identify Review the equations for the production of sodium, bromine, and iodine found on pages R2 and R28 of the Elements Handbook. Identify the oxidizing agent and the reducing agent in each reaction.

Mineral Colors

Beryl is a rather unassuming colorless mineral on its own. But when impurities caused by trace amounts of certain elements are present in the crystal, beryl transforms into brilliant green emeralds, pale blue aquamarines, light pink morganites, golden yellow heliodors, and ruby-toned red beryls.

Transition metal elements, such as iron, chromium, and manganese, are the most common causes of color in minerals. The type, amount, and oxidation number of the transition metal as well as the compound it forms determine the color. Most transition metals have two or more oxidation numbers, each of which can be responsible for a different color in a mineral. For example, Fe^{2+} gives aquamarine its blue color, while Fe^{3+} makes heliodor yellow. Mn^{2+} is responsible for morganite's pink hue, and Mn^{3+} turns beryl a rich red.

Changing the oxidation state of the impurity can change the color of the mineral. Heating a yellow beryl, for example, changes the Fe^{3+} in the stone to Fe^{2+}, turning the beryl blue. And heating a purple amethyst (quartz colored by Fe^{3+}) produces yellow-brown citrine (Fe^{2+}).

ADDING COLOR TO GEMS
Transition elements are responsible for creating different colors of beryl.

ONE STATE, DIFFERENT COLORS
Chromium(III) produces both the red of rubies and the green of emeralds by forming different compounds in the base mineral.

DIGGING IN THE DIRT
Beryl is obtained through mining. In this mine in Madagascar, workers are digging by hand to find beryl.

Take It Further

1. Identify Determine the oxidation number for each of the following transition metal ions: Fe^{2+}, Fe^{3+}, Mn^{2+}, Mn^{3+}.

2. Apply Concepts When amethyst is heated to produce citrine, is the iron in the mineral oxidized or reduced? Explain your answer.

Small-Scale Lab

Half-Reactions

Purpose
To observe redox reactions and to write half-reactions that describe them

Materials
- ruler
- reaction surface
- chemicals listed in the grid

Procedure
1. On separate sheets of paper, draw two grids similar to the one below.

	HCl	HNO₃	H₂SO₄
Zn			
Mg			
Cu			
Fe			

2. Make each square 2 cm on each side. Place a reaction surface over one of the grids and add one drop of each acid solution to one piece of each metal, as shown above. Use the second grid as a data table to record your observations for each solution.

Analyze
Using your data, answer the following questions.
1. Explain Which metal is the most reactive? How do you know? Which metal did not react with any of the acids?
2. Infer List the metals in order of decreasing reactivity.

3. Infer What is the chemical formula of the gas produced in each reaction?
4. Calculate An active metal reacts with an acid to produce hydrogen gas and a salt. Write chemical equations and net ionic equations to describe the reactions you observed. Are all of these redox reactions? Explain.
5. Calculate The half-reaction for the oxidation of zinc is shown below.

$$Zn(s) \longrightarrow Zn^{2+}(aq) + 2e^-$$

Write the oxidation half-reaction for the other metals that react.
6. Calculate The half-reaction for the reduction of hydrogen from the acid is shown below.

$$2H^+ + 2e^- \longrightarrow H_2(g)$$

Notice that this half-reaction is the same for all the acids. Demonstrate how adding this half-reaction to each oxidation half-reaction results in the overall net ionic equations.

You're the Chemist
The following small-scale activities allow you to develop your own procedures and analyze the results.
1. Analyze Data Pennies minted after 1982 are made of zinc with a thin copper coating. Use a penny that has been damaged so that a portion of the zinc shows through to compare the reactivity of the zinc and the copper toward various acids.
2. Design an Experiment Many household products, such as toilet-bowl cleaners and vinegar, contain acids. Design and carry out experiments to find out if these products also react with metals.

20 **Study** Guide

BIGIDEA REACTIONS

Oxidation-reduction reactions always occur simultaneously in redox reactions. Losing electrons is oxidation. Gaining electrons is reduction. If oxygen is involved in the reaction, then the substance gaining oxygen is oxidized, while the substance losing oxygen is reduced. The species that is reduced is the oxidizing agent, while the oxidized species is the reducing agent. Redox reactions are identified by changes in oxidation number. Redox equations can be balanced by two methods, the oxidation-number-change method and by balancing the oxidation and reduction half-reactions.

20.1 The Meaning of Oxidation and Reduction

🔑 A substance that undergoes oxidation gains oxygen or loses electrons, while a substance that undergoes reduction loses oxygen or gains electrons.

🔑 The presence of salts and acids accelerates corrosion by producing conductive solutions that make electron transfer easier.

- oxidation-reduction reaction (693)
- oxidation (694)
- reduction (694)
- reducing agent (695)
- oxidizing agent (695)

20.2 Oxidation Numbers

🔑 As a general rule, a bonded atom's oxidation number is the charge that it would have if the electrons in the bond were assigned to the atom of the more electronegative element.

🔑 An increase in the oxidation number of an atom or ion indicates oxidation. A decrease in the oxidation number of an atom or ion indicates reduction.

- oxidation number (701)

20.3 Describing Redox Equations

🔑 One class of chemical reactions is oxidation-reduction (redox) reactions, in which electrons are transferred from one reacting species to another. The other class includes all other reactions, in which no electron transfer occurs.

🔑 To balance a redox equation using the oxidation-number change method, the total increase in oxidation number of the species oxidized must be balanced by the total decrease in the oxidation number of the species reduced.

🔑 To balance a redox reaction using half-reactions, write separate half-reactions for the oxidation and the reduction. After you balance atoms in each half-reaction, balance electrons gained in the reduction with electrons lost in the oxidation.

- oxidation-number-change method (710)
- half-reaction (712)
- half-reaction method (712)

Skills Tune-Up: Redox Reactions

Problem

Use the changes in oxidation number to identify which atoms are oxidized and which are reduced in each reaction.

$$2ZnS(s) + 3O_2(g) \longrightarrow 2ZnO(s) + 2SO_2(g)$$

The following reaction takes place in a basic solution. Use the half-reaction method to write a balanced ionic equation.

$$MnO_4^-(aq) + I^-(aq) \longrightarrow MnO_2(s) + I_2(s)$$

① Analyze

Assign an oxidation number to each atom on both sides of the equation. A decrease in oxidation number indicates reduction. An increase in oxidation number indicates oxidation.

Follow the steps of the half-reaction method to balance the equation. Write separate half-reactions for the oxidation and the reduction. After you balance atoms in each half-reaction, balance electrons gained in the reduction with electrons lost in the oxidation.

② Solve

Use the Rules for Assigning Oxidation Numbers to identify the oxidation number of each atom.

$$2\overset{+2\ -2}{ZnS}(s) + 3\overset{0}{O_2}(g) \longrightarrow 2\overset{+2\ -2}{ZnO}(s) + 2\overset{+4-2}{SO_2}(g)$$

The oxidation number of sulfur increases from +2 to +4, so sulfur is oxidized.

The oxidation number of oxygen decreases from 0 to −2, so oxygen is reduced.

> Remember that the sum of the oxidation numbers of the atoms in a neutral compound must equal zero.

Perform the steps below.

Step 1:
$$MnO_4^-(aq) + I^-(aq) \longrightarrow MnO_2(s) + I_2(s)$$

Step 2:
Oxidation half-reaction: $I^-(aq) \longrightarrow I_2(s)$
Reduction half-reaction: $MnO_4^-(aq) \longrightarrow MnO_2(s)$

> Hint: First, balance the equation as though it is an acidic solution, using H^+ ions and H_2O. Then, add as many OH^- ions to each side of the equation as there are H^+ ions on one side.

Step 3:
Balance the oxidation half-reaction.
$$I^-(aq) \longrightarrow I_2(s)$$
$$2I^-(aq) \longrightarrow I_2(s)$$

Balance the reduction half-reaction.
$$MnO_4^-(aq) \longrightarrow MnO_2(s) + 2H_2O$$
$$4H^+ + MnO_4^-(aq) \longrightarrow MnO_2(s) + 2H_2O$$
$$4OH^- + 4H^+ + MnO_4^-(aq) \longrightarrow MnO_2(s) + 2H_2O + 4OH^-$$
$$4H_2O + MnO_4^-(aq) \longrightarrow MnO_2(s) + 2H_2O + 4OH^-$$
$$2H_2O + MnO_4^-(aq) \longrightarrow MnO_2(s) + 4OH^-$$

Step 4:
Oxidation: $2I^-(aq) \longrightarrow I_2(s) + 2e^-$
Reduction: $3e^- + 2H_2O + MnO_4^-(aq) \longrightarrow MnO_2(s) + 4OH^-$

Step 5:
Oxidation: $6I^-(aq) \longrightarrow 3I_2(s) + 6e^-$
Reduction: $6e^- + 4H_2O + 2MnO_4^-(aq) \longrightarrow 2MnO_2(s) + 8OH^-$

Step 6:
$$6I^-(aq) + 6e^- + 4H_2O + 2MnO_4^-(aq) \longrightarrow 3I_2(s) + 6e^- + 2MnO_2(s) + 8OH^-$$
$$6I^-(aq) + 4H_2O + 2MnO_4^-(aq) \longrightarrow 3I_2(s) + 2MnO_2(s) + 8OH^-$$

 **20 Assessment**

Lesson by Lesson

20.1 The Meaning of Oxidation and Reduction

32. What chemical process must always accompany a reduction process?

33. What happens to an oxidizing agent during a redox reaction?

★34. Balance each redox equation and identify whether the first substance in each equation was oxidized or reduced.

a. $Ba(s) + O_2(g) \longrightarrow BaO(s)$
b. $CuO(s) + H_2(g) \longrightarrow Cu(s) + H_2O(l)$
c. $C_2H_4(g) + O_2(g) \longrightarrow CO_2(g) + H_2O(l)$
d. $CaO(s) + Al(s) \longrightarrow Al_2O_3(s) + Ca(s)$

35. Identify each process as either oxidation or reduction.

a. $Al \longrightarrow Al^{3+} + 3e^-$
b. $2Cl^- \longrightarrow Cl_2 + 2e^-$
c. $S^{2-} \longrightarrow S + 2e^-$
d. $Sr \longrightarrow Sr^{2+} + 2e^-$

★36. Which of the following would most likely be oxidizing agents, and which would most likely be reducing agents? (*Hint:* Think in terms of tendencies to lose or gain electrons.)

a. Cl_2
b. K
c. Ag^+
d. Zn^{2+}

★ 37. Refer to the electronegativity values in Table 6.2 to determine which reactant is oxidized and which reactant is reduced in each reaction.

a. $H_2(g) + S(s) \longrightarrow H_2S(g)$
b. $N_2(g) + 3H_2(g) \longrightarrow 2NH_3(g)$
c. $S(s) + O_2(g) \longrightarrow SO_2(g)$
d. $2H_2(g) + O_2(g) \longrightarrow 2H_2O(l)$

38. Identify the oxidizing agent and the reducing agent for each of the reactions in Problem 37.

20.2 Oxidation Numbers

39. In your own words, what is an oxidation number?

40. Which of these statements is false?

a. The oxidation number of an uncombined element is zero.
b. The sum of the oxidation numbers of the atoms in a polyatomic ion must equal the charge of the ion.
c. Every element has a single oxidation number.
d. The oxidation number of oxygen in a compound or a polyatomic ion is almost always −2.

41. Determine the oxidation number of each metal atom.

a. Ca^{2+} **c.** Na_2CrO_4 **e.** MnO_4^-
b. Al_2S_3 **d.** V_2O_5

★42. Assign oxidation numbers to the atoms in the following ions:

a. OH^- **c.** IO_3^- **e.** HSO_4^-
b. PO_4^{3-} **d.** $H_2PO_4^-$

20.3 Describing Redox Equations

43. Use the changes in oxidation numbers to identify which atoms are oxidized and which are reduced in each reaction.

a. $Al(s) + MnO_2(s) \longrightarrow Al_2O_3(s) + Mn(s)$
b. $K(s) + H_2O(l) \longrightarrow KOH(aq) + H_2(g)$
c. $HgO(s) \longrightarrow Hg(l) + O_2(g)$
d. $P_4(s) + O_2(g) \longrightarrow P_4O_{10}(s)$

★44. Balance each redox equation.

a. $Al(s) + Cl_2(g) \longrightarrow AlCl_3(s)$
b. $Al(s) + Fe_2O_3(s) \longrightarrow Al_2O_3(s) + Fe(s)$
c. $Cl_2(g) + KOH(aq) \longrightarrow$
$\qquad KClO_3(aq) + KCl(aq) + H_2O(l)$
d. $HNO_3(aq) + H_2S(g) \longrightarrow$
$\qquad S(s) + NO(g) + H_2O(l)$
e. $KIO_4(aq) + KI(aq) + HCl(aq) \longrightarrow$
$\qquad KCl(aq) + I_2(s) + H_2O(l)$

★45. Identify which of these unbalanced equations represent redox reactions.

a. $Li(s) + H_2O(l) \longrightarrow LiOH(aq) + H_2(g)$
b. $K_2Cr_2O_7(aq) + HCl(aq) \longrightarrow$
$\qquad KCl(aq) + CrCl_3(aq) + H_2O(l) + Cl_2(g)$
c. $Al(s) + HCl(aq) \longrightarrow AlCl_3(aq) + H_2(g)$
d. $Cl_2(g) + H_2O(l) \longrightarrow HCl(aq) + HClO(aq)$
e. $I_2O_5(s) + CO(g) \longrightarrow I_2(s) + CO_2(g)$
f. $H_2O(l) + SO_3(g) \longrightarrow H_2SO_4(aq)$

*46. Use the half-reaction method to write a balanced ionic equation for each reaction. All occur in acidic solutions.

a. $CuS(s) + NO_3^-(aq) \longrightarrow$
$$Cu(NO_3)_2(aq) + NO_2(g) + SO_2(g)$$

b. $I^-(aq) + NO_3^-(aq) \longrightarrow I_2(s) + NO(g)$

*47. Use the half-reaction method to write a balanced ionic equation for each reaction. All occur in basic solutions.

a. $MnO_4^-(aq) + ClO_2^-(aq) \longrightarrow$
$$MnO_2(s) + ClO_4^-(aq)$$

b. $Cr^{3+}(aq) + ClO^-(aq) \longrightarrow$
$$CrO_4^{2-}(aq) + Cl^-(aq)$$

c. $Mn^{3+}(aq) + I^-(aq) \longrightarrow$
$$Mn^{2+}(aq) + IO_3^-(aq)$$

Understand Concepts

48. Balance the equations in Problem 43 by an appropriate method.

49. Balance the equations in Problem 45 by an appropriate method.

*50. Determine the oxidation number of phosphorus in each substance.

a. P_4O_8 **d.** P_4O_6

b. PO_4^{3-} **e.** $H_2PO_4^-$

c. P_2O_5 **f.** PO_3^{3-}

51. What is the oxidation number for chromium in each of these compounds?

a. K_2CrO_4 **b.** Cr_2O_3

52. Identify the element oxidized, the element reduced, the oxidizing agent, and the reducing agent in each unbalanced redox equation.

a. $MnO_2(s) + HCl(aq) \longrightarrow$
$$MnCl_2(aq) + Cl_2(g) + H_2O(l)$$

b. $Cu(s) + HNO_3(aq) \longrightarrow$
$$Cu(NO_3)_2(aq) + NO_2(g) + H_2O(l)$$

c. $P(s) + HNO_3(aq) + H_2O(l) \longrightarrow$
$$NO(g) + H_3PO_4(aq)$$

d. $Bi(OH)_3(s) + Na_2SnO_2(aq) \longrightarrow$
$$Bi(s) + Na_2SnO_3(aq) + H_2O(l)$$

53. Balance each redox equation in Problem 52 by using the oxidation-number-change method.

*54. An alcohol-content measuring device is used to test a person's breath for the alcohol ethanol, C_2H_5OH. In this test, ethanol reacts with an acidic solution of orange dichromate ion to form green chromium(III) ion.

$$Cr_2O_7^{2-}(aq) + C_2H_5OH(aq) \longrightarrow$$
$$Cr^{3+}(aq) + CO_2(g)$$

The amount of color change is proportional to the amount of ethanol in the exhaled breath.

a. Balance this equation by the half-reaction method.

b. Is dichromate ion an oxidizing agent or a reducing agent?

55. The metallic element tungsten, used as a filament in incandescent light bulbs, is obtained by heating tungsten(VI) oxide with hydrogen.

$$WO_3(s) + H_2(g) \longrightarrow W(s) + H_2O(g)$$

a. Balance the equation.

b. What is the reducing agent in this reaction?

c. Which element undergoes an increase in oxidation number?

56. Silver tarnishes when it reacts with hydrogen sulfide in the air.

$$Ag(s) + H_2S(g) \longrightarrow Ag_2S(s) + H_2(g)$$

a. Is silver oxidized or reduced in this reaction?

b. Identify the oxidizing agent and the reducing agent.

c. Balance the equation.

57. The following equation represents an oxidation-reduction reaction that uses oxygen. Show how this reaction can also be defined as an oxidation-reduction reaction in terms of electron transfer.

$$Pb(s) + O_2(g) \longrightarrow PbO(s)$$

58. Does each of the following equations represent a redox reaction? Explain how you know.

a. $Bi_2O_3(s) + 3C(s) \longrightarrow 2Bi(s) + 3CO(g)$

b. $Cr_2O_3(s) + 3H_2S(g) \longrightarrow Cr_2S_3(s) + 3H_2O(l)$

c. $BCl_3(g) + 3H_2O(l) \longrightarrow H_3BO_3(s) + 3HCl(g)$

59. Write chemical equations for the following redox reactions. Balance each equation using the oxidation-number-change method.

   a. Solid barium chlorate decomposes when heated, yielding solid barium chloride and gaseous oxygen.

   b. Solid lead(II) sulfide reacts with gaseous oxygen to produce solid lead(II) oxide and gaseous sulfur dioxide.

60. The following unbalanced equation represents a reaction that can occur when dinitrogen tetroxide, N_2O_4, is combined with hydrazine, N_2H_4.

$$N_2O_4(l) + N_2H_4(l) \longrightarrow N_2(g) + H_2O(g)$$

Balance the equation and describe in words the electron transfer that takes place.

61. Examine the following hypothetical redox equation.

$$2X + 3H_2Y \longrightarrow X_2Y_3 + 3H_2$$

   a. What is the oxidation number of element X on each side of the equation?

   b. What is the oxidation number of element Y on each side of the equation?

   c. What is oxidized in this equation?

   d. What is reduced in this equation?

Think Critically

62. **Explain** Why must the number of electrons lost equal the number of electrons gained in every redox reaction.

63. **Explain** The highest possible oxidation number that chlorine exhibits in any compound is +7, whereas its most negative oxidation number is −1. Write the electron configuration of chlorine, and explain why these are the limiting oxidation numbers for chlorine.

64. **Explain** Why is a sodium atom a reducing agent but a sodium ion is not?

65. **Explain** Many decomposition, single-replacement, combination, and combustion reactions are also redox reactions. Why is a double-replacement reaction never a redox reaction?

66. **Make Generalizations** Why must every redox reaction have a reducing agent and an oxidizing agent?

67. **Infer** Humankind began to make and use iron tools more than 3000 years ago, but few iron artifacts from ancient times have survived. Explain.

68. **Identify** Which substance in each pair is more likely to be an oxidizing agent?

   a. S^{2-} or SO_4^{2-}

   b. H_2O or H_2O_2

   c. NO_2^- or NO_3^-

   d. $Cr_2O_7^{2-}$ or Cr^{3+}

   e. H_2 or H_2O

69. **Identify** Which is more likely to be a strong reducing agent, a group 1A metal or a group 7A nonmetal? Explain.

70. **Predict** Predict the product(s) and write the balanced equation for each of these redox reactions. Identify the oxidizing agent in each reaction.

   a. rubidium + iodine $\longrightarrow$

   b. barium + water $\longrightarrow$

   c. aluminum + iron(II) sulfate $\longrightarrow$

   d. butene (C_4H_8) + oxygen $\longrightarrow$

   e. zinc + hydrobromic acid $\longrightarrow$

   f. magnesium + bromine $\longrightarrow$

71. **Explain** The electronegativity of rhenium, Re, is 1.9, and the electronegativity of selenium is 2.4. If rhenium were to react with selenium to form a compound, which element would be oxidized and which element would be reduced? Explain.

72. **Explain** Which of the following ions is most likely to be an oxidizing agent? Explain your choice.

$$MnO_4^-, \ MnO_4^{2-}, \ Mn^{+2}$$

Enrichment

73. **Calculate** How many grams of copper are needed to reduce completely the silver ions in 85.0 mL of 0.150M $AgNO_3(aq)$ solution?

74. **Calculate** How many milliliters of 0.280M $K_2Cr_2O_7(aq)$ solution are needed to oxidize 1.40 g of sulfur? First, balance the equation.

$$K_2Cr_2O_7(aq) + H_2O(l) + S(s) \longrightarrow$$
$$SO_2(g) + KOH(aq) + Cr_2O_3(s)$$

75. **Calculate** Carbon monoxide can be removed from the air by passing it over solid diiodine pentoxide.

$$CO(g) + I_2O_5(s) \longrightarrow I_2(s) + CO_2(g)$$

a. Balance the equation.

b. Identify the element being oxidized and the element being reduced.

c. How many grams of carbon monoxide can be removed from the air by 0.55 g of diiodine pentoxide (I_2O_5)?

76. **Calculate** What is the oxidation number of nitrogen in each of these species?

a. HNO_3 c. N_2O_3 e. N_2O g. NO

b. NH_3 d. NO_2^- f. NH_4Cl h. NO_2

77. **Calculate** The elements fluorine and oxygen can react to form fluorine monoxide, F_2O. Write the balanced chemical equation for this reaction. Check electronegativity values, and then identify the elements oxidized and reduced.

78. **Explain** The oxidation number of nitrogen can range from a minimum of −3 to a maximum of +5. Use this information to explain why the nitride ion, N^{3-}, can act only as a reducing agent, and why the nitrate ion, NO_3^-, can act only as an oxidizing agent.

79. **Calculate** Oxidation-reduction reactions form the basis for chemical analysis by redox titration. Potassium permanganate, a good oxidizing agent, is sometimes used as a titrant because it undergoes a color change as it is reduced.

$$\underset{\text{(purple)}}{MnO_4^-(aq)} \longrightarrow \underset{\text{(colorless)}}{Mn^{2+}(aq)}$$

Write a balanced redox equation for the oxidation of stannous ion to stannic ion in acidic solution using permanganate as the oxidizing agent.

*80. **Describe** There are a number of anions that are commonly used as oxidizing or reducing agents in the laboratory. Balance each of these half reactions. Identify each of the anions as an oxidizing or reducing agent.

a. $Cr_2O_7^{2-}(aq) \rightarrow Cr^{3+}(aq)$ [acidic solution]

b. $S_2O_3^{2-}(aq) \rightarrow SO_4^{2-}(aq)$ [acidic solution]

c. $CrO_4^{2-}(aq) \rightarrow Cr(OH)_3(aq)$ [basic solution]

d. $MnO_4^-(aq) \rightarrow Mn^{2+}(aq)$ [acidic solution]

e. $C_2O_4^{2-}(aq) \rightarrow CO_2(g)$ [acidic solution]

f. $MnO_4^-(aq) \rightarrow MnO_2(s)$ [basic solution]

81. **Calculate** Combine each of the following pairs of half-reactions into a complete, balanced, ionic redox equation.

a. $Hg^{2+} + 2e^- \longrightarrow Hg$
$Al \longrightarrow Al^{3+} + 3e^-$

b. $MnO_2 + 4H^+ + 2e^- \longrightarrow Mn^{2+} + 2H_2O$
$Fe \longrightarrow Fe^{2+} + 2e^-$

c. $Fe^{3+} + e^- \longrightarrow Fe^{2+}$
$Cd \longrightarrow Cd^{2+} + 2e^-$

Write About Science

82. **Explain** Silver recovered from shipwrecks may have layers of black tarnish. Research and write a report on how the thick layers of tarnish are removed from the silver artifacts.

83. **Connect to the BIGIDEA** Write a paragraph about five different real-world examples of oxidation-reduction reactions.

CHEMYSTERY

Tarnished Treasure

Gold and silver coins recovered from the same shipwrecked Spanish galleons were exposed to the same elements of the sea. However, the silver coins corrode faster than gold coins because silver is more easily oxidized than gold. Oxidation reactions cause silver coins to corrode, eventually causing their surface to become black and crumbly. Since gold is not as easily oxidized, the gold coins retain their gold color and do not show as many signs of oxidation.

84. **Infer** Suppose there were two types of coins, one made of magnesium and one made of iron. Which coin would you expect to tarnish faster if they were both exposed to the same conditions?

85. **Connect to the BIGIDEA** Why would it be helpful for shipbuilders to have a knowledge of redox reactions?

*86. The complete combustion of hydrocarbons involves the oxidation of both carbon and hydrogen atoms by oxygen. The following table lists the moles of O_2 used, and the moles of CO_2 and moles of H_2O produced, when a series of hydrocarbons called alkanes are burned.

Alkane burned	O_2 used (mol)	CO_2 produced (mol)	H_2O produced (mol)
CH_4	2	1	2
C_2H_6	3.5	2	3
C_3H_8	5	3	4
C_4H_{10}	a. _____	d. _____	g. _____
C_5H_{12}	b. _____	e. _____	h. _____
C_6H_{14}	c. _____	f. _____	i. _____

a. Complete the table.
b. Based on the data, write a balanced generalized equation for the complete oxidation of any alkane. Use the following form, and write the coefficients in terms of x and y:

$$C_xH_y + \_\_\_ O_2 \longrightarrow \_\_\_ CO_2 + \_\_\_ H_2O$$

87. Name a change of state that does not involve a liquid.

*88. A gas cylinder has a volume of 6.8 L and is filled with 13.8 g of N_2. Calculate the pressure of N_2 at 25°C.

89. A particular paint must be stirred before using. Is the stirred paint a solution or a suspension? Explain.

90. Which of these are nonelectrolytes?
   a. $S(s)$ c. $SiO_2(s)$
   b. $NH_4Cl(aq)$ d. $F_2(g)$

*91. How would you make 440 mL of 1.5M HCl solution from a stock solution of 6.0M HCl?

92. One mole of LiF and $Ca(NO_3)_2$ are each dissolved in 1.0 L of water. Which solution has the higher boiling point? Explain.

93. What is the molarity of the solution prepared by dissolving 46.4 g H_3PO_4 in enough water to make 1.25 L of solution?

*94. The K_{sp} of lead(II) bromide ($PbBr_2$) at 25°C is 2.1×10^{-6}. What is the solubility of $PbBr_2$ (in mol/L) at this temperature?

95. A reaction goes essentially to completion. Do you expect the value of K to be large or small?

96. Bottles containing 0.1M solutions of Na_2SO_4, $BaCl_2$, and NaCl have had their labels accidentally switched. To discover which bottle contains the NaCl, you place a clear saturated solution of $BaSO_4$ ($K_{sp} = 1.1 \times 10^{-10}$) into three test tubes. To each test tube you add a few drops of each mislabeled solution. The results are shown below. To which tube was NaCl added? Explain.

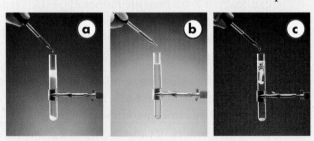

97. What is the hydrogen-ion concentration of solutions with the following pH?
   a. 2.00   b. 11.00   c. 8.80

98. How many milliliters of a 4.00M KOH solution are needed to neutralize 45.0 mL of 2.50M H_2SO_4 solution?

99. Identify the conjugate acid-base pairs in each equation.
   a. $NH_4^+(aq) + H_2O(l) \longrightarrow$
      $$NH_3(aq) + H_3O^+(aq)$$
   b. $H_2SO_3(aq) + NH_2^-(aq) \longrightarrow$
      $$HSO_3^-(aq) + NH_3(aq)$$
   c. $HNO_3(aq) + I^-(aq) \longrightarrow$
      $$HI(aq) + NO_3^-(aq)$$

*100. Calculate the pH of solutions with the following hydrogen-ion or hydroxide-ion concentrations. Classify each as acidic, basic, or neutral.
   a. $[H^+] = 0.000\ 010M$
   b. $[OH^-] = 1.0 \times 10^{-4}M$
   c. $[OH^-] = 1.0 \times 10^{-1}M$
   d. $[H^+] = 3.0 \times 10^{-7}M$

If You Have Trouble With . . .

Question	86	87	88	89	90	91	92	93	94	95	96	97	98	99	100
See Chapter	12	13	14	15	15	16	16	16	18	18	19	19	19	19	19

Standardized Test Prep

Select the choice that best answers each question or completes each statement.

1. Which of these processes is not an oxidation?
   (A) a decrease in oxidation number
   (B) a complete loss of electrons
   (C) a gain of oxygen
   (D) a loss of hydrogen by a covalent molecule

2. In which of these pairs of nitrogen-containing ions and compounds is the oxidation number of nitrogen in the ion higher than in the nitrogen compound?

   I. N_2H_4 and NH_4^+
   II. NO_3^- and N_2O_4
   III. N_2O and NO_2^-

   (A) I only
   (B) I and II only
   (C) I and III only
   (D) II and III only
   (E) I, II, and III

3. Identify the elements oxidized and reduced in this reaction.

   $$2ClO^- + H_2 + 2e^- \longrightarrow 2Cl^- + 2OH^-$$

   (A) Cl is oxidized; H is reduced
   (B) H is oxidized; Cl is reduced
   (C) Cl is oxidized; O is reduced
   (D) O is oxidized; Cl is reduced

4. Which of these half-reactions represents a reduction?

   I. $Fe^{2+} \longrightarrow Fe^{3+}$
   II. $Cr_2O_7^{2-} \longrightarrow Cr^{3+}$
   III. $MnO_4^- \longrightarrow Mn^{2-}$

   (A) I and II only
   (B) II and III only
   (C) I and III only
   (D) I, II, and III

5. Which of these general types of reactions is not a redox reaction?
   (A) single replacement
   (B) double replacement
   (C) combustion
   (D) combination

6. What is the reducing agent in this reaction?

   $$MnO_4^- + SO_2 \longrightarrow Mn^{2+} + SO_4^{2-}$$

   (A) SO_2
   (B) SO_4^{2-}
   (C) Mn^{2+}
   (D) MnO_4^-

Tips for Success

Interpreting Data Tables To interpret the content in a table, start by reading the title (if there is one). Then, read the headings. Try to figure out the relationship between the different columns and rows of information. Ask yourself: *What information is related in the table? How are the relationships represented?*

Use the table to answer Questions 7–9.

Metal	Metal ion
K	K^+
3 Ca	Ca^{2+}
Na	Na^+
Mg	Mg^{2+}
4 Fe	Fe^{2+}
Sn	Sn^{2+}
Pb	Pb^{2+}
Cu	Cu^{2+}
5 Ag	Ag^+

7. Which arrow indicates increasing ease of oxidation? Of reduction?

8. Which numbered group of metals are the strongest reducing agents? Which numbered group of metals are the most difficult to oxidize?

9. Which is a stronger oxidizing agent, Na or Fe?

Use this diagram to answer Questions 10 and 11. It shows the formation of an ion from an atom.

Atom → Ion

10. Does the diagram represent oxidation or reduction? Does the oxidation number increase or decrease when the ion forms?

11. Draw a diagram showing the formation of a sulfide ion from a sulfur atom. Make the relative sizes of the atom and ion realistic. Does your drawing represent an oxidation or a reduction?

If You Have Trouble With . . .

Question	1	2	3	4	5	6	7	8	9	10	11
See Lesson	20.1	20.2	20.2	20.2	20.3	20.3	20.2	20.2	20.2	20.2	20.1

21

Electrochemistry

INSIDE:

- **21.1** Electrochemical Cells
- **21.2** Half-Cells and Cell Potentials
- **21.3** Electrolytic Cells

PearsonChem.com

An electrochemical process was used to produce the shiny chrome finish on this car.

MATTER AND ENERGY

Essential Questions:

1. *How is energy produced in an electrochemical process?*

2. *How can energy be used to drive an electrochemical process?*

CHEMYSTERY

Trash or Treasure?

Maria and her friend decided to spend the Saturday browsing a local flea market. At one vendor's display, Maria spotted a beautiful, shiny gold ring. The vendor told Maria that the ring was an antique from the 1800s and made from solid gold. Enamored by the ring, Maria purchased it and placed it on her finger.

Several weeks later, while taking off the ring, Maria noticed that the ring was discolored in many places. It almost looked like the gold was peeling off the ring. Maria was disturbed because the ring was expensive, and she believed that it was a valuable antique. She decided to take the ring to a jeweler to see if it could be polished and restored to its original gold color. However, Maria became upset when the jeweler revealed the truth about her "gold" ring.

▶ Connect to the **BIG**IDEA As you read about electrochemical processes, think about how a ring could be made to look like it was made out of pure gold when it was not.

NATIONAL SCIENCE EDUCATION STANDARDS

A-1, B-3, B-5, E-2, G-1, G-3

21.1 Electrochemical Cells

Q: *Why do some kinds of jellyfish glow?* On a summer evening, fireflies glow to attract their mates. In the ocean depths, angelfish emit light to attract prey. Luminous shrimp, squid, jellyfish, and even bacteria also exist. These organisms, and others, are able to give off energy in the form of light as a result of redox reactions.

Key Questions

🔑 What type of chemical reaction is involved in all electrochemical processes?

🔑 How does a voltaic cell produce electrical energy?

🔑 What current applications use electrochemical processes to produce electrical energy?

Vocabulary

- electrochemical process
- electrochemical cell
- voltaic cell • half-cell
- salt bridge • electrode
- anode • cathode • dry cell
- battery • fuel cell

Electrochemical Processes

🔑 What type of chemical reaction is involved in all electrochemical processes?

Chemical processes can either release energy or absorb energy. The energy can sometimes be in the form of electricity. An **electrochemical process** is any conversion between chemical energy and electrical energy. 🔑 **All electrochemical processes involve redox reactions.** Electrochemical processes have many applications in the home as well as in industry. Flashlight and automobile batteries are familiar examples of devices used to generate electricity. The manufacture of sodium and aluminum metals and the silver-plating of tableware involve the use of electricity. Biological systems also use electrochemistry to carry nerve impulses.

Redox Reactions and the Activity Series When a strip of zinc metal is dipped into an aqueous solution of blue copper(II) sulfate, the zinc becomes copper-plated, as shown in Figure 21.1. The net ionic equation involves only zinc and copper.

$$Zn(s) + Cu^{2+}(aq) \longrightarrow Zn^{2+}(aq) + Cu(s)$$

Figure 21.1
Redox Reaction
Zinc metal oxidizes spontaneously in a copper-ion solution. **a.** A zinc strip is immersed in a solution of copper(II) sulfate. **b.** As the copper plates out onto the zinc, the blue copper(II) sulfate solution is replaced by a colorless solution of zinc sulfate. The copper appears black because it is in a finely divided state.

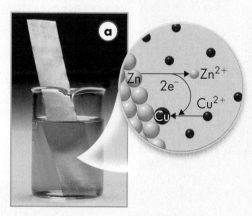

Activity Series of Metals

	Element	Oxidation half-reaction
Most active and most easily oxidized	Lithium	$Li(s) \longrightarrow Li^+(aq) + e^-$
	Potassium	$K(s) \longrightarrow K^+(aq) + e^-$
	Barium	$Ba(s) \longrightarrow Ba^{2+}(aq) + 2e^-$
	Calcium	$Ca(s) \longrightarrow Ca^{2+}(aq) + 2e^-$
	Sodium	$Na(s) \longrightarrow Na^+(aq) + e^-$
	Magnesium	$Mg(s) \longrightarrow Mg^{2+}(aq) + 2e^-$
Decreasing activity	Aluminum	$Al(s) \longrightarrow Al^{3+}(aq) + 3e^-$
	Zinc	$Zn(s) \longrightarrow Zn^{2+}(aq) + 2e^-$
	Iron	$Fe(s) \longrightarrow Fe^{2+}(aq) + 2e^-$
	Nickel	$Ni(s) \longrightarrow Ni^{2+}(aq) + 2e^-$
	Tin	$Sn(s) \longrightarrow Sn^{2+}(aq) + 2e^-$
	Lead	$Pb(s) \longrightarrow Pb^{2+}(aq) + 2e^-$
	Hydrogen*	$H_2(g) \longrightarrow 2H^+(aq) + 2e^-$
	Copper	$Cu(s) \longrightarrow Cu^{2+}(aq) + 2e^-$
	Silver	$Ag(s) \longrightarrow Ag^+(aq) + e^-$
	Mercury	$Hg(s) \longrightarrow Hg^{2+}(aq) + 2e^-$
Least active and least easily oxidized	Gold	$Au(s) \longrightarrow Au^{3+}(aq) + 3e^-$

*Hydrogen is included for reference purposes.

Table 21.1 The half-reaction for the oxidation of each metal is shown.

a. Read Tables What is the half-reaction for the oxidation of nickel?

b. Compare Which metal is more readily oxidized, lead or magnesium?

c. Relate Cause and Effect What will happen if a strip of copper is dipped in a solution of silver nitrate? If a reaction occurs, write the half-reactions.

Remember: The more active metal will be oxidized; the less active metal will be reduced.

Electrons are transferred from zinc atoms to copper ions. This is a spontaneous redox reaction. Zinc atoms lose electrons as they are oxidized to zinc ions, while copper ions in solution gain the electrons lost by the zinc. The copper ions are reduced to copper atoms and are deposited as metallic copper. As the copper ions in solution are gradually replaced by zinc ions, the blue color of the solution fades. The balanced half-reactions for this redox reaction can be written as follows:

Oxidation: $Zn(s) \longrightarrow Zn^{2+}(aq) + 2e^-$

Reduction: $Cu^{2+}(aq) + 2e^- \longrightarrow Cu(s)$

In the activity series of metals in Table 21.1, zinc is above copper on the list. For any two metals in an activity series, the more active metal is the more readily oxidized. Zinc is more readily oxidized than copper. When zinc is dipped into a copper(II) sulfate solution, zinc becomes plated with copper. In contrast, when a copper strip is dipped into a solution of zinc sulfate, the copper does not spontaneously become plated with zinc. This is because copper metal is not oxidized by zinc ions.

Electrochemical Cells When a zinc strip is dipped into a copper(II) sulfate solution, electrons are transferred from zinc atoms to copper ions. This flow of electrons is an electric current. If a redox reaction is to be used as a source of electrical energy, the two half-reactions must be physically separated. In the case of the zinc-metal–copper-ion reaction, the electrons released by the zinc atoms must pass through an external circuit to reach the copper ions if useful electrical energy is to be produced. In that situation, the system serves as an electrochemical cell. Alternatively, an electric current can be used to produce a chemical change. That system also serves as an electrochemical cell. Any device that converts chemical energy into electrical energy or electrical energy into chemical energy is an **electrochemical cell.** Redox reactions occur in all electrochemical cells.

Voltaic Cells

How does a voltaic cell produce electrical energy?

In 1800, the Italian physicist Alessandro Volta built the first electrochemical cell that could be used to generate a direct electric current (DC). Named after its inventor, a **voltaic cell** is an electrochemical cell used to convert chemical energy into electrical energy. **Electrical energy is produced in a voltaic cell by a spontaneous redox reaction within the cell.** You can find voltaic cells everywhere. They power your flashlight and your mp3 player, as shown in Figure 21.2.

Constructing a Voltaic Cell A voltaic cell consists of two half-cells. A **half-cell** is one part of a voltaic cell in which either oxidation or reduction occurs. A typical half-cell consists of a piece of metal immersed in a solution of its ions. Figure 21.3 on the following page shows a voltaic cell that makes use of the zinc–copper reaction. In this cell, one half-cell is a zinc strip immersed in a solution of zinc sulfate. The other half-cell is a copper strip immersed in a solution of copper(II) sulfate.

The half-cells are connected by a **salt bridge,** which is a tube containing a strong electrolyte, often potassium sulfate (K_2SO_4). Salt bridges also contain agar, a gelatinous substance. A porous plate may be used instead of a salt bridge. The salt bridge or porous plate allows ions to pass from one half-cell to the other but prevents the solutions from mixing completely. A wire carries the electrons in the external circuit from the zinc strip to the copper strip. A voltmeter or light bulb can be connected in the circuit. The driving force of such a voltaic cell is the spontaneous redox reaction between zinc metal and copper ions in solution.

The zinc and copper strips in this voltaic cell serve as the electrodes. An **electrode** is a conductor in a circuit that carries electrons to or from a substance other than a metal. The reaction at the electrode determines whether the electrode is labeled as an anode or a cathode. The electrode at which oxidation occurs is called the **anode.** Electrons are produced at the anode. Therefore, the anode is labeled the negative electrode in a voltaic cell. The electrode at which reduction occurs is called the **cathode.** Electrons are consumed at the cathode in a voltaic cell. As a result, the cathode is labeled the positive electrode. Neither electrode is actually charged, however. All parts of the voltaic cell remain balanced in terms of charge at all times. The moving electrons balance any charge that might build up as oxidation and reduction occur.

Figure 21.2 Voltaic Cell
A voltaic cell powers this mp3 player.
Predict *What other items contain voltaic cells?*

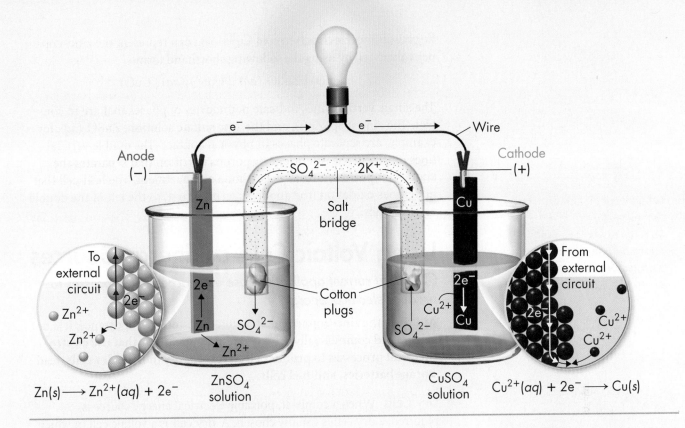

$$Zn(s) \longrightarrow Zn^{2+}(aq) + 2e^-$$

$$Cu^{2+}(aq) + 2e^- \longrightarrow Cu(s)$$

How a Voltaic Cell Works The electrochemical process that occurs in a zinc–copper voltaic cell can best be described in a number of steps. These steps actually occur at the same time.

Step 1 Electrons are produced at the zinc strip according to the oxidation half-reaction:

$$Zn(s) \longrightarrow Zn^{2+}(aq) + 2e^-$$

Zinc is oxidized at the zinc strip, so the zinc strip is the anode, or negative electrode, in the voltaic cell.

Step 2 The electrons leave the zinc anode and pass through the external circuit to the copper strip. (If a bulb is in the circuit, the electron flow will cause it to light. If a voltmeter is present, it will indicate a voltage.)

Step 3 Electrons enter the copper strip and interact with copper ions in solution. There, the following reduction half-reaction occurs:

$$Cu^{2+}(aq) + 2e^- \longrightarrow Cu(s)$$

Copper ions are reduced at the copper strip, so the copper strip is the cathode, or positive electrode, in the voltaic cell.

Step 4 To complete the circuit, both positive and negative ions move through the aqueous solutions via the salt bridge. The two half-reactions can be summed to show the overall cell reaction. Note that the electrons must cancel.

$$Zn(s) \longrightarrow Zn^{2+}(aq) + \cancel{2e^-}$$

$$Cu^{2+}(aq) + \cancel{2e^-} \longrightarrow Cu(s)$$

$$\overline{Zn(s) + Cu^{2+}(aq) \longrightarrow Zn^{2+}(aq) + Cu(s)}$$

Figure 21.3 Zinc–Copper Voltaic Cell

In this voltaic cell, the electrons generated from the oxidation of Zn to Zn^{2+} flow through the external circuit (the wire) into the copper strip. These electrons reduce the surrounding Cu^{2+} to Cu. To maintain neutrality in the electrolytes, anions flow through the salt bridge.

Explain *What is the purpose of the salt bridge?*

> **See** voltaic cells animated online.

Representing Electrochemical Cells You can represent the zinc–copper voltaic cell by using the following shorthand form.

$$Zn(s) \mid ZnSO_4(aq) \parallel CuSO_4(aq) \mid Cu(s)$$

The single vertical lines indicate boundaries of phases that are in contact. The zinc strip, $Zn(s)$, and the zinc sulfate solution, $ZnSO_4(aq)$, for example, are separate phases in physical contact. The double vertical lines represent the salt bridge or porous partition that separates the anode compartment from the cathode compartment. The half-cell that undergoes oxidation (the anode) is written first, to the left of the double vertical lines.

Using Voltaic Cells as Energy Sources

🔑 *What current applications use electrochemical processes to produce electrical energy?*

Although the zinc–copper voltaic cell is of historical importance, it is no longer used commercially. 🔑 **Current applications that use electrochemical processes to produce electrical energy include dry cells, lead storage batteries, and fuel cells.**

Dry Cells When a compact, portable electrical energy source is required, a dry cell is usually chosen. A **dry cell** is a voltaic cell in which the electrolyte is a paste. In one type of dry cell, a zinc container is filled with a thick, moist electrolyte paste of manganese(IV) oxide (MnO_2), zinc chloride ($ZnCl_2$), ammonium chloride (NH_4Cl), and water (H_2O). As shown in Figure 21.4a, a graphite rod is embedded in the paste. The zinc container is the anode, and the graphite rod is the cathode. The thick paste and its surrounding paper liner prevent the contents of the cell from freely mixing, so a salt bridge is not needed. The half-reactions for this cell are shown below.

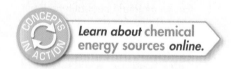
Learn about chemical energy sources **online.**

Oxidation: $Zn(s) \longrightarrow Zn^{2+}(aq) + 2e^-$ (at anode)

Reduction: $2MnO_2(s) + 2NH_4^+(aq) + 2e^- \longrightarrow$
$$Mn_2O_3(s) + 2NH_3(aq) + H_2O(l) \text{ (at cathode)}$$

Figure 21.4 Dry Cells
Both dry cells and alkaline batteries are single electrochemical cells that produce about 1.5 V. **a.** The dry cell is inexpensive, has a short shelf life, and suffers from voltage drop when in use. **b.** The alkaline battery has a longer shelf life and does not suffer from voltage drop.

Apply Concepts *What is oxidized in these cells and what is reduced?*

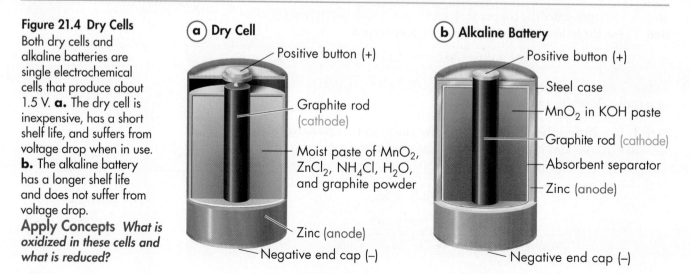

ⓐ Dry Cell
- Positive button (+)
- Graphite rod (cathode)
- Moist paste of MnO_2, $ZnCl_2$, NH_4Cl, H_2O, and graphite powder
- Zinc (anode)
- Negative end cap (–)

ⓑ Alkaline Battery
- Positive button (+)
- Steel case
- MnO_2 in KOH paste
- Graphite rod (cathode)
- Absorbent separator
- Zinc (anode)
- Negative end cap (–)

In an ordinary dry cell, the graphite rod serves only as a conductor and does not undergo reduction, even though it is the cathode. The manganese in MnO_2 is the species that is actually reduced. The electrical potential of this cell starts out at 1.5 V but decreases steadily during use to about 0.8 V. Dry cells of this type are not rechargeable because the cathode reaction is not reversible.

The alkaline battery, shown in Figure 21.4b on the previous page, is an improved dry cell. In the alkaline battery, the reactions are similar to those in the common dry cell, but the electrolyte is a basic KOH paste. This change in design eliminates the buildup of ammonia gas and maintains the zinc electrode, which corrodes more slowly under basic, or alkaline, conditions.

Lead Storage Batteries People depend on lead storage batteries to start their cars. A **battery** is a group of voltaic cells connected together. A 12-V car battery consists of six voltaic cells connected together. Each cell produces about 2 V and consists of lead grids, as shown in Figure 21.5. One set of grids, the anode, is packed with spongy lead. The other set, the cathode, is packed with lead(IV) oxide (PbO_2). The electrolyte for both half-cells in a lead storage battery is sulfuric acid. Using the same electrolyte for both half-cells allows the cell to operate without a salt bridge or porous separator. The half-reactions are as follows:

Oxidation: $Pb(s) + SO_4^{2-}(aq) \longrightarrow PbSO_4(s) + 2e^-$

Reduction: $PbO_2(s) + 4H^+(aq) + SO_4^{2-}(aq) + 2e^- \longrightarrow$
$$PbSO_4(s) + 2H_2O(l)$$

When a lead storage battery discharges, it produces the electrical energy needed to start a car. The overall spontaneous redox reaction that occurs is the sum of the oxidation and reduction half-reactions.

$$Pb(s) + PbO_2(s) + 2H_2SO_4(aq) \longrightarrow 2PbSO_4(s) + 2H_2O(l)$$

This equation shows that lead(II) sulfate forms during discharge. The sulfate slowly builds up on the plates, and the concentration of the sulfuric acid electrolyte decreases.

READING SUPPORT

Build Reading Skills: *Compare and Contrast* An alkaline battery is actually a dry cell, whereas a lead storage battery is considered to be a true battery. *How are alkaline batteries and lead storage batteries similar? How are they different?*

Figure 21.5 Lead Storage Battery One cell of a 12-V lead storage battery is illustrated here. Current is produced when lead at the anode and lead(IV) oxide at the cathode are both converted to lead(II) sulfate. These processes decrease the sulfuric acid concentration in the battery. Reversing the reaction recharges the battery.

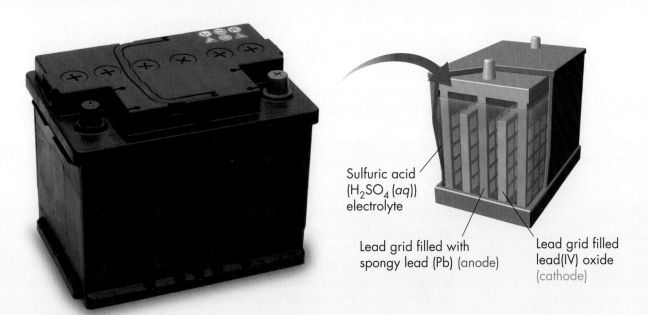

Sulfuric acid (H_2SO_4 (aq)) electrolyte

Lead grid filled with spongy lead (Pb) (anode)

Lead grid filled lead(IV) oxide (cathode)

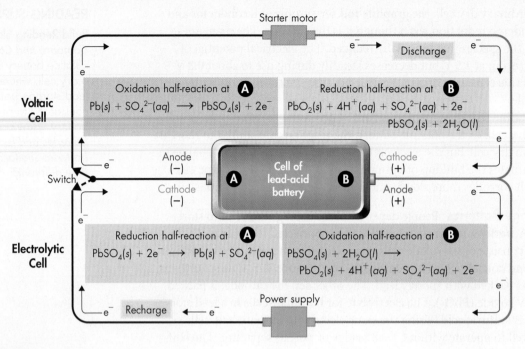

Figure 21.6 Discharge and Recharge of a Lead-Acid Battery
The lead-acid battery in an automobile acts as a voltaic cell (top) when it supplies current to start the engine. Some of the power from the running engine is used to recharge the battery, which then acts as an electrolytic cell (bottom). You will learn more about electrolytic cells in Lesson 21.3.

The reverse reaction occurs when a lead storage battery is recharged. This reaction occurs whenever the car's generator is working properly.

$$2PbSO_4(s) + 2H_2O(l) \longrightarrow Pb(s) + PbO_2(s) + 2H_2SO_4(aq)$$

This is not a spontaneous reaction. To make the reaction proceed as written, a direct current must pass through the cell in a direction opposite that of the current flow during discharge. The processes that occur during the discharge and recharge of a lead-acid battery are summarized in Figure 21.6. In theory, a lead storage battery can be discharged and recharged indefinitely, but in practice its lifespan is limited. Small amounts of lead(II) sulfate fall from the electrodes and collect on the bottom of the cell. Eventually, the electrodes lose so much lead(II) sulfate that the recharging process is ineffective or the cell is shorted out. The battery must then be replaced.

Fuel Cells To overcome the disadvantages associated with lead storage batteries, cells with renewable electrodes have been developed. Such cells, called **fuel cells,** are voltaic cells in which a fuel substance undergoes oxidation and from which electrical energy is continuously obtained. Fuel cells do not have to be recharged. They can be designed to emit no air pollutants and to operate more quietly and more cost-effectively than a conventional electrical generator.

Perhaps the simplest fuel cell involves the reaction of hydrogen gas and oxygen gas. The only product of the reaction is liquid water. In the hydrogen–oxygen fuel cell shown in Figure 21.7a, there are three compartments separated from one another by two electrodes. The electrodes are usually made of carbon. Oxygen (the oxidizing agent) from the air flows into the cathode compartment. Hydrogen (the fuel) flows into the anode compartment. The anode and cathode are separated by a thin membrane that allows hydrogen ions to pass through but not electrons. The membrane therefore acts as a salt bridge. Electrons from the oxidation half-reaction at the anode pass through an external circuit to enter the reduction half-reaction at the cathode.

The half-reactions in this type of hydrogen–oxygen fuel cell are as follows:

Oxidation: $2H_2(g) \longrightarrow 4H^+(aq) + 4e^-$ (at anode)

Reduction: $O_2(g) + 4H^+(aq) + 4e^- \longrightarrow 2H_2O(g)$ (at cathode)

The overall reaction is the oxidation of hydrogen to form water.

$$2H_2(g) + O_2(g) \longrightarrow 2H_2O(g)$$

Other fuels, such as methane (CH_4) and ammonia (NH_3), can be used in place of hydrogen. Other oxidizing agents, such as chlorine (Cl_2) and ozone (O_3), can be used in place of oxygen.

Since the 1960s, astronauts have used fuel cells as an energy source aboard spacecraft. Hydrogen–oxygen fuel cells with a mass of approximately 100 kg each were used in the Apollo spacecraft missions. Fuel cells are well suited for extended space missions because they offer a continuous energy source that releases no pollutants. On space shuttle missions, for example, astronauts drink the water produced by onboard hydrogen–oxygen fuel cells.

The use of fuel cells is no longer limited to space travel. Scientists and engineers have developed fuel-cell cars. These vehicles, such as the one shown in Figure 21.7b, are propelled by electric motors, which are powered by fuel cells. Fuel-cell vehicles can be fueled with pure hydrogen gas, which is stored in high-pressure tanks. However, more research and development is needed before fuel-cell vehicles will predominate the roadways. Currently, fuel cells are expensive to make, and it is difficult to store hydrogen. Nevertheless, you may soon be seeing fuel-cell cars, buses, and bicycles. You may even one day own a cellphone or laptop that is powered by a miniature fuel cell.

Figure 21.7 Hydrogen–Oxygen Fuel Cell
The hydrogen–oxygen fuel cell is a clean source of power. **a.** The membrane allows $H^+(aq)$ ions produced by the oxidation of $H_2(g)$ at the anode to migrate to the cathode, where $H_2O(g)$ is formed. **b.** Such cells can be used to fuel vehicles.

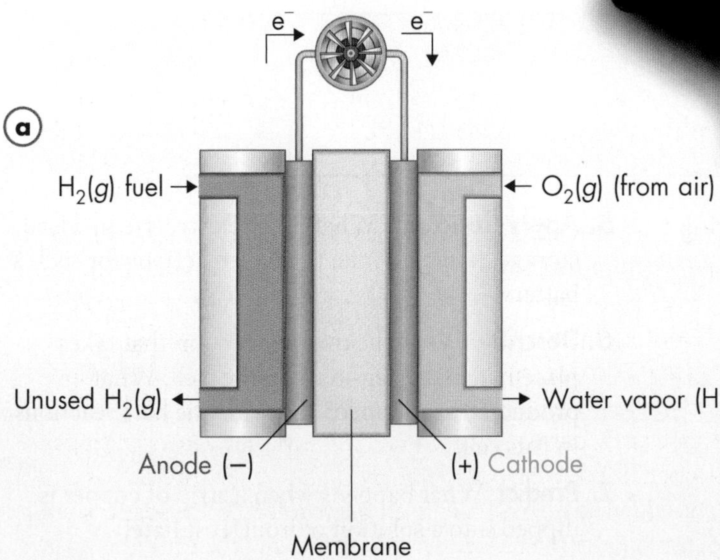

CHEMISTRY & YOU: HISTORY

Alessandro Volta

In the late 1770s, Italian physicist Alessandro Volta (1745–1827) discovered that contact between two different metals could produce electricity. Using this knowledge, Volta began experimenting with ways to produce a steady electric current. In 1799, he built a stack of alternating zinc and copper discs, separated by pasteboard soaked in saltwater. When he connected a wire to both ends of the pile, a steady current flowed. This device, called the "voltaic pile," was the first battery.

Volta found that different types of metals could change the amount of current produced and that he could increase the current by adding disks to the stack. Later, he improved on the pile by creating a "crown of cups"— separate cups of salt solution linked by metal straps. In 1810, Napoleon Bonaparte gave Volta the title of Count in honor of his work, and in 1881 the unit of electrical potential was named the "volt" in Volta's honor.

THE BATTERY REINVENTED Modern batteries look much different from Volta's alternating zinc and copper discs.

Take It Further

1. Explain What was the function of the pasteboard soaked in saltwater in Volta's battery?

2. Infer What is one possible reason why Volta's "crown of cups" would generate more current than a "voltaic pile"?

21.1 LessonCheck

1. Identify What type of reaction occurs during an electrochemical process?

2. Describe What is the source of electrical energy produced in a voltaic cell?

3. List What are three examples of technologies that use electrochemical processes to supply electrical energy?

4. Compare Which metal is more easily oxidized, lead or calcium?

5. Apply Concepts What is the electrolyte in a lead storage battery? Write the half-reactions for such a battery.

6. Describe Write the overall reaction that takes place in a hydrogen–oxygen fuel cell. What product(s) are formed? Describe the half-reactions in this cell.

7. Predict What happens when a strip of copper is dipped into a solution of iron(II) sulfate?

736 Chapter 21 • Lesson 1

21.2 Half-Cells and Cell Potentials

CHEMISTRY & YOU

Q: *How can you calculate the electrical potential of a cell in a laptop battery?* Batteries provide current to power lights and many kinds of electronic devices—such as the laptop shown here. The electrical potential between the negative and positive terminals of a lithium laptop battery is 3.7 V. In this lesson, you will learn how to calculate electrical potential.

Key Questions

▣ What causes the electrical potential of an electrochemical cell?

▣ How can you determine the standard reduction potential of a half-cell?

▣ How can you determine if a redox reaction is spontaneous?

Vocabulary

• electrical potential
• reduction potential
• cell potential
• standard cell potential
• standard hydrogen electrode

Electrical Potential

▣ **What causes the electrical potential of an electrochemical cell?**

The **electrical potential** of a voltaic cell is a measure of the cell's ability to produce an electric current. Electrical potential is usually measured in volts (V). The potential of an isolated half-cell cannot be measured. For example, you cannot measure the electrical potential of a zinc half-cell or of a copper half-cell separately. When these two half-cells are connected to form a voltaic cell, however, the difference in potential can be measured.

▣ **The electrical potential of a cell results from a competition for electrons between two half-cells.** The half-cell that has a greater tendency to acquire electrons is the one in which reduction occurs. Oxidation occurs in the other half-cell. The tendency of a given half-reaction to occur as a reduction is called the **reduction potential.** The half-cell in which reduction occurs has a greater reduction potential than the half-cell in which oxidation occurs. The difference between the reduction potentials of the two half-cells is called the **cell potential.**

$$\text{cell potential} = \left(\begin{array}{c} \text{reduction potential} \\ \text{of half-cell in which} \\ \text{reduction occurs} \end{array} \right) - \left(\begin{array}{c} \text{reduction potential} \\ \text{of half-cell in which} \\ \text{oxidation occurs} \end{array} \right)$$

$$\text{or } E_{\text{cell}} = E_{\text{red}} - E_{\text{oxid}}$$

The **standard cell potential** (E_{cell}°) is the measured cell potential when the ion concentrations in the half-cells are $1M$, any gases are at a pressure of 101 kPa, and the temperature is 25°C. The symbols E_{red}° and E_{oxid}° represent the standard reduction potentials for the reduction and oxidation half-cells, respectively. The relationship between these values follows the general relationship for cell potential above.

$$E_{\text{cell}}^{\circ} = E_{\text{red}}^{\circ} - E_{\text{oxid}}^{\circ}$$

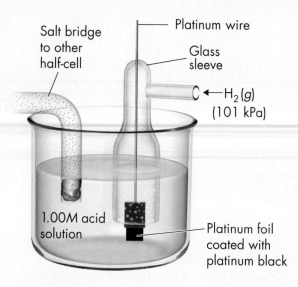

Figure 21.8 Standard Hydrogen Electrode
The standard hydrogen electrode is arbitrarily assigned a standard reduction potential of 0.00 V at 25°C.

Half-cell potentials cannot be measured directly, so scientists have chosen an arbitrary electrode to serve as a reference. The **standard hydrogen electrode** is used with other electrodes, so the reduction potentials of the other cells can be measured. The standard reduction potential of the hydrogen electrode has been assigned a value of 0.00 V. The standard hydrogen electrode, which is illustrated in Figure 21.8, consists of a platinum electrode immersed in a solution with a hydrogen-ion concentration of $1M$. The solution is at 25°C. The electrode itself is a small square of platinum foil coated with finely divided platinum, known as platinum black. Hydrogen gas at a pressure of 101 kPa is bubbled around the platinum electrode. The half-cell reaction that occurs at the platinum black surface is as follows:

$$2H^+(aq, 1M) + 2e^- \rightleftharpoons H_2(g, 101\text{ kPa}) \quad E^\circ_{H^+} = 0.00\text{ V}$$

The double arrows in the equation indicate that the reaction is reversible. The symbol $E^\circ_{H^+}$ represents the standard reduction potential of H^+. The standard reduction potential of H^+ is the tendency of H^+ ions to acquire electrons and be reduced to $H_2(g)$. Whether this half-cell reaction occurs as a reduction or as an oxidation is determined by the reduction potential of the half-cell to which the standard hydrogen electrode is connected.

Standard Reduction Potentials

🔑 How can you determine the standard reduction potential of a half-cell?

A voltaic cell can be made by connecting a standard hydrogen half-cell to a standard zinc half-cell, as shown in Figure 21.9. To determine the overall reaction for this cell, first identify the half-cell in which reduction takes place. In all electrochemical cells, reduction takes place at the cathode, and oxidation takes place at the anode. A voltmeter gives a reading of +0.76 V when the zinc electrode is connected to the negative terminal and the hydrogen electrode is connected to the positive terminal. The zinc is oxidized, which means that it is the anode. Hydrogen ions are reduced, which means that the hydrogen electrode is the cathode. You can now write the half-reactions and the overall cell reaction.

Oxidation: $\quad Zn(s) \longrightarrow Zn^{2+}(aq) + 2e^-$ (at anode)

Reduction: $\quad 2H^+(aq) + 2e^- \longrightarrow H_2(g)$ (at cathode)

Cell reaction: $\overline{Zn(s) + 2H^+(aq) \longrightarrow Zn^{2+}(aq) + H_2(g)}$

🔑 **You can determine the standard reduction potential of a half-cell by using a standard hydrogen electrode and the equation for standard cell potential.** In the zinc–hydrogen cell, zinc is oxidized and hydrogen ions are reduced. Let $E^\circ_{red} = E^\circ_{H^+}$ and $E^\circ_{oxid} = E^\circ_{Zn^{2+}}$ in the standard cell potential equation.

$$E^\circ_{cell} = E^\circ_{red} - E^\circ_{oxid}$$
$$E^\circ_{cell} = E^\circ_{H^+} - E^\circ_{Zn^{2+}}$$

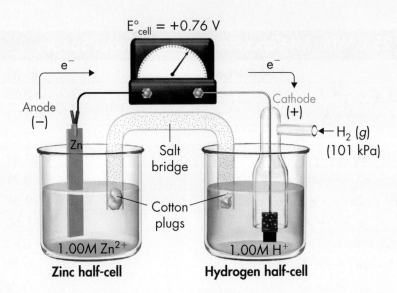

$$E^{\circ}_{cell} = +0.76 \text{ V}$$

e⁻

Anode
(−)

Zn

Salt bridge

Cotton plugs

1.00M Zn²⁺

Zinc half-cell

e⁻

Cathode
(+)

H₂ (g)
(101 kPa)

1.00M H⁺

Hydrogen half-cell

Figure 21.9 Zinc–Hydrogen Cell
This voltaic cell consists of zinc and hydrogen half-cells.
Interpret Diagrams *Where does reduction occur? What species is reduced in this cell?*

The cell potential (E°_{cell}) is measured at +0.76 V. The reduction potential of the hydrogen half-cell is a defined standard: $E^{\circ}_{H^+}$ always equals 0.00 V. Substituting these values into the preceding equation will give the standard reduction potential for the zinc half-cell.

$$+0.76 \text{ V} = 0.00 \text{ V} - E^{\circ}_{Zn^{2+}}$$

$$E^{\circ}_{Zn^{2+}} = -0.76 \text{ V}$$

The standard reduction potential for the zinc half-cell is −0.76 V. The value is negative because the tendency of zinc ions to be reduced to zinc metal in this cell is less than the tendency of hydrogen ions to be reduced to hydrogen gas.

Many different half-cells can be paired with the hydrogen half-cell in a similar manner. Using this method, the standard reduction potential for each half-cell can be obtained. For a standard copper half-cell, for example, the measured standard cell potential is +0.34 V when the copper electrode is connected to the positive electrode and the hydrogen electrode is connected to the negative terminal. Copper is the cathode, and copper ions are reduced to copper metal when the cell operates. The hydrogen half-cell is the anode, and hydrogen gas is oxidized to hydrogen ions. You can calculate the standard reduction potential for copper as follows:

$$E^{\circ}_{cell} = E^{\circ}_{red} - E^{\circ}_{oxid}$$

$$E^{\circ}_{cell} = E^{\circ}_{Cu^{2+}} - E^{\circ}_{H^+}$$

$$+0.34 \text{ V} = E^{\circ}_{Cu^{2+}} - 0.00 \text{ V}$$

$$E^{\circ}_{Cu^{2+}} = +0.34 \text{ V}$$

This value is positive because the tendency for copper ions to be reduced in the cell is greater than the tendency of hydrogen ions to be reduced.

Table 21.2 on the following page lists some standard reduction potentials at 25°C. The half-reactions are arranged in increasing order of their tendency to occur in the forward direction—that is, as a reduction. Thus, the half-reactions at the top of the table have the least tendency to occur as reductions. The half-reactions at the bottom of the table have the greatest tendency to occur as reductions.

CHEMISTRY & YOU

Q: *What do you need to know to calculate the electrical potential of a cell in a laptop battery?*

Table 21.2

Reduction Potentials at 25°C With 1M Concentrations of Aqueous Species

	Electrode	Half-reaction	$E°$ (V)
Least tendency to occur as a reduction	Li^+/Li	$Li^+ + e^- \longrightarrow Li$	−3.05
	K^+/K	$K^+ + e^- \longrightarrow K$	−2.93
	Ba^{2+}/Ba	$Ba^{2+} + 2e^- \longrightarrow Ba$	−2.90
	Ca^{2+}/Ca	$Ca^{2+} + 2e^- \longrightarrow Ca$	−2.87
	Na^+/Na	$Na^+ + e^- \longrightarrow Na$	−2.71
	Mg^{2+}/Mg	$Mg^{2+} + 2e^- \longrightarrow Mg$	−2.37
	Al^{3+}/Al	$Al^{3+} + 3e^- \longrightarrow Al$	−1.66
	H_2O/H_2	$2H_2O + 2e^- \longrightarrow H_2 + 2OH^-$	−0.83
	Zn^{2+}/Zn	$Zn^{2+} + 2e^- \longrightarrow Zn$	−0.76
	Cr^{3+}/Cr	$Cr^{3+} + 3e^- \longrightarrow Cr$	−0.74
	Fe^{2+}/Fe	$Fe^{2+} + 2e^- \longrightarrow Fe$	−0.44
	H_2O/H_2 (pH 7)	$2H_2O + 2e^- \longrightarrow H_2 + 2OH^-$	−0.42
	Cd^{2+}/Cd	$Cd^{2+} + 2e^- \longrightarrow Cd$	−0.40
	$PbSO_4/Pb$	$PbSO_4 + 2e^- \longrightarrow Pb + SO_4^{2-}$	−0.36
	Co^{2+}/Co	$Co^{2+} + 2e^- \longrightarrow Co$	−0.28
	Ni^{2+}/Ni	$Ni^{2+} + 2e^- \longrightarrow Ni$	−0.25
	Sn^{2+}/Sn	$Sn^{2+} + 2e^- \longrightarrow Sn$	−0.14
	Pb^{2+}/Pb	$Pb^{2+} + 2e^- \longrightarrow Pb$	−0.13
	Fe^{3+}/Fe	$Fe^{3+} + 3e^- \longrightarrow Fe$	−0.036
	H^+/H_2	$2H^+ + 2e^- \longrightarrow H_2$	0.000
	$AgCl/Ag$	$AgCl + e^- \longrightarrow Ag + Cl^-$	+0.22
	Hg_2Cl_2/Hg	$Hg_2Cl_2 + 2e^- \longrightarrow 2Hg + 2Cl^-$	+0.27
	Cu^{2+}/Cu	$Cu^{2+} + 2e^- \longrightarrow Cu$	+0.34
	O_2/OH^-	$O_2 + 2H_2O + 4e^- \longrightarrow 4OH^-$	+0.40
	Cu^+/Cu	$Cu^+ + e^- \longrightarrow Cu$	+0.52
	I_2/I^-	$I_2 + 2e^- \longrightarrow 2I^-$	+0.54
	Fe^{3+}/Fe^{2+}	$Fe^{3+} + e^- \longrightarrow Fe^{2+}$	+0.77
	Hg_2^{2+}/Hg	$Hg_2^{2+} + 2e^- \longrightarrow 2Hg$	+0.79
	Ag^+/Ag	$Ag^+ + e^- \longrightarrow Ag$	+0.80
	O_2/H_2O (pH 7)	$O_2 + 4H^+ + 4e^- \longrightarrow 2H_2O$	+0.82
	Hg^{2+}/Hg	$Hg^{2+} + 2e^- \longrightarrow Hg$	+0.85
	Br_2/Br^-	$Br_2 + 2e^- \longrightarrow 2Br^-$	+1.07
	O_2/H_2O	$O_2 + 4H^+ + 4e^- \longrightarrow 2H_2O$	+1.23
	MnO_2/Mn^{2+}	$MnO_2 + 4H^+ + 2e^- \longrightarrow Mn^{2+} + 2H_2O$	+1.28
	$Cr_2O_7^{2-}/Cr^{3+}$	$Cr_2O_7^{2-} + 14H^+ + 6e^- \longrightarrow 2Cr^{3+} + 7H_2O$	+1.33
	Cl_2/Cl^-	$Cl_2 + 2e^- \longrightarrow 2Cl^-$	+1.36
	PbO_2/Pb^{2+}	$PbO_2 + 4H^+ + 2e^- \longrightarrow Pb^{2+} + 2H_2O$	+1.46
	MnO_4^-/Mn^{2+}	$MnO_4^- + 8H^+ + 5e^- \longrightarrow Mn^{2+} + 4H_2O$	+1.51
Greatest tendency to occur as a reduction	$PbO_2/PbSO_4$	$PbO_2 + 4H^+ + SO_4^{2-} + 2e^- \longrightarrow PbSO_4 + 2H_2O$	+1.69
	F_2/F^-	$F_2 + 2e^- \longrightarrow 2F^-$	+2.87

Increasing tendency to occur as a reduction (stronger oxidizing agent)

Calculating Standard Cell Potentials

> How can you determine if a redox reaction is spontaneous?

In an electrochemical cell, the half-cell reaction having the more positive (or less negative) reduction potential occurs as a reduction in the cell. You can use the known standard reduction potentials for the half-cells (from Table 21.2) to predict the half-cells in which reduction and oxidation will occur and to find the $E°_{cell}$ value without having to actually assemble the cell. **If the cell potential for a given redox reaction is positive, then the reaction is spontaneous as written. If the cell potential is negative, then the reaction is non-spontaneous.** This latter reaction will be spontaneous in the reverse direction, and the cell potential will then have a numerically equal but positive value.

Sample Problem 21.1

Determining Reaction Spontaneity

Show that the following redox reaction between zinc metal and silver ions is spontaneous.

$$Zn(s) + 2Ag^+(aq) \longrightarrow Zn^{2+}(aq) + 2Ag(s)$$

❶ Analyze List the knowns and the unknown. Identify the half-reactions, and calculate the standard cell potential ($E°_{cell} = E°_{red} - E°_{oxid}$). If $E°_{cell}$ is positive, the reaction is spontaneous.

KNOWNS

cell reaction: $Zn(s) + 2Ag^+(aq) \longrightarrow Zn^{2+}(aq) + 2Ag(s)$

UNKNOWN

Is the reaction spontaneous?

❷ Calculate Solve for the unknown.

First, identify the half-reactions.

Oxidation: $Zn(s) \longrightarrow Zn^{2+}(aq) + 2e^-$

Reduction: $Ag^+(aq) + e^- \longrightarrow Ag(s)$

Write both half-cells as reductions with their standard reduction potentials.

$Zn^{2+}(aq) + 2e^- \longrightarrow Zn(s)$ $\quad E°_{Zn^{2+}} = -0.76\ V$

$Ag^+(aq) + e^- \longrightarrow Ag(s)$ $\quad E°_{Ag^+} = +0.80\ V$

Calculate the standard cell potential.

$E°_{cell} = E°_{red} - E°_{oxid} = E°_{Ag^+} - E°_{Zn^{2+}}$

$= +0.80\ V - (-0.76\ V) = +1.56\ V$

$E°_{cell} > 0$, so the reaction is spontaneous.

❸ Evaluate Does the result make sense? Zinc is above silver in the activity series for metals. It makes sense that zinc is oxidized in the presence of silver ions.

Use Table 21.2 to look up the standard reduction potentials for the half-cells.

---

8. Determine whether the following redox reaction will occur spontaneously:

$3Zn^{2+}(aq) + 2Cr(s) \longrightarrow 3Zn(s) + 2Cr^{3+}(aq)$

9. Is this redox reaction spontaneous as written?

$Co^{2+}(aq) + Fe(s) \longrightarrow Fe^{2+}(aq) + Co(s)$

SampleProblem 21.2

Writing the Cell Reaction

Determine the cell reaction for a voltaic cell composed of the following half-cells:

$$Fe^{3+}(aq) + e^- \longrightarrow Fe^{2+}(aq) \quad E^\circ_{Fe^{3+}} = +0.77 \text{ V}$$

$$Ni^{2+}(aq) + 2e^- \longrightarrow Ni(s) \quad E^\circ_{Ni^{2+}} = -0.25 \text{ V}$$

❶ **Analyze** **Identify the relevant concepts.** The half-cell with the more positive reduction potential is the one in which reduction occurs (the cathode). The oxidation reaction occurs at the anode. Add the half-reactions, making certain that the number of electrons lost equals the number of electrons gained.

❷ **Solve** **Apply the concepts to this problem.**

| First, identify the cathode and the anode. | The Fe^{3+} half-cell has the more positive reduction potential, so it is the cathode. The Ni^{2+} half-cell has the more negative reduction potential, so it is the anode. In this voltaic cell, Fe^{3+} is reduced and Ni is oxidized. |

Write the half-cell reactions in the direction in which they actually occur.

Oxidation: $Ni(s) \longrightarrow Ni^{2+}(aq) + 2e^-$ (at anode)

Reduction: $Fe^{3+}(aq) + e^- \longrightarrow Fe^{2+}(aq)$ (at cathode)

If necessary, multiply the half-reactions by the appropriate factor(s) so that the electrons cancel when the half-reactions are added.

$$Ni(s) \longrightarrow Ni^{2+}(aq) + 2e^-$$
$$2[Fe^{3+}(aq) + e^- \longrightarrow Fe^{2+}(aq)]$$

Multiply the Fe^{3+} half-cell equation by 2 so that the number of electrons are present in equal numbers on both sides of the equation.

Add the half-reactions.

$$Ni(s) \longrightarrow Ni^{2+}(aq) + 2e^-$$
$$2Fe^{3+}(aq) + 2e^- \longrightarrow 2Fe^{2+}(aq)$$
$$Ni(s) + 2Fe^{3+}(aq) \longrightarrow Ni^{2+}(aq) + 2Fe^{2+}(aq)$$

The electrons lost by the species that is oxidized must be equal to the electrons gained by the species that is reduced.

The half-cell with the more positive reduction potential is the cathode.

10. A voltaic cell is constructed using the following half-reactions:

$$Cu^{2+}(aq) + 2e^- \longrightarrow Cu(s)$$
$$E^\circ_{Cu^{2+}} = +0.34 \text{ V}$$
$$Al^{3+}(aq) + 3e^- \longrightarrow Al(s)$$
$$E^\circ_{Al^{3+}} = -1.66 \text{ V}$$

Determine the cell reaction.

11. A voltaic cell is constructed using the following half-reactions:

$$Ag^+(aq) + e^- \longrightarrow Ag(s)$$
$$E^\circ_{Ag^+} = +0.80 \text{ V}$$
$$Cu^{2+}(aq) + 2e^- \longrightarrow Cu(s)$$
$$E^\circ_{Cu^{2+}} = +0.34 \text{ V}$$

Determine the cell reaction.

Calculating the Standard Cell Potential

Calculate the standard cell potential for the voltaic cell described in Sample Problem 21.2. The half-reactions are as follows:

$$Fe^{3+}(aq) + e^- \longrightarrow Fe^{2+}(aq) \quad E^\circ_{Fe^{3+}} = +0.77 \text{ V}$$

$$Ni^{2+}(aq) + 2e^- \longrightarrow Ni(s) \quad E^\circ_{Ni^{2+}} = -0.25 \text{ V}$$

① Analyze List the knowns and the unknown. Use the equation $E^\circ_{cell} = E^\circ_{red} - E^\circ_{oxid}$ to calculate the standard cell potential.

KNOWNS	UNKNOWN
$E^\circ_{Fe^{3+}} = +0.77$ V	$E^\circ_{cell} = ?$
$E^\circ_{Ni^{2+}} = -0.25$ V	
anode: Ni^{2+} half-cell	
cathode: Fe^{3+} half-cell	

② Calculate Solve for the unknown.

First, write the equation for the standard cell potential.

$$E^\circ_{cell} = E^\circ_{red} - E^\circ_{oxid} = E^\circ_{Fe^{3+}} - E^\circ_{Ni^{2+}}$$

Substitute the values for the standard reduction potentials and solve the equation.

$$E^\circ_{cell} = +0.77 \text{ V} - (-0.25 \text{ V}) = +1.02 \text{ V}$$

③ Evaluate Does the result make sense? The reduction potential of the reduction is positive, and the reduction potential of the oxidation is negative. Therefore, E°_{cell} must be positive.

12. Calculate the standard cell potential of a voltaic cell constructed using the half-reactions described in Problem 10.

If you did Problem 10, you know what the anode and cathode are in this cell.

13. Calculate the standard cell potential of a voltaic cell constructed using the half-reactions described in Problem 11.

If you did Problem 11, you know what the anode and cathode are in this cell.

⊚ 21.2 LessonCheck

14. 🔑 **Explain** What causes the electrical potential of a cell?

15. 🔑 **Describe** How can you find the standard reduction potential of a half-cell?

16. 🔑 **Review** What cell potential values indicate a spontaneous reaction? What cell potential values indicate a nonspontaneous reaction?

17. Calculate Determine whether the following redox reaction will occur spontaneously:

$$2Al^{3+}(aq) + 3Mg(s) \longrightarrow 2Al(s) + 3Mg^{2+}(aq)$$

18. Calculate Determine the cell reaction and standard cell potential for a voltaic cell composed of the following half-cells:

$$Li^+(aq) + e^- \longrightarrow Li(s) \quad E^\circ_{Li^+} = -3.05 \text{ V}$$

$$Mg^{2+}(aq) + 2e^- \longrightarrow Mg(s) \quad E^\circ_{Mg^{2+}} = -2.37 \text{ V}$$

BIGIDEA MATTER AND ENERGY

19. Why does a lead-acid battery produce energy? Calculate the standard cell potential of one voltaic cell in a lead-acid battery.

A Lemon Battery

Batteries provide power to many of the electronic devices you may use in your daily life, including laptops, cellphones, and mp3 players. Batteries come in all different shapes and sizes, from the large 12-V battery in cars, to the AAA batteries in calculators, to the tiny batteries in watches.

A battery is essentially a container that contains an anode, where oxidation occurs, a cathode, where reduction occurs, and an electrolyte. Electrons flow from the anode to the cathode through an external circuit, which is usually the device to which the battery is supplying energy. Positive and negative ions move through the electrolyte to complete the circuit.

Did you know that you can make a battery at home with only nails or wires and fruit? Try this activity at home and see how much of a voltage you can generate.

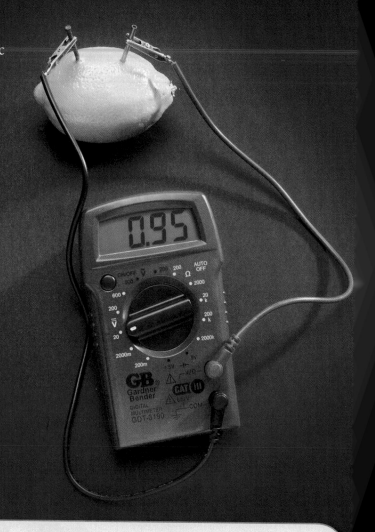

On Your Own

1. For this activity, you will need a **copper nail, screw, or wire** (about 5 cm long) and a **zinc or galvanized nail or screw** (about 5 cm long). These will serve as your electrodes. You will also need a **whole lemon** and a **multimeter** set to measure voltage (if you have one). Clean the electrodes with hot, soapy water, rinse, and dry them. Soften the lemon by rolling it on a table. Be careful not to break the skin.

2. Insert the zinc and copper electrodes into the lemon. The electrodes should not touch and should be about 2–3 cm apart.

3. Briefly touch both electrodes at the same time with your tongue and observe what happens.

4. Measure the voltage of your lemon battery with the multimeter. Attach the positive (red) lead to the copper electrode and the negative (black) lead to the zinc electrode.

Think About It

1. Observe Describe the sensation you felt on your tongue.

2. Measure What was the voltage of your battery? What would happen if you attached the positive lead of the multimeter to the zinc electrode and the negative lead to the copper electrode?

3. Predict Could you generate enough voltage to start a car if you connected 12 lemon batteries together in series? Explain.

21.3 Electrolytic Cells

Q: *How can an aluminum bottle be colored?* You probably know that aluminum is a metal that is silver in color. How then can objects made from aluminum be colored? If an aluminum object has a color other than silver, it was anodized before it was dyed. In the anodizing process, the aluminum object is the anode in an electrolytic cell. The electrolyte is a dilute acid. When an electric current flows through the cell, aluminum oxide forms on the surface of the aluminum. In this lesson, you will learn about electrochemical processes that require electrical energy.

Key Questions

🔑 How do voltaic and electrolytic cells differ?

🔑 What are some applications that use electrolytic cells?

Vocabulary

• electrolysis
• electrolytic cell

Electrolytic vs. Voltaic Cells

🔑 **How do voltaic and electrolytic cells differ?**

In Lesson 21.1, you learned how a spontaneous chemical reaction can be used to generate a flow of electrons (an electric current). In this lesson, you will learn how an electric current can be used to make a nonspontaneous redox reaction occur. The process in which electrical energy is used to bring about such a chemical change is called **electrolysis.** Although you may not have realized it, you are already familiar with some results of electrolysis, such as gold-plated jewelry and chrome-plated automobile parts. Figure 21.10 shows some silver-plated dishes.

The apparatus in which electrolysis is carried out is an electrolytic cell. An **electrolytic cell** is an electrochemical cell used to cause a chemical change through the application of electrical energy. An electrolytic cell uses electrical energy (direct current) to make a nonspontaneous redox reaction proceed to completion.

Figure 21.10
Products of Electrolysis
Pure silver can be plated onto steel using electrolysis.

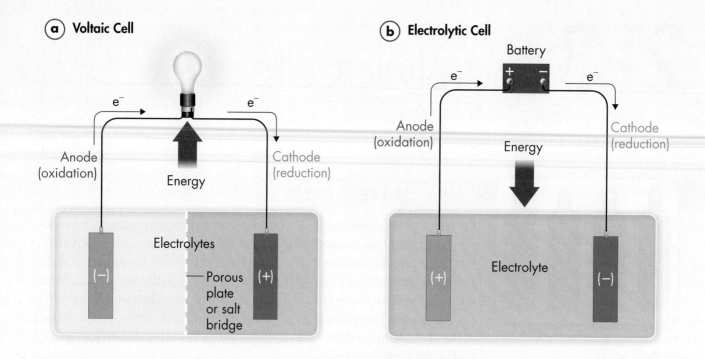

(a) Voltaic Cell

Anode (oxidation)

Energy

Cathode (reduction)

Electrolytes

(−)

(+)

Porous plate or salt bridge

(b) Electrolytic Cell

Battery

Anode (oxidation)

Energy

Cathode (reduction)

Electrolyte

(+)

(−)

Figure 21.11 Voltaic and Electrolytic Cells
Electrochemical cells can be classified as voltaic or electrolytic. **a.** In a voltaic cell, energy is released from a spontaneous redox reaction. The system (cell) does work on the surroundings (light bulb). **b.** In an electrolytic cell, energy is absorbed to drive a nonspontaneous reaction. The surroundings (battery or power supply) do work on the system (cell).

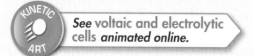

See voltaic and electrolytic cells **animated online.**

In both voltaic and electrolytic cells, electrons flow from the anode to the cathode in the external circuit. As shown in Figure 21.11, for both types of cells, the electrode at which reduction occurs is the cathode. The electrode at which oxidation occurs is the anode.

The key difference between voltaic and electrolytic cells is that in a voltaic cell, the flow of electrons is the result of a spontaneous redox reaction, whereas in an electrolytic cell, electrons are caused to flow by an outside power source, such as a battery. The redox process in the voltaic cell is spontaneous; in the electrolytic cell, the redox process is nonspontaneous. Electrolytic and voltaic cells also differ in the assignment of charge to the electrodes. In a voltaic cell, the anode is the negative electrode and the cathode is the positive electrode. In an electrolytic cell, the cathode is considered to be the negative electrode because it is connected to the negative electrode of the battery. The anode in the electrolytic cell is considered to be the positive electrode because it is connected to the positive electrode of the battery. It is important to remember these conventions about the two kinds of cells.

Driving Nonspontaneous Processes

What are some applications that use electrolytic cells?

Electrolysis can be used to drive otherwise nonspontaneous reactions that are of commercial importance. **Electrolysis of a solution or of a melted, or molten, ionic compound can result in the separation of elements from compounds. Electrolytic cells are also commonly used in the plating, purifying, and refining of metals.**

Electrolysis of Water When a current is applied to two electrodes immersed in pure water, nothing happens. There is no current flow and no electrolysis. However, when an electrolyte such as H_2SO_4 or KNO_3 in low concentration is added to the pure water, the solution conducts an electric current and electrolysis occurs. This process is illustrated in Figure 21.12. The products of the electrolysis of water are hydrogen gas and oxygen gas. This process is sometimes used to produce hydrogen gas for fuel cells.

Water is oxidized at the anode according to the following oxidation half-reaction:

Oxidation: $2H_2O(l) \longrightarrow O_2(g) + 4H^+(aq) + 4e^-$ (at anode)

Water is reduced to hydrogen at the cathode according to the following reduction half-reaction:

Reduction: $2H_2O(l) + 2e^- \longrightarrow H_2(g) + 2OH^-(aq)$ (at cathode)

The region around the anode turns acidic due to an increase in H^+ ions. The region around the cathode turns basic due to the production of OH^- ions. The overall cell reaction is obtained by adding the half-reactions (after doubling the reduction half-reaction equation to balance electrons).

$$
\begin{array}{rl}
\text{Oxidation:} & 2H_2O(l) \longrightarrow O_2(g) + 4H^+(aq) + 4e^- \\
\text{Reduction:} & 2[2H_2O(l) + 2e^- \longrightarrow H_2(g) + 2OH^-(aq)] \\
\hline
\text{Overall cell reaction:} & 6H_2O(l) \longrightarrow 2H_2(g) + O_2(g) + \\
& 4H^+(aq) + 4OH^-(aq)
\end{array}
$$

The ions produced tend to recombine to form water.

$$4H^+(aq) + 4OH^-(aq) \longrightarrow 4H_2O(l)$$

Therefore, the net reaction can be written as follows:

$$2H_2O(l) \longrightarrow 2H_2(g) + O_2(g)$$

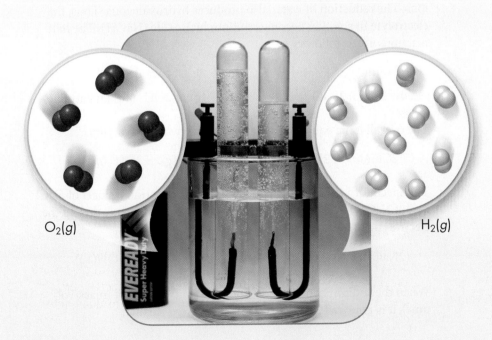

$O_2(g)$

$H_2(g)$

Figure 21.12 Electrolysis of Water
When an electric current is passed through water, the water decomposes into oxygen gas and hydrogen gas.
Interpret Photos *Which electrode in the photograph is the cathode? Which is the anode?*

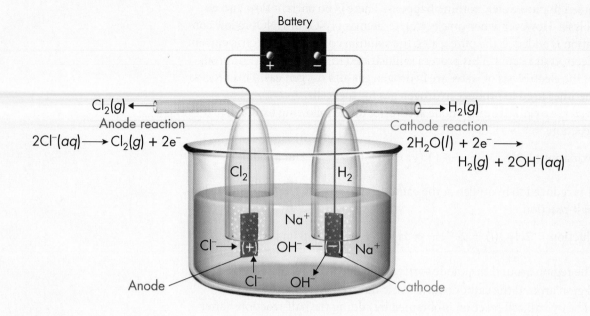

Battery

$Cl_2(g)$ ←
Anode reaction
$2Cl^-(aq) \longrightarrow Cl_2(g) + 2e^-$

→ $H_2(g)$
Cathode reaction
$2H_2O(l) + 2e^- \longrightarrow$
$H_2(g) + 2OH^-(aq)$

Cl_2 H_2

Na^+

$Cl^- \rightarrow$ (+) $OH^- \leftarrow$ (−) Na^+

Anode Cl^- OH^- Cathode

Figure 21.13 Electrolysis of Brine
Chlorine gas, hydrogen gas, and sodium hydroxide are produced when an electric current is passed through an aqueous solution of sodium chloride.
Interpret Diagrams *Which substances are produced by oxidation? Which substances are produced by reduction?*

Electrolysis of Brine If the electrolyte in an aqueous solution is more easily oxidized or reduced than water, then the products of electrolysis will be substances other than hydrogen and oxygen. An example is the electrolysis of brine, a concentrated aqueous solution of sodium chloride. This process simultaneously produces three important industrial chemicals: chlorine gas, hydrogen gas, and sodium hydroxide. The electrolytic cell for the electrolysis of brine is shown in Figure 21.13.

During electrolysis of brine, chloride ions are oxidized to produce chlorine gas at the anode. Water is reduced to produce hydrogen gas at the cathode. Sodium ions are not reduced to sodium metal in the process because water molecules are more easily reduced than are sodium ions. The reduction of water also produces hydroxide ions. Thus, the electrolyte in solution becomes sodium hydroxide (NaOH). The half-reactions are as follows:

Oxidation: $2Cl^-(aq) \longrightarrow Cl_2(g) + 2e^-$ (at anode)

Reduction: $2H_2O(l) + 2e^- \longrightarrow H_2(g) + 2OH^-(aq)$ (at cathode)

The overall ionic equation is the sum of the two half-reactions.

$$2Cl^-(aq) + 2H_2O(l) \longrightarrow Cl_2(g) + H_2(g) + 2OH^-(aq)$$

The spectator ion Na^+ can be included in the equation (as part of NaCl and of NaOH) to show the formation of sodium hydroxide during the electrolytic process.

$$2NaCl(aq) + 2H_2O(l) \longrightarrow Cl_2(g) + H_2(g) + 2NaOH(aq)$$

When the sodium hydroxide solution is about 10 percent (mass/volume), it is removed from the cell and processed further.

Electrolysis of Molten Sodium Chloride Both sodium and chlorine are commercially important. Sodium is used in sodium vapor lamps and as the coolant in some nuclear reactors. Chlorine, a greenish-yellow gas, is used to sterilize drinking water and is important in the manufacture of polyvinyl chloride (PVC) and various pesticides. These two elements are produced through the electrolysis of pure molten sodium chloride, rather than an aqueous solution of NaCl. Chlorine gas is produced at the anode, and molten sodium collects at the cathode. The half-reactions for the electrolysis of molten sodium chloride are as follows:

Oxidation: $2Cl^-(l) \longrightarrow Cl_2(g) + 2e^-$ (at anode)

Reduction: $2Na^+(l) + 2e^- \longrightarrow 2Na(l)$ (at cathode)

The overall equation is the sum of the two half-reactions.

$$2NaCl(l) \longrightarrow 2Na(l) + Cl_2(g)$$

The electrolytic cell in which this commercial process is carried out is called the Downs cell and is shown in Figure 21.14. The cell operates at a temperature of 801°C so that the sodium chloride is maintained in the molten state. A perforated iron screen separates the circular cathode from the graphite anode. The sodium, with a melting point of 97.8°C, remains in liquid form. The liquid sodium floats on the more dense molten sodium chloride and is drawn off as it is formed. The chlorine gas is collected after it bubbles up and out of the molten salt. The design of the Downs cell allows fresh sodium chloride to be added as required. The design also separates the products so they will not recombine to re-form sodium chloride.

Figure 21.14 Downs Cell
The Downs cell produces sodium metal and chlorine gas from the electrolysis of molten sodium chloride.

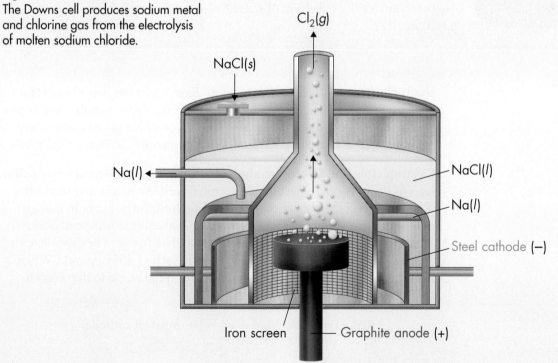

$Cl_2(g)$

$NaCl(s)$

$Na(l)$

$NaCl(l)$

$Na(l)$

Steel cathode (−)

Iron screen — Graphite anode (+)

Quick Lab

Purpose To electrochemically oxidize metals and identify the products

Materials
- reaction surface
- aluminum foil
- filter paper
- micropipette or dropper
- sodium sulfate (Na_2SO_4) solution
- penny
- 9-volt battery
- nickel coin
- iron nail

Electrochemical Analysis of Metals

Procedure

1. Stack the following in order on a reaction surface: a 3-cm square of aluminum foil, a 2-cm square of filter paper, 1 drop of Na_2SO_4 solution, and a penny. The penny should be roughly centered on the filter paper, which should be roughly centered on the foil.

2. Apply the negative (−) terminal of the 9-volt battery to the aluminum foil and the positive (+) terminal to the penny for no more than three seconds.

3. Remove the penny and observe the filter paper.

4. Repeat Steps 1–3, replacing the penny with the nickel coin.

5. Repeat Steps 1–3, replacing the penny with the iron nail.

Analyze and Conclude

1. Observe What colors formed on the filter paper for each object?

2. Describe For each metal object you tested, the battery oxidized the metal atoms to form metal cations with a 2+ charge. Write a half-reaction for each metal oxidation you observed. Did these reactions take place at the anode or the cathode?

3. Relate Cause and Effect Explain in your own words why the colors formed on the filter paper.

4. Describe The aluminum foil serves as the cathode, where the reduction of water takes place. Write the half-reaction for the reduction of water.

5. Describe Combine the half-reaction for the oxidation of copper with the half-reaction for the reduction of water to form the overall equation for the cell reaction.

Using Electrolysis in Metal Processing Electrolysis has many important applications in the field of metallurgy. Many of the shiny, metallic objects you see every day—such as chrome-plated fixtures or nickel-plated coins—were manufactured with the help of electrolytic processes.

Electroplating and Electroforming Electroplating is the deposition of a thin layer of a metal on an object in an electrolytic cell. An object may be electroplated to protect the surface of the base metal from corrosion or to make it more attractive. An object that is to be silver-plated is made the cathode in an electrolytic cell. The anode is the metallic silver that is to be deposited, and the electrolyte is a solution of a silver salt, such as silver cyanide. When a direct current is applied, silver ions move from the anode to the object to be plated.

$$\text{Reduction:} \quad Ag^+(aq) + e^- \longrightarrow Ag(s) \text{ (at cathode)}$$

The net result is that silver transfers from the silver anode to the object being plated. Figure 21.15 shows statuettes that were electroplated with copper, nickel, and 24-carat gold. Many factors contribute to the quality of the metal coating that forms. In the plating solution, the concentration of the cations to be reduced must be carefully controlled. The solution must also contain compounds to control the acidity and to increase the conductivity. Other compounds may be used to make the metal coating brighter or smoother.

Electroforming is a process in which an object is reproduced by making a metal mold of it at the cathode of a cell. For example, a mold of an object can be coated with metal so it will conduct a current. It is then electroplated with a thick coating of metal. This coating can then be stripped off of the mold. Electroforming is used to make jewelry and tubing for chemical instrumentation, such as gas chromatographs.

Electrowinning and Electrorefining In a process called electrowinning, impure metals can be purified in electrolytic cells. The cations of molten salts or aqueous solutions are reduced at the cathode to give very pure metals. A common use of electrowinning is in the extraction of aluminum from its ore, bauxite. Bauxite is impure alumina (Al_2O_3). In a method known as the Hall-Heroult process, purified alumina is dissolved in molten cryolite (Na_3AlF_6), and heated to above 1000°C in a carbon-lined tank. The carbon lining, connected to a direct current, serves as the cathode. The anode consists of carbon rods dipped into the tank. At the cathode, Al^{3+} ions are reduced, forming molten aluminum. At the anode, carbon is oxidized, forming carbon dioxide gas. The overall reaction is as follows:

$$2Al_2O_3(l) + 3C(s) \longrightarrow 4Al(l) + 3CO_2(g)$$

In the process of electrorefining, a piece of impure metal is made the anode of the cell. It is oxidized to the cation and then reduced to the pure metal at the cathode. This technique is used to obtain ultrapure silver, lead, and copper.

Other Processes Other electrolytic processes are centered on the anode rather than the cathode. In electropolishing, for example, the surface of an object at the anode is dissolved selectively to give it a high polish. In electromachining, a piece of metal at the anode is partially dissolved until the remaining portion is an exact copy of the object at the cathode.

Figure 21.15 Electroplating
Copper, nickel, and gold were electroplated onto pewter to produce these statuettes.

CHEMISTRY & YOU

Q: *In the process of anodizing aluminum, the aluminum object serves as the anode. To which electrode of the power source is the anode connected?*

21.3 LessonCheck

20. ▣ **Describe** What is the difference between an electrolytic cell and a voltaic cell?

21. ▣ **List** What are some applications of electrolytic cells?

22. Compare What is the charge on the anode of an electrolytic cell? What is the charge on the anode of a voltaic cell?

23. Apply Concepts Which process, oxidation or reduction, always occurs at the cathode of an electrolytic cell?

24. Explain Read about the Hall-Heroult process on page R13. Write the half-reactions for the electrolysis that takes place, and explain the function of cryolite in the process.

BIGIDEA MATTER AND ENERGY

25. Does the redox reaction in a voltaic cell release free energy? If no electrical energy is supplied, does the redox reaction in an electrolytic cell release free energy? Explain.

Small-Scale Lab

Electrolysis of Water

Purpose
To electrolyze solutions and interpret your observations in terms of chemical reactions and equations

Materials
- reaction surface • micropipettes or droppers
- electrolysis device • water
- sodium sulfate (Na_2SO_4) solution
- bromothymol blue (BTB) solution

Procedure

1. On separate sheets of paper, draw two grids similar to Figure A. Make each square 2 cm on each side.

2. Place a reaction surface over one of the grids and add one drop of each solution shown in Figure A.

3. Apply the leads of the electrolysis device to each solution. Be sure to clean the leads between each experiment. Look carefully at the cathode (negative lead) and the anode (positive lead).

4. Use the second grid as a data table to record your observations for each solution.

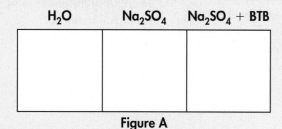

H_2O	Na_2SO_4	Na_2SO_4 + BTB

Figure A

Analyze and Conclude

1. Relate Cause and Effect Explain why pure water does not conduct an electric current and does not undergo electrolysis.

2. Relate Cause and Effect Explain why water with sodium sulfate conducts an electric current and undergoes electrolysis.

3. Analyze Data The cathode provides electrons to water, and the following half-reaction occurs:

$$2H_2O(l) + 2e^- \longrightarrow H_2(g) + 2OH^-(aq)$$

Explain how your observations correspond to the products shown in this reaction.

4. Analyze Data The anode removes electrons from water, and the following half-reaction occurs:

$$H_2O(l) \longrightarrow \tfrac{1}{2}O_2(g) + 2H^+(aq) + 2e^-$$

Explain how your observations correspond to the products shown in this reaction.

5. Summarize Add the two half-reactions to obtain the overall reaction for the electrolysis of water. Simplify the result by adding the OH^- and H^+ ions to get H_2O, and then canceling anything that appears on both sides of the equation.

You're the Chemist

1. Analyze Data Perform the above experiment using the solutions shown in Figure B. Record your results. The cathode and anode reactions are

$$2H_2O(l) + 2e^- \longrightarrow H_2(g) + 2OH^-(aq) \text{ (at cathode)}$$

$$2I^-(aq) \longrightarrow I_2(aq) + 2e^- \text{ (at anode)}$$

Explain how your observations correspond to the products shown in these half-reactions.

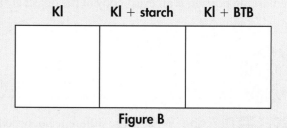

KI	KI + starch	KI + BTB

Figure B

2. Analyze Data For each half-reaction listed above, look up the $E°$ values in Table 21.2. Show that the $E°$ values are consistent with what you observe.

3. Design an Experiment Design an experiment to explore what happens when you electrolyze NaCl, KBr, and $CuSO_4$ with and without BTB. Write half-reactions to predict your results.

21 Study Guide

BIGIDEA MATTER AND ENERGY

The two types of electrochemical cells are voltaic cells and electrolytic cells. In a voltaic cell, electric current is produced by a spontaneous redox reaction. Voltaic cells are used in batteries and fuel cells. In an electrolytic cell, a nonspontaneous redox reaction is driven by the application of electrical energy. Electrolytic cells are used to produce commercially important chemicals and to plate, purify, and refine metals.

21.1 Electrochemical Cells

🔑 All electrochemical processes involve redox reactions.

🔑 Electrical energy is produced in a voltaic cell by a spontaneous redox reaction within the cell.

🔑 Current applications that use electrochemical processes to produce electrical energy include dry cells, lead storage batteries, and fuel cells.

- electrochemical process (728)
- electrochemical cell (730)
- voltaic cell (730)
- half-cell (730)
- salt bridge (730)
- electrode (730)
- anode (730)
- cathode (730)
- dry cell (732)
- battery (733)
- fuel cell (734)

21.2 Half-Cells and Cell Potentials

🔑 The electrical potential of a cell results from a competition for electrons between two half-cells.

🔑 You can determine the standard reduction potential of a half-cell by using a standard hydrogen electrode and the equation for standard cell potential.

🔑 If the cell potential for a given redox reaction is positive, then the reaction is spontaneous as written. If the cell potential is negative, then the reaction is nonspontaneous.

- electrical potential (737)
- reduction potential (737)
- cell potential (737)
- standard cell potential (737)
- standard hydrogen electrode (738)

Key Equation

$$E^\circ_{cell} = E^\circ_{red} - E^\circ_{oxid}$$

21.3 Electrolytic Cells

🔑 The key difference between voltaic and electrolytic cells is that in a voltaic cell, the flow of electrons is the result of a spontaneous redox reaction, whereas in an electrolytic cell, electrons are caused to flow by an outside power source, such as a battery.

🔑 Electrolysis of a solution or of a melted, or molten, ionic compound can result in the separation of elements from compounds. Electrolytic cells are also commonly used in the plating, purifying, and refining of metals.

- electrolysis (745)
- electrolytic cell (745)

ONLINE PROBLEMS

Lesson by Lesson

21.1 Electrochemical Cells

26. If the relative activities of two metals are known, which metal is more easily oxidized?

27. Write the half-reactions that occur when a strip of aluminum is dipped into a solution of copper(II) sulfate.

⋆**28.** For each pair of metals listed below, decide which metal is more readily oxidized.

   a. Hg, Cu   **d.** Sn, Ag
   b. Ca, Al   **e.** Pb, Zn
   c. Ni, Mg   **f.** Cu, Al

29. What would you expect to happen when a strip of lead is placed in an aqueous solution of magnesium nitrate?

30. What is meant by the term *half-cell*?

31. Explain the function of the salt bridge in a voltaic cell.

32. At which electrode in a voltaic cell does reduction always occur?

⋆**33.** Describe the structure of a dry cell. What substance is oxidized? What substance is reduced?

34. How are dry cells and alkaline batteries similar? How are they different?

35. Explain why the density of the electrolyte in a lead storage battery decreases during the discharge process.

⋆**36.** Use the shorthand method to represent the electrochemical reaction in a lead storage battery.

37. List the advantages of a fuel cell over a lead storage battery.

38. Fuel cells can be designed to generate electrical energy while emitting no air pollutants, yet they are not widely used. Explain.

21.2 Half-Cells and Cell Potentials

39. What is the electrical potential of a voltaic cell?

⋆**40.** What is the difference between standard cell potential and standard reduction potential?

41. What is the electrical potential of a standard hydrogen electrode? How was it determined?

42. Explain how to determine the standard reduction potential for the aluminum half-cell.

43. How does the order of the metals in Table 21.1 compare with the order in Table 21.2? Explain.

⋆**44.** Determine whether these redox reactions will occur spontaneously. Calculate the standard cell potential in each case.

   a. $Cu(s) + 2H^+(aq) \longrightarrow Cu^{2+}(aq) + H_2(g)$
   b. $2Ag(s) + Fe^{2+}(aq) \longrightarrow 2Ag^+(aq) + Fe(s)$

45. Use the information in Table 21.2 to calculate standard cell potentials for these voltaic cells.

   a. $Zn \mid Zn^{2+} \parallel Cu^{2+} \mid Cu$
   b. $Ni \mid Ni^{2+} \parallel Cl_2 \mid Cl^-$
   c. $Sn \mid Sn^{2+} \parallel Ag^+ \mid Ag$

21.3 Electrolytic Cells

⋆**46.** Distinguish between voltaic and electrolytic cells.

Use the diagram to answer Problems 47–49.

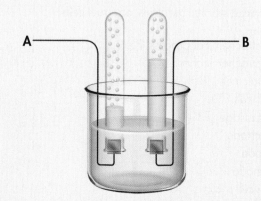

47. Write the equation for the decomposition of water by electrolysis.

48. At which electrode, A or B, is hydrogen produced?

49. The equation for the electrolysis of brine is

$$2NaCl(aq) + 2H_2O(l) \longrightarrow$$
$$Cl_2(g) + H_2(g) + 2NaOH(aq)$$

How would you modify the electrolysis diagram to make it quantitatively represent the formation of hydrogen and chlorine?

⋆**50.** What chemical changes occur during the electrolysis of brine?

51. What are the products of the electrolysis of molten sodium chloride?

52. What are some applications of electrolysis in the field of metallurgy?

53. Describe briefly how you would electroplate a teaspoon with silver.

Understand Concepts

54. Describe the composition of the anode, cathode, and electrolyte in the following:
   a. a fully charged lead storage battery
   b. a fully discharged lead storage battery

*****55.** Predict what will happen, if anything, when an iron nail is dipped into a solution of copper(II) sulfate. Write the oxidation and reduction half-reactions for this process and the balanced equation for the overall reaction.

56. The standard reduction potential for a cadmium half-cell is -0.40 V. What does this mean?

***** 57.** Calculate $E°_{cell}$ and write the overall cell reaction for these cells.
   a. $Sn \mid Sn^{2+} \parallel Pb^{2+} \mid Pb$
   b. $H_2 \mid H^+ \parallel Br_2 \mid Br^-$

58. Why is it not possible to measure the potential of an isolated half-cell?

59. Complete the data table below for the electrolysis of water.

H₂O used	H₂ formed	O₂ formed
a. 2.0 mol	_____ mol	_____ mol
b. _____ g	_____ g	16.0 g
c. _____ mL	10.0 g	_____ g
d. 44.4 g	_____ g	_____ g
e. _____ g	8.80 L (STP)	_____ L (STP)
f. 66.0 mL	_____ g	_____ L (STP)

*****60.** What is the relationship between the voltage produced by a redox reaction and the spontaneity of the reaction?

61. The reactions that take place in voltaic cells produce electric current, and the reactions in electrolytic cells can be made to take place when an electric current is applied. What common feature do these redox reactions share?

*****62.** In one process used to produce aluminum metal, ore containing aluminum oxide is converted to aluminum chloride. Aluminum metal and chlorine gas are then produced by the electrolysis of molten aluminum chloride ($AlCl_3$).
   a. Write the half-reactions that take place at the cathode and the anode.
   b. Write the equation for the overall cell reaction.
   c. Identify the products produced at the cathode and the anode.

63. Use the information in Table 21.2 to determine which of the following cell reactions will proceed spontaneously.
   a. $Zn + Pb^{2+} \longrightarrow ?$
   b. $Cu + Fe^{2+} \longrightarrow ?$
   c. $Ag + Cu^{2+} \longrightarrow ?$
   d. $H_2 + Cu \longrightarrow ?$
   e. $Fe + Pb^{2+} \longrightarrow ?$
   f. $Na + Cl_2 \longrightarrow ?$

64. For each spontaneous reaction in Problem 63, write the half-reaction that takes place at the anode. Write the half-reaction that takes place at the cathode.

65. Write the overall balanced equation for each spontaneous reaction in Problem 63.

66. Determine the standard cell potential for each spontaneous reaction in Problem 63.

67. In certain cases, more than one reaction is possible at an electrode. How can you determine which reaction actually takes place?

*****68.** Answer the following questions for the electrolysis of brine (concentrated sodium chloride solution).
   a. Write the equations for the two possible reactions that can take place at the anode.
   b. Write the equations for the two possible reactions that can take place at the cathode.
   c. Which reaction actually takes place at the anode? Explain why this reaction takes place in preference to the other possible reaction.
   d. Which reaction actually takes place at the cathode? Explain why this reaction takes place in preference to the other possible reaction.

*****69.** Identify the stronger oxidizing agent in each of the following pairs:
   a. Li^+, Ca^{2+} **c.** Cu^{2+}, Cu^+
   b. Fe^{3+}, Hg_2^{2+} **d.** Hg^{2+}, I_2

70. Gold is not included in Table 21.2. Where in the table does gold belong?

✱71. Why is direct current, not alternating current, used in the electroplating of metals?

72. Write the overall cell reactions and calculate $E°_{cell}$ for voltaic cells composed of the following sets of half-reactions.

    a. $Ag^+(aq) + e^- \longrightarrow Ag(s)$
        $Cr^{3+}(aq) + 3e^- \longrightarrow Cr(s)$
    b. $Al^{3+}(aq) + 3e^- \longrightarrow Al(s)$
        $Cd^{2+}(aq) + 2e^- \longrightarrow Cd(s)$

Think Critically

✱73. Relate Cause and Effect Lead storage batteries can be recharged. Why are dry cells not rechargeable?

74. Infer For any voltaic cell, chemists consider the electrode that produces electrons to be negative, and they call it the anode. Most dictionaries, however, define the anode as the positively charged electrode. Explain.

✱75. Interpret Diagrams Describe the process that is occurring in the illustration below.

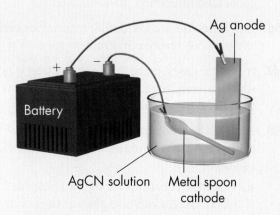

Ag anode

Battery

AgCN solution   Metal spoon cathode

76. Relate Cause and Effect In most voltaic cells, the half-cells are connected by a salt bridge or a porous barrier instead of a piece of wire made of copper or some other metal. Why is a metal wire not suitable for connecting the half-cells of a voltaic cell? Explain your answer.

77. Infer What property do lead(II) sulfate and lead(IV) oxide have that makes salt bridges unnecessary in a lead storage battery?

78. Interpret Diagrams An electrolytic cell is shown below. The substance MX is an ionic compound.

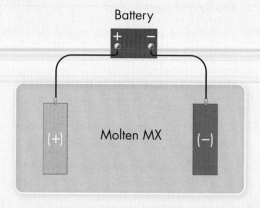

Battery

Molten MX

    a. At which electrode does reduction occur?
    b. At which electrode are electrons being released by ions?
    c. At which electrode are electrons entering the cell?
    d. At which electrode does elemental M form?

✱79. Interpret Graphs Which plot is characteristic of a dry cell? Explain your answer.

a.

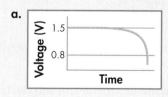

b.

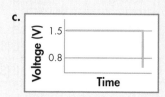

c.

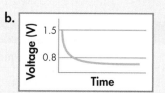

d.

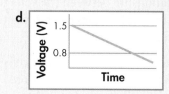

Enrichment

★**80. Calculate** Write the overall cell reactions and calculate E°_{cell} for voltaic cells composed of the following sets of half-reactions.

a. $AgCl(s) + e^- \longrightarrow Ag(s) + Cl^-(aq)$
$Ni^{2+}(aq) + 2e^- \longrightarrow Ni(s)$

b. $Al^{3+}(aq) + 3e^- \longrightarrow Al(s)$
$Cl_2(g) + 2e^- \longrightarrow 2Cl^-(aq)$

81. Evaluate An engineer has proposed a new battery design that uses silver as the electrode in both half-cells. As a chemist, what would you tell the engineer about the proposal?

82. Apply Concepts Impure copper is purified in an electrolytic cell. Design an electrolytic cell, with H_2SO_4 as the electrolyte, that will allow you to carry out this process. Give the oxidation and reduction half-reactions and a balanced equation for the overall reaction.

83. Apply Concepts This spontaneous redox reaction occurs in the voltaic cell illustrated below.

$$Ni^{2+}(aq) + Fe(s) \longrightarrow Ni(s) + Fe^{2+}(aq)$$

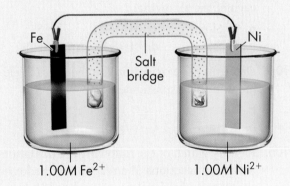

1.00M Fe²⁺   1.00M Ni²⁺

a. Identify the anode and the cathode.
b. Assign charges to the electrodes.
c. Write the half-reactions.
d. Calculate the standard cell potential when the half-cells are at standard conditions.

★**84. Relate Cause and Effect** The cells in an automobile battery are separated from each other. However, the electrolyte is the same in all the cells. What would be the consequence of placing all the cells into a single container of electrolyte solution rather than into separate compartments?

Write About Science

85. Explain Write a paragraph explaining how a zinc–copper voltaic cell works. Make sure to mention the half-reactions and the overall reaction in your explanation. (*Hint:* Use Figure 21.3 as a reference.)

86. Compare and Contrast What do voltaic cells and electrolytic cells have in common? How do they differ?

CHEMYSTERY

Trash or Treasure?

The jeweler informed Maria that she did not purchase a pure gold antique ring but an inexpensive piece of costume jewelry. The ring was in fact made of stainless steel that was electroplated with gold. As Maria wore the ring, the thin layer of gold began to wear off, revealing the stainless steel underneath. However, the jeweler offered to re-plate the inexpensive ring with more gold to restore its original color.

The process by which gold is plated onto another metal is similar to the process by which silver is plated onto an object. The object that is to be gold-plated is the cathode in the electrolytic cell. The anode is metallic gold, which supplies the gold to be deposited onto the object. The electrolyte is a solution of a gold compound. Electroplating of the object occurs when a direct current is applied.

87. Describe Draw the electrolytic cell that is used to plate gold onto an object. Label the anode and the cathode and assign charges to the electrodes. Indicate the direction of electron flow and write the half-reactions.

★**88. Infer** How could you remove the gold from a gold-plated object using an electrolytic cell?

89. Connect to the BIGIDEA Will the half-reactions in an electrochemical cell used to plate gold onto an object occur if no electric current is supplied to the cell? Explain.

90. Balance each equation.

a. $H_2S(g) + HNO_3(aq) \longrightarrow$
$$S(s) + NO(g) + H_2O(l)$$

b. $AgNO_3(aq) + Pb(s) \longrightarrow$
$$Pb(NO_3)_2(aq) + Ag(s)$$

c. $Cl_2(g) + NaOH(aq) \longrightarrow$
$$NaCl(aq) + NaClO_3(aq) + H_2O(l)$$

*91. A sample of oxygen gas has a volume of 425 mL at 30°C. What is the new volume of the gas if the temperature is raised to 60°C while the pressure is kept constant?

92. Write formulas for these hydrates.

a. tin(IV) chloride pentahydrate
b. magnesium sulfate heptahydrate
c. iron(III) phosphate tetrahydrate
d. calcium chloride dihydrate

*93. Calculate the grams of solute required to make the following solutions:

a. 250 g of 0.90% NaCl (m/m)
b. 500 mL of $2.0M$ KNO_3

94. Concentrated nitric acid is $16M$. How would you prepare 500 mL of $1.0M$ HNO_3 from the concentrated acid?

95. Convert the following:

a. 4.32×10^5 joules to kilojoules
b. 255 Calories to calories
c. 645 calories to joules

96. Calculate the quantity of heat lost or gained in the following changes:

a. 0.625 mol NaOH(s) dissolves in water
b. 1.17 mol water freezes at 0°C
c. 0.30 mol $C_2H_6O(l)$ vaporizes
d. 0.66 mol of steam condenses at 100°C

*97. The combustion of natural gas, methane (CH_4), is an exothermic reaction.

$$CH_4(g) + 2O_2(g) \longrightarrow CO_2(g) + 2H_2O(l)$$
$$\Delta H = -890 \text{ kJ}$$

Calculate the amount of heat liberated when 4.80 g CH_4 reacts with an excess of oxygen.

*98. Four reactions have the following equilibrium constants. Identify in which of these reactions the reactants are favored over products. Why?

a. $K_{eq} = 0.006$
b. $K_{eq} = 5.3$
c. $K_{eq} = 8 \times 10^{-4}$
d. $K_{eq} = 2 \times 10^3$

99. Give the equilibrium-constant expression for the decomposition of ammonia to nitrogen and hydrogen.

$$2NH_3(g) \rightleftharpoons N_2(g) + 3H_2(g)$$

*100. Determine the pH for each solution.

a. $[H^+] = 1.0 \times 10^{-8}M$
b. $[H^+] = 0.000010M$
c. $[OH^-] = 1.0 \times 10^{-4}M$
d. $[OH^-] = 1.0 \times 10^{-9}M$

101. Three solutions have the following pH values. What are the hydroxide-ion concentrations of these solutions?

a. pH = 7.0   **b.** pH = 4.0   **c.** pH = 9.0

102. Write a balanced equation for the reaction of each of the following metals with water:

a. sodium   **b.** calcium

*103. Determine the oxidation number of sulfur in each of the following:

a. H_2SO_4 **c.** SO_2 **e.** S
b. H_2S **d.** $Na_2S_2O_3$ **f.** SO_3^{2-}

104. Determine the oxidation number of each element in these substances.

a. $CaCr_2O_7$ **c.** $Ca(NO_3)_2$
b. $KMnO_4$ **d.** $Al(OH)_3$

*105. Identify which of the following are oxidation-reduction reactions. If a reaction is a redox reaction, name the element oxidized and the element reduced.

a. $CaCO_3(s) \longrightarrow CaO(s) + CO_2(g)$
b. $Ca(s) + Cl_2(g) \longrightarrow CaCl_2(s)$
c. $Ca(s) + 2H_2O(l) \longrightarrow Ca(OH)_2(aq) + H_2(g)$

106. Balance each redox equation.

a. $Br_2(g) + NaOH(aq) \longrightarrow$
$$NaBrO_3(aq) + NaBr(aq) + H_2O(l)$$
b. $Fe_2O_3(s) + H_2(g) \longrightarrow Fe(s) + H_2O(l)$

If You Have Trouble With . . .

Question	90	91	92	93	94	95	96	97	98	99	100	101	102	103	104	105	106
See Chapter	11	14	15	16	16	17	17	17	18	18	19	19	19	20	20	20	20

Standardized Test Prep

Select the choice that best answers each question or completes each statement.

1. Which statement describes electrolysis?
   (A) Reduction occurs at the anode.
   (B) Energy is produced.
   (C) Oxidation occurs at the cathode.
   (D) Positive ions move to the cathode.

2. A voltaic cell is constructed using the following half-reactions:

   $Cd^{2+}(aq) + 2e^- \longrightarrow Cd(s) \quad E°_{Cd^{2+}} = -0.40\ V$
   $Sn^{2+}(aq) + 2e^- \longrightarrow Sn(s) \quad E°_{Sn^{2+}} = -0.14\ V$

   What is the standard cell potential for this voltaic cell?
   (A) −0.54 V   (C) +0.26 V
   (B) −0.26 V   (D) +0.54 V

3. Which of the following is a product of the reaction that occurs in a hydrogen–oxygen fuel cell?
   (A) $CO(g)$ (C) $H_2O(g)$
   (B) $CO_2(g)$ (D) $H_2O_2(l)$

4. Magnesium metal is prepared by the electrolysis of molten $MgCl_2$. One half-reaction is

   $$Mg^{2+}(l) + 2e^- \longrightarrow Mg(l)$$

   Which of the following statements is true?
   (A) This half-reaction occurs at the cathode.
   (B) Magnesium ions are oxidized.
   (C) Chloride ions are reduced at the anode.
   (D) Chloride ions gain electrons during this process.

5. If the cell potential for a redox reaction is positive,
   (A) the redox reaction is spontaneous.
   (B) the redox reaction is not spontaneous.
   (C) the reaction only occurs during electrolysis.
   (D) More than one statement is correct.

Use the data table to answer Questions 6–12. Hydrogen is included as a reference point for the metals.

Activity Series of Selected Metals	
Element	**Oxidation half-reaction**
Lithium	$Li(s) \longrightarrow Li^+(aq) + e^-$
Potassium	$K(s) \longrightarrow K^+(aq) + e^-$
Sodium	$Na(s) \longrightarrow Na^+(aq) + e^-$
Aluminum	$Al(s) \longrightarrow Al^{3+}(aq) + 3e^-$
Zinc	$Zn(s) \longrightarrow Zn^{2+}(aq) + 2e^-$
Iron	$Fe(s) \longrightarrow Fe^{2+}(aq) + 2e^-$
Hydrogen	$H_2(g) \longrightarrow 2H^+(aq) + 2e^-$
Copper	$Cu(s) \longrightarrow Cu^{2+}(aq) + 2e^-$

6. Which metal will more easily lose an electron, sodium or potassium?

7. Which metal is more easily oxidized, copper or aluminum?

8. What is the relationship between ease of oxidation and the activity of a metal?

9. Describe what would happen if you placed a clean strip of aluminum in a solution of copper(II) sulfate. Explain your answer.

10. Would a copper strip placed in a solution containing zinc ions react spontaneously with the zinc ions? Explain your reasoning.

11. Based on the positions of zinc and iron in the table, explain how attaching zinc blocks to a steel ship hull protects the steel from corrosion.

12. Write the half-reaction for the reduction of aluminum ions.

13. An electrolytic cell is shown at the right. Draw this cell on a separate piece of paper and label the anode, cathode, and direction of electron flow.

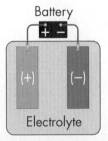

If You Have Trouble With . . .													
Question	1	2	3	4	5	6	7	8	9	10	11	12	13
See Lesson	21.3	21.2	21.1	21.3	21.2	21.1	21.1	21.1	21.1	21.1	21.1	21.1	21.3

22

Hydrocarbon Compounds

INSIDE:

- **22.1** Hydrocarbons
- **22.2** Unsaturated Hydrocarbons
- **22.3** Isomers
- **22.4** Hydrocarbon Rings
- **22.5** Hydrocarbons From Earth's Crust

PearsonChem.com

Turkmenistan has some of the world's largest deposits of natural gas. This natural gas deposit in the city of Darvaza has been burning for over three decades!

CARBON CHEMISTRY

Essential Questions:

1. *How are hydrocarbons named?*

2. *What are the general properties of hydrocarbons?*

CHEMYSTERY

Nose for Hire

Walking home from school one day, Anthony spotted a poster soliciting participants for a smell test. The poster offered participants "$50 for less than an hour of your time." So he decided to go for it.

When Anthony reported for the study, after filling out some paperwork, a researcher asked him to smell two chemical samples. The first one smelled like a freshly cut orange. The second had an odor that reminded him of pine trees.

Anthony was curious. "What am I smelling?" he asked. "Limonene," the researcher answered. "What about the second one?" Anthony asked. The researcher gave the same reply: "Limonene." Anthony was perplexed. How could two substances, both with the name limonene, smell so different?

▶ **Connect to the BIGIDEA** As you read about hydrocarbons, think about what could make this phenomenon possible.

NATIONAL SCIENCE EDUCATION STANDARDS

A-1, A-2, B-2, D-3, E-1, E-2, F-3, F-4, F-5, F-6, G-1, G-3

22.1 Hydrocarbons

Q: *Why are some fossil fuels gases, some liquids, and some solids?* The gasoline used to fuel this motorcycle is a liquid at STP. So are the diesel fuel used in trucks and buses, and the kerosene used in lanterns. Other fuels are gases or solids. For example, the fuel used in a furnace might be natural gas or a solid such as coal. All these fuels contain mixtures of compounds called hydrocarbons. In this lesson, you will learn about the structure and properties of hydrocarbons.

Key Questions

🔑 Why does a carbon atom form four covalent bonds?

🔑 What are two possible arrangements of carbon atoms in an alkane?

Vocabulary

- hydrocarbon
- alkane
- straight-chain alkane
- homologous series
- condensed structural formula
- substituent
- alkyl group
- branched-chain alkane

Organic Chemistry and Hydrocarbons

🔑 **Why does a carbon atom form four covalent bonds?**

Fewer than 200 years ago, it was thought that only living organisms could synthesize the carbon compounds found in their cells. So these compounds were classified as organic compounds, and the study of these compounds was known as organic chemistry. Many people thought that a mysterious vital force directed the formation of carbon compounds. A German chemist, Friedrich Wöhler (1800–1882), refuted this idea in 1828. He was able to use inorganic substances to synthesize urea—an organic compound found in urine. Today, organic chemistry includes the chemistry of almost all carbon compounds, regardless of their origin.

Introduction to Hydrocarbons In a reference book that lists properties of common compounds, the list of organic compounds is much longer than the list of inorganic compounds. In fact, new organic compounds are synthesized every day. The simplest organic compounds are called hydrocarbons. By definition, a compound contains at least two elements. A **hydrocarbon** is an organic compound that contains only carbon and hydrogen. The two simplest hydrocarbons are methane and ethane.

Methane (CH_4) is the major component of natural gas. It is sometimes called marsh gas because it is formed by the action of bacteria on decaying plants in swamps and other marshy areas. Livestock and termites also emit substantial quantities of methane as a product of digestion.

Recall that a carbon atom has four valence electrons and a hydrogen atom has one valence electron. So one carbon atom can form a single covalent bond with four hydrogen atoms as shown below.

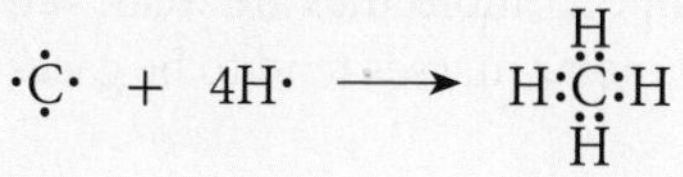

$$\cdot \overset{\displaystyle \cdot}{\underset{\displaystyle \cdot}{C}} \cdot \; + \; 4H\cdot \; \longrightarrow \; H\!:\!\overset{\displaystyle H}{\underset{\displaystyle H}{C}}\!:\!H$$

Carbon   Hydrogen   Methane
atom   atoms   molecule

Because carbon has four valence electrons, a carbon atom always forms four covalent bonds. Remembering this principle will help you to write correct structures for organic compounds.

Methane is not typical of the vast majority of organic compounds because there isn't a bond between carbon atoms in a methane molecule. But there is a carbon-carbon bond in ethane. In an ethane molecule, two carbon atoms share a pair of electrons. The remaining six valence electrons form bonding pairs with the electrons from six hydrogen atoms.

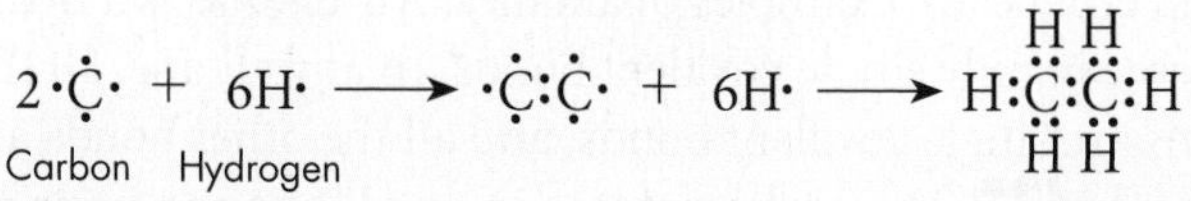

$$2\,\cdot\!C\!\cdot \; + \; 6H\cdot \; \longrightarrow \; \cdot C\!:\!C\cdot \; + \; 6H\cdot \; \longrightarrow \; H\!:\!\overset{\displaystyle H\;\;H}{\underset{\displaystyle H\;\;H}{C\!:\!C}}\!:\!H$$

Carbon   Hydrogen   Ethane
atoms   atoms   molecule

The ability of carbon to form stable carbon-carbon bonds is one reason that carbon can form so many different compounds.

Representing Hydrocarbons Table 22.1 shows the structural formulas, ball-and-stick models, and space-filling models for methane and ethane. Structural formulas are a convenient way to show the arrangement of atoms in a molecule. But two-dimensional structural formulas do not provide accurate information about how the atoms in a molecule are arranged in space. Three-dimensional molecular models represent the shapes of molecules more accurately. Throughout this chapter and the next, ball-and-stick models and space-filling models will be used along with structural formulas to represent organic molecules. Hybrid orbital theory and VSEPR theory are used to predict the molecular shapes.

READING SUPPORT

Build Study Skills: *Cluster Diagram* As you read through the chapter, construct a cluster diagram organizing the different types of hydrocarbons. Use color-coding to distinguish among the groups. *How will this diagram help you learn about hydrocarbons?*

Table 22.1

Different Ways of Representing Hydrocarbons

Name	Structural formula	Ball-and-stick model	Space-filling model
Methane	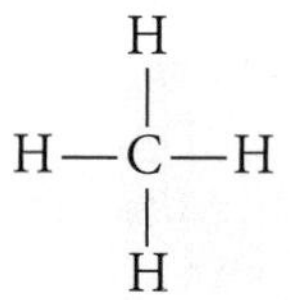 H—C—H with H above and H below	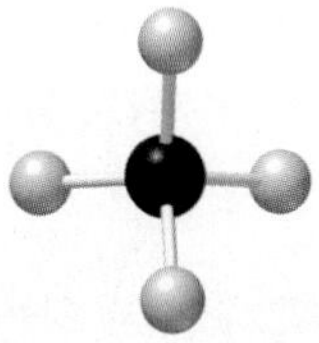	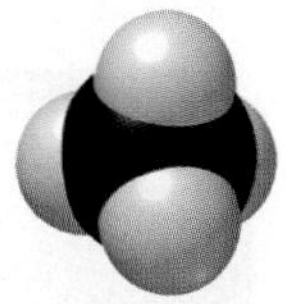
Ethane	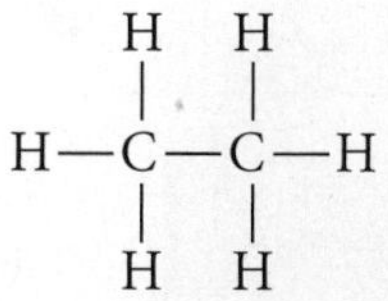 H—C—C—H with H above and H below each C	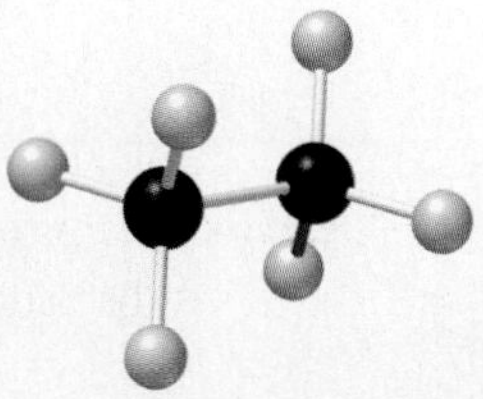	

Properties of Hydrocarbons

The electron pair in a carbon-hydrogen bond or a carbon-carbon bond is shared almost equally by the nuclei of the atoms forming the bond. Thus, hydrocarbons are nonpolar molecules. The attractions between nonpolar molecules are weak van der Waals forces. So hydrocarbons with low molar masses tend to be gases or liquids that boil at a low temperature.

Recall the general rule "like dissolves like." Two nonpolar compounds will form a solution, as will two polar compounds. But a nonpolar compound and a polar compound will not form a solution. For example, because oil is a mixture of hydrocarbons, oil and water do not mix. So oil will float on top of water, as shown in Figure 22.1.

Alkanes

What are two possible arrangements of carbon atoms in an alkane?

Methane and ethane are examples of alkanes. An **alkane** is a hydrocarbon in which there are only single covalent bonds. In any alkane, all the carbon-carbon bonds are single covalent bonds, and all the other bonds are carbon-hydrogen bonds. **The carbon atoms in an alkane can be arranged in a straight chain or in a chain that has branches.**

Straight-Chain Alkanes Ethane is the simplest **straight-chain alkane,** which is an alkane that contains any number of carbon atoms, one after the other, in a chain. Propane (C_3H_8) has three carbon atoms bonded in a chain with eight electrons shared with eight hydrogen atoms. Butane (C_4H_{10}) has a chain of four carbons and ten hydrogens. Figure 22.2 shows how propane and butane can be used.

Figure 22.1 Oil and Water
The nonpolar molecules in this cooking oil are not attracted to the polar water molecules, so they do not mix.
Interpret Photos *What evidence of insolubility do you see in the photo?*

Figure 22.2 Hydrocarbon Fuels
Hydrocarbons are commonly used as fuels. **a.** Pressurized tanks of propane are used to fuel the burners in hot-air balloons. **b.** Butane serves as the fuel for many kitchen torches.

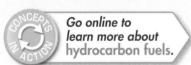
Go online to learn more about hydrocarbon fuels.

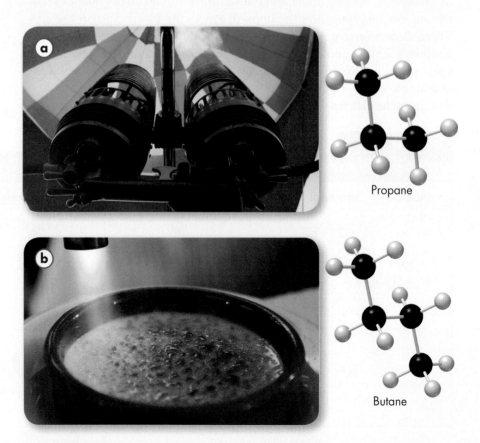

Propane

Butane

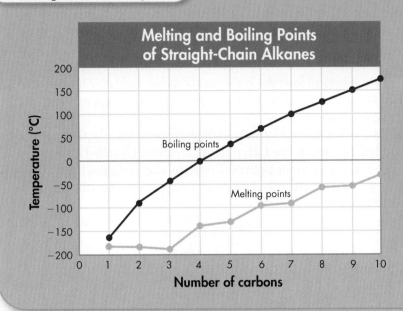

Melting and Boiling Points of Straight-Chain Alkanes

Boiling points

Melting points

Temperature (°C)

Number of carbons

Figure 22.3 The graph illustrates how the melting and boiling points vary with the number of carbons in straight-chain alkanes.

a. Describe Determine whether each alkane is a solid, liquid, or gas at room temperature.

b. Read Graphs How do the added carbons affect the boiling points of the straight-chain alkanes?

c. Predict Estimate a boiling point for undecane, the straight-chain alkane with eleven carbons.

Figure 22.3 shows the melting and boiling points for straight-chain alkanes containing up to ten carbons. The straight-chain alkanes are an example of a homologous series. A group of compounds forms a **homologous series** if there is a constant increment of change in molecular structure from one compound in the series to the next. A CH_2 group is the increment of change in straight-chain alkanes. This change is summarized below for the initial part of the homologous series.

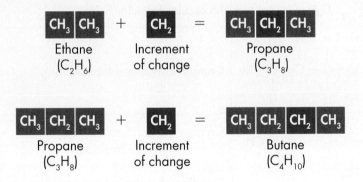

| CH₃ | CH₃ | + | CH₂ | = | CH₃ | CH₂ | CH₃ |

Ethane
(C_2H_6)

Increment of change

Propane
(C_3H_8)

Propane
(C_3H_8)

Increment of change

Butane
(C_4H_{10})

Notice in Figure 22.3 that the boiling points of the straight-chain alkanes increase as the number of carbons in the chain increase. The melting points increase in a similar way.

Naming Straight-Chain Alkanes The names of straight-chain alkanes follow rules established by the International Union of Pure and Applied Chemistry (IUPAC). Every alkane has a name that ends with the suffix *-ane*. For the straight-chain alkanes with one to four carbon atoms, the official names and the common names are the same. They are methane, ethane, propane, and butane, respectively. A mixture of Latin and Greek prefixes are used to name the hydrocarbons having straight chains longer than four carbon atoms. The prefixes are *pent-* for 5, *hex-* for 6, *hept-* for 7, and so on. Use Table 22.2 to memorize the names of the first ten straight-chain alkanes.

Table 22.2

Straight-Chain Alkanes

Name	Formula
Methane	CH_4
Ethane	C_2H_6
Propane	C_3H_8
Butane	C_4H_{10}
Pentane	C_5H_{12}
Hexane	C_6H_{14}
Heptane	C_7H_{16}
Octane	C_8H_{18}
Nonane	C_9H_{20}
Decane	$C_{10}H_{22}$

Q: *Hydrocarbons such as alkanes can be used as fuels. You just learned that the boiling and melting points of straight-chain alkanes increase as the number of carbons increase. Now explain why some hydrocarbon fuels are gases and others are liquids.*

Drawing Structural Formulas for Straight-Chain Alkanes To draw the structural formula for a straight-chain alkane, write the symbol for carbon as many times as necessary to get the proper chain length. Then complete the formula with hydrogens and lines representing covalent bonds. Complete structural formulas show all the atoms and bonds in a molecule. Sometimes, however, shorthand or condensed structural formulas work just as well. In a **condensed structural formula,** some bonds and/or atoms are left out of the structural formula. Although the bonds and atoms do not appear, you must understand that they are there.

A condensed structural formula in the form of $CH_3(CH_2)_nCH_3$ uses a different kind of shorthand. The CH_2 unit in parentheses is called a methylene group. The subscript n to the right of the parentheses indicates the number of methylene groups that are linked together. This shorthand method applies to butane as follows:

$$CH_3(CH_2)_2CH_3$$

Methylene unit — Subscript

The subscript after the parentheses in the condensed structural formula for butane is 2. This means two methylene groups are linked together in the structure. Table 22.3 shows several ways to draw condensed structural formulas, using butane as an example.

In each condensed structural formula, certain features of the complete structural formula are left out.

Table 22.3

Formulas for Butane	
Formula	**Description**
C_4H_{10}	Molecular formula
H—C—C—C—C—H (with H above and below each C)	Complete structural formula
$CH_3—CH_2—CH_2—CH_3$	Condensed structural formula (C—H bonds understood)
$CH_3CH_2CH_2CH_3$	Condensed structural formula (C—H and C—C bonds understood)
$CH_3(CH_2)_2CH_3$	Condensed structural formula (all bonds understood)
C—C—C—C	Carbon skeleton (hydrogens and C—H bonds understood)
⌇ (line-angle)	Line-angle formula (carbons and hydrogens understood) Carbon atoms are located at each intersection and at the ends of lines.

Drawing Structural Formulas for Alkanes

Draw complete structural formulas for the straight-chain alkanes that have
a. three carbon atoms. **b.** four carbon atoms.

❶ Analyze **Identify the relevant concepts.** In an alkane, each carbon atom forms four covalent bonds to hydrogen or to other carbon atoms. Because these are straight-chain alkanes, write the appropriate number of carbons in a straight line, connected to each other by single bonds. Then add the appropriate number of hydrogen atoms.

❷ Solve **Apply the concepts to this problem.**

Start with the number of carbons.	**a.** C—C—C	**b.** C—C—C—C

Each center carbon bonds to two hydrogens. Each end carbon bonds to three hydrogens.

a.
```
      H   H   H
      |   |   |
  H — C — C — C — H
      |   |   |
      H   H   H
```

b.
```
      H   H   H   H
      |   |   |   |
  H — C — C — C — C — H
      |   |   |   |
      H   H   H   H
```

Make sure that each carbon has 4 bonds.

1. Draw complete structural formulas for the straight-chain alkanes with five and six carbon atoms.

2. How many single bonds are there in a propane molecule?

Branched-Chain Alkanes Alkanes and other hydrocarbons do not always have carbon atoms bonded in straight chains. Because a carbon atom forms four covalent bonds, it can bond not only to one or two other carbon atoms, but also to three or even four other carbons, resulting in branched chains. In organic chemistry, branches on a hydrocarbon chain are discussed as if they were substituted for a hydrogen atom on the chain. An atom or group of atoms that can take the place of a hydrogen atom on a parent hydrocarbon molecule is called a **substituent.** Look at the diagrams below. The longest continuous carbon chain of a branched-chain hydrocarbon is called the parent alkane. All other carbon atoms or groups of carbon atoms are regarded as substituents. In Chapter 23, you will study compounds in which atoms such as halogens, oxygen, and nitrogen can take the place of a hydrogen atom on the carbon chain.

Substituent
```
        C
        |
  C — C — C
```
Parent alkane (propane)

Substituents
```
      C   C   C
      |   |   |
  C — C — C — C — C — C
```
Parent alkane (hexane)

A hydrocarbon substituent that is derived from an alkane is called an **alkyl group.** You can think of an alkyl group as just an alkane with one of the hydrogens removed. An alkyl group can be one carbon or several carbons long. Alkyl groups are named by removing the *-ane* ending from the parent hydrocarbon name and adding *-yl*. The three smallest alkyl groups are the methyl group (— CH_3), the ethyl group (— CH_2CH_3), and the propyl group (— $CH_2CH_2CH_3$).

When a substituent alkyl group is attached to a straight-chain hydrocarbon, branches are formed. An alkane with one or more alkyl groups is called a **branched-chain alkane.** Each carbon in an organic molecule can be categorized as a primary, secondary, tertiary, or quaternary carbon. If the carbon in question has only one carbon attached to it, then the carbon is a primary carbon. If two carbons are attached to the carbon in question, the carbon is a secondary carbon; if three carbons, a tertiary carbon; and if four carbons, a quaternary carbon. Examples of primary, secondary, tertiary, and quaternary carbons are labeled in the structural formulas below.

$$CH_3—CH_3 \qquad CH_3—CH_2—CH_3 \qquad CH_3—CH—CH_3 \qquad CH_3—C—CH_3$$

Primary carbons   Secondary carbon   Tertiary carbon   Quaternary carbon

Isooctane is a hydrocarbon that contains each of these types of carbons. You have probably seen labels for octane ratings in gasoline as shown in Figure 22.4. Isooctane is the standard for determining octane ratings of the mixtures of hydrocarbons that make up gasoline. A gasoline's octane rating is a measure of its ability to prevent engine knock, which is the sound an internal combustion engine makes when gasoline ignites too soon. Knocking reduces a vehicle's performance and can eventually lead to engine damage.

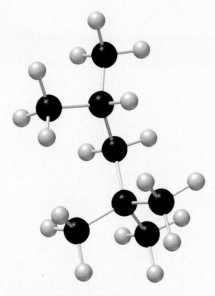

Figure 22.4 Isooctane
Octane ratings of gasoline are relative to that of isooctane, a good anti-knock fuel, which is assigned a value of 100.
Interpret Diagrams *Find each type of carbon—primary, secondary, tertiary, and quaternary—in the model of isooctane.*

Naming Branched-Chain Alkanes The IUPAC rules for naming branched-chain alkanes are quite straightforward. The name of a branched-chain alkane is based on the name of the longest continuous carbon chain. Each substituent is named according to the length of its chain and numbered according to its position on the main chain. The compound with the structural formula shown to the right can be used as an example.

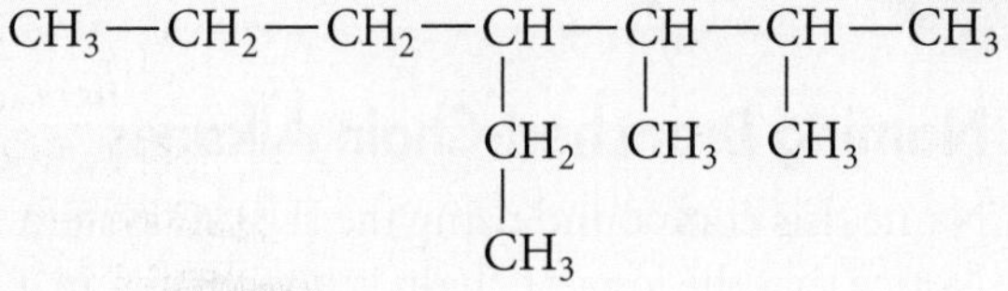

$$CH_3-CH_2-CH_2-CH-CH-CH-CH_3$$

with CH_2, CH_3, CH_3 branches, and CH_3 below CH_2.

---

1. Find the longest continuous chain of carbons in the molecule. This chain is considered the parent hydrocarbon.

> The longest chain is highlighted in the example. It contains seven carbon atoms. So, the parent hydrocarbon is heptane.

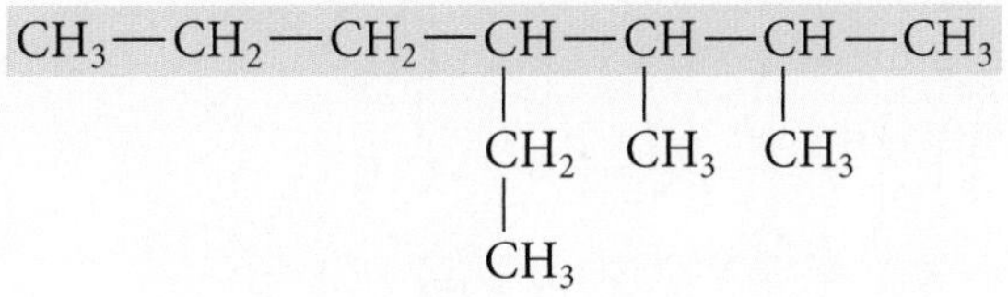

$$CH_3-CH_2-CH_2-CH-CH-CH-CH_3$$

with CH_2, CH_3, CH_3 branches, and CH_3 below CH_2.

---

2. Number the carbons in the main chain in sequence. To do this, start at the end that will give the substituent groups attached to the chain the smallest numbers.

> Numbering the chain from right to left gives the substituents the lowest numbers (2, 3, and 4). Numbering the chain the other way violates the rule.

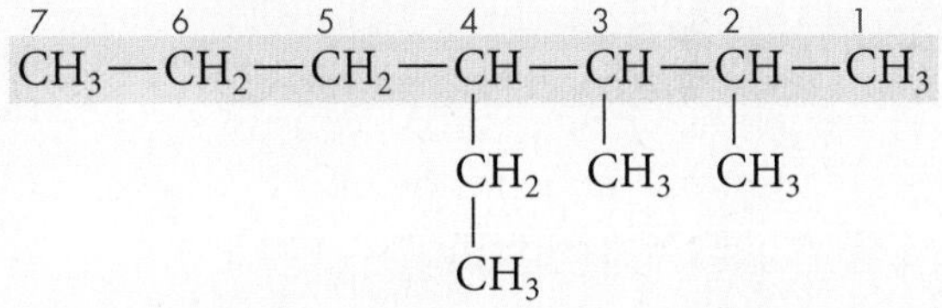

$$\overset{7}{CH_3}-\overset{6}{CH_2}-\overset{5}{CH_2}-\overset{4}{CH}-\overset{3}{CH}-\overset{2}{CH}-\overset{1}{CH_3}$$

with CH_2, CH_3, CH_3 branches, and CH_3 below CH_2.

---

3. Add numbers to the names of the substituent groups to identify their positions on the chain. These numbers become prefixes to the name of the substituent group.

> The substituents and positions are 2-methyl, 3-methyl, and 4-ethyl.

---

4. Use prefixes to indicate the appearance of the same group more than once in the structural formula. Common prefixes are *di-* (twice), *tri-* (three times), and *tetra-* (four times).

> The two methyl groups are combined as 2,3-dimethyl.

---

5. List the names of alkyl substituents in alphabetical order. For purposes of alphabetizing, ignore the prefixes *di-*, *tri-*, and so on.

> The 4-ethyl group is listed first, followed by 2,3-dimethyl.

---

6. Combine all the parts and use proper punctuation. Write the entire name without any spaces. Use commas to separate numbers and use hyphens to separate numbers and words.

> The correct name of the compound is 4-ethyl-2,3-dimethylheptane. It is incorrect to write the name as 4-ethyl-2,3-dimethyl heptane.

Sample Problem 22.2

Naming Branched-Chain Alkanes

Name this compound using the IUPAC system. Notice that the longest chain is not written in a straight line.

$$CH_3-CH_2-\underset{\underset{\underset{\underset{CH_3}{|}}{\underset{CH_2}{|}}}{\overset{\overset{CH_3}{|}}{C}}-CH_3$$

① Analyze **Identify the relevant concepts.** The parent structure is the longest chain of carbons. All other groups are substituents. Number the carbons to give the first substituent the lowest possible number. These location numbers become part of the name as prefixes. List the names of the substituents in alphabetical order with numbers separated by commas, and numbers and words separated by hyphens.

② Solve **Apply the concepts to this problem.**

Identify the longest carbon chain in the molecule.	The longest chain has six carbons, so the name ends with hexane.
Identify the substituents and their positions on the parent hydrocarbon.	There are two methyl substituents on carbon 3, so the prefix is 3,3-dimethyl.
Put everything together. You can skip the alphabetizing step because there is only one type of substituent.	The correct IUPAC name is 3,3-dimethylhexane.

substituents

$$\overset{1}{C}H_3-\overset{2}{C}H_2-\overset{3}{C}-CH_3$$
with CH_3 above C3 and below: $\overset{4}{C}H_2$, $\overset{5}{C}H_2$, $\overset{6}{C}H_3$

Remember to start numbering at the end that gives the substituents the smallest numbers!

3. Name these compounds according to the IUPAC system.

a. $$CH_2-CH_2-\underset{\underset{\underset{CH_3}{|}}{\underset{CH_2}{|}}}{CH}-CH_2-CH_3$$
with CH_3 below first carbon

b. $$CH_3-CH_2-\underset{\underset{CH_3}{|}}{CH}-CH_3$$

4. Name the following compound according to the IUPAC system.

$$CH_3-CH_2-CH_2-\underset{\underset{\underset{CH_3-CH}{|}}{\underset{CH_2}{|}}}{CH}-CH_2-CH_3$$
with CH_3 below CH

Drawing Structural Formulas for Branched-Chain Alkanes With the name of a branched-chain alkane and knowledge of the IUPAC rules, it is easy to reconstruct the structural formula. First, find the root word (ending in -ane) in the hydrocarbon name. Then, draw the longest carbon chain to create the parent hydrocarbon, and number the carbons on the chain. Next, identify the substituent groups in the hydrocarbon name. Attach the substituents to the numbered parent chain at the proper positions. Complete the structural formula by adding hydrogens as needed.

Drawing Structural Formulas for Branched-Chain Alkanes

Draw the structural formula for 2,2,4-trimethylpentane, or isooctane.

❶ **Analyze Identify the relevant concepts.** The part of the name that ends in *-ane* indicates the parent structure. Prefixes indicate the types of substituents, the number of times each appears, and their locations on the parent chain. Hydrogens are added as needed.

❷ **Solve Apply the concepts to this problem.**

Draw the number of carbons needed to represent the parent structure indicated in the name, and number the carbons on the chain.	The parent structure is pentane, which has five carbon atoms.
Attach each substituent as indicated in the prefix.	There are two methyl groups on carbon 2 and one on carbon 4.
Finish by adding hydrogens where needed in the formula.	A total of nine hydrogens need to be added to complete the structure.

C—C—C—C—C
1 2 3 4 5

$$\begin{array}{c} \quad\ CH_3 \qquad CH_3 \\ \ \ \ \ | \qquad\ \ \ | \\ C-C-C-C-C \\ 1\ \ |2\ \ 3\ \ 4\ \ 5 \\ \ \ \ CH_3 \end{array}$$

$$\begin{array}{c} \qquad CH_3 \qquad\ CH_3 \\ \qquad\ | \qquad\quad\ | \\ CH_3-C-CH_2-CH-CH_3 \\ \qquad\ | \\ \qquad CH_3 \end{array}$$

Be careful: Each carbon has four, and only four, bonds.

---

5. Draw the structural formula for 2,3-dimethylhexane.

6. Draw the structural formula for 4-ethyl-2,3,4-trimethyloctane.

22.1 LessonCheck

7. 🔑 **Review** Why do carbon atoms form four covalent bonds?

8. 🔑 **Identify** What are two ways that carbon atoms can be arranged in an alkane?

9. Infer Explain why mineral oil, which is a mixture of hydrocarbons, is not soluble in water.

10. Describe Draw complete structural formulas for the following alkanes:
  a. octane
  b. 3-ethylhexane

11. Describe Write a condensed structural formula for 2,2-dimethylbutane.

12. Identify Name the following alkanes using the IUPAC system.

a.
$$\begin{array}{c} \ \ \ H\ \ \ H\ \ \ H \\ \ \ \ |\ \ \ \ |\ \ \ \ | \\ H-C-C-C-H \\ \ \ \ |\ \ \ \ |\ \ \ \ | \\ \ \ \ H\ \ \ H\ \ \ H \end{array}$$

b. $CH_3-CH-CH-CH_2-CH_3$
  $\qquad\quad | \quad\ \ |$
  $\qquad\ CH_3\ CH_3$

BIGIDEA CARBON CHEMISTRY

13. How would you characterize alkanes in terms of bond polarity?

22.2 Unsaturated Hydrocarbons

CHEMISTRY & YOU

Q: *What does it mean if a fat is unsaturated?* You've probably read nutrition labels listing saturated and unsaturated fat content. For example, olives are high in unsaturated fat but low in saturated fat. In this lesson, you'll find out what the terms *saturated* and *unsaturated* mean.

Key Questions

🔑 What are the structural characteristics of alkenes?

🔑 What are the structural characteristics of alkynes?

Vocabulary

• saturated compound
• unsaturated compound
• alkene • alkyne

Figure 22.5 Ethene
Because rotation is restricted around the double bond, atoms in ethene lie in one plane.

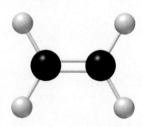

CHEMISTRY & YOU

Q: *You just read about saturated and unsaturated compounds. Use what you have learned to describe how saturated and unsaturated fats differ structurally.*

Alkenes

🔑 What are the structural characteristics of alkenes?

An organic compound that contains the maximum number of hydrogen atoms per carbon atom is called a **saturated compound.** Alkanes are saturated compounds because the only bonds in alkanes are single covalent bonds. An organic compound that contains double or triple carbon-carbon bonds is called an **unsaturated compound.** The ratio of hydrogen atoms to carbon atoms is lower in an unsaturated compound than in a saturated compound. An **alkene** is a hydrocarbon that contains one or more carbon-carbon double covalent bonds. A carbon-carbon double bond is shown in structural formulas as two parallel lines. 🔑 **At least one carbon-carbon bond in an alkene is a double covalent bond. Other bonds may be single carbon-carbon bonds and carbon-hydrogen bonds.**

Ethene (C_2H_4) is the simplest alkene. It is often called by the common name ethylene. Figure 22.5 shows the ball-and-stick model of ethene. To name an alkene by the IUPAC system, find the longest chain in the molecule that contains the double bond. This chain is the parent alkene. It has the root name of the alkane with the same number of carbons plus the ending *-ene*. The chain is numbered so that the carbon atoms of the double bond have the lowest possible numbers. Substituents on the chain are named and numbered in the same way they are for alkanes. Some examples of the structures and IUPAC names of simple alkenes are shown below.

$$CH_2{=}CH_2$$
Ethene

$$CH_3{-}\overset{\overset{\displaystyle H}{|}}{C}{=}\overset{\overset{\displaystyle H}{|}}{C}{-}H$$
Propene

$$CH_2{=}CH{-}CH_2{-}CH_3$$
1-butene

$$CH_3{-}\overset{\overset{\displaystyle H}{|}}{C}{=}\overset{\overset{\displaystyle H}{|}}{C}{-}CH_3$$
2-butene

$$CH_3{-}\overset{\overset{\displaystyle CH_3}{|}}{CH}{-}\overset{\overset{\displaystyle H}{|}}{C}{=}\overset{\overset{\displaystyle H}{|}}{C}{-}CH_3$$
4-methyl-2-pentene

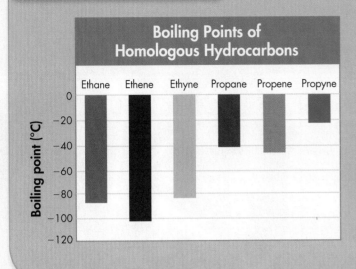

Boiling Points of Homologous Hydrocarbons

Figure 22.6 The graph shows the relationship between the boiling points and the degree of saturation for some hydrocarbons.

a. Read Graphs Determine the boiling point for each hydrocarbon in the graph.

b. Identify Draw a condensed structural formula for each hydrocarbon.

c. Make Generalizations How does the degree of saturation affect the boiling points of hydrocarbons with the same number of carbon atoms?

Note: The *degree of saturation* refers to the ratio of hydrogen atoms to carbon atoms.

Alkynes

What are the structural characteristics of alkynes?

A hydrocarbon that contains one or more carbon-carbon triple covalent bonds is called an **alkyne.** A carbon-carbon triple bond is shown in structural formulas as three parallel lines. **At least one carbon-carbon bond in an alkyne is a triple covalent bond. Other bonds may be single or double carbon-carbon bonds and carbon-hydrogen bonds.** Like alkenes, alkynes are unsaturated compounds.

Alkynes are not plentiful in nature. The simplest alkyne is ethyne (C_2H_2), which has the common name acetylene. Acetylene is the fuel burned in oxy-acetylene torches used for welding. Figure 22.7 shows that the single bonds that extend from the carbons in the carbon-carbon triple bond of ethyne are separated by an angle of 180°, which makes ethyne a linear molecule.

Like alkanes, the major attractions between alkenes and alkynes are weak van der Waals forces. As a result, the introduction of a double or triple bond into a hydrocarbon does not have a dramatic effect on physical properties such as boiling point. Compare the boiling points for alkanes, alkenes, and alkynes with two and three carbons in Figure 22.6.

Figure 22.7 Ethyne
The triple bond restricts rotation in an ethyne molecule, which has a linear shape.
Identify *What is the ratio of hydrogen to carbon in ethyne?*

22.2 LessonCheck

14. **Review** Describe the bonding between atoms in an alkene.

15. **Identify** What types of bonds are present in an alkyne?

16. Explain What is the difference between saturated and unsaturated hydrocarbons?

17. Make Generalizations How do the boiling points of alkenes and alkynes compare to those of alkanes?

18. Apply Concepts Draw electron dot structures for ethene and ethyne. Use your knowledge of bonding theories to describe the shape of each molecule.

Arson Investigator

Arson is a dangerous crime in which a person starts a fire with the intent to cause property damage or to harm another person. The person responsible, an arsonist, often uses an accelerant to initiate the fire. Gasoline and lighter fluid—both ignitable fluids composed of hydrocarbons—are two of the most commonly used accelerants. If arson is suspected, an arson investigator carefully examines the fire scene and looks for evidence of a crime.

Arson investigators often collect debris from the scene to take back to the laboratory to analyze for accelerants. Investigators frequently analyze the samples with an instrument called a gas chromatograph. The output of the analysis is sometimes called a "fingerprint" because, like a human fingerprint, each accelerant shows a characteristic pattern. With the knowledge of the molecules in each accelerant, the investigator can identify the accelerant from the fingerprint. Knowing which accelerant was used in the crime can help police narrow the search for the arsonist.

WHO'S YOUR PARTNER? Trained dogs with keen noses are often used to guide the evidence collection.

Gas Chromatographic Analysis

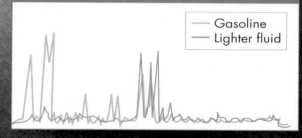

— Gasoline
— Lighter fluid

ACCELERANTS Gasoline and lighter fluid are complex mixtures of hydrocarbons. Each peak in the chromatograph represents a different chemical compound.

Take It Further

1. Describe One of the hydrocarbons found in gasoline is the branched-chain alkane 3-methylhexane. Write the condensed structural formula for this compound.

2. Analyze Data Use the data in the gas chromatographic analysis above to compare the number of hydrocarbon compounds in gasoline and lighter fluid.

22.3 Isomers

CHEMISTRY & YOU

Q: *How do isomers help you see?* Like many other biological processes, vision involves chemistry. Light entering the eye causes a change in the three-dimensional structure of retinal molecules in your eye. The overall structure of retinal molecules appears bent before the light strikes; afterward the structure appears relatively straight. This structural change results in vision.

Key Questions

🔑 How do the properties of constitutional isomers differ?

🔑 What are two types of stereoisomers?

Vocabulary

• isomer
• constitutional isomer
• stereoisomer
• *cis-trans* isomer
• *cis* configuration
• *trans* configuration
• asymmetric carbon
• enantiomer

Constitutional Isomers

🔑 How do the properties of constitutional isomers differ?

You may have noticed that the structures of some hydrocarbons differ only in the positions of substituents or of multiple bonds. Look at the structural formulas for butane and 2-methylpropane and at the models in Figure 22.8.

$$CH_3—CH_2—CH_2—CH_3$$

Butane (C_4H_{10})
(bp −0.5°C)

$$CH_3—\overset{\overset{\displaystyle CH_3}{|}}{CH}—CH_3$$

2-methylpropane (C_4H_{10})
(bp −11.7°C)

Even though both compounds have the formula C_4H_{10}, their boiling points and other properties differ. Because their structures are different, they are different substances. Compounds that have the same molecular formula but different molecular structures are called **isomers.**

Butane and 2-methylpropane represent a category of isomers called constitutional isomers, or structural isomers. **Constitutional isomers** are compounds that have the same molecular formula, but the atoms are joined together differently. 🔑 **Constitutional isomers differ in physical properties such as boiling point and melting point. They also have different chemical reactivities.** In general, the more highly branched the hydrocarbon structure is, the lower the boiling point of the isomer will be compared with less branched isomers.

Figure 22.8 Constitutional Isomers
Both butane and 2-methylpropane have the molecular formula C_4H_{10}. But the atoms in each compound are arranged differently.

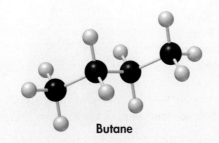

Butane

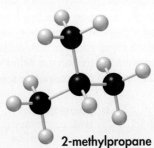

2-methylpropane

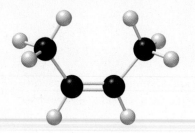

Cis configuration

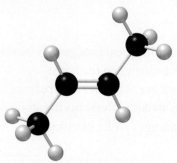

Trans configuration

Figure 22.9 Cis-Trans Isomers
The properties of *cis-trans* isomers are different. The boiling point of *cis*-2-butene is 3.7°C, and the boiling point of *trans*-2-butene is 0.8°C.

Compare *How are the* cis *and* trans *configurations different?*

Stereoisomers

🔑 What are two types of stereoisomers?

Remember that molecules are three-dimensional structures. So molecules with the same molecular formula and with atoms joined in exactly the same order may still be isomers. **Stereoisomers** are molecules in which the atoms are joined in the same order, but the positions of the atoms in space are different. 🔑 **Two types of stereoisomers are *cis-trans* isomers and enantiomers.**

Cis-Trans Isomers A double bond between two carbon atoms prevents other atoms in the molecule from rotating, or spinning, with respect to each other. Because of this lack of rotation, groups on either side of the double bond can have different orientations in space. **Cis-trans isomers,** also known as geometric isomers, have atoms joined in the same order, but the spatial orientation of the groups differs. Although *cis-trans* isomerism is possible in other molecules, the most common example occurs in molecules with double bonds. Look at the models of 2-butene in Figure 22.9. Two arrangements are possible for the methyl groups and hydrogen atoms with respect to the rigid double bond. In the **cis configuration,** similar groups are on the same side of the double bond. But, when similar groups extend from opposite sides of the double bond, the isomer is in the **trans configuration.** *Cis-trans* isomers have different physical and chemical properties.

You should be able to identify *cis-trans* isomers of alkenes when each carbon of the double bond has one substituent and one hydrogen. Notice that the substituent groups attached to the carbons of the double bond do not need to be the same as illustrated in the structures below.

$$CH_3 \diagdown \qquad \diagup H$$
$$C=C$$
$$H \diagup \qquad \diagdown CH_2CH_3$$
trans-2-pentene

$$CH_3 \diagdown \qquad \diagup CH_2CH_3$$
$$C=C$$
$$H \diagup \qquad \diagdown H$$
cis-2-pentene

$$CH_3 \diagdown \qquad \diagup H$$
$$C=C$$
$$CH_3CH_2 \diagup \qquad \diagdown H$$
2-methyl-1-butene
(no *cis, trans* isomers)

Enantiomers The second category of stereoisomerism occurs whenever a central atom has four different atoms or groups attached. Most commonly the central atom is carbon. A carbon with four different atoms or groups attached is an **asymmetric carbon.** Look at the molecular models in Figure 22.10. Because H, F, Cl, and Br atoms are attached to a single carbon atom, the carbon is an asymmetric carbon. The relationship between the two molecules is similar to the relationship between right and left hands. Sometimes the terms *right-handed* and *left-handed* are used to describe compounds with an asymmetric carbon.

Figure 22.10 Asymmetric Carbons
When a carbon atom has four different substituents, as in the compound CHFClBr, it is an asymmetric carbon. Molecules with an asymmetric carbon are either right-handed or left-handed and cannot be superimposed.

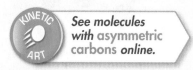

See molecules with asymmetric **carbons** *online.*

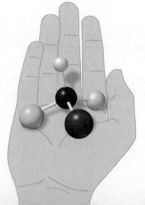

To understand the stereoisomerism that involves asymmetric carbons, you need to visualize the relationship between an object and its mirror image. If the object is symmetrical, like a ball, then its mirror image can be super-imposed. That is, the appearance of the ball and its reflection are indistin-guishable. By contrast, a pair of hands is distinguishable even though the hands have identical parts. The right hand reflects as a left hand, and the left hand reflects as a right hand. When you try to stack your hands on top of one another, the thumb of one hand lines up with the little finger of the other hand. No matter how you turn your hands, you can't get them to look exactly alike.

Pairs of molecules that are mirror images and not superimposable are called **enantiomers,** or optical isomers. The molecules shown in Figure 22.10 are examples of enantiomers. Unlike other isomers, enantiomers have identi-cal physical properties such as boiling points and densities. Enantiomers do, however, behave differently when they interact with other molecules that have asymmetric carbons. In Chapter 24, you will learn that many molecules in your body have asymmetric carbons. As a result, each enantiomer can have a different effect on the body.

CHEMISTRY & YOU

Q: *What kind of isomerism aids in vision? Look at Figure 22.9. Explain how the overall structure of a retinal molecule would appear relatively straight or bent depend-ing on which cis-trans isomer it is.*

Sample Problem 22.4

Identifying Asymmetric Carbon Atoms

Which compound has an asymmetric carbon?

a. CH₃CHCH₃
          |
         OH

b. CH₃CHCH₂CH₃
          |
         OH

> The central carbon in compound (a) has two CH₃ groups attached, so the carbon is not asymmetric.

❶ **Analyze** Identify the relevant concepts.
An asymmetric carbon has four different substituents attached.

❷ **Solve** Apply the concepts to this problem.

> Draw the structure in a way that makes it easier to compare the four different groups attached to the central carbon.

> Compare the groups. If all four groups are unique, the central carbon is asymmetric. If any two are the same, the central carbon is not asymmetric.

Compound (b) has an asymmetric carbon.

19. Identify the asymmetric carbon, if any, in each of the following compounds:

   a. CH₃CHCHO
              |
              Cl

   b. CH₃CHOH
              |
              CH₃

20. Identify any asymmetric carbons in the following compounds:

                    CH₃
                     |
   a. CH₃CH₂—C—Br   **b.** CH₂Cl₂
                     |
                     F

Purpose To build ball-and-stick models and name the nine constitutional isomers of heptane (C_7H_{16})

Materials

- **ball-and-stick molecular model kit** (Colors used to represent elements in the kit may not match colors used to represent elements in this book.)
- **pencil and paper**

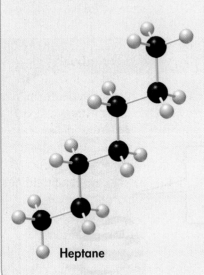

Heptane

Isomers of Heptane

Procedure

1. Build a model for the straight-chain isomer of C_7H_{16}. Draw the structural formula for this isomer.

2. Remove one carbon atom from the end of the chain and reattach it as a methyl substituent to form a branched-chain alkane. Draw the structural formula for this isomer.

3. Move the methyl group to a new position on the chain. Then draw this third isomer. Is there another position that the methyl group can be placed on the chain of six carbons to form yet another isomer?

4. Make other constitutional isomers by shortening the longest straight chain and using the removed carbons as substituents. Draw the structural formulas for each isomer.

Analyze and Conclude

1. List What are the names of the nine constitutional isomers of C_7H_{16}?

2. Identify What is the shortest possible straight carbon chain in the group of heptane isomers?

3. Explain Why does each constitutional isomer have its own unique name?

4. Use Models Look carefully at the structural formulas you drew for the nine constitutional isomers. Identify any that have an asymmetric carbon.

22.3 LessonCheck

21. 🔑 **Explain** Why would you expect two constitutional isomers to have different properties such as boiling points?

22. 🔑 **Review** Name two types of stereoisomers.

23. Apply Concepts Draw structural formulas for the following alkenes. If a compound has *cis-trans* isomers, draw both the *cis* and *trans* forms.
  a. 1-pentene
  b. 2-hexene
  c. 2-methyl-1-butene
  d. 2,5-dimethyl-3-hexene

24. Compare How are constitutional isomers and stereoisomers similar? How are they different?

25. Explain How can you identify an asymmetric carbon?

26. Use Analogies Think of an analogy to describe the relationship between two molecules that are enantiomers.

27. Summarize Draw a concept map to show how the following vocabulary words are related: isomers, constitutional isomers, stereoisomers, *cis-trans* isomers, and enantiomers.

22.4 Hydrocarbon Rings

Q: *Does a compound have to be smelly in order to be classified as aromatic?* When you hear the word *aromatic*, you may think of perfume or flowers. But in organic chemistry, *aromatic* means something else.

Key Questions

🔑 What is the general structure of a cyclic hydrocarbon?

🔑 What is the most accurate description of bonding in benzene?

Vocabulary

- cyclic hydrocarbon
- cycloalkane
- aromatic compound
- aliphatic compound

Cyclic Hydrocarbons

🔑 **What is the general structure of a cyclic hydrocarbon?**

Not all hydrocarbons are straight chains or branched chains. 🔑 **In some hydrocarbon compounds, the carbon chain is in the form of a ring.** A compound that contains a hydrocarbon ring is called a **cyclic hydrocarbon.** Figure 22.11 shows the structures of some examples. Many molecules found in nature contain cyclic hydrocarbons. Rings with five and six carbons are the most abundant.

Just as straight-chain and branched-chain alkanes can be either saturated or unsaturated, so can cyclic hydrocarbons. A cyclic hydrocarbon that contains only single bonds, and is therefore saturated, is called a **cycloalkane.** To determine the IUPAC name of a cycloalkane, first count the number of carbons in the ring and assign the corresponding alkane name. Then simply add the prefix *cyclo-* to the alkane name. For example, the three-carbon ring in Figure 22.11 is named cyclopropane.

Figure 22.11 Cycloalkanes
These illustrations show the first four members of the homologous series of cycloalkanes.
Predict *How would you expect the boiling point of cycloheptane to compare to the boiling points of these cycloalkanes?*

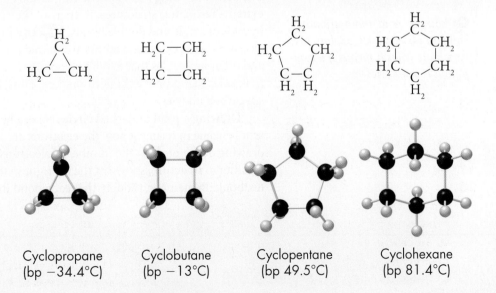

Cyclopropane (bp −34.4°C) Cyclobutane (bp −13°C) Cyclopentane (bp 49.5°C) Cyclohexane (bp 81.4°C)

Figure 22.12 Benzene

All the atoms in the aromatic compound benzene lie in a single plane.
Use Models *What is the molecular formula for benzene?*

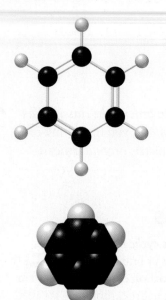

Aromatic Hydrocarbons

 *What is the most accurate description of bonding in benzene?*

There is a class of unsaturated cyclic hydrocarbons that are responsible for the aromas of spices such as vanilla, cinnamon, cloves, and ginger. These compounds were originally called aromatic compounds because they have distinct, pleasant aromas. However, not all compounds classified as aromatic have pleasant odors. In fact, many do not have an odor at all.

Benzene is the simplest aromatic compound. An **aromatic compound,** or arene, is now defined as an organic compound that contains a benzene ring or other ring in which the bonding is like that of benzene. Any compound not classified as an aromatic compound is an **aliphatic compound.** The compounds you studied earlier in this chapter—alkanes, alkenes, alkynes, and cycloalkanes—are aliphatic compounds. The properties of aromatic compounds are quite different from those of aliphatic compounds.

The Structure of Benzene Friedrich Kekulé (1829–1896) made a major contribution to chemistry. He was the first to describe the structure of a benzene molecule. Look at the models of benzene shown in Figure 22.12. The benzene molecule is a six-membered carbon ring with one hydrogen atom attached to each carbon. This arrangement leaves one electron from each carbon free to participate in a double bond. Two different structures with alternating double bonds can be written for benzene.

These structural formulas show only the extremes in electron sharing between any two adjacent carbons in benzene. One extreme is a normal single bond. The other extreme is a normal double bond. Recall that when two or more equally valid structures can be drawn for a molecule, resonance occurs. The actual bonding in a benzene ring doesn't alternate between the two extreme resonance structures. Rather, all the bonds in the ring are identical hybrids of single and double bonds.  **In a benzene molecule, the bonding electrons between carbon atoms are shared evenly around the ring.** Benzene and other molecules that exhibit resonance are more stable than similar molecules that do not exhibit resonance. Thus, benzene is not as reactive as six-carbon alkenes.

Drawing a solid or dashed circle inside a hexagon is a good way to represent benzene in terms of how the electrons are distributed. However, such a drawing does not show the number of electrons involved. For this reason, the traditional structure, shown at the far right in the series below, is used in this textbook. Remember, though, that each bond in the ring is identical.

CHEMISTRY & YOU

Q: *You just read about aromatic compounds. Can you explain to a classmate what it means if a compound is aromatic?*

Substituted Aromatic Compounds Many dyes used to produce the intense colors of your clothing, such as the blue shown in Figure 22.13 are substituted aromatic compounds. Compounds containing substituents attached to a benzene ring are named using benzene as the parent hydrocarbon. When the benzene ring is a substituent, the C_6H_5 group is called a phenyl group.

Figure 22.13 Dyes
Many dye molecules have phenyl groups. For example, indigo, which is used to color blue jeans, has two phenyl groups.

Methylbenzene (toluene)   Ethylbenzene   3-phenylhexane

Some derivatives of benzene have two substituents. These derivatives are called disubstituted benzenes. Dimethylbenzene, also called xylene, is an example of a disubstituted benzene. There are three constitutional isomers for dimethylbenzene ($C_6H_4(CH_3)_2$). The boiling points of the three compounds are a reminder that constitutional isomers have different physical properties.

1,2-dimethylbenzene
(*o*-xylene)
(bp 144°C)

1,3-dimethylbenzene
(*m*-xylene)
(bp 139°C)

1,4-dimethylbenzene
(*p*-xylene)
(bp 138°C)

In the IUPAC naming system, the possible positions of two substituents in disubstituted benzene are designated as 1,2; 1,3; or 1,4. Common names for disubstituted benzenes use the terms *ortho*, *meta*, and *para* (abbreviated as *o*, *m*, and *p*) in place of numbers.

22.4 LessonCheck

28. **Define** What is a cyclic hydrocarbon?

29. **Review** Describe the bonding between carbon atoms in benzene.

30. Identify Name the following compounds using the IUPAC system.

a. CH₂CH₃

b.

c. CH₂CH₃
CH₂CH₂CH₃

31. Evaluate The alternate name for an aromatic compound is arene. Do you think arene is a good option? Consider what the suffix -*ene* means when used with aliphatic compounds.

BIGIDEA CARBON CHEMISTRY

32. Hexane, 1-hexene, cyclohexane, and benzene each have six carbon atoms. What is the difference between these hydrocarbons? Use the words *aliphatic*, *aromatic*, *saturated*, and *unsaturated* to explain your answer.

22.5 Hydrocarbons From Earth's Crust

Q: *Where does gasoline come from?* You might think gasoline comes from the gas station, but what about before that? In this lesson, you'll find out where gasoline comes from and how it is refined.

Key Questions

○ What hydrocarbons are in natural gas?

○ What is the first step in the refining of petroleum?

○ What characteristics are used to classify coal?

Vocabulary

• cracking

Natural Gas

○ What hydrocarbons are in natural gas?

The burning of fossil fuels produces much of the world's energy. Fossil fuels are carbon based because they are derived from the decay of organisms. Millions of years ago, marine organisms died, settled on the ocean floor, and were buried in ocean sediments. Heat, pressure, and bacteria changed the residue into petroleum and natural gas, which contain mostly aliphatic hydrocarbons. Figure 22.14 shows how natural gas is often found overlaying oil deposits or in separate pockets in rock.

○ Natural gas is an important source of alkanes of low molar mass. Typically, natural gas is composed of about 80 percent methane, 10 percent ethane, 4 percent propane, and 2 percent butane. The remaining 4 percent consists of nitrogen and hydrocarbons of higher molar mass. Natural gas also contains a small amount of the noble gas helium. In fact, natural gas is a major source of helium. Methane, the major constituent of natural gas, is especially prized for combustion because it burns with a hot, clean flame.

$$CH_4(g) + 2O_2(g) \longrightarrow CO_2(g) + 2H_2O(g) + \text{heat}$$

Propane and butane are separated from the other gases in natural gas by liquefaction. These heating fuels are sold in liquid form in pressurized tanks as liquid petroleum gas (LPG).

Oxygen is necessary for the efficient combustion of a hydrocarbon. If there is not enough oxygen available, the combustion is incomplete. Complete combustion of a hydrocarbon produces a blue flame. Incomplete combustion produces a yellow flame. The yellow color is due to the formation of small, glowing carbon particles that are deposited as soot when they cool. Carbon monoxide, a toxic gas, also forms along with carbon dioxide and water during incomplete combustion.

Natural gas

Petroleum

Water

Figure 22.14 Oil and Gas Wells
Wells are drilled to reach natural gas and petroleum deposits.

Petroleum

What is the first step in the refining of petroleum?

The organic compounds found in petroleum, or crude oil, are more complex than those in natural gas. Most of the hydrocarbons in petroleum are straight-chain and branched-chain alkanes. But petroleum also contains small amounts of aromatic compounds and sulfur-, oxygen-, and nitrogen-containing organic compounds.

Humans have known about petroleum for centuries; ancient peoples found it seeping from the ground in certain areas. In the late 1850s, a vast deposit of petroleum was discovered in Pennsylvania when a well was drilled to obtain petroleum for use as a fuel. Within decades, petroleum deposits had also been found in the Middle East, Europe, and the East Indies. Petroleum has since been found in other parts of the world as well.

Crude oil is a mixture of hydrocarbons having anywhere from 1 carbon atom to more than 40 carbon atoms. Without further treatment, crude oil is not very useful. The mixture must be separated, or refined, into parts called fractions, which have many commercial uses. **Petroleum refining begins with the distillation of crude oil into fractions according to boiling point.** Figure 22.15 shows a schematic of a petroleum refining distillation tower. Each distillation fraction contains several different hydrocarbons.

Note that the gasoline fraction makes up just 40 percent of the crude oil mixture. However, gasoline is by far the most commonly used petroleum product. To make the supply meet the demand, other processes such as cracking are used. **Cracking** is a controlled process by which hydrocarbons are broken down or rearranged into smaller, more useful molecules. For example, fractions containing compounds of higher molar mass are "cracked" to produce the more useful short-chain components of gasoline and kerosene. Hydrocarbons are cracked with the aid of a catalyst and with heat. This process also produces low-molar-mass alkanes, which are used to manufacture paints and plastics. Other catalytic processes besides cracking are used to increase the amounts of components that improve the performance of gasoline.

Figure 22.15 Fractional Distillation of Crude Oil
The crude oil is heated so that it vaporizes and rises through the fractionating column. Compounds with the highest boiling points condense near the bottom. Compounds with the lowest boiling points condense near the top. **Infer** *In which fraction would you expect to find decane?*

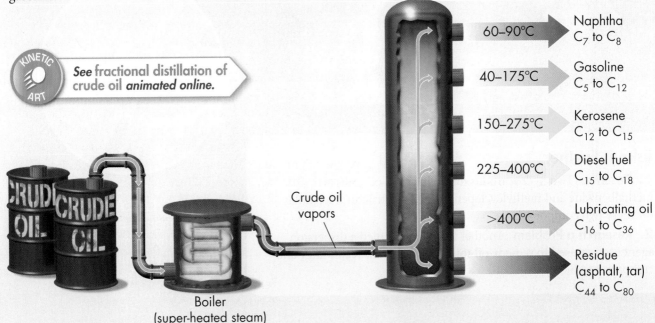

See fractional distillation of crude oil animated online.

60–90°C — Naphtha C_7 to C_8

40–175°C — Gasoline C_5 to C_{12}

150–275°C — Kerosene C_{12} to C_{15}

225–400°C — Diesel fuel C_{15} to C_{18}

>400°C — Lubricating oil C_{16} to C_{36}

Residue (asphalt, tar) C_{44} to C_{80}

Crude oil vapors

Boiler (super-heated steam)

Bioremediation

Oil and water don't mix. You may have witnessed this fact watching footage of an oil spill in the news. Oil spills can lead to the deaths of seabirds and marine mammals and can contaminate soil and drinking water.

One tool being used to clean up spilled oil is a relatively new technology called bioremediation. The technology uses "oil-eating" microbes—particularly bacteria—to remedy the spill. For these microbes, the hydrocarbons in crude oil are not a contaminant but a food source. During the digestion process, harmful hydrocarbons are converted to less harmful products—mainly carbon dioxide and water. Bioremediation is a safe, simple, and relatively inexpensive method of dealing with spilled oil. However, the process takes time to work. In addition, it is usually only effective on residual oil on shorelines, after part of the spill has been removed by other means.

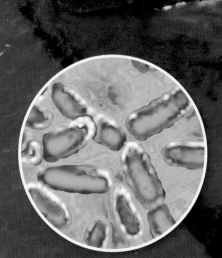

HIGH-TECH . . . AND ALIVE The degradation of petroleum in the marine environment is carried out by diverse microorganisms, including the *Pseudomonas* species shown here.

Take It **Further**

1. Describe Two hydrocarbons found in crude oil spills are methylbenzene and methylcyclopentane. Draw structural formulas for these two compounds.

2. Research a Problem Another technology called a dispersion agent is often used to remedy oil spills. Research this technology and compare it to bioremediation.

Coal

What characteristics are used to classify coal?

Geologists think that coal had its origin some 300 million years ago when huge tree ferns and mosses grew abundantly in swampy tropical regions. When the plants died, they formed thick layers of decaying vegetation. Layer after layer of soil and rock eventually covered the decaying vegetation, which caused a buildup of intense pressure. This pressure, together with heat from Earth's interior, slowly turned the plant remains into coal.

Coal Formation The first stage in the formation of coal is an intermediate material known as peat. Peat, shown in Figure 22.16, is a soft, brown, spongy, fibrous material. When first dug out of a bog, peat has a very high water content. After it has been allowed to dry, it produces a low-cost but smoky fuel. If peat is left in the ground, it continues to change. After a long period of time, peat loses most of its fibrous texture and becomes lignite, or brown coal. **Coal is classified by its hardness and carbon content.** For example, lignite is much harder than peat and has a higher carbon content (about 30 percent). The water content, however, is still high. Continued pressure and heat slowly change lignite into bituminous coal, or soft coal, which is harder than lignite. Bituminous coal has a lower water content and higher carbon content (35 percent to 85 percent) than lignite. In some regions of Earth's crust, even greater pressures have been exerted. In those places, such as the earth beneath eastern Pennsylvania, soft coal has been changed into anthracite, or hard coal. Anthracite has a carbon content that exceeds 85 percent, making it an excellent fuel source.

Coal, which is usually found in seams from 1 to 3 meters thick, is obtained from both underground and surface mines. In North America, coal mines are usually less than 100 meters underground. Much of the coal is so close to the surface that it is strip mined. By contrast, many coal mines in Europe and Asia extend 1000 to 1500 meters below Earth's surface.

CHEMISTRY & YOU

Q: *Where does gasoline come from? Where does coal come from? Use Figures 22.14, 22.15, and 22.16 to explain your answers.*

Figure 22.16 Coal Formation
When tree ferns and mosses die, their decomposing remains build up. Over millions of years, layers of decaying organic material pile up and form peat. Continued pressure and heat transform peat into lignite, bituminous coal, and anthracite coal.
Identify *What three variables contribute to coal formation?*

Time, heat, pressure

Peat   Lignite   Bituminous   Anthracite

Composition of Coal Coal consists largely of condensed aromatic compounds of extremely high molar mass. These compounds have a high proportion of carbon compared with hydrogen. Due to the high proportion of aromatic compounds, coal leaves more soot when burned than the more aliphatic fuels obtained from petroleum. Coal also contains a small amount of sulfur. As coal burns, the sulfur oxidizes to form SO_2 and SO_3, two major air pollutants that contribute to acid rain and the smog shown in Figure 22.17. In order to reduce air pollution, the majority of sulfur is removed before the coal is burned. Any sulfur oxides present after combustion are generally captured before the emissions leave the smokestack.

Coal may be distilled to obtain a variety of products: coal gas, coal tar, ammonia, and coke. Coke is the solid material left after coal distillation. It is used as a fuel in many industrial processes and is the crucial reducing agent in the smelting of iron ore. Coal gas consists mainly of hydrogen, methane, and carbon monoxide. Coal tar can be distilled further into benzene, toluene, naphthalene, phenol, and pitch. The ammonia from distilled coal is converted to ammonium sulfate for use as a fertilizer.

Figure 22.17 Smog in Beijing
Sulfur oxides from emissions of coal-fired plants in China often contribute to dense smog.

22.5 LessonCheck

33. ▭ **Describe** Which type of hydrocarbons can be found in natural gas?

34. ▭ **Review** Describe the first process used in the refining of petroleum.

35. ▭ **Identify** What are the two characteristics used to classify coal?

36. Compare How do the combustion products differ for complete and incomplete combustion of hydrocarbons?

37. Explain Why is cracking a necessary step in the petroleum refining process?

38. List What are some common products made from natural gas, petroleum, and coal?

39. Summarize How did each of the three major fossil fuels form?

40. Compare How do the chemical compositions of natural gas, petroleum, and coal differ?

Hydrocarbon Isomers

Purpose

To draw line-angle formulas and name some of the isomers in gasoline

Materials

- toothpicks
- modeling clay
- pencil
- paper

Procedure

Gasoline is a complex mixture of hydrocarbon molecules. Generally, each molecule contains between five and twelve carbon atoms. Many of the components of gasoline are isomers with the same molecular formula. These components include the isomers of pentane. Study the formulas and names of the constitutional isomers of C_5H_{12} in the table below. Make a model of each isomer using toothpicks and modeling clay, using the space-filling models as a guide. Compare the models for each isomer.

Isomers of C_5H_{12}		
Condensed formula	**Line-angle formula**	**Space-filling model**
$CH_3CH_2CH_2CH_2CH_3$ pentane		
$CH_3CHCH_2CH_3$ $\|$ CH_3 2-methylbutane		
CH_3 $\|$ CH_3CCH_3 $\|$ CH_3 2,2-dimethylpropane		

Analyze and Conclude

1. Describe Draw the complete structural formula for each isomer of C_5H_{12} in the table.

2. Infer In a line-angle formula, each line represents a carbon-carbon bond. Each end of a line, as well as the intersection of lines, represents a carbon atom. Knowing that carbon always forms four covalent bonds, explain how to determine the number of hydrogen atoms bonded to each carbon in a line-angle formula.

3. Describe Because butane can vaporize readily, it is used in the formulations of gasolines in cold climates during winter. Draw condensed structural formulas and line-angle formulas for the two isomers of butane (C_4H_{10}).

You're the Chemist

1. Analyze Data Gasoline contains isomers of hexane, too. Draw the line-angle formulas and name the five isomers of C_6H_{14}. Make a model of each isomer.

2. Design an Experiment Gasoline also contains small amounts of the six isomers of pentene. Two of the isomers are *cis* and *trans* configurations of the same constitutional isomer. Experiment with your models to make the six isomers. Use two toothpicks to represent a double bond. Draw line-angle formulas for each isomer. Name each compound.

22 Study Guide

BIGIDEA CARBON CHEMISTRY

Hydrocarbons are named using the IUPAC system, although sometimes common names are used for certain familiar compounds. All hydrocarbons are nonpolar molecules. In general, the fewer carbon atoms in a hydrocarbon, the lower its melting and boiling points. Hydrocarbons with the same molecular formula but different molecular structures can have different properties.

22.1 Hydrocarbons

Because carbon has four valence electrons, a carbon atom always forms four covalent bonds.

The carbon atoms in an alkane can be arranged in a straight chain or in a chain that has branches.

- hydrocarbon (762)
- alkane (764)
- straight-chain alkane (764)
- homologous series (765)
- condensed structural formula (766)
- substituent (767)
- alkyl group (768)
- branched-chain alkane (768)

22.2 Unsaturated Hydrocarbons

At least one carbon-carbon bond in an alkene is a double covalent bond. Other bonds may be single carbon-carbon bonds and carbon-hydrogen bonds.

At least one carbon-carbon bond in an alkyne is a triple covalent bond. Other bonds may be single or double carbon-carbon bonds and carbon-hydrogen bonds.

- saturated compound (772)
- unsaturated compound (772)
- alkene (772)
- alkyne (773)

22.3 Isomers

Constitutional isomers differ in physical properties such as boiling point and melting point. They also have different chemical reactivities.

Two types of stereoisomers are *cis-trans* isomers and enantiomers.

- isomer (775)
- constitutional isomer (775)
- stereoisomer (776)
- *cis-trans* isomer (776)
- *cis* configuration (776)
- *trans* configuration (776)
- asymmetric carbon (776)
- enantiomer (777)

22.4 Hydrocarbon Rings

In some hydrocarbon compounds, the carbon chain is in the form of a ring.

In a benzene molecule, the bonding electrons between carbon atoms are shared evenly around the ring.

- cyclic hydrocarbon (779)
- cycloalkane (779)
- aromatic compound (780)
- aliphatic compound (780)

22.5 Hydrocarbons From Earth's Crust

Natural gas is an important source of alkanes of low molar mass.

Petroleum refining begins with the distillation of crude oil into fractions according to boiling point.

Coal is classified by its hardness and carbon content.

- cracking (783)

Skills Tune-Up: Structural Formulas

Problem	❶ Analyze	❷ Solve
Name this compound using the IUPAC system. CH₃ | CH₂ | CH₂ | CH₂ | CH—CH₂—CH₃ | CH—CH₃ | CH—CH₃ | CH₃	• The carbons on the parent hydrocarbon should be numbered to give the substituents the lowest possible numbers. • The location numbers for the substituents are included in the prefix. If there are multiple substituents of the same type, include that information in the prefix as well, for example, *di-* or *tri-* for two or three substituents, respectively. • The names of the substituents should be listed in alphabetical order with correct punctuation. Hint: Review Sample Problem 22.2 if you have trouble naming branched-chain alkanes.	Parent hydrocarbon: eight carbon atoms (octane) Substituents and their locations: • methyl group on carbon 2 • methyl group on carbon 3 • ethyl group on carbon 4 8 CH₃ | 7 CH₂ | 6 CH₂ | 5 CH₂ | 4 CH—[CH₂—CH₃] | 3 CH—[CH₃] ← Substituents | 2 CH—[CH₃] | 1 CH₃ Prefix: 4-ethyl-2,3-dimethyl The IUPAC name is 4-ethyl-2,3-dimethyloctane.
Draw a condensed structural formula for 4-ethyl-2-methylheptane. Hint: Review Sample Problem 22.3 if you have trouble drawing structural formulas for branched-chain alkanes.	• The part of the name that ends in *-ane* identifies the parent hydrocarbon. • Prefixes identify the substituents, how many times they appear, and the location of each on the parent hydrocarbon. • Each carbon atom must have four covalent bonds. Hydrogens should be added to meet this need.	Parent hydrocarbon: heptane (seven carbon atoms) Substituents and their locations: • ethyl group on carbon 4 • methyl group on carbon 2 The structural formula for 4-ethyl-2-methylheptane is CH₃ | CH—CH₃ | CH₂ | CH—CH₂—CH₃ | CH₂ | CH₂ | CH₃

ONLINE PROBLEMS

Lesson by Lesson

22.1 Hydrocarbons

41. Why are alkane molecules nonpolar?

*42. Draw condensed structural formulas for pentane and hexane. Assume that the C—H and C—C bonds are understood.

43. Name the alkanes that have the following molecular or structural formulas.

a. $CH_3CH_2CH_3$
b. $CH_3(CH_2)_6CH_3$
c.
$$H-\overset{\overset{\displaystyle H}{|}}{\underset{\underset{\displaystyle H}{|}}{C}}-\overset{\overset{\displaystyle H}{|}}{\underset{\underset{\displaystyle H}{|}}{C}}-\overset{\overset{\displaystyle H}{|}}{\underset{\underset{\displaystyle H}{|}}{C}}-\overset{\overset{\displaystyle H}{|}}{\underset{\underset{\displaystyle H}{|}}{C}}-\overset{\overset{\displaystyle H}{|}}{\underset{\underset{\displaystyle H}{|}}{C}}-H$$

44. Draw structures for the alkyl groups derived from methane, ethane, and propane.

*45. Give the IUPAC name for each compound.

a.
$$CH_3-\overset{}{\underset{\underset{\displaystyle CH_3}{|}}{CH}}-\overset{}{\underset{\underset{\displaystyle CH_3}{|}}{CH_2}}$$

b.
$$CH_3-\overset{}{\underset{\underset{\displaystyle CH_3}{|}}{CH}}-\overset{}{\underset{\underset{\displaystyle CH_3}{|}}{CH}}-CH_3$$

c.
$$CH_3-\overset{}{\underset{\underset{\underset{\underset{\displaystyle CH_3}{|}}{\displaystyle CH_2}}{|}}{CH}}-CH_2-\overset{}{\underset{\underset{\displaystyle CH_3}{|}}{CH_2}}$$

22.2 Unsaturated Hydrocarbons

46. Give the IUPAC name for these alkenes.

a. $CH_3CH=CH_2$
b.
$$\underset{H}{\overset{CH_3}{>}}C=C\underset{CH_2CH_3}{\overset{H}{<}}$$
c.
$$CH_3\underset{\underset{\displaystyle CH_3}{|}}{CH}CH_2CH=CH_2$$
d.
$$\underset{CH_3}{\overset{CH_3}{>}}C=C\underset{CH_2CH_3}{\overset{CH_2CH_3}{<}}$$

*47. Classify each of the following compounds as saturated or unsaturated. Explain.

a. $CH_3CH=CHCH_2CH_3$
b. $CH_3CH_2CH_3$

22.3 Isomers

48. Draw and name all the constitutional isomers with the molecular formula C_6H_{14}.

49. Draw one constitutional isomer of each compound.

a.
$$CH_3-\overset{\overset{\displaystyle CH_3}{|}}{\underset{\underset{\displaystyle CH_3}{|}}{C}}-CH_3$$

b.
$$CH_3-\overset{\overset{\displaystyle CH_3}{|}}{CH}-\overset{}{\underset{\underset{\underset{\displaystyle CH_3}{|}}{\displaystyle CH_2}}{CH}}-CH_3$$

50. Draw a structural formula or carbon skeleton for each of the following alkenes. If *cis* and *trans* forms are present, include both forms.

a. 2-pentene
b. 2-methyl-2-pentene
c. 3-ethyl-2-pentene

51. Can you draw a constitutional isomer of hexane that has an asymmetric carbon? Explain.

*52. Do all molecules have enantiomers? Explain.

22.4 Hydrocarbon Rings

53. Give the IUPAC name for the following cyclic hydrocarbons.

a.

b.

54. Explain why both of these structures represent 1,2-diethylbenzene.

$$\underset{CH_2CH_3}{\overset{CH_2CH_3}{\bigcirc}} \qquad \underset{CH_2CH_3}{\overset{CH_2CH_3}{\bigcirc}}$$

*55. Draw a structural formula for each compound.

a. 1,4-diethylbenzene
b. 2-methyl-3-phenylpentane
c. 1,3-dimethylbenzene

22.5 Hydrocarbons From Earth's Crust

56. Rank these materials in order of increasing carbon content: bituminous coal, peat, lignite, and anthracite coal.

57. How are catalysts used in petroleum refining?

★58. What happens to the sulfur when coal burns?

Understand Concepts

59. Why are the following names incorrect? What are the correct names?
  a. 2-dimethylpentane
  b. 1,3-dimethylpropane
  c. 3-methylbutane
  d. 3,4-dimethylbutane

★60. For each hydrocarbon shown, identify the type of covalent bonds and name the compound.

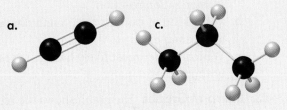

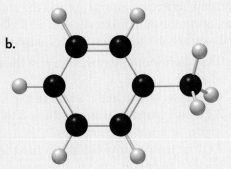

61. Write structural formulas for these compounds.
  a. propyne
  b. cyclohexane
  c. 2-phenylpropane
  d. 2,2,4-trimethylpentane

★62. After ethane, what are the next three members of the homologous series of alkanes?

63. Compare *cis-trans* isomers and enantiomers.

64. Draw electron dot structures for each compound.
  a. propene   **c.** propyne
  b. propane   **d.** cyclobutane

65. Write an equation for the combustion of octane.

★66. Compare these three molecular structures. Which would you expect to be most stable? Explain your answer.

67. The four hydrocarbons produced in the largest amounts in the United States in a recent year are listed in the table below. Answer the following questions based on the data given.

Chemical	Amount produced (billions of kg)
Ethene	15.9
Propene	8.4
Benzene	5.3
Ethylbenzene	4.3

  a. How many billion kilograms of aromatic compounds were produced?
  b. Of the total mass of all four compounds produced, what percent by mass was made up of aliphatic compounds?

★68. Are these two structures *cis-trans* isomers? Explain your answer.

$$CH_3 \quad CH_3 \qquad\qquad H \qquad H$$
$$C=C \qquad\qquad C=C$$
$$H \qquad H \qquad\qquad CH_3 \qquad CH_3$$

69. Use the labeled features in the molecular structure below to answer the following questions.

❷
$CH_2CH_2CH_3$
❶
C_6H_5 H
❺   ❸
CH_3 $CH=CH_2$
$Cl—C—Br$
F ❹

  a. Which label identifies a double bond?
  b. Which label identifies a phenyl group?
  c. Which label identifies a methyl group?
  d. Which label identifies an asymmetric carbon?
  e. Which label identifies a propyl group?

70. Does ethylcyclohexane have an asymmetric carbon? Explain.

★ 71. Use the labeled features in the molecular structure below to answer the following questions.

$$CH_3-\underset{\underset{\underset{CH_3}{|}}{\underset{①}{\overset{CH_3}{\overset{|}{C}}}}}{}-CH_2\underset{②}{}-\underset{\underset{③}{\overset{CH_3}{\overset{|}{CH}}}}{}-CH_3\underset{④}{}$$

a. Which label identifies a primary carbon?
b. Which label identifies a secondary carbon?
c. Which label identifies a tertiary carbon?
d. Which label identifies a quaternary carbon?

Think Critically

★ 72. Infer Methane (CH_4), a widely used fuel, has a heat of combustion (ΔH) of -890 kJ/mol. The ΔH for benzene (C_6H_6) is much higher, -3268 kJ/mol, yet benzene alone is never used as a fuel. Suggest some reasons why benzene is a less desirable fuel than methane.

73. Analyze Explain why you cannot draw a structural formula for methene.

74. Use Models Use the isomers of 2-pentene to show how lack of rotation about a carbon-carbon double bond leads to *cis-trans* isomers.

75. Infer Most cyclic hydrocarbons have higher boiling points than alkanes with the same number of carbons. Suggest a possible explanation for this general difference in boiling points.

★ 76. Apply Concepts Alkadienes are hydrocarbons with two double bonds. Draw the structural formula of the alkadiene with the molecular formula C_3H_4.

77. Predict The molecular formula C_4H_6 could represent an alkyne, a cycloalkene, or a hydrocarbon with two double bonds. Write a condensed structural formula for each. Which compound do you think is the least stable? Why?

★ 78. Apply Concepts Draw structural formulas for the following compounds:

a. 3,4-dimethyl-3-hexene
b. 1-ethyl-2-methylcyclopentane
c. 5,5-dipropyldecane

79. Compare What structural feature is associated with each of these hydrocarbons: an alkane, an alkene, an aromatic hydrocarbon, and a cycloalkane?

80. Evaluate and Revise Draw a correct structure for any of the choices below that are incorrect.

a. $CH_3-CH=CH-CH_2-CH_3$
b.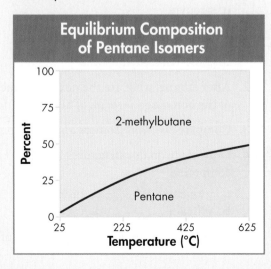
c. $CH_3-C\equiv CH-CH_2-CH_3$
d. $CH_3=CH-CH_2-CH_3$

81. Apply Concepts Upon complete combustion, a gaseous alkane gives a volume of carbon dioxide that is twice the volume of the starting alkane at the same temperature and pressure. Identify the alkane and write the balanced equation for its combustion.

★ 82. Apply Concepts The alkanes 2-methylbutane and pentane are readily interconverted, or isomerized, in the presence of a catalyst.

a. Write a balanced chemical equation for this isomerization reaction.
b. What kind of isomers are 2-methylbutane and pentane?
c. Which isomer most likely has the lowest boiling point?

83. Interpret Graphs The graph shows the relationship between temperature and the composition of equilibrium mixtures of 2-methylbutane and pentane in the presence of a catalyst.

a. The equilibrium mixtures contain the most of which isomer?
b. Could you obtain better yields of the isomer 2-methylbutane by running the reaction at higher or lower temperatures?
c. At what temperature could you run the reaction to obtain a mixture that contains about 25 percent pentane and 75 percent 2-methylbutane?

Equilibrium Composition of Pentane Isomers

84. Predict Use the graph in Figure 22.3 to predict the boiling point of dodecane, the straight-chain alkane containing twelve carbons. Then use a chemistry handbook to find the actual boiling point of dodecane. Compare the actual boiling point with your prediction.

85. Apply Concepts Correct each of the following names and draw the correct structural formulas.

a. 4-methylhexane
b. 1,4-diethyl cyclopentane
c. 3,3methyl-4-ethyloctane
d. 4,4-dimethylpentane
e. 2-ethylheptane
f. phenylmethane

★86. Interpret Graphs The graph shows the number of constitutional isomers for alkanes with three to ten carbon atoms.

a. How many constitutional isomers are there for the C_6, C_7, C_8, C_9, and C_{10} alkanes?

b. The difference between the number of isomers for C_7 and C_8 is 9. The difference between the number of isomers for C_9 and C_{10} is 40. In each case, one additional carbon atom is added to the molecule. Why is the change in the number of isomers so different?

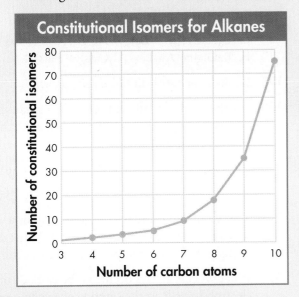

Constitutional Isomers for Alkanes

Number of constitutional isomers (y-axis: 0–80)
Number of carbon atoms (x-axis: 3–10)

87. Evaluate Fossil fuels such as oil and natural gas are the raw materials for many consumer products. Should this information affect the decision to develop energy sources other than fossil fuels? Explain.

88. Research a Problem When fossil fuels burn in an internal combustion engine, the exhaust contains more than carbon dioxide gas and water vapor. Research how catalytic converters work, and write a paragraph explaining what happens to pollutants in a catalytic converter.

89. Connect to the BIGIDEA You've probably seen the instruction "Shake well before using" on a salad dressing bottle. These instructions usually appear on dressings that contain olive oil and water as two of the main ingredients. The molecules in olive oil have long hydrocarbon tails. Explain why you need to shake these types of salad dressings before pouring them onto your salad.

CHEMYSTERY

Nose for Hire

After finishing up with the smell test, Anthony immediately went home and jumped on the Internet to research limonene. He discovered that the two limonene compounds were enantiomers. The right-handed enantiomer smells like oranges, and the left-handed one smells like pine trees. He read on to learn that a nose, like all human tissue, is composed of molecules with asymmetric carbons. As a result, the molecules in your nose that are responsible for detecting smell react differently to the two enantiomers of limonene.

This phenomenon is common in compounds with asymmetric carbons. Another example is the two enantiomers of the compound carvone. One enantiomer smells like spearmint and the other enantiomer smells like the spice caraway.

★90. Infer Do physical properties such as color, density, and boiling point differ for the two enantiomers of limonene?

91. Connect to the BIGIDEA Many medications have asymmetric carbons. There are cases in which one enantiomer helps, while the other causes severe harm. How is this occurrence possible?

*92. Calculate the following quantities:

a. The number of liters occupied at STP by 6.20×10^{-1} mol $Cl_2(g)$

b. The volume of a gas at 3 kPa of pressure if the same gas has a volume of 6 L at 0.5 kPa and the temperature is constant

c. The partial pressure of gas X (P_x) in a mixture of three gases, X, Y, and Z, if the total pressure (P_{total}) is 50 kPa and the sum of the partial pressures of Y and Z is 30 kPa

*93. How many moles of solute are in 750 mL of $1.50M$ KNO_3? How many grams of KNO_3 is this?

94. How many calories are absorbed when 56.0 g of liquid water at 100°C is vaporized to steam?

95. A silver dollar is heated and placed in a foam cup calorimeter containing 50.0 mL of water at 26.5°C. The water reached a maximum temperature of 27.3°C. How many joules of heat were released by the silver dollar?

96. What is the relationship between a calorie and a joule? How many joules is 1 kcal?

97. How does (a) particle size and (b) temperature affect the rate of a chemical reaction?

*98. Explain how the equilibrium position of this reaction is affected by (a) decreasing the temperature and (b) removing CO_2.

$$CaCO_3(s) + heat \rightleftharpoons CaO(s) + CO_2(g)$$

99. Write equilibrium constant expressions for the following reactions:

a. $Cl_2(g) + I_2(g) \rightleftharpoons 2ICl(g)$
b. $2HBr(g) \rightleftharpoons H_2(g) + Br_2(g)$
c. $2S_2Cl_2(g) + 2H_2O(g) \rightleftharpoons$
$$4HCl(g) + 3S(g) + SO_2(g)$$
d. $N_2(g) + 3H_2(g) \rightleftharpoons 2NH_3(g)$

*100. What are the pH values for aqueous solutions containing each of the following hydroxide-ion concentrations?

a. $1.0 \times 10^{-4}M$ **c.** $0.010M$
b. $3.9 \times 10^{-7}M$ **d.** $0.0050M$

101. A colorless solution of unknown pH turns blue when tested with the acid-base indicator bromothymol blue. It remains colorless when tested with phenolphthalein.

a. What is the approximate pH of the solution?
b. How could you determine the pH more accurately?

*102. Write the formula for each acid or base.

a. phosphoric acid   **c.** carbonic acid
b. cesium hydroxide   **d.** barium hydroxide

103. Write the reaction for the dissociation of each of the following compounds in water.

a. sodium hydroxide   **b.** barium hydroxide

*104. Give the oxidation number of each element in the following substances:

a. $CaCO_3$ **c.** $LiIO_3$
b. Cl_2 **d.** Na_2SO_3

105. Are these processes oxidation or reduction?

a. $Fe^{3+} + e^- \rightarrow Fe^{2+}$
b. $Cl_2 + 2e^- \rightarrow 2Cl^-$
c. $Fe^{3+} + 3e^- \rightarrow Fe$
d. $Zn \rightarrow Zn^{2+} + 2e^-$

106. Determine the oxidation number of nitrogen in the following compounds and ions:

a. N_2O_4 **c.** NO_2 **e.** NH_3
b. NO_3^- **d.** NH_4^+ **f.** NO

107. Balance these redox equations.

a. $C_3H_7OH(l) + O_2(g) \rightarrow CO_2(g) + H_2O(l)$
b. $BaO(s) + Al(s) \rightarrow Al_2O_3(s) + Ba(s)$

108. Explain the term *standard cell potential*.

109. A voltaic cell is made of the following half-cells. Determine the cell reaction and calculate the standard cell potential.

$Al^{3+}(aq) + 3e^- \rightarrow Al(s)$ $E^\circ_{Al^{3+}} = -1.66V$

$Ni^{2+}(aq) + 2e^- \rightarrow Ni(s)$ $E^\circ_{Ni^{2+}} = -0.25V$

*110. The calculated standard cell potential for a redox reaction is a negative number. What does a negative number tell you about the reaction?

111. What process always occurs at the cathode of an electrolytic cell? At the cathode of a voltaic cell?

If You Have Trouble With . . .

Question	92	93	94	95	96	97	98	99	100	101	102	103	104	105	106	107	108	109	110	111
See Chapter	14	16	17	17	17	18	18	18	19	19	19	19	20	20	20	20	21	21	21	21

Standardized Test Prep

Select the choice that best answers each question or completes each statement.

1. What is the name of the compound with the following structural formula?

$$CH_3-C-C-C-CH_3$$

with CH_3, H, CH_3 on top and H, H, H on bottom

   (A) 1,2,3,3-tetramethylpropane
   (B) heptane
   (C) 2,4-dimethylpentane
   (D) 1,5-dimethylbutane

2. Which of these are characteristic of all alkenes?
   I. unsaturated
   II. carbon-carbon double bond
   III. enantiomers

   (A) I and II only
   (B) II and III only
   (C) I and III only
   (D) I, II, and III

3. How many carbon atoms are in a molecule of 4,5-diethyloctane?
   (A) 10   (C) 14
   (B) 12   (D) 16

4. *Cis-trans* isomerism is possible in
   (A) 2-pentene.   (C) propyne.
   (B) 2-butane.   (D) benzene.

> ### Tips for Success
>
> **Eliminate Wrong Answers** If you don't know which response to a question is correct, start by eliminating those you know are wrong. If you can rule out some choices, you'll have fewer choices left to consider, which will increase your chances of choosing the correct answer.

5. A constitutional isomer of heptane is
   (A) methylbenzene.
   (B) 3,3-dimethylpentane.
   (C) cycloheptane.
   (D) 3-methylhexene.

6. Which molecule can have enantiomers?
   (A) CH_4 (C) $CFClBrI$
   (B) CF_2H_2 (D) CF_2ClH

7. Draw structural formulas for three constitutional isomers of pentane, C_5H_{12}. Name each isomer.

8. Write structural formulas for the four constitutional isomers of cyclopentane. Name each of the isomers.

The lettered choices below refer to Questions 9–12. A lettered choice may be used once, more than once, or not at all.
   (A) alkene
   (B) arene
   (C) alkyne
   (D) alkane

To which of the above classes of hydrocarbons does each of the following compounds belong?

9. C_7H_{16}

10. C_5H_8

11. C_6H_6

12. C_8H_{16}

Use the molecular structures below to answer Questions 13–16. A molecular structure may be used once, more than once, or not at all.

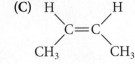

(A)   (C)

(B) $CH_3CH_2CH_2CH_3$ (D)

13. Which structure is a cycloalkane?

14. Which structure is a saturated hydrocarbon?

15. Which structure is a *cis*-isomer?

16. Which structure is a *trans*-isomer?

If You Have Trouble With . . .

Question	1	2	3	4	5	6	7	8	9	10	11	12	13	14	15	16
See Lesson	22.1	22.2	22.1	22.3	22.3	22.3	22.3	22.3	22.1	22.2	22.4	22.2	22.4	22.2	22.3	22.3

23

Functional Groups

INSIDE:

- **23.1** Introduction to Functional Groups
- **23.2** Alcohols, Ethers, and Amines
- **23.3** Carbonyl Compounds
- **23.4** Polymers

PearsonChem.com

The unique flavors and aromas of spices are due to organic compounds with various functional groups.

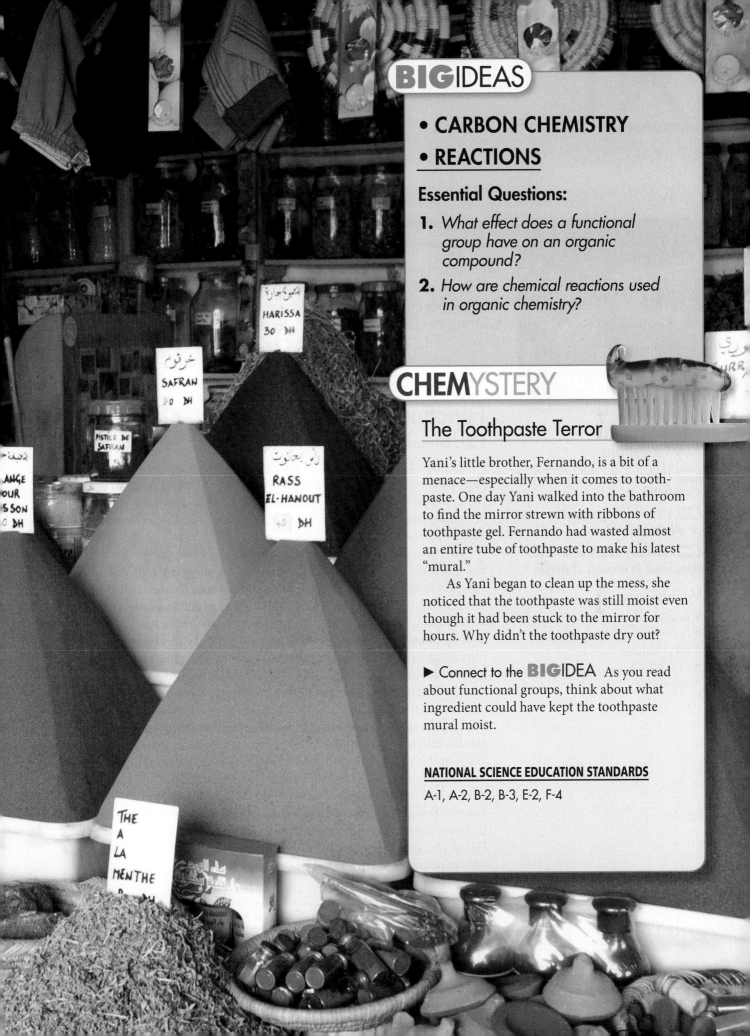

BIGIDEAS

- **CARBON CHEMISTRY**
- **REACTIONS**

Essential Questions:

1. *What effect does a functional group have on an organic compound?*

2. *How are chemical reactions used in organic chemistry?*

CHEMYSTERY

The Toothpaste Terror

Yani's little brother, Fernando, is a bit of a menace—especially when it comes to toothpaste. One day Yani walked into the bathroom to find the mirror strewn with ribbons of toothpaste gel. Fernando had wasted almost an entire tube of toothpaste to make his latest "mural."

As Yani began to clean up the mess, she noticed that the toothpaste was still moist even though it had been stuck to the mirror for hours. Why didn't the toothpaste dry out?

▶ Connect to the **BIGIDEA** As you read about functional groups, think about what ingredient could have kept the toothpaste mural moist.

NATIONAL SCIENCE EDUCATION STANDARDS

A-1, A-2, B-2, B-3, E-2, F-4

23.1 Introduction to Functional Groups

Q: *How can you tell the difference between one organic compound and another?* If you've ever seen a marching band, you know that all the members wear the same uniform. From a distance, all the musicians look nearly identical. But are they? If you look more closely, you can distinguish their differences by the instruments they hold. In a similar way, one hydrocarbon is nearly identical to another until it is distinguished by a functional group.

Key Questions

🔑 How are organic compounds classified?

🔑 What is the general formula of a halocarbon?

🔑 How are substitution reactions used in organic chemistry?

Vocabulary

- functional group
- halocarbon
- alkyl halide
- aryl halide
- substitution reaction

Functional Groups

🔑 *How are organic compounds classified?*

In Chapter 22, you learned about the essential components of every organic compound: hydrocarbon chains and rings. In most organic reactions, the saturated hydrocarbon skeletons of molecules are chemically inert, or nonreactive. So how, then, can there be hundreds of different kinds of organic reactions?

Most organic chemistry involves substituents, which are groups attached to hydrocarbon chains or rings. The substituents of organic molecules often contain oxygen, nitrogen, sulfur, and/or phosphorus. They are called functional groups because they are the chemically functional parts of the molecules. A **functional group** is a specific arrangement of atoms in an organic compound that is capable of characteristic chemical reactions. Most organic chemistry involves the functional groups of organic molecules. Note that the double and triple bonds of alkenes and alkynes are chemically reactive. Therefore, double and triple carbon-carbon bonds are considered functional groups.

🔑 **Organic compounds can be classified according to their functional groups.** Table 23.1 identifies the functional groups that you will learn about in this chapter. You will find it helpful to refer to this table as new functional groups are introduced. In each general structure listed, the symbol R represents any carbon chains or rings attached to the functional group. In some cases, R can be a hydrogen atom. When more than one R group is shown in the structural formula, the groups do not need to be the same. Figure 23.1 shows several consumer products containing organic compounds with various functional groups.

CONCEPTS IN ACTION

Go online to learn more about products containing organic compounds.

Table 23.1

Organic Compounds Classified by Functional Group

Compound type	General structure	Functional group
Halocarbon	R—X (X = F, Cl, Br, or I)	Halogen
Alcohol	R—OH	Hydroxy
Ether	R—O—R	Ether
Amine	R—NH$_2$	Amino
Aldehyde	$\underset{R-C-H}{\overset{O}{\parallel}}$	Carbonyl
Ketone	$\underset{R-C-R}{\overset{O}{\parallel}}$	Carbonyl
Carboxylic acid	$\underset{R-C-OH}{\overset{O}{\parallel}}$	Carboxyl
Ester	$\underset{R-C-O-R}{\overset{O}{\parallel}}$	Ester
Amide	$\underset{R-C-N-R}{\overset{O\qquad R}{\parallel\quad\ \ \mid}}$	Amide

Figure 23.1 Consumer Products
Many items contain hydrocarbon derivatives. The hydrocarbon skeletons in these products are chemically similar. Functional groups give each product unique properties and uses.

ASPIRIN

250 TABLETS
MG EACH

Figure 23.2 Halocarbons A halocarbon is a carbon-containing compound with a halogen substituent.
Classify *Are these halocarbons alkyl halides or aryl halides?*

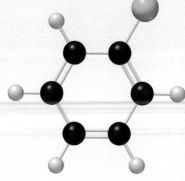

Chloromethane   Chloroethene   Chlorobenzene

Halocarbons

What is the general formula of a halocarbon?

A **halocarbon** is an organic compound that contains at least one covalently bonded fluorine, chlorine, bromine, or iodine atom. **The general formula of a halocarbon is RX, where X is a halogen substituent.** The IUPAC rules for naming halocarbons are based on the name of the parent hydrocarbon. The halogen groups are named as substituents. Examples of IUPAC names for some simple halocarbons are shown below. The common names are given in parentheses. Figure 23.2 shows the ball-and-stick models for these halocarbons.

$$CH_3 - Cl$$

Chloromethane
(methyl chloride)

Chloroethene
(vinyl chloride)

Chlorobenzene
(phenyl chloride)

Common names of halocarbons consist of two parts. The first part names the hydrocarbon portion of the molecule as an alkyl group, such as *methyl-* or *ethyl-*. The second part names the halogen with an *-ide* ending. On the basis of their common names, a halocarbon in which a halogen is attached to a carbon of an aliphatic chain is called an **alkyl halide.** A halocarbon in which a halogen is attached to a carbon of an arene ring is called an **aryl halide.** Table 23.2 lists the names of some substituent groups other than methyl, ethyl, and propyl.

The attractions between halocarbon molecules are primarily the result of the weak van der Waals interactions. Generally, these attractions increase with the degree of halogen substitution. This means that more highly halogenated organic compounds have higher boiling points, as illustrated in Table 23.3.

Very few halocarbons are found in nature, but they can be readily prepared and used for many purposes. For example, hydrofluorocarbons (HFCs) are used as refrigerants in automobile air-conditioning systems. Halocarbons are also used as solvents and as ingredients of stretchable polymers.

Table 23.2

Some Common Substituent Groups

Name	Group structure
Isopropyl	$CH_3 - \overset{\displaystyle CH_3}{\underset{\displaystyle H}{C}} -$
Isobutyl	$CH_3 - \overset{\displaystyle CH_3}{CH} - CH_2 -$
Secondary butyl (*sec*-butyl)	$CH_3 - CH_2 - \overset{}{CH} - CH_3$
Tertiary butyl (*tert*-butyl)	$CH_3 - \overset{\displaystyle CH_3}{\underset{\displaystyle CH_3}{C}} -$
Vinyl	$\overset{H}{\underset{H}{C}} = \overset{}{\underset{H}{C}}$
Phenyl	

Table 23.3

Comparing Methane and Chloromethanes

Molecular formula	Name	Molar mass (g)	Boiling point (°C)
CH_4	Methane	16.0	−161
CH_3Cl	Chloromethane (methyl chloride)	50.5	−24
CH_2Cl_2	Dichloromethane (methylene chloride)	85.0	40
$CHCl_3$	Trichloromethane (chloroform)	119.5	61
CCl_4	Tetrachloromethane (carbon tetrachloride)	154.0	74

Substitution Reactions

🔑 *How are substitution reactions used in organic chemistry?*

Organic reactions often proceed more slowly than inorganic reactions because organic reactions commonly involve the breaking of relatively strong covalent bonds. They often require catalysts. Many organic reactions are complex, and they usually give a mixture of products. The desired product must then be separated by distillation, crystallization, or other means. A common type of organic reaction is a **substitution reaction,** in which an atom, or a group of atoms, replaces another atom or group of atoms.

🔑 **Substitution reactions are an important method of introducing new functional groups to organic molecules.** For example, a halogen atom can replace a hydrogen atom on an alkane to produce a halocarbon. The symbol X stands for a halogen in this generalized equation.

$$R-H \quad + \quad X_2 \quad \longrightarrow \quad R-X \quad + \quad HX$$
Alkane · Halogen · Halocarbon · Hydrogen halide

From the generalized equation, you can write a specific one. This type of reaction is also called a halogenation reaction because the reaction introduces a halogen atom into the molecule. Sunlight or another source of ultraviolet radiation usually serves as a catalyst.

$$CH_4 \quad + \quad Cl_2 \quad \xrightarrow{UV\ light} \quad CH_3Cl \quad + \quad HCl$$
Methane · Chlorine · Chloromethane · Hydrogen chloride

Even under controlled conditions, this simple substitution reaction produces a mixture of mono-, di-, tri-, and tetrachloromethanes.

Halogenation of benzene in the presence of a catalyst causes the substitution of a hydrogen atom on the ring. Iron compounds are often used as catalysts for substitution reactions in aromatic compounds.

Benzene · Bromine · Bromobenzene · Hydrogen bromide

CHEMISTRY & YOU

Q: *Earlier you learned that adding a halogen substituent to a hydrocarbon affects certain physical properties. How can you distinguish between hydrocarbons and halocarbons in terms of structures and properties?*

Halocarbons can be converted to other types of compounds by substitution reactions. For example, hydroxide ions can displace halogen atoms on carbon chains to form an alcohol. (Fluorine is one exception. Because fluoro groups are not easily displaced, they are seldom used to prepare alcohols.) The general reaction for the formation of an alcohol from a halocarbon is as follows:

$$\underset{\text{Halocarbon}}{R—X} + \underset{\text{Hydroxide ion}}{OH^-} \xrightarrow[\text{100°C}]{H_2O} \underset{\text{Alcohol}}{R—OH} + \underset{\text{Halide ion}}{X^-}$$

Chemists usually use aqueous solutions of sodium hydroxide or potassium hydroxide as the source of hydroxide ions. The chemical equation for two specific examples are shown below.

$$\underset{\text{Iodomethane}}{CH_3—I(l)} + \underset{\substack{\text{Potassium}\\\text{hydroxide}}}{KOH(aq)} \xrightarrow{\text{100°C}} \underset{\text{Methanol}}{CH_3—OH(l)} + \underset{\substack{\text{Potassium}\\\text{iodide}}}{KI(aq)}$$

$$\underset{\text{Bromoethane}}{CH_3CH_2Br(l)} + \underset{\substack{\text{Sodium}\\\text{hydroxide}}}{NaOH(aq)} \xrightarrow{\text{100°C}} \underset{\text{Ethanol}}{CH_3CH_2OH(l)} + \underset{\substack{\text{Sodium}\\\text{Bromide}}}{NaBr(aq)}$$

Halocarbons can also be converted to other halocarbons, amines, or ethers by similar substitution reactions.

23.1 LessonCheck

ONLINE PROBLEMS

1. **Review** How are organic compounds classified?

2. **Identify** What is the general formula of a halocarbon?

3. **Explain** Why are substitution reactions useful in organic chemistry?

4. **Classify** Identify the functional group in each structure. Then classify the compound according to its functional group.
   a. $CH_3—OH$
   b. $CH_3—CH_2—NH_2$
   c.
   d. $CH_3—CH_2—CH_2—Br$
   e. $CH_3—CH_2—O—CH_2—CH_3$
   f. $CH_3—CH_2—I$

5. **Describe** Draw a structural formula for each compound listed below.
   a. isopropyl chloride
   b. 1-iodo-2,2-dimethylpentane
   c. *p*-bromotoluene
   d. bromoethene
   e. 2-bromo-2-chloro-1,1,1-trifluoroethane
   f. vinyl iodide

6. **Compare** How would you expect the boiling points of ethane and chloroethane to compare? Explain your answer.

7. **Apply Concepts** Draw the structural formulas and write the IUPAC names of all possible dichloropropanes that could result from a substitution reaction involving chlorine and propane.

8. **Describe** Write a balanced chemical equation for the preparation of 2-propanol from potassium hydroxide and 2-bromopropane.

PCBs: A Persistent Pollutant

Even though that tuna you're eating for dinner might be freshly caught, it still could be contaminated by a toxic industrial chemical that hasn't been manufactured in the U.S. in over 30 years! These chemicals, called polychlorinated biphenyls (PCBs), do not break down easily, and therefore persist wherever they end up for long periods of time.

PCBs are aromatic halocarbons that were used in a variety of industrial applications, including electrical transformers, hydraulic fluids, and carbonless copy paper. The chemicals, which were banned in 1979, accumulated as waste in the sediments and water of rivers, lakes, and oceans. Organisms that live in the water ingest the chemicals, which can build up over time in their fatty tissues. This buildup can be passed up the food chain. At the top of the food chain, PCBs levels can be from 100,000 to 1,000,000 times higher than the original environmental levels.

Although the amount of PCBs from a single meal is not harmful, continued low levels of exposure may lead to various health issues, including cancer.

MAGNIFYING THE EFFECT

Organisms that are higher up in the food chain can accumulate greater PCB concentrations than organisms that are lower in the food chain. The series to the right shows typical PCB levels for each member in units of parts per billion (ppb).

Bluefin tuna
89 ppb

Squid
14 ppb

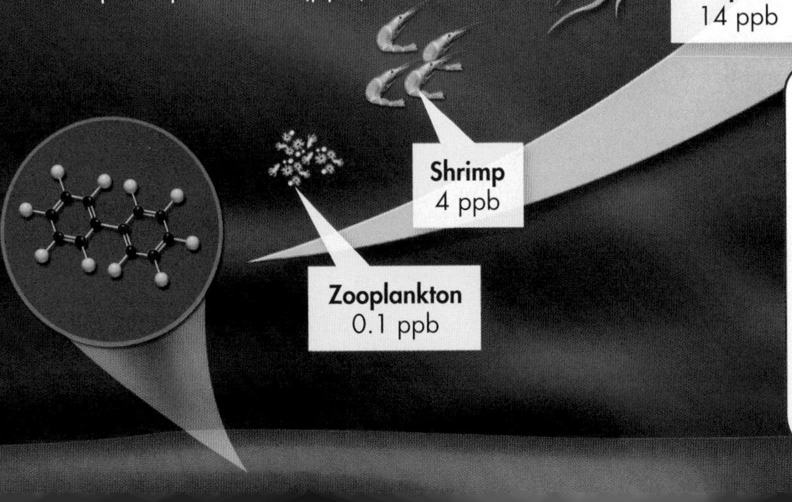

Shrimp
4 ppb

Zooplankton
0.1 ppb

Take It Further

1. Identify PCBs are biphenyls with one to ten chlorine atoms attached. Draw structural formulas of five different PCBs.

2. Infer Polychlorinated biphenyls are heat stable, nonflammable, and have high electrical resistance. Based on these properties, why might companies have used PCBs as insulating materials and thermal conductors?

23.2 Alcohols, Ethers, and Amines

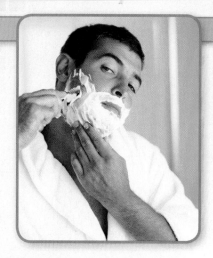

Q: *How can organic chemistry cool you down?* Aftershave lotion contains a certain organic compound that imparts a cooling sensation on the skin. The same ingredient can be found in mint-flavored candy, cough drops, and muscle rubs. In this lesson, you'll read about three classes of organic compounds that have a wide variety of uses.

Alcohols

⚲ What is the general formula of an alcohol?

What do mouthwash, perfume, and hairspray have in common? They all contain an alcohol of some type. An **alcohol** is an organic compound with an —OH group. ⚲ **The general formula of an alcohol is ROH.**

Alcohol

The —OH functional group in alcohols is called a **hydroxy group,** sometimes called a hydroxyl group. The oxygen atom in the —OH group has two pairs of nonbonding electrons, which compress the R—O—H bond angle. As a result, an alcohol functional group has a bent shape.

Aliphatic alcohols can be classified into structural categories according to the number of carbons attached to the carbon with the hydroxy group. If only one carbon (or no carbon) is attached to C—OH, the latter carbon is considered a primary carbon, and the alcohol is a primary alcohol. If two carbons are attached, the carbon is a secondary carbon, which gives a secondary alcohol; if three carbons, a tertiary carbon, and a tertiary alcohol. This nomenclature is summarized below using R to represent any carbon chains or rings.

Primary alcohol	$R-CH_2-OH$	Only one R group is attached to C—OH of a primary (abbreviated 1°) alcohol.
Secondary alcohol	$R-\overset{\displaystyle R}{\underset{\displaystyle \vert}{C}}H-OH$	Two R groups are attached to C—OH of a secondary (2°) alcohol.
Tertiary alcohol	$R-\overset{\displaystyle R}{\underset{\displaystyle \underset{\displaystyle R}{\vert}}{\overset{\displaystyle \vert}{C}}}-OH$	Three R groups are attached to C—OH of a tertiary (3°) alcohol.

Key Questions

⚲ What is the general formula of an alcohol?

⚲ How are addition reactions used in organic chemistry?

⚲ What is the general formula of an ether?

⚲ What is the general formula of an amine?

Vocabulary

- alcohol
- hydroxy group
- fermentation
- addition reaction
- hydration reaction
- hydrogenation reaction
- ether
- amine

Naming Alcohols Both IUPAC and common names are used for alcohols. To name aliphatic alcohols using the IUPAC system, drop the *-e* ending of the parent hydrocarbon name and add the ending *-ol.* The parent hydrocarbon is the longest continuous chain of carbons that includes the carbon attached to the hydroxy group. In numbering the parent hydrocarbon, the position of the hydroxy group is given the lowest possible number. Some alcohols have more than one hydroxy group. To name these alcohols using the IUPAC system, simply add the ending *-diol* or *-triol,* to the parent hydrocarbon name if the alcohol has two or three hydroxy groups, respectively.

The common names of aliphatic alcohols are written in the same way as those of halocarbons. The alkyl group ethyl, for example, is named and followed by the word *alcohol,* as in *ethyl alcohol.* The common name for an alcohol with two hydroxy groups is a glycol.

When the hydroxy group is attached directly to an aromatic ring, the compound is called a phenol. To assign the IUPAC name, phenol is used as the parent hydrocarbon. For example, a phenol with a methyl group attached is called a methylphenol. Cresol is the common name for the *o, m,* and *p* constitutional isomers of methylphenol. Table 23.4 lists the names, structural formulas, and ball-and-stick models of some simple alcohols and phenols.

Table 23.4		
Some Common Alcohols and Phenols		
IUPAC name (common name)	**Structural formula**	**Ball-and-stick model**
Ethanol (ethyl alcohol)	$CH_3—CH_2—OH$	
2-propanol (isopropyl alcohol)	$CH_3—\overset{\displaystyle OH}{\overset{\displaystyle \vert}{CH}}—CH_3$	
1,2-ethanediol (ethylene glycol)	$\underset{\displaystyle OH}{\underset{\displaystyle \vert}{CH_2}}—\underset{\displaystyle OH}{\underset{\displaystyle \vert}{CH_2}}$	
1,2,3-propanetriol (glycerol)	$\underset{\displaystyle OH}{\underset{\displaystyle \vert}{CH_2}}—\underset{\displaystyle OH}{\underset{\displaystyle \vert}{CH}}—\underset{\displaystyle OH}{\underset{\displaystyle \vert}{CH_2}}$	
2-methylphenol (*o*-cresol)	CH_3 / OH	

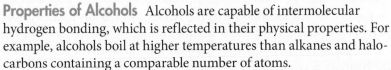

Properties of Alcohols Alcohols are capable of intermolecular hydrogen bonding, which is reflected in their physical properties. For example, alcohols boil at higher temperatures than alkanes and halocarbons containing a comparable number of atoms.

Because alcohols are derivatives of water (the hydroxy group is part of a water molecule), they are somewhat soluble in water. Alcohols with up to four carbons are completely soluble in water. The solubility of alcohols with more than four carbons in the chain is usually much lower. This is because alcohols consist of two parts—the carbon chain and the hydroxy group. The carbon chain is nonpolar and is not attracted to water. The hydroxy group is polar and strongly interacts with water through hydrogen bonding. For alcohols of up to four carbons, the polarity of the hydroxy group overpowers the nonpolarity of the carbon chain. As a result, these alcohols are soluble in water. As the number of carbon atoms increases above four, however, the nonpolarity of the carbon chain dominates, and the solubility of the alcohol decreases.

Uses of Alcohols Figure 23.3 illustrates some common uses of alcohols. For example, 2-propanol, which is more familiarly known as rubbing alcohol, is often used as an antiseptic. It is also used as a base for perfumes, creams, lotions, and other cosmetics. Another alcohol, 1,2,3-propanetriol, is highly soluble in water because it has three hydroxy groups. It also has a tendency to absorb water from its surroundings. This quality makes 1,2,3-propanetriol a valuable moistening agent in cosmetics, foods, and pharmaceuticals.

Some antifreezes use 1,2-ethanediol as the main ingredient. This alcohol has a high boiling point, 197°C, which helps prevent vehicle engines from overheating. Its advantages over other liquids with high boiling points are its solubility in water and its low freezing point, −17.4°C. When water is added to 1,2-ethanediol, the mixture freezes at even lower temperatures. For example, a 50% (v/v) aqueous solution of 1,2-ethanediol freezes at −36°C. This property also makes 1,2-ethanediol an effective anti-icing agent.

Figure 23.3 Uses of Alcohols
Alcohols are used in many common products. **a.** Isopropyl alcohol (IUPAC: 2-propanol) is an effective antiseptic. **b.** Many cosmetic products, including lip gloss, contain 1,2,3-propanetriol. **c.** Aircraft anti-icing fluids are about 65 percent 1,2-ethanediol.
Infer *Why does anti-icing fluid prevent water on the aircraft from freezing at 0°C?*

Figure 23.4 Fermentation in Bread
Yeasts, which are part of a bread recipe, break down sugars in the dough mixture. The carbon dioxide gas that is produced diffuses and causes the dough to rise. Tiny holes remain in the baked bread as evidence of the carbon dioxide gas.

Ethanol is an important industrial chemical. Most ethanol is produced by yeast fermentation of sugar. **Fermentation** is the production of ethanol from sugars by the action of yeasts or bacteria. The enzymes of the yeasts or bacteria serve as catalysts for the transformation. The bread in Figure 23.4 rises because of fermentation. Glucose molecules in the dough are broken down by the following fermentation reaction.

$$C_6H_{12}O_6(aq) \longrightarrow 2CH_3CH_2OH(aq) + 2CO_2(g)$$
Glucose   Ethanol   Carbon dioxide

The ethanol in alcoholic beverages is generally produced by fermentation. Ethanol is an intoxicating substance; it is a depressant that can be fatal if taken in large doses at once.

The ethanol used in many industrial applications is denatured. Denatured alcohol is ethanol that is unsuitable for consumption due to the presence of an additive. That added substance, or denaturant, is often methanol. Methanol is extremely toxic. As little as 10 mL has been reported to cause blindness, and as little as 30 mL has been known to cause death.

READING SUPPORT

Build Study Skills: *Compare/Contrast Table* As you read about addition reactions, use a compare/contrast table to organize the information. In total, three kinds of addition reactions are discussed. Include a column in your table for each kind. *What do the reactions have in common?*

Addition Reactions

How are addition reactions used in organic chemistry?

The carbon–carbon single bonds in alkanes are not easy to break. In an alkene, however, one of the bonds in the double bond is somewhat weaker. This bond is easier to break than a carbon–carbon single bond. So it is sometimes possible for a compound of general structure X—Y to add to a double bond. In an **addition reaction,** a substance is added at the double or triple bond of an alkene or alkyne. **Addition reactions are an important method of introducing new functional groups to organic molecules. They are also used to convert alkenes to alkanes.** In the general addition reaction shown below, X and Y represent the two parts of the reagent that are added to the alkene.

$$\underset{\text{Alkene}}{\diagdown C=C \diagup} + \underset{\text{Reagent}}{X-Y} \longrightarrow \underset{\text{Product}}{-\overset{\overset{\displaystyle X}{|}}{C}-\overset{\overset{\displaystyle Y}{|}}{C}-}$$

Hydration Reactions

The addition of water to an alkene is a **hydration reaction.** A hydration reaction results in the formation of an alcohol. Hydration reactions usually occur when the alkene and water are heated to about 100°C in the presence of a small amount of a strong acid. The acid, usually hydrochloric acid or sulfuric acid, serves as a catalyst for the reaction. The addition of water to ethene to form ethanol is a typical hydration reaction. The parts of ethanol that come from the addition of water are shown in blue in the equation below.

$$\underset{\text{Ethene}}{\overset{\text{H}\quad\quad\text{H}}{\text{C}=\text{C}}} + \underset{\text{Water}}{\text{H}-\text{OH}} \xrightarrow[100°C]{\text{H}^+} \underset{\text{Ethanol}}{\overset{\text{H}\quad\text{OH}}{\text{H}-\text{C}-\text{C}-\text{H}}}$$

Halogenation Reactions

When the reagent X—Y is a halogen molecule such as chlorine or bromine, the product of the reaction is a disubstituted halocarbon. The addition of bromine to ethene to form the disubstituted halocarbon 1,2-dibromoethane is an example.

$$\underset{\substack{\text{Ethene}\\\text{(colorless)}}}{\text{C}=\text{C}} + \underset{\substack{\text{Bromine}\\\text{(orange)}}}{\text{Br}-\text{Br}} \longrightarrow \underset{\substack{\text{1,2-dibromoethane}\\\text{(colorless)}}}{\overset{\text{Br}\quad\text{Br}}{\text{H}-\text{C}-\text{C}-\text{H}}}$$

The addition of bromine to carbon–carbon multiple bonds is often used as a chemical test for unsaturation in an organic molecule. Bromine has an orange color, but most bromine-substituted organic compounds are colorless. The test for unsaturation is performed by adding a few drops of a 1% solution of bromine in tetrachloromethane to the suspected alkene. As Figure 23.5 shows, the loss of the orange color is a positive test for unsaturation. If the orange color remains, the sample is completely saturated.

Hydrogen halides, such as HBr or HCl, also can add to a double bond. Because the product contains only one substituent, it is called a monosubstituted halocarbon. The addition of hydrogen chloride to ethene is an example.

$$\underset{\text{Ethene}}{\text{C}=\text{C}} + \underset{\substack{\text{Hydrogen}\\\text{chloride}}}{\text{H}-\text{Cl}} \longrightarrow \underset{\text{Chloroethane}}{\overset{\text{H}\quad\text{Cl}}{\text{H}-\text{C}-\text{C}-\text{H}}}$$

Figure 23.5 Test for Unsaturation
Bromine solution can be used to identify unsaturated organic compounds. **a.** After mixing, if the solution remains colorless, the compound is positive for unsaturation. **b.** If the solution remains orange, the compound is negative for unsaturation.

Hydrogenation Reactions The addition of hydrogen to a carbon–carbon double bond to produce an alkane is called a **hydrogenation reaction.** Hydrogenation usually requires a catalyst. A platinum (Pt) or palladium (Pd) catalyst is often used. The manufacture of margarine or spreads from various oils is a common application of hydrogenation. As shown in Figure 23.6, adding hydrogen to unsaturated fats in oils results in the formation of saturated fats. Saturated fats have higher melting points than unsaturated fats. This is why margarine remains solid at room temperature.

The hydrogenation of a double bond is a reduction reaction. In the examples below, ethene is reduced to ethane, and cyclohexene is reduced to cyclohexane.

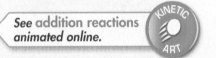

See addition reactions *animated online.*

Ethene   Hydrogen   Ethane

Cyclohexene   Hydrogen   Cyclohexane

Under normal conditions, benzene resists hydrogenation. It also resists the addition of a halogen or a hydrogen halide. However, under conditions of high temperatures and high pressures of hydrogen, and with certain catalysts, three molecules of hydrogen gas can reduce one molecule of benzene to form cyclohexane.

Benzene   Hydrogen   Cyclohexane

Ethers

🔑 What is the general formula of an ether?

Another class of organic compounds may sound familiar to you—ethers. An **ether** is an organic compound in which oxygen is bonded to two carbon groups. 🔑 **The general formula of an ether is ROR.** Like an alcohol, an ether molecule is bent because of the unshared pairs of electrons on the oxygen atom.

$$R \overset{\overset{\displaystyle \cdot\cdot}{O}}{\diagdown} R$$

Ether

To name an ether using the IUPAC system, first you need to identify the two R groups. The smaller R group is treated as part of the substituent and the *-ane* or *-ene* ending is replaced with *-oxy*. The larger R group is the parent hydrocarbon. In the common names of ethers, both R groups are treated as substituents. The *-ane* or *-ene* endings are replaced with *-yl* for both R groups. To form the common name, list the names of the two R groups in alphabetical order and follow with the word *ether*. Two simple ethers are shown below along with their IUPAC and common names.

$$CH_3CH_2 — O — CH_3 \qquad CH_3 — O — \bigcirc$$

Methoxyethane
(ethyl methyl ether)

Methoxybenzene
(methyl phenyl ether)

Ethyl methyl ether and methyl phenyl ether are nonsymmetric molecules. This is because the R groups attached to the oxygen atom are different. When both R groups are the same, the ether is symmetric. The same rules apply when naming symmetric ethers with the IUPAC system as shown in the examples below. The common names of symmetric ethers use the prefix *di-*. Sometimes, however, the prefix *di-* is dropped and a compound such as diethyl ether is simply called ethyl ether.

$$CH_3CH_2 — O — CH_2CH_3 \qquad \bigcirc — O — \bigcirc$$

Ethoxyethane
(diethyl ether)

Phenoxybenzene
(diphenyl ether)

Diethyl ether was the first reliable general anesthetic. Doctors used it for more than a century. However, because diethyl ether is highly flammable and often causes nausea, it was eventually replaced by other anesthetics such as isoflurane shown in Figure 23.7. Diphenyl ether is used in the manufacture of perfumes and soaps for its characteristic geranium smell.

Ethers usually have lower boiling points than alcohols of comparable molar mass, but higher boiling points than comparable hydrocarbons and halocarbons. Unlike alcohols, ethers are not capable of forming hydrogen bonds with other ether molecules. The oxygen atom in an ether is a hydrogen acceptor. But recall that ethers have no hydroxy hydrogen atoms to donate in hydrogen bonding. Ethers can, however, form hydrogen bonds with water. So ethers are more soluble in water than hydrocarbons and halocarbons. Ethers are less soluble in water than alcohols because they form fewer hydrogen bonds than alcohols do when interacting with water.

Figure 23.7 Isoflurane
Isoflurane ($C_3H_2ClF_5O$) is a halogenated ether that is used as an inhaled anesthetic. This veterinarian is administering an inhaled anesthetic to a koala.
Observe *Is isoflurane a symmetric or a nonsymmetric ether?*

Amines

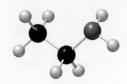

 What is the general formula of an amine?

An **amine** is an organic compound in which nitrogen is bonded to a carbon group. Amines are similar to ammonia (NH_3). When one, two, or three of the hydrogens in ammonia are replaced by carbon groups, the compound is classified as an amine. **The general formula of an amine is RNH_2, R_2NH, or R_3N.** Amines can be classified according to the number of R groups attached to the nitrogen atom. An amine with the general formula RNH_2 is a primary amine because one R group is attached to the nitrogen atom. Amines with two and three R groups attached to the nitrogen atom are secondary and tertiary amines, respectively.

The IUPAC system for naming primary amines is similar to that of alcohols. The *-e* ending of the parent hydrocarbon is changed to *-amine*. For example, CH_3NH_2 is named methanamine. The common names of primary amines are similar to the IUPAC names. The alkyl or aryl group is named and followed by *-amine*. The common name for methanamine is methylamine. Figure 23.8 shows ball-and-stick models of the two simple primary amines ethanamine and benzenamine.

Ethanamine

Benzenamine

$CH_3CH_2NH_2$

Ethanamine
(ethylamine)

Benzenamine
(phenylamine)

Like alcohols, primary amines form intermolecular hydrogen bonds. Because nitrogen is less electronegative than oxygen, the hydrogen bonds in amines are not as strong as those of alcohols. As a result, primary amines have lower boiling points than alcohols with a comparable number of carbons. Amines can also hydrogen bond with water. So smaller amines are soluble in water, but as the number of carbons increase, the solubility in water decreases.

Figure 23.8 Primary Amines Ethanamine is used to make plastics, pharmaceuticals, and pesticides. Benzenamine is used to make furniture foam and some of the dyes that give clothing their colors.
Explain *Why are these compounds primary amines?*

23.2 LessonCheck

9. **Review** What is the general formula of an alcohol?

10. **Review** How are addition reactions commonly used in organic chemistry?

11. **Describe** Write the general formula of an ether.

12. **List** What are three possible general formulas of an amine?

13. **Identify** Write the IUPAC and common names of each compound below.
    a. $CH_3CH_2CHCH_3$
       $|$
       OH
    b. $CH_3CH_2CH_2NH_2$
    c. $CH_3CH_2CH_2OCH_2CH_2CH_2CH_3$

14. **Predict** Give the structure for the expected organic product from each of the following addition reactions.
    a. $CH_3CH=CHCH_3 + H_2O \xrightarrow[100°C]{H^+}$
    b. $CH_2=CHCH_3 + Cl_2 \longrightarrow$
    c. $CH_3CH=CHCH_3 + HBr \longrightarrow$
    d. $CH_3CH=CHCH_3 + H_2 \xrightarrow{catalyst}$

BIGIDEA REACTIONS

15. Write a short paragraph in which you compare and contrast substitution reactions and addition reactions. Include at least two examples of each reaction type, and describe your examples with balanced equations.

23.3 Carbonyl Compounds

CHEMISTRY & YOU

Q: *What gives a banana its characteristic smell?* Many organic molecules have pleasant aromas. These molecules provide the fragrances of certain foods and flowers. You will learn about a number of them in this lesson.

Key Questions

🔑 What structural characteristic do an aldehyde and a ketone share?

🔑 What is the general formula of a carboxylic acid?

🔑 Why is dehydrogenation classified as an oxidation reaction?

🔑 What is the general formula of an ester?

Vocabulary

• carbonyl group
• aldehyde
• ketone
• carboxyl group
• carboxylic acid
• fatty acid
• dehydrogenation reaction
• ester

Aldehydes and Ketones

🔑 **What structural characteristic do an aldehyde and a ketone share?**

Remember that in an alcohol, an oxygen atom is bonded to a carbon group and a hydrogen atom. In an ether, an oxygen atom is bonded to two carbon groups. An oxygen atom can also be bonded to a single carbon atom by a double covalent bond. Such an arrangement is called a carbonyl group. A **carbonyl group** is a functional group with the general structure C=O.

🔑 **The C=O functional group is present in aldehydes and ketones.** An **aldehyde** is an organic compound in which the carbon of the carbonyl group is joined to at least one hydrogen. The general formula of an aldehyde is RCHO. A **ketone** is an organic compound in which the carbon of the carbonyl group is joined to two other carbons. The general formula of a ketone is RCOR. The structures of an aldehyde and a ketone are summarized below.

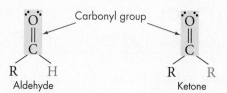

The IUPAC system may be used for naming aldehydes and ketones. For either class of compounds, first identify the longest carbon chain that contains the carbonyl group. Replace the -e ending of the parent structure with -al to designate an aldehyde. In the IUPAC system, the continuous-chain aldehydes are named methanal, ethanal, propanal, butanal, and so forth.

Ketones are named by changing the ending of the longest continuous carbon chain that contains the carbonyl group from -e to -one. If the carbonyl group of a ketone could occur at more than one place on the chain, then its position is designated by the lowest possible number. Table 23.5 illustrates the naming of some common aldehydes and ketones.

Table 23.5			
Some Common Aldehydes and Ketones			
Compound type	**IUPAC name (common name)**	**Structural formula**	**Ball-and-stick model**
Aldehyde	Methanal (formaldehyde)	$H-\overset{\overset{\displaystyle O}{\|\|}}{C}-H$	
Aldehyde	Ethanal (acetaldehyde)	$CH_3-\overset{\overset{\displaystyle O}{\|\|}}{C}-H$	
Aldehyde	Benzaldehyde (benzaldehyde)	$\overset{\overset{\displaystyle O}{\|\|}}{C}-H$ attached to benzene ring	
Ketone	Propanone (acetone)	$CH_3-\overset{\overset{\displaystyle O}{\|\|}}{C}-CH_3$	
Ketone	Diphenylmethanone (benzophenone)	$\overset{\overset{\displaystyle O}{\|\|}}{C}$ between two benzene rings	

Uses of Aldehydes and Ketones The simplest aldehyde is methanal (HCHO), also called formaldehyde. Methanal is very important industrially. Its greatest use is in the manufacture of synthetic resins. Methanal is usually available as a 40% aqueous solution, known as formalin. Formalin can be used to preserve biological specimens. The methanal in solution combines with protein in tissues to make the tissues hard and insoluble in water. This prevents the specimen from decaying.

The most common industrial ketone is propanone, also called acetone. Propanone is a colorless, volatile liquid that boils at 56°C. Propanone is used in industry as a solvent for resins, plastics, and varnishes. Many nail-polish removers contain propanone, too.

Some Organic Compounds with Three Carbons			
Compound	Formula	Boiling point (°C)	Primary intermolecular interactions
Propane	$CH_3CH_2CH_3$	–42	Dispersion forces
Propanal	CH_3CH_2CHO	49	Polar-polar interactions
Propanone	CH_3COCH_3	56	Polar-polar interactions
1-Propanol	$CH_3CH_2CH_2OH$	97	Hydrogen bonding

Table 23.6 These four organic compounds have the same number of carbon atoms. Yet their boiling points are different.
a. Classify Determine the type of each organic compound.
b. Compare Use your knowledge of intermolecular interactions to explain the similarities and differences in the boiling points of the four compounds.

A wide variety of aldehydes and ketones have been isolated from plants and animals. Many of them, particularly those with high molar masses, have fragrant odors. They are usually known by their common names, which can indicate their natural sources or perhaps a characteristic property. Benzaldehyde is the simplest aromatic aldehyde. It's also known as oil of bitter almond because it is largely responsible for the taste and aroma of almonds. Many flavoring agents, including vanilla bean extract and the cinnamon sticks shown in Figure 23.9, contain aromatic aldehydes.

Figure 23.9 Cinnamaldehyde
The cinnamon sticks in this drink contain an aldehyde with the common name cinnamaldehyde.

Properties of Aldehydes and Ketones Aldehydes and ketones cannot form intermolecular hydrogen bonds because they lack —OH and —NH groups. Consequently, they have boiling points that are lower than those of corresponding alcohols. Aldehydes and ketones can attract each other, however, through polar–polar interactions of their carbonyl groups. As a result, their boiling points are higher than those of the corresponding alkanes. These attractive forces account for the fact that nearly all aldehydes and ketones are either liquids or solids at room temperature. The exception is methanal, which is a gas. Table 23.6 compares the boiling points of an alkane, an aldehyde, a ketone, and an alcohol with the same number of carbon atoms.

Aldehydes and ketones can form weak hydrogen bonds between the carbonyl oxygen and the hydrogen atoms of water. The lower members of the series—up to three carbons—are soluble in water in all proportions. As the length of the hydrocarbon chain increases above four, however, water solubility decreases. When the carbon chain exceeds five or six carbons, the solubility of both aldehydes and ketones is very low. As might be expected, all aldehydes and ketones are soluble in nonpolar solvents.

Carboxylic Acids

What is the general formula of a carboxylic acid?

A **carboxyl group** is a functional group that consists of a carbonyl group attached to a hydroxy group. It can be written as —COOH or —CO_2H. A **carboxylic acid** is an organic compound with a carboxyl group. **The general formula of a carboxylic acid is RCOOH.**

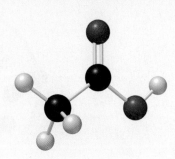

Figure 23.10 Ethanoic Acid
Ethanoic acid is a simple carboxylic acid. It is a colorless, volatile liquid.
Identify *What R group is attached to the carboxyl group in ethanoic acid?*

As you may have guessed from their name, carboxylic acids are acidic. Carboxylic acids are considered weak acids because they ionize weakly in solution. In water, they can lose a hydrogen ion and form a carboxylate ion, as shown in the following reaction.

In the IUPAC system, carboxylic acids are named by replacing the *-e* ending of the parent structure with the ending *-oic acid*. Remember, the parent hydrocarbon of a carboxylic acid is the longest continuous carbon chain containing the carboxyl group. So, for example, the carboxylic acid CH_3COOH is named ethanoic acid. Figure 23.10 shows the ball-and-stick model of ethanoic acid. Table 23.7 lists the names and formulas of some common saturated aliphatic carboxylic acids.

Table 23.7

Some Saturated Aliphatic Carboxylic Acids

Molecular formula	Carbon atoms	IUPAC name	Common name	Melting point (°C)
HCOOH	1	Methanoic acid	Formic acid	8
CH_3COOH	2	Ethanoic acid	Acetic acid	17
CH_3CH_2COOH	3	Propanoic acid	Propionic acid	−22
$CH_3(CH_2)_2COOH$	4	Butanoic acid	Butyric acid	−6
$CH_3(CH_2)_4COOH$	6	Hexanoic acid	Caproic acid	−3
$CH_3(CH_2)_6COOH$	8	Octanoic acid	Caprylic acid	16
$CH_3(CH_2)_8COOH$	10	Decanoic acid	Capric acid	31
$CH_3(CH_2)_{10}COOH$	12	Dodecanoic acid	Lauric acid	44
$CH_3(CH_2)_{12}COOH$	14	Tetradecanoic acid	Myristic acid	58
$CH_3(CH_2)_{14}COOH$	16	Hexadecanoic acid	Palmitic acid	63
$CH_3(CH_2)_{16}COOH$	18	Octadecanoic acid	Stearic acid	70

Figure 23.11 Citric Acid
A common carboxylic acid is citric acid, which is found in lemons and limes.
Use Models *How many carboxyl groups does a citric acid molecule have?*

Carboxylic acids are abundant and widely distributed in nature. The lemons and limes in Figure 23.11 contain citric acid, a carboxylic acid that gives citrus fruits their sour flavor. The IUPAC name for citric acid is 2-hydroxypropane-1,2,3-tricarboxylic acid. Many carboxylic acids have common names derived from a Greek or Latin word that describes their natural sources. For example, the common name for ethanoic acid is acetic acid, which comes from the Latin word *acetum,* meaning vinegar. Common household vinegar contains about 5% (v/v) acetic acid. Many carboxylic acids were first isolated from fats and are called **fatty acids.** Propionic acid, the three-carbon acid, literally means first fatty acid.

Like alcohols, carboxylic acids form intermolecular hydrogen bonds. Thus, carboxylic acids have higher boiling and melting points than other compounds of similar molar mass. The low-molar-mass members of the aliphatic carboxylic acid series are colorless, volatile liquids. The higher members of the series are nonvolatile, waxy solids with low melting points. All aromatic carboxylic acids are solids at room temperature.

The carboxyl group in carboxylic acids is polar and readily forms hydrogen bonds with water molecules. As a result, methanoic, ethanoic, propanoic, and butanoic acids are completely soluble in water. After four carbons, however, the solubility drops sharply. Most carboxylic acids are also soluble in organic solvents such as ethanol or propanone.

Oxidation-Reduction Reactions

🔑 **Why is dehydrogenation classified as an oxidation reaction?**

The classes of organic compounds you have just studied—aldehydes, ketones, and carboxylic acids—are related by oxidation and reduction reactions. Recall from Chapter 20 that oxidation is the gain of oxygen, loss of hydrogen, or loss of electrons and reduction is the loss of oxygen, gain of hydrogen, or gain of electrons. Also remember that one does not occur without the other.

In organic chemistry, the number of oxygen atoms and hydrogen atoms attached to carbon indicates the degree of oxidation of a compound. The fewer hydrogens on a carbon–carbon bond, the more oxidized the bond. Thus, a triple bond is more oxidized than a double bond, which is more oxidized than a single bond.

The loss of a molecule of hydrogen from an organic molecule is called a **dehydrogenation reaction.** It is the opposite of a hydrogenation reaction. Strong heating and a catalyst are usually needed to make dehydrogenation reactions occur. 🔑 **Dehydrogenation is an oxidation reaction because the loss of each molecule of hydrogen involves the loss of two electrons from the organic molecule.** The remaining carbon electrons pair to make a second or third bond, as shown in the reactions below.

See oxidation reactions *animated* online.

$$H-\underset{\underset{H}{|}}{\overset{\overset{H}{|}}{C}}-\underset{\underset{H}{|}}{\overset{\overset{H}{|}}{C}}-H \xrightarrow[\text{oxidation}]{\substack{\text{loss of hydrogen} \\ \text{(dehydrogenation)}}} \underset{H}{\overset{H}{C}}=\underset{H}{\overset{H}{C}} \xrightarrow[\text{oxidation}]{\substack{\text{loss of hydrogen} \\ \text{(dehydrogenation)}}} H-C\equiv C-H$$

Least oxidized
(most reduced)

Most oxidized
(least reduced)

Oxidation in organic chemistry also involves the number and degree of oxidation of oxygen atoms attached to a carbon atom. For example, methane, a saturated hydrocarbon, can be oxidized in steps to carbon dioxide. This occurs if it alternately gains oxygen atoms and loses hydrogen atoms. Methane is oxidized to methanol, then to methanal, then to methanoic acid, and finally to carbon dioxide. The carbon dioxide is most oxidized or least reduced, and methane is least oxidized or most reduced.

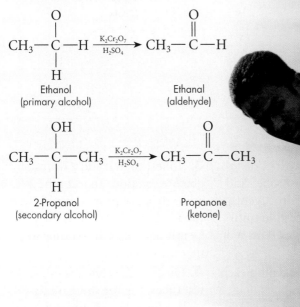

Methane
(most energetic molecule)   Methanol   Methanal   Methanoic acid   Carbon dioxide
(least energetic molecule)

The more reduced a carbon compound is, the more energy it can release upon its complete oxidation to carbon dioxide. The oxidation of organic compounds is exothermic. The energy-releasing properties of oxidation reactions are extremely important for the production of energy in living systems. To play a sport, such as the one shown in Figure 23.12, your body must produce energy by oxidation reactions.

Primary alcohols can be oxidized to aldehydes, and secondary alcohols can be oxidized to ketones by warming them with acidified potassium dichromate ($K_2Cr_2O_7$). Tertiary alcohols, however, cannot be oxidized because there is no hydrogen atom present on the carbon atom attached to the hydroxy group. Examples of oxidation of a primary and secondary alcohol are shown below.

Ethanol
(primary alcohol)   Ethanal
(aldehyde)

2-Propanol
(secondary alcohol)   Propanone
(ketone)

Figure 23.12
Oxidation in Living Systems
Oxidation reactions occur in many daily activities. These athletes are energized by oxidation reactions taking place within the cells of their bodies.

Aldehydes are so easily oxidized that it is difficult to prevent further oxidation to carboxylic acids as shown in the reaction below.

$$R-\overset{\overset{\displaystyle O}{\|}}{C}-H \xrightarrow[\text{H}_2\text{SO}_4]{\text{K}_2\text{Cr}_2\text{O}_7} R-\overset{\overset{\displaystyle O}{\|}}{C}-OH$$

Aldehyde   Carboxylic acid

Further oxidation is avoided by removing them from the reaction mixture as they are formed. Unlike aldehydes, ketones are relatively resistant to further oxidation, so there is no need to remove them from the mixture during the reaction.

Tests for aldehydes make use of the ease with which these compounds are oxidized. Benedict's and Fehling's reagents are deep-blue alkaline solutions of copper(II) sulfate. Figure 23.13 illustrates Fehling's test for an aldehyde. When an aldehyde is oxidized with Benedict's or Fehling's reagent, a red precipitate of copper(I) oxide (Cu_2O) is formed. The aldehyde is oxidized to its acid, and copper(II) ions (Cu^{2+}) are reduced to copper(I) ions (Cu^+).

Figure 23.13 Fehling's Test
When an aldehyde is mixed with Fehling's reagent (left test tube) and heated, the blue copper(II) ions in Fehling's reagent are reduced to form Cu_2O, a red precipitate (right test tube). **Infer** *What is the oxidation state of copper in the product?*

Quick Lab

Purpose To distinguish an aldehyde from an alcohol or a ketone using Tollens' reagent

Materials
- $1M$ sodium hydroxide
- 5% silver nitrate
- $6M$ aqueous ammonia
- 4 small test tubes
- test tube rack
- plastic droppers
- glucose solution
- propanone
- ethanol

Testing for an Aldehyde

Procedure

1. Add 1 drop of $1M$ sodium hydroxide to 2 mL of 5% silver nitrate in a test tube. Add $6M$ aqueous ammonia drop by drop, gently agitating the tube after each addition until the brownish precipitate dissolves. This will be your Tollens' reagent.

2. Place 10 drops of Tollens' reagent in each of three clean, labeled test tubes.

3. To test tube 1, add 2 drops of glucose solution. To test tube 2, add 2 drops of propanone. To test tube 3, add 2 drops of ethanol. Gently agitate each test tube to mix the contents.

4. Observe the contents of the test tubes, leaving them undisturbed for at least 5 minutes.

Analyze and Conclude

1. Observe What evidence of a chemical reaction did you observe in test tube 1? In test tube 2? In test tube 3?

2. Describe Write the equation for any chemical reaction you observed.

3. Infer If you observed a chemical reaction in one or more of the test tubes, what practical uses might the reaction have?

Esters

🔑 What is the general formula of an ester?

Esters are probably the most pleasant and delicious organic compounds one can study. Many esters have pleasant, fruity odors. Esters give blueberries, pineapples, apples, pears, bananas, and many other fruits their characteristic aromas. They also give many perfumes their fragrances. An **ester** is an organic compound in which the —OH of the carboxyl group has been replaced by an —OR from an alcohol. Esters contain a carbonyl group and an ether link to the carbonyl carbon. 🔑 **The general formula of an ester is RCOOR.**

Q: *The smell of straw-berries is largely due to benzyl acetate. The smell of almonds is largely due to benzaldehyde. How are the general formulas of these compounds similar? How are they different?*

Carbonyl group (from the acid) →

Alkyl or aryl group (from the alcohol)

$$R \quad O—R$$

Ester

Figure 23.14 shows the esters that contribute to the characteristic odors of bananas and strawberries. Simple esters are neutral substances. Although the molecules are polar, they cannot form hydrogen bonds with one another because they do not contain hydrogen attached to oxygen or another electronegative atom. As a result, only weak attractions hold ester molecules to one another. As you might expect, esters have much lower boiling points than carboxylic acids. The low-molar-mass esters are somewhat soluble in water, but esters containing more than four or five carbons have very limited solubility.

Esters may be prepared from a carboxylic acid and an alcohol. The process is called esterification. The reactants, usually a carboxylic acid and a primary or secondary alcohol, are heated with an acid as a catalyst. The synthesis of ethyl ethanoate from ethanoic acid and ethanol is an example of esterification.

$$CH_3—\overset{\overset{\displaystyle O}{\|}}{C}—OH + CH_3CH_2O—H \underset{}{\overset{H^+}{\rightleftharpoons}} CH_3—\overset{\overset{\displaystyle O}{\|}}{C}—OCH_2CH_3 + H_2O$$

Ethanoic acid   Ethanol   Ethyl ethanoate

Figure 23.14 Esters
The characteristic aromas of many fruits are due to esters. Isopentyl acetate is an ester found in bananas. Strawberries contain the ester benzyl acetate.

Benzyl acetate

Isopentyl acetate

If an ester is heated with water for several hours, usually very little happens. In strong acid or base solutions, however, the ester breaks down. An ester is hydrolyzed by the addition of water to produce a carboxylic acid and an alcohol. The reaction is rapid in acidic solution.

$$CH_3-\overset{\overset{\displaystyle O}{\|}}{C}-OCH_2CH_3 + H_2O \underset{}{\overset{H^+}{\rightleftharpoons}} CH_3-\overset{\overset{\displaystyle O}{\|}}{C}-OH + HOCH_2CH_3$$

Ethyl ethanoate   Ethanoic acid   Ethanol

Hydroxide ions also promote this reaction. Usually aqueous solutions of sodium hydroxide or potassium hydroxide are the source of hydroxide ions. Because many esters do not dissolve in water, a solvent such as ethanol is added to make the solution homogeneous. The reaction mixture is usually heated. All of the ester is converted to products. The carboxylic acid product is in solution as its sodium or potassium salt as shown in the example below.

$$CH_3-\overset{\overset{\displaystyle O}{\|}}{C}-OCH_2CH_3 + NaOH \longrightarrow CH_3-\overset{\overset{\displaystyle O}{\|}}{C}-O^-Na^+ + HOCH_2CH_3$$

Ethyl ethanoate   Sodium ethanoate   Ethanol

If the reaction mixture is acidified, the carboxylic acid forms.

$$CH_3-\overset{\overset{\displaystyle O}{\|}}{C}-O^-Na^+ + HCl \longrightarrow CH_3-\overset{\overset{\displaystyle O}{\|}}{C}-OH + NaCl$$

Sodium ethanoate   Ethanoic acid

23.3 LessonCheck

16. **Review** Describe the structure of the carbonyl groups that are characteristic of aldehydes and ketones.

17. **Identify** What is the general formula of a carboxylic acid?

18. **Explain** Why is dehydrogenation an oxidation reaction?

19. **Describe** What is the general formula of an ester?

20. **Predict** What products are expected when the following compounds are oxidized?
a. $CH_3CH_2CH_2CH_2OH$
b. $\underset{CH_3CH_2CHCH_3}{\overset{\overset{\displaystyle OH}{|}}{}}$
c. $\underset{\underset{\displaystyle CH_3}{|}}{\overset{\overset{\displaystyle OH}{|}}{CH_3CH_2CCH_3}}$

21. **Classify** Write the IUPAC name for each of the following compounds:
a. CH_3CH_2CHO
b. $CH_3CH_2CH_2\overset{\overset{\displaystyle O}{\|}}{C}CH_2CH_3$
c. $CH_3CH_2CH_2CH_2COOH$

22. **Describe** Draw structural formulas for the following organic compounds:
a. hexanoic acid
b. butanal
c. 2-pentanone

BIGIDEA CARBON CHEMISTRY

23. How can you describe the degree of oxidation of an organic compound?

Scratch and Sniff Stickers

When you were a kid, you may have been rewarded with a scratch and sniff sticker for an A+ assignment. Many scratch and sniff stickers smell like fruits such as cherries, strawberries, or grapes. Others smell like root beer, pickles, pizza, or even stinky sneakers. Have you ever wondered where the scents come from?

Esters are usually the smelly component used in scratch and sniff sticker technology. The esters used in the stickers are volatile liquids, which explains why you are able to smell them. A single ester or a mixture of esters with the desired odor is contained in numerous tiny brittle capsules that are glued onto the surface of the sticker paper. The capsules are so small that you can barely notice the rough texture of the sticker. When you scratch the sticker, you break some of the capsules and allow the ester molecules to make their way to your nose.

SNIFF IT The volatile ester molecules that are contained in the capsules are released from each ruptured capsule.

SCRATCH IT When your finger exerts sufficient pressure on the capsules, they rupture.

Take It Further

1. Explain Why does the smell get more faint as the sticker is continually scratched?

2. Describe Methyl butanoate can be used to impart a pineapple aroma. Write a condensed structural formula for this ester.

3. Infer Which carboxylic acid and alcohol would you use to prepare ethyl heptanoate, the ester that smells like grapes?

23.4 Polymers

Q: *How do organic molecules bond together to form long chains?* Similar to the way these skydivers are linked together in a chain, organic molecules can bond together to form long molecular chains. As more molecules bond together, the molecular chains grow longer and longer.

Key Questions

🔑 How does an addition polymer form?

🔑 How are condensation polymers formed?

Vocabulary

• polymer
• monomer

Addition Polymers

🔑 **How does an addition polymer form?**

Most of the reactions that you have learned about so far involve reactants and products of low molar mass. Some of the most important organic compounds that exist, however, are giant molecules called polymers. Each day, you see many different polymers. For example, the materials you know as plastics are polymers. The kinds and uses of plastics are numerous indeed!

A **polymer** is a large molecule formed by the covalent bonding of repeating smaller molecules. The smaller molecules that combine to form a polymer are called **monomers.** Some polymers contain only one type of monomer. Others contain two or more types of monomers. The reaction that joins monomers to form a polymer is called polymerization. Most polymerization reactions require a catalyst.

🔑 **An addition polymer forms when unsaturated monomers react to form a polymer.** Ethene undergoes addition polymerization. The ethene molecules bond to one another to form the long-chain polymer polyethylene as described in the equation below.

$$x\text{CH}_2{=}\text{CH}_2 \longrightarrow \text{H}{+}\text{CH}_2{-}\text{CH}_2{+}_x\text{H}$$

Ethene
(ethylene)

Polyethylene

Figure 23.15 Polyethylene
Many familiar household items, including this unsinkable duck, are made of polyethylene.

Note that the letter x on the reactant side of the equation refers to the number of monomers (in this case, ethene) that combine to form the polymer. The x on the product side indicates the number of repeating units in the polymer. Parentheses are used to identify the repeating unit (in this case, $-\text{CH}_2-\text{CH}_2-$).

Polyethylene, which is chemically resistant and easy to clean, is an important industrial product. It is used to make plastic bottles, containers, and even toys, such as the one in Figure 23.15.

Figure 23.16 Polymer Products
a. Polypropylene is used in the manufacture of a variety of items that require stiffness, including these kazoos.
b. Polystyrene foam is used to make protective helmets.
Infer *How does the polystyrene foam in a helmet protect a cyclist during an accident?*

The physical properties of polyethylene can be controlled by shortening or lengthening the carbon chains. Polyethylene that contains relatively short chains ($x = 100$) has the consistency of paraffin wax. Polyethylene with long chains ($x = 1000$) is harder and more rigid.

Figure 23.16 shows some items made from polymers of substituted ethenes. Polypropylene, a stiffer polymer than polyethylene, is used extensively in utensils and beverage containers. Polypropylene is prepared by the polymerization of propene.

$$x CH_2 = CH\text{—}CH_3 \longrightarrow (CH_2\text{—}CH)_x\text{—}CH_3$$

Propene
(propylene)

Polypropylene

Polystyrene, in the form of a rigid foam, is a poor heat conductor. This makes it useful for insulating homes and for manufacturing molded items such as coffee cups and picnic coolers. Polystyrene is prepared by the polymerization of styrene as shown in the reaction below.

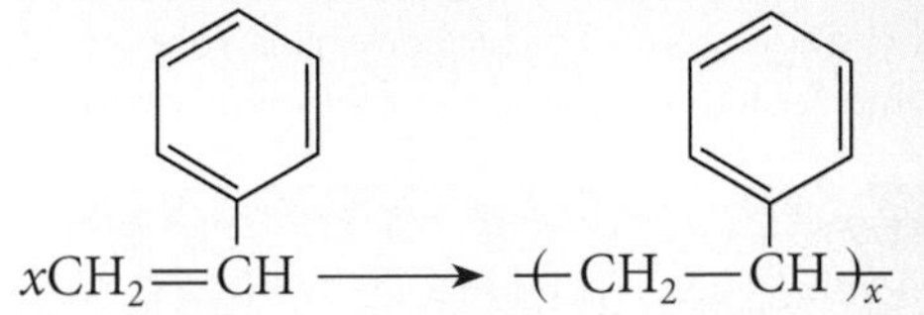

$$x CH_2 = CH \longrightarrow (CH_2\text{—}CH)_x$$

Styrene
(vinyl benzene)

Polystyrene

Many halocarbon polymers, including polyvinyl chloride (PVC), have useful properties. For example, polyvinyl chloride is used to make plumbing pipes, rainwear, and garden hoses. It is also produced in sheets, sometimes with a fabric backing, for use as a tough plastic upholstery covering. Vinyl chloride is the monomer of polyvinyl chloride.

$$x CH_2 = CH\text{—}Cl \longrightarrow (CH_2\text{—}CH)_x\text{—}Cl$$

Chloroethene
(vinyl chloride)

Polyvinyl chloride
(PVC)

Polytetrafluoroethene (PTFE) is the product of the polymerization of tetrafluoroethene monomers. PTFE is very resistant to heat and chemical corrosion. You are probably familiar with this polymer as a coating on nonstick cookware. PTFE is also used to insulate wires and cables. Because PTFE is very durable and slick, it is formed into bearings and bushings used in chemical reactors. It also is suspended in motor oils as a friction-reducing agent.

$$x CF_2{=}CF_2 \longrightarrow {+}CF_2{-}CF_2{+}_x$$

Tetraflouroethene   PTFE

Polyisoprene is the polymer that constitutes natural rubber. The monomer of polyisoprene, isoprene, is harvested from tropical plants such as the rubber tree. Polyisoprene is used to make rubber bands, soles of athletic shoes, and many other common items. Figure 23.17 shows how isoprene is used in the manufacture of tires.

$$x CH_2{=}CCH{=}CH_2 \longrightarrow \begin{array}{c} {+}CH_2 \qquad\quad CH_2{+}_x \\ C{=}C \\ CH_3 \qquad\qquad H \end{array}$$

Isoprene: CH_3

Figure 23.17 Natural Rubber

Isoprene   Polyisoprene

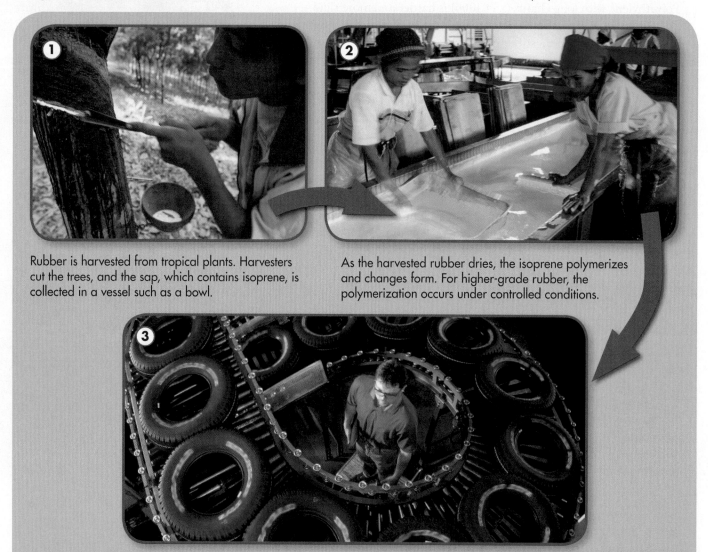

① Rubber is harvested from tropical plants. Harvesters cut the trees, and the sap, which contains isoprene, is collected in a vessel such as a bowl.

② As the harvested rubber dries, the isoprene polymerizes and changes form. For higher-grade rubber, the polymerization occurs under controlled conditions.

③ Finally, the manufacturer processes and molds the polymer to form the desired product.

Condensation Polymers

How are condensation polymers formed?

The formation of a polyester is a common example of condensation polymerization. **Condensation polymers are formed by the joining of monomers with the loss of a small molecule such as water.** Polyesters are polymers that consist of many repeating units of dicarboxylic acids and dihydroxy alcohols joined by ester bonds.

The formation of a polyester can be represented by a block diagram, which shows only the functional groups involved in the polymerization reaction. The squares and circles represent unreactive parts of the organic molecules. Condensation polymerization requires that there be two functional groups on each monomer molecule.

$$x\text{HO}-\overset{\overset{\text{O}}{\|}}{\text{C}}-\square-\overset{\overset{\text{O}}{\|}}{\text{C}}-\text{OH} + x\text{HO}-\bigcirc-\text{OH} \longrightarrow$$

Dicarboxylic acid Dihydroxy alcohol

$$\left(\overset{\overset{\text{O}}{\|}}{\text{C}}-\square-\overset{\overset{\text{O}}{\|}}{\text{C}}-\text{O}-\bigcirc-\text{O}\right)_x + 2x\text{H}_2\text{O}$$

Representative polymer unit of a polyester

The polyester polyethylene terephthalate (PET) is formed from terephthalic acid and ethylene glycol as shown in the reaction below.

$$x\text{HO}-\overset{\overset{\text{O}}{\|}}{\text{C}}-\bigcirc-\overset{\overset{\text{O}}{\|}}{\text{C}}-\text{OH} + x\text{HO}-\text{CH}_2\text{CH}_2-\text{OH} \longrightarrow$$

Terephthalic acid Ethylene glycol

$$\left(\overset{\overset{\text{O}}{\|}}{\text{C}}-\bigcirc-\overset{\overset{\text{O}}{\|}}{\text{C}}-\text{O}-\text{CH}_2\text{CH}_2-\text{O}\right)_x + 2x\text{H}_2\text{O}$$

Representative polymer unit of PET

Figure 23.18 shows two very different products made from PET: water bottles and a fleece jacket. But, in fact, the fabric of the jacket is made from recycled PET bottles. PET fibers form when the compound is melted and forced through tiny holes in devices called spinnerettes. The fibers are used for tire cord and permanent-press clothing. PET fibers are often blended with cotton to make clothing that is more comfortable on hot, humid days than those containing 100% polyester. These clothes retain the wrinkle resistance of 100% polyester. Woven PET fiber tubing can be used to replace major blood vessels. PET melts may also be forced through a narrow slit to produce sheets of film that are used extensively on credit cards and as coverings for frozen dinners.

CHEMISTRY & YOU

Q: *Polymers make up most of the bottles, containers, and packaging that you see around you. Try to identify the polymers in some of these items. How would you classify them—as additional polymers or condensation polymers?*

Figure 23.18 Recycling PET
Plastic bottles from which you sip your drink may one day be part of someone else's wardrobe. It only takes about a dozen large bottles that are made from PET to make one fleece jacket.

Many important polymers are formed by the reaction of carboxylic acids and amines. The amines used to make polymers generally contain the amino functional group (—NH$_2$). The condensation of a carboxylic acid and an amine produces an amide.

$$R-\overset{\overset{O}{\|}}{C}-OH + H-\overset{\overset{H}{|}}{N}-R \longrightarrow R-\overset{\overset{O}{\|}}{C}-\overset{\overset{H}{|}}{N}-R + H_2O$$

Carboxylic acid   Amine   Amide

Polyamides are polymers in which the carboxylic acid and amine monomer units are linked by amide bonds. The many types of nylon are polyamides. You are probably familiar with a range of nylon products. The representative polymer unit of nylon is derived from 6-aminohexanoic acid, a compound that contains both carboxyl and amino functional groups. The long polymer chain is formed by the successive attachment of the carboxyl group of one molecule of the monomer to the amino group of the next monomer by the formation of an amide bond.

$$x H_2N-CH_2 \left(CH_2\right)_4 \overset{\overset{O}{\|}}{C}-OH \xrightarrow{heat} \left(CH_2 \left(CH_2\right)_4 \overset{\overset{O}{\|}}{C}-\overset{\overset{H}{|}}{N}\right)_x + x H_2O$$

6-Aminohexanoic acid   Representative polymer unit of nylon

The melted polymer can be spun into very fine, yet very strong, fibers. Nylon fibers are used for carpeting, tire cord, fishing lines, sheer hosiery, and textiles. Nylon is also molded into gears, bearings, zippers, and the ropes being used in Figure 23.19.

Polyamides that contain aromatic rings are extremely tough and flame resistant. The aromatic rings make the resulting fiber stiffer and tougher. Kevlar^{TM} is a polyamide with a carbon skeleton consisting of aromatic rings derived from terephthalic acid and p-phenylenediamine. A properly constructed vest made of Kevlar is strong enough to stop high-speed bullets, yet is light and flexible enough to be worn under normal clothing.

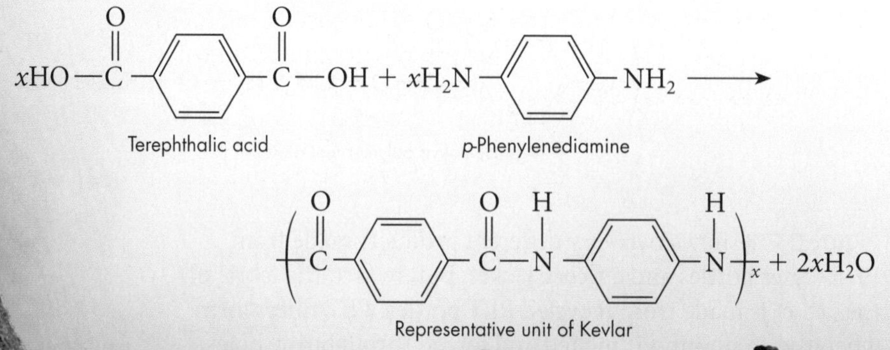

$$x HO-\overset{\overset{O}{\|}}{C}-\bigcirc-\overset{\overset{O}{\|}}{C}-OH + x H_2N-\bigcirc-NH_2 \longrightarrow$$

Terephthalic acid   p-Phenylenediamine

$$\left(\overset{\overset{O}{\|}}{C}-\bigcirc-\overset{\overset{O}{\|}}{C}-\overset{\overset{H}{|}}{N}-\bigcirc-\overset{\overset{H}{|}}{N}\right)_x + 2x H_2O$$

Representative unit of Kevlar

Figure 23.19
Nylon Rope
Many climbers use climbing rope with cores that are composed of nylon. *Infer* *What quality makes nylon a good choice for the construction of climbing rope?*

Nomex™ is another polyamide that contains aromatic rings. It is used in the fabrication of flame-resistant building materials and in the manufacture of the flame-resistant clothing the firefighter wears in Figure 23.20. Nomex is a poor conductor of electricity. Because it is also rigid, it is used to make parts for electrical fixtures. Nomex is a polyamide made from isophthalic acid and *m*-phenylenediamine as shown in the reaction below.

Figure 23.20 Nomex Clothing
Flame-resistant clothing is made of Nomex, a polyamide with aromatic rings.

Isophthalic acid   *m*-Phenylenediamine

Representative unit of Nomex

Proteins, which are polyamides of naturally occurring molecules, rank among the most important of all biological molecules. You will learn about these polymers in more detail in Chapter 24.

23.4 LessonCheck

ONLINE PROBLEMS

24. 🔑 **Review** Describe how addition polymers form.

25. 🔑 **Review** How do condensation polymers form?

26. Compare What is a polymer? A monomer?

27. Describe What structure must a monomer have if it is to undergo addition polymerization?

28. Identify What is formed when a carboxylic acid and an amine combine? Give an example of the type of polymer that is formed by this reaction.

29. Explain How is water involved in the formation of a condensation polymer?

30. Use Analogies Write an analogy that you can use to describe to a middle-school student how a polymer is constructed from monomers. Use diagrams as well as words to describe your analogy.

31. Identify Give names and uses for three polymers you encounter in your home.

Small-Scale Lab

Polymers

Purpose
To cross-link some polymers and examine their properties

Materials
- 3½-oz plastic cup
- soda straw
- guar gum powder
- plastic spoon
- 4% borax solution
- pipet
- food coloring (optional)

Procedure
1. Half fill a 3½-oz cup with water. Add food coloring to the water if you want the polymer to be colored.

2. Use a soda straw as a measuring scoop to obtain approximately 2 cm of powdered guar gum. **CAUTION** *Do not use your mouth to draw up the guar gum into the straw.* Gently sprinkle the guar gum powder into the water while stirring with a plastic spoon. Add the guar gum powder slowly to prevent it from clumping. Stir the mixture well.

3. While stirring, add one full pipet (about 4 mL) of borax solution. Continue to stir until a change occurs.

Analyze
1. Is the polymer you just made a liquid or a solid? What special characteristics does it have?

2. Guar gum is a carbohydrate, a polymer with many repeating alcohol functional groups (—OH). Draw a zigzag line to represent a crude polymer chain. Add —OH groups along the chain to represent the alcohol functional groups.

3. Borate ions combine with alcohol to form water and borate complexes of the alcohol as shown below. Write a similar equation that replaces all of the —OH groups on the borate with —OR groups.

$$\left[\begin{array}{c} HO \quad OH \\ B \\ HO \quad OH \end{array}\right]^{-} + R-OH \longrightarrow \left[\begin{array}{c} HO \quad OH \\ B \\ HO \quad OR \end{array}\right]^{-} + H_2O$$

4. If two polymer chains each contain two nearby —OH groups, borate will cross-link the polymer chains by forming a complex with two alcohols on each chain. Draw a structure similar to the one you drew for Question 3, but replace your four R groups with two polymer chains.

You're the Chemist
1. Design an Experiment! Try using borax to cross-link other common carbohydrate polymers, such as cornstarch or liquid laundry starch. For each polymer, half fill a 3-oz cup with the chosen carbohydrate polymer and add enough water to bring the liquid to within about 1 cm of the rim. Stir carefully and thoroughly. Add one full pipet (about 4 mL) of borax solution while stirring. Describe the similarities and differences between this cross-linked polymer and the polymer you made previously. Compare the properties of these polymers.

2. Analyze Data! Cut a 1 cm × 15 cm strip of paper. Use a drop of glue or a stapler to fasten one end of the paper strip to the other end to form a ring. Now cut out some identical-sized strips of paper, and glue or staple them together into an interlocking chain of paper rings. Explain how this chain is like a polymer. Make another paper ring that cross-links your chain to one of your classmates' chains. Explain how these linked chains are like cross-linked polymers.

BIGIDEAS
CARBON CHEMISTRY AND REACTIONS

Functional groups affect the physical and chemical properties of organic compounds. Chemical reactions can be used to change the structure of organic molecules, often by introducing a new functional group. Substitution, addition, oxidation-reduction, and polymerization reactions are commonly used in organic chemistry.

23.1 Introduction to Functional Groups

🔑 Organic compounds can be classified according to their functional groups.

🔑 The general formula of a halocarbon is RX, where X is a halogen substituent.

🔑 Substitution reactions are an important method of introducing new functional groups to organic molecules.

....

- functional group (798)
- halocarbon (800)
- alkyl halide (800)
- aryl halide (800)
- substitution reaction (801)

23.2 Alcohols, Ethers, and Amines

🔑 The general formula of an alcohol is ROH.

🔑 Addition reactions are an important method of introducing new functional groups to organic molecules. They are also used to convert alkenes to alkanes.

🔑 The general formula of an ether is ROR.

🔑 The general formula of an amine is RNH_2, R_2NH, or R_3N.

....

- alcohol (804)
- hydroxy group (804)
- fermentation (807)
- addition reaction (807)
- hydration reaction (808)
- hydrogenation reaction (809)
- ether (810)
- amine (811)

23.3 Carbonyl Compounds

🔑 The $C = O$ functional group is present in aldehydes and ketones.

🔑 The general formula of a carboxylic acid is RCOOH.

🔑 Dehydrogenation is an oxidation reaction because the loss of each molecule of hydrogen involves the loss of two electrons from the organic molecule.

🔑 The general formula of an ester is RCOOR.

....

- carbonyl group (812)
- aldehyde (812)
- ketone (812)
- carboxyl group (815)
- carboxylic acid (815)
- fatty acid (816)
- dehydrogenation reaction (816)
- ester (819)

23.4 Polymers

🔑 An addition polymer forms when unsaturated monomers react to form a polymer.

🔑 Condensation polymers are formed by the joining of monomers with the loss of a small molecule such as water.

....

- polymer (822)
- monomer (822)

Lesson by Lesson

23.1 Introduction to Functional Groups

32. What does R in the formula RCH_2Cl represent?

*****33.** Write a structural formula for each compound.

   a. 1,2,2-trichlorobutane
   b. 1,3,5-tribromobenzene
   c. 1,2-dichlorocyclohexane

34. Name the following halocarbons:

   a. $CH_2\!\!=\!\!CHCH_2Cl$

   b. $CH_3\underset{\underset{CH_3}{|}}{C}HCH_2\underset{\underset{Cl}{|}}{C}HCH_2Cl$

   c.

35. Write structural formulas and give IUPAC names for all the isomers of the following compounds:

   a. $C_3H_6Cl_2$ **b.** C_4H_9Br

36. What organic products are formed in the following reactions?

   a. ⬡—Br + $NaOH$ $\xrightarrow{heat}$ ____ + $NaBr$

   b. ⬡—Cl + $NaOH$ ⟶ ____ + $NaCl$

   c. $CH_3\underset{\underset{CH_3}{|}}{C}HCl$ + $NaOH$ ⟶ ____ + $NaCl$

   d. ⬡ + Br_2 $\xrightarrow{catalyst}$ ____ + HBr

23.2 Alcohols, Ethers, and Amines

***37.** Give the IUPAC names for these alcohols.

   a. $CH_3\!-\!\underset{\underset{OH}{|}}{C}H\!-\!CH_3$

   b. $\underset{\underset{OH}{|}}{C}H_2\!-\!\underset{\underset{OH}{|}}{C}H\!-\!CH_3$

   c. $CH_3\!-\!\underset{\underset{OH}{|}}{\overset{\overset{CH_3}{|}}{C}}\!-\!CH_3$

*****38.** Write structures and names of the products obtained upon addition of each of the following reagents to ethene.

   a. HBr   **b.** Cl_2 **c.** H_2O **d.** H_2 **e.** HCl

39. Write the structure for the expected product from each reaction.

   a. $CH_2\!\!=\!\!CHCH_2CH_3 + Br_2 \longrightarrow$

   b. $CH_3CH\!\!=\!\!CHCH_3 + I_2 \longrightarrow$

   c. $CH_3CH\!\!=\!\!CHCH_3 + HBr \longrightarrow$

   d. $CH_3CH\!\!=\!\!CHCH_3 + H_2 \longrightarrow$

   e. ⬡ (with double bond) + $Cl_2 \longrightarrow$

40. Give the IUPAC and common names for the following ethers:

   a. $CH_3OCH_2CH_3$

   b. ⬡$-O-CH_2CH_3$

   c. $CH_2\!\!=\!\!CHOCH\!\!=\!\!CH_2$

   d. $CH_3\underset{\underset{CH_3}{|}}{C}HO\underset{\underset{CH_3}{|}}{C}HCH_3$

41. Name the following amines:

   a. $CH_3CH_2CH_2CH_2NH_2$
   b. $CH_3CH_2NH_2$

23.3 Carbonyl Compounds

*****42.** Give the IUPAC names for the following carbonyl compounds:

   a. $CH_3\overset{\overset{O}{\|}}{C}CH_3$ **d.** $CH_3CH_2\overset{\overset{O}{\|}}{C}CH_2CH_2CH_3$

   b. CH_3CHO **e.** ⬡$-CH_2CHO$

   c. $CH_3\underset{\underset{CH_3}{|}}{C}HCH_2CHO$ **f.** $CH_3(CH_2)_3COOH$

43. Write the structure for the expected organic product from each reaction.

   a. $CH_3CH_2OH \xrightarrow[H_2SO_4]{K_2Cr_2O_7}$

   b. $CH_3CHO \xrightarrow[H_2SO_4]{K_2Cr_2O_7}$

   c. $CH_3CH_2CH_2CHO \xrightarrow[H_2SO_4]{K_2Cr_2O_7}$

   d. $CH_3\!-\!CH_2\!-\!\underset{\underset{OH}{|}}{C}H\!-\!CH_3 \xrightarrow[H^+]{K_2Cr_2O_7}$

23.4 Polymers

44. Different samples of a polymer such as polyethylene can have different properties. Explain.

★45. Draw the structure of the repeating units in a polymer that has the following monomers:

    a. 1-butene
    b. 1,2-dichloroethene

Understand Concepts

46. Write a general formula for each type of compound.

    a. halocarbon   **d.** ester
    b. ketone   **e.** amide
    c. aldehyde   **f.** ether

47. Place the following compounds in order from lowest boiling point to highest boiling point. Molar masses are given in parentheses.

    a. CH_3CHO (44 g)
    b. CH_3CH_2OH (46 g)
    c. $CH_3CH_2CH_3$ (44 g)

48. Write the structure and name of the expected products for each reaction.

    a. $CH_3COOH + CH_3OH \xrightarrow{\text{H}^+}$

    b. $CH_3CH_2CH_2COOCH_2CH_3 + H_2O \xrightarrow{\text{H}^+}$

    c. $CH_3CH_2OH \xrightarrow[\text{H}^+]{\text{K}_2\text{Cr}_2\text{O}_7}$

49. Explain why a carbon–carbon double bond is nonpolar, but a carbon–oxygen double bond is very polar.

★50. Classify each compound as an alcohol, a phenol, or an ether.

    a.

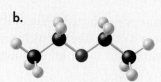

    d.

    b.

    e. CH_3CH_2CHOH
               |
               CH_3

    c.

    f. $CH_3CH_2OCH_3$

51. Explain why 2-methyl-1-propanol can be oxidized, but 2-methyl-2-propanol cannot be oxidized.

---

52. Write the structural formulas for the products of these reactions.

    a. $CH_3CH_2CH{=}CH_2 + Cl_2 \longrightarrow$
    b. $CH_3CH_2CH{=}CH_2 + Br_2 \longrightarrow$

    c. ⬡ + HBr ⟶

★53. For each compound pictured below, identify the functional group and name the compound. The red atoms represent oxygen.

    a. 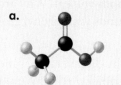   **c.**

    b.   **d.**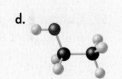

54. Write the name and structure for the alcohol that must be oxidized to make each carbonyl compound.

    a. HCHO   **c.** CH_3
                            |
                       CH_3CHCHO

    b.   O   **d.**
           ||
     CH_3CCH_3

55. Write the structures of the expected products for the following reactions:

    a. $CH_3CH_2COOCH_2CH_3 + NaOH \longrightarrow$

    b. CH_3COO-⬡$ + KOH \longrightarrow$

    c. $CH_3CH_2COOCH_2CH_2CH_3 + H_2O \xrightarrow{\text{H}^+}$

    d. $CH_3CH_2COOCH_2CHCH_3 + H_2O \xrightarrow{\text{HCl}}$
                               |
                             CH_3

56. Apply Concepts Draw the structures of the expected products and name the reactants and products for each reaction below.

a. $CH_3COOCH_3 + H_2O \xrightarrow{HCl}$

b. $CH_3CH_2COOCH_2CH_2CH_3 + H_2O \xrightarrow{H^+}$

c. $HCOOCH_2CH_3 + KOH \longrightarrow$

⋆57. Draw Conclusions Benzene is poisonous and a proven carcinogen. Yet many compounds containing benzene rings, such as benzaldehyde, are common in the foods you eat. Why are some organic compounds with phenyl groups safe to eat?

58. Compare Explain why diethyl ether is more soluble in water than dihexyl ether. Would you expect propane or diethyl ether to be more soluble in water? Why?

59. Compare Explain why 1-butanol has a higher boiling point than diethyl ether. Which compound would you expect to be more soluble in water? Why?

60. Evaluate Propane ($CH_3CH_2CH_3$) and acetaldehyde (CH_3CHO) have the same molar mass, but propane boils at –42°C and acetaldehyde boils at 21°C. Account for this difference.

⋆61. Compare and Contrast How would you expect the water solubility of ethanoic and decanoic acids to compare?

62. Infer The processes used to synthesize many organic compounds often use compounds that contain double or triple bonds as reactants. Explain why using unsaturated reactants might be advantageous over using saturated reactants.

⋆63. Classify Cadaverine (1,5-pentanediamine) and putrescine (1,4-butanediamine) are unpleasant-smelling compounds that are formed by bacteria in rotting flesh. Draw their structures. What class of organic compounds are these two chemicals?

64. Graph Use the data in Table 23.3 to make a graph of boiling point versus number of chlorine atoms for the five compounds listed in the table. Is the graph a straight line? Use the graph to describe the relationship between boiling point and degree of halogen substitution.

65. Apply Concepts For the following structures, write a chemical equation showing how to produce the compound.

a.   b.

⋆66. Infer Tetrahydrofuran (THF) is an important industrial organic solvent. THF is a cyclic ether containing four carbon atoms in the ring. Draw a structural formula of this cyclic ether.

67. Predict Write structures and names of the organic products obtained when the following compounds react with Fehling's reagent.

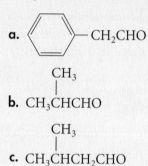

a.

$$CH_3$$
$$|$$
b. CH_3CHCHO

$$CH_3$$
$$|$$
c. CH_3CHCH_2CHO

68. Interpret Graphs The graph shows the boiling points of the C_2–C_{10} straight-chain 1-hydroxy alcohols and straight-chain 1-chloroalkanes plotted versus their molar masses.

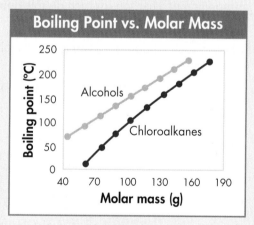

Boiling Point vs. Molar Mass

a. Explain why the boiling points of the alcohols are consistently higher than those of the chloroalkanes of similar molar mass.

b. Why does the gap in boiling point between the alcohols and chloroalkanes decrease with increasing chain length?

*69. **Interpret Diagrams** Cholesterol is a compound in your diet and is also synthesized in the liver. Sometimes it is deposited on the inner walls of blood vessels, causing hardening of the arteries. Describe the structural features and functional groups of this important molecule.

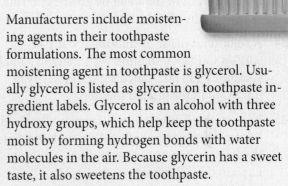

70. **Propose a Solution** Hydrocarbons from petroleum are an important source of raw material for the chemical industry. Using reactions covered in this chapter, propose a scheme for the synthesis of ethylene glycol, a major component of antifreeze, from petrochemical ethene.

*71. **Draw Conclusions** Human hair is composed of long-chain polymers. Some of the monomers in these polymers contain sulfur atoms. When two sulfur atoms are adjacent to one another, they form strong, covalent disulfide (S—S) bonds that can link two polymer molecules together. The location of these bonds between the hair polymers affects how curly or straight the hair is and helps to hold the polymers in their shape. Waving lotion that is used in permanent waves is a reducing agent, and neutralizing agent is an oxidizing agent. Using this information, explain in terms of chemistry how a permanent wave can change the shape of hair. Describe what chemical steps should be taken to change the shape of someone's hair from straight to curly.

72. **Infer** Which of the following monomers can be used to produce the addition polymer $-(CF_2)_x-$: $CH_2=CF_2$, $CH_2=CHF$, CF_4, $CF_2=CF_2$, or $CHF=CHF$?

73. **Analyze Data** An unidentified compound of molecular formula $C_5H_{10}O$ produced a red precipitate when treated with Fehling's reagent. Further testing showed that the compound does not contain a hydrocarbon ring. Write structural formulas for all of the compounds that this unknown substance might be.

74. **Research a Problem** Methyl tert-butyl ether (MTBE) is a commonly used gasoline additive. Recently, regulatory agencies have begun to limit its use. Write a paragraph about MTBE, in which you explain the function of MTBE in gasoline and why its use is now limited.

75. **Connect to the BIGIDEA** Acetylsalicylic acid (aspirin) and ibuprofen are both active ingredients of over-the-counter pain relievers. They work by preventing certain proteins from sending pain signals to the brain. Look up the structures of these two active ingredients. Write a short report, in which you compare the structures and functional groups of the two compounds.

CHEMYSTERY

The Toothpaste Terror

Manufacturers include moistening agents in their toothpaste formulations. The most common moistening agent in toothpaste is glycerol. Usually glycerol is listed as glycerin on toothpaste ingredient labels. Glycerol is an alcohol with three hydroxy groups, which help keep the toothpaste moist by forming hydrogen bonds with water molecules in the air. Because glycerin has a sweet taste, it also sweetens the toothpaste.

*76. **Compare** Counterfeiters have been known to manufacture cheap toothpaste by substituting diethylene glycol for glycerol. Like glycerol, diethylene glycol is a moistening agent, but it is also toxic. Compare the structures of diethylene glycol and glycerol.

77. **Connect to the BIGIDEA** Often there is more than one moistening agent in toothpaste. Look at the ingredient list on your toothpaste container. Are there any other alcohols besides glycerol that may serve as moistening agents? Search the Internet to find the structures of each alcohol, and identify the number of hydroxy groups.

✶78. What is the maximum number of orbitals in the p sublevel of an atom?

a. 1   **b.** 3   **c.** 5   **d.** 9

79. Using electron dot structures, illustrate the formation of F^- from a fluorine atom and OH^- from atoms of hydrogen and oxygen.

80. Calculate the mass, in grams, of one liter of SO_2 at standard temperature and pressure.

81. A sample of 1.40 L of nitrogen gas in a sealed container at 25.0°C and 1.00×10^2 kPa is heated to 68.7°C. What is the new pressure?

✶82. Sodium carbonate is often sold as the anhydrous compound $[Na_2CO_3(s)]$ or as the decahydrate $[Na_2CO_3 \cdot 10H_2O(s)]$. If the price per kilogram of the anhydrous and decahydrate forms are the same, which compound is the better value?

83. Assume that water enters a power plant at 20°C and leaves at 30°C. Will the amount of dissolved oxygen in the water be greater entering or leaving the plant?

84. A solution is made by diluting 250 mL of $0.210M$ $Ca(NO_3)_2$ solution with water to a final volume of 450 mL. Calculate the molarity of $Ca(NO_3)_2$ in the diluted solution.

85. In a saturated solution containing undissolved solute, the solute is continually dissolving, but the solution concentration remains constant. Explain this statement.

✶86. A 500-g aluminum tray at 22°C is heated to 180°C in an oven. How many kJ of heat does the aluminum tray absorb if the specific heat of aluminum is 0.90 J/(g·°C)?

87. Predict the direction of shift in the equilibrium position for each change in conditions.

$$2NO_2(g) \rightleftharpoons 2NO(g) + O_2(g)$$

a. O_2 partial pressure decrease
b. total pressure increase
c. O_2 partial pressure increase
d. NO partial pressure increase

✶88. List these K_a values for weak acids in order of increasing acid strength.

a. 3.5×10^{-6}
b. 2.7×10^{-3}
c. 1.5×10^{-5}
d. 6.6×10^{-5}

89. Assign an oxidation number to each atom in these compounds.

a. $NaNO_2$
b. $CoSO_4$
c. SeO_2
d. $Zn(OH)_2$
e. K_2PtCl_4

90. Solid sodium borohydride ($NaBH_4$) is being studied as a possible source of hydrogen fuel for hydrogen-powered vehicles. The borohydride reacts with water to produce hydrogen gas and sodium metaborate. Identify which atoms of the reactants are oxidized, which atoms are reduced, and which atoms are unaffected in this reaction.

$$NaBH_4(s) + 2H_2O(l) \longrightarrow 4H_2(g) + NaBO_2(aq)$$

91. What is the source of the electrical energy produced in a voltaic cell?

✶92. At which electrode in an electrolytic cell does reduction always occur? What is the charge on this electrode?

93. Draw a condensed structural formula for each compound.

a. 1,2-dimethylcyclobutane
b. 2-methyl-2-pentene
c. 2-butene
d. 2-pentyne
e. 2-methylhexene

✶94. Is petroleum or coal most likely to be a good source of aromatic compounds?

95. Which of these statements applies to ethene?

a. saturated hydrocarbon
b. $H—C—H$ bond angle of 120°
c. alkene
d. aromatic compound

If You Have Trouble With . . .

Question	78	79	80	81	82	83	84	85	86	87	88	89	90	91	92	93	94	95
See Chapter	5	7	10	14	15	16	16	16	17	18	19	20	20	21	21	22	22	22

Standardized Test Prep

Select the choice that best answers each question or completes each statement.

1. The acid-catalyzed hydrolysis of an ester gives a carboxylic acid and
   - **(A)** an amine.
   - **(B)** an ether.
   - **(C)** an alcohol.
   - **(D)** an alkene.

2. Ethane, methanal, and methanol have similar molar masses. Which series lists the compounds in order of increasing boiling point?
   - **(A)** ethane, methanal, methanol
   - **(B)** methanal, methanol, ethane
   - **(C)** methanol, methanal, ethane
   - **(D)** ethane, methanol, methanal

3. A carbonyl group is characterized by a
   - **(A)** carbon–carbon double bond.
   - **(B)** carbon–oxygen double bond.
   - **(C)** carbon–nitrogen single bond.
   - **(D)** carbon–oxygen single bond.

The lettered choices below refer to Questions 4–7. A lettered choice may be used once, more than once, or not at all.
   - **(A)** alcohol
   - **(B)** ketone
   - **(C)** carboxylic acid
   - **(D)** ether

To which class of organic compounds does each of the following compounds belong?

4. CH_3CH_2COOH

5. $CH_3CH_2CH_2OH$

6. $CH_3CH_2OCH_3$

7. CH_3COCH_3

Use the following models with Question 8.

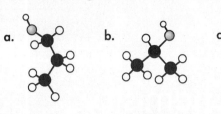

a.　　b.　　c.

8. The molecular formula for each compound is C_3H_8O. Write the name for each compound.

9. There are two compounds with a carbonyl group that have the molecular formula C_3H_6O. Write a complete structural formula for each compound. Name each compound.

Tips for Success

Eliminate Wrong Answers If you don't know which choice is correct, eliminate those you know are wrong. If you can rule out some choices, you'll increase your chances of choosing the correct answer.

Characterize the reactions in Questions 10–14 as an addition, esterification, oxidation, polymerization, or substitution reaction.

10. $CH_3CHO \xrightarrow[H_2SO_4]{K_2Cr_2O_7} CH_3COOH$

11. $CH_2{=}CH_2 + HCl \longrightarrow CH_3CH_2Cl$

12. $CH_3CO_2H + CH_3CH_2OH \xrightarrow{H^+} CH_3COOCH_2CH_3 + H_2O$

13. $xCH_2{=}CH_2 \longrightarrow H{+}CH_2{-}CH_2{-}{)_x}H$

14. ⬡ $+ Br_2 \xrightarrow{catalyst}$ ⬡Br $+ HBr$

For each question there are two statements. Decide whether each statement is true or false. Then decide whether Statement II is a correct explanation for Statement I.

	Statement I		Statement II
15.	The addition of hydrogen to an alkene is a reduction reaction.	BECAUSE	The addition of hydrogen to any molecule is a reduction reaction.
16.	Aldehydes are easily oxidized.	BECAUSE	Oxidation of aldehydes produces alcohols.
17.	Ethanol (CH_3CH_2OH) is immiscible in water in all proportions.	BECAUSE	Ethanol molecules can form hydrogen bonds with other ethanol molecules.

If You Have Trouble With . . .

Question	1	2	3	4	5	6	7	8	9	10	11	12	13	14	15	16	17
See Lesson	23.3	23.3	23.3	23.3	23.2	23.2	23.3	23.2	23.3	23.3	23.2	23.3	23.4	23.1	23.2	23.3	23.2

24

The Chemistry of Life

INSIDE:

PearsonChem.com

All organisms, including you and your classmates, are made of the same types of molecules: carbohydrates, proteins, lipids, and nucleic acids.

836

CHEMISTRY AS THE CENTRAL SCIENCE

Essential Questions:

1. *What are the characteristics of the four main types of biological molecules?*

2. *What is the function of anabolism and catabolism in a cell?*

CHEMYSTERY

Phenyl-what?

Do you ever look at the labels on food and wonder what they mean? In the United States, the Food and Drug Administration (FDA) regulates the requirements for how foods are labeled. Information that you might see on foods includes a nutrition label, the quantity of the food, the ingredients the food contains, and an expiration date.

Some food labels also contain warnings about the ingredients in the food. Some labels warn you about something common, like nuts or milk. But other times the warning may leave you wondering what it means. The warning on the label shown here says the product "Contains phenylalanine." What is phenylalanine? Why would people need to know that phenylalanine is in their food?

▶ Connect to the **BIG**IDEA As you read about molecules involved in life's processes, think about how the chemistry of these molecules is central to living things.

NATIONAL SCIENCE EDUCATION STANDARDS

C-1, C-2, C-3, C-5, F-1

24.1 A Basis for Life

Q: *Where do fish get their oxygen?* All animals need oxygen to survive. Most fish obtain oxygen as water flows across their gills. We breathe in oxygen from the air around us. The air you breathe is composed mainly of nitrogen (N_2) and oxygen (O_2). Earth's early atmosphere may have been very different, with very little oxygen, and most inhospitable to life. It is thought that the atmosphere changed over time. In this lesson, you will learn how oxygen in both the air and water is produced.

Key Questions

▷ What are the two major types of cells that occur in nature?

▷ What compound is reduced during photosynthesis? What compounds are formed?

Vocabulary

• photosynthesis

Figure 24.1 Cell Types
Typical prokaryotic and eukaryotic cells are shown here. Note that only the eukaryotic cell has a nucleus.
Compare and Contrast *How do prokaryotic and eukaryotic cells compare in size?*

The Structure of Cells

▷ **What are the two major types of cells that occur in nature?**

Life! You are certainly familiar with it, but what does it really mean? Until recently, life was defined as the ability of an organism to grow and to reproduce its own kind. However, recent discoveries made at the fringes of life seem to blur this simple definition. As difficult as it is to define life, you can generally regard tiny structures called cells as the fundamental units of life.

Organisms are composed of as few as one cell or as many as billions of cells. ▷ **Two major cell types occur in nature: prokaryotic cells and eukaryotic cells.** The prokaryotic cell is the more ancient of the two. Microscopic examination of fossilized remains shows that prokaryotic cells were present on Earth at least 3 billion years ago. Eukaryotic cells did not appear until about 1 billion years ago. Figure 24.1 shows both types of cells.

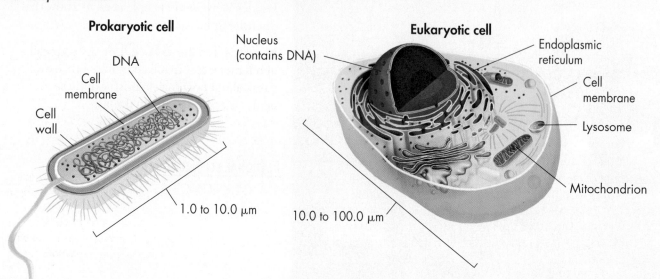

Prokaryotic cell

- DNA
- Cell membrane
- Cell wall

1.0 to 10.0 μm

Eukaryotic cell

- Nucleus (contains DNA)
- Endoplasmic reticulum
- Cell membrane
- Lysosome
- Mitochondrion

10.0 to 100.0 μm

Both eukaryotic and prokaryotic cells contain all the chemicals necessary for life, encased in a cell membrane. The cell membrane is a sack that holds the contents of a cell and acts as a selective barrier for the passage of substances into and out of the cell. Eukaryotic cells are considerably larger and more complex than prokaryotic cells, but the chemical processes carried out by both types of cells are very similar.

One major feature that distinguishes eukaryotic cells from prokaryotic cells is that eukaryotic cells contain membrane-enclosed organelles. Organelles, meaning little organs, are small structures suspended in the interior cellular fluid, or cytoplasm. The organelles are the sites of many specialized functions in eukaryotic cells. For example, the nucleus, a structure that is important in eukaryotic cell reproduction, is not present in prokaryotic cells. Mitochondria (singular: mitochondrion) are the source of cellular energy in eukaryotic cells that use oxygen. Mitochondria are often referred to as the powerhouses of the cell. Lysosomes are the sites for the digestion of substances taken into a cell. Yet another membrane-enclosed structure in eukaryotic cells is the highly folded, netlike endoplasmic reticulum (ER). Among its various functions, the ER serves as an attachment site for ribosomes. The ribosomes, small organelles that are not membrane-enclosed, are the sites where essential substances called proteins are made.

The Energy and Carbon Cycle

What compound is reduced during photosynthesis? What compounds are formed?

Organisms must have energy to survive. The ultimate source of this energy is the sun. Cells of green plants and certain algae contain organelles called chloroplasts that are able to capture solar energy and make food. Within a chloroplast is a light-capturing system of membranes, shown in Figure 24.2, that converts light energy into chemical energy by a process called **photosynthesis**. In addition to sunlight, photosynthetic organisms require carbon dioxide and water. **Photosynthesis uses the energy from sunlight to reduce carbon dioxide to compounds that contain C—H bonds, mainly in the form of glucose ($C_6H_{12}O_6$).** The following equation summarizes the process:

$$6CO_2 \ + \ 6H_2O \ + \ \text{Energy} \longrightarrow C_6H_{12}O_6 \ + \ 6O_2$$

Carbon dioxide (carbon in more oxidized state) Water from sunlight Glucose (carbon in more reduced state) Oxygen

Figure 24.3 on the next page illustrates the relationship between photosynthesis and the carbon compounds used by all organisms. In the energy and carbon cycle, photosynthetic organisms produce necessary carbon compounds. Animals, which do not carry out photosynthesis, get these carbon compounds by eating plants or by eating animals that feed on plants. Both plants and animals get energy by unleashing the energy stored in the chemical bonds of these carbon compounds. The nutrients are oxidized back to carbon dioxide and water in the process.

$$C_6H_{12}O_6 \ + \ 6O_2 \longrightarrow 6CO_2 \ + \ 6H_2O \ + \ \text{Energy}$$

Glucose (carbon in more reduced state) Oxygen Carbon dioxide (carbon in more oxidized state) Water

Figure 24.2 Chloroplast
The reactions of photosynthesis take place on the inner membranes and in the spaces between membranes of a chloroplast. The pigments in chloroplasts are why leaves are green in color.

Q: *Fish, like all animals, need oxygen to survive. What process produces oxygen?*

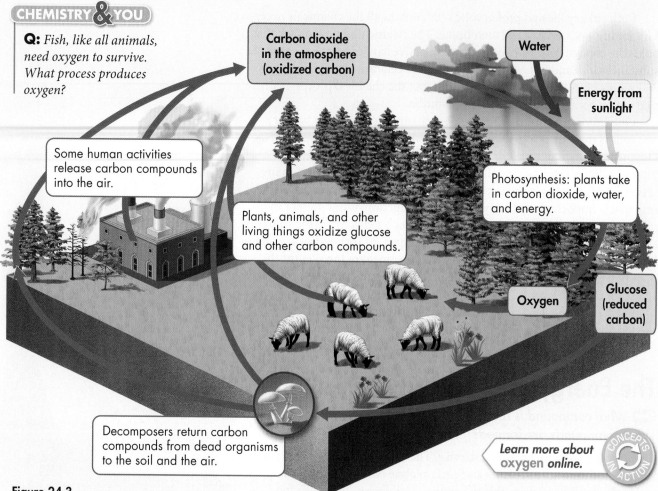

Carbon dioxide in the atmosphere (oxidized carbon)

Water

Energy from sunlight

Some human activities release carbon compounds into the air.

Photosynthesis: plants take in carbon dioxide, water, and energy.

Plants, animals, and other living things oxidize glucose and other carbon compounds.

Oxygen

Glucose (reduced carbon)

Decomposers return carbon compounds from dead organisms to the soil and the air.

Learn more about oxygen online.

CONCEPTS IN ACTION

Figure 24.3
Energy and Carbon Cycles
In the energy and carbon cycle, photosynthesis and the oxidation of glucose are responsible for the major transformations and movements of carbon. Plants release oxygen into the atmosphere through photosynthesis.
Interpret Diagrams *In which parts of the cycle is oxygen consumed?*

Although plant life could survive without animals, animal life could never survive without plants. Without photosynthesis, the supply of carbon compounds that animals need to get energy would not exist.

Oxygen is another important product of photosynthesis. Photosynthetic land-dwelling and aquatic organisms produce the oxygen found in Earth's atmosphere, oceans, and lakes. Oxygen is needed for most organisms to live. The importance of photosynthetic organisms is a major reason for the concern about the loss of such organisms through the destruction of forests.

All biological processes, including photosynthesis, are based on certain essential kinds of chemical substances. Surprisingly, the great complexity of life arises from just a few types of biological molecules. In the remainder of this chapter, you will learn about the molecular structures of the great classes of biological molecules and the roles they play in living things.

24.1 LessonCheck

ONLINE PROBLEMS

1. Identify What two types of cells occur in nature?

2. Review What chemical changes occur during photosynthesis?

3. Identify What are the fundamental units of life?

4. Describe Describe the structure of a eukaryotic cell.

5. Describe What is the function of chloroplasts in green plants and algae?

6. Identify Write an equation that describes the oxidation of glucose.

7. Explain Explain how carbon moves through the environment.

24.2 Carbohydrates

CHEMISTRY & YOU

Q: *Why does a cow chew all day?* Cows spend most of their day chewing their food. A cow's diet is rich in cellulose, which belongs to a class of organic molecules known as carbohydrates. In this lesson, you will learn about the structures and functions of carbohydrates.

Key Question

🔑 **What is the general formula of carbohydrates?**

Vocabulary

- carbohydrate
- monosaccharide
- disaccharide
- polysaccharide

Figure 24.4 Carbohydrates in Food Carbohydrates are the most abundant sources of energy in food. But some sources are healthier than others. Vegetables, fruits, beans, and whole-grain pastas are a healthier source of carbohydrates than white breads, cookies, and sodas.

Classifying Carbohydrates

🔑 *What is the general formula of carbohydrates?*

Long-distance runners often prepare for a big race by eating a great deal of bread and pasta, a process known as carbohydrate loading. Breads and pastas are excellent sources of the family of important molecules called carbohydrates. **Carbohydrates** are monomers and polymers of aldehydes and ketones that have numerous hydroxyl groups attached; they are made up of carbon, hydrogen, and oxygen. 🔑 **Most carbohydrates have the general formula $C_n(H_2O)_n$.** The name *carbohydrate* comes from the early observation that because of the formula, $C_n(H_2O)_n$, the compounds appear to be hydrates of carbon. But, carbohydrates are not true hydrates.

Carbohydrates are the main source of energy for the body. They are found in most foods, including fruits, breads, and the pasta and legumes in Figure 24.4. Carbohydrates are also in many sweets, such as cookies and pies. In this lesson, you will learn about the similarities and differences among some well-known types of carbohydrates.

Monosaccharides The simplest carbohydrate molecules are called simple sugars, or **monosaccharides.** Glucose and fructose are examples of simple sugars. Glucose is abundant in plants and animals. Glucose is the primary energy source for our bodies. Depending on the source, glucose has also been called corn sugar, grape sugar, or blood sugar. Fructose occurs in a large number of fruits and in honey. Glucose and fructose both have the molecular formula $C_6H_{12}O_6$. However, glucose has an aldehyde functional group, whereas fructose has a ketone functional group. Therefore, glucose and fructose are constitutional isomers. Both undergo many of the same reactions as ordinary aldehydes and ketones.

In aqueous solution, simple sugars such as glucose and fructose exist in a dynamic equilibrium between straight-chain and cyclic forms. The cyclic form predominates. The structures for each sugar in both forms are below.

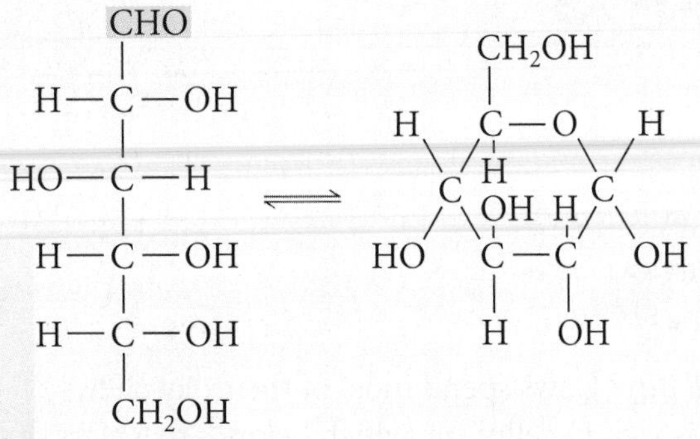

Straight-chain and cyclic forms of glucose

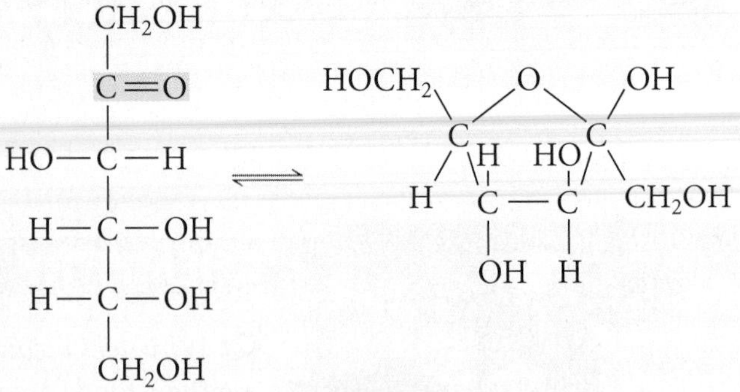

Straight-chain and cyclic forms of fructose

READING SUPPORT

Build Vocabulary:
Prefixes The word *saccharide* is from the Sanskrit *sarkara*, which means "sugar." The prefixes *mono-, di-,* and *poly-* mean one, two and many, respectively. *How does knowing this help you remember the meanings of monosaccharide, disaccharaide, and polysaccharide?*

Note the aldehyde functional group (—CHO) on the straight-chain form of glucose and the ketone functional group $\left(-\underset{\underset{O}{\parallel}}{C}-\right)$ on the straight-chain form of fructose.

Disaccharides Simple sugars form the building blocks of more complex carbohydrates. The cyclic forms of two simple sugars can be linked by means of a condensation reaction. For example, the linking of glucose and fructose with the loss of a water molecule produces sucrose—common table sugar. Sugar cane plants, such as those in Figure 24.5, are a major source of sucrose. A sugar such as sucrose that forms from the condensation of two monosaccharides is known as a **disaccharide.** The reaction by which it forms is as follows:

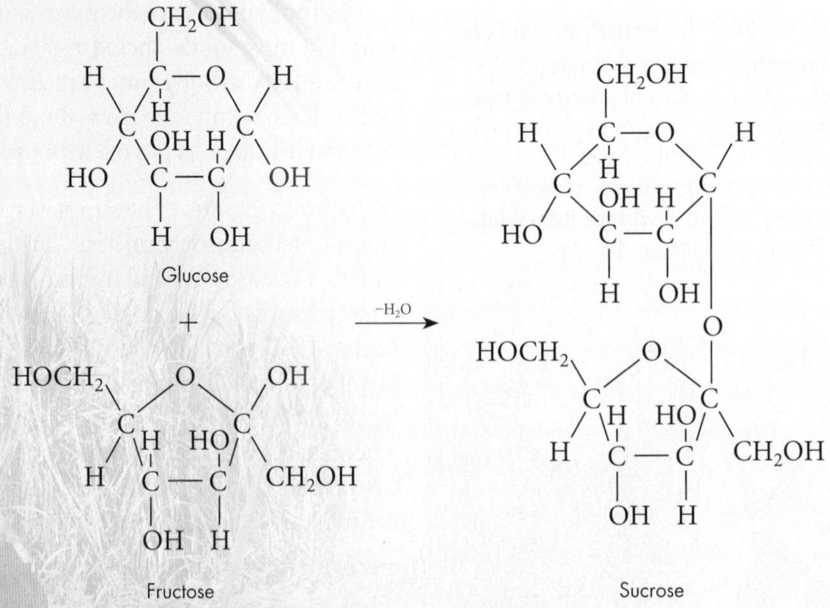

Glucose

+

Fructose

$\xrightarrow{-H_2O}$

Sucrose

Figure 24.5 Sugar Cane
Sucrose is obtained commercially mainly from the juice of sugar cane and sugar beets. Sugar cane, shown here, grows as a tall grass and is often harvested by hand.

Polysaccharides The formation of a disaccharide is sometimes the first step in a condensation polymerization reaction that produces extremely large molecules. The polymers produced by the linkage of many monosaccharide monomers are called **polysaccharides.** Starches, the major storage form of glucose in plants, are polysaccharide polymers that consist of glucose monomers. Figure 24.6 shows a portion of a starch molecule.

A typical linear starch molecule contains hundreds of glucose monomers. Other starches are branched molecules, each branch containing about a dozen glucose units. Glycogen, the energy source stored in the liver and muscle cells of animals, is a more highly branched molecule than plant starches. Glycogen, too, consists of glucose monomers.

Cellulose is probably the most abundant biological molecule on Earth. As you can see in Figure 24.6, cellulose also is a polymer of glucose. The orientation of the bond that links the glucose monomers in cellulose is different from the bond orientation in starch and in glycogen. Starch can be digested by most organisms and is partially soluble in water. Cellulose, however, can be digested by only a few kinds of microorganisms, such as those that live in the digestive tracts of cattle and termites. Cellulose is insoluble in water and is an important structural polysaccharide that provides form, hardness, and rigidity in plants. Plant cell walls are made of cellulose. Cotton is about 80 percent cellulose.

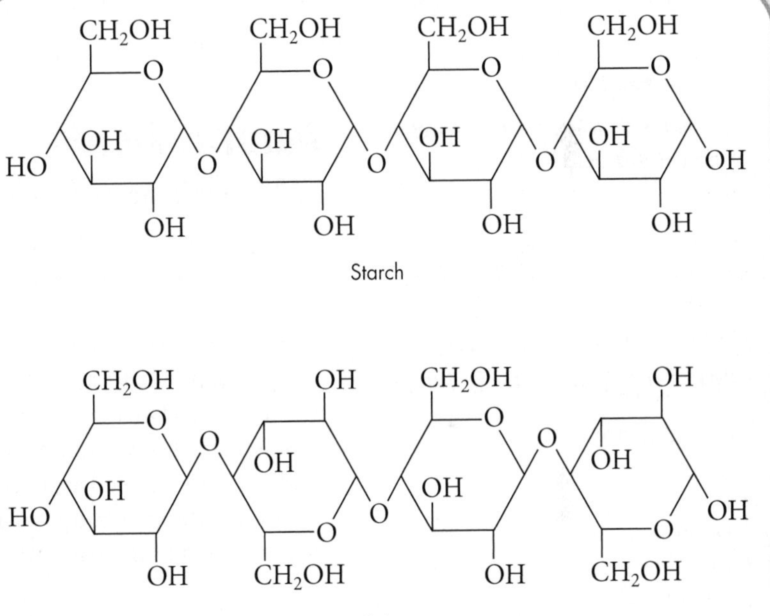

Figure 24.6 Polysaccharides
Starch and cellulose are similar polymers made up of hundreds of glucose monomers. They differ in the orientation of the bond between the glucose units. Because of this difference, starch is readily digestible, but cellulose is indigestible by most organisms.
Use Models *What are the differences between the complete structural formulas used in Figure 24.5 and the formulas used in Figure 24.6?*

CHEMISTRY & YOU

Q: *A cow's diet consists mostly of cellulose. A cow's stomach contains several parts. Food enters the first part of the stomach and is then regurgitated so the cow can chew it again. The regurgitated food then goes to a later part of the stomach where special bacteria live. Why is chewing and regurgitating necessary for a cow to digest cellulose?*

Starch

Cellulose

24.2 LessonCheck

8. Review What is the general formula for carbohydrates?

9. Identify Where is glucose found in nature?

10. Explain How can the cyclic forms of two simple sugars be combined?

11. Compare Distinguish between the important structural features of sucrose, glucose, and fructose.

12. Describe Describe the main characteristics of monosaccharides, disaccharides, and polysaccharides.

13. Compare Starch and cellulose have different properties, but both are composed of glucose units. Explain what makes them different.

14. Review Name a source for each polysaccharide:
a. starch
b. cellulose
c. glycogen

15. Identify What is the most abundant carbohydrate on Earth, and where is it found?

24.3 Amino Acids and Their Polymers

CHEMISTRY & YOU

Q: *Why do your muscles need amino acids?* Your muscles are constantly in use. For example, muscles in your stomach aid in digestion of the food you eat, and muscles in your fingers allow you to turn pages in a book or manipulate a computer mouse. Strength-building exercises can cause your muscles to become larger and stronger. This could not happen without amino acids. In this lesson, you will learn about amino acids and some of their functions.

Key Questions

▸ What is the general structure of an amino acid?

▸ What determines the differences in the chemical and physiological properties of peptides and proteins?

▸ How do enzymes affect the rates of reactions in living things?

Vocabulary

• amino acid
• peptide
• peptide bond
• protein
• enzyme
• substrate
• active site

Amino Acids

▸ **What is the general structure of an amino acid?**

Many biological compounds contain nitrogen in addition to carbon, oxygen, and hydrogen. Some of the most important nitrogen-containing molecules in organisms are amino acids. In fact, the polymers of amino acids make up more than one half of the dry weight of your body.

An **amino acid** is any compound that contains an amino group ($-NH_2$) and a carboxyl group ($-COOH$) in the same molecule. For chemists and biochemists, however, the term is usually reserved for the 20 common amino acids that are formed and used by living organisms. ▸ **Amino acids consist of a carboxyl group, an amino group, a hydrogen, and an R group side chain that are all covalently bonded to a central carbon atom.**

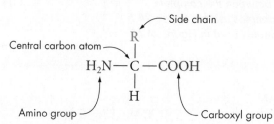

The chemical nature of the side-chain group accounts for the differences in properties of the 20 amino acids. In some amino acids, the side chains are nonpolar aliphatic or aromatic hydrocarbons. In other amino acids, the side chains are neutral but polar. In still others, the side chains are acidic or basic.

Because the central carbon of amino acids is asymmetric, these compounds can exist as enantiomers. As you may recall from Lesson 22.3, enantiomers may be right- or left-handed. Nearly all the amino acids found in nature are of the left-handed, or L, form.

Table 24.1 gives the names of amino acids with their three-letter abbreviations. Examine the abbreviations. You will use them as shortcuts when you read or write about protein structure.

Table 24.1

Common Amino Acids							
Name	Symbol	Name	Symbol	Name	Symbol	Name	Symbol
Alanine	Ala	Glutamine	Gln	Leucine	Leu	Serine	Ser
Arginine	Arg	Glutamic acid	Glu	Lysine	Lys	Threonine	Thr
Asparagine	Asn	Glycine	Gly	Methionine	Met	Tryptophan	Trp
Aspartic acid	Asp	Histidine	His	Phenylalanine	Phe	Tyrosine	Tyr
Cysteine	Cys	Isoleucine	Ile	Proline	Pro	Valine	Val

Peptides and Proteins

What determines the differences in the chemical and physiological properties of peptides and proteins?

A **peptide** is any combination of amino acids in which the amino group of one amino acid is united with the carboxyl group of another amino acid. The amide bond between the carboxyl group of one amino acid and the nitrogen in the amino group of the next amino acid in the peptide chain is called a **peptide bond.** Peptide bonds always involve the central amino and central carboxyl groups. The side chains are not involved in the bonding.

$$H_2N-\underset{\underset{H}{|}}{\overset{\overset{R}{|}}{C}}-\overset{\overset{O}{\|}}{C}-OH \; + \; H-\underset{\underset{H}{|}}{\overset{\overset{R}{|}}{N}}-\underset{\underset{H}{|}}{\overset{\overset{|}{|}}{C}}-\overset{\overset{O}{\|}}{C}-OH \longrightarrow H_2N-\underset{\underset{H}{|}}{\overset{\overset{R}{|}}{C}}-\overset{\overset{O}{\|}}{C}-\underset{\underset{H}{|}}{\overset{}{N}}-\underset{\underset{H}{|}}{\overset{\overset{R}{|}}{C}}-\overset{\overset{O}{\|}}{C}-OH \; + \; H_2O$$

Peptide bond

Amino acid   Amino acid   Peptide

A free amino group is at one end of the peptide. The convention is to write the peptide formula so that the free amino group is at the left end. There is also a free carboxyl group, which appears at the right end of the molecule.

More amino acids may be added to the peptide in the same fashion to form long chains by condensation polymerization. The order in which the amino acids of a peptide molecule are linked is called the amino acid sequence of that molecule. The amino acid sequence of a peptide is conveniently expressed using the three-letter abbreviations for the amino acids. For example, Asp—Glu—Gly represents a peptide containing three amino acids. This tri-peptide contains aspartic acid, glutamic acid, and glycine, in that order, with the free amino group assumed to be on the left end (on the Asp) and the free carboxyl group on the right end (on the Gly). Note that Asp—Glu—Gly is a different peptide from Gly—Glu—Asp because the order of amino acids is reversed, and thus the free amino group and free carboxyl group are on different amino acids.

In theory, the process of adding amino acids to a peptide chain can continue indefinitely. A peptide with more than ten amino acids is a polypeptide. A peptide with more than about 100 amino acids is a **protein.** On average, a molecule of 100 amino acids has a molecular mass of about 10,000 amu. Proteins are an important class of biomolecules. For example, your skin, hair, nails, and muscles are all made of proteins. Proteins are needed for almost all chemical reactions that occur in the body. We can make some of the amino acids that our cells use to make proteins. Other amino acids must be obtained by eating foods rich in proteins, such as the beans in Figure 24.7.

**Figure 24.7
Amino Acids in Your Diet**
Beans and brown rice are good sources of amino acids.

Figure 24.8 Peptide Structures
Peptides form three-dimensional shapes. **a.** This is a representation of amino acids in a peptide chain. **b.** The chain may coil into a helix. **c.** Two peptide chains may become arranged in a pleated, sheetlike structure.

Apply Concepts *What types of bonds determine the three-dimensional shape of a protein?*

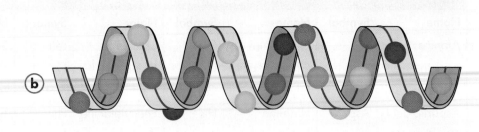
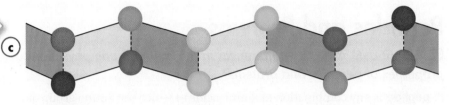

(a) (b) (c)

See peptide structure *animated online.*

CHEMISTRY & YOU

Q: *Why do your muscles need amino acids?*

Figure 24.9 Myoglobin
The three-dimensional structure of myoglobin, the oxygen storage protein of muscle tissue, is shown here. Most of the peptide chain of myoglobin is wound into helixes. Myoglobin also contains a nonprotein structure called heme. Heme contains four linked rings with an iron(II) ion (Fe^{2+}) at the center. Molecular oxygen binds to the heme iron. Marine animals, such as this dolphin, have a large concentration of myoglobin in their muscles which allows them to store oxygen during long dives.

🔑 **Differences in the chemical and physiological properties of peptides and proteins result from differences in the amino acid sequence.** Twenty amino acids can be linked in an enormous number of ways in a protein molecule. As many as 20^{100} different amino acid sequences are possible for a protein of 100 amino acids containing a combination of the 20 different amino acids.

Protein molecules are folded into relatively stable three-dimensional shapes. Figure 24.8a represents a long peptide chain of a protein, and Figure 24.8b shows how sections of peptide chain may coil into a regular spiral, known as a helix. Peptide chains may also be arranged side by side to form a pleated sheet, as shown in Figure 24.8c. Irregular folding of the chains also can occur. The three-dimensional shape of a protein is determined by interactions among the amino acids in its peptide chains. Protein shape is partly maintained by hydrogen bonds between adjacent folded chains. Covalent bonds also form between sulfur atoms of cysteine side chains that are folded near each other. In that way, separate polypeptide chains may be joined into a single protein. Figure 24.9 traces the shape of myoglobin, a protein that stores oxygen in muscle cells. The peptide chains of most of the myoglobin molecule are twisted into helixes.

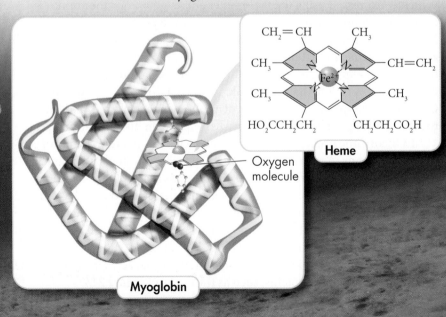

Oxygen molecule

Heme

Myoglobin

Enzymes

How do enzymes affect the rates of reactions in living things?

Enzymes are proteins that act as biological catalysts. **Enzymes increase the rates of chemical reactions in living things.** In 1926, the American chemist James B. Sumner reported the first isolation and crystallization of an enzyme. The enzyme he isolated was urease. Urease hydrolyzes urea, a constituent of urine, into ammonia and carbon dioxide. The strong ammonia smell of wet diapers that sit for a long time is the result of the action of bacteria that contain this enzyme. The equation for the reaction is shown below.

$$\underset{\text{Urea}}{H_2N-\overset{\overset{\displaystyle O}{\|}}{C}-NH_2(aq)} + \underset{\text{Water}}{H_2O(l)} \xrightarrow{\text{urease}} \underset{\text{Ammonia}}{2NH_3(g)} + \underset{\substack{\text{Carbon}\\\text{dioxide}}}{CO_2(g)}$$

Since the discovery of urease, thousands of enzymes have been isolated and structurally characterized as proteins.

In addition to being able to promote reactions, enzymes have two other properties of true catalysts. First, they are unchanged by the reaction they catalyze. Second, they do not change the normal equilibrium position of a chemical system. The same amount of product is eventually formed whether or not an enzyme is present. Few reactions in cells ever reach equilibrium, however. The products tend to convert rapidly to another substance in a subsequent enzyme-catalyzed reaction. According to Le Châtelier's principle, such removal of a product pulls the reaction toward completion.

How Enzymes Work Enzymes catalyze most of the chemical changes that occur in the cell. **Substrates** are the molecules on which an enzyme acts. In a typical enzymatic reaction, shown in Figure 24.10, the substrate interacts with side chains of the amino acids on the enzyme. These interactions cause the making and breaking of bonds. A substrate molecule must make contact with, and bind to, an enzyme molecule before the substrate can be transformed into product. The place on an enzyme where a substrate binds is called the **active site.** An active site is usually a pocket or crevice formed by folds in the peptide chains of the enzyme protein. The peptide chain of an enzyme is folded in a unique way to accommodate the substrate at the active site.

Figure 24.10 Enzyme and Substrate
A substrate fits into a distinctively shaped active site on an enzyme. Bond-breaking occurs at the active site to produce the products of the reaction.
Predict *What would happen if access to the active site were blocked by another molecule?*

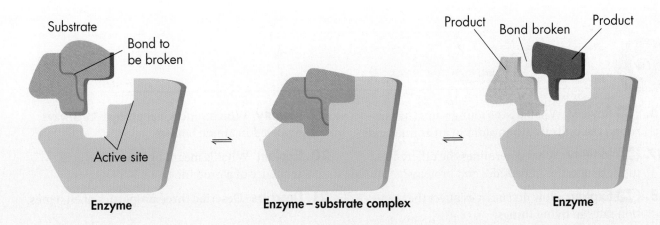

Substrate
Bond to be broken
Active site
Enzyme ⇌ **Enzyme–substrate complex** ⇌ **Enzyme**
Product   Bond broken   Product

**Figure 24.11
Carbonic Anhydrase
a.** Carbonic anhydrase (blue) has only one substrate, carbonic acid (red). **b.** An enzyme-substrate complex of carbonic anhydrase and carbonic acid. Notice how the substrate fits snugly into the active site.

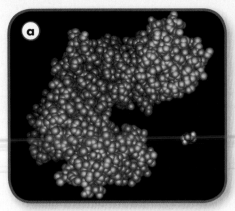
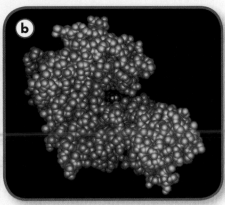

Since the active site of each enzyme has a distinctive shape, only a specific substrate molecule can fit into the enzyme, similar to how only one key shape will fit into a certain lock. Thus, each enzyme can catalyze only one chemical reaction at a time. An enzyme-substrate complex is formed when an enzyme molecule and a substrate molecule are joined. Figure 24.11 shows a model of the enzyme-substrate complex formed between the enzyme carbonic anhydrase and its substrate, carbonic acid.

To see the efficiency of enzymes, consider the effects of carbonic anhydrase on carbonic acid. Carbonic anhydrase catalyzes the reversible breakdown of carbonic acid to carbon dioxide and water. One molecule of carbonic anhydrase can catalyze the breakdown of 36 million molecules of carbonic acid in one minute!

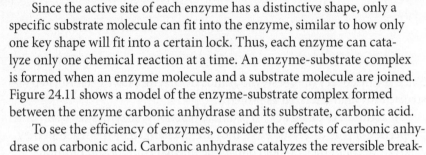

$$\underset{\text{Carbonic acid}}{H_2CO_3(aq)} \xrightleftharpoons{\text{carbonic anhydrase}} \underset{\substack{\text{Carbon}\\\text{dioxide}}}{CO_2(g)} + \underset{\text{Water}}{H_2O(l)}$$

Coenzymes Some enzymes can directly catalyze the transformation of biological substrates without assistance from other substances. Other enzymes need nonprotein coenzymes, also called cofactors, to assist the transformation. Coenzymes are metal ions or small organic molecules that must be present for an enzyme-catalyzed reaction to occur. Many water-soluble vitamins, such as B vitamins, are coenzymes. Metal ions that act as coenzymes include the cations of magnesium, potassium, iron, and zinc. The enzyme catalase includes an iron(III) ion in its structure. Catalase catalyzes the breakdown of hydrogen peroxide to water and oxygen, as shown in Figure 24.12 and in the reaction below.

$$2H_2O_2(aq) \xrightarrow{\text{catalase}} 2H_2O(l) + O_2(g)$$

Figure 24.12 Catalase
Liver contains high levels of the enzyme catalase. When a small amount of crushed liver cells is added to a solution of hydrogen peroxide, oxygen gas is rapidly evolved.

24.3 LessonCheck

16. ▣ **Review** What are the four groups that surround the central carbon atom in an amino acid?

17. ▣ **Identify** What determines the differences in the properties of peptides and proteins?

18. ▣ **Explain** How do enzymes affect the reaction rates in living things?

19. Identify Which functional groups are always involved in amide bonds?

20. Explain What is meant by the amino acid sequence of a protein?

21. Describe Describe three properties of enzymes.

Small-Scale Lab

The Egg: A Biochemical Storehouse

Purpose
To explore some physical and chemical properties of a chicken egg

Materials
- chicken egg
- ruler
- balance

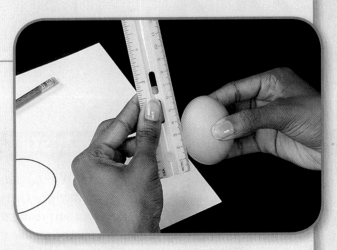

Procedure
Obtain a chicken egg. Examine the egg's shape, and measure its length and width in centimeters. Measure the mass of the egg. Make an accurate, life-size sketch of your egg and record all of your data on the sketch.

Analyze and Conclude
Using your experimental data, record the answers to the following questions below your drawing.

1. Calculate One way to compare the shapes of eggs is by using a shape index. The shape index is the width (w) of an egg expressed as a percentage of its length (l). Calculate the shape index of your egg.

$$\text{Shape index} = \frac{w}{l} \times 100\%$$

2. Calculate The volume, original mass (when freshly laid), and surface area of an egg can easily be estimated by using the following equations.

$V = (0.5236)(lw^2) \quad m = (0.5632)(lw^2)$
$A = (3.138)(lw^2)^{2/3}$
$V = \text{volume} \qquad m = \text{original mass}$
$A = \text{surface area}$

Use your data to calculate the volume, original mass, and surface area of your egg. Show your work, and record your results.

3. Compare Which is greater, the measured mass or the calculated mass of your egg? Suggest why the mass of an egg might change over time.

4. Compare Using your measured mass and your calculated volume, calculate the density of your egg. Compare this value with the density of a freshly laid egg (density of freshly laid egg = 1.075 g/cm³).

You're the Chemist
The following small-scale activities allow you to develop your own procedures and analyze the results.

1. Design an Experiment Design an experiment to answer the following question: Does the mass of an egg change over time?

2. Analyze Data Using your measured mass, your calculated original mass, and your experiments on the mass loss of an egg over time, estimate the age of your egg. What assumptions must you make?

3. Design an Experiment Design and carry out an experiment to measure the volume of your egg. Write down what you did and what you found.

4. Design an Experiment Carry out a series of experiments, or consult with your classmates and use their data, to determine if and how the shape index varies with the size of the egg (small, medium, large, extra large, jumbo).

5. Analyze Data Determine how the mass of an egg varies with its size (small, medium, large, extra large, jumbo).

6. Analyze Data An eggshell contains a calcium carbonate matrix with a protein cuticle. Place one drop of HCl on an eggshell and observe what happens. Write a chemical equation for this reaction. **CAUTION** *HCl is caustic and can burn skin.*

7. Analyze Data Proteins can be detected by adding aqueous solutions of copper(II) sulfate and sodium hydroxide to a sample. A violet color indicates the presence of protein. Test powdered milk and an eggshell for protein. What are your results?

8. Design an Experiment Design and carry out an experiment to answer the following question: Does temperature affect the mass of an egg over time?

24.4 Lipids

Q: *Why is fat an important part of our diet?* The media often portray fat as something that should be avoided because it is bad for you. It is probably not surprising that red meat can be high in fat. But you might not expect avocadoes like the one shown here to be high in fat. In this lesson, you will learn why fats are actually necessary in our diet.

Key Question

What physical property distinguishes lipids from other classes of biological molecules?

Vocabulary

- lipids
- triglyceride
- saponification
- phospholipid
- wax

Figure 24.13 Fats in Foods
Moderate levels of dietary fats and oils are essential to health.

Describing Lipids

What physical property distinguishes lipids from other classes of biological molecules?

Fats, oils, and other water-insoluble compounds are called **lipids.**
Carbohydrates and proteins tend to dissolve in water. Whereas, lipids tend to dissolve readily in organic solvents, such as ether and chloroform. Most fats, such as the butter in Figure 24.13, are obtained from animals. The fats from palm kernels and coconuts, however, are exceptions. Most oils, such as olive oil, are plant products.

Although excessive dietary fat is harmful, you do need some lipids in your diet to stay healthy. Experts recommend that your lipid intake make up less than 30 percent of your daily caloric intake of food. Lipids provide an efficient way for your body to store energy. They are also needed to keep your cell membranes healthy.

Triglycerides Natural fats and oils exist as triesters of glycerol with fatty acids, which are long-chain carboxylic acids (C_{12} through C_{24}). This form of lipid is known as a **triglyceride.** Triglycerides are important as the long-term storage form of energy in the human body. The following equation shows the general reaction for the formation of triglycerides.

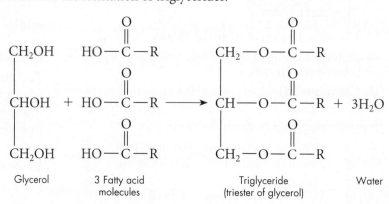

Glycerol | 3 Fatty acid molecules → Triglyceride (triester of glycerol) + Water

A fat, such as beef tallow or coconut oil, is mixed with an excess of sodium hydroxide and heated.

Sodium chloride is added to the saponification mixture. This causes the sodium salts of the fatty acids to separate as a thick curd of crude soap.

The crude soap is purified and can then be processed as desired.

Figure 24.14 Soapmaking
These photographs illustrate soapmaking. Once the soap is formed, it is poured into molds. Later it may be milled, or shredded, with scent or color added, and then remolded to produce a finished product.

Like other esters, fats and oils are easily hydrolyzed in the presence of acids and bases. The hydrolysis of oils or fats by boiling with an aqueous solution of an alkali-metal hydroxide is called **saponification.** Saponification is used to make soap. Soaps are thus the alkali metal (Na, K, or Li) salts of fatty acids. A typical saponification reaction is shown below.

$$
\begin{array}{c}
CH_2-O-\overset{\overset{\displaystyle O}{\|}}{C}-(CH_2)_{16}CH_3 \\
CH-O-\overset{\overset{\displaystyle O}{\|}}{C}-(CH_2)_{16}CH_3 \quad + \quad 3NaOH \quad \longrightarrow \\
CH_2-O-\overset{\overset{\displaystyle O}{\|}}{C}-(CH_2)_{16}CH_3
\end{array}
\qquad
\begin{array}{c}
CH_2OH \\
CHOH \\
CH_2OH
\end{array}
\quad + \quad 3CH_3(CH_2)_{16}-\overset{\overset{\displaystyle O}{\|}}{C}-O^-Na^+
$$

Tristearin (triester of glycerol and stearic acid)　　　　Glycerol　　　　Sodium stearate (a soap)

As shown in Figure 24.14, soap can be made from a fat, such as beef tallow or coconut oil. Glycerol is an important byproduct of saponification reactions. It is recovered by evaporating the water layer.

Phospholipids Lipids that contain phosphate groups are called **phospholipids.** Phospholipids are abundant in cells. Figure 24.15 shows a typical phospholipid molecule, lecithin. The lecithin molecule has a hydrophilic (water-loving) ionic head and oily or hydrophobic (water-hating) hydrocarbon tails. Recall the solubility rule, "Like dissolves like." Lecithin, which is partly hydrophobic and partly hydrophilic, behaves in water like both an insoluble hydrocarbon and a soluble ionic compound. In water, the hydrophobic carbon chains of lecithin aggregate to exclude water. The hydrophilic part is drawn to water, which can solvate it. In water, phospholipids spontaneously form a spherical double layer, called a lipid bilayer, in which the hydrophobic tails of phospholipid molecules are sandwiched between two layers of hydrophilic heads.

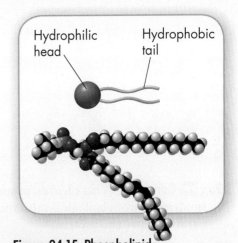

Figure 24.15 Phospholipid
In the simplified diagram, the hydrophilic head is shown as a sphere and the hydrophobic tails as wavy lines. The space-filling model is the phospholipid lecithin.

The Chemistry of Life **851**

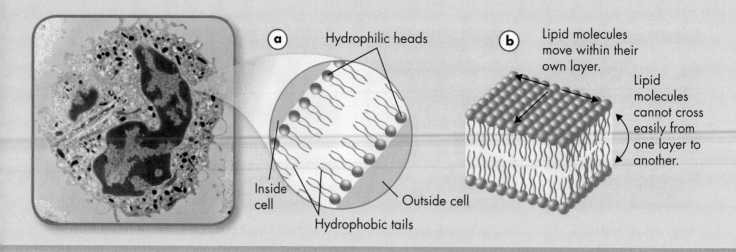

a. Hydrophilic heads

Inside cell

Hydrophobic tails

Outside cell

b. Lipid molecules move within their own layer.

Lipid molecules cannot cross easily from one layer to another.

Figure 24.16 Lipid Bilayer
A cell membrane has a lipid bilayer structure. **a.** The hydrophilic heads are in contact with water, but the hydrophobic tails are not. **b.** The lipid molecules move easily within their own layer but do not readily move to the other layer.
Apply Concepts *What prevents a lipid molecule from crossing to the opposite side of the bilayer?*

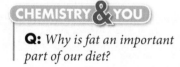

Q: *Why is fat an important part of our diet?*

Cell membranes, such as the one shown in Figure 24.16, consist primarily of lipid bilayers. The lipid bilayer of a cell membrane acts as a barrier against the passage of molecules and ions into and out of the cell. However, cells do need to take in certain ions and molecules, such as nutrients, while excluding other materials. Selective absorption is accomplished by the protrusion of protein molecules through the lipid bilayer. These proteins form channels through which specific ions and molecules can selectively pass. Not all membrane proteins extend all the way through the membrane. Proteins, such as enzymes, may be bound to the interior surface of the membrane. Many membrane proteins have attached carbohydrate molecules. The carbohydrate portion is on the exterior of the lipid bilayer, where it can hydrogen-bond with water. The protein portion is on the interior of the lipid bilayer, so it does not contact the water.

Waxes Another type of lipids are **waxes.** Waxes are esters of long-chain fatty acids and long-chain alcohols. The hydrocarbon chains for both the acid and the alcohol usually contain from 10 to 30 carbon atoms. Waxes are low-melting, stable solids. In many plants, a wax coat protects the surfaces of leaves from water loss and attack by microorganisms. For example, carnauba wax, a major ingredient in car wax and floor polish, is found on the leaves of a South American palm tree. In animals, waxes coat the skin, hair, and feathers and help keep these structures pliable and waterproof.

⊚ 24.4 LessonCheck

ONLINE PROBLEMS

22. 🔑 Compare What physical property sets lipids apart from biological substances such as carbohydrates and proteins?

23. Compare Compare the molecular structures of the three main types of lipids.

24. Identify What are the products of a saponification reaction?

25. Explain What role do phospholipids and proteins play in cell membranes?

26. Explain How do phospholipids behave in water?

27. Identify What two classes of organic compounds combine to form a wax?

28. Identify What is the function of waxes in plants? In animals?

Biochemists

Biochemistry is the chemistry of life, and biochemists combine the fields of chemistry, microbiology, cell biology, genetics, and physics to study the chemical and physical processes of cells and organisms.

Biochemists often work in medical, agricultural, and food-related fields. Those working in medical fields may investigate the causes of diseases and genetic disorders and develop new drugs and medications. They might also research the chemical changes that take place in cells to identify how substances such as drugs, hormones, and household chemicals affect cells, tissues, and body functions. Biochemists working in agriculture may develop new techniques for such tasks as crop cultivation and pest control. Biochemists working in food science may analyze the effects of cooking, canning, and processing on the nutritional value of foods, or they may study the effects of certain foods and nutrients on the human body.

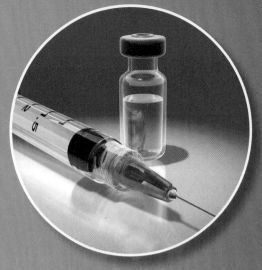

FLU FIGHTERS Biochemists investigate the chemical aspects of the immune system and viruses to create vaccines that help prevent viral diseases such as known strands of influenza viruses.

MONITORING THE ENVIRONMENT
Biochemists analyze the effects of environmental conditions on plants and animals such as these corals in the Indian Ocean.

CREATING BIOFUELS Understanding both plant genetics and chemistry allows biochemists to research how plants such as corn and soy can be used as renewable fuel sources.

Take It Further

1. Identify What are three life processes that depend on chemistry? Explain your answer.

2. Evaluate the Impact on Society What is one way in which understanding the chemical processes involved in aging might help future generations?

24.5 Nucleic Acids

Q: *Why do children often look similar to their parents?* Maybe people have told you that you have your mother's eyes or your father's nose. Although this is not literally true (your eyes and nose are your own), you do inherit some traits from your parents. In this lesson, you will learn about molecules that are involved in the inheritance of traits from parents.

Key Questions

📋 What are the functions of DNA and RNA?

📋 How many bases of DNA are required to specify one amino acid in a peptide chain?

📋 What are gene mutations?

📋 What are two examples of DNA technologies used today?

Vocabulary

• nucleic acid
• nucleotide
• gene

DNA and RNA

📋 **What are the functions of DNA and RNA?**

More than 100 years ago, a Swiss biochemist discovered a class of nitrogen-containing compounds in the nuclei of cells. The nuclei were first obtained from dead white blood cells in the pus of infected wounds. The eventual understanding of the biological role of the compounds has led to a revolution in biochemistry.

These nitrogen-containing compounds, called **nucleic acids,** are polymers that are found primarily in a cell's nucleus. They are indispensable components of every living thing. Two kinds of nucleic acids are in cells—*deoxyribo*nucleic *acid* (DNA) and *ribo*nucleic *acid* (RNA). 📋 **DNA stores the information needed to make proteins and governs the reproduction and growth of cells and new organisms. RNA has a key role in the transmission of the information stored in DNA and in the synthesis of proteins.**

The monomers that make up the DNA and RNA polymers are called **nucleotides.** Nucleic acids are therefore polynucleotides. As shown below, each nucleotide consists of a phosphate group, a five-carbon sugar, and a nitrogen-containing unit called a nitrogen base.

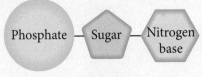

Nucleotide

The sugar unit in the nucleotides of DNA is the five-carbon monosaccharide known as deoxyribose. There are four different nitrogen bases in DNA—adenine, guanine, thymine, and cytosine. These four bases are abbreviated A, G, T, and C, respectively, and are shown in a short segment of a DNA molecule in Figure 24.17. Notice that adenine and guanine each contains a double ring and that thymine and cytosine each contains a single ring. Ribose, which has one more oxygen atom than deoxyribose, is the sugar found in the nucleotide monomers of RNA. The base thymine is never found in RNA. Instead, it is replaced by a fifth nitrogen base, called uracil, which is abbreviated U.

Figure 24.17 DNA
The nucleotide monomers of DNA are linked together through their sugar-phosphate groups. Two strands of DNA coil into a helix.

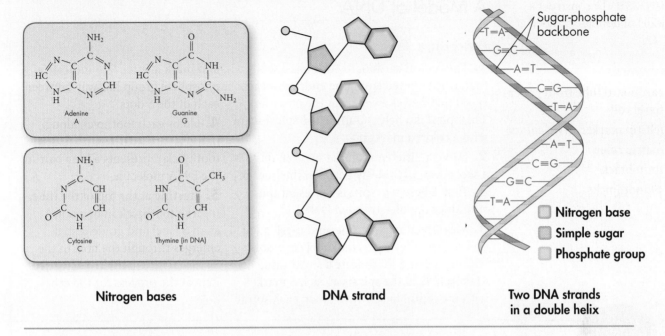

Nitrogen bases   **DNA strand**   **Two DNA strands in a double helix**

   Chemists studying nucleic acids discovered that the amount of adenine in DNA always equals the amount of thymine (A = T). Similarly, the amount of guanine always equals the amount of cytosine (G = C). The significance of these facts was not apparent until 1953, when James Watson and Francis Crick proposed that the structure of DNA consists of two polynucleotide chains wrapped into a spiral shape, as in Figure 24.17. This spiral is the famous double helix of DNA. For the nitrogen bases to fit neatly into the double helix, every double-ringed base on one strand must be paired with a single-ringed base on the opposing strand. The pairing of A with T and G with C not only provides the best possible fit; it also allows the maximum number of hydrogen bonds to form between the opposing bases, as Figure 24.18 shows. Thus, the pairing of A and T (with two hydrogen bonds between the opposing bases) and of G and C (with three hydrogen bonds) makes for the most stable arrangement in the double helix.

Figure 24.18
Hydrogen Bonding in DNA
The two DNA strands in a double helix are held together by many hydrogen bonds; there are two hydrogen bonds between each thymine (T) and adenine (A) and three hydrogen bonds between each cytosine (C) and guanine (G).
Interpret Diagrams *In the pairing of C with G, how many hydrogen bonds involve nitrogen? How many involve oxygen?*

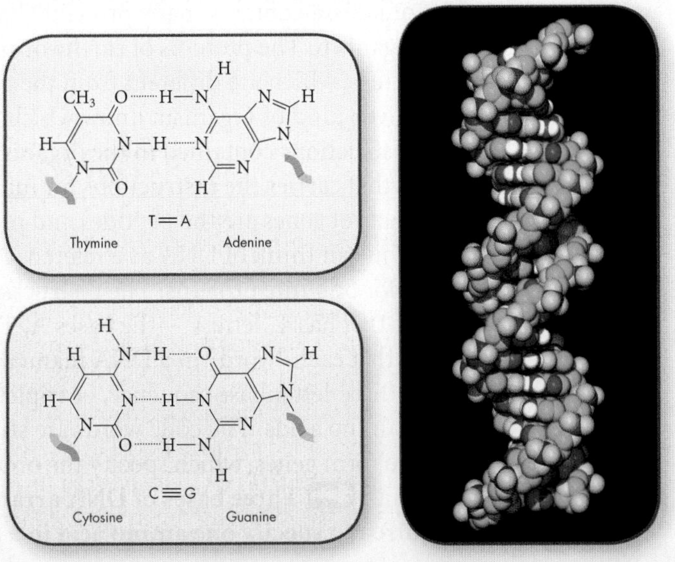

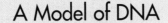

Purpose To construct a model of double-stranded DNA

Materials

- cardboard tube from paper-towel roll
- felt-tip markers (two colors)
- metric ruler
- thumbtack
- 10 toothpicks

A Model of DNA

Procedure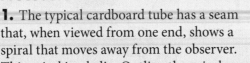

1. The typical cardboard tube has a seam that, when viewed from one end, shows a spiral that moves away from the observer. This spiral is a helix. Outline the spiral seam with a colored marker.

2. Using a different-colored marker, draw a second spiral midway between the lines of the first. These two spirals represent the two strands of double-stranded DNA.

3. Measure along the tube, and mark a dot on each spiral every 5 cm. Label each dot with the letter *S* to indicate a sugar unit. Make a hole in the spirals at each *S* mark with the thumbtack. Move down each spiral

and mark a letter *P* to indicate a phosphate group halfway between each of the *S* dots.

4. Color each toothpick along half its length with a marker. A toothpick represents a base pair in the DNA molecule.

5. Starting at the top of the tube, insert a toothpick in one hole at an *S* label and guide it so it emerges through the hole in the *S* on the opposite side of the tube. Repeat the process for the other holes.

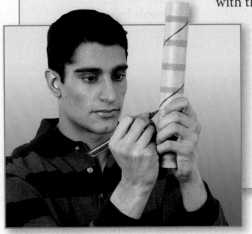

Analyze and Conclude

1. Use Models Are the bases on the interior or the exterior of the double helix? Are they randomly arranged or neatly stacked?

2. Analyze Data Are the phosphate groups on the exterior or the interior of the DNA structure?

3. Analyze Data Are the sugar groups on the interior or the exterior of the DNA molecule?

The Genetic Code

🔑 *How many bases of DNA are required to specify one amino acid in a peptide chain?*

An organism contains many proteins that are characteristic of that particular organism. The proteins of earthworms are different from the proteins of pine trees, which are different from the proteins of humans. How do cells in a given kind of organism know which proteins to make? The cells use the instructions contained in the organism's DNA. A **gene** is a segment of DNA that carries the instructions for making one peptide chain. Thus, the products of genes are the peptides and proteins found in an organism.

You can think of DNA as a reference manual that stores the instructions for building proteins. The instructions are written in a simple language that has 4 "letters"—the bases A, T, G, and C. Experimental data show that each "word" in a DNA manual is exactly three letters in length. Each three-letter base sequence, or triplet, codes for one of the 20 common amino acids. The code words are strung together in the DNA molecule to form genes, which specify the order of amino acids in peptides and proteins. 🔑 **Three bases of DNA arranged in a specific sequence are required to specify one amino acid in a peptide or protein chain.**

Table 24.2 provides the DNA code words for the 20 common amino acids. For example, you can see that the DNA code word AAA specifies the amino acid phenylalanine (Phe) and that the DNA code word CGA specifies the amino acid alanine (Ala). Note that most amino acids are specified by more than one code word, but a code word never specifies more than one amino acid. With DNA code words of three letters, 900 bases arranged in a specific sequence would be required to code for a peptide chain made up of 300 amino acids arranged in a specific sequence.

One of the the code words (TAC) signifies the initiation of a peptide. Three code words (ATT, ATC, and ACT) are reserved as end, or termination, code words. The translation of a base sequence of DNA in a gene into the amino acid sequence of a peptide begins with the initiation code word and runs continuously until a termination code word is reached. The termination code word signals a stop to the addition of amino acids in the production of the peptide. You can think of a termination code as being similar to the period at the end of a sentence.

The molecular masses of DNA molecules reach into the millions and possibly billions. Even with only four bases, the number of possible sequences of nucleotides in a DNA chain is enormous. The sequence of the nitrogen bases A, T, G, and C in the DNA of an organism constitutes the genetic plan, or blueprint, for that organism. This genetic plan is inherited from parents and passed to offspring. Differences in the number and sequence of the bases in DNA ultimately are responsible for the great diversity of living creatures found on Earth.

CHEMISTRY & YOU

Q: *Why do children often look similar to their parents?*

Table 24.2

Three-Letter DNA Code Words for the Amino Acids

First Letter in Code Word	Second Letter in Code Word				Third Letter in Code Word
	A	**G**	**T**	**C**	
A	AAA Phe AAG Phe	AGA Ser AGG Ser	ATA Tyr ATG Tyr	ACA Cys ACG Cys	**A G**
	AAT Leu AAC Leu	AGT Ser AGC Ser	ATT End ATC End	ACT End ACC Trp	**T C**
G	GAA Leu GAG Leu	GGA Pro GGG Pro	GTA His GTG His	GCA Arg GCG Arg	**A G**
	GAT Leu GAC Leu	GGT Pro GGC Pro	GTT Gln GTC Gln	GCT Arg GCC Arg	**T C**
T	TAA Ile TAG Ile	TGA Thr TGG Thr	TTA Asn TTG Asn	TCA Ser TCG Ser	**A G**
	TAT Ile TAC Met	TGT Thr TGC Thr	TTT Lys TTC Lys	TCT Arg TCC Arg	**T C**
C	CAA Val CAG Val	CGA Ala CGG Ala	CTA Asp CTG Asp	CCA Gly CCG Gly	**A G**
	CAT Val CAC Val	CGT Ala CGC Ala	CTT Glu CTC Glu	CCT Gly CCC Gly	**T C**

Gene Mutations

🔑 What are gene mutations?

When a change occurs in a DNA code word, the result is a mutation in the DNA. 🔑 **Substitutions, additions, or deletions of one or more nucleotides in the DNA molecule are called gene mutations.** The effect of the deletion of a single base from a gene can be illustrated by the following analogy. Suppose a string of letters of the alphabet goes as follows:

PATTHEREDCAT

The letters may not make sense at first glance. However, if you separate them into three-letter words, they form a perfectly sensible statement:

PAT THE RED CAT

Now delete the first letter, and again separate the string into three-letter segments:

ATT HER EDC AT

This last sequence is nonsensical. Similarly, the deletion of a base in the DNA base sequence can turn the information into nonsense. A sequence that once may have coded for the proper sequence of amino acids in a necessary protein may be replaced by a sequence that produces a useless or damaging amino acid sequence. The same sort of harmful effect may be produced by mutations involving substitutions or additions of nucleotides.

Such mutations might result in the production of a faulty protein or of no protein at all. Diseases that result from gene mutations are called genetic disorders. Thousands of genetic disorders have been identified. Galactosemia is an example of a genetic disorder that affects about 1 in 55,000 newborn babies. Galactosemia results from a mutation in an enzyme called GALT (galactose-1-phosphate uridyl transferase). GALT is needed to break down the sugar galactose into glucose, as shown in Figure 24.19. Without normal GALT, galactose can build up in the body and cause kidney failure, an enlarged liver, cataracts, and brain damage. Newborns are usually tested for galactosemia at birth. The only way to treat galactosemia is to avoid foods that contain galactose, such as milk, cheese, and dried beans.

Not all gene mutations are harmful. Occasionally, a mutation can result in the synthesis of a protein that is more efficient than the version that previously existed. Such a mutation could thus be beneficial to the survival of the affected organism.

Figure 24.19 Galactosemia
Persons with galactosemia have mutations in the gene for the enzyme GALT. They cannot complete the breakdown of lactose. Any food containing galactose or lactose, including milk and products containing milk, should be avoided.

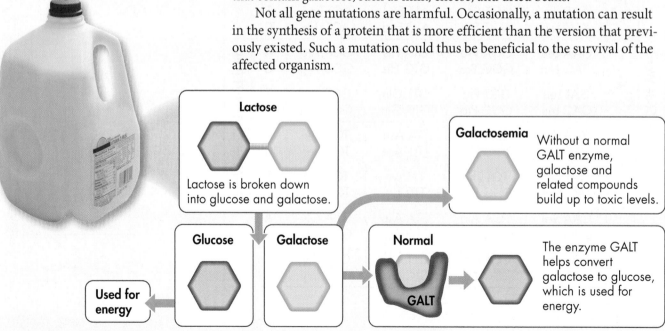

Lactose
Lactose is broken down into glucose and galactose.

Galactosemia Without a normal GALT enzyme, galactose and related compounds build up to toxic levels.

Glucose

Galactose

Normal The enzyme GALT helps convert galactose to glucose, which is used for energy.

GALT

Used for energy

DNA Technologies

🔑 **What are two examples of DNA technologies used today?**

Since DNA is such an important part of living things, it may not be surprising that DNA technology has had a significant impact on our society. In the following pages, you will learn about some of these technologies.

DNA Typing Only a small fraction of a human's DNA is used for coding the information needed for protein synthesis. The rest consists of repeating, noncoding base sequences that separate or sometimes interrupt gene coding sequences. The role of these stretches of noncoding DNA is unclear. The noncoding sequences are similar for members of the same family but are slightly different for almost every individual. Differences also exist in the coding portions of DNA. The base sequences of DNA are slightly different for different individuals, except for identical twins. Identical twins look similar because they have identical DNA.

🔑 **DNA typing uses the variation in the DNA of individuals as a basis for creating DNA profiles to identify a person from samples of his or her hair, skin cells, or body fluid.** Because DNA sequences, like fingerprints, are unique for each individual, DNA typing has also been called DNA fingerprinting. To construct a DNA profile, scientists first isolate the DNA in a sample. Only a tiny sample is needed. A sample can be anything that contains DNA, including teeth, fingernails, blood, hair, saliva, and skin cells. Figure 24.20 shows some items that investigators obtained from a crime scene.

Samples can be typed in several different ways, but the method used most commonly by the Federal Bureau of Investigation (FBI) is short tandem repeat (STR) analysis. A short tandem repeat is a short segment of DNA that is repeated several times. For example, one of the regions of DNA used by the FBI contains repeats of the sequence AGAT. To obtain a profile, the FBI looks at 13 different STR regions.

The DNA profile can then be compared with a sample of DNA from a known individual, as Figure 24.21 shows. The FBI has a technology system called the Combined DNA Indexing Systems (CODIS) that allows laboratories throughout the country to share and search DNA profiles. The chances of two people (except for identical twins) having the same DNA profile for these 13 regions is 1 in 1 billion.

Figure 24.20
Crime Scene Evidence
These scientists are analyzing items taken from a crime scene. DNA may be isolated from blood on the items, in this case clothing and an axe.

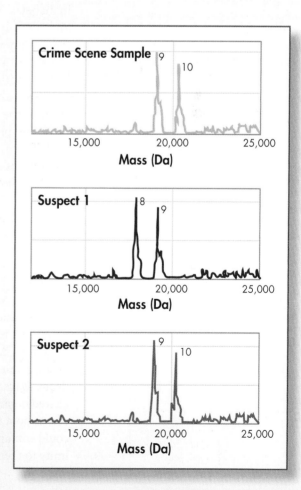

Figure 24.21 DNA Profile
This is an example of what a DNA profile for one STR region might look like. The DNA from the crime scene has a segement with 9 repeats and a segment with 10 repeats. Suspect 1 can be eliminated because the length of that person's segments does not match the crime scene sample.

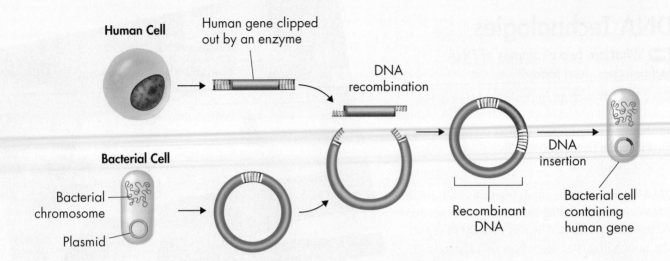

Human Cell

Human gene clipped out by an enzyme

DNA recombination

Bacterial Cell

Bacterial chromosome

Plasmid

DNA insertion

Recombinant DNA

Bacterial cell containing human gene

Figure 24.22
Recombinant DNA
Included here are the elements of an experiment involving recombinant DNA. In this experiment, DNA from one organism is inserted into the DNA of a different organism.

Recombinant DNA Technology Scientists have learned to manipulate genes by various methods. 🔵 **Recombinant DNA technology consists of methods for cleaving a DNA chain, inserting a new piece of DNA into the gap created by the cleavage, and resealing the chain.** Figure 24.22 illustrates such a method. The altered DNA formed by this method is known as recombinant DNA.

Applications in Medicine The first practical application of recombinant DNA technology was to insert the gene for making human insulin into bacteria. Most people naturally make insulin, a polypeptide that controls levels of blood sugar. However, insufficient insulin production results in diabetes. The symptoms of diabetes can often be controlled by insulin injections. In the past, human insulin was not available for this purpose. Pig insulin, which is quite similar in structure to human insulin, was used as a substitute. Some patients, however, were allergic to pig insulin. Today, diabetic patients use the human form of insulin produced by bacteria that have been altered by recombinant DNA technology. Use of this insulin removes the need for the potentially dangerous use of pig insulin.

Other proteins produced by recombinant DNA technology are used as medicinal drugs. For example, an enzyme called tissue plasminogen activator (TPA) is used to dissolve blood clots in patients who have suffered heart attacks. Another protein, interferon, is thought to relieve or delay some of the debilitating effects of multiple sclerosis. Recombinant DNA technology is also being applied to the cure of genetic disorders in an experimental treatment known as gene therapy.

Applications in Agriculture In agriculture, new recombinant DNA techniques can make plants resistant to pests and weed killers and produce fruits and vegetables that are better suited for shipping and storage. The most common traits in genetically modified crops are herbicide resistance and insect resistance in corn, cotton, soybean, and canola.

Crops have also been genetically modified for pharmaceutical purposes. These so-called pharma crops are genetically modified to produce drugs to treat or prevent diseases such as cancer or AIDs. Genetically altered organisms have many potential benefits, but some people have concerns about their safety. There is also concern that genetically modified crops could contaminate other crops if they are grown and processed in close proximity to them.

Cloning Ethical concerns were raised in 1997 when Scottish scientists announced the birth of a lamb named Dolly, shown in Figure 24.23. In normal animal reproduction, an offspring is a genetic mixture of the characteristics of both parents. Dolly, however, was a clone—an offspring of a single individual. A clone is an exact genetic copy of its parent because it is formed using the DNA of only that parent. Since the cloning of Dolly, other animals have also been successfully cloned, including cows, mice, and cats. The birth of cloned animals has raised the question of whether humans might eventually be cloned. Many people are concerned about some of the possible outcomes of cloning identical individuals. These situations are one aspect of more general concerns about the uniqueness of life.

Figure 24.23 Cloning
Polly and Dolly had no fathers. Dolly was cloned from a single cell taken from her mother. Polly was also cloned from a single cell that was genetically modified.
Infer *How did Dolly's DNA compare with the DNA in her mother's cells?*

Cloning without genetic modification

DOLLY was a female domestic sheep remarkable for being the first mammal to be cloned from an adult cell.

Cloning plus genetic modification

POLLY and her sister Molly were the first mammals to have been successfully cloned from an adult cell and to be genetically modified at the same time.

24.5 LessonCheck

29. Review What functions are performed by DNA and RNA?

30. Review What does a three-letter base sequence of DNA specify?

31. Identify What are three types of gene mutations?

32. Identify What methods are used in recombinant DNA technology?

33. Describe Describe how scientific methods might be applied to the process of DNA fingerprinting.

34. Evaluate Why do you think cloning is controversial? What are your personal thoughts on this matter?

24.6 Metabolism

Q: *Why does a hummingbird eat so much?* A hummingbird eats more than its weight in food each day. Hummingbirds have a high body temperature, fast heart rate, and a fast breathing rate. All of these factors affect the hummingbird's metabolism. In this lesson, you will learn about the reactions that are part of an organism's metabolism.

Key Questions

▸ What is the function of ATP in living cells?

▸ What happens to biological molecules and energy during catabolism and anabolism?

▸ How do nitrogen-fixing bacteria provide plants with a usable form of nitrogen?

Vocabulary

• adenosine triphosphate (ATP)
• metabolism
• catabolism
• anabolism

ATP

▸ **What is the function of ATP in living cells?**

All living things need energy to function. **Adenosine triphosphate (ATP),** shown in Figure 24.24, is a molecule that transmits this energy in the cells of living organisms. The function of ATP can be compared to a belt connecting an electric motor to a pump. The motor generates energy capable of operating the pump. But if a belt does not connect the motor to the pump, the energy produced by the motor is wasted. You can think of ATP as the belt that connects the production and use of energy by cells. ▸ **In living cells, ATP is the energy carrier between the spontaneous reactions that release energy and nonspontaneous reactions that use energy.**

Recall that oxidation reactions, such as the combustion of methane in a furnace or the oxidation of glucose in a living cell, are spontaneous reactions that release energy. This energy can be captured when adenosine diphosphate (ADP) condenses with an inorganic phosphate group to become ATP. The addition of a phosphate group, called phosphorylation, occurs during certain biochemical oxidation reactions.

Figure 24.24 ATP
ATP is made of adenine, ribose, and three phosphate groups. ATP provides energy to muscles for moving the body.
Compare and Contrast *How is the structure of ATP similar to that of a DNA nucleotide?*

The reaction diagram at the top:

$$\text{Adenosine} - \overset{\overset{\displaystyle O}{\|}}{\underset{\underset{\displaystyle OH}{|}}{P}} - O - \overset{\overset{\displaystyle O}{\|}}{\underset{\underset{\displaystyle OH}{|}}{P}} - OH \; + \; HO - \overset{\overset{\displaystyle O}{\|}}{\underset{\underset{\displaystyle OH}{|}}{P}} - OH \longrightarrow \text{Adenosine} - \overset{\overset{\displaystyle O}{\|}}{\underset{\underset{\displaystyle OH}{|}}{P}} - O - \overset{\overset{\displaystyle O}{\|}}{\underset{\underset{\displaystyle OH}{|}}{P}} - O - \overset{\overset{\displaystyle O}{\|}}{\underset{\underset{\displaystyle OH}{|}}{P}} - OH \; + \; H_2O$$

Adenosine diphosphate (ADP) Inorganic phosphate (Pi) Adenosine triphosphate (ATP) Water

The formation of ATP efficiently captures energy produced by the oxidation reactions in living cells. Every mole of ATP produced by the phosphorylation of ADP stores about 30.5 kJ of energy. The reverse happens when ATP is hydrolyzed back to ADP: Every mole of ATP that is hydrolyzed back to ADP releases about 30.5 kJ of energy. Cells use this released energy to drive processes that would ordinarily be nonspontaneous. Because of its ability to capture energy from one process and transmit it to another, ATP is sometimes referred to as a high-energy compound; however, the energy produced by the breakdown of ATP to ADP is not particularly high for the breaking of a covalent bond. ATP is important because it occupies an intermediate position in the energetics of the cell. It can be formed by using the energy obtained from a few higher-energy oxidation reactions. The energy that is contained in the bonds of ATP can then be used to drive other cellular processes.

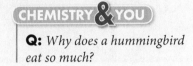

Metabolism Reactions

What happens to biological molecules and energy during catabolism and anabolism?

Thousands of chemical reactions take place in the cells of a living organism. The entire set of chemical reactions carried out by an organism is known as the organism's **metabolism.** The reactions that occur in metabolism can be divided into two main processes, catabolism and anabolism.

Catabolism In metabolism, unneeded cellular components and the nutrients in food are broken down into simpler compounds by chemical reactions collectively called **catabolism.** Catabolic reactions release energy as well as produce simple compounds. **The degradation of complex biological molecules such as carbohydrates, lipids, proteins, and nucleic acids during catabolism provides the energy and the building blocks for the construction of new biological compounds needed by the cell.** Through the formation of ATP, catabolic reactions provide the energy for such needs as body motion and the transport of nutrients to cells where they are required. The oxidation reactions of catabolism also provide energy in the form of heat. These reactions help keep your body temperature constant at 37°C.

The complete oxidation of glucose to carbon dioxide and water is one of the most important energy-yielding processes of catabolism. Study Figure 24.25, which summarizes the major steps in the degradation of one glucose molecule to six molecules of carbon dioxide. The complete oxidation actually involves many reactions that are not shown. As you can see in the figure, the major carbon-containing reactants and products are named, and they are also referred to according to the number of carbons they contain.

Figure 24.25 Glucose Catabolism
The breakdown of glucose to carbon dioxide and water is one of the most important energy-yielding processes of catabolism.
Make Generalizations *What happens to the number of carbon-carbon bonds from one step to the next?*

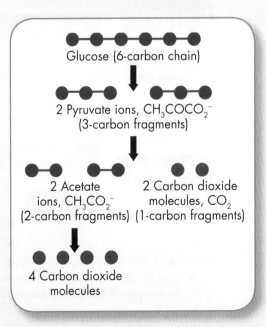

Glucose (6-carbon chain)

2 Pyruvate ions, $CH_3COCO_2^-$ (3-carbon fragments)

2 Acetate ions, $CH_3CO_2^-$ (2-carbon fragments) 2 Carbon dioxide molecules, CO_2 (1-carbon fragments)

4 Carbon dioxide molecules

Figure 24.26 Animal Metabolism
Organisms such as this mouse use the energy stored in the chemical bonds of food molecules to power their body processes.

The combustion of one mole of glucose to six moles of carbon dioxide and six moles of water, either by fire or by oxidation in a living cell, produces 2.82×10^3 kJ of energy. Cells that use oxygen may produce up to 38 moles of ATP by capturing the energy released by the complete oxidation of a single mole of glucose! The large amount of ATP produced from the oxidation of glucose makes it the likeliest mode of energy production for most kinds of cells. In fact, if glucose is available, brain cells use no other source of carbon compounds for energy production. The need for energy and building blocks is the reason why all organisms, such as the field mouse shown in Figure 24.26, require food.

Anabolism Some of the simple compounds produced by catabolism are used to synthesize more-complex biological molecules—carbohydrates, lipids, proteins, and nucleic acids—necessary for the health and growth of an organism. The synthesis reactions of metabolism are called **anabolism.** Unlike catabolism, which releases energy, anabolism uses energy.

Figure 24.27 gives an overview of the relationship between catabolism and anabolism. Nutrients and unneeded cell components are degraded to simpler components by the reactions of catabolism. The oxidative reactions of catabolism yield energy captured in the formation of ATP. **In anabolism, the products and the energy of catabolism are used to make new compounds and cell parts needed for cellular life and growth.** You already know that energy produced by physical and chemical processes is of little value unless the energy can be captured to do work. If it is not captured, the energy is lost as heat. The chemical energy produced by catabolism must have some means of being used for the chemical work of anabolism. The ATP molecule is that means of transmitting energy.

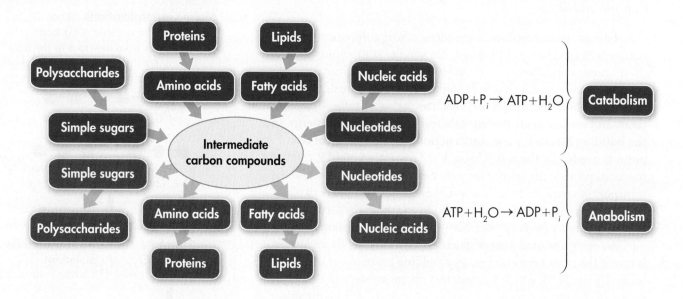

Figure 24.27 Catabolism and Anabolism
Simple compounds produced by catabolism are used in the synthesis reactions of anabolism.
Apply Concepts *What part of metabolism releases energy? What part uses energy?*

The Nitrogen Cycle

How do nitrogen-fixing bacteria provide plants with a usable form of nitrogen?

You have learned that the biological molecules taken into an organism's body as nutrients in food are broken down during catabolism. Food contains carbohydrates, proteins, lipids, nucleic acids, vitamins, and minerals. These nutrients are composed mainly of carbon, hydrogen, and oxygen atoms. Many biological compounds, such as proteins, contain nitrogen as well. Although Earth's atmosphere is 78 percent nitrogen gas, no animals and only a few plants can use this form of nitrogen to make nitrogen-containing compounds. However, certain bacteria can convert nitrogen gas into usable forms in a process called nitrogen fixation. **Nitrogen-fixing bacteria reduce atmospheric nitrogen ($N_2(g)$) to ammonia ($NH_3(g)$), a water-soluble form of nitrogen that can be used by plants.** In soil and biological fluids, most ammonia is present as ammonium ions.

Plants incorporate ammonia into biological nitrogen compounds such as proteins, nucleic acids, and ATP. Because animals cannot synthesize these compounds, they get them by eating plants or other animals that eat plants. When these plants and animals die, they decay with the aid of bacteria. Decaying matter returns nitrogen to the soil as ammonia, nitrite ions (NO_2^-), or nitrate ions (NO_3^-). Moreover, some nitrogen gas is returned to the atmosphere. This flow of nitrogen between the atmosphere and Earth and its living creatures is the nitrogen cycle, shown in Figure 24.28.

Figure 24.28 Nitrogen Cycle
Nitrogen moves between the atmosphere and the biosphere in the nitrogen cycle.

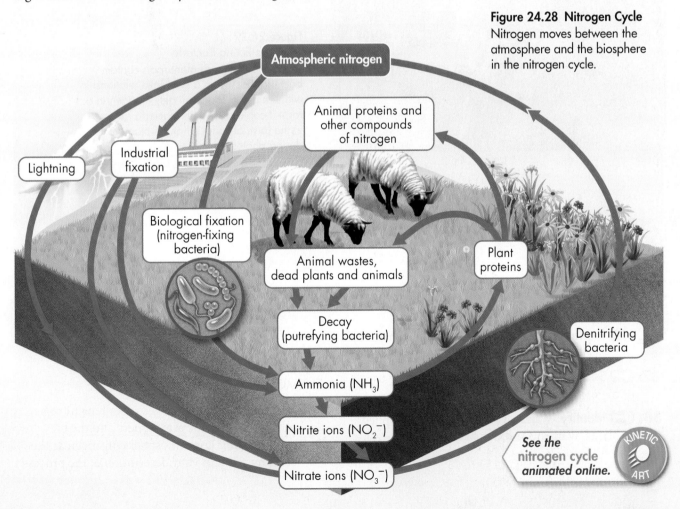

See the nitrogen cycle animated online.

Biological Nitrogen Fixation There are two types of nitrogen-fixing bacteria: free-living and symbiotic. Free-living bacteria lead an independent existence in soil. Symbiotic bacteria, such as *Rhizobium,* live in a mutually beneficial arrangement with plants. Symbiotic bacteria live in nodules on the roots of legumes, such as alfalfa, clover, peas, and beans. These root nodules are shown in Figure 24.29. Soil fertility can be improved by plowing nitrogen-rich legumes back into the ground instead of harvesting them.

Industrial Nitrogen Fixation Modern agriculture uses an enormous quantity of nitrogen, which plays a role in the nitrogen cycle. For the past several years, the daily amount of atmospheric nitrogen fixed by industrial processes in the production of fertilizers has probably exceeded the amount fixed by living organisms in Earth's forests and oceans. Nitrogen fertilizers enter the biosphere when they are taken up by plants. In addition, a small amount of atmospheric nitrogen is fixed by lightning discharges, which produce the soluble nitrogen oxides (NO, NO_2, N_2O_4, and N_2O_5).

Figure 24.29
Nitrogen-Fixing Bacteria
The bumps on these plant roots contain bacteria that live in a symbiotic relationship with the plant. The plant gets nitrogen in a form it can use, and the bacteria get food in the form of sugars that the plant makes during photosynthesis.

  # 24.6 LessonCheck

35. **Explain** What is the role of ATP in energy production and energy use in living cells?

36. **Explain** What is the function of catabolism in the cells of living organisms?

37. **Sequence** How does anabolism make use of the products of catabolism?

38. **Identify** What form of nitrogen is supplied to plants by nitrogen-fixing bacteria?

39. **Identify** How many moles of ATP are formed from the complete oxidation of one mole of glucose in a cell that uses oxygen?

BIGIDEA
CHEMISTRY AS THE CENTRAL SCIENCE

40. Write a paragraph that describes how nitrogen moves between the atmosphere and the biosphere. (*Hint:* Use atmospheric nitrogen as the starting point in your description of the process.)

DNA Testing

Would you want to know if you are predisposed to a treatable disease, such as diabetes or breast cancer? What about an incurable disease, such as Huntington's disease? The answers to these questions, and many more, are only a drop of saliva away.

In the past few years, researchers have learned how to test for hundreds of genetic disorders using genetic testing. Genetic testing involves analyzing a person's DNA to determine changes in genes that may indicate a specific disorder. The DNA used for the tests can be obtained from a sample of blood, urine, or even saliva. In fact, today you can mail a saliva sample to a lab, and then view your test results online!

Genetic testing can be valuable in determining a person's likelihood of developing a treatable disease. However, learning of a genetic predisposition for a disease that currently has no treatments or cures can cause anxiety or despair. In addition, there are many ethical concerns involved in genetic testing, including who gets access to the test results and how many actual tests are performed on the DNA. The information in DNA is much greater than just the specific disease a lab could test for. Because of these concerns, it is important to consider all the consequences of knowing your genetic information before getting tested.

DNA MUTATIONS Alterations in the order of the bases in DNA cause gene mutations, which can lead to diseases.

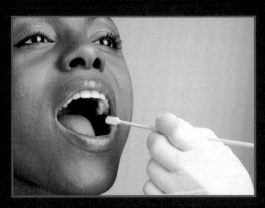

TESTING FROM HOME At-home tests involve collecting saliva or blood samples. The sample is then sent to a lab, which analyzes the DNA for mutations known to correspond to different diseases and disorders.

Take It Further

1. Identify What are some of the possible benefits of genetic testing? What are some of the possible risks?

2. Form an Opinion Would you want to be tested for potential genetic disorders? Why or why not?

24 **Study** Guide

BIGIDEA
CHEMISTRY AS THE CENTRAL SCIENCE

There are four main types of biological molecules. Most carbohydrates are polymers that release energy when broken down. Proteins are polymers of amino acids and are needed for most chemical reactions in cells. Lipids are water-insoluble and can be used for long-term energy storage. Nucleic acids are polymers of nucleotides. The nucleic acid DNA carries the instructions for a cell. Catabolic reactions break down biological molecules to provide energy and building blocks for the cell. Anabolic reactions build biological molecules to store energy and make new cell parts.

24.1 A Basis for Life

🔑 The two major cell types that occur in nature are prokaryotic cells and eukaryotic cells.

🔑 Photosynthesis uses sunlight to reduce CO_2 to compounds that contain C—H bonds, mainly in the form of glucose.

• photosynthesis (839)

24.2 Carbohydrates

🔑 Most carbohydrates have the general formula $C_n(H_2O)_n$.

• carbohydrate (841)   • disaccharide (842)
• monosaccharide (841)   • polysaccharide (843)

24.3 Amino Acids and Their Polymers

🔑 An amino acid has a carboxyl group, an amino group, a hydrogen atom, and an R group bonded to a central carbon atom.

🔑 Differences in the amino acid sequence result in differences in the properties of peptides.

🔑 Enzymes increase reaction rates.

• amino acid (844)   • enzyme (847)
• peptide (845)   • substrate (847)
• peptide bond (845)   • active site (847)
• protein (845)

24.4 Lipids

🔑 Lipids tend to dissolve readily in organic solvents, whereas carbohydrates and proteins tend to dissolve in water.

• lipid (850)   • phospholipid (851)
• triglyceride (850)   • wax (852)
• saponification (851)

24.5 Nucleic Acids

🔑 DNA stores information needed to make proteins and governs the reproduction of cells. RNA transmits information stored in DNA during protein synthesis.

🔑 A sequence of three bases of DNA is required to specify one amino acid in a peptide.

🔑 Gene mutations occur when one or more nucleotides in DNA are substituted, added, or deleted.

🔑 Examples of DNA technology include DNA typing, production of bacteria that make human proteins, genetically modifying foods and animals, and cloning.

• nucleic acid (854)   • gene (856)
• nucleotide (854)

24.6 Metabolism

🔑 In living cells, ATP is the energy carrier between the spontaneous reactions that release and the nonspontaneous reactions that use energy.

🔑 The degradation of biological molecules during catabolism provides the energy and the building blocks for making new compounds. In anabolism, new compounds needed for cellular life and growth are made from the products of catabolism.

🔑 Nitrogen-fixing bacteria reduce atmospheric nitrogen to ammonia, a water-soluble form of nitrogen that can be used by plants.

• adenosine triphosphate   • catabolism (863)
  (ATP) (862)   • anabolism (864)
• metabolism (863)

 **24 Assessment**

★ Solutions appear in Appendix E

Lesson by Lesson

24.1 A Basis for Life

41. What is the main difference between a prokaryotic and a eukaryotic cell?

★**42.** Explain what happens in photosynthesis.

43. Write a balanced equation for the complete oxidation of glucose.

44. Describe three organelles found in eukaryotic cells. Give a function of each organelle.

24.2 Carbohydrates

45. Name two important monosaccharides.

46. Where in nature are glucose and fructose found?

★**47.** How does the carbonyl functional group differ in glucose and fructose?

48. Which monosaccharides combine to form the disaccharide sucrose?

49. What is the product of the complete hydrolysis of starch? Of glycogen?

50. What product is formed when cellulose is broken down?

24.3 Amino Acids and Their Polymers

51. What is the name given to the bond connecting two amino acids in a peptide chain?

52. How many peptide bonds does the tripeptide Ser—Gly—Phe have? Explain.

★**53.** Describe two common patterns found in the folding of protein chains.

54. Are the structures of the following two tripeptides the same? Explain.
   a. Ala—Ser—Gly   **b.** Gly—Ser—Ala

55. Describe the function of an enzyme.

56. What is an enzyme-substrate complex? How does it form?

24.4 Lipids

57. Distinguish between a fat and an oil.

58. What is a triglyceride?

59. What is a soap?

60. Draw structural formulas for the products of the complete hydrolysis of tristearin.

61. Draw a simple representation of a lipid bilayer.

62. What two types of compounds combine to form a wax?

24.5 Nucleic Acids

63. What two types of nucleic acids do cells have?

★**64.** What are the components of a nucleotide?

65. What is the structural difference between the sugar unit in RNA and the sugar unit in DNA?

66. What type of bonding helps hold a DNA double helix together?

67. Which of the following base pairs are found in a DNA molecule: A—A, A—T, C—G, G—A, A—U, T—U?

68. How many bases specify an amino acid in the genetic code?

★**69.** What are the consequences of a substitution of one base for another in DNA? Give an example.

★**70.** What is the basis for identifying an individual by DNA profiling?

71. What is recombinant DNA?

24.6 Metabolism

72. Write an abbreviated, balanced equation for the hydrolysis of ATP to ADP.

73. Where do the complex biomolecules your body degrades during catabolism come from?

★**74.** How are catabolism and anabolism related?

75. Describe the nitrogen cycle in your own words.

76. What is the source of raw materials used in anabolic reactions?

77. What is meant by industrial nitrogen fixation? What is produced during this process?

Understand Concepts

★**78.** The formula for palmitic acid is $CH_3(CH_2)_{14}CO_2H$. A popular soap is mostly sodium palmitate. Draw a structural formula for sodium palmitate.

79. Why are the hydrophilic heads located on the outsides of the cell membrane?

80. Consider the following sequence of DNA: GCC–CCA–ACG–TTA.

    a. Using the code words for amino acids in Table 24.2 on page 857, write the amino acid sequence formed by translation of the DNA sequence into a peptide.

    b. What amino acid sequence would result from the substitution of adenine (A) for the second cytosine (C)?

81. Identify or classify each of the following biological molecules.

    a.

    b.

    c.

*82. Use Table 24.2 on page 857 to write a base sequence for DNA that codes for the tripeptide Ala — Gly — Ser. Why might your answer be different from the answers of your classmates?

83. A segment of a DNA strand has the following base sequence: CGATCCA. Write the base sequence that would be found on the other strand in the double helix.

84. Which type of monomer produces each of the following polymers?

    a. protein   **c.** nucleic acid
    b. polysaccharide

85. What is one function of membrane proteins?

*86. Does every code word in DNA specify an amino acid in protein synthesis? Explain.

87. What are some of the outcomes of recombinant DNA research?

*88. The complete oxidation of glucose releases 2.82×10^3 kJ/mol of energy, and the formation of ATP from ADP requires 30.5 kJ/mol. What percent of the energy released in the complete oxidation of glucose is captured in the formation of ATP?

*89. An average adult expends about 8400 kJ of energy every day. How many moles of ATP must be converted to ADP to provide this amount of energy?

90. Why can't humans digest cellulose, considering that it is made of the same monomers as starch?

91. How is an enzyme-substrate complex formed in the enzyme's active site?

92. What role do coenzymes play in metabolism?

93. Suggest a reason why prokaryotic cells are thought to be more ancient than eukaryotic cells.

94. What are the possible consequences of an error in DNA sequence?

95. Explain why photosynthesis might be considered the most important chemical process on Earth.

*96. Describe the differences among monosaccharides, disaccharides, and polysaccharides. Give examples of each type of carbohydrate.

97. Describe how amino acids join to form a peptide bond.

*98. What is base pairing? How does base pairing relate to the structure of DNA?

Think Critically

99. **Explain** Interpret this statement: "Carbon dioxide is an energy-poor molecule, but glucose is an energy-rich molecule."

100. **Sequence** In the DNA double helix, where are the base pairs located in relation to the backbone structure: inside the double helix or outside the double helix? What must happen before the protein-making machinery of the cell can "read" the code words formed by the DNA bases?

101. **Explain** Which type of gene mutation do you think will do more damage to an organism: a substitution mutation in which one base is substituted for another base or an addition mutation in which a base is added to a sequence of bases? Explain.

102. **Predict** Suggest a reason why a bean plant might not grow well if planted in sterilized soil.

103. **Identify** What class of polymer is formed from each of the following monomers?

   a. amino acids
   b. monosaccharides
   c. nucleotides

*104. **Interpret Diagrams** Complete the following equation by drawing the structural formulas of the products:

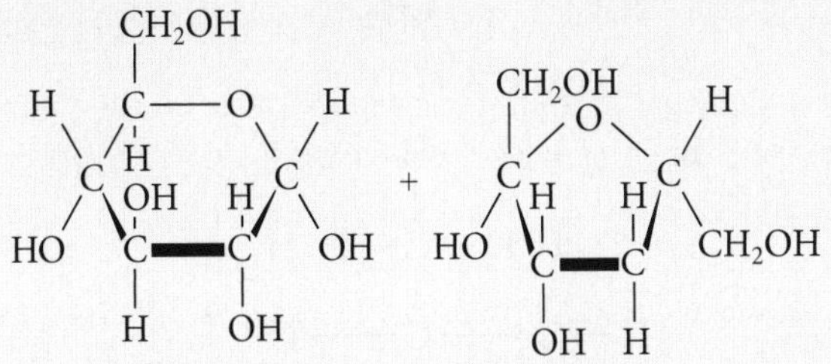

Enrichment

105. **Compare and Contrast** Compare the structure of a DNA nucleotide with an RNA nucleotide.

106. **Compare** Describe the structural features all amino acids have in common. What structural features differ among the amino acids?

*107. **Identify** Using structural formulas, write a chemical equation for the formation of a dipeptide from two amino acids. What functional group does the reaction create?

108. **Cause and Effect** Explain why cell growth stops when the dietary intake of nutrients is insufficient.

109. **Interpret Diagrams** The following compound is hydrolyzed by boiling with sodium hydroxide. What are the saponification products?

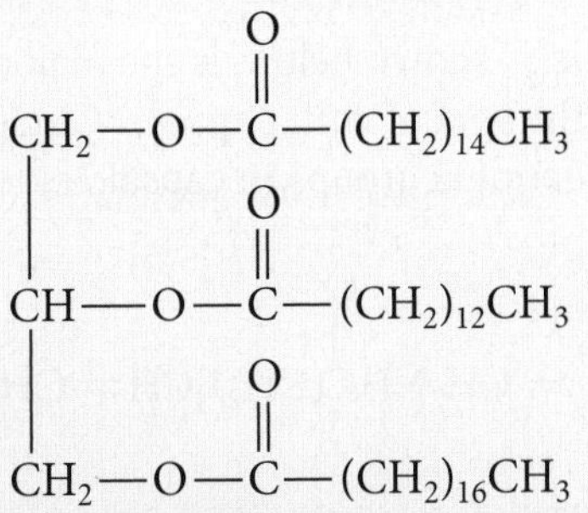

110. **Identify** What causes the spontaneous formation of a lipid bilayer?

111. **Explain** Peptide chains fold and bend into three-dimensional shapes. Suggest how a peptide chain is held in this 3-D shape.

*112. **Interpret Diagrams** A sequence of nine bases in a gene codes for the amino acid sequence Trp-Met-Met. What is the sequence of bases in this DNA fragment? Use Table 24.2 on page 857 to help you. Could you determine the base sequence for certain if the amino acid sequence were Trp-Met-Leu? Why or why not?

Write About Science

113. **Explain** Write a paragraph explaining how cells are able to selectively absorb certain ions and molecules while excluding other materials.

114. **Connect to the BIGIDEA** Choose one of the biological molecules discussed in this chapter. Write a paragraph describing how the elements and structure of the molecules relate to the function of the molecules.

CHEMYSTERY

Phenyl-what?

Phenylalanine is an amino acid, a monomer of proteins. So, how could phenylalanine be hazardous to your health? For most people, phenylalanine is not a health concern. But it is a concern for people who have the genetic disorder phenylketonuria, or PKU. Normally, phenylalanine is converted by the body to another amino acid, tyrosine. People with PKU lack the enzyme that is required to convert phenylalanine to tyrosine. When this happens, phenylalanine accumulates to toxic levels in the body. PKU is treated by eating a diet low in phenylalanine (the body still needs a small amount phenylalanine).

115. **Infer** Given that phenylalanine is an amino acid, which types of foods would you expect to be high in phenylalanine?

116. **Connect to the BIGIDEA** Why does a nutritionist need to understand chemistry?

117. Describe two factors that cause real gases to depart from the ideal gas law.

118. Characterize these compounds as electrolytes or nonelectrolytes.

a. NaCl   **c.** CCl_4
b. $CuSO_4$ **d.** H_2O

*__119.__ Calculate the boiling-point elevation for these aqueous solutions.

a. $0.507m$ NaCl   **c.** $0.155m$ $CaCl_2$
b. $0.204m$ NH_4Cl **d.** $0.222m$ $NaHSO_4$

*__120.__ How much heat (in kJ) is released or absorbed when 0.265 mol of sodium bicarbonate is decomposed according to the reaction below?

$$2NaHCO_3(s) \rightarrow Na_2CO_3(s) + H_2O(g) + CO_2(g)$$

$$\Delta H = 129 \text{ kJ}$$

121. Explain why the needles on a dried-out fir tree can burn with almost explosive rapidity.

122. What must be true at the end point of an acid-base titration?

123. Calculate the pH of each of the following solutions:

a. $[H^+] = 7.0 \times 10^{-5}M$
b. $[OH^-] = 1.8 \times 10^{-9}M$
c. $[OH^-] = 6.1 \times 10^{-2}M$
d. $[H^+] = 4.4 \times 10^{-11}M$

124. Identify the oxidizing agent in each reaction.

a. xenon + fluorine $\longrightarrow$ xenon tetrafluoride
b. sulfur + oxygen $\longrightarrow$ sulfur trioxide
c. gaseous chlorine + aqueous sodium bromide $\longrightarrow$ aqueous bromine + aqueous sodium chloride

125. At which electrode in a voltaic cell does oxidation always occur? What is the charge on this electrode?

126. What would you observe when a length of nickel wire is immersed in an aqueous solution of silver nitrate?

127. For each pair of metals shown below, decide which metal is more readily reduced.

a. Cu, Mg   **c.** Ag, Sn   **e.** Ni, Cd
b. Cd, Ni   **d.** Zn, Fe   **f.** Al, Cu

*__128.__ Write a molecular structure for each compound.

a. heptane   **c.** 2-phenylbutane
b. 2-methyl-3-hexene   **d.** 1,3-diethylbenzene

129. Name the next highest homolog of each of these compounds.

a. 1-butene   **c.** pentane
b. cyclooctane   **d.** nonane

*__130.__ Give the IUPAC name for these compounds.

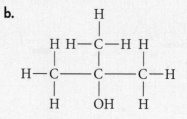

131. Write a molecular formula for each compound.

a. methyl acetate
b. 2-hydroxypropanoic acid

132. Name each polymer and state at least one of its uses.

a. $+CF_2-CF_2+_x$ **c.** $H+CH_2-CH_2+H$

b. $+CH_2-\underset{\underset{Cl}{|}}{CH}+_x$ **d.** $+CH_2-CH+_x$

133. Capsaicin, shown below, is the major contributor to the heat of chili peppers. Circle and name the functional groups in capsaicin.

$$CH_3O$$
$$HO-\bigcirc-CH_2NHC(CH_2)_4CH=CHCH(CH_3)_2$$

If You Have Trouble With . . .

Question	117	118	119	120	121	122	123	124	125	126	127	128	129	130	131	132	133
See Chapter	14	15	16	17	18	19	19	20	21	21	21	22	22	23	23	23	23

Standardized Test Prep

Select the choice that best answers each question or completes each statement.

1. What phrase best describes ATP?
   (A) energy producer
   (B) energy consumer
   (C) energy pump
   (D) energy transmitter

For Questions 2–5, match the category of organic compounds listed below that is most closely identified with each biological molecule.

    I. monosaccharides
    II. amino acids
    III. fatty acids
    IV. nucleotides

2. proteins
3. nucleic acids
4. lipids
5. carbohydrates

6. Which element is not found in amino acids?
   (A) phosphorus   (C) oxygen
   (B) nitrogen   (D) hydrogen

7. For any enzyme to function, the substrate must bind to the
   (A) product.   (C) active site.
   (B) cofactor.   (D) peptide.

Use the paragraph to answer Questions 8–10.
Because an amino acid contains both a carboxyl group and an amino group, it is amphoteric, that is, it can act as either an acid or a base. Crystalline amino acids have some properties—relatively high melting points and high water solubilities—that are more characteristic of ionic substances than of molecular substances.

8. Write an equation showing glycine acting as an acid in a reaction with water. (Glycine is the simplest amino acid. Its side chain is R = H.)

9. Write an equation showing glycine acting as a base in a reaction with water.

10. It is possible for glycine to undergo an internal Brønsted-Lowry acid-base neutralization reaction. Write the resulting structural formula. Explain how this reaction would account for the ionic properties of glycine.

For each question, there are two statements. Decide whether each statement is true or false. Then decide whether Statement II is a correct explanation for Statement I.

	Statement I		Statement II
11.	Lipids tend to be insoluble in water.	BECAUSE	Lipids have mainly nonpolar bonds.
12.	Starch and cellulose are both digestible by most organisms.	BECAUSE	Glucose is the monomer in both starch and cellulose.
13.	Many of the reactions in catabolism are oxidation reactions.	BECAUSE	Oxidation reactions tend to be energy-producing reactions.
14.	The sequence of bases in DNA contains the code for making proteins.	BECAUSE	Each pair of bases in DNA codes for a specific amino acid.

If You Have Trouble With . . .

Question	1	2	3	4	5	6	7	8	9	10	11	12	13	14
See Lesson	24.6	24.3	24.5	24.4	24.2	24.3	24.3	24.3	24.3	24.3	24.4	24.2	24.6	24.5

25

Nuclear
Chemistry

INSIDE:

- **25.1 Nuclear Radiation**
- **25.2 Nuclear Transformations**
- **25.3 Fission and Fusion**
- **25.4 Radiation in Your Life**

PearsonChem.com

A nuclear submarine uses energy released by nuclear reactions.

ELECTRONS AND THE STRUCTURE OF ATOMS

Essential Questions:

1. *What happens when an unstable nucleus decays?*

2. *How is the structure of atoms altered during fission and fusion?*

3. *How does nuclear chemistry affect your life?*

CHEMYSTERY

An Ice-Age Baby

In 2007, a reindeer herder in north-central Russia thought he spotted the frozen remains of a reindeer. What he found was a perfectly preserved baby wooly mammoth about the size of a large dog. The only thing missing was its shaggy coat. Scientists named the mammoth Lyuba, which means "love" in Russian.

Wooly mammoths are an extinct species related to modern elephants. These large mammals had curly tusks and long hair. They lived on Earth from about 1.8 million years ago until about 11,500 years ago. How do scientists know when Lyuba lived and died?

▶ **Connect to the BIGIDEA** As you read about nuclear reactions, think about which type of reaction could be used to find the age of a wooly mammoth fossil.

NATIONAL SCIENCE EDUCATION STANDARDS

B-1, B-6

25.1 Nuclear Radiation

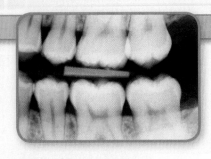

Q: *What makes some types of radiation more dangerous than other types?* Atoms emit electromagnetic radiation when an electron moves from a higher energy level to a lower energy level. Most electromagnetic radiation, such as visible light, has low energy and is not dangerous. X-rays are an exception. Lengthy or frequent exposure to X-rays can damage cells in your body. This lesson will explain why exposure is also a concern with nuclear radiation.

Key Questions

⊂⊐ *How do nuclear reactions differ from chemical reactions?*

⊂⊐ *What are three types of nuclear radiation?*

Vocabulary

- radioactivity
- nuclear radiation
- radioisotope
- alpha particle
- beta particle
- gamma ray

Figure 25.1 Marie Curie
Marie Curie and her husband Pierre shared the 1903 Nobel Prize in physics with Becquerel for their pioneering work on radioactivity.

Radioactivity

⊂⊐ **How do nuclear reactions differ from chemical reactions?**

In 1896, the French chemist Antoine Henri Becquerel made an accidental discovery. He was studying the ability of uranium salts that had been exposed to sunlight to fog photographic film plates. During bad weather, when Becquerel could not expose a sample to sunlight, he left the sample on top of the photographic plate. When he developed the plate, he discovered that the uranium salt still fogged the film. At the time, two of Becquerel's associates were Marie and Pierre Curie. The Curies were able to show that rays emitted by uranium atoms caused the film to fog. Marie Curie is shown in Figure 25.1. She used the term **radioactivity** to refer to the spontaneous emission of rays or particles from certain elements, such as uranium. The rays and particles emitted from a radioactive source are called **nuclear radiation.**

Radioactivity, which is also called radioactive decay, is an example of a nuclear reaction. In both chemical reactions and nuclear reactions, atoms become more stable. The word *stable* means "constant" or "not likely to change." In a chemical reaction, atoms tend to attain a more stable electron configuration by transferring or sharing electrons. Nuclear reactions begin with unstable isotopes, or **radioisotopes.** Atoms of these isotopes become more stable when changes occur in their nuclei. The changes are always accompanied by the emission of large amounts of energy. ⊂⊐ **Unlike chemical reactions, nuclear reactions are not affected by changes in temperature, pressure, or the presence of catalysts. Also, nuclear reactions of a given radioisotope cannot be slowed down, speeded up, or stopped.**

Radioactive decay is a spontaneous process that does not require an input of energy. If the product of a nuclear reaction is unstable, it will decay too. The process continues until unstable isotopes of one element are changed, or transformed, into stable isotopes of a different element. These stable isotopes are not radioactive.

Table 25.1

Characteristics of Some Types of Radiation						
Type	**Consists of**	**Symbol**	**Charge**	**Mass (amu)**	**Common source**	**Penetrating power**
Alpha radiation	Alpha particles (helium nuclei)	α, $^4_2$He	2+	4	Radium-226	Low (0.05 mm body tissue)
Beta radiation	Beta particles (electrons)	β, $^0_{-1}$e	1−	1/1837	Carbon-14	Moderate (4 mm body tissue)
Gamma radiation	High-energy electromagnetic radiation	γ	0	0	Cobalt-60	Very high (penetrates body easily)

Types of Radiation

🔑 *What are three types of nuclear radiation?*

Radiation is emitted during radioactive decay. 🔑 **Three types of nuclear radiation are alpha radiation, beta radiation, and gamma radiation.** Table 25.1 summarizes the characteristics of these three types of radiation.

Alpha Radiation Some radioactive sources emit helium nuclei, which are also called alpha particles. Each **alpha particle** contains two protons and two neutrons and has a double positive charge. In nuclear equations, an alpha particle is written $^4_2$He or α. The electric charge symbol is usually omitted.

The radioisotope uranium-238 emits alpha radiation and is transformed into another radioisotope, thorium-234. Figure 25.2 illustrates this process.

$$^{238}_{92}\text{U} \xrightarrow{\text{Radioactive decay}} {}^{234}_{90}\text{Th} + {}^4_2\text{He (}\alpha\text{ emission)}$$

Uranium-238   Thorium-234   Alpha particle

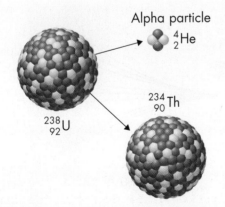

Alpha particle
$^4_2$He

$^{234}_{90}$Th

$^{238}_{92}$U

Figure 25.2 Alpha Decay
Uranium-238 decays and forms thorium-234. The radiation emitted is an alpha particle.
Interpret Diagrams *Describe the structure of an alpha particle.*

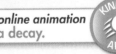

See an online animation of alpha decay.

KINETIC ART

When an atom loses an alpha particle, the atomic number of the product is lower by two and its mass number is lower by four. In a balanced nuclear equation, the sum of the mass numbers (superscripts) on the right must equal the sum on the left. The same is true for the atomic numbers (subscripts).

Because of their large mass and charge, alpha particles do not travel very far and are not very penetrating. A sheet of paper or the surface of your skin can stop them. But radioisotopes that emit alpha particles can cause harm when ingested. Once inside the body, the particles don't have to travel far to penetrate soft tissue.

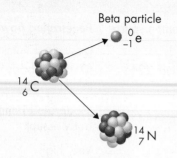

Figure 25.3 Beta Decay
When a carbon-14 atom decays, the products are nitrogen-14 and a beta particle.

Beta Radiation An electron resulting from the breaking apart of a neutron in an atom is called a **beta particle.** The neutron breaks apart into a proton, which remains in the nucleus, and a fast-moving electron, which is released.

$$\underset{\text{Neutron}}{{}^{1}_{0}\text{n}} \longrightarrow \underset{\text{Proton}}{{}^{1}_{1}\text{p}} + \underset{\substack{\text{Electron}\\\text{(beta particle)}}}{{}^{0}_{-1}\text{e}}$$

The symbol for the electron has a subscript of –1 and a superscript of 0. The –1 represents the charge on the electron. The 0 represents the extremely small mass of the electron compared to the mass of a proton.

Carbon-14 is a radioisotope. It emits a beta particle as it decays and forms nitrogen-14. Figure 25.3 illustrates this reaction.

$$\underset{\substack{\text{Carbon-14}\\\text{(radioactive)}}}{{}^{14}_{6}\text{C}} \longrightarrow \underset{\substack{\text{Nitrogen-14}\\\text{(stable)}}}{{}^{14}_{7}\text{N}} + \underset{\substack{\text{Beta particle}}}{{}^{0}_{-1}\text{e}} \;\;(\beta\text{ emission})$$

The nitrogen-14 atom has the same mass number as carbon-14, but its atomic number has increased by 1. It contains an additional proton and one fewer neutron. The nuclear equation is balanced.

A beta particle has less charge than an alpha particle and much less mass than an alpha particle. Thus, beta particles are more penetrating than alpha particles. Beta particles can pass through paper but are stopped by aluminum foil or thin pieces of wood. Because of their opposite charges, alpha and beta radiation can be separated by an electric field, as shown in Figure 25.4.

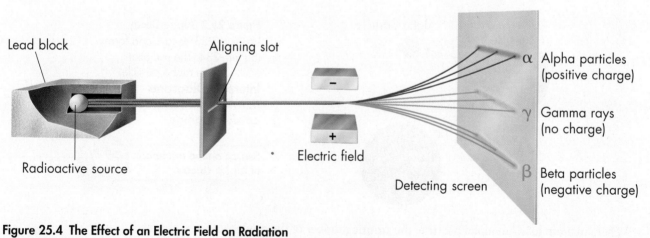

Figure 25.4 The Effect of an Electric Field on Radiation
An electric field has a different effect on each type of radiation. Alpha and beta particles move in opposite directions. Alpha particles move toward the negative plate and beta particles move toward the positive plate. Gamma rays are not deflected as they pass between the plates.
Applying Concepts *Why are gamma rays not deflected?*

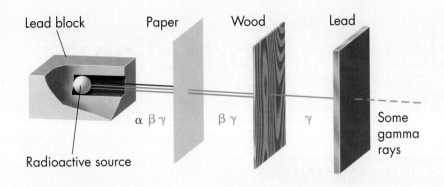

Lead block Paper Wood Lead

α β γ   β γ   γ

Radioactive source

Some gamma rays

Figure 25.5 Relative Penetrating Power of Nuclear Radiation
Because of their large mass and charge, alpha particles (red) are the least penetrating of the three main types of nuclear radiation. Gamma rays (yellow) have no mass or charge and are the most penetrating.
Infer *How penetrating are beta particles (green) compared to alpha particles and gamma rays?*

Gamma Radiation A high-energy photon emitted by a radioisotope is called a **gamma ray.** The high-energy photons are a form of electromagnetic radiation. Nuclei often emit gamma rays along with alpha or beta particles during radioactive decay. The following examples demonstrate this process.

$$^{230}_{90}\text{Th} \longrightarrow {}^{226}_{88}\text{Ra} + {}^{4}_{2}\text{He} + \gamma$$

Thorium-230   Radium-226   Alpha   Gamma
                                particle   ray

$$^{234}_{90}\text{Th} \longrightarrow {}^{234}_{91}\text{Pa} + {}^{0}_{-1}\text{e} + \gamma$$

Thorium-234   Protactinium-234   Beta   Gamma
                                     particle   ray

Gamma rays have no mass and no electrical charge. So the emission of gamma radiation does not alter the atomic number or mass number of an atom. Because gamma rays are extremely penetrating, they can be very dangerous. For example, gamma rays pass easily through paper, wood, and the human body. They can be stopped, although not completely, by several meters of concrete or several centimeters of lead, as shown in Figure 25.5.

CHEMISTRY & YOU

Q: *Gamma rays can be dangerous because of their penetrating power. What property determines the relative penetrating power of electromagnetic radiation?*

25.1 LessonCheck

1. **Compare** What factors do not affect nuclear reactions, but do affect chemical reactions?

2. **Describe** Briefly describe the three main types of nuclear radiation.

3. **Identify** What part of an atom undergoes change during radioactive decay?

4. **Compare and Contrast** How is the atomic number of a nucleus changed by alpha decay? By beta decay? By gamma decay?

5. **Describe** What two items must be equal for a nuclear equation to be balanced?

6. **Relate Cause and Effect** How does alpha decay affect the mass number of a nucleus? How does beta decay affect the mass number?

7. **Identify** Which of the three types of radiation described in this lesson is the most penetrating, and why?

8. **Predict** When polonium-210 decays by alpha radiation, what isotope is formed?

CHEMISTRY & YOU

Q: *What is the source of radon in homes?* All the isotopes of radon gas are unstable and emit radiation. Inhaled radon is the second leading cause of lung cancer in the United States. Radon may accumulate in a basement that is not well ventilated. Because radon is a colorless, odorless gas, people often do not know that they are being exposed to high levels of radon. Test kits are available to measure the levels of radon in a building. In this lesson, you will study the decay series that produces this hazardous gas.

Key Questions

🔑 What determines the type of decay a radioisotope undergoes?

🔑 How much of a radioactive sample remains after each half-life?

🔑 What are two ways in which transmutation can occur?

Vocabulary

• nuclear force
• band of stability
• positron
• half-life
• transmutation
• transuranium elements

Nuclear Stability and Decay

🔑 **What determines the type of decay a radioisotope undergoes?**
All atomic nuclei, except those of hydrogen atoms, consist of neutrons and two or more protons. If a force did not hold these subatomic particles together, the like-charged protons would repel one another and fly apart. The **nuclear force** is an attractive force that acts between *all* nuclear particles that are extremely close together, such as protons and neutrons in a nucleus. At these short distances, the nuclear force dominates over electromagnetic repulsions and holds the nucleus together.

More than 1,500 different nuclei are known. Only 264 of the known nuclei are stable and do not decay. The rest are unstable and will change over time. The stability of a nucleus depends on the ratio of neutrons to protons. Figure 25.6 shows a graph of the number of neutrons vs. the number of protons for all known stable nuclei. The region of the graph in which these points are located is called the **band of stability.** For elements of low atomic number (below about 20), this ratio is about 1. Above atomic number 20, stable nuclei have more neutrons than protons.

A nucleus may be unstable and undergo spontaneous decay for different reasons. 🔑 **The neutron-to-proton ratio in a radioisotope determines the type of decay that occurs.** Some nuclei are unstable because they have too many neutrons relative to the number of protons. When one of these nuclei decays, a neutron emits a beta particle (fast-moving electron) from the nucleus. A neutron that emits an electron becomes a proton.

$$\ce{^1_0n -> ^1_1p + ^0_{-1}e}$$

This process is known as beta emission. It increases the number of protons while decreasing the number of neutrons. Radioisotopes that undergo beta emission include the following.

$$\ce{^{66}_{29}Cu -> ^{66}_{30}Zn + ^0_{-1}e}$$

$$\ce{^{14}_6C -> ^{14}_7N + ^0_{-1}e}$$

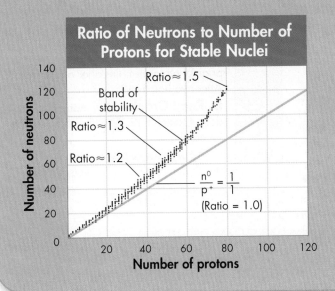

Ratio of Neutrons to Number of Protons for Stable Nuclei

Figure 25.6 A plot of neutrons vs. protons for all stable nuclei forms a pattern called the band of stability, which is shown in purple. The green line shows what the pattern would be if the ratio were 1 for every nucleus.

a. Identify What does each dot represent?

b. Read Graphs What is the ratio of neutrons to protons for tin (Sn, atomic number = 50)?

c. Describe How does the neutron-to-proton ratio change as the number of protons increases in stable nuclei?

Other nuclei are unstable because they have too few neutrons relative to the number of protons. These nuclei increase their stability by converting a proton to a neutron. An electron is captured by a nucleus during this process, which is called electron capture. Here are two examples of electron capture.

$$^{59}_{28}\text{Ni} + ^{0}_{-1}\text{e} \longrightarrow ^{59}_{27}\text{Co}$$

$$^{37}_{18}\text{Ar} + ^{0}_{-1}\text{e} \longrightarrow ^{37}_{17}\text{Cl}$$

A **positron** is a particle with the mass of an electron but a positive charge. Its symbol is $^{0}_{+1}\text{e}$. During positron emission, a proton changes to a neutron, just as in electron capture. Here are two examples of positron emission.

$$^{8}_{5}\text{B} \longrightarrow ^{8}_{4}\text{Be} + ^{0}_{+1}\text{e}$$

$$^{15}_{8}\text{O} \longrightarrow ^{15}_{7}\text{N} + ^{0}_{+1}\text{e}$$

When a proton is converted to a neutron, the atomic number decreases by 1 and the number of neutrons increases by 1.

All nuclei that have an atomic number greater than 83 are radioactive. These nuclei have both too many neutrons and too many protons to be stable. Therefore, they undergo radioactive decay. Most of them emit alpha particles. Alpha emission increases the neutron-to-proton ratio, which tends to increase the stability of the nucleus. In alpha emission the mass number decreases by four and the atomic number decreases by two.

$$^{226}_{88}\text{Ra} \longrightarrow ^{222}_{86}\text{Rn} + ^{4}_{2}\text{He}$$

$$^{232}_{90}\text{Th} \longrightarrow ^{228}_{88}\text{Ra} + ^{4}_{2}\text{He}$$

Recall that conservation of mass is an important property of chemical reactions. In contrast, mass is not conserved during nuclear reactions. An extremely small quantity of mass is converted into the energy released during radioactive decay.

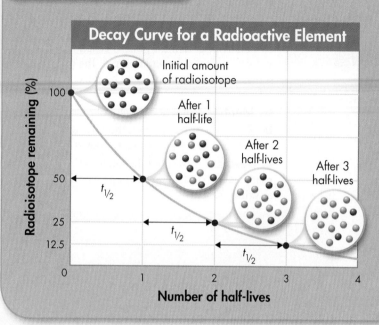

Decay Curve for a Radioactive Element

Radioisotope remaining (%)

Initial amount of radioisotope

After 1 half-life

After 2 half-lives

After 3 half-lives

$t_{1/2}$

Number of half-lives

Figure 25.7 This decay curve shows that during each half-life, half of the radioactive atoms decay into atoms of another element.

a. Read Graphs What percent of the original atoms remains after one half-life? After two half-lives?

b. Read Graphs How many half-lives does it take for 12.5% of the radioisotope to remain?

c. Apply Concepts Explain why this graph can apply to all radioisotopes.

Half-Life

🗝 *How much of a radioactive sample remains after each half-life?*

Every radioisotope has a characteristic rate of decay, which is measured by its half-life. A **half-life** ($t_{\frac{1}{2}}$) is the time required for one-half of the nuclei in a radioisotope sample to decay to products, as shown in Figure 25.7. 🗝 **During each half-life, half of the remaining radioactive atoms decay into atoms of a new element.**

Comparing Half-Lives Half-lives can be as short as a second or as long as billions of years. Table 25.2 shows the half-lives of some radioisotopes that occur in nature. Scientists use the half-lives of some long-term radioisotopes to determine the age of ancient objects. Many artificially produced radioisotopes have short half-lives, which makes them useful in nuclear medicine. Short-lived isotopes are not a long-term radiation hazard for patients.

Q: *Uranium compounds are found in rocks and in soils that form from these rocks. How can these uranium compounds lead to a build up of radon in homes and other buildings?*

Table 25.2

Half-Lives of Some Naturally Occurring Radioisotopes

Isotope	Half-life	Radiation emitted
Carbon-14	5.730×10^3 years	β
Potassium-40	1.25×10^9 years	β, γ
Radon-222	3.8 days	α
Radium-226	1.6×10^3 years	α, γ
Thorium-234	24.1 days	β, γ
Uranium-235	7.0×10^8 years	α, γ
Uranium-238	4.5×10^9 years	α

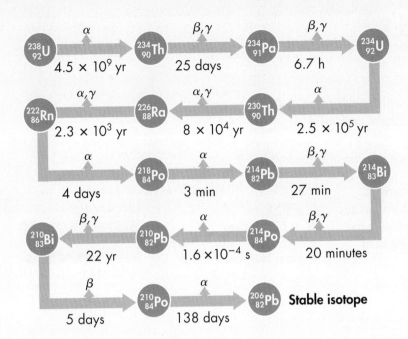

Figure 25.8 Decay Series of U-238
Uranium-238 decays through a series of radioactive intermediates, including radon (Rn) gas.
Interpret Diagrams *What is the stable end product of this series?*

One isotope that has a long half-life is uranium-238. It decays through a complex series of unstable isotopes to the stable isotope lead-206. Figure 25.8 summarizes this process. The age of uranium-containing minerals can be estimated by measuring the ratio of uranium-238 to lead-206. Because the half-life of uranium-238 is 4.5×10^9 years, it is possible to use its half-life to date rocks as old as the solar system.

Radiocarbon Dating Scientists often find the age of an object that was once part of a living system by measuring the amount of carbon-14 ($^{14}_{6}C$) it contains. Carbon-14 has a half-life of 5730 years. Most of Earth's carbon, however, consists of the more stable isotopes $^{12}_{6}C$ and $^{13}_{6}C$. The ratio of $^{14}_{6}C$ to the other carbon isotopes in the environment is fairly constant because high-energy cosmic rays from space constantly produce $^{14}_{6}C$ in carbon dioxide in the upper atmosphere.

Plants use carbon dioxide to produce carbon compounds, such as glucose. In those compounds, the ratio of carbon isotopes is the same as in the air. The same ratio is maintained as animals consume the plants, and other animals. Thus, the ratio of carbon-14 to other carbon isotopes is constant during an organism's lifetime. When an organism dies, it stops exchanging carbon with the environment and its radioactive $^{14}_{6}C$ atoms decay without being replaced. Therefore, the ratio of $^{14}_{6}C$ to stable carbon in the remains of an organism changes in a predictable way. Archaeologists can use this data to estimate when an organism died.

Exponential Decay Function You can use the following equation to calculate how much of an isotope will remain after a given number of half-lives.

$$A = A_0 \times \left(\tfrac{1}{2}\right)^n$$

In the formula, A stands for the amount remaining, A_0 for the initial amount, and n for the number of half-lives. The exponent n indicates how many times A_0 must be multiplied by $\tfrac{1}{2}$ to determine A. Table 25.3 shows examples in which $n = 1$ and $n = 2$.

Go online to learn more about half-life.

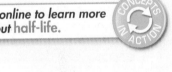

Table 25.3

Decay of Initial Amount (A_0) of Radioisotope

Half-Life	Amount Remaining
0	$A_0 \times \left(\tfrac{1}{2}\right)^0 = A_0$
1	$A_0 \times \left(\tfrac{1}{2}\right)^1 = A_0 \times \tfrac{1}{2}$
2	$A_0 \times \left(\tfrac{1}{2}\right)^2 = A_0 \times \tfrac{1}{2} \times \tfrac{1}{2}$

Sample Problem 25.1

Using Half-lives in Calculations

Carbon-14 emits beta radiation and decays with a half-life ($t_{\frac{1}{2}}$) of 5730 years. Assume you start with a mass of 2.00×10^{-12} g of carbon-14.

a. How long is three half-lives?

b. How many grams of the isotope remain at the end of three half-lives?

❶ Analyze List the knowns and the unknowns.

To calculate the length of three half-lives, multiply the half-life by three. To find the mass of the radioisotope remaining, multiply the original mass by $\frac{1}{2}$ for each half-life that has elapsed.

KNOWNS	UNKNOWNS
$t_{\frac{1}{2}} = 5730$ years	3 half-lives $= ?$ years
initial mass(A_O) 2.00×10^{-12}g	mass remaining $= ?$ g
number of half-lives (n) $= 3$	

❷ Calculate Solve for the unknowns.

Multiply the half-life of carbon-14 by the total number of half-lives.

a. $t_{\frac{1}{2}} \times n = 5730$ years $\times 3 = \boxed{17{,}190 \text{ years}}$

The initial mass of carbon-14 is reduced by one half for each half-life. So multiply by $\frac{1}{2}$ three times.

b. Remaining mass $= 2.00 \times 10^{-12}$ g $\times \dfrac{1}{2} \times \dfrac{1}{2} \times \dfrac{1}{2}$

$= 0.250 \times 10^{-12}$ g

$= \boxed{2.50 \times 10^{-13} \text{ g}}$

You can get the same answer by using the equation for an exponential decay function.

c. $A = A_O\left(\dfrac{1}{2}\right)^n = (2.00 \times 10^{-12} \text{ g})\left(\dfrac{1}{2}\right)^3$

$= (2.00 \times 10^{-12} \text{ g})\left(\dfrac{1}{8}\right)$

$= 0.250 \times 10^{-12}$ g

$= \boxed{2.50 \times 10^{-13} \text{ g}}$

❸ Evaluate Do the results make sense? The mass of carbon-14 after three half-lives should be one-eighth of the original mass. If you divide 2.50×10^{-13} g by 2.00×10^{-12} g, you will get 12.5%, or $\frac{1}{8}$.

For Problem 9, first figure out the number of half-lives.

9. Manganese-56 is a beta emitter with a half-life of 2.6 h. What is the mass of manganese-56 in a 1.0-mg sample of the isotope at the end of 10.4 h?

10. Thorium-234 has a half-life of 24.1 days. Will all the thorium atoms in a sample decay in 48.2 days? Explain.

Transmutation Reactions

What are two ways in which transmutation can occur?

For thousands of years, alchemists tried to change lead into gold, an element which is more highly valued than lead. Despite much effort, they were not able to achieve their goal. What they wanted to achieve is **transmutation,** or the conversion of an atom of one element into an atom of another element. This change can occur in at least two ways. **Transmutation can occur by radioactive decay or when particles bombard the nucleus of an atom.** The particles may be protons, neutrons, alpha particles, or small atoms.

Transmutations are common in nature. The production of carbon-14 from nitrogen-14 that takes place in the upper atmosphere is one example. Recall the decay series of uranium-238, which was described in Figure 25.8. In this series, 14 transmutations occur before a stable isotope of lead is produced. Some transmutations that do not occur in nature can be forced to occur in a laboratory or in a nuclear reactor. Ernest Rutherford performed the earliest artificial transmutation in 1919. He bombarded nitrogen gas with alpha particles. The results of this action are shown in Figure 25.9. As the nitrogen atoms absorb the alpha particles, they form fluorine-18 atoms.

$$\underset{\text{Nitrogen-14}}{^{14}_{7}\text{N}} + \underset{\substack{\text{Alpha} \\ \text{particle}}}{^{4}_{2}\text{He}} \longrightarrow \underset{\text{Fluorine-18}}{^{18}_{9}\text{F}}$$

The unstable fluorine atoms quickly decay to form a stable isotope of oxygen and a proton.

$$\underset{\text{Fluorine-18}}{^{18}_{9}\text{F}} \longrightarrow \underset{\text{Oxygen-17}}{^{17}_{8}\text{O}} + \underset{\text{Proton}}{^{1}_{1}\text{p}}$$

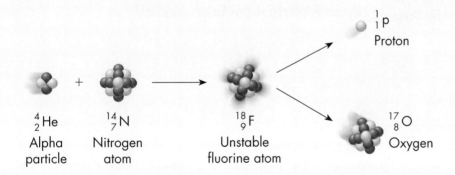

$$\underset{\substack{\text{Alpha} \\ \text{particle}}}{^{4}_{2}\text{He}} + \underset{\substack{\text{Nitrogen} \\ \text{atom}}}{^{14}_{7}\text{N}} \longrightarrow \underset{\substack{\text{Unstable} \\ \text{fluorine atom}}}{^{18}_{9}\text{F}}$$

$^{1}_{1}\text{p}$ Proton

$^{17}_{8}\text{O}$ Oxygen

Figure 25.9 The Transmutation of Nitrogen-14
The first artificial transmutation reaction involved bombarding nitrogen gas with alpha particles. **Interpret Diagrams** *Which particle is the intermediate in this nuclear reaction?*

Rutherford's experiment eventually led to the discovery of the proton. He and other scientists noticed a pattern as they did different transmutation experiments. In every case, hydrogen nuclei were emitted. Scientists realized that these hydrogen nuclei (protons) must have a fundamental role in atomic structure. James Chadwick's discovery of the neutron in 1932 also involved a transmutation experiment. Neutrons were produced when beryllium-9 was bombarded with alpha particles.

$$\underset{\text{Beryllium-9}}{^{9}_{4}\text{Be}} + \underset{\substack{\text{Alpha} \\ \text{particle}}}{^{4}_{2}\text{He}} \longrightarrow \underset{\text{Carbon-12}}{^{12}_{6}\text{C}} + \underset{\text{Neutron}}{^{1}_{0}\text{n}}$$

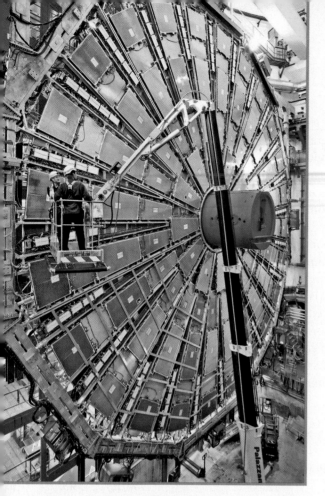

Figure 25.10 Particle Accelerator
The Large Hadron Collider is the most powerful accelerator in the world. It has a circumference of about 27 kilometers and is about 100 meters underground. The accelerator is designed to mimic the conditions that existed right after the Big Bang.

Elements with atomic numbers above 92, the atomic number of uranium, are called **transuranium elements.** All of these elements are radioactive. All transuranium elements undergo transmutation. These elements are synthesized in nuclear reactors and nuclear accelerators. Reactors produce beams of low-energy particles. Accelerators are used to increase the speed of bombarding particles to very high speeds. Sometimes particles must pass through a series of accelerators before they reach the desired speed. The European Organization for Nuclear Research, known as CERN, has a number of accelerators at its site on the border between France and Switzerland. Figure 25.10 shows CERN's largest accelerator.

When uranium-238 is bombarded with the relatively slow neutrons from a nuclear reactor, some uranium nuclei capture these neutrons. The product is uranium-239.

$$^{238}_{92}U + ^{1}_{0}n \longrightarrow ^{239}_{92}U$$

Uranium-239 is radioactive and emits a beta particle. The other product is an isotope of the artificial radioactive element neptunium (atomic number 93).

$$^{239}_{92}U \longrightarrow ^{239}_{93}Np + ^{0}_{-1}e$$

Neptunium is unstable and decays, emitting a beta particle and a second artificial element, plutonium (atomic number 94).

$$^{239}_{93}Np \longrightarrow ^{239}_{94}Pu + ^{0}_{-1}e$$

Plutonium and neptunium are both transuranium elements. The majority of these elements do not occur in nature. Scientists in Berkeley, California, synthesized the first two artificial elements in 1940. Since that time, more than 20 additional transuranium elements have been produced artificially.

25.2 LessonCheck

11. Identify What factor determines the type of decay that occurs in a radioisotope?

12. Predict How much of a sample of radioisotope remains after one half-life? After two half-lives?

13. Explain How can transmutation occur in a stable isotope?

14. Apply Concepts Complete the following nuclear equations. Use what you know about balanced nuclear equations to identify the missing particles.
a. $^{27}_{13}Al + ^{4}_{2}He \longrightarrow ^{30}_{14}Si + ?$
b. $^{214}_{83}Bi \longrightarrow ^{4}_{2}He + ?$
c. $^{27}_{14}Si \longrightarrow ^{0}_{-1}e + ?$
d. $^{66}_{29}Cu \longrightarrow ^{66}_{30}Zn + ?$

15. Calculate A radioisotope has a half-life of 4 days. How much of a 20-gram sample of this radioisotope remains at the end of each time period?
a. 4 days
b. 8 days

16. Calculate The mass of cobalt-60 in a sample decreased from 0.800 g to 0.200 g over a period of 10.5 years. From this information, calculate the half-life of cobalt-60.

17. Interpret Graphs Suppose the variable on the x-axis in Figure 25.7 were time instead of number of half-lives. Could the same graph be used to represent all radioisotopes? Why or why not?

Small-Scale Lab

Radioactivity and Half-Lives

Purpose
To simulate the transformation of a radioactive isotope over time, graph the data, and relate the data to radioactive decay and half-lives

Materials
- coin
- graph paper

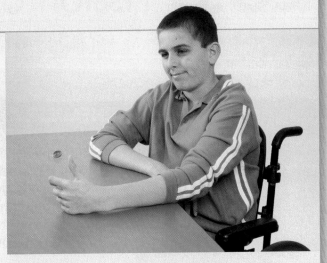

Procedure
1. On a sheet of paper, make a data table similar to the one below.

2. For trial 1, flip a coin 100 times. In your table, record the total number of heads that result.

3. For trial 2, flip the coin the same number of times as the number of heads in trial 1. Record the number of flips and the number of heads that result.

4. Continue the procedure until you obtain no more heads.

Trial	Number of flips	Number of heads
1	100	
2		
3		
4		
5		
6		
7		
8		

Analyze

1. Graph Use graph paper to plot the number of flips (*y*-axis) versus the trial number (*x*-axis). Draw a smooth line to connect the points.

2. Interpret Graphs Is the rate of the number of heads produced over time linear or nonlinear? Is the rate constant over time or does it change?

3. Relate Cause and Effect Why does each trial reduce the number of heads by about one-half?

4. Use Models A half-life is the time required for one-half of the atoms of a radioisotope to decay to products. What value represents one half-life for the process of flipping coins?

You're the Chemist

1. Design an Experiment Design and carry out an experiment using a single die to model radioactive decay. Plot your data.

2. Calculate Radon-222 undergoes alpha decay, emitting an alpha particle (helium nucleus),

$$^{222}_{86}\text{Rn} \longrightarrow {}^{218}_{84}\text{Po} + {}^{4}_{2}\text{He}$$

Find the half-life of radon-222 in Table 25.2 and determine how long it takes for only one eighth of a sample of radon-222 to remain.

3. Calculate Carbon-14 undergoes beta decay, emitting a beta particle (electron),

$$^{14}_{6}\text{C} \longrightarrow {}^{14}_{7}\text{N} + {}^{0}_{-1}\text{e}$$

Find the half-life of carbon-14 in Table 25.2 and determine what fraction of the carbon-14 in a sample will remain after 11,460 years.

25.3 Fission and Fusion

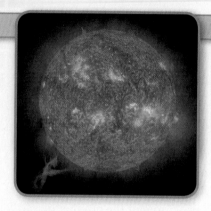

Q: *Where does the sun's energy come from?* The sun appears as a bright, fiery ball in the sky. The sun is so bright that you should never look at it directly without eye protection. The sun is about halfway through its life cycle. It has been producing energy for about 5 billion years and is expected to continue to produce energy for about 5 billion more. In this lesson, you will study the nuclear reaction that takes place in the sun.

Key Questions

 What happens in a nuclear chain reaction?

 How do fission reactions and fusion reactions differ?

Vocabulary

• fission
• neutron moderation
• neutron absorption
• fusion

Nuclear Fission

What happens in a nuclear chain reaction?

When the nuclei of certain isotopes are bombarded with neutrons, the nuclei split into smaller fragments. This process is called **fission.** Uranium-235 and plutonium-239, for example, are fissionable isotopes. Figure 25.11 shows how uranium-235 breaks into two smaller fragments of roughly the same size when struck by a slow-moving neutron. At the same time, more neutrons are released by the fission. These neutrons strike the nuclei of other uranium-235 atoms, which causes a chain reaction. **In a chain reaction, some of the emitted neutrons react with other fissionable atoms, which emit neutrons that react with still more fissionable atoms.**

Nuclear fission can release enormous amounts of energy. The fission of 1 kg of uranium-235, for example, yields an amount of energy equal to that produced when 20,000 tons of dynamite explode. In an uncontrolled nuclear chain reaction, all the energy is released in fractions of a second. An atomic bomb is a device that can trigger an uncontrolled nuclear chain reaction.

Figure 25.11 Fission of Uranium
When struck by a slow-moving neutron, a uranium-235 nucleus breaks into two smaller nuclei and releases three neutrons.
Predict *What happens when the released neutrons strike other uranium-235 nuclei?*

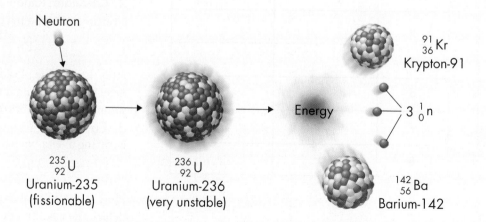

Neutron

$^{235}_{92}U$
Uranium-235
(fissionable)

$^{236}_{92}U$
Uranium-236
(very unstable)

Energy

$^{91}_{36}Kr$
Krypton-91

$3\,^{1}_{0}n$

$^{142}_{56}Ba$
Barium-142

Fission can be controlled so energy is released more slowly. Nuclear reactors, such as the one shown in Figure 25.12, use controlled fission to produce useful energy. The reaction takes place within uranium-235 or plutonium-239 fuel rods. Much of the energy produced in this reaction is in the form of heat. A fluid, usually liquid sodium or water, removes heat from the core, or central part, of the reactor. Thus, the fluid is called a coolant. The heated fluid is used to change water to steam, which drives a turbine that generates electricity. The control of fission in a nuclear reactor involves two steps, neutron moderation and neutron absorption.

Neutron Moderation

Neutron moderation is a process that slows down neutrons so the reactor fuel can capture them to continue the chain reaction. Moderation is necessary because most of the neutrons produced move so fast that they would pass right through a nucleus without being captured. Water and carbon in the form of graphite are good moderators.

Neutron Absorption

To prevent the chain reaction from going too fast, some of the slowed neutrons must be trapped before they hit fissionable atoms. **Neutron absorption** is a process that decreases the number of slow-moving neutrons. Control rods, made of materials such as cadmium, are used to absorb neutrons. When the control rods extend almost all the way into the reactor core, they absorb many neutrons, and fission occurs slowly. As the rods are pulled out, they absorb fewer neutrons and the fission process speeds up. If the chain reaction were to go too fast, heat might be produced faster than the coolant could remove it. The reactor core would overheat, which could lead to mechanical failure and release of radioactive materials into the atmosphere. Ultimately, a meltdown of the reactor core might occur.

Figure 25.12 Nuclear Reactor
A nuclear reactor is used to produce electricity. A coolant absorbs heat produced by the controlled fission reaction and transfers the heat to water, which changes to steam. The steam drives a turbine, which drives a generator that produces electricity.
Interpret Diagrams *What happens to the steam after it drives the turbine?*

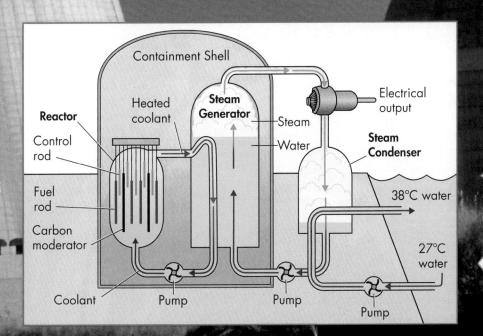

See a nuclear reactor animated online.

KINETIC ART

Nuclear Waste Fuel rods from nuclear power plants are one major source of nuclear waste. The fuel rods are made from a fissionable isotope, either uranium-235 or plutonium-239. The rods are long and narrow—typically 3 meters long with a 0.5-cm diameter. In a typical reactor, three hundred fuel rods are bundled together to form an assembly, and one hundred assemblies are arranged to form the reactor core. During fission, the amount of fissionable isotope in each fuel rod decreases. Eventually the rods no longer have enough fuel to ensure that the output of the power station remains constant. The isotope-depleted, or spent, fuel rods must be removed and replaced with new fuel rods.

Spent fuel rods are classified as high-level nuclear waste. They contain a mixture of highly radioactive isotopes, including fission products and what remains of the nuclear fuel. Some of these fission products have very short half-lives, on the order of fractions of seconds. Others have half-lives of hundreds or thousands of years. All nuclear power plants have holding tanks, or "swimming pools," for spent fuel rods. Water cools the spent rods, and also acts as a radiation shield to reduce the radiation levels. The pools, like the one shown in Figure 25.13, are typically 12 meters deep. Storage racks at the bottom of these pools are designed to hold the spent fuel assemblies. The rods continue to produce heat for years after their removal from the core.

The spent fuel rods may spend a decade or more in a holding tank. In the past, plant operators expected spent fuel rods to be reprocessed. Any leftover fissionable isotope in the rods would be recycled in the manufacture of new fuel rods. However, with large deposits of uranium ore available—many in the United States—it is less expensive to mine new fuel than to reprocess depleted fuel. At some nuclear plants, the storage pool has no space left. In order to keep these plants open, their fuel rods must be moved to off-site storage facilities. Finding appropriate storage sites is difficult because high-level waste may need be stored for a long time. Plutonium-239, for example, will not decay to safe levels for 240,000 years. Often, people are concerned about having nuclear waste stored nearby or shipped through their communities.

Figure 25.13 Storage of Fuel Rods
Racks at the bottom of this pool contain spent fuel rods.

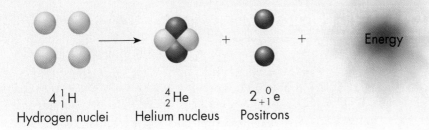

$4\,^{1}_{1}\text{H}$
Hydrogen nuclei

$^{4}_{2}\text{He}$
Helium nucleus

$2\,^{0}_{+1}\text{e}$
Positrons

Energy

Figure 25.14 Fusion in the Sun
In the sun, hydrogen nuclei fuse to produce helium nuclei.
Interpret Diagrams *What are the other products of this reaction?*

Nuclear Fusion

How do fission reactions and fusion reactions differ?

The sun, directly and indirectly, is the source of most energy used on Earth. The energy emitted by the sun results from nuclear fusion. **Fusion** occurs when nuclei combine to produce a nucleus of greater mass. In solar fusion, hydrogen nuclei (protons) fuse to make helium nuclei. Figure 25.14 shows that the reaction also produces two positrons. **Fusion reactions, in which small nuclei combine, release much more energy than fission reactions, in which large nuclei split apart and form smaller nuclei.** However, fusion reactions occur only at very high temperatures—in excess of 40,000,000°C.

The use of controlled nuclear fusion as an energy source on Earth is appealing. The potential fuels are inexpensive and readily available. Some scientists are studying a reaction in which a deuterium (hydrogen-2) nucleus and a tritium (hydrogen-3) nucleus combine to form a helium nucleus.

$$^{2}_{1}\text{H} + ^{3}_{1}\text{H} \longrightarrow ^{4}_{2}\text{He} + ^{1}_{0}\text{n} + \text{energy}$$

The problems with fusion lie in achieving the high temperatures needed to start the reaction and in containing the reaction once it has started. The high temperatures required to start fusion reactions have been achieved by using a fission bomb. Such a bomb is the triggering device used for setting off a hydrogen bomb, which is an uncontrolled-fusion device. This process is of no use, however, as a controlled generator of power.

CHEMISTRY & YOU

Q: *The high temperatures needed to support fusion exist within the sun's core. Late in the sun's life cycle, other fusion reactions will occur. What element would form when two helium nuclei fuse?*

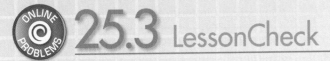

25.3 LessonCheck

18. **Relate Cause and Effect** Explain what happens in a nuclear chain reaction.

19. **Compare** How are fusion reactions different from fission reactions?

20. **Explain** What is neutron moderation, and why is it necessary in a nuclear reactor?

21. **Identify** What are two sources of the radioactive nuclei present in spent fuel rods?

22. **Evaluate** Suppose the technical problems with fusion reactors could be overcome. What are some advantages to using a fusion reactor to produce electricity?

23. **Interpret Diagrams** Review the diagram of a reactor in Figure 25.12. What role does water play in a typical nuclear reactor?

24. **Infer** Some nuclear waste is stored about 600 meters below the desert in New Mexico inside caverns dug out of an ancient bed of rock salt. The land above the storage site is owned by the federal government. Why do you think this location was chosen?

25. **Describe** Read about heavy water reactors on page R35 of the Elements Handbook. What is the advantage of using heavy water instead of ordinary water as a neutron moderator?

Small-Scale Nuclear Power

About 20 percent of the electricity generated each year in the United States comes from nuclear power. Operating costs for nuclear power plants are lower than for plants that burn fossil fuels. However, a nuclear power plant, like the one shown in the photo, costs more and takes longer to build than a coal-burning plant. Also, people have concerns about the safety of these plants.

Plants that burn fossil fuels also have issues. Concerns about global warming have made the reduction of carbon emissions a priority for many countries. To meet this goal, plants that burn fossil fuels must install technology to trap the carbon dioxide produced when coal or natural gas burn. A greater reliance on nuclear power can help reduce carbon emissions.

Researchers at Oregon State University have proposed a new kind of nuclear power plant to address some of the problems presented by traditional plants. The large above-ground reactor of a traditional plant would be replaced by self-contained modules, which would be located sixty-five feet below ground level. The plant could open with only a few modules. More modules can be added as needed.

Old vs. New

	Traditional Plant	Small-Scale Plant
Construction	Single-unit plants must be built onsite. Construction time is 7–10 years.	Modular units are factory-built and shipped to the site. Construction time is 3–3.5 years.
Coolant method	Valves and pumps circulate the coolant around the reactor core.	Gravity, condensation, evaporation, and convection circulate the coolant.
Safety	The reactor is above ground. A backup electricity source is needed for coolant systems. If the reactor must be shut down, no electricity is generated.	The modules are underground, in self-contained steel chambers, immersed in a pool of water. One module can be shut down without affecting the other modules.
Facility size	Many traditional single-unit plants require about 20 acres.	A plant that provides as much electricity as a small traditional plant would require about 4 acres.

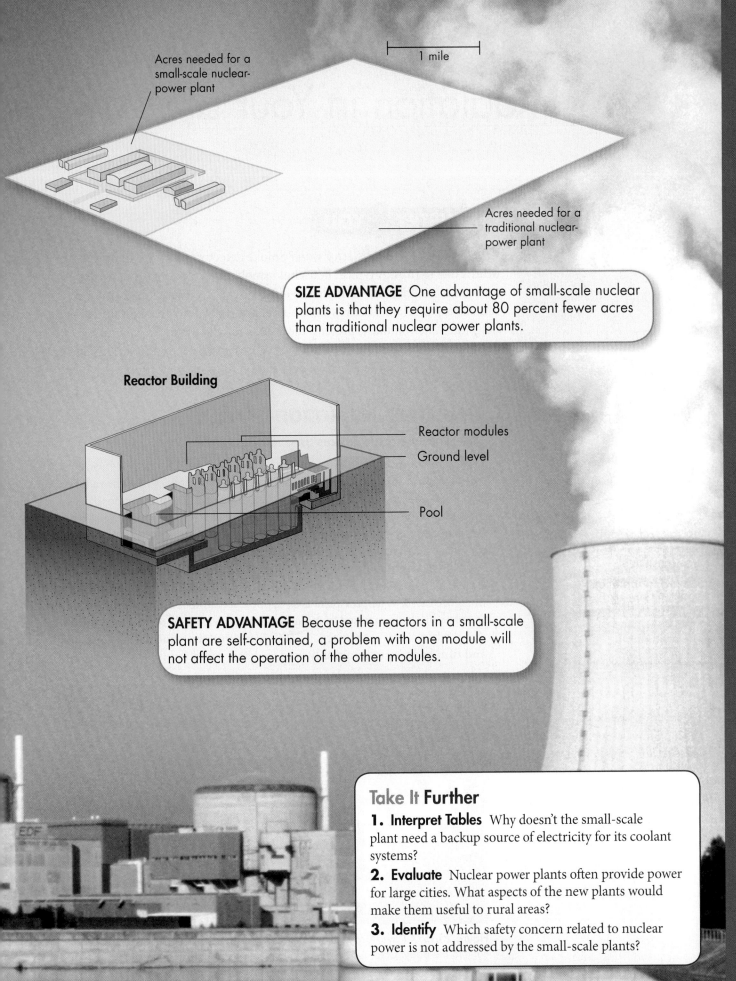

Acres needed for a small-scale nuclear-power plant

1 mile

Acres needed for a traditional nuclear-power plant

SIZE ADVANTAGE One advantage of small-scale nuclear plants is that they require about 80 percent fewer acres than traditional nuclear power plants.

Reactor Building

Reactor modules

Ground level

Pool

SAFETY ADVANTAGE Because the reactors in a small-scale plant are self-contained, a problem with one module will not affect the operation of the other modules.

Take It Further

1. Interpret Tables Why doesn't the small-scale plant need a backup source of electricity for its coolant systems?

2. Evaluate Nuclear power plants often provide power for large cities. What aspects of the new plants would make them useful to rural areas?

3. Identify Which safety concern related to nuclear power is not addressed by the small-scale plants?

25.4 Radiation in Your Life

Key Questions

🔑 What are three devices used to detect radiation?

🔑 What are some practical uses of radioisotopes?

Vocabulary

• ionizing radiation

Q: *How does a smoke detector work?* Smoke detectors can limit injuries or deaths due to fires. A typical household smoke detector contains a small amount of americium, $^{241}_{95}Am$, in the form of AmO_2. Americium-241 is a radioisotope. When the air is smoke-free, a current flows through the smoke detector. When smoke is present, there is a drop in current. This drop is detected by an electronic circuit, which causes an alarm to sound. This lesson will help you understand the role of radiation in smoke detection.

Detecting Radiation

🔑 **What are three devices used to detect radiation?**

Radiation emitted by radioisotopes has enough energy to knock electrons off some atoms of a bombarded substance, producing ions. Thus, the radiation emitted by radioisotopes is called **ionizing radiation.** It is not possible for humans to see, hear, smell, or feel ionizing radiation. So people must rely on detection devices to alert them to the presence of radiation and to monitor its level. These devices work because of the effects of the radiation when it strikes atoms or molecules in the detector. For example, the radiation can expose a photographic plate, which produces an image such as the one shown in Figure 25.15. When the plate is developed, its darkened areas show where the plate has been exposed to radiation. Some devices rely on the current produced when atoms are ionized. 🔑 **Geiger counters, scintillation counters, and film badges are commonly used to detect radiation.**

Q: *Radiation emitted in a smoke detector ionizes the nitrogen and oxygen in air, and a current flows. When smoke particles attach to the ions, the ions lose their charge. What happens next?*

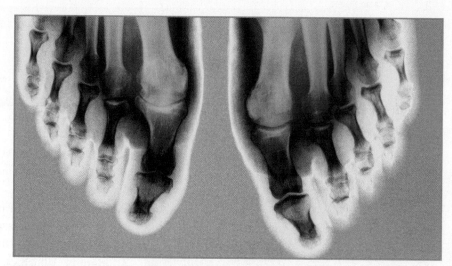

Figure 25.15 X-Rays X-rays allow doctors to see inside the body without having to cut into the body. Color was added to highlight parts of the image.

Geiger Counter A Geiger counter uses a gas-filled metal tube to detect radiation. The tube has a central wire electrode that is connected to a power supply. When ionizing radiation penetrates a thin window at one end of the tube, the gas inside the tube becomes ionized. Because of the ions and free electrons produced, the gas is able to conduct electricity. Each time a Geiger tube is exposed to radiation, current flows. The bursts of current drive electronic counters or cause audible clicks from a built-in speaker. Geiger counters can detect alpha, beta, and gamma radiation. The first small, hand-held Geiger counters were developed in the 1930s.

Astronomers use Geiger counters to detect cosmic rays from outer space. Geologists use Geiger counters to search for radioactive minerals, such as uranium ores. These devices are also used to check for leaks in hospitals and other places that use radiation. Figure 25.16 shows one use for a Geiger counter.

Scintillation Counter A scintillation counter uses a phosphor-coated surface to detect radiation. When ionizing radiation strikes the surface, the phosphor produces bright flashes of light, or scintillations. The number of flashes and energies are detected electronically. The data is then converted into electronic pulses, which are measured and recorded. Scintillation counters are more sensitive than Geiger counters. This means that they can detect some radiation that would not be detected by a Geiger counter. Scintillation counters are used to track the path of radioisotopes through the body. They are also used to monitor the possible transport of radioactive materials across national borders and through airports.

Film Badge Figure 25.17 is a diagram of a typical film badge. The badge contains layers of photographic film covered with black light-proof paper. The film is sealed in a plastic or metal holder. To reach the film, radiation must pass through a filter, which absorbs some radiation, or a transparent area through which radiation can pass easily. People who work with or near ionizing radiation must wear a film badge to monitor their exposure while they are at work. At specific intervals, the film is removed and developed. The strength and type of radiation exposure are determined by comparing the darkness of the film in all the exposed areas. Records are kept of the results. Film badges do not protect a person from radiation, but they do monitor the degree of exposure. To protect themselves, workers must keep a safe distance from the source and use adequate shielding.

Figure 25.16 Geiger Counters
This person is using a Geiger counter to check for pockets of radiation in contaminated dirt at a spill site.

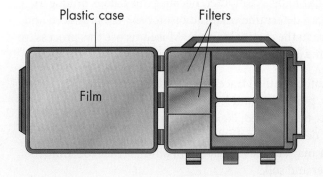

Plastic case   Filters

Film

Figure 25.17 Film Badge
In a film badge, radiation passes through one of several filters or through a transparent area before it strikes the film. Different amounts of radiation pass through each area.

Purpose To demonstrate the relationship between radiation intensity and the distance from the radiation source

Materials
- flashlight
- strips of duct tape
- scissors
- poster board, white (50 cm × 50 cm)
- meter ruler or tape measure
- flat surface, long enough to hold the meter ruler
- graph paper

Inverse-Square Relationships

Procedure

1. Estimate and record the distance (*A*) from the bulb filament to the front surface of the flashlight.

2. Cover the end of a flashlight with strips of duct tape. Leave a 1 cm × 1 cm square slit in the center of the tape.

3. Place the flashlight on its side on a flat surface. Turn on the flashlight. Darken the room.

4. Mount a large piece of white poster board in front of the flashlight, perpendicular to the horizontal surface.

5. Move the flashlight away from the board in short increments. At each

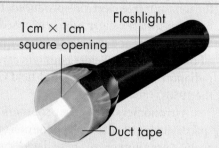
1cm × 1cm square opening
Flashlight
Duct tape

position, record the distance (*B*) from the flashlight to the board and the length (*L*) of one side of the square image on the board.

6. On a sheet of graph paper, plot *L* on the *y*-axis versus *A* + *B* on the *x*-axis. On another sheet, plot L^2 on the *y*-axis versus *A* + *B* on the *x*-axis.

Analyze and Conclude

1. Make Generalizations As the flashlight is moved away from the board, what happens to the intensity of the light in the square image? Use your graphs to describe the relationship between intensity and distance.

2. Explain When the distance of the flashlight from the board (*B*) is doubled and tripled, what happens to the areas and intensities of the squares?

Using Radiation

➤ What are some practical uses of radioisotopes?

Although radiation can be harmful, it can be used safely and has many important applications. ➤ **Radioisotopes are used to analyze matter, study plant growth, diagnose medical problems, and treat diseases.**

Analyzing Matter Scientists use radiation to detect trace amounts of elements in samples. The process is called neutron activation analysis. A sample is bombarded with neutrons from a radioactive source. Some atoms in the sample become radioactive. The half-life and type of radiation emitted can be detected and analyzed by a computer. Because this data is unique for each isotope, scientists can determine what radioisotopes were produced and infer what elements were in the original sample. Museums use this process to detect art forgeries. Crime laboratories use it to analyze gunpowder residues.

Using Tracers Radioisotopes called tracers are used in agriculture to test the effects of herbicides, pesticides, and fertilizers on plants. A tracer is introduced into the substance being tested. Next, plants are treated with the tagged substance. Devices that detect radioactivity are used to locate the substance in the plants. The tracer may also be monitored in animals that consume the plants, as well as in water and soil.

Diagnosing Medical Problems Radioisotopes can be used to detect disorders of the thyroid gland, which is located in the throat. The main function of this gland is to control the rate at which your cells release energy from food. The thyroid gland extracts iodide ions from blood and uses them to make the hormone thyroxine. To diagnose thyroid disease, the patient is given a drink containing a small amount of the radioisotope iodine-131. After about two hours, the amount of iodide uptake is measured by scanning the patient's throat with a radiation detector. Figure 25.18 shows the results of such a scan. In a similar way, the radioisotope technetium-99m is used to detect brain tumors and liver disorders. Phosphorus-32 is used to detect skin cancer.

Treating Diseases Radiation is one method used in the treatment of some cancers. Cancer is a disease in which abnormal cells in the body are produced at a rate far beyond the rate for normal cells. The mass of cancer cells that result from this runaway growth is called a tumor. Fast-growing cancer cells are more susceptible to damage by high-energy radiation such as gamma rays than are healthy cells. Thus, radiation can be used to kill the cancer cells in a tumor. Some normal cells are also killed, however, and cancer cells at the center of the tumor may be resistant to the radiation. Therefore, the benefits of the treatment and the risks to the patient must be carefully evaluated before radiation treatment begins. Cobalt-60 and cesium-137 are typical radiation sources for cancer therapy.

Salts of radioisotopes can also be sealed in gold tubes and directly inserted in tumors. This method of treatment is called seeding. The salts emit beta and gamma rays that kill the surrounding cancer cells. Because the radioisotope is in a sealed container, it is prevented from traveling to other parts of the body.

Prescribed drugs containing radioisotopes of gold, iodine, or phosphorus are sometimes used in radiation therapy. For example, a dose of iodine-131 larger than that used to detect thyroid diseases can be given to a patient to treat the disease. The radioactive iodine passes through the digestive system into the blood, which carries it to the thyroid. The iodine that collects in the gland emits beta particles and gamma rays , which provide therapy.

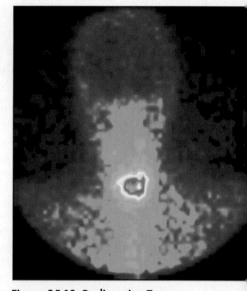

Figure 25.18 Radioactive Tracer
This scanned image of a thyroid gland shows where radioactive iodine-131 has been absorbed. Doctors use these images to identify thyroid disorders.

 **25.4** LessonCheck

26. ⚷ **Compare** In each of the three detection devices described in the lesson, what is used to detect the radiation?

27. ⚷ **Review** What are two ways radioisotopes can be used in medicine?

28. Define Why is the radiation emitted by radioisotopes called ionizing radiation?

29. Explain Suppose you worked with or near a radiation source. Why might your employer use a film badge rather than a Geiger counter to monitor your exposure to radiation?

30. Infer Why do airports use scintillation counters and not Geiger counters to search for radioactive materials?

31. Compare Of Geiger counters, scintillation counters, and film badges, which device is most similar to a smoke detector? Explain your choice.

32. Sequence Briefly describe the three steps that occur when iodine-131 is used to diagnose thyroid disease?

33. Explain What is one advantage of using sealed tubes, or seeds, to treat a tumor?

25 Study Guide

BIGIDEA ELECTRONS AND THE STRUCTURE OF ATOMS

Unstable atomic nuclei decay by emitting alpha or beta particles. Often gamma rays are emitted, too. During fission and fusion, atoms change their chemical identity as the number of protons in their nuclei change. In fission, large nuclei split into two or more smaller nuclei. In fusion, smaller nuclei combine to form larger nuclei at extremely high temperature and pressure. The ability to detect particles emitted when nuclei decay helps scientists study processes that take place in living organisms, This ability also allows scientists to determine the age of fossils and other objects.

25.1 Nuclear Radiation

🔑 Unlike chemical reactions, nuclear reactions are not affected by changes in temperature, pressure, or the presence of catalysts. Also, nuclear reactions of a given radioisotope cannot be slowed down, speeded up, or stopped.

🔑 Three types of nuclear radiation are alpha radiation, beta radiation, and gamma radiation.

- radioactivity (876)
- nuclear radiation (876)
- radioisotope (876)
- alpha particle (877)
- beta particle (878)
- gamma ray (879)

25.2 Nuclear Transformations

🔑 The neutron-to-proton ratio in a radioisotope determines the type of decay that occurs.

🔑 During each half-life, half of the remaining radioactive atoms decay into atoms of a new element.

🔑 Transmutation can occur by radioactive decay, or when particles bombard the nucleus of an atom.

- nuclear force (880)
- band of stability (880)
- positron (881)
- half-life (882)
- transmutation (885)
- transuranium elements (886)

Key Equation

$$A = A_0 \times \left(\frac{1}{2}\right)^n$$

25.3 Fission and Fusion

🔑 In a chain reaction, some of the emitted neutrons react with other fissionable atoms, which emit neutrons that react with still more fissionable atoms.

🔑 Fusion reactions, in which small nuclei combine, release much more energy than fission reactions, in which large nuclei split apart to form smaller nuclei.

- fission (888)
- neutron moderation (889)
- neutron absorption (889)
- fusion (891)

25.4 Radiation in Your Life

🔑 Geiger counters, scintillation counters, and film badges are commonly used to detect radiation.

🔑 Radioisotopes are used to analyze the composition of matter, study plant growth, diagnose medical problems, and treat diseases.

- ionizing radiation (894)

Math Tune-Up: Nuclear Reactions

Problem	❶ Analyze	❷ Calculate	❸ Evaluate
Plutonium-239 decays by emitting an alpha particle. What is the product of this reaction? $^{239}_{94}\text{Pu} \longrightarrow {}^{4}_{2}\text{He} + \text{X}$	Knowns: mass number of Pu = 239 mass number of α = 4 atomic number of Pu = 94 atomic number of α = 2 Unknowns: Mass number of X = ? Atomic number of X = ? Identity of X = ? In an equation for a nuclear reaction, mass numbers and atomic numbers must be balanced.	The mass number of X must equal the mass number of Pu minus the mass number of α. The atomic number of X must equal the atomic number of Pu minus the atomic number of α. $^{239}_{94}\text{Pu} \longrightarrow {}^{4}_{2}\text{He} + {}^{239-4}_{94-2}\text{X}$ $\longrightarrow {}^{4}_{2}\text{He} + {}^{235}_{92}\text{X}$ The element with atomic number 92 is uranium. $^{239}_{94}\text{Pu} \longrightarrow {}^{4}_{2}\text{He} + {}^{235}_{92}\text{U}$	The mass numbers total 239 on both sides of the equation. The atomic numbers total 94 on both sides of the equation. The isotope uranium-235 is a well-known radioisotope.
Thorium-234 has a half-life of 24.1 days. If a thorium-234 sample has a mass of 6.4×10^{-12} g, how much of the sample is left after 72.3 days?	Knowns: Original mass of Th = 6.4×10^{-12} g Decay time = 72.3 days $t_{\frac{1}{2}}$ = 24.1 days Unknowns: Mass of Th remaining = ? The mass of thorium-234 decreases by half with each half-life. Find the number of half-lives in 72.3 days and multiply the mass of thorium by $\frac{1}{2}$ for each half-life.	Divide the decay time by the half-life of thorium to find the number of half-lives. $\dfrac{72.3 \text{ days}}{24.1 \text{ days/half-life}} = 3 \text{ half-lives}$ Multiply the mass of thorium by $\frac{1}{2}$ three times. $6.4 \times 10^{-12}\text{g} \times \frac{1}{2} \times \frac{1}{2} \times \frac{1}{2} =$ $8.0 \times 10^{-13}\text{g}$	After three half-lives, the number of atoms of a radioisotope will decrease to $\frac{1}{8}$ of the original number. Hint: Review Sample Problem 25.1 for another calculation involving half-life.
Carbon-14 undergoes beta decay and produces nitrogen-14. The half-life for this process is 5730 years. In a sample from an ancient piece of pottery, the ratio of carbon-14 atoms to nitrogen-14 atoms is 25%. How old is the pottery?	Knowns: $t_{\frac{1}{2}}$ = 5730 yr Ratio of C-14 to N-14 = 25% Unknown: Age of sample = ? The number of C-14 atoms decreases by half every 5730 years. Find the number of half-lives that reduce the number of C-14 atoms to $\frac{1}{4}$ (25%) and multiply by 5730.	A ratio of C-14 atoms to N-14 atoms of $\frac{1}{4}$ means that C-14 has decayed for two half-lives: $\dfrac{1}{4} = \dfrac{1}{2} \times \dfrac{1}{2} = \left(\dfrac{1}{2}\right)^{2}$ Convert two half-lives to years. 5730 years $\times$ 2 = 11,460 years	The pottery sample is 11,460 years old, which is equal to two half-lives or the time required for 75% of the carbon-14 atoms to decay.

25 Assessment

★ Solutions appear in Appendix E

Lesson by Lesson

25.1 Nuclear Radiation

34. Explain how radioisotopes are different from other isotopes.

35. The decay of radium-226 produces an isotope of the element radon and alpha radiation. The atomic number of radium (Ra) is 88; the atomic number of radon (Rn) is 86. Write a balanced equation for this transformation.

★36. An isotope of the element lead (Pb) decays to an isotope of the element bismuth (Bi) by emission of a beta particle. Complete the equation for the reaction by supplying the missing atomic number and mass number.

$$^{210}_{?}\text{Pb} \longrightarrow \, ^{?}_{83}\text{Bi} + \, ^{0}_{-1}\text{e}$$

37. Write the symbol and charge for each item.
  a. alpha particle
  b. beta particle
  c. gamma ray

★38. Alpha radiation is emitted during the decay of the following isotopes. Write balanced nuclear equations to describe each decay process. Name the element produced in each case.
  a. uranium-238 ($^{238}_{92}\text{U}$)   **c.** uranium-235 ($^{235}_{92}\text{U}$)
  b. thorium-230 ($^{230}_{90}\text{Th}$)   **d.** radon-222 ($^{222}_{86}\text{Rn}$)

39. The following radioisotopes are beta emitters. Write balanced nuclear equations to describe each decay process.
  a. carbon-14 ($^{14}_{6}\text{C}$)   **c.** potassium-40 ($^{40}_{19}\text{K}$)
  b. strontium-90 ($^{90}_{38}\text{Sr}$)   **d.** nitrogen-13 ($^{13}_{7}\text{N}$)

★40. How are the mass number and atomic number of a nucleus affected by the loss of the following?
  a. beta particle
  b. alpha particle
  c. gamma ray

41. The following radioactive nuclei decay by emitting alpha particles. Write the product of the decay process for each isotope.
  a. $^{238}_{94}\text{Pu}$ **c.** $^{210}_{84}\text{Po}$
  b. $^{210}_{83}\text{Bi}$ **d.** $^{230}_{90}\text{Th}$

25.2 Nuclear Transformations

★42. What happens to an atom with a nucleus that falls outside the band of stability?

43. Write an equation for the radioactive decay of fluorine-17 by positron emission.

44. Identify the more stable isotope in each pair.
  a. $^{14}_{6}\text{C}$, $^{13}_{6}\text{C}$ **c.** $^{15}_{8}\text{O}$, $^{16}_{8}\text{O}$
  b. $^{3}_{1}\text{H}$, $^{1}_{1}\text{H}$ **d.** $^{13}_{7}\text{N}$, $^{14}_{7}\text{N}$

45. Define *half-life*.

46. Why is it important that radioactive isotopes used for diagnosis or treatment of medical problems have relatively short half-lives?

★47. A patient is given 20 mg of iodine-131. The half-life of iodine-131 is 8 days. How much of the isotope will remain in the patient's body after 40 days?

48. What is the difference between natural and artificial radioactivity?

49. What are the transuranium elements? Why are they unusual?

25.3 Fission and Fusion

50. Describe the process of nuclear fission, and define a nuclear chain reaction.

51. Why are spent fuel rods removed from a reactor core? What do they contain? What happens to them after they are removed?

52. Fusion reactions produce enormous amounts of energy. Why is fusion not used to generate electrical power?

25.4 Radiation in Your Life

53. Why are X-rays and the radiation emitted by radioisotopes called ionizing radiation?

54. Why must people rely on devices such as Geiger counters to detect radiation?

55. What type of people are required to wear a film badge and what is the purpose of this device?

56. Why are cancer cells more easily damaged by high-energy radiation than healthy cells are?

Understand Concepts

* 57. Write balanced nuclear equations for these transmutations.

a. $^{30}_{15}P$ to $^{30}_{14}Si$
b. $^{13}_{6}C$ to $^{14}_{6}C$
c. $^{131}_{53}I$ to $^{131}_{54}Xe$

58. How are the nuclear reactions that take place in the sun different from the nuclear reactions that take place in a nuclear reactor?

59. Complete these nuclear equations.

a. $^{32}_{15}P \longrightarrow \boxed{} + {}^{0}_{-1}e$
b. $\boxed{} \longrightarrow {}^{14}_{7}N + {}^{0}_{-1}e$
c. $^{238}_{92}U \longrightarrow {}^{234}_{90}Th + \boxed{}$
d. $^{141}_{56}Ba \longrightarrow \boxed{} + {}^{0}_{-1}e$
e. $\boxed{} \longrightarrow {}^{181}_{77}Ir + {}^{4}_{2}He$

60. Write nuclear equations for the beta decay of the following isotopes.

a. $^{90}_{38}Sr$ **b.** $^{14}_{6}C$ **c.** $^{137}_{55}Cs$ **d.** $^{239}_{93}Np$ **e.** $^{50}_{22}Ti$

61. The graph shows the radioactive decay curve for thorium-234. Use the graph to answer the questions below.

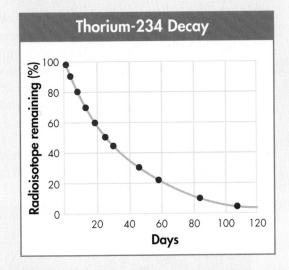

Thorium-234 Decay

a. What percentage of the isotope remains after 60 days?
b. After 40 days have passed, how many grams of a 250-g sample of thorium-234 would remain?
c. How long would it take in days for 44 g of thorium-234 to decay to 4.4 g of thorium-234?
d. What is the half-life of thorium-234?

62. Write a balanced nuclear equation for each word equation.

a. Radon-222 emits an alpha particle to form polonium-218.
b. Radium-230 is produced when thorium-234 emits an alpha particle.
c. When polonium-210 emits an alpha particle, the product is lead-206.

63. Briefly describe the contributions the following people made to the study of radioactivity and nuclear chemistry.

a. Marie Curie
b. Antoine Henri Becquerel
c. James Chadwick
d. Ernest Rutherford

64. How many protons and how many neutrons are in each of the following nuclei?

a. $^{60}_{27}Co$ **b.** $^{206}_{82}Pb$ **c.** $^{233}_{90}Th$ **d.** $^{3}_{1}H$

*65. A sample of matter has 32 million radioactive atoms. How many of these atoms would be left after five half-lives?

66. Write balanced nuclear equations for alpha emission by each of these isotopes.

a. $^{231}_{91}Pa$ **b.** $^{241}_{95}Am$ **c.** $^{226}_{88}Ra$ **d.** $^{252}_{99}Es$

* 67. Write balanced nuclear equations for beta emission by each of these isotopes.

a. $^{3}_{1}H$ **b.** $^{28}_{12}Mg$ **c.** $^{131}_{53}I$ **d.** $^{75}_{34}Se$

68. Use the concept of stability to compare chemical reactions with nuclear reactions.

69. The ratio of carbon-14 to carbon-12 in a chunk of charcoal from an archaeological dig is one-half the ratio of carbon-14 to carbon-12 in a piece of freshly cut wood. How old is the chunk of charcoal?

70. How are a positron and an electron similar? How are they different?

*71. Use what you know about balanced nuclear reaction equations to complete the following equations.

a. $^{38}_{19}K \longrightarrow {}^{38}_{20}Ca + ?$
b. $^{242}_{94}Pu \longrightarrow ? + {}^{4}_{2}He$
c. $^{68}_{31}Ga \longrightarrow ? + {}^{0}_{-1}e$
d. $^{68}_{32}Ge \longrightarrow {}^{68}_{31}Ga + ?$

Think Critically

*72. **Classify** Name the elements represented by the following symbols and indicate which of them would have no stable isotopes.

a. Pt   b. Th   c. Fr   d. Ti

e. Xe   f. Cf   g. V   h. Pd

73. **Interpret Graphs** Use the graph to determine which of these isotopes have stable nuclei: neon-21, zirconium-90, and neodymium-130.

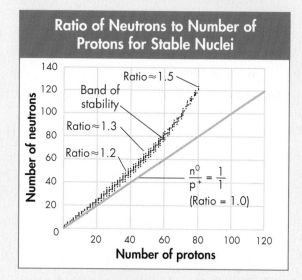

74. **Use Analogies** Compare the half-life of an element to a single-elimination sports tournament. *Hint:* What happens in each round of the tournament?

75. **Infer** A radioactive nucleus decays to give a bismuth-211 ($^{211}_{83}$Bi) nucleus and an alpha particle. What was the original nucleus?

*76. **Calculate** The carbon-14 content of an object produces 4 counts per minute per gram of carbon. Living matter has a carbon-14 content that produces 16 counts per minute per gram of carbon. What is the age of the object?

77. **Relate Cause and Effect** Why is an alpha particle less penetrating than a beta particle?

78. **Infer** Why might radioisotopes of C, N, and O be especially harmful to living creatures?

79. **Compare and Contrast** Iodine-131 is used to diagnose and treat thyroid disorders. What is the main difference between the two processes?

80. **Apply Concepts** Should a radioisotope with a half-life measured in days be used in a smoke detector? Why or why not?

81. **Calculate** Bismuth-209 was bombarded with iron-58 for several days. Meitnerium ($^{266}_{109}$Mt) was produced. How many neutrons were released per atom?

$$^{209}_{83}\text{Bi} + ^{58}_{26}\text{Fe} \longrightarrow ^{266}_{109}\text{Mt} + ?^1_0\text{n}$$

*82. **Predict** When neutrons strike magnesium-24 ($^{24}_{12}$Mg), a neutron is captured and photons are ejected. What new element is formed?

83. **Make Generalizations** Plutonium-239 emits alpha particles, which do not penetrate a thin sheet of paper or skin. Under what conditions would plutonium-239 be especially hazardous for organisms?

*84. **Calculate** Tritium (hydrogen-3) has a half-life of 12.3 years. How old is a bottle of wine if the tritium content is 25% that of new wine?

85. **Apply Concepts** What properties of isotopes make it possible to use neutron activation analysis to identify the composition of matter?

86. **Relate Cause and Effect** What effect did the discovery of radioactivity have on Dalton's model of the atom?

87. **Analyze Data** A sample of californium-249 ($^{249}_{98}$Cf) was used as the target in the synthesis of seaborgium ($^{236}_{106}$Sg). Four neutrons were emitted for each transformed $^{249}_{98}$Cf. The result was a nucleus with 106 protons and a mass of 263 amu. What type of particle struck the target?

$$^{249}_{98}\text{Cf} + ? \longrightarrow 4^1_0\text{n} + ^{263}_{106}\text{Sg}$$

88. **Use Models** Explain how the falling dominoes in the photograph can be used as a model for a chain reaction.

89. Calculate The radioisotope cesium-137 has a half-life of 30 years. A sample decayed at the rate of 544 counts per minute in the year 1985. In what year will the decay rate be 17 counts per minute?

90. Interpret Graphs Use the graph below to answer the questions.

   a. Describe the process that is being depicted in the graph.

   b. Suggest an appropriate title for the graph.

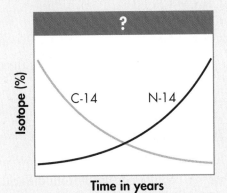

91. Apply Concepts Bismuth-211 decays by alpha emission to yield another radioisotope, which emits beta radiation as it decays to a stable isotope. Write equations for the nuclear reactions and name the decay products.

92. Analyze Data What isotope remains after three beta particles and five alpha particles are lost from a thorium-234 isotope?

93. Evaluate In the following argument, the third statement is based on the first two statements. Is the reasoning logical? Why or why not?

   (1) Radiation kills fast-growing cells.

   (2) Cancer cells are fast-growing.

   (3) Therefore, radiation kills only cancer cells.

∗94. Calculate Uranium has a density of 19 g/cm^3. What volume does a mass of 8.0 kg of uranium occupy?

95. Make Generalizations Element 107 (Bh) is formed when nuclei of element 109 (Mt) each emit an alpha particle. Nuclei of element 107, in turn, each emit an alpha particle, forming an atom with a mass number of 262. Write balanced equations for these two nuclear reactions.

96. Summarize Research methods used to date materials such as pottery, coral, and stone. Prepare a written report that summarizes your findings on the radioisotopes used, their half-lives, and their limitations.

97. Explain Research how technetium-99m is produced. What does the letter *m* at the end of its name stand for? How is the isotope used in bone imaging?

CHEMYSTERY

An Ice-Age Baby

Scientists were able to use carbon-14 dating to determine the age of the baby mammoth discovered in 2007. During Lyuba's short time on Earth, the ratio of carbon-14 to other carbon isotopes in her body was constant. After she died, the unstable carbon-14 atoms began to decay. The ratio of carbon-14 atoms to other carbon atoms was no longer fixed. Based on the ratio of carbon isotopes in the preserved sample, Lyuba lived and died about 40,000 years ago.

Archaeologists use the same method to date artifacts left behind by ancient cultures. An artifact is an object made or shaped by humans. Examples of artifacts are tools, weapons, and ornaments.

98. Calculate Approximately how many half-lives does 40,000 years represent? The half-life for carbon-14 is 5730 years.

99. Apply Concepts Archaeologists find a wooden bowl, a stone arrowhead, and a bone bead at a site that they suspect is about 40,000 years old. Which objects can they use to test their hypothesis? Explain.

100. Connect to the BIGIDEA Describe what happens to the structure of carbon-14 atoms as this isotope decays.

101. How many protons, neutrons, and electrons are in an atom of each isotope?

  a. iron-59

  b. uranium-235

  c. chromium-52

102. What is the Pauli exclusion principle? What is Hund's rule?

103. Identify the bonds between each pair of atoms as ionic or covalent.

  a. carbon and silicon

  b. calcium and fluorine

  c. sulfur and nitrogen

  d. bromine and cesium

104. The diagram below shows a water molecule. Identify the location of any partial positive and partial negative charges on the molecule. Then explain how the partial charges and their locations produce an attraction between different water molecules.

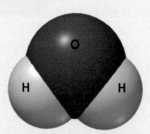

★105. A piece of magnesium with a mass of 10.00 g is added to sulfuric acid. How many cubic centimeters of hydrogen gas (at STP) will be produced if the magnesium reacts completely? How many moles of hydrogen gas are in this volume?

106. Balance the following equations.

  a. $Ca(OH)_2 + HCl \longrightarrow CaCl_2 + H_2O$

  b. $Fe_2O_3 + H_2 \longrightarrow Fe + H_2O$

  c. $NaHCO_3 + H_2SO_4 \longrightarrow$
                          $Na_2SO_4 + CO_2 + H_2O$

  d. $C_2H_6 + O_2 \longrightarrow CO_2 + H_2O$

★107. You have a 0.30M solution of sodium sulfate. What volume (in mL) must be measured to give 0.0020 mol of sodium sulfate?

108. Draw the structural formula for each compound.

  a. 2,2-dimethylhexane

  b. 1,2-dimethylcyclopentane

  c. 2-methyl-2-heptene

  d. 2-butyne

  e. 1,4-dimethylbenzene

  f. 3-ethyloctane

109. Name each compound.

  a. CH_3CH_2COOH

  b. CH_3CH_2CHO

  c. $CH_3CH_2CH_2OH$

  d. $CH_3CH_2CH_2NH_2$

  e. $CH_3CH_2CH_2Cl$

  f. $CH_3CH_2OCH_3$

110. For each pair of compounds, which is the more highly oxidized?

  a. ethanol and ethanal

  b. ethane and ethene

  c. ethanoic acid and ethanal

  d. ethyne and ethane

111. What two compounds result from the acid-catalyzed hydrolysis of propyl ethanoate?

112. Which of these classes of compounds does not contain a carbon–oxygen double bond?

  a. amide

  b. ketone

  c. aldehyde

  d. carboxylic acid

113. Match a numbered item with each term.

  a. amino acid   **(1)** carbohydrate

  b. fat   **(2)** nucleic acid

  c. monosaccharide   **(3)** lipid

  d. peptide bond   **(4)** protein

  e. sugar

  f. DNA

  g. saponification

  h. genetic code

  i. enzyme

  j. triglyceride

If You Have Trouble With...

Question	101	102	103	104	105	106	107	108	109	110	111	112	113
See Chapter	4	5	8	8	12	11	16	22	23	23	23	23	24

Standardized Test Prep

Tips for Success

Anticipate the Answer Use what you know to decide what you think the answer should be. Then see if your answer, or one similar to it, is given as a choice.

Select the choice that best answers each question.

1. If a radioisotope undergoes beta emission,
   (A) the atomic number changes.
   (B) the number of neutrons remains constant.
   (C) the isotope loses a proton.
   (D) the mass number changes.

2. The radioisotope radon-222 has a half-life of 3.8 days. How much of an initial 20.0-g sample of radon-222 would remain after 15.2 days?
   (A) 5.00 g   (C) 1.25 g
   (B) 12.5 g   (D) 2.50 g

3. Spent fuel rods from nuclear reactors
   (A) are no longer radioactive.
   (B) are stored under water for at least a decade.
   (C) contain only one isotope of uranium, ^{238}U.
   (D) remain radioactive for less than 100 years.

4. What particle is needed to balance this equation?
   $$^{27}_{13}\text{Al} + ^{4}_{2}\text{He} \longrightarrow ? + ^{30}_{15}\text{P}$$

For each nuclear equation in Questions 5–8, name the particle that is being emitted or captured.

5. $^{59}_{26}\text{Fe} \longrightarrow ^{59}_{27}\text{Co} + ^{0}_{-1}e$

6. $^{185}_{79}\text{Au} \longrightarrow ^{181}_{77}\text{Ir} + ^{4}_{2}\text{He}$

7. $^{59}_{27}\text{Co} + ^{1}_{0}n \longrightarrow ^{60}_{27}\text{Co}$

8. $^{118}_{54}\text{Xe} \longrightarrow ^{118}_{53}\text{I} + ^{0}_{+1}e$

Use the drawings of atomic nuclei to answer Questions 9 and 10.

9. Write the name and symbol for each isotope.

10. Which isotope is radioactive?

(A)   (B)   (C)

● Proton   ● Neutron

Use the graph to answer Questions 11–13.

Estimate the percent remaining of the radioisotope after the given number of half-lives.

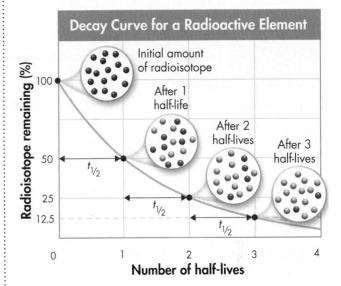

11. 0.5 $t_{1/2}$

12. 1.25 $t_{1/2}$

13. 3.75 $t_{1/2}$

The lettered choices below refer to Questions 14–17. A lettered choice may be used once, more than once, or not at all.
   (A) film badge
   (B) radioactive tracer
   (C) radiation therapy
   (D) neutron activation analysis
   (E) Geiger counter

Which of the above items or processes is best described by each of the following applications?

14. treating some cancers

15. detecting ionizing radiation

16. monitoring exposure to radiation

17. diagnosing some diseases

If You Have Trouble With...

Question	1	2	3	4	5	6	7	8	9	10	11	12	13	14	15	16	17
See Lesson	25.1	25.2	25.3	25.3	25.1	25.1	25.3	25.2	25.1	25.2	25.2	25.2	25.2	25.4	25.4	25.4	25.4

Appendix A

Elements Handbook

ELEMENTS AROUND YOU AND WITHIN YOU

Elements in Earth's Crust

Element	Parts per million
Oxygen	466,000
Silicon	277,000
Aluminum	82,000
Iron	41,000
Calcium	41,000
Sodium	23,000
Potassium	21,000
Magnesium	21,000
Titanium	4400
Hydrogen	1400

Elements in the Atmosphere

Element	Parts per million*
Nitrogen	780,900
Oxygen	209,500
Argon	9300
Neon	18
Helium	5.2
Krypton	1.14
Hydrogen	0.5
Xenon	0.086
Radon	Traces

*Data is for dry air.

Elements Dissolved in the Oceans

Element	Parts per million
Chlorine	19,400
Sodium	10,800
Magnesium	1300
Sulfur	904
Calcium	411
Potassium	392
Bromine	67
Carbon	28
Strontium	8
Boron	5

Elements in the Human Body

Element	Percent of total body mass
Oxygen	61
Carbon	23
Hydrogen	10
Nitrogen	2.6
Calcium	1.4
Phosphorus	1.1
Sulfur	0.2
Potassium	0.2
Sodium	0.14
Chlorine	0.12

GROUP 1A

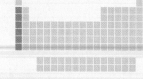

3	2 1
Li	
Lithium	
6.941	

Lithium discovered in 1817 by Johan August Arfvedson

11	2 8 1
Na	
Sodium	
22.990	

Sodium discovered in 1807 by Sir Humphry Davy

19	2 8 8 1
K	
Potassium	
39.098	

Potassium discovered in 1807 by Sir Humphry Davy

37	2 8 18 8 1
Rb	
Rubidium	
85.468	

Rubidium discovered in 1861 by Robert Bunsen & Gustav Kirchhoff

55	2 8 18 18 8 1
Cs	
Cesium	
132.91	

Cesium discovered in 1860 by Robert Bunsen & Gustav Kirchhoff

87	2 8 18 32 18 8 1
Fr	
Francium	
(223)	

Francium discovered in 1939 by Marguerite Perey

Physical Properties

- Alkali metals are silver-gray solids that are soft enough to cut with a knife. They are soft because they have only one valence electron.

- The presence of a single valence electron also explains the low melting points and boiling points of alkali metals.

Pure alkali metals are stored under oil because they will react with oxygen and moisture in air.

Melting and Boiling Points

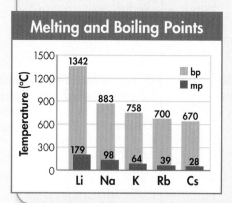

Density

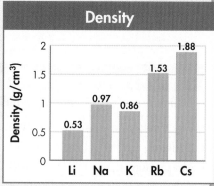

Sources

- Alkali metals do not occur uncombined in nature because they are highly reactive.

- Sodium occurs widely as sodium chloride in underground salt and brine deposits. It is a major component of seawater.

- Sodium is the only alkali metal manufactured on a large scale. It is generally produced by the electrolysis of molten sodium chloride.

$$2NaCl(l) \longrightarrow 2Na(l) + Cl_2(g)$$

Lithium and potassium are produced by a similar process.

- The mineral sylvite, KCl, is a source of potassium.

Manufacture of Sodium

NaCl(s)

Cl₂(g)

Na(l)

Molten NaCl

Molten Na

Steel cathode (–)

Iron screen

Graphite anode (+)

Atomic Properties

- Alkali metals have an electron configuration that ends in ns^1.
- The alkali metals are the most reactive metals.
- Alkali metals form ions with a 1+ charge.
- The atoms of alkali metals are the largest in their periods.
- Cesium is a good reducing agent because its first ionization energy is very low.

First Ionization Energy

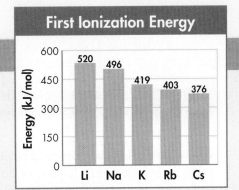

Li	Na	K	Rb	Cs
520	496	419	403	376

Energy (kJ/mol)

Electronegativity

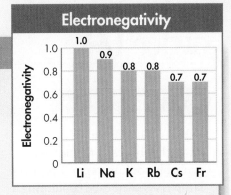

Li	Na	K	Rb	Cs	Fr
1.0	0.9	0.8	0.8	0.7	0.7

Electronegativity

	Li	Na	K	Rb	Cs
Atomic radius (pm)	156	191	238	255	273
Ionic radius (pm)	60 Li^+	95 Na^+	133 K^+	148 Rb^+	169 Cs^+

Alkali metals can be identified by the colors produced when their compounds are heated in a flame.

Lithium   Sodium   Potassium   Rubidium   Cesium

Important Compounds and Reactions

- All alkali metals react with water to form an alkaline solution. Example:

$$2K(s) + 2H_2O(l) \longrightarrow 2KOH(aq) + H_2(g)$$

- All alkali metals react with halogens to form an ionic halide. Example:

$$2Cs(s) + Cl_2(g) \longrightarrow 2CsCl(s)$$
$$\Delta H = -442.8 \text{ kJ/mol}$$

- When heated, sodium hydrogen carbonate (baking soda) produces $CO_2(g)$ and steam, which causes baked goods to rise.

$$2NaHCO_3(s) \xrightarrow{\Delta} Na_2CO_3(s) + CO_2(g) + H_2O(g)$$
$$\Delta H = 129 \text{ kJ/mol}$$

- Lithium hydride is a convenient source for preparing hydrogen.

$$LiH(s) + H_2O(l) \longrightarrow LiOH(aq) + H_2(g)$$

- Potassium superoxide, KO_2, is a source of oxygen in submarines. It removes CO_2 from the atmosphere as it produces oxygen.

$$4KO_2(s) + 2CO_2(g) \longrightarrow 2K_2CO_3(s) + 3O_2(g).$$

- Sodium hypochlorite, NaClO, is used as a bleach and to disinfect swimming pools.
- Sodium hydrogen carbonate, $NaHCO_3$, is used in fire extinguishers.
- Potassium nitrate, KNO_3, is used in matches and chemical fertilizers.
- Sodium hydroxide, NaOH, is used as a drain cleaner. It is also used to produce other chemicals and in many industrial processes.

Uses of NaOH

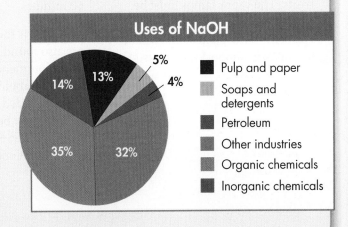

■ Pulp and paper	5%
■ Soaps and detergents	4%
■ Petroleum	13%
■ Other industries	14%
■ Organic chemicals	35%
■ Inorganic chemicals	32%

GROUP 1A

Na Vapor Lamps

When streetlights have a golden glow, the source of the light is probably sodium vapor. Inside the lamp is a sealed tube containing a sodium-mercury alloy and a starter gas, such as xenon. Electrodes at each end of the tube are connected to an electric circuit. When the lamp is on, a spark, or arc, forms between the electrodes. The arc produces enough heat to vaporize the sodium and mercury atoms. Within the arc, atoms ionize. Outside the arc, ions recombine with electrons and light is emitted—yellow for sodium and blue-green for mercury.

A sodium vapor lamp uses less energy than most other light sources and costs less to operate. But the lamp isn't a perfect light source. The color of an object is visible only when light of that color is reflected off the object. So yellow lines on the pavement appear yellow under a sodium vapor lamp, but a red stop sign appears gray.

People who grow plants under artificial light may use sodium vapor lamps to stimulate the production of flowers and fruits. The vapor lamps must be combined with other light sources. Otherwise, the plant stems will be too weak to support the plants.

Na K Restoring Electrolytes

"Don't sweat it" may be good advice for handling stress, but not for maintaining a healthy body. The sweat you produce on a hot day or during exercise cools your body as it evaporates. Sweat consists mainly of water, sodium chloride, and small amounts of other inorganic salts. The salts are electrolytes that help keep the volume of body fluids constant. Electrolytes produce ions when they dissolve in water.

Body fluids contain sodium ions and potassium ions. Potassium ions are the principal cations inside cells. Sodium ions are the principal cations in the fluids outside of cells. The transmission of nerve impulses depends on the movement of sodium and potassium ions across the membranes of nerve cells. Potassium ions cause the heart muscle to relax between heartbeats.

Replacing the water lost during exercise is important, but not sufficient. Electrolytes must be replaced too. Some signs of electrolyte depletion are muscle cramps, nausea, and an inability to think clearly. Many athletes use sports drinks to replace electrolytes. Some experts recommend these drinks for people who lose more than 8 liters of sweat daily or exercise continuously for more than 60 minutes.

Bananas account for about one-third of the fresh fruit consumed in the United States.

Table salt is the chief source of sodium in the diet. But large amounts are also found in unexpected places, such as eggs. For a healthy adult, the recommended daily intake of sodium chloride is about 5 grams per day—about half the amount many people consume. The daily recommended amount of potassium is about 1 gram. The word *daily* is important because your kidneys excrete potassium even when the supply is low. Eating foods high in potassium and low in sodium is ideal. Such foods include bananas, chicken, and orange juice.

Cs Cesium Atomic Clock

Some watches contain a quartz crystal that vibrates at a constant rate. The vibration provides the "beat" that is translated into the time you see displayed. A clock with a quartz crystal is more accurate than a mechanical clock, which has moving parts that can be worn down by friction. But a quartz crystal isn't accurate enough for modern communication and navigation systems.

For greater accuracy, you need an atomic clock, which may gain or lose only one second in a million years! In most atomic clocks, cesium-133 atoms provide the "beat." Unlike quartz crystals, all cesium-133 atoms are identical and they don't wear out with use. The clock is designed so that the atoms repeatedly absorb and emit radiation. The emitted radiation has a frequency of exactly 9,192,631,770 cycles per second. The cycles are counted and translated into seconds, minutes, and hours.

There are four cesium atomic clocks at the National Institute of Standards and Technology in Fort Collins, Colorado. Short-wave radio waves are useds to transmit accurate time signals from these clocks to most of North America. Clocks and watches advertised as "radio controlled" contain a tiny antenna and receiver that pick up the signal and decode the information. The owner sets the time zone. The radio signal sets the time.

Global Positioning System (GPS) receivers can pinpoint any location on Earth to within a few meters. The system depends on accurate time signals from atomic clocks in 24 Earth-orbiting satellites.

The GPS receiver in this car compares signals sent at exactly the same time from three different satellites to determine a location.

Na Salt of the Earth

In the ancient world, table salt (NaCl) was an extremely valuable commodity. Before refrigeration, salt was used to preserve foods such as meats and fish. As salt draws the water out of bacteria, they shrivel up and die. Sailors ("salty dogs") especially depended on salt pork and fish to survive long voyages.

Trade routes were established and roads were built to transport salt. In ancient China, coins were made of salt and taxes were levied on salt. Roman soldiers were paid an allotment called a *salarium argentum,* or "salt silver," from which the word *salary* is derived.

Li Bipolar Disorder

Millions of people in the United States experience the extreme mood swings of bipolar disorder. During a manic phase, they think they can conquer the world. During a depression, they may feel hopeless. The ionic compound lithium carbonate can be used to control these symptoms.

Exactly how the treatment works is not known. Scientists do know that lithium ions can increase the level of serotonin. Serotonin is one of the chemical messengers (neurotransmitters) that transmit messages between brain cells.

Did You Know?

Most alkali metals are stored under oil. But **lithium** has such a low density that it floats on oil. So a coat of petroleum jelly is applied to lithium before it is stored.

GROUP 2A

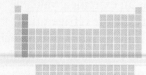

4	2 2
Be	
Beryllium 9.0122	

Beryllium discovered in 1798 by Nicholas Vauquelin

12	2 8 2
Mg	
Magnesium 24.305	

Magnesium isolated in 1808 by Sir Humphry Davy

20	2 8 8 2
Ca	
Calcium 40.08	

Calcium discovered in 1808 by Sir Humphry Davy

38	2 8 18 8 2
Sr	
Strontium 87.62	

Strontium discovered in 1808 by Sir Humphry Davy

56	2 8 18 18 2
Ba	
Barium 137.33	

Barium discovered in 1808 by Sir Humphry Davy

88	2 8 18 32 18 8 2
Ra	
Radium (226)	

Radium discovered in 1898 by Marie Curie & Pierre Curie

Physical Properties

- Alkaline earth metals are relatively soft, but harder than alkali metals.
- Alkaline earth metals have a gray white luster when freshly cut. When exposed to air, they quickly form a tough, thin oxide coating.
- Densities, melting points, and boiling points tend to be higher than for the alkali metal in the same period.
- Magnesium alloys are strong and lightweight. They are used in cameras, lawnmowers, aircraft, and automobiles.

Melting and Boiling Points

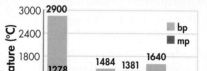

Density

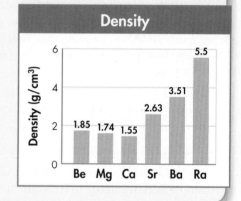

Sources

- Alkaline earth metals are not found in nature in the elemental state.
- Many mountain ranges contain alkaline earth carbonates—limestone ($CaCO_3$) and dolomite ($CaCO_3 \cdot MgCO_3$).
- Barium is produced by reducing its oxide with aluminum at high temperature.

$$3BaO(s) + 2Al(s) \longrightarrow 3Ba(l) + Al_2O_3(s)$$

- Salts of highly radioactive radium are by-products of uranium refining.

Oyster shells containing $CaCO_3$ are used to extract magnesium from seawater. The chlorine gas produced during the electrolysis of magnesium chloride is fed back into the process.

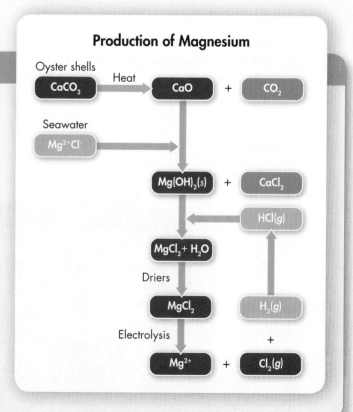

Production of Magnesium

Atomic Properties

- Alkaline earth metals have an electron configuration that ends in ns^2.

- The alkaline earth metals are strong reducing agents, losing 2 electrons and forming ions with a 2+ charge.

- Because radium is luminous, it was once used to make the hands and numbers on watches glow in the dark.

- The ratio of ^{87}Sr to ^{86}Sr varies with location. This data is used to solve puzzles, such as the source of timber used in prehistoric buildings.

First Ionization Energy

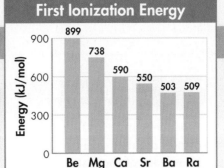

Energy (kJ/mol)

Be	Mg	Ca	Sr	Ba	Ra
899	738	590	550	503	509

Electronegativity

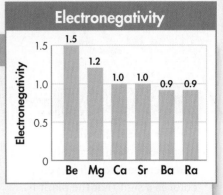

Electronegativity

Be	Mg	Ca	Sr	Ba	Ra
1.5	1.2	1.0	1.0	0.9	0.9

	Be	Mg	Ca	Sr	Ba	Ra
Atomic radius (pm)	113	160	197	215	224	223
Ionic radius (pm)	44 Be^{2+}	66 Mg^{2+}	99 Ca^{2+}	112 Sr^{2+}	134 Ba^{2+}	143 Ra^{2+}

Calcium, strontium, and barium can be identified by the colors produced when their compounds are heated in a flame.

Calcium   Strontium   Barium

Important Compounds and Reactions

- Alkaline earth metals are less reactive than alkali metals.

- Alkaline earth metals react with halogens to form ionic halides. Example:

$$Mg(s) + Br_2(l) \longrightarrow MgBr_2(s)$$

- All Group 2A metals (except Be) react with water to form an alkaline solution. Example:

$$Sr(s) + 2H_2O(l) \longrightarrow Sr(OH)_2(aq) + H_2(g)$$

- Alkaline earth metals react with oxygen to form binary oxides. Example:

$$2Ca(s) + O_2(g) \longrightarrow 2CaO(s)$$
$$\Delta H = -635.1 \text{ kJ/mol}$$

- Heating limestone produces lime, CaO.

$$CaCO_3(s) \xrightarrow{\Delta} CaO(s) + CO_2(g)$$
$$\Delta H = 176 \text{ kJ/mol}$$

- Slaked lime, $Ca(OH)_2$, reacts with carbon dioxide to form limestone.

$$Ca(OH)_2(s) + CO_2(g) \longrightarrow CaCO_3(s) + H_2O(g)$$

- Barium peroxide is used as a dry powdered bleach. It reacts with water to form the bleaching agent, hydrogen peroxide.

$$BaO_2(s) + 2H_2O(l) \longrightarrow H_2O_2(aq) + Ba(OH)_2(aq)$$

- Gypsum, calcium sulfate dihydrate, $CaSO_4 \cdot 2H_2O$, is used to make plasterboard.

- Calcium phosphate, $Ca_3(PO_4)_2$, is the major component of bone and tooth enamel.

Slaked lime is an ingredient in plaster, cement, and the mortar used in this stone wall.

GROUP 2A

Mg Chlorophyll

A plant that is deprived of magnesium will turn yellow and eventually die. The yellow color is a sign that the plant is not producing enough of the green pigment chlorophyll, which is found in structures called chloroplasts. One square millimeter of a leaf's surface contains about half a million chloroplasts. In chloroplasts, light energy is changed to chemical energy.

Chlorophyll molecules absorb wavelengths of blue light and red light, and reflect green light. There is a magnesium ion at the center of each chlorophyll molecule. It is embedded like a jewel in a crown-like ring. The magnesium ion forms a bond with each nitrogen atom.

Chlorophyll a

Chlorophyll is typical of a family of compounds called porphyrins, which contain a central metal ion. In heme, the ion is Fe^{2+}. There are four heme molecules in hemoglobin, which transports oxygen in the blood.

Sr Ba Fireworks

Producing an aerial fireworks display requires skill and knowledge of chemistry. Shells are stored in steel pipes anchored in sand. A typical shell contains two charges, one to launch the shell and one to cause the shell to burst. When the lifting charge explodes, the shell is blown out of the pipe and the fuse attached to the bursting charge ignites. The shell travels for a few seconds before it bursts.

The name of this fireworks effect is chrysanthemum.

The explosions that launch the shells and cause them to burst are exothermic redox reactions. The reducing agent, or fuel, may be aluminum, magnesium, or sulfur. The oxidizing agent may be a nitrate, a chlorate, or a perchlorate, such as potassium perchlorate ($KClO_4$).

When a shell bursts, it releases tiny pellets called "stars," which produce the colors. Only a few elements are needed to produce these colors. Two are alkaline earth metals, strontium for bright red and barium for light green. These same colors are produced when strontium and barium compounds are heated in a flame. Flame tests can identify elements because an element emits characteristic wavelengths of light when its electrons absorb energy and then return to the ground state.

Labels for shells used in a fireworks display describe the color and effect produced by the shell.

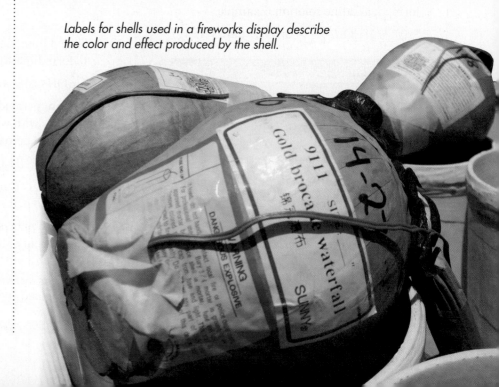

Ca Limestone Caves

The chemical reactions that form a limestone cave are simple. Carbon dioxide in the air dissolves in rain to form weak carbonic acid, H_2CO_3. As rain passes through soil, it dissolves carbon dioxide produced by decaying plants and becomes even more acidic. The rainwater seeps into limestone, $CaCO_3$, beneath the soil. The $CaCO_3$ dissolves in the carbonic acid, forming a solution of calcium hydrogen carbonate, $Ca(HCO_3)_2$.

$$CaCO_3(s) + H_2CO_3(aq) \longrightarrow Ca^{2+}(aq) + 2HCO_3^-(aq)$$

Over millions of years, as more and more limestone dissolves, a cave forms and slowly grows in size. Once the cave stops growing, another process may occur. Calcium hydrogen carbonate solution drips through the cave's roof. Carbon dioxide is released from solution, leaving behind a tiny deposit of solid calcium carbonate.

$$Ca^{2+}(aq) + 2HCO_3^-(aq) \longrightarrow$$
$$CaCO_3(s) + CO_2(g) + H_2O(l)$$

The deposit slowly grows into a stalactite, which hangs from the ceiling like an icicle. Drops of solution that fall from the ceiling form stalagmites on the cave floor. Calcium carbonate is white. So any color in the deposits is due to traces of metal ions, such as copper (blue-green) and iron (red-brown). The growth rate of the formations depends mainly on the volume of water that drips through the roof and the concentration of calcium hydrogen carbonate in the water. In many caves, the rate of growth is measured in centimeters per hundreds or thousands of years.

Stalactites and stalagmites may join together to form columns.

Ca Building Strong Bones

As a young adult, you can have a major effect on the health of your bones later in life. You acquire 90% of the bone tissue in your skeleton before age 18 as females and age 20 as males. Physical activity and the amount of calcium in your diet are factors that affect the buildup of bone mass.

To maintain a constant level of calcium in your blood, your body may release calcium from bone tissue. If enough calcium is lost from bones, they become brittle and tend to break easily. This condition, known as osteoporosis, is most common in older people. However, it can occur in young and middle-aged adults.

The recommended daily intake of calcium from age 9 to age 18 is 1.3 g per day. This is the amount of calcium in a liter of milk. Calcium-fortified foods, such as orange juice, are a good choice for those who cannot digest the lactose in milk.

Vitamin D helps your body absorb calcium. The vitamin D your skin produces when exposed to sunlight is usually not enough to meet your daily requirement. So orange juice is also fortified with vitamin D.

Did You Know?

Calcium oxide (lime) emits a bright white light when it is heated. Before electric lights, theaters could spotlight a single actor by focusing the light from heated lime. Thus, the expression *in the limelight* describes a person in a prominent position.

GROUP 3A

5	$^2_3$
B	
Boron	
10.81	

Boron discovered in 1808 by Sir Humphry Davy and by Joseph-Louis Gay-Lussac & Louis-Jacques Thénard

13	$^2_8$ $_3$
Al	
Aluminum	
26.982	

Aluminum discovered in 1825 by Hans Christian Oersted

31	$^2_8$ $^{18}_3$
Ga	
Gallium	
69.72	

Gallium discovered in 1875 by Paul-Emile Lecoq de Boisbaudran

49	$^2_8$ $^{18}_{18}$ $_3$
In	
Indium	
114.82	

Indium discovered in 1863 by Ferdinand Reich & Hieronymus T. Richter

81	$^2_8$ $^{18}_{32}$ $^{18}_3$
Tl	
Thallium	
204.37	

Thallium discovered in 1861 by Sir William Crookes

Physical Properties

- Boron is a metalloid. The rest of the Group 3A elements are metals.

- Aluminum is a valuable structural material because of its strength, especially in alloys with silicon or iron. These alloys have a low density and resist corrosion.

- Gallium has an extremely wide liquid temperature range (30°C to 2204°C). Solid gallium floats in liquid gallium, which is unusual for a metal.

Boron is black, lustrous, and extremely hard, but brittle.

Melting and Boiling Points

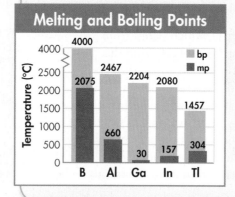

Density

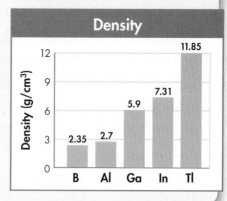

Sources

- Boron is always combined with oxygen in nature. Boron can be prepared by the reaction of its oxide with magnesium metal.

$$B_2O_3(s) + 3Mg(s) \longrightarrow 2B(s) + 3MgO(s)$$

- Bauxite is a common ore of aluminum. The primary mineral in bauxite is alumina, Al_2O_3, which is reduced to aluminum by electrolysis.

- Gallium, indium, and thallium are quite rare. They are typically extracted from ores being processed to extract other metals.

The conveyor belt is being used to unload bauxite from a train. Bauxite is a major source of aluminum. It is also a source of gallium.

Atomic Properties

- Group 3A elements have an electron configuration that ends in ns^2np^1.

- The most common oxidation number for boron, aluminum, gallium, and indium is +3. For thallium, it is +1.

- Group 3A elements become more metallic from top to bottom within the group.

- Radioactive thallium-201 is injected into patients taking a stress test used in the diagnosis of heart disease.

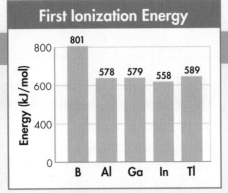

First Ionization Energy

Energy (kJ/mol)

B	Al	Ga	In	Tl
801	578	579	558	589

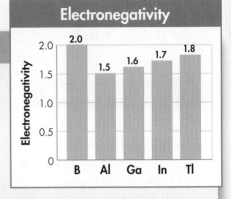

Electronegativity

Electronegativity

B	Al	Ga	In	Tl
2.0	1.5	1.6	1.7	1.8

	B	Al	Ga	In	Tl
Atomic radius (pm)	83	143	141	166	172
Ionic radius (pm)	23 B^{3+}	51 Al^{3+}	62 Ga^{3+}	81 In^{3+}	95 Tl^{3+}

Important Compounds and Reactions

- Group 3A elements react with halogens to form halides. Example:

$$2Al(s) + 3Cl_2(g) \longrightarrow 2AlCl_3(s)$$

Aluminum chloride is used as a catalyst in organic reactions.

- Group 3A elements react with oxygen to form oxides. Example:

$$4Al(s) + 3O_2(g) \longrightarrow 2Al_2O_3(s)$$
$$\Delta H = -1676 \text{ kJ/mol}$$

Because this reaction is so exothermic, powdered aluminum is a component of some explosives, fireworks, and rocket fuels.

- Aluminum sulfate (alum), $Al_2(SO_4)_3 \cdot 18H_2O$, is used as a coagulant in water treatment plants.

- Gallium arsenide, GaAs, converts electric current to light in light-emitting diodes (LEDs). It is produced as follows.

$$(CH_3)_3Ga(g) + AsH_3(g) \longrightarrow GaAs(s) + 3CH_4(g)$$

This LED is shown at about five times actual size.

Corundum is a mineral form of aluminum oxide. Rubies are corundum in which a few aluminum ions have been replaced by chromium ions.

- Borax, $Na_2B_4O_7 \cdot 10H_2O$, is used to soften water and is found in glasses and glazes. When a mixture of borax and hydrochloric acid is heated, boric acid is produced.

$$Na_2B_4O_7(aq) + 2HCl(aq) + 5H_2O(l) \longrightarrow$$
$$4H_3BO_3(aq) + 2NaCl(aq)$$

- Boric acid is poisonous if ingested. The solid is used as an insecticide against cockroaches. A dilute solution of boric acid is an eyewash.

- Boron carbide, B_4C, is almost as hard as diamond. It is used for items that must resist wear, such as cutting tools.

- Laboratory glassware is made of heat-resistant glass containing 12% to 15% boric oxide.

In | Uses of Indium

Indium is a soft metal with a low melting point of 157°C. One useful property of liquid indium is its ability to "wet" glass. It spreads out and forms a thin layer on the glass instead of beading up. This property allows indium to be deposited on glass to make mirrors that are as reflective, but more corrosion-resistant, than silvered mirrors.

Low-melting alloys that contain indium are used as solders to join glass to glass. They also can join a metal to a metal at low temperatures. There are products, such as electronics components, that could be damaged if joined at a high temperature. The seals of some fire sprinkler heads are held in place by indium alloys. When heat from a fire melts the alloy, the seal is released, which allows water to pour from the sprinkler head.

Al | Recycling Aluminum

Lightweight, durable aluminum has many uses. When aluminum parts replace steel parts in vehicles, less fuel is needed to travel the same distance. About 20% of the aluminum produced is used for packaging, including foil and cans.

In the United States, over 80 billion aluminum soft drink cans are sold each year. More than 50% of these cans are recycled. The energy saved by recycling just one of these cans could be used to operate a television for three hours. The energy needed to recycle aluminum is 5% of the energy needed to obtain new aluminum from ore. An added benefit of recycling is a reduction in solid waste.

Recycled aluminum cans are shredded, crushed, and heated to remove materials other than aluminum. Aluminum pieces about the size of a potato chip are placed in furnaces where they are mixed with new aluminum and melted. Then, the molten aluminum is poured into 7.6-m ingots that have a mass of about 13,600 kg. The ingots pass through rolling mills that reduce their thickness from about 0.5 m to about 0.25 mm. The thin sheets are coiled and shipped to a manufacturer who produces the bodies and tops of the cans. Aluminum from a recycled can is part of a new can within 60 days.

Aluminum is used in durable consumer goods such as baseball bats.

Aluminum cans are compressed before being shipped to aluminum companies for recycling.

Al Manufacturing Aluminum

Aluminum is the most abundant metal in Earth's crust (8.3% by mass). It is found in minerals such as bauxite (impure aluminum oxide, Al_2O_3). But for years after its discovery, there wasn't a practical way to extract aluminum from its ores. This rare and expensive metal was used, like gold, mainly for decoration.

A professor at Oberlin College in Ohio challenged his class to find an inexpensive way to produce aluminum. In 1885, Charles Hall responded to the challenge. He set up a laboratory in a woodshed. He knew that other chemists had tried to decompose aluminum oxide by electrolysis. This method was not practical because the melting point of aluminum oxide is quite high (2045°C). Hall found that mixing aluminum oxide with cryolite (Na_3AlF_6) produced a mixture that melted at a much lower temperature of 1012°C.

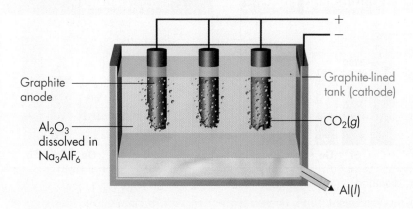

Graphite anode

Al_2O_3 dissolved in Na_3AlF_6

Graphite-lined tank (cathode)

$CO_2(g)$

$Al(l)$

The process Hall invented is often called the Hall-Heroult process. Paul Heroult, a 23-year-old Frenchman, developed the same process almost simultaneously. It is still used today. Pure aluminum oxide is extracted from bauxite through heating to a temperature above 1000°C. The aluminum oxide is dissolved in molten cryolite and contained in a graphite-lined iron tank. The graphite rods used as an anode are consumed during the process.

$$\text{Anode: } C(s) + 2O^{2-}(l) \longrightarrow CO_2(g) + 4e^-$$

$$\text{Cathode: } 3e^- + Al^{3+}(l) \longrightarrow Al(l)$$

The products are carbon dioxide and molten aluminum metal. Because the aluminum is more dense than the aluminum oxide-cryolite mixture, it collects at the bottom of the tank and is drawn off periodically.

Al Anodized Aluminum

If an aluminum object, such as a flashlight, has a color other than silver, it was anodized before it was dyed. The main goal of anodizing is to protect the aluminum from corrosion by coating it with aluminum oxide. The ability to be dyed is an added benefit.

The aluminum object becomes the anode in an electrolytic cell. The electrolyte is a dilute acid. When an electric current flows through the cell, aluminum oxide forms on the surface of the aluminum.

The oxide layer is thin, hard, and dense. It contains tiny pores, which can absorb an organic dye. If a dyed piece is placed in boiling water, the oxide layer absorbs water and swells. The swelling closes the pores and seals in the dye. Because the oxide layer is so thin, the silver of the aluminum base is visible through the dye and gives the object a metallic sheen.

Did You Know?

Indium's name comes from indigo, a bright line in its emission spectrum. Indium will emit a high-pitched sound when it is bent. Tin and gallium also "cry" when bent.

GROUP 4A

Carbon known since ancient times

6	2 4
C	
Carbon	
12.011	

Silicon discovered in 1824 by Jöns Jacob Berzelius

14	2 8 4
Si	
Silicon	
28.086	

Germanium discovered in 1886 by Clemens Winkler

32	2 8 18 4
Ge	
Germanium	
72.59	

Tin known since ancient times

50	2 8 18 18 4
Sn	
Tin	
118.69	

Lead known since ancient times

82	2 8 18 32 18 4
Pb	
Lead	
207.2	

Physical Properties

- Group 4A elements are all solids at room temperature.
- The metallic properties of Group 4A elements increase from carbon to lead.
- Diamond, graphite, and buckminsterfullerene are three allotropes of carbon.

Phase Diagram of Carbon

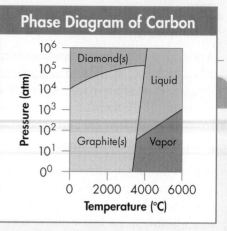

Graphite is more stable than diamond at STP, but the activation energy is too high for diamond to change to graphite at these conditions.

Melting and Boiling Points

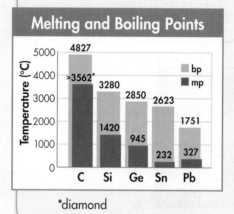

*diamond

Density

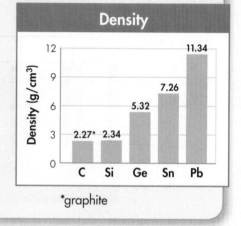

*graphite

Sources

- Carbon is found in nature as an element, in Earth's atmosphere as carbon dioxide, in Earth's crust as carbonate minerals, and in organic compounds produced in cells.

- Silicon can be produced by the reduction of silicon dioxide (silica) with magnesium, carbon, or aluminum. Example:

$$SiO_2(s) + 2Mg(s) \longrightarrow Si(s) + 2MgO(s)$$

- Tin is prepared by reduction of the mineral cassiterite, SnO_2.

$$SnO_2(s) + 2C(s) \longrightarrow 2CO(g) + Sn(s)$$

- Lead is refined from the mineral galena, PbS. Galena is heated in air to form a mixture of PbO and $PbSO_4$. Lead is produced through further reaction of these compounds with PbS.

Al_2SiO_5
andalusite

$AlSi_2O_5OH$
pyrophyllite

About 90% of the minerals in Earth's crust are silica and silicates. In silicates, each silicon atom is surrounded by three or four oxygen atoms. These units can be linked together in chains, sheets, rings, or crystals.

Atomic Properties

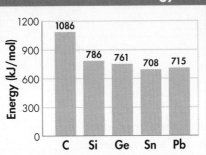

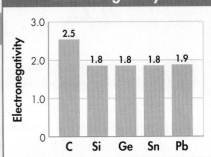

- Group 4A elements have an electron configuration that ends in ns^2np^2.

- For Group 4A elements, the most common oxidation numbers are $+4$ and $+2$. For carbon, -4 is also common.

- Silicon and germanium are semiconductors.

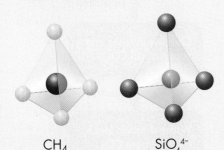

CH$_4$
methane molecule

SiO$_4^{4-}$
silicate ion

	C	Si	Ge	Sn	Pb
Atomic radius (pm)	77	109	122	139	175
Ionic radius (pm)	15 C^{4+}	41 Si^{4+}	53 Ge^{4+}	71 Sn^{4+}	84 Pb^{4+}

When carbon and silicon form four covalent bonds, there is often sp^3 hybridization. The result is compounds and ions with tetrahedral structures.

Important Compounds and Reactions

- Group 4A elements are oxidized by halogens.

$$Ge(s) + 2Cl_2(g) \longrightarrow GeCl_4(l)$$

- Group 4A elements combine with oxygen to form oxides. Example:

$$Sn(s) + O_2(g) \longrightarrow SnO_2(s)$$

- Complete combustion of hydrocarbons yields carbon dioxide and water. Example:

$$CH_4(g) + 2O_2(g) \longrightarrow CO_2(g) + 2H_2O(l)$$
$$\Delta H = -890 \text{ kJ/mol}$$

- Plants use carbon dioxide to produce carbohydrates and oxygen.

- Aqueous sodium silicate, Na_2SiO_3, is used as an adhesive for paper, as a binder in cement, and to stabilize shale during oil drilling.

$$SiO_2(s) + 2NaOH(aq) \longrightarrow Na_2SiO_3(aq) + H_2O(l)$$

- Acetylene is a fuel used for welding. It forms when calcium carbide and water react.

$$CaC_2(s) + 2H_2O(l) \longrightarrow C_2H_2(g) + Ca(OH)_2(aq)$$

- Tungsten carbide, WC, is used on the cutting surfaces of drill bits and saw blades.

- Tin(II) fluoride, SnF_2, is used in some toothpastes to prevent tooth decay.

Silicon dioxide, SiO$_2$, is the sand on many beaches. It is used to make glass, including glass that is "stained" with metallic salts. The pieces of glass in this window are held together with strips of lead.

GROUP 4A

C Green Chemistry

The term *green chemistry* was coined in 1992. It describes the effort to design chemical processes that don't use or produce hazardous substances. The goal is to protect the environment and conserve resources. For example, if a catalyst is used to reduce the temperature at which a reaction occurs, the process requires less energy.

Carbon dioxide is at the center of a green chemistry success story. Organic solvents are used to dissolve substances that are insoluble in water. Many of these solvents are toxic. It can be difficult to remove all traces of the toxic solvent from reaction products and safely recycle or dispose of the solvent. Supercritical carbon dioxide can replace some organic solvents.

A gas becomes a supercritical fluid at a temperature and pressure called its critical point. For carbon dioxide, this occurs at 31.1°C and about 100 atmospheres. At its critical point, carbon dioxide is in a hybrid state. It has a high density (like a liquid) but it is easily compressed (like a gas). Many organic compounds dissolve in supercritical carbon dioxide. The solvent is easily separated from a reaction mixture because it evaporates at room temperature and atmospheric pressure. It is also used to separate substances from mixtures. It can extract caffeine from coffee beans, dry-clean clothes, or clean circuit boards.

Decaffeinating Coffee

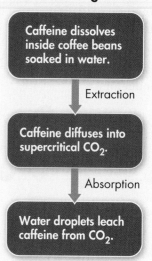

Caffeine dissolves inside coffee beans soaked in water.

↓ Extraction

Caffeine diffuses into supercritical CO_2.

↓ Absorption

Water droplets leach caffeine from CO_2.

After the caffeine is extracted, the coffee beans are dried and roasted. The aqueous solution of caffeine is sold to soft drink manufacturers.

Si Optical Glass

Glass is a material with the structure of a liquid, but the hardness of a solid. In most solids, the particles are arranged in an orderly lattice. In solid glass, the molecules remain disordered, as in a liquid. The main ingredient in most glass is silica (SiO_2), which is one of the few substances that can cool without crystallizing.

The glass used in eyeglasses, microscopes, and telescopes is called optical glass. This type of glass is purer than window glass and transmits more light. Optical glass can be drawn into long fibers that are used like tiny periscopes to view tissues deep within the human body.

In an optical fiber, light travels through a thin glass center called the core. A second glass layer reflects light back into the core.

An outer plastic layer protects the fiber from damage. The transmission of light signals through glass is called fiber optics.

When the fibers are bundled into cables, they often replace electrical cables in computer networks. They are also used to transmit television signals and phone calls over long distances.

With a cellular phone, you can call or text your friends from almost any location. Most phones also let you read and send e-mails, get directions, take a photograph, listen to music, or access the latest news. How can such a complex device be small enough to fit in your pocket? Semiconductor technology is responsible.

Silicon is a semiconductor. In its pure form, it conducts an electric current better than most nonmetals but not as well as metals. But its ability to conduct can be changed dramatically by doping, or adding traces of other elements, to the silicon crystal.

Doping with arsenic produces a donor, or n-type, semiconductor. Each arsenic atom has five valence electrons, compared with four for silicon. So there are extra electrons in the crystal. Doping with boron produces an acceptor, or p-type, semiconductor. Because boron has only three valence electrons, there is a positive "hole" in the crystal for every boron atom. The extra electrons or holes are free to move and conduct an electric current.

Combinations of n-type and p-type semiconductors are used to build tiny electronic components. An integrated circuit containing millions of components can fit on a small semiconductor wafer. The resulting "chip" can be used to control devices such as computers, calculators, DVD players, televisions, and phones.

Pure silicon

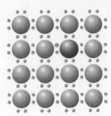

n-type (with arsenic)

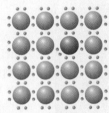

p-type (with boron)

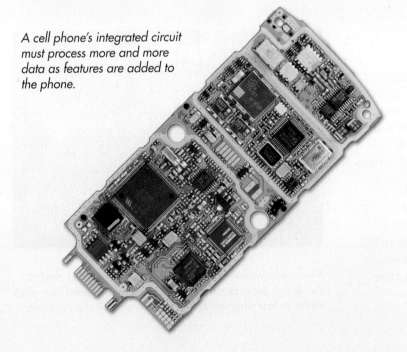

A cell phone's integrated circuit must process more and more data as features are added to the phone.

Buckminsterfullerene (C_{60}) is one member of a family of fullerenes. These structures are closed-cage spherical or nearly spherical forms of elemental carbon. The cages are networks of 20 to 600 carbon atoms.

Scientists have verified the existence of nesting spheres of fullerenes. C_{60} can be nested inside C_{240}, and this pair can be nested inside C_{540}. These nesting structures are sometimes called bucky-onions because they resemble the layers of an onion.

Dr. Sumio Iijima discovered a tubular fullerene, or carbon nanotube, in Japan in 1991.

Did You Know?

One name for diamonds is "ice." A diamond can quickly draw heat from your hand when you touch it. Such a high thermal conductivity is unusual for a substance containing covalent bonds.

GROUP 4A

There are gases in Earth's atmosphere that are called greenhouse gases because they act like the glass in a greenhouse. Sunlight easily passes through these gases to Earth's surface. Some of the solar energy is reflected off the surface as infrared radiation. This radiation is absorbed by greenhouse gases and radiated back to Earth. By trapping infrared radiation, the greenhouse gases keep Earth's surface about 33°C warmer than it would be otherwise.

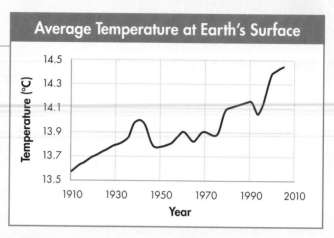

Average Temperature at Earth's Surface

With an increase in greenhouse gases, more infrared radiation is trapped, causing global warming.

The glass in a greenhouse traps infrared radiation.

Carbon dioxide (CO_2) is the most abundant greenhouse gas. It is released into the air as a product of cellular respiration and removed from the air during photosynthesis. Such interactions normally keep the amount of atmospheric CO_2 in check. But the burning of fossil fuels releases more than 20 billion metric tons of CO_2 every year. Also, as forests are cleared for agriculture, the ability of plants to remove CO_2 from the atmosphere is reduced.

Scientists agree that a rise of only a few degrees in Earth's temperature could cause problems. They disagree on how severe the problems could be. Could climates change so that farmlands become deserts? Could the melting of ice caps cause sea levels to rise until coastal cities are under water?

Si   Composite Materials

Most composites contain two distinctly different materials. The materials can be arranged in layers as when a sheet of plastic is sealed between panes of glass. Or a composite may consist of a matrix in which fibers of a second material are embedded. Often, the matrix is plastic. The fibers can be carbon.

Composites reinforced with carbon fibers are stronger than steel, yet light in weight. These composites are used in sports equipment, such as hockey sticks and golf clubs. It is less tiring to swing a tennis racket made from a carbon-fiber composite than one made from wood or metal. Carbon-fiber baseball bats act more like wood bats than do aluminum bats.

New aircraft often rely on composite materials. As part of the design process, a model of the plane is placed in a wind tunnel to test what will happen to the aircraft during flight.

C Recycling Plastics

At about 2 kg of waste per person per day, the United States leads the world in the production of solid waste. Luckily, the United States is also a leader in recycling. It is important to recycle plastics because they are made from crude oil, a non-renewable resource. Also, some plastics release toxic gases, such as hydrogen cyanide (HCN) and hydrogen chloride (HCl), when they burn in an incinerator. Finally, plastics are used for packaging material because they do not decay when exposed to sunlight, water, or microorganisms. The downside of this resistance to decay is that plastics can remain unchanged in dumps and landfills for decades.

Plastics are usually sorted by type before they are melted and reprocessed. The plastics industry has a code to identify types of plastics. The numeral 1 is assigned to polyethylene terephthalate (PET), which is used in soft-drink bottles. The numeral 2 refers to high-density polyethylene (HDPE), which is used in milk jugs and shampoo bottles. These are the two types in greatest demand. Carpets and clothing are made from recycled PET fibers. Recycled HDPE is used as a wood substitute for decks and benches.

Fleece clothing often contains post-consumer recycled (PCR) plastic.

Si Silicone Polymers

If you have worn hard contact lenses or used shaving cream, you have used a silicone. Silicone polymers have chains in which silicon and oxygen alternate. The properties of silicones depend on the groups that are bonded to the silicon atoms and the length of the chains.

In silicone rubber and resins, there are cross-links between the chains. These silicones repel water and remain elastic, even at low temperatures. They are used in space suits, as gaskets in airplane windows, and as sealants that are squeezed into place and left to harden.

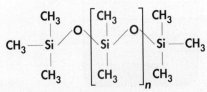

Polydimethylsiloxane

In polydimethylsiloxane, two methyl groups are bonded to each silicon atom in the chain. Polydimethylsiloxane is used as a lubricant in skin and suntan lotions.

C Carbon Monoxide

It is hard to detect colorless, odorless carbon monoxide gas. When it is inhaled, its molecules bind to the hemoglobin in red blood cells. They bind about 200 times more effectively than oxygen molecules do. So less oxygen reaches body tissues. Headaches, dizziness, nausea, and drowsiness are symptoms of low-level carbon monoxide poisoning. Higher levels of carbon monoxide are fatal.

The incomplete combustion of fuel in gas furnaces and space heaters produces carbon monoxide. It also forms, to some degree, in all internal combustion engines. In the United States, cars have catalytic converters, which convert carbon monoxide to carbon dioxide. In most communities, home owners are required to install devices that monitor the carbon monoxide concentration.

Cigarette smoke contains carbon monoxide. The carbon monoxide from one cigarette can remain in a smoker's blood for several hours. Smoking increases the risk of heart attacks because the heart must pump harder to deliver oxygen to cells when the level of oxygen in the blood is reduced.

Did You Know?

Members of the Scott expedition to the South Pole in 1912 may have died because of **tin.** Their supply of paraffin fuel leaked out through tiny holes in the tin-soldered joints of the storage cans because tin slowly changes to a powder below 13°C.

GROUP 5A

Nitrogen discovered in 1772 by Daniel Rutherford

7	2 5
N	
Nitrogen 14.007	

Phosphorus discovered in 1669 by Hennig Brand

15	2 8 5
P	
Phosphorus 30.974	

Arsenic discovered in 1250 by Albertus Magnus

33	2 8 18 5
As	
Arsenic 74.922	

Antimony discovered in 1600s or earlier

51	2 8 18 18 5
Sb	
Antimony 121.75	

Bismuth described in 1450 by Basil Valentine; shown to be a distinct element in 1753 by Claude-François Geoffroy

83	2 8 18 32 18 5
Bi	
Bismuth 208.98	

Physical Properties

- Except for nitrogen gas, Group 5A elements are solid at room temperature.
- The metallic properties of Group 5A elements increase from top to bottom within the group. N and P are nonmetals. As and Sb are metalloids. Bi is a metal.
- Liquid nitrogen is a cryogen, a liquid refrigerant that boils below −190°C.
- Phosphorus has 10 allotropes including white and red.

White phosphorus is very reactive and must be stored under water. Red phosphorus is much more stable.

Melting and Boiling Points

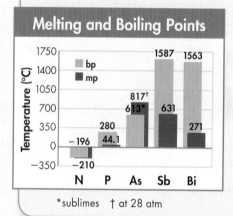

*sublimes   † at 28 atm

Density

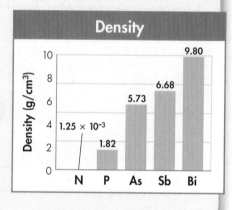

Sources

- Nitrogen is obtained from the fractional distillation of liquefied air.
- Phosphorus is derived from phosphate minerals. Example:

$$Ca_3(PO_4)_2(s) + 3SiO_2(s) + 5C(s) \longrightarrow 2P(l) + 3CaSiO_3(s) + 5CO(g)$$

- Arsenic is prepared by heating a mixture of $FeAs_2$ and FeS_2 in the absence of air.
- Antimony is prepared by roasting the ore stibnite, Sb_2S_3.

Fractional Distillation of Air

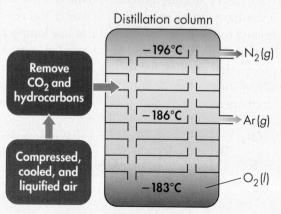

Distillation column

Atomic Properties

- Group 5A elements have an electron configuration that ends in ns^2np^3.

- The most common oxidation numbers for Group 5A elements are +3, +5, and −3.

- Nitrogen has oxidation numbers from −3 to +5 (and all numbers in between) in a variety of stable compounds.

- Elemental nitrogen, N_2, is highly unreactive due to its strong N-to-N triple bond.

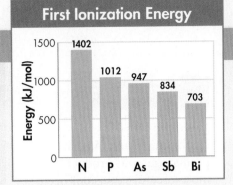

First Ionization Energy

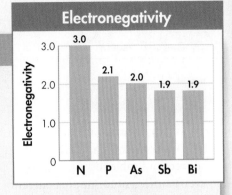

Electronegativity

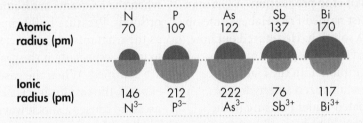

	N	P	As	Sb	Bi
Atomic radius (pm)	70	109	122	137	170
Ionic radius (pm)	146 N^{3-}	212 P^{3-}	222 As^{3-}	76 Sb^{3+}	117 Bi^{3+}

Important Compounds and Reactions

- Nitrous oxide, N_2O, (laughing gas) is an anesthetic. It is made from ammonium nitrate.

$$NH_4NO_3(s) \xrightarrow{\Delta} N_2O(g) + 2H_2O(g)$$

- Nitrogen dioxide, NO_2, is an air pollutant produced when fossil fuels burn at high temperatures.

- Lightning causes the nitrogen and oxygen in air to react and form nitric oxide, NO.

- Poisonous hydrazine, N_2H_4, is used as a rocket fuel. It is prepared by the following reaction.

$$2NH_3(aq) + OCl^-(aq) \longrightarrow$$
$$N_2H_4(aq) + Cl^-(aq) + H_2O(l)$$

The reaction is complex. One intermediate is chloramine, NH_2Cl, which is also poisonous. The labels on bottles of household ammonia and chlorine bleach warn you not to mix these solutions. If you ignore the warning, chloramine will be produced.

- Nitric acid, HNO_3, is used to make fertilizers and explosives. It is produced by the Ostwald process.

- Phosphoric acid is used in soft drinks and fertilizers. It is made by a double-replacement reaction.

$$Ca_3(PO_4)_2(s) + 3H_2SO_4(aq) \longrightarrow$$
$$3CaSO_4(aq) + 2H_3PO_4(aq)$$

Dentists use phosphoric acid to etch the exposed dentine layer of a drilled tooth to help a filling adhere to the tooth.

- Ammonia is synthesized directly from its elements by the Haber-Bosch process.

$$3H_2(g) + N_2(g) \longrightarrow 2NH_3(g)$$

- Amino acids such as glycine, H_2NCH_2COOH, are the building blocks of proteins.

- Bismuth subsalicylate, $BiO(C_7H_5O_3)$, is the active ingredient of a pink liquid antacid.

- Arsenic trioxide, As_2O_3, is powerful poison. Its use as a weed killer and insecticide has been restricted.

- Antimony is added to alloys to increase their hardness.

Ostwald Process

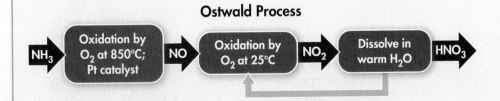

Ammonia is oxidized to nitrogen dioxide in two stages. The nitrogen dioxide forms nitric acid as it passes through warm water.

GROUP 5A

N Ammonia

The nitrogen in air is not in a form that is useful for plants. Natural sources of usable nitrogen in soil aren't sufficient to support current levels of crop production. A German chemist named Fritz Haber came up with a solution. He figured out how to convert atmospheric nitrogen into ammonia. In the Haber process, nitrogen and hydrogen are heated under pressure in the presence of iron.

$$N_2(g) + 3H_2(g) \longrightarrow 2NH_3(g)$$
$$\Delta H = 46.19 \text{ kJ/mol}$$

The ammonia is liquefied. Liquid ammonia, aqueous solutions of ammonia, and ammonium salts are used as fertilizers. Liquid ammonia is also used as a refrigerant. Many cleaning products contain aqueous ammonia, which is a weak base. Ammonia is also used to manufacture explosives.

Haber Process

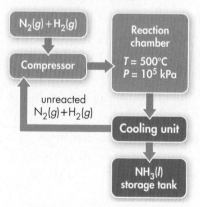

When the reaction mixture is cooled, the liquefied ammonia can be separated from the nitrogen and hydrogen.

N Explosives

Explosions are extremely rapid exothermic reactions that produce gaseous products. The most forceful explosions occur when the reactants are liquids or solids. Pressure builds up as the reactants are converted to gases, especially if the gases are confined. When the gases expand, the resulting release of pressure causes a shock wave. The kinetic energy of this wave, the wind that follows it, and the heat is the destructive force of the explosion.

Engineers use a series of small controlled explosions to force a building to collapse inward, or implode.

An explosion requires fuel and an oxidizer. If the oxidizer and fuel are separate, the reaction is a combustion reaction. This type of explosion could occur if natural gas leaking in a building was ignited by a spark or flame.

$$CH_4 + 2O_2(g) \longrightarrow CO_2(g) + 2H_2O(g) \qquad \Delta H = 890 \text{ kJ/mol}$$

If the fuel is its own oxidizer, a decomposition reaction takes place. Nitroglycerine, $C_3H_5(NO_3)_3$, is a thick, pale, oily liquid. It decomposes to form a mixture of gaseous products.

$$4C_3H_5(NO_3)_3(l) \longrightarrow 6N_2(g) + O_2(g) + 12CO_2(g) + 10H_2O(g)$$
$$\Delta H = -1427 \text{ kJ/mol}$$

Self-oxidizing explosives are often unstable. Jarring them may be enough to cause detonation. Alfred Nobel, a Swedish chemist and inventor, found a way to use nitroglycerine with less risk. After his family's nitroglycerine factory exploded in 1864, he moved his experiments to a barge in the middle of a lake. One day he found a cask of nitroglycerine that had leaked. Luckily, the diatomite in which the cask was packed had absorbed the liquid. Nobel found that the mixture was stable until detonated by a blasting cap. Plus, the mixture was as explosive as the pure liquid. Nobel named his invention dynamite.

In his will, Nobel established a fund to provide annual prizes in chemistry, physics, physiology and medicine, literature, and peace.

N Acid Rain

Normal rainfall has a pH of about 5.6. It is mildly acidic because carbon dioxide in the air dissolves in tiny water droplets and forms carbonic acid (H_2CO_3). In acid rain, the pH is lower due to the emission of nitrogen oxides and sulfur oxides into the atmosphere. Some natural sources, such as volcanoes, emit these oxides. But most come from the burning of fossil fuels. In the atmosphere, the oxides form nitric acid (HNO_3) and sulfuric acid (H_2SO_4), which fall to Earth in rain or snow.

Because acid rain dissolves and washes away nutrients from soil, trees are dying in the Appalachian Mountains. Because aquatic species are highly sensitive to changes in pH, some lakes once full of fish and frogs are nearly lifeless.

Power plants are one source of sulfur oxides and nitrogen oxides. Devices called scrubbers are used to remove these pollutants from smoke. In one type of scrubber, smoke passes through an aqueous suspension of lime (CaO). The lime reacts with SO_2 to form solid calcium sulfite ($CaSO_3$).

Another type of scrubber can be used to remove nitrogen oxides. Ammonia is sprayed onto a surface covered with a mixture of catalysts. As smoke passes over the surface, nitrogen oxides react with ammonia and oxygen, forming nitrogen and water.

Another way to deal with nitrogen oxides is to keep them from forming in the first place. The method involves burning a fuel, such as coal, at a high temperature. When the burner contains more fuel than air, most of the oxygen in the air reacts with the fuel rather than the nitrogen.

This map is based on analysis of samples collected from field stations in 2008.

pH Ranges of Rain

> 5.3	4.8 – 4.9
5.2 – 5.3	4.7 – 4.8
5.1 – 5.2	4.6 – 4.7
5.0 – 5.1	4.5 – 4.6
4.9 – 5.0	4.4 – 4.5

N P Fertilizers

5-6-5 blend

Most fertilizers contain salts of nitrogen, phosphorus, and potassium. These elements are essential to plant growth. On the label, the percents by mass of these nutrients are always listed in the order N-P-K.

Because the salts in a fertilizer can vary, there are rules for reporting the content. Nitrogen is always reported as the percent by mass of elemental nitrogen. Phosphorus and potassium are reported as the percent by mass of phosphorus pentoxide, P_2O_5, and potassium oxide, K_2O.

This system makes it easy to compare fertilizers. For example, a fertilizer labeled 20-10-10 has twice the mass of nitrogen as one labeled 10-10-10. But they both have the same mass of phosphorus and potassium. The numbers may not add up to 100% because fertilizers always contain ingredients not included in the N-P-K analysis.

Did You Know?

If nail polish or lipstick contains **bismuth** oxychloride (BiOCl), it appears lustrous and pearly.

GROUP 6A

Oxygen discovered in 1772 by Carl Scheele and in 1774 by Joseph Priestly

8	2 6
O	
Oxygen	
15.999	

Sulfur known since ancient times

16	2 8 6
S	
Sulfur	
32.06	

Selenium discovered in 1817 by Jöns Jacob Berzelius

34	2 8 18 6
Se	
Selenium	
78.96	

Tellurium discovered in 1782 by Franz Joseph Müller von Reichenstein

52	2 8 18 18 6
Te	
Tellurium	
127.60	

Polonium discovered in 1898 by Marie Curie

84	2 8 18 32 18 6
Po	
Polonium	
(209)	

Physical Properties

- Except for oxygen gas, O_2, Group 6A elements are solid at room temperature.
- The metallic properties of Group 6A elements increase from top to bottom within the group.
- Polonium is a radioactive metal.

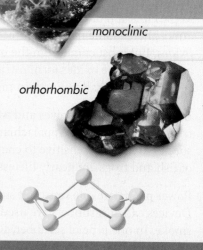

monoclinic

orthorhombic

The unit cell in crystalline sulfur is an S_8 molecule.

Melting and Boiling Points

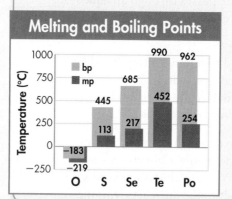

Temperature (°C) — bp, mp

O: −183, −219
S: 445, 113
Se: 685, 217
Te: 990, 452
Po: 962, 254

Density

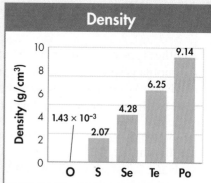

Density (g/cm³)

O: 1.43×10^{-3}
S: 2.07
Se: 4.28
Te: 6.25
Po: 9.14

Sources

- Large-scale production of oxygen is by fractional distillation of liquid air. Liquid oxygen is stored and shipped at its boiling point of −183°C in vacuum-walled bottles.

- The Frasch process is used to mine sulfur from underground deposits. A well is drilled into a sulfur bed and a set of concentric tubes installed. Superheated water melts the sulfur. Compressed air forces it to the surface.

- Sulfur is also produced from hydrogen sulfide, H_2S, and sulfur dioxide, SO_2.

  $$2H_2S(g) + SO_2(g) \longrightarrow 2H_2O(l) + 3S(s)$$

- Selenium and tellurium are by-products of the processing of sulfide ores for other metals.

- Polonium is formed by the radioactive decay of radium in minerals such as pitchblende.

The Frasch Process

Compressed air →

Hot sulfur froth

Superheated water (180°C) →

Quicksand

Sulfur-bearing rock

Superheated water

Solid sulfur

Air

Liquid sulfur (119°C)

Atomic Properties

- Group 6A elements have an electron configuration that ends in ns^2np^4.
- For Group 6A elements, the most common oxidation numbers are +4, +6, and −2.
- Oxygen is paramagnetic because there are unpaired electrons in O_2 molecules.

First Ionization Energy

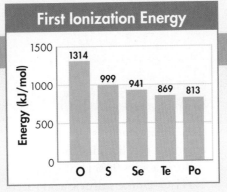

Energy (kJ/mol)

O	S	Se	Te	Po
1314	999	941	869	813

Electronegativity

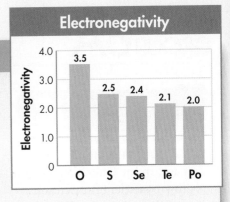

Electronegativity

O	S	Se	Te	Po
3.5	2.5	2.4	2.1	2.0

	O	S	Se	Te	Po
Atomic radius (pm)	66	105	120	139	168
Ionic radius (pm)	140 O^{2-}	184 S^{2-}	198 Se^{2-}	221 Te^{2-}	94 Po^{4+}

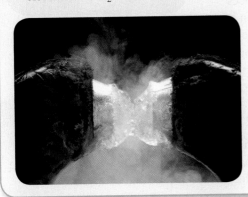

Liquid oxygen is held between the poles of a magnet because of its attraction to the magnet.

Important Compounds and Reactions

- Oxygen reacts with almost all other elements to form oxides. Example:

$$4K(s) + O_2(g) \longrightarrow 2K_2O(s) \quad \Delta H = -363.2 \text{ kJ/mol}$$

- Ozone, O_3, is produced directly from oxygen, O_2, during lightning strikes.

$$3O_2(g) \longrightarrow 2O_3(g) \quad \Delta H = +285 \text{ kJ/mol}$$

- Oxygen is necessary for releasing energy from fuels, such as glucose, in organisms.

$$C_6H_{12}O_6(s) + 6O_2(g) \longrightarrow 6CO_2(g) + 6H_2O(g)$$
$$\Delta H = -2808 \text{ kJ/mol}$$

- Oxygen is used to produce steel and to oxidize hydrogen in fuel cells.
- Sulfur compounds often have unpleasant odors. Hydrogen sulfide, H_2S, smells like a rotten egg. It forms when metallic sulfides and hydrochloric acid react. Example:

$$FeS(s) + 2HCl(aq) \longrightarrow H_2S(g) + FeCl_2(aq)$$

- Concentrated sulfuric acid, H_2SO_4, is a strong dehydrating agent. Example:

$$C_{12}H_{22}O_{11}(s) \xrightarrow{H_2SO_4} 12C(s) + 11H_2O(g)$$

When concentrated sulfuric acid is added to sucrose, water vapor and carbon are produced. The release of the vapor causes the carbon to expand.

- Ethyl mercaptan, CH_3CH_2SH, is commonly called "stench." It is added to supplies of odorless natural gas so people will know when the gas is leaking.
- Sodium thiosulfate, $Na_2S_2O_3$, also known as *hypo*, is used in the development of dental X-rays.
- The addition of cadmium selenide, CdSe, gives glass a beautiful ruby color.

GROUP 6A

Se Selenium In Food

Selenium is an antioxidant that protects cell membranes from damage. In the United States, grain is grown on selenium-rich soils. Livestock and people who eat those grains are unlikely to be deficient in selenium.

An essential nutrient may be harmful in large doses. Too much selenium can damage the nervous system. It may also cause anxiety and fatigue.

This milkvetch (Astragalus bisulcatus) accumulates high levels of selenium.

Soils in the Great Plains and Rocky Mountain regions often contain high levels of selenium. If cattle graze on plants that grow in those soils, they may develop chronic selenium poisoning. The symptoms include loss of hair, sore hoofs, lameness, and a lack of energy.

Acute selenium poisoning causes cattle to lose their vision and stumble aimlessly before dying from respiratory failure. Cowboys called this condition the "blind staggers."

S Sulfuric Acid

Pure sulfuric acid is a dense, colorless, oily liquid. Concentrated sulfuric acid is 98% H_2SO_4 and 2% H_2O. Dilute sulfuric acid reacts with metals, oxides, hydroxides, or carbonates to form sulfates. The reaction with metals also releases hydrogen gas. Sulfuric acid can be used to produce other acids from their salts. For example, hydrogen chloride can be produced from sulfuric acid and sodium chloride.

$$H_2SO_4(l) + 2NaCl(s) \longrightarrow Na_2SO_4(s) + 2HCl(g)$$

Sulfuric acid is produced mainly from sulfur dioxide. The process is called the contact process because the key reaction takes place when the reactants are in contact with the surface of the solid catalyst.

(1) Melted sulfur is burned in air.

$$S(l) + O_2(g) \longrightarrow SO_2(g)$$

(2) Sulfur dioxide is oxidized in the presence of a vanadium oxide catalyst, V_2O_5.

$$2SO_2(g) + O_2(g) \xrightarrow{V_2O_5} 2SO_3(g)$$

(3) Sulfur trioxide dissolves in water and forms sulfuric acid.

Much of the sulfuric acid produced in North America is used to make fertilizers. Sulfuric acid is also used in petroleum refining, the production of other chemicals, and for pickling iron and steel. During pickling, oxides are removed from the surface of a metal.

When sulfur burns in air, the product is the irritating gas sulfur dioxide, SO_2.

This marine slug of the species Berthella martensi produces sulfuric acid, which discourages predators.

O Ozone

Near Earth's surface, ozone (O_3) is a pollutant. In the stratosphere, ozone is literally a lifesaver. The ozone layer in the stratosphere absorbs 99% of the sun's harmful ultraviolet (UV) radiation. In the 1970s, scientists began to suspect that the ozone layer might be threatened. They based their concerns on laboratory models. In 1985, their suspicions were confirmed when British researchers discovered a "hole" in the ozone layer over Antarctica. In the winter, the amount of ozone was reduced by almost one half.

The scientists traced the thinning of the ozone layer to chemicals called chlorofluorocarbons (CFCs). These chemicals were used mainly as propellants in aerosol spray cans and as coolants in refrigerators and air conditioners. CFCs are highly stable and inert in the lower atmosphere. Over time, they drift up into the stratosphere, where they are broken down by solar radiation. Through a repeated cycle of reactions (2) and (3), a single chlorine atom can destroy as many as 100,000 molecules of ozone.

$$(1) \quad CCl_3F \longrightarrow Cl\bullet + \bullet CCl_2F$$
$$(2) \quad Cl\bullet + O_3 \longrightarrow ClO\bullet + O_2$$
$$(3) \quad ClO\bullet + O \longrightarrow Cl\bullet + O_2$$

In 1978, the United States banned the use of CFCs in aerosols. In 2007, most countries agreed to stop producing CFCs by 2020. The ban has had an effect. Concentrations of CFCs have begun to level off in the stratosphere and even decline in the lower atmosphere.

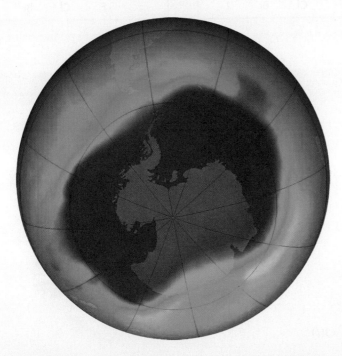

In September 2006, the "hole" over Antarctica was record size. The amount of ozone is low in the blue areas. It may take decades for the ozone layer to reach pre-1980 levels.

S Thiols

Skunks use a foul-smelling liquid to repel predators. The compounds in the mixture are mainly sulfur-containing molecules. One type of sulfur compound called a thiol is responsible for the foul odor. Thiols are organic compounds in which the oxygen of an alcohol has been replaced by sulfur. The general formula for a thiol is RSH.

The foul liquid is secreted and stored in glands until the skunk feels threatened. When it is threatened, the skunk contracts the muscles around the glands and sprays the liquid in the direction of the threat. A skunk can propel the liquid for about three meters! Other than smelling bad for a while, the "attacker" is not harmed.

Did You Know?

Organic compounds containing **sulfur** give onions their taste and smell. When an onion is cut, reactions occur that produce propanethial-S-oxide. When receptors in your eyes are exposed to this irritating gas, they trigger the production of tears.

GROUP 7A

Fluorine discovered in 1886 by Henri Moissan

9	2 7
F	
Flourine	
18.998	

Chlorine discovered in 1774 by Carl Wilhelm Scheele

17	2 8 7
Cl	
Chlorine	
35.453	

Bromine discovered in 1826 by Antoine-Jérôme Balard

35	2 8 18 7
Br	
Bromine	
79.904	

Iodine discovered in 1811 by Bernard Courtois

53	2 8 18 18 7
I	
Iodine	
126.90	

Astatine discovered in 1940 by Dale R. Corson, K. R. Mackenzie, & Emilio Segrè

85	2 8 18 32 18 7
At	
Astatine	
(210)	

Physical Properties

- Halogens are nonmetals. At room temperature, fluorine and chlorine are gases and bromine is a liquid. Iodine and astatine are solids.

- Halogens are very reactive. The reactivity decreases from fluorine to astatine. Halogens do not exist in the elemental form in nature.

- Astatine isotopes are radioactive with short half-lives.

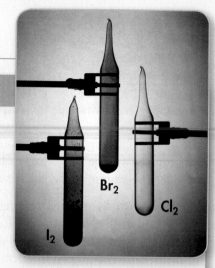

The colorful vapors of bromine and iodine are visible because bromine is volatile and iodine sublimes easily at room temperature.

Melting and Boiling Points

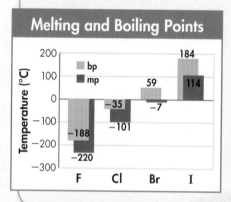

Density

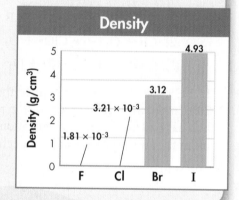

Sources

- Chlorine gas is made commercially by the electrolysis of brine.

$$2NaCl(aq) + 2H_2O(l) \longrightarrow Cl_2(g) + H_2(g) + 2NaOH(aq)$$

- Bromine is obtained from seawater by a displacement reaction with chlorine.

$$2NaBr(aq) + Cl_2(g) \longrightarrow 2NaCl(aq) + Br_2(l)$$

- Iodine is found in brine and in sodium iodate, $NaIO_3$, in deposits of sodium nitrate. Iodine is produced from $NaIO_3$ by this redox reaction.

$$2NaIO_3(aq) + 5NaHSO_3(aq) \longrightarrow I_2(g) + 2Na_2SO_4(aq) + 3NaHSO_4(aq) + H_2O(l)$$

- Fluorine is manufactured by the electrolysis of potassium fluoride, KF, dissolved in liquid hydrogen fluoride, HF.

Fluorite, CaF_2, is the principal mineral of fluorine. The term fluorescent comes from this mineral, which glows in the presence of UV radiation.

Atomic Properties

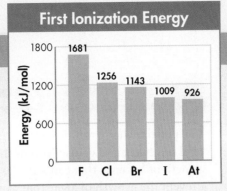

First Ionization Energy

Energy (kJ/mol)

1681, 1256, 1143, 1009, 926

F Cl Br I At

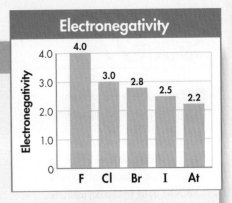

Electronegativity

Electronegativity

4.0, 3.0, 2.8, 2.5, 2.2

F Cl Br I At

- Group 7A elements have an electron configuration that ends in ns^2np^5.
- Halogens exist as diatomic molecules.
- Each halogen has the highest electronegativity in its period.
- The most common ionic charge for halogens is $1-$. Except for fluorine, halogens also have positive oxidation numbers of $+1$, $+3$, $+5$, and $+7$.

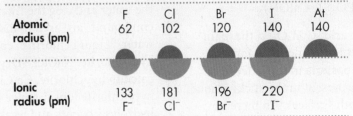

	F	Cl	Br	I	At
Atomic radius (pm)	62	102	120	140	140
Ionic radius (pm)	133 F^-	181 Cl^-	196 Br^-	220 I^-	

Chlorine forms four anions with oxygen. The oxidation number of chlorine is different in each anion.

Hypochlorite ion   Chlorite ion   Chlorate ion   Perchlorate ion

Important Compounds and Reactions

- Halogens form metal halides. Example:

$$2Na(s) + Cl_2(g) \longrightarrow 2NaCl(s) \quad \Delta H = -411 \text{ kJ/mol}$$

- Halogens form hydrogen halides. Example:

$$H_2(g) + Cl_2(g) \longrightarrow 2HCl(g) \quad \Delta H = -92.3 \text{ kJ/mol}$$

- Dry bleach is a mixture of compounds represented by the formula CaCl(ClO). Dry bleach is used to bleach paper and textiles. It also removes stains and disinfects laundry.

$$Ca(OH)_2(aq) + Cl_2(g) \longrightarrow$$
$$CaCl(ClO)(aq) + H_2O(l)$$

- Small amounts of oxygen are produced in the laboratory by heating potassium chlorate, $KClO_3$. Potassium chlorate is an oxidizing agent in fireworks, matches, and explosives.

$$2KClO_3(s) \longrightarrow 2KCl(s) + 3O_2(g)$$

- Canisters of sodium chlorate are used on submarines to produce oxygen. They are carried on airplanes in case of an emergency.

- Chlorine is used to make the monomer vinyl chloride, $CH_2 = CHCl$, which reacts to form the polymer polyvinyl chloride (PVC).

Chlorine reacts vigorously with sodium to form solid sodium chloride.

- Hydrofluoric acid (HF) is made from the mineral fluorite and sulfuric acid. Although HF is extremely dangerous, it has many uses, including cleaning metals and frosting glass.

$$CaF_2(s) + H_2SO_4(aq) \longrightarrow 2HF(g) + CaSO_4(s)$$

- Nonstick pans are coated with a polymer of tetrafluoroethene, $F_2C = CF_2$.

- Tincture of iodine is a solution of iodine, I_2, and potassium iodide, KI, in alcohol. It is an example of an iodine-based skin disinfectant.

GROUP 7A

F Tooth Decay

Your teeth have a hard outer layer called enamel. This layer is mainly calcium carbonate, $CaCO_3$, and hydroxyapatite, $[Ca_3(PO_4)_2]_3 \cdot Ca(OH)_2$.

Lactic acid, $C_3H_6O_3$, is the main cause of tooth decay. It forms when bacteria in saliva feed on sugars present in the sticky plaque on tooth surfaces. An increase in H^+ concentration causes the minerals in tooth enamel to decay faster. One source of this increased acidity is the phosphoric acid in soft drinks.

Fluoride ions are added to the water supply in many cities. Most toothpastes contain fluoride ions. The ions replace hydroxide ions in hydroxyapatite to form fluoroapatite, $[Ca_3(PO_4)_2]_3 \cdot CaF_2$. This replacement makes the enamel more resistant.

Fluoride ions alone will not prevent tooth decay. You need to brush your teeth and floss to keep plaque from building up on your tooth enamel.

Cl Swimming Pool Chemistry

The person who maintains a swimming pool has two main goals. Prevent the growth of bacteria that cause diseases. Prevent the growth of algae that can foul the water and clog the filters. Chlorine compounds are used to disinfect pool water. "Liquid chlorine" contains sodium hypochlorite, $NaClO$. "Dry chlorine" is calcium hypchlorite, $Ca(ClO)_2$. When hypochlorite ions dissolve in water, hydrolysis occurs and weak hypochlorous acid, $HClO$, is produced.

$$ClO^-(aq) + H_2O(l) \rightleftharpoons HOCl(aq) + OH^-(aq)$$

The amount of undissociated hypochlorous acid in the pool water depends on the pH. If the pH is too high, the hydrolysis reaction will shift toward the reactants and reduce the concentration of $HClO$. If the pH is too low, too much acid will form. A high concentration of acid can cause eye irritation, damage plaster, and corrode the metal piping and filters in the pool.

If the pH of the pool water is too high, solid sodium hydrogen sulfate can be used to react with the OH^- ions.

$$NaHSO_4(s) + OH^-(aq) \longrightarrow Na^+(aq) + SO_4^{2-}(aq) + H_2O(l)$$

If the pH is too low, sodium carbonate can be used to neutralize some of the acid.

$$Na_2CO_3(s) + 2H^+(aq) \longrightarrow 2Na^+(aq) + H_2O(l) + CO_2(aq)$$

The use of fluorides in drinking water and toothpastes has caused such a drastic reduction in tooth decay that many young adults have never had a cavity.

F Blood Substitutes

The most important function of blood is its ability to deliver oxygen from the lungs to cells throughout the body and carry carbon dioxide from the cells to the lungs. Blood transfusions have been the traditional response to blood loss due to severe injuries or surgery. Blood transfusions have saved millions of lives. But it takes time to determine the recipient's blood type and less common blood types may not be available. Also, blood can carry disease-causing bacteria and viruses.

Scientists have tried for years to develop an effective and profitable blood substitute. One approach focused on perfluorocarbons (PFCs). PFCs are organic compounds in which all the hydrogen has been replaced by fluorine. PFCs can dissolve and transport oxygen. They are fairly inexpensive to manufacture, their purity can be controlled, and they don't react with other substances in the body.

Some problems with PFCs were revealed during clininal trials. Because PFCs are insoluble in water, they must be mixed with lipids to form an emulsion. The emulsion can be unstable in blood, which means that it is not effective for long. Because PFCs carry less oxygen than hemoglobin does, the patient must breathe oxygen-rich air.

Because blood is so complex, scientists may never find a substitute to perform all its functions. Therefore, there is still a great need for donations of human blood.

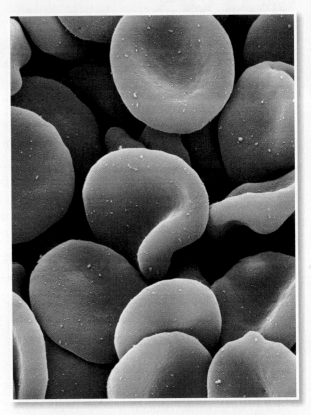

Hemoglobin is the molecule in red blood cells that transports oxygen. For a blood substitute to be effective, it has to perform this same function.

I Iodized Salt

The thyroid gland produces hormones that help to control the body's growth and the energy produced by cells. Trace amounts of iodine are needed to produce thyroid hormones. An adult needs about 150 mg of iodine daily.

Ocean fish are a good source of iodine. When people used to get most of their food from local sources, a person who lived far from the ocean often had an iodine deficiency. To compensate for the lack of iodine, the thyroid gland might enlarge. A severe deficiency causes some forms of mental disability. Adding potassium iodide to table salt proved to be a simple solution to this public health problem.

In the United States, iodized salt was first sold in 1924. There is about 400 mg of iodine in a teaspoon of iodized salt. The use of iodized salt has virtually eliminated the problem of iodine deficiency in the United States.

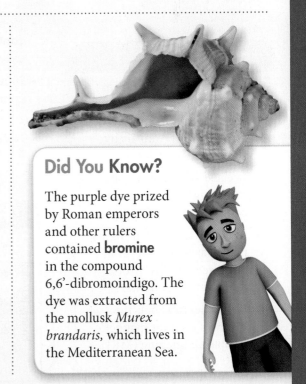

Did You Know?

The purple dye prized by Roman emperors and other rulers contained **bromine** in the compound 6,6'-dibromoindigo. The dye was extracted from the mollusk *Murex brandaris,* which lives in the Mediterranean Sea.

GROUP 8A

2 2 **He** Helium 4.0026	**Helium** discovered in 1868 by Pierre Janssen
10 2 8 **Ne** Neon 20.179	**Neon** discovered in 1898 by Sir William Ramsay & Morris Travers
18 2 8 8 **Ar** Argon 39.948	**Argon** discovered in 1894 by Lord Rayleigh & Sir William Ramsay
36 2 18 8 **Kr** Krypton 83.80	**Krypton** discovered in 1898 by Sir William Ramsay & Morris Travers
54 2 8 18 18 8 **Xe** Xenon 131.30	**Xenon** discovered in 1898 by Sir William Ramsay & Morris Travers
86 2 8 18 32 18 8 **Rn** Radon (222)	**Radon** discovered in 1900 by Friedrich E. Dorn

Sources

- Helium is separated from natural gas deposits. Neon, argon, krypton, and xenon are separated from air by fractional distillation.

- Because of its low density, helium is used in weather balloons and airships.

- In addition to "neon" lights, noble gases are used in fluorescent bulbs, strobe lights, and headlights.

- Liquid helium cools the magnets used for magnetic resonance imaging (MRI).

Physical and Chemical Properties

- All Group 8A elements are monatomic gases at STP.

- Noble gases are colorless, odorless, and tasteless.

- The first compound of a noble gas, $XePtF_6$, was made in 1962. More than 100 compounds of fluorine and xenon are now known.

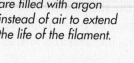

Incandescent light bulbs are filled with argon instead of air to extend the life of the filament.

- A compound of argon, HArF, exists only at temperatures below −246°C.

Melting and Boiling Points

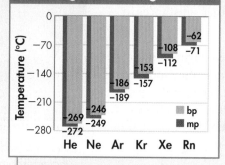

Density

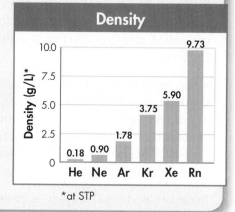

*at STP

Atomic Properties

- Noble gases have an electron configuration that ends in ns^2np^6, except for helium ($1s^2$).

- In noble gas compounds, the most common oxidation number for the gas is +2.

- Noble gases have the highest ionization energies because their energy levels are filled.

First Ionization Energy

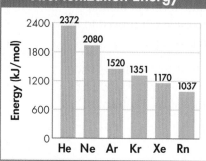

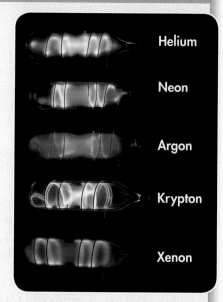

Each noble gas emits a characteristic color in a gas discharge tube.

Ne Neon Lights

By 1855, scientists could produce light by passing an electric current through a gas under low pressure in a sealed glass tube. With the discovery of the noble gases, a new technology emerged. In 1910, George Claude displayed the first neon lamp in Paris, France.

In 1923, a car dealer from Los Angeles bought two signs that spelled out "Packard" for $24,000 (about $250,000 in today's dollars). When he displayed the signs in Los Angeles, people described the light as "liquid fire." By the 1930s, businesses were using neon lights to draw the attention of customers.

Neon and argon are the gases most often used in neon lights. Orange-red lights contain only neon. Other colors are produced by adding a bit of mercury to the noble gas. The tube is coated with a material that glows when exposed to UV light emitted by mercury vapor.

Ar Taken For a Ride By Argon

Whether riding on a paved city street or on an unpaved mountain trail, a bicyclist is likely to find rough patches. When faced with rough terrain, the cyclist may worry about the tires, but probably not about the bicycle frame. The metal frames are made of steel, aluminum alloy, or titanium tubes that are joined together.

The tubes are joined together by Tungsten Inert Gas (TIG) welding. An electric arc is struck between a tungsten electrode and the parts to be welded. Heat from the arc melts the ends of the tubes and fuses them together. Filler may be placed between the ends of the tubes to increase the strength of the joint or to produce a smoother joint.

During welding in air, there is a danger that the metal tubes or electrode will oxidize. To prevent oxidation, the area around the arc is filled with an inert gas, most often argon. Welding with argon has an added benefit. Because argon is a poor conductor of heat, the arc that forms is narrow. This narrow arc produces a weld that is both neat in appearance and mechanically strong.

Xe Xenon-Ion Engine

The signals for a television program may bounce off a communication satellite. The satellite is in orbit above the equator. The position of the satellite may be maintained by a xenon-ion propulsion system.

When electrons strike xenon atoms in a xenon-ion engine, the atoms lose electrons and form positive ions. The ions are accelerated by a charged grid and shot from the engine at about 105 km/h. This action pushes, or thrusts, the satellite in the opposite direction. With multiple engines facing in different directions, a satellite can be moved in any direction.

Although a xenon-ion engine produces a relatively small amount of thrust, it can provide thrust for months or years. This makes xenon-ion engines a good choice for lengthy space missions. In addition, an inert gas poses no hazard for the satellite or the people who handle the propellant tanks.

Did You Know?

When liquid **helium** is cooled to below 2 K, its viscosity drops to zero. It will escape from an unsealed container by flowing up the sides of the container.

Hydrogen

1	1
H	
Hydrogen	
1.0079	

Hydrogen discovered in 1766 by Henry Cavendish

Sources

- Hydrogen is rarely found on Earth in an uncombined state.

- Electrolysis of water produces the purest hydrogen, but the process requires too much energy to be economical.

$$2H_2O(l) \longrightarrow 2H_2(g) + O_2(g)$$
$$\Delta H = +572 \text{ kJ}$$

- Hydrogen is produced when methane and steam react at 1100°C over a nickel catalyst.

$$H_2O(g) + CH_4(g) \xrightarrow{\text{Ni}} CO(g) + 3H_2(g)$$
$$\Delta H = +206 \text{ kJ}$$

The products pass over a metal oxide catalyst at 400°C. As carbon monoxide reacts with added steam, more hydrogen is produced.

$$CO(g) + H_2O(g) \longrightarrow CO_2(g) + H_2(g)$$
$$\Delta H = -41 \text{ kJ}$$

Carbon dioxide is removed as the gases flow through a basic solution.

$$CO_2(g) + 2OH^-(aq) \longrightarrow CO_3^{2-}(aq) + H_2O(l)$$

Atomic and Physical Properties

- Hydrogen has an electron configuration of $1s^1$.

- The most common oxidation numbers for hydrogen are +1 and −1.

- Most hydrogen (99.985%) is protium, or hydrogen-1.

- The other stable isotope is deuterium (hydrogen-2), which has the symbol D. Harold Urey discovered heavy hydrogen, D_2, in 1931.

- Tritium (hydrogen-3) was discovered in 1934. Its half-life is 12.3 years.

Properties of Hydrogen

Property	Value
Density at STP	0.09 g/L
Melting point	−259°C
Boiling point	−253°C
Ionization energy	1.312×10^3 kJ/mol
Electronegativity	2.1

Atomic radius (pm)	H 30
Ionic radius (pm)	1.2 H^+

Atomic and Physical Properties

- Hydrogen forms molecular binary hydrides with nonmetals. Example:

$$H_2(g) + Cl_2(g) \longrightarrow 2HCl(g)$$

- Two thirds of the hydrogen produced in the U.S. is used to synthesize the molecular binary compound ammonia.

- Hydrogen forms ionic hydrides with alkali metals and alkaline earth metals. These hydrides are powerful reducing agents. Example:

$$Ca(s) + H_2(g) \longrightarrow CaH_2(s)$$

- Hydrogen is used to make methanol, CH_3OH. The reaction takes place at 200–300 atm and 400°C in the presence of a metal oxide catalyst.

$$CO(g) + 2H_2(g) \longrightarrow CH_3OH(g)$$

Methanol is an industrial solvent. It is used to make formaldehyde, CH_2O, which is used to make plastics.

Hydrogen is used to turn liquid oils such as corn oil into solid margarine. Hydrogen is added to carbon–carbon double bonds during hydrogenation.

H Heavy Water Reactors

Because 1 in 6400 hydrogen atoms is deuterium, 1 in 41 million water molecules is D_2O. D_2O is called heavy water because it is about 10% heavier than ordinary water. In heavy water nuclear reactors, D_2O is used in place of H_2O as a neutron moderator. Both types of water are good moderators, but D_2O is more efficient than H_2O because D_2O absorbs fewer neutrons. So in a heavy water reactor, the uranium used to make the fuel doesn't have to be enriched. The initial cost of separating the heavy water from light water is offset by the lower cost of the uranium fuel.

Water passes through a series of extraction towers in which D_2O is separated from H_2O.

H Hydrogen Economy

Hydrogen is a pollution-free fuel. When it burns in air, the only product is water with trace amounts of nitrogen oxides. No carbon dioxide, carbon monoxide, oxides of sulfur, or unburned hydrocarbons are emitted. In a *hydrogen economy,* hydrogen would replace fossil fuels as the energy source for heating, transportation, and industrial processes. Achieving this goal will require new technology for the production, distribution, and storage of hydrogen.

Cars that run on hydrogen are being built. In one model, hydrogen is stored under pressure in a tank. The hydrogen is fed into a fuel cell, where it combines with oxygen to produce electricity. The electricity runs an electric motor that in turn drives the wheels. The valves to the hydrogen tank are designed to shut down if sensors detect a leak.

Large-scale production of hydrogen currently begins with fossil fuels. But in a true hydrogen economy, the source of the hydrogen would not be fossil fuels. Some scientists are working on a process that uses enzymes to extract hydrogen from wood chips or grass. Others are focused on algae that produce hydrogen in the presence of sunlight.

At the Los Angeles auto show in 2008, one auto manufacturer presented this design concept for a hydrogen-powered sports car.

H Hydrogen Peroxide

The strips used to whiten teeth usually contain hydrogen peroxide, H_2O_2. It is a powerful oxidizer that doesn't produce toxic gases or unwanted residues. A 3% aqueous solution is safe for use at home. Stronger concentrations are used to treat wastewater, bleach paper, and make germ-fighting detergents.

Hydrogen peroxide can inhibit the growth of bacteria in water pipes and increase the growth of bacteria that clean up polluted soils. How is this possible? The answer is *selectivity.* Scientists can adjust variables such as pH, temperature, and concentration so that hydrogen peroxide oxidizes one pollutant and not another.

Did You Know?

Hydrogen in the center of the sun has a density of about 200 g/mL. The temperature is about 13 million degrees Celsius. Radiation released when hydrogen nuclei fuse takes about a million years to reach the sun's surface.

Hydrogen **R35**

Transition Metals

Before 1700

Au gold

Ag silver

Cu copper

Fe iron

Hg mercury

Zn zinc

1700–1799

Co cobalt (1735)

Pt platinum (1735)

Ni nickel (1751t)

Mn manganese (1774)

Mo molybdenum (1778)

W tungsten (1783)

Ti titanium (1791)

Y yttrium (1794)

Cr chromium (1797)

1800–1899

V vanadium (1801)

Nb niobium (1801)

Ta tantalum (1802)

Pd palladium (1803)

Rh rhodium (1803)

Os osmium (1803)

Ir iridum (1803)

Cd cadmium (1817)

Zr zirconium (1824)

Ru ruthenium (1844)

Sc scandium (1878)

After 1900

Lu lutetium (1907)

Hf hafnium (1923)

Re rhenium (1925)

Physical Properties

- Most transition metals are ductile, malleable, and good conductors of heat and electric current.

- For transition metals, density tends to increase across a period, while melting point increases to a peak in Group 6B and then decreases.

Except for copper and gold, transition metals, including platinum, have a silvery luster.

- Compounds of transition metals tend to have color.

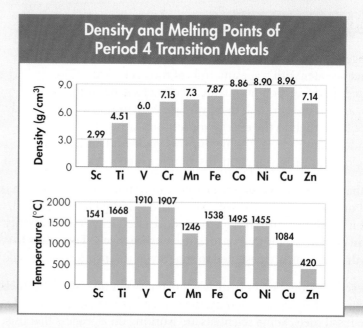

Density and Melting Points of Period 4 Transition Metals

Density (g/cm³)

Sc	Ti	V	Cr	Mn	Fe	Co	Ni	Cu	Zn
2.99	4.51	6.0	7.15	7.3	7.87	8.86	8.90	8.96	7.14

Temperature (°C)

Sc	Ti	V	Cr	Mn	Fe	Co	Ni	Cu	Zn
1541	1668	1910	1907	1246	1538	1495	1455	1084	420

Sources

- Transition metals come from mineral deposits in Earth's crust. Minerals that are used for the commercial production of metals are called ores.

- For centuries, people have developed techniques for separating metals from ores. The ore is concentrated and the metal removed by reduction. Then the metal is refined and purified.

Gold exists as an element in nature. But its ore needs to be concentrated before the gold can be extracted and purified.

Atomic Properties

- Among the transition metals, as atomic number increases, there is an increase in the number of electrons in the second-to-highest occupied energy level.

- In periods 5 and 6, transition metals in the same group have identical or almost identical atomic radii. Thus, these pairs of elements have very similar chemical properties. They tend to occur together in nature and are difficult to separate.

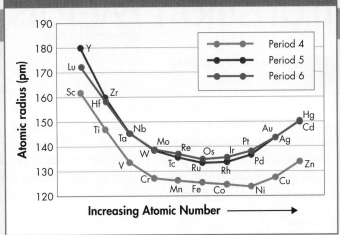

Trends in Atomic Size for Transition Metals

Chemical Properties

- There is great variation in reactivity among transition metals. Scandium and yttrium are similar to Group 1A and 2A metals. They are easily oxidized on exposure to air and react with water to release hydrogen. Platinum and gold are extremely unreactive and resist oxidation.

- In general, transition metals have multiple oxidation states. Compounds in which these elements are in their highest oxidation states are powerful oxidizing agents.

- Most transition metals form compounds with distinctive colors. The color of a transition metal compound or solution can indicate the oxidation state of the metal.

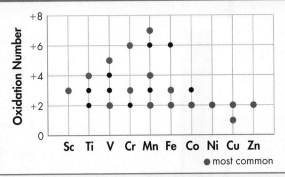

Oxidation Numbers of Period 4 Transition Metals

VO_3^-

$Cr_2O_7^{2-}$

MnO_4^-

In these aqueous solutions, vanadium, chromium, and manganese are in their highest oxidation states.

The oxidation number of vanadium is +5 in the yellow solution, +4 in the blue solution, +3 in the green solution, and +2 in the purple solution.

Transition Metals

Cu Copper Alloys

Copper was one of the first metals to be widely used. It is found uncombined in nature or easily reduced from its ores. The Roman supply of copper came mainly from Cyprus and was known as *aes Cyprium* (metal of Cyprus). This name evolved to *cyprium* and then *cuprium*, which is why copper has the symbol Cu. Pure copper is valued both for its ability to conduct an electric current and its ability to resist corrosion.

Around 3500 BC, people began to add tin to copper to form bronze. This alloy is harder than pure copper and easier to melt for casting. Metalworkers could produce bronze with different properties by varying the amount of tin. Bronze used to make statues might contain as little as 10% tin by mass. Bronze used to make bells would contain 13% to 25% tin. Most copper coins are bronze with 4% tin and 1% zinc.

When a bronze bell is struck, the clear, loud tone lasts for several seconds. This ancient Chinese bell was probably part of a set of graduated chimes.

Historically, brass was used to make high-quality scientific instruments like this microscope.

Brass is an alloy of copper and zinc. Brass is harder than pure copper and more malleable than bronze. Brass containing at least 65% copper can be worked when it is cold. Brass with 55% to 65% copper can be worked when it is hot. Before large amounts of gold and silver reached Europe in the 1500s, brass was the metal used for decorative items.

Copper that is exposed to oxygen and water forms a patina of basic copper salts. This thin film protects the underlying metal from further oxidation. The composition of the patina, its color, and the rate at which it forms vary with the climate. The rate is faster near the ocean.

The exterior of this science museum near the harbor in Amsterdam is copper, which has formed a patina.

Fe Iron and Steel

Carbon is used to extract iron from its ores. At first, people used charcoal from burnt wood. In 1709, Abraham Darby invented a process that used coke instead of charcoal. Coke is almost pure carbon. It is produced when coal is heated in the absence of air and the impurities removed as gases. With coke, producing iron became less costly and more efficient.

Iron ore is reduced to metallic iron in a blast furnace. Ore, coke, and limestone are added at the top of the furnace. Molten iron and slag collect at the bottom. The "pig" iron produced contains 3% to 5% carbon and smaller amounts of other impurities, which make the iron brittle. Pig iron can't be rolled or welded, but it can be cast. Cast iron is used to make stoves and engine blocks for cars.

Most pig iron is used to make steel. The methods for making steel differ, but they all lower the carbon content to less than 2% and remove other impurities. About 90% of the steel produced is carbon steel, which contains no other metals. Mild steel, which is malleable and ductile, contains less than 0.2% carbon. Medium steel (0.2% to 0.6% carbon) is used for structural components, such as beams and girders. Because high-carbon steel (0.8% to 1.5% carbon) is harder than other carbon steels, it is used to make items such as drill bits and knives.

Transition metals are used to produce alloy steels with a specific set of properties. The most common stainless steel contains about 18% chromium and 8% nickel.

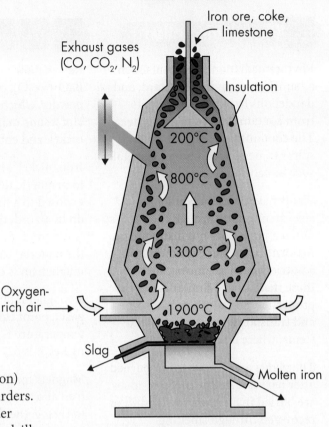

Blast Furnace

Iron ore, coke, limestone

Exhaust gases (CO, CO_2, N_2)

Insulation

200°C

800°C

1300°C

Oxygen-rich air

1900°C

Slag

Molten iron

Iron ore typically contains Fe_2O_3, and SiO_2. When heated, limestone produces CaO, which reacts with SiO_2 to form slag. Slag is used to manufacture Portland cement.

In 1779, Abraham Darby III built the world's first cast-iron bridge across the River Severn in England. The bridge is still used by pedestrians.

Did You Know?

Swords made with Damascus steel were highly valued. The source of this quality was the 0.02% **vanadium** in the iron ore that the steel makers used. When they began to use a different source of iron ore, the quality of their steel declined.

Transition Metals

Cd Phytoremediation

Phytoremediation uses plants such as sunflowers, Indian mustard, and dandelions to remove pollutants from contaminated soil and water. The contaminants include organic solvents, pesticides, and toxic metals such as cadmium and chromium.

Plants have a natural ability to absorb nutrients through their roots. Often a plant does not distinguish a toxic metal such as cadmium from a nutrient such as zinc because these metals have similar chemical properties. So cadmium is absorbed and transported to the leaves and stems, where it accumulates.

The plants are composted or burned after harvesting. The metal residues are buried in an approved landfill or recovered through smelting.

Fe Ni Co Permanent Magnets

Refrigerator magnets contain a barium ferrite, $BaO \cdot 6Fe_2O_3$, or strontium ferrite, $SrO \cdot 6Fe_2O_3$, powder, which is embedded in plastic or rubber. Horseshoe magnets usually contain an alloy of aluminum, nickel, and cobalt.

Iron, nickel, and cobalt are strongly attracted to magnetic fields. When these metals are exposed to a magnetic field, their cations line up in an orderly arrangement. When the field is removed, the ions remain lined up, and the material can act as a magnet. This type of magnetism is called ferromagnetism.

A magnet retains its strength unless it is heated past a point called the Curie temperature. For iron, this temperature is 1043 K. For cobalt, it is 1388 K. For nickel, it is 627 K.

Magnets made from a neodymium, boron, and iron alloy are very powerful. If they are allowed to fly together, they will shatter. They are used to check for counterfeit bills because they can detect tiny magnetic particles placed in the ink of genuine bills.

The shapes formed by this collection of small neodymium-iron-boron spheres are retained because the spheres are strongly attracted to each other.

Au Gold

Gold occurs chiefly as small flecks of free metal in veins of quartz. About 5 g of gold is produced from a metric ton (10^6 g) of gold-bearing rock.

Gold can be pounded into sheets so thin that they will transmit light. These sheets, called gold leaf, are used for lettering and decoration in general. Gold is used on the outside surfaces of satellites because it resists corrosion. Its high electrical and thermal conductivity make gold a good choice to plate contacts in microcircuits.

Pure gold is alloyed to make it harder and more durable. Gold alloys are safe to use as fillings for teeth because gold is highly unreactive.

Units called karats (k) are used to describe the purity of gold. Pure gold is 24k or 100% gold. Gold in coins is usually 22k or 92% gold. Gold in rings is often 14k (58% gold).

Connectors in electronics cables may be gold-plated to enhance signal transfer and minimize corrosion.

Micronutrients

Trace amounts of some transition metals are essential for human health.

Iron is found mainly in hemoglobin and myoglobin. Hemoglobin is the protein that transports oxygen in blood. Myoglobin is the protein that stores oxygen in muscle tissue. Vitamin C helps the absorption of iron by promoting the reduction of Fe^{3+} ions to Fe^{2+} ions.

Zinc is a cofactor in many enzymes. It helps protect the immune system. Hormones that control growth and reproduction do not function properly without zinc. A lack of zinc impairs the sense of taste and reduces the appetite.

Copper is a component of enzymes that control the synthesis of melanin, hemoglobin, and phospholipids in the sheath that protects nerves.

Molybdenum affects the absorption of copper. It is also needed for the oxidation of lipids and the metabolism of sulfur and nitrogen.

Chromium assists in the metabolism of glucose and may help to control adult-onset diabetes. A lack of chromium may affect growth.

Manganese is required for the proper function of the nervous system and the thyroid gland. It is needed for glucose metabolism. It helps maintain healthy bones and cartilage.

Cobalt is a component of vitamin B_{12}, which is required for the synthesis of red blood cells.

Transition Metal Micronutrients

Element	RDA or AI*	Dietary Sources
Iron	10 mg RDA (M) 20 mg RDA (F)	liver, green vegetables, egg yolk, fish, whole wheat, nuts, oatmeal, molasses, and beans
Zinc	11 mg RDA (M) 8 mg RDA (F)	liver, eggs, meat, milk, whole grains, and shellfish
Copper	900 μg RDA	beans, peas, and shellfish
Molybdenum	45 μg RDA	beans, peas, and whole grains
Chromium	35 μg AI (M) 25 μg AI (F)	meat and whole grains
Manganese	2.3 mg AI (M) 1.8 mg AI (F)	nuts, whole grains, dried fruits, and green leafy vegetables

*Recommended Dietary Allowance or Adequate Intake

Ti Sunscreens

You need some exposure to sunlight so your skin cells can make vitamin D, which is needed for healthy bones and teeth. Yet the UV radiation in sunlight can damage skin cells and even lead to skin cancer. The best way to protect your skin is to limit your time in the sun. The next best way is to use a sunscreen.

All the active ingredients in sunscreens protect against UVB light (280–320 nm), which is the primary cause of sunburn. Some ingredients protect against UVA light (320–400 nm), which penetrates deeper and causes long-term damage. A sun protective factor rating (SPF) measures only how effective a sunscreen is against UVB, not UVA.

Titanium dioxide, TiO_2, can reflect and scatter UV light. This stable and nonirritating oxide has one drawback. It looks like white paint on the skin. One manufacturer has addressed this problem by decreasing the size of the TiO_2 particles to a diameter of about 21 nm. At this size, TiO_2 appears transparent because its particles are smaller than wavelengths of visible light and light isn't reflected by the particles.

Did You Know?

An octopus has blood that is blue, not red, because the compound that transports oxygen in an octopus contains **copper,** not iron. Snails, oysters, and spiders are also bluebloods.

Appendix B

Table B.1

Some Properties of the Elements

Element	Symbol	Atomic number	Atomic mass	Melting point (°C)	Boiling point (°C)	Density (g/cm³) (gases at STP)	Oxidation numbers
Actinium	Ac	89	(227)	1050	3200	10.07	+3
Aluminum	Al	13	26.98154	660.37	2467	2.6989	+3
Americium	Am	95	243	994	2607	13.67	+3, +4, +5, +6
Antimony	Sb	51	121.75	630.74	1587	6.691	−3, +3, +5
Argon	Ar	18	39.948	−189.2	−185.7	0.0017837	
Arsenic	As	33	74.9216	817	613	5.73	−3, +3, +5
Astatine	At	85	(210)	302	337	−	
Barium	Ba	56	137.33	725	1640	3.5	+2
Berkelium	Bk	97	(247)	986	−	14.78	
Beryllium	Be	4	9.01218	1278	2970	1.848	+2
Bismuth	Bi	83	208.9804	271.3	1560	9.747	+3, +5
Bohrium	Bh	107	(264)	−	−	−	
Boron	B	5	10.81	2075	3675	2.34	+3
Bromine	Br	35	79.904	−7.2	58.78	3.12	−1, +1, +5
Cadmium	Cd	48	112.41	320.9	765	8.65	+2
Calcium	Ca	20	40.08	839	1484	1.55	+2
Californium	Cf	98	(251)	900	−	14	
Carbon	C	6	12.011	3550	4827	2.267	−4, +2, +4
Cerium	Ce	58	140.12	799	3426	6.657	+3, +4
Cesium	Cs	55	132.9054	28.40	669.3	1.873	+1
Chlorine	Cl	17	35.453	−100.98	−34.6	0.003214	−1, +1, +5, +7
Chromium	Cr	24	51.996	1907	2672	7.18	+2, +3, +6
Cobalt	Co	27	58.9332	1495	2870	8.9	+2, +3
Copernicium	Cn	112	(277)	−	−	−	
Copper	Cu	29	63.546	1083.4	2567	8.96	+1, +2
Curium	Cm	96	(247)	1340	−	13.51	+3
Darmstadtium	Ds	110	(269)	−	−	−	
Dubnium	Db	105	(262)	−	−	−	
Dysprosium	Dy	66	162.50	1412	2562	8.550	+3
Einsteinium	Es	99	(252)	−	−	−	
Erbium	Er	68	167.26	159	2863	9.066	+3
Europium	Eu	63	151.96	822	1597	5.243	+2, +3
Fermium	Fm	100	(257)	−	−	−	
Fluorine	F	9	18.998403	−219.62	−188.54	0.00181	−1
Francium	Fr	87	(223)	27	677	−	+1
Gadolinium	Gd	64	157.25	1313	3266	7.9004	+3
Gallium	Ga	31	69.72	29.78	2204	5.904	+3
Germanium	Ge	32	72.59	937.4	2830	5.323	+2, +4
Gold	Au	79	196.9665	1064.43	2856	19.3	+1, +3
Hafnium	Hf	72	178.49	2227	4602	13.31	+4
Hassium	Hs	108	(265)	−	−	−	
Helium	He	2	4.00260	−272.2	−268.934	0.001785	
Holmium	Ho	67	164.9304	1474	2695	8.795	+3
Hydrogen	H	1	1.00794	−259.14	−252.87	0.00008988	−1, +1
Indium	In	49	114.82	156.61	2080	7.31	+1, +3
Iodine	I	53	126.9045	113.5	184.35	4.93	−1, +1, +5, +7
Iridium	Ir	77	192.22	2410	4130	22.42	+3, +4
Iron	Fe	26	55.847	1535	2750	7.874	+2, +3
Krypton	Kr	36	83.80	−156.6	−152.30	0.003733	
Lanthanum	La	57	138.9055	921	3457	6.145	+3
Lawrencium	Lr	103	(262)	−	−	−	+3
Lead	Pb	82	207.2	327.502	1740	11.35	+2, +4

Some Properties of the Elements (cont.)

Element	Symbol	Atomic number	Atomic mass	Melting point (°C)	Boiling point (°C)	Density (g/cm³) (gases at STP)	Oxidation numbers
Lithium	Li	3	6.941	180.54	1342	0.534	+1
Lutetium	Lu	71	174.967	1663	3395	9.840	+3
Magnesium	Mg	12	24.305	648.8	1107	1.738	+2
Manganese	Mn	25	54.9380	1244	1962	7.32	+2, +3, +4, +7
Meitnerium	Mt	109	(268)	—	—	—	
Mendelevium	Md	101	257	—	—	—	+2, +3
Mercury	Hg	80	200.59	−38.842	356.58	13.55	+1, +2
Molybdenum	Mo	42	95.94	2617	4612	10.22	+6
Neodymium	Nd	60	144.24	1021	3068	6.90	+3
Neon	Ne	10	20.179	−248.67	−246.048	0.0008999	
Neptunium	Np	93	(237)	640	3902	20.25	+3, +4, +5, +6
Nickel	Ni	28	58.69	1453	2732	8.902	+2, +3
Niobium	Nb	41	92.9064	2468	4742	8.57	+3, +5
Nitrogen	N	7	14.0067	−209.86	−195.8	0.0012506	−3, +3, +5
Nobelium	No	102	(259)	—	—	—	+2, +3
Osmium	Os	76	190.2	3045	5027	22.57	+3, +4
Oxygen	O	8	15.9994	−218.4	−182.962	0.001429	−2
Palladium	Pd	46	106.42	1554	2970	12.02	+2, +4
Phosphorus	P	15	30.97376	44.1	280	1.82	−3, +3, +5
Platinum	Pt	78	195.08	1772	3627	21.45	+2, +4
Plutonium	Pu	94	(244)	641	3232	19.84	+3, +4, +5, +6
Polonium	Po	84	(209)	254	962	9.32	+2, +4
Potassium	K	19	39.0982	63.25	760	0.862	+1
Praseodymium	Pr	59	140.9077	931	3512	6.64	+3
Promethium	Pm	61	(145)	1168	2460	7.22	+3
Protactinium	Pa	91	231.0359	1560	4027	15.37	+4, +5
Radium	Ra	88	(226)	700	1140	5.5	+2
Radon	Rn	86	(222)	−71	−61.8	0.00973	
Rhenium	Re	75	186.207	3180	5627	21.02	+4, +6, +7
Rhodium	Rh	45	102.9055	1966	3727	12.41	+3
Roentgenium	Rg	111	(272)	—	—	—	
Rubidium	Rb	37	85.4678	38.89	686	1.532	+1
Ruthenium	Ru	44	101.07	2310	3900	12.41	+3
Rutherfordium	Rf	104	(261)	—	—	—	
Samarium	Sm	62	150.36	1077	1791	7.520	+2, +3
Scandium	Sc	21	44.9559	1541	2831	2.989	+3
Seaborgium	Sg	106	(263)	—	—	—	
Selenium	Se	34	78.96	217	684.9	4.79	−2, +4, +6
Silicon	Si	14	28.0855	1410	2355	2.33	−4, +2, +4
Silver	Ag	47	107.8682	961.93	2212	10.50	+1
Sodium	Na	11	22.98977	97.81	882.9	0.971	+1
Strontium	Sr	38	87.62	769	1381	2.63	+2
Sulfur	S	16	32.06	112.8	444.7	2.07	−2, +4, +6
Tantalum	Ta	73	180.9479	2996	5425	16.654	+5
Technetium	Tc	43	(98)	2172	4877	11.50	+4, +6, +7
Tellurium	Te	52	127.60	449.5	989.8	6.24	−2, +4, +6
Terbium	Tb	65	158.9254	1356	3123	8.229	+3
Thallium	Tl	81	204.383	303.5	1457	11.85	+1, +3
Thorium	Th	90	232.0381	1750	4790	11.72	+4
Thulium	Tm	69	168.9342	1545	1947	9.321	+3
Tin	Sn	50	118.69	231.968	2270	7.31	+2, +4
Titanium	Ti	22	47.88	1660	3287	4.54	+2, +3, +4
Tungsten	W	74	183.85	3410	5660	19.3	+6
Uranium	U	92	238.0289	1132.3	3818	18.95	+3, +4, +5, +6
Vanadium	V	23	50.9415	1890	3380	6.11	+2, +3, +4, +5
Xenon	Xe	54	131.29	−111.9	−107.1	0.005887	
Ytterbium	Yb	70	173.04	819	1194	6.965	+2, +3
Yttrium	Y	39	88.9059	1522	3338	4.469	+3
Zinc	Zn	30	65.38	419.58	907	7.133	+2
Zirconium	Zr	40	91.22	1852	4377	6.506	+4

Electron Configuration of the Elements

	Element	Sublevels																		
		1s	2s	2p	3s	3p	3d	4s	4p	4d	4f	5s	5p	5d	5f	6s	6p	6d	7s	7p
1	Hydrogen	1																		
2	Helium	2																		
3	Lithium	2	1																	
4	Beryllium	2	2																	
5	Boron	2	2	1																
6	Carbon	2	2	2																
7	Nitrogen	2	2	3																
8	Oxygen	2	2	4																
9	Fluorine	2	2	5																
10	Neon	2	2	6																
11	Sodium	2	2	6	1															
12	Magnesium	2	2	6	2															
13	Aluminum	2	2	6	2	1														
14	Silicon	2	2	6	2	2														
15	Phosphorus	2	2	6	2	3														
16	Sulfur	2	2	6	2	4														
17	Chlorine	2	2	6	2	5														
18	Argon	2	2	6	2	6														
19	Potassium	2	2	6	2	6		1												
20	Calcium	2	2	6	2	6		2												
21	Scandium	2	2	6	2	6	1	2												
22	Titanium	2	2	6	2	6	2	2												
23	Vanadium	2	2	6	2	6	3	2												
24	Chromium	2	2	6	2	6	5	1												
25	Manganese	2	2	6	2	6	5	2												
26	Iron	2	2	6	2	6	6	2												
27	Cobalt	2	2	6	2	6	7	2												
28	Nickel	2	2	6	2	6	8	2												
29	Copper	2	2	6	2	6	10	1												
30	Zinc	2	2	6	2	6	10	2												
31	Gallium	2	2	6	2	6	10	2	1											
32	Germanium	2	2	6	2	6	10	2	2											
33	Arsenic	2	2	6	2	6	10	2	3											
34	Selenium	2	2	6	2	6	10	2	4											
35	Bromine	2	2	6	2	6	10	2	5											
36	Krypton	2	2	6	2	6	10	2	6											
37	Rubidium	2	2	6	2	6	10	2	6			1								
38	Strontium	2	2	6	2	6	10	2	6			2								
39	Yttrium	2	2	6	2	6	10	2	6	1		2								
40	Zirconium	2	2	6	2	6	10	2	6	2		2								
41	Niobium	2	2	6	2	6	10	2	6	4		1								
42	Molybdenum	2	2	6	2	6	10	2	6	5		1								
43	Technetium	2	2	6	2	6	10	2	6	5		2								
44	Ruthenium	2	2	6	2	6	10	2	6	7		1								
45	Rhodium	2	2	6	2	6	10	2	6	8		1								
46	Palladium	2	2	6	2	6	10	2	6	10										
47	Silver	2	2	6	2	6	10	2	6	10		1								
48	Cadmium	2	2	6	2	6	10	2	6	10		2								
49	Indium	2	2	6	2	6	10	2	6	10		2	1							
50	Tin	2	2	6	2	6	10	2	6	10		2	2							
51	Antimony	2	2	6	2	6	10	2	6	10		2	3							
52	Tellurium	2	2	6	2	6	10	2	6	10		2	4							
53	Iodine	2	2	6	2	6	10	2	6	10		2	5							
54	Xenon	2	2	6	2	6	10	2	6	10		2	6							
55	Cesium	2	2	6	2	6	10	2	6	10		2	6			1				
56	Barium	2	2	6	2	6	10	2	6	10		2	6			2				

Table B.2

Electron Configuration of the Elements (cont.)

#	Element	1s	2s	2p	3s	3p	3d	4s	4p	4d	4f	5s	5p	5d	5f	6s	6p	6d	7s	7p
57	Lanthanum	2	2	6	2	6	10	2	6	10		2	6	1		2				
58	Cerium	2	2	6	2	6	10	2	6	10	1	2	6	1		2				
59	Praseodymium	2	2	6	2	6	10	2	6	10	3	2	6			2				
60	Neodymium	2	2	6	2	6	10	2	6	10	4	2	6			2				
61	Promethium	2	2	6	2	6	10	2	6	10	5	2	6			2				
62	Samarium	2	2	6	2	6	10	2	6	10	6	2	6			2				
63	Europium	2	2	6	2	6	10	2	6	10	7	2	6			2				
64	Gadolinium	2	2	6	2	6	10	2	6	10	7	2	6	1		2				
65	Terbium	2	2	6	2	6	10	2	6	10	9	2	6			2				
66	Dysprosium	2	2	6	2	6	10	2	6	10	10	2	6			2				
67	Holmium	2	2	6	2	6	10	2	6	10	11	2	6			2				
68	Erbium	2	2	6	2	6	10	2	6	10	12	2	6			2				
69	Thulium	2	2	6	2	6	10	2	6	10	13	2	6			2				
70	Ytterbium	2	2	6	2	6	10	2	6	10	14	2	6			2				
71	Lutetium	2	2	6	2	6	10	2	6	10	14	2	6	1		2				
72	Hafnium	2	2	6	2	6	10	2	6	10	14	2	6	2		2				
73	Tantalum	2	2	6	2	6	10	2	6	10	14	2	6	3		2				
74	Tungsten	2	2	6	2	6	10	2	6	10	14	2	6	4		2				
75	Rhenium	2	2	6	2	6	10	2	6	10	14	2	6	5		2				
76	Osmium	2	2	6	2	6	10	2	6	10	14	2	6	6		2				
77	Iridium	2	2	6	2	6	10	2	6	10	14	2	6	7		2				
78	Platinum	2	2	6	2	6	10	2	6	10	14	2	6	9		1				
79	Gold	2	2	6	2	6	10	2	6	10	14	2	6	10		1				
80	Mercury	2	2	6	2	6	10	2	6	10	14	2	6	10		2				
81	Thallium	2	2	6	2	6	10	2	6	10	14	2	6	10		2	1			
82	Lead	2	2	6	2	6	10	2	6	10	14	2	6	10		2	2			
83	Bismuth	2	2	6	2	6	10	2	6	10	14	2	6	10		2	3			
84	Polonium	2	2	6	2	6	10	2	6	10	14	2	6	10		2	4			
85	Astatine	2	2	6	2	6	10	2	6	10	14	2	6	10		2	5			
86	Radon	2	2	6	2	6	10	2	6	10	14	2	6	10		2	6			
87	Francium	2	2	6	2	6	10	2	6	10	14	2	6	10		2	6		1	
88	Radium	2	2	6	2	6	10	2	6	10	14	2	6	10		2	6		2	
89	Actinium	2	2	6	2	6	10	2	6	10	14	2	6	10		2	6	1	2	
90	Thorium	2	2	6	2	6	10	2	6	10	14	2	6	10		2	6	2	2	
91	Protactinium	2	2	6	2	6	10	2	6	10	14	2	6	10	2	2	6	1	2	
92	Uranium	2	2	6	2	6	10	2	6	10	14	2	6	10	3	2	6	1	2	
93	Neptunium	2	2	6	2	6	10	2	6	10	14	2	6	10	4	2	6	1	2	
94	Plutonium	2	2	6	2	6	10	2	6	10	14	2	6	10	6	2	6		2	
95	Americium	2	2	6	2	6	10	2	6	10	14	2	6	10	7	2	6		2	
96	Curium	2	2	6	2	6	10	2	6	10	14	2	6	10	7	2	6	1	2	
97	Berkelium	2	2	6	2	6	10	2	6	10	14	2	6	10	9	2	6		2	
98	Californium	2	2	6	2	6	10	2	6	10	14	2	6	10	10	2	6		2	
99	Einsteinium	2	2	6	2	6	10	2	6	10	14	2	6	10	11	2	6		2	
100	Fermium	2	2	6	2	6	10	2	6	10	14	2	6	10	12	2	6		2	
101	Mendelevium	2	2	6	2	6	10	2	6	10	14	2	6	10	13	2	6		2	
102	Nobelium	2	2	6	2	6	10	2	6	10	14	2	6	10	14	2	6		2	
103	Lawrencium	2	2	6	2	6	10	2	6	10	14	2	6	10	14	2	6	1	2	
104	Rutherfordium	2	2	6	2	6	10	2	6	10	14	2	6	10	14	2	6	2	2	
105	Dubnium	2	2	6	2	6	10	2	6	10	14	2	6	10	14	2	6	3	2	
106	Seaborgium	2	2	6	2	6	10	2	6	10	14	2	6	10	14	2	6	4	2	
107	Bohrium	2	2	6	2	6	10	2	6	10	14	2	6	10	14	2	6	5	2	
108	Hassium	2	2	6	2	6	10	2	6	10	14	2	6	10	14	2	6	6	2	
109	Meitnerium	2	2	6	2	6	10	2	6	10	14	2	6	10	14	2	6	7	2	
110	Darmstadium	2	2	6	2	6	10	2	6	10	14	2	6	10	14	2	6	9	1	
111	Roentgenium	2	2	6	2	6	10	2	6	10	14	2	6	10	14	2	6	10	1	
112	Copernicium	2	2	6	2	6	10	2	6	10	14	2	6	10	14	2	6	10	2	

Physical Constants

Atomic mass unit	$1 \text{ amu} = 1.6605 \times 10^{-24} \text{ g}$
Avogadro's number	$N = 6.0221 \times 10^{23} \text{ particles/mol}$
Gas constant	$R = 8.31 \text{ L} \cdot \text{kPa/K} \cdot \text{mol}$
Ideal gas molar volume	$V_m = 22.414 \text{ L/mol}$
Masses of subatomic particles	
Electron (e^-)	$m_e = 0.0005486 \text{ amu} = 9.1096 \times 10^{-28} \text{ g}$
Proton (p^+)	$m_p = 1.007277 \text{ amu} = 1.67261 \times 10^{-24} \text{ g}$
Neutron (n^0)	$m_n = 1.008665 \text{ amu} = 1.67492 \times 10^{-24} \text{ g}$
Speed of light (in vacuum)	$c = 2.997925 \times 10^8 \text{ m/s}$

Table B.4

SI Units and Equivalents

Quantity	SI unit	Common equivalents		
Length	meter (m)	1 meter	=	1.0936 yards
		1 centimeter	=	0.39370 inch
		1 inch	=	2.54 centimeters
		1 mile	=	5280 feet
			=	1.6093 kilometers
Volume	cubic meter (m^3)	1 liter	=	10^{-3} m^3
			=	1.0567 quarts
		1 gallon	=	4 quarts
			=	8 pints
			=	3.7854 liters
		1 quart	=	32 fluid ounces
			=	0.94635 liter
Temperature	kelvin (K)	1 kelvin	=	1 degree Celsius
		$^\circ$C	=	$\frac{5}{9}$ (F − 32)
		K	=	$^\circ$C + 273.15
Mass	kilogram (kg)	1 kilogram	=	1000 grams
			=	mass weighing 2.2046 pounds
		1 amu	=	$1.66057 \times 10^{-27} \text{ kilograms}$
Time	second (s)	1 hour	=	60 minutes
		1 hour	=	3600 seconds
Energy	joule (J)	1 joule	=	$1 \text{ kg} \cdot \text{m}^2/\text{s}^2$ (exact)
		1 joule	=	0.23901 calorie
		1 calorie	=	4.184 joules
Pressure	pascal (Pa)	1 atmosphere	=	101.3 kilopascals
			=	760 mm Hg (torr)
			=	14.70 pounds per square inch

Table B.5

Other Symbols and Abbreviations

α	alpha rays	ΔH_f	heat of formation	m	molality
β	beta rays	h	hour	mL	milliliter (*volume*)
γ	gamma rays	h	Planck's constant	mm	millimeter (*length*)
Δ	change in	Hz	hertz (*frequency*)	mol	mole (*amount*)
$\delta+, \delta-$	partial ionic charge	J	joule (*energy*)	mp	melting point
λ	wavelength	K	kelvin (*temperature*)	N	normality
π	pi bond	K_a	acid dissociation constant	n^0	neutron
σ	sigma bond	K_b	base dissociation constant	n	number of moles
ν	frequency	K_b	molal boiling point elevation constant	n	principal quantum number
amu	atomic mass unit				
(*aq*)	aqueous solution	K_{eq}	equilibrium constant	P	pressure
atm	atmosphere (*pressure*)	K_f	molal freezing point depression constant	p^+	proton
bp	boiling point			Pa	pascal (*pressure*)
				R	ideal gas constant
°C	degree Celsius (*temperature*)	K_w	ion product constant for water	S	entropy
c	speed of light in a vacuum			s	second
		K_{sp}	solubility product constant	(*s*)	solid
cm	centimeter (*length*)	kcal	kilocalorie (*energy*)	SI	International System of Units
E	energy				
e^-	electron	kg	kilogram (*mass*)		
fp	freezing point	kPa	kilopascal (*pressure*)	STP	standard temperature and pressure
G	Gibbs free energy	L	liter (*volume*)		
g	gram (*mass*)	(*l*)	liquid	T	temperature
(*g*)	gas	M	molarity	$t_{\frac{1}{2}}$	half-life
gfm	gram formula mass	m	meter (*length*)	V	volume
H	enthalpy	m	mass	v	velocity

Table B.6

Common Polyatomic Ions

Charge	Name	Formula	Charge	Name	Formula
1−	Chlorate	ClO_3^-	2−	Carbonate	CO_3^{2-}
	Chlorite	ClO_2^-		Chromate	CrO_4^{2-}
	Cyanide	CN^-		Dichromate	$Cr_2O_7^{2-}$
	Dihydrogen phosphate	$H_2PO_4^-$		Oxalate	$C_2O_4^{2-}$
	Ethanoate	CH_3COO^-		Peroxide	O_2^{2-}
	Hydroxide	OH^-		Silicate	SiO_3^{2-}
	Hydrogen carbonate	HCO_3^-		Sulfate	SO_4^{2-}
	Hydrogen sulfate	HSO_4^-		Sulfite	SO_3^{2-}
	Hydrogen sulfite	HSO_3^-		Thiosulfate	$S_2O_3^{2-}$
	Hypochlorite	ClO^-			
	Nitrate	NO_3^-	3−	Phosphate	PO_4^{3-}
	Nitrite	NO_2^-		Phosphite	PO_3^{3-}
	Perchlorate	ClO_4^-			
	Permanganate	MnO_4^-	1+	Ammonium	NH_4^+
	Thiocyanate	SCN^-			

Solubilities of Compounds at 25°C and 101.3 kPa

	ethanoate	bromide	carbonate	chlorate	chloride	hydroxide	iodide	nitrate	oxide	perchlorate	phosphate	sulfate	sulfide
aluminum	S	S	X	S	S	I	S	S	I	S	I	S	d
ammonium	S	S	S	S	S	X	S	S	X	S	S	S	S
barium	S	S	I	S	S	S	S	S	sS	S	I	I	d
calcium	S	S	I	S	S	S	S	S	sS	S	I	sS	I
copper(II)	S	S	X	S	S	I	S	S	I	S	I	S	I
iron(II)	S	S	I	S	S	I	S	S	I	S	I	S	I
iron(III)	S	S	X	S	S	I	S	S	I	S	I	sS	d
lithium	S	S	sS	S	S	S	S	S	S	S	sS	S	S
magnesium	S	S	I	S	S	I	S	S	I	S	I	S	d
potassium	S	S	S	S	S	S	S	S	S	S	S	S	S
silver	sS	I	I	S	I	X	I	S	I	S	I	sS	I
sodium	S	S	S	S	S	S	S	S	S	S	S	S	S
strontium	S	S	I	S	S	S	S	S	S	S	I	I	I
zinc	S	S	I	S	S	I	S	S	I	S	I	S	I

Key: S = soluble   d = decomposes in water
sS = slightly soluble   X = no such compound
I = insoluble

Appendix C

Safety in the Chemistry Lab

The experiments in this book have been carefully designed to minimize the risk of injury. However, safety is also your responsibility. The following rules are essential for keeping you safe in the laboratory. The rules address pre-lab preparation, proper laboratory practices, and post-lab procedures.

Pre-Lab Preparation

1. Read the entire procedure before you begin. Listen to all of your teacher's instructions. When in doubt about a procedure, ask your teacher.

2. Do only the assigned experiments. Do any experiment only when your teacher is present and has given you permission to work.

3. Know the location and operation of the following safety equipment: fire extinguisher, fire blanket, emergency shower, and eye wash station.

4. Know the location of emergency exits and escape routes. To make it easy to exit quickly, do not block walkways with furniture. Keep your work area orderly and free of personal belongings such as coats and backpacks.

5. Protect your clothing and hair from chemicals and sources of heat. Tie back long hair and roll up loose sleeves when working in the laboratory. Avoid wearing bulky or loose-fitting clothing. Remove dangling jewelry. Wear closed-toe shoes at all times in the laboratory.

Proper Laboratory Practices

6. Even with well-designed and tested laboratory procedures, an accident may occur while you are working in the lab. Report any accident, no matter how minor, to your teacher.

7. Wear chemical splash goggles at all times when working in the laboratory. These goggles are designed to protect your eyes from injury. While working in the lab, do not rub your eyes, because chemicals are easily transferred from your hands to your eyes.

⚠ If, despite these precautions, a chemical gets in your eye, remove any contact lenses and immediately wash your eye with a continuous stream of lukewarm water for at least 15 minutes.

8. To reduce danger, waste, and cleanup, always use the minimal amounts of chemicals specified for an experiment.

9. Never taste any chemical used in the laboratory, including food products that are the subject of an investigation. Treat all items as though they are contaminated with unknown chemicals that may be toxic. Keep all food and drink that is not part of an experiment out of the laboratory. Do not eat, drink, or chew gum in the laboratory.

⚠ If you accidentally ingest a substance, notify your teacher immediately.

10. Don't use chipped or cracked glassware. Don't handle broken glass. If glassware breaks, tell your teacher and nearby classmates. Discard broken glass as instructed by your teacher.

⚠ If, despite these precautions, you receive a minor cut, allow it to bleed for a short time. Wash the injured area under cold, running water and notify your teacher. More serious cuts or puncture wounds require immediate medical attention.

11. Do not handle hot glassware or equipment. You can prevent burns by being aware that hot and cold equipment can look exactly the same.

⚠ If you are burned, immediately run cold water over the burned area for several minutes until the pain is reduced. Cooling helps the burn heal. Ask a classmate to notify your teacher.

12. Recognize that the danger of an electrical shock is greater in the presence of water. Keep electrical appliances away from sinks and faucets to minimize the risk of electrical shock. Be careful not to spill water or other liquids in the vicinity of an electrical appliance.

⚠ If, despite these precautions, you spill water near an electrical appliance, stand back, notify your teacher, and warn other students in the area.

13. Report any chemical spills immediately to your teacher. Follow your teacher's instructions for cleaning up spills. Warn other students about the identity and location of spilled chemicals.

⚠ If, despite these precautions, a corrosive chemical gets on your skin or clothing, notify your teacher. Then wash the affected area with cold, running water for several minutes.

Post-Lab Procedures

14. Dispose of chemicals in a way that protects you, your classmates, and the environment. Always follow your teacher's directions for cleanup and disposal. Clean your small-scale reaction surface by draining the contents onto a paper towel. Then wipe the surface with a damp paper towel and dry the surface completely. Dispose of the paper towels in the waste bin.

15. Wash your hands thoroughly with soap and water before leaving the laboratory.

A Materials Safety Data Sheet (MSDS) for a chemical describes any safety issues. A diagram summarizes risks related to flammability, health, and reactivity. A number scale indicates the level of risk.

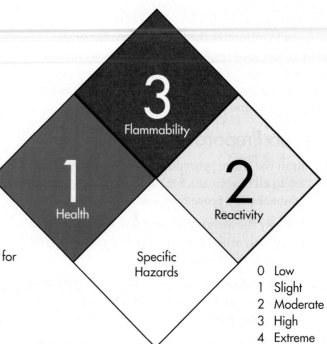

3 Flammability
1 Health
2 Reactivity
Specific Hazards

0 Low
1 Slight
2 Moderate
3 High
4 Extreme

Take appropriate precautions when any of the following safety symbols appears in an experiment.

Safety Symbols

 Eye Safety Wear safety goggles.

 Clothing Protection Wear a lab coat or apron when using corrosive chemicals or chemicals that can stain clothing.

 Skin Protection Wear plastic gloves when using chemicals that can irritate or stain your skin.

 Broken Glass Do not use chipped or cracked glassware. Do not heat the bottom of a test tube.

 Open Flame Tie back hair and loose clothing. Never reach across a lit burner.

 Flammable Substance Do not have a flame near flammable materials.

 Corrosive Substance Wear safety goggles, an apron, and gloves when working with corrosive chemicals.

 Poison Don't chew gum, drink, or eat in the laboratory. Never taste a chemical in the laboratory.

 Fume Avoid inhaling substances that can irritate your respiratory system.

 Thermal Burn Do not touch hot glassware or equipment.

 Electrical Equipment Keep electrical equipment away from water or other liquids.

 Sharp Object To avoid a puncture wound, use scissors or other sharp objects only as intended.

 Disposal Dispose of chemicals only as directed.

 Hand Washing Wash your hands thoroughly with soap and water.

Appendix D

Chapter 2

1. Are intensive or extensive properties most helpful in identifying a substance? Explain your choice.

2. Classify the following mixtures as homogeneous or heterogeneous.

   a. a toaster

   b. a calculator

   c. the air on a clear day

   d. a copper coin

3. Identify the following as a mixture or a substance.

   a. tomato juice

   b. a rusty, iron fence post

   c. a drop of mercury

   d. a milkshake

4. Classify the following as a physical change or a chemical change.

   a. salad dressing separates into layers after standing

   b. spilled acid burns a hole in cotton jeans

   c. alcohol freezes

   d. ice sublimes

5. Classify the following properties of an aluminum bar as either physical or chemical.

   a. burns in pure oxygen

   b. melts at 660°C

   c. bends easily

   d. is nonmagnetic

Chapter 3

6. How many significant figures are in each measurement?

   a. 786.32 mg

   b. 0.0004 s

   c. 5.060 kg

   d. 7006.0 g

   e. 0.0500 s

   f. 66.066 mg

   g. 4000 m

   h. 40.0×10^3 m

7. Write each of the measurements in Problem 6 in scientific notation.

8. What is the total mass of three gold bars that weigh 5543 mg, 23.45 mg, and 697.4 mg?

9. The normal daily high temperature on the planet Zork is −85°C. Express this temperature in kelvins.

10. Methane, a gas that contributes to global warming, has a density of 0.714 g/L. What is the mass, in grams, of 25.0 L of methane?

11. The density of zinc is 9.394 g/cm^3 at 20°C. What is the volume (in cubic centimeters) of a sphere of zinc metal that has a mass of 15.6 g?

12. Calculate the mass in kilograms of 964 mL of the element mercury. The density of mercury is 13.6 g/mL.

13. Make the following conversions:

    a. 55 mg to grams

    b. 5.76 dL to liters

    c. 0.96 m to micrometers

    d. 5.26 ns to seconds

    e. 87 kg to milligrams

    f. 846 mmol to centimoles

    g. 3.4 nm to picometers

    h. 6.66×10^3 kg to megagrams

    i. 2.34×10^{-5} mL to microliters

14. When you donate a unit of blood to the Red Cross, you "give" about 0.55 L of blood. How many cubic centimeters (cm^3) of blood is this?

15. The recommended daily amount (RDA) of vitamin B$_6$ for adults is 0.2 cg. How many micrograms of vitamin B$_6$ should be consumed each day?

16. A person develops jaundice (characterized by yellowing of the skin) when the concentration of bilirubin in his or her blood is 18 mg bilirubin per liter of blood. Assuming a total blood volume of 5.2 L, what is the number of grams of bilirubin in the person's blood?

17. Mites are small eight-legged "bugs" in the same family as spiders. A particularly small mite has a mass of 0.0043 dg. What is the mass of this mite expressed in micrograms?

18. A runner covers a 3.00-mile course in 35.0 minutes. What is her average speed in kilometers/hour?

19. You are going to carry out a chemical reaction in which you need 16 g of oxygen for every 7.0 g of nitrogen that will be used. If you have 0.554 kg of oxygen, how many milligrams of nitrogen do you need?

20. If your heart beats at an average rate of 72 times per minute, how many times will your heart beat each year?

21. Four empty beakers weigh a total of 1.84 kg. Each beaker when full holds 0.75 kg of water. How much do two full beakers of water weigh?

22. How many days would it take you to count a million pennies if you could count one penny each second? Express the answer to 3 significant figures.

23. A soap bubble film is 8.0×10^2 nm thick. Express this thickness in the following units:

   a. centimeters   **c.** decimeters

   b. micrometers   **d.** millimeters

24. The pitcher's mound on a regulation baseball field is 60 feet 6 inches from home plate. How many seconds does it take a 96 mph fastball to reach home plate? (5280 ft = 1 mile)

25. Gemstones such as diamonds are measured in carats, where 1 carat = 2.00 dg. How many kilograms of diamonds were produced if 12.5 million carats of diamonds were mined in a recent year?

26. How many meters does a car moving at 95 km/hour travel in 1.0 second?

27. A milliliter of water is equal to 20 drops of water. If water is dripping from a faucet at the rate of 7 drops per minute, how many days will it take to completely fill a 2.00-L soda bottle?

28. A prescription for a certain drug calls for a dose of 0.200 mg/kg of body weight, four times a day. The drug is packaged in capsules of 5 mg. How many capsules per dose should be given to a patient who weighs 75 kg?

29. A certain low-tar cigarette contains 11.0 mg of tar per cigarette.

   a. If all the tar gets into the lungs, how many packs of cigarettes (20 cigarettes per pack) would have to be smoked to produce 0.500 lb of tar? (454 g = 1 lb)

   b. If a person smoked two packs per day, how many years would it take to accumulate 0.500 lb of tar?

30. A chemist needs 25.0 mL of a liquid compound.

   a. What mass of the compound is necessary if the density is 0.718 g/cm^3?

   b. If the compound costs \$1.75/gram, what is the cost of this amount of the compound?

31. What volume of sodium has the same mass as 22.0 cm^3 of silicon? The density of sodium is 0.97 g/cm^3; the density of silicon is 2.33 g/cm^3.

32. What is the mass, in kilograms, of a block of platinum that measures 23.0 cm by 78.4 cm by 122 cm? The density of platinum is 22.5 g/cm^3.

33. Sulfuric acid sold for laboratory use consists of 96.7% sulfuric acid, H_2SO_4, by mass. The density of the solution is 1.845 g/cm^3. Compute the number of kilograms of H_2SO_4 in a 2.20-L bottle of laboratory sulfuric acid.

34. How many kilograms of dry air are in a room that measures 15.0 ft by 18.0 ft by 8.00 ft? Use an average density of air of 1.168 g/L. There are 30.48 cm in one foot.

35. Calculate the number of cubic centimeters in each of the following:

   a. 1 m^3 **c.** 5 nm^3

   b. 1 dm^3 **d.** 2×10^{-3} km^3

Chapter 4

36. In which of these atom(s) is the number of protons equal to the number of neutrons?

   a. germanium-72   **c.** silicon-28

   b. calcium-40   **d.** hydrogen-1

37. Give the total number of subatomic particles (protons, electrons, and neutrons) in each atom.

   a. vanadium-51   **c.** tin-120

   b. aluminum-27   **d.** hafnium-178

38. Identify the element name and mass number of an atom with the given composition.

    a. 42 protons, 56 neutrons, 42 electrons

    b. 2 protons, 1 neutron, 2 electrons

    c. 76 protons, 113 neutrons, 76 electrons

    d. 31 protons, 40 neutrons, 31 electrons

39. Use the mass and percent abundance of the four isotopes of strontium to calculate the atomic mass of strontium.

Isotope	Mass (amu)	Abundance (%)
Strontium-84	83.193	0.560
Strontium-86	85.909	9.86
Strontium-87	86.908	7.00
Strontium-88	87.906	82.58

40. An atom of carbon and an atom of element Z together weigh 6 amu less than double the weight of an atom of oxygen. If an atom of oxygen weighs 16 amu and an atom of carbon weighs 12 amu, what does an atom of element Z weigh?

Chapter 5

41. What is the maximum number of electrons in each of the following?

    a. the fourth energy level

    b. the $5p$ energy sublevel

    c. a single $4f$ orbital

    d. the first three energy levels

42. Write the electron configuration of each atom.

    a. nickel

    b. sulfur

    c. arsenic

    d. rubidium

43. Identify the symbols of the elements with the following electron configurations:

    a. $1s^2 2s^2 2p^6 3s^2 3p^6 3d^{10} 4s^1$

    b. $1s^2 2s^2 2p^6 3s^2 3p^5$

    c. $1s^2 2s^2 2p^6 3s^2 3p^6 3d^{10} 4s^2 4p^6 4d^2 5s^2$

    d. $1s^2 2s^2 2p^6 3s^2 3p^6 3d^{10} 4s^2 4p^6$

44. How many electrons are in the

    a. third energy level of an indium atom?

    b. second energy level of an oxygen atom?

    c. third energy level of a vanadium atom?

    d. first energy level of a barium atom?

45. Calculate the wavelength (in meters) of each of these frequencies of electromagnetic radiation.

    a. 9.82×10^{19}/s

    b. 2.24×10^{14}/s

    c. 5.31×10^7/s

    d. 7.78×10^{10}/s

46. Order the wavelengths in Problem 45 from highest to lowest energy.

Chapter 6

47. Based on their relative positions on the periodic table, which atom in each pair has the smaller atomic radius?

    a. Na, K

    b. Cl, Br

    c. K, Br

    d. Ne, Na

48. Based on their relative positions on the periodic table, which atom in each pair has the greater electronegativity?

    a. B, C

    b. Na, Al

    c. Li, Cs

    d. As, F

49. Based on their relative positions on the periodic table, which atom in each pair has the highest first ionization energy?

    a. F, Br

    b. Li, F

    c. Ca, Be

    d. K, Ar

50. Here are the first, second, and third ionization energies (kJ/mol) respectively for the representative elements "X" and "Y."

Element	First ionization energy (kJ/mol)	Second ionization energy (kJ/mol)	Third ionization energy (kJ/mol)
X	738	1450	7732
Y	496	4565	6912

In what group on the periodic table would these elements most likely be found?

51. Would the ion formed from each element be larger or smaller than the atom from which it was formed?

a. calcium

b. aluminum

c. bromine

d. nitrogen

Chapter 7

52. In any group of representative elements on the periodic table, how does the number of valence electrons vary as the elements within the group increase in mass?

53. How many valence electrons are lost by the metallic element when forming each of these ionic compounds?

a. BaS

b. In_2Se_3

c. GaP

d. SrI_2

54. Write the formulas for two cations of representative elements that have the electron configuration $1s^2 2s^2 2p^6 3s^2 3p^6$.

55. If "X" is the formula for any halogen and "M" is the formula for any metal, which of these is a valid formula of an ionic compound formed between "M" and "X"? What is the electron dot structure for "M" in each of the compounds that can be formed?

a. MX_2

b. M_2X_2

c. MX_3

d. M_2X_3

56. How many electrons are in each ion?

a. Pb^{4+}

c. Te^{2-}

b. Cr^{3+}

d. C^{4-}

Chapter 8

57. Draw an electron dot structure for each substance.

a. H_2Te

b. AsH_3

c. $SiBr_4$

d. I_2

58. How many electrons are in the electron dot structure for each of these polyatomic ions?

a. cyanide, CN^-

b. bromate ion, BrO_3^-

c. phosphite ion, PO_3^{3-}

d. nitrite, NO_2^-

59. Use VSEPR theory to predict the shape of each molecule in Problem 57.

60. Classify each of the molecules in Problem 57 as polar or nonpolar.

Chapter 9

61. Classify each of these compounds as molecular or ionic.

a. CF_4

b. PtO_2

c. SrI_2

d. NH_4Br

e. K_2CO_3

f. NI_3

g. $C_5H_{10}O_5$

h. $Ba(OH)_2$

62. Name or write the formulas for these molecular compounds.

a. $SiCl_4$

b. phosphorus triiodide

c. Br_2O_7

d. iodine monofluoride

e. BrF_5

f. diarsenic trioxide

g. NCl_3

h. diphosphorus pentoxide

63. Write the formulas for these ionic compounds.

    a. barium iodide

    b. iron(III) acetate

    c. potassium dichromate

    d. ammonium bromide

    e. cesium nitride

    f. cobalt(III) nitrate

    g. aluminum oxalate

    h. mercurous chloride

64. Name these ionic compounds.

    a. Rb_2S **e.** $HgCl_2$

    b. LiI   **f.** $CuClO_3$

    c. $Pb(C_2H_3O_2)_2$ **g.** NaCN

    d. Mg_3N_2 **h.** $Cr(ClO_4)_3$

65. Name these compounds.

    a. Cs_2O **e.** H_2CrO_4

    b. SnS_2 **f.** CaC_2O_4

    c. N_4S_4 **g.** $(NH_4)_3PO_4$

    d. B_2O_3 **h.** As_4O_{10}

66. Write the formulas for these compounds.

    a. calcium oxide

    b. sulfurous acid

    c. diboron tetrachloride

    d. calcium hydrogen phosphate

    e. tin(II) chromate

    f. ferric hydroxide

    g. manganese(II) chlorite

    h. iodine monochloride

67. Explain why it is not fair to be asked to write a formula for each named "compound."

    a. iron bromide

    b. sulfur oxide

    c. lead hypochlorite

    d. phosphorus chloride

68. Iron forms two compounds with oxygen. One compound consists of 1.396 g of iron and 0.400 grams of oxygen. The other has 0.582 g iron and 0.250 g oxygen. Show by calculation whether this pair of compounds obeys the law of multiple proportions.

Chapter 10

69. How many of each kind of atom are in a formula unit of each compound?

    a. $(NH_4)_2SO_3$

    b. $AlPO_4$

    c. $Ca(C_2H_3O_2)_2$

    d. $Fe_2(SO_4)_3$

70. How many of each kind of atom are in a molecule of each compound?

    a. $C_3H_7O_2$

    b. $C_3H_5(OH)_3$

    c. $C_2H_4(COOH)_2$

    d. $C_7H_5(NO_3)_3$

71. Calculate the molar mass of each of these binary ionic compounds.

    a. MgO   **c.** Hg_2I_2

    b. $AlCl_3$ **d.** Sr_3N_2

72. Calculate the molar mass of each of these ionic compounds.

    a. $(NH_4)_2C_2O_4$

    b. $Ca(OH)_2$

    c. Na_2HPO_4

    d. $Mg(HSO_4)_2$

73. Calculate the molar mass of each of these molecular compounds.

    a. N_2O_5

    b. C_3H_7OH

    c. SO_3

    d. XeF_6

74. Calculate the molar mass of each of these compounds.

    a. DEET, $C_{12}H_{17}ON$, an insect repellent

    b. aspartame, $C_{14}H_{18}N_2O_5$, a sugar substitute

    c. codeine, $C_{18}H_{21}NO_3$, an analgesic (painkiller)

    d. sodium benzoate, $NaC_7H_5O_2$, a food preservative

75. What is the mass, in grams, of each of the following?

    a. 5.000 mol Ar

    b. 1.64 mol $NaNO_2$

    c. 0.886 mol $(NH_4)_2SO_4$

    d. 18.3 mol SiF_4

76. How many moles is each of the following?

a. 579 g Pt

b. 0.0426 g NO_2

c. 56.8 g H_2SO_3

d. 6.78×10^3 g CsH_2PO_4

77. Find the number of representative particles in each of the following:

a. 4.40 mol Pd

b. 0.284 mol NaI

c. 1.62 mol NH_3

d. 12.8 mol $Fe(C_2H_3O_2)_2$

78. How many moles is each of the following?

a. 7.26×10^{22} atoms Zr

b. 1.48×10^{24} molecules C_2H_6O

c. 4.00×10^{23} formula units $KClO_3$

d. 9.02×10^{24} molecules OF_2

79. Calculate the volume, in liters, of each of these gases at STP.

a. 3.64 mol H_2

b. 0.0648 mol C_2H_6

c. 8.44 mol SO_3

d. 1.26 mol Xe

80. How many moles is each of the following at STP?

a. 56.4 L He

b. 7.64 L N_2

c. 0.888 L CO

d. 126 L SO_2

81. Calculate the number of representative particles in each mass.

a. 14.6 g CO_2

b. 68.3 g Os

c. 0.847 g KCl

d. 174 g Au_2O_3

82. Calculate the mass of each of the following samples.

a. 7.00×10^9 molecules Br_2

b. 9.22×10^{22} formula units NaF

c. 4.8×10^{24} atoms Li

d. 2.66×10^{20} molecules H_2CO

83. Find the mass of each of the gases at STP.

a. 2.44 L O_2

b. 777 L CH_4

c. 78.0 L SO_3

d. 0.0642 L H_2

84. Calculate the volume of each of these gases at STP.

a. 0.469 g Cl_2

b. 44.8 g NO

c. 2.76 g N_2O_3

d. 93.2 g F_2

85. Calculate the number of representative particles in each volume.

a. 64.0 L H_2S

b. 3.36 L C_3H_8

c. 4.78×10^4 L HF

d. 6.88×10^{-2} L Kr

86. Find the volume at STP of the following:

a. 3.66×10^{21} molecules F_2

b. 6.11×10^{22} molecules PH_3

c. 1.16×10^{25} atoms Ne

d. 4.48×10^{24} molecules C_2H_2

87. Calculate the number of oxygen atoms in each of the following:

a. 7 molecules of the explosive nitroglycerine, $C_3H_5(NO_3)_3$

b. 3.00 mol of the antiseptic hydrogen peroxide, H_2O_2

c. a balloon filled with 2.00 L O_2

d. 8.04 g of the fertilizer, NH_4NO_3

88. Calculate the number of grams of hydrogen in each of the following.

a. a balloon filled with 7.06×10^{24} hydrogen molecules

b. a balloon filled with 14.0 L of methane, CH_4, at STP

c. a 2.00-L bottle of water (density of $H_2O = 1.00$ g/mL)

d. a 69.5-g ice cube (density of ice = 0.917 g/cm³)

89. Calculate the percent composition of each compound.

a. PbO_2

b. $(CH_3)_2CO$

c. KIO_3

d. $Na_2S_2O_3$

e. IF_5

f. $HBrO_4$

g. P_4O_6

h. C_3H_7COOH

90. Use the answers from Problem 89 to calculate the number of grams of the indicated element in the compound.

   a. lead in 63.8 g PbO_2

   b. carbon in 1.664 g $(CH_3)_2CO$

   c. oxygen in 36.8 g KIO_3

   d. sulfur in 6.26 g $Na_2S_2O_3$

   e. fluorine in 594 g IF_5

   f. bromine in 82.7 g $HBrO_4$

   g. phosphorus in 2.66 g P_4O_6

   h. carbon in 55.0 g C_3H_7COOH

91. Which of these are empirical formulas?

   a. $Al_2(SO_4)_3$

   b. $C_6H_4Cl_2$

   c. $C_2H_4(OH)_2$

   d. $K_2Cr_2O_7$

92. What is the empirical formula of

   a. $C_6H_{16}N_2$, a compound used to make nylon?

   b. $C_6H_8N_2$, a component of chocolate?

   c. C_8H_8, used to make polystyrene foam plastics?

   d. C_3H_7OH, rubbing alcohol?

93. Determine the empirical formula for each compound from the percent composition data.

   a. 85.71% C, 14.29% H

   b. 60.94% Ba, 10.65% C, 28.41% O

   c. 37.50% C, 12.50% H, 50.00% O

   d. 27.87% P, 72.13% S

   e. 67.61% U, 32.39% F

   f. 74.19% Na, 25.79% O

   g. 32.43% C, 5.41% H, 43.24% O, 18.92% N

   h. 18.70% Li, 16.26% C, 65.04% O

94. Find the molecular formula from the given empirical formula and molar mass.

Empirical formula	Molar mass (g/mol)	Molecular formula
C_2H_3	54.0	**a.** _____
C_2H_2Cl	123.0	**b.** _____
$C_3H_4O_3$	176.0	**c.** _____
C_5H_7N	162.0	**d.** _____

95. A compound with a molar mass of 312.2 g/mol contains 69.23% C, 3.85% H, and 26.92% N. What is the molecular formula of this compound?

96. The molar mass of caffeine, the stimulant found in coffee, is 194.0 g/mol. The percent composition of caffeine is 49.48% C, 5.19% H, 28.85% N, and 16.48% O. What is the molecular formula of caffeine?

97. Linoleic acid, which has a molar mass of 280.0 g/mol, is found in many vegetable oils. The percent composition of this compound is 77.1% carbon, 11.4% hydrogen, and 11.4% oxygen. Find the empirical formula and molecular formula of this compound.

98. A 2.716-g sample of a compound of C, H, N, and O was found to contain 0.7580 g C, 0.0633 g H, and 0.8843 g N. The molar mass of the compound is 129 g/mol. Calculate the compound's empirical and molecular formula.

Chapter 11

99. What is the function of the element platinum in this reaction?

$$2H_2 + O_2 \xrightarrow{\text{Pt}} 2H_2O$$

100. Balance the following equations:

   a. $Hg(NO_3)_2 + NH_4SCN \longrightarrow Hg(SCN)_2 + NH_4NO_3$

   b. $CH_4O + O_2 \longrightarrow CO_2 + H_2O$

   c. $Ca + Cl_2 \longrightarrow CaCl_2$

   d. $Na_3PO_4 + CoCl_2 \longrightarrow Co_3(PO_4)_2 + NaCl$

   e. $Fe + AgNO_3 \longrightarrow Fe(NO_3)_2 + Ag$

   f. $N_2H_4 \longrightarrow NH_3 + N_2$

   g. $C_{12}H_{26} + O_2 \longrightarrow CO_2 + H_2O$

   h. $CuCl + Mg \longrightarrow Cu + MgCl_2$

101. Classify each of the equations in Problem 100 by type.

102. Write balanced equations for each of these reactions. Indicate states of matter in your equations.

   a. Potassium metal reacts with water to form hydrogen gas and aqueous potassium hydroxide.

   b. Nitrogen monoxide gas reacts with gaseous carbon monoxide to form carbon dioxide gas and nitrogen gas.

c. Hydrochloric acid reacts with oxygen gas to form liquid water and chlorine gas.

d. Aqueous calcium hydroxide reacts with acetic acid to form water and aqueous calcium acetate.

e. Oxygen gas reacts with solid lead(II) sulfide to form sulfur dioxide gas and lead(II) oxide.

f. Solid lithium oxide reacts with water to form aqueous lithium hydroxide.

g. Solid manganese dioxide reacts with oxalic acid to form solid manganese(II) oxide, water, and gaseous carbon dioxide.

h. Gaseous diboron hexahydride reacts with oxygen gas to form liquid water and solid diboron trioxide.

103. Complete and then balance each of these equations.

a. $HCl(aq) \xrightarrow{\text{electricity}}$

b. $Br_2(l) + AlI_3(aq) \longrightarrow$

c. $Na(s) + S(s) \longrightarrow$

d. $Ba(OH)_2(aq) + HNO_3(aq) \longrightarrow$

e. $C_7H_{14}O_2(l) + O_2(g) \longrightarrow$

f. $Ni(NO_3)_2(aq) + Na_2CO_3(aq) \longrightarrow$

104. Balance each of these equations.

a. $MnO_2 + HCl \longrightarrow MnCl_2 + Cl_2 + H_2O$

b. $PCl_5 + H_2O \longrightarrow H_3PO_4 + HCl$

c. $Ca_3P_2 + H_2O \longrightarrow PH_3 + Ca(OH)_2$

d. $Li_3N + H_2O \longrightarrow LiOH + NH_3$

e. $H_2O_2 + N_2H_4 \longrightarrow N_2 + H_2O$

f. $SiCl_4 + Mg \longrightarrow MgCl_2 + Si$

g. $V_2O_5 + H_2 \longrightarrow V_2O_3 + H_2O$

h. $HBr + KHSO_3 \longrightarrow KBr + H_2O + SO_2$

105. Use Table 11.3 to predict whether a precipitate will form when aqueous solutions of these pairs of salts are mixed. If a precipitate forms, write its formula.

a. ammonium sulfate and barium bromide

b. chromium(II) chloride and lithium carbonate

c. potassium nitrate and sodium chloride

d. sodium sulfide and mercury(II) nitrate

106. Write a balanced complete ionic equation for each of these double-replacement reactions. All the reactants are in aqueous solution.

a. nickel(II) chloride + potassium phosphate

b. acetic acid + calcium hydroxide

c. calcium iodide + sodium sulfate

d. sodium hydroxide + lead(II) nitrate

107. Identify the spectator ions in each of the reactions in Problem 106.

108. Write net ionic equations for each of the reactions in Problem 106.

Chapter 12

109. Interpret each equation in terms of interacting particles.

a. $H_2 + F_2 \longrightarrow 2HF$

b. $2K_3PO_4 + 3CoCl_2 \longrightarrow Co_3(PO_4)_2 + 6KCl$

c. $2PbS + 3O_2 \longrightarrow 2PbO + 2SO_2$

d. $Fe + S \longrightarrow FeS$

110. Write all possible mole ratios for these equations.

a. $2NO + Cl_2 \longrightarrow 2NOCl$

b. $2KClO_3 \longrightarrow 2KCl + 3O_2$

c. $3N_2H_4 \longrightarrow 4NH_3 + N_2$

d. $2Na + O_2 \longrightarrow Na_2O_2$

111. Show by calculation that the following equations obey the law of conservation of mass:

a. $3NO_2 + H_2O \longrightarrow 2HNO_3 + NO$

b. $4HCl + O_2 \longrightarrow 2H_2O + 2Cl_2$

c. $2Li + S \longrightarrow Li_2S$

d. $2CH_4O + 3O_2 \longrightarrow 2CO_2 + 4H_2O$

112. Nitric acid, HNO_3, is produced by a process that allows nitrogen dioxide to react with water.

$$3NO_2(g) + H_2O(l) \longrightarrow 2HNO_3(aq) + NO(g)$$

a. How many moles of nitrogen dioxide, NO_2, are required to produce 3.56 mol of nitric acid?

b. How many moles of water react with 0.946 mol of nitrogen dioxide?

113. Calcium hydroxide reacts with nitric acid to produce an aqueous solution of calcium nitrate.

$$Ca(OH)_2(aq) + 2HNO_3(aq) \longrightarrow$$
$$2H_2O(l) + Ca(NO_3)_2(aq)$$

a. How many moles of calcium hydroxide are needed to react with 5.88 mol of nitric acid?

b. How many moles of calcium nitrate are produced when 2.30 mol of water are made in this reaction?

114. Chromium combines with oxygen to form chromium(III) oxide.

$$4Cr(s) + 3O_2(g) \longrightarrow 2Cr_2O_3(s)$$

a. How many moles of chromium are needed to react with 45.6 g of oxygen?

b. How many moles of chromium(III) oxide are produced when 2.86 g of chromium react?

115. Sodium hydroxide is formed when sodium oxide reacts with water.

$$Na_2O(s) + H_2O(l) \longrightarrow 2NaOH(aq)$$

a. Calculate the grams of sodium hydroxide formed when 2.24 moles of sodium oxide react with water.

b. What mass of water (in centigrams) is needed to react with 0.126 mol of sodium oxide?

116. The reaction of nitrogen monoxide with carbon monoxide produces carbon dioxide and nitrogen.

$$2NO(g) + 2CO(g) \longrightarrow 2CO_2(g) + N_2(g)$$

a. How many liters of nitrogen monoxide at STP are needed to produce 3.40 mol of nitrogen gas?

b. When 2.18 moles of nitrogen are made in this reaction, how many liters of carbon dioxide at STP are produced?

117. Hydrogen fluoride gas is produced directly from its component elements.

$$H_2(g) + F_2(g) \longrightarrow 2HF(g)$$

a. When 40.0 L of fluorine at STP reacts with an excess of hydrogen, how many moles of hydrogen fluoride are made?

b. How many moles of fluorine are needed to make 8.04 L of hydrogen fluoride at STP?

118. Rust (iron(III) oxide) is formed by the reaction of oxygen with iron.

$$4Fe(s) + 3O_2(g) \longrightarrow 2Fe_2O_3(s)$$

a. Calculate the mass of oxygen required to react with 10.0 g of iron.

b. How many grams of rust form when 2.48 g of iron reacts with an excess of oxygen?

119. Silver chloride precipitates when aqueous solutions of calcium chloride and silver nitrate are mixed.

$$CaCl_2(aq) + 2AgNO_3(aq) \longrightarrow$$
$$2AgCl(s) + Ca(NO_3)_2(aq)$$

a. How many grams of calcium nitrate are formed when 0.500 g of calcium chloride reacts with an excess of silver nitrate?

b. How many grams of calcium chloride are required to react completely with 34.8 g of silver nitrate?

120. The complete combustion of octane, a component of gasoline, forms carbon dioxide and water.

$$2C_8H_{18}(l) + 25O_2(g) \longrightarrow$$
$$16CO_2(g) + 18H_2O(l)$$

a. How many grams of C_8H_{18} must be reacted to give 5.00 g of CO_2?

b. How many liters of oxygen gas at STP are required to burn 2.20 g C_8H_{18}?

121. A precipitate of nickel(II) carbonate forms when aqueous solutions of sodium carbonate and nickel(II) nitrate are mixed.

$$Ni(NO_3)_2(aq) + Na_2CO_3(aq) \longrightarrow$$
$$NiCO_3(s) + 2NaNO_3(aq)$$

a. How many grams of each reactant must be used to form 67.2 g of the precipitate?

b. When 1.88 g of nickel(II) carbonate are formed, how many grams of sodium nitrate are produced?

122. One way to make ethanol is to react ethene with water at high pressure.

$$C_2H_4(g) + H_2O(g) \longrightarrow C_2H_6O(l)$$

a. How many grams of each reactant are needed to produce 8.84 g of ethanol?

b. How many liters of ethanol are produced when 1.00 kg of ethene is reacted with an excess of water? The density of ethanol is 0.789 g/mL.

123. Balance the equation for the formation of aluminum hydroxide, a common ingredient in some antacid tablets.

$$Al_2(SO_4)_3(aq) + NaOH(aq) \longrightarrow$$
$$Al(OH)_3(s) + Na_2SO_4(aq)$$

  a. How many grams of sodium hydroxide are required to react completely with 6.22 g of aluminum sulfate?

  b. When 32.0 grams of sodium hydroxide reacts with an excess of aluminum sulfate, how many grams of aluminum hydroxide are formed?

124. One source of elemental oxygen in the laboratory is the decomposition of hydrogen peroxide.

$$2H_2O_2(l) \longrightarrow 2H_2O(l) + O_2(g)$$

  a. How many grams of hydrogen peroxide are needed to produce 5.00 g of oxygen?

  b. When 16.8 g of hydrogen peroxide are decomposed, how many liters (at STP) of oxygen are produced?

125. One source of acid rain is the production of nitric acid from nitrogen dioxide and water in the atmosphere.

$$3NO_2(g) + H_2O(l) \longrightarrow NO(g) + 2HNO_3(aq)$$

  a. How many kilograms of nitric acid are produced when 5.60 kg of nitrogen dioxide reacts with an excess of water?

  b. Calculate the mass in grams of nitrogen monoxide produced when 0.648 kg of nitric acid is formed by this reaction.

126. Steel rails for trains are welded together with the liquid (molten) iron formed by the immense heat generated by this reaction.

$$2Al(s) + Fe_2O_3(s) \longrightarrow Al_2O_3(s) + 2Fe(l)$$

  a. How many grams of aluminum are needed to react completely with 0.500 kg of iron(III) oxide?

  b. How many milliliters of molten iron are produced when 80.0 g of iron(III) oxide are reacted with an excess of aluminum? The density of iron is 7.87 g/cm^3. Assume the densities of molten iron and solid iron are the same.

127. Chlorine gas is made by reacting oxygen with hydrochloric acid.

$$4HCl(aq) + O_2(g) \longrightarrow 2Cl_2(g) + 2H_2O(l)$$

  a. How many grams of each of the reactants are required to produce 44.0 g of chlorine?

  b. At STP, how many liters of oxygen are needed to react completely with 125 g of hydrochloric acid?

128. Hydrogen fluoride is made by reacting sulfuric acid with calcium fluoride.

$$H_2SO_4(l) + CaF_2(s) \longrightarrow 2HF(g) + CaSO_4(s)$$

  a. How many grams of hydrogen fluoride and calcium sulfate are produced when 2.86 g of calcium fluoride reacts with an excess of sulfuric acid?

  b. Calculate the number of kilograms of calcium fluoride that must react with an excess of sulfuric acid to produce 1.00 kg of hydrogen fluoride.

129. When solid dinitrogen pentoxide is heated, it produces oxygen and nitrogen dioxide.

  a. Write the balanced equation for this reaction.

  b. How many grams of each product are formed when 4.00 g of dinitrogen pentoxide is completely decomposed?

130. Laundry bleach (NaClO) is made by reacting chlorine with sodium hydroxide.

$$Cl_2(g) + 2NaOH(aq) \longrightarrow$$
$$NaClO(aq) + NaCl(aq) + H_2O(l)$$

  a. How many grams of chlorine must react with an excess of sodium hydroxide to produce 2.50 kg of sodium hypochlorite?

  b. At room temperature, chlorine gas has a density of 2.95 g/L. How many dL of chlorine gas are needed to react completely with 66.8 g of sodium hydroxide?

131. Bubbling oxygen gas through liquid acetaldehyde (C_2H_4O) forms a single product, acetic acid.

  a. Write a balanced equation for this reaction.

  b. How many grams of oxygen are needed to react completely with 542 g of acetaldehyde?

132. Water is decomposed into its elements by an electric current.

    a. Write a balanced equation for the reaction.

    b. What is the total volume (in liters at STP) of gases produced when 222 g of water are decomposed?

133. Oxygen is generated in a rebreathing gas mask by a reaction of water vapor with potassium superoxide, KO_2.

$$4KO_2(s) + 2H_2O(l) \longrightarrow 3O_2(g) + 4KOH(s)$$

    a. How many liters of oxygen gas at STP are produced when 56.0 g of potassium superoxide react completely with water vapor?

    b. How many grams of potassium hydroxide are produced when the 56.0 g of KO_2 react with an excess of water?

134. Find the limiting reagent for each set of reactants. Then calculate the number of moles of each reactant remaining and the amount of each product formed after the reaction.

$$4NH_3(g) + 3O_2(g) \longrightarrow 2N_2(g) + 6H_2O(l)$$

    a. 4.00 mol NH_3 + 4.00 mol O_2

    b. 2.00 mol NH_3 + 1.00 mol O_2

    c. 7.00 mol NH_3 + 5.00 mol O_2

    d. 3.25 mol NH_3 + 2.75 mol O_2

135. Diboron trioxide is formed by reacting 14.0 g of diboron hexahydride with 68.0 g of oxygen.

$$B_2H_6(g) + 3O_2(g) \longrightarrow 3H_2O(l) + B_2O_3(s)$$

    a. Identify the limiting reagent.

    b. Calculate the mass of diboron trioxide produced.

136. When hydrochloric acid is added to calcium carbonate, bubbles of carbon dioxide gas are produced.

$$CaCO_3(s) + 2HCl(aq) \longrightarrow$$
$$CaCl_2(aq) + H_2O(l) + CO_2(g)$$

    a. What is the limiting reagent when 1.68 g of HCl is added to 4.82 g $CaCO_3$?

    b. In the reaction, how many milliliters of water are produced? (density = 1.00 g/cm^3)

    c. What is the volume, in liters, of carbon dioxide produced? Assume STP.

137. The elements phosphorus and chlorine react to form phosphorus trichloride.

$$P_4(s) + 6Cl_2(g) \longrightarrow 4PCl_3(l)$$

    a. What is the limiting reagent when 100.0 g of phosphorus reacts with 200.0 g of chlorine?

    b. How many grams of phosphorus trichloride are formed?

138. Hydrogen gas is one of the products of the reaction of aluminum with hydrochloric acid.

$$2Al(s) + 6HCl(aq) \longrightarrow AlCl_3(aq) + 3H_2(g)$$

How many grams of H_2 are produced when 20.0 g of Al reacts with 60.0 g of HCl?

139. When copper(I) oxide, Cu_2O, is heated in oxygen, copper(II) oxide is formed.

$$2Cu_2O(s) + O_2(g) \longrightarrow 4CuO(s)$$

When 4.00 mol of copper(I) oxide reacts with 2.00 mol of oxygen, 7.44 mol of CuO is obtained. What is the percent yield of this reaction?

140. When 7.00 mol C reacts with 5.00 mol SO_2, 1.80 mol CS_2 is formed.

$$3C(s) + 2SO_2(g) \longrightarrow CS_2(l) + 2CO_2(g)$$

What is the percent yield of this reaction?

141. An excess of water is reacted with 25.0 g of calcium carbide. A mass of 7.20 g of C_2H_2 is obtained.

$$CaC_2(s) + 2H_2O(l) \longrightarrow$$
$$C_2H_2(g) + Ca(OH)_2(aq)$$

What is the percent yield of C_2H_2?

142. An excess of sulfur dioxide was reacted with 0.150 g of oxygen gas. A mass of 0.725 g of sulfur trioxide was recovered.

$$2SO_2(g) + O_2(g) \longrightarrow 2SO_3(g)$$

What is the percent yield of sulfur trioxide?

143. When 30.0 g CH_4 reacts with 90.0 g O_2 and 30.0 g NH_3, 94.4 g H_2O is formed.

$$2CH_4(g) + 3O_2(g) + 2NH_3(g) \longrightarrow$$
$$2HCN(g) + 6H_2O(l)$$

What is the percent yield of this reaction?

Chapter 13

144. Make the following pressure conversions:

　　a. 364 kPa to atm

　　b. 815 mm Hg to kPa

　　c. 0.260 atm to mm Hg

　　d. 1555 mm Hg to atm

　　e. 85.8 kPa to mm Hg

　　f. 0.440 atm to kPa

145. Water evaporates much more slowly at room temperature than acetone. How does the relative strength of intermolecular forces compare in these two compounds?

146. In the same location, equal quantities of water are poured into a drinking glass and a glass pie pan. In which container will the water evaporate first? Explain your choice.

147. Equal masses of liquid and solid wax are placed in an oven maintained at a temperature exactly at the melting point of the wax. How would the relative amounts of liquid and solid wax change over time?

Chapter 14

148. A sample of gas at a pressure of 124 kPa has a volume of 3.00 L. If the gas is compressed to a volume of 1.26 L, what is its new pressure? (Assume constant temperature.)

149. A scuba tank has a volume of 11.0 L. What volume of gas in liters at 0.950 atm is required to completely fill the tank to a pressure of 45.0 atm, assuming no change in the temperature of the gas?

150. A syringe contains 2.60 mL of gas at 20.0°C. What is the volume of gas after the temperature is increased to 68.0°C?

151. A contained gas has a volume of 120.0 mL at −183°C. What volume does this gas occupy at 47.0°C?

152. To what temperature must a contained gas at a pressure of 464 mm Hg and a temperature of 40.0°C be raised to increase the pressure to 994 mm Hg?

153. The pressure of a gas in a cylinder at 27.0°C is 846 kPa. What is the pressure in the cylinder when the temperature is increased to 54.0°C?

154. Calculate the final pressure of a gas initially at 122 kPa pressure that is expanded from 4.50 L at 56°C to 18.0 L at 124°C.

155. A weather balloon has a volume of 3.5 kL at 1.01 atm and 18°C. What is the balloon's volume at a pressure of 0.420 atm and −18°C?

156. A cylinder contains 4.50 L of nitrogen at 35°C and a pressure of 644 kPa. How many moles of N_2 are in the cylinder?

157. A balloon containing 1.46 mol of neon gas has a volume of 36.2 L.

　　a. Under the same conditions, what is the volume of the balloon if an additional 0.34 mol of Ne is added to the balloon?

　　b. Would the answer change if 0.34 mol of He were added instead of neon?

158. What is the pressure (in kPa) in a 5.00-L tank containing 0.240 mol of oxygen gas at a temperature of 17°C?

159. Calculate the volume of 0.880 mol of fluorine gas at 26°C and 88.8 kPa.

160. A metal cylinder contains 0.440 mol of nitrogen gas at a pressure of 34.0 kPa. What is the pressure in the container after 0.128 mol of nitrogen are removed?

161. All the neon gas from a 10.0-L container at a pressure of 202 kPa is added to a 20.0-L container of argon at a pressure of 505 kPa. After the transfer, what are the partial pressures of neon and argon?

162. A child buys a balloon filled with 3.50 L of helium on a very hot day when it's 39.0°C outside. Assuming a constant pressure, what is the volume of the balloon when the child brings the balloon home to an air-conditioned house at 20.0°C?

163. Suppose you have a 0.500-L cylinder that contains 0.150 mol of oxygen gas, O_2, at 25°C.

　　a. What is the pressure inside the cylinder?

　　b. How would the pressure inside the cylinder change if you substituted 0.150 mol of sulfur dioxide gas, SO_2, for the 0.150 mol of oxygen gas?

　　c. How would the pressure inside the cylinder change if you added 0.150 mol of sulfur dioxide gas, SO_2, to the oxygen already in the cylinder?

164. In a typical automobile engine, the gas mixture in a cylinder is compressed and the pressure increases from 1.00 atm to 9.50 atm. If the uncompressed volume of the cylinder is 755 mL, what is the volume when fully compressed? (Assume constant temperature.)

165. What is the new pressure when an aerosol can with an initial pressure of 4.50 atm at 25°C is heated in a fire to 650°C?

166. How many moles of air are in the lungs of an average person with a total lung capacity of 3.8 L? Assume that the person is at sea level (1.00 atm) and has a normal body temperature of 37°C.

167. Two containers of equal size are filled with 4.0 g of He and 32.0 g of O_2, respectively. Assuming a constant temperature, would you expect the pressures of these two gases to be identical? Explain your answer.

168. Lithium nitride is formed from its elements.
$$6Li(s) + N_2(g) \longrightarrow 2Li_3N(s)$$
How many milliliters of nitrogen gas at STP are needed to react with 0.246 g of lithium?

169. Nitrogen and hydrogen react to form ammonia.
$$3H_2(g) + N_2(g) \longrightarrow 2NH_3(g)$$
How many liters of hydrogen gas measured at 86.4 kPa pressure and 245°C are needed to react completely with 6.44 g N_2?

170. Auto air bags are inflated by nitrogen gas formed through this decomposition reaction:
$$2NaN_3(s) \longrightarrow 2Na(s) + 3N_2(g)$$
How many grams of NaN_3 are needed to inflate an air bag to a volume of 10.6 L, assuming STP?

Chapter 15

171. Which of these molecules can form hydrogen bonds with water?

a. H_2 c. HCl

b. CH_3OH d. C_2H_6

172. Classify each substance as an electrolyte or a nonelectrolyte.

a. NH_4NO_3 c. $NaBr_2$

b. C_2H_6O d. Cl_2

173. Calculate the percent by mass of water in lithium perchlorate trihydrate.

174. An experiment requires making a solution that contains 34.6 g of $CaCl_2$. Your only source is the hydrate, $CaCl_2 \cdot 2H_2O$. How many grams of the hydrate do you need to use to obtain the required mass of $CaCl_2$?

175. A 19.97-g sample of a hydrate contains 5.08 g Cu, 2.57 g S, 5.12 g O, and 7.20 g H_2O. What is the empirical formula of this hydrate?

Chapter 16

176. The solubility of carbon dioxide gas at 50°C and 1.00 atm pressure is 7.6×10^{-2} g/100 g H_2O. Assuming constant temperature, calculate the solubility of CO_2 when the pressure is increased to 2.50 atm.

177. Calculate the molarity of each of these solutions.

a. 4.24 mol NaCl in 2.00 L of solution

b. 0.164 mol of $C_5H_{10}O_5$ in 125 mL of solution

c. 0.0056 mol CsBr in 50.0 mL of solution

d. 2.84 mol C_2H_6O in 0.650 L of solution

178. What is the molarity of each of these solutions?

a. 3.34 g $CuNO_2$ in 0.150 L of solution

b. 0.0688 g CoF_2 in 20.0 mL of solution

c. 88.8 g KOH in 0.755 L of solution

d. 1.66 g $LiNO_3$ in 455 mL of solution

179. Find the moles of solute in the following solutions:

a. 650 mL of $0.28M$ $NaNO_3$

b. 1.4 L of $0.35M$ KI

c. 0.340 L of $2.22M$ $CaCl_2$

d. 148 mL of $0.0068M$ LiF

180. Calculate the mass of solute in each of these solutions.

a. 2.00 L of $0.440M$ MgF_2

b. 6.80 dL of $1.88M$ CH_4O

c. 65.0 mL of $0.0360M$ $NaNO_3$

d. 5.00 mL of $1.48M$ HCl

181. How many milliliters of a stock solution of $2.50M$ $SrCl_2$ solution are required to make each diluted solution?

   a. 50.0 mL of $1.00M$ $SrCl_2$

   b. 1.0 L of $0.40M$ $SrCl_2$

   c. 750 mL of $0.25M$ $SrCl_2$

   d. 65.0 dL of $0.146M$ $SrCl_2$

182. An aqueous solution is 65% (v/v) rubbing alcohol. How many milliliters of alcohol are in a 97-mL sample of this solution?

183. Calculate the percent by mass of each of these solutions.

   a. 6.50 g CsI in 266 g H_2O

   b. 246 g NaOH in 1.40 kg H_2O

   c. 0.428 g K_2CO_3 in 8.58 g H_2O

   d. 1.20 kg $NaNO_3$ in 2.00 kg H_2O

184. Calculate the mole fraction of each component of the following solutions:

   a. 2.40 mol CH_4O and 5.36 mol C_2H_6O

   b. 1.25 mol H_2O and 87.6 g HCl

   c. 24.0 g C_2H_6O and 10.0 g H_2O

   d. 0.464 g C_2H_6O and 2.36 g CH_4O

185. Potassium bromide is dissolved in water. Which statements are true when comparing the solution to pure water?

   a. The boiling point of the solution is higher.

   b. The vapor pressure of the solution is higher.

   c. The freezing point of the solution is higher.

186. Calculate the molality of these solutions.

   a. 0.246 mol KCl in 1.66 kg solvent

   b. 0.116 mol $LiNO_3$ in 844 g solvent

   c. 56.6 mmol CsI in 1.06 kg solvent

   d. 6.66 mol $MgBr_2$ in 2.50 kg solvent

187. Calculate the freezing and boiling points of each of these aqueous solutions.

   a. $2.34m$ NH_4Br

   b. $1.17m$ $CaCl_2$

   c. 24.4 g LiCl in 0.400 kg H_2O

   d. 44.8 g $MgCl_2$ in 1.20 kg H_2O

188. When aqueous solutions of sodium carbonate and nickel(II) nitrate are mixed, nickel(II) carbonate precipitates.

$$Ni(NO_3)_2(aq) + Na_2CO_3(aq) \longrightarrow$$
$$NiCO_3(s) + 2NaNO_3(aq)$$

   a. What volume of $0.366M$ $Ni(NO_3)_2$ is required to completely react with 55.8 mL of $0.500M$ Na_2CO_3?

   b. How many grams of nickel(II) carbonate precipitate in this reaction?

189. Aluminum hydroxide precipitates when aqueous solutions of aluminum sulfate and sodium hydroxide are mixed.

$$Al_2(SO_4)_3(aq) + 6NaOH(aq) \longrightarrow$$
$$2Al(OH)_3(s) + 3Na_2SO_4(aq)$$

   a. What volume of $0.136M$ $Al_2(SO_4)_3$ is needed to completely react with 26.0 mL of $1.20M$ NaOH?

   b. What mass of aluminum hydroxide precipitates in this reaction?

190. A conductivity meter quantitatively measures the ability of an aqueous solution to conduct electrical current. The magnitude of the conductivity value is proportional to the number of ions in the solution. Data from an experiment are given in the table.

Solutions (0.2M)	Conductivity (μS/cm)
KCl	2050
$AlCl_3$	4500
$CaCl_2$	3540
NaOH	2080
C_2H_6O	0

   a. Which two of the solutions have similar conductivities? Why would you expect this?

   b. The ratio of the conductivity of the aluminum chloride solution to the conductivity of the potassium chloride solution is approximately two to one. Why would you expect this result?

Chapter 17

191. As the mass of a substance increases,

  a. does its heat capacity increase, decrease, or remain constant?

  b. does its specific heat increase, decrease, or remain constant?

192. The temperature of a 6.42-gram piece of glass is 15°C. How many calories would it take to increase the temperature of the glass to 96°C? The specific heat of glass is 0.12 cal/(g·°C).

193. Ethanol has a specific heat of 2.43 J/(g·°C). If 468 J of heat is added to 29.0 g of ethanol initially at 25.0°C, what is the final temperature of the liquid?

194. When 1564 J of energy is added to a sample of gold at 25.0°C, the temperature of the gold increases by 424.0°C. What is the mass of the gold? The specific heat of gold is 0.129 J/(g·°C).

195. Identical masses of aluminum and lead at the same temperature absorb identical amounts of heat energy. The specific heat of aluminum is 0.901 J/(g·°C); the specific heat of lead is 0.129 J/(g·°C). Which gets hotter, the aluminum or the lead?

196. Suppose your diet provides 2100 Cal (kcal) in a day, and your body weight is 68 kg. Start with an initial body temperature of a normal 37°C. Calculate the maximum temperature that your body would reach by absorbing all 2100 kcal at once. For purposes of this problem, assume that your body is 100% water. The specific heat of water is 1.00 cal/(g·°C).

197. Nitrogen monoxide is formed from its elements.

$$N_2(g) + O_2(g) \longrightarrow 2NO(g)$$
$$\Delta H = 181 \text{ kJ/mol}$$

  a. Is this reaction exothermic or endothermic?

  b. How many kilojoules of energy are needed to form 8.70 mol NO?

198. Carbon dioxide and water are produced by the complete combustion of propane, C_3H_8.

$$C_3H_8(g) + 5O_2(g) \longrightarrow$$
$$3CO_2(g) + 4H_2O(g) + 526 \text{ kcal}$$

  a. Is this reaction exothermic or endothermic?

  b. How many kcal of energy are produced when 14.4 g C_3H_8 burns in an excess of oxygen?

199. The following reaction was used to fuel the rockets in the Apollo mission landing module.

$$2N_2H_4(l) + N_2O_4(l) \longrightarrow 3N_2(g) + 4H_2O(g)$$
$$\Delta H = -1049 \text{ kJ}$$

  a. Is this reaction endothermic or exothermic?

  b. How many grams of N_2H_4 must be reacted with an excess of N_2O_4 to produce 645 kJ of energy?

  c. How many kilojoules of energy are produced when 5.40 g N_2O_4 reacts with an excess of N_2H_4?

200. The heat of fusion of mercury is 2.30 kJ/mol. How much heat (in J) is released when 24.0 g Hg changes from the liquid state to the solid state at its freezing point?

201. How much heat energy is required to change 50.0 g of liquid water at 100°C to water vapor at 100°C? The molar heat of fusion is 6.01 kJ/mol, and the molar heat of vaporization is 40.7 kJ/mol.

202. There is a dramatic temperature change when solid ammonium nitrate is dissolved in water.

$$NH_4NO_3(s) \longrightarrow NH_4^+(aq) + NO_3^-(aq)$$
$$\Delta H_{soln} = 25.7 \text{kJ/mol}$$

  a. Is there a temperature increase or decrease when ammonium nitrate dissolves in water?

  b. Calculate the heat change when 55.0 g $NH_4NO_3(s)$ dissolves in water.

203. Use the data in Table 17.4 and the additional values for $\Delta H°$ given below to calculate the standard heat of reaction ($\Delta H°$) for each of these reactions.

Substance	$\Delta H_f°$ (kJ/mol)
$N_2H_4(l)$	50.63
$HNO_3(aq)$	−207.4

  a. $2SO_2(g) + O_2(g) \longrightarrow 2SO_3(g)$
  b. $3N_2H_4(l) \longrightarrow 4NH_3(g) + N_2(g)$
  c. $3NO_2(g) + H_2O(g) \longrightarrow 2HNO_3(aq) + NO(g)$
  d. $2NO(g) + 2CO(g) \longrightarrow 2CO_2(g) + N_2(g)$

204. Ethanol is manufactured by reacting water with ethane, C_2H_4.

$$C_2H_4(g) + H_2O(l) \longrightarrow C_2H_6O(l)$$

Use the following equations to calculate the $\Delta H°$ for this reaction.

$$C_2H_6O(l) + 3O_2(g) \longrightarrow 2CO_2(g) + 3H_2O(l)$$
$$\Delta H = -1367 \text{ kJ}$$

$$C_2H_4(g) + 3O_2(g) \longrightarrow 2CO_2(g) + 2H_2O(l)$$
$$\Delta H = -1411 \text{ kJ}$$

205. Use the following equations to calculate the standard heat of formation, in kJ/mol, of magnesium nitrate:

$$2MgO(s) \longrightarrow 2Mg(s) + O_2(g) \quad \Delta H = 1203 \text{ kJ}$$
$$Mg_3N_2(s) \longrightarrow 3Mg(s) + N_2(g) \quad \Delta H = 463 \text{ kJ}$$
$$Mg(NO_3)_2(s) + 8Mg(s) \longrightarrow 6MgO(s) + Mg_3N_2(s)$$
$$\Delta H = -3884 \text{ kJ}$$

206. The heat of sublimation of dry ice (solid CO_2) is 25.2 kJ/mol. How many grams of water at 0.0°C would be frozen by the complete sublimation of 48.0 g of dry ice that is dropped into the water? The heat of fusion of water is 6.01 kJ/mol.

Chapter 18

207. Nitric oxide reacts with hydrogen to form nitrogen gas and water.

$$2NO(g) + 2H_2(g) \longrightarrow N_2(g) + 2H_2O(g)$$

In an experiment, doubling the H_2 concentration causes the rate of reaction to double. When the NO concentration is doubled, the rate of the reaction increases by a factor of eight. Write the rate law for the reaction.

208. At equilibrium, are the reactants or the products favored for reactions that have the following equilibrium constants?

a. $K_{eq} = 5.6 \times 10^{-7}$ **c.** $K_{eq} = 5.6 \times 10^{-14}$
b. $K_{eq} = 5.6 \times 10^{21}$ **d.** $K_{eq} = 5.6 \times 10^5$

209. Write the expression for the equilibrium constant for each reaction.

a. $2PCl_3(g) + O_2(g) \rightleftharpoons 2POCl_3(g)$
b. $2HOCl(g) \rightleftharpoons Cl_2O(g) + H_2O(g)$
c. $Br_2(g) + 5F_2(g) \rightleftharpoons 2BrF_5(g)$
d. $N_2H_4(g) + 6H_2O_2(g) \rightleftharpoons$
$$2NO_2(g) + 8H_2O(g)$$

210. Using the equations in Problem 209, calculate the value of K_{eq} when the following amounts of reactants and products are present in a 1-L container at equilibrium.

a. 1.44 mol PCl_3, 1.44 mol O_2, and 2.60 mol $POCl_3$
b. 0.220 mol HOCl, 4.68 mol Cl_2O, and 6.82 mol H_2O
c. 0.0500 mol Br_2, 1.00 mol F_2, and 0.0465 mol BrF_5
d. 0.400 mol N_2H_4, 0.100 mol H_2O_2, 1.20 mol NO_2, and 1.00 mol H_2O

211. List three ways to cause a shift in this equilibrium to the right, forming more $CH_4O(g)$.

$$CO(g) + 2H_2(g) \rightleftharpoons CH_4O(g) + \text{heat}$$

212. A yellow gas (Y) reacts with a colorless gas (C) to produce a blue gas (B), according to this equation:

$$C(g) + 3Y(g) \rightleftharpoons 2B(g) + \text{heat}$$

The system is initially at equilibrium and has a green color. What happens to the color of the system if the following stresses are placed on the system? Note: Blue and yellow mix to form green.

a. A large amount of colorless C is removed from the reaction container.
b. The reaction container is heated.

213. Assume that the following chemical system is originally at equilibrium and the color of the liquid is purplish (a mixture of the colors pink and blue):

$$\text{heat} + [Co(H_2O)_6]^{2+}(aq) + 4 Cl^-(aq) \rightleftharpoons$$
$$\underset{\text{pink}}{} \quad [CoCl_4]^{2-}(aq) + 6 H_2O(l)$$
$$\underset{\text{blue}}{}$$

a. How does the color change if chloride ion is added to the system?
b. How does the color change if the reaction mixture is cooled?

214. Use Table 18.1 to predict whether a precipitate will form when the following pairs of substances are mixed.

a. $K_2S(aq) + Cu(NO_3)_2(aq)$
b. $NH_4Cl(aq) + Pb(NO_3)_2(aq)$
c. $Na_2CO_3(aq) + ZnCl_2(aq)$
d. $KNO_3(aq) + BaCl_2(aq)$

215. Find the equilibrium concentrations of zinc and sulfide ions in a saturated solution of zinc sulfide with $K_{sp} = 3.0 \times 10^{-23}$.

216. For each change, does the entropy increase or decrease?

    a. A gold nugget melts.

    b. Liquid wax solidifies.

    c. Liquid water forms from water vapor.

    d. Liquid water forms from hydrogen and oxygen gas.

Chapter 19

217. Identify each of the species in each equation as a Brønsted-Lowry acid or a Brønsted-Lowry base.

    a. $H_2O(aq) + CN^-(aq) \rightleftharpoons OH^-(aq) + HCN(aq)$

    b. $HClO_3(aq) + H_2O(aq) \rightleftharpoons ClO_3^-(aq) + H_3O^+(aq)$

    c. $C_5H_5NH^+(aq) + OH^-(aq) \rightleftharpoons C_5H_5N(aq) + H_2O(aq)$

    d. $HSO_4^-(aq) + H_3O^+(aq) \rightleftharpoons H_2SO_4(aq) + H_2O(aq)$

218. Which of the following are conjugate acid-base pairs?

    a. NH_4^+, NH_3

    b. $H_3PO_4, H_2PO_4^-$

    c. HSO_4^-, SO_4^{2-}

    d. H_3O^+, OH^-

219. Ammonia can act as a Lewis base toward which of these compounds?

    a. CH_4

    b. BCl_3

    c. NF_3

    d. OF_2

220. Calculate the pH of each solution and classify it as acidic or basic.

    a. $[H^+] = 4.6 \times 10^{-4}M$

    b. $[H^+] = 1.2 \times 10^{-8}M$

    c. $[OH^-] = 8.3 \times 10^{-4}M$

    d. $[OH^-] = 2.8 \times 10^{-11}M$

    e. $[H^+] = 3.9 \times 10^{-2}M$

    f. $[OH^-] = 1.5 \times 10^{-9}M$

221. Calculate the $[H^+]$ and the $[OH^-]$ from the pH of each solution.

    a. pH = 6.03

    b. pH = 1.18

    c. pH = 12.68

    d. pH = 4.33

    e. pH = 9.16

    f. pH = 3.46

222. Rank these acids from strongest to weakest.

    a. HX, $K_a = 1 \times 10^{-4}$

    b. HY, $K_a = 1 \times 10^{-11}$

    c. HP, $K_a = 1 \times 10^{-2}$

    d. HQ, $K_a = 1 \times 10^{-9}$

223. Acetylsalicylic acid (aspirin) has a K_a of 3×10^{-4}. A $0.00056M$ solution of aspirin would be best described by which terms: weak, strong, dilute, concentrated?

224. A $0.10000M$ solution of an unknown acid, HX, has a hydrogen ion concentration of $3.65 \times 10^{-4}M$. Calculate the value of K_a for this acid.

225. Name and write the formula for the salt formed in each of the following acid-base neutralizations.

    a. aluminum hydroxide with phosphoric acid

    b. oxalic acid with magnesium hydroxide

    c. sulfurous acid with lithium hydroxide

    d. sodium hydroxide with carbonic acid

226. How many moles of sulfuric acid are required to neutralize 1.40 mol of potassium hydroxide?

$$2KOH(aq) + H_2SO_4(aq) \longrightarrow K_2SO_4(aq) + 2H_2O(l)$$

227. What is the molarity of a hydrochloric acid solution if 25.0 mL of the solution reacts completely with 1.66 g $NaHCO_3$?

$$HCl(aq) + NaHCO_3(s) \longrightarrow NaCl(aq) + H_2O(l) + CO_2(g)$$

228. In an acid base titration, how many mL of $0.180M$ HCl are required to neutralize 20.0 mL of $0.220M$ NaOH?

229. How many milliliters of $0.456M$ $Ca(OH)_2$ are needed to neutralize 25.0 mL of $0.300M$ HCl?

230. A buffer (HBrO/BrO⁻) solution is made by mixing together equal quantities of hypobromous acid (HBrO) and sodium hypobromite (NaBrO).

    a. Write an equation for the reaction that occurs when an acid is added to this buffer.

    b. Write an equation for the reaction that occurs when a base is added to this buffer.

Chapter 20

231. What is the oxidation number of sulfur in each of these species?

    a. SF_6 **d.** SO_3

    b. CaS_2O_3 **e.** S

    c. K_2SO_3 **f.** H_2SO_4

232. What is the oxidation number of bromine in each of the following?

    a. CsBr   **d.** Br_2

    b. $NaBrO_3$ **e.** BrCl

    c. BrO_2^- **f.** NaBrO

233. Consider the following reaction:

$$CuCl_2(aq) + Fe(s) \longrightarrow Cu(s) + FeCl_2(aq)$$

    a. Which reactant lost electrons?

    b. What is the oxidizing agent?

    c. Which reactant was oxidized in this reaction?

    d. What is the reducing agent?

234. In each of these reactions, is sulfur oxidized or reduced?

    a. $HgS(s) \longrightarrow Hg(l) + S(s)$

    b. $S(s) + O_2(g) \longrightarrow SO_3(g)$

    c. $H_2SO_4(aq) + Ca(s) \longrightarrow H_2S(g) + Ca^{2+}(aq)$

    d. $Al(s) + S(s) \longrightarrow Al_2S_3(s)$

235. Balance each of the equations in Problem 234.

236. Balance each of the following redox reactions and classify each as a combination, decomposition, or single-replacement reaction.

    a. $Mg(s) + H_2O(l) \longrightarrow Mg(OH)_2 + H_2(g)$

    b. $PF_3(g) + F_2(g) \longrightarrow PF_5(g)$

    c. $C_2H_2(g) + H_2(g) \longrightarrow C_2H_6(g)$

    d. $NaNO_3(s) \longrightarrow NaNO_2(s) + O_2(g)$

237. Iron(II) sulfite reacts with an acid solution of permanganate ion.

$$5FeSO_3 + 14H^+ + 3MnO_4^- \longrightarrow$$
$$3Mn^{2+} + 5Fe^{3+} + 5SO_4^{2-} + 7H_2O$$

    a. What is the oxidation number of iron and of manganese in the reactants?

    b. What is the oxidation number of sulfur and of oxygen in SO_4^{2-}?

    c. Identify the oxidizing agent in this reaction.

    d. What is reduced in this reaction?

238. Write a balanced chemical equation for each of these reactions, and identify the element oxidized and the element reduced.

    a. Nitrogen monoxide reacts with hydrogen to form nitrogen and water.

    b. Potassium permanganate, iron(II) sulfate, and sulfuric acid react, producing manganese(II) sulfate, iron(III) sulfate, potassium sulfate, and water.

    c. Elemental phosphorus (P_4) and nitrogen monoxide react to form tetraphosphorus hexoxide and nitrogen.

    d. Sulfur dioxide, nitric acid, and water react to produce sulfuric acid and nitrogen monoxide.

239. Balance each redox equation by the oxidation-number-change method. Identify the oxidizing agent and the reducing agent.

    a. $KMnO_4(aq) + NaNO_2(aq) + H_2O(l) \longrightarrow$
$$MnO_2(s) + NaNO_3(aq) + KOH(aq)$$

    b. $I_2(s) + Na_2S_2O_3(aq) \longrightarrow$
$$Na_2S_4O_6(aq) + NaI(aq)$$

    c. $HCl(aq) + NH_4Cl(aq) + K_2Cr_2O_7(aq) \longrightarrow$
$$CrCl_3(aq) + KCl(aq) + N_2(g) + H_2O(l)$$

    d. $FeCl_2(aq) + H_2O_2(aq) + HCl(aq) \longrightarrow$
$$FeCl_3(aq) + H_2O(l)$$

240. Use the half-reaction method to write a balanced ionic equation for each reaction. Identify the species oxidized and the species reduced.

    a. $Cr_2O_7^{2-}(aq) + I^-(aq) \longrightarrow$
$$Cr^{3+}(aq) + I_2(s) \text{ (in acidic solution)}$$

    b. $MnO_4^-(aq) + SO_3^{2-}(aq) \longrightarrow$
$$Mn^{2+}(aq) + SO_4^{2-}(aq) \text{ (in acidic solution)}$$

    c. $C_2O_4^{2-}(aq) + MnO_4^-(aq) \longrightarrow$
$$CO_3^{2-}(aq) + MnO_2(s) \text{ (in basic solution)}$$

    d. $CN^-(aq) + 2MnO_4^-(aq) \longrightarrow$
$$MnO_2(s) + CNO^-(aq) \text{ (in basic solution)}$$

Chapter 21

241. What happens when a strip of zinc is dipped into a solution of aluminum chloride?

242. A strip of aluminum is dipped into a solution of nickel(II) sulfate. Explain the result.

243. A voltaic cell is constructed using the following half-reactions:

$$Ag^+(aq) + e^- \longrightarrow Ag(s) \quad E^\circ_{Ag^+} = +0.80 \text{ V}$$
$$Al^{3+}(aq) + 3e^- \longrightarrow Al(s) \quad E^\circ_{Al^{3+}} = -1.66 \text{ V}$$

Determine the cell reaction.

244. Calculate the standard cell potential for the voltaic cell described in Problem 243.

245. What process, reduction or oxidation, always occurs at the anode of an electrolytic cell?

Chapter 22

246. What bonding properties make carbon uniquely suited to make a very large number of organic compounds?

247. Draw structural formulas for these compounds.

   a. 3-phenylpentane

   b. 2-phenyl-1-butene

248. Describe the structural features of an alkene molecule that permits the existence of *cis-trans* isomers.

249. How is an asymmetric carbon produced in an organic molecule?

250. Which of these structures are *cis* isomers?

a.

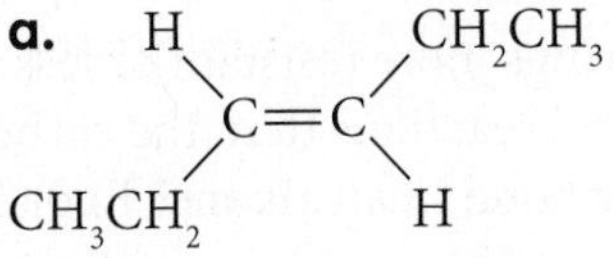

b.

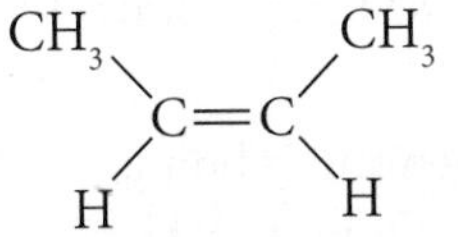

c.

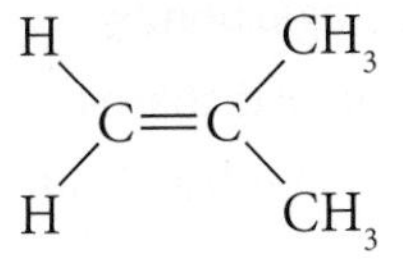

d.

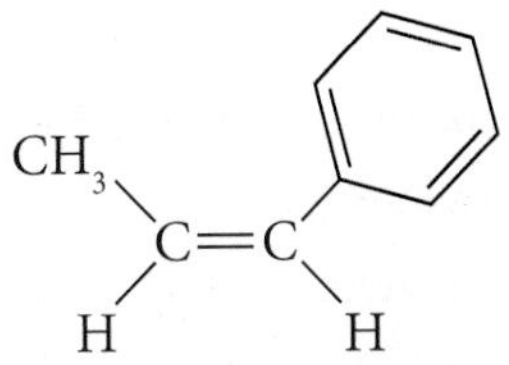

e.

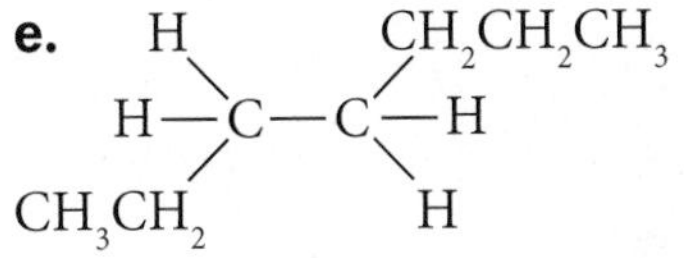

251. Write the IUPAC names for these structures. Use *cis* and *trans* prefixes when appropriate.

a.

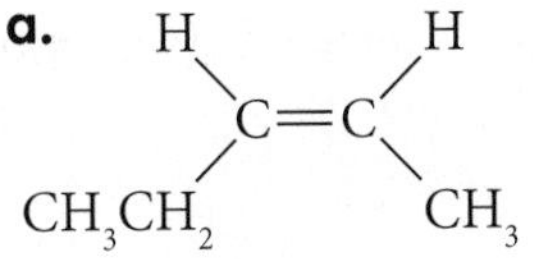

b.

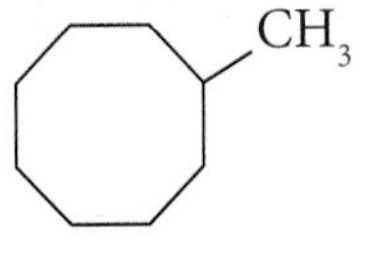

c.

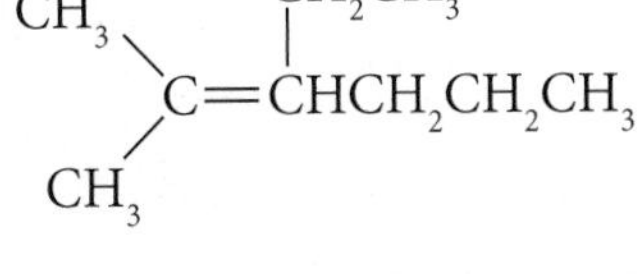

d.

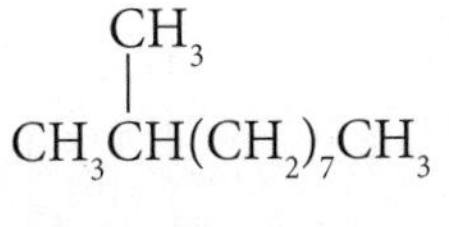

$$CH_3CH(CH_2)_7CH_3$$

e.

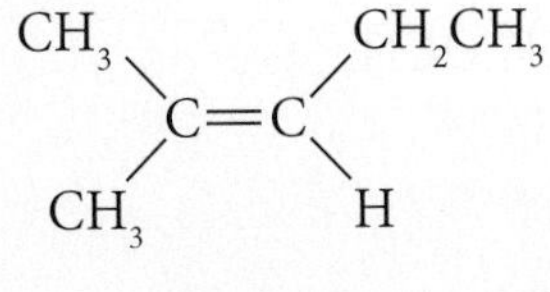

252. What name is given to a benzene ring when it is a substituent in an organic molecule?

253. Are benzene rings more resistant or less resistant to chemical reactions than the carbon-carbon double bond in an alkane? Explain your answer.

254. Which structural feature(s) characterize alkanes?

    a. carbon-hydrogen single bonds

    b. carbon-carbon double bonds

    c. carbon-carbon single bonds

    d. may contain branched chains

    e. may contain phenyl substituents

255. Draw structural formulas for these compounds.

    a. 1,3-diethylbenzene

    b. 1-ethyl-4-propylbenzene

    c. 1,3,5-triethylbenzene

256. If you want to devise an industrial process to prepare methylbenzene, would you prefer petroleum or coal as your starting material? Explain your choice.

Chapter 23

257. Name the functional group in these molecular structures.

    a. CH_3CH_2Br

    b. 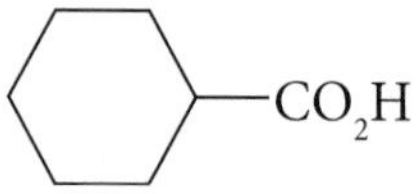 $-CO_2H$

    c. 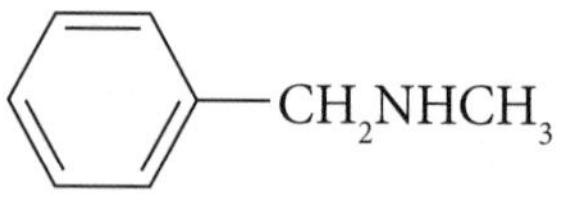 $-CH_2NHCH_3$

    d. 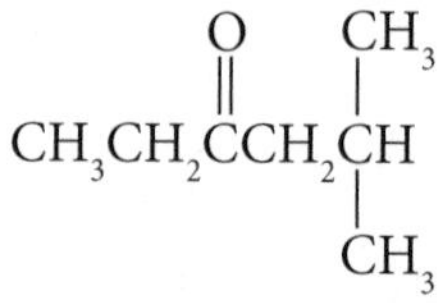 $CH_3CH_2CCH_2CH$ with $=O$ and CH_3, CH_3

    e. $CH_3CH_2CH_2OCH_3$

258. Which of these structures represent aryl halides?

    a.

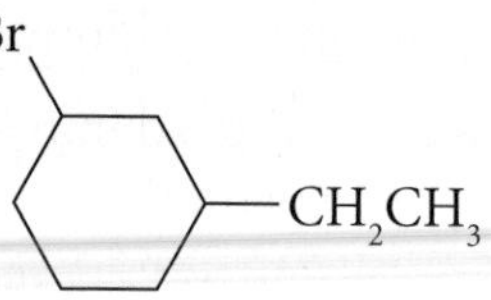

    b.

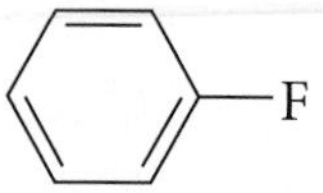

    c.

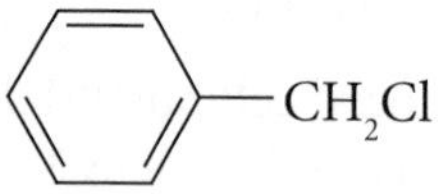

    d.

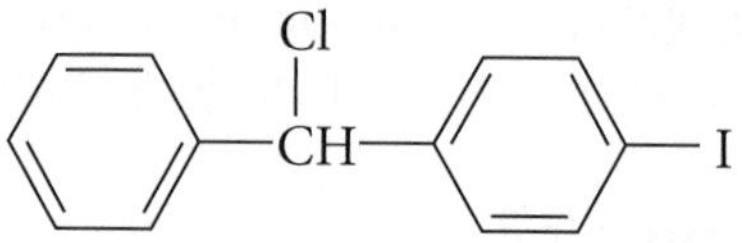

    e.

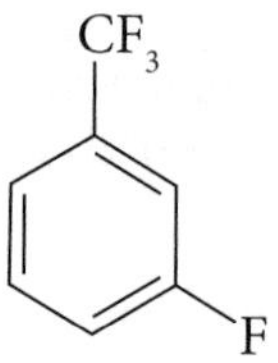

259. If 5.23 g of an alkene is required to completely decolorize 9.92 g of bromine, what is the molar mass of the alkene?

260. Write structural formulas for the organic product of these reactions.

    a. $CH_2=CHCH_2CH_3 + Cl_2 \longrightarrow$

    b. 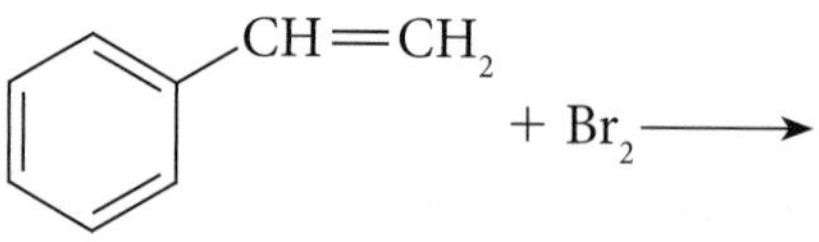 $+ Br_2 \longrightarrow$

    c. 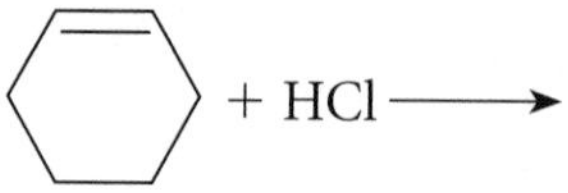 $+ HCl \longrightarrow$

    d. 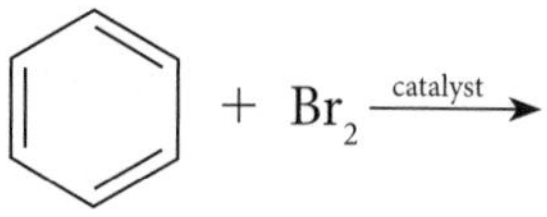 $+ Br_2 \xrightarrow{catalyst}$

261. Treatment of 7.57 g of pentanoic acid with a large excess of ethanol in the presence of a catalytic amount of hydrochloric acid produced 8.21 g of ethyl pentanoate after purification. Write a balanced equation for the reaction and calculate the percent yield of the ester.

262. Classify these reactions as oxidation or reduction.

a.

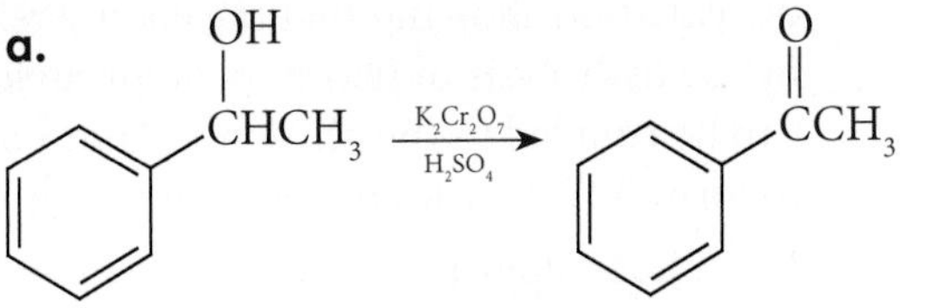

$$\underset{H_2SO_4}{\overset{K_2Cr_2O_7}{\longrightarrow}}$$

b. $CH_3CH_2CH_2CH_2CHO \xrightarrow{CuSO_4}$

$CH_3CH_2CH_2CH_2CO_2H$

c.

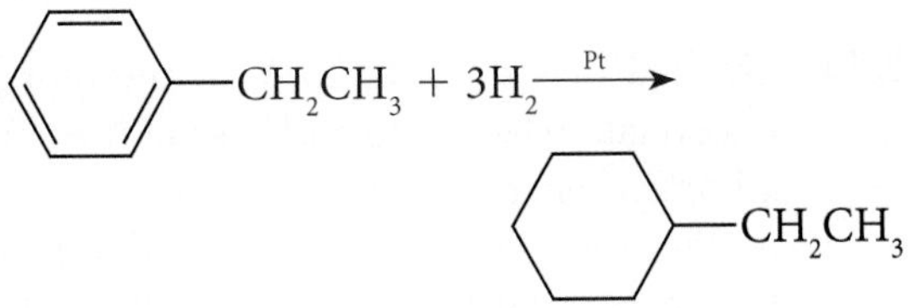

$-CH_2CH_3 + 3H_2 \xrightarrow{Pt}$

$-CH_2CH_3$

d. $CH_4 + 2O_2 \longrightarrow CO_2 + 2H_2O$

263. How many liters of hydrogen gas at STP are required to saturate 0.150 mole of benzene?

264. Write complete equations for the following organic reactions. Be sure to include all reactants and catalysts required for the transformations.

a. 1-pentene to pentane

b. 2,3-dimethyl-2-butene to 2-chloro-2,3-dimethylbutane

c. ethane to chloroethane

d. cyclohexene to 1,2-dibromocyclohexane

265. A sample of benzaldehyde is oxidized to produce the crystalline white solid, benzoic acid. Write the structural formula of benzoic acid.

266. Complete these reactions.

a. $CH_3CH_2CH_2I + KOH \xrightarrow[100°C]{H_2O}$

b.

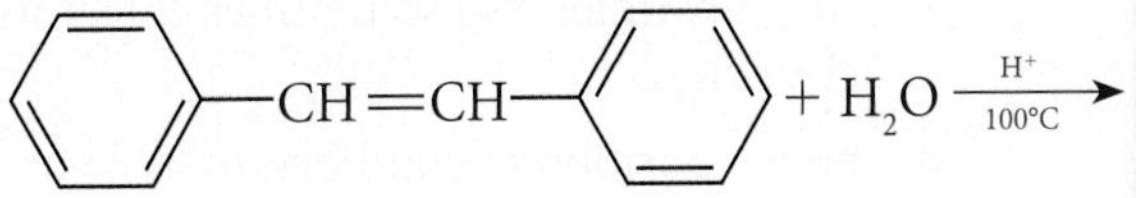

$-CH=CH- + H_2O \xrightarrow[100°C]{H^+}$

c. $CH_3CH_2CHO \xrightarrow{K_2Cr_2O_7}$

d.

$\xrightarrow{K_2Cr_2O_7}$

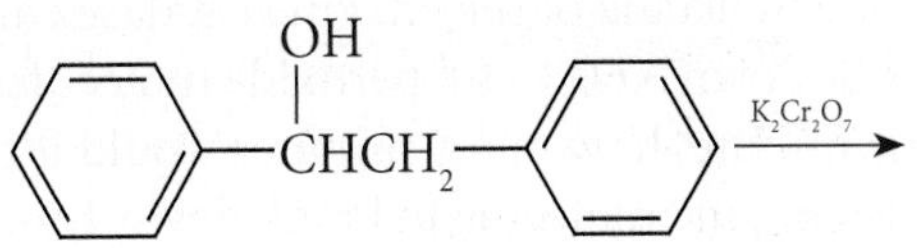

267. Classify each of these reactions as a hydration, hydrogenation, hydrolysis, or substitution.

a.

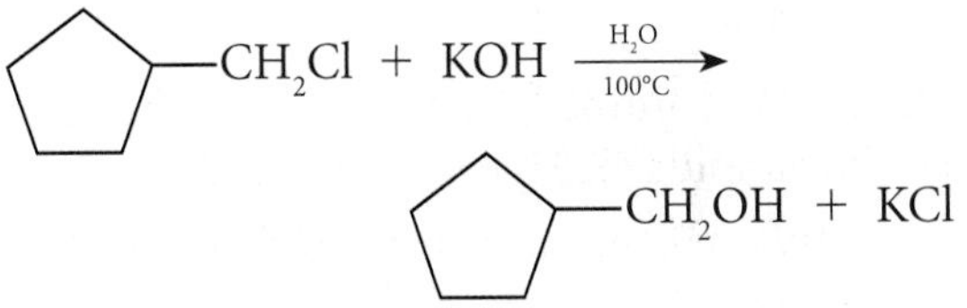

$-CH_2Cl + KOH \xrightarrow[100°C]{H_2O}$

$-CH_2OH + KCl$

b.

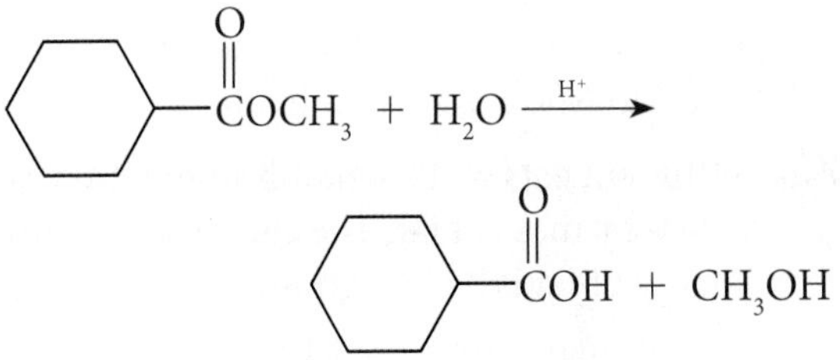

$+ H_2O \xrightarrow{H^+}$

$-COH + CH_3OH$

c.

$+ H_2O \xrightarrow[100°C]{H^+}$

$-OH$

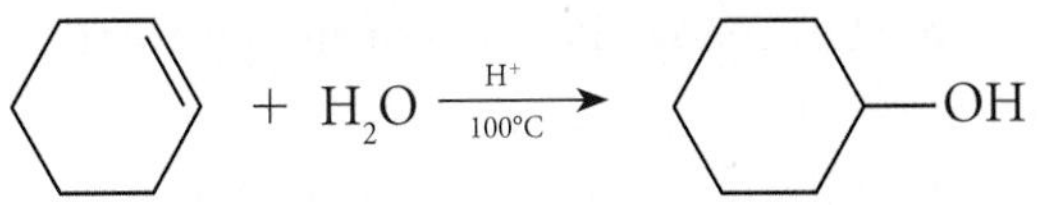

d.

$-C\equiv CH + 2H_2 \xrightarrow{Pt}$

$-CH_2CH_3$

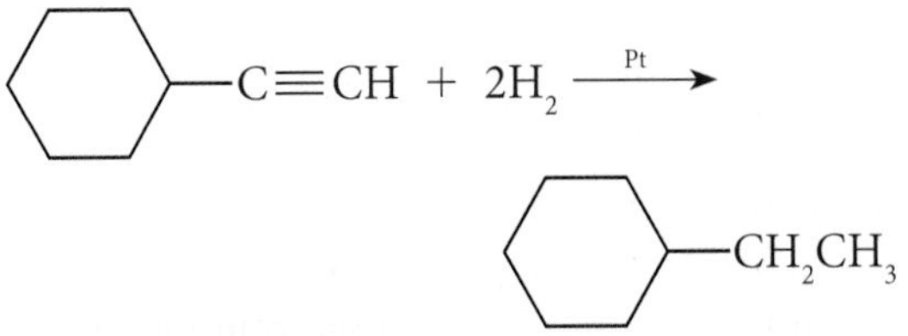

Chapter 24

268. Saliva contains an enzyme called amylase, which catalyzes the breakdown of starch to its monomers. Suggest a reason why a piece of bread begins to taste sweet when it has been chewed for a short time.

269. Which of these statements apply to enzymes?

    a. do not change position of equilibrium

    b. catalyze biological reactions

    c. bind substrates and sometimes cofactors at active sites

    d. change position of equilibrium to favor products

    e. are almost always nucleic acids

270. If one molecule of the enzyme catalase can break down 3.60×10^6 peroxide molecules in one minute, how many minutes would it take this enzyme molecule to break down 1 mole of peroxide? How many hours?

271. The level of glucose in the blood is normally 70–120 mg/dL. If a student's volume of blood is 4.5 L and her blood glucose level is 90 mg/dL, what is the total number of grams of glucose in her blood?

272. Sucrose, ordinary table sugar, has the molecular formula $C_{12}H_{22}O_{11}$.

    a. What is the molar mass of sucrose?

    b. What is the molarity of an aqueous solution containing 7.12 g/L of sucrose?

    c. Write a balanced equation for the complete combustion of sucrose in air.

273. A student eats a 115-g hamburger that contains 20.0% by mass of fat. The chemical potential energy of fat is 37.7 kJ/gram.

    a. How many grams of fat does the hamburger contain?

    b. How many kilojoules of energy are stored in the fat?

    c. What is this amount of energy in dietary Calories?

    d. What percentage of total Calories does this amount of energy represent in a 2.00×10^3 Calorie/day diet?

274. Walnuts, rich in fats and oils and with a chemical potential energy of 25.8 kJ/g, are a nutritious treat for many people. Suppose you eat 27.3 g of walnuts and then take a brisk walk. If you burn 3.76×10^2 kJ of kinetic energy for each kilometer you walk, how far will you need to walk to use up the energy provided by the walnuts?

275. There are 3.4 base pairs in every complete turn of the double helix in a DNA molecule. How many turns are in a DNA molecule that contains 5.0×10^8 base pairs?

276. ATP is not the only biological molecule capable of transmitting energy. For example, hydrolysis of the molecule phosphoenolpyruvic acid releases even more free energy than the hydrolysis of ATP. Use the equations below to write a net equation showing that the energy released by the hydrolysis of phosphoenolpyruvic acid can be coupled to the phosphorylation of ADP to form ATP in a spontaneous reaction.

$$\text{Phosphoenolpyruvic acid} + H_2O \longrightarrow$$
$$\text{pyruvic acid} + P_i$$
$$\Delta G = -61.4 \text{ kJ/mol}$$

$$\text{ADP} + P_i + \longrightarrow \text{ATP} + H_2O$$
$$\Delta G = 30.5 \text{ kJ/mol}$$

277. The hydrolysis of ATP to ADP and inorganic phosphate releases 30.5 kJ/mol of free energy. If all of this energy is wasted as heat, how many moles of ATP must be hydrolyzed to raise the temperature of 1 L of water at 20°C to 37°C?

Chapter 25

278. How do the mass number and the atomic number of radioactive atom A change if it first emits an alpha particle and the resulting atom then emits a beta particle to finally give atom C?

279. A radioactive active atom undergoes beta decay to yield cesium-133. Write a balanced equation for this nuclear reaction.

280. Which nuclei would you predict to be stable? Explain your answer.

    a. $^{9}_{3}\text{Li}$ **c.** $^{20}_{8}\text{O}$

    b. $^{59}_{27}\text{Co}$ **d.** $^{146}_{60}\text{Nd}$

281. Write a balanced nuclear equation for the following:

    a. beta decay of sodium-26

    b. alpha decay of $^{234}_{92}\text{U}$

282. Plutonium-239 presents a serious nuclear waste disposal problem. If seven half-lives are required for the radioactivity from the waste to reach a tolerable level and if Pu-239 has a $t_{1/2} = 2.41 \times 10^4$ years, how long must the Pu-239 be stored?

Appendix E

Selected
Solutions

Chapter 1

25. $12 \text{ blocks} \times \dfrac{1 \text{ mi}}{10 \text{ blocks}} \times \dfrac{20 \text{ min}}{1 \text{ mi}} = 24 \text{ min}$

26. $48 \text{ min} \times \dfrac{1 \text{ mi}}{20 \text{ min}} \times \dfrac{10 \text{ blocks}}{1 \text{ mi}} = 24 \text{ blocks}$

27. Algebra II would be scheduled during the 2nd period instead of 1st period.

28. No, Manny's schedule would not change. Algebra II would not be scheduled during 2nd period because Art must be scheduled during this time. Algebra II would not be scheduled during 3rd period because Chemistry must be scheduled during this time. Therefore, Algebra II would still be scheduled during 1st period.

35. Chemistry is concerned with the changes that matter undergoes.

37. A scientist who is studying cancer with the goal of finding an effective treatment is doing applied research because the research is directed toward a practical goal or application.

38. A firefighter needs to know which chemicals to use to fight different types of fires; a knowledge of chemistry will help a reporter gather information during an interview with a chemist.

42. Scientists can study the composition of distant stars by analyzing the light they transmit to Earth.

44. The most powerful tool that any scientist can have is the scientific method.

46. c

48. Repeat the experiment. If you get the same result, you must propose a new hypothesis.

49. A scientific law summarizes the results of many experiments; a theory explains the results of the experiments.

51. Good problem solvers do b, c, and d.

54. Two games won out of three games played means that one game is lost out of three games played:
$162 \text{ games played} \times \dfrac{1 \text{ loss}}{3 \text{ games played}} = 54 \text{ losses}$

56. $1{,}000{,}000 \text{ pennies} \times \dfrac{1 \text{ sec}}{1 \text{ penny}} \times \dfrac{1 \text{ min}}{60 \text{ sec}} \times \dfrac{1 \text{ h}}{60 \text{ min}} \times$
$\dfrac{1 \text{ day}}{24 \text{ h}} = 11.6 \text{ days (about 12 days)}$

57. Answers vary; possible answers: 1c, 2d, 3e, 4b, 5a

58. One possible answer is the development of materials to produce artificial limbs.

61. The doctor's hypothesis is that the sore throat is the result of bacteria that cause strep throat. The experiment she performs to test the hypothesis is to test the sample for the presence of the bacteria that causes strep.

62. Your experiment may be correct, but your hypothesis may be wrong. You should reexamine your hypothesis and repeat the experiment.

65. **a.** Independent variable: amount of salt added
   b. Dependent variable: freezing point of the salt water
   c. Changing the volume of the water would also change the relative amount of salt per volume of water and would affect the results.
   d. Yes, to a point. The freezing point appears to be leveling off at about 15°C.

66. $40 \text{ mi by bicycle} \times \dfrac{30 \text{ mi by car}}{4 \text{ mi by bicycle}} = 300 \text{ mi by car}$

70. A person who is educated in the theories and practice of chemistry is more likely to recognize the significance of an accidental discovery and have the means and motivation to develop that accidental discovery into an important scientific contribution.

71. Method 1: Divide the weight of four beakers by 2; 2.0 lb/2 = 1.0 lb. Method 2: Multiply the weight of one beaker by 2; 0.5 lb × 2 = 1.0 lb. The answers are the same.

72. A theory can never be proven. It is a well-tested explanation of a broad set of observations. A theory may need to be changed in the future to explain new observations.

73. c

75. Number of crates = 5 × 6 × 5 = 150 crates
$150 \text{ crates} \times \dfrac{4 \text{ boxes}}{1 \text{ crate}} \times \dfrac{20 \text{ cartons}}{1 \text{ box}} \times \dfrac{12 \text{ eggs}}{1 \text{ carton}}$
$= 144{,}000 \text{ eggs}$

77. **a.** $1 \text{ package} \times \dfrac{1 \text{ carton}}{6 \text{ packages}} \times \dfrac{1 \text{ box}}{12 \text{ cartons}} \times \dfrac{1 \text{ crate}}{8 \text{ boxes}} \times$
$\dfrac{\$576.00}{1 \text{ crate}} = \$1.00$
   b. number of envelopes in a package

80. Answers will vary, but possible answers are as follows: Factors: (1) PLA is made from natural resources; (2) producing PLA requires less energy than producing petroleum-based plastics; (3) compost facility availability. Factors (1) and (2) make PLA products a good choice, but factor (3) may make it difficult to choose PLA products.

Chapter 2

10. Iron is magnetic; table salt is not. Table salt will dissolve in water; iron will not.

11. By lowering the temperature to below the boiling point of each gas, you could condense each substance and separate the gases.

20. Liquid A is probably a substance. Liquid B is a mixture because a solid remained after evaporation.

21. The liquid was not an element because a solid was left when the liquid evaporated. A physical process, such as evaporation, cannot be used to break down a compound. Therefore, the liquid was a mixture.

42. State; both are gases.

44. A vapor; the term *vapor* is used to refer to the gaseous state of a substance which normally exists as a liquid or solid at room temperature.

47. Sharpening a pencil is an irreversible change. Making ice cubes is a reversible change.

50. **a.** heterogeneous
   b. homogeneous
   c. depends on how well the batter is mixed
   d. homogeneous
   e. heterogeneous
   f. homogeneous
   g. heterogeneous
   h. homogeneous

53. **a.** Sodium chloride (table salt) is a compound because it is made of two elements, sodium and chloride.
   b. Salt water is a mixture because it is made of two compounds, water (H_2O) and NaCl.
   c. Sodium is an element because it is not combined with any other element.

57. The compound water contains two parts hydrogen to one part oxygen.

60. **a.** physical
   b. chemical (color change)
   c. chemical (production of a gas)
   d. physical

62. $40 \text{ g NH}_4\text{NO}_3 - 14 \text{ g N} - 8 \text{ g O} = 18 \text{ g H}_2\text{O}$

66. Sulfur, which is the only substance in the table that is a solid at room temperature

67. Mass is an extensive property, which depends only on the amount of matter in the sample, not on the composition of the sample.

70. The particles in solids are packed tightly together so it is difficult to compress them. The particles in a gas are spaced relatively far apart.

76. **a.** gas produced
   b. formation of a precipitate
   c. color and texture change
   d. energy change, odor change
   e. gas produced
   f. color change, odor change

80. The wax appears to disappear because the products of the reaction—carbon dioxide and water vapor—are colorless gases.

81. Add sufficient water to dissolve all of the sugar. Separate the charcoal and sand from the sugar water by filtration. Large pieces of charcoal could be separated on the basis of color or size. Small pieces of charcoal could be burned.

85. **a.** Yes; because the graph is a straight line, the proportion of iron to oxygen is a constant, which is true for a compound.
   b. No; a point for the values given wouldn't fall on the line. The mass ratio of iron to oxygen is different.

88. **a.** oxygen and calcium
   b. silicon, aluminum, and iron
   c. Different; the second most abundant element in Earth's crust, silicon, is not abundant in the human body, and the second most abundant element in the human body, carbon, is not among the most abundant elements in Earth's crust. If the elements are different, then the compounds must also be different.

Chapter 3

1. **a.** $(6.6 \times 10^{-8}) + (5.0 \times 10^{-9}) =$
   $(6.6 \times 10^{-8}) + (0.5 \times 10^{-8}) =$
   $(6.6 + 0.5) \times 10^{-8} = 7.1 \times 10^{-8}$
   b. $(9.4 \times 10^{-2}) - (2.1 \times 10^{-2}) =$
   $(9.4 - 2.1) \times 10^{-2} = 7.3 \times 10^{-2}$

2. $\dfrac{6.6 \times 10^6}{(8.8 \times 10^{-2}) \times (2.5 \times 10^3)} = 0.30 \times 10^5 = 3.0 \times 10^4$

3. Error = experimental value − accepted value = 2.04 m − 2.00 m = 0.04 m

$$\% \text{ error} = \frac{|\text{error}|}{\text{accepted value}} \times 100\% = \frac{|0.04 \text{ m}|}{2.00 \text{ m}} \times 100\%$$
$$= 2\%$$

4. a. 4 **b.** 4 **c.** 2 **d.** 5

5. a. 3 **b.** 2 **c.** 4 **d.** 4

6. a. 8.71×10^1 m **d.** 9.01×10^3 m
b. 4.36×10^8 m **e.** 1.78×10^{-3} m
c. 1.55×10^{-2} m **f.** 6.30×10^2 m

7. a. 9×10^1 m **d.** 9×10^3 m
b. 4×10^8 m **e.** 2×10^{-3} m
c. 2×10^{-2} m **f.** 6×10^2 m

8. a. 61.2 m + 9.35 m + 8.6 m = 79.15 m = 79.2 m
b. 9.44 m − 2.11 m = 7.33 m
c. 1.36 m + 10.17 m = 11.53 m
d. 34.61m − 17.3 m = 17.3 m

9. 14.2 g + 8.73 g + 0.912 g = 23.842 g = 23.8 g

10. a. 8.3 m × 2.22 m = $18.4 \text{ m}^2 = 18 \text{ m}^2 = 1.8 \times 10^1 \text{ m}^2$
b. 8432 m^2 ÷ 12.5 m = 675 m = 6.75×10^2 m
c. $35.2 \text{ s} \times \dfrac{1 \text{ min}}{60 \text{ s}} = 0.587 \text{ min} = 5.87 \times 10^{-1} \text{ min}$

11. $V = l \times w \times h$ = 22.4 m × 11.3 m × 5.2 m = 1316.2 $\text{m}^3 = 1.3 \times 10^3 \text{ m}^3$

19. mp: K = °C + 273 = 960.8 + 273 = 1234 K
bp: K = °C + 273 = 2212 + 273 = 2485 K

20. °C = K − 273 = 77.2 − 273 = −196°C

21. $\text{Density} = \dfrac{\text{mass}}{\text{volume}} = \dfrac{612 \text{ g}}{245 \text{ cm}^3} = 2.50 \text{ g/cm}^3$

No, because the density of aluminum is 2.7 g/cm^3.

22. $\text{Density} = \dfrac{\text{mass}}{\text{volume}} = \dfrac{68.0 \text{ g}}{6.48 \text{ cm}^3} = 10.5 \text{ g/cm}^3$

36. $1 \text{ wk} \times \dfrac{7 \text{ d}}{1 \text{ wk}} \times \dfrac{24 \text{ h}}{1 \text{ d}} \times \dfrac{60 \text{ min}}{1 \text{ h}} = 10{,}080 \text{ min} = 1.0080 \times 10^4 \text{ min}$

37. $40 \text{ h} \times \dfrac{60 \text{ min}}{1 \text{ h}} \times \dfrac{60 \text{ s}}{1 \text{ min}} = 144{,}000 \text{ s} = 1.44000 \times 10^5 \text{ s}$

38. $570 \text{ cm ribbon} \times \dfrac{1 \text{ student}}{8.5 \text{ cm ribbon}} = 67 \text{ students}$

39. $48.0°\text{C change} \times \dfrac{1.80°\text{F change}}{1.00°\text{C change}} = 86.4°\text{F change}$

40. $5.00 \text{ g Au} \times \dfrac{1 \text{ atom Au}}{3.271 \times 10^{-22} \text{ g Au}} = 1.53 \times 10^{22} \text{ atoms Au}$

41. a. $0.044 \text{ km} \times \dfrac{10^3 \text{ m}}{1 \text{ km}} = 44 \text{ m}$

b. $4.6 \text{ mg} \times \dfrac{1 \text{ g}}{10^3 \text{ mg}} = 4.6 \times 10^{-3} \text{ g}$

c. $0.107 \text{ g} \times \dfrac{10^2 \text{ cg}}{1 \text{ g}} = 10.7 \text{ cg}$

42. a. $15 \text{ cm}^3 \times \dfrac{1 \text{ L}}{10^3 \text{ cm}^3} = 0.015 \text{ L} = 1.5 \times 10^{-2} \text{ L}$

b. $7.38 \text{ g} \times \dfrac{1 \text{ kg}}{10^3 \text{ g}} = 7.38 \times 10^{-3} \text{ kg}$

c. $6.7 \text{ s} \times \dfrac{10^3 \text{ ms}}{1 \text{ s}} = 6.7 \times 10^3 \text{ ms}$

d. $94.5 \text{ g} \times \dfrac{10^6 \text{ μg}}{1 \text{ g}} = 9.45 \times 10^7 \text{ μg}$

43. a. $14.8 \text{ g B} \times \dfrac{1 \text{ cm}^3}{2.34 \text{ g B}} = 6.32 \text{ cm}^3$

b. $4.62 \text{ g Hg} \times \dfrac{1 \text{ cm}^3}{13.5 \text{ g Hg}} = 0.342 \text{ cm}^3 = 3.42 \times 10^{-1} \text{ cm}^3$

44. a. $\text{Volume} = \dfrac{\text{mass}}{\text{density}} = \dfrac{14.8 \text{ g B}}{2.34 \text{ g B/cm}^3} = 6.32 \text{ cm}^3$

b. $\text{Volume} = \dfrac{\text{mass}}{\text{density}} = \dfrac{4.62 \text{ g Hg}}{13.5 \text{ g Hg/cm}^3} = 0.342 \text{ cm}^3$
$= 3.42 \times 10^{-1} \text{ cm}^3$

45. $50.0 \text{ cm}^3 \times \dfrac{0.950 \text{ g}}{1 \text{ cm}^3} = 47.5 \text{ g}$

46. $0.227 \text{ nm} \times \dfrac{1 \text{ m}}{10^9 \text{ nm}} = 0.227 \times 10^{-9} \text{ m} = 2.27 \times 10^{-8} \text{ m}$

47. $1.3 \times 10^4 \text{ km} \times \dfrac{10^3 \text{ m}}{1 \text{ km}} \times \dfrac{10 \text{ dm}}{1 \text{ m}} = 1.3 \times 10^{4+3+1} \text{ dm}$
$= 1.3 \times 10^8 \text{ dm}$

48. $\dfrac{19.3 \text{ g}}{1 \text{ cm}^3} \times \dfrac{10^6 \text{ cm}^3}{1 \text{ m}^3} \times \dfrac{1 \text{ kg}}{10^3 \text{ g}} = 19.3 \times 10^{6-3} \text{ kg/m}^3$
$= 19.3 \times 10^3 \text{ kg/m}^3 = 1.93 \times 10^4 \text{ kg/m}^3$

49. $\dfrac{7.0 \times 10^6 \text{ RBCs}}{1 \text{ mm}^3} \times \dfrac{10^9 \text{ mm}^3}{1 \text{ m}^3} \times \dfrac{1 \text{ m}^3}{10^3 \text{ dm}^3} \times \dfrac{1 \text{ dm}^3}{1 \text{ L}}$
$= 7.0 \times 10^{6+9-3} \text{ RBCs/L} = 7.0 \times 10^{12} \text{ RBCs/L}$

59. a. 43 g **d.** 92.0 m
b. 7.3 cm^2 **e.** 32.4 m^3
c. 225.8 L **f.** 104 m^3

60. (58) **a.** 9.85×10^1 L **d.** 1.22×10^{10}°C
b. 7.63×10^{-4} cg **e.** 7.50×10^{-3} mm
c. 5.70×10^1 m **f.** 1.76×10^3 mL
(59) **a.** 4.3×10^1 g **d.** 9.20×10^1 m
b. 7.3×10^0 cm^2 **e.** 3.24×10^1 m^3
c. 2.258×10^2 L **f.** 1.04×10^2 m^3

63. pm, nm, μm, mm, cm, dm, m, km;
$1 \text{ pm} = 10^{-12} \text{ m}$, $1 \text{ nm} = 10^{-9} \text{ m}$, $1 \text{ μm} = 10^{-6} \text{ m}$,
$1 \text{ mm} = 10^{-3} \text{ m}$, $1 \text{ cm} = 10^{-2} \text{ m}$, $1 \text{ dm} = 10^{-1} \text{ m}$,
$1 \text{ km} = 10^3 \text{ m}$

66. $K = °C + 273 = 962 + 273 = 1235 \text{ K}$

69. $\text{Density} = \dfrac{\text{mass}}{\text{volume}} = \dfrac{57.3 \text{ g}}{4.7 \text{ cm}^3} = 12 \text{ g/cm}^3$

No; the density of the metal bar is 12 g/cm^3, but the density of gold is 19 g/cm^3.

74. a. $157 \text{ cs} \times \dfrac{1 \text{ s}}{100 \text{ cs}} = 1.57 \text{ s}$

b. $42.7 \text{ L} \times \dfrac{10^3 \text{ mL}}{1 \text{ L}} = 42{,}700 \text{ mL} = 4.27 \times 10^4 \text{ mL}$

c. $261 \text{ nm} \times \dfrac{1 \text{ m}}{10^9 \text{ nm}} \times \dfrac{10^3 \text{ mm}}{1 \text{ m}} = 261 \times 10^{3-9} \text{ mm}$

$= 261 \times 10^{-6} \text{ mm} = 2.61 \times 10^{-4} \text{ mm}$

d. $0.065 \text{ km} \times \dfrac{10^3 \text{ m}}{1 \text{ km}} \times \dfrac{10 \text{ dm}}{1 \text{ m}} = 650 \text{ dm} =$

$6.5 \times 10^2 \text{ dm}$

e. $642 \text{ cg} \times \dfrac{1 \text{ g}}{10^2 \text{ cg}} \times \dfrac{1 \text{ kg}}{10^3 \text{ g}} = \dfrac{642 \text{ kg}}{10^{2+3}} = \dfrac{642 \text{ kg}}{10^5}$

$= 642 \times 10^{-5} \text{ kg} = 6.42 \times 10^{-3} \text{ kg}$

f. $8.25 \times 10^2 \text{ cg} \times \dfrac{1 \text{ g}}{10^2 \text{ cg}} \times \dfrac{10^9 \text{ ng}}{1 \text{ g}} = 8.25 \times 10^9 \text{ ng}$

75. a. $\dfrac{0.44 \text{ mL}}{1 \text{ min}} \times \dfrac{1 \text{ L}}{10^3 \text{ mL}} \times \dfrac{10^6 \text{ μL}}{1 \text{ L}} \times \dfrac{1 \text{ min}}{60 \text{ s}}$

$= (7.3 \times 10^{-3}) \times 10^3 \text{ μL/s} = 7.3 \text{ μL/s}$

b. $\dfrac{7.86 \text{ g}}{1 \text{ cm}^2} \times \dfrac{10^4 \text{ cm}^2}{1 \text{ m}^2} \times \dfrac{1 \text{ m}^2}{10^6 \text{ mm}^2} \times \dfrac{10^3 \text{ mg}}{1 \text{ g}}$

$= 7.86 \times 10^1 \text{ mg/mm}^2 = 78.6 \text{ mg/mm}^2$

c. $\dfrac{1.54 \text{ kg}}{1 \text{ L}} \times \dfrac{10^3 \text{ g}}{1 \text{ kg}} \times \dfrac{1 \text{ L}}{10^3 \text{ mL}} \times \dfrac{1 \text{ mL}}{1 \text{ cm}^3} = 1.54 \text{ g/cm}^3$

77. a. $28.3 \text{ cg} \times \dfrac{1 \text{ g}}{10^2 \text{ cg}} \times \dfrac{10^3 \text{ mg}}{\text{g}} = 28.3 \times 10^1 \text{ mg}$

$= 283 \text{ mg}$

b. $283 \text{ mg} \times \dfrac{1 \text{ g}}{10^3 \text{ mg}} = 0.283 \text{ g}$

c. $0.283 \text{ g} \times \dfrac{1 \text{ kg}}{10^3 \text{ g}} = 0.000283 \text{ kg}$

d. $6.6 \times 10^3 \text{ mg} \times \dfrac{1 \text{ g}}{10^3 \text{ mg}} = 6.6 \text{ g}$

e. $6.6 \text{ g} \times \dfrac{10^2 \text{ cg}}{1 \text{ g}} = 660 \text{ cg} = 6.6 \times 10^2 \text{ cg}$

f. $6.6 \text{ g} \times \dfrac{1 \text{ kg}}{10^3 \text{ g}} = 6.6 \times 10^{-3} \text{ kg}$

g. $2.8 \times 10^{-4} \text{ g} \times \dfrac{10^3 \text{ mg}}{\text{g}} = 2.8 \times 10^{-1} \text{ mg}$

h. $2.8 \times 10^{-4} \text{ g} \times \dfrac{10^2 \text{ cg}}{\text{g}} = 2.8 \times 10^{-2} \text{ cg}$

i. $2.8 \times 10^{-4} \text{ g} \times \dfrac{1 \text{ kg}}{10^3 \text{ g}} = 2.8 \times 10^{-7} \text{ kg}$

86. $125 \text{ kg coal} \times \dfrac{1.30 \text{ kg C}}{2.00 \text{ kg coal}} = 81.25 \text{ kg C} = 81.3 \text{ kg C}$

87. $50 \text{ g air} \times \dfrac{1 \text{ cm}^3 \text{ air}}{1.19 \times 10^{-3} \text{ g air}} = 42.0 \times 10^3 \text{ cm}^3 \text{ air}$

$= 4.20 \times 10^4 \text{ cm}^3 \text{ air}$

89. $\text{Volume} = 158 \text{ g H}_2\text{O} \times \dfrac{1 \text{ cm}^3}{1.000 \text{ g H}_2\text{O}} = 158 \text{ cm}^3$

$\text{Density} = \dfrac{\text{mass}}{\text{volume}} = \dfrac{127 \text{ g}}{158 \text{ cm}^3} = 0.804 \text{ g/cm}^3$

90. $\dfrac{0.15 \text{ s}}{1 \text{ min}} \times \dfrac{60 \text{ min}}{1 \text{ h}} \times \dfrac{24 \text{ h}}{1 \text{ day}} \times \dfrac{1 \text{ min}}{60 \text{ s}}$

$= 0.15 \times 24 \text{ min/day} = 3.6 \text{ min/day lost}$

91. $V = 28.6 \text{ cm} \times (73.0 \times 10^{-1} \text{ cm}) \times (0.72 \times 10^2 \text{ cm})$
$= 1.50 \times 10^4 \text{ cm}^3$

$\text{Density} = \dfrac{\text{mass}}{\text{volume}} =$

$\dfrac{1.38 \times 10^4 \text{ g}}{1.50 \times 10^4 \text{ cm}^3} \times \dfrac{1 \text{ kg}}{10^3 \text{ g}} \times \dfrac{10^3 \text{ cm}^3}{1 \text{ L}} = 0.92 \text{ kg/L}$

93. $1.5 \times 10^8 \text{ km} \times \dfrac{10^3 \text{ m}}{1 \text{ km}} \times \dfrac{1 \text{ s}}{3.0 \times 10^8 \text{ m}} \times \dfrac{1 \text{ min}}{60 \text{ s}}$

$= 8.3 \text{ min}$

94. $\dfrac{5.52 \text{ g}}{1 \text{ cm}^3} \times \dfrac{1 \text{ kg}}{10^3 \text{ g}} \times \dfrac{10^6 \text{ cm}^3}{1 \text{ m}^3} \times \dfrac{1 \text{ m}^3}{10^3 \text{ dm}^3} = \dfrac{5.52 \times 10^6 \text{ kg}}{10^6 \text{ dm}^3}$

$= 5.52 \text{ kg/dm}^3$

97. $\text{Mass}_{\text{amalgam}} = 26.0 \text{ g} + 10.8 \text{ g} + 2.4 \text{ g} + 0.8 \text{ g} = 40.0 \text{ g}$

$25.0 \text{ g amalgam} \times \dfrac{26.0 \text{ g Ag}}{40.0 \text{ g amalgam}} = 16.3 \text{ g Ag}$

98. $\dfrac{112 \text{ km}}{1 \text{ hr}} \times \dfrac{10^3 \text{ m}}{1 \text{ km}} \times \dfrac{1 \text{ hr}}{60 \text{ min}} \times \dfrac{1 \text{ min}}{60 \text{ s}} =$

$0.0311 \times 10^3 \text{ m/s} = 31.1 \text{ m/s}$

103. $\text{Volume of Fe} = 355 \text{ g Fe} \times \dfrac{1 \text{ cm}^3 \text{ Fe}}{7.87 \text{ g Fe}} = 45.1 \text{ cm}^3 \text{ Fe}$

$\text{Mass} = \text{volume} \times \text{density} = 45.1 \text{ cm}^3 \times \dfrac{11.3 \text{ g Pb}}{1 \text{ cm}^3}$

$= 510 \text{ g Pb}$

104. $\dfrac{8.0 \times 10^{-1} \text{ cg Sr}}{1 \text{ kg seawater}} \times \dfrac{1 \text{ kg seawater}}{10^3 \text{ g seawater}} \times \dfrac{1.0 \text{ g seawater}}{1 \text{ cm}^3 \text{ seawater}}$

$\times \dfrac{10^6 \text{ cm}^3 \text{ seawater}}{1 \text{ m}^3 \text{ seawater}} \times \dfrac{1 \text{ g Sr}}{10^2 \text{ cg Sr}} = 8.0 \text{ g Sr/m}^3 \text{ seawater}$

107. $34.5 \text{ g Au} \times \dfrac{1 \text{ cm}^3 \text{ Au}}{19.3 \text{ g Au}} \times \dfrac{1 \text{ mL Au}}{1 \text{ cm}^3 \text{ Au}} = 1.79 \text{ mL Au}$

Chapter 4

16. a. 9 protons and 9 electrons

b. 20 protons and 20 electrons

c. 13 protons and 13 electrons

d. 19 protons and 19 electrons

17. a. 16 b. 16 c. 23 d. 23 e. B f. 5 g. 5

18. a. neutrons = mass number − atomic number
$= 80 - 35 = 45$

b. neutrons = mass number − atomic number
$= 32 - 16 = 16$

c. neutrons = mass number − atomic number
$= 108 - 47 = 61$

d. neutrons = mass number − atomic number
$= 207 - 82 = 125$

19. a. $^{12}_{6}\text{C}$ b. $^{11}_{5}\text{B}$ c. $^{9}_{4}\text{Be}$ d. $^{16}_{8}\text{O}$

20. $^{16}_{8}\text{O}, ^{17}_{8}\text{O}, ^{18}_{8}\text{O}$

21. neutrons = mass number − atomic number
$= 50 - 24 = 26$; chromium-50 has 26 neutrons.

neutrons = mass number − atomic number
$= 52 - 24 = 28$; chromium-52 has 28 neutrons.

neutrons = mass number − atomic number
$= 53 - 24 = 29$; chromium-53 has 29 neutrons.

22. Boron's atomic mass (10.81 amu) is closer to 11 than it is to 10, so boron-11 is more abundant than boron-10.

23. Silicon's atomic mass (28.086 amu) is closest to 28 and closer to 29 than it is to 30. Therefore, silicon-28 is more abundant than silicon-29, and silicon-29 is more abundant than silicon-30.

24. for ^{63}Cu: 62.93 amu $\times$ 0.692 = 43.5 amu
for ^{65}Cu: 64.93 amu $\times$ 0.308 = 20.0 amu
atomic mass = 43.5 amu + 20.0 amu = 63.5 amu

25. for ^{79}Br: 78.92 amu $\times$ 0.5069 = 40.00 amu
for ^{81}Br: 80.92 amu $\times$ 0.4931 = 39.90 amu
atomic mass = 40.00 amu + 39.90 amu = 79.90 amu

40. repel

44. He did not expect alpha particles to be deflected at a large angle.

51. a. 19 b. 9 c. 14 d. 29
e. 22 f. 22 g. 25 h. 30

53. for ^{6}Li: 6.015 amu $\times$ 0.075 = 0.45 amu
for ^{7}Li: 7.016 amu $\times$ 0.925 = 6.49 amu
atomic mass = 0.45 amu + 6.49 amu = 6.94 amu

54. because of the existence of isotopes

60. 5 protons and 6 neutrons in the nucleus; 5 electrons outside the nucleus

64. $[(82 + 122) \times 0.014] + [(82 + 124) \times 0.241]$
$+ [(82 + 125) \times 0.221] + [(82 + 126) \times 0.524]$
$= 207 \text{ amu}$

66. a. $8,289,000 + 502,570 + 120,570 + 7800 + 1435$
$+ 477 + 211 + 198 = 8,922,261$

$8,289,000 \div 8,922,261 = 0.929 = 92.9\%$

b. $(8,289,000 + 502,570 + 120,570) \div 8,922,261$
$= 0.9989 = 99.89\%$

c. $(477 + 211 + 198) \div 8,922,261$
$= 0.0000993 = 0.00993\%$

67. $^{14}_{7}\text{N}$: 14.003 amu; 99.63%
$^{15}_{7}\text{N}$: 15.000 amu; 0.37%
average atomic mass = 14.01 amu

74. The following are reasonable hypotheses: (*i*) The space in an individual atom is large relative to the volume of the atom but very small relative to an object the size of a hand. (*ii*) There are many layers of atoms in a wall or a desk. The space that exists is distributed evenly throughout the solid, similar to the distribution of air pockets in foam insulation.

78. $6.941 = [6.015 \times (1 - A)] + (7.016 \times A)$
$6.941 = 6.015 - 6.015A + 7.016A$
$6.941 - 6.015 = 7.016A - 6.015A$

$A = \dfrac{0.926}{1.001} = 0.925 = 92.5\%$

79. $17(1.67 \times 10^{-24} \text{ g}) + 18(1.67 \times 10^{-24} \text{ g})$
$+ 17(9.11 \times 10^{-28} \text{ g}) = 5.857 \times 10^{-23} \text{ g}$
$5.857 \times 10^{-23} \text{ g} - (5.81 \times 10^{-23} \text{ g}) = 4.70 \times 10^{-25} \text{ g}$

86. $54 \text{ g H}_2\text{O} - 6 \text{ g H} = 48 \text{ g O}$

88. $4.42 \text{ cm}^3 \times \dfrac{22.5 \text{ g Pt}}{1 \text{ cm}^3} = 99.5 \text{ g Pt}$

Chapter 5

8. a. $1s^2 2s^2 2p^2$

b. $1s^2 2s^2 2p^6 3s^2 3p^6$

c. $1s^2 2s^2 2p^6 3s^2 3p^6 3d^8 4s^2$

9. a. $1s^2 2s^2 2p^1$; 1 unpaired electron

b. $1s^2 2s^2 2p^6 3s^2 3p^2$; 2 unpaired electrons

c. $1s^2 2s^2 2p^6 3s^2 3p^4$; 2 unpaired electrons

15. $\lambda = \dfrac{c}{\nu} = \dfrac{2.998 \times 10^8 \text{ m/s}}{1.50 \times 10^{13}\text{/s}} = 2.00 \times 10^{-5}\text{m}$; longer

wavelength than red light

16. $\nu = \dfrac{c}{\lambda} = \dfrac{2.998 \times 10^8 \text{ m/s}}{5.00 \times 10^{-8} \text{ m}} = 6.00 \times 10^{15}/\text{s};$

ultraviolet

17. $E = h\nu = (6.626 \times 10^{-34} \text{ J} \cdot \text{s}) \times (5.00 \times 10^{11}/\text{s}) = 3.31 \times 10^{-22} \text{ J}$

18. $\nu = \dfrac{c}{\lambda} = \dfrac{2.998 \times 10^8 \text{ m/s}}{260 \text{ nm}} \times \dfrac{10^9 \text{ nm}}{1 \text{ m}} = 1.2 \times 10^{15}/\text{s}$

$E = h\nu = (6.626 \times 10^{-34} \text{ J} \cdot \text{s}) \times (1.2 \times 10^{15}/\text{s})$
$= 8.0 \times 10^{-19} \text{ J}$

28. Bohr proposed that electrons traveled in circular paths around the nucleus.

30. An electron is found 90% of the time inside this boundary.

33. The $2p$ sublevel contains three orbitals: $2p_x$, $2p_y$, and $2p_z$.

34. a. 1 ($1s$)   **c.** 3 ($3s$, $3p$, $3d$)

    b. 2 ($2s$, $2p$)   **d.** 4 ($4s$, $4p$, $4d$, $4f$)

35. Aufbau principle: Electrons occupy the lowest possible energy levels. Pauli Exclusion Principle: An atomic orbital can hold at most two electrons. Hund's Rule: One electron occupies each of a set of orbitals with equal energies before any pairing of electrons occurs.

36. $2s$, $3p$, $4s$, $3d$

37. a. valid   **b.** invalid   **c.** invalid   **d.** valid

39. The p orbitals in the third quantum level have three electrons.

42. a. 2   **b.** 3   **c.** 1   **d.** 6

44. a. $1s^2 2s^2 2p^6 3s^2 3p^6 3d^{10} 4s^2 4p^4$

    b. $1s^2 2s^2 2p^6 3s^2 3p^6 3d^2 4s^2$

    c. $1s^2 2s^2 2p^6 3s^2 3p^6 3d^3 4s^2$

    d. $1s^2 2s^2 2p^6 3s^2 3p^6 4s^2$

47. a. v, vi, iv, iii, i, ii

    b. It is the reverse.

50. A quantum is a discrete amount of energy. Photons are light quanta.

51. A photon of ultraviolet light has a higher frequency (smaller wavelength) than a photon of infrared light. Therefore, a photon of ultraviolet light has more energy than a photon of infrared light.

52. $E = h\nu = (6.626 \times 10^{-34} \text{ J} \cdot \text{s}) \times (5.80 \times 10^{14}/\text{s}) = 3.84 \times 10^{-19} \text{ J}$

53. Classical physics views energy changes as continuous. In the quantum concept, energy changes occur in tiny discrete units called quanta.

54. The electron of the hydrogen atom is raised (excited) to a higher energy level.

57. $1s^2 2s^2 2p^6 3s^2 3p^6 3d^{10} 4s^2 4p^3$; $n = 1$, 2 electrons; $n = 2$, 8 electrons; $n = 3$, 18 electrons; $n = 4$, 5 electrons; the fourth energy level ($n = 4$) is not filled.

59. $1s^2 2s^2 2p^3$; nitrogen (7 electrons); 3 unpaired electrons (in the $2p$ sublevel)

60. a. Na, sodium (11 electrons)

    b. N, nitrogen (7 electrons)

    c. Si, silicon (14 electrons)

    d. O, oxygen (8 electrons)

    e. K, potassium (19 electrons)

    f. Ti, titanium (22 electrons)

63. a. $\lambda = 4.36 \times 10^{-7} \text{ m} \times \dfrac{10^2 \text{ cm}}{1 \text{ m}} = 4.36 \times 10^{-5} \text{ cm}$

    b. visible

    c. $\nu = \dfrac{c}{\lambda} = \dfrac{2.998 \times 10^8 \text{ m/s}}{4.36 \times 10^{-7} \text{ m}} = 6.88 \times 10^{14}/\text{s}$

65. a. Electrons with a low velocity will be emitted.

    b. More electrons will be emitted but with a low velocity.

    c. Electrons will be emitted with a higher velocity.

66. $\nu = \dfrac{c}{\lambda} = \dfrac{2.998 \times 10^8 \text{ m/s}}{6.45 \times 10^{-7} \text{ cm}} \times \dfrac{10^2 \text{ cm}}{1 \text{ m}}$
$= 4.65 \times 10^{14}/\text{s}$

$E = h\nu = (6.626 \times 10^{-34} \text{ J} \cdot \text{s}) \times (4.65 \times 10^{14}/\text{s})$
$= 3.08 \times 10^{-19} \text{ J}$

Red light is lower energy than green light.

69. a. emits energy

    b. requires the absorption of energy

    c. requires the absorption of energy

    d. requires the absorption of energy

70. The outermost electron of sodium absorbs photons of wavelength 589 nm as it jumps to a higher energy level, but the electron is not energetic enough to emit a photon at this wavelength. Therefore, the white light spectrum exhibits a dark line at 589 nm.

72. a. $E = h\nu = h \times \dfrac{c}{\lambda} = 6.626 \times 10^{-34} \text{ J} \cdot \text{s}$

$\times \dfrac{2.998 \times 10^8 \text{ m/s}}{1.2 \times 10^{-4} \text{ m}} = 1.7 \times 10^{-21} \text{ J}$

    b. $E = h\nu = h \times \dfrac{c}{\lambda} = 6.626 \times 10^{-34} \text{ J} \cdot \text{s}$

$\times \dfrac{2.998 \times 10^8 \text{ m/s}}{5.1 \times 10^{-7} \text{ m}} = 3.9 \times 10^{-19} \text{ J}$

c. $E = hv = h \times \dfrac{c}{\lambda} = 6.626 \times 10^{-34} \text{ J} \cdot \text{s}$

$$\times \dfrac{2.998 \times 10^8 \text{ m/s}}{1.4 \times 10^{-8} \text{ m}} = 1.7 \times 10^{-17} \text{ J}$$

The energy of the photon of light increases as its wavelength decreases.

73. An orbit confines the electron to a fixed circular path around the nucleus; an orbital is a region around the nucleus in which electrons are likely to be found.

75. Answers will vary. Students may note that radio waves have the lowest energy in the electromagnetic spectrum and, thus, would not be energetic enough to cook food. Others may reason that if microwaves cook food faster than infrared radiation, then radio waves would cook food even faster.

78. **a.** atom with electron in $n = 1$ level
   b. atom with electron in $n = 4$ level
   c. atom with electron in $n = 4$ level
   d. atom with electron in $n = 1$ level

79. The element is potassium (19 electrons).
   a. excited state, valence electron has been promoted from $4s$ to $5p$
   b. ground state, lowest energy electron configuration
   c. impossible configuration, $3p$ orbitals can hold a maximum of 6 electrons, not 7

81. **a.** $v_1 = \dfrac{c}{\lambda} = \dfrac{2.998 \times 10^8 \text{ m/s}}{5.77 \times 10^{-3} \text{ cm}} \times \dfrac{10^2 \text{ cm}}{1 \text{ m}}$

$= 5.20 \times 10^{12}/\text{s}$

$v_2 = \dfrac{c}{\lambda} = \dfrac{2.998 \times 10^8 \text{ m/s}}{6.82 \times 10^{-4} \text{ cm}} \times \dfrac{10^2 \text{ cm}}{1 \text{ m}}$

$= 4.40 \times 10^{13}/\text{s}$

$v_3 = \dfrac{c}{\lambda} = \dfrac{2.998 \times 10^8 \text{ m/s}}{3.16 \times 10^{-4} \text{ cm}} \times \dfrac{10^2 \text{ cm}}{1 \text{ m}}$

$= 9.49 \times 10^{13}/\text{s}$

$v_4 = \dfrac{c}{\lambda} = \dfrac{2.998 \times 10^8 \text{ m/s}}{1.76 \times 10^{-4} \text{ cm}} \times \dfrac{10^2 \text{ cm}}{1 \text{ m}}$

$= 1.70 \times 10^{14}/\text{s}$

$v_5 = \dfrac{c}{\lambda} = \dfrac{2.998 \times 10^8 \text{ m/s}}{1.36 \times 10^{-4} \text{ cm}} \times \dfrac{10^2 \text{ cm}}{1 \text{ m}}$

$= 2.20 \times 10^{14}/\text{s}$

$v_6 = \dfrac{c}{\lambda} = \dfrac{2.998 \times 10^8 \text{ m/s}}{6.38 \times 10^{-5} \text{ cm}} \times \dfrac{10^2 \text{ cm}}{1 \text{ m}}$

$= 4.70 \times 10^{14}/\text{s}$

b.

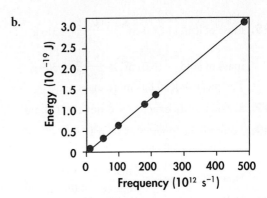

c. $6.63 \times 10^{-34} \text{ J} \cdot \text{s}$
d. The slope is Planck's constant.

83. Hydrogen atom ($Z = 1$), $n = 1$:

$$E = 1^2 \times \dfrac{2.18 \times 10^{-18} \text{ J}}{1^2} = 2.18 \times 10^{-18} \text{ J}$$

Hydrogen atom ($Z = 1$), $n = 2$:

$$E = 1^2 \times \dfrac{2.18 \times 10^{-18} \text{ J}}{2^2} = 5.45 \times 10^{-19} \text{ J}$$

Li^{2+} ion ($Z = 3$), $n = 1$:

$$E = 3^2 \times \dfrac{2.18 \times 10^{-18} \text{ J}}{1^2} = 1.96 \times 10^{-17} \text{ J}$$

85. Two magnets would push each other apart. In the same way, electrons with the same spin would push apart and be unable to occupy the same orbital.

88. The light emitted from an incandescent bulb has wavelengths from 300 nm to 700 nm, which corresponds to a frequency range of about $4 \times 10^{14} \text{ s}^{-1}$ to $1 \times 10^{15} \text{ s}^{-1}$:

$$v = \dfrac{c}{\lambda} = \dfrac{2.998 \times 10^8 \text{ m/s}}{700 \text{ nm}} \times \dfrac{10^9 \text{ nm}}{1 \text{ m}} = 4 \times 10^{14} \text{ s}^{-1}$$

$$v = \dfrac{c}{\lambda} = \dfrac{2.998 \times 10^8 \text{ m/s}}{300 \text{ nm}} \times \dfrac{10^9 \text{ nm}}{1 \text{ m}} = 1 \times 10^{15} \text{ s}^{-1}$$

This means that the energy absorbed by the photons is in the range of about $3 \times 10^{-19} \text{ J}$ to $7 \times 10^{-19} \text{ J}$:

$E = hv = (6.626 \times 10^{-34} \text{ J} \cdot \text{s}) \times (4 \times 10^{14}/\text{s})$
$\quad = 3 \times 10^{-19} \text{ J}$

$E = hv = (6.626 \times 10^{-34} \text{ J} \cdot \text{s}) \times (1 \times 10^{15}/\text{s})$
$\quad = 7 \times 10^{-19} \text{ J}$

89. **a.** heterogeneous
   b. heterogeneous
   c. homogeneous

91. A compound has constant composition; the composition of a mixture can vary.

93. $77 \text{ pm} \times \dfrac{1 \text{ m}}{10^{12} \text{ pm}} \times \dfrac{10^6 \text{ μm}}{1 \text{ m}} = 7.7 \times 10^{-5} \text{ μm}$

95. mass of lead $= 28.0\,\text{cm}^3 \times \dfrac{11.3\,\text{g}}{1\,\text{cm}^3} = 316\,\text{g}$

mass of gold $= 16.0\,\text{cm}^3 \times \dfrac{19.3\,\text{g}}{1\,\text{cm}^3} = 309\,\text{g}$

The piece of lead has more mass.

97. a. exact   **b.** exact   **c.** not exact **d.** not exact

99. Volume of copper $= 24.08\,\text{mL} - 20.00\,\text{mL} = 4.08\,\text{mL} = 4.08\,\text{cm}^3$

Density of copper $= \dfrac{\text{mass}}{\text{volume}} = \dfrac{36.4\,\text{g}}{4.08\,\text{cm}^3} = 8.92\,\text{g/cm}^3$

101. Helium gas is less dense than the nitrogen gas and oxygen gas in the air.

102. Accuracy is a measure of how close the value is to the true value; precision is a measure of how close a series of measurements are to one another.

105. Neon-20 has 10 neutrons in the nucleus; neon-21 has 11 neutrons in the nucleus.

Chapter 6

9. a. $1s^2 2s^2 2p^2$

b. $1s^2 2s^2 2p^6 3s^2 3p^6 3d^{10} 4s^2 4p^6 5s^2$

c. $1s^2 2s^2 2p^6 3s^2 3p^6 3d^3 4s^2$

10. a. B, Al, Ga, In, Tl

b. F, Cl, Br, I, At

c. Ti, Zr, Hf, Rf

27. The close match between the predicted properties and the actual properties of gallium helped gain wider acceptance for Mendeleev's periodic table.

34. helium

38. a. sodium   **c.** germanium

b. strontium   **d.** selenium

43. The ionic radius of a metal cation is smaller than the atomic radius of the metal atom.

47. a. O   **b.** F   **c.** O   **d.** S

51. b; nitrogen and phosphorus are in the same group (Group 5A).

56. a. H, Li, Na, K, Rb, Cs, Fr

b. O, S, Se, Te, Po

c. Zn, Cd, Hg, Uub

60. It is relatively easy to remove two electrons from magnesium; it is much more difficult to remove a third electron. It is relatively easy to remove three electrons from aluminum; it is much more difficult to remove a fourth electron.

65. a. The electrons in calcium are removed from the same energy level. In potassium, the second electron is removed from a lower energy level.

b. Because cesium has a larger atomic radius than lithium, the nuclear charge in a cesium atom has a smaller effect on the electrons in the highest occupied energy level.

c. The third electron removed from a magnesium atom is in a lower energy level.

66. Zinc has a greater nuclear charge (more protons) than calcium.

68. a. $1s^2 2s^2 2p^6 3s^2 3p^6 3d^{10} 4s^2 4p^6$

b. $1s^2 2s^2 2p^6$

c. $1s^2 2s^2 2p^6$

d. $1s^2 2s^2 2p^6$

75. Electron affinity increases (becomes more negative) from left to right across a period because the nuclear charge increases and the shielding effect is constant.

78. a. Possible cations are Rb^+ and Sr^{2+}; possible anions are Br^-, Se^{2-}, and As^{3-}.

b. No, a cation is isoelectronic with the noble gas in the preceding period, and an anion is isoelectronic with the noble gas in the same period.

85. a. physical change   **c.** physical change

b. chemical change   **d.** chemical change

90. a. $2.24\,\text{nm} \times \dfrac{1\,\text{m}}{10^9\,\text{nm}} = 2.24 \times 10^{-9}\,\text{m}$

b. $8.13\,\text{cm} \times \dfrac{1\,\text{m}}{10^2\,\text{cm}} = 8.13 \times 10^{-2}\,\text{m}$

c. $7.4\,\text{pm} \times \dfrac{1\,\text{m}}{10^{12}\,\text{pm}} = 7.4 \times 10^{-12}\,\text{m}$

d. $9.37\,\text{mm} \times \dfrac{1\,\text{m}}{10^3\,\text{mm}} = 9.37 \times 10^{-3}\,\text{m}$

93. The density of the olive is $1.05\,\text{g/cm}^3$. The olive will sink because its density is greater than that of water.

98. a. 48   **b.** 44   **c.** 114   **d.** 110

100. a. none   **b.** one, $2p$ **c.** none   **d.** none

Chapter 7

10. a. In order to have a completely filled valence shell, the iodine atom must gain 1 electron. This electron comes from 1 potassium atom, which loses 1 electron. The formula is KI.

b. Each oxygen atom needs 2 electrons to have an octet, but each aluminum atom loses 3 electrons; so, 2 aluminum atoms are needed for every 3 oxygen atoms. The formula is Al_2O_3.

11. A calcium atom loses 2 valence electrons to form a Ca^{2+} cation. A chlorine atom gains 1 electron to form a Cl^- anion. The formula of the compound that forms is $CaCl_2$.

28. a. Group 5A; 5 valence electrons

b. Group 1A; 1 valence electron

c. Group 5A; 5 valence electrons

d. Group 2A; 2 valence electrons

e. Group 7A; 7 valence electrons

f. Group 4A; 4 valence electrons

31. a. 2; a calcium atom has 2 valence electrons, which it can lose.

b. 3; an aluminum atom has 3 valence electrons, which it can lose.

c. 1; a lithium atom has 1 valence electron, which it can lose.

d. 2; a barium atom has 2 valence electrons, which it can lose.

34. a. 3; a nitrogen atom has 5 valence electrons. It achieves an octet by gaining 3 electrons.

b. 2; a sulfur atom has 6 valence electrons. It achieves an octet by gaining 2 electrons.

c. 1; a chlorine atom has 7 valence electrons. It achieves an octet by gaining 1 electron.

d. 3; a phosphorus atom has 5 valence electrons. It achieves an octet by gaining 3 electrons.

35. a. A sulfur atom has 6 valence electrons and gains 2 electrons to attain a noble-gas configuration. The formula of the ion formed is S^{2-}.

b. A sodium atom has 1 valence electron and loses 1 electron to attain a noble-gas configuration. The formula of the ion formed is Na^{+}.

c. A fluorine atom has 7 valence electrons and gains 1 electron to attain a noble-gas configuration. The formula of the ion formed is F^{-}.

d. A phosphorus atom has 5 valence electrons and gains 3 electrons to attain a noble-gas configuration. The formula of the ion formed is P^{3-}.

40. a, c, e (ionic compounds form between atoms of metals and nonmetals)

43. a. Ca^{2+}, F^{-} **d.** Al^{3+}, S^{2-}

b. Al^{3+}, Br^{-} **e.** K^{+}, N^{3-}

c. Li^{+}, O^{2-}

47. Atoms in metals are arranged in a compact and orderly manner.

49. body-centered cubic: Na, K, Fe, Cr, or W; face-centered cubic: Cu, Ag, Au, Al, or Pb; hexagonal close-packed: Mg, Zn, or Cd

55. It has lost valence electrons.

58. a. sulfide ion (anion), S^{2-}

b. aluminum ion (cation), Al^{3+}

c. nitride ion (anion), N^{3-}

d. calcium ion (cation), Ca^{2+}

59. a. $1s^2\,2s^2\,2p^6\,3s^2\,3p^6\,3d^6$

b. $1s^2\,2s^2\,2p^6\,3s^2\,3p^6\,3d^7$

c. $1s^2\,2s^2\,2p^6\,3s^2\,3p^6\,3d^8$

62. All have the noble-gas configuration of $1s^2\,2s^2\,2p^6\,3s^2\,3p^6$.

67. a, c, e, f (these substances are not composed of metals and nonmetals)

68. a. $BaBr_2$ **b.** Al_2S_3 **c.** K_3N

72. 12

75. a. Cu, Zn   **c.** Cu, Sn

b. Ag, Cu   **d.** Fe, Cr, Ni, C

76. Each dot in the electron dot structure represents a valence electron in the electron configuration diagram.

79. a. 6A (the Ca^{2+} cation must be balanced by an anion with a charge of $2-$)

b. 7A (the Mg^{2+} cation must be balanced by 2 anions with a charge of $1-$)

c. 1A (the N^{3-} anion must be balanced by 3 cations with a charge of $1+$)

d. 6A (the 2 Al^{3+} cations must be balanced by 3 anions with a charge of $2-$)

e. 1A (the F^{-} anion must be balanced by a cation with a charge of $1+$)

f. 2A (the S^{2-} anion must be balanced by a cation with a charge of $2+$)

83. Both metals and ionic compounds are composed of ions. Both are held together by electrostatic attractions. Metals always conduct an electric current, and ionic compounds conduct an electric current only when melted or dissolved in water. Ionic compounds are composed of cations and anions, but metals are composed of cations and free-floating valence electrons. Metals are ductile, but ionic compounds are brittle.

86. a. Lithium is a metal; a lithium atom will form a cation by losing 1 electron.

b. Sodium is a metal; a sodium atom will form a cation by losing 1 electron.

c. Neon is a noble gas; it is chemically nonreactive.

d. Chlorine is a nonmetal; a chlorine atom will form an anion by gaining 1 electron.

e. Magnesium is a metal; a magnesium atom will form a cation by losing 2 electrons.

89. a. CaO; the electrostatic forces of attraction between the Ca^{2+} cations and O^{2-} anions in CaO are much stronger than the forces between the Na^{+} cations and Cl^{-} anions in NaCl.

b. Yes; CaO has stronger electrostatic attractions than NaCl, which must be overcome to melt the compound.

92. The charge on the copper cation is 2+. Its electron configuration is $1s^2 2s^2 2p^6 3s^2 3p^6 3d^9$.

98. a. chemical   c. physical
b. chemical   d. chemical

100. a. liquid, vapor   c. liquid, vapor
b. vapor   d. liquid, vapor

102. a. $6 \times 10^4 \, \text{cm} \times \dfrac{1 \, \text{m}}{10^2 \, \text{cm}} = 600 \, \text{m}$

b. $6 \times 10^6 \, \text{mm} \times \dfrac{1 \, \text{m}}{10^3 \, \text{mm}} = 6000 \, \text{m}$

c. $0.06 \, \text{km} \times \dfrac{10^3 \, \text{m}}{1 \, \text{km}} = 60 \, \text{m}$

d. $6 \times 10^9 \, \text{nm} \times \dfrac{1 \, \text{m}}{10^9 \, \text{nm}} = 6 \, \text{m}$

Distance (b) is the longest.

104. $\text{volume} = \dfrac{\text{mass}}{\text{density}} = \dfrac{62.9 \, \text{g}}{2.33 \, \text{g/cm}^3} = 27.0 \, \text{cm}^3$

108. a. 1   b. 3   c. 1   d. 5

111. a. $500 \, \text{nm} \times \dfrac{1 \, \text{m}}{10^9 \, \text{nm}} = 5 \times 10^{-7} \, \text{m}$

b. ultraviolet

112. a. K, $1s^2 2s^2 2p^6 3s^2 3p^6 4s^1$
b. Al, $1s^2 2s^2 2p^6 3s^2 3p^1$
c. S, $1s^2 2s^2 2p^6 3s^2 3p^4$
d. Ba, $1s^2 2s^2 2p^6 3s^2 3p^6 3d^{10} 4s^2 4p^6 4d^{10} 5s^2 5p^6 6s^2$

Chapter 8

7. a. :C̈l:C̈l: b. :B̈r:B̈r: c. :Ï:Ï:

8. a. H:Ö:Ö:H   b. :C̈l:P̈:C̈l:
:C̈l:

9. [H:Ö:]⁻

10. $\left[\begin{array}{c} \ddot{\text{O}}: \\ :\ddot{\text{O}}:\ddot{\text{S}}:\ddot{\text{O}}: \\ \ddot{\text{O}}: \end{array}\right]^{2-}$ $\left[\begin{array}{c} \ddot{\text{O}}: \\ :\ddot{\text{O}}:\ddot{\text{C}}: \\ \ddot{\text{O}}: \end{array}\right]^{2-}$

29. a. 0.7; moderately polar covalent
b. 2.2; ionic
c. 1.0; moderately to very polar covalent
d. 1.0; moderately to very polar covalent
e. 2.5; ionic
f. 0; nonpolar covalent

30. c and d (tie at 0.4), b (0.7), a (0.9)

48. One atom contributes both electrons to a coordinate covalent bond, as in CO.

50. An unshared pair of electrons is needed for a coordinate covalent bond. There are no unshared pairs in compounds with only C—H and C—C bonds.

54. b and c; assuming only single bonds, the P and S atoms each have 10 valence electrons.

58. a. H:N̈:H   b. :B̈r:C̈l: c. H:Ö:Ö:H   d. H:S̈i:H
H   H

60. a. linear   d. bent
b. tetrahedral   e. linear
c. trigonal planar   f. bent

63. a. sp^3 b. sp^2 c. sp d. sp

65. c (1.9), d (1.4), a (.09), f (0.5), b (0.4), e (0.0)

69. $1 \, \text{mol CH}_4 \times \dfrac{393 \, \text{kJ}}{1 \, \text{mol CH}_4} \times 4 = 1572 \, \text{kJ}$

71. The $3s$ and three $3p$ orbitals of phosphorus hybridize to form four sp^3 atomic orbitals. The resulting shape is pyramidal with a bond angle of 107° between the sigma bonds.

78. a (the phosphorus atom in PBr_5 has 10 valence electrons)

82. Ethyl alcohol can form intermolecular hydrogen bonds between its polar —OH groups, but dimethyl ether cannot form hydrogen bonds.

84. a. bent   b. tetrahedral   c. pyramidal

91. a. :F̈—Be—F̈:   (Be has only 4 valence electrons.)

b. (S has 12 valence electrons.)

c. (Cl has only 7 valence electrons.)

d. (B has only 6 valence electrons.)

e. :F̈—Xe—F̈:   (Xe has 10 valence electrons.)

97. a. $66.5 \, \text{mm} \times \dfrac{1 \, \text{m}}{10^3 \, \text{mm}} \times \dfrac{10^6 \, \mu\text{m}}{1 \, \text{m}} = 6.65 \times 10^4 \, \mu\text{m}$

b. $4 \times 10^{-2} \, \text{g} \times \dfrac{100 \, \text{cg}}{1 \, \text{g}} = 4 \, \text{cg}$

c. $\dfrac{5.62 \, \text{mg}}{1 \, \text{mL}} \times \dfrac{1 \, \text{g}}{10^3 \, \text{mg}} \times \dfrac{10 \, \text{dg}}{1 \, \text{g}} \times \dfrac{10^3 \, \text{mL}}{1 \, \text{L}} = 56.2 \, \text{dg/L}$

d. $\dfrac{85 \, \text{km}}{1 \, \text{h}} \times \dfrac{1 \, \text{h}}{60 \, \text{min}} \times \dfrac{1 \, \text{min}}{60 \, \text{s}} \times \dfrac{10^3 \, \text{m}}{1 \, \text{km}} = 2.4 \times 10^1 \, \text{m/s}$

101. Protons (positive charge) and electrons (negative charge) must be equal.

109. a. barium   b. silicon   c. sodium

111. All have the same number of electrons as a noble gas.

Chapter 9

1. a. selenide ion   **c.** phosphide ion
   b. barium ion   **d.** iodide ion

2. a. three electrons lost   **c.** one electron lost
   b. two electrons gained   **d.** two electrons lost

10. a. BaS   **b.** Li_2O **c.** Ca_3N_2 **d.** CuI_2

11. a. NaI   **b.** $SnCl_2$ **c.** K_2S **d.** CaI_2

12. a. zinc sulfide   **c.** barium oxide
   b. potassium chloride   **d.** copper(II) bromide

13. a. calcium oxide   **c.** iron(II) sulfide
   b. copper(I) selenide   **d.** aluminum fluoride

14. a. $(NH_4)_2SO_3$ **b.** $Ca_3(PO_4)_2$

15. a. $LiHSO_4$ **b.** $Cr(NO_2)_3$

16. a. calcium oxalate
   b. potassium hypochlorite
   c. potassium permanganate
   d. lithium sulfite

17. a. aluminum hydroxide   **c.** tin(II) phosphate
   b. sodium chlorate   **d.** sodium chromate

27. a. oxygen difluoride   **c.** sulfur trioxide
   b. disulfur decafluoride   **d.** sulfur hexafluoride

28. a. N_2O_4 **b.** XeF_4 **c.** S_2F_{10} **d.** IF_7

37. a. hydrofluoric acid
   b. nitric acid
   c. sulfurous acid

38. a. $HClO_4$ **b.** HI   **c.** $HClO_2$

39. a. barium hydroxide
   b. calcium hydroxide
   c. rubidium hydroxide

40. a. CsOH   **b.** $Be(OH)_2$ **c.** $Mn(OH)_3$

48. $\dfrac{2.98 \text{ g Pb}}{0.461 \text{ g O}} = \dfrac{x}{1.00 \text{ g O}}$

$x = \dfrac{2.98 \text{ g Pb} \times 1.00 \text{ g O}}{0.461 \text{ g O}} = 6.46 \text{ g Pb}$

$\dfrac{9.89 \text{ g Pb}}{0.763 \text{ g O}} = \dfrac{y}{1.00 \text{ g O}}$

$y = \dfrac{9.89 \text{ g Pb} \times 1.00 \text{ g O}}{0.763 \text{ g O}} = 13.0 \text{ g Pb}$

$\text{mass ratio} = \dfrac{6.46 \text{ g Pb}}{13.0 \text{ g Pb}} = 1{:}2$

49. Since $\dfrac{7 \text{ Fe}}{3 \text{ O}} = 2.3$ and $\dfrac{23 \text{ g Fe}}{10 \text{ g O}} = 2.3$, the compound must be iron(III) oxide.

58. a. 2+   **b.** 2+   **c.** 3+   **d.** 1+

64. Determine the charge of the anion, and then work the formula backward to find the charge of the transition metal cation needed to give a net charge of zero for the formula unit.

70. a. tri-   **c.** di-   **e.** penta-
   b. mono-   **d.** hexa-   **f.** tetra-

76. a. lead(II) hydroxide   **c.** $Cu(OH)_2$
   b. cobalt(II) hydroxide   **d.** $Fe(OH)_2$

79. No, the ratio of nitrogen to oxygen is 42:26, which is not a 7:4 ratio.

82. a. sodium chlorate
   b. mercury(I) bromide
   c. potassium chromate
   d. perchloric acid
   e. tin(IV) oxide
   f. iron(III) acetate
   g. potassium hydrogen sulfate
   h. calcium hydroxide
   i. barium sulfide

86. binary molecular compound

88. $SnCl_4$

96. a. N_2O, dinitrogen monoxide
   b. NO_2, nitrogen dioxide
   c. NO, nitrogen monoxide
   d. N_2O_4, dinitrogen tetroxide

98. a. The charges do not balance; CsCl.
   b. Neon does not form compounds.
   c. The charges do not balance; ZnO.
   d. The subscripts are not the lowest whole-number ratio; BaS.

100. binary ionic compounds: d and g; binary molecular compounds: a and f; compounds with polyatomic ions: b, c, e, h, and i; acids: b and e; base: c

101. a. 3.60 g solid/1.40 g gas = 2.57 and
6.48 g solid/2.52 g gas = 2.57
The compound obeys the law of definite proportions.
   b. % gas = 1.40/5.00 and 2.52/9.00 = 28.0% gas
0.28 × 14.0 g = 3.92 g colorless gas

102. law of conservation of mass

106. a. Potassium carbonate has a greater water solubility than $CaCO_3$, so you could see which one dissolves in water more readily.

b. The copper compound is blue; the iron compound is white.

c. Add water to dissolve the NH_4Cl, and then filter out the insoluble $BaSO_4$.

d. chlorine (nonmetal), sulfur (nonmetal), bromine (nonmetal), barium (metal), iodine (nonmetal), mercury (metal)

e. barium sulfate, calcium carbonate, potassium carbonate, copper(II) sulfate pentahydrate, iron(II) sulfate pentahydrate, ammonium chloride

f. mass = density × volume

mass = $47.0 \, cm^3 \times 13.59 \, g/cm^3 = 639 \, g \, Hg$

g. volume = $\dfrac{mass}{density} = \dfrac{16.6 \, g}{2.07 \, g/cm^3} = 8.02 \, cm^3$

h. color, density, melting point, and boiling point

111. ionic; $Ca(OH)_2$

113. a. 4   **b.** 2   **c.** 2   **d.** 4   **e.** 2   **f.** 1

118. a. 2   **b.** protons   **c.** electrons   **d.** neutrons

119. a. neon   **b.** carbon   **c.** boron   **d.** helium

124. a. 1   **b.** 6   **c.** 8   **d.** 2   **e.** 7   **f.** 5

127. b and c; molecular compounds formed by two nonmetals have covalent bonds.

Chapter 10

1. $0.50 \, \text{bushel apples} \times \dfrac{1 \, \text{dozen apples}}{0.20 \, \text{bushel apples}} \times$
$\dfrac{2.0 \, \text{kg apples}}{1 \, \text{dozen apples}} = 5.0 \, \text{kg apples}$

2. $14 \, \text{kg apples} \times \dfrac{1 \, \text{dozen apples}}{2.0 \, \text{kg apples}} \times \dfrac{12 \, \text{apples}}{1 \, \text{dozen apples}} \times$
$\dfrac{8 \, \text{seeds}}{1 \, \text{apple}} = 670 \, \text{seeds}$

3. $2.80 \times 10^{24} \, \text{atoms Si} \times \dfrac{1 \, \text{mol Si}}{6.02 \times 10^{23} \times \text{atoms Si}} =$
$4.65 \, \text{mol Si}$

4. $2.17 \times 10^{23} \, \text{molecules Br}_2 \times$
$\dfrac{1 \, \text{mol Br}_2}{6.02 \times 10^{23} \, \text{molecules Br}_2} = 0.360 \, \text{mol Br}_2$

5. $1.14 \, \text{mol SO}_3 \times \dfrac{6.02 \times 10^{23} \, \text{molecules SO}_3}{1 \, \text{mol SO}_3} \times$
$\dfrac{4 \, \text{atoms}}{1 \, \text{molecule SO}_3} = 2.75 \times 10^{24} \, \text{atoms}$

6. $2.12 \, \text{mol C}_3\text{H}_8 \times \dfrac{6.02 \times 10^{23} \, \text{molecules C}_3\text{H}_8}{1 \, \text{mol C}_3\text{H}_8} \times$
$\dfrac{3 \, \text{C atoms}}{1 \, \text{molecule C}_3\text{H}_8} = 3.83 \times 10^{24} \, \text{C atoms}$

$2.12 \, \text{mol C}_3\text{H}_8 \times \dfrac{6.02 \times 10^{23} \, \text{molecules C}_3\text{H}_8}{1 \, \text{mol C}_3\text{H}_8} \times$
$\dfrac{8 \, \text{H atoms}}{1 \, \text{molecule C}_3\text{H}_8} = 1.02 \times 10^{25} \, \text{H atoms}$

7. $1 \, \text{mol P} \times \dfrac{31.0 \, \text{g P}}{1 \, \text{mol P}} = 31.0 \, \text{g P}$

$3 \, \text{mol Cl} \times \dfrac{35.5 \, \text{g Cl}}{1 \, \text{mol Cl}} = 106.5 \, \text{g Cl}$

mass of 1 mol PCl_3 = 31.0 g P + 106.5 g Cl = 138.0 g

molar mass of PCl_3 = 138 g/mol

8. $1 \, \text{mol Na} \times \dfrac{23.0 \, \text{g Na}}{1 \, \text{mol Na}} = 23.0 \, \text{g Na}$

$1 \, \text{mol H} \times \dfrac{1.0 \, \text{g H}}{1 \, \text{mol H}} = 1.0 \, \text{g H}$

$1 \, \text{mol C} \times \dfrac{12.0 \, \text{g C}}{1 \, \text{mol C}} = 12.0 \, \text{g C}$

$3 \, \text{mol O} \times \dfrac{16.0 \, \text{g O}}{1 \, \text{mol O}} = 48.0 \, \text{g O}$

mass of 1 mol $NaHCO_3$ = 23.0 g + 1.0 g + 12.0 g + 48.0 g = 84.0 g

molar mass of $NaHCO_3$ = 84.0 g/mol

16. $20 \, \text{mol C} \times \dfrac{12.0 \, \text{g C}}{1 \, \text{mol C}} = 240.0 \, \text{g C}$

$42 \, \text{mol H} \times \dfrac{1.0 \, \text{g H}}{1 \, \text{mol H}} = 42.0 \, \text{g H}$

1 mol $C_{20}H_{42}$ = 240.0 g C + 42.0 g H = 282.0 g $C_{20}H_{42}$

$4.52 \times 10^{-3} \, \text{mol C}_{20}\text{H}_{42} \times \dfrac{282.0 \, \text{g C}_{20}\text{H}_{42}}{1 \, \text{mol C}_{20}\text{H}_{42}} = 1.27 \, \text{g}$

17. $1 \, \text{mol Fe} \times \dfrac{55.8 \, \text{g Fe}}{1 \, \text{mol Fe}} = 55.8 \, \text{g Fe}$

$2 \, \text{mol O} \times \dfrac{16.0 \, \text{g O}}{1 \, \text{mol O}} = 32.0 \, \text{g O}$

$2 \, \text{mol H} \times \dfrac{1.0 \, \text{g H}}{1 \, \text{mol H}} = 2.0 \, \text{g H}$

1 mol $Fe(OH)_2$ = 55.8 g Fe + 32.0 g O + 2.0 g H = 89.8 g $Fe(OH)_2$

$2.50 \, \text{mol Fe(OH)}_2 \times \dfrac{89.8 \, \text{g}}{1 \, \text{mol Fe(OH)}_2} = 225 \, \text{g Fe(OH)}_2$

18. $3.70 \times 10^{-1} \, \text{g B} \times \dfrac{1 \, \text{mol B}}{10.8 \, \text{g B}} = 3.43 \times 10^{-2} \, \text{mol B}$

19. $2 \text{ mol N} \times \dfrac{14.0 \text{ g N}}{1 \text{ mol N}} = 28 \text{ g N}$

$3 \text{ mol O} \times \dfrac{16.0 \text{ g O}}{1 \text{ mol O}} = 48.0 \text{ g O}$

$1 \text{ mol N}_2\text{O}_3 = 28 \text{ g N} + 48.0 \text{ g O} = 76.0 \text{ g N}_2\text{O}_3$

$75.0 \text{ g N}_2\text{O}_3 \times \dfrac{1 \text{ mol N}_2\text{O}_3}{76.0 \text{ g N}_2\text{O}_3} = 0.987 \text{ mol N}_2\text{O}_3$

20. a. $3.20 \times 10^{-3} \text{ mol CO}_2 \times \dfrac{22.4 \text{ L CO}_2}{1 \text{ mol CO}_2} =$

$7.17 \times 10^{-2} \text{ L CO}_2$

b. $3.70 \text{ mol N}_2 \times \dfrac{22.4 \text{ L N}_2}{1 \text{ mol N}_2} = 82.9 \text{ L N}_2$

c. $0.960 \text{ mol CH}_4 \times \dfrac{22.4 \text{ L CH}_4}{1 \text{ mol CH}_4} = 21.5 \text{ L CH}_4$

21. a. $67.2 \text{ L SO}_2 \times \dfrac{1 \text{ mol SO}_2}{22.4 \text{ L SO}_2} = 3.00 \text{ mol SO}_2$

b. $0.880 \text{ L He} \times \dfrac{1 \text{ mol He}}{22.4 \text{ L He}} = 0.039 \text{ mol He}$

c. $1.00 \times 10^3 \text{ L C}_2\text{H}_6 \times \dfrac{1 \text{ mol C}_2\text{H}_6}{22.4 \text{ L C}_2\text{H}_6} = 44.6 \text{ mol C}_2\text{H}_6$

22. $\dfrac{3.58 \text{ g}}{\text{L}} \times \dfrac{22.4 \text{ L}}{1 \text{ mol}} = 80.2 \text{ g/mol}$

23. molar mass of Kr = 83.8 g/mol

$\dfrac{83.8 \text{ g}}{1 \text{ mol Kr}} \times \dfrac{1 \text{ mol Kr}}{22.4 \text{ L}} = 3.74 \text{ g/L}$

33. mass of compound = 9.03 g + 3.48 g = 12.51 g

$\% \text{ Mg} = \dfrac{\text{mass of Mg}}{\text{mass of compound}} \times 100\% = \dfrac{9.03 \text{ g}}{12.51 \text{ g}} \times 100\%$

$= 72.2\% \text{ Mg}$

$\% \text{ N} = \dfrac{\text{mass of N}}{\text{mass of compound}} \times 100\% = \dfrac{3.48 \text{ g}}{12.51 \text{ g}} \times 100\%$

$= 27.8\% \text{ N}$

34. mass of oxygen = 14.2 g − 13.2 g = 1.0 g

$\% \text{ Hg} = \dfrac{\text{mass of Hg}}{\text{mass of compound}} \times 100\% = \dfrac{13.2 \text{ g}}{14.2 \text{ g}} \times 100\%$

$= 93.0\% \text{ Hg}$

$\% \text{ O} = \dfrac{\text{mass of O}}{\text{mass of compound}} \times 100\% = \dfrac{1.0 \text{ g}}{14.2 \text{ g}} \times 100\%$

$= 7.0\% \text{ O}$

35. a. mass of N in 1 mol NH_3 = 1 mol × 14.0 g/mol
= 14.0 g

molar mass of NH_3 = 14.0 g + 3 × 1.0 g = 17.0 g

$\% \text{ N} = \dfrac{\text{mass of N in 1 mol NH}_3}{\text{molar mass of NH}_3} \times 100\% =$

$\dfrac{14.0 \text{ g}}{17.0 \text{ g}} \times 100\% = 82.4\% \text{ N}$

b. mass of N in 1 mol NH_4NO_3 = 1 mol ×
14.0 g/mol = 14.0 g

molar mass of NH_4NO_3 = 14.0 g + 4 × 1.0 g +
14.0 g + 3 × 16.0 g = 80.0 g

$\% \text{ N} = \dfrac{\text{mass of N in 1 mol NH}_4\text{NO}_3}{\text{molar mass of NH}_4\text{NO}_3} \times 100\% =$

$\dfrac{28.0 \text{ g}}{80.0 \text{ g}} \times 100\% = 35.0\% \text{ N}$

36. a. mass of C in 1 mol C_2H_6 = 2 mol × 12.0 g/mol
= 24.0 g

mass of H in 1 mol C_2H_6 = 6 mol × 1.0 g/mol
= 6.0 g

molar mass of C_2H_6 = 24.0 g + 6.0 g = 30.0 g

$\% \text{ C} = \dfrac{\text{mass of C in 1 mol C}_2\text{H}_6}{\text{molar mass of C}_2\text{H}_6} \times 100\% =$

$\dfrac{24.0 \text{ g}}{30.0 \text{ g}} \times 100\% = 80.0\% \text{ C}$

$\% \text{ H} = \dfrac{\text{mass of H in 1 mol C}_2\text{H}_6}{\text{molar mass of C}_2\text{H}_6} \times 100\% =$

$\dfrac{6.0 \text{ g}}{30.0 \text{ g}} = 20.0\% \text{ H}$

b. mass of Na in 1 mol $NaHSO_4$ = 1 mol ×
23.0 g/mol = 23.0 g

mass of H in 1 mol $NaHSO_4$ = 1 mol ×
1.0 g/mol = 1.0 g

mass of S in 1 mol $NaHSO_4$ = 1 mol ×
32.1 g/mol = 32.1 g

mass of O in 1 mol $NaHSO_4$ = 4 mol ×
16.0 g/mol = 64.0 g

molar mass of $NaHSO_4$ = 23.0 g + 1.0 g + 32.1 g
+ 64.0 g = 120.1 g

$\% \text{Na} = \dfrac{\text{mass of Na in 1 mol NaHSO}_4}{\text{molar mass of NaHSO}_4} \times 100\%$

$= \dfrac{23.0 \text{ g}}{120.1 \text{ g}} = 19.2\% \text{ Na}$

$\% \text{ H} = \dfrac{\text{mass of H in 1 mol NaHSO}_4}{\text{molar mass of NaHSO}_4} \times 100\%$

$= \dfrac{1.0 \text{ g}}{120.1 \text{ g}} = 0.80\% \text{ H}$

$\% \text{ S} = \dfrac{\text{mass of S in 1 mol NaHSO}_4}{\text{molar mass of NaHSO}_4} \times 100\%$

$= \dfrac{32.1 \text{ g}}{120.1 \text{ g}} = 26.7\% \text{ S}$

$\% \text{ O} = \dfrac{\text{mass of O in 1 mol NaHSO}_4}{\text{molar mass of NaHSO}_4} \times 100\%$

$= \dfrac{64.0 \text{ g}}{120.1 \text{ g}} = 53.3\% \text{ O}$

37. a. $125 \text{ g NH}_3 \times \dfrac{82.4 \text{ g N}}{100 \text{ g NH}_3} = 103 \text{ g N}$

b. $125 \text{ g NH}_4\text{NO}_3 \times \dfrac{35.0 \text{ g N}}{100 \text{ g NH}_4\text{NO}_3} = 43.8 \text{ g N}$

38. a. $350 \text{ g C}_2\text{H}_6 \times \dfrac{2.0 \text{ g} \times 10^1 \text{ g H}}{100 \text{ g C}_2\text{H}_6} = 7.0 \times 10^1 \text{ g H}$

b. $20.2 \text{ g NaHSO}_4 \times \dfrac{0.83 \text{ g H}}{100 \text{ g NaHSO}_4} = 0.17 \text{ g H}$

39. a. $94.1 \text{ g O} \times \dfrac{1 \text{ mol O}}{16.0 \text{ g O}} = 5.88 \text{ mol O}$

$5.9 \text{ g H} \times \dfrac{1 \text{ mol H}}{1.0 \text{ g H}} = 5.9 \text{ mol H}$

The mole ratio of O to H is $O_{5.88}H_{5.9}$

$\dfrac{5.88 \text{ mol O}}{5.88} = 1 \text{ mol O}$

$\dfrac{5.9 \text{ mol H}}{5.88} = 1 \text{ mol H}$

The mole ratio of O to H is OH.
The empirical formula is OH.

b. $67.6 \text{ g Hg} \times \dfrac{1 \text{ mol Hg}}{200.6 \text{ g Hg}} = 0.337 \text{ mol Hg}$

$10.8 \text{ g S} \times \dfrac{1 \text{ mol S}}{32.1 \text{ g S}} = 0.336 \text{ mol S}$

$21.6 \text{ g O} \times \dfrac{1 \text{ mol O}}{16.0 \text{ g O}} = 1.35 \text{ mol O}$

The mole ratio of Hg to S to O is $Hg_{0.337}S_{0.336}O_{1.35}$.

$\dfrac{0.337 \text{ mol Hg}}{0.336} = 1 \text{ mol Hg}$

$\dfrac{0.336 \text{ mol S}}{0.336} = 1 \text{ mol S}$

$\dfrac{1.35 \text{ mol O}}{0.336} = 4 \text{ mol O}$

The mole ratio of Hg to S to O is $HgSO_4$.
The empirical formula is $HgSO_4$.

40. $62.1 \text{ g C} \times \dfrac{1 \text{ mol C}}{12.0 \text{ g C}} = 5.18 \text{ mol C}$

$13.8 \text{ g H} \times \dfrac{1 \text{ mol H}}{1.0 \text{ g H}} = 13.8 \text{ mol H}$

$24.1 \text{ g N} \times \dfrac{1 \text{ mol N}}{14.0 \text{ g N}} = 1.72 \text{ mol N}$

$\dfrac{5.18 \text{ mol C}}{1.72} = 3 \text{ mol C}$

$\dfrac{13.8 \text{ mol H}}{1.72} = 8 \text{ mol H}$

$\dfrac{1.72 \text{ mol N}}{1.72} = 1 \text{ mol N}$

The empirical formula is C_3H_8N.

41. efm of CClN $= 12.0 \text{ g/mol} + 35.5 \text{ g/mol} + 14.0 \text{ g/mol} = 61.5 \text{ g/mol}$

$\dfrac{\text{molar mass}}{\text{efm}} = \dfrac{184.5 \text{ g/mol}}{61.5 \text{ g/mol}} = 3$

$(\text{CClN}) \times 3 = C_3Cl_3N_3$.

42. efm $= 12.0 \text{ g/mol} + 3(1.0 \text{ g/mol}) + 16.0 \text{ g/mol} = 31.0 \text{ g/mol}$

$\dfrac{\text{molar mass}}{\text{efm of CH}_3\text{O}} = \dfrac{62.0 \text{ g/mol}}{31.0 \text{ g/mol}} = 2$

$(\text{CH}_3\text{O}) \times 2 = C_2H_6O_2$

51. a. molecule
b. formula unit
c. molecule
d. atom

52. a. 3
b. 2
c. 9
d. 10

54. a. 2.41×10^{24} formula units of NaCl $\times$

$\dfrac{1 \text{ mol NaCl}}{6.02 \times 10^{23} \text{ formula units NaCl}} = 0.400 \times 10^1 = 4.00 \text{ mol NaCl}$

b. 9.03×10^{24} atoms of Hg $\times \dfrac{1 \text{ mol Hg}}{6.02 \times 10^{23} \text{ atoms Hg}}$

$= 15.0 \text{ mol Hg}$

c. 4.65×10^{24} molecules of $NO_2^- \times$

$\dfrac{1 \text{ mol NO}_2}{6.02 \times 10^{23} \text{ molecules NO}_2} = 0.772 \times 10^1 = 7.72 \text{ molecules NO}_2$

57. a. $3.00 \text{ mol Sn} \times \dfrac{6.02 \times 10^{23} \text{ atoms Sn}}{1 \text{ mol Sn}} = 1.81 \times 10^{24} \text{ atoms Sn}$

b. $0.400 \text{ mol KCl} \times \dfrac{6.02 \times 10^{23} \text{ formula units KCl}}{1 \text{ mol KCl}}$

$= 2.41 \times 10^{23} \text{ formula units KCl}$

c. $7.50 \text{ mol SO}_2 \times \dfrac{6.02 \times 10^{23} \text{ molecules SO}_2}{1 \text{ mol SO}_2} = 4.52 \times 10^{24} \text{ molecules SO}_2$

d. $4.80 \times 10^{-3} \text{ mol NaI} \times$

$\dfrac{6.02 \times 10^{23} \text{ formula units NaI}}{1 \text{ mol NaI}} = 2.89 \times 10^{21} \text{ formula units NaI}$.

60. a. $(3 \times 1.0 \text{ g/mol}) + (1 \times 31.0 \text{ g/mol}) + (4 \times 16.0 \text{ g/mol}) = 98.0 \text{ g/mol}$

b. $(2 \times 14.0 \text{ g/mol}) + (3 \times 16.0 \text{ g/mol}) = 76.0 \text{ g/mol}$

c. $(1 \times 40.1 \text{ g/mol}) + (1 \times 12.0 \text{ g/mol}) + (3 \times 16.0 \text{ g/mol}) = 100.1 \text{ g/mol}$

d. $2 \times [(1 \times 14.0 \text{ g/mol}) + (4 \times 1.0 \text{ g/mol})] + (1 \times 32.1 \text{ g/mol}) + (4 \times 16.0 \text{ g/mol}) = 132.1 \text{ g/mol}$

e. $(4 \times 12.0 \text{ g/mol}) + (9 \times 1.0 \text{ g/mol}) + (2 \times 16.0 \text{ g/mol}) = 89.0 \text{ g/mol}$

f. $2 \times 79.9 \text{ g/mol} = 159.8 \text{ g/mol}$

63. a. mass C in 1 mol $C_{12}H_{22}O_{11} = 12$ mol $\times$ 12.0 g/mol $= 144.0$ g

mass H in 1 mol $C_{12}H_{22}O_{11} = 22$ mol $\times$ 1.0 g/mol $= 22.0$ g

mass O in 1 mol $C_{12}H_{22}O_{11} = 11$ mol $\times$ 16.0 g/mol $= 176.0$ g

molar mass $C_{12}H_{22}O_{11} = 144.0$ g $+ 22.0$ g $+ 176.0$ g $= 342.0$ g

$$0.250 \text{ mol } C_{12}H_{22}O_{11} \times \frac{342.0 \text{ g } C_{12}H_{22}O_{11}}{1 \text{ mol } C_{12}H_{22}O_{11}} = 85.5 \text{ g } C_{12}H_{22}O_{11}$$

b. mass Na in 1 mol NaCl $= 1$ mol $\times$ 23.0 g/mol $= 23.0$ g

mass Cl in 1 mol NaCl $= 1$ mol $\times$ 35.5 g/mol $= 35.5$ g

molar mass of NaCl $= 23.0$ g $+ 35.5$ g $= 58.5$ g

$$0.250 \text{ mol NaCl} \times \frac{58.5 \text{ g NaCl}}{1 \text{ mol NaCl}} = 14.6 \text{ g NaCl}$$

c. mass K in 1 mol $KMnO_4 = 1$ mol $\times$ 39.1 g/mol $= 39.1$ g

mass Mn in 1 mol $KMnO_4 = 1$ mol $\times$ 54.9 g/mol $= 54.9$ g

mass O in 1 mol $KMnO_4 = 4$ mol $\times$ 16.0 g/mol $= 64.0$ g

molar mass $KMnO_4 = 39.1$ g $+ 54.9$ g $+ 64.0$ g $= 158.0$ g

$$0.250 \text{ mol } KMnO_4 \times \frac{158.0 \text{ g } KMnO_4}{1 \text{ mol } KMnO_4} = 39.5 \text{ g } KMnO_4$$

64. a. $1.00 \times 10^2 \text{ g } C_{12}H_{22}O_{11} \times \dfrac{1 \text{ mol } C_{12}H_{22}O_{11}}{342.0 \text{ g } C_{12}H_{22}O_{11}} = 0.292 \text{ mol } C_{12}H_{22}O_{11}$

b. $1.00 \times 10^2 \text{ g NaCl} \times \dfrac{1 \text{ mol NaCl}}{58.5 \text{ g NaCl}} = 1.71 \text{ mol NaCl}$

c. $1.00 \times 10^2 \text{ g } KMnO_4 \times \dfrac{1 \text{ mol } KMnO_4}{158.0 \text{ g } KMnO_4} = 0.633 \text{ mol } KMnO_4$

67. a. $7.64 \text{ mol Ar} \times \dfrac{22.4 \text{ L Ar}}{1 \text{ mol Ar}} = 171 \text{ L Ar}$

b. $1.34 \text{ mol } SO_2 \times \dfrac{22.4 \text{ L } SO_2}{1 \text{ mol } SO_2} = 30.0 \text{ L } SO_2$

c. $0.442 \text{ mol } C_2H_6 \times \dfrac{22.4 \text{ L } C_2H_6}{1 \text{ mol } C_2H_6} = 9.90 \text{ L } C_2H_6$

d. $2.45 \times 10^{-3} \text{ mol } H_2S \times \dfrac{22.4 \text{ L } H_2S}{1 \text{ mol } H_2S} = 5.49 \times 10^{-2} \text{ L } H_2S$

68. $\dfrac{0.902 \text{ g}}{1 \text{ L}} \times \dfrac{22.4 \text{ L}}{1 \text{ mol}} = 20.2 \text{ g/mol}$

72. Total mass $= 13.3$ g $+ 5.7$ g $= 19.0$ g

% Fe $= \dfrac{13.3 \text{ g}}{19.0 \text{ g}} \times 100\% = 70.0\%$ Fe

% O $= \dfrac{5.7 \text{ g}}{19.0 \text{ g}} \times 100\% = 3.0 \times 10^1\%$ O

73. a. % H $= \dfrac{2.0 \text{ g}}{34.1 \text{ g}} \times 100\% = 5.9\%$ H

% S $= \dfrac{32.1 \text{ g}}{34.1 \text{ g}} \times 100\% = 94.1\%$ S

b. % N $= \dfrac{28.0 \text{ g}}{124.0 \text{ g}} \times 100\% = 22.6\%$ N

% H $= \dfrac{8.0 \text{ g}}{124.0 \text{ g}} \times 100\% = 6.5\%$ H

% C $= \dfrac{24.0 \text{ g}}{124.0 \text{ g}} \times 100\% = 19.4\%$ C

% O $= \dfrac{64.0 \text{ g}}{124.0 \text{ g}} \times 100\% = 51.6\%$ O

c. % Mg $= \dfrac{24.3 \text{ g}}{58.3 \text{ g}} \times 100\% = 41.7\%$ Mg

% O $= \dfrac{32.0 \text{ g}}{58.3 \text{ g}} \times 100\% = 54.9\%$ O

% H $= \dfrac{2.0 \text{ g}}{58.3 \text{ g}} \times 100\% = 3.4\%$ H

d. % Na $= \dfrac{69.0 \text{ g}}{164.0 \text{ g}} \times 100\% = 42.1\%$ Na

% P $= \dfrac{31.0 \text{ g}}{164.0 \text{ g}} \times 100\% = 18.9\%$ P

% O $= \dfrac{64.0 \text{ g}}{164.0 \text{ g}} \times 100\% = 39.0\%$ O

74. a. $3.54 \text{ g } H_2S \times \dfrac{94.1 \text{ g S}}{100 \text{ g } H_2S} = 3.33 \text{ g S}$

b. $25.0 \text{ g } (NH_4)_2C_2O_4 \times \dfrac{22.6 \text{ g N}}{100 \text{ g } (NH_4)_2C_2O_4} = 5.65 \text{ g N}$

c. $97.4 \text{ g } Mg(OH)_2 \times \dfrac{41.7 \text{ g Mg}}{100 \text{ g } Mg(OH)_2} = 40.6 \text{ g Mg}$

d. $804 \text{ g } Na_3PO_4 \times \dfrac{18.9 \text{ g P}}{100 \text{ g } Na_3PO_4} = 152 \text{ g P}$

76. An empirical formula has the lowest whole-number ratio of elements.

    a. molecular   **c.** molecular and empirical

    b. molecular   **d.** molecular and empirical

79. a. efm of $CH_2O = 12.0 \text{ g/mol} + 2 \times (1.0 \text{ g/mol}) + 16.0 \text{ g/mol} = 30.0 \text{ g/mol}$

$$\frac{\text{molar mass}}{\text{efm}} = \frac{90 \text{ g/mol}}{30.0 \text{ g/mol}} = 3$$

$(CH_2O) \times 3 = C_3H_6O_3$

b. efm of $HgCl = 200.6 \text{ g/mol} + 35.5 \text{ g/mol} = 236.1 \text{ g/mol}$

$$\frac{\text{molar mass}}{\text{efm}} = \frac{472.2 \text{ g/mol}}{236.1 \text{ g/mol}} = 2$$

$(HgCl) \times 2 = Hg_2Cl_2$

80. a. $1.00 \text{ mol } C_{12}H_{22}O_{11} \times$

$$\frac{6.02 \times 10^{23} \text{ molecules } C_{12}H_{22}O_{11}}{1 \text{ mol } C_{12}H_{22}O_{11}} \times$$

$$\frac{45 \text{ atoms}}{1 \text{ molecule } C_{12}H_{22}O_{11}} = 2.71 \times 10^{25} \text{ atoms}$$

b. $2.00 \text{ mol } C_{12}H_{22}O_{11} \times$

$$\frac{6.02 \times 10^{23} \text{ molecules } C_{12}H_{22}O_{11}}{1 \text{ mol } C_{12}H_{22}O_{11}} \times$$

$$\frac{12 \text{ C atoms}}{1 \text{ molecule } C_{12}H_{22}O_{11}} = 1.44 \times 10^{25} \text{ C atoms}$$

c. $2.00 \text{ mol } C_{12}H_{22}O_{11} \times$

$$\frac{6.02 \times 10^{23} \text{ molecules } C_{12}H_{22}O_{11}}{1 \text{ mol } C_{12}H_{22}O_{11}} \times$$

$$\frac{22 \text{ H atoms}}{1 \text{ molecule } C_{12}H_{22}O_{11}} = 2.65 \times 10^{25} \text{ H atoms}$$

d. $3.65 \text{ mol } C_{12}H_{22}O_{11} \times$

$$\frac{6.02 \times 10^{23} \text{ molecules } C_{12}H_{22}O_{11}}{1 \text{ mol } C_{12}H_{22}O_{11}} \times$$

$$\frac{11 \text{ O atoms}}{1 \text{ molecule } C_{12}H_{22}O_{11}} = 2.42 \times 10^{25} \text{ O atoms}$$

82. a. efm of $CH_2O = 12.0 \text{ g/mol} + 2 \times (1.0 \text{ g/mol}) + 16.0 \text{ g/mol} = 30.0 \text{ g/mol}$

Compound A: $\dfrac{\text{molar mass of A}}{\text{efm}} = \dfrac{60.0 \text{ g/mol}}{30.0 \text{ g/mol}} = 2$

$(CH_2O) \times 2 = C_2H_4O_2$

Compound D: $\dfrac{\text{molar mass of D}}{\text{efm}} = \dfrac{150.0 \text{ g/mol}}{30.0 \text{ g/mol}} = 5$

$(CH_2O) \times 5 = C_5H_{10}O_5$

Compound E: $\dfrac{\text{molar mass of E}}{\text{efm}} = \dfrac{180.0 \text{ g/mol}}{30.0 \text{ g/mol}} = 6$

$(CH_2O) \times 6 = C_6H_{12}O_6$

b. $\text{slope} = \dfrac{\Delta \text{ molar mass}}{\Delta \text{ mass of C}} = \dfrac{150.0 - 60.0}{60.0 - 24.0} = \dfrac{2.5}{1}$

The slope is the ratio of the empirical formula mass to the mass of carbon in the empirical formula: $30.0 \text{ g} / 12.0 \text{ g} = 2.5/1$.

c. The two other data points occur when molar mass/efm = 3 and 4. These data points correspond to compounds with molecular formulas $C_3H_6O_3$ and $C_4H_8O_4$, respectively. Thus, the x, y values are (36, 90) and (48, 120).

85. molar mass of $Cl_2O = 2 \times (35.5 \text{ g/mol}) + 16.0 \text{ g/mol} = 87.0 \text{ g/mol}$

$$90.0 \text{ g } Cl_2O \times \frac{1 \text{ mol } Cl_2O}{87.0 \text{ g } Cl_2O} \times \frac{1 \text{ mol } O}{1 \text{ mol } Cl_2O} \times \frac{16.0 \text{ g } O}{1 \text{ mol } O}$$

$$= 16.6 \text{ g } O$$

87. $150.0 \text{ mg } C_{17}H_{18}FN_3O_3 \times \dfrac{1 \text{ g } C_{17}H_{18}FN_3O_3}{1000 \text{ mg } C_{17}H_{18}FN_3O_3}$

$$\times \frac{1 \text{ mol } C_{17}H_{18}FN_3O_3}{331.0 \text{ g } C_{17}H_{18}FN_3O_3} \times$$

$$\frac{6.02 \times 10^{23} \text{ molecules } C_{17}H_{18}FN_3O_3}{1 \text{ mol } C_{17}H_{18}FN_3O_3} \times$$

$$\frac{1 \text{ F atom}}{1 \text{ molecule } C_{17}H_{18}FN_3O_3} = 2.73 \times 10^{20} \text{ F atoms}$$

89. a. $94.1 \text{ g } O \times \dfrac{1 \text{ mol } O}{16.0 \text{ g } O} = 5.88 \text{ mol } O$

$5.9 \text{ g } H \times \dfrac{1 \text{ mol } H}{1.0 \text{ g } H} = 5.9 \text{ mol } H$

$\dfrac{5.88 \text{ mol } O}{5.88} = 1.00 \text{ mol } O; \dfrac{5.9 \text{ mol } H}{5.88} = 1.00 \text{ mol } H;$

The empirical formula is HO.

$$\frac{\text{molar mass}}{\text{efm}} = \frac{34 \text{ g/mol}}{17.0 \text{ g/mol}} = 2$$

$(HO) \times 2 = H_2O_2$

b. $50.7 \text{ g } C \times \dfrac{1 \text{ mol } C}{12.0 \text{ g } C} = 4.23 \text{ mol } C$

$4.2 \text{ g } H \times \dfrac{1 \text{ mol } H}{1.0 \text{ g } H} = 4.2 \text{ mol } H$

$45.1 \text{ g } O \times \dfrac{1 \text{ mol } O}{16.0 \text{ g } O} = 2.83 \text{ mol } O$

$\dfrac{4.23 \text{ mol } C}{2.83} = 1.49 \text{ mol } C; \dfrac{4.2 \text{ mol } H}{2.83} = 1.5 \text{ mol } H;$

$\dfrac{2.83 \text{ mol } O}{2.83} = 1.00 \text{ mol } O$

$1.49 \text{ mol C} \times 2 = 3 \text{ mol C}; 1.5 \text{ mol H} \times 2 = 3 \text{ mol H}; 1.00 \text{ mol O} \times 2 = 2 \text{ mol O}$. The empirical formula is $C_3H_3O_2$.

$$\frac{\text{molar mass}}{\text{efm}} = \frac{142 \text{ g/mol}}{71.0 \text{ g/mol}} = 2$$

$(C_3H_3O_2) \times 2 = C_6H_6O_4$

c. $56.6 \text{ g K} \times \dfrac{1 \text{ mol K}}{39.1 \text{ g K}} = 1.45 \text{ mol K}$

$8.7 \text{ g C} \times \dfrac{1 \text{ mol C}}{12.0 \text{ g C}} = 0.73 \text{ mol C}$

$34.7 \text{ g O} \times \dfrac{1 \text{ mol O}}{16.0 \text{ g O}} = 2.17 \text{ mol O}$

$\dfrac{1.45 \text{ mol K}}{0.73} = 2.00 \text{ mol K}; \dfrac{0.73 \text{ mol C}}{0.73} = 1.00 \text{ mol C};$

$\dfrac{2.17 \text{ mol O}}{0.73} = 3.00 \text{ mol O}$

The empirical formula is K_2CO_3.

$\dfrac{\text{molar mass}}{\text{efm}} = \dfrac{138.2 \text{ g/mol}}{138.2 \text{ g/mol}} = 1$

$(K_2CO_3) \times 1 = K_2CO_3$

90. a. Atomic mass of boron = 10.8 amu

$15 \text{ atoms B} \times \dfrac{10.8 \text{ amu}}{1 \text{ atom B}} = 162 \text{ amu}$

$\dfrac{162 \text{ amu}}{6} = 27.0 \text{ amu}$

b. aluminum

91. $6.02 \times 10^{23} \text{ particles} \times \dfrac{5 \times 10^{-6} \text{ cm}}{1 \text{ particle}} \times \dfrac{1 \text{ m}}{100 \text{ cm}} \times$

$\dfrac{1 \text{ km}}{1000 \text{ m}} = 3 \times 10^{13} \text{ km}$

94. $5.50 \text{ L} \times \dfrac{1 \text{ mol He}}{22.4 \text{ L}} \times \dfrac{4.0 \text{ g He}}{1 \text{ mol He}} = 0.98 \text{ g He}$

96. Let the number of carbon atoms = x. Then, the empirical formula is $C_xH_{3x}O_{x/2}$. The smallest value of x that will give whole number subscripts is 2. Therefore, the empirical formula is C_2H_6O.

100. a. $68 \text{ g C} \times \dfrac{1 \text{ mol C}}{12.0 \text{ g C}} = 5.7 \text{ mol C}$

$7 \text{ g H} \times \dfrac{1 \text{ mol H}}{1.0 \text{ g H}} = 7.0 \text{ mol H}$

$20 \text{ g O} \times \dfrac{1 \text{ mol O}}{16.0 \text{ g O}} = 1.3 \text{ mol O}$

$9 \text{ g N} \times \dfrac{1 \text{ mol N}}{14.0 \text{ g N}} = 0.64 \text{ mol N}$

$\dfrac{5.7 \text{ mol C}}{0.64} = 9 \text{ mol C}; \dfrac{7 \text{ mol H}}{0.64} = 11 \text{ mol H};$

$\dfrac{1.3 \text{ mol O}}{0.64} = 2 \text{ mol O}; \dfrac{0.6 \text{ mol N}}{0.64} = 1 \text{ mol N}$

The empirical formula is $C_9H_{11}O_2N$.

b. $\dfrac{\text{molar mass}}{\text{efm}} = \dfrac{165.2 \text{ g/mol}}{165.0 \text{ g/mol}} = 1$

The molecular formula is $C_9H_{11}O_2N$.

101. From the given information, the ratio of atoms is $C_{0.6}H_1O_{1.8}N_{0.6}$. The empirical formula is $(C_{0.6}H_1O_{1.8}N_{0.6}) \times 5 = C_3H_5O_9N_3$.

efm $= 3 \times (12.0 \text{ g/mol}) + 5 \times (1.0 \text{ g/mol}) + 9 \times (16.0 \text{ g/mol}) + 3 \times (14.0 \text{ g/mol}) = 227.0 \text{ g/mol}$

$\text{molar mass} = \dfrac{1.00 \text{ g}}{0.00441 \text{ mol}} = 227 \text{ g/mol}$

$\dfrac{\text{molar mass}}{\text{efm}} = \dfrac{227}{227.0} = 1$

The molecular formula is also $C_3H_5O_9N_3$.

103. $75.0 \text{ g air} \times \dfrac{1 \text{ L air}}{1.19 \text{ g air}} \times \dfrac{20.95 \text{ L } O_2}{100 \text{ L air}} \times \dfrac{1 \text{ mol } O_2}{22.4 \text{ L } O_2} \times$

$\dfrac{6.02 \times 10^{23} \text{ molecules } O_2}{1 \text{ mol } O_2} = 3.54 \times 10^{23} \text{ molecules } O_2$

105. Consider a cube containing 1 mol of NaCl. The mass of the cube (to 4 significant figures) would then be 22.99 g + 35.45 g = 58.44 g. The volume of the cube can be calculated using the density of solid NaCl:

$58.44 \text{ g NaCl} \times \dfrac{1 \text{ cm}^3}{2.165 \text{ g NaCl}} = 26.99 \text{ cm}^3$

The length of one side of the cube is then

$\sqrt[3]{26.99 \text{ cm}^3} = 3.000 \text{ cm}$

The number of ions per side is as follows:

$3.000 \text{ cm} \times \dfrac{1 \text{ ion}}{2.819 \times 10^{-8} \text{ cm}} = 1.064 \times 10^8 \text{ ions}$

The total number of ions in the cube is then $(1.064 \times 10^8 \text{ ions})^3 = 1.205 \times 10^{24} \text{ ions}$

To calculate Avogadro's number, determine the number of formula units in the cube:

$1.205 \times 10^{24} \text{ ions} \times \dfrac{1 \text{ formula unit}}{2 \text{ ions}} =$

$6.025 \times 10^{23} \text{ formula units}$

108. $30.0 \text{ mg} \times \dfrac{1 \text{ g}}{1000 \text{ mg}} \times \dfrac{1 \text{ mol of compound}}{312 \text{ g}} \times$

$\dfrac{6.02 \times 10^{23} \text{ molecules}}{1 \text{ mol of compound}} = 5.79 \times 10^{19} \text{ molecules}$

110. chemical change: wax burning

physical changes: wax melting, wax vaporizing

111. a. physical change   **d.** physical change

   b. chemical change   **e.** chemical change

   c. chemical change   **f.** physical change

114. $\dfrac{84.0 \text{ g}}{2.75 \text{ cm} \times 4.80 \text{ cm} \times 7.5 \text{ cm}} = 0.85 \text{ g/cm}^3$

The block will float because its density (0.85 g/cm^3) is less than the density of water (1.00 g/cm^3).

115. a. $4.72 \cancel{g} \times \dfrac{1000 \text{ mg}}{1 \cancel{g}} = 4.72 \times 10^3 \text{ mg}$

b. $\dfrac{2.7 \times 10^3 \cancel{cm}}{\cancel{s}} \times \dfrac{1 \cancel{m}}{100 \cancel{cm}} \times \dfrac{1 \text{ km}}{1000 \cancel{m}} \times \dfrac{60 \cancel{s}}{1 \cancel{min}} \times$

$\dfrac{60 \cancel{min}}{1 \text{ h}} = 97 \text{ km/h}$

c. $4.4 \cancel{mm} \times \dfrac{1 \cancel{m}}{1000 \cancel{mm}} \times \dfrac{10 \text{ dm}}{1 \cancel{m}} = 4.4 \times 10^{-2} \text{ dm}$

116. a. 40 protons, 40 electrons, 50 neutrons

b. 46 protons, 46 electrons, 62 neutrons

c. 35 protons, 35 electrons, 46 neutrons

d. 51 protons, 51 electrons, 72 neutrons

117. a. $1s^2 2s^2 2p^5$

b. $1s^2 2s^1$

c. $1s^2 2s^2 2p^6 3s^2 3p^6 3d^{10} 4s^2 4p^6 5s^1$

119. Cr, Cd, Cu, Co

126. d. CaS_2 **f.** $Ba(OH)$

127. a. iron(III) hydroxide **c.** sodium carbonate
b. ammonium iodide **d.** carbon tetrachloride

128. a. KNO_3 **b.** CuO **c.** Mg_3N_2 **d.** AgF

Chapter 11

1. When solid sodium is dropped in water, hydrogen gas and aqueous sodium hydroxide are produced.

2. $S(s) + O_2(g) \longrightarrow SO_2(g)$

3. $3CO + Fe_2O_3 \longrightarrow 2Fe + 3CO_2$

4. $2C + O_2 \longrightarrow 2CO$

5. a. $FeCl_3 + 3NaOH \longrightarrow Fe(OH)_3 + 3NaCl$

b. $CS_2 + 3Cl_2 \longrightarrow CCl_4 + S_2Cl_2$

c. $2KI + Pb(NO_3)_2 \longrightarrow PbI_2 + 2KNO_3$

d. $2C_2H_2 + 5O_2 \longrightarrow 4CO_2 + 2H_2O$

6. a. $Ca(OH)_2 + H_2SO_4 \longrightarrow CaSO_4 + 2H_2O$

b. $Na + H_2O \longrightarrow NaOH + H$

12. HBr

13. $2HI \longrightarrow H_2 + I_2$

14. $3Mg + N_2 \longrightarrow Mg_3N_2$

15. a. $Fe(s) + Pb(NO_3)_2(aq) \longrightarrow Fe(NO_3)_2(aq) + Pb(s)$

b. $Cl_2(aq) + 2NaI(aq) \longrightarrow 2NaCl(aq) + I_2(aq)$

c. $Ca(s) + 2H_2O(l) \longrightarrow Ca(OH)_2(aq) + H_2(g)$

d. $Zn(s) + H_2SO_4(aq) \longrightarrow ZnSO_4(aq) + H_2(g)$

16. a. $3NaOH(aq) + Fe(NO_3)_3(aq) \longrightarrow$
$Fe(OH)_3(s) + 3NaNO_3(aq)$

b. $3Ba(NO_3)_2(aq) + 2H_3PO_4(aq) \longrightarrow$
$Ba_3(PO_4)_2(s) + 6HNO_3(aq)$

c. $FeS(s) + 2HCl(aq) \longrightarrow H_2S(g) + FeCl_2(aq)$

17. a. $3KOH(aq) + H_3PO_4(aq) \longrightarrow$
$K_3PO_4(aq) + 3H_2O(l)$

b. $AgNO_3(aq) + NaCl(s) \longrightarrow AgCl(s) + NaNO_3(aq)$

c. $3Ca(OH)_2(aq) + 2H_3PO_4(aq) \longrightarrow$
$Ca_3(PO_4)_2(aq) + 6H_2O(l)$

d. $2KI(aq) + Pb(NO_3)_2(aq) \longrightarrow$
$2KNO_3(aq) + PbI_2(s)$

e. $3H_2SO_4(aq) + 2Al(OH)_3(aq) \longrightarrow$
$Al_2(SO_4)_3(aq) + 6H_2O(l)$

18. a. $CH_2O(g) + O_2(g) \longrightarrow CO_2(g) + H_2O(g)$

b. $C_7H_{16}(l) + 11O_2(g) \longrightarrow 7CO_2(g) + 8H_2O(g)$

c. $2C_6H_6(l) + 15O_2(g) \longrightarrow 12CO_2(g) + 6H_2O(g)$

19. a. $C_6H_{12}O_6(s) + 6O_2(g) \longrightarrow 6CO_2(g) + 6H_2O(g)$

b. $C_3H_6O(l) + 4O_2(g) \longrightarrow 3CO_2(g) + 3H_2O(g)$

c. $2C_5H_{12}O(l) + 15O_2(g) \longrightarrow 10CO_2(g) + 12H_2O(g)$

25. $OH^-(aq) + H^+(aq) \longrightarrow H_2O(l)$

26. Complete ionic equation:
$3Ca^{2+}(aq) + 6OH^-(aq) + 6H^+(aq) + 2PO_4^{3-}(aq)$
$\longrightarrow Ca_3(PO_4)_2(s) + 6H_2O(l)$

Net ionic equation: same as complete ionic equation

27. The precipitate formed is lead chloride.
$Pb^{2+}(aq) + 2Cl^-(aq) \longrightarrow PbCl_2(s)$

28. Complete ionic equation:
$Fe^{3+}(aq) + NO_3^-(aq) + 3Na^+(aq) + 3OH^-(aq) \longrightarrow$
$3Na^+(aq) + NO_3^-(aq) + Fe(OH)_3(s)$
Net ionic equation:
$Fe^{3+}(aq) + OH^-(aq) \longrightarrow Fe(OH)_3(s)$

37. a. $2PbO_2(s) \longrightarrow 2PbO(s) + O_2(g)$

b. $2Fe(OH)_3(s) \longrightarrow Fe_2O_3(s) + 3H_2O(l)$

c. $(NH_4)_2CO_3(s) \longrightarrow 2NH_3(g) + H_2O(g) + CO_2(g)$

d. $CaCl_2(aq) + H_2SO_4(aq) \longrightarrow$
$CaSO_4(s) + 2HCl(aq)$

38. a. $2Mg(s) + O_2(g) \longrightarrow 2MgO(s)$

b. $4P(s) + 5O_2(g) \longrightarrow 2P_2O_5(s)$

c. $Ca(s) + S(s) \longrightarrow CaS(s)$

46. a. $H^+(aq) + OH^-(aq) \longrightarrow H_2O(l)$

b. $Ag^+(aq) + Cl^-(aq) \longrightarrow AgCl(s)$

51. a. $Na_2O(s) + H_2O(l) \longrightarrow 2NaOH(aq)$

b. $H_2(g) + Br_2(g) \longrightarrow 2HBr(g)$

c. $Cl_2O_7(l) + H_2O(l) \longrightarrow 2HClO_4(aq)$

53. a. tube A

b. $2Na(s) + 2H_2O(l) \longrightarrow 2NaOH(aq) + H_2(g)$
single-replacement

57. a. $CdS(s)$

b. $Na^+(aq)$ and $NO_3^-(aq)$

c. $Cd^{2+}(aq) + S^{2-}(aq) \longrightarrow CdS(s)$

60. a. single-replacement

b. $Cl_2(g) + 2I^-(aq) \longrightarrow I_2(aq) + 2Cl^-(aq)$

62. a. $2K(s) + 2H_2O(l) \longrightarrow 2KOH(aq) + H_2(g)$

b. $C_2H_5OH(l) + 3O_2(g) \longrightarrow 2CO_2(g) + 3H_2O(g)$

c. $2Bi(NO_3)_3(aq) + 3H_2S(g) \longrightarrow$
$Bi_2S_3(s) + 6HNO_3(aq)$

d. $2Al(s) + 3Br_2(l) \longrightarrow 2AlBr_3(s)$

65. Smoking is not permitted near an oxygen source because a fire will burn faster in an area of high oxygen concentration. However, if a match were struck in a room full of oxygen and isolated from combustible material, it would only burn more vigorously.

70. 22 protons, 28 neutrons, and 22 electrons

74. a. K_2CrO_4 **c.** permanganic acid

b. $NaHSO_3$ **d.** potassium oxalate

77. First, determine the empirical formula.

$$49.5 \text{ g C} \times \frac{1 \text{ mol C}}{12.0 \text{ g C}} = 4.13 \text{ mol C}$$

$$5.20 \text{ g H} \times \frac{1 \text{ mol H}}{1.01 \text{ g H}} = 5.15 \text{ mol H}$$

$$16.5 \text{ g O} \times \frac{1 \text{ mol O}}{16.0 \text{ g O}} = 1.03 \text{ mol O}$$

$$28.9 \text{ g N} \times \frac{1 \text{ mol N}}{14.0 \text{ g N}} = 2.06 \text{ mol N}$$

Then, divide each value by 1.03. The empirical formula is $C_4H_5ON_2$. The mass of the empirical formula is 97 g.

$$\frac{gfm}{efm} = \frac{194.1 \text{ g}}{97 \text{ g}} = 2$$

$$(C_4H_5ON_2) \times 2 = C_8H_{10}O_2N_4$$

Chapter 12

1. $288 \text{ ESW}_3\text{HP}_2 \times \dfrac{1 \text{ seat}}{1 \text{ ESW}_3\text{HP}_2} = 288 \text{ seats}$

$288 \text{ ESW}_3\text{HP}_2 \times \dfrac{3 \text{ wheels}}{1 \text{ ESW}_3\text{HP}_2} = 864 \text{ wheels}$

$288 \text{ ESW}_3\text{HP}_2 \times \dfrac{2 \text{ pedals}}{1 \text{ ESW}_3\text{HP}_2} = 576 \text{ pedals}$

2. Answers will vary but should include the correct number of "parts" to make the product. For example, 1 deck + 2 trucks + 4 wheels $\longrightarrow DT_2W_4$. Note: The truck (T) of a skateboard holds the wheels (W). The deck (D) of a skateboard is the part that a skateboarder stands on when riding.

3. 2 molecules H_2 + 1 molecule $O_2 \longrightarrow$
2 molecules H_2O

2 moles H_2 + 1 mole $O_2 \longrightarrow$ 2 moles H_2O

44.8 L H_2 + 22.4 L $O_2 \longrightarrow$ 44.8 L H_2O

4. $C_2H_4(g) + 3O_2 \longrightarrow 2CO_2(g) + 2H_2O(g)$;

1 mol C_2H_4 + 3 mol $O_2 \longrightarrow$
2 mol CO_2 + 2 mol H_2O;

22.4 L C_2H_4 + 67.2 L $O_2 \longrightarrow$
44.8 L CO_2 + 44.8 L H_2O;

$$\left(1 \text{ mol} \times \frac{28.0 \text{ g}}{\text{mol}}\right) + \left(3 \text{ mol} \times \frac{32.0 \text{ g}}{\text{mol}}\right) \longrightarrow$$
$$\left(2 \text{ mol} \times \frac{44.0 \text{ g}}{\text{mol}}\right) + \left(2 \text{ mol} \times \frac{18.0 \text{ g}}{\text{mol}}\right)$$

28.0 g C_2H_4 + 96.0 g $O_2 \longrightarrow$ 88.0 g CO_2 + 36.0 g H_2O

124 g = 124 g

11. a. $\dfrac{4 \text{ mol Al}}{3 \text{ mol O}_2}$ $\dfrac{3 \text{ mol O}_2}{4 \text{ mol Al}}$ $\dfrac{4 \text{ mol Al}}{2 \text{ mol Al}_2O_3}$

$\dfrac{2 \text{ mol Al}_2O_3}{4 \text{ mol Al}}$ $\dfrac{3 \text{ mol O}_2}{2 \text{ mol Al}_2O_3}$ $\dfrac{2 \text{ mol Al}_2O_3}{3 \text{ mol O}_2}$

b. $3.7 \text{ mol Al}_2O_3 \times \dfrac{4 \text{ mol Al}}{2 \text{ mol Al}_2O_3} = 7.4 \text{ mol Al}$

12. a. $14.8 \text{ mol Al} \times \dfrac{3 \text{ mol O}_2}{4 \text{ mol Al}} = 11.1 \text{ mol O}_2$

b. $0.78 \text{ mol O}_2 \times \dfrac{2 \text{ mol Al}_2O_3}{3 \text{ mol O}_2} = 0.52 \text{ mol Al}_2O_3$

13. $5.00 \text{ g CaC}_2 \times \dfrac{1 \text{ mol CaC}_2}{64.1 \text{ g CaC}_2} \times \dfrac{1 \text{ mol C}_2H_2}{1 \text{ mol CaC}_2}$
$\times \dfrac{26.0 \text{ g C}_2H_2}{1 \text{ mol C}_2H_2} = 2.03 \text{ g C}_2H_2$

14. $49.0 \text{ g H}_2O \times \dfrac{1 \text{ mol H}_2O}{18.0 \text{ g H}_2O} \times \dfrac{1 \text{ mol CaC}_2}{2 \text{ mol H}_2O}$
$= 1.36 \text{ mol CaC}_2$

15. $6.54 \text{ g KClO}_3 \times \dfrac{1 \text{ mol KClO}_3}{122.6 \text{ g KClO}_3} \times \dfrac{3 \text{ mol O}_2}{2 \text{ mol KClO}_3} \times$

$\dfrac{6.02 \times 10^{23} \text{ molecules O}_2}{1 \text{ mol O}_2} = 4.82 \times 10^{22} \text{ molecules O}_2$

16. $5.00 \times 10^{22} \text{ molecules NO} \times \dfrac{1 \text{ mol NO}}{6.02 \times 10^{23} \text{ molecules NO}}$

$\times \dfrac{3 \text{ mol NO}_2}{1 \text{ mol NO}} \times \dfrac{46.0 \text{ g NO}_2}{1 \text{ mol NO}_2} = 11.5 \text{ g NO}_2$

17. $3.86 \text{ L CO} \times \dfrac{1 \text{ mol CO}}{22.4 \text{ L CO}} \times \dfrac{1 \text{ mol O}_2}{2 \text{ mol CO}} \times \dfrac{22.4 \text{ L O}_2}{1 \text{ mol O}_2}$
$= 1.93 \text{ L O}_2$

18. $0.42 \text{ L H}_2 \times \dfrac{1 \text{ mol H}_2}{22.4 \text{ L H}_2} \times \dfrac{4 \text{ mol PH}_3}{6 \text{ mol H}_2} \times \dfrac{22.4 \text{ L PH}_3}{1 \text{ mol PH}_3}$
$= 0.28 \text{ L PH}_3$

19. $27.9 \text{ mL O}_2 \times \dfrac{2 \text{ mL SO}_2}{3 \text{ mL O}_2} = 18.6 \text{ mL SO}_2$

20. $0.38 \text{ L SO}_2 \times \dfrac{1 \text{ L CO}_2}{2 \text{ L SO}_2} \times \dfrac{10 \text{ dL CO}_2}{1 \text{ L CO}_2} = 1.9 \text{ dL CO}_2$

26. $2.70 \text{ mol C}_2\text{H}_4 \times \dfrac{3 \text{ mol O}_2}{1 \text{ mol C}_2\text{H}_4} = 8.10 \text{ mol O}_2$

8.10 mol O_2 are needed to react with $2.70 \text{ mol C}_2\text{H}_4$, but there are only 6.30 mol O_2 given for the reaction. Therefore, O_2 is the limiting reagent.

27. $6.00 \text{ g HCl} \times \dfrac{1 \text{ mol HCl}}{36.5 \text{ g HCl}} = 0.160 \text{ mol HCl}$

$5.00 \text{ g Mg} \times \dfrac{1 \text{ mol Mg}}{24.3 \text{ g Mg}} = 0.210 \text{ mol Mg}$

$0.16 \text{ mol HCl} \times \dfrac{1 \text{ mol Mg}}{2 \text{ mol HCl}} = 0.080 \text{ mol Mg}$

HCl is the limiting reagent.

28. a. $2.70 \text{ mol C}_2\text{H}_4 \times \dfrac{2 \text{ mol O}_2}{1 \text{ mol C}_2\text{H}_4} = 5.40 \text{ mol O}_2$

C_2H_4 is the limiting reagent.

b. $2.70 \text{ mol C}_2\text{H}_4 \times \dfrac{2 \text{ mol H}_2\text{O}}{1 \text{ mol C}_2\text{H}_4} = 5.40 \text{ mol H}_2\text{O}$

29. $2.40 \text{ mol C}_2\text{H}_2 \times \dfrac{5 \text{ mol O}_2}{2 \text{ mol C}_2\text{H}_2} = 6.00 \text{ mol O}_2$

C_2H_2 is the limiting reagent.

$2.40 \text{ mol C}_2\text{H}_2 \times \dfrac{2 \text{ mol H}_2\text{O}}{2 \text{ mol C}_2\text{H}_2} \times \dfrac{18.0 \text{ g H}_2\text{O}}{1 \text{ mol H}_2\text{O}}$
$= 43.2 \text{ g H}_2\text{O}$

30. $84.8 \text{ g Fe}_2\text{O}_3 \times \dfrac{1 \text{ mol Fe}_2\text{O}_3}{159.9 \text{ g Fe}_2\text{O}_3} \times \dfrac{2 \text{ mol Fe}}{1 \text{ mol Fe}_2\text{O}_3}$
$\times \dfrac{55.9 \text{ g Fe}}{1 \text{ mol Fe}} = 59.3 \text{ g Fe}$

31. $Cu(s) + 2AgNO_3(aq) \longrightarrow 2Ag(s) + Cu(NO_3)_2(aq)$

$5.00 \text{ g Cu} \times \dfrac{1 \text{ mol Cu}}{63.6 \text{ g Cu}} \times \dfrac{2 \text{ mol Ag}}{1 \text{ mol Cu}} \times \dfrac{107.9 \text{ g Ag}}{1 \text{ mol Ag}}$
$= 17.0 \text{ g Ag}$

32. $50.0 \text{ g SiO}_2 \times \dfrac{1 \text{ mol SiO}_2}{60.1 \text{ g SiO}_2} \times \dfrac{1 \text{ mol SiC}}{1 \text{ mol SiO}_2} \times \dfrac{40.1 \text{ g SiC}}{1 \text{ mol SiC}}$
$= 33.36 \text{ g SiC}$

$\% \text{ yield} = \dfrac{27.9 \text{ g SiC}}{33.4 \text{ g SiC}} \times 100\% = 83.5\%$

33. $N_2 + 3H_2 \longrightarrow 2NH_3$

$15.0 \text{ g N}_2 \times \dfrac{1 \text{ mol N}_2}{28.0 \text{ g N}_2} \times \dfrac{3 \text{ mol H}_2}{1 \text{ mol N}_2} \times \dfrac{2.0 \text{ g H}_2}{1 \text{ mol H}_2} = 3.2 \text{ g H}_2$

N_2 is the limiting reagent, so use the given mass of nitrogen to find the theoretical yield of NH_3.

$15.0 \text{ g N}_2 \times \dfrac{1 \text{ mol N}_2}{28.0 \text{ g N}_2} \times \dfrac{2 \text{ mol NH}_3}{1 \text{ mol N}_2} \times \dfrac{17.0 \text{ g NH}_3}{1 \text{ mol NH}_3}$
$= 18.2 \text{ g NH}_3$

$\% \text{ yield} = \dfrac{10.5 \text{ g NH}_3}{18.2 \text{ g NH}_3} \times 100\% = 57.7\%$

45. a. $2.7 \text{ mol C} \times \dfrac{1 \text{ mol CS}_2}{5 \text{ mol C}} = 0.54 \text{ mol CS}_2$

b. $5.44 \text{ mol SO}_2 \times \dfrac{5 \text{ mol C}}{2 \text{ mol SO}_2} = 13.6 \text{ mol C}$

c. $0.246 \text{ mol CS}_2 \times \dfrac{4 \text{ mol CO}}{1 \text{ mol CS}_2} = 0.984 \text{ mol CO}$

d. $118 \text{ mol CS}_2 \times \dfrac{2 \text{ mol SO}_2}{1 \text{ mol CS}_2} = 236 \text{ mol SO}_2$

46. a. $3.60 \times 10^2 \text{ g CH}_3\text{OH} \times \dfrac{1 \text{ mol CH}_3\text{OH}}{32.0 \text{ g CH}_3\text{OH}}$
$\times \dfrac{1 \text{ mol CO}}{1 \text{ mol CH}_3\text{OH}} = 11.3 \text{ mol CO}$

$3.60 \times 10^2 \text{ g CH}_3\text{OH} \times \dfrac{1 \text{ mol CH}_3\text{OH}}{32.0 \text{ g CH}_3\text{OH}}$
$\times \dfrac{2 \text{ mol H}_2}{1 \text{ mol CH}_3\text{OH}} = 22.5 \text{ mol H}_2$

b. $4.00 \text{ mol CH}_3\text{OH} \times \dfrac{1 \text{ mol CO}}{1 \text{ mol CH}_3\text{OH}} \times \dfrac{28.0 \text{ g CO}}{1 \text{ mol CO}}$
$= 112 \text{ g CO}$

$4.00 \text{ mol CH}_3\text{OH} \times \dfrac{2 \text{ mol H}_2}{1 \text{ mol CH}_3\text{OH}} \times \dfrac{2.0 \text{ g H}_2}{1 \text{ mol H}_2}$
$= 16 \text{ g H}_2$

c. $2.85 \text{ mol CO} \times \dfrac{2 \text{ mol H}_2}{1 \text{ mol CO}} \times \dfrac{2.0 \text{ g H}_2}{1 \text{ mol H}_2} = 11 \text{ g H}_2$

50. a. $32.9 \text{ g Li}_3\text{N} \times \dfrac{1 \text{ mol Li}_3\text{N}}{34.7 \text{ g Li}_3\text{N}} \times \dfrac{3 \text{ mol H}_2\text{O}}{1 \text{ mol Li}_3\text{N}}$
$\times \dfrac{18.0 \text{ g H}_2\text{O}}{1 \text{ mol H}_2\text{O}} = 51.2 \text{ g H}_2\text{O}$

b. $32.9 \text{ g Li}_3\text{N} \times \dfrac{1 \text{ mol Li}_3\text{N}}{34.7 \text{ g Li}_3\text{N}} \times \dfrac{1 \text{ mol NH}_3}{1 \text{ mol Li}_3\text{N}}$

$\times \dfrac{6.02 \times 10^{23} \text{ molecules NH}_3}{1 \text{ mol NH}_3}$

$= 5.71 \times 10^{23} \text{ molecules NH}_3$

c. $15.0 \text{ L NH}_3 \times \dfrac{1 \text{ mol NH}_3}{22.4 \text{ L NH}_3} \times \dfrac{1 \text{ mol Li}_3\text{N}}{1 \text{ mol NH}_3}$

$\times \dfrac{34.7 \text{ g Li}_3\text{N}}{1 \text{ mol Li}_3\text{N}} = 23.2 \text{ g Li}_3\text{N}$

53. a. $3.0 \text{ mol Al} \times \dfrac{3 \text{ mol Cl}_2}{2 \text{ mol Al}} = 4.5 \text{ mol Cl}_2$

Al is the limiting reagent.

b. $3.0 \text{ mol Al} \times \dfrac{2 \text{ mol AlCl}_3}{2 \text{ mol Al}} = 3.0 \text{ mol AlCl}_3$

c. $5.3 \text{ mol Cl}_2 - 4.5 \text{ mol Cl}_2 = 0.80 \text{ mol Cl}_2$

54. $15.0 \text{ g Sb}_2\text{S}_3 \times \dfrac{1 \text{ mol Sb}_2\text{S}_3}{339.9 \text{ g Sb}_2\text{S}_3} \times \dfrac{2 \text{ mol Sb}}{1 \text{ mol Sb}_2\text{S}_3}$

$\times \dfrac{121.8 \text{ g Sb}}{1 \text{ mol Sb}} = 10.8 \text{ g Sb}$

$\% \text{ yield} = \dfrac{9.84 \text{ g Sb}}{10.8 \text{ g Sb}} \times 100\% = 91.1\%$

57. a. $1.49 \text{ g HNO}_3 \times \dfrac{1 \text{ mol HNO}_3}{63.0 \text{ g HNO}_3} \times \dfrac{4 \text{ mol Zn}}{10 \text{ mol HNO}_3}$

$\times \dfrac{6.02 \times 10^{23} \text{ atoms Zn}}{1 \text{ mol Zn}} = 5.70 \times 10^{21} \text{ atoms Zn}$

b. $29.1 \text{ g NH}_4\text{NO}_3 \times \dfrac{1 \text{ mol NH}_4\text{NO}_3}{80.0 \text{ g NH}_4\text{NO}_3}$

$\times \dfrac{4 \text{ mol Zn}}{1 \text{ mol NH}_4\text{NO}_3} \times \dfrac{65.4 \text{ g Zn}}{1 \text{ mol Zn}} = 95.2 \text{ g Zn}$

60. a. $1.0 \text{ kg N}_2\text{H}_4 \times \dfrac{10^3 \text{ g N}_2\text{H}_4}{1.0 \text{ kg N}_2\text{H}_4} \times \dfrac{1 \text{ mol N}_2\text{H}_4}{32.0 \text{ g N}_2\text{H}_4}$

$\times \dfrac{1 \text{ mol N}_2}{1 \text{ mol N}_2\text{H}_4} \times \dfrac{22.4 \text{ L N}_2}{1 \text{ mol N}_2} = 7.0 \times 10^2 \text{ L N}_2$

$1.2 \text{ kg O}_2 \times \dfrac{10^3 \text{ g O}_2}{1 \text{ kg O}_2} \times \dfrac{1 \text{ mol O}_2}{32.0 \text{ g O}_2} \times \dfrac{1 \text{ mol N}_2}{1 \text{ mol O}_2}$

$\times \dfrac{22.4 \text{ L N}_2}{1 \text{ mol N}_2} = 8.4 \times 10^2 \text{ L N}_2$

Since $7.0 \times 10^2 \text{ L N}_2 < 8.4 \times 10^2 \text{ L N}_2$, the limiting reagent is N_2H_4 and O_2 is in excess.

b. $1.0 \text{ kg N}_2\text{H}_4 \times \dfrac{10^3 \text{ g N}_2\text{H}_4}{1 \text{ kg N}_2\text{H}_4} \times \dfrac{1 \text{ mol N}_2\text{H}_4}{32.0 \text{ g N}_2\text{H}_4} \times$

$\dfrac{1 \text{ mol O}_2}{1 \text{ mol N}_2\text{H}_4} \times \dfrac{32.0 \text{ g O}_2}{1 \text{ mol O}_2} = 1.0 \times 10^3 \text{ g O}_2 \text{ used}$

$1.0 \times 10^3 \text{ g O}_2 \times \dfrac{1 \text{ kg O}_2}{10^3 \text{ g O}_2} = 1.0 \text{ kg O}_2$

$1.2 \text{ kg O}_2 - 1.0 \text{ kg O}_2 = 0.2 \text{ kg O}_2$

The excess remaining reagent is 0.2 kg O_2.

64. $158 \text{ g CH}_4 \times \dfrac{1 \text{ mol CH}_4}{16.0 \text{ g CH}_4} \times \dfrac{3 \text{ mol H}_2}{1 \text{ mol CH}_4}$

$\times \dfrac{6.02 \times 10^{23} \text{ molecules H}_2}{1 \text{ mol H}_2} = 1.78 \times 10^{25} \text{ molecules H}_2$

67. a. $\text{SF}_2\,(l) + 2\text{F}_2\,(g) \longrightarrow \text{SF}_6\,(g)$

b. $5.00 \text{ mg SF}_2 \times \dfrac{1 \text{ g SF}_2}{10^3 \text{ mg SF}_2} \times \dfrac{1 \text{ mol SF}_2}{70.1 \text{ g SF}_2}$

$\times \dfrac{2 \text{ mol F}_2}{1 \text{ mol SF}_2} \times \dfrac{6.02 \times 10^{23} \text{ molecules F}_2}{1 \text{ mol F}_2}$

$= 8.59 \times 10^{19} \text{ molecules}$

c. $6.66 \text{ g SF}_2 \times \dfrac{1 \text{ mol SF}_2}{70.1 \text{ g SF}_2} \times \dfrac{2 \text{ mol F}_2}{1 \text{ mol SF}_2} \times \dfrac{22.4 \text{ L F}_2}{1 \text{ mol F}_2}$

$= 4.26 \text{ L F}_2$

69. $B \longrightarrow C$:

$\% \text{ yield} = \dfrac{\text{actual yield}}{\text{theoretical yield}} \times 100\%$

$= \dfrac{2.00 \text{ mol C}}{4.00 \text{ mol C}} \times 100\% = 50.0\%$

$C \longrightarrow D$:

Let x represent the actual yield of compound D.

$\% \text{ yield} = 25.0\% = \dfrac{x}{2 \text{ mol D}} \times 100\%$

$x = 0.250 \times 2 \text{ mol D}$
$x = 0.500 \text{ mol D}$

$D \longrightarrow E$:

Let y represent the actual yield of compound E.

$\% \text{ yield} = 10.0\% = \dfrac{y}{0.500 \text{ mol E}} \times 100\%$

$y = 0.100 \times 0.500 \text{ mol E}$
$y = 0.0500 \text{ mol E}$

$E \longrightarrow F$:

$\% \text{ yield} = \dfrac{\text{actual yield}}{\text{theoretical yield}} \times 100\%$

$= \dfrac{0.0100 \text{ mol F}}{0.0500 \text{ mol F}} \times 100\% = 20.0\%$

72. a. $2Ca_3(PO_4)_2 + 6SiO_2 \longrightarrow P_4O_{10} + 6CaSiO_3$

$P_4O_{10} + 10C \longrightarrow P_4 + 10CO$

b. $5.5 \times 10^5 \text{ g } Ca_3(PO_4)_2 \times \dfrac{1 \text{ mol } Ca_3(PO_4)_2}{310.3 \text{ g } Ca_3(PO_4)_2}$

$\times \dfrac{1 \text{ mol } P_4O_{10}}{2 \text{ mol } Ca_3(PO_4)_2} = 8.9 \times 10^2 \text{ mol } P_4O_{10}$

$2.3 \times 10^5 \text{ g } SiO_2 \times \dfrac{1 \text{ mol } SiO_2}{60.1 \text{ g } SiO_2} \times \dfrac{1 \text{ mol } P_4O_{10}}{6 \text{ mol } SiO_2}$

$= 6.4 \times 10^2 \text{ mol } P_4O_{10}$

Since 6.4×10^2 mol $P_4O_{10} < 8.9 \times 10^2$ mol P_4O_{10}, SiO_2 is the limiting reagent.

c. $6.4 \times 10^2 \text{ mol } P_4O_{10} \times \dfrac{1 \text{ mol } P_4}{1 \text{ mol } P_4O_{10}} \times \dfrac{124.0 \text{ g } P_4}{1 \text{ mol } P_4}$

$= 7.9 \times 10^4 \text{ g } P_4$

d. $6.4 \times 10^2 \text{ mol } P_4O_{10} \times \dfrac{10 \text{ mol } C}{1 \text{ mol } P_4O_{10}} \times \dfrac{12.0 \text{ g } C}{1 \text{ mol } C}$

$= 7.7 \times 10^4 \text{ g } C$

75. The balanced equation is:

$C_6H_{12}O_6 \longrightarrow 2C_2H_5OH + 2CO_2$

$1.0 \times 10^3 \text{ kg } C_6H_{12}O_6 \times \dfrac{10^3 \text{ g } C_6H_{12}O_6}{1 \text{ kg } C_6H_{12}O_6}$

$\times \dfrac{1 \text{ mol } C_6H_{12}O_6}{180.0 \text{ g } C_6H_{12}O_6} \times \dfrac{2 \text{ mol } C_2H_5OH}{1 \text{ mol } C_6H_{12}O_6} \times \dfrac{46.0 \text{ g } C_2H_5OH}{1 \text{ mol } C_2H_5OH}$

$\times \dfrac{1 \text{ kg } C_2H_5OH}{10^3 \text{ g } C_2H_5OH} \times \dfrac{5.0 \text{ K}}{8 \text{ kg } C_2H_5OH} \times \dfrac{1 \text{ day}}{24 \text{ K}} = 13 \text{ days}$

78. First calculate the amount of $CaCO_3$ needed to produce 81.8 g of $CaCl_2$:

$81.8 \text{ g } CaCl_2 \times \dfrac{1 \text{ mol } CaCl_2}{111.0 \text{ g } CaCl_2} \times \dfrac{1 \text{ mol } CaCO_3}{1 \text{ mol } CaCl_2}$

$\times \dfrac{100.1 \text{ g } CaCO_3}{1 \text{ mol } CaCO_3} = 73.8 \text{ g } CaCO_3$

Then calculate % $CaCO_3$ in the limestone:

$\dfrac{73.8 \text{ g } CaCO_3}{84.4 \text{ g limestone}} \times 100\% = 87.4\% \text{ } CaCO_3$

82. a. $4NH_3 + 5O_2 \longrightarrow 4NO + 6H_2O$

$2NO + O_2 \longrightarrow 2NO_2$

$3NO_2 + H_2O \longrightarrow 2HNO_3 + NO$

b. $88.0 \text{ g } NH_3 \times \dfrac{14.0 \text{ g } N}{17.0 \text{ g } NH_3} \times \dfrac{63.0 \text{ g } HNO_3}{14.0 \text{ g } N} = 326 \text{ g } HNO_3$

c. 70.0% of 1 kg HNO_3 = 700 g HNO_3

$700 \text{ g } HNO_3 \times \dfrac{88.0 \text{ g } NH_3}{326 \text{ g } HNO_3} = 189 \text{ g } NH_3$

---

88. a. 22, 22, 25   **c.** 8, 8, 10

b. 50, 50, 70   **d.** 12, 12, 14

99. $(3 \times 9.0) + (2 \times 27.0) + (6 \times 28.1) + (18 \times 16.0)$

$= 537.6$

$147 \text{ g } Be_3Al_2Si_6O_{18} \times \dfrac{27.0 \text{ g } Be}{537.6 \text{ g } Be_3Al_2Si_6O_{18}} = 7.38 \text{ g } Be$

101. $90 \text{ g} \times 0.267 = 24 \text{ g } C$

$24 \text{ g } C \times \dfrac{1 \text{ mol } C}{12.0 \text{ g } C} = 2.0 \text{ mol } C$

$90 \text{ g} \times 0.022 = 2.0 \text{ g } H$

$2.0 \text{ g } H \times \dfrac{1 \text{ mol } H}{1.0 \text{ g } H} = 2.0 \text{ mol } H$

$90 \text{ g} \times 0.711 = 64 \text{ g } O$

$64 \text{ g } O \times \dfrac{1 \text{ mol } O}{16.0 \text{ g } O} = 4.0 \text{ mol } O$

The empirical formula is $C_2H_2O_4$.

Chapter 13

1. $385 \text{ mm Hg} \times \dfrac{101.3 \text{ kPa}}{760 \text{ mm Hg}} = 51.3 \text{ kPa}$

$51.3 \text{ kPa} \times \dfrac{1 \text{ atm}}{101.3 \text{ kPa}} = 0.507 \text{ atm}$

2. $33.7 \text{ kPa} \times \dfrac{1 \text{ atm}}{101.3 \text{ kPa}} = 0.33 \text{ atm} > 0.25 \text{ atm}$

31. In an elastic collision, energy is transferred between particles.

35. a. $190 \text{ mm Hg} \times \dfrac{101.3 \text{ kPa}}{760 \text{ mm Hg}} = 25 \text{ kPa}$

b. $190 \text{ mm Hg} \times \dfrac{1 \text{ atm}}{760 \text{ mm Hg}} = 0.25 \text{ atm}$

40. Since the Kelvin temperature is directly proportional to the average kinetic energy and the temperature increased from 300 K to 900 K, then the average kinetic energy triples as well.

43. Two opposing processes are occurring at identical rates.

49. Escaping molecules have more kinetic energy than the average. Thus, the average kinetic energy and temperature of the remaining molecules are lower.

52. The intermolecular attractions between molecules are weaker than the attractions between ions.

53. Water from the food sublimed and then condensed on the lid.

55. The average kinetic energy of the molecules is greater because, by definition, a fever is a state of increased body temperature.

60. Decrease; as the attractions become stronger, it becomes more difficult for molecules to overcome the attractions and vaporize.

63. The Kelvin temperature is directly proportional to the average kinetic energy. As the temperature rises, the air particles speed up and increase in kinetic energy which causes the raft to expand. As the temperature drops, the air particles slow down resulting in a decrease in kinetic energy, which causes the raft to not be fully inflated.

65. Possible answer: Since the beaker is an open container, the water should boil at 100°C at or close to sea level. Your partner probably misread the thermometer and should recheck the value.

72. No; at 15 kPa, water would boil at a temperature of about 50°C, which is much higher than room temperature.

76. No; if (a) > (b) then water vapor will condense at a greater rate than the liquid evaporates.

79. a. body-centered cubic

b. 8

c. CsCl (one Cl^- ion and $8 \times \frac{1}{8}$ equals one Cs^+ ion)

85. a. $1s^2 2s^2 2p^6 3s^2 3p^6$

b. $1s^2 2s^2 2p^6 3s^2 3p^6$

c. $1s^2$

93. a. $56.2 \text{ g } HClO_4 \times \dfrac{1 \text{ mol } HClO_4}{100.5 \text{ g } HClO_4} \times \dfrac{1 \text{ mol } Cl_2O_7}{2 \text{ mol } HClO_4}$

$\times \dfrac{183.0 \text{ g } Cl_2O_7}{1 \text{ mol } Cl_2O_7} = 51.2 \text{ g } Cl_2O_7$

b. $3.40 \text{ mol } HClO_4 \times \dfrac{1 \text{ mol } H_2O}{2 \text{ mol } HClO_4} \times \dfrac{22.4 \text{ L } H_2O}{1 \text{ mol } H_2O}$

$\times \dfrac{1000 \text{ mL } H_2O}{1 \text{ L } H_2O} = 3.81 \times 10^4 \text{ mL } H_2O$

95. $H_2S(aq) + Cd(NO_3)_2(aq) \longrightarrow 2HNO_3(aq) + CdS(s)$

99. a. $1 \text{ mol } C_{12}H_{22}O_{11} \times \dfrac{11 \text{ mol } H_2O}{1 \text{ mol } C_{12}H_{22}O_{11}} \times \dfrac{18.0 \text{ g } H_2O}{1 \text{ mol } H_2O}$
$= 198 \text{ g } H_2O$

b. $11 \text{ mol } H_2O + 12 \text{ mol } C = 23 \text{ mol}$

c. $1 \text{ mol } C_{12}H_{22}O_{11} \times \dfrac{12 \text{ mol } C}{1 \text{ mol } C_{12}H_{22}O_{11}} \times \dfrac{12.0 \text{ g } C}{1 \text{ mol } C}$
$= 144 \text{ g } C$

100. $40.0 \text{ g } C_2H_4 \times \dfrac{1 \text{ mol } C_2H_4}{28.0 \text{ g } C_2H_4} \times \dfrac{1 \text{ mol } H_2}{1 \text{ mol } C_2H_4} \times$
$\dfrac{2.0 \text{ g } H_2}{1 \text{ mol } H_2} = 2.86 \text{ g } H_2$

C_2H_4 is the limiting reagent.

9. $V_2 = \dfrac{P_1 \times V_1}{P_2} = \dfrac{105 \text{ kPa} \times 2.50 \text{ L}}{40.5 \text{ kPa}} = 6.48 \text{ L}$

10. $P_2 = \dfrac{P_1 \times V_1}{V_2} = \dfrac{205 \text{ kPa} \times 4.00 \text{ L}}{12.0 \text{ L}} = 68.3 \text{ kPa}$

11. $T_1 = 325°C + 273 = 598 \text{ K}$

$T_2 = 25°C + 273 = 298 \text{ K}$

$V_2 = \dfrac{V_1 \times T_2}{T_1} = \dfrac{6.80 \text{ L} \times 298 \text{ K}}{598 \text{ K}} = 3.39 \text{ L}$

12. $T_1 = -50.0°C + 273 = 223 \text{ K}$

$T_2 = 100.0°C + 273 = 373 \text{ K}$

$V_2 = \dfrac{V_1 \times T_2}{T_1} = \dfrac{5.00 \text{ L} \times 373 \text{ K}}{223 \text{ K}} = 8.36 \text{ L}$

13. $T_1 = 41°C + 273 = 314 \text{ K}$

$T_2 = 22°C + 273 = 295 \text{ K}$

$P_2 = \dfrac{P_1 \times T_2}{T_1} = \dfrac{108 \text{ kPa} \times 295 \text{ K}}{314 \text{ K}} = 101 \text{ kPa}$

14. $T_1 = 27°C + 273 = 300 \text{ K}$

$T_2 = \dfrac{P_2 \times T_1}{P_1} = \dfrac{225 \text{ kPa} \times 300 \text{ K}}{198 \text{ kPa}} = 341 \text{ K } (68°C)$

15. $T_1 = 25°C + 273 = 298 \text{ K}$

$T_2 = 125°C + 273 = 398 \text{ K}$

$V_2 = \dfrac{P_1 \times V_1 \times T_2}{T_1 \times P_2} = \dfrac{155 \text{ kPa} \times 1.00 \text{ L} \times 398 \text{ K}}{298 \text{ kPa} \times 605 \text{ K}}$
$= 0.342 \text{ L}$

16. $T_1 = -50°C + 273 = 223 \text{ K}$

$T_2 = 102°C + 273 = 375 \text{ K}$

$P_2 = \dfrac{P_1 \times V_1 \times T_2}{T_1 \times V_2} = \dfrac{107 \text{ kPa} \times 5.00 \text{ L} \times 375 \text{ K}}{223 \text{ K} \times 7.00 \text{ L}}$
$= 129 \text{ kPa}$

26. $n = \dfrac{P \times V}{R \times T}$

$n = \dfrac{1.89 \times 10^3 \text{ kPa} \times 685 \text{ L}}{8.31 \dfrac{\text{L} \cdot \text{kPa}}{\text{K} \cdot \text{mol}} \times 621 \text{ K}} = 251 \text{ mol He}$

27. $T = 25°C + 273 = 298 \text{ K}$

$P = \dfrac{n \times R \times T}{V}$

$P = \dfrac{0.450 \text{ mol} \times 8.31 \dfrac{\text{L} \cdot \text{kPa}}{\text{K} \cdot \text{mol}} \times 298 \text{ K}}{0.650 \text{ L}}$

$= 1.71 \times 10^3 \text{ kPa}$

28. $T = 37°C + 273 = 310$ K

$$n = \frac{P \times V}{R \times T} = \frac{102 \text{ kPa} \times 2.20 \text{ L}}{8.31 \frac{\text{L} \cdot \text{kPa}}{\text{K} \cdot \text{mol}} \times 310 \text{ K}}$$

$$= 0.0871 \text{ mol air}$$

$$0.0871 \text{ mol air} \times \frac{29 \text{ g air}}{1 \text{ mol air}} = 2.5 \text{ g air}$$

29. $T = 25°C + 273 = 298$ K

$$n = 12.0 \text{ g O}_2 \times \frac{1 \text{ mol O}_2}{32.0 \text{ g O}_2} = 0.375 \text{ mol O}_2$$

$$V = \frac{n \times R \times T}{P}$$

$$V = \frac{0.375 \text{ mol} \times 8.31 \frac{\text{L} \cdot \text{kPa}}{\text{K} \cdot \text{mol}} \times 298 \text{ K}}{52.7 \text{ kPa}} = 17.6 \text{ L}$$

37. $P_{total} = P_{O_2} + P_{N_2} + P_{CO_2}$

$$P_{CO_2} = P_{total} - (P_{O_2} + P_{N_2})$$

$$P_{CO_2} = 32.9 \text{ kPa} - 6.6 \text{ kPa} - 23.0 \text{ kPa}$$

$$P_{CO_2} = 3.3 \text{ kPa}$$

38. $P_{total} = P_{O_2} + P_{N_2} + P_{He}$

$$P_{total} = 20.0 \text{ kPa} + 46.7 \text{ kPa} + 26.7 \text{ kPa}$$

$$P_{total} = 93.4 \text{ kPa}$$

39. $\dfrac{\text{Rate}_{H_2}}{\text{Rate}_{CO_2}} = \sqrt{\dfrac{\text{molar mass}_{CO_2}}{\text{molar mass}_{H_2}}} = \sqrt{\dfrac{44.0 \text{ g}}{2.0 \text{ g}}} = \sqrt{22} = 4.7$

The ratio is 4.7:1.

54. $P_2 = \dfrac{P_1 \times T_2}{T_1} = \dfrac{300 \text{ kPa} \times 101 \text{ K}}{303 \text{ K}} = 100 \text{ kPa}$

57. $T_1 = 150.0°C + 273 = 423$ K

$$T_2 = \frac{T_1 \times V_2}{T_1} = \frac{423 \text{ K} \times 600 \text{ mL}}{300 \text{ mL}} = 846 \text{ K} \ (573°C)$$

58. $T_1 = 327.0°C + 273 = 600$ K

$$T_2 = \frac{T_1 \times V_2}{T_1} = \frac{600 \text{ K} \times 5 \text{ L}}{15 \text{ L}} = 200 \text{ K} \ (-73°C)$$

61. $P_2 = \dfrac{P_1 \times T_2}{T_1} = \dfrac{6.58 \text{ kPa} \times 211 \text{ K}}{539 \text{ K}} = 2.58 \text{ kPa}$

65. $T = 35°C + 273 = 308$ K

$$V = \frac{n \times R \times T}{P}$$

$$V = \frac{1.24 \text{ mol} \times 8.31 \frac{\text{L} \cdot \text{kPa}}{\text{K} \cdot \text{mol}} \times 308 \text{ K}}{96.2 \text{ kPa}} = 33.0 \text{ L}$$

67. $T = 35°C + 273 = 308$ K

$$n = 4.50 \text{ g CH}_4 \times \frac{1 \text{ mol CH}_4}{16.0 \text{ g CH}_4} = 0.281 \text{ mol CH}_4$$

$$P = \frac{n \times R \times T}{V}$$

$$P = \frac{0.281 \text{ mol} \times 8.31 \frac{\text{L} \cdot \text{kPa}}{\text{K} \cdot \text{mol}} \times 308 \text{ K}}{2.00 \text{ L}}$$

$$= 360 \text{ kPa} = 3.60 \times 10^2 \text{ kPa}$$

69. $T = 0°C + 273 = 273$ K

$$n = \frac{P \times V}{R \times T} = \frac{99 \text{ kPa} \times 240 \text{ L}}{8.31 \frac{\text{L} \cdot \text{kPa}}{\text{K} \cdot \text{mol}} \times 273 \text{ K}} = 10.5 \text{ mol He}$$

$$10.5 \text{ mol He} \times \frac{4.0 \text{ g He}}{1 \text{ mol He}} = 42 \text{ g He}$$

73. $\dfrac{\text{Rate}_{He}}{\text{Rate}_{Ne}} = \dfrac{\sqrt{\text{molar mass}_{Ne}}}{\sqrt{\text{molar mass}_{He}}} = \dfrac{\sqrt{20.2 \text{ g}}}{\sqrt{4.0 \text{ g}}} = \sqrt{5.05} = 2.25$

The ratio is 2.25:1.

83. $T_1 = 20°C + 273 = 293$ K

$$T_2 = \frac{T_1 \times P_2 \times V_2}{P_1 \times V_1}$$

$$T_2 = \frac{293 \text{ K} \times 56.7 \text{ kPa} \times 8.00 \text{ L}}{86.7 \text{ kPa} \times 3.50 \text{ L}} = 438 \text{ K} \ (165°C)$$

87. Let g represent a certain gas.

$$\text{Rate}_g = 4 \times \text{Rate}_{O_2}$$

$$\frac{\text{Rate}_g}{\text{Rate}_{O_2}} = \sqrt{\frac{\text{molar mass}_{O_2}}{\text{molar mass}_g}}$$

$$\frac{4 \times \text{Rate}_{O_2}}{\text{Rate}_{O_2}} = \sqrt{\frac{32.0 \text{ g}}{\text{molar mass}_g}}$$

$$4^2 = \left(\sqrt{\frac{32.0 \text{ g}}{\text{molar mass}_g}} \right)^2$$

$$16 = \frac{32.0 \text{ g}}{\text{molar mass}_g}$$

$$\text{molar mass}_g = \frac{32.0 \text{ g}}{16} = 2.0 \text{ g}$$

88. Let g represent an unknown gas.
Let n = the number of moles of gas.

$$\frac{\text{Rate}_g}{\text{Rate}_{O_2}} = \sqrt{\frac{\text{molar mass}_{O_2}}{\text{molar mass}_g}}$$

$$\frac{\dfrac{n}{75 \text{ s}}}{\dfrac{n}{30 \text{ s}}} = \sqrt{\frac{32.0 \text{ g}}{\text{molar mass}_g}}$$

$$\left(\frac{30}{75} \right)^2 = \frac{32.0 \text{ g}}{\text{molar mass}_g}$$

$$900 \times \text{molar mass}_g = 5625 \times 32.0 \text{ g}$$

$$\text{molar mass}_g = \frac{180,000 \text{ g}}{900} = 200 \text{ g}$$

94. a. $T = 120°C + 273 = 393$ K

$$34.0 \text{ g NH}_3 \times \frac{1 \text{ mol NH}_3}{17.0 \text{ g NH}_3} = 2 \text{ mol NH}_3$$

$$96.0 \text{ g O}_2 \times \frac{1 \text{ mol O}_2}{32.0 \text{ g O}_2} = 3 \text{ mol O}_2$$

$$2 \text{ mol NH}_3 \times \frac{5 \text{ mol O}_2}{4 \text{ mol NH}_3} = 2.5 \text{ mol O}_2$$

2.5 mol O_2 < 3 mol O_2, so NH_3 is limiting reagent.

$$n_{NO} = 2 \text{ mol NH}_3 \times \frac{4 \text{ mol NO}}{4 \text{ mol NH}_3} = 2 \text{ mol NO}$$

$$P = \frac{n \times R \times T}{V}$$

$$P_{NO} = \frac{2 \text{ mol} \times 8.31 \frac{L \cdot kPa}{K \cdot mol} \times 393 \text{ K}}{40.0 \text{ L}} = 163 \text{ kPa}$$

b. $n_{H_2O} = 2 \text{ mol NH}_3 \times \frac{6 \text{ mol H}_2O}{4 \text{ mol NH}_3} = 3 \text{ mol H}_2O$

$$P_{H_2O} = \frac{3 \text{ mol} \times 8.31 \frac{L \cdot kPa}{K \cdot mol} \times 393 \text{ K}}{40.0 \text{ L}} = 245 \text{ kPa}$$

O_2 is in excess by 0.5 mol.

$$P_{O_2} = \frac{0.5 \text{ mol} \times 8.31 \frac{L \cdot kPa}{K \cdot mol} \times 393 \text{ K}}{40.0 \text{ L}} = 41 \text{ kPa}$$

$$P_{total} = P_{O_2} + P_{NO} + P_{H_2O}$$
$$= 41 \text{ kPa} + 163 \text{ kPa} + 245 \text{ kPa} = 449 \text{ kPa}$$

96. b. 700 mm Hg

c. directly proportional

d. The pressure rises 2.4 mm of Hg for every 1°C.

$$\text{slope of line } (m) = \frac{750 \text{ mm Hg} - 726 \text{ mm Hg}}{20°C - 10°C}$$
$$= \frac{24 \text{ mm Hg}}{10°C} = 2.4 \text{ mm Hg/°C}$$

e. $m = 2.4$; y-intercept = 700 mm Hg;
equation of line:
$P = (2.4 \text{ mm Hg/°C})T + 700 \text{ mm Hg}$

f. Gay-Lussac's law; sample data points:
$(T_1, P_1) = (10°C, 726 \text{ mm Hg})$
$(T_2, P_2) = (20°C, 750 \text{ mm Hg})$

$T_1 = 10°C + 273 = 283$ K
$T_1 = 20°C + 273 = 293$ K

$$\frac{P_1}{T_1} = \frac{P_2}{T_2}$$

$$\frac{726 \text{ mm Hg}}{283 \text{ K}} = \frac{750 \text{ mm Hg}}{293 \text{ K}} = 2.6 \text{ mm Hg/K}$$

99. Let $n_{initial}$ represent moles of methane/ethyne.

$n_{initial} = n_{CH_4} + n_{C_2H_2}$ [equation 1]

Let n_{CO_2} represent final moles of CO_2. $PV = nRT$, so
$V = nRT/P$. At constant volume and temperature:

$$V = \frac{n_{CO_2} \times R \times T}{25.2 \text{ kPa}} = \frac{n_{initial} \times R \times T}{16.8 \text{ kPa}}$$

$n_{CO_2} \times 16.8 \text{ kPa} = 25.2 \text{ kPa} \times n_{initial}$

$$n_{CO_2} = \frac{25.2 \text{ kPa}}{16.8 \text{ kPa}} \times n_{initial}$$

$n_{CO_2} = 1.5 n_{initial}$ [equation 2]

Chemical equations for combustion:
$CH_4 + 2O_2 \longrightarrow CO_2 + 2H_2O$
(Each mol CH_4 burned yields 1 mol CO_2.)

$C_2H_2 + \frac{5}{2}O_2 \longrightarrow 2CO_2 + H_2O$
(Each mol C_2H_2 burned yields 2 mol CO_2.)

Therefore, $n_{CO_2} = n_{CH_4} + 2n_{C_2H_2}$ [equation 3]

Substitute equation 2 into equation 3:
$1.5 n_{initial} = n_{CH_4} + 2n_{C_2H_2}$

Substitute for $n_{initial}$ using equation 1:

$1.5(n_{CH_4} + n_{C_2H_2}) = n_{CH_4} + 2n_{C_2H_2}$

$n_{CH_4} = n_{C_2H_2}$

So, in terms of moles, the initial mixture is equal parts methane and ethyne, or 50% methane (CH_4).

100. Let x be the percentage of total gas volume occupied by its molecules.

$$V_{H_2 \text{ molecules}} = 3.0 \times 10^{20} \text{ molecules H}_2 \times$$
$$\frac{6.7 \times 10^{-24} \text{ mL}}{1 \text{ molecule H}_2} \times \frac{1 \text{ L}}{10^3 \text{ mL}} = 2.0 \times 10^{-6} \text{ L}$$

a. $\frac{V_{molecules}}{V_{gas}} \times 100\% = \frac{2.0 \times 10^{-6} \text{ L}}{0.10 \text{ L}} \times 100\%$
$$= 2.0 \times 10^{-3}\%$$

b. $\frac{V_{molecules}}{V_{gas}} \times 100\% = \frac{2.0 \times 10^{-6} \text{ L}}{1 \times 10^{-4} \text{ L}} \times 100\% = 2.0\%$

107. $h = 1.60$ mm $= 0.160$ cm

$V = l \times w \times h = 4.50 \text{ cm} \times 1.30 \text{ cm} \times 0.160 \text{ cm} = 0.936 \text{ cm}^3$

$\text{Density} = \frac{\text{mass}}{\text{volume}} = \frac{9.92 \text{ g}}{0.936 \text{ cm}^3} = 10.6 \text{ g/cm}^3$

113. a. tin(II) bromide   **c.** magnesium hydroxide

b. barium sulfate   **d.** iodine pentafluoride

115. a. molar mass of $Ca(CH_3CO_2)_2 = (1 \times 40.1$ g/mol$)$ $+ (4 \times 12.0$ g/mol$) + (6 \times 1.0$ g/mol$) +$ $(4 \times 16.0$ g/mol$) = 158.1$ g/mol

b. molar mass of $H_3PO_4 = (3 \times 1.0$ g/mol$) + (1 \times$ 31.0 g/mol$) + (4 \times 16.0$ g/mol$) = 98.0$ g/mol

c. molar mass of $C_{12}H_{22}O_{11} = (12 \times 12.0$ g/mol$)$ $+ (22 \times 1.0$ g/mol$) + (11 \times 16.0$ g/mol$) =$ 342.0 g/mol

d. molar mass of $Pb(NO_3)_2 = (1 \times 207.2$ g/mol$)$ $+ (2 \times 14.0$ g/mol$) + (6 \times 16.0$ g/mol$) =$ 331.2 g/mol

117. a. efm of $C_2H_4O = (2 \times 12.0$ g/mol$) + (4 \times$ 1.0 g/mol$) + (1 \times 16.0$ g/mol$) = 44.0$ g/mol

$$\frac{\text{molar mass}}{\text{efm}} = \frac{88 \text{ g/mol}}{44.0 \text{ g/mol}} = 2$$
$(C_2H_4O) \times 2 = C_4H_8O_2$

b. efm of $CH = 12.0$ g/mol $+ 1.0$ g/mol $= 13.0$ g/mol

$$\frac{\text{molar mass}}{\text{efm}} = \frac{104 \text{ g/mol}}{13.0 \text{ g/mol}} = 8$$
$(CH) \times 8 = C_8H_8$

c. $\%C = 26.7\% = \dfrac{\text{mass of C}}{90 \text{ g}} \times 100\%$

mass of C $= 0.267 \times 90$ g $= 24$ g
$24 \text{ g C} \times \dfrac{1 \text{ mol C}}{12.0 \text{ g C}} = 2.0$ mol C

$\%O = 71.1\% = \dfrac{\text{mass of O}}{90 \text{ g}} \times 100\%$

mass of O $= 0.711 \times 90$ g $= 64$ g
$64 \text{ g O} \times \dfrac{1 \text{ mol O}}{16.0 \text{ g O}} = 4.0$ mol O

$\%H = 2.2\% = \dfrac{\text{mass of H}}{90 \text{ g}} \times 100\%$

mass of H $= 0.022 \times 90$ g $= 2.0$ g
$2.0 \text{ g H} \times \dfrac{1 \text{ mol H}}{1.0 \text{ g H}} = 2.0$ mol H

The empirical formula is $C_2H_2O_4$. Since molar mass/efm $= 1$, $C_2H_2O_4$ is both the empirical formula and molecular formula

121. a. $4Al(s) + 3O_2(g) \longrightarrow 2Al_2O_3(s)$

b. $583 \text{ g Al}_2O_3 \times \dfrac{1 \text{ mol Al}_2O_3}{102 \text{ g Al}_2O_3} = 5.72$ mol Al_2O_3

$5.72 \text{ g Al}_2O_3 \times \dfrac{4 \text{ mol Al}}{2 \text{ mol Al}_2O_3} \times \dfrac{27.0 \text{ g Al}}{1 \text{ mol Al}} = 309$ g Al

$5.72 \text{ g Al}_2O_3 \times \dfrac{3 \text{ mol O}_2}{2 \text{ mol Al}_2O_3} \times \dfrac{32.0 \text{ g O}_2}{1 \text{ mol O}_2} = 275$ g O_2

Chapter 15

8. mass of 5 mol $H_2O = 5[(2 \times 1.0$ g$) + 16.0$ g$]$ $= 90.0$ g

molar mass of $CuSO_4 \cdot H_2O = 63.5$ g $+ 32.1$ g $+$ $(4 \times 16.0$ g$) + 90.0$ g $= 249.6$ g

$\%$ by mass $H_2O = \dfrac{\text{mass of water}}{\text{mass of hydrate}} \times 100\% =$

$\dfrac{90.0 \text{ g}}{249.6 \text{ g}} \times 100\% = 36.1\%$

9. $5.00 \text{ g Na}_2CO_3 \times \dfrac{100.0 \text{ g Na}_2CO_3 \cdot 10 \text{ H}_2O}{37.06 \text{ g Na}_2CO_3} =$

13.5 g $Na_2CO_3 \cdot 10H_2O$

25. Surface molecules are attracted to the liquid molecules below but not to the air. Molecules inside the liquid are attracted in all directions.

28. A surfactant is a wetting agent such as soap or detergent. A surfactant interferes with hydrogen bonding between water molecules and reduces surface tension.

31. Water has low vapor pressure.

35. Bodies of water would freeze from the bottom up. This would kill many forms of aquatic life.

38. Solvent: water; solute: sugar

39. No; the molecules and ions are smaller than the pores of the filter and would therefore pass through the filter.

40. Solvent molecules surround positively charged and negatively charged ions.

43. a. HCl (polar) dissolves.

b. K_2SO_4 (ionic) dissolves.

c. NaI (ionic) dissolves.

d. C_2H_6 (nonpolar) will not dissolve.

e. NH_3 (polar) dissolves.

f. $CaCO_3$ (strong ionic forces) will not dissolve.

45. Its ions are free to move toward positively and negatively charged electrodes.

48. **a.** $Na_2SO_4 \cdot 10H_2O$

    b. $CaCl_2 \cdot 2H_2O$

    c. $Ba(OH)_2 \cdot 8H_2O$

49. **a.** tin(IV) chloride pentahydrate

    b. iron(II) sulfate heptahydrate

    c. barium bromide tetrahydrate

    d. iron(III) phosphate tetrahydrate

50. $MgSO_4 \cdot 7H_2O(s) \longrightarrow MgSO_4 \cdot H_2O(s) + 6H_2O(g)$

52. Hygroscopic substances absorb water vapor from the air and create a dry environment in a sealed container.

54. solutions, colloids, suspensions

55. Colloids and suspensions exhibit the Tyndall effect, but solutions do not. The particles in a suspension will settle out over time.

59. Brownian motion and repulsion between like-charged ions adsorbed on the surfaces of colloidal particles.

62. hexane, ethanol, water

63. **a.** 1.0000 g/mL   **b.** 4°C

    c. No; there would be a break in the curve at 0°C as liquid water at 0°C changes to ice at 0°C.

65. Hydrobromic acid disassociates into hydrogen and bromide ions when dissolved in water, but methanol does not.

66. **a.** Water expands when it freezes to ice.

    b. Water is polar, and wax is nonpolar; water has a higher surface tension.

    c. Water has a lower vapor pressure than alcohol.

68. **a.** gasoline   **c.** water

    b. gasoline   **d.** water

69. **a.** No, both form clear, colorless solutions.

    b. Evaporate the water to examine the crystals; test for electrical conductivity; do a flame test.

72. **a.** $NH_4Cl(s) \longrightarrow NH_4^+(aq) + Cl^-(aq)$

    b. $C_2H_4O_2(s) \longrightarrow H^+(aq) + C_2H_3O_2^-(aq)$

    c. $Cu(NO_3)_2(s) \longrightarrow Cu^{2+}(aq) + 2NO_3^-(aq)$

    d. $HgCl_2(s) \longrightarrow Hg^{2+}(aq) + 2Cl^-(aq)$

73. **a.** sodium carbonate monohydrate;

    mass of 1 mol $H_2O = (2 \times 1.0 \text{ g}) + 16.0 \text{ g} = 18.0 \text{ g}$

    molar mass of $Na_2CO_3 \cdot H_2O = (2 \times 23.0 \text{ g}) + 12.0 \text{ g} + (3 \times 16.0 \text{ g}) + 18.0 \text{ g} = 124.0 \text{ g}$

    % by mass $H_2O = \dfrac{18.0 \text{ g}}{124.0 \text{ g}} \times 100\% = 14.5\%$

b. magnesium sulfate heptahydrate;

    mass of 7 mol $H_2O = 7[(2 \times 1.0 \text{ g}) + 16.0 \text{ g}]$
    $= 126.0 \text{ g}$

    molar mass of $MgSO_4 \cdot 7H_2O = 24.3 \text{ g} + 32.1 \text{ g} + (4 \times 16.0 \text{ g}) + 126.0 \text{ g} = 246.4 \text{ g}$

    % by mass $H_2O = \dfrac{126.0 \text{ g}}{246.4 \text{ g}} \times 100\% = 51.14\%$

75. **a.** $Ba(OH)_2(s) + 8H_2O(l) \longrightarrow Ba(OH)_2 \cdot 8H_2O(s)$

    b. mass of 8 mol $H_2O = 8[(2 \times 1.0 \text{ g}) + 16.0 \text{ g}] = 144.0 \text{ g}$

    molar mass of $Ba(OH)_2 \cdot 8H_2O = 137.3 \text{ g} + 2(16.0 \text{ g} + 1.0 \text{ g}) + 144.0 \text{ g} = 315.3 \text{ g}$

    % by mass $H_2O = \dfrac{144.0 \text{ g}}{315.3 \text{ g}} \times 100\% = 45.67\%$

76. From Practice Problem 8, the percent H_2O in $CuSO_4 \cdot 5H_2O$ is 36.1%. This means that for every 100.0 g of hydrate, there are $100.0 \text{ g} - 36.1 \text{ g} = 63.9 \text{ g}$ of anhydrous $CuSO_4$.

$$10.0 \text{ g } CuSO_4 \times \dfrac{100.0 \text{ g } CuSO_4 \cdot 5H_2O}{63.9 \text{ g } CuSO_4} =$$

$$15.6 \text{ g } CuSO_4 \cdot 5H_2O$$

78. **a.** (1), (3), (6), (8)

    b. (1), (2), (5), (6), (7), (9)

    c. (2), (4), (5)

80. **a.** nonelectrolyte

    b. weak electrolyte

    c. strong electrolyte

81. The container would break because water expands as it freezes.

83. The surface tension of water keeps the strider from sinking. The surfactant would reduce the surface tension and the strider would shrink.

85. The hydrogen-bonded structures in liquid water are disrupted when ethyl alcohol is added because the alcohol competes for hydrogen bonds with water molecules and the water structure collapses. Thus, mixtures of water and ethyl alcohol have less volume than the sum of the volumes of the components. Mixing two liquids could result in a volume greater than the sum of the volumes of the components if the structural ordering in the mixture is greater than in the separated components.

86. Most of the important chemical reactions of life take place in aqueous solutions inside cells.

89. a. pink   **b.** pink   **c.** blue

d. mass of 6 mol $H_2O = 6[(2 \times 1.0\text{ g}) + 16.0\text{ g}] =$ 108.0 g

molar mass of $CoCl_2 \cdot 6H_2O = 58.9\text{ g} + (2 \times 35.5\text{ g})$ + 108.0 g = 237.9 g

% by mass $H_2O = \dfrac{108.0\ \cancel{g}}{237.9\ \cancel{g}} \times 100\% = 45.40\%$

e. water or water vapor

91. In spring, when the ice melts and the temperature of the surface water increases to 4°C, it becomes heavier than the water below it and sinks. The downward movement of surface water forces water in the deeper parts of the lake upward, where it is warmed.

92. A surfactant helps to wet the burning material, so less water is needed to put out the fire. Thus, less water carries pollutants into the environment.

93. Water enters cracks in pavement and expands when it freezes, creating larger cracks. Continuous freeze-thaw cycles cause pavement to break up and form potholes.

97. The molecules in the dirt and grease dissolve in the water.

100. a. 5   **b.** 2   **c.** 2   **d.** 4

102. $H^+ + H{:}\ddot{\underset{\cdot\cdot}{O}}{:}H \longrightarrow H{:}\ddot{\underset{H}{O}}{:}H^{\ +}$

104. a. $6CO_2(g) + 6H_2O(l) \longrightarrow C_6H_{12}O_6(s) + 6O_2(g)$

b. $2Na(s) + 2H_2O(l) \longrightarrow$
$$Na^+(aq) + 2OH^-(aq) + H_2(g)$$

106. $2.00 \times 10^{-3}\ \cancel{\text{mol }H_2O_2} \times \dfrac{2\ \cancel{\text{mol }H_2O}}{2\ \cancel{\text{mol }H_2O_2}} \times \dfrac{18.0\text{ g }H_2O}{1\ \cancel{\text{mol }H_2O}}$

$$= 0.0360\text{ g }H_2O$$

$2.00 \times 10^{-3}\ \cancel{\text{mol }H_2O_2} \times \dfrac{1\ \cancel{\text{mol }O_2}}{2\ \cancel{\text{mol }H_2O_2}} \times \dfrac{22.4\text{ L }O_2}{1\ \cancel{\text{mol }O_2}}$

$$= 0.0224\text{ L }O_2$$

107. $2.60 \times 10^2\ \cancel{\text{g }H_2O} \times \dfrac{1\ \cancel{\text{mol }H_2O}}{18.0\ \cancel{\text{g }H_2O}} \times \dfrac{1\ \cancel{\text{mol }C_2H_4O}}{1\ \cancel{\text{mol }H_2O}} \times$

$\dfrac{44.0\text{ g }C_2H_4O}{1\ \cancel{\text{mol }C_2H_4O}} = 636\text{ g }C_2H_4O$

109. a. $40\ \cancel{cm^3} \times \dfrac{1\ \cancel{mL}}{1\ \cancel{cm^3}} \times \dfrac{1\ \cancel{L}}{1000\ \cancel{mL}} \times \dfrac{1\text{ mol }O_2}{22.4\ \cancel{L}}$

$$= 1.8 \times 10^{-3}\text{ mol }O_2$$

$60\ \cancel{cm^3} \times \dfrac{1\ \cancel{mL}}{1\ \cancel{cm^3}} \times \dfrac{1\ \cancel{L}}{1000\ \cancel{mL}} \times \dfrac{1\text{ mol }H_2}{22.4\ \cancel{L}}$

$$= 2.7 \times 10^{-3}\text{ mol }H_2$$

$1.8 \times 10^{-3}\ \cancel{\text{mol }O_2} \times \dfrac{2\text{ mol }H_2}{1\ \cancel{\text{mol }O_2}} = 3.6 \times 10^{-3}\text{ mol }H_2$

Since $2.7 \times 10^{-3}\text{ mol }H_2 < 3.6 \times 10^{-3}\text{ mol }H_2$, hydrogen is the limiting reagent.

b. $2.7 \times 10^{-3}\ \cancel{\text{mol }H_2} \times \dfrac{2\ \cancel{\text{mol }H_2O}}{2\ \cancel{\text{mol }H_2}} \times \dfrac{18.0\text{ g }H_2O}{1\ \cancel{\text{mol }H_2O}}$

$$= 0.049\text{ g }H_2O$$

c. oxygen

d. $2.7 \times 10^{-3}\ \cancel{\text{mol }H_2} \times \dfrac{1\text{ mol }O_2}{2\ \cancel{\text{mol }H_2}} = 1.4 \times 10^{-3}\text{ mol }O_2$

Excess $O_2 = (1.8 \times 10^{-3} - 1.4 \times 10^{-3})\text{ mol }O_2 =$ $0.4 \times 10^{-3}\text{ mol }O_2$

$0.4 \times 10^{-3}\ \cancel{\text{mol }O_2} \times \dfrac{22.4\text{ L}}{1\ \cancel{\text{mol }O_2}} = 9 \times 10^{-3}\text{ L}$

111. $T_1 = 100°C + 273\text{ K} = 373\text{ K}$
$T_2 = 200°C + 273\text{ K} = 473\text{ K}$

$P_2 = \dfrac{P_1 \times T_2}{T_1} = \dfrac{1.00\text{ atm} \times 473\ \cancel{K}}{373\ \cancel{K}} = 1.27\text{ atm}$

Chapter 16

1. $S_2 = \dfrac{S_1 \times P_2}{P_1} = \dfrac{0.16\text{ g/L} \times 288\ \cancel{kPa}}{104\ \cancel{kPa}} = 0.44\text{ g/L}$

2. $P_2 = \dfrac{P_1 \times S_2}{S_1} = \dfrac{1.0\text{ atm} \times 9.5\ \cancel{g/L}}{3.6\ \cancel{g/L}} = 2.6\text{ atm}$

10. $\dfrac{36.0\ \cancel{\text{g }C_6H_{12}O_6}}{2.0\text{ L}} \times \dfrac{1\text{ mol }C_6H_{12}O_6}{180\ \cancel{\text{g }C_6H_{12}O_6}} = 0.10\text{ mol/L}$
$= 0.10M$

11. $\dfrac{0.70\text{ mol NaCl}}{250\ \cancel{mL}} \times \dfrac{10^3\ \cancel{mL}}{1\text{ L}} = 2.8\text{ mol/L} = 2.8M$

12. $335\ \cancel{mL} \times \dfrac{1\ \cancel{L}}{10^3\ \cancel{mL}} \times \dfrac{0.425\text{ mol }NH_4NO_3}{1\ \cancel{L}} =$
$$0.142\text{ mol }NH_4NO_3$$

13. $250\ \cancel{mL} \times \dfrac{1\ \cancel{L}}{10^3\ \cancel{mL}} \times \dfrac{2.0\text{ mol }CaCl_2}{1\ \cancel{L}} = 0.50\text{ mol }CaCl_2$

$0.50\ \cancel{\text{mol }CaCl_2} \times \dfrac{111.1\text{ g }CaCl_2}{1\ \cancel{\text{mol }CaCl_2}} = 56\text{ g }CaCl_2$

14. $V_1 = \dfrac{M_2 \times V_2}{M_1} = \dfrac{0.760M \times 250\text{ mL}}{4.00M} = 47.5\text{ mL}$

15. $V_2 = \dfrac{M_1 \times V_1}{M_2} = \dfrac{0.20\ \cancel{M} \times 250\text{ mL}}{1.0\ \cancel{M}} = 50\text{ mL}$

Use a pipet to transfer 50 mL (calculation above) of the $1.0M$ solution to a 250-ml volumetric flask. Then add distilled water up to the mark.

16. $\dfrac{10\ \cancel{mL}\text{ propanone}}{200\ \cancel{mL}} \times 100\% = 5.0\ \%\text{ propanone (v/v)}$

17. $3.0\%(\text{v/v}) = \dfrac{V_{\text{H}_2\text{O}_2}}{V_{\text{soln}}} \times 100\%$

$V_{\text{H}_2\text{O}_2} = \dfrac{3.0\%}{100\%} \times 400.0 \text{ mL} = 12 \text{ mL}$

18. $250 \text{ g solution} \times \dfrac{10 \text{ g MgSO}_4}{100 \text{ g solution}} = 25 \text{ g MgSO}_4$

34. $750 \text{ g H}_2\text{O} \times \dfrac{0.400 \text{ mol NaF}}{10^3 \text{ g H}_2\text{O}} \times \dfrac{42.0 \text{ g NaF}}{1 \text{ mol NaF}} =$
12.6 g NaF

35. $\dfrac{10.0 \text{ g NaCl}}{600 \text{ g H}_2\text{O}} \times \dfrac{1 \text{ mol NaCl}}{58.5 \text{ g NaCl}} \times \dfrac{10^3 \text{ g H}_2\text{O}}{1 \text{ kg H}_2\text{O}} =$
$0.285m \text{ NaCl}$

36. $n_{\text{C}_2\text{H}_6\text{O}} = 300 \text{ g C}_2\text{H}_6\text{O} \times \dfrac{1 \text{ mol C}_2\text{H}_6\text{O}}{46.0 \text{ g C}_2\text{H}_6\text{O}} =$
$6.52 \text{ mol C}_2\text{H}_6\text{O}$

$n_{\text{H}_2\text{O}} = 500 \text{ g H}_2\text{O} \times \dfrac{1 \text{ mol H}_2\text{O}}{18.0 \text{ g H}_2\text{O}} = 27.8 \text{ mol H}_2\text{O}$

$X_{\text{C}_2\text{H}_6\text{O}} = \dfrac{n_{\text{C}_2\text{H}_6\text{O}}}{n_{\text{C}_2\text{H}_6\text{O}} + n_{\text{H}_2\text{O}}} = \dfrac{6.52 \text{ mol}}{27.8 \text{ mol} + 6.52 \text{ mol}} = 0.190$

$X_{\text{H}_2\text{O}} = \dfrac{n_{\text{H}_2\text{O}}}{n_{\text{C}_2\text{H}_6\text{O}} + n_{\text{H}_2\text{O}}} = \dfrac{27.8 \text{ mol}}{27.8 \text{ mol} + 6.52 \text{ mol}} = 0.810$

37. $n_{\text{CCl}_4} = 50.0 \text{ g CCl}_4 \times \dfrac{1 \text{ mol CCl}_4}{153.8 \text{ g CCl}_4} = 0.325 \text{ mol CCl}_4$

$n_{\text{CHCl}_3} = 50.0 \text{ g CHCl}_3 \times \dfrac{1 \text{ mol CHCl}_3}{119.4 \text{ g CHCl}_3}$
$= 0.419 \text{ mol CHCl}_3$

$X_{\text{CCl}_4} = \dfrac{n_{\text{CCl}_4}}{n_{\text{CCl}_4} + n_{\text{CHCl}_3}} = \dfrac{0.325 \text{ mol}}{0.325 \text{ mol} + 0.419 \text{ mol}}$
$= 0.437$

$X_{\text{CHCl}_3} = \dfrac{n_{\text{CHCl}_3}}{n_{\text{CCl}_4} + n_{\text{CHCl}_3}} = \dfrac{0.419 \text{ mol}}{0.325 \text{ mol} + 0.419 \text{ mol}}$
$= 0.563$

38. $10.0 \text{ g C}_6\text{H}_{12}\text{O}_6 \times \dfrac{1 \text{ mol C}_6\text{H}_{12}\text{O}_6}{180.0 \text{ g C}_6\text{H}_{12}\text{O}_6} =$
$0.0556 \text{ mol C}_6\text{H}_{12}\text{O}_6$

$m = \dfrac{0.0556 \text{ mol C}_6\text{H}_{12}\text{O}_6}{50.0 \text{ g H}_2\text{O} \times \dfrac{1 \text{ kg H}_2\text{O}}{10^3 \text{ g H}_2\text{O}}} = 1.11m \text{ C}_6\text{H}_{12}\text{O}_6$

$\Delta T_f = K_f \times m = 1.86°\text{C/}m \times 1.11m = 2.06°\text{C}$

39. $200 \text{ g C}_3\text{H}_6\text{O} \times \dfrac{1 \text{ mol C}_3\text{H}_6\text{O}}{58.0 \text{ g C}_3\text{H}_6\text{O}} = 3.45 \text{ mol C}_3\text{H}_6\text{O}$

$m = \dfrac{3.45 \text{ mol C}_3\text{H}_6\text{O}}{400 \text{ g benzene} \times \dfrac{1 \text{ kg benzene}}{10^3 \text{ g benzene}}} = 8.63m \text{ C}_3\text{H}_6\text{O}$

$\Delta T_f = K_f \times m = 5.12°\text{C/}m \times 8.62m = 44.2°\text{C}$

40. $m = \dfrac{1.25 \text{ mol CaCl}_2}{1400 \text{ g H}_2\text{O} \times \dfrac{1 \text{ kg H}_2\text{O}}{10^3 \text{ g H}_2\text{O}}} = 0.893m \text{ CaCl}_2$

Each formula unit of $CaCl_2$ disassociates into 3 particles, so molality of total particles is:

$3 \times 0.893m = 2.68m$

$\Delta T_b = K_b \times m = 0.512°\text{C/}m \times 2.68m = 1.37°\text{C}$

$T_b = 100°\text{C} + 1.37°\text{C} = 101.37°\text{C}$

41. $m = \dfrac{\Delta T_b}{K_b} = \dfrac{2.00°\text{C}}{0.512°\text{C}/m} = 3.91m$
(molality of total particles)

Each formula unit of NaCl disassociates into 2 particles, so the solution concentration is:

$3.91m/2 = 1.96m$

Mass of NaCl needed per 1 kg of H_2O is:

$1.96 \text{ mol NaCl} \times \dfrac{58.5 \text{ g NaCl}}{1 \text{ mol NaCl}} = 115 \text{ g NaCl}$

55. a. $S_2 = \dfrac{S_1 \times P_2}{P_1} = \dfrac{0.026 \text{ g/L} \times 0.60 \text{ atm}}{1.00 \text{ atm}} = 0.016 \text{ g/L}$

b. $S_2 = \dfrac{S_1 \times P_2}{P_1} = \dfrac{0.026 \text{ g/L} \times 1.80 \text{ atm}}{1.00 \text{ atm}} = 0.047 \text{ g/L}$

58. $V_1 = \dfrac{M_2 \times V_2}{M_1} = \dfrac{0.100M \times 100.0 \text{ mL}}{0.500M} = 20.0 \text{ mL}$

59. $\dfrac{0.50 \text{ g NaCl}}{100 \text{ mL}} \times \dfrac{1 \text{ mol NaCl}}{58.5 \text{ g NaCl}} \times \dfrac{10^3 \text{ mL}}{1 \text{ L}} = 0.085M$

61. a. $2500 \text{ g solution} \times \dfrac{0.90 \text{ g NaCl}}{100 \text{ g solution}} = 23 \text{ g NaCl}$

b. $0.050 \text{ kg solution} \times \dfrac{1000 \text{ g solution}}{1 \text{ kg solution}} \times \dfrac{4.0 \text{ g MgCl}_2}{100 \text{ g solution}}$
$= 2.0 \text{ g MgCl}_2$

63. a. $\dfrac{25 \text{ mL ethanol}}{150 \text{ mL}} \times 100\% = 17\% \text{ (v/v) ethanol}$

b. $\dfrac{175 \text{ mL isopropyl alcohol}}{275 \text{ mL}} \times 100\% =$
$63.6\% \text{ (v/v) isopropyl alcohol}$

72. a. Molality of $Na_2SO_4 = \dfrac{1.40 \text{ mol } Na_2SO_4}{1750 \text{ g } H_2O \times \dfrac{1 \text{ kg } H_2O}{10^3 \text{ g } H_2O}}$

$= 0.800m \; Na_2SO_4$

Each mol of Na_2SO_4 that dissolves yields 3 mol of particles.

Molality of total particles $= 3 \times 0.800m = 2.40m$

$\Delta T_f = K_f \times m = 1.86°C/m \times 2.40\,m = 4.46°C$

$T_f = 0°C - 4.46°C = -4.46°C$

b. Molality of $MgSO_4 = \dfrac{0.060 \text{ mol } MgSO_4}{100 \text{ g } H_2O \times \dfrac{1 \text{ kg } H_2O}{10^3 \text{ g } H_2O}}$

$= 0.60m \; MgSO_4$

Each mol of $MgSO_4$ that dissolves yields 2 mol of particles.

Molality of total particles $= 2 \times 0.60m = 1.2m$

$\Delta T_f = K_f \times m = 1.86°C/m \times 1.2\,m = 2.2°C$

$T_f = 0°C - 22°C = -2.2°C$

76. $12.0 \text{ g } C_{10}H_8 \times \dfrac{1 \text{ mol } C_{10}H_8}{128.0 \text{ g } C_{10}H_8} = 0.0938 \text{ mol } C_{10}H_8$

$m = \dfrac{0.0938 \text{ mol } C_{10}H_8}{50.0 \text{ g } C_6H_6 \times \dfrac{1 \text{ kg } C_6H_6}{1000 \text{ g } C_6H_6}} = 1.88m \; C_{10}H_8$

$\Delta T_f = K_f \times m = 5.12°C/m \times 1.88\,m = 9.63°C$

$\Delta T_b = K_b \times m = 2.53°C/m \times 1.88\,m = 4.76°C$

85. a. At 20°C, the solubility of KCl in water is 34.0 g/100 g H_2O, or 44.2 g/130 g H_2O. Therefore, 44.2 g KCl remain dissolved.

b. 50.0 g KCl − 44.2 g KCl = 5.8 g KCl

87. $S = \dfrac{36.0 \text{ g NaCl}}{100 \text{ g } H_2O} \times \dfrac{0.750}{0.750} = \dfrac{27.0 \text{ g NaCl}}{75.0 \text{ g } H_2O}$

The solution contains 26.5 g NaCl/75.0 g H_2O and is therefore unsaturated.

91. $m = \dfrac{\Delta T_f}{K_f} = \dfrac{0.460°C}{5.12°C/m} = 0.898m$

Let x = molar mass of the nondissociating solute.

$\dfrac{5.76 \text{ g}/x}{750 \text{ g benzene}} \times \dfrac{1000 \text{ g benzene}}{1 \text{ kg benzene}} = 0.898m$

$7.68 \text{ g}/x = 0.0898 \text{ mol}$

$x = 7.68 \text{ g}/0.0898 \text{ mol} = 85.5 \text{ g/mol}$

92. $1000 \text{ g } H_2O \times \dfrac{1 \text{ mol}}{18.0 \text{ g } H_2O} = 55.6 \text{ mol } H_2O$

$m_{C_{12}H_{22}O_{11}} = 1.62m = 1.62 \text{ mol } C_{12}H_{22}O_{11}/\text{kg } H_2O$

$X_{H_2O} = \dfrac{55.6 \text{ mol } H_2O}{55.6 \text{ mol } H_2O + 1.62 \text{ mol } C_{12}H_{22}O_{11}} = 0.972$

$X_{C_{12}H_{22}O_{11}} = \dfrac{1.62 \text{ mol } C_{12}H_{22}O_{11}}{55.6 \text{ mol } H_2O + 1.62 \text{ mol } C_{12}H_{22}O_{11}}$

$= 0.0283$

100. $Na_2SO_4(aq) + BaCl(aq) \longrightarrow BaSO_4(s) + 2NaCl(aq)$

$5.28 \text{ g } BaSO_4 \times \dfrac{1 \text{ mol } BaSO_4}{233.4 \text{ g } BaSO_4} \times \dfrac{1 \text{ mol } Na_2SO_4}{1 \text{ mol } BaSO_4}$

$= 0.0226 \text{ mol } Na_2SO_4$

Molarity $= \dfrac{0.0226 \text{ mol } Na_2SO_4}{250 \times 10^{-3} \text{ L}} = 0.090M \; Na_2SO_4$

103. $V_1 = \dfrac{M_2 \times V_2}{M_1} = \dfrac{0.50M \times 100 \text{ mL}}{2.0M} = 25 \text{ mL}$

Step 1: Start with a stock solution that is 2.0M KCl.

Step 2: Transfer 25 mL of 2.0M KCl to a 100-mL volumetric flask.

Step 3: Add distilled water up to the 100-mL mark.

108. atomic mass of Rb $= (0.72165)(84.912 \text{ amu}) + (0.27835)(86.909 \text{ amu}) = 61.277 \text{ amu} + 24.191 \text{ amu}$
$= 85.468 \text{ amu}$

114. a. 1 mol Fe = 55.8 g Fe

1 mol Cu = 63.5 g Cu

1 mol Hg = 200.6 g Hg

1 mol S = 32.1 g S

b. Each sample contains 6.02×10^{23} atoms.

c. $25.0 \text{ g Fe} \times \dfrac{1 \text{ mol Fe}}{55.8 \text{ g Fe}} = 0.448 \text{ mol Fe}$

$25.0 \text{ g Fe} \times \dfrac{1 \text{ mol Cu}}{63.5 \text{ g Cu}} = 0.394 \text{ mol Cu}$

$25.0 \text{ g Fe} \times \dfrac{1 \text{ mol Hg}}{200.6 \text{ g Hg}} = 0.125 \text{ mol Hg}$

$25.0 \text{ g Fe} \times \dfrac{1 \text{ mol S}}{32.1 \text{ g S}} = 0.779 \text{ mol S}$

115. $1500 \text{ g } H_2 \times \dfrac{1 \text{ mol } H_2}{2.0 \text{ g } H_2} \times \dfrac{22.4 \text{ L } H_2}{1 \text{ mol } H_2} = 1.7 \times 10^4 \text{ L}$

120. $T_1 = 25°C + 273 = 298 \text{ K}$

$T_1 = 45°C + 273 = 318 \text{ K}$

$P_2 = \dfrac{P_1 \times T_2}{T_1} = \dfrac{101.3 \text{ kPa} \times 318 \text{ K}}{298 \text{ K}} = 108 \text{ kPa}$

Chapter 17

1. Heat flows from the system (wax) to the surroundings (air). The process is exothermic.

2. Since the beaker becomes cold, heat is absorbed by the system (chemicals within the beaker) from the surroundings (beaker and surrounding air). The process is endothermic.

3. $\Delta T = 85°C - 21°C = 64°C$

$C_{\text{olive oil}} = \dfrac{q}{m \times \Delta T} = \dfrac{435 \text{ J}}{3.4 \text{ g} \times 64°C} = 2.0 \text{ J/(g} \cdot °C)$

4. $q = C_{Hg} \times m \times \Delta T = (0.14 \text{ J}/(\text{g} \cdot {}^\circ\text{C}))(250.0 \text{ g})(52{}^\circ\text{C})$
$= 1800 \text{ J} = 1.8 \text{ kJ}$

12. $V_{water} = 50.0 \text{ mL} + 50.0 \text{ mL} = 100.0 \text{ mL}$

$m_{water} = 100.0 \text{ mL} \times \dfrac{1.00 \text{ g}}{1 \text{ mL}} = 100.0 \text{ g}$

$\Delta T = 26.0{}^\circ\text{C} - 22.5{}^\circ\text{C} = 3.5{}^\circ\text{C}$

$\Delta H = -q_{surr} = -m_{water} \times C_{water} \times \Delta T = -(100.0 \text{ g})$
$\times (4.18 \text{ J}/(\text{g} \cdot {}^\circ\text{C}))(3.5{}^\circ\text{C}) = -1460 \text{ J} = -1.46 \text{ kJ}$
(1.46 kJ of heat was released)

13. $\Delta T = 26.4{}^\circ\text{C} - 25.0{}^\circ\text{C} = 1.4{}^\circ\text{C}$

$\Delta H = -q_{surr} = -m_{water} \times C_{water} \times \Delta T = -(25.0 \text{ g})$
$\times (4.18 \text{ J}/(\text{g} \cdot {}^\circ\text{C}))(1.4{}^\circ\text{C}) = -150 \text{ J}$
(150 J of heat is released by the pebble)

14. $\Delta H = 3.40 \text{ mol Fe}_2\text{O}_3 \times \dfrac{26.3 \text{ kJ}}{1 \text{ mol Fe}_2\text{O}_3} = 89.4 \text{ kJ}$

15. $\Delta H = 5.66 \text{ g CS}_2 \times \dfrac{1 \text{ mol CS}_2}{76.2 \text{ g CS}_2} \times \dfrac{89.3 \text{ kJ}}{1 \text{ mol CS}_2} = 6.63 \text{ kJ}$

22. $m_{\text{H}_2\text{O}(s)} = 0.400 \text{ kJ} \times \dfrac{1 \text{ mol H}_2\text{O}(s)}{6.01 \text{ kJ}} \times \dfrac{18.0 \text{ g H}_2\text{O}(s)}{1 \text{ mol H}_2\text{O}(s)}$
$= 1.20 \text{ g H}_2\text{O}(s)$

23. $\Delta H = 50.0 \text{ g H}_2\text{O}(l) \times \dfrac{1 \text{ mol H}_2\text{O}(l)}{18.0 \text{ g H}_2\text{O}(l)} \times \dfrac{-6.01 \text{ kJ}}{1 \text{ mol H}_2\text{O}(l)}$
$= 16.7 \text{ kJ}$

24. $\Delta H = 63.7 \text{ g H}_2\text{O}(l) \times \dfrac{1 \text{ mol H}_2\text{O}(l)}{18.0 \text{ g H}_2\text{O}(l)} \times \dfrac{40.7 \text{ kJ}}{1 \text{ mol H}_2\text{O}(l)}$
$= 144 \text{ kJ}$

25. $\Delta H = 0.46 \text{ g C}_2\text{H}_5\text{Cl} \times \dfrac{1 \text{ mol C}_2\text{H}_5\text{Cl}}{64.5 \text{ g C}_2\text{H}_5\text{Cl}} \times \dfrac{24.7 \text{ kJ}}{1 \text{ mol C}_2\text{H}_5\text{Cl}}$
$= 0.18 \text{ kJ}$

26. $\Delta H = 0.677 \text{ mol NaOH}(s) \times \dfrac{-44.5 \text{ kJ}}{1 \text{ mol NaOH}(s)} = -30.1 \text{ kJ}$

27. moles of $\text{NH}_4\text{NO}_3(s) = 88.0 \text{ kJ} \times \dfrac{1 \text{ mol NH}_4\text{NO}_3(s)}{25.7 \text{ kJ}}$
$= 3.42 \text{ mol NH}_4\text{NO}_3(s)$

35. $\Delta H_f{}^\circ(\text{reactants}) = 1 \text{ mol Br}_2(g) \times \dfrac{30.91 \text{ kJ}}{1 \text{ mol Br}_2(g)}$
$= 30.91 \text{ kJ}$

$\Delta H_f{}^\circ(\text{products}) = 1 \text{ mol Br}_2(l) \times \dfrac{0 \text{ kJ}}{1 \text{ mol Br}_2(l)} = 0 \text{ kJ}$

$\Delta H{}^\circ = \Delta H_f{}^\circ(\text{products}) - \Delta H_f{}^\circ(\text{reactants})$
$= 0 \text{ kJ} - 30.91 \text{ kJ} = -30.91 \text{ kJ}$

36. $2\text{NO}(g) + \text{O}_2(g) \longrightarrow 2\text{NO}_2(g)$

$\Delta H_f{}^\circ(\text{reactants}) = 2 \text{ mol NO}(g) \times \dfrac{90.37 \text{ kJ}}{1 \text{ mol NO}(g)}$
$+ 1 \text{ mol O}_2(g) \times \dfrac{0 \text{ kJ}}{1 \text{ mol O}_2(g)} = 180.7 \text{ kJ}$

$\Delta H_f{}^\circ(\text{products}) = 2 \text{ mol NO}_2(g) \times \dfrac{33.85 \text{ kJ}}{1 \text{ mol NO}_2(g)}$
$= 67.70 \text{ kJ}$

$\Delta H{}^\circ = \Delta H_f{}^\circ(\text{products}) - \Delta H_f{}^\circ(\text{reactants})$
$= 67.70 \text{ kJ} - 180.7 \text{ kJ} = -113.0 \text{ kJ}$

47. a. exothermic
b. The immediate surroundings are the glass beaker and the air. If one or more of the substances is in water, the water is also considered part of the surroundings.

48. a. exothermic   **c.** exothermic
b. endothermic   **d.** endothermic

51. a. $8.50 \times 10^2 \text{ cal} \times \dfrac{1 \text{ Cal}}{1000 \text{ cal}} = 0.85 \text{ Cal}$

b. $444 \text{ cal} \times \dfrac{4.18 \text{ J}}{1 \text{ cal}} = 1.86 \times 10^3 \text{ J}$

c. $1.8 \text{ kJ} \times \dfrac{1000 \text{ J}}{1 \text{ kJ}} = 1.8 \times 10^3 \text{ J}$

d. $45 \times 10^{-1} \text{ kJ} \times \dfrac{1000 \text{ J}}{1 \text{ kJ}} \times \dfrac{1 \text{ cal}}{4.18 \text{ J}} = 1.1 \times 10^2 \text{ cal}$

53. $q = C \times m \times \Delta T = (0.24 \text{ J}/g \cdot {}^\circ\text{C})(400.0 \text{ g})(45{}^\circ\text{C})$
$= 4.3 \times 10^3 \text{ J}$

59. $\Delta H = 0.75 \text{ mol Mg} \times \dfrac{-1204 \text{ kJ}}{2 \text{ mol Mg}} = -4.5 \times 10^2 \text{ kJ}$

62. a. $\Delta H = 3.50 \text{ mol H}_2\text{O}(l) \times \dfrac{-6.01 \text{ kJ}}{1 \text{ mol H}_2\text{O}(l)} = -21.0 \text{ kJ}$

b. $\Delta H = 0.44 \text{ mol H}_2\text{O}(g) \times \dfrac{-40.7 \text{ kJ}}{1 \text{ mol H}_2\text{O}(g)} = -18 \text{ kJ}$

c. $\Delta H = 1.25 \text{ mol NaOH} \times \dfrac{-44.5 \text{ kJ}}{1 \text{ mol NaOH}} = -55.6 \text{ kJ}$

d. $\Delta H = 0.15 \text{ mol C}_2\text{H}_6\text{O} \times \dfrac{5.8 \text{ kJ}}{1 \text{ mol C}_2\text{H}_6\text{O}} = 6.5 \text{ kJ}$

65. a. $\Delta H = 1 \text{ mol Al}_2\text{O}_3(s) \times \dfrac{-3352 \text{ kJ}}{2 \text{ mol Al}_2\text{O}_3(s)} = -1676 \text{ kJ}$

b. ΔH is negative so the reaction is exothermic.

66. Reverse the second equation and change the sign of ΔH. Then add the equations and the values of ΔH.

$\text{Pb}(s) + 2\text{Cl}_2 \longrightarrow \text{PbCl}_4(l) \qquad \Delta H = -329.2 \text{ kJ}$
$\text{PbCl}_2(s) \longrightarrow \text{Pb}(s) + \text{Cl}_2(g) \qquad \Delta H = 359.4 \text{ kJ}$
$\overline{\text{PbCl}_2(s) + \text{Cl}_2(g) \longrightarrow \text{PbCl}_4(l) \quad \Delta H = 30.2 \text{ kJ}}$

70. Substance B; for equal masses, the substance with the greater specific heat undergoes the smaller temperature change.

74. $C_{\text{stainless steel}} = \dfrac{q}{m \times \Delta T} = \dfrac{141 \text{ J}}{1.55 \text{ g} \times 178°\text{C}} = 0.511 \text{ J/(g·°C)}$

76. a. $\Delta H_f°(\text{reactants}) = 1 \text{ mol CH}_4(g) \times \dfrac{-74.86 \text{ kJ}}{1 \text{ mol CH}_4(g)}$

$+ \dfrac{3}{2} \text{ mol O}_2(g) \times \dfrac{0 \text{ kJ}}{1 \text{ mol O}_2(g)} = -74.86 \text{ kJ}$

$\Delta H_f°(\text{products}) = 1 \text{ mol CO}(g) \times \dfrac{-110.5 \text{ kJ}}{1 \text{ mol CO}(g)}$

$+ 2 \text{ mol H}_2\text{O}(l) \times \dfrac{-285.8 \text{ kJ}}{1 \text{ mol H}_2\text{O}(l)} = -682.1 \text{ kJ}$

$\Delta H° = \Delta H_f°(\text{products}) - \Delta H_f°(\text{reactants})$
$= (-682.1 \text{ kJ}) - (-74.86 \text{ kJ}) = -607.2 \text{ kJ}$

b. $\Delta H_f°(\text{reactants}) = 2 \text{ mol CO}(g) \times \dfrac{-110.5 \text{ kJ}}{1 \text{ mol CO}(g)}$

$+ 1 \text{ mol O}_2(g) \times \dfrac{0 \text{ kJ}}{1 \text{ mol O}_2(g)} = -221.0 \text{ kJ}$

$\Delta H_f°(\text{products}) = 2 \text{ mol CO}_2(g) \times \dfrac{-393.5 \text{ kJ}}{1 \text{ mol CO}(g)}$

$= -787.0 \text{ kJ}$

$\Delta H° = \Delta H_f°(\text{products}) - \Delta H_f°(\text{reactants})$
$= (-787.0 \text{ kJ}) - (-221.0 \text{ kJ}) = -566.0 \text{ kJ}$

78. Multiply the first equation by 2, reverse it, and change the sign of ΔH.

$2\text{PCl}_3(g) + 2\text{Cl}_2(g) \longrightarrow 2\text{PCl}_5(s) \qquad \Delta H = (2)(-87.9 \text{ kJ})$

$2\text{P}(s) + 3\text{Cl}_2(g) \longrightarrow 2\text{PCl}_3(s) \qquad \Delta H = -574 \text{ kJ}$

$\overline{2\text{P}(s) + 5\text{Cl}_2(g) \longrightarrow 2\text{PCl}_5(s) \qquad \Delta H = -750 \text{ kJ}}$

81. $q = 106 \text{ Cal} \times \dfrac{1000 \text{ cal}}{1 \text{ Cal}} = 1.06 \times 10^5 \text{ cal}$

$\Delta T = 100.0°\text{C} - 25.0°\text{C} = 75.0°\text{C}$

$m_{\text{water}} = \dfrac{q}{C_{\text{water}} \times \Delta T} = \dfrac{1.06 \times 10^5 \text{ cal}}{(1.00 \text{ cal/}(g·°\text{C}))(75.0°\text{C})}$

$= 1.41 \times 10^3 \text{ g}$

85. Calculate the grams of ice that melt when 3.20 kcal is absorbed.

$3.20 \text{ kcal} \times \dfrac{4.18 \text{ kJ}}{1 \text{ kcal}} \times \dfrac{1 \text{ mol H}_2\text{O}}{6.01 \text{ kJ}} \times \dfrac{18.0 \text{ g H}_2\text{O}}{1 \text{ mol H}_2\text{O}}$

$= 40.1 \text{ g ice melts}$

The amount of ice remaining is:

$1.0 \text{ kg} - 0.401 \text{ kg} = 0.96 \text{ kg ice} = 9.6 \times 10^2 \text{ g ice}$

89. a. This equation is the original equation multiplied by 2, so multiply ΔH by 2:

$\Delta H = 2 \times (-92.38 \text{ kJ}) = -184.76 \text{ kJ}$

b. This equation is the original equation multiplied by $\dfrac{3}{2}$, so multiply ΔH by $\dfrac{3}{2}$:

$\Delta H = \dfrac{3}{2} \times (-92.38 \text{ kJ}) = -138.6 \text{ kJ}$

c. This equation is the original equation multiplied by $\dfrac{1}{2}$, so multiply ΔH by $\dfrac{1}{2}$:

$\Delta H = \dfrac{1}{2} \times (-92.38 \text{ kJ}) = -46.19 \text{ kJ}$

91. a. Calculate the heat absorbed by the melting ice:

$40.0 \text{ g H}_2\text{O}(l) \times \dfrac{1 \text{ mol H}_2\text{O}(s)}{18.0 \text{ g H}_2\text{O}(s)} \times \dfrac{6.01 \text{ kJ}}{1 \text{ mol H}_2\text{O}(l)}$

$\times \dfrac{1000 \text{ J}}{1 \text{ kJ}} = 1.34 \times 10^4 \text{ J}$

Convert to calories:

$1.34 \times 10^4 \text{ J} \times \dfrac{1 \text{ cal}}{4.18 \text{ J}} = 3.21 \times 10^4 \text{ cal}$

Convert to kilocalories:

$3.21 \times 10^3 \text{ cal} \times \dfrac{1 \text{ kcal}}{1000 \text{ cal}} = 3.21 \text{ kcal}$

b. $m_{\text{water}} = \dfrac{q}{C_{\text{water}} \times \Delta T} = \dfrac{1.34 \times 10^4 \text{ J}}{4.18 \text{ J/(g·°C)} \times (25.0°\text{C})}$

$= 128 \text{ g}$

94. $\Delta H_f°(\text{reactants}) = 1 \text{ mol C}_6\text{H}_{12}\text{O}_6(s) \times$

$\dfrac{-1260 \text{ kJ}}{1 \text{ mol C}_6\text{H}_{12}\text{O}_6(s)} + 6 \text{ mol O}_2(g) \times \dfrac{0 \text{ kJ}}{1 \text{ mol O}_2(g)}$

$= -1260 \text{ kJ}$

$\Delta H_f°(\text{products}) = 6 \text{ mol CO}_2(g) \times \dfrac{-393.5 \text{ kJ}}{1 \text{ mol CO}_2(g)}$

$+ 6 \text{ mol H}_2\text{O}(l) \times \dfrac{-285.8 \text{ kJ}}{1 \text{ mol H}_2\text{O}(l)} = -4075.8 \text{ kJ}$

$\Delta H° = \Delta H_f°(\text{products}) - \Delta H_f°(\text{reactants}) =$
$(-4075.8 \text{ kJ}) - (-1260 \text{ kJ}) = -2820 \text{ kJ}$

97. The heat released as the glass cools equals the heat absorbed by the water.

$q_{\text{glass}} = -q_{\text{water}}$ and $T_{f,\text{glass}} = T_{f,\text{water}} = T_f$, so:

$C_{\text{glass}}m_{\text{glass}}(T_f - T_{i,\text{glass}}) = -C_{\text{water}}m_{\text{water}}(T_f - T_{i,\text{water}})$

$T_f(C_{\text{glass}}m_{\text{glass}} + C_{\text{water}}m_{\text{water}}) = C_{\text{water}}m_{\text{water}}T_{i,\text{water}}$
$+ C_{\text{glass}}m_{\text{glass}}T_{i,\text{glass}}$

$T_f = \dfrac{C_{\text{water}}m_{\text{water}}T_{i,\text{water}} + C_{\text{glass}}m_{\text{glass}}T_{i,\text{glass}}}{C_{\text{glass}}m_{\text{glass}} + C_{\text{water}}m_{\text{water}}} =$

$\dfrac{(1.00 \text{ cal/}(g·°\text{C}))(175 \text{ g})(21°\text{C}) + (2.1 \text{ cal/}(g·°\text{C}))(41.0 \text{ g})(95°\text{C})}{(2.1 \text{ cal/}(g·°\text{C}))(41.0 \text{ g}) + (1.00 \text{ cal/}(g·°\text{C}))(175 \text{ g})}$

$= \dfrac{3700 \text{ cal} + 8200 \text{ cal}}{86 \text{ cal/°C} + 175 \text{ cal/°C}} = \dfrac{11900 \text{ cal}}{261 \text{ cal/°C}} = 45.6°\text{C}$

102. Evaporation is an endothermic process. As the water evaporates, it absorbs heat from the trees and fruit, causing their temperature to decrease. This can lead to the branches, leaves and fruit freezing.

106. **a.** 6.99 m^2 **c.** $3.6 \times 10^2 \text{ m/s}$

  b. 10.68 g **d.** $4.44°\text{C}$

108. $\lambda = \dfrac{c}{v} = \dfrac{2.998 \times 10^8 \text{ m/s}}{93.1 \times 10^6 \text{ s}^{-1}} = 3.22 \text{ m}$

112. **a.** K_3N **c.** $Ca(NO_3)_2$

  b. Al_2S_3 **d.** $CaSO_4$

113. $44.8 \text{ L} \times \dfrac{1 \text{ mol } H_2}{22.4 \text{ L}} \times \dfrac{6.02 \times 10^{23} \text{ H}_2 \text{ molecules}}{1 \text{ mol } H_2}$
$$= 1.20 \times 10^{24} \text{ H}_2 \text{ molecules}$$

115. $N_2(g) + O_2(g) \longrightarrow 2NO(g)$

  $2NO(g) + O_2(g) \longrightarrow 2NO_2(g)$

118. $V_2 = \dfrac{V_1 \times T_2}{T_1} = \dfrac{8.57 \text{ L} \times 355 \text{ K}}{273 \text{ K}} = 11.1 \text{ L}$

Chapter 18

7. $\text{Rate}_1 = 0.5 \text{ mol/(L·s)}$

  $\text{Rate}_2 = x$

  $\dfrac{\text{Rate}_2}{\text{Rate}_1} = \dfrac{x^1}{0.5^1} = \left(\dfrac{1}{2}\right)^1$

  $2x = 0.5 \text{ mol/(L·s)}$

  $x = \dfrac{0.5 \text{ mol/(L·s)}}{2} = 0.25 \text{ mol/(L·s)}$;

  $\dfrac{\text{Rate}_2}{\text{Rate}_1} = \dfrac{x^1}{0.5^1} = \left(\dfrac{1}{4}\right)^1$

  $4x = 0.5 \text{ mol/(L·s)}$

  $x = \dfrac{0.5 \text{ mol/(L·s)}}{4} = 0.125 \text{ mol/(L·s)}$

8. $\text{Rate} = k[A]$

  $k = \dfrac{\text{Rate}}{[A]} = \dfrac{\frac{\text{mol}}{(\text{L·s})}}{\frac{\text{mol}}{\text{L}}} = \dfrac{1}{\text{s}} = \text{s}^{-1}$

17. **a.** favors products **c.** favors reactants

  b. favors reactants **d.** favors reactants

18. **a.** favors reactants **c.** favors products

  b. favors reactants **d.** favors products

19. $K_{eq} = \dfrac{[NH_3]^2}{[N_2][H_2]^3} = \dfrac{(0.10M)^2}{(0.25M) \times (0.15M)^3} = 12$

20. $K_{eq} = \dfrac{[N_2][H_2]^3}{[NH_3]^2} = \dfrac{(0.25M) \times (0.15M)^3}{(0.10M)^2} = 8.4 \times 10^{-2}$;
One is the inverse of the other.

21. $K_{eq} = \dfrac{[NO]^2}{[N_2][O_2]} = \dfrac{(0.02M)^2}{0.50M \times 0.50M} = 1.6 \times 10^{-3}$

22. $0.047 \text{ mol } H_2O \times \dfrac{1 \text{ mol } H_2}{1 \text{ mol } H_2O} = 0.047 \text{ mol } H_2$

  $0.10 - 0.047 = 0.053 \text{ mol } H_2$ at equilibrium
  (mol H_2 = mol CO_2)

  $K_{eq} = \dfrac{[H_2O][CO]}{[H_2][CO_2]} = \dfrac{(0.047M) \times (0.047M)}{(0.053M) \times (0.053M)} = 0.79$

23. $K_{eq} = \dfrac{[N_2O_4]}{[NO_2]^2}$

  $5.6 = \dfrac{0.66M}{[NO_2]^2}$

  $[NO_2]^2 = \dfrac{0.66M}{5.6}$

  $[NO_2] = \sqrt{\dfrac{0.66M}{5.6}} = 0.34M$

24. $[H_2] = [I_2] = 0.50M$;

  $K_{eq} = \dfrac{[H_2][I_2]}{[HI]^2}$

  $0.020 = \dfrac{0.50M \times 0.50M}{[HI]^2}$

  $[HI]^2 = \dfrac{0.50M \times 0.50M}{0.020} = \dfrac{0.25M^2}{0.020} = 12.5M^2$

  $[HI] = \sqrt{12.5M^2} = 3.5M$

33. $K_{sp} = [Pb^{2+}] \times [S^{2-}]$

  $3.0 \times 10^{-28} = [Pb^{2+}]^2$

  $[Pb^{2+}] = \sqrt{3.0 \times 10^{-28}M^2} = 2 \times 10^{-14}M$

34. $K_{sp} = [Ca^{2+}] \times [CO_3^{2-}]$

  $4.5 \times 10^{-9} = [Ca^{2+}]^2$

  $[Ca^{2+}] = \sqrt{4.5 \times 10^{-9}M^2} = 6.7 \times 10^{-5}M$

35. $K_{sp} = [Pb^{2+}] \times [S^{2-}]$

  $[S^{2-}] = \dfrac{K_{sp}}{[Pb^{2+}]} = \dfrac{(8 \times 10^{-19})}{0.04} = 2 \times 10^{-17}M$

36. $K_{sp} = [Sr^{2+}] \times [SO_4^{2-}]$

  $[SO_4^{2-}] = \dfrac{K_{sp}}{[Sr^{2+}]} = \dfrac{(3.2 \times 10^{-7})}{0.10} = 3.2 \times 10^{-6}M$

54. Atoms, ions, or molecules can react to form products, or they can bounce apart unchanged.

58. A catalyst increases the rate of reactions by providing an alternative reaction mechanism with a lower activation energy.

61.

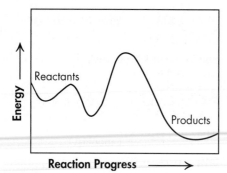

The intermediate is $N_2O_2(g)$.

66. a. $K_{eq} = \dfrac{[CH_4] \times [H_2S]^2}{[H_2]^4 \times [CS_2]}$

    b. $K_{eq} = \dfrac{[PCl_3] \times [Cl_2]}{[PCl_5]}$

71. c, b, d, a

77. a. Entropy increases.   **b.** Entropy decreases.

81. c

85. Since the total energy change for the forward reaction (-20 kJ) is negative, energy is released, and the reaction is exothermic. The reverse reaction is endothermic (energy is absorbed). The reaction progress curve for the reverse reaction is as follows:

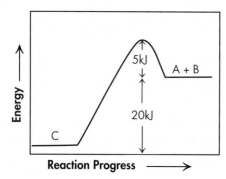

The activation energy of the reverse reaction is the total height of the peak (20 kJ + 5 kJ = 25 kJ).

89. increase in products

91. $K_{eq} = \dfrac{[CO] \times [H_2O]}{[CO_2] \times [H_2]} = \dfrac{0.448 \times 0.448}{0.552 \times 0.552} = 6.59 \times 10^{-1}$

92. The product of the concentrations of the ions must be greater than the ion-product constant (K_{sp}).

97. a. favors products   **c.** favors reactants

    b. no effect   **d.** no effect

100. a. IO^-

    b. two

    c. the slow reaction

    d. $2H_2O_2 \longrightarrow 2H_2O + O_2$

    e. No, the I^- is changed in the reaction. A catalyst would not appear in the reaction as a reactant, an intermediate, or a product.

103. first order in NO_2^-, first order in NH_4^+, second order overall

105. Increase pressure, cool the reaction mixture, and remove NH_3

109. a. about 3 g

    b. about 1.3 g

    c. The rate of decomposition slows down over time.

115. Potassium chloride is an ionic compound, not a molecular compound.

117. a. sodium perchlorate, 1−

    b. potassium permanganate, 1−

    c. calcium phosphate, 3−

    d. magnesium carbonate, 2−

    e. sodium sulfate, 2−

    f. potassium dichromate, 2−

121. a. $2KClO_3(s) + \text{heat} \longrightarrow 2KCl(s) + 3O_2(g)$

    b. molar mass = 39.1 + 35.5 + (3 × 16.0) = 122.6 g

$$4.88 \text{ g } \cancel{KClO_3} \times \frac{1 \text{ mol } \cancel{KClO_3}}{122.6 \text{ g } \cancel{KClO_3}} \times \frac{3 \text{ mol } \cancel{O_2}}{2 \text{ mol } \cancel{KClO_3}}$$
$$\times \frac{32 \text{ g } O_2}{1 \text{ mol } \cancel{O_2}} = 1.91 \text{ g } O_2$$

129. $2.40 \text{ } \cancel{L\ KCl} \times \dfrac{0.66 \text{ mol KCl}}{1 \text{ } \cancel{L\ KCl}} = 1.58 \text{ mol KCl}$

133. The process is exothermic because heat is released.

Chapter 19

1. a. H^+ is the Lewis acid; H_2O is the Lewis base.

    b. $AlCl_3$ is the Lewis acid; Cl^- is the Lewis base.

2. Lewis base; it has a nonbonding pair of electrons that it can donate.

10. a. basic   **c.** acidic

    b. basic   **d.** neutral

11. $[H^+] = \dfrac{K_w}{[OH^-]} = \dfrac{1.0 \times 10^{-14}}{1 \times 10^{-3}M} = 1 \times 10^{-11}M$; basic

12. a. $pH = -\log[H^+] = -\log(0.045M) = 1.35$

    b. $pH = -\log[H^+] = -\log(8.7 \times 10^{-6}M) = 5.06$

    c. $pH = -\log[H^+] = -\log(0.0015M) = 2.82$

    d. $pH = -\log[H^+] = -\log(1.2 \times 10^{-3}M) = 2.92$

13. a. $pH = -\log[H^+] = -\log(1.0 \times 10^{-12}M) = 12$

    b. $pH = -\log[H^+] = -\log(1 \times 10^{-4}M) = 4$

14. a. $pH = -\log[H^+]$

$$5.00 = -\log[H^+]$$
$$-5.00 = \log[H^+]$$
$$[H^+] = 10^{-5.00} = 1.00 \times 10^{-5}M$$

b. $pH = -\log[H^+]$

$12.83 = -\log[H^+]$

$-12.83 = \log[H^+]$

$[H^+] = 10^{-12.83} = 1.48 \times 10^{-13} M$

15. a. $pH = -\log[H^+]$

$4.00 = -\log[H^+]$

$-4.00 = \log[H^+]$

$[H^+] = 10^{-4.00} = 1.00 \times 10^{-4} M$

b. $pH = -\log[H^+]$

$11.55 = -\log[H^+]$

$-11.55 = \log[H^+]$

$[H^+] = 10^{-11.55} = 2.82 \times 10^{-12} M$

16. a. $[H^+] = \dfrac{K_w}{[OH^-]} = \dfrac{1.0 \times 10^{-14}}{4.3 \times 10^{-5} M} = 0.23 \times 10^{-9} M$

$pH = -\log[H^+] = -\log(0.23 \times 10^{-9} M) = 9.64$

b. $[H^+] = \dfrac{K_w}{[OH^-]} = \dfrac{1.0 \times 10^{-14}}{4.5 \times 10^{-11} M} = 0.22 \times 10^{-3} M$

$pH = -\log[H^+] = -\log(0.22 \times 10^{-3} M) = 3.66$

17. a. $[H^+] = \dfrac{K_w}{[OH^-]} = \dfrac{1.0 \times 10^{-14}}{5.0 \times 10^{-9} M} = 0.20 \times 10^{-5} M$

$pH = -\log[H^+] = -\log(0.20 \times 10^{-5} M) = 5.70$

b. $[H^+] = \dfrac{K_w}{[OH^-]} = \dfrac{1.0 \times 10^{-14}}{8.3 \times 10^{-4} M} = 0.12 \times 10^{-10} M$

$pH = -\log[H^+] = -\log(0.12 \times 10^{-10} M) = 10.91$

25. $0.1000 M - 4.2 \times 10^{-3} M = 0.0958 M$

$K_a = \dfrac{(4.2 \times 10^{-3}) \times (4.2 \times 10^{-3})}{(0.0958)} = 1.8 \times 10^{-4}$

26. $0.2000 M - 9.86 \times 10^{-4} M = 0.199 M$

$K_a = \dfrac{(9.86 \times 10^{-4}) \times (9.86 \times 10^{-4})}{(0.199)} = 4.89 \times 10^{-6}$

35. $H_3PO_4(aq) + 3KOH(aq) \longrightarrow K_3PO_4(aq) + 3H_2O(l)$

$1.56 \; \text{mol } H_3PO_4 \times \dfrac{3 \; \text{mol KOH}}{1 \; \text{mol } H_3PO_4} = 4.68 \; \text{mol KOH}$

36. $HNO_3(aq) + NaOH(aq) \longrightarrow NaNO_3(aq) + H_2O(l)$

$0.20 \; \text{mol } HNO_3 \times \dfrac{1 \; \text{mol NaOH}}{1 \; \text{mol } HNO_3} = 0.20 \; \text{mol NaOH}$

37. $25.0 \; \text{mL KOH} \times \dfrac{1.00 \; \text{mol KOH}}{1000 \; \text{mL KOH}} \times \dfrac{1 \; \text{mol HCl}}{1 \; \text{mol KOH}}$

$\times \dfrac{1000 \; \text{mL HCl}}{0.45 \; \text{mol HCl}} = 56 \; \text{mL HCl}$

38. $38.5 \; \text{mL NaOH} \times \dfrac{0.150 \; \text{mol NaOH}}{1000 \; \text{mL NaOH}} \times \dfrac{1 \; \text{mol } H_3PO_4}{3 \; \text{mol NaOH}}$

$= 0.00193 \; \text{mol } H_3PO_4$

$\dfrac{0.00193 \; \text{mol } H_3PO_4}{0.0150 \; \text{L } H_3PO_4} = 0.129 M \; H_3PO_4$

44. a. $HPO_4{}^{2-}(aq) + H^+(aq) \longrightarrow H_2PO_4{}^-(aq)$

b. $H_2PO_4{}^-(aq) + OH^-(aq) \longrightarrow$

$\qquad\qquad\qquad HPO_4{}^{2-}(aq) + H_2O(l)$

45. $HCOO^-(aq) + H^+(aq) \longrightarrow HCOOH(aq)$

52. Acids ionize to give hydrogen ions in aqueous solution. Bases ionize to give hydroxide ions in aqueous solution.

55. a. $2Li(s) + 2H_2O(l) \longrightarrow 2LiOH(aq) + H_2(g)$

b. $Ba(s) + 2H_2O(l) \longrightarrow Ba(OH)_2(s) + H_2(g)$

63. a. $pH = -\log[H^+] = -\log\left(\dfrac{K_w}{[OH^-]}\right)$

$= -\log\left(\dfrac{1 \times 10^{-14}}{1 \times 10^{-2} M}\right) = 12; \; \text{basic}$

b. $pH = -\log[H^+] = -\log(1 \times 10^{-2} M) = 2; \; \text{acidic}$

66. a. strong base   **c.** strong acid

b. weak base   **d.** strong acid

73. a. $NaOH(aq) + HCl(aq) \longrightarrow NaCl(aq) + H_2O(l)$

$28.0 \; \text{mL HCl} \times \dfrac{1 \; \text{L HCl}}{10^3 \; \text{mL HCl}} \times \dfrac{1 \; \text{mol HCl}}{1 \; \text{L HCl}}$

$\times \dfrac{1 \; \text{mol NaOH}}{1 \; \text{mol HCl}} = 0.028 \; \text{mol NaOH}$

$\dfrac{0.028 \; \text{mol NaOH}}{20.0 \; \text{mL}} \times \dfrac{10^3 \; \text{mL}}{1 \; \text{L}} = 1.40 M$

b. $3NaOH(aq) + H_3PO_4(aq) \longrightarrow$

$\qquad\qquad\qquad Na_3PO_4(aq) + 3H_2O(l)$

$17.4 \; \text{mL } H_3PO_4 \times \dfrac{1 \; \text{L } H_3PO_4}{10^3 \; \text{mL } H_3PO_4} \times \dfrac{1 \; \text{mol } H_3PO_4}{1 \; \text{L } H_3PO_4}$

$\times \dfrac{3 \; \text{mol NaOH}}{1 \; \text{mol } H_3PO_4} = 0.0522 \; \text{mol NaOH}$

$\dfrac{0.0522 \; \text{mol NaOH}}{20.0 \; \text{mL}} \times \dfrac{10^3 \; \text{mL}}{1 \; \text{L}} = 2.61 M$

75. $HCO_3{}^-(aq) + H_2O(l) \longrightarrow H_2CO_3(aq) + OH^-(aq)$

81. $HPO_4{}^{2-}(aq) \longrightarrow H^+(aq) + PO_4{}^{3-}(aq)$
(acting as an acid)

$HPO_4{}^{2-}(aq) + H^+(aq) \longrightarrow H_2PO_4{}^-(aq)$
(acting as a base)

85. a. $HClO_2$, chlorous acid

b. H_3O^+, hydronium ion

c. H_3PO_4, phosphoric acid

d. $NH_4{}^+$, ammonium ion

91. a. $2HCl(aq) + Mg(OH)_2(aq) \longrightarrow$

$\qquad\qquad\qquad MgCl_2(aq) + 2H_2O(l)$

b. $2HCl(aq) + CaCO_3(aq) \longrightarrow$

$\qquad\qquad\qquad H_2O(l) + CO_2(g) + CaCl_2(aq)$

c. $3HCl(aq) + Al(OH)_3(aq) \longrightarrow AlCl_3(aq) + 3H_2O(l)$

95. b, c, d, a

100. $HOCN(aq) + OH^-(aq) \longrightarrow H_2O(l) + OCN^-(aq)$

$OCN^-(aq) + H^+(aq) \longrightarrow HOCN(aq)$

101. The y-axis might correspond to [H$^+$] because HCl is a strong acid.

106. pOH $= -\log[\text{OH}^-]$

110. $K_w = K_a K_b = \dfrac{[\text{H}^+][\cancel{\text{A}^-}]}{[\cancel{\text{HA}}]} \times \dfrac{[\cancel{\text{HA}}][\text{OH}^-]}{[\cancel{\text{A}^-}]} = [\text{H}^+][\text{OH}^-]$

113. Rapid breathing releases more CO_2. The shift in equilibrium causes H_2CO_3 and H$^+$ concentrations to decrease. The loss of H$^+$ increases the basicity of the blood and alkalosis results. Slow breathing does not release enough CO_2. The CO_2 buildup increases the H_2CO_3 and H$^+$ concentrations. The H$^+$ concentration increases the acidity of the blood and acidosis results.

118. neutralization; raised

121. liquid

126. hydrogen bond

129. $V_1 = \dfrac{M_2 \times V_2}{M_1} = \dfrac{2.5\cancel{M} \times 1.50\ \text{L}}{8.0\cancel{M}} = 0.47\ \text{L}$

132. a. $34.5\ \cancel{\text{cal}} \times \dfrac{1\ \text{J}}{0.239\ \cancel{\text{cal}}} = 144\ \text{J}$

b. $250\ \cancel{\text{Cal}} \times \dfrac{10^3\ \cancel{\text{cal}}}{1\ \cancel{\text{Cal}}} \times \dfrac{1\ \cancel{\text{J}}}{0.239\ \cancel{\text{cal}}} \times \dfrac{1\ \text{kJ}}{10^3\ \cancel{\text{J}}}$
$$= 1.05 \times 10^3\ \text{kJ}$$

c. $0.347\ \cancel{\text{kJ}} \times \dfrac{10^3\ \cancel{\text{J}}}{1\ \cancel{\text{kJ}}} \times \dfrac{0.239\ \text{cal}}{1\ \cancel{\text{J}}} = 82.9\ \text{cal}$

137. a. NaCl(aq)　　**b.** CO_2(g)　　**c.** hot water

Chapter 20

1. a. Na: oxidized, loses electrons (reducing agent); S: reduced, gains electrons (oxidizing agent)

b. Al: oxidized, loses electrons (reducing agent); O_2: reduced, gains electrons (oxidizing agent)

2. a. oxidation (loss of 1 electron)

b. oxidation (loss of 2 electrons)

c. reduction (gain of 2 electrons)

d. reduction (gain of 2 electrons)

10. a. S, +3; O, −2　　**c.** P, +5; O, −2

b. Na, +1; O, −1　　**d.** N, +5; O, −2

11. a. $\overset{+1+5-2}{\text{KClO}_3}$; +5　　**c.** $\overset{+2\ +7-2}{\text{Ca(ClO}_4)_2}$; +7

b. 0　　**d.** $\overset{+1\ -2}{\text{Cl}_2\text{O}}$; +1

12. a. H_2 is oxidized (0 to +1); O_2 is reduced (0 to −2).

b. N is reduced (+5 to +3); O is oxidized (−2 to 0).

13. a. H_2 is the reducing agent; O_2 is the oxidizing agent.

b. N is the oxidizing agent; O is the reducing agent.

14. a. N in NH$_4$$^+$ is oxidized (−3 to 0); H is unchanged; N in NO$_2$$^-$ is reduced (+3 to 0); O is unchanged.

b. Pb is reduced (+4 to +2); O is unchanged; H is unchanged; I is oxidized (−1 in HI to 0 in I_2).

15. a. N in NH$_4$$^+$ is the reducing agent; N in NO$_2$$^-$ is the oxidizing agent.

b. Pb is the oxidizing agent; I is the reducing agent.

21. a. redox reaction: Mg is oxidized (0 to +2), Br$_2$ is reduced (0 to −1)

b. not a redox reaction

22. a. not a redox reaction

b. redox reaction: H_2 is oxidized (0 to +1), Cu is reduced (+2 to 0)

23. a.
$$\overbrace{\overset{+1+5-2}{\text{KClO}_3}(s) \longrightarrow \overset{+1\ -1}{\text{KCl}}(s) + \overset{0}{\text{O}_2}(g)}$$
$(1)(-6) = -6$　$(3)(+2) = +6$

One K atom must be reduced for every 3 oxygen atoms oxidized.

$\text{KClO}_3(s) \longrightarrow \text{KCl}(s) + \text{O}_2(g)$

Balance by inspection; put the coefficient 3 in front of O_2, and the coefficient 2 in front of $KClO_3$ and KCl:

$2\text{KClO}_3(s) \longrightarrow 2\text{KCl}(s) + 3\text{O}_2(g)$

b. $2\text{HNO}_2(aq) + 2\text{HI}(aq) \longrightarrow$
$$2\text{NO}(g) + \text{I}_2(s) + 2\text{H}_2\text{O}(l)$$

24. a.
$(2)(-3) = -6$
$$\overset{+3\ -2}{\text{Bi}_2\text{S}_3}(s) + \overset{+1+5-2}{\text{HNO}_3}(aq) \longrightarrow$$
$$\overset{+3\ +5-2}{\text{Bi(NO}_3)_3}(aq) + \overset{+2\ -2}{\text{NO}}(g) + \overset{0}{\text{S}}(s) + \overset{+1\ -2}{\text{H}_2\text{O}}(l)$$
$(3)(+2) = +6$

2 N atoms must be reduced for every 3 sulfur atoms oxidized.

$\text{Bi}_2\text{S}_3(s) + 2\text{HNO}_3(aq) \longrightarrow$
$$\text{Bi(NO}_3)_3(aq) + 2\text{NO}(g) + 3\text{S}(s) + \text{H}_2\text{O}(l)$$

Balance by inspection; put the coefficient 2 in front of $Bi(NO_3)_3$, the coefficient 8 in front of HNO_3, and the coefficient 4 in front of H_2O:

$\text{Bi}_2\text{S}_3(s) + 8\text{HNO}_3(aq) \longrightarrow$
$$2\text{Bi(NO}_3)_3(aq) + 2\text{NO}(g) + 3\text{S}(s) + 4\text{H}_2\text{O}(l)$$

b. $\text{SbCl}_5(aq) + 2\text{KI}(aq) \longrightarrow$
$$\text{SbCl}_3(aq) + 2\text{KCl}(aq) + \text{I}_2(s)$$

25. Oxidation half-reaction: $\overset{+2}{Sn^{2+}} \longrightarrow \overset{+4}{Sn^{4+}}$

Reduction half-reaction: $\overset{+6}{Cr_2O_7^{2-}} \longrightarrow \overset{+3}{Cr^{3+}}$

Oxidation: $Sn^{2+}(aq) \longrightarrow Sn^{4+}(aq)$ (atoms balanced)

Reduction: $Cr_2O_7^{2-}(aq) + 14H^+ \longrightarrow$
$$2Cr^{3+}(aq) + 7H_2O(l)$$
(atoms balanced)

Oxidation: $Sn^{2+}(aq) \longrightarrow Sn^{4+}(aq) + 2e^-$
(charges balanced)

Reduction: $Cr_2O_7^{2-}(aq) + 14H^+ + 6e^- \longrightarrow$
$$2Cr^{3+}(aq) + 7H_2O(l)$$
(charges balanced)

Oxidation: $3Sn^{2+}(aq) \longrightarrow 3Sn^{4+}(aq) + 6e^-$

Reduction: $Cr_2O_7^{2-}(aq) + 14H^+ + 6e^- \longrightarrow$
$$2Cr^{3+}(aq) + 7H_2O(l)$$

$3Sn^{2+}(aq) + Cr_2O_7^{2-}(aq) + 14H^+ + \cancel{6e^-} \longrightarrow$
$$3Sn^{4+}(aq) + \cancel{6e^-} + 2Cr^{3+}(aq) + 7H_2O(l)$$

$3Sn^{2+}(aq) + Cr_2O_7^{2-}(aq) + 14H^+ \longrightarrow$
$$3Sn^{4+}(aq) + 2Cr^{3+}(aq) + 7H_2O(l)$$

26. $Zn(s) + NO_3^-(aq) + H_2O(l) + OH^-(aq) \longrightarrow$
$$Zn^{2+} + OH^-(aq) + NH_3(aq)$$

Oxidation half-reaction: $\overset{0}{Zn} \longrightarrow \overset{+2}{Zn^{2+}}$

Reduction half-reaction: $\overset{+5}{NO_3^-} \longrightarrow \overset{-3}{NH_3}$

Oxidation: $Zn(s) \longrightarrow Zn^{2+}(aq)$ (atoms balanced)

Reduction: $NO_3^-(aq) + 6H_2O(l) \longrightarrow$
$$NH_3(aq) + 9OH^-(aq)$$
(atoms balanced)

Oxidation: $Zn(s) \longrightarrow Zn^{2+}(aq) + 2e^-$
(charges balanced)

Reduction: $NO_3^-(aq) + 6H_2O(l) + 8e^- \longrightarrow$
$$NH_3(aq) + 9OH^-(aq)$$
(charges balanced)

Oxidation: $Zn(s) \longrightarrow Zn^{2+}(aq) + 2e^-$
(charges balanced)

Reduction: $NO_3^-(aq) + 6H_2O(l) + 8e^- \longrightarrow$
$$NH_3(aq) + 9OH^-(aq)$$
(charges balanced)

Oxidation: $4Zn(s) \longrightarrow 4Zn^{2+}(aq) + 8e^-$
(charges balanced)

Reduction: $NO_3^-(aq) + 6H_2O(l) + 8e^- \longrightarrow$
$$NH_3(aq) + 9OH^-(aq)$$
(charges balanced)

$4Zn(s) + NO_3^-(aq) + 6H_2O(l) + \cancel{8e^-} \longrightarrow$
$$4Zn^{2+}(aq) + \cancel{8e^-} + NH_3(aq) + 9OH^-(aq)$$

$4Zn(s) + NO_3^-(aq) + 6H_2O(l) \longrightarrow$
$$4Zn^{2+}(aq) + NH_3(aq) + 9OH^-(aq)$$

$4Zn(s) + NO_3^-(aq) + 6H_2O(l) + 16OH^-(aq) \longrightarrow$
$$4Zn^{2+}(aq) + NH_3(aq) + 9OH^-(aq) + 16OH^-(aq)$$
(spectator ions added)

$4Zn(s) + NO_3^-(aq) + 6H_2O(l) + 16OH^-(aq) \longrightarrow$
$$4Zn(OH)_4^{2-}(aq) + NH_3(aq) + 9OH^-(aq)$$

$4Zn(s) + NO_3^-(aq) + 6H_2O(l) + 7OH^-(aq) \longrightarrow$
$$4Zn(OH)_4^{2-}(aq) + NH_3(aq)$$

34. a. $2Ba(s) + O_2(g) \longrightarrow 2BaO(s)$; barium is oxidized

b. $CuO(s) + H_2(g) \longrightarrow Cu(s) + H_2O(l)$; copper is reduced

c. $C_2H_4(g) + 3O_2(g) \longrightarrow 2CO_2(g) + 2H_2O(l)$; carbon is oxidized

d. $3CaO(s) + 2Al(s) \longrightarrow Al_2O_3(s) + 3Ca(s)$; calcium is reduced

36. a. oxidizing agent **c.** oxidizing agent

b. reducing agent **d.** oxidizing agent

37. a. H_2 is oxidized; S is reduced.

b. N_2 is reduced; H_2 is oxidized.

c. S is oxidized; O_2 is reduced.

d. H_2 is oxidized; O_2 is reduced.

42. a. O, -2; H, $+1$ **d.** H, $+1$; P, $+5$; O, -2

b. P, $+5$; O, -2 **e.** H, $+1$; S, $+6$; O, -2

c. I, $+5$; O, -2

44. a. $2Al(s) + 3Cl_2(g) \longrightarrow 2AlCl_3(s)$

b. $2Al(s) + Fe_2O_3(s) \longrightarrow Al_2O_3(s) + 2Fe(s)$

c. $3Cl_2(g) + 6KOH(aq) \longrightarrow$
$$KClO_3(aq) + 5KCl(aq) + 3H_2O(l)$$

d. $2HNO_3(aq) + 3H_2S(aq) \longrightarrow$
$$3S(s) + 2NO(g) + 4H_2O(l)$$

e. $KIO_4(aq) + 7KI(aq) + 8HCl(aq) \longrightarrow$
$$8KCl(aq) + 4I_2(s) + 4H_2O(l)$$

45. redox: a, b, c, d, e

46. a. $CuS(s) + 8NO_3^-(aq) + 8H^+(aq) \longrightarrow$
$$Cu(NO_3)_2(aq) + SO_2(g) + 6NO_2(g) + 4H_2O(l)$$

b. $6I^-(aq) + 2NO_3^-(aq) + 8H^+(aq) \longrightarrow$
$$3I_2(s) + 2NO(g) + 4H_2O(l)$$

47. a. $4MnO_4^-(aq) + 3ClO_2^-(aq) + 2H_2O(l) \longrightarrow$
$$4MnO_2(s) + 3ClO_4^-(aq) + 4OH^-(aq)$$

b. $2Cr^{3+}(aq) + 3ClO^-(aq) + 10OH^-(aq) \longrightarrow$
$$2CrO_4^{2-}(aq) + 3Cl^-(aq) + 5H_2O(l)$$

c. $6Mn^{3+}(aq) + I^-(aq) + 6OH^-(aq) \longrightarrow$
$$6Mn^{2+}(aq) + IO_3^-(aq) + 3H_2O(l)$$

50. a. $+4$ **b.** $+5$ **c.** $+5$ **d.** $+3$ **e.** $+5$ **f.** $+3$

54. a. $16H^+(aq) + 2Cr_2O_7^{2-}(aq) + C_2H_5OH(aq) \longrightarrow$
$$4Cr^{3+}(aq) + 2CO_2(g) + 11H_2O(l)$$

b. oxidizing agent

59. a. $Ba(ClO_3)_2(s) \longrightarrow BaCl_2(s) + 3O_2(g)$

b. $2PbS(s) + 3O_2(g) \longrightarrow 2PbO(s) + 2SO_2(g)$

63. $1s^2 2s^2 2p^6 3s^2 3p^5$; a chlorine atom can "lose" its 7 valence electrons or it can gain 1 electron to fill the last $3p$ orbital.

66. In every redox reaction one species loses one or more electrons and is a reducing agent. Another substance gains one or more electrons and is an oxidizing agent.

70. a. $Rb(s) + I_2(s) \longrightarrow RbI_2(s)$; oxidizing agent is I

b. $Ba(s) + 2H_2O(l) \longrightarrow Ba(OH)_2(aq) + H_2(g)$; oxidizing agent is H

c. $2Al(s) + 3FeSO_4(aq) \longrightarrow Al_2(SO_4)_3(aq) + 3Fe(s)$; oxidizing agent is Fe

d. $C_4H_8(g) + 6O_2(g) \longrightarrow 4CO_2(g) + 4H_2O(l)$; oxidizing agent is O

e. $Zn(s) + 2HBr(aq) \longrightarrow ZnBr_2(aq) + H_2(g)$; oxidizing agent is H

f. $Mg(s) + Br_2(l) \longrightarrow MgBr_2(s)$, oxidizing agent is Br

73. $2AgNO_3(aq) + Cu(s) \longrightarrow Cu(NO_3)_2(aq) + 2Ag(s)$

$$85.0 \text{ mL} \times \frac{1 \text{ L}}{1000 \text{ mL}} \times \frac{0.150 \text{ mol AgNO}_3}{1 \text{ L AgNO}_3}$$

$$\times \frac{1 \text{ mol Cu}}{2 \text{ mol AgNO}_3} \times \frac{63.5 \text{ g Cu}}{1 \text{ mol Cu}} = 0.405 \text{ g Cu}$$

80. a. $Cr_2O_7{}^{2-}(aq) + 14H^+ + 6e^- \longrightarrow$
$$2Cr^{3+}(aq) + 7H_2O(l)$$
$Cr_2O_7{}^{2-}$ is an oxidizing agent.

b. $S_2O_3{}^{2-}(aq) + 5H_2O(l) \longrightarrow$
$$2SO_4{}^{2-}(aq) + 10H^+ + 8e^-$$
$S_2O_3{}^{2-}$ is a reducing agent.

c. $CrO_4{}^{2-}(aq) + 4H_2O(l) + 3e^- \longrightarrow$
$$Cr(OH)_3(aq) + 5OH^-(aq)$$
$CrO_4{}^{2-}$ is an oxidizing agent.

d. $MnO_4{}^-(aq) + 8H^+ + 5e^- \longrightarrow$
$$Mn^{2+}(aq) + 4H_2O(l)$$
$MnO_4{}^-$ is an oxidizing agent.

e. $C_2O_4{}^{2-}(aq) \longrightarrow 2CO_2(g) + 2e^-$
$C_2O_4{}^{2-}$ is a reducing agent.

f. $2H_2O(l) + MnO_4{}^-(aq) + 3e^- \longrightarrow$
$$MnO_2(s) + 4OH^-(aq)$$
$MnO_4{}^-$ is an oxidizing agent.

86. a.

Alkane burned	O_2 used (mol)	CO_2 produced (mol)	H_2O produced (mol)
CH_4	2	1	2
C_2H_6	3.5	2	3
C_3H_8	5	3	4
C_4H_{10}	6.5	4	5
C_5H_{12}	8	5	6
C_6H_{14}	9.5	6	7

b. $C_xH_y + [x + (y/4)]O_2 \longrightarrow xCO_2 + (y/2)H_2O$

88. $T = 25°C + 273 = 298 \text{ K}$

$$P = \frac{n \times R \times T}{V}$$

$$= \frac{\left(13.8 \text{ g N}_2 \times \frac{1 \text{ mol N}_2}{28.0 \text{ g N}_2}\right) \times 8.31\left(\frac{\text{L} \cdot \text{kPa}}{\text{K} \cdot \text{mol}}\right) \times 298 \text{ K}}{6.8 \text{ L}}$$

$$= 1.8 \times 10^2 \text{ kPa}$$

91. $V_2 = \dfrac{M_1 \times V_1}{M_2} = \dfrac{1.5 M \text{ HCl} \times 440 \text{ mL HCl}}{6.0 M \text{ HCl}}$
$= 110 \text{ mL } 6.0 M \text{ HCl}$

Dilute 110 mL of $6.0M$ HCl to 440 mL total volume.

94. $PbBr_2(s) \longrightarrow Pb^{2+} + 2Br^-$

$K_{sp} = [Pb^{2+}][Br^-] = 2.1 \times 10^{-6}$

Let $x = [Pb^{2+}]$.

Then $2x = [Br^-]$.

$(x)(2x)^2 = 2.1 \times 10^{-6}$

$4x^3 = 2.1 \times 10^{-6}$

$x = [Pb^{2+}] = 8.1 \times 10^{-3}$

The solubility of $PbBr_2$ is $8.1 \times 10^{-3}M$.

100. a. $pH = -\log[H^+] = -\log(0.000010) = -\log(10^{-5})$
$= 5.00$ (acidic)

b. $[H^+] = \dfrac{K_w}{[OH^-]} = \dfrac{1.0 \times 10^{-14}M^2}{1 \times 10^{-4}M} = 1.0 \times 10^{-10}M$

$pH = -\log[H^+] = -\log(1.0 \times 10^{-10}M)$
$= 10.00$ (basic)

c. $[H^+] = \dfrac{K_w}{[OH^-]} = \dfrac{1.0 \times 10^{-14}M^2}{1 \times 10^{-1}M} = 1.0 \times 10^{-13}M$

$pH = -\log[H^+] = -\log(1.0 \times 10^{-13}M)$
$= 13.00$ (basic)

d. $pH = -\log[H^+] = -\log(3.0 \times 10^{-7})$
$= 6.50$ (acidic)

Chapter 21

8. The half-reactions are
Oxidation: $Cr(s) \longrightarrow Cr^{3+}(aq) + 3e^-$
Reduction: $Zn^{2+}(aq) + 2e^- \longrightarrow Zn(s)$
Writing both half-cells as reductions:
$Cr^{3+}(aq) + 3e^- \longrightarrow Cr(s) \qquad E°_{Cr^{3+}} = -0.74 \text{ V}$
$Zn^{2+}(aq) + 2e^- \longrightarrow Zn(s) \qquad E°_{Zn^{2+}} = -0.76 \text{ V}$
$E°_{cell} = E°_{red} - E°_{oxid} = E°_{Zn^{2+}} - E°_{Cr^{3+}}$
$= -0.76 \text{ V} - (-0.74 \text{ V}) = -0.02 \text{ V}$
$E°_{cell} < 0$, so the reaction is not spontaneous.

9. The half-reactions are

Oxidation: $Fe(s) \longrightarrow Fe^{2+}(aq) + 2e^-$

Reduction: $Co^{2+}(aq) + 2e^- \longrightarrow Co(s)$

Writing both half-cells as reductions:

$Fe^{2+}(aq) + 2e^- \longrightarrow Fe(s) \qquad E°_{Fe^{2+}} = -0.44 \text{ V}$

$Co^{2+}(aq) + 2e^- \longrightarrow Co(s) \qquad E°_{Co^{2+}} = -0.28 \text{ V}$

$E°_{cell} = E°_{red} - E°_{oxid} = E°_{Co^{2+}} - E°_{Fe^{2+}}$

$= -0.28 \text{ V} - (-0.44 \text{ V}) = +0.16 \text{ V}$

$E°_{cell} > 0$, so the reaction is spontaneous.

10. Cu^{2+} is reduced, and Al is oxidized.

Oxidation: $Al(s) \longrightarrow Al^{3+}(aq) + 3e^-$

Reduction: $Cu^{2+}(aq) + 2e^- \longrightarrow Cu(s)$

Writing both half-cells as reductions:

$2[Al(s) \longrightarrow Al^{3+}(aq) + 3e^-]$

$3[Cu^{2+}(aq) + 2e^- \longrightarrow Cu(s)]$

$2Al(s) \longrightarrow 2Al^{3+}(aq) + \cancel{6e^-}$

$3Cu^{2+}(aq) + \cancel{6e^-} \longrightarrow 3Cu(s)$

$2Al(s) + 3Cu^{2+}(aq) \longrightarrow 2Al^{3+}(aq) + 3Cu(s)$

11. Ag^+ is reduced, and Cu is oxidized.

The half-reactions are

Oxidation: $Cu(s) \longrightarrow Cu^{2+}(aq) + 2e^-$

Reduction: $Ag^+(aq) + e^- \longrightarrow Ag(s)$

Writing both half-cells as reductions:

$Cu(s) \longrightarrow Cu^{2+}(aq) + 2e^-$

$2[Ag^+(aq) + e^- \longrightarrow Ag(s)]$

$Cu(s) \longrightarrow Cu^{2+}(aq) + \cancel{2e^-}$

$2Ag^{2+}(aq) + \cancel{2e^-} \longrightarrow 2Ag(s)$

$Cu(s) + 2Ag^{2+}(aq) \longrightarrow Cu^{2+}(aq) + 2Ag(s)$

12. $E°_{cell} = E°_{red} - E°_{oxid} = E°_{Cu^{2+}} - E°_{Al^{3+}}$

$= 0.34 \text{ V} - (-1.66 \text{ V}) = +2.00 \text{ V}$

13. $E°_{cell} = E°_{red} - E°_{oxid} = E°_{Ag^+} - E°_{Cu^{2+}}$

$= 0.80 \text{ V} - (+0.34 \text{ V}) = +0.46 \text{ V}$

28. Using Table 21.1, the more active element is the most readily oxidized.

a. Cu **b.** Ca **c.** Mg **d.** Sn **e.** Zn **f.** Al

33. A zinc container (anode) filled with electrolyte paste; the cathode is a graphite rod embedded in the paste; Zn is oxidized; MnO_2 is reduced.

36. $Pb(s) \mid PbSO_4(aq) \parallel PbO_2(s) \mid PbSO_4(s)$

40. The standard reduction potential of a half-cell is a measure of the tendency of a given half-reaction to occur as a reduction under standard conditions. The difference between the standard reduction potentials of the two half-cells is called the standard cell potential.

44. a. Cu is oxidized, and H^+ is reduced.

Writing both half-reactions as reductions:

$Cu(s) \longrightarrow Cu^{2+}(aq) + 2e^- \qquad E°_{Cu^{2+}} = +0.34 \text{ V}$

$2H^+(aq) + 2e^- \longrightarrow H_2(g) \qquad E°_{H^+} = 0.000 \text{ V}$

$E°_{cell} = E°_{red} - E°_{oxid} = E°_{H^+} - E°_{Cu^{2+}}$

$= 0.000 \text{ V} - (+0.34 \text{ V}) = -0.34 \text{ V}$

$E°_{cell} < 0$, so the reaction will not occur spontaneously.

b. Ag is oxidized, and Fe^{2+} is reduced.

Writing both half-reactions as reductions:

$Ag(s) \longrightarrow Ag^+(aq) + e^- \qquad E°_{Ag^+} = +0.80 \text{ V}$

$Fe^{2+}(aq) + 2e^- \longrightarrow Fe(s) \qquad E°_{Fe^{2+}} = -0.44 \text{ V}$

$E°_{cell} = E°_{red} - E°_{oxid} = E°_{Fe^{2+}} - E°_{Ag^+}$

$= -0.44 \text{ V} - (+0.80 \text{ V}) = -1.24 \text{ V}$

$E°_{cell} < 0$, so the reaction will not occur spontaneously.

46. Voltaic cells convert chemical energy into electrical energy. Electrolytic cells use electrical energy to cause a chemical reaction.

50. Chloride ions are oxidized to produce chlorine gas, and water is reduced to produce hydrogen gas.

55. The iron nail will become copper-plated as Fe is oxidized to Fe^{2+} and Cu^{2+} is reduced to Cu.

Oxidation: $Fe(s) \longrightarrow Fe^{2+}(aq) + \cancel{2e^-}$

Reduction: $Cu^{2+}(aq) + \cancel{2e^-} \longrightarrow Cu(s)$

Overall cell reaction:

$Fe(s) + Cu^{2+}(aq) \longrightarrow Fe^{2+}(aq) + Cu(s)$

57. a. $Sn(s) + Pb^{2+}(aq) \longrightarrow Sn^{2+}(aq) + Pb(s)$

Oxidation: $Sn(s) \longrightarrow Sn^{2+}(aq) + \cancel{2e^-}$

Reduction: $Pb^{2+}(aq) + \cancel{2e^-} \longrightarrow Pb(s)$

Overall cell reaction:

$Sn(s) + Pb^{2+}(aq) \longrightarrow Sn^{2+}(aq) + Pb(s)$

$E°_{cell} = E°_{red} - E°_{oxid} = E°_{Pb^{2+}} - E°_{Sn^{2+}}$

$= -0.13 \text{ V} - (-0.14 \text{ V}) = +0.01 \text{ V}$

b. $H_2(g) + Br_2(l) \longrightarrow 2H^+(aq) + 2Br^-(aq)$

Oxidation: $H_2(g) \longrightarrow 2H^+(aq) + \cancel{2e^-}$

Reduction: $Br_2(l) + \cancel{2e^-} \longrightarrow 2Br^-(aq)$

Overall cell reaction:

$H_2(g) + Br_2(l) \longrightarrow 2H^+(aq) + 2Br^-(aq)$

$E°_{cell} = E°_{red} - E°_{oxid} = E°_{Br^-} - E°_{H^+}$

$= +1.07 \text{ V} - 0.00 \text{ V} = +1.07 \text{ V}$

60. If the cell potential for a redox reaction is positive, the reaction is spontaneous as written.

62. **a.** oxidation: $2Cl^-(l) \longrightarrow Cl_2(g) + 2e^-$ (at anode)

reduction: $Al^{3+}(l) + 3e^- \longrightarrow Al(l)$ (at cathode)

b. Multiply the oxidation half-reaction by 3 and the reduction half-reaction by 2 to balance the electrons:

$6Cl^-(l) \longrightarrow 3Cl_2(g) + \cancel{6e^-}$

$2Al^{3+}(l) + \cancel{6e^-} \longrightarrow 2Al(l)$

Overall cell reaction:

$2AlCl_3(l) \longrightarrow 2Al(l) + 3Cl_2(g)$

c. Chlorine gas is produced at the anode. Liquid aluminum is produced at the cathode.

68. **a.** Possible oxidation reactions at anode:

(i) $2Cl^-(aq) \longrightarrow Cl_2(g) + 2e^-$

(ii) $2H_2O(l) \longrightarrow O_2(g) + 4H^+(aq) + 4e^-$

b. Possible reduction reactions at cathode:

(i) $Na^+(aq) + e^- \longrightarrow Na(s)$

(ii) $2H_2O(l) + 2e^- \longrightarrow H_2(g) + 2OH^-(aq)$

c. (i) Chloride ions are more readily oxidized to chlorine gas than water molecules are oxidized to oxygen.

d. (ii) Water molecules are more easily reduced than sodium ions.

69. The stronger oxidizing agent will have the more positive standard reduction potential ($E°$).

a. Ca^{2+} **b.** Hg_2^{2+} **c.** Cu^+ **d.** Hg^{2+}

71. A direct current flows in one direction only. If an alternating current is used, the reactions at the anode and cathode would constantly be reversed.

73. The cathode reaction in a dry cell is not reversible, so dry cells are not rechargeable. The anode and cathode reactions in a lead storage battery are reversible. Therefore, lead storage batteries are rechargeable when electrical energy is applied.

75. The spoon is being electroplated with silver in an electrolytic cell. The spoon serves as the cathode, and the anode is metallic silver. The electrolyte is a solution of silver cyanide. When a direct current is applied, silver ions move from the anode to the spoon, where they are reduced to silver metal.

79. d; the voltage of a dry cell decreases steadily.

80. **a.** The standard reduction potential for AgCl (+0.22 V) is more positive than the standard reduction potential for Ni^{2+} (−0.25 V), so AgCl is reduced and Ni is oxidized.

Oxidation: $Ni(s) \longrightarrow Ni^{2+}(aq) + 2e^-$

Reduction: $2[AgCl(s) + e^- \longrightarrow Ag(s) + Cl^-(aq)]$

Overall cell reaction:

$Ni(s) + 2AgCl(s) \longrightarrow 2Ag(s) + NiCl_2(aq)$

$E°_{cell} = E°_{red} - E°_{oxid} = E°_{AgCl} - E°_{Ni^{2+}}$

$= +0.22 \text{ V} - (-0.25 \text{ V}) = +0.47 \text{ V}$

b. The standard reduction potential for Cl^- (+1.36 V) is more positive than the standard reduction potential for Al^{3+} (−1.66 V), so Cl^- is reduced and Al^{3+} is oxidized.

Oxidation: $2[Al(s) \longrightarrow Al^{3+}(aq) + 3e^-]$

Reduction: $3[Cl_2(g) + 2e^- \longrightarrow 2Cl^-(aq)]$

Overall cell reaction:

$2Al(s) + 3Cl_2(s) \longrightarrow 2AlCl_3(s)$

$E°_{cell} = E°_{red} - E°_{oxid} = E°_{Cl^-} - E°_{Al^{3+}}$

$= +1.36 \text{ V} - (-1.66 \text{ V}) = +3.02 \text{ V}$

84. The battery output would not be 12 V.

88. Connect the positive electrode of the power source to the gold object and the negative electrode to another metal. The gold object will then serve as the anode and the gold will be oxidized.

91. $T_1 = 30°C + 273 = 303 \text{ K}$

$T_2 = 60°C + 273 = 333 \text{ K}$

$V_2 = \dfrac{V_1 \times T_2}{T_1} = \dfrac{425 \text{ mL} \times 333 \text{ K}}{303 \text{ K}} = 467 \text{ mL}$

93. **a.** $250 \cancel{\text{ g}} \times \dfrac{0.90 \text{ g NaCl}}{100 \cancel{\text{ g}}} = 2.3 \text{ g NaCl}$

b. $500 \cancel{\text{ mL}} \times \dfrac{1 \cancel{\text{ L}}}{1000 \cancel{\text{ mL}}} \times \dfrac{2 \cancel{\text{ mol KNO}_3}}{1 \cancel{\text{ L}}}$

$\times \dfrac{101.1 \text{ g KNO}_3}{1 \cancel{\text{ mol KNO}_3}} = 101 \text{ g KNO}_3$

97. $4.80 \cancel{\text{ g CH}_4} \times \dfrac{1 \cancel{\text{ mol CH}_4}}{16.0 \cancel{\text{ g CH}_4}} \times \dfrac{-890 \text{ kJ}}{1 \cancel{\text{ mol CH}_4}} = -267 \text{ kJ}$

98. a and c; $K_{eq} < 1$

100. **a.** $pH = -\log[H^+] = -\log(1.0 \times 10^{-8}M) = 8.00$

b. $pH = -\log[H^+] = -\log(0.000010M) = 5.00$

c. $[H^+] = \dfrac{K_w}{[OH^-]} = \dfrac{1.0 \times 10^{-14}}{1.0 \times 10^{-4}M} = 1.0 \times 10^{-10}M$

$pH = -\log[H^+] = -\log(1.0 \times 10^{-10}M) = 10.00$

d. $[H^+] = \dfrac{K_w}{[OH^-]} = \dfrac{1.0 \times 10^{-14}}{1.0 \times 10^{-9}M} = 1.0 \times 10^{-5}M$

$pH = -\log[H^+] = -\log(1.0 \times 10^{-5}M) = 5.00$

103. **a.** +6   **b.** −2   **c.** +4   **d.** +2   **e.** 0   **f.** +4

105. b; Ca is oxidized to Ca^{2+}, and Cl_2 is reduced to Cl^-.

c; Ca is oxidized to Ca^{2+}, and H^+ is reduced to H_2.

Chapter 22

1.

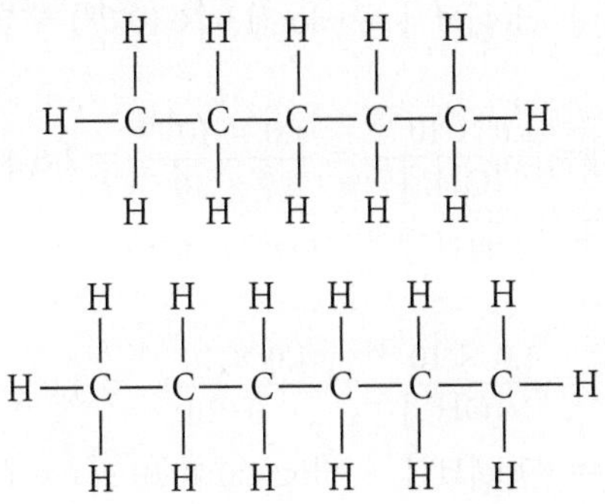

2. 10 single bonds

3. a. 3-ethylhexane   **b.** 2-methylbutane

4. 4-ethyl-2-methylheptane

5.

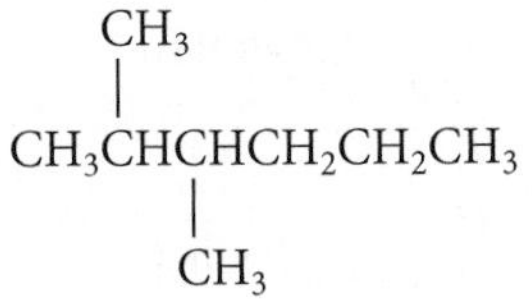

6.

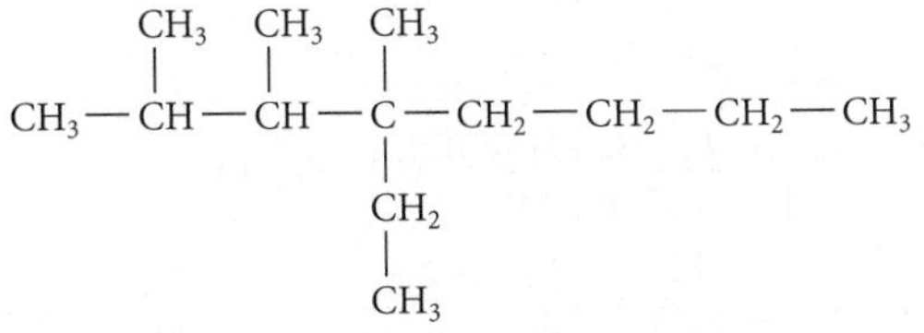

19. a.

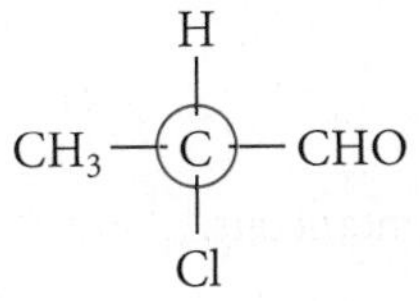

    b. no asymmetric carbon

20. a.

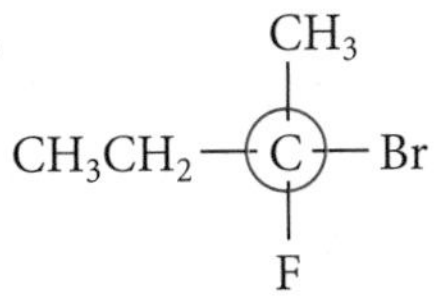

    b. no asymmetric carbon

42. pentane: $CH_3CH_2CH_2CH_2CH_3$
hexane: $CH_3CH_2CH_2CH_2CH_2CH_3$

45. a. 2-methylbutane

    b. 2,3-dimethylbutane

    c. 3-methylhexane

47. a. unsaturated, because there is a double carbon-carbon bond

    b. saturated, because the compound contains the maximum number of hydrogen atoms per carbon atom

52. No, only molecules with at least one asymmetric carbon can have enantiomers.

55. a.

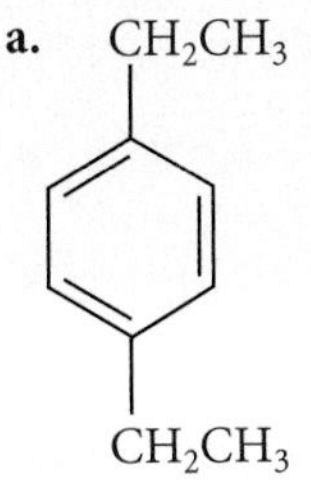

    c.

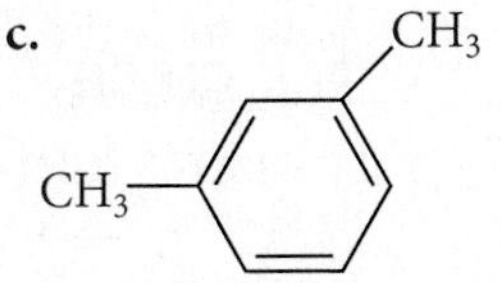

    b.

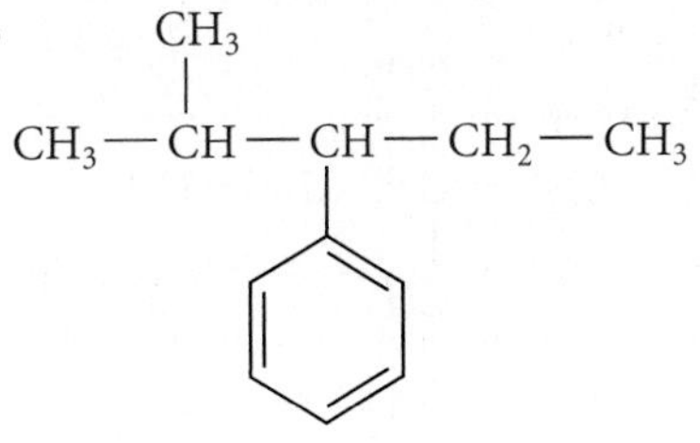

58. The combustion of sulfur in coal produces the air pollutants SO_2 and SO_3.

60. a. Ethyne (acetylene) has one triple carbon-carbon bond and two single carbon-hydrogen bonds.

    b. In methylbenzene, there are hybrid bonds within the ring. All other bonds are single bonds.

    c. All the bonds in propane are single bonds.

62. propane, butane, pentane

66. The middle structure is most stable due to resonance within the ring.

68. No, the structures are identical; one has been flipped over.

71. a. 4   **b.** 2   **c.** 3   **d.** 1

72. The amount of heat per carbon is higher for methane (-890 kJ/mol of carbon burned) than for benzene ($-3268 \div 6$ carbons $= -545$ kJ/mol of carbon burned). Burning aromatic compounds produces more soot.

76. $CH_2{=}C{=}CH_2$

78. a. $CH_3-CH_2-\underset{\underset{CH_3}{|}}{C}=\underset{\underset{CH_3}{|}}{C}-CH_2-CH_3$

b.

c.

82. a.

$$CH_3CH_2CH_2CH_2CH_3 \rightleftharpoons CH_3\underset{\underset{CH_3}{|}}{C}HCH_2CH_3$$

b. constitutional

c. 2-methylbutane

86. a. $C_6 = 5$, $C_7 = 9$, $C_8 = 18$, $C_9 = 35$, $C_{10} = 75$

b. As the size of the alkane molecule gets larger, the number of different ways that the carbon atoms can be bonded together (to form constitutional isomers) increases dramatically.

90. No, enantiomers have identical physical properties.

92. a. $6.20 \times 10^{-1} \text{ mol Cl}_2 \times \dfrac{22.4 \text{ L}}{1 \text{ mol Cl}_2} = 13.9 \text{ L}$

b. $V_2 = \dfrac{P_1 \times V_1}{P_2} = \dfrac{0.5 \text{ kPa} \times 6 \text{ L}}{3 \text{ kPa}} = 1 \text{ L}$

c. $P_X + P_Y + P_Z = P_{\text{total}}$
$P_X + 30 \text{ kPa} = 50 \text{ kPa}$
$P_X + 30 \text{ kPa} - 30 \text{ kPa} = 50 \text{kPa} - 30\text{kPa}$
$P_X = 20 \text{ kPa}$

93. $750 \text{ mL KNO}_3 \times \dfrac{1 \text{ L KNO}_3}{1000 \text{ mL KNO}_3} \times \dfrac{1.50 \text{ mol KNO}_3}{1 \text{ L KNO}_3}$
$= 1.13 \text{ mol KNO}_3$;

$1.13 \text{ mol KNO}_3 \times \dfrac{101.1 \text{ g KNO}_3}{1.000 \text{ mol KNO}_3} = 114 \text{ g KNO}_3$

98. a. favors reactants   **b.** favors products

100. a. $[H^+] = \dfrac{1.0 \times 10^{-14}}{[OH^-]} = \dfrac{1.0 \times 10^{-14}}{1.0 \times 10^{-4}} = 1.0 \times 10^{-10} M$

pH $= -\log[H^+] = -\log(1.0 \times 10^{-10}) = 10.00$

b. $[H^+] = \dfrac{1.0 \times 10^{-14}}{[OH^-]} = \dfrac{1.0 \times 10^{-14}}{3.9 \times 10^{-7}} = 2.6 \times 10^{-8} M$

pH $= -\log[H^+] = -\log(2.6 \times 10^{-8}) = 7.59$

c. $[H^+] = \dfrac{1.0 \times 10^{-14}}{[OH^-]} = \dfrac{1.0 \times 10^{-14}}{0.010} = 1.0 \times 10^{-12} M$

pH $= -\log[H^+] = -\log(1.0 \times 10^{-12}) = 12.00$

d. $[H^+] = \dfrac{1.0 \times 10^{-14}}{[OH^-]} = \dfrac{1.0 \times 10^{-14}}{5.0 \times 10^{-3}} = 2.0 \times 10^{-12} M$

pH $= -\log[H^+] = -\log(2.0 \times 10^{-12}) = 11.70$

102. a. H_3PO_4 **c.** H_2CO_3
b. $CsOH$ **d.** $Be(OH)_2$

104. a. $2 + C + 3(-2) = 0$
$-4 + C = 0$
$C = +4$
Ca, $+2$; C, $+4$; O, -2

b. Cl, 0

c. $1 + I + 3(-2) = 0$
$I - 5 = 0$
$I = +5$
Li, $+1$; I, $+5$; O, -2

d. $2(+1) + S + 3(-2) = 0$
$S - 4 = 0$
$S = +4$
Na, $+1$; S, $+4$; O, -2

110. The reaction is nonspontaneous.

Chapter 23

33. a.

$ClCH_2\underset{\underset{Cl}{|}}{\overset{\overset{Cl}{|}}{C}}CH_2CH_3$

c.

b.

37. a. 2-propanol

b. 1,2-propanediol

c. 2-methyl-2-propanol

38. a.

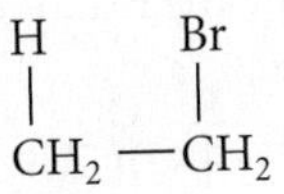

$$CH_2\!-\!CH_2$$
with H and Br above

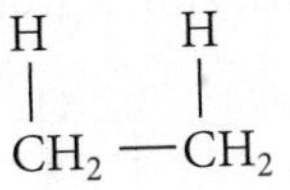

bromoethane

b.

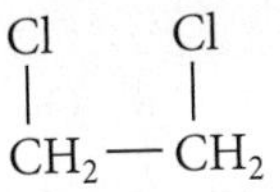

$$CH_2\!-\!CH_2$$
with Cl and Cl above

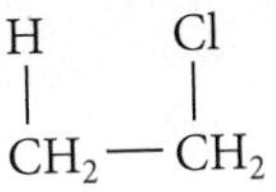

1,2–dichloroethane

c.

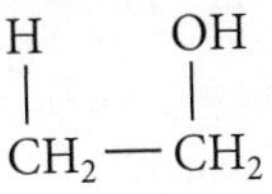

$$CH_2\!-\!CH_2$$
with H and OH above

ethanol

d.

$$CH_2\!-\!CH_2$$
with H and H above

ethane

e.

$$CH_2\!-\!CH_2$$
with H and Cl above

chloroethane

42. a. propanone
b. ethanal
c. 3-methylbutanal
d. 3-hexanone
e. 2-phenylethanal
f. pentanoic acid

45. a. 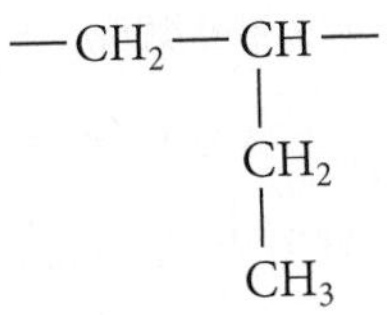
$$-CH_2\!-\!CH\!-$$
with CH_2 and CH_3 below

b. 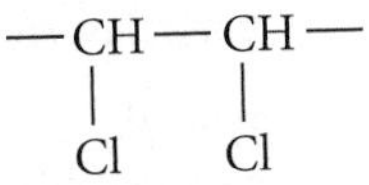
$$-CH\!-\!CH\!-$$
with Cl and Cl below

50. a. phenol
b. ether
c. alcohol
d. phenol
e. alcohol
f. ether

53. a. carboxyl group, ethanoic acid (acetic acid)
b. ether, diethyl ether (ethyl ether)
c. ketone (carbonyl group), propanone (acetone)
d. alcohol (hydroxy group), ethanol (ethyl alcohol)

57. The chemical properties (and toxicity) of organic compounds are determined by the compound as a whole. As a substituent in a molecule, a phenyl group ring does not have the same properties as benzene.

61. Ethanoic acid (two carbons long) is more soluble in water than decanoic acid (ten carbons long).

63. cadaverine, $H_2N(CH_2)_5NH_2$;
putrescine, $H_2N(CH_2)_4NH_2$
Both compounds are amines.

66.

69. Cholesterol is an alcohol with a hydroxy group on a cycloalkane. It has four nonaromatic rings. It has a double bond in one of its rings, as well as a large alkyl group, making the molecule nonpolar.

71. Waving lotion reduces —S—S— bonds to —SH bonds. Hair can be placed in curlers to form the hair in the desired shape. The neutralizing agent is an oxidizing agent that reforms —S—S— bonds, locking the hair into its curly shape. Similar steps could be used to straighten curly hair.

76. The two molecules are similar in size. Diethylene glycol has four carbons, and glycerol has three carbons. Diethylene glycol is an ether with two hydroxy groups. Glycerol has three hydroxy groups.

diethylene glycol

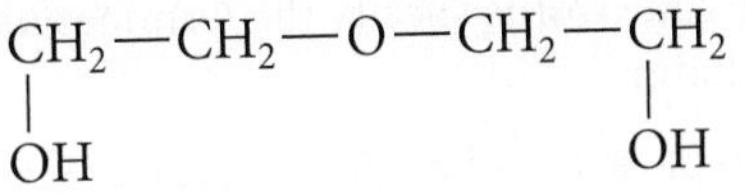

$$CH_2\!-\!CH_2\!-\!O\!-\!CH_2\!-\!CH_2$$
with OH below the first and last carbons

glycerol

$$CH_2\!-\!CH\!-\!CH_2$$
with OH below each carbon

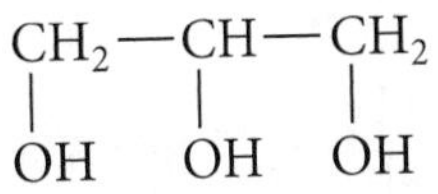

78. b, 3

82. Anhydrous $Na_2CO_3(s)$ is the better value because the decahydrate is 63.0% water.

86. $\Delta T = 180°C - 22°C = 158°C$

$q = C_{Al} \times m \times \Delta T$

$$q = \frac{0.90 \text{ J} \times \dfrac{1 \text{ kJ}}{10^3 \text{ J}} \times 500 \text{ g} \times 158°C}{(\text{g}\cdot°C)} = 71 \text{ kJ}$$

88. a, c, d, b

92. Reduction always occurs at the cathode. In an electrolytic cell, the cathode is the negative electrode.

94. coal

Chapter 24

42. Photosynthetic organisms use the sun's energy to synthesize carbon compounds, such as glucose, from CO_2 and H_2O.

47. Glucose is an aldehyde; fructose is a ketone.

53. Peptide chains fold into helixes or into pleated sheets in which peptide chains lie side by side.

64. phosphate group, sugar unit, nitrogen base

69. A substitution of one base for another may have no effect because the amino acid specified by the DNA code is not changed. Or a substitution of one base for another can result in a gene mutation in which the amino specified by the DNA code is changed.

70. Each individual's DNA is unique.

74. In catabolism, biological molecules are broken down and energy is released. In anabolism, energy and the products of catabolism are used to make biological molecules.

78.

$$CH_3(CH_2)_{14}-\overset{\overset{\displaystyle O}{\|}}{C}-O^-Na^+$$
(sodium palmitate)

82. C-G-x-C-C-x-T-C-A(or G)
Answers vary because there are multiple codes for the same amino acid.

86. No; three code words specify the termination of a peptide chain.

88. Oxidation of each mol of glucose yields 38 mol ATP, so:

$$\frac{38 \text{ mol ATP} \times 30.5 \text{ kJ/mol ATP}}{2.82 \times 10^3 \text{ kJ}} \times 100\% = 41.1\%$$

89. $8400 \text{ kJ} \times \dfrac{1 \text{ mol ATP}}{30.5 \text{ kJ}} = 275 \text{ mol ATP}$

96. A monosaccharide (such as glucose and fructose) consists of a single simple sugar unit. A disaccharide (such as sucrose) consists of two linked monosaccharide units. A polysaccharide (such as starch or glycogen) consists of many linked monosaccharide units.

98. Base-pairing describes the hydrogen bonding that occurs between thymine (T) and adenine (A) and between cytosine (C) and guanine (G) in DNA. Base-pairing helps hold together the two DNA strands in a double helix.

104.

107. An amide group is formed by the reaction.

112. A-C-C-T-A-C-T-A-C
No; Leu has 6 possible code words.

119. a. Each formula unit of NaCl disassociates into 2 particles, so $0.507m \times 2 = 1.014m$.

$$\Delta T_b = K_b \times m = \frac{0.512°C}{\cancel{m}} \times 1.014\cancel{m} = 0.519°C$$

b. Each formula unit of NH_4Cl disassociates into 2 particles, so $0.204m \times 2 = 0.408m$.

$$\Delta T_b = K_b \times m = \frac{0.512°C}{\cancel{m}} \times 0.408\cancel{m} = 0.209°C$$

c. Each formula unit of $CaCl_2$ disassociates into 3 particles, so $0.155m \times 3 = 0.465m$.

$$\Delta T_b = K_b \times m = \frac{0.512°C}{\cancel{m}} \times 0.465\cancel{m} = 0.238°C$$

d. Each formula unit of $NaHSO_4$ disassociates into 2 particles, so $0.222m \times 2 = 0.444m$.

$$\Delta T_b = K_b \times m = \frac{0.512°C}{\cancel{m}} \times 0.444\cancel{m} = 0.227°C$$

120. $\Delta H = 0.265 \text{ mol NaHCO}_3 \times \dfrac{129 \text{ kJ}}{2 \text{ mol NaHCO}_3}$

$= 17.1 \text{ kJ heat absorbed}$

128. a. $CH_3-CH_2-CH_2-CH_2-CH_2-CH_2-CH_3$

b.

$$CH_3-\overset{\overset{\displaystyle CH_3}{|}}{CH}-CH=CH-CH_2-CH_3$$

c.

$CH_3-CH-CH_2-CH_3$

d.

130. a. cyclopentane
b. 2-methyl-2-propanol
c. 3-pentanone

Chapter 25

9. $10.4 \text{ h} \div 2.6 \text{ h/half-life} = 4 \text{ half-lives}$

$A = A_0 \left(\frac{1}{2}\right)^4 = 1.0 \text{ mg} \times \frac{1}{16} = 0.063 \text{ mg Mn-56}$

10. $48.2 \text{ days} \div 24.1 \text{ days/half-life} = 2 \text{ half-lives}$

$(\text{Th-234 atoms}) \times \left(\frac{1}{2}\right)^2 = (\text{Th-234 atoms}) \times \frac{1}{4}$

No, $\frac{1}{4}$ of the Th-234 sample will remain.

36. $^{210}_{82}\text{Pb} \longrightarrow ^{210}_{83}\text{Bi} + ^{0}_{-1}\text{e}$

38. **a.** $^{238}_{92}\text{U} \longrightarrow ^{234}_{90}\text{Th} + ^{4}_{2}\text{He}$; thorium-234

b. $^{230}_{90}\text{Th} \longrightarrow ^{226}_{88}\text{Ra} + ^{4}_{2}\text{He}$; radium-226

c. $^{235}_{92}\text{U} \longrightarrow ^{231}_{90}\text{Th} + ^{4}_{2}\text{He}$; thorium-231

d. $^{222}_{86}\text{Rn} \longrightarrow ^{218}_{84}\text{Po} + ^{4}_{2}\text{He}$; polonium-218

40. **a.** mass number is unchanged; atomic number increases by 1

b. mass number decreases by 4; atomic number decreases by 2

c. Mass number and atomic number are both unchanged.

42. The atom undergoes radioactive decay.

47. $n = 40 \text{ days} \div 8 \text{ days/half-life} = 5 \text{ half-lives}$

$A = A_0 \left(\frac{1}{2}\right)^n = (20 \text{ mg}) \left(\frac{1}{2}\right)^5 = \frac{20}{32} = 0.625 \text{ mg}$

0.625 mg of I-131 remains.

57. **a.** $^{30}_{15}\text{P} + ^{0}_{-1}\text{e} \longrightarrow ^{30}_{14}\text{Si}$

b. $^{13}_{6}\text{C} + ^{1}_{0}\text{n} \longrightarrow ^{14}_{6}\text{C}$

c. $^{131}_{53}\text{I} \longrightarrow ^{131}_{54}\text{Xe} + ^{0}_{-1}\text{e}$

65. $A = A_0 \left(\frac{1}{2}\right)^n = (3.2 \times 10^7 \text{ atoms}) \left(\frac{1}{2}\right)^5$

$= \frac{3.2 \times 10^7 \text{ atoms}}{32} = 1 \times 10^6 \text{ atoms}$

67. **a.** $^{3}_{1}\text{H} \longrightarrow ^{3}_{2}\text{H} + ^{0}_{-1}\text{e}$ **c.** $^{131}_{53}\text{I} \longrightarrow ^{131}_{54}\text{Xe} + ^{0}_{-1}\text{e}$

b. $^{28}_{12}\text{Mg} \longrightarrow ^{28}_{13}\text{Al} + ^{0}_{-1}\text{e}$ **d.** $^{75}_{34}\text{Se} \longrightarrow ^{75}_{35}\text{Br} + ^{0}_{-1}\text{e}$

71. **a.** $^{0}_{-1}\text{e}$ **b.** $^{238}_{92}\text{U}$ **c.** $^{68}_{32}\text{Ge}$ **d.** $^{0}_{+1}\text{e}$

72. **a.** platinum   **d.** titanium   **g.** vanadium

b. thorium   **e.** xenon   **h.** palladium

c. francium   **f.** californium

Thorium (b), francium (c), and californium (f) have no stable isotopes.

76. Carbon-14 has decayed $\frac{4 \text{ counts/min}}{16 \text{ counts/min}} = \frac{1}{4}$.

Since $\frac{1}{4} = \left(\frac{1}{2}\right)^2$, the artifact is 2 half-lives old.

One half-life is 5.73×10^3 years.

2 half-lives $= (5.73 \times 10^3) \times 2 = 11,460$ years.

82. $^{25}_{12}\text{Mg}$

84. $25\% = \frac{25}{100} = \frac{1}{4}$.

$\left(\frac{1}{2}\right)^n = \frac{1}{4}$, so $n = 2$ half-lives.

12.3 years $\times$ 2 half-lives $= 24.6$ years.

94. $\text{volume} = \frac{\text{mass}}{\text{density}} = \frac{8.0 \text{ kg} \times \dfrac{1000 \text{ g}}{1 \text{ kg}}}{\dfrac{19 \text{ g}}{1 \text{ cm}^3}} = 4.2 \times 10^2 \text{ cm}^3$

105. $10.00 \text{ g Mg} \times \dfrac{1 \text{ mol Mg}}{24.3 \text{ g Mg}} \times \dfrac{1 \text{ mol H}_2}{1 \text{ mol Mg}} = 0.412 \text{ mol H}_2$

$0.412 \text{ mol H}_2 \times \dfrac{22.4 \text{ L H}_2}{1 \text{ mol H}_2} \times \dfrac{1000 \text{ mL H}_2}{1 \text{ L H}_2} \times \dfrac{1 \text{ cm}^3 \text{ H}_2}{1 \text{ mL H}_2}$

$= 9.22 \times 10^3 \text{ cm}^3 \text{ H}_2$

107. $\text{volume} = \dfrac{\text{moles}}{\text{molarity}} = \dfrac{0.0020 \text{ mol Na}_2\text{SO}_4}{\dfrac{0.30 \text{ mol Na}_2\text{SO}_4}{1 \text{ L}} \times \dfrac{1 \text{ L}}{1000 \text{ mL}}}$

$= 6.7 \text{ mL}$

Glossary

A

absolute zero: the zero point on the Kelvin temperature scale, equivalent to $-273.15°C$ *(79)*

    cero absoluto: punto cero en la escala de temperatura Kelvin; equivale a $-273.15°C$

accepted value: a quantity used by general agreement of the scientific community *(65)*

    valor aceptado: cantidad que se usa por acuerdo general de la comunidad científica

accuracy: the closeness of a measurement to the true value of what is being measured *(64)*

    exactitud: qué tan cerca está una medición del valor real de lo que se mide

acid: a compound that produces hydrogen ions in solution; see also hydrogen-ion donor, Lewis acid *(285)*

    ácido: compuesto que, en solución, produce iones hidrógeno; ver también donante iones hidrógeno, ácido de Lewis

acid dissociation constant (K_a): the ratio of the concentration of the dissociated form of an acid to the undissociated form; stronger acids have larger K_a values than weaker acids *(665)*

    constante de disociación ácida (K_a): razón de la concentración de la forma disociada de un ácido a la concentración de la forma no disociada; los ácidos fuertes tienen valores K_a más altos que los ácidos débiles

acidic solution: any solution in which the hydrogen-ion concentration is greater than the hydroxide-ion concentration *(654)*

    solución ácida: cualquier solución en la que la concentración de iones hidrógeno es mayor que la de iones hidróxido

activated complex: an unstable arrangement of atoms that exists momentarily at the peak of the activation-energy barrier; an intermediate or transitional structure formed during the course of a reaction *(596)*

    complejo activado: acomodo inestable de átomos que existe momentáneamente en el punto más alto de la barrera de energía de activación; estructura intermedia o de transición que se forma en el curso de una reacción

activation energy: the minimum energy colliding particles must have in order to react *(596)*

    energía de activación: energía mínima que deben tener las partículas para que, al chocar, reaccionen

active site: a groove or pocket in an enzyme molecule into which the substrate (reactant molecule) fits; where the substrate is converted to products *(847)*

    sitio activo: hendidura o bolsa en una molécula de enzima, en la que embona el sustrato (molécula que reacciona); donde el sustrato se convierte en productos

activity series: a list of elements in order of decreasing activity; the activity series of halogens is Fl, Cl, Br, I *(360)*

    serie de actividad: lista de elementos en orden de actividad decreciente; la serie de actividad de los halógenos es F, Cl, Br, I

actual yield: the amount of product that forms when a reaction is carried out in the laboratory *(405)*

    rendimiento real: cantidad de producto que se forma cuando se lleva a cabo una reacción en el laboratorio

addition reaction: a reaction in which a substance is added at the double bond of an alkene or at the triple bond of an alkyne *(807)*

    reacción de adición: reacción en la que una sustancia se añade al doble enlace de un alqueno o al triple enlace de un alquino

adenosine triphosphate (ATP): a molecule that transmits the energy needed by cells of all living things *(862)*

    trifosfato de adenosina (ATP): molécula que transmite la energía que necesitan las células de todos los seres vivos

alcohol: an organic compound having an —OH (hydroxy) group; the general structure is R—OH *(804)*

    alcohol: compuesto orgánico que posee un grupo —OH (hidroxilo); su estructura general es R—OH

aldehyde: an organic compound in which the carbon of the carbonyl group is joined to at least one hydrogen; the general formula is RCHO *(812)*

    aldehído: compuesto orgánico en el que el carbono del grupo carbonilo está unido a por lo menos un hidrógeno; su fórmula general es RCHO

aliphatic hydrocarbon: any straight-chain or branched-chain alkane, alkene, or alkyne *(780)*

    hidrocarburo alifático: cualquier alcano, alqueno o alquino de cadena lineal o cadena ramificada

alkali metal: any metal in Group 1A of the periodic table *(167)*

    metal alcalino: cualquier metal del grupo 1A de la tabla periódica

alkaline earth metal: any metal in Group 2A of the periodic table *(167)*

    metal alcalinotérreo: cualquier metal del grupo 2A de la tabla periódica

alkane: a hydrocarbon containing only single covalent bonds; alkanes are saturated hydrocarbons *(764)*

    alcano: hidrocarburo que sólo contiene enlaces covalentes sencillos; los alcanos son hidrocarburos saturados

alkene: a hydrocarbon containing one or more carbon–carbon double bonds; alkenes are unsaturated hydrocarbons *(772)*

    alqueno: hidrocarburo que contiene uno o más enlaces dobles carbono–carbono; los alquenos son hidrocarburos insaturados

alkyl group: a hydrocarbon substituent; the methyl group ($-CH_3$) is an alkyl group *(768)*

    grupo alquilo: un hidrocarburo sustituto; el grupo metilo ($-CH_3$) es un grupo alquilo

alkyl halide: a halocarbon in which one or more halogen atoms are attached to the carbon atoms of an aliphatic chain *(800)*

    haluro de alquilo: compuesto halocarbonado en el que uno o más átomos de halógeno están unidos a los átomos de carbono de una cadena alifática

alkyne: a hydrocarbon containing a carbon–carbon triple bond; alkynes are unsaturated hydrocarbons *(773)*

    alquino: hidrocarburo que contiene un triple enlace carbono–carbono; los alquinos son hidrocarburos insaturados

allotrope: one of two or more different molecular forms of an element in the same physical state; oxygen (O_2) and ozone (O_3) are allotropes of the element oxygen *(434)*

    alótropo: una de dos o más formas moleculares distintas de un elemento en el mismo estado físico; el oxígeno (O_2) y el ozono (O_3) son alótropos del elemento oxígeno

alloy: a mixture composed of two or more elements, at least one of which is a metal *(211)*

    aleación: mezcla formada por dos o más elementos, donde al menos uno de ellos es un metal

alpha particle: a positively charged particle emitted from certain radioactive nuclei; it consists of two protons and two neutrons and is identical to the nucleus of a helium atom *(877)*

    partícula alfa: partícula con carga positiva emitida por ciertos núcleos radiactivos; consta de dos protones y dos neutrones, y es idéntica al núcleo de un átomo de helio

amine: an organic compound in which nitrogen is bonded to a carbon group *(811)*

    amina: compuesto orgánico en el cual el nitrógeno se enlaza a un grupo de carbonos

amino acid: an organic compound having amino ($-NH_2$) and carboxyl ($-COOH$) groups in the same molecule; proteins are made from the 20 naturally occurring amino acids *(844)*

    aminoácido: compuesto orgánico que posee grupos amino ($-NH_2$) y carboxilo ($-COOH$) en la misma molécula; las proteínas se forman a partir de los 20 aminoácidos naturales

amorphous solid: describes a solid that lacks an ordered internal structure; denotes a random arrangement of atoms *(434)*

    sólido amorfo: describe un sólido que carece de una estructura interna ordenada; denota un acomodo aleatorio de átomos

amphoteric: a substance that can act as both an acid and a base *(651)*

    anfótero: una sustancia que puede actuar como ácido y también como base

amplitude: the height of a wave's crest *(138)*

    amplitud: altura de la cresta de una onda

anabolism: synthesis processes in the metabolism of cells; these processes usually require the expenditure of energy *(864)*

    anabolismo: procesos de síntesis dentro del metabolismo de las células; por lo regular, esos procesos requieren gasto de energía

analytical chemistry: the area of chemistry that focuses on the composition of matter *(3)*

    química analítica: rama de la química que estudia la composición de la materia

anhydrous: describes a substance that does not contain water *(498)*

    anhidro: se refiere a una sustancia que no contiene agua

anion: any atom or group of atoms with a negative charge *(176)*

    anión: cualquier átomo o grupo de átomos que posee carga negativa

anode: the electrode at which oxidation occurs *(730)*

    ánodo: electrodo en el que hay oxidación

applied chemistry: research that is directed toward a practical goal or application *(3)*

    química aplicada: investigaciones que tienen una meta o aplicación práctica

aqueous solution: water that contains dissolved substances *(494)*

    solución acuosa: agua que contiene sustancias disueltas

aromatic compound: an organic compound that contains a benzene ring or other ring in which the bonding is like that of benzene; aromatic compounds are also known as arenes *(780)*

    compuesto aromático: compuesto orgánico que contiene un anillo bencénico u otro anillo con enlaces similares a los del benceno; los compuestos aromáticos también se conocen como arenos

aryl halide: a halocarbon in which one or more halogens are attached to the carbon atoms of an arene ring *(800)*

    haluro de arilo: compuesto en el que uno o más átomos de halógeno están unidos a átomos de carbono de un anillo de areno

asymmetric carbon: a carbon atom that has four different atoms or groups attached *(776)*

    carbono asimétrico: átomo de carbono unido a cuatro átomos o grupos distintos

atmospheric pressure: the pressure exerted by atoms and molecules in the atmosphere surrounding Earth, resulting from collisions of these particles with objects *(421)*

    presión atmosférica: presión ejercida por átomos y moléculas de la atmósfera que rodea a la Tierra y que resulta de los choques de dichas partículas con los objetos

atom: the smallest particle of an element that retains its identity in a chemical reaction *(102)*

    átomo: partícula más pequeña de un elemento que conserva su identidad en una reacción química

atomic emission spectrum: the pattern formed when light passes through a prism or diffraction grating to separate it into the different frequencies of light it contains *(140)*

    espectro de emisión atómica: patrón que se forma cuando la luz atraviesa un prisma o una rejilla de difracción que la separa en las dife-rentes frecuencias de luz que contiene

atomic mass: the weighted average of the masses of the isotopes of an element *(117)*

    masa atómica: promedio ponderado de las masas de los isótopos de un elemento

atomic mass unit (amu): a unit of mass equal to one-twelfth the mass of a carbon-12 atom *(116)*

    unidad de masa atómica (uma): unidad de masa igual a un doceavo de la masa de un átomo de carbono 12

atomic number: the number of protons in the nucleus of an atom of an element *(112)*

    número atómico: número de protones que hay en el núcleo del átomo de un elemento

atomic orbital: a mathematical expression describing the probability of finding an electron at various locations; usually represented by the region of space around the nucleus where there is a high probability of finding an electron *(131)*

    orbital atómico: expresión matemática que describe la probabilidad de hallar un electrón en diversos lugares; se suele representar como la región del espacio en torno al núcleo donde hay una probabilidad elevada de hallar un electrón

atomic radius: one-half the distance between the nuclei of two atoms of the same element when the atoms are joined *(174)*

    radio atómico: mitad de la distancia entre los núcleos de dos átomos del mismo elemento cuando dichos átomos están unidos

aufbau principle: the rule that electrons occupy the orbitals of lowest energy first *(134)*

    principio de aufbau: regla según la cual los electrones primero ocupan los orbitales de energía más baja

Avogadro's hypothesis: equal volumes of gases at the same temperature and pressure contain equal numbers of particles *(320)*

    hipótesis de Avogadro: volúmenes iguales de gases a la misma temperatura y presión contienen el mismo número de partículas

Avogadro's number: the number of representative particles contained in one mole of a substance; equal to 6.02×10^{23} particles *(308)*

    número de Avogadro: número de partículas representativas contenidas en un mol de una sustancia; es igual a 6.02×10^{23} partículas

B

balanced equation: a chemical equation in which mass is conserved; each side of the equation has the same number of atoms of each element *(350)*

    ecuación balanceada: ecuación química en la que se conserva la masa; cada lado de la ecuación tiene el mismo número de átomos de cada elemento

band of stability: the location of stable nuclei on a neutron-vs.-proton plot *(880)*

    banda de estabilidad: región ocupada por los núcleos estables en un diagrama neutrones-protones

barometer: an instrument used to measure atmospheric pressure *(421)*

    barómetro: instrumento que sirve para medir la presión atmosférica

base: a compound that produces hydroxide ions in solution; see also hydrogen-ion acceptor, Lewis base *(287)*

    base: compuesto que, en solución, produce iones hidróxido, ver también receptor de iones hidrógeno, base de Lewis

base dissociation constant (K_b): the ratio of the concentration of the conjugate acid times the concentration of the hydroxide ion to the concentration of the base *(668)*

    constante de disociación básica (K_b): razón de la concentración del ácido combinado multiplicada por la concentración del ion hidróxido, a la concentración de la base

basic solution: any solution in which the hydroxide-ion concentration is greater than the hydrogen-ion concentration *(654)*

    solución básica: cualquier solución en la que la concentración de ion hidróxido es mayor que la concentración de ion hidrógeno

battery: a group of voltaic cells that are connected to one another *(733)*

    batería: grupo de celdas voltaicas conectadas entre sí

beta particle: an electron resulting from the breaking apart of neutrons in an atom *(878)*

    partícula beta: electrón que se produce al descomponerse los neutrones de un átomo

binary compound: a compound composed of two elements; NaCl and Al_2O_3 are binary compounds *(272)*

    compuesto binario: compuesto integrado por dos elementos; NaCl y Al_2O_3 son compuestos binarios

biochemistry: the area of chemistry that focuses on processes that take place in organisms *(3)*

    bioquímica: rama de la química que se concentra en los procesos que se dan en los organismos

boiling point (bp): the temperature at which the vapor pressure of a liquid is just equal to the external pressure on the liquid *(428)*

    punto de ebullición (p. eb.): temperatura en la que la presión de vapor de un líquido es apenas igual a la presión externa sobre el líquido

boiling-point elevation: the difference in temperature between the boiling point of a solution and the boiling point of the pure solvent *(537)*

    incremento del punto de ebullición: diferencia de temperatura entre el punto de ebullición de una solución y el punto de ebullición del disolvente puro

bond dissociation energy: the energy required to break the bond between two covalently bonded atoms; this value is usually expressed in kJ per mol of substance *(236)*

    energía de disociación de enlaces: energía requerida para romper el enlace entre dos átomos unidos de forma covalente; este valor suele expresarse en kJ por mol de sustancia

bonding orbital: a molecular orbital that can be occupied by two electrons of a covalent bond *(240)*

    orbital de enlace: orbital molecular que puede ser ocupado por los dos electrones de un enlace covalente

Boyle's law: for a given mass of gas at constant temperature, the volume of the gas varies inversely with pressure *(456)*

    ley de Boyle: para una masa dada de gas a temperatura constante, el volumen del gas varía en proporción inversa con la presión

branched-chain alkane: an alkane with one or more alkyl groups attached to the parent structure *(768)*

    alcano de cadena ramificada: alcano con uno o más grupos alquilo unidos a la estructura madre

Brownian motion: the chaotic movement of colloidal particles, caused by collision with particles of the solvent in which they are dispersed *(506)*

    movimiento browniano: movimiento caótico de partículas coloidales, debido a los choques con las partículas del disolvente en el que están dispersas

buffer: a solution in which the pH remains relatively constant when small amounts of acid or base are added; a buffer can be either a solution of a weak acid and the salt of a weak acid or a solution of a weak base with the salt of a weak base *(678)*

    solución amortiguadora: solución cuyo pH permanece relativamente constante si se le añaden pequeñas cantidades de ácido o base; una solución amortiguadora puede ser una solución de un ácido débil y la sal de un ácido débil o una solución de una base débil y la sal de una base débil

buffer capacity: a measure of the amount of acid or base that may be added to a buffer solution before a significant change in pH occurs *(679)*

    capacidad amortiguadora: medida de la cantidad de ácido o base que se puede añadir a una solución amortiguadora sin que haya un cambio importante del pH

C

calorie (cal): the quantity of heat needed to raise the temperature of 1 g of pure water 1°C *(77)*

    caloría (cal): cantidad de calor necesaria para elevar 1°C la temperatura de 1 g de agua pura

calorimeter: an insulated device used to measure the absorption or release of heat in chemical or physical processes *(562)*

    calorímetro: aparato con material aislante que sirve para medir la absorción o desprendimiento de calor durante procesos químicos o físicos

calorimetry: the precise measurement of heat flow out of a system for chemical and physical processes *(562)*

    calorimetría: medición precisa del cambio del calor durante procesos químicos y físicos

carbohydrate: the name given to monomers and polymers of aldehydes and ketones that have numerous hydroxyl groups; sugars and starches are carbohydrates *(841)*

    carbohidrato: nombre dado a monómeros y polímeros de aldehídos y cetonas que tienen muchos grupos hidroxilo; los azúcares y almidones son carbohidratos

carbonyl group: a functional group having a carbon atom and an oxygen atom joined by a double bond; it is found in aldehydes, ketones, esters, and amides *(812)*

    grupo carbonilo: grupo funcional que consiste en un átomo de carbono y uno de oxígeno unidos por un doble enlace; se le encuentra en aldehídos, cetonas, ésteres y amidas

carboxyl group: a functional group consisting of a carbonyl group attached to a hydroxyl group; it is found in carboxylic acids *(815)*

    grupo carboxilo: grupo funcional que consiste en un grupo carbonilo unido a un grupo hidroxilo; se le encuentra en los ácidos carboxílicos

carboxylic acid: an organic acid containing a carboxyl group; the general formula is RCOOH *(815)*

ácido carboxílico: ácido orgánico que contiene un grupo carboxilo; su fórmula general es RCOOH

catabolism: the reactions in living cells in which substances are broken down and energy is produced *(863)*

catabolismo: reacción, dentro de las células vivas, por la que diversas sustancias se descomponen y producen energía

catalyst: a substance that increases the rate of reaction by lowering the activation-energy barrier; the catalyst is not used up in the reaction *(348)*

catalizador: sustancia que aumenta la velocidad de reacción disminuyendo la barrera de energía de activación; el catalizador no se consume en la reacción

cathode: the electrode at which reduction occurs *(730)*

cátodo: electrodo en el que hay reducción

cathode ray: a stream of electrons produced at the negative electrode (cathode) of a tube containing a gas at low pressure *(105)*

rayo catódico: haz de electrones producido en el electrodo negativo (cátodo) de un tubo que contiene un gas a baja presión

cation: any atom or group of atoms with a positive charge *(176)*

catión: cualquier átomo o grupo de átomos que posee carga positiva

cell potential: the difference between the reduction potentials of two half-cells *(737)*

potencial de celda: diferencia entre los potenciales de reducción de dos medias celdas

Celsius scale: the temperature scale on which the freezing point of water is 0°C and the boiling point is 100°C *(78)*

escala Celsius: escala de temperatura en la que el punto de congelación del agua es 0°C y el punto de ebullición del agua es 100°C

Charles's law: the volume of a fixed mass of gas is directly proportional to its Kelvin temperature if the pressure is kept constant *(458)*

ley de Charles: el volumen de una masa fija de gas es directamente proporcional a su temperatura Kelvin si la presión se mantiene constante

chemical change: a change that produces matter with a different composition than the original matter *(43)*

cambio químico: cambio que produce materia con una composición diferente que la de la materia original

chemical equation: an expression representing a chemical reaction; the formulas of the reactants (on the left) are connected by an arrow with the formulas for the products (on the right) *(348)*

ecuación química: expresión que representa una reacción química; las fórmulas de los reactantes (a la izquierda) se unen mediante una flecha a las fórmulas de los productos (a la derecha)

chemical equilibrium: a state of balance in which the rates of the forward and reverse reactions are equal; no net change in the amount of reactants and products occurs in the chemical system *(610)*

equilibrio químico: estado de equilibrio en el que las velocidades de la reacción de evolución y la reacción inversa son iguales; no hay un cambio total en la cantidad de reactantes y productos en el sistema químico

chemical formula: an expression that indicates the number and type of atoms present in the smallest representative unit of a substance *(202)*

fórmula química: expresión que indica el número y tipo de átomos que están presentes en la unidad más pequeña representativa de una sustancia

chemical potential energy: energy stored in chemical bonds *(556)*

energía potencial química: energía almacenada en los enlaces químicos

chemical property: the ability of a substance to undergo a specific chemical change *(48)*

propiedad química: capacidad de una sustancia para sufrir un cambio químico específico

chemical reaction: a change in which one or more reactants change into one or more products; characterized by the breaking of bonds in reactants and the formation of bonds in products *(48)*

reacción química: cambio en el que uno o más reactantes se convierten en uno o más productos; se caracteriza por la ruptura de enlaces en los reactantes y la formación de enlaces en los productos

chemical symbol: a one- or two-letter representation of an element *(45)*

símbolo químico: representación de un elemento que emplea una o dos letras

chemistry: the study of the composition of matter and the changes that matter undergoes *(2)*

química: estudio de la composición de la materia y los cambios que ésta sufre

cis configuration: the configuration in which substituent groups are on the same side of a double bond *(776)*

configuración cis: configuración en la cual los grupos sustitutos están del mismo lado de un doble enlace

cis-trans isomers: compounds that have atoms in the same order, but differ in the orientation of groups around a double bond *(776)*

isómeros cis-trans: compuestos cuyos átomos tienen el mismo orden, pero difieren con respecto a la orientación de los grupos alrededor de un enlace doble

coefficient: a small whole number that appears in front of a formula in a balanced chemical equation *(350)*

coeficiente: número entero pequeño que aparece antepuesto a una fórmula en una ecuación química balanceada

coenzyme: a small organic molecule or metal ion necessary for an enzyme's biological activity *(848)*

coenzima: pequeña molécula orgánica o ion metálico que se requiere para que una enzima tenga actividad biológica

colligative property: a property of a solution that depends only upon the number of solute particles, and not upon their identities; boiling-point elevation, freezing-point depression, and vapor-pressure lowering are colligative properties *(534)*

propiedad coligativa: propiedad de una solución que depende únicamente del número de partículas de soluto, y no del tipo de soluto; el incremento del punto de ebullición, la disminución del punto de congelación y el descenso de la presión de vapor son propiedades coligativas

collision theory: atoms, ions, and molecules can react to form products when they collide, provided that the particles have enough kinetic energy *(596)*

teoría de choques: los átomos, iones y moléculas pueden reaccionar para formar productos cuando chocan, siempre que las partículas tengan suficiente energía cinética

colloid: a mixture whose particles are intermediate in size between those of a suspension and a solution *(505)*

coloide: mezcla cuyas partículas tienen un tamaño intermedio entre las de una suspensión y una solución

combination reaction: a chemical change in which two or more substances react to form a single new substance; also called a synthesis reaction *(356)*

reacción de combinación: cambio químico en el que dos o más sustancias reaccionan para formar una sola sustancia nueva; también llamado reacción de síntesis

combined gas law: the law that describes the relationship among the pressure, temperature, and volume of an enclosed gas *(462)*

ley combinada de los gases: ley que describe las relaciones entre la presión, la temperatura y el volumen de un gas encerrado

combustion reaction: a chemical change in which an element or a compound reacts with oxygen, often producing energy in the form of heat and light *(363)*

reacción de combustión: cambio químico en el que un elemento o un compuesto reacciona con oxígeno y por lo regular produce energía en forma de luz y calor

common ion: an ion that is common to both salts in a solution; in a solution of silver nitrate and silver chloride, Ag^+ would be a common ion *(624)*

ion común: ion que es común a dos sales disueltas en una solución; en una solución de nitrato de plata y cloruro de plata, Ag^+ sería un ion común

common ion effect: a decrease in the solubility of an ionic compound caused by the addition of a common ion *(624)*

efecto de ion común: disminución en la solubilidad de un compuesto iónico debida a la adición de un ion común

complete ionic equation: an equation that shows dissolved ionic compounds as dissociated free ions *(370)*

ecuación iónica completa: ecuación que muestra los compuestos iónicos disueltos en forma de iones disociados libres

compound: a substance that contains two or more elements chemically combined in a fixed proportion *(42)*

compuesto: sustancia que contiene dos o más elementos combinados químicamente en una proporción fija

compressibility: a measure of how much the volume of matter decreases under pressure *(450)*

compresibilidad: medida de cuánto disminuye el volumen de la materia cuando se le aplica presión

concentrated solution: a solution containing a large amount of solute *(525)*

solución concentrada: solución que contiene una gran cantidad de soluto

concentration: a measurement of the amount of solute that is dissolved in a given quantity of solvent; usually expressed as mol/L *(525)*

concentración: medida de la cantidad de soluto que está disuelto en una cantidad específica de disolvente; suele expresarse en mol/L

condensed structural formula: a structural formula that leaves out some bonds and/or atoms; the presence of these atoms or bonds is understood *(766)*

fórmula estructural condensada: fórmula estructural que no muestra algunos enlaces o átomos; se sobreentiende la presencia de estos enlaces o átomos

conjugate acid: the particle formed when a base gains a hydrogen ion; NH_4^+ is the conjugate acid of the base NH_3 *(650)*

ácido conjugado: partícula que se forma cuando una base gana un ion hidrógeno; NH_4^+ es el ácido conjugado de la base NH_3

conjugate acid-base pair: two substances that are related by the loss or gain of a single hydrogen ion; ammonia (NH_3) and the ammonium ion (NH_4^+) are a conjugate acid-base pair *(650)*

par conjugado ácido-base: dos sustancias relacionadas entre sí por la pérdida o ganancia de un solo ion hidrógeno; el amoníaco (NH_3) y el ion amonio (NH_4^+) son un par conjugado ácido-base

conjugate base: the particle that remains when an acid has donated a hydrogen ion; OH^- is the conjugate base of the acid water *(650)*

base conjugada: partícula que queda cuando un ácido transfiere un ion hidrógeno; OH^- es la base conjugada del ácido agua

constitutional isomers: compounds that have the same molecular formula, but whose atoms are bonded in a different order *(775)*

isómeros constitucionales: compuestos que tienen la misma fórmula molecular, pero cuyos átomos están enlazados en distinto orden

conversion factor: a ratio of equivalent measurements used to convert a quantity from one unit to another *(84)*

    factor de conversión: razón de medidas equivalentes usadas para convertir una cantidad de una unidad a otra

coordinate covalent bond: a covalent bond in which one atom contributes both bonding electrons *(232)*

    enlace covalente coordinado: enlace covalente en el que un átomo aporta dos electrones de enlace

coordination number: the number of ions of opposite charge that surround each ion in a crystal *(205)*

    número de coordinación: número de iones de carga opuesta que rodean a cada ion en un cristal

covalent bond: a bond formed by the sharing of electrons between atoms *(215)*

    enlace covalente: enlace que se forma cuando dos átomos comparten electrones

cracking: the controlled process by which hydrocarbons are broken down or rearranged into smaller, more useful molecules *(783)*

    pirólisis: proceso controlado por el cual los hidrocarburos se descomponen o reacomodan para obtener moléculas más pequeñas y útiles

crystal: a solid in which the atoms, ions, or molecules are arranged in an orderly, repeating, three-dimensional pattern called a crystal lattice *(432)*

    cristal: sólido en el que los átomos, iones o moléculas están dispuestos en un patrón tridimensional ordenado y repetitivo llamado red cristalina

cycloalkane: cyclic hydrocarbon that contains only single bonds *(779)*

    cicloalcano: hidrocarburo cíclico que solamente contiene enlaces simples

cyclic hydrocarbon: an organic compound that contains a hydrocarbon ring *(779)*

    hidrocarburo cíclico: compuesto orgánico que contiene un anillo de hidrocarburo

D

Dalton's atomic theory the first theory to relate chemical changes to events at the atomic level *(103)*

    teoría atómica de Dalton: primera teoría en relacionar los cambios químicos con sucesos a nivel atómico

Dalton's law of partial pressures: at constant volume and temperature, the total pressure exerted by a mixture of gases is equal to the sum of the partial pressures of the component gases *(470)*

    teoría de Dalton de las presiones parciales: a volumen y temperatura constantes, la presión total ejercida por una mezcla de gases es igual a la suma de las presiones parciales de los gases componentes

decomposition reaction: a chemical change in which a single compound is broken down into two or more simpler products *(358)*

    reacción de descomposición: cambio químico en el que un solo compuesto se descompone en dos o más productos más simples

dehydrogenation reaction: a reaction in which hydrogen is lost *(816)*

    reacción de deshidrogenación: reacción en la que se pierde hidrógeno

deliquescent: describes a substance that removes sufficient water from the air to form a solution; the solution formed has a lower vapor pressure than that of the water in the air *(501)*

    delicuescente: término que describe una sustancia que absorbe suficiente humedad del aire como para formar una solución; la solución formada tiene una presión de vapor más baja que la de la humedad del aire

density: the ratio of the mass of an object to its volume *(80)*

    densidad: razón de la masa de un objeto a su volumen

dependent variable: the variable that is observed during an experiment; also called responding variable *(16)*

    variable dependiente: variable que se observa durante un experimento; también llamada variable de repuesta

desiccant: a hygroscopic substance used as a drying agent *(499)*

    desecante: sustancia higroscópica empleada como agente secante

diatomic molecule: a molecule consisting of two atoms *(223)*

    molécula diatómica: molécula que cons-ta de dos átomos

diffusion: the tendency of molecules to move toward areas of lower concentration until the concentration is uniform throughout *(472)*

    difusión: tendencia de las moléculas a moverse hacia áreas de baja concentración hasta que la concentración es uniforme en todo el medio

dilute solution: a solution that contains a small amount of solute *(525)*

    solución diluida: solución que contiene muy poco soluto

dimensional analysis: a technique of problem-solving that uses the units that are part of a measurement to help solve the problem *(86)*

    análisis dimensional: técnica para resolver problemas que se apoya en las unidades de las mediciones para resolver el problema

dipole: a molecule that has two poles, or regions, with opposite charges *(249)*

    dipolo: molécula que tiene dos polos o regiones de carga opuesta

dipole interactions: intermolecular forces resulting from the attraction of oppositely charged regions of polar molecules (250)

   interacción dipolar: fuerzas intermoleculares que resultan de la atracción de regiones de moléculas polares que tienen cargas opuestas

diprotic acid: any acid that contains two ionizable protons (hydrogen ions); sulfuric acid (H_2SO_4) is a diprotic acid (647)

   ácido diprótico: cualquier ácido que contenga dos protones (iones hidrógeno) ionizables; el ácido sulfúrico (H_2SO_4) es un ácido diprótico

disaccharide: a carbohydrate formed from two monosaccharide units; common table sugar (sucrose) is a disaccharide (842)

   disacárido: carbohidrato formado por dos unidades de monosacárido; el azúcar de mesa común (sacarosa) es un disacárido

dispersion forces: attractions between molecules caused by the electron motion on one molecule affecting the electron motion on the other through electrical forces; these are the weakest interactions between molecules (251)

   fuerzas de dispersión: atracciones entre moléculas que se dan cuando el movimiento de los electrones de una molécula afecta el movimiento de los electrones de la otra mediante fuerzas eléctricas; se trata de las interacciones más débiles entre moléculas

displacement reaction: see single-replacement reaction

   reacción de desplazamiento: véase reacción de sustitución sencilla

distillation: a process used to separate components of a mixture using differences in boiling points (40)

   destilación: proceso que se emplea para separar las sustancias de una mezcla por medio de diferentes puntos de ebullición

double covalent bond: a bond in which two atoms share two pairs of electrons (230)

   enlace covalente doble: enlace en el que dos átomos comparten dos pares de electrones

double-replacement reaction: a chemical change that involves an exchange of positive ions between two compounds (362)

   reacción de sustitución doble: cambio químico que implica un intercambio de iones positivos entre dos compuestos

dry cell: a commercial voltaic cell in which the electrolyte is a moist paste; despite their name, the compact, portable batteries used in flashlights are dry cells (732)

   pila seca: celda voltaica comercial en la que, a pesar del nombre, el electrolito es una pasta húmeda; las baterías compactas y portátiles que se usan en las linternas son pilas secas

E

effloresce: to lose water of hydration; the process occurs when the hydrate has a vapor pressure higher than that of water vapor in the air (499)

   eflorecerse: perder agua de hidratación; el proceso se presenta cuando la presión de vapor del hidrato es más alta que la del vapor de agua en el aire

effusion: the process that occurs when a gas escapes through a tiny hole in its container (472)

   efusión: proceso en el cual un gas escapa por un agujero diminuto en su recipiente

electrical potential: the ability of a voltaic cell to produce an electric current (737)

   potencial eléctrico: capacidad de una celda voltaica para producir corriente eléctrica

electrochemical cell: any device that converts chemical energy into electrical energy or electrical energy into chemical energy (730)

   celda electroquímica: cualquier dispositivo que convierte energía química en energía eléctrica o energía eléctrica en energía química

electrochemical process: the conversion of chemical energy into electrical energy or electrical energy into chemical energy; all electrochemical processes involve redox reactions (728)

   proceso electroquímico: conversión de energía química en energía eléctrica o energía eléctrica en energía química; en todos los procesos electroquímicos intervienen reacciones redox

electrode: a conductor in a circuit that carries electrons to or from a substance other than a metal (730)

   electrodo: en un circuito, un conductor que transporta electrones hacia o desde una sustancia que no es un metal

electrolysis: a process in which electrical energy is used to bring about a chemical change; the electrolysis of water produces hydrogen and oxygen (745)

   electrolisis: proceso en el que se usa energía eléctrica para realizar un cambio químico; la electrolisis del agua produce hidrógeno y oxígeno

electrolyte: a compound that conducts an electric current when it is in an aqueous solution or in the molten state; all ionic compounds are electrolytes, but most covalent compounds are not (496)

   electrolito: compuesto que conduce una corriente eléctrica cuando está en solución acuosa o está derretido; todos los compuestos iónicos son electrolitos, pero muy pocos compuestos covalentes lo son

electrolytic cell: an electrochemical cell used to cause a chemical change through the application of electrical energy (745)

   celda electrolítica: celda electroquímica que se usa para efectuar un cambio químico mediante la aplicación de energía eléctrica

electromagnetic radiation: energy waves that travel in a vacuum at a speed of 2.998×10^8 m/s; includes radio waves, microwaves, infrared waves, visible light, ultraviolet waves, X-rays, and gamma rays *(139)*

   radiación electromagnética: ondas de energía que viajan en el vacío a una velocidad de 2.998×10^8 m/s; incluye las ondas de radio, microondas, ondas infrarrojas, luz visible, ondas ultravioleta, rayos X y rayos gamma

electron: a negatively charged subatomic particle *(105)*

   electrón: partícula subatómica con carga negativa

electron configuration: the arrangement of electrons of an atom in its ground state into various orbitals around the nuclei of atoms *(134)*

   configuración electrónica: distribución de los electrones de un átomo en su estado basal, en diversos orbitales alrededor del núcleo del átomo

electron dot structure: a notation that depicts valence electrons as dots around the atomic symbol of the element; the symbol represents the inner electrons and atomic nucleus; also called Lewis dot structure *(195)*

   estructura de punto electrón: notación que muestra los electrones de valencia como puntos alrededor del símbolo atómico del elemento; el símbolo representa los electrones internos y el núcleo atómico; también se conoce como estructura de puntos de Lewis

electronegativity: the ability of an atom to attract electrons when the atom is in a compound *(181)*

   electronegatividad: capacidad de un átomo para atraer electrones cuando el átomo está en un compuesto

element: the simplest form of matter that has a unique set of properties; an element cannot be broken down into simpler substances by chemical means *(42)*

   elemento: forma más simple de materia que posee un conjunto único de propiedades; un elemento no puede descomponerse en sustancias más simples usando métodos químicos

elementary reaction: a reaction in which reactants are converted to products in a single step *(607)*

   reacción básica: reacción en la que los reactantes se convierten en productos en un solo paso

empirical formula: a formula with the lowest whole-number ratio of elements in a compound; the empirical formula of hydrogen peroxide (H_2O_2) is HO *(330)*

   fórmula empírica: fórmula que muestra las proporciones de los elementos en un compuesto con los números enteros más pequeños posibles; la fórmula empírica del peróxido de hidrógeno (H_2O_2) es HO

emulsion: the colloidal dispersion of one liquid in another *(507)*

   emulsión: dispersión coloidal de un líquido en otro

enantiomers: molecules that differ from one another in the way that four different groups are arranged around a carbon atom *(777)*

   enantiómero: moléculas que se diferencian entre sí por la forma en que cuatro grupos diferentes están dispuestos alrededor de un átomo de carbono

endothermic process: a process that absorbs heat from the surroundings *(557)*

   proceso endotérmico: proceso en el que se absorbe calor del entorno

end point: the point in a titration at which the indicator changes color *(674)*

   punto final: punto de una valoración química en cual el indicador cambia de color

energy: the capacity for doing work or producing heat *(77)*

   energía: capacidad para efectuar trabajo o producir calor

energy level: the specific energies an electron in an atom or other system can have *(129)*

   nivel energético: las energías específicas que puede tener un electrón en un átomo u otro sistema

enthalpy (H): the heat content of a system at constant pressure *(562)*

   entalpía (H): cantidad de calor en un sistema a presión constante

entropy (S): a measure of the disorder of a system; systems tend to go from a state of order (low entropy) to a state of maximum disorder (high entropy) *(630)*

   entropía (S): medida del desorden de un sistema; los sistemas tienden a pasar de un estado ordenado (baja entropía) a un estado de máximo desorden (alta entropía)

enzyme: a protein that acts as a biological catalyst *(847)*

   enzima: proteína que actúa como catalizador biológico

enzyme–substrate complex: the structure formed when a substrate molecule joins an enzyme at its active site *(847)*

   complejo enzima-sustrato: estructura que se forma cuando una molécula de sustrato se une a una enzima en su sitio activo

equilibrium constant (K_{eq}): the ratio of product concentrations to reactant concentrations at equilibrium, with each concentration raised to a power equal to the number of moles of that substance in the balanced chemical equation *(616)*

   constante de equilibrio (K_{eq}): razón de las concentraciones de los productos a las concentraciones de los reactantes en el equilibrio, con cada concentración elevada a una potencia igual al número de moles de esa sustancia en la ecuación química balanceada

equilibrium position: the relative concentrations of reactants and products of a reaction that has reached equilibrium; indicates whether the reactants or products are favored in the reversible reaction *(611)*

   posición de equilibrio: las concentraciones relativas de reactantes y productos de una reacción que ha alcanzado el equilibrio; indica si se favorecen los reactantes o productos en la reacción reversible

equivalence point: the point in a titration where the number of moles of hydrogen ions equals the number of moles of hydroxide ions *(674)*

    punto de equivalencia: punto de una valoración química en la que el número de moles de iones hidrógeno es igual al número de moles de iones hidróxido

error: the difference between the accepted value and the experimental value *(65)*

    error: diferencia entre el valor aceptado y el valor experimental

ester: a derivative of a carboxylic acid in which the —OH of the carboxyl group has been replaced by the —OR from an alcohol; the general formula is RCOOR *(819)*

    éster: derivado de un ácido carboxílico en el que el —OH del grupo carboxilo ha sido sustituido por el —OR de un alcohol; la fórmula general es RCOOR

ether: an organic compound in which oxygen is bonded to two carbon groups; the general formula is R—O—R *(810)*

    éter: compuesto orgánico en el que el oxígeno está unido a dos grupos carbono; la fórmula general es R—O—R

evaporation: vaporization that occurs at the surface of a liquid that is not boiling *(426)*

    evaporación: vaporización que se da en la superficie de un líquido que no está en ebullición

excess reagent: a reagent present in a quantity that is more than sufficient to react with a limiting reagent; any reactant that remains after the limiting reagent is used up in a chemical reaction *(401)*

    reactivo excesivo: reactivo que está presente en una cantidad más que suficiente para reaccionar con un reactivo limitante; cualquier reactante que queda después de que se ha usado todo el reactivo limitante en una reacción química

exothermic process: a process that releases heat to its surroundings *(557)*

    proceso exotérmico: proceso en el que se desprende calor hacia el entorno

experiment: a repeatable procedure that is used to test a hypothesis *(16)*

    experimento: procedimiento repetido que sirve para probar una hipótesis

experimental value: a quantitative value measured during an experiment *(65)*

    valor experimental: valor cuantitativo que se mide durante un experimento

extensive property: a property that depends on the amount of matter in a sample *(34)*

    propiedad extensiva: propiedad que depende de la cantidad de materia en una muestra

F

fatty acid: the name given to continuous-chain carboxylic acids that were first isolated from fats *(816)*

    ácido graso: nombre que se da a los ácidos carboxílicos de cadena continua que se aislaron originalmente de las grasas

fermentation: the production of ethanol from sugars by the action of yeast or bacteria *(807)*

    fermentación: producción de etanol a partir de azúcares por la acción de levaduras o bacterias

filtration: a process that separates a solid from the liquid in a heterogeneous mixture *(40)*

    filtración: proceso para separar un sólido de un líquido en una mezcla heterogénea

first-order reaction: a reaction in which the reaction rate is proportional to the concentration of only one reactant *(605)*

    reacción de primer orden: reacción cuya velocidad de reacción es proporcional a la concentración de un solo reactante

fission: the splitting of a nucleus into smaller fragments, accompanied by the release of neutrons and a large amount of energy *(888)*

    fisión: división de un núcleo en fragmentos más pequeños, acompañada por desprendimiento de neutrones y una gran cantidad de energía

formula unit: the lowest whole-number ratio of ions in an ionic compound; in magnesium chloride, the ratio of magnesium ions to chloride ions is 1:2 and the formula unit is $MgCl_2$ *(202)*

    unidad de fórmula: razón más baja, expresada en números enteros, de los iones de un compuesto iónico; en el cloruro de magnesio, la razón de iones magnesio a iones cloruro es de 1:2, así que la unidad de fórmula es $MgCl_2$

free energy: the energy available to do work *(627)*

    energía libre: energía que está disponible para realizar trabajo

freezing point: the temperature at which a liquid changes to a solid *(431)*

    punto de congelación: temperatura a la cual un líquido se convierte en un sólido

freezing-point depression: the difference in temperature between the freezing point of a solution and the freezing point of the pure solvent *(536)*

    disminución del punto de congelación: diferencia de temperatura entre el punto de congelación de una solución y el del disolvente puro

frequency (v): the number of wave cycles that pass a given point per unit of time; frequency and wavelength are inversely proportional to each other *(138)*

    frecuencia (v): número de ciclos de onda que pasan por un punto específico en la unidad de tiempo; la fre... y la longitud de onda son inversamente proporci...

fuel cell: a voltaic cell that does not need to be recharged; the fuel is oxidized to produce a continuous supply of electrical energy *(734)*

    celda de combustible: celda voltaica que no necesita recargarse; el combustible se oxida para producir un suministro continuo de energía eléctrica

functional group: a specific arrangement of atoms in an organic compound that is capable of characteristic chemical reactions; the chemistry of an organic compound is determined by its functional groups *(798)*

    grupo funcional: distribución específica de átomos en un compuesto orgánico que puede participar en reacciones químicas características; la química de un compuesto orgánico está determinada por sus grupos funcionales

fusion: the process of combining nuclei to produce a nucleus of greater mass *(891)*

    fusión: proceso en el que se combinan núcleos para producir un núcleo con mayor masa

G

gamma ray: a high-energy photon emitted by a radioisotope *(879)*

    rayo gamma: fotón de alta energía emitido por un radioisótopo

gas: a form of matter that takes the shape and volume of its container; a gas has no definite shape or volume *(37)*

    gas: estado de la materia que adopta la forma y el volumen del recipiente que la contiene; los gases no tienen forma ni volumen definidos

gas pressure: results from the force exerted by a gas per unit surface area of an object; due to collisions of gas particles with the object *(421)*

    presión de gas: resultado de la fuerza que ejerce un gas por unidad de área total de un objeto; se debe a los choques de las partículas de gas contra el objeto

Gay-Lussac's law: the pressure of a gas is directly proportional to the Kelvin temperature if the volume is constant *(460)*

    ley de Gay-Lussac: la presión de un gas es directamente proporcional a su temperatura Kelvin si se mantiene constante el volumen

gene: a segment of DNA that codes for a single peptide chain *(856)*

    gen: segmento de ADN que contiene el código para una sola cadena péptida

glass: transparent fusion product of inorganic materials that have cooled to a rigid state without crystallizing *(434)*

    vidrio: producto transparente que resulta de la fusión de materiales inorgánicos que se han enfriado hasta solidificarse sin cristalizarse

Graham's law of effusion: the rate of effusion of a gas is inversely proportional to the square root of its molar mass; this relationship is also true for the diffusion of gases *(472)*

    ley de efusión de Graham: la velocidad de efusión de un gas es inversamente proporcional a la raíz cuadrada de su masa molar; esta relación también se cumple en la difusión de gases

gram (g): a metric mass unit equal to the mass of 1 cm^3 of water at $4°C$ *(77)*

    gramo (g): unidad métrica de masa equivalente a la masa de 1 cm^3 de agua a $4°C$

ground state: the lowest possible energy of an atom described by quantum mechanics *(145)*

    estado fundamental: energía más baja que puede tener un átomo descrito por la mecánica cuántica

group: a vertical column of elements in the periodic table; the constituent elements of a group have similar chemical and physical properties *(47)*

    grupo: columna vertical de elementos en la tabla periódica; los elementos de un grupo tienen propiedades físicas y químicas similares

H

half-cell: the part of a voltaic cell in which either oxidation or reduction occurs; it consists of a single electrode immersed in a solution of its ions *(730)*

    semicelda: parte de una celda voltaica en la que se lleva a cabo la oxidación o reducción; consta de un solo electrodo sumergido en una solución de sus iones

half-life ($t_{1/2}$): the time required for one-half of the nuclei of a radioisotope sample to decay to products *(882)*

    semivida ($t_{1/2}$): tiempo que tarda en desintegrarse la mitad de los núcleos de una muestra de un radioisótopo

half-reaction: an equation showing either the oxidation or the reduction that takes place in a redox reaction *(712)*

    semirreacción: ecuación que muestra la oxidación o bien la reducción que se da en una reacción redox

half-reaction method: a method of balancing a redox equation by balancing the oxidation and reduction half-reactions separately before combining them into a balanced redox equation *(712)*

    método de semirreacción: método para balancear una ecuación redox equilibrando por separado las semirreacciones de oxidación y reducción antes de combinarlas para obtener una ecuación redox balanceada

halide ion: a negative ion formed when a halogen atom gains an electron *(199)*

    ion haluro: ion negativo que se forma cuando un átomo de halógeno gana un electrón

halocarbon: any member of a class of organic compounds containing covalently bonded fluorine, chlorine, bromine, or iodine *(800)*

   compuesto halocarbonado: cualquier miembro de una clase de compuestos orgánicos que contienen flúor, cloro, bromo o yodo unidos mediante enlaces covalentes

halogen: a nonmetal in Group 7A of the periodic table *(167)*

   halógeno: no metal del grupo 7A de la tabla periódica

heat (q): energy that transfers from one object to another because of a temperature difference between the objects *(556)*

   calor (q): energía que fluye de un objeto a otro debido a la diferencia de temperatura entre los objetos

heat capacity: the amount of heat needed to increase the temperature of an object exactly 1°C *(559)*

   capacidad calorífica: cantidad de calor necesaria para elevar exactamente 1°C la temperatura de un objeto

heat of combustion: the heat of reaction for the complete burning of one mole of a substance *(568)*

   calor de combustión: calor de reacción al quemarse totalmente un mol de una sustancia

heat of reaction: the enthalpy change for a chemical equation exactly as it is written *(565)*

   calor de reacción: cambio de entalpía correspondiente a una ecuación química en la forma exacta en que está escrita

Heisenberg uncertainty principle: it is impossible to know exactly both the velocity and the position of a particle at the same time *(148)*

   principio de incertidumbre de Heisenberg: es imposible conocer con exactitud la velocidad y la posición de una partícula al mismo tiempo

Henry's law: at a given temperature the solubility of a gas in a liquid is directly proportional to the pressure of the gas above the liquid *(523)*

   ley de Henry: a una temperatura determinada, la solubilidad de un gas en un líquido es directamente proporcional a la presión del gas sobre el líquido

hertz (Hz): the unit of frequency, equal to one cycle per second *(138)*

   hertz (Hz): unidad de frecuencia, equivalente a un ciclo por segundo

Hess's law of heat summation: if you add two or more thermochemical equations to give a final equation, then you also add the heats of reaction to give the final heat of reaction *(578)*

   ley de Hess de la suma de los calores: ley según la cual, si se suman dos o más ecuaciones termoquímicas para obtener una ecuación final, también se suman los calores de reacción para obtener el calor de reacción final

heterogeneous mixture: a mixture that is not uniform in composition; components are not evenly distributed throughout the mixture *(39)*

   mezcla heterogénea: mezcla cuya composición no es uniforme; sus componentes no están distribuidos de forma equitativa en toda la mezcla

homogeneous mixture: a mixture that is uniform in composition; components are evenly distributed and not easily distinguished *(39)*

   mezcla homogénea: mezcla cuya composición es uniforme; sus componentes están distribuidos de forma equitativa y no es fácil distinguirlos

homologous series: a group of compounds in which there is a constant increment of change in molecular structure from one compound in the series to the next *(765)*

   serie homóloga: grupo de compuestos en el que se observa un incremento constante de cambio en la estructura molecular de un compuesto al siguiente

Hund's rule: electrons occupy orbitals of the same energy in a way that makes the number or electrons with the same spin direction as large as possible *(134)*

   regla de Hund: los electrones ocupan orbitales de la misma energía haciendo que el número de electrones cuyo espín tiene la misma dirección sea lo más grande posible

hybridization: the mixing of several atomic orbitals to form the same total number of equivalent hybrid orbitals *(244)*

   hibridización: combinación de varios orbitales atómicos para formar el mismo número total de orbitales híbridos equivalentes

hydrate: a compound that has a specific number of water molecules bound to each formula unit *(498)*

   hidrato: compuesto que tiene un número específico de moléculas de agua unidas a cada unidad de fórmula

hydration reaction: a reaction in which water is added to an alkene *(808)*

   reacción de hidratación: reacción en la que se añade agua a un alqueno

hydrocarbon: an organic compound that contains only carbon and hydrogen *(762)*

   hidrocarburo: compuesto orgánico que contiene sólo carbono e hidrógeno

hydrogenation reaction: a reaction in which hydrogen is added to a carbon–carbon double bond to give an alkane *(809)*

   reacción de hidrogenación: reacción en la que se añade hidrógeno a un doble enlace carbono–carbono para obtener un alcano

hydrogen bonds: attractive forces in which a hydrogen covalently bonded to a very electronegative atom is also weakly bonded to an unshared electron pair of another electronegative atom *(251)*

enlaces de hidrógeno: fuerzas de atracción en las que un átomo de hidrógeno, unido por un enlace covalente a un átomo muy electronegativo, también se une débilmente a un par no compartido de electrones de otro átomo electronegativo

hydrogen-ion acceptor: a base, according to the Brønsted-Lowry theory; ammonia acts as a base when it accepts hydrogen ions from water *(649)*

receptor de iones hidrógeno: una base, según la teoría de Brønsted-Lowry; el amoniaco actúa como base cuando acepta iones hidrógeno del agua

hydrogen-ion donor: an acid, according to the Brønsted-Lowry theory *(649)*

donador de iones hidrógeno: un ácido, según la teoría de Brønsted-Lowry

hydronium ion (H_3O^+): the positive ion formed when a water molecule gains a hydrogen ion *(647)*

ion hidronio (H_3O^+): ion positivo que se forma cuando una molécula de agua gana un ion hidrógeno

hydroxy group: the —OH functional group in alcohols *(804)*

grupo hidroxilo: el grupo funcional —OH de los alcoholes

hygroscopic: a term describing salts and other compounds that remove moisture from the air *(499)*

higroscópico: se llama así a las sales y otros compuestos que absorben humedad del aire

hypothesis: a proposed explanation for an observation *(16)*
hipótesis: explicación propuesta para una observación

I

ideal gas constant: the constant in the ideal gas law with the symbol R and the value 8.31 (L·kPa)/(K·mol) *(465)*

constante del gas ideal: constante de la ley del gas ideal; se representa con el símbolo R y tiene un valor de 8.31 (L·kPa)/(K·mol)

ideal gas law: the relationship $PV = nRT$, which describes the behavior of an ideal gas *(465)*

ley del gas ideal: relación $PV = nRT$, que describe el comportamiento del gas ideal

immiscible: describes liquids that are insoluble in one another; oil and water are immiscible *(521)*

inmiscible: se dice de los líquidos que son insolubles uno en el otro; el aceite y el agua son inmiscibles

independent variable: the variable that is changed during an experiment; also called manipulated variable *(16)*

variable independiente: variable que cambia durante un experimento; también se llama variable manipulada

inhibitor: a substance that interferes with the action of a catalyst *(601)*

inhibidor: sustancia que interfiere la acción de un catalizador

inner transition metal: an element in the lanthanide or actinide series; the highest occupied *s* sublevel and nearby *f* sublevel of its atoms generally contain electrons; also called inner transition element *(172)*

metal de transición interna: elemento de las series de los lantánidos o los actínidos; el subnivel *s* más alto ocupado y el subnivel *f* cercano de sus átomos contienen electrones; también se llama elemento de transición interna

inorganic chemistry: the study of substances that, in general, do not contain carbon *(3)*

química inorgánica: estudio de sustancias que, en general, no contienen carbono

intensive property: a property that depends on the type of matter in a sample, not the amount of matter *(34)*

propiedad intensiva: propiedad que depende del tipo de materia de una muestra, no de la cantidad de materia

intermediate: a product of one of the steps in a reaction mechanism; it becomes a reactant in the next step *(607)*

intermediario: producto de uno de los pasos de un mecanismo de reacción; se convierte en reactante en el siguiente paso

International System of Units (SI): the revised version of the metric system, adopted by international agreement in 1960 *(74)*

Sistema Internacional de Unidades (SI): versión modificada del sistema métrico, adoptada por acuerdo internacional en 1960

ion: an atom or group of atoms that has a positive or negative charge *(176)*

ion: átomo o grupo de átomos que tiene carga positiva o negativa

ionic bond: the electrostatic attraction that binds oppositely charged ions together *(201)*

enlace iónico: atracción electrostática que une a iones con carga opuesta

ionic compound: a compound composed of positive and negative ions *(201)*

compuesto iónico: compuesto formado por iones positivos y negativos

ionization energy: the energy required to remove an electron from an atom in its gaseous state *(177)*

energía de ionización: energía necesaria para sacar un electrón de un átomo en su estado gaseoso

ionizing radiation: radiation with enough energy to knock electrons off some atoms of a bombarded substance to produce ions *(894)*

radiación ionizante: radiación que tiene la energía suficiente para desprender electrones de algunos átomos de una sustancia bombardeada, produciendo así iones

ion-product constant for water (K_w): the product of the concentrations of hydrogen ions and hydroxide ions in water; it is 1×10^{-14} at 25°C *(654)*

   constante de producto iónico del agua (K_w): producto de las concentraciones de iones hidrógeno y de iones hidróxido del agua; es 1×10^{-14} a 25°C

isomers: compounds that have the same molecular formula but different molecular structures *(775)*

   isómeros: compuestos que tienen la misma fórmula molecular, pero diferentes estructuras moleculares

isotopes: atoms of the same element that have the same atomic number but different atomic masses due to a different number of neutrons *(114)*

   isótopos: átomos del mismo elemento que tienen el mismo número atómico pero diferentes masas atómicas porque tienen un distinto número de neutrones

J

joule (J): the SI unit of energy; 4.184 J equal one calorie *(77)*

   julio (J): unidad de energía en el SI; 4.184 J equivalen a una caloría

K

Kelvin scale: the temperature scale in which the freezing point of water is 273 K and the boiling point is 373 K; 0 K is absolute zero *(78)*

   escala Kelvin: escala de temperatura en la que el punto de congelación del agua es 273 K, y el de ebullición, 373 K; 0 K es el cero absoluto

ketone: an organic compound in which the carbon of the carbonyl group is joined to two other carbons; the general formula is RCOR *(812)*

   cetona: compuesto orgánico en el que el carbono del grupo carbonilo está unido a otros dos carbonos: la fórmula general es RCOR

kilogram (kg): the mass of 1 L of water at 4°C; it is the base unit of mass in SI *(77)*

   kilogramo (kg): masa de 1 L de agua a 4°C; es la unidad base de masa en el SI

kinetic energy: the energy an object has because of its motion *(420)*

   energía cinética: energía que tienen los objetos de acuerdo con su movimiento

kinetic theory: a theory explaining the states of matter, based on the concept that all matter consists of tiny particles that are in constant motion *(420)*

   teoría cinética: teoría que explica los estados de la materia basándose en el concepto de que toda la materia está formada por pequeñas partículas que están en constante movimiento

L

law of conservation of energy: in any chemical or physical process, energy is neither created nor destroyed *(557)*

   ley de conservación de la energía: ley según la cual en ningún proceso químico o físico se crea ni se destruye energía

law of conservation of mass: in any physical change or chemical reaction, mass is conserved; mass can be neither created nor destroyed *(50)*

   ley de conservación de la masa: en cualquier cambio físico o reacción química, la masa se conserva; la masa no puede crearse ni destruirse

law of definite proportions: in samples of any chemical compound, the masses of the elements are always in the same proportion *(289)*

   ley de las proporciones definidas: en muestras de cualquier compuesto químico, las masas de los elementos siempre están en la misma proporción

law of disorder: it is a natural tendency of systems to move in the direction of maximum chaos or disorder *(630)*

   ley del desorden: tendencia natural de los sistemas a desplazarse en la dirección hacia el máximo caos o desorden

law of multiple proportions: whenever two elements form more than one compound, the different masses of one element that combine with the same mass of the other element are in the ratio of small whole numbers *(290)*

   ley de las proporciones múltiples: siempre que dos elementos forman más de un compuesto, las diferentes masas de un elemento que se combinan con la misma masa del otro elemento están en razón de números enteros pequeños

Le Châtelier's principle: when a stress is applied to a system in dynamic equilibrium, the system changes in a way that relieves the stress *(612)*

   principio de Le Châtelier: cuando se aplica una tensión a un sistema que está en equilibrio dinámico, el sistema cambia a modo de aliviar dicha tensión

Lewis acid: any substance that can accept a pair of electrons to form a covalent bond *(651)*

   ácido de Lewis: cualquier sustancia capaz de aceptar un par de electrones para formar un enlace covalente

Lewis base: any substance that can donate a pair of electrons to form a covalent bond *(651)*

   base de Lewis: cualquier sustancia capaz de ceder un par de electrones para formar un enlace covalente

limiting reagent: any reactant that is used up first in a chemical reaction; it determines the amount of product that can be formed in the reaction *(401)*

   reactivo limitante: cualquier reactante que se haya consumido primero en una reacción química; determina la cantidad de producto que se puede formar en la reacción

lipid: a member of a large class of relatively water-insoluble organic compounds; fats, oils, and waxes are lipids *(850)*

lípido: miembro de una clase amplia de compuestos orgánicos relativamente insolubles en agua; las grasas, aceites y ceras son lípidos

liquid: a form of matter that flows, has a fixed volume, and an indefinite shape *(36)*

líquido: forma de materia que fluye; tiene volumen fijo pero forma indefinida

liter (L): the volume of a cube measuring 10 centimeters on each edge (1000 cm^3); it is the common unprefixed unit of volume in the metric system *(76)*

litro (L): volumen de un cubo cuyas aristas miden 10 centímetros cada una (1000 cm^3); es la unidad común de volumen en el sistema métrico

M

manipulated variable: *see* independent variable *(16)*

variable manipulada: *véase* variable independiente

mass: a measure of the amount of matter that an object contains; the SI base unit of mass is the kilogram *(34)*

masa: medida de la cantidad de materia contenida en un objeto; la unidad base de masa en el SI es el kilogramo

mass number: the total number of protons and neutrons in the nucleus of an atom *(113)*

número de masa: número total de protones y neutrones que contiene el núcleo de un átomo

matter: anything that has mass and occupies space *(2)*

materia: todo lo que tiene masa y ocupa espacio

measurement: a quantitative description that includes both a number and a unit *(62)*

medición: descripción cuantitativa que incluye tanto números como unidades

melting point (mp): the temperature at which a substance changes from a solid to a liquid; the melting point of water is 0°C *(431)*

punto de fusión (p.f.): temperatura a la que una sustancia cambia del estado sólido al líquido; el punto de fusión del agua es 0°C

metabolism: all the chemical reactions carried out by an organism; includes energy-producing (catabolism) reactions and energy-absorbing (anabolism) reactions *(863)*

metabolismo: todas las reacciones químicas llevadas a cabo por los organismos; incluyen reacciones que producen energía (catabolismo) y reacciones que consumen energía (anabolismo)

metal: one of a class of elements that are good conductors of heat and electric current; metals tend to be ductile, malleable, and shiny *(165)*

metal: miembro de una clase de elementos que son buenos conductores del calor y la electricidad; los metales suelen ser dúctiles, maleables y brillantes

metallic bond: the force of attraction that holds metals together; it consists of the attraction of free-floating valence electrons for positively charged metal ions *(209)*

enlace metálico: fuerza de atracción que mantiene unidos los átomos de un metal; se debe a la atracción entre los electrones de valencia, que flotan libremente, y los iones metálicos de carga positiva

metalloid: an element that tends to have properties that are similar to those of metals and nonmetals *(166)*

metaloide: elemento cuyas propiedades son similares a las de los metales y de los no metales

meter (m): the base unit of length in SI *(75)*

metro (m): unidad base de longitud en el SI

miscible: describes liquids that dissolve in one another in all proportions *(521)*

miscible: se les llama así a los líquidos que se disuelven uno en el otro en todas las proporciones

mixture: a physical blend of two or more substances that are not chemically combined *(38)*

mezcla: incorporación física de dos o más sustancias que no se combinan químicamente

model: a representation of an object or event *(16)*

modelo: representación de un objeto o evento

molal boiling-point elevation constant (K_b): the change in boiling point for a 1-molal solution of a nonvolatile molecular solute *(543)*

constante molal de la elevación del punto de ebullición (K_b): cambio en el punto de ebullición de una solución 1-molal de un soluto molecular no volátil

molal freezing-point depression constant (K_f): the change in freezing point for a 1-molal solution of a nonvolatile molecular solute *(542)*

constante molal de la disminución del punto de congelación (K_f): cambio en el punto de congelación de una solución 1-molal de un soluto molecular no volátil

molality (m): the concentration of solute in a solution expressed as the number of moles of solute dissolved in 1 kilogram (1000 g) of solvent *(538)*

molalidad (m): concentración de soluto en una solución expresada como el número de moles de soluto disueltos en 1 kilogramo (1000 g) de disolvente

molar heat of condensation (ΔH_{cond}): the amount of heat released by one mole of a vapor as it condenses to a liquid at a constant temperature *(572)*

calor molar de condensación (ΔH_{cond}): cantidad de calor que un mol de vapor desprende al condensarse, convirtiéndose en líquido, a temperatura constante

molar heat of fusion (ΔH_{fus}): the amount of heat absorbed by one mole of a solid substance as it melts to a liquid at a constant temperature *(569)*

calor molar de fusión (ΔH_{fus}): cantidad de calor que un mol de una sustancia sólida absorbe al fundirse, convirtiéndose en líquido, a temperatura constante

molar heat of solidification (ΔH_{solid}): the amount of heat lost by one mole of a liquid as it solidifies at a constant temperature *(569)*

calor molar de solidificación (ΔH_{solid}): cantidad de calor que un mol de un líquido pierde al solidificarse a temperatura constante

molar heat of solution (ΔH_{soln}): the enthalpy change caused by the dissolution of one mole of a substance *(574)*

calor molar de disolución (ΔH_{soln}): cambio de calor debido a la disolución de un mol de una sustancia

molar heat of vaporization (ΔH_{vap}): the amount of heat absorbed by one mole of a liquid as it vaporizes at a constant temperature *(571)*

calor molar de vaporización (ΔH_{vap}): cantidad de calor absorbida por un mol de un líquido al evaporarse a temperatura constante

molarity (M): the concentration of solute in a solution expressed as the number of moles of solute dissolved in 1 liter of solution *(525)*

molaridad (M): concentración de soluto en una solución expresada como el número de moles de soluto disueltos en 1 litro de solución

molar mass: a term used to refer to the mass of a mole of any substance *(313)*

masa molar: término empleado para referirse a la masa de un mol de cualquier sustancia

molar volume: the volume occupied by 1 mole of a gas at standard temperature and pressure (STP); 22.4 L *(320)*

volumen molar: volumen ocupado por 1 mol de un gas a temperatura y presión estándar (TPE); 22.4 L

mole (mol): the amount of a substance that contains 6.02×10^{23} representative particles of that substance *(308)*

mol: cantidad de una sustancia que contiene 6.02×10^{23} partículas representativas de esa sustancia

molecular compound: a compound that is composed of molecules *(223)*

compuesto molecular: compuesto formado por moléculas

molecular formula: a chemical formula of a molecular compound that shows the kinds and numbers of atoms present in a molecule of a compound *(223)*

fórmula molecular: fórmula química de un compuesto molecular que indica los tipos y números de átomos presentes en una molécula de un compuesto

molecular orbital: an orbital that applies to the entire molecule *(240)*

orbital molecular: orbital que abarca toda la molécula

molecule: a neutral group of atoms joined together by covalent bonds *(215)*

molécula: grupo neutro de átomos unidos por enlaces covalentes

mole fraction: the ratio of the moles of solute in solution to the total number of moles of both solvent and solute *(540)*

fracción molar: razón de los moles de soluto en solución al número total de moles de disolvente y soluto

mole ratio: a conversion factor derived from the coefficients of a balanced chemical equation interpreted in terms of moles *(390)*

razón molar: factor de conversión derivado de los coeficientes de una ecuación química equilibrada interpretada en términos de moles

monatomic ion: a single atom with a positive or negative charge resulting from the loss or gain of one or more valence electrons *(264)*

ion monoatómico: un solo átomo con carga positiva o negativa debido a la pérdida o ganancia de uno o más electrones de valencia

monomer: a simple molecule that repeatedly combines to form a polymer *(822)*

monómero: molécula sencilla que se combina repetidamente para formar un polímero

monoprotic acid: any acid that contains one ionizable proton (hydrogen ion); nitric acid (HNO_3) is a monoprotic acid *(647)*

ácido monoprótico: ácido que sólo contiene un protón (ion hidrógeno) ionizable; el ácido nítrico (HNO_3) es un ácido monoprótico

monosaccharide: a carbohydrate consisting of one sugar unit; also called a simple sugar *(841)*

monosacárido: carbohidrato que consta de una sola unidad de azúcar; también llamado azúcar simple

N

net ionic equation: an equation for a reaction in solution showing only those particles that are directly involved in the chemical change *(370)*

ecuación iónica neta: ecuación de una reacción en solución que sólo muestra las partículas que intervienen directamente en el cambio químico

network solid: a solid in which all of the atoms are covalently bonded to each other *(252)*

sólido en cadena: sólido en el que todos los átomos están unidos entre sí por enlaces covalentes

neutralization reaction: a reaction in which an acid and a base react in an aqueous solution to produce a salt and water *(672)*

reacción de neutralización: reacción en la que un ácido y una base reaccionan en una solución acuosa para producir una sal y agua

neutral solution: an aqueous solution in which the concentrations of hydrogen and hydroxide ions are equal; it has a pH of 7.0 (653)

solución neutral: solución acuosa en la que las concentraciones de iones hidrógeno e iones hidróxido son iguales; tiene un pH de 7.0

neutron: a subatomic particle with no charge and a mass of 1 amu; found in the nucleus of an atom (107)

neutrón: partícula subatómica sin carga que tiene una masa de 1 uma; se le encuentra en el núcleo de los átomos

neutron absorption: a process that decreases the number of slow-moving neutrons in a nuclear reactor; this is accomplished by using control rods made of a material such as cadmium, which absorbs neutrons (889)

absorción de neutrones: proceso que reduce el número de neutrones lentos en un reactor nuclear; esto se logra mediante el uso de varillas de control hechas con un material como el cadmio, que absorbe neutrones

neutron moderation: a process used in nuclear reactors to slow down neutrons so the reactor fuel captures them to continue the chain reaction (889)

moderación de neutrones: proceso empleado en reactores nucleares para frenar los neutrones de modo que el combustible del reactor los capture para continuar la reacción en cadena

noble gas: an element in Group 8A of the periodic table; the *s* and *p* sublevels of the highest occupied energy level are filled (170)

gas noble: elemento del grupo 8A de la tabla periódica; los subniveles *s* y *p* del nivel energético ocupado más alto están totalmente llenos

nonelectrolyte: a compound that does not conduct an electric current in aqueous solution or in the molten state (496)

no electrolito: compuesto que no conduce una corriente eléctrica en solución acuosa ni en estado fundido

nonmetal: an element that tends to be a poor conductor of heat and electric current; nonmetals generally have properties opposite to those of metals (165)

no metal: elemento que suele ser mal conductor del calor y la electricidad; las propiedades de los no metales generalmente son opuestas a las de los metales

nonpolar covalent bond: a covalent bond in which the electrons are shared equally by the two atoms (247)

enlace covalente no polar: enlace covalente en el que los dos átomos comparten equitativamente los electrones

nonspontaneous reaction: a reaction that does not favor the formation of products at the specified conditions (628)

reacción no espontánea: reacción que no favorece la formación de productos en las condiciones especificadas

normal boiling point: the boiling point of a liquid at a pressure of 101.3 kPa or 1 atm (430)

punto normal de ebullición: el punto de ebullición de un líquido a una presión de 101.3 kPa o 1 atm

nuclear force: an attractive force that acts between all nuclear particles that are extremely close together, such as protons and neutrons in a nucleus (880)

fuerza nuclear: fuerza de atracción que actúa entre todas las partículas nucleares que están extremadamente cerca unas de otras, como los protones y los neutrones en un núcleo

nuclear radiation: the penetrating rays and particles emitted by a radioactive source (876)

radiación nuclear: rayos y partículas penetrantes que una fuente radiactiva emite

nucleic acid: a polymer of ribonucleotides (RNA) or deoxyribonucleotides (DNA) found primarily in cell nuclei; nucleic acids play an important role in the transmission of hereditary characteristics, protein synthesis, and the control of cell activities (854)

ácido nucleico: polímero de ribonucleótidos (ARN) o desoxirribonucleótidos (ADN) que se encuentra primordialmente en el núcleo de las células; los ácidos nucleicos desempeñan un papel importante en la transmisión de las características hereditarias, en la síntesis de proteínas y en el control de las actividades celulares

nucleotide: one of the monomers that make up DNA and RNA; it consists of a nitrogen-containing base (a purine or pyrimidine), a sugar (ribose or deoxyribose), and a phosphate group (854)

nucleótido: uno de los monómeros que constituyen el ADN y el ARN; consiste en una base nitrogenada (una purina o una pirimidina), un azúcar (ribosa o desoxirribosa) y un grupo fosfato

nucleus: the tiny, dense central portion of an atom, composed of protons and neutrons (108)

núcleo: la diminuta porción central densa de un átomo; se compone de protones y neutrones

observation: information obtained through the senses; observation in science often involves a measurement (15)

observación: información obtenida a través de los sentidos; en la ciencia, la observación suele implicar la medición

octet rule: atoms react by gaining or losing electrons so as to acquire the stable electron structure of a noble gas, usually eight valence electrons (195)

regla del octeto: los átomos reaccionan ganando o perdiendo electrones a modo de adquirir la estructura electrónica estable de un gas noble, que por lo regular consta de ocho electrones de valencia

organic chemistry: the study of compounds containing carbon *(3)*

química orgánica: estudio de los compuestos que contienen carbono

oxidation: a process that involves complete or partial loss of electrons or a gain of oxygen; it results in an increase in the oxidation number of an atom *(694)*

oxidación: proceso que implica la pérdida total o parcial de electrones o la ganancia de oxígeno; conduce a un aumento en el número de oxidación de un átomo

oxidation number: a positive or negative number assigned to an atom to indicate its degree of oxidation or reduction; the oxidation number of an uncombined element is zero *(701)*

número de oxidación: número positivo o negativo que se asigna a un átomo para indicar su grado de oxidación o reducción; el número de oxidación de un elemento no combinado es cero

oxidation-number-change method: a method of balancing a redox equation by comparing the increases and decreases in oxidation numbers *(710)*

método de cambio del número de oxidación: método para balancear una ecuación redox comparando los incrementos y reducciones de los números de oxidación

oxidation-reduction reaction: a reaction that involves the transfer of electrons between reactants *(693)*

reacción de oxidación–reducción: reacción en la que hay transferencia de electrones entre los reactantes

oxidizing agent: the substance in a redox reaction that accepts electrons; in the reaction, the oxidizing agent is reduced *(695)*

agente oxidante: en una reacción redox, la sustancia que acepta electrones; en la reacción, el agente oxidante se reduce

P

partial pressure: the contribution each gas in a mixture of gases makes to the total pressure *(469)*

presión parcial: contribución de cada gas de una mezcla de gases a la presión total

pascal (Pa): the SI unit of pressure *(422)*

pascal (Pa): unidad de presión en el SI

Pauli exclusion principle: an atomic orbital may describe at most two electrons, each with opposite spin direction *(134)*

principio de exclusión de Pauli: orbital atómico puede describir como máximo a dos electrones, los cuales deben tener espín opuesto

peptide: an organic compound formed by a combination of amino acids in which the amino group of one acid is united with the carboxyl group of another through an amide bond *(845)*

péptido: compuesto orgánico formado por la combinación de aminoácidos de modo que el grupo amino de un ácido se une al grupo carboxilo de otro creando un enlace amida

peptide bond: the bond between the carbonyl group of one amino acid and the nitrogen of the next amino acid in the peptide chain; the structure is

$$\begin{array}{cc} O & H \\ \parallel & | \\ -C- & N- \end{array}$$

(845)

enlace péptido: enlace que hay entre el grupo carbonilo de un aminoácido y el nitrógeno del siguiente aminoácido de la cadena péptida; la estructura es

$$\begin{array}{cc} O & H \\ \parallel & | \\ -C- & N- \end{array}$$

percent composition: the percent by mass of each element in a compound *(325)*

composición porcentual: porcentaje en masa de cada elemento de un compuesto

percent error: the percent that a measured value differs from the accepted value *(65)*

error porcentual: porcentaje en que un valor medido difiere del valor aceptado

percent yield: the ratio of the actual yield to the theoretical yield for a chemical reaction expressed as a percentage; a measure of the efficiency of a reaction *(405)*

rendimiento porcentual: razón del rendimiento real al rendimiento teórico de una reacción química, expresado como porcentaje; es una medida de la eficiencia de la reacción

period: a horizontal row of elements in the periodic table *(46)*

periodo: fila horizontal de elementos en la tabla periódica

periodic law: when the elements are arranged in order of increasing atomic number, there is a periodic repetition of their physical and chemical properties *(162)*

ley periódica: si los elementos se acomodan en orden de menor a mayor número atómico, se observa una repetición periódica de sus propiedades físicas y químicas

periodic table: an arrangement of elements in which the elements are separated into groups based on a set of repeating properties *(46)*

tabla periódica: distribución de los elementos dividiéndolos en grupos según un conjunto de propiedades repetidas

pH: a number used to denote the hydrogen-ion concentration, or acidity, of a solution; it is the negative logarithm of the hydrogen-ion concentration of a solution *(656)*

    pH: número empleado para denotar la concentración de ion hidrógeno (acidez) de una solución; es el logaritmo negativo de la concentración de ion hidrógeno en una solución

phase: any part of a sample with uniform composition and properties *(39)*

    fase: cualquier parte de una muestra que tiene composición y propiedades uniformes

phase diagram: a graph showing the conditions at which a substance exists as a solid, liquid, or vapor *(438)*

    diagrama de fases: gráfica que muestra las condiciones en las que una sustancia existe como sólido, líquido o vapor

phospholipid: a lipid that contains a phosphate group; because phospholipids have hydrophilic heads and hydrophobic tails, they form the lipid bilayers found in cell membranes *(851)*

    fosfolípido: lípido que contiene un grupo fosfato; como los fosfolípidos tienen una cabeza hidrofílica y una cola hidrofóbica, pueden formar las bicapas lípidas de las membranas celulares

photoelectric effect: the ejection of electrons by certain metals when they absorb light with a frequency above a threshold frequency *(143)*

    efecto fotoeléctrico: liberación de electrones por algunos metales cuando absorben la luz con una frecuencia superior a un umbral (o frecuencia mínima)

photon: a quantum of light; a discrete bundle of electromagnetic energy that interacts with matter similarly to particles *(144)*

    fotón: cuanto de luz; paquete discreto de energía electromagnética que interactúa con la materia de forma similar a como lo hacen las partículas

photosynthesis: the process by which green plants and algae use radiant energy from the sun to synthesize glucose from carbon dioxide and water *(839)*

    fotosíntesis: proceso por el cual las plantas y algas verdes aprovechan la energía radiante del Sol para sintetizar glucosa a partir de dióxido de carbono y agua

physical change: a change during which some properties of a material change, but the composition of the material does not change *(37)*

    cambio físico: cambio durante el cual se alteran algunas propiedades de un material, pero sin que se altere la composición del material

physical chemistry: the area of chemistry that deals with the mechanism, the rate, and the energy transfer that occurs when matter undergoes a change *(3)*

    fisicoquímica: área de la química que se relaciona con el mecanismo, la velocidad y la transferencia de energía que ocurre cuando la materia sufre un cambio

physical property: a quality or condition of a substance that can be observed or measured without changing the substance's composition *(35)*

    propiedad física: cualidad o condición de una sustancia que se puede observar o medir sin alterar la composición de la sustancia

pi bond (π bond): a covalent bond in which the bonding electrons are most likely to be found in sausage-shaped regions above and below the bond axis of the bonded atoms *(241)*

    enlace pi (enlace π): enlace covalente en el que hay una alta probabilidad de encontrar los electrones de enlace en regiones alargadas que están arriba y abajo del eje de enlace de los átomos enlazados

Planck's constant (h): a number used to calculate the radiant energy (E) absorbed or emitted by a body based on the frequency of radiation (143)

    constante de Planck (h): número que se usa para calcular la energía radiante (E) que un cuerpo absorbe o emite basándose en la frecuencia de radiación

polar covalent bond (polar bond): a covalent bond between atoms in which the electrons are shared unequally *(248)*

    enlace covalente polar (enlace polar): enlace covalente entre átomos que no comparten equitativamente sus electrones

polar molecule: a molecule in which one side of the molecule is slightly negative and the opposite side is slightly positive *(249)*

    molécula polar: molécula que tiene un lado ligeramente negativo y el otro ligeramente positivo

polyatomic ion: a tightly bound group of atoms that behaves as a unit and has a positive or negative charge *(232)*

    ion poliatómico: grupo fuertemente enlazado de átomos, que se comporta como una unidad y tiene carga positiva o negativa

polymer: a very large molecule formed by the covalent bonding of repeating small molecules, known as monomers *(822)*

    polímero: molécula muy grande formada por la unión, mediante enlaces covalentes, de moléculas pequeñas repetidas, llamadas monómeros

polysaccharide: a complex carbohydrate polymer formed by the linkage of many monosaccharide monomers; starch, glycogen, and cellulose are polysaccharides *(843)*

    polisacárido: carbohidrato complejo formado por el encadenamiento de muchos monómeros monosacáridos; el almidón, el glucógeno y la celulosa son polisacáridos

positron: a particle with the mass of an electron but a positive charge *(881)*

    positrón: partícula con la misma masa que un electrón pero con carga positiva

precipitate: a solid that forms and settles out of a liquid mixture (49)

  precipitado: sólido que se forma a partir de una mezcla líquida y se asienta

precision: describes the closeness, or reproducibility, of a set of measurements taken under the same conditions (64)

  precisión: cifra que describe la variabilidad de una serie de mediciones efectuadas en las mismas condiciones

product: a substance produced in a chemical reaction (48)

  producto: sustancia que se obtiene en una reacción química

protein: any peptide with more than 100 amino acids (845)

  proteína: cualquier péptido que tiene más de 100 aminoácidos

proton: a positively charged subatomic particle found in the nucleus of an atom (107)

  protón: partícula subatómica con carga positiva que se encuentra en el núcleo de los átomos

pure chemistry: the pursuit of chemical knowledge for its own sake (3)

  química pura: búsqueda de conocimientos químicos por sí mismos

pure substance: *see* substance

  sustancia pura: *véase* sustancia

Q

quantum: the amount of energy needed to move an electron from one energy level to another (129)

  cuanto: cantidad de energía necesaria para desplazar un electrón de un nivel energético a otro

quantum mechanical model: the modern description, primarily mathematical, of the behavior of electrons in atoms (130)

  modelo según la mecánica cuántica: descripción moderna, primordialmente matemática, del comportamiento de los electrones en los átomos

R

radioactivity: the process by which nuclei emit particles and rays (876)

  radiactividad: proceso por el cual los núcleos emiten partículas y rayos

radioisotope: an isotope that has an unstable nucleus and undergoes radioactive decay (876)

  radioisótopo: isótopo cuyo núcleo es inestable y sufre desintegración radiactiva

rate: describes the speed of change over an interval of time (595)

  velocidad (de reacción): cifra que describe la velocidad de cambio a lo largo de un intervalo de tiempo

rate law: an expression relating the rate of a reaction to the concentration of the reactants (604)

  ley de velocidad de reacción: expresión que relaciona la velocidad de una reacción con la concentración de los reactantes

reactant: a substance present at the start of a reaction (48)

  reactante: sustancia presente al principio de una reacción

reaction mechanism: a series of elementary reactions that take place during the course of a complex reaction (607)

  mecanismo de reacción: serie de reacciones básicas que se dan durante el curso de una reacción compleja

reducing agent: the substance in a redox reaction that donates electrons; in the reaction, the reducing agent is oxidized (695)

  agente reductor: en una reacción redox, la sustancia que cede electrones; en la reacción, el agente reductor se oxida

reduction: a process that involves a complete or partial gain of electrons or the loss of oxygen; it results in a decrease in the oxidation number of an atom (694)

  reducción: proceso que implica una ganancia total o parcial de electrones o pérdida de oxígeno; provoca una disminución en el número de oxidación de un átomo

reduction potential: a measure of the tendency of a given half-reaction to occur as a reduction (gain of electrons) in an electrochemical cell (737)

  potencial de reducción: medida de la tendencia que tiene una semirreacción específica de efectuarse como reducción (con ganancia de electrones) en una celda electroquímica

representative element: an element in an "A" group in the periodic table; as a group these elements display a wide range of physical and chemical properties. In their atoms, the *s* and *p* sublevels in the highest occupied energy level are partially filled (171)

  elemento representativo: elemento de un grupo "A" de la tabla periódica; en conjunto, estos elementos exhiben una amplia gama de propiedades físicas y químicas. En sus átomos, los subniveles *s* y *p* del nivel energético ocupado más alto están parcialmente llenos

representative particle: the smallest unit into which a substance can be broken down without a change in composition, usually atoms, molecules, or ions (308)

  partícula representativa: unidad más pequeña en que puede dividirse una sustancia sin que cambie su composición; por lo regular es un átomo, molécula o ion

resonance structure: one of the two or more equally valid electron dot structures of a molecule or polyatomic ion (237)

  estructura de resonancia: una de las dos o más estructuras electrón-punto igualmente válidas de una molécula o ion poliatómico

responding variable: *see* dependent variable (16)

  variable de respuesta: *véase* variable dependiente

reversible reaction: a reaction in which the conversion of reactants into products and the conversion of products into reactants occur simultaneously *(609)*

   reacción reversible: reacción en la que se da en forma simultánea la conversión de reactantes en productos y la conversión de productos en reactantes

S

salt bridge: a tube containing a strong electrolyte used to separate the half-cells in a voltaic cell; it allows the passage of ions from one half-cell to the other but prevents the solutions from mixing completely *(730)*

   puente salino: tubo que contiene un electrolito fuerte y se usa para separar las semiceldas de una celda voltaica; permite el paso de iones de una semicelda a la otra, pero impide que las soluciones se mezclen totalmente

salt hydrolysis: a process in which the cations or anions of a dissociated salt accept hydrogen ions from water or donate hydrogen ions to water *(677)*

   hidrólisis de sales: proceso por el cual los cationes o aniones de una sal disociada aceptan iones hidrógeno del agua o ceden iones hidrógeno al agua

saponification: the hydrolysis of fats or oils by a hot aqueous alkali-metal hydroxide; soaps are made by saponification *(851)*

   saponificación: hidrólisis de grasas o aceites con una solución acuosa caliente de un hidróxido de metal alcalino; los jabones se hacen mediante la saponificación

saturated compound: an organic compound in which all carbon atoms are joined by single covalent bonds; it contains the maximum number of hydrogen atoms per carbon atom *(772)*

   compuesto saturado: compuesto orgánico en el que todos los átomos de carbono están unidos unos a otros por enlaces covalentes sencillos; contiene el número máximo de átomos de hidrógeno por átomo de carbono

saturated solution: a solution containing the maximum amount of solute for a given amount of solvent at a constant temperature and pressure; an equilibrium exists between undissolved solute and ions in solution *(520)*

   solución saturada: solución que contiene la cantidad máxima de soluto para una cantidad dada de disolvente a temperatura y presión constantes; existe equilibrio entre el soluto no disuelto y los iones en solución

scientific law: a concise statement that summarizes the results of many observations and experiments *(17)*

   ley científica: expresión concisa que resume los resultados de muchas observaciones y experimentos

scientific notation: an expression of numbers in the form $m \times 10^n$, where m is equal to or greater than 1 and less than 10, and n is an integer *(62)*

   notación científica: convención por la cual los números se expresan en la forma $m \times 10^n$, donde m es un número mayor o igual que 1 y menor que 10, y n es un entero

self-ionization: a term describing the reaction in which two water molecules react to produce ions *(653)*

   autoionización: reacción en la que dos moléculas de agua reaccionan para producir iones

sigma bond (σ bond): a bond formed when two atomic orbitals combine for form a molecular orbital that is symmetrical around the axis connecting the two atomic nuclei *(240)*

   enlace sigma (enlace σ): enlace que se forma cuando dos orbitales atómicos se combinan para formar un orbital molecular que es simétrico respecto al eje que conecta a los dos núcleos atómicos

significant figures: all the digits that can be known precisely in a measurement, plus a last estimated digit *(66)*

   dígitos significativos: todos los dígitos de una medición que se pueden conocer con precisión, más un último dígito estimado

single covalent bond: a bond formed when two atoms share a pair of electrons *(226)*

   enlace covalente sencillo: enlace que se forma cuando dos átomos comparten un par de electrones

single-replacement reaction: a chemical change in which one element replaces a second element in a compound; also called a displacement reaction *(360)*

   reacción de sustitución sencilla: cambio químico en el que un elemento reemplaza a un segundo elemento en un compuesto; también llamado reacción de desplazamiento

skeleton equation: a chemical equation that does not indicate the relative amounts of reactants and products *(348)*

   ecuación esqueleto: ecuación química que no indica las cantidades relativas de los reactantes y productos

solid: a form of matter that has a definite shape and volume *(36)*

   sólido: estado de la materia que tiene forma y volumen definidos

solubility: the amount of a substance that dissolves in a given quantity of solvent at specified conditions of temperature and pressure to produce a saturated solution *(520)*

    solubilidad: cantidad de una sustancia que se disuelve en una cantidad dada de disolvente, bajo condiciones específicas de temperatura y presión, para producir una solución saturada

solubility product constant (K_{sp}): an equilibrium constant applied to the solubility of electrolytes; it is equal to the product of the concentrations of the ions each raised to a power equal to the coefficient of the ion in the dissociation equation *(622)*

    constante del producto de solubilidad (K_{sp}): constante de equilibrio aplicada a la capacidad disoluble de electrolitos; es igual al producto de las concentraciones de los iones, cada una elevada a una potencia igual al coeficiente que tiene ese ion en la ecuación de disociación

solute: dissolved particles in a solution *(494)*

    soluto: partículas disueltas en una solución

solution: a homogeneous mixture; consists of solutes dissolved in a solvent *(39)*

    solución: mezcla homogénea que consiste en solutos disueltos en un disolvente

solvation: a process that occurs when an ionic solute dissolves; in solution, solvent molecules surround the positive and negative ions *(495)*

    solvatación: proceso que tiene lugar cuando se disuelve un soluto iónico; en solución, las moléculas de disolvente rodean a los iones positivos y negativos

solvent: the dissolving medium in a solution *(494)*

    disolvente: medio dispersor en una solución

specific heat: the amount of heat needed to increase the temperature of 1 g of a substance 1°C; also called specific heat capacity *(559)*

    calor específico: cantidad de calor requerida para elevar 1°C la temperatura de 1 g de una sustancia

specific rate constant: a proportionality constant relating the concentrations of reactants to the rate of the reaction *(604)*

    constante específica de velocidad de reacción: constante de proporcionalidad que relaciona las concentraciones de los reactantes con la velocidad de la reacción

spectator ion: an ion that is not directly involved in a chemical reaction; an ion that does not change oxidation number or composition during a reaction *(370)*

    ion espectador: ion que no interviene directamente en una reacción química; ion que no cambia de número de oxidación ni de composición durante una reacción

spectrum: wavelengths of visible light that are separated when a beam of light passes through a prism; range of wavelengths of electromagnetic radiation *(139)*

    espectro: longitudes de onda de la luz visible que se separan cuando un haz de luz atraviesa un prisma; gama de longitudes de onda de radiación electromagnética

spin: a quantum mechanical property of electrons that may be thought of as clockwise or counterclockwise *(134)*

    espín: propiedad de los electrones según la mecánica cuántica en la cual la rotación se considera en sentido de las agujas del reloj o en sentido contrario a las agujas del reloj

spontaneous reaction: a reaction that favors the formation of products at the specified conditions; spontaneity depends on enthalpy and entropy changes *(628)*

    reacción espontánea: reacción que favorece la formación de productos, bajo las condiciones especificadas; la espontaneidad depende de los cambios de entalpía y de entropía

standard atmosphere (atm): a unit of pressure; it is the pressure required to support 760 mm of mercury in a mercury barometer at 25°C *(422)*

    atmósfera estándar (atm): unidad de presión; es la presión necesaria para sostener 760 mm de mercurio en un barómetro de mercurio a 25°C

standard cell potential (E_{cell}°): the measured cell potential when the ion concentration in the half-cells are 1.00M at 1 atm of pressure and 25°C *(737)*

    potencial estándar de celda (E_{cell}°): potencial de celda que se mide cuando las concentraciones de los iones en las semiceldas son 1.00M a 1 atm de presión y 25°C

standard heat of formation (ΔH_f°): the change in enthalpy that accompanies the formation of one mole of a compound from its elements with all substances in their standard states at 25°C *(580)*

    calor estándar de formación (ΔH_f°): cambio de entalpía que acompaña a la formación de un mol de un compuesto a partir de sus elementos, estando todas las sustancias en su estado estándar a 25°C

standard hydrogen electrode: an arbitrary reference electrode (half-cell) used with another electrode (half-cell) to measure the standard reduction potential of that cell; the standard reduction potential of the hydrogen electrode is assigned a value of 0.00 V *(738)*

    electrodo estándar de hidrógeno: electrodo (semicelda) arbitrario de referencia que se usa junto con otro electrodo (semicelda) para medir el potencial estándar de reducción de esa celda; se asigna al potencial estándar de reducción del electrodo de hidrógeno el valor de 0.00 V

standard solution: a solution of known concentration used in carrying out a titration *(674)*

    solución estándar: solución cuya concentración se conoce; se usa para efectuar valoraciones químicas

standard temperature and pressure (STP): the conditions under which the volume of a gas is usually measured; standard temperature is 0°C, and standard pressure is 101.3 kPa, or 1 atmosphere (atm) *(320)*

    temperatura y presión estándar (TPE): las condiciones en las que normalmente se mide el volumen de un gas; la temperatura estándar es 0°C y la presión estándar es 101.3 kPa, o sea, 1 atmósfera (atm)

stereoisomers: molecules that have atoms in the same order, but which differ in the arrangement of the atoms in space (776)

 estereoisómeros: moléculas cuyos átomos están en el mismo orden, pero que difieren en la distribución de los átomos en el espacio

stoichiometry: that portion of chemistry dealing with numerical relationships in chemical reactions; the calculation of quantities of substances involved in chemical equations (386)

 estequiometría: rama de la química que se ocupa de las relaciones numéricas en las ecuaciones químicas; el cálculo de las cantidades de sustancias presentes en las ecuaciones químicas

straight-chain alkane: a saturated hydrocarbon that contains any number of carbon atoms arranged one after the other in a chain (764)

 alcano de cadena lineal: hidrocarburo saturado que contiene cualquier número de átomos de carbono acomodados uno tras otro en una cadena

strong acid: an acid that is completely (or almost completely) ionized in aqueous solution (664)

 ácido fuerte: ácido que se ioniza casi totalmente en solución acuosa

strong base: a base that completely dissociates into metal ions and hydroxide ions in aqueous solution (668)

 base fuerte: base que se disocia totalmente en una solución acuosa para dar iones metálicos y iones hidróxido

strong electrolyte: a solution in which a large portion of the solute exists as ions (497)

 electrolito fuerte: solución en la que una porción considerable del soluto existe en forma de iones

structural formula: a chemical formula that shows the arrangement of atoms in a molecule or a polyatomic ion; each dash between a pair of atoms indicates a pair of shared electrons (227)

 fórmula estructural: fórmula química que indica la distribución de los átomos en una molécula o ion poliatómico; cada raya entre un par de átomos indica un par de electrones compartidos

sublimation: the process in which a solid changes to a gas or vapor without passing through the liquid state (436)

 sublimación: proceso por el cual un sólido cambia a gas o vapor sin pasar por el estado líquido

substance: matter that has a uniform and definite composition; either an element or a compound; also called pure substance (35)

 sustancia: materia que tiene una composición uniforme y definida; puede ser un elemento o un compuesto; también llamada sustancia pura

substituent: an atom or group of atoms that can take the place of a hydrogen atom on a parent hydrocarbon molecule (767)

 sustituto: átomo o grupo de átomos que puede ocupar el lugar de un átomo de hidrógeno en una molécula precursora de hidrocarburo

substitution reaction: a common type of organic reaction; involves the replacement of an atom or group of atoms by another atom or group of atoms (801)

 reacción de sustitución: tipo común de reacción orgánica; implica el reemplazo de un átomo o grupo de átomos por otro átomo o grupo de átomos

substrate: a molecule on which an enzyme acts (847)

 sustrato: molécula sobre la que actúa una enzima

supersaturated solution: a solution that contains more solute than it can theoretically hold at a given temperature; excess solute precipitates if a seed crystal is added (522)

 solución sobresaturada: solución que contiene más soluto del que en teoría puede contener a una temperatura específica; el soluto en exceso se precipita si se añade un cristal que actúa como semilla

surface tension: an inward force that tends to minimize the surface area of a liquid; it causes the surface to behave as if it were a thin skin (490)

 tensión superficial: fuerza que tiende a reducir al mínimo la superficie total de un líquido y actúa hacia el seno de éste; hace que la superficie se comporte como si fuera una membrana elástica

surfactant: any substance that interferes with the hydrogen bonding between water molecules and thereby reduces surface tension; soaps are surfactants (490)

 tensoactivo: cualquier sustancia que perturba la formación de enlaces de hidrógeno entre las moléculas de agua y así reduce la tensión superficial; los jabones y detergentes son tensoactivos

surroundings: everything in the universe outside of the system (557)

 entorno: todo lo que no forma parte del sistema, es decir, el resto del universo

suspension: a mixture from which some of the particles settle out slowly upon standing (504)

 suspensión: mezcla de la que se separan lentamente algunas partículas por asentamiento cuando no se agita

synthesis reaction: *see* combination reaction

 reacción de síntesis: *véase* reacción de combinación

system: a part of the universe on which you focus your attention (557)

 sistema: parte del universo en la que centramos nuestra atención

T

technology: the means by which a society provides its members with those things needed and desired *(8)*

    tecnología: los medios por los cuales una sociedad proporciona a sus miembros las cosas que necesitan y desean

temperature: a measure of the average kinetic energy of particles in matter; temperature determines the direction of heat transfer *(78)*

    temperatura: medida de la energía cinética promedio de las partículas de la materia; la temperatura determina la dirección de la transferencia de calor

tetrahedral angle: a bond angle of 109.5° that results when a central atom forms four bonds directed toward the center of a regular tetrahedron *(242)*

    ángulo tetraédrico: ángulo de enlace de 109.5° que se forma cuando un átomo central forma cuatro enlaces dirigidos hacia el centro de un tetraedro regular

theoretical yield: the amount of product that could form during a reaction calculated from a balanced chemical equation; it represents the maximum amount of product that could be formed from a given amount of reactant *(405)*

    rendimiento teórico: cantidad de producto que podría formarse durante una reacción, calculada a partir de una ecuación química balanceada; representa la cantidad máxima de producto que podría formarse a partir de una cantidad determinada de reactantes

theory: a well-tested explanation for a broad set of observations *(17)*

    teoría: explicación, probada exhaustivamente, de un conjunto amplio de observaciones

thermochemical equation: a chemical equation that includes the enthalpy change *(565)*

    ecuación termoquímica: ecuación química que incluye el cambio de calor

thermochemistry: the study of energy changes that occur during chemical reactions and changes in state *(556)*

    termoquímica: estudio de los cambios de calor que acompañan a las reacciones químicas y a los cambios de estado físico

titration: process used to determine the concentration of a solution (often an acid or base) in which a solution of known concentration (the standard) is added to a measured amount of the solution of unknown concentration until an indicator signals the end point *(673)*

    valoración química: proceso empleado para determinar la concentración de una solución (a menudo un ácido o base) por el cual una solución de concentración conocida (solución estándar) se añade a una cantidad medida de una solución cuya concentración se desconoce, hasta que un indicador marca el punto final

***trans* configuration:** the configuration in which substituent groups are on the opposite sides of a double bond *(776)*

    configuración *trans*: configuración en la que los grupos sustitutos están en lados opuestos de un doble enlace

transition metal: one of the Group B elements in which the highest occupied *s* sublevel and a nearby *d* sublevel generally contain electrons *(172)*

    metal de transición: uno de los elementos del grupo B en el que el subnivel *s* ocupado más alto y un subnivel *d* cercano generalmente contienen electrones

transmutation: the conversion of an atom of one element to an atom of another element *(885)*

    transmutación: conversión de un átomo de un elemento en un átomo de otro elemento

transuranium element: any elements in the periodic table with atomic number above 92, the atomic number of uranium *(886)*

    elemento transuránico: cualquier elemento de la tabla periódica cuyo número atómico es mayor que 92, el número atómico del uranio

triglyceride: an ester in which all three hydroxyl groups on a glycerol molecule have been replaced by long-chain fatty acids; fats are triglycerides *(850)*

    triglicérido: éster en el que los tres grupos hidroxilo de una molécula de glicerol han sido sustituidos por ácidos grasos de cadena larga; las grasas son triglicéridos

triple covalent bond: a covalent bond in which three pairs of electrons are shared by two atoms *(230)*

    enlace covalente triple: enlace covalente en el que dos átomos comparten tres pares de electrones

triple point: the point on a phase diagram that represents the only set of conditions at which all three phases exist in equilibrium with one another *(402)*

    punto triple: punto de un diagrama de fases que representa el único conjunto de condiciones en el que las tres fases existen en equilibrio

triprotic acid: any acid that contains three ionizable protons (hydrogen ions); phosphoric acid (H_3PO_4) is a triprotic acid *(647)*

    ácido triprótico: ácido que contiene tres protones (iones hidrógeno) ionizables; el ácido fosfórico (H_3PO_4) es un ácido triprótico

Tyndall effect: scattering of light by particles in a colloid or suspension, which causes a beam of light to become visible *(506)*

    efecto Tyndall: dispersión de la luz por las partículas de un coloide o una suspensión, que hace que un haz de luz se vuelva visible

U

unit cell: the smallest group of particles within a crystal that retains the geometric shape of the crystal *(433)*

  celda unitaria: grupo más pequeño de partículas dentro de un cristal que conserva la forma geométrica del cristal

unsaturated solution: a solution that contains less solute than a saturated solution at a given temperature and pressure *(520)*

  solución insaturada: se dice de una solución que contiene menos soluto que una solución saturada a una temperatura y presión específicas

unsaturated compound: an organic compound with one or more double or triple carbon–carbon bonds *(772)*

  compuesto insaturado: compuesto orgánico que tiene uno o más dobles o triples enlaces carbono–carbono

unshared pair: a pair of valence electrons that is not shared between atoms *(227)*

  par no compartido: par de electrones de valencia que no es compartido por dos átomos

V

vacuum: a space where no particles of matter exist *(421)*

  vacío: espacio en el que no existen partículas de materia

valence electron: an electron in the highest occupied energy level of an atom *(194)*

  electrón de valencia: electrón que está en el nivel energético ocupado más alto de un átomo

van der Waals forces: the two weakest intermolecular attractions—dispersion interactions and dipole forces *(250)*

  fuerzas de van der Waals: las dos atracciones intermoleculares más débiles—interacciones de dispersión y fuerzas dipolares

vapor: describes the gaseous state of a substance that is generally a liquid or solid at room temperature *(37)*

  vapor: estado gaseoso de una sustancia que suele ser líquida o sólida a temperatura ambiente

vaporization: the conversion of a liquid to a gas or a vapor *(426)*

  vaporización: conversión de un líquido en gas o vapor

vapor pressure: a measure of the force exerted by a gas above a liquid in a sealed container; a dynamic equilibrium exists between the vapor and the liquid *(427)*

  presión de vapor: medida de la fuerza que ejerce un gas sobre un líquido en un contenedor sellado; equilibrio dinámico que existe entre el vapor y el líquido

voltaic cell: an electrochemical cell used to convert chemical energy into electrical energy; the energy is produced by a spontaneous redox reaction *(730)*

  celda voltaica: celda electroquímica empleada para convertir energía química en energía eléctrica; la energía se produce por una reacción redox espontánea

volume: a measure of the space occupied by a sample of matter *(34)*

  volumen: medida del espacio ocupado por una muestra de materia

VSEPR theory: valence-shell electron-pair repulsion theory; because electron pairs repel, molecules adjust their shapes so that valence electron pairs are as far apart as possible *(242)*

  teoría RPENV: teoría de repulsión de pares de electrones del nivel de valencia; como los pares de electrones se repelen, las moléculas ajustan su forma de modo que los pares de electrones de valencia estén lo más alejados posible entre sí

W

water of hydration: water molecules that are an integral part of a crystal structure *(498)*

  agua de hidratación: moléculas de agua que forman parte integral de una estructura cristalina

wavelength (λ): the distance between adjacent crests of a wave *(138)*

  longitud de onda (λ): distancia entre crestas adyacentes de una onda

wax: an ester of a long-chain fatty acid and a long-chain alcohol *(852)*

  cera: éster de un ácido graso de cadena larga y un alcohol de cadena larga

weak acid: an acid that is only slightly ionized in aqueous solution *(664)*

  ácido débil: ácido que se ioniza poco en solución acuosa

weak base: a base that reacts with water to form the hydroxide ion and the conjugate acid of the base *(668)*

  base débil: base que reacciona con agua para formar el ion hidróxido y el ácido combinado de la base

weak electrolyte: a solution that conducts electricity poorly because only a fraction of the solute exists as ions *(497)*

  electrolito débil: solución que apenas conduce la electricidad porque sólo una fracción del soluto existe en forma de iones

weight: a force that measures the pull of gravity on a given mass *(77)*

  peso: fuerza que mide la atracción de la gravedad sobre una masa específica

Index

The page on which a term is defined is indicated in **boldface** type. Page numbers for appendices begin with R.

pulp 687
pure chemistry **3**
pyrite 194

Q

quantum **129**
quantum mechanical model **130**
quantum mechanics 147–148
quarks 107

R

radiation
    nuclear 877–879
    electromagnetic 139
    ionizing 894
radioactive decay 876
radioactivity **876**, 887
radiocarbon dating 883
radioisotopes **876,** 896, 897
radium R6
    radium-226 isotope 882
radon R1, R32
    radon-222 isotope 882
Ramsay, William 11
rate-determining steps 608
rate laws **604**–605
rates **595**
ratios of units, converting 91
reactants **48,** 346
reaction mechanisms **607**–608
reaction rates
    describing 594–597
    factors affecting 598–601
reactions
    in calculating enthalpy change 567
    coupled 629
    determining spontaneity 741
    elementary 607
    examples of 347
    finding order of, from experimental
      data 606
    first-order 605
    heat of 565–566
    higher-order 605
    limiting reagent in 402
    percent yield of 404–406, 408
    reversible 609–611
    standard heat of 581–582
    theoretical yield of 406
recombinant DNA technology 860–861
recycling 52–53
redox reactions 728
    activity series and 728–729
    balancing equations in 709–715
    with molecular compounds 696
    electron shift in 694

    in forming ions 694–695
    identifying 707–709
    with oxygen 692–693
reducing agents **695**
    in fireworks 700
reduction 692–696, **694,** 710
    processes leading to 696
reduction potential **737**
representative elements **171**
representative particle **308**
resolution 110
resonance 237
reverse osmosis desalination 502–503
reversible reactions **609**–611, 628
rhenium R36
rhodium R36
ribonucleic acid (RNA) 854–856
ribose 854
ribosomes 839
rounding 68–69
Royal Society of London for the
    Promotion of Natural Knowledge
    15
rubber 824
rubidium R2
Ruska, Ernst 110
rusting 348
ruthenium R36
Rutherford, Daniel R20
Rutherford, Ernest 107–109, 128, 133,
    885
Rutherford atomic model 108–109,
    128, 130
rutile 205

S

saccharin 12
safety, laboratory 20–21, R49–50
salt bridge **730**
salt hydrolysis 676–678, **677**
salts in solution 676–680
saponification **851**
saturated compound **772**
saturated solution **520,** 623
scandium R36, R37
scanning electron microscopes (SEM)
    100, 104, 110
Scheele, Carl Wilhelm R24, R28
Schrödinger, Erwin 130, 133
scientific law **17**
scientific methodology 15–17
scientific notation **62**–63
scintillation counter 895
screening machines 52
scrubbers R23
Seaborg, Glenn 159
seaborgium 163

seeding 897
Segrè, Emilio R28
selenium R24, R26
self-ionization **653**
semiconductors R17
serine 845
sigma bond **240**–241
significant figures **66**–71
silicates R14
silicon 166, R1, R14
silicon carbide 252
silicon dioxide R15
silicone polymers R19
silver R36
    ions 197, 266
    tarnish removal from 354
Silver, Spencer 13
silver chloride 622
silver hallide 370
single covalent bonds **226**–229,
    244–245
single-replacement reactions **360**–361,
    366
single-replacement redox reactions 707
sinkhole 517, 551
skeletal system 183
skeleton equation **348,** 349
slag 440
smog 237, 455, 786
soapmaking 851
Sobrero, Ascanio 368
sodium 749, R2
    ion 176, 196, 264
    manufacture of R2
    properties of 43
sodium azide 397
sodium bromide 274
sodium carbonate 649
sodium chloride 201, 204, 208, 225,
    535, R2
    coordination number of 205
    electrolysis of molten 749
    formation of 202
    melting point of 431
    name and formula of 264
    properties of 35, 43
    solubility of 522, 535
sodium cyanide 345, 363
sodium ethanoate 677
sodium hydrogen carbonate R3
sodium hydroxide 287, 345, 501, 646,
    648, R3
sodium hypochlorite 278, 693, R3
sodium perborate 693
sodium percarbonate 693
sodium silicate 664, R15
sodium sulfite 274

Credits

Periodic Table of the Elements

Representative Elements

- Alkali metals
- Alkaline earth metals
- Other metals
- Metalloids
- Nonmetals
- Noble gases

Transition Elements

- Transition metals
- Inner transition metals

Key

C	Solid
Br	Liquid
He	Gas
Tc	Not found in nature

Key to element box:
Atomic number — 13
Electrons in each energy level — 2 8 3
Element symbol — Al
Element name — Aluminum
Atomic mass† — 26.982

†The atomic masses in parentheses are the mass numbers of the longest-lived isotope of elements for which a standard atomic mass cannot be defined.

*Discovery reported but not verified

Elements 104–118 are the transactinide elements.

Group 1A (1)

Z	Symbol	Name	Mass	Electrons
1	H	Hydrogen	1.0079	1
3	Li	Lithium	6.941	2,1
11	Na	Sodium	22.990	2,8,1
19	K	Potassium	39.098	2,8,8,1
37	Rb	Rubidium	85.468	2,8,18,8,1
55	Cs	Cesium	132.91	2,8,18,18,8,1
87	Fr	Francium	(223)	2,8,18,32,18,8,1

Group 2A (2)

Z	Symbol	Name	Mass	Electrons
4	Be	Beryllium	9.0122	2,2
12	Mg	Magnesium	24.305	2,8,2
20	Ca	Calcium	40.08	2,8,8,2
38	Sr	Strontium	87.62	2,8,18,8,2
56	Ba	Barium	137.33	2,8,18,18,8,2
88	Ra	Radium	(226)	2,8,18,32,18,8,2

Transition metals (groups 3B–2B)

3B (3)
- 21 Sc Scandium 44.956 — 2,8,9,2
- 39 Y Yttrium 88.906 — 2,8,18,9,2
- 71 Lu Lutetium 174.97 — 2,8,18,32,9,2
- 103 Lr Lawrencium (262) — 2,8,18,32,32,9,2

4B (4)
- 22 Ti Titanium 47.90 — 2,8,10,2
- 40 Zr Zirconium 91.22 — 2,8,18,10,2
- 72 Hf Hafnium 178.49 — 2,8,18,32,10,2
- 104 Rf Rutherfordium (261) — 2,8,18,32,32,10,2

5B (5)
- 23 V Vanadium 50.941 — 2,8,11,2
- 41 Nb Niobium 92.906 — 2,8,18,12,1
- 73 Ta Tantalum 180.95 — 2,8,18,32,11,2
- 105 Db Dubnium (262) — 2,8,18,32,32,11,2

6B (6)
- 24 Cr Chromium 51.996 — 2,8,13,1
- 42 Mo Molybdenum 95.94 — 2,8,18,13,1
- 74 W Tungsten 183.85 — 2,8,18,32,12,2
- 106 Sg Seaborgium (263) — 2,8,18,32,32,12,2

7B (7)
- 25 Mn Manganese 54.938 — 2,8,13,2
- 43 Tc Technetium (98) — 2,8,18,14,1
- 75 Re Rhenium 186.21 — 2,8,18,32,13,2
- 107 Bh Bohrium (264) — 2,8,18,32,32,13,2

8B (8)
- 26 Fe Iron 55.847 — 2,8,14,2
- 44 Ru Ruthenium 101.07 — 2,8,18,15,1
- 76 Os Osmium 190.2 — 2,8,18,32,14,2
- 108 Hs Hassium (265) — 2,8,18,32,32,14,2

8B (9)
- 27 Co Cobalt 58.933 — 2,8,15,2
- 45 Rh Rhodium 102.91 — 2,8,18,16,1
- 77 Ir Iridium 192.22 — 2,8,18,32,15,2
- 109 Mt Meitnerium (268) — 2,8,18,32,32,15,2

8B (10)
- 28 Ni Nickel 58.71 — 2,8,16,2
- 46 Pd Palladium 106.4 — 2,8,18,18
- 78 Pt Platinum 195.09 — 2,8,18,32,17,1
- 110 Ds Darmstadtium (269) — 2,8,18,32,32,17,1

1B (11)
- 29 Cu Copper 63.546 — 2,8,18,1
- 47 Ag Silver 107.87 — 2,8,18,18,1
- 79 Au Gold 196.97 — 2,8,18,32,18,1
- 111 Rg Roentgenium (272) — 2,8,18,32,32,18,1

2B (12)
- 30 Zn Zinc 65.38 — 2,8,18,2
- 48 Cd Cadmium 112.41 — 2,8,18,18,2
- 80 Hg Mercury 200.59 — 2,8,18,32,18,2
- 112 Cn Copernicium (277) — 2,8,18,32,32,18,2

Group 3A (13)

Z	Symbol	Name	Mass
5	B	Boron	10.81
13	Al	Aluminum	26.982
31	Ga	Gallium	69.72
49	In	Indium	114.82
81	Tl	Thallium	204.37
113	Uut*	Ununtrium	(284)

Group 4A (14)

Z	Symbol	Name	Mass
6	C	Carbon	12.011
14	Si	Silicon	28.086
32	Ge	Germanium	72.59
50	Sn	Tin	118.69
82	Pb	Lead	207.2
114	Fl	Flerovium	(289)

Group 5A (15)

Z	Symbol	Name	Mass
7	N	Nitrogen	14.007
15	P	Phosphorus	30.974
33	As	Arsenic	74.922
51	Sb	Antimony	121.75
83	Bi	Bismuth	208.98
115	Uup*	Ununpentium	(288)

Group 6A (16)

Z	Symbol	Name	Mass
8	O	Oxygen	15.999
16	S	Sulfur	32.06
34	Se	Selenium	78.96
52	Te	Tellurium	127.60
84	Po	Polonium	(209)
116	Lv	Livermorium	(293)

Group 7A (17)

Z	Symbol	Name	Mass
9	F	Fluorine	18.998
17	Cl	Chlorine	35.453
35	Br	Bromine	79.904
53	I	Iodine	126.90
85	At	Astatine	(210)
117	Uus*	Ununseptium	(294)

Group 8A (18)

Z	Symbol	Name	Mass
2	He	Helium	4.0026
10	Ne	Neon	20.179
18	Ar	Argon	39.948
36	Kr	Krypton	83.80
54	Xe	Xenon	131.30
86	Rn	Radon	(222)
118	Uuo*	Ununoctium	(299)

Lanthanide Series

Z	Symbol	Name	Mass
57	La	Lanthanum	138.91
58	Ce	Cerium	140.12
59	Pr	Praseodymium	140.91
60	Nd	Neodymium	144.24
61	Pm	Promethium	(145)
62	Sm	Samarium	150.4
63	Eu	Europium	151.96
64	Gd	Gadolinium	157.25
65	Tb	Terbium	158.93
66	Dy	Dysprosium	162.50
67	Ho	Holmium	164.93
68	Er	Erbium	167.26
69	Tm	Thulium	168.93
70	Yb	Ytterbium	173.04

Actinide Series

Z	Symbol	Name	Mass
89	Ac	Actinium	(227)
90	Th	Thorium	232.04
91	Pa	Protactinium	231.04
92	U	Uranium	238.03
93	Np	Neptunium	(237)
94	Pu	Plutonium	(244)
95	Am	Americium	(243)
96	Cm	Curium	(247)
97	Bk	Berkelium	(247)
98	Cf	Californium	(251)
99	Es	Einsteinium	(252)
100	Fm	Fermium	(257)
101	Md	Mendelevium	(258)
102	No	Nobelium	(259)